Herzog, Johann Jacob; Schaff, Philip; Hauck, Albert

The new Schaff-Herzog encyclopedia of religious knowledge

Vol. 3

Herzog, Johann Jacob; Schaff, Philip; Hauck, Albert

The new Schaff-Herzog encyclopedia of religious knowledge

Vol. 3

Inktank publishing, 2018

www.inktank-publishing.com

ISBN/EAN: 9783747768402

THE NEW
SCHAFF-HERZOG ENCYCLOPEDIA
OF
RELIGIOUS KNOWLEDGE

EDITED BY

SAMUEL MACAULEY JACKSON, D.D., LL.D.
(Editor-in-Chief)

WITH THE ASSISTANCE OF

CHARLES COLEBROOK SHERMAN
AND
GEORGE WILLIAM GILMORE, M.A.
(Associate Editors)

AND THE FOLLOWING DEPARTMENT EDITORS

CLARENCE AUGUSTINE BECKWITH, D.D.
(Department of Systematic Theology)

HENRY KING CARROLL, LL.D.
(Department of Minor Denominations)

JAMES FRANCIS DRISCOLL, D.D.
(Department of Liturgics and Religious Orders)

JAMES FREDERIC McCURDY, PH.D., LL.D.
(Department of the Old Testament)

HENRY SYLVESTER NASH, D.D.
(Department of the New Testament)

ALBERT HENRY NEWMAN, D.D., LL.D.
(Department of Church History)

FRANK HORACE VIZETELLY, F.S.A.
(Department of Pronunciation and Typography)

VOLUME III
CHAMIER — DRAENDORF

FUNK AND WAGNALLS COMPANY
NEW YORK AND LONDON

EDITORS

SAMUEL MACAULEY JACKSON, D.D., LL.D.
(EDITOR-IN-CHIEF.)
Professor of Church History, New York University.

ASSOCIATE EDITORS

CHARLES COLEBROOK SHERMAN
Editor in Biblical Criticism and Theology on "The New International Encyclopedia," New York.

GEORGE WILLIAM GILMORE, M.A.
New York, Formerly Professor of Biblical History and Lecturer on Comparative Religion, Bangor Theological Seminary.

DEPARTMENT EDITORS, VOLUME III

CLARENCE AUGUSTINE BECKWITH, D.D.
(*Department of Systematic Theology.*)
Professor of Systematic Theology, Chicago Theological Seminary.

HENRY KING CARROLL, LL.D.
(*Department of Minor Denominations.*)
Formerly a Corresponding Secretary of the Board of Foreign Missions of the Methodist Episcopal Church, New York.

JAMES FRANCIS DRISCOLL, D.D.
(*Department of Liturgics and Religious Orders.*)
President of St. Joseph's Seminary, Yonkers, N. Y.

JAMES FREDERICK McCURDY, Ph.D., LL.D.
(*Department of the Old Testament.*)
Professor of Oriental Languages, University College, Toronto.

HENRY SYLVESTER NASH, D.D.
(*Department of the New Testament.*)
Professor of the Literature and Interpretation of the New Testament, Episcopal Theological School, Cambridge, Mass.

ALBERT HENRY NEWMAN, D.D., LL.D.
(*Department of Church History.*)
Professor of Church History, Baylor Theological Seminary (Baylor University), Waco, Tex.

FRANK HORACE VIZETELLY, F.S.A.
(*Department of Pronunciation and Typography.*)
Managing Editor of the STANDARD DICTIONARY, etc., New York City.

CONTRIBUTORS AND COLLABORATORS, VOLUME III

JUSTIN EDWARDS ABBOTT, D.D.,
Missionary in Bombay, India.

HANS ACHELIS, Ph.D., Th.D.,
Professor of Church History, University of Halle.

RUDOLF ANSTEIN (†),
Late Pastor in Basel.

FRANKLIN CARL ARNOLD, Ph.D., Th.D.,
Professor of Church History, University of Breslau.

WILHELM BAUR (†), Th.D.,
Late General Superintendent in Bonn.

GEORGE JAMES BAYLES, Ph.D.,
Writer on Civil and Ecclesiastical Law.

CLARENCE AUGUSTINE BECKWITH, D.D.,
Professor of Systematic Theology, Chicago Theological Seminary.

KARL BENRATH, Ph.D., Th.D.,
Professor of Church History, University of Königsberg.

IMMANUEL GUSTAV ADOLF BENZINGER, Ph.D., Th.Lic.,
German Orientalist and Vice-Consul for Holland in Jerusalem.

CARL BERTHEAU, Th.D.,
Pastor of St. Michael's, Hamburg.

BERNHARD BESS, Th.Lic.,
Librarian, University of Halle.

RUDOLPH MICHAEL BINDER, Ph.D.,
Lecturer in Sociology, New York University.

EMIL BLOESCH (†), Th.D.,
Late Professor of Theology, Bern.

HEINRICH BOEHMER, Ph.D., Th.Lic.,
Professor of Church History, University of Bonn.

AMY GASTON CHARLES AUGUSTE BONET-MAURY, D.D., LL.D.,
Professor of Church History, Independent School of Divinity, Paris.

GOTTLIEB NATHANAEL BONWETSCH, Th.D.,
Professor of Church History, University of Göttingen.

FRIEDRICH BOSSE, Ph.D., Th.Lic.,
Assistant Librarian, University Library, Marburg.

GUSTAV BOSSERT, Ph.D., Th.D.,
Retired Pastor, Stuttgart.

PERCY HOLMES BOYNTON,
Secretary of Instruction in the Chautauqua Institution, Chautauqua, N. Y.

JOHANNES FRIEDRICH THEODOR BRIEGER, Ph.D., Th.D.,
Professor of Church History, University of Leipsic.

FRANTS PEDER WILLIAM BUHL, Ph.D., Th.D.,
Professor of Oriental Languages, University of Copenhagen.

KARL BURGER (†), Th.D.,
Late Supreme Consistorial Councilor in Munich.

HENRY KING CARROLL, LL.D.,
Formerly Corresponding Secretary of the Methodist Missionary Society.

WALTER CASPARI, Ph.D., Th.Lic.,
University Preacher and Professor of Practical Theology, University of Erlangen.

JACQUES EUGÈNE CHOISY, Th.D.,
Pastor in Geneva.

FERDINAND COHRS, Th.Lic.,
Consistorial Councilor, Ilfeld, Germany.

AUGUST HERMANN CREMER (†), Th.D.,
Late Professor of Systematic Theology, University of Greifswald.

WALTER EWING CRUM, M.A.,
Coptic Scholar, London.

FRIEDRICH WILHELM CUNO (†), Th.Lic.,
Late Pastor at Eddigehausen, Hanover.

SAMUEL MARTIN DEUTSCH, Th.D.,
Professor of Church History, University of Berlin.

MORTON DEXTER, M.A.,
Congregational Clergyman and Author, Boston.

DEODAT DISSELHOFF,
Pastor at Kaiserswerth, Germany.

BERNHARD DOMBART (†), Ph.D.,
Formerly Gymnasial Rector, Ansbach, Germany.

JAMES FRANCIS DRISCOLL, D.D.,
President of St. Joseph's Seminary, Yonkers, N. Y.

HENRY JAY DUCKWORTH, D.D.,
Secretary of Education for the Ohio Central Christian Conference.

LUDWIG ALFRED ERICHSON (†), Ph.D., Th.D.,
Late Preacher at St. Thomas', Strasburg, Germany.

HUBERT EVANS, Ph.D.,
Member of the Editorial Staff of the Encyclopedia Britannica Company, New York.

THEODOR FOERSTER (†), Th.D.,
Late Professor of Church History, University of Halle.

CHRISTIAN HENRY FORNEY, D.D., LL.D.,
Editor of the *Church Advocate*, Harrisburg, Pa.

RUDOLF FOSS (†),
Late Councilor in Grosslichterfelde, Germany.

GUSTAV WILHELM FRANK (†), Th.D.,
Late Professor of Dogmatics, Symbolics, and Christian Ethics, University of Vienna.

EMIL ALBERT FRIEDBERG, Th.D., Dr.Jur.,
Professor of Ecclesiastical, Public, and German Law, University of Leipsic.

JOHANN FRIEDRICH, Ph.D., Th.D.,
Professor of Church History, University of Munich.

THEODOR GEROLD, Th.D.,
President of the Consistory, Strasburg.

JOHANNES ABRAHAM GERTH VAN WIJK (†), Th.D.,
Late Reformed Church Clergyman at The Hague, Holland.

CHRISTIAN GEYER, Ph.D.,
Clergyman in Nuremberg, Germany.

GEORGE WILLIAM GILMORE, M.A.,
Former Professor of Biblical History and Lecturer on Comparative Religion, Bangor Theological Seminary.

WILHELM GOETZ, Ph.D.,
Honorary Professor of Geography, Technical High School, and Professor, Military Academy, Munich, Germany.

CASPAR RENÉ GREGORY, Ph.D., Dr.Jur., Th.D., D.D., LL.D.,
Professor of New Testament Exegesis, University of Leipsic.

GEORG GRUETZMACHER, Ph.D., Th.Lic.,
Extraordinary Professor of Church History, University of Heidelberg.

KARL RUDOLF HAGENBACH (†), Ph.D., Th.D.,
Late Professor of Theology, University of Basel.

ADOLF HARNACK, M.D., Ph.D., Th.D., Dr.Jur.,
General Director of the Royal Library and Professor of Church History, University of Berlin.

ALBERT HAUCK, Ph.D., Th.D., Dr.Jur.,
Professor of Church History, University of Leipsic, Editor-in-Chief of the Hauck-Herzog *Realencyklopädie*.

HERMAN HAUPT, Ph.D.,
Professor and Director of the University Library, Giessen.

CARL FRIEDRICH GEORG HEINRICI, Ph.D., Th.D.,
Professor of New Testament Exegesis, University of Leipsic.

ERNST HENKE (†), Ph.D., Th.D.,
Late Professor of Theology, University of Marburg.

HERMANN HERING, Th.D.,
Professor of Philosophy of Religion and Homiletics, University of Halle.

JOHANN JAKOB HERZOG (†), Ph.D., Th.D.,
Late Professor of Reformed Theology, University of Erlangen.

PAUL HINSCHIUS (†), Dr.Jur., Th.D.,
Late Professor of Ecclesiastical Law, University of Berlin.

KARL HOLL, Ph.D., Th.D.,
Professor of Church History, University of Berlin.

GEORGE ELLIOTT HOWARD, Ph.D.,
Professor of Institutional History, University of Nebraska.

EDUARD JACOBS, Ph.D.,
Privy Councilor, Wernigerode, Prussian Saxony.

HEINRICH FRIEDRICH JACOBSON (†),
Late Professor of Law, University of Königsberg.

HERMANN JACOBY, Th.D.,
Professor of Homiletics, University of Königsberg.

MARTIN KAEHLER, Th.D.,
Professor of Dogmatics and New Testament Exegesis, University of Halle.

FRIEDRICH WILHELM FERDINAND KATTENBUSCH, Th.D.,
Professor of Dogmatics, University of Halle.

EMIL FRIEDRICH KAUTZSCH, Ph.D., Th.D.,
Professor of Old Testament Exegesis, University of Halle.

PETER GUSTAV KAWERAU, Th.D.,
Consistorial Councilor, University Preacher, and Professor of Practical Theology, University of Breslau.

HUGO WILHELM PAUL KLEINERT, Ph.D., Th.D.,
Professor of Old Testament Exegesis and Practical Theology, University of Berlin.

HEINRICH AUGUST KLOSTERMANN, Th.D.,
Professor of Old Testament Exegesis, University of Kiel.

FRIEDRICH EDUARD KOENIG, Ph.D., Th.D.,
Professor of Old Testament Exegesis, University of Bonn.

JULIUS KOESTLIN (†), Ph.D., Th.D., Dr.Jur.,
Late Professor of Theology, University of Halle.

THEODOR FRIEDRICH HERMANN KOLDE, Ph.D., Th.D.,
Professor of Church History, University of Erlangen.

HERMANN GUSTAV EDUARD KRUEGER, Ph.D., Th.D.,
Professor of Church History, University of Giessen.

JOHANNES WILHELM KUNZE, Ph.D., Th.D.,
Professor of Systematic and Practical Theology, University of Greifswald.

MAXIMILIAN ALBERT LANDERER (†), Ph.D., Th.D.,
Late Professor of Theology, University of Tübingen.

WILLIAM HENRY LARRABEE, LL.D.,
Plainfield, N. J.

MORITZ LAUTERBURG,
Professor of Practical Theology, University of Bern.

KARL LUDWIG LEIMBACH (†), Ph.D., Th.D.,
Late Provincial Councilor for Schools, Hanover, Germany.

LUDWIG LEMME, Th.D.,
Professor of Systematic Theology, University of Heidelberg.

EDUARD LEMPP, Ph.D.,
Chief Inspector of the Royal Orphan Asylum, Stuttgart, Germany.

BRUNO LINDNER, Ph.D.,
Professor of Aryan Languages, University of Leipsic.

THOMAS MARTIN LINDSAY, M.A., D.D.,
Principal United Free Church College, Glasgow.

GEORG LOESCHE, Ph.D., Th.D.,
Professor of Church History, Evangelical Theological Faculty, Vienna.

WILHELM LOTZ, Ph.D., Th.D.,
Professor of Old Testament Exegesis, University of Erlangen.

JAMES FREDERICK McCURDY, Ph.D., LL.D.,
Professor of Oriental Languages, University of Toronto.

OTTO MEJER (†), Ph.D., Th.D.,
Late President of the Consistory, Hanover.

PHILIPP MEYER, Th.D.,
Supreme Consistorial Councilor, Hanover.

CARL THEODOR MIRBT, Th.D.,
Professor of Church History, University of Marburg.

ERNST FRIEDRICH KARL MUELLER, Th.D.,
Professor of Reformed Theology, University of Erlangen.

GEORG MUELLER, Ph.D., Th.D.,
Inspector of Schools, Leipsic.

FRIEDRICH WILHELM REINHARD MUMM, Th.Lic.,
General Secretary of the Free Ecclesiastical-Social Conference, Berlin.

HENRY SYLVESTER NASH, D.D.,
Professor of the Literature and Interpretation of the New Testament, Episcopal Theological School, Cambridge, Massachusetts.

MARTIN VON NATHUSIUS (†), Th.D.,
Late Professor of Practical Theology, University of Greifswald.

ALBERT HENRY NEWMAN, D.D., LL.D.,
Professor of Church History, Baylor Theological Seminary (Baylor University), Waco, Texas.

THEODOR JULIUS NEY, Th.D.,
Supreme Consistorial Councilor, Speyer, Bavaria.

FREDERICK CHRISTIAN NIELSEN (†), D.D.,
Late Bishop of Aarhus, Denmark.

CONRAD VON ORELLI, Ph.D., Th.D.,
Professor of Old Testament Exegesis and History of Religion, University of Basel.

CHARLES PFENDER,
Pastor of St. Paul's Evangelical Lutheran Church, Paris.

FREDERICK DUNGLISON POWER, M.A., LL.D.,
Pastor of Garfield Memorial Church, Washington, D. C.

ERWIN PREUSCHEN, Ph.D., Th.Lic.,
Pastor at Hirschhorn-on-the-Neckar, Germany.

HERMANN RAHLENBECK,
Pastor in Cologne.

K. RÉVÉSZ,
Senior of the Reformed Church, Kaschau, Hungary.

GEORG CHRISTIAN RIETSCHEL, Th.D.,
University Preacher and Professor of Practical Theology, University of Leipsic.

HENDRIK CORNELIS ROGGE (†), Th.D.,
Late Professor of History, University of Amsterdam.

EUGEN SACHSSE, Th.D.,
Professor of Practical Theology, University of Bonn.

HUGO SACHSSE, Ph.D., Th.Lic., Dr.Jur.,
Professor of Ecclesiastical Law, University of Rostock.

FERDINAND SANDER,
Councilor for Schools in Bremen, Germany.

ELIAS BENJAMIN SANFORD, D.D.,
General Secretary of the National Federation of Churches and Christian Workers.

THEODOR SCHAEFER, Th.D.,
Head of the Deaconesses' Institute, Altona.

DAVID SCHLEY SCHAFF, D.D.,
Professor of Church History, Western Theological Seminary, Allegheny, Pennsylvania.

PHILIP SCHAFF (†), D.D., LL.D.,
Late Professor of Church History, Union Theological Seminary, New York.

ADOLPH FREDERICK SCHAUFFLER, D.D.,
President of New York City Mission and Tract Society.

CHRISTOPH THEODOR GOTTLOB VON SCHEURL (†), Ph.D., Th.D.,
Late Professor in Nuremberg.

REINHOLD SCHMID, Th.Lic.,
Pastor in Oberholzheim, Württemberg.

HEINRICH SCHMIDT (†),
Late Professor of Theology, University of Erlangen.

KARL SCHMIDT, Th.D.,
Pastor at Goldberg, Mecklenburg.

THEODOR SCHOTT (†), Ph.D., Th.D.,
Late Librarian and Professor of Theology, University of Stuttgart.

JOHANN FRIEDRICH RITTER VON SCHULTE, Dr.Jur.,
Professor of Law, University of Bonn.

VICTOR SCHULTZE, Th.D.,
Professor of Church History and Christian Archeology, University of Greifswald.

LUDWIG THEODOR SCHULZE, Ph.D., Th.D.,
Professor of Systematic Theology, University of Rostock.

OTTO SEEBASS, Ph.D.,
Educator, Leipsic, Germany.

REINHOLD SEEBERG, Th.D.,
Professor of Systematic Theology, University of Berlin.

EMIL SEHLING, Dr.Jur.,
Professor of Ecclesiastical and Commercial Law, University of Erlangen.

CHARLES COLEBROOK SHERMAN,
Editor in Biblical Criticism and Theology on *The New International Encyclopedia*, New York.

ALBERT B SIMPSON,
President Christian and Missionary Alliance.

ARTHUR HENDERSON SMITH, M.A.,
American Missionary, P'ang Chuang, China.

ROBERT WALTER STEWART, B.Sc., B.D.,
Glasgow, Scotland.

JOSEPH JAMES SUMMERBELL,
Editor of *The Herald of Gospel Liberty*, Dayton, Ohio.

KARL THIEME, Ph.D., Th.D.,
Professor of Dogmatics, University of Leipsic.

ERNST PETER WILHELM TROELTSCH, Ph.D., Th.D.,
Professor of Systematic Theology, University of Heidelberg.

PAUL TSCHACKERT, Ph.D., Th.D.,
Professor of Church History, University of Göttingen.

JOHANN GERHARD WILHELM UHLHORN (†), Th.D.,
Late Consistorial Councilor, Hanover.

SIETRE DOUWES VAN VEEN, Th.D.,
Professor of Church History and Christian Archeology, University of Utrecht.

MARVIN RICHARDSON VINCENT, D.D.,
Professor of New Testament Exegesis and Criticism, Union Theological Seminary, New York.

JOHANNES WEISS, Th.D.,
Professor of New Testament Exegesis, University of Heidelberg.

AUGUST WILHELM ERNST WERNER, Th.D.,
Pastor Primarius, Guben, Prussia.

FRIEDRICH LUDWIG LEONHARD WIEGAND, Ph.D., Th.D.,
Professor of Church History, University of Greifswald.

SAMUEL WELLS WILLIAMS (†), LL.D.,
Late Professor of Chinese Language and Literature, Yale College.

JOSEPH DAWSON WILSON, D.D.,
Professor of Ecclesiastical History in Reformed Episcopal Seminary, Philadelphia, Pa.

RICHARD PAUL WUELKER, Ph.D.,
Professor of English Philology, University of Leipsic.

OTTO ZOECKLER (†), Ph.D., Th.D.,
Late Professor of Church History and Apologetics, University of Greifswald.

BIBLIOGRAPHICAL APPENDIX—VOLS. I—III

The following list of books is supplementary to the bibliographies given at the end of the articles contained in volumes I.–III., and brings the literature down to January, 1909. In this list each vocabulary entry is printed in capital letters.

ADAM OF BREMEN: W. P. Kohlmann, *Adam von Bremen*, Leipsic, 1908.

ADAMNAN: *An Irish Precursor of Dante. A Study on the Vision of Heaven and Hell ascribed to the 8th-century Saint Adamnan, with Translation of the Irish Text* by C. S. Boswell, London, 1908.

AKED, C. F.: *Old Events and Modern Meanings and Other Sermons*, New York, 1908; *Wells and Palm Trees: cool Water and abundant Rest on Life's rough Way*, ib., 1908.

ALCUIN: G. F. Browne, *Alcuin of York. Lectures delivered in the Cathedral Church of Bristol in 1907 and 1908*, London, 1908.

ALFRED THE GREAT: *Asser's Life of King Alfred*, ed. L. C. Jane, London, 1908.

ALLEN, W.: D. B. Camm, *William Cardinal Allen, Founder of the Seminaries*, London, 1908.

AMOS: J. Touzard, *Le Livre d'Amos*, Paris, 1909.

APHRAATES: P. Schroen, *Aprahat, seine Person und sein Verständnis des Christentums*, Berlin, 1907.

APOLLONIUS OF TYANA: F. W. G. Campbell, *Apollonius of Tyana. A Study of his Life and Times*, London, 1908.

APOLOGETICS: W. Ernst, *Aufgabe und Arbeitsmethode der Apologetik für die Gegenwart*, Berlin, 1908.

ARABIA: M. Hartmann, *Die arabische Frage mit einen Versuche der Archäologie Jemens*, Leipsic, 1909.

ARISTOTLE: *Works*, Eng. transl., vol. viii., *Metaphysics*, London, 1909.

ART AND CHURCH: H. B. Walters, *The Arts of the Church*, Oxford, 1908.

ASSYRIA: R. W. Rogers, *Religion of Babylonia and Assyria*, New York, 1908.

ATONEMENT: J. Stalker, *The Atonement*, London, 1908.

J. Grimal, *Le Sacerdoce et le sacrifice de . . . Jésus-Christ*, Paris, 1908.

AUGUSTINE: H. Becker, *Augustin. Studien zu einer geistigen Entwicklung*, Leipsic, 1908.

W. Thimme, *Augustins geistige Entwickelung . . . 386–391*, Berlin, 1908.

AUSTRIA: J. R. Kusej, *Joseph II. und die äussere Kirchenverfassung Innerösterreichs (Bistums,- Pfarr- und Klosterregulierung). Ein Beitrag zur Geschichte des österreich. Staats kirchenrechtes*, Stuttgart, 1908.

AVILA, JUAN DE: *Letters of Blessed John of Avila, translated and selected from the Spanish by the Benedictines of Stanbrook, with Preface by Gasquet*, London, 1904.

BABYLONIA: See ASSYRIA, ut sup.

BARRY, A.: *Do we Believe? The Law of Faith perfected in Christ*, London, 1908.

BAUR, F. C.: G. Schneider, *F. C. Baur in seiner Bedeutung für die Theologie*, Munich, 1909.

BEHAISM: S. Sprague, *The Story of the Bahai Movement*, London, 1908; *A Year with the Bahais in India and Burma*, ib., 1908.

BIBLE TEXT: *Biblia Hebraica*, ed. R. Kittel, Leipsic, 1906.

A. B. Ehrlich, *Randglossen zur hebräischen Bibel*, vol. i., *Genesis und Exodus*, Leipsic, 1908.

C. R. Gregory, *Die griechischen Handschriften des N. T.*, Leipsic, 1908.

H. C. Vedder, *Our New Testament; how did we get it?* Philadelphia, 1908.

Transcript of the Turin Manuscript of the " Dodekapropheton "; tr. and collated by Rev. W. C. Oesterley, New York, 1908.

BIBLE VERSIONS, B. IV.: *The Gospel of St. John in West Saxon*, Boston, 1904; *The Gospel of St. Matthew in West Saxon*, Boston, 1904; *The Gospel of St. Mark in West Saxon*, 1905; *The Gospel of St. Luke in West Saxon*, Boston, 1906, ed. J. W. Bright. *The West Saxon Psalms, being the Prose Portion, or the " first fifty," of the so-called Paris Psalter*, ed. J. W. Bright, Catherine Donovan, and R. L. Ramsay, Boston, 1907.

The Coptic (Sahidic) Version of Certain Books of the Old Testament from a Papyrus in the British Museum, ed. H. Thompson, New York, 1908.

BIBLICAL INTRODUCTION: C. R. Gregory, *Einleitung in das N. T.*, Leipsic, 1909.

BIBLICAL THEOLOGY: W. E. Orchard, *The Evolution of the Old Testament Religion*, London, 1908.

W. H. Bennett, *Religion of the Post-exilic Prophets*, Edinburgh, 1908.

BONIFACE: An Eng. transl. of the correspondence of Boniface, ed. E. J. Kylie, London, 1908.

BUDDHISM: E. Windisch, *Buddhas Geburt und die Lehre von der Seelenwanderung*, Leipsic, 1908.

CALVIN, J.: P. Bess, *Unsere religiösen Erzieher*, vol. ii., Leipsic, 1908.

R. Schwarz has edited a collection of 670 letters of Calvin in Germ. transl., Tübingen, 1908.

CAMPION, EDMUND: W. Allen, *A Briefe Historie of the Glorious Martyrdom of twelve Reverend Priests. Father Edmund Campion and his Companions; with contemporary Verses by the venerable H. Walpole, and the earliest Engravings of the Martyrdom;* ed. J. H. Pollen, Saint Louis, 1908.

L. J. Guiney, *Blessed Edmond Campion*, London, 1908.

Carmelites: *The Ascent of Mt. Carmel by St. John of the Cross, transl. by D. Lewis, with prefatory Essay on the Development of Mysticism in the Carmelite Order*, by B. Zimmermann, London, 1906.

Catechisms, § 16: *Luther's Small Catechism Developed and Explained, Prepared and Published by Authority of the General Synod of the Evangelical Synod of the Ev. Luth. Church, U. S. A.*, Philadelphia (current).

Cemeteries: E. Calve, *Bibliografia delle catacombe e delle chiese di Roma*, Rome, 1908.

Charity, Sisters of: L. Bougaud, *Hist. of St. Vincent de Paul, . . . and of the Sisters of Charity*, New York, 1908.

Chile: G. F. S. Elliot, *Chile, its Hist. and Development*, London, 1907.

China: D. Mac Gillivray, *A Century of Protestant Missions in China*, London, 1908.
M. Bromhall, *The Chinese Empire, a General and Missionary Survey*, London, 1908.
A. Launay, *Hist. des missions étrangères*, vols. i.—iii., Vannes, 1907–08.
F. L. Norris, *China*, London, 1908.
J. Speicher, *Conquests of the Cross in China*, New York, 1907.
R. W. Thompson, *The Story of Fifty Years in China*, London, 1908.

Christology: S. Faut, *Die Christologie seit Schleiermacher, ihre Geschichte und ihre Begründung*, Tübingen, 1907.

Chrysostom: *Chrysostomika. Studi e ricerche intorno a S. Giovanni Crisostomo a cura del comitato per il XV centenario della sua morte*, Rome, 1908.

Church and State: S. Coit, *National Idealism and a State Church*, London, 1907.
H. von der Goltz, *Kirche und Staat*, Berlin, 1907.

Clement of Alexandria: J. Gabrielson, *Ueber die Quellen des Clemens von Alexandrien*, Leipsic, 1906.

Clement of Rome: C. Schmidt, *Der erste Clemensbrief in altkoptischer Uebersetzung*, Leipsic, 1908 (in *TU*, xxxii. 1.).
G. A. van den Bergh van Eysinga, *Onderzoek naar de echtheid van Clemens erste brief aan de Corinthiërs*, Leyden, 1908.

Clifford, John: D. Crane, *John Clifford, God's Soldier and the People's Tribune*, London, 1908.

Collyer, R.: *Some Memories*, Boston, 1908.

Common Prayer, Book of: S. Coit, *National Idealism and the Book of Common Prayer. An Essay in Re-interpretation and Revision*, London, 1908.

Communism: W. A. Hinds, *American Communities*, 2d ed., Chicago, 1908.

Comparative Religion: F. B. Jevons, *An Introduction to the Study of Comparative Religion*, 2d ed., New York, 1908.
H. Webster, *Primitive Secret Societies. A Study in early Politics and Religion*, London, 1908.
A. van Gennep, *Tabou et totémisme à Madagascar*, Paris, 1904.
R. de la Grasserie, *Des Phénomènes religieux dits mystères (triades ou dédoublements divins; anthroposes ou incarnations; apothysioses ou redemptions par sacrifice, avec leur aboutissement dans le culte)*, Paris, 1908.
E. Doutté, *Magie et religion dans l'Afrique du Nord*, Paris, 1908.
B. Thompson, *The Fijians. A Study of the Decay of Custom*, London, 1908.

Concordances: *A Textual Concordance of the Holy Scriptures; arranged especially for Use in Preaching*, New York, 1908.

Concordats: H. Rudorff, *Zur Erklärung des Wormser Konkordats*, Weimar, 1906.

Confirmation: C. R. Ball, *Confirmation, Before and After*, London, 1909.

Congregationalists: D. Macfadyen, *Constructive Congregational Ideals*, London, 1908.

Conscience: F. Le Dantec, *Science et conscience*, Paris, 1908.

Constantine the Great and His Sons: Joannes M. Pfättisch, *Die Rede Konstantins des Grossen an die Versammlung der Heiligen auf ihre Echtheit untersucht*, Freiburg and St. Louis, 1908. [A defense.]

Conway, Moncure Daniel: E. C. Walker, *A Sketch and an Appreciation of Moncure Daniel Conway, Freethinker and Humanitarian*, New York, 1908.

Copleston, R. S.: *Buddhism, Primitive and Present*, new ed., 1908.

Covenant: F. V. Norton, *A Lexicographical and Historical Study of Διαθήκη*, Chicago, 1908.

Covenanters: J. K. Hewison, *The Covenanters. A History of the Church in Scotland from the Reformation to the Revolution*, Glasgow, 1908.
J. Willcock, *A Scots Earl in Covenanting Times, Being the Life and Times of Archibald, 9th Earl of Argyll (1629–85)*, Edinburgh, 1908.

Cross and its Use as a Symbol: W. M. Clow, *The Cross in Christian Experience*, London, 1908.

Crowther, S. A.: J. Page, *The Black Bishop. Samuel Adjai Crowther*, London, 1908.

Damascus: Ibn al-Qalasani, *Hist. of Damascus*, ed. M. H. F. Amedrog, Leyden, 1908.

David: B. Baentsch, *David und sein Zeitalter*, Leipsic, 1907.

Death, Dance of: K. Künstle, *Die Legende der drei Lebenden und der drei Toten und der Totentanz*, Freiburg, 1908.

Deism: I. W. Riley, *American Philosophy; the early Schools*, pp. 191 sqq., New York, 1907.

Descartes, R.: K. Jungmann, *René Descartes. Eine Einführung in seine Werke*, Leipsic, 1908.

Diaspora: E. W. Bussmann, *Evangelische Diasporakunde. Handbuch für Pfarrer und Freunde deutscher Auslandsgemeinden*, Marburg, 1908.

Didache: A. Seeberg, *Die Beiden Wege und das Aposteldekret*, Leipsic, 1908.

Diseases and the Healing Art, Hebrew: A series of articles by E. M. Merrins, M.D. in *Bibliotheca Sacra*, April, 1904, to October, 1908.

Dogma, Dogmatics: F. Ballard, *Christian Essentials*, New York, 1908.
H. H. Wendt, *System der christlichen Lehre*, Göttingen, 1907.
A. H. Strong, vol. ii., Philadelphia, 1908.
F. J. Hall, *Dogmatic Theology. Vol. ii., Authority, Ecclesiastical and Biblical*, Chicago, 1908.

Donellan (Donnelan) Lectures: 1906–07. H. J. Dukinfield Astley, *Prehistoric Archaeology and the O. T.*, Edinburgh, 1908.

LIST OF ABBREVIATIONS

Abbreviations in common use or self-evident are not included here. For additional information concerning the works listed, see vol. i., pp. viii.-xx., and the appropriate articles in the body of the work.

ADB............ *Allgemeine deutsche Biographie*, Leipsic, 1875 sqq., vol. 53, 1907
Adv............ *adversus*, "against"
AJP............ *American Journal of Philology*, Baltimore, 1880 sqq.
AJT............ *American Journal of Theology*, Chicago, 1897 sqq.
AKR............ *Archiv für katholisches Kirchenrecht*, Innsbruck, 1857-61, Mainz, 1872 sqq.
ALKG............ *Archiv für Litteratur- und Kirchengeschichte des Mittelalters*, Freiburg, 1885 sqq.
Am............ American
AMA............ *Abhandlungen der Münchener Akademie*, Munich, 1763 sqq.
ANF............ *Ante-Nicene Fathers*, American edition by A. Cleveland Coxe, 8 vols. and index, Buffalo, 1887; vol. ix., ed. Allan Menzies, New York, 1897
Apoc............ Apocrypha, apocryphal
Apol............ *Apologia*, *Apology*
Arab............ Arabic
Aram............ Aramaic
art............ article
Art. Schmal............ Schmalkald Articles
ASB............ *Acta sanctorum*, ed. J. Bolland and others, Antwerp, 1643 sqq.
ASM............ *Acta sanctorum ordinis S. Benedicti*, ed. J. Mabillon, 9 vols., Paris, 1668-1701
Assyr............ Assyrian
A. T............. *Altes Testament*, "Old Testament"
Augs. Con............ Augsburg Confession
A. V............ Authorized Version (of the English Bible)
AZ............ *Allgemeine Zeitung*, Augsburg, Tübingen, Stuttgart, and Tübingen, 1798 sqq.
Baldwin, *Dictionary*............ J. M. Baldwin, *Dictionary of Philosophy and Psychology*, 3 vols. in 4, New York, 1901-05
Benzinger, *Archäologie*............ I. Benzinger, *Hebräische Archäologie*, 2d ed., Freiburg, 1907
Bertholdt, *Einleitung*............ L. Bertholdt, *Historisch-Kritische Einleitung . . . des Alten und Neuen Testaments*, 6 vols., Erlangen, 1812-19
BFBS............ British and Foreign Bible Society
Bingham, *Origines*............ J. Bingham, *Origines ecclesiasticæ*, 10 vols., London, 1708-22; new ed., Oxford, 1855
Bouquet, *Recueil*............ M. Bouquet, *Recueil des historiens des Gaules et de la France*, continued by various hands, 23 vols., Paris, 1738-76
Bower, *Popes*............ Archibald Bower, *History of the Popes . . . to 1758, continued by S. H. Cox*, 3 vols., Philadelphia, 1845-47
BQR............ *Baptist Quarterly Review*, Philadelphia, 1867 sqq.
BRG............ See Jaffé
Cant............ Canticles, Song of Solomon
cap............ *caput*, "chapter"
Ceillier, *Auteurs sacrés*............ R. Ceillier, *Histoire des auteurs sacrés et ecclésiastiques*, 16 vols. in 17, Paris, 1858-69
Chron............ *Chronicon*, "Chronicle"
I Chron............ I Chronicles
II Chron............ II Chronicles
CIG............ *Corpus inscriptionum Græcarum*, Berlin, 1825 sqq.
CIL............ *Corpus inscriptionum Latinarum*, Berlin, 1863 sqq.
CIS............ *Corpus inscriptionum Semiticarum*, Paris, 1881 sqq.
cod............ codex
cod. D............ *codex Bezæ*
cod. Theod............ *codex Theodosianus*
Col............ Epistle to the Colossians
col., cols............ column, columns
Conf............ *Confessiones*, "Confessions"
I Cor............ First Epistle to the Corinthians
II Cor............ Second Epistle to the Corinthians
COT............ See Schrader
CQR............ *The Church Quarterly Review*, London, 1875 sqq.
CR............ *Corpus reformatorum*, begun at Halle, 1834, vol. lxxxix., Berlin and Leipsic, 1905 sqq.
Creighton, *Papacy*............ M. Creighton, *A History of the Papacy from the Great Schism to the Sack of Rome*, new ed., 6 vols., New York and London, 1897
CSEL............ *Corpus scriptorum ecclesiasticorum Latinorum*, Vienna, 1867 sqq.
CSHB............ *Corpus scriptorum historiæ Byzantinæ*, 49 vols., Bonn, 1828-78
Currier, *Religious Orders*............ C. W. Currier, *History of Religious Orders*, New York, 1896
D............ Deuteronomist
DACL............ F. Cabrol, *Dictionnaire d'archéologie chrétienne et de liturgie*, Paris, 1903 sqq.
Dan............ Daniel
DB............ J. Hastings, *Dictionary of the Bible*, 4 vols. and extra vol., Edinburgh and New York, 1898-1904
DCA............ W. Smith and S. Cheetham, *Dictionary of Christian Antiquities*, 2 vols., London, 1875-80
DCB............ W. Smith and H. Wace, *Dictionary of Christian Biography*, 4 vols., Boston, 1877-87
DCG............ J. Hastings, J. A. Selbie, and J. C. Lambert, *A Dictionary of Christ and the Gospels*, 2 vols., Edinburgh and New York, 1906-08
Deut............ Deuteronomy
De vir. ill............ *De viris illustribus*
De Wette-Schrader, *Einleitung*............ W. M. L. de Wette, *Lehrbuch der historisch-kritischen Einleitung in die Bibel*, vol. i. *A. T.*, ed. E. Schrader, Berlin, 1869
DGQ............ See Wattenbach
DNB............ L. Stephen and S. Lee, *Dictionary of National Biography*, 63 vols. and supplement 3 vols., London, 1885-1901
Driver, *Introduction*............ S. R. Driver, *Introduction to the Literature of the Old Testament*, 5th ed., New York, 1894
E............ Elohist
EB............ T. K. Cheyne and J. S. Black, *Encyclopædia Biblica*, 4 vols., London and New York, 1899-1903
Eccl............ *Ecclesia*, "Church"; *ecclesiasticus*, "ecclesiastical"
Eccles............ Ecclesiastes
Ecclus............ Ecclesiasticus
ed............ edition; *edidit*, "edited by"
Eph............ Epistle to the Ephesians
Epist............ *Epistola*, *Epistolæ*, "Epistle," "Epistles"
Ersch and Gruber, *Encyklopädie*............ J. S. Ersch and J. G. Gruber, *Allgemeine Encyklopädie der Wissenschaften und Künste*, Leipsic, 1818 sqq.
E.V............ English versions (of the Bible)
Ex............ Exodus
Ezek............ Ezekiel
fasc............ *fasciculus*
Friedrich, *KD*............ J. Friedrich, *Kirchengeschichte Deutschlands*, 2 vols., Bamberg, 1867-69
Fritzsche, *Exegetisches Handbuch*............ O. F. Fritzsche and C. L. W. Grimm, *Kurzgefasstes exegetisches Handbuch zu den Apocryphen des Alten Testaments*, 6 parts, Leipsic, 1851-60
Gal............ Epistle to the Galatians
Gams, *Series episcoporum*............ P. B. Gams, *Series episcoporum ecclesiae Catholicae*, Regensburg, 1873, and supplement, 1886
Gee and Hardy, *Documents*............ H. Gee and W. J. Hardy, *Documents Illustrative of English Church History*, London, 1896
Gen............ Genesis

Germ ... German
GGA ... *Göttingische Gelehrte Anzeigen*, Göttingen, 1824 sqq.
Gibbon, *Decline and Fall* ... E. Gibbon, *History of the Decline and Fall of the Roman Empire*, ed. J. B. Bury, 7 vols., London, 1896–1900
Gk ... Greek, Grecized
Gross, *Sources* ... C. Gross, *The Sources and Literature of English History . . . to 1485*, London, 1900
Hab ... Habakkuk
Haddan and Stubbs, *Councils* ... A. W. Haddan and W. Stubbs, *Councils and Ecclesiastical Documents Relating to Great Britain and Ireland*, 3 vols., Oxford, 1869–78
Har ... Refers to patristic works on heresies or heretics, Tertullian's *De præscriptione*, the *Pros haireseis* of Irenæus, the *Panarion* of Epiphanius, etc.
Hag ... Haggai
Harduin, *Concilia* ... J. Harduin, *Conciliorum collectio regia maxima*, 12 vols., Paris, 1715
Harnack, *Dogma* ... A. Harnack, *History of Dogma . . . from the 3d German edition*, 7 vols., Boston, 1895–1900
Harnack, *Litteratur* ... A. Harnack, *Geschichte der altchristlichen Litteratur bis Eusebius*, 2 vols. in 3, Leipsic, 1893–1904
Hauck, *KD* ... A. Hauck, *Kirchengeschichte Deutschlands*, vol. i., Leipsic, 1904; vol. ii., 1900; vol. iii., 1906; vol. iv., 1903
Hauck-Herzog, *RE* ... *Realencyklopädie für protestantische Theologie und Kirche*, founded by J. J. Herzog, 3d ed. by A. Hauck, Leipsic, 1896–1909
Heb ... Epistle to the Hebrews
Hebr ... Hebrew
Hefele, *Conciliengeschichte* ... C. J. von Hefele, *Conciliengeschichte*, continued by J. Hergenröther, vols. i.–vi., viii.–ix., Freiburg, 1883–93
Heimbucher, *Orden und Kongregationen* ... M. Heimbucher, *Die Orden und Kongregationen der katholischen Kirche*, 2d ed. 3 vols., Paderborn, 1907
Helyot, *Ordres monastiques* ... P. Helyot, *Histoire des ordres monastiques, religieux et militaires*, 8 vols., Paris, 1714–19; new ed., 1839–42
Henderson, *Documents* ... E. F. Henderson, *Select Historical Documents of the Middle Ages*, London, 1892
Hist ... History, *historie*, *historia*
Hist. eccl ... *Historia ecclesiastica*, *ecclesiæ*, "Church History"
Hom ... *Homilia*, *homiliai*, "homily, homilies"
Hos ... Hosea
Isa ... Isaiah
Ital ... Italian
J ... Jahvist (Yahwist)
JA ... *Journal Asiatique*, Paris, 1822 sqq.
Jaffé, *BRG* ... P. Jaffé, *Bibliotheca rerum Germanicarum*, 6 vols., Berlin, 1864–73
Jaffé, *Regesta* ... P. Jaffé, *Regesta pontificum Romanorum . . . ad annum 1198*, Berlin, 1851; 2d ed., Leipsic, 1881–88
JAOS ... *Journal of the American Oriental Society*, New Haven, 1849 sqq.
JBL ... *Journal of Biblical Literature and Exegesis*, first appeared as *Journal of the Society of Biblical Literature and Exegesis*, Middletown, 1882–88, then Boston, 1890 sqq.
JE ... *The Jewish Encyclopedia*, 12 vols., New York, 1901–06
JE ... The combined narrative of the Jahvist (Yahwist) and Elohist
Jer ... Jeremiah
Josephus, *Ant* ... Flavius Josephus, "Antiquities of the Jews"
Josephus, *Apion* ... Flavius Josephus, "Against Apion"
Josephus, *Life* ... Life of Flavius Josephus
Josephus, *War* ... Flavius Josephus, "The Jewish War"
Josh ... Joshua
JPT ... *Jahrbücher für protestantische Theologie*, Leipsic, 1875 sqq.
JQR ... *The Jewish Quarterly Review*, London, 1888 sqq.
JTS ... *Journal of Theological Studies*, London, 1899 sqq.
Julian, *Hymnology* ... J. Julian, *A Dictionary of Hymnology*, revised edition, London, 1907
JWT ... *Jaarboeken voor Wetenschappelijke Theologie*, Utrecht, 1845 sqq.
KAT ... See Schrader
KB ... See Schrader
KD ... See Friedrich, Hauck, Rettberg
KL ... *Wetzer und Welte's Kirchenlexikon*, 2d ed., by J. Hergenröther and F. Kaulen, 12 vols., Freiburg, 1882–1903
Krüger, *History* ... G. Krüger, *History of Early Christian Literature in the First Three Centuries*, New York, 1897
Krumbacher, *Geschichte* ... K. Krumbacher, *Geschichte der byzantinischen Litteratur*, 2d ed., Munich, 1897
Labbe, *Concilia* ... P. Labbe, *Sacrorum conciliorum nova et amplissima collectio*, 31 vols., Florence and Venice, 1759–98
Lam ... Lamentations
Lanigan, *Eccl. Hist* ... J. Lanigan, *Ecclesiastical History of Ireland to the 13th Century*, 4 vols., Dublin, 1829
Lat ... Latin, Latinized
Leg ... *Leges*, *Legum*
Lev ... Leviticus
Lichtenberger, *ESR* ... F. Lichtenberger, *Encyclopédie des sciences religieuses*, 13 vols., Paris, 1877–1882
Lorenz, *DGQ* ... O. Lorenz, *Deutschlands Geschichtsquellen im Mittelalter*, 3d. ed., Berlin, 1887
LXX ... The Septuagint
I Macc ... I Maccabees
II Macc ... II Maccabees
Mai, *Nova collectio* ... A. Mai, *Scriptorum veterum nova collectio*, 10 vols., Rome, 1825–38
Mal ... Malachi
Mann, *Popes* ... R. C. Mann, *Lives of the Popes in the Early Middle Ages*, London, 1902 sqq.
Mansi, *Concilia* ... G. D. Mansi, *Sanctorum conciliorum collectio nova*, 31 vols., Florence and Venice, 1728
Matt ... Matthew
MGH ... *Monumenta Germaniæ historica*, ed. G. H. Pertz and others, Hanover and Berlin, 1826 sqq. The following abbreviations are used for the sections and subsections of this work: *Ant.*, *Antiquitates*, "Antiquities"; *Auct. ant.*, *Auctores antiquissimi*, "Oldest Writers"; *Chron. min.*, *Chronica minora*, "Lesser Chronicles"; *Dip.*, *Diplomata*, "Diplomas, Documents"; *Epist.*, *Epistolæ*, "Letters"; *Gest. pont. Rom.*, *Gesta pontificum Romanorum*, "Deeds of the popes of Rome"; *Leg.*, *Leges*, "Laws"; *Lib. de lite*, *Libelli de lite inter regnum et sacerdotium sæculorum xi et xii conscripti*, "Books concerning the Strife between the Civil and Ecclesiastical Authorities in the Eleventh and Twelfth Centuries"; *Nec.*, *Necrologia Germaniæ*, "Necrology of Germany"; *Poet. Lat. ævi Car.*, *Poetæ Latini ævi Carolini*, "Latin Poets of the Caroline Time"; *Poet. Lat. med. ævi*, *Poetæ Latini medii ævi*, "Latin Poets of the Middle Ages"; *Script.*, *Scriptores*, "Writers"; *Script. rer. Germ.*, *Scriptores rerum Germanicarum*, "Writers on German Subjects"; *Script. rer. Langob.*, *Scriptores rerum Langobardicarum et Italicarum*, "Writers on Lombard and Italian Subjects"; *Script. rer. Merov.*, *Scriptores rerum Merovingicarum*, "Writers on Merovingian Subjects"
Mic ... Micah
Milman, *Latin Christianity* ... H. H. Milman, *History of Latin Christianity, Including that of the Popes to . . . Nicholas V.*, 8 vols., London, 1860–61
Mirbt, *Quellen* ... C. Mirbt, *Quellen zur Geschichte des Papsttums und des römischen Katholicismus*, Tübingen, 1901
Moeller, *Christian Church* ... W. Moeller, *History of the Christian Church*, 3 vols., London, 1892–1900
MPG ... J. P. Migne, *Patrologiæ cursus completus, series Græca*, 162 vols., Paris, 1857–66
MPL ... J. P. Migne, *Patrologiæ cursus completus, series Latina*, 221 vols., Paris, 1844–64
MS., MSS ... Manuscript, Manuscripts
Muratori, *Scriptores* ... L. A. Muratori, *Rerum Italicarum scriptores*, 28 vols., 1723–51
NA ... *Neues Archiv der Gesellschaft für ältere deutsche Geschichtskunde*, Hanover, 1876 sqq.
Nah ... Nahum
n.d ... no date of publication
Neander, *Christian Church* ... A. Neander, *General History of the Christian Religion and Church*, 6 vols. and index, Boston, 1872–81
Neh ... Nehemiah
Niceron, *Mémoires* ... R. P. Niceron, *Mémoires pour servir à l'histoire des hommes illustres . . .*, 43 vols., Paris, 1729–45
NKZ ... *Neue kirchliche Zeitschrift*, Leipsic, 1890 sqq.
Nowack, *Archäologie* ... W. Nowack, *Lehrbuch der hebräischen Archäologie*, 2 vols., Freiburg, 1894
n.p ... no place of publication

NPNF	*The Nicene and Post-Nicene Fathers*, 1st series, 14 vols., New York, 1887–92; 2d series, 14 vols., New York, 1890–1900
N. T.	New Testament, *Novum Testamentum*, *Nouveau Testament*, *Neues Testament*
Num	Numbers
Ob	Obadiah
O. S. B.	*Ordo sancti Benedicti*, "Order of St. Benedict"
O. T.	Old Testament
OTJC	See Smith
P	Priestly document
Pastor, *Popes*	L. Pastor, *The History of the Popes from the Close of the Middle Ages*, 8 vols., London, 1891–1908
PEA	*Patres ecclesiæ Anglicanæ*, ed. J. A. Giles, 34 vols., London, 1838–46
PEF	Palestine Exploration Fund
I Pet	First Epistle of Peter
II Pet	Second Epistle of Peter
Pliny, *Hist. nat.*	Pliny, *Historia naturalis*
Potthast, *Wegweiser*	A. Potthast, *Bibliotheca historica medii ævi. Wegweiser durch die Geschichtswerke*, Berlin, 1896
Prov	Proverbs
Ps	Psalms
PSBA	*Proceedings of the Society of Biblical Archeology*, London, 1880 sqq.
q.v., qq.v.	quod (quæ) vide, "which see"
R	Redactor
Ranke, *Popes*	L. von Ranke, *History of the Popes*, 3 vols., London, 1906
RDM	*Revue des deux mondes*, Paris, 1831 sqq.
RE	See Hauck-Herzog
Reich, *Documents*	E. Reich, *Select Documents Illustrating Mediæval and Modern History*, London, 1905
REJ	*Revue des études Juives*, Paris, 1880 sqq.
Rettberg, *KD*	F. W. Rettberg, *Kirchengeschichte Deutschlands*, 2 vols., Göttingen, 1846–48
Rev	Book of Revelation
RHR	*Revue de l'histoire des religions*, Paris, 1880 sqq.
Richter, *Kirchenrecht*	A. L. Richter, *Lehrbuch des katholischen und evangelischen Kirchenrechts*, 8th ed. by W. Kahl, Leipsic, 1886
Robinson, *Researches*, and *Later Researches*	E. Robinson, *Biblical Researches in Palestine*, Boston, 1841, and *Later Biblical Researches in Palestine*, 3d ed. of the whole, 3 vols., 1867
Robinson, *European History*	J. H. Robinson, *Readings in European History*, 2 vols., Boston, 1904–06
Robinson and Beard, *Modern Europe*	J. H. Robinson and C. A. Beard, *Development of Modern Europe*, 2 vols., Boston, 1907
Rom	Epistle to the Romans
RSE	*Revue des sciences ecclésiastiques*, Arras, 1860–74, Amiens, 1875 sqq.
RTP	*Revue de théologie et de philosophie*, Lausanne, 1873
R. V.	Revised Version (of the English Bible)
sæc.	*sæculum*, "century"
I Sam	I Samuel
II Sam	II Samuel
SBA	*Sitzungsberichte der Berliner Akademie*, Berlin, 1882 sqq.
SBE	F. Max Müller and others, *The Sacred Books of the East*, Oxford, 1879 sqq., vol. xlviii., 1904
SBOT	*Sacred Books of the Old Testament* ("Rainbow Bible"), Leipsic, London, and Baltimore, 1894 sqq.
Schaff, *Christian Church*	P. Schaff, *History of the Christian Church*, vols. i.–iv., vi., vii., New York, 1882–92, vol. v., part 1, by D. S. Schaff, 1907
Schaff, *Creeds*	P. Schaff, *The Creeds of Christendom*, 3 vols. New York, 1877–84
Schrader, *COT*	E. Schrader, *Cuneiform Inscriptions and the Old Testament*, 2 vols., London, 1885–88
Schrader, *KAT*	E. Schrader, *Die Keilinschriften und das Alte Testament*, 2 vols., Berlin, 1902–03
Schrader, *KB*	E. Schrader, *Keilinschriftliche Bibliothek*, 6 vols., Berlin, 1889–1901
Schürer, *Geschichte*	E. Schürer, *Geschichte des jüdischen Volkes im Zeitalter Jesu Christi*, 4th ed., 3 vols., Leipsic, 1902 sqq.; Eng. transl., 6 vols., New York, 1891
Script	*Scriptores*, "writers"
Scrivener, *Introduction*	F. H. A. Scrivener, *Introduction to New Testament Criticism*, 4th ed., London, 1894
Sent	*Sententiæ*, "Sentences"
S. J.	*Societas Jesu*, "Society of Jesus"
SK	*Theologische Studien und Kritiken*, Hamburg, 1826 sqq.
SMA	*Sitzungsberichte der Münchener Akademie*, Munich, 1860 sqq.
Smith, *Kinship*	W. R. Smith, *Kinship and Marriage in Early Arabia*, London, 1903
Smith, *OTJC*	W. R. Smith, *The Old Testament in the Jewish Church*, London, 1892
Smith, *Prophets*	W. R. Smith, *Prophets of Israel . . . to the Eighth Century*, London, 1895
Smith, *Rel. of Sem.*	W. R. Smith, *Religion of the Semites*, London, 1894
S. P. C. K.	Society for the Promotion of Christian Knowledge
S. P. G.	Society for the Propagation of the Gospel in Foreign Parts
sq., sqq.	and following
Strom	*Stromata*, "Miscellanies"
s.v.	sub voce, or sub verbo
Swete, *Introduction*	H. B. Swete, *Introduction to the Old Testament in Greek*, London, 1900
Syr	Syriac
TBS	Trinitarian Bible Society
Thatcher and McNeal, *Source Book*	O. J. Thatcher and E. H. McNeal, *A Source Book for Mediæval History*, New York, 1905
I Thess	First Epistle to the Thessalonians
II Thess	Second Epistle to the Thessalonians
ThT	*Theologische Tijdschrift*, Amsterdam and Leyden, 1867 sqq.
Tillemont, *Mémoires*	L. S. le Nain de Tillemont, *Mémoires . . . ecclésiastiques des six premiers siècles*, 16 vols., Paris, 1693–1712
I Tim	First Epistle to Timothy
II Tim	Second Epistle to Timothy
TJB	*Theologischer Jahresbericht*, Leipsic, 1882–1887, Freiburg, 1888, Brunswick, 1889–1897, Berlin, 1898 sqq.
TLB	*Theologisches Litteraturblatt*, Bonn, 1866 sqq.
TLZ	*Theologische Litteraturzeitung*, Leipsic, 1876 sqq.
Tob	Tobit
TQ	*Theologische Quartalschrift*, Tübingen, 1819 sqq.
TS	J. A. Robinson, *Texts and Studies*, Cambridge, 1891 sqq.
TSBA	*Transactions of the Society of Biblical Archæology*, London, 1872 sqq.
TSK	*Theologische Studien und Kritiken*, Hamburg, 1826 sqq.
TU	*Texte und Untersuchungen zur Geschichte der altchristlichen Litteratur*, ed. O. von Gebhardt and A. Harnack, Leipsic, 1882 sqq.
TZT	*Tübinger Zeitschrift für Theologie*, Tübingen, 1838–40
Ugolini, *Thesaurus*	B. Ugolinus, *Thesaurus antiquitatum sacrarum*, 34 vols., Venice, 1744–69
V. T.	*Vetus Testamentum*, *Vieux Testament*, "Old Testament"
Wattenbach, *DGQ*	W. Wattenbach, *Deutschlands Geschichtsquellen*, 5th ed., 2 vols., Berlin, 1885; 6th ed., 1893–94
Wellhausen, *Heidentum*	J. Wellhausen, *Reste arabischen Heidentums*, Berlin, 1887
Wellhausen, *Prolegomena*	J. Wellhausen, *Prolegomena zur Geschichte Israels*, 6th ed., Berlin, 1905, Eng. transl., Edinburgh, 1885
ZA	*Zeitschrift für Assyriologie*, Leipsic, 1886–88, Berlin, 1889 sqq.
Zahn, *Einleitung*	T. Zahn, *Einleitung in das Neue Testament*, 3d ed., Leipsic, 1907
Zahn, *Kanon*	T. Zahn, *Geschichte des neutestamentlichen Kanons*, 2 vols., Leipsic, 1888–92
ZATW	*Zeitschrift für die alttestamentliche Wissenschaft*, Giessen, 1881 sqq.
ZDAL	*Zeitschrift für deutsches Alterthum und deutsche Literatur*, Berlin, 1876 sqq.
ZDMG	*Zeitschrift der deutschen morgenländischen Gesellschaft*, Leipsic, 1847 sqq.
ZDP	*Zeitschrift für deutsche Philologie*, Halle, 1869 sqq.
ZDPV	*Zeitschrift des deutschen Palästina-Vereins*, Leipsic, 1878 sqq.
Zech	Zechariah
Zeph	Zephaniah
ZHT	*Zeitschrift für die historische Theologie*, published successively at Leipsic, Hamburg, and Gotha, 1832–75
ZKG	*Zeitschrift für Kirchengeschichte*, Gotha, 1876 sqq.
ZKR	*Zeitschrift für Kirchenrecht*, Berlin, Tübingen, Freiburg, 1861 sqq.
ZKT	*Zeitschrift für katholische Theologie*, Innsbruck, 1877 sqq.
ZKW	*Zeitschrift für kirchliche Wissenschaft und kirchliches Leben*, Leipsic, 1880–89
ZNTW	*Zeitschrift für die neutestamentliche Wissenschaft*, Giessen, 1900 sqq.
ZPK	*Zeitschrift für Protestantismus und Kirche*, Erlangen, 1838–76
ZWT	*Zeitschrift für wissenschaftliche Theologie*, Jena, 1858–60, Halle, 1861–67, Leipsic, 1868 sqq.

SYSTEM OF TRANSLITERATION

The following system of transliteration has been used for Hebrew:

א = ' or omitted at the beginning of a word.	ז = z	ע = '
בּ = b	ח = ḥ	פּ = p
ב = bh or b	ט = ṭ	פ = ph or p
גּ = g	י = y	צ = ẓ
ג = gh or g	כּ = k	ק = ḳ
דּ = d	כ = kh or k	ר = r
ד = dh or d	ל = l	שׂ = s
ה = h	מ = m	שׁ = sh
ו = w	נ = n	תּ = t
	ס = s	ת = th or t

The vowels are transcribed by a, e, i, o, u, without attempt to indicate quantity or quality. Arabic and other Semitic languages are transliterated according to the same system as Hebrew. Greek is written with Roman characters, the common equivalents being used.

KEY TO PRONUNCIATION

When the pronunciation is self-evident the titles are not respelled; when by mere division and accentuation it can be shown sufficiently clearly the titles have been divided into syllables, and the accented syllables indicated.

a as in *sofa*	o as in not	iu as in duration
ä " " *arm*	ô " " nor	c = k " " cat
a " " *at*	u " " full[2]	ch " " *church*
â " " *fare*	û " " rule	cw = qu as in *queen*
e " " pen[1]	u " " but	dh (*th*) " " *the*
ê " " *fate*	ū " " burn	f " " *fancy*
i " " *tin*	ai " " pine	g (hard) " " *go*
î " " machine	au " " *out*	H " " *loch* (Scotch)
o " " *obey*	oi " " *oil*	hw (*wh*) " " *why*
ō " " *no*	iû " " *few*	j " " *jaw*

[1] In accented syllables only; in unaccented syllables it approximates the sound of e in over. The letter ṇ, with a dot beneath it, indicates the sound of n as in ink. Nasal n (as in French words) is rendered n.
[2] In German and French names û approximates the sound of u in dune.

THE NEW SCHAFF-HERZOG
ENCYCLOPEDIA OF RELIGIOUS KNOWLEDGE

CHAMIER, shā″myē′, **DANIEL**: French preacher (Reformed); b. at the castle of Le Mont, near Mocas (in the district of Saint-Marcellin, 23 m. w. of Grenoble), 1565; killed at Montauban Oct. 17, 1621. He belonged to an old Roman Catholic family of Avignon, but his father had embraced the Protestant faith and gained many converts in the south of France, especially at Montélimar, where he became pastor. Daniel studied at the University of Orange and at Geneva under Beza and De la Faye (1583–89). He was ordained minister at Montpellier, and about 1595 succeeded his father at Montélimar. His intelligence and the firmness of his character led the provincial synod to appoint him deputy to the national synod at Saumur and the political gathering at Loudun in 1596, and thenceforth he was a frequent delegate to such assemblies. He succeeded in preventing the addition of certain limitations to the Edict of Nantes, and brought the Edict to the Synod of Montpellier in 1598. In 1601 and 1602 he took part in two celebrated discussions at Montpellier with the Jesuits Cotton and Gaultier. In 1603 he presided over the National Synod at Gap, when an article was added to the Reformed confession of faith declaring the pope to be the Antichrist foretold in the Scriptures. In 1607 Henry IV. granted him permission as representative of the Church of Dauphiné to establish an academy at Montpellier, and he became professor, returning, however, after a short time to Montélimar. In 1612 he became pastor and professor at Montauban. When Louis XIII. besieged the city in 1621 Chamier sent his students to the walls, shared himself in all the dangers and misfortunes of the citizens, and was mortally wounded during the defense. In theology he held fast to Calvin's dogma of predestination, even to supralapsarianism; in some other respects he differed from Calvin, e.g., concerning Christ's descent into hell and the doctrine of angels. His works were: *Dispute de la vocation des ministres de l'Église réformée* (La Rochelle, 1589); *Epistolæ jesuiticæ* (Geneva, 1599); *La Confusion des disputes papistes* (1600); *Disputatio scholastico-theologica de œcumenico pontifice* (1601); *La Honte de Babylone* (Sédan, 1612); *La Jésuitomanie* (Montauban, 1618); *Journal du voyage de M. D. Chamier à Paris et à la cour de Henri IV. en 1607* (ed. C. Read, Paris, 1858).

G. Bonet-Maury.

Bibliography: J. Quick, *Memoir of D. Chamier, with Notices of his Descendants*, London, 1852, also in Read's edition of the *Journal*, u.s.

III.—1

CHANCEL: In the narrowest sense the sanctuary of a church, i.e., an enclosure beyond or within the choir containing the altar. As the distinction between clergy and laity developed, it became customary to reserve an ever larger space for the former, and separate it from the body of the church, as by a screen. Their space then came to be designated as the chancel, and the word is often employed in modern usage for all beyond the nave and transepts. See Altar.

CHANCERY, APOSTOLIC (*Cancellaria Apostolica*). See Curia, § 3.

CHANDIEU, shān″dyū′, **ANTOINE DE LA ROCHE**: French Reformed theologian; b. at the castle of Chabot (near Macon) 1534; d. at Geneva Feb. 23, 1591. His trend toward the Reformed was strengthened during his study of law at Toulouse, and after a theological course at Geneva he became the pastor of the Reformed congregation of Paris, 1556–62. When in the night of Sept. 4, 1557, a Protestant meeting was attacked and 140 persons were imprisoned, Chandieu published his *Remonstrance au Roi* and his *Apologie des bons Chrétiens contre les ennemis de l'église catholique*. In consequence, he was arrested, but was soon released at the intervention of Anthony of Navarre. In 1558 he went to Orléans, but soon returned to Paris. He took an active part in the deliberations of the first national synod of the Reformed Church in France which was held at Paris May 26–28, 1559, and assisted in preparing a confession of faith. He presided at the third national synod at Orléans, Apr. 25, 1562, where Morelli's doctrine regarding the general right of voting at ecclesiastical elections was condemned. The controversy nevertheless continued, and Chandieu wrote a rejoinder, *La confirmation de la discipline ecclésiastique observée en églises réformées de France* (Geneva, 1566). At the eighth national synod, held at Nîmes, May 6, 1572, the matter of Morelli, who was seconded by Pierre Ramus, De Rosier, Bergeron, and others, was again taken up and again condemned. After the massacre of St. Bartholomew (1572), Chandieu fled to Switzerland, and lived first at Geneva and afterward at Lausanne and Aubonne, everywhere advocating and defending the cause of his countrymen, many of whom lived in Switzerland. In the religious war of 1585 he was field-chaplain to Henry of Navarre; but in May, 1588, he returned to his family at Geneva, where he died three years later, lamented by the Protestants of Geneva and France and by Beza. Chandieu was a prolific author, writing under the pseudonyms of Zamariel, Theopsaltes, La Croix, and, after 1577, of Sadeel. Among his works special mention may be made of the following: *Meditationes in Psalmum xxxii.* (Geneva, 1578; Eng. transl. by W. Watkinson, London, 1579); *De verbo Dei scripto* (1580); *De vera peccatorum remissione* (1580); *De unico Christi sacerdotio* (Geneva, 1581); *De veritate naturæ humanæ Christi* (1585); *De spirituali manducatione corporis Christi* (1589; Eng. transl., London, 1859); and *De sacramentali manducatione corporis Christi* (Geneva, 1589). A collected edition appeared at Geneva in 1592 under the title *Antonii Sadælis viri nobilissimi opera theologica.* Of great importance was his *Histoire des persécutions et martyrs de l'église de Paris depuis l'an 1557 jusqu'au temps de Charles IX.* (Lyons, 1563), in which he described his residence at Paris (1557–60). He also distinguished himself as a poet, and in 1563 defended his Church in verse against the attacks of the poet Pierre de Ronsard. (Theodor Schott†.)

Bibliography: A. Bernus, *Le Ministre A. de Chandieu*, in *Bulletin de la société de l'histoire du protestantisme français*, xxxvii (1888), 2 sqq.; J. Senebier, *Histoire littéraire de Genève*, i. 322 sqq., Geneva, 1786; E. and É. Haag, *La France protestante*, ed. H. L. Bordier, iii. 1049 sqq., Paris, 1852, Lichtenberger, *ESR*, iii. 33–41, Paris, 1878.

CHANDLER, EDWARD: Church of England bishop; b. in Dublin about 1670; d. in London July 20, 1750. He studied at Emmanuel College, Cambridge (M.A., 1693; D.D., 1701); was consecrated bishop of Lichfield 1717, and in 1730 was translated to Durham. He gained his reputation by his *Defence of Christianity from the Prophecies of the Old Testament* (London, 1725), a reply to *A Discourse on the Grounds and Reasons of the Christian Religion* (1724) by Anthony Collins (q.v.). Collins replied with *The Scheme of Literal Prophecy Considered* (1726), and Chandler then published *A Vindication of the Defence of Christianity from the Prophecies of the Old Testament* (2 vols., 1728). The chief point of their debate was whether or not there was general expectation of the coming of a messiah at the time of the birth of Jesus, Collins denying this and Chandler affirming it. Chandler has been charged with having bought his see, and with dying "shamefully rich."

CHANDLER, SAMUEL: English Presbyterian; b. at Hungerford (26 m. w.s.w. of Reading), Berkshire, 1693; d. in London May 8, 1766. He was educated at Bridgewater and at Gloucester, where he formed lifelong friendships with Bishop Butler and Archbishop Secker. He finished his studies at Leyden; became pastor of the Presbyterian church at Peckham, Surrey (a suburb of London), 1716; assistant at the Old Jewry, London, 1726, and in 1728 pastor. He was a learned and talented man, and is said to have refused offers of preferment in the Established Church. In 1760 he preached a sermon on the death of George II., in which he compared the deceased king to David. This called forth an anonymous pamphlet in which David was described as a bad man, and the comparison objected to as an insult to the late king. Chandler made a brief reply in 1762, and then prepared *A Critical History of the Life of David* (2 vols., London, 1766), which is his best known and most valuable work. His other publications were numerous, and are for the most part controversial, directed against the Deists or the Roman Catholics. Four volumes of sermons were published posthumously (1768). In theology he was a semi-Arian, or, as he expressed it, "a moderate Calvinist."

CHANGE OF CONFESSION: The change from one Christian Church to another. The expression is not equivalent to change of religion, and the subject has practical interest mainly as concerns conversions from Roman Catholicism to Protestantism and vice versa in certain European countries where legal complications are involved.

Where only one confession is recognized by law, there can be no change of confession. Thus there was none before the time of the Reformation; not only was it true that every secession from the Church was considered an offense, but no such thing was recognized either by ecclesiastical or secular law. In Germany rules of procedure in cases of confessional change first began to be formulated after the Evangelical princes and the German Empire ceased to acknowledge the law against heretics by the Religious Peace of Augsburg in 1555, and after the Empire decreed at the Peace of Westphalia in 1648 that under certain conditions Protestants in Roman Catholic territories and Roman Catholics in Protestant territories might be tolerated and possess civil rights. These rules were further developed under the modern principle of toleration, according to which the State recognizes in the Churches only more or less favored associations, and treats them accordingly from the legal point of view.

The Roman Catholic Church, however, still clings to the state of affairs before the Reformation, and still considers itself the only existing Church. According to the Roman view, every one who goes over to Protestantism is a heretic, and every one who changes from Protestantism to the Roman Catholic Church returns from an error of faith to the knowledge of truth or rather to the churchly authority which possesses this truth. The ban is imposed upon every one who leaves the Church; even every born Protestant is under the ban; and every one who goes over to Catholicism is required not only to make the Catholic confession of faith, but also to confess that as Protestant he was a heretic, and to renounce his heresy and ask for absolution.

The Protestant Churches admit the right of change, although a person who makes use of this right is regarded as unfaithful. The declaration of an intention to make a change, regular attendance at the services of another church, or at its communion table, are considered sufficient to sever old connections. Whoever comes over from another Church is not required to abjure his former faith, but simply to make a confession according to the new doctrine, whereupon he is admitted to the Lord's Supper as the *signum communionis.*

It is the task of the State to regulate the existence of different confessions side by side, as well as to protect the liberty of conscience of the individual. Accordingly the legal ordinances concerning change of confession proceed from the State. The law of Prussia forbids the making of proselytes, but this is interpreted to mean that no religious party has the right "to seduce members of another confession by force or cunning to join its own Church," and that "nobody is allowed to disturb the peace of a family or impair its rights under the pretense of religious zeal." In Austria Protestants were, until 1868, forbidden to convert Roman Catholics. The modern State has generally fixed a certain age before which conversion can not take place, in order to exclude disputes as to the capacity of judgment of the convert. The State leaves the conditions of admission to the church organizations, but sometimes regulates the form of withdrawal for the sake of keeping accurate ecclesiastical statistics. The person who leaves has sometimes been required to announce his withdrawal to the pastor, and sometimes a certificate of dismissal is required. The Austrian interconfessional law of May 25, 1868, and the Prussian law of May 14, 1873, require only a declaration before the proper state official, who notifies the Church. (A. HAUCK.)

CHANNING, WILLIAM ELLERY.

Life (§ 1).
His Views as Stated by Himself (§ 2).
His Doctrines, Influence, and Character (§ 3).
Works (§ 4).

William Ellery Channing, the most celebrated and influential Unitarian theologian America has produced, was born at Newport, R. I., Apr. 7, 1780; d. at Bennington, Vt., Oct. 2, 1842. His father was an honored judge and a moderate Calvinist; his mother, a refined and pious woman. Under such influences he early manifested a deeply religious nature, and chose the clerical profession. He traced his conversion to the influence of the funeral of his father, and a religious revival which then swept over New England. After his father's death he passed under the tuition of his uncle at New London, the Rev. Henry Channing, and then went to Harvard College, being graduated in 1798. For two years he acted as private tutor in Richmond, Va., and while there had such mental agony from religious doubts that he was physically enfeebled, and returned to Newport in 1800 "thin and pallid," with a constitution permanently impaired. At home he associated much with the Rev. Dr. Samuel Hopkins—the famous Calvinist, and pupil of Jonathan Edwards—for whose character he felt the deepest reverence. In 1802 he returned to Harvard, where he had been elected regent. The same year he was licensed to preach, and at once distinguished himself by his fire, his unction, and his elegant style. On June 1, 1803, he was ordained and installed pastor of the Congregational Church in Federal Street, Boston, his only pastoral settlement. Here he introduced a new era in preaching, and enlivened the pulpit by themes of Christian philanthropy and social reform. A new edifice was erected in 1809 to accommodate the increased congregations. At the close of his sermons Channing was often physically exhausted. In the earlier period of his ministry he was as indefatigable in pastoral visitation as in his pulpit.

1. Life.

Not long after this time, it became apparent that many of the Congregational churches of New England, especially in Boston and its neighborhood, had, through various influences, become Antitrinitarian and Anti-Calvinistic (see CONGREGATIONALISTS, I., 4, § 8; UNITARIANS). In the separation which followed, Channing allied himself with the so-called "Liberal" party, and became its acknowledged head. In a famous sermon at the installation of Rev. Jared Sparks as pastor of the Unitarian Society in Baltimore in 1819 he gave a clear statement of the points wherein he diverged from the orthodox churches of the time. He is commonly called a Unitarian; but, in his own language, he wished to regard himself as "belonging not to a sect, but to the community of free minds, of lovers of truth, and followers of Christ, both on earth and in heaven. I desire to escape the narrow walls of a particular church" (Sermon at the installation of Rev. M. J. Motte, 1828). This catholicity of spirit secured him the esteem of men of all schools and parties. In a letter of May 8, 1841, he declared: "I have little or no interest in Unitarianism as a sect. I can endure no sectarian bonds. With Dr. Priestley, a good and great man who had much to do in producing the late Unitarian movement, I have less sympathy than with many of the 'Orthodox'" (*Memoir*, ii. 105). In a letter of Aug. 29, 1841, addressed to an Englishman, he expressed the noble sentiment: "As I grow older . . . I distrust sectarian influence more and more. I am more detached from a denomination, and strive to feel more my connection with the Universal Church, with all good and holy men. I am little of a Unitarian, have little sympathy with the system of Priestley and Belsham, and stand aloof from all but those who strive and pray for clearer light, and look for a purer and more effectual manifestation of Christian truth" (*Memoir*, ii. 106). From this confession some have inferred that toward the close of his life he leaned more to orthodoxy; but this is emphatically denied by his nephew and biographer, and by E. S. Gannett, his colleague and successor. In another letter written three months later (Nov., 1841), he says: "I value Unitarianism, not because I regard it as in itself a perfect system, but as freed from many great and pernicious errors of the older systems, as encouraging freedom of thought, as raising us above the despotism of the Church, and as breathing a mild and tolerant spirit into all the members of the Christian body" (*Memoir*, ii. 121).

2. His Views as Stated by Himself.

Channing opposed, on the one hand, the stiff, cold, Puritan orthodoxy of his day, and combated vigorously the traditional views on the Trinity, the atonement, and total depravity; on the other hand, he opposed equally the rationalistic and radical Unitarianism, and sought a middle way. He was averse to creeds and precise doctrinal statements, and laid stress on freedom and individuality in belief and religious experience. He insisted upon

3. His Doctrines, Influence, and Character.

the expression of Christian belief in virtuous action and humanitarian sympathies. He dwelt much upon love as expressing God's purpose in the mission of Christ and as the supreme manifestation of Christian character. He emphasized the human element in Christ and Christianity, which was too much overlooked by Calvinism, and paid one of the most beautiful and eloquent tributes to the perfection of the moral character of Christ. He held up his example as the great ideal to be followed. He found in Christ a perfect manifestation of God to men, and at the same time the ideal of humanity, who spoke with divine authority. He firmly believed in his sinlessness, miracles, and resurrection. He was "always inclined," he wrote as late as Mar. 31, 1832, "to the doctrine of the preexistence of Christ" (*Memoir*, ii. 133). He was, therefore, not a humanitarian, like Priestley, but rather an Arian, as his nephew calls him. His talent and generous cast of mind were averse to controversy, and he paid little attention to metaphysical questions. He preferred to dwell upon "Christ's spirit, his distinguishing moral attributes, the purposes of his mission" (letter of Mar. 31, 1832, *Memoir*, ii. 133), and the problems of practical Christianity. He remained a supernaturalist to the end; and his last utterances on the Gospels and the character of Jesus are among the strongest and noblest. Of the resurrection he said (letter, Nov. 20, 1839, *Memoir*, ii. 145): "The resurrection of Christ, related as it is to his character and religion, and recorded as it is in the Gospels, is a fact which comes to me with a certainty which I find in few ancient histories." In a letter, July 6, 1841, regretting omissions in a recent sermon of Theodore Parker, he wrote: "Without miracles the historical Christ is gone. . . . In regard to miracles I never had the least difficulty. The grand miracle is the perfect divine character of Christ, and to such a being a miraculous mode of manifestation seems natural. It is by no figure of speech that I call Christ miraculous." Channing, however, was not so much a theologian as a preacher and a philanthropist. He was no dreamer, but a practical reformer. He labored for the purification of life and society, and entered heartily into schemes for the abolition of slavery, of intemperance, of prison-abuses, and of war, and for the circulation of the Bible. He had an exalted idea of the nobility of human nature, and an undying faith in freedom and progress.

4. Works.

Channing's works have been published in various forms (complete ed., 6 vols., Boston, 1848; 1 vol., 1875; London, 1880; etc.), and have been widely circulated in English and translations. The best known are *Evidences of Christianity*, addresses delivered at Cambridge, 1821; a treatise on *Slavery*, 1841; discourses on the *Character of Christ;* and critical essays on *Milton*, *Fénelon*, *Bonaparte*, and *Self-culture*. The centenary of his birth was celebrated at Newport on Apr. 7, 1880, and memorial meetings were also held in New York, Brooklyn, Washington, and several cities of New England. The corner-stone of the Channing Memorial Church at Newport (dedicated Oct. 19, 1881) was laid at this time. (P. SCHAFF†) D. S. SCHAFF.

BIBLIOGRAPHY: *Memoir of W. E. Channing, with Extracts from his Correspondence and Manuscripts*, by his nephew, W. H. Channing, 3 vols., Boston, 1848; *Channing, sa vie et ses œuvres*, with preface by C. de Rémusat, Paris, 1857, enlarged ed., 1861; C. A. Bartol, *Principles and Portraits*, Boston, 1880; C. T. Brooks, *William Ellery Channing, a Centennial Memory*, ib. 1880; Elizabeth Palmer Peabody, *Reminiscences of William Ellery Channing*, ib. 1880; *The Channing Centenary*, ed. R. M. Bellows, ib. 1881; W. W. Fenn, *W. E. Channing and the Growth of Spiritual Christianity*, in *Pioneers of Religious Liberty in America*, ib. 1903. Also J. H. Allen, *The Unitarians*, in the *American Church History Series*, New York, 1894; G. W. Cooke, *Unitarianism in America*, Boston, 1902; J. W. Chadwick, *William Ellery Channing, Minister of Religion*, ib. 1903; and other works mentioned under UNITARIANS.

CHANNING, WILLIAM HENRY: Unitarian, nephew of William Ellery Channing; b. in Boston May 25, 1810; d. in London Dec. 23, 1884. He was graduated at Harvard, 1829, and at the Cambridge Divinity School, 1833. He filled many pastorates, most of them of short duration, the longer and more important being at Cincinnati, 1838–41; Rochester, N. Y., 1852–54; Liverpool, England, 1854–61 (Renshaw Street Chapel, 1854–1857; Hope Street Chapel, 1857–61, where he succeeded Dr. James Martineau); Washington, D. C., 1861–65. He returned to England in 1865 and spent the rest of his life there, making several visits, however, to his native land. He was an eloquent speaker, but more successful as a lecturer and occasional preacher than as pastor; an earnest, spiritual, and enthusiastic man, but visionary and impractical. The chief elements of his creed were faith in God, belief in Jesus Christ as the perfect man, and a boundless hope for humanity to be realized through organization and external remedies. Schemes of social reform captivated him, he sympathized with the Brook Farm experiment, and adopted many of the ideas of Fourier. The antislavery struggle in America enlisted his ardent support, and, while pastor in Washington during the Civil War, he labored untiringly for the Union cause and for the relief of the wounded in the field. He was chaplain of Congress, 1863–64. In 1869 he delivered a course of Lowell lectures at Boston on the "Progress of Civilization." He published many sermons, addresses, and articles, and edited several short-lived periodicals; translated Jouffroy's *Introduction to Ethics* (2 vols., Boston, 1841); prepared a *Memoir* of his uncle, William Ellery Channing (3 vols., 1848), and edited a volume of his discourses, *The Perfect Life* (1873); edited the *Memoir and Writings* of his cousin, J. H. Perkins (2 vols., 1851); and, with James Freeman Clarke and R. W. Emerson, edited the *Memoirs* of Margaret Fuller (2 vols., 1852).

BIBLIOGRAPHY: O. B. Frothingham, *Life of William Henry Channing*, Boston, 1886.

CHANTAL, JEANNE FRANÇOISE FREMIOT DE. See VISITATION, ORDER OF THE.

CHANTEPIE DE LA SAUSSAYE, shān″te-pī′ de lā sō″sê′, **PIERRE DANIEL:** Dutch Protestant; b. at Leeuwarden (16 m. e.n.e. of Harlingen) Apr. 9, 1848. He was educated at the University of

Utrecht (D.D., 1871), and after being a pastor of the Reformed Church from 1872 to 1878, was appointed professor of the history of religions at Amsterdam, where he remained until 1899. Since the latter year he has been professor of ethics at Leyden. He is a member of the Royal Academy of Sciences at Amsterdam and several other learned societies, and, in addition to many briefer contributions to periodicals and a number of sermons, has written: *Lehrbuch der Religionsgeschichte* (2 vols., Freiburg, 1887-79, 3d ed., 1905; Eng. transl. of vol. i. by B. S. Colyer-Fergusson, London, 1892); *Zekerheid en Twijfel* (Haarlem, 1893); and *Religion of the Ancient Teutons* (Boston, 1901).

CHANTRY: A chapel or an aisle in a church endowed for the purpose of having masses said for the soul of the founder, or of others nominated by him; also the money left for such purposes. The chantry priest was one employed on such a foundation. There were 1,000 chantries in England when Henry VIII., in 1545, issued his order for their suppression (37 Hen. VIII., cap. 4), on the ground that their possessions were generally misapplied. The death of the king soon ensuing, their suppression was apparently not carried out. At all events, in the first year of Edward VI. (1 Edward VI., cap. 14, 1547) a very long act was passed dissolving the chantries, along with free chapels, hospitals, fraternities, brotherhoods, gilds, and other promotions, and devoting their revenues to charitable and educational purposes. The reason given for such appropriation was the alleged maintenance of superstition and ignorance by these foundations. The text of this article is in Gee and Hardy, *Documents*, pp. 328-357.

CHAPEL: A small building used for divine worship. It may be entirely detached, to supply the needs of people at a distance from the parish church; or form a separate apartment in a large building, such as a convent or a nobleman's house; or run out of and form part of a large church, with an altar of its own. In this last sense some of the largest Gothic churches have small chapels entirely surrounding the east end or choir, the "Lady Chapel," dedicated to the Blessed Virgin, being usually directly behind the high altar (see ARCHITECTURE, ECCLESIASTICAL). In modern English usage the word chapel is commonly applied to non-conformist places of worship, those of the Establishment alone being known as churches; but the term "chapel of ease" is occasionally applied to Established places of worship coming under the meaning first given above, and without parochial boundaries.

CHAPIN, EDWIN HUBBELL: American Universalist; b. at Union Village, Washington County, N. Y., Dec. 29, 1814; d. in New York Dec. 26, 1880. He studied four years at the Bennington (Vermont) Academy, began the study of law, but abandoned it in 1837 to become assistant editor of the *Evangelical Magazine and Gospel Advocate*, a Universalist paper published at Utica, N. Y. He was ordained in 1838. He was pastor at Richmond, Va., 1838-39; at Charlestown, Mass., 1840-45; and assistant to Hosea Ballou in Boston, 1845-48. In 1848 he went to the Fourth Universalist Church, New York, and remained there till death. During his pastorate the society moved from Murray Street to new and more commodious church buildings on Broadway near Spring Street (1852), and then to the corner of Fifth Avenue and Forty-fifth Street (1866), and adopted the name "Church of the Divine Paternity." He was one of the prominent clergymen of New York, and his services were much in demand as lecturer and on special occasions. His sympathies and creed were broad, his preaching was eloquent and popular. He possessed a ready wit and no slight poetical talent; an admirable ordination-hymn, "Father, at this altar bending," is from his pen. His publications, chiefly sermons, include *Discourses on the Lord's Prayer* (Boston, 1850); *Moral Aspects of City Life* (New York, 1853); *Lessons of Faith and Life* (1877); *The Church of the Living God* (1881).

BIBLIOGRAPHY: S. Ellis, *Life of Edwin H. Chapin*, Boston, 1882.

CHAPLAIN: A term which, with its equivalents (Lat. *Capellanus*, Germ. *Kaplan*, Fr. *Desservant*), designates members of the clergy assigned to some kinds of special service. In the Roman Catholic Church a chaplain is a priest who acts as assistant to the pastor of a parish. According to both Tridentine and earlier law, each parish has but one priest in full charge; if it is too large to be properly administered by him alone, he is supposed to appoint a sufficient number of chaplains, with the approval of the bishop.

In the Roman Catholic Church.

These serve directly under him, are maintained by him, and may be dismissed at his pleasure. There are cases, however, in which a beneficed foundation exists within a parish, with chapels or altars at which the incumbent is bound to say a certain number of masses. Such beneficed chaplains (*capellani curati*) are either bound to assist the parish priest, or may be specially directed to do so by the bishop. As beneficed clergy, they can not be removed at the latter's will; but he is not obliged to avail himself of their services, unless certain parochial duties are assigned to them by the terms of their foundation. Such cases occur most frequently in chapels situated at a considerable distance from the parish church, or in hospitals and similar institutions. In case the parish priest fails to appoint chaplains, or does not appoint enough, when directed to do so by the bishop, the latter, in accordance with the law of Devolution (q.v.), may proceed to appoint. In some places, by either written law or custom, the bishop has a general right of appointment on his own motion; and then the chaplains are removable not by the parish priest but by the bishop—unless they have beneficed rights as mentioned above.

In France the chaplains were called *desservants*. The old French law distinguishes between parish churches (*parochiales ecclesiæ*) and subsidiary (*succursales*) chapels which supplement them. The system of the seventeenth century drew a distinction between parish priests who were independent in their functions and chaplains who officiated only by the license of the bishop, revocable at any time. This system struck Napoleon when he was thinking of restoring the Church after the destruction wrought by the Revolution. The Concordat of 1801 laid down only the fundamental principles, especially regarding the bishops, who were permitted to name incumbents approved by the government to the parish churches. The "organic articles" of 1802 went further into detail, and dealt with the support of the churches. As the payment of parish priests was undertaken by the State, it was desirable to limit their number, and provision was made for the establishment of one in each district. But as these districts were far too large to be administered by one priest, as many others as were necessary were to be chosen for *succursales*, and supported by their pensions and the voluntary offerings of the congregations. Their appointment was to be made by the bishop, and revocable at his pleasure. Imperial decrees of May and December, 1804, rearranged the assignments and provided a stipend of five hundred francs apiece. The *desservants* made increasing claims to independence; but the bishops were not inclined to give up their powers, and Gregory XVI. sanctioned the existing arrangement until further order. Repeated controversies arose over the position of these priests, who were by far the larger number in France, Belgium, and the provinces on the left bank of the Rhine; and while still theoretically removable, they succeeded in establishing the rule in practise that they should not be displaced except for cause, after an investigation by diocesan officials.

The French Desservants.

Historically, also, the name chaplain was early applied to priests who served private chapels, in castles and royal palaces. Bishops also had their private chaplains, who served partly as secretaries. The popes, too, have always had their own chaplains, who have as a rule acted as their confessors. By present use these latter are divided into three classes: honorary, ceremonial, and private.

(O. Meier†.)

The clergymen employed in the army and navy of all Christian countries are called "chaplains," and are under different rules and regulations. Thus in the British army they are under a chaplain-general of the forces; are not attached to particular regiments or corps, but to garrisons and military stations at home and abroad. They are according to their length of service divided into four classes, corresponding to colonels, lieutenant-colonels, majors, and captains, respectively; and after twenty-five years' service are entitled to retire on a pension. They are not all from the Church of England or Ireland, but some come from the Presbyterian and Roman Catholic churches. In the United States chaplains are appointed by the president, and assigned or transferred by the secretary of war, but report monthly to the adjutant-general, especially as to the baptism, marriages, and funerals at which they have officiated. During the Civil War there was in the Northern army a chaplain to each regiment, but at its conclusion all were discharged. Later, thirty were engaged and sent to posts, generally on the frontier. To-day there are no regimental chaplains, but only chaplains attached to posts. Much depends upon the post commander whether the chaplain can be efficient or not. In 1907, Major-General Frederick D. Grant reports, there were fifty-three chaplains in the whole army, from different denominations and ranked as follows: Majors 4, Captains 41, First Lieutenants 8. He adds: "In general their duties are to have charge of religious instruction, visit the sick, baptize children, officiate at marriages and funerals, and by statute they have charge of post schools in the English branches." The number of chaplains in the United States navy on July 1st, 1907, was twenty-five, with rank as follows. Captains 4, Commanders 7, Lieutenant-Commanders 5, Lieutenants (junior grade) 2. Their duties are thus set forth in the regulations of 1905, communicated by the commandant of the New York Navy Yard. (1) The chaplain shall perform divine service and offer prayers on board of the ship to which he is attached, at such times as the captain may prescribe; and on board other ships to which chaplains are not attached, or at shore stations and naval hospitals, when so directed by the senior officer present. (2) He shall be permitted to conduct public worship according to the manner and forms of the church of which he is a minister. (3) He shall facilitate, so far as possible, the performance of divine service by clergymen of churches other than his own, who may be permitted by the captain to visit the ship for that purpose. (4) He may, with the sanction of the captain, form voluntary classes for religious instruction. (5) He shall visit the sick frequently, unless the condition of the sick renders such visits unadvisable. (6) Under the direction of the captain, he shall supervise the instruction of such persons in the navy as may need to be taught the elementary principles of reading, writing, arithmetic, and geography. He shall report in writing to the captain at the end of each quarter the character of instruction given, the number of hours of instruction, and the progress made by each person. He shall always report at quarters when on board. His duty in battle is to aid the wounded, and his station at quarters for battle and for inspection shall be as the captain may direct. Chaplains shall report annually to the secretary of the navy the official services performed by them. The pay of these army and navy chaplains varies according to their length of service and rank, and in navy according to whether they are at sea or on shore. In the French army and navy attendance upon the chaplains' services is voluntary, but in all other European countries it is compulsory. In the United States navy the penalty of disturbing a church service is three months' imprisonment.

In Military and Naval Service.

Chaplains are also attached to militia regiments in the United States. They are chosen by the regiments, generally on the strength of their outside reputation, so that it is a distinct compliment and recognition of ability and popularity to be asked. They preach an occasional sermon, and clad in a distinctive uniform appear on the parades of their regiments.

Chaplains are attached to parliamentary bodies and to state and national societies. Their duties in congress, the state legislatures, and the British parliament are mainly connected with the religious service at the beginning of each day's session. In the case of societies they preach before the body once a year and say grace at the annual banquet. Prisons, almshouses, asylums, and similar institutions also have chaplains, who commonly live in the building and conduct regular services. Where a chaplain is a man of the right stamp, he is of the utmost help to the officers, as he can do much to promote good feeling between them and the subordinates, beneficiaries, or inmates, as the case may be, for he is by education and manner of life the equal of the chief, and by profession and intercourse the friend of all the rest. It is good policy in a government or institution to make this branch of service attractive to the clerical profession, and to maintain it by strict discipline.

Bibliography: L. Ferraris, *Prompta bibliotheca canonica*, s.v "capellanus." Venice, 1782-94; Z. B. van Espen, *Jus ecclesiasticum universum*, part 2, tit. 3, chap. 2, Louvain, 1700; D. Bouix, *Tractatus de Parocho*, pp. 426 sqq., 444 sqq., 645 sqq., Paris, 1856; A. L. Richter, *Lehrbuch des . . . Kirchenrechts*, ed. W. Kahl, p. 468, Leipsic, 1886; E. Friedberg, *Lehrbuch des Kirchenrechts*, pp. 175 sqq., ib. 1895

CHAPMAN, (J) WILBUR: Presbyterian; b. at Richmond, Ind., June 17, 1859. He was educated at Lake Forest University (B.A., 1879) and Lane Theological Seminary (1882), and was pastor of the First Reformed Church, Albany, N. Y., from 1883 to 1888. He was pastor of Bethany Presbyterian Church, Philadelphia, in 1888-93, and then engaged in evangelistic work until 1899, when he became pastor of the Fourth Presbyterian Church, New York City, where he remained until 1903. In the latter year he was chosen executive secretary of the General Assembly's Committee on Evangelistic Work for the Presbyterian Church. His works include: *Ivory Palaces of the King* (Chicago, 1893); *Received Ye the Holy Ghost?* (1894); "*And Peter*" (1895); *Present-Day Parables* (Cleveland, O., 1900); *Revivals and Missions* (New York, 1900); *Present-Day Evangelism* (1903); *Fishing for Men* (Chicago, 1904); and *Samuel Hopkins Hadley of Water Street* (New York, 1906); *Another Mile* (1908).

CHAPTER.

A chapter is an ecclesiastical corporation of a collegiate nature, whose principal function is to provide for public worship in the cathedral or other church to which it is attached. The origin of chapters may be traced back to the early period when the bishop had for a council or senate his *presbyterium*, i.e., the total number of the priests and deacons belonging to his own particular church. The further development has been largely influenced since the fourth century by the extension of monastic institutions in some degree to the secular clergy. Eusebius of Vercelli and Augustine established a community life for their clergy under one roof, and at Hippo there was even a monastic vow of poverty. These examples were imitated in Africa, Spain, and Gaul; in the last-named the expression *mensa canonica* was used as early as Gregory of Tours. The phrase is explained by the fact that all the clergy of a church were inscribed in a special list (*matricula* or *canon*), from which regularly appointed clergy were known as *canonici*. This use of the term occurs in the canons of the Synod of Laodicea (c. 360), and in the sixth century was general in the Frankish kingdom. The *mensa canonica*, accordingly, was the common table of the clergy of a particular church, and the *vita canonica* their life in common. There was originally no reference in the term to any rule of life, as some have thought from another use of the word *canon*. By the middle of the eighth century, this community life for the clergy had become very general throughout the Frankish kingdom, usually following the regulations laid down by Chrodegang of Metz for his clergy. At the Synod of Aachen in 816 Louis the Pious caused a new code of rules to be drawn up, based on Chrodegang's, as that had been on the Benedictine rule, and relating to churches other than cathedrals which had several clergy, later known as collegiate churches. According to both rules, the clergy lived with the bishop or other superior in a prescribed house (*claustrum*), and were required to recite together the canonical hours and to render obedience to their head. In this capacity, besides the bishop, the archdeacon appears in Chrodegang's rule, the provost in that of Aachen. The organization differed from the monastic system in being conditioned by differences of clerical rank and by the permission of private property. In the ninth and early tenth centuries, this became the approved form of clerical life in cathedrals and other larger churches, and the name chapter was applied to the organization. In the rule of Chrodegang *capitulum* designated originally the chapter to be read at the daily gatherings of the clergy, then the place in which the reading occurred, then the gathering, and finally the community as a whole.

1. Origin and Development of the Common Life.

As a result of the gradual redistribution of the revenues which had originally served for the maintenance of the community life, and the permission of separate residences (*mansiones*) for individual clergy, the *vita canonica* decayed during the eleventh century in many churches where it had formerly obtained. There were, however, numerous efforts directed to its restoration, in the spirit of the new ascetic movement and on the theory that the possession of private property had caused the decay. Supported by men like Hildebrand, Peter Damian, and Gerhoh of Reichersberg, and favored by the popes, these efforts were decidedly successful, and led to an enforcement of the common life by the Lateran Council of 1059 under Nicholas II., which extended the community principle to property. In the later

2. In the Eleventh and Twelfth Centuries.

eleventh and the twelfth centuries the former secular canons were in many localities replaced by regular canons, living under a stricter rule, especially that known as of Saint Augustine, though it is not his composition, but a collection of excerpts from mainly pseudo-Augustinian sermons. These Augustinian canons, in their turn, were not seldom replaced from the twelfth century on by Premonstratensians. But the ascetic tendency was not strong or enduring enough to reform all the chapters. The independence given by the possession of property prevented their reconstruction on the original model; and the worldliness of the higher clergy made such regulation oppressive, so that the institution once more fell into decay in the thirteenth century.

The functions of the *presbyterium* as the bishop's council were assumed, during the period of the prevalence of the *vita canonica*, not by the whole body of the clergy living in community, but by those of the higher orders; and, on the other hand, room was found for the cooperation (in important matters affecting the diocese) of the clergy of the other churches in the see city besides the cathedral, and for representatives of the lay population of the city. The actual current administration was indeed conducted by the cathedral chapter; but when the distribution of revenues above alluded to made a division between the interests of the bishop and those of the chapter, the former was very apt to neglect to consult the latter, or to rely, for support in his measures, on the other clergy and prominent laity. The Decretals of Gregory IX. enforced the right of the chapter to a consultative voice; and it was finally established as common law that the chapter was the only body with an independent right to advise the bishop in the conduct of diocesan affairs. From the beginning of the thirteenth century the chapters succeeded in excluding the other clergy and the lay nobility from any voice in the election of bishops.

3. Canons.

A full or capitular canon was one who had a vote in the chapter, a stall in the choir, and commonly, though not necessarily, a prebend, i.e., a fixed income derived either from a share of the community revenues or from certain specially assigned property, tithes, etc. In contrast with the full rights of the *canonici seniores*, who were in major orders, was the position of the *juniores*—clerks in minor orders or youths receiving education in the capitular school, who had no voice in the chapter. The number of both classes was limited only by the amount of the community property. Later, especially in Germany from the thirteenth century, the number of canonries and prebends was limited in many chapters, at first for various economic reasons and then for the purpose of assuring a richer livelihood to their members. The custom still, however, prevailed of receiving youths to be trained for canonries. A special fund was set aside for their support, and they were bound on their side to the *vita communis*. They were known as *juniores canonici non capitulares, domicelli, domicellares*. In chapters with fixed numbers *canonici supranumerarii* were those waiting for a prebend to be vacated The Lateran Council of 1179 had indeed forbidden the conferring of Expectancies (q.v.); but under the lax papal interpretation of the application of this prohibition to capitular positions, and the definite concession of four expectancies to each chapter by Alexander IV. (1254), the practise continued, and admission among the *domicellares* was regularly the title to a full canonry in order of seniority.

Qualifications for admission had long been fixed by the chapters themselves before the common law took cognizance of the question. The Clementina required the possession of holy orders, and the Council of Trent decreed that half the canonries should be given to doctors, masters, or licentiates in theology or canon law, and that in cathedral chapters half should be held by priests. The older statutes of the chapters themselves required (besides the possession of a "title") that the candidate should have received at least the tonsure, and be free from notable bodily defects, and of unblemished honor, of legitimate, and sometimes of noble, birth; fourteen years commonly, sometimes less, was the minimum of age. While all canons were theoretically equal, there were offices among them to which special functions were attached. Such were the *præbendæ doctorales* for those holding doctor's degrees, others destined to provide support for university professors, *præbendæ parochiales* connected with a parochial cure, *præbendæ presbyterales* for those in priest's orders who performed the requisite sacerdotal functions when the majority of the canons were deacons or subdeacons, *præbendæ exemptæ* or *liberæ* to which the obligation of residence was not attached, and *præbendæ regiæ*, either those to which sovereigns had the right of presentation from having founded them, or which were held by the sovereigns themselves as honorary canons. Besides the canons, who were frequently hindered by political position or disinclination from performing their spiritual functions, there were often a number of *vicarii, mansionarii*, or *capellani*, who had charge of the services and represented the canons in them.

4. Modern Organization.

The organization of chapters in modern times is usually a simpler one, especially owing to their loss of political importance in modern states. They usually consist of a number of *capitulares* or *numerarii*, who enter upon their rights as soon as they are nominated; the *canonici exspectantes, juniores*, and *domicellares* have almost ceased to exist. The requirements are: priestly or (in some cases) any major orders; the age of thirty in some places, in others that requisite for the subdiaconate or twenty-two, unless they must be priests, when it would be twenty-four; practical experience in ecclesiastical service or in an educational position, or at least a notable degree of learning; and in some cases native birth, either within the country or the diocese. Besides the full canons, there are in some countries honorary canons; in Austria and France deserving clerics who hold merely an honorary title without effective membership in the chapter, while in Prussia, although the obligation of residence is not imposed, they have a sort of membership, extending at least as far as participation in episcopal elections. The office of vicar still exists; but in the modern chapter its holders are assistants rather than, as formerly, representatives of the canons.

5. Officers. As to the officers of the chapter, after the redistribution of revenues to which allusion has been made and the acquisition of property, the provost generally retained only the right of presiding over the chapter and administering its property. The enforcement of discipline and the conduct of public worship was usually in charge of the dean, who had a certain disciplinary power, to be exercised with the counsel and assent of the chapter; in the Middle Ages his functions were frequently combined with those of the archpriest. Other officials were the *primicerius*, *cantor*, or *præcentor*, in charge of the services and music; the *scholasticus*, in charge of the chapter school, and often of other schools in the see city or the diocese; the *sacrista* or *thesaurarius*, in charge of the sacred vessels, vestments, and other things used in divine worship; the *cellerarius*, who in the days of the *vita communis* provided for the housekeeping, and the *portarius*, who in the same period regulated the intercourse of the members of the chapter with the outside world. In the nineteenth-century reorganization of capitular life this whole system of official administration has been much simplified in some countries, especially in Germany, while others, such as Italy and Spain, retain more of the medieval arrangements. In accordance with the provisions of the Council of Trent, a theologian and a penitentiary are appointed for each chapter.

In the early period of the *vita communis* the decision as to the reception of new members into the community rested with its head, either bishop or provost, though the *seniores* sometimes had a consultative voice. After the dissolution of the common life, the chapter had the right in some cases to confirm or reject a nomination made by the bishop, and in others to nominate independently to certain canonries, while others, again, especially those founded by a bishop, were wholly in his gift. Further modifications were introduced by the papal claim of reservation, and by the patronal rights of founders. The emperors from the thirteenth century, and later other sovereigns and secular and ecclesiastical princes in their own countries, claimed the *jus primariarum precum*, the right to appoint one person to each chapter after their coronation or consecration. Opposed to this diversity is the principle of the present common law that cathedral canonries are in the joint gift of the bishop and the chapter, while in collegiate churches they are filled by the chapter with subsequent institution at the hands of the bishop.

The chapter is now, since the dissolution of the *vita communis* and the distribution of what was originally common property, a corporation with a separate legal existence of its own apart from the bishop, competent to deal with both ecclesiastical matters and matters of property, and to ordain and manage its own internal affairs independently, as by altering its former statutes and making new ones. By common law the consent of the bishop is not necessary for this, though it is by special provision in some of the newer reorganized systems.

6. Legal Provisions and Duties. The duties of the chapter as a whole include the daily performance of divine service, both mass and choir offices. Cathedral chapters have the further duty of assisting the bishop in pontifical functions and in the administration of the diocese. The right corresponding to the last-named duty finds expression in various ways. The bishop is required to have the assent of the chapter for any alienation of the property of the cathedral or diocesan institutions, for any notable change in the system of benefices, for the appointment of a coadjutor, for any measures which are prejudicial to the rights or privileges of the chapter, and for the introduction into the diocese of a new feast of obligation. He is further required to seek their counsel in the appointment or deposition of ecclesiastical dignitaries, in the granting of dispensations or confirmations, in matters which touch the interests of the chapter, in the more important questions of diocesan administration, etc. For the rights of the chapter during the vacancy of a see or the incapacity of a bishop, see SEDES VACANS. According to the Roman Catholic theory, cathedral chapters are not essential and fundamental parts of the constitution of the Church, but the product of historic development. Accordingly, church law leaves a great deal to local usage in regard to the part to be played by them in the administration of a diocese; and they are lacking entirely in many dioceses, as in the "missionary" districts of North America, while in others (as in England, Ireland, and Canada) their organization is very loose.

Little need be said here about the survival of chapters in the Protestant churches. For the English system, see ENGLAND, CHURCH OF, III., § 3. A few scattered chapters, of either cathedral or collegiate type, still exist in evangelical Germany, such as those of Brandenburg, Naumburg, Merseburg, and Zeitz in Prussia, and Meissen and Wurzen in Saxony.

7. In Protestant Churches. After the Reformation the chapters which came over to the new doctrine with their bishops were usually dissolved; but a few of them succeeded in maintaining their existence in spite of the local sovereign, especially those which did not become wholly Protestant and went on as "mixed chapters" (Osnabrück, Halberstadt, Minden), with a system of alternation as to the bishopric between the two religions, lasting even through the Peace of Westphalia. The connection of the others with the bishops who had become Protestants did not last long, and most of them were sooner or later incorporated with the territories of the sovereigns who had at first been their administrators; and only those named above survived the general secularization of 1803. Even these, however, are not properly church bodies, but corporations for the preservation and administration of certain property and revenues; and steps have been taken toward the abolition of the Prussian chapters. (A. HAUCK.)

BIBLIOGRAPHY: D. Bouix, *De capitulis*, Paris, 1852; P. Schneider, *Die bischöflichen Domkapitel*, Mains, 1855; idem, *Die Entwickelung der bischöflichen Domkapitel bis zum vierzehnten Jahrhunderte*, Würzburg, 1882; G. A. Huller, *Die juristische Persönlichkeiten der Domkapitel in Deutschland*, Bamberg, 1860; G. Finazzi, *Dei capituli cathedrali*, Lucca, 1863; P. Hinschius, *Kirchenrecht der Katholiken und Protestanten*, ii. 49–161, Berlin, 1871; A. L. Richter, *Lehrbuch des katholischen und evangelischen Kirchenrechts*, 8th ed. by W. Kahl, pp. 440 sqq., 528, Leipsic, 1877–86; W. F. Hook, *Church Dictionary*, s.vv. *Chapter* and *Dean*, London, 1887; E. Hatch, *Growth of Church Institutions*, ib. 1887; idem, *Organization of Early Christian Churches*, ib. 1888; E. Friedberg, *Lehrbuch des katholischen und protestantischen Kirchenrechts*, p. 164, Leipsic, 1895; H. D. M. Spence, *The White Robe of Churches*, London, 1900; H. Schaefer, *Pfarrkirche und Stift*, Stuttgart, 1903; A. Werminghoff, *Kirchenverfassung Deutschlands im Mittelalter*, Hanover, 1905.

CHAPTER AND VERSE DIVISION IN THE BIBLE. See BIBLE TEXT, III.

CHAPTER-COURTS (*Chorgerichte*): The name applied, in the canton of Bern after the Reformation, to the tribunals having charge of matrimonial causes and the execution of church discipline. As early as 1470, the town council of Bern had seriously attempted to take in hand the moral condition of the inhabitants, neglected by the Church. In the same spirit, the Reformation here was rather one of practise than of doctrine. Thus, after the issue of the first reforming decree, it was naturally one of the concerns of the Bernese authorities to replace the suppressed episcopal courts by a new tribunal which should represent the civil government but regard questions coming before it from a religious standpoint. On May 29, 1528, the new court began its work. It was composed of six members—two from the greater and two from the lesser council, with two preachers. It met in the building belonging to the old chapter, whence it probably took its name. In September it set forth principles to govern matrimonial causes, and in November the other matters coming under its jurisdiction. These were offenses against the law of God which could not be punished as violations of express civil statutes—such things as drunkenness, incontinence, usury, atheism, superstition, witchcraft, blasphemy, and gambling, which latter was strictly forbidden as unworthy of Christian people. An appeal had been intended to lie to the council, but this was abrogated in Jan., 1529. In March of this year the first formal regulations were put forth, evidently based on those adopted at Zurich in 1525. The punishments prescribed consisted of deprivation of honors and offices, imprisonment, banishment—not often money fines, which became more usual later. The strictness of the judges caused no little murmuring at first, and the "Great Synod" of Jan., 1532, was obliged to promise that greater mildness should be shown. The attendance of the preachers was even for a time partially dispensed with, but in 1536 they were recalled, since so many questions came up in which their judgment, as expositors of God's word, was needed. In the same year Bern conquered Vaud and the other Savoyard lands to the southwest, and proceeded to introduce the Reformation on its own principles. The ministers of Vaud, especially Viret and Beza, wished to set up a system of strict church discipline on the Geneva model; but this did not agree with the Bernese view of the unity of the State, including the Church within itself, so that ultimately chapter-courts were set up in each church district of the conquered territory. The ministers, under Calvin's influence, stood out obstinately for strictly ecclesiastical discipline, with excommunication for its principal weapon. Things finally came to an open breach, and the banishment of a number of the clergy. All this attracted greater attention to the system of chapter-courts; and greater severity than ever was shown against wanton dress, fortune-telling, gambling, and immoral dances and songs. The rules of the chapter-courts were enforced in the old local tribunals, which were gradually abolished (1561) in the interest of administrative unity; the same thing happened (1566) in certain cities, such as Brugg and Zofingen, where the magistrates had for a time dealt with matrimonial causes and general morality.

Viret and his friends had, however, been right in a way. The chapter-courts were, after all, of the nature of civil government and police. As such, they had done a good deal for external morality and order; but they could do little for the promotion of vital piety; their connection with the Church was loose and external. The duty of examining and licensing candidates for church offices, which had been originally given to them, fell to another body very soon; the clergy managed their own discipline in their own assemblies; and in the end the chapter-courts had nothing but questions of marriage and paternity and an external *police des mœurs*. After 1704 appeals were granted to the town council or the Two Hundred; and in 1708 the number was changed to eight secular judges with two clerical assessors. They had now a formal code of their own, with purely secular penalties, which was revised or enlarged at need. They continued to exist (except in the period of the Helvetic Republic, 1798–1803) until the revision of the constitution in 1831. By the law of 1874 most of the duties of the chapter-courts were given to the "church-councils," which now regulate questions of morality in so far as the modern State permits. (E. BLÖSCH†.)

BIBLIOGRAPHY: C. B. Hundeshagen, *Die Konflikte in der Bern. Landeskirche*, in C. Trechsel, *Beiträge*, Bern, 1841–1842; Frickert, *Die Kirchengebräuche in Bern*, Aarau, 1846; Von Stürler, in *Archiv des historischen Vereins von Bern*, 1862; E. Egli, *Actensammlung zur Geschichte der Zürcher Reformation*, Zurich, 1879.

CHARACTER: The composite of definite moral and personal traits which serves to distinguish an individual and to mark the type to which he belongs. Morality is essentially a matter of will, and thus of free agency. The will is, therefore, closely associated with character; but it exists, in the true sense of the word, only in so far as it is free and accepts the new modification voluntarily, instead of possessing it by nature, or being constrained to it by external influences. The criterion of character, in Kantian phrase, is "not what nature makes of man, but what man makes of himself." Character must, therefore, differ essentially from the original disposition of man. The different forces and impulses of the mental life form the basis, means, and material for will and character, but in themselves they are only anteethical. They may, furthermore, be devoted either to lofty or to low ethical ends. Such a naturalistic basis can not be allowed to condition the principle of decision for or against the will of God, nor can it be permitted to control the moral demand and aims. In terms of Christian ethics the fundamental requirements for a noble character are that, as divine revelation demands and renders possible, it should obtain a heart established with grace through faith (Heb. xiii. 9), that it be strengthened with might by the Spirit and become rooted and grounded in self-denying love (Eph. iii. 16 sqq.), that it come unto a perfect man, unto the measure of the stature of the fulness of Christ (Eph. iv. 13; I Cor. xvi. 13), and that it be ready to perform faithfully every duty which its special ability and position in the world requires. The natural dispositions, however, retain their importance for the weal or wo of character, and influences of the temperament may facilitate or aggravate the change for good or bad. On this account the will must influence nature lest it should destroy the formation of character and check the fulfilment of certain individual duties, so that the natural man must accordingly become subject to righteous will. Even where it is impossible to overcome certain natural dispositions, character must at least oppose them, and assert its authority by discipline. On the other hand, the natural elements of psychic life should be allowed a certain influence on the will, in case their tendency is good. Additional influences and factors arise from external conditions and social positions, so that character may be defined, with Scharling, "as the impress of the will on the basis of natural individuality." Thus arises an endless variety and diversity of characters, owing partly to moral and immoral free will, partly to varying temperaments, and partly to the manifold relations between the will, natural disposition, and personal experience. True ethical goodness of the character, however, always lies in that will which resigns itself to the moral principles, subjects the natural man to them, and at the same time endeavors to become fit for the tasks assigned to it individually, ever striving to become better adapted to its endowment and position. Christian ethics must naturally be directed from the very first toward developing and strengthening the character. Success here implies not only a mature discretion and insight into the basal principles of morality, but also a thorough understanding of one's own temperament and of mankind and the world.

(J. Köstlin†.)

CHARIOT. See War.

CHARISMATA, cā-ris'mā-tā: The term used by theologians to designate the remarkable signs of the divine favor and power which accompanied the work of the primitive Church, beginning with the gift of tongues on the day of Pentecost. The belief in such signs exists to-day among large numbers of Protestants as well as in the Roman Catholic Church, with the difference that the latter sees in the miracles of the saints the continuation of these miraculous powers, while on the evangelical side they are supposed to have ceased at the latest with the first three centuries, either through the fault of the Church or by God's design. The question of the continuance of the charismata is in many modern treatises connected with that of the continuance of miracles, the writers regarding the gift of supernatural power to effect supernatural operations as a fulfilment of Mark xvi. 17, 18. Baur, on the other hand, saw in the charismata only the gifts and dispositions which the individual converts brought to Christianity, transformed by the working of the Spirit into the various forms of Christian consciousness and life. This view, which excludes any giving of power to work miracles, as well as any new divine gift or divine reenforcement of natural gifts, is demonstrably not (as Baur claims) Pauline, but can not here be controverted at length. The word *charisma* itself does not tell anything as to the nature of the gifts. Except in one passage of Philo and in I Pet. iv. 10, it is only found in Paul's use of it, though probably not formed by him. In most of the places where he employs it, it denotes an extraordinary evidence of God's favor; in II Cor. i. 11, his own deliverance from death; in Rom. i. 11 a gift of the Holy Spirit, such as comfort or illumination. In other places it refers to special gifts bestowed upon the Christian (I Tim. iv. 14; II Tim. i. 6) as signs and tokens of the grace received by belief in the message of redemption (I Cor. i. 6, 7), which render him capable of a particular kind of action, in order to render some special service to the whole body (I Cor. xii. 4 sqq.). The place, therefore, that each member has in the community he has by virtue of a *charisma*, which he is to administer to his brethren (I Pet. iv. 10). Natural powers as such are useless to the life of the body of Christ; what it needs must, like itself, be spiritual. Charismata, then, may be defined as powers and capacities necessary for the edification of the Church, bestowed by the Holy Spirit upon its members, in virtue of which they are enabled to employ their natural faculties in the service of the Church, or are endowed with new abilities for this purpose. According to I Cor. xii. 16; Rom. xii. 5–8; Eph. iv. 11, the charismata form the basis of the offices in the Church. There can be no office without a charisma; but not all charismata are applicable to the exercise of an office. Those which correspond to permanent and invariable needs of the Church form the basis of offices, the others do not. To the latter class belong those of a miraculous or extraordinary character, like those which are peculiar to the apostles or to the apostolic period. Since the number of the charismata must correspond to the needs of the Church, it follows that the lists in I Cor. xii., Eph. iv., and Rom. xii. can not be taken as exhaustive.

(H. Cremer†.)

Bibliography: W. J. Conybeare and J. S. Howson, *Life and Epistles of St. Paul*, chap. xiii., New York, 1869; Schaff, *Christian Church*, i. 230–242, 430–444 (reviews the opinions); Neander, *Christian Church*, i. 180–188 et passim; M. Lauterburg, *Der Begriff des Charisma*, in A. Schlatter and H. Cremer, *Beiträge zur Forderung christlicher Theo-*

logie, Gütersloh, 1898; *KL*, iii. 82-89; *DCA*, i. 349-350; commentaries on Acts, Romans, Corinthians, and Ephesians.

CHARITY, BROTHERS OF (*Fratres caritatis*): A name common to several benevolent orders of the Western Church during the Middle Ages. It is applied especially to the society founded about 1280 by a landowner Guido at Joinville, the *Frères de la Charité de la bienheureuse Marie*, to which Clement VI. gave an Augustinian rule and which took charge of the great Parisian hospital Les Billets from the fourteenth century until about 1640. In 1540, almost contemporaneous with the rise of the Jesuits, an order was founded in Grenada by the Portuguese Juan Ciudad, called John of God (b. 1495; d. Mar. 8, 1550), which was generally known under the name of Brothers of Charity. After a life of dissipation and wild adventures in the army of the Hungarian King Ferdinand I. in his campaigns against the Turks, John was converted by a sermon of the famous Juan d'Avila, and underwent the most excessive penances, on which account he was regarded as a madman. Learning by his own experience how the insane were treated in the hospitals of those days, he resolved to devote himself especially to the nursing of these unfortunates and others in special need. In the house which he rented at Grenada, and which became the first scene of his self-sacrificing work of love, he received only the sick from the poorest classes. Soon he gathered around himself and his first two associates, Martino and Velasco, a number of sympathetic laymen. After ten years' activity he died, and Martino took charge of the institution, which as yet had neither a written rule nor a monastic organization. The number of houses soon increased, especially after the establishment of the large hospital at Madrid, which was richly endowed by Philip II., to which others were soon added in different cities of Spain, Italy, and, after the seventeenth century, in France and Germany. The bull of authorization issued by Pius V. (Jan. 1, 1572) elevated the lay society to an order with the Augustinian rule, and placed their houses under episcopal jurisdiction, although the brethren were permitted to elect their directors (*majores*, not *priores* or *abbates*) and to present some of their number for the priesthood. A general chapter held at Rome by Sixtus V. prepared the outlines of the constitution of the order. These articles were first published in 1589, and were enlarged under Paul V., Alexander VII., and Clement XI. (cf. the final redaction dating from 1718, in Holstenius-Brockie, *Codex regularum*, vi. 293-362). The statutes included in their requirements a thorough medical knowledge on the part of the hospital staff. The secular head master and the chief tender of the sick had to be an experienced physician and surgeon, respectively. Of the eleven provinces in which the order is found, ten belong to the old world, one to America. The number of houses is at present about 120. (O. Zöckler†.)

Bibliography: The early *Vita* of John of God are given in *ASB*, March, i. 814-858. Consult the more modern treatments: L. Saglier, *Vie de S. Jean de Dieu, avec l'histoire . . . de la fondation et du développement de son ordre*, Paris, 1877; C. Wilmet, *Lebensbeschreibung des . . . Johannes von Gott*, Regensburg, 1860. Further, on the order, consult: Helyot, *Ordres monastiques*, iv. 131-147; Heimbucher, *Orden und Kongregationen*, ii. 491-496.

CHARITY, CHRISTIAN: As distinguished from mere compassion, which may be but a transitory emotion or a desire without accomplishment, charity requires the cooperation of the will; it presupposes a permanent willingness to help one's neighbor in his need. If love comprehends the whole of Christian moral obligations (Rom. xiii. 9), charity is its manifestation toward our fellows, whether in temporal or in spiritual need. It is a permanent attribute of God (II Cor. i. 3), because human misery is always before his eyes, and has been operative in him from all eternity, in his plan of redemption. Under the old covenant, God, revealing himself as merciful and gracious, required his people to show mercy toward their needy brethren (Zech. vii. 9). It has, however, a deeper foundation in the New Testament. As the children of God by their brotherhood with Jesus Christ, the disciples could not but imitate the mercy of God (Luke vi. 36); he who failed in this regard showed that he was unworthy of membership in the new kingdom (Matt. xviii. 33; James ii. 13). The ethical organization of men is founded upon charity, and destroyed by its absence (Luke x. 37; Heb. ii. 17, iv. 15). Thus the true Good Samaritan is not only the model, but the source of all real charity, and his disciples show their fellowship with him by it (Matt. ix. 13; Rom. xii. 4-5). It is the characteristic difference between the Christian and the non-Christian world, which knows little of it. Nothing in primitive Christianity so struck the outside observer; even the emperor Julian was obliged to admit its force, while he strove in vain to imitate it. Step by step it did away with heathen customs—infanticide, removal of the weak and sickly, brutality to slaves; it built hospitals and asylums everywhere.

In the Roman Catholic Church, according to the development of ethics since Ambrose in the form of a system of virtues and duties, charity is considered under both heads. Thomas Aquinas reckons it among the so-called "theological virtues," and says that it is the highest of the virtues which go out to our neighbor. He enumerates seven corporal works of mercy (feeding the hungry, giving drink to the thirsty, clothing the naked, ransoming the captive, sheltering the homeless, visiting the sick, and burying the dead), and seven spiritual (admonishing sinners, instructing the ignorant, counseling the doubtful, comforting the sorrowful, bearing wrongs patiently, forgiving all injuries, praying for the living and the dead).

(L. Lemme.)

Bibliography: The standard work is G. Uhlhorn, *Die christliche Liebesthätigkeit*, 3 vols., Stuttgart, 1882-90, Eng. transl. of vol. i., New York, 1883.

CHARITY, SISTERS OF: A name applied loosely to various female communities in the Roman Catholic Church devoted especially to the care of the sick and the poor. Some associations of this kind will be treated in the article Women, Congregations of. For the Irish Sisters of Charity see English Ladies. It will be necessary here to treat only of the two best known and most influential of these communities.

1. The Sisters of Charity of St. Vincent de Paul: The title of *Confrérie de la charité pour l'assistance spirituelle et corporelle des pauvres malades* was given by Vincent de Paul (q.v.) originally to the association of women which he organized in 1617 in his small parish of Châtillon-les-Dombes, in the diocese of Lyons, and which, after approval of its statutes by the archbishop, spread also to other places. After the final transfer of its headquarters to Paris (1618), he founded similar associations in the capital and its neighborhood. He entrusted the direction of these *Dames de la Charité*, after the death of his patroness the Countess of Gondy (1625), to the devoted Louise Marillac, under whose guidance the development of the rapidly growing association into a community of unmarried women began in 1633, in which year the first of such members were admitted to the confraternity. On the Feast of the Annunciation in the following year a number of these *Filles servantes des pauvres de la charité* (later commonly known as *Sœurs Grises* from their gray habit) took their vows at the village of La Chapelle near Paris. Eight years later they were transferred to the city itself, where, by the time of the death of Vincent and Louise Marillac (both in 1660), they had already twenty-eight houses. The rule drawn up by the founder was confirmed by Clement IX. in 1668. It includes the obligation of rising daily at four o'clock, making a meditation twice daily, willingly tending all the sick, even the most repulsive, and rendering unconditional obedience to superiors. Life-vows were not taken by the sisters, but after a probation of five years a vow of obedience was pronounced which was to be renewed from year to year. The order was placed in a sort of dependence on the "Priests of the Mission," or Lazarists, whose superior was to be their director. The order spread during the seventeenth and eighteenth centuries principally in France and Poland, and reached the number of 500 houses. With the other religious orders it was suppressed at the Revolution, but continued its self-sacrificing labors none the less, until it was formally reestablished by Napoleon in 1807, and began a new and wider growth. In France alone it had about 400 houses in 1890; but the laicizing of the hospitals carried out by the government in the last few years has considerably weakened it since. Its total membership in all countries is supposed at present to be about 30,000. [The sisters of charity of St. Vincent de Paul were established in the United States in 1809 by Elizabeth Seton (q.v.). In 1907 this branch of the order numbered 4,698 professed sisters and had charge of 27 asylums, 33 orphanages, 27 academies, and 103 parochial schools.]

2. The Sisters of Charity of St. Charles: A community of similar nature and purpose grew up under this name in 1626 in the great hospital of St. Charles Borromeo at Nancy. The general of the Premonstratensians, Epiphanius Ludovicus, abbot of Estival, drew up in 1652 a rule for it, according to which the members were to take the three usual monastic vows, together with a fourth binding them to devote themselves for life to the care of the sick poor and friendless children. From the mother house at Nancy they spread first through France, and in the nineteenth century through a large part of Germany and Austria. At the end of this century they numbered about 450 houses with nearly 3,000 members, divided into four congregations at Nancy, Prague, Trebnitz, and Treves.

(O. Zöckler†.)

Bibliography: F. Bournaud, *Les Sœurs, 1633–1900*, Paris, 1900; F. F. Buss, *Der Orden der barmherzigen Schwestern*, Schaffhausen, 1847; D. Wulf, *Das segensreiche Wirken der Schwestern*, Münster, 1851; *Sisters of Charity, Catholic and Protestant*, London, 1855; G. Uhlhorn, *Die christliche Liebesthätigkeit seit der Reformation*, pp. 210–227, Stuttgart, 1882; F. Hervé-Basin, *Les Grands Ordres des femmes*, Paris, 1889; C. de Richemont, *Histoire de Mme. le Gras*, ib. 1894; L. Baunard, *La Vénérable Louise de Marillac*, Paris, 1898; B. R. Parkes, *Historic Nuns*, London, 1898; Currier, *Religious Orders*, pp. 446–452; Heimbucher, *Orden und Kongregationen*, ii. 430–438.

CHARLEMAGNE.

Charlemagne or Charles the Great (Lat. *Carolus Magnus*), founder of the Holy Roman Empire, was the son of Pepin, the first of the Carolingian line of Frankish kings, and grandson of Charles Martel, the powerful mayor of the palace under the last Merovingian kings. He was born c. 742, perhaps at Aachen or Ingelheim; d. at Aachen Jan. 28, 814.

1. Ecclesiastical Policy of the Frankish Kings. With his father and younger brother, Karlman, he was anointed king of the Franks by Pope Stephen II. in 754. He ruled jointly with Karlman after Pepin's death in 768, and alone after Karlman's death in 771. He was crowned emperor of the Romans at Rome by Pope Leo III. on Christmas Day, 800. In both civil and ecclesiastical matters Charlemagne carried out with consummate ability the policy of his father. From Clovis, the first Merovingian king (481–511; see Franks), onward the Frankish rulers pursued the policy of endowing and extending the Roman Church as a means of consolidating and strengthening the civil administration. The conquest of heathen peoples was not thought complete until they were Christianized and the newly acquired territory had been provided with a well-ordered and comprehensive ecclesiastical establishment. Resources devoted to ecclesiastical equipment and endowment were supposed to yield the best possible results in assimilating and loyalizing the communities in which they were expended. Where land was abundant it cost little to endow with landed estates archbishoprics, bishoprics, abbacies, etc., especially as the incumbents owed allegiance to their benefactors and could be relied upon for any kind of needful service.

The Lombards (q.v.) had long been a thorn in the side of the papacy. In 739 Pope Gregory III. had entreated Charles Martel to come to his relief, but Charles was not ready for so great an undertaking.

In 753 Stephen II. gained permission to visit Pepin for secret conference. Pepin sent his young sons Charles and Karlman to meet him, and received him (754) with the utmost cordiality. The conference was epoch-making. With the concurrence of his nobles, Pepin made with the pope an offensive and defensive alliance, recognized the pope's ecclesiastical headship, and undertook to deliver the papal territory from Lombard oppression and to promote the papal cause in all Frankish possessions and dependencies; while the pope commended Rome and the Romans to the protection of the king, crowned him *patricius Romanorum* and king of the Franks, crowned his two sons, and undertook to support the Frankish kingdom in every possible way. A successful campaign against the Lombards (754) led to the bestowal on the pope of the territory claimed as the patrimony of Peter (see PAPAL STATES) and the exarchate of Ravenna, but the conquest did not prove permanent, and it was left for Charlemagne to complete it (774).

2. Charlemagne's Policy.

From his childhood Charlemagne was carefully instructed by his father in warfare and in statecraft, and in early youth was associated with his father in the government of the realm. When crowned at St. Denis (754) he was made to promise to Peter and his vicar or his successors to be a friend to their friends and an enemy to their enemies. As ruler his policy was to extend his kingdom as widely as possible by conquest and to bring the whole domain into a well-ordered and homogeneous organism by diffusing throughout Christian civilization. His five campaigns against the Lombards (773, 774, 776, 780, and 784) had for their object the emancipation of the Church from Lombard oppression and encroachment and the inclusion of their territory in his own domain. The bestowment of a portion of the territory upon the Roman See and the apparent recognition of the alleged Donation of Constantine (q.v.) involved no surrender of his own sovereignty. His eighteen expeditions against the Saxons (770–784) had for their object the subjugation of their territory to Frankish rule and the Christianization of the entire population. He regarded the latter work, with the establishment of a full ecclesiastical system dependent on the Roman See, as necessary to the permanence and effectiveness of the former. His five campaigns against the Saracens in Italy were for the protection of Frankish territory and of Roman Christianity. The same may be said of his seven campaigns against the Arabs in Spain. Many of his wars were for the protection of frontiers already established; but when territory was once definitely acquired and incorporated in his realm his first thought was to provide for the speedy Christianization of its population by covering the territory with Christian institutions and by compelling the people to submit to baptism and conform to the cultus of the Church. Free forms of Christianity fared little better with Charlemagne and his predecessors than paganism, uniformity and articulation with the Holy Catholic Church being regarded as essential for the purposes of the State. The infliction of the death penalty for attempts to evade baptism, for desecration or destruction of church property, and for the celebration of pagan rites was based upon his conviction that the Christianization of the entire population was essential to the accomplishment of his political ends.

3. Coronation as Emperor.

In 799 Pope Leo III., sorely beset by a hostile faction and driven from Rome, made his way to the king's court at Paderborn. He was received with all honor and sent back with a royal guard and assurance of ample protection. Near the end of 800 Charlemagne visited Rome to complete the restoration of order and of the pope's authority, and on Dec. 25, while engaged in a religious service, he was crowned emperor by the grateful pope. This coronation was prized by Charlemagne as involving a recognition by the Roman See, the most influential surviving representative of Roman dignity and authority, of his right to be regarded as the legitimate successor of the Cæsars and as a solemn expression of the pope's determination to make common cause with him in the work of building up a world-wide empire in which the Roman form of religion should have exclusive sway. It is evident that he had no thought of subordinating the civil to the ecclesiastical authority. After the coronation as before, he legislated as freely in ecclesiastical as in civil matters. His capitularies and laws abound in minute regulations for every department of ecclesiastical life and work.

4. His Services to Learning.

Of primary importance was the educational movement begun by Pepin and carried forward with unremitting zeal and vast expenditure by Charlemagne. He had a deep personal interest in all forms of knowledge, and throughout his reign was diligent in his efforts to learn. The most eminent scholars of Britain and of Italy were drawn into his service. Something like a university was maintained in the court, and by an educational system under the guidance of Alcuin (q.v.) he sought to diffuse civilization throughout his realm. The monasteries and the churches were the chosen channels for the spread of enlightenment. It is probable that no other ruler ever accomplished so much for the diffusion of learning. A statement by Einhard (*Vita*, xxv.) that the emperor could not write can not fairly be taken to mean more than that he neglected to acquire a skilful use of the pen, preferring the services of amanuenses. He is said to have had a speaking knowledge of Latin, to have understood Greek, and to have had some acquaintance with Hebrew.

5. The Iconoclastic Controversy.

Charlemagne followed in the footsteps of Pepin in his attitude toward the worship of images. The Caroline Books (q.v.), put forth in the name of Charlemagne and with his authority, combated the decisions of the Second Nicene Council in favor of image-worship, approved by the pope, while at the same time condemning iconoclasm. Images are declared to be useful for the ornamentation of the churches and the perpetuation of holy deeds, yet they are by no means necessary. Christians having fellowship with Christ ought always to have him present in their hearts and to be able to look beyond the sensible into the spiritual. The Scriptures and not images are the proper outward means for gaining acquaintance with Christ. The Synod of Frankfort (794), called and controlled by Charlemagne, condemned the adoration and service of images (see IMAGES AND IMAGE-WORSHIP, II.). The negotiations between Charlemagne and the empress Irene looking toward the marriage of the two sovereigns and the reuniting of the East and the West, which were brought to an end by the overthrow of the empress (802), no doubt had in view the world-wide unification of ecclesiastical as well as civil administration.

Charlemagne paid little heed to moral or ecclesiastical considerations in contracting and annulling his marriages, and had no idea of limiting himself to one wife at a time. Besides several regular marriages, he sustained semimarital relations with a number of women, whose children he recognized and provided for.

A. H. NEWMAN.

BIBLIOGRAPHY: A convenient list of sources is given in Potthast, *Wegweiser*, pp. 192–194, 1234–35. The *Opera Omnia*, including letters, are in *MPL*, xcvii.–xcviii. The *Capitularia*, ed. G. H. Pertz, are in *MGH, Leg.*, i (1835), 32–194, and the *Leges Langobardorum* are in the same, iv (1868), 485–514. Other important early sources are given in *MGH, Script.*, i.–ii., 1826–29. Several short documents are given in the original in S. Mathews, *Select Medieval Documents*, pp. 10–14, Boston, 1892; a capitulary is in Eng. transl. in E. F. Henderson, *Documents*, pp. 189–200; several documents are in Thatcher and McNeal, *Source Book*, pp. 35–38. Excellent illustrative extracts are given in English, with a bibliography, in Robinson, *European History*, pp. 126–149.

The fundamental life is the *Vita Karoli Magni* by Einhard: it is in *ASB*, Jan., ii. 877–888; also, ed. Pertz, in *MGH, Script.*, ii (1829), 443–463; ed. G. Waitz, in *Script. rer. Germ.*, Hanover, 1880; in *MPL*, xcvii. 25–62; a good edition is by A. Holder, Freiburg, 1882; there is an Eng. transl. by S. E. Turner, New York, 1880, and in Thatcher and McNeal, *Source Book*, pp. 38–48. Modern treatments of the life are: P. A. Thijm, *Karl der Grosse und seine Zeit*, Münster, 1868; E. L. Cutts, *Charlemagne and his Times*, London, 1887; J. I. Mombert, *Hist. of Charles the Great*, London, 1888 (scholarly, discusses the sources); J. I. Humbert, *Hist. of Charles the Great*, ib. 1889; R. Foss, *Karl der Grosse*, Gütersloh, 1897; T. Hodgkin, *Charles the Great*, New York, 1897; H. W. C. Davis, *Charlemagne*, New York, 1900.

Shorter treatments or discussions of various phases of his life and activities are: A. Ebert, *Allgemeine Geschichte der Literatur des Mittelalters*, ii. 3–108, Leipsic, 1880; A. West, *Alcuin and the Rise of the Christian Schools*, New York, 1893; E. F. Henderson, *Germany in the Middle Ages*, pp. 56 sqq., New York, 1894; F. Gregorovius, *Rome in the Middle Ages*, vol. ii., book iv., chaps. 4–7, vol. iii., book v., chap. 1, London, 1894–95; J. A. Ketterer, *Karl der Grosse und die Kirche*, Munich, 1898; C. L. Wells, *The Age of Charlemagne*, New York, 1898; J. Nover, *Karl der Grosse und seine Paladine*, Glogau, 1900; J. Bryce, *The Holy Roman Empire*, especially chap. v., New York, 1904; J. B. Mullinger, *The Schools of Charles the Great*, ib. 1904; H. Prutz, *The Age of Charlemagne*, vol. viii. of *History of All Nations*, ed. J. H. Wright, Philadelphia, 1905; Milman, *Latin Christianity*, book iv., chap. xii., book v., chap i.; Neander, *Christian Church*, vol. iii., passim; Schaff, *Christian Church*, iv. 236–249; Moeller, *Christian Church*, ii. 90–98. Consult also: S. Abel and B. Simson, *Jahrbücher des fränkischen Reichs*, 2 vols., Leipsic, 1883; Wattenbach, *DGQ*; and the literature under ALCUIN.

CHARLES V.

Charles's Policy. The Diet of Worms (§ 1).
Political Events Favor the Protestant Cause (§ 2).
Attempts at Religious Unity. Diet of Augsburg (§ 3).
Efforts for a General Council (§ 4).
Renewal of Hostilities; Failure to Secure Unity (§ 5).
Abdication (§ 6).

Charles V., emperor of the Holy Roman Empire 1519–56 and king of Spain (as Charles I.), was born at Ghent Feb. 24, 1500; d. at the monastery of San Jerónimo de Yuste (124 m. by rail w.s.w. of Madrid), in Estramadura, Sept. 21, 1558. He was the son of Philip the Handsome of Austria and Joan of Aragon, grandson on the paternal side of the emperor Maximilian I. and Mary of Burgundy, on the maternal side of Ferdinand and Isabella, who had united Aragon and Castile into the kingdom of Spain. In 1516 he succeeded Ferdinand and Isabella as king of Spain, and ruler of the Netherlands, of the kingdom of Naples (including Sicily and Sardinia), Milan, Luxemburg, and Franche-Comté. As a member of the house of Hapsburg he was archduke of Austria. Thus as a youth of sixteen he was by far the most powerful sovereign in Europe. In 1519 he was elected emperor in competition with Francis I. of France, largely through the influence of Frederick of Saxony (see FREDERICK III., THE WISE).

1. Charles's Policy. The Diet of Worms.

From the beginning of his reign as king of Spain Charles was beset with difficulties. It required the most strenuous efforts of Ximenes, chief counselor of Ferdinand, to prevent open revolt in Spain, where Charles's right to the succession was considered doubtful and where, because of his Dutch training and Dutch counselors, he was unpopular. He entered upon his imperial administration amid the throes of the Protestant revolution, threatened in the West by the jealousy and ambition of the king of France and in the East by the attacks of the Ottoman Turks, who were encouraged by France to do their worst. The necessity of protecting the Netherlands, his Italian and other Western possessions from French voracity, and the Eastern domains of the house of Hapsburg from Turkish aggression, lay at the basis of Charles's policy in ecclesiastical matters. Immediately after his coronation as emperor at Aachen (Oct., 1520) the necessity of vigorous measures for the suppression of Lutheranism became manifest. The Diet of Worms followed (Jan. 28–May 25, 1521), but Charles, influenced by his confessor, Quintana, and having a wholesome dread of civil war, refused to deal as summarily with Luther as the papal nuncio, Girolamo Aleandro, wished. The Edict of Worms, representing the extent to which Charles was prepared to go in the direction of coercion, prohibited the printing, sale, and reading of Luther's books, and the giving of comfort and support to him; but the safe-conduct under which he had come to Worms was respected (see WORMS).

On May 8 a secret treaty was made at Worms between the emperor and the pope against France. Henry VIII. of England joined the alliance, hoping to acquire territory lost to France and to increase his own importance by having Wolsey, his chief counselor, elected pope. War broke out almost immediately. The duke of Bourbon espoused the imperial cause. The pope, expecting the French to win and fearing the increase of imperial power in Italy, transferred his allegiance to Francis, and thus angered the emperor, who proved victorious and took Francis prisoner in the battle of Pavia (1524).

2. Political Events Favor the Protestant Cause.

The marriage of Charles to the infanta of Portugal rather than to Mary, daughter of Henry VIII., caused the latter to withdraw from the imperial alliance and make peace with France. Availing themselves of the emperor's absorption in extra-German enterprises, many German princes ignored the Edict of Worms and openly promoted the Lutheran cause. In July, 1525, Duke George of Saxony, the elector of Brandenburg, the archbishop-elector of Mainz, and the duke of Brunswick met at Dessau and formed a Catholic league to cooperate with the emperor in exterminating "the accursed Lutheran sect." In Feb., 1526, the elector of Saxony and the landgrave of Hesse (joined later by seven other princes) formed the Gotha-Torgau alliance for the defense of Lutheranism. The manifest strength of the evangelical cause and his breach with the pope caused Charles to assume a conciliatory attitude, and the Diet of Speyer (June, 1526; see SPEYER, DIETS OF) left the German princes free to deal with religious questions each according to his sense of duty. Turkish invasion in the east and the need of a German army for the chastisement of the pope promoted this policy of toleration. In May, 1526, a secret league was formed by the pope, France, England, Venice, Milan, and Florence, against the emperor, who (Sept. 17) declared the pope no pastor, but a usurper, and appealed from him to a general council. In 1527 Charles sent a German Lutheran army led by Georg von Frundsberg and a Spanish army led by the duke of Bourbon against the pope and his allies. The imperial troops forced their way into Rome at the cost of the lives of about five thousand of its defenders and for eight days reveled in pillage, drunkenness, and outrage. The pope took refuge in the castle of St. Angelo. Cardinals were dragged through the city and forced to pay ransom. St. Peter's was used for a stable. Just before the sack of Rome England and France had agreed to unite in demanding of the emperor the release of the French princes held by him as hostages and the payment to England of certain indemnities, and to make war on him immediately in case of his refusal. The sack of Rome and maltreatment of the pope augmented the hostility of England and France. Henry VIII. hoped, by succoring the pope and antagonizing the emperor, to secure the good offices of the former in the matter of the divorce from Catherine of Aragon, a relative of the latter. Charles felt it advisable to come to terms with the pope. He restored most of the territory taken from him and received a promise to convene a general council for the pacification of Christendom and the reformation of the Church.

In 1528 the duke of Bavaria sought the cooperation of England, France, and Lorraine in an effort to depose Charles; and Philip of Hesse sought the assistance of France, Silesia, Poland, and others against the house of Hapsburg.

3. Attempts at Religious Unity. Diet of Augsburg.

Charles's decisive victory over the French led to the Peace of Cambrai (July, 1529), and was followed by an agreement between him and the French king to cooperate in efforts for religious unification. The Second Diet of Speyer (1529; see SPEYER, DIETS OF) nullified the tolerant policy of the first. The manifest determination of Charles to crush Lutheranism led the Lutheran princes to unite in a protest—whence the designation "Protestants." The failure of Lutherans and Zwinglians to unite for the defense of the Evangelical cause (see MARBURG, CONFERENCE OF) and the retreat of the army of Suleiman from the gates of Vienna caused the emperor, now at peace with France and the papacy, to feel that at last he was master of the situation. He was, in fact, now at the height of his power, and all that was lacking to complete success was the restoration of religious unity. He planned to visit Germany, call a diet for religious pacification, summon the different Evangelical parties to present their views, and have them confuted by Roman Catholic theologians invited for the purpose. He announced his intention to leave all past errors to the judgment of Christ, and to give due consideration to every man's opinions; yet he did not conceal his determination to bring all the people of his empire into one commonwealth and one Church. Arriving in Augsburg for the diet of 1530, he sought to intimidate the German princes, insisting that they should keep their preachers silent during the sessions of the diet and requesting them to join him in the Corpus Christi procession. They stanchly refused compliance. The irenic confession of faith prepared by Melanchthon (see AUGSBURG CONFESSION AND ITS APOLOGY) was attacked by the Roman Catholic theologians. Charles objected to the harsh polemics in which they indulged and insisted on a more conciliatory statement than they at first prepared.

The confession of Zwingli and that of the four cities (see TETRAPOLITAN CONFESSION) were treated with even less consideration. Lorenzo Campeggi, representing the pope, urged drastic measures for the extirpation of heresy; but Charles was too much of a statesman not to see that in case of a conflict the Evangelical princes and cities would be supported by France, Bavaria, and other anti-Hapsburg powers, and again assumed a conciliatory attitude. The Schmalkald League (1531; see SCHMALKALD ARTICLES) soon had as its members all the Lutheran princes and cities and gained the support of France, England, Denmark, Hungary, and the duchy of Gelders; and Charles was again embarrassed by Turkish aggression. By the Religious Peace of Nuremberg (q.v.; 1532) he renewed the toleration of 1526.

Charles spent the following nine years in Spain, and from this time onward was unwearied in his efforts to secure the convocation of a general council which should thoroughly reform the ecclesiastical administration, redress the grievances of the Protestants, and make possible the reunion of Christendom. His overtures to the

4. Efforts for a General Council.

Lutheran princes for the settlement of differences by a free council were repelled, and for the next few years he had the mortification of seeing Protestantism advancing more rapidly than ever before. In 1541 he conferred in person with Paul III. regarding a council, and Trent was selected as being outside of, but near Italy and in Catholic Austria (see TRENT, COUNCIL OF). Charles insisted that reformation should have precedence of doctrinal definition, while the pope and his advisers thought the latter the matter of supreme importance. As a compromise it was arranged that alternate sessions should be devoted to reformation and doctrine. Charles's interest in reformation was political rather than moral or religious. He thought efforts at coercion without antecedent reformation would result in war and render unification impossible. He repeatedly invited the Protestants to send representatives to the council, with promises of safe-conduct and fair treatment. At the Fourth Diet of Speyer (1544) a dispute between the duke of Brunswick and the elector of Saxony and the landgrave of Hesse that had resulted in the imprisonment of the former and the seizure of his estates, was settled by the emperor, and he secured the promise of a large German army for a campaign against the Turks. With the help of the English and the Germans Charles gained such advantages over the king of France as to be able to make a favorable peace (Crespy, Sept., 1544). The peace involved an agreement on the part of the two sovereigns to unite in promoting the council and in reunifying Christendom.

At the Diet of Worms (May, 1545) the impossibility of reconciling the Protestants became more manifest to the emperor than ever before, and he began to prepare for the inevitable

5. Renewal of Hostilities; Failure to Secure Unity.

conflict. War was immediately renewed between the duke of Brunswick and the elector of Saxony and the landgrave of Hesse. It resulted disastrously to the former. The elector of the Palatinate showed Protestant leanings early in 1546 and the death of the elector-archbishop of Mainz (Sept., 1545) precipitated a struggle for ascendency between supporters of the emperor and the Protestants. At the Diet of Regensburg (June, 1546) the Schmalkald allies protested against the council and petitioned for continuance of peace. The emperor treated their overtures with contempt and expressed his purpose to vindicate his imperial authority. In July he declared war against the allies as outlaws and rebels. The defection of Maurice of Saxony gave a marked advantage to the imperial cause, and by June, 1547, Charles had destroyed the Schmalkald League and had the Protestants at his mercy. Yet even now he was too prudent to attempt the sudden and violent extirpation of the Evangelical faith. He secured the concurrence of the Lutheran princes and theologians in the Augsburg and Leipsic Interims (see INTERIM) in a scheme for the partial and gradual restoration of Roman Catholicism. The return of Maurice to the support of the Lutheran cause, disagreement between the emperor and the pope, and the intervention of France deprived the imperial cause of the advantages that had been gained. In the Treaty of Passau (Aug., 1552) Charles felt obliged to grant amnesty and religious toleration to the Lutherans, and by 1554 the imperial authority had become so weakened that Charles allowed his brother Ferdinand to make peace (1555) with the Lutherans on terms recognizing complete equality of rights for Lutheran and Roman Catholic princes (see AUGSBURG, RELIGIOUS PEACE OF).

Deeply humiliated and utterly discouraged, Charles abdicated (1556), leaving to his son Philip his hereditary possessions. He was

6. Abdication.

succeeded in the imperial office by his brother Ferdinand. He retired to the monastery of Yuste, where, broken in health and depressed in spirit, he spent the two remaining years of his life. Shortly before his death, seeing in Luther the cause of all his woes, he expressed regret that he had not burned the archheretic at the Diet of Worms. Charles was unquestionably a statesman of more than average ability, self-possessed, comparatively tolerant, free from fanatical zeal for the Roman Catholic faith, less treacherous than most of the rulers of his time, and supremely concerned to conserve and extend the Hapsburg possessions and power and to effect religious unification as a means to this end. Circumstances beyond his control made his position an extremely difficult one. From his point of view, it probably would have been advisable to crush Lutheranism in its infancy. A. H. NEWMAN.

BIBLIOGRAPHY: A very extensive bibliography may be found in the *British Museum Catalogue* under "Charles V. Emperor of Germany." Among the voluminous sources may be mentioned: K. Lanz, *Correspondenz des Kaisers Karl V. aus dem kaiserlichen Archiv*, 3 vols., Leipsic, 1844-1846; *Staatspapiere zur Geschichte des Kaisers Karl V.*, Stuttgart, 1845; *Actenstücke und Briefe zur Geschichte Karls V.*, Vienna, 1853-57; J. J. I. von Döllinger, *Dokumente zur Geschichte Karls V.*, in *Beiträge*, vol. i., Regensburg, 1862. A French version of a Portuguese transl. of the lost autobiography of Charles was published by K. de Lettenhove, *Commentaires de Charles-Quint*, Brussels, 1862, Eng. transl., *Autobiography of the Emperor Charles V.*, London, 1862 (covers, 1516-48). Early lives are by: A. Ulloa, Venice, 1560; Sandoval, Valladolid, 1606; Sepulveda, Madrid, 1780; A. de Musica, Leipsic, 1728. An English classic and standard authority is W. Robertson, *Hist. of Charles V.*, ed. W. H. Prescott, best ed. Philadelphia, 1857, new ed. London, 1882. Consult further: D. G. van Male, *Lettres sur la vie intérieure de l'empereur Charles-Quint*, Brussels, 1843; W. Bradford, *Correspondence of Charles V. and his Ambassadors in England and France*, London, 1850; J. J. Hannusch, *Kaiser Karl V., seine Zeit und seine Zeitgenossen*, Vienna, 1853; A. Pichot, *Charles-Quint, Chronique de sa vie intérieure et de sa vie politique*, Paris, 1854; W. Maurenbrecher, *Karl V. und die deutsche Protestanten, 1545-55*, Düsseldorf, 1865; O. C. Krabbe, *Kaiser Karl V. und das Augsburger Interim*, Rostock, 1872; A. von Druffel, *Kaiser Karl V. und die römische Curie, 1544-46*, 3 parts, Munich, 1877 sqq.; H. Baumgarten, *Geschichte Karls V.*, Stuttgart, 1885; W. Stirling-Maxwell, *Cloister Life of Charles V.*, ed. J. Stirling-Maxwell, London, 1891; Baumgarten, *Karl V. und die deutsche Reformation*, Coburg, 1893; O. Waltz, *Die Denkwürdigkeiten Kaiser Karls V.*, Bonn, 1901; J. Bryce, *The Holy Roman Empire*, chap. xix., New York, 1904; E. Armstrong, *The Emperor Charles*

V., 2 vols., London, 1902; Pastor, *Popes*, vi. 379, 421; Creighton, *Papacy*, vi. 109–127 et passim; Schaff, *Christian Church*, vi. 262 et passim; Moeller, *Christian Church*, iii. 23 sqq. et passim (worth consulting). The subject is treated necessarily in works on the Reformation and on the church history of the period.

CHARLES (née RUNDLE), ELIZABETH: Church of England authoress; b. at Tavistock (13 m. n. of Plymouth), Devonshire, Jan. 2, 1828; d. at Hampstead (a suburb of London) Mar. 28, 1896. She was educated at home, and commenced to write at an early age, her work winning the approval of such authors as James Anthony Froude and Tennyson. In 1851 she married Andrew Paton Charles (d. June 4, 1868), a chandler, and did much philanthropic work among the poor of Wapping. After 1894 she resided at Hampstead, where she continued her interest in philanthropy, attending the meetings of the North London Hospital for Consumption, and taking an active interest in the Metropolitan Association for Befriending Young Servants, while as early as 1885 she had founded at Hampstead a home for incurables called Friedenheim. Mrs. Charles was a prolific writer, but her fame rests chiefly on her *Chronicles of the Schönberg-Cotta Family*, first published at London in 1863. This is a historical romance of the time of Luther, and gained wide popularity, running through many editions and being translated into most European and several Oriental languages. Among her other works special mention may be made of her *Rest in Christ, or the Crucifix and the Cross* (London, 1848); *Tales and Sketches of Christian Life in Different Lands and Ages* (1850); *The Two Vocations* (1853); *The Voice of Christian Life in Song* (1858); *The Martyrs of Spain and Liberators of Holland* (1862); *Wanderings over Bible Lands and Seas* (1862); *Sketches of Christian Life in England in the Olden Time* (1864); *Sketches of the Women of Christendom* (1880); *An Old Story of Bethlehem* (1884); *The True Vine* (1885); *The Great Prayer of Christendom: Thoughts on the Lord's Prayer* (1886); *Wanderings over Lands and Seas* (1887); *Martyrs and Saints of the First Twelve Centuries* (1887); *"By the Coming of the Holy Ghost"* (1888); *"By Thy Glorious Resurrection and Ascension"* (1888); and the autobiographical *Our Seven Homes*, edited by Mary Davidson (1896).

CHARLES, ROBERT HENRY: Anglican theologian and Ethiopic scholar; b. at Cookstown (21 m. w. of Armagh), County Tyrone, Ireland, Aug. 6, 1855. He was educated at Queen's University, Ireland (B.A., 1877), and Trinity College, Dublin (B.A., 1881); and was incorporated M.A. at Exeter College, Oxford, in 1892. He was ordered deacon in 1883 and ordained priest in 1884, and was successively curate of St. Mark's, Whitechapel (1883–1885), St. Philip's, Kensington (1885–86), and St. Mark's, Kennington, Surrey (1886–89). In 1898–1906 he was professor of Biblical Greek in Trinity College, Dublin, and in 1905 was also appointed Grinfeld lecturer on the Septuagint at Oxford. He was Hibbert lecturer at Oxford in 1898, Jowett lecturer in London in 1898–99, and select preacher at Dublin in 1889–1900 and 1902–03, and was elected a fellow of the British Academy in 1906. In addition to numerous contributions to theological periodicals and encyclopedias, he has written *Forgiveness and Other Sermons* (London, 1886); *The Book of Enoch* (Ethiopic text; 1903); *Ethiopic Version of the Hebrew Book of Jubilees* (Oxford, 1894); *The Apocalypse of Baruch* (Syriac text and translation; London, 1896); *The Assumption of Moses* (Latin text and translation; 1897); *Critical History of the Doctrine of a Future Life in Israel, in Judaism, in Christianity* (Jowett lectures for 1898–99; 1899); *The Ascension of Isaiah* (Ethiopic, Greek, and Latin texts and translation; 1900); *The Book of Jubilees: or, The Little Genesis* (translation; 1902); *The Ethiopic Version of the Book of Enoch* (1905); *Greek Version of the Testaments of the Twelve Patriarchs with the Variants of the Armenian and Slavonic Versions and the Hebrew and Aramaic Fragments* (Oxford, 1906); *Testament of the Twelve Patriarchs* (1908); and, with W. R. Morfill, translation of the Slavonic text of *The Book of the Secrets of Enoch* (1896).

CHARLES, SAINT, SISTERS OF CHARITY OF. See CHARITY, SISTERS OF.

CHARLES, THOMAS: Welsh Methodist; b. at Pantdwfn, near St. Clears (8 m. w.s.w. of Carmarthen), Carmarthenshire, Oct. 14, 1755; d. at Bala, Merionethshire, Oct. 5, 1814. He was educated under Methodist influences in Wales and at Jesus College, Oxford (1775–78; B.A., 1779), was ordained deacon and priest in the Church of England, and held a curacy in Somersetshire; but his opinions and style of preaching unfitted him for service as an English curate, and in 1783 he settled at Bala and soon became a leader of the Welsh Methodists. He made long preaching tours over all North Wales, instituted "circulating schools" and Sunday-schools, and trained teachers at his own expense. The revival which began in 1791 and spread from Bala as a center was a direct result of his labors. He maintained close connections with the English Methodists and extended his efforts to Ireland in 1807. In 1802 he helped to found the British and Foreign Bible Society (see BIBLE SOCIETIES, I., 2). He wrote tracts and books in Welsh for the religious instruction of his countrymen, including a catechism, which in English translation was recommended by the Countess of Huntingdon for use in her chapels, and a "Scriptural Dictionary" in Welsh (4 vols., Bala, 1805–08) which went through seven editions. A printing-press which he established at Bala in 1803 issued more than 300,000 copies before his death.

BIBLIOGRAPHY: Edward Morgan, *Memoir of the Life and Labours of Thomas Charles*, London, 1828; William Hughes, *Life and Letters of Thomas Charles*, Rhyl, 1881; *Essays, Letters, and Interesting Papers of Thomas Charles*, ed. E. Morgan, London, 1836.

CHARNOCK, STEPHEN: Puritan; b. in London 1628; d. there July 27, 1680. He studied at Emmanuel College, Cambridge, took his degree there, and became minister in Southwark; in 1649 he went to Oxford and became fellow of New College (1650) and proctor (M.A., 1652); went to Ireland with Henry Cromwell as chaplain (1655); returned to England soon after the death of Oliver

Cromwell, and lived for fifteen years in London in retirement and without regular charge; in 1675 he was appointed joint pastor with Thomas Watson of a Presbyterian congregation in Bishopsgate Street, London. He was a grave and impressive preacher and a man of fervent piety. His chief work was *On the Existence and Attributes of God*, published posthumously, ed. Richard Adams and Edward Veal (London, 1681; many subsequent editions; American ed., with biographical sketch by William Symington, 2 vols., New York, 1874); there is an edition of his *Works* with memoir by Edward Parsons (9 vols., London, 1815), and another with introduction by James McCosh, in *Nichol's Series of Standard Divines* (5 vols., Edinburgh, 1864).

BIBLIOGRAPHY: Notices additional to those mentioned in the text are A. à Wood, *Athenæ Oxonienses*, ed. P. Bliss, iii. 1234–36, 4 vols., London, 1813–20; *DNB*, x. 134–135.

CHARRON, shär"rōn', PIERRE: French Roman Catholic ecclesiastic and theologian; b. at Paris 1541; d. there Nov. 16, 1603. He studied law at Orléans and Bourges, and practised for several years, after which he entered the Church and soon became a pulpit orator of note. He preached for a number of years in various cities of southern France, and was finally appointed preacher to Queen Margaret. In his forty-seventh year he returned to Paris and wished to enter a monastic order, but was rejected on account of his age. He then resumed his activity as a preacher, and in Bordeaux made the acquaintance of Montaigne. In 1594 he was appointed vicar-general by the bishop of Cahors, and in the following year was sent as a deputy to a convention of the French clergy, where he was so highly esteemed that he was chosen first secretary. Charron was the author of three works. The first of these was his *Traité des trois vérités, contre tous athées, idolâtres, juifs, mahométans, hérétiques et schismatiques* (Bordeaux, 1594), in which he maintained against the atheists that there is a God and a religion; against the pagans, Jews, and Mohammedans that the Christian religion alone is true; and against heretics and schismatics that salvation can be found only in the Roman Catholic Church. He likewise wrote a collection of sixteen *Discours chrétiens* (1600), on the mass, the knowledge of God, salvation, and the communion of the saints. Still more famous was his *Traité de la sagesse* (1601; Eng. transl. by S. Lennard, London, 1612 [?]), in which he proceeded from the thesis that the true understanding of man consists in knowledge of himself and of the nature and limits of his powers, so that this wisdom should direct his inward and his outward life. Truth, on the other hand, can be found with God alone, and man is unable to gain it by himself. This agnostic tendency led Charron to express himself with such freedom concerning all positive religions, including Christianity, that the Jesuit Garasse branded him as an atheist. The *Traité* was accordingly expurgated by Jeannin for the edition of 1604, but in this form the book found few readers, and three years later the text was restored with Jeannin's notes. Shortly before his death Charron published a compendium of his work with an apology under the title *Petit traité de la sagesse* (Paris, 1606). (C. PFENDER.)

BIBLIOGRAPHY: The works, with a Life by M. de la Roche-Maillet, were published, Paris, 1635. Consult: C. A. Sainte-Beuve, *Causeries de Lundi*, vol. xi., 4th ed., 16 vols., Paris, 1882–85.

CHARTERIS, ARCHIBALD HAMILTON: Church of Scotland; b. at Wamphray (15 m. n.e. of Dumfries), Dumfriesshire, Dec. 13, 1835. He studied at Edinburgh (B.A., 1853), Tubingen (1870) and Bonn (1871); d. at Edinburgh Apr. 24, 1908. He was minister of St. Quivox, Ayrshire (1858–59), New Abbey, Dumfriesshire (1859–63), and The Park Parish, Edinburgh (1863–68). From 1868 to 1898 he was professor of Biblical criticism in Edinburgh University. He was chairman of the General Assembly's Committee on Christian Life and Work, 1869–94, and was instrumental in establishing the Young Men's Guild, the Woman's Guild, and the Deaconesses' Hospital, and in reviving the order of deaconesses as a part of the organization of the Church of Scotland. He was appointed a chaplain to the queen in 1869, and was moderator of the General Assembly of the Church of Scotland in 1892. From 1901 to 1908 he was chaplain in ordinary to the king in Scotland. In theology he was a conservative. He has written *Life of Professor James Robertson* (Edinburgh, 1863); *Canonicity: A Collection of Early Testimonies to the Canonical Books of the New Testament* (London, 1880); *The New Testament Scriptures* (1888); and *The Church of Christ* (1905).

CHASE, FREDERIC HENRY: Anglican bishop of Ely; b. in London Feb. 21, 1853; studied at Christ's College, Cambridge (B.A., 1876); was curate of Sherborne, Dorset (1876–79), and of St. Michael's, Cambridge (1879–84). He was tutor of the Clergy Training School, Cambridge, from 1884 to 1887, and its principal from 1887 to 1901, and was lecturer in theology in Pembroke College, Cambridge, from 1881 to 1890, and in Christ's College from 1893 to 1901, as well as examining chaplain to the archbishop of York in 1894–1905. He was Hulsean lecturer in 1900, and was Norrisian professor of divinity in Cambridge University and president of Queen's College, Cambridge, from 1901 to 1905, as well as vice-chancellor of the university from 1902 to 1904. In 1905 he was consecrated bishop of Ely. He has written *Chrysostom* (London, 1887); *The Old Syriac Element in the Text of Codex Bezæ* (1893); *The Lord's Prayer in the Early Church* (Cambridge, 1891); *The Syro-Latin Text of the Gospels* (London, 1895); *Credibility of the Book of Acts* (Hulsean lectures for 1900–1901; 1902); and *The Gospels in the Light of Historical Criticism* (1905). He also edited F. J. A. Hort's *Commentary on I Peter* (London, 1898).

CHASE, IRAH: American Baptist; b. at Stratton, Vt., Oct. 5, 1793; d. at Newton Center, Mass., Nov. 1, 1864. He was graduated at Middlebury College, Vt., 1814, and Andover 1817; he was ordained 1817, and preached for a year as missionary in Virginia; in 1818 he became professor of languages and Biblical literature in the first Baptist theological school in the country, then at Philadelphia, in 1822 incorporated with Columbian University at Washington; he resigned in 1825 and was one of the founders of the Newton Theological Institution and professor of Biblical theology there till 1836, of ecclesiastical history, 1836-45. The latter part of his life was spent in literary work. He wrote much for the religious periodicals and published, with other books, *Remarks on the Book of Daniel* (Boston, 1844); *The Work Claiming to be the Constitutions of the Holy Apostles, including the Canons, Whiston's Version, revised from the Greek, with a prize essay upon their original contents translated from the German* (New York, 1848); *The Design of Baptism Viewed in its Relation to the Christian Life* (Boston, 1851); *Infant Baptism an Invention of Man* (Philadelphia, n.d.).

CHASIDIM (Heb. *Ḥasidhim*, "Pious"): **1.** A Jewish religious party important during the time of the Maccabean wars. They advocated the strictest ideals of Judaism prescribed by the scribes, opposed the Grecizing tendencies of the age, and for a long time supported the Maccabees in the struggle with the Seleucidæ for independence. They were the precursors of the Pharisees. See HASMONEANS, § 1.

2. The adherents of a religious movement which arose among the Polish Jews in the seventeenth century. It was essentially a pietistic and mystic reaction against Talmudism, and thus presents a certain analogue to the pietism current in Christian circles about the same period, though there was no actual relation between the two. The founder of the Chasidim was an obscure Polish rabbi named Israel ben-Eleazar, who received the epithet of Baal Shem-Tob or "Master of the good name" (i.e., the mystic name of God), whence he was frequently termed Besht (from the initial letters *b-sh-t*). Teaching a religion of the heart, and discarding Talmudic formalism for personal faith and love of God, he gathered about him-

The Founder of the Chasidim and his Teachings.

self an enormous following which numbered many rabbis whom the legalism of the Talmud had failed to satisfy. About 1740 he made his headquarters in Miedzybos in Podolia, and there developed his two cardinal doctrines that God is everywhere, and that man may commune with God. The first tenet was pantheistic and the second cabalistic. To attain perfect communion with the deity ecstatic prayer and meditation, often induced by violent physical motions or even by the use of intoxicants, were necessary, while thus a direct influence might be brought to bear upon God himself. Formalism was altogether discarded by Chasidism, and in a like spirit the non-Jewish asceticism grafted on Talmudic ritualism by the "practical Cabala" was rejected. The Chasidim were to serve and worship God with gladness and in the freedom of the spirit, while reason was distinctly subordinate to faith.

He who realized Chasidic ideals was "righteous" (*ẓaddiḳ*) and had preeminence over lesser souls. Therein lay the danger of the system, for the *ẓaddiḳ* came, in increasing measure, to be regarded as a quasimediator with God, who could influence the deity to bestow blessings on those that had not achieved perfect righteousness and communion with the divinity. This concept was

The Zaddikim.

thoroughly non-Jewish, nor was such homage ever rendered to any rabbi as to the ordinary *ẓaddiḳ*. The cleavage between the orthodox Jews and the Chasidim grew wider; separate synagogues were formed, and changes were made in the arrangements of the prayers, the rules for slaughtering, and other ancient Jewish customs. It was not until after the death of Besht, however, that the power of the *ẓaddiḳ* gained full development, but then the rule was evolved that the "righteous" should be supported by less holy souls in return for his mediation with God. From a sincere, though often ignorant, leader of his flock he became only too frequently a mere thaumaturgist, healing the sick and performing other miracles with his amulets and the penances which he imposed. Yet Chasidism was not a homogeneous system, but developed, in course of time, into two distinct schools, one finding its center in South Russia and Poland, and the other in Lithuania and White Russia. The cause of this demarcation was, in the main, intellectual. In South Russia and in Poland the mystical and pietistic trend was no new thing. It had already been exemplified in the movements headed by Jacob Frank (q.v.) and in the religious upheaval caused in Oriental Judaism by the pseudo-Messiah Shabbethai Zebi. It had been augmented, moreover, by the religious anarchy consequent on the political disturbances in Poland and by the savage persecutions of Chmielnicki and the Haidamacks. The result was a combination of ignorance and despair, which furnished a fallow soil for an optimistic mysticism freed from all restraints of the ritual law. In these regions, then, the *ẓaddiḳ* flourished and worked his miracles at the expense of the still more benighted Chasidim. In White Russia and Lithuania, on the other hand, these destructive factors had not been at work, and the Talmud retained its position of honor and its conservative power. There, moreover, the Jews

History of Chasidism.

centered in the cities, and thus were under the intellectual restraint and stimulus of the scholars of the Talmud, while in the villages of Poland and South Russia imagination could run riot, devoid of the restraint of scholarship. For all these reasons Chasidism did not gain in the north the exclusive dominance which it possessed in the south, and its break with rabbinical Judaism was far less radical. The *ẓaddiḳ* of White Russia and Lithuania was little more than a heterodox rabbi, and was deeply influenced by the "rational Chasidism" taught by Zalman of Liozna (1747-1812), who postulated the need of an intelligent faith rather than absolute subjection of reason, and reduced the *ẓaddiḳ* to the place of a teacher instead of a thaumaturgist.

Chasidism, being suspected (and not without some probability) of an affinity with the vagaries of Frank and Shabbethai Zebi, was everywhere bitterly opposed by orthodox Judaism, represented by the *mitnaggedim* ("opponents"). In the north, where the hold of Chasidism was so slight, the hostility was extreme, and the sectarians were denounced to the government, although without success. The result was the existence of the two schools side by side, but in the south rabbinical Judaism was completely routed, and the *ẓaddiḳim* took the place of the rabbis. The Chasidim, however, met with their most formidable opponents when the *maskilim* ("enlightened") arose in the nineteenth century. This movement, inspired by Moses Mendelssohn and his followers, was fatal, in its importation of Occidental Christian learning and criticism, to the ignorant mysticism of Chasidism. Its power is now confined to the uneducated Jews of southern Russia, where the *maskilim* meet the stubborn resistance of stagnation and a reactionary tendency which is more intense, because less enlightened, than that of rabbinical Judaism.

Opposition to the System.

This trend is not improbably increased by the attitude of the Russian government toward the Jews, but elsewhere the despair which evoked it no longer exists, and with the absence of the cause the effect has vanished. Yet in passing judgment on Chasidism, it should not be forgotten that, with all its faults, it possessed one important element which was the secret of its power, the insistence on personal piety and faith as the means of salvation, rather than on the intellectualism of rabbinical legalism, a teaching by no means new in Judaism, but revived and fostered by this sect in a time of need.

Bibliography: H. Graetz, *Geschichte der Juden*, vol. xi., chap 3, Leipsic, 1891 (the fullest account); J. M. Jost, *Geschichte des Judenthums und seiner Sekten*, iii. 184, 3 parts, ib. 1857–59; L. Löw, *Vergangenheit und Gegenwart der Chasidäer*, Budapest, 1859; J. R. Ehrlich, *Der Weg meines Lebens*, Vienna, 1874; S. Schechter, *Studies in Judaism*, Philadelphia, 1896; *KL*, iii. 102–103; *JE*, vi. 251–256.

CHASTEL, shās"tel', ÉTIENNE LOUIS: Swiss church historian; b. at Geneva July 11, 1801; d. there Feb. 24, 1886. He was educated at Geneva, and subsequently studied in France, Italy, and England. In 1832 he became a pastor in his native city, where, seven years later, he was appointed professor of church history in the theological faculty of the university. He was a prolific author, his chief works being as follows: *Conférences sur l'histoire du Christianisme* (2 vols., Geneva, 1839–47); *Histoire de la destruction du paganisme dans l'empire d'Orient* (1850); *Études historiques sur l'influence de la charité durant les premiers siècles chrétiens* (Paris, 1853; Eng. transl. by G. A. Matile, Philadelphia, 1857); *Le Christianisme au dix-neuvième siècle* (Geneva, 1874; Eng. transl. by J. R. Beard, London, 1875), this forming, in a new edition, part of his *Histoire du Christianisme depuis son origine jusqu'à nos jours* (5 vols., Paris, 1881–84); and *Lettres inédites de Madame de Maintenon au lieutenant de Baville* (1875). His *Mélanges historiques et religieux* appeared posthumously, together with a biographical sketch by A. Bouvier (Paris, 1888).

CHASTITY: Chastity in the modern acceptation of the word is a condition and a virtue—the state of physical and moral purity in sexual relations, and self-preservation from unallowed sexual desires. As a virtue it was highly esteemed early in heathen antiquity, by the Romans, and among the Germanic tribes—all the more as it was uncommon. Even to the present day it has been required more strictly from women than from men, and there are traces of this inequality in the Mosaic law. Indeed it can not be said that as concerns chastity Israel rose much above the general level of the pre-Christian period; the nation's moral consciousness of sexual purity was not acute. Christianity first gave to chastity its full value. The New Testament writers use the word *hagnos* in this connection, which originally meant "dedicated," "holy," then "pure," "chaste." The New Testament idea is based upon the entirely new, Christian, conception of the value and significance of the human body and of its life. Included in the plan of salvation, destined to eternal communion with God, called to future transfiguration in celestial existence, the body to the Christian is an object of solicitude and conscientious care (I Cor. vi. 19).

In the performance of this duty the Christian must fight all carnal desires (I Pet. ii. 11), especially the sexual instinct, which in all times and places has been recognised and felt by men as one of the fiercest and most invincible. That the instinct in itself is not sinful may be inferred from God's institution of wedlock. But any transgression of this limit is unchastity, whether in thought (Matt. v. 28), in word (Eph. v. 3, 12), or in deed (I Cor. vi. 15). The destructive effect of incontinence extends not only to the body, but to the soul as well, which is thereby polluted, made unfit for all good, and irretrievably estranged from spiritual intercourse with God, hence these sins exclude from the future communion of heaven (I Cor. vi. 9, 10; Eph. v. 5; Rev. xxi. 8, 27).

For the attainment of chastity training is necessary. For the Christian this training has its root in the grace of regeneration. The guidance and support of the Holy Spirit is indispensable and assured (Rom. viii. 13; Gal. v. 22–23), but is ineffectual without personal exertion and self-discipline on the part of the individual (I Cor. ix. 27; Eph. iv. 29, v. 4; Phil. iv. 8; I Tim. v. 22). The duty of prayer, watchfulness, and the other means of self-training is incumbent on all without respect to sex or age, and rests in an especial degree upon those whose calling is to educate others. While wedlock is a holy defense of chastity (I Cor. vii. 2), it is no guaranty of purity (I Cor. vii. 3–5; I Pet. iii. 1–7). Celibacy, too, has its dangers; it is imposed upon many by circumstances in modern times, but incontinence is not excused thereby. Finally the successful result of Christian training and discipline, made possible by the Christian's inward relation to Jesus Christ, is something different from the natural sense of shame and outward decorum, also from the particular gifts of chastity referred to in Matt. xix. 12, which Paul attributes to himself (I Cor. vii. 7), for which the tradition of the Church praises the Apostle John, and which is mentioned in the Apocalypse (xiv. 4).

Karl Burger†.

CHASUBLE (Lat. *casula*): The principal vestment worn by Roman Catholic priests when celebrating mass. See Vestments and Insignia, Ecclesiastical.

CHÂTEL, shā''tel', **FERDINAND FRANÇOIS**: Founder of the Église catholique-française; b. at Gannat (34 m. s.s.w. of Moulins) Jan. 9, 1795; d. at Paris Feb. 18, 1857. At first chaplain of a regiment of the line, he was called by the July Revolution of 1830 to a place of importance at Paris. An adherent of the liberalism of the period, he sought to found a Church based on reason rather than on Rome, retaining, for the most part, the forms of Roman Catholic ritual, yet changing their meaning and rendering them patriotic in tendency. His theological education was but superficial, and it is clear that at first he was rationalistic and later pantheistic in tendency, while he preserved traces of the cult of Reason in the sense that term bore during the French Revolution. Châtel soon won a considerable following in his movement for reform, and in 1831 he was able to announce the establishment of the Église catholique-française, a temple for several thousand persons being erected at Paris in the Faubourg St. Martin two years later. On the high altar was a representation of Reason in the form of a woman who supported another holding a cross and typifying Religion, while near them was a lion as a symbol of the strength of Reason. The sides of the altar were adorned with pictures of Fénelon and St. Vincent de Paul, with the words *gloire* and *patrie*. The service had the form of a mass; feasts were celebrated in honor of great men, especially Frenchmen; and at Christmas Châtel himself was honored as a "reformer" by the side of Christ. About 1837 the community reached its height, although the majority of its adherents were confined to Paris, but in 1842 it came to an end. The government of Louis Philippe favored it at first, but later became hostile to it. Châtel long survived the organization which he had founded, and died in poverty and neglect. He expounded his views in a series of works, none of which was of any spiritual importance. F. Kattenbusch.

Bibliography: A. Theiner, in *TQ*, 1832, pp. 651 sqq.; H. Reuchlin, *Das Christentum in Frankreich*, pp. 293 sqq., Hamburg, 1837; F. F. Fleck, *Wissenschaftliche Reise durch . . . Frankreich*, vol. ii., part 2, pp. 65 sqq., Leipsic, 1838; F. Kunstmann, in *Zeitschrift für Theologie*, iii (1840), 57 sqq.; R. Holzapfel, in *ZHT*, xiv (1844), 103 sqq.; A. Martin, *Châtel et l'église française*, Montauban, 1904; *KL*, iii. 108-110.

CHAUNCY, CHARLES: 1. Second president of Harvard College; b. at Ardeley or Yardley Bury (10 m. n. of Hertford), Hertfordshire, England, 1592 (baptized Nov. 5); d. in Cambridge, Mass., Feb. 19, 1672. He studied at Trinity College, Cambridge (B.A., 1613; M.A., 1617; B.D., 1624), and became fellow and lecturer in Greek (or professor); was vicar of Ware, Hertfordshire, 1627–33, and of Marston St. Lawrence, Northamptonshire, 1633–37. His stern Puritanism brought him into difficulties with the church authorities in both parishes, and in 1634 he was suspended and imprisoned; after some months' confinement he made submission, but regretted the act ever afterward. He decided to go to America, and before sailing wrote *The Retraction of Charles Chauncy formerly minister of Ware in Hertfordshire* (London, 1641), published, as he says, "for the satisfaction of all such who either are, or justly might be, offended with his scandalous submission, made before the High Commission Court, Feb. 11, 1635." He arrived at Plymouth, Dec., 1637, and acted as assistant there till 1641, when he went to Scituate; he was invited to return to Ware in 1654 and was making preparations for departure when he was offered the presidency of Harvard to succeed Henry Dunster; he accepted with reluctance, was inaugurated Nov. 29, and filled the position faithfully and well. He was a good scholar and, in addition to his attainments as a theologian, had considerable knowledge of medicine; he is said to have been an admirable preacher and was esteemed for his piety. He published *The Doctrine of the Sacrament, with the right use thereof, catechetically handled by way of question and answer* (London, 1642); a volume of sermons on justification (1659); and *Antisynodalia scripta Americana, or a proposal of the judgement of the dissenting ministers of the churches of New England assembled Mar. 10, 1662* (Cambridge, 1662). He had six sons, who were all graduated at Harvard, all became ministers, and all are believed, like their father, to have been physicians as well. His eldest son **Isaac** (b. at Ware Aug. 23, 1632; d. in London Feb. 28, 1712) was ejected as rector of Woodborough, Wiltshire, by the Act of Uniformity in 1662, and in 1687 became minister of the independent congregation in Bury Street, London, formerly served by John Owen; on his resignation in 1701 he was succeeded by his assistant, Isaac Watts; for the rest of his life he practised medicine and taught. He was a voluminous writer.

Bibliography: William Chauncey Fowler, *Memorials of the Chaunceys*, Boston, 1858; Cotton Mather, in his *Magnalia*, gives a chapter to President Chauncy under the title *Cadmus Americanus*, bk. iii., chap. xxiii., vol. i., pp. 463–476, Hartford, 1855; James Savage, *Genealogical Dictionary of the First Settlers of New England*, i. 366–369, Boston, 1860.

2. New England clergyman, great-grandson of President Chauncy; b. in Boston Jan. 1. 1705; d. there Feb. 10, 1787. He was graduated at Harvard, 1721; ordained assistant minister of the First Church of Boston, 1727, and remained there till his death. He cultivated a plain and matter-of-fact style in preaching, and was noted for scrupulous integrity. He tried to check the extreme excitement attending the preaching of Whitefield, and wrote in reference to it *Seasonable Thoughts on the State of Religion in New England* (Boston, 1743), and two or three open letters to Whitefield (1744–1745). He stoutly opposed the establishment of episcopacy in the colonies, and published *The Validity of Presbyterian Ordination Asserted and Maintained* (1762) and *A Complete View of Episcopacy until the Close of the Second Century* (1771). He believed in the final restoration of all, or Universalism, and advocated it in *The Salvation for All Men Illustrated and Vindicated as a Scripture Doctrine* (1782); *Divine Glory Brought to View in the Final Salvation of All Men* (1783); *The Benevo-*

lence of the Deity Fairly and Impartially Considered (1784); *Five Dissertations on the Scripture Account of the Fall and its Consequences* (1787).

BIBLIOGRAPHY: W. C. Fowler, *Memorials of the Chaunceys*, pp. 49–70, Boston, 1858.

CHAUTAUQUA INSTITUTION: An institution on Chautauqua Lake (post-office, Chautauqua, N. Y.), founded in 1874 as a Sunday-school teachers' normal institute by John H. Vincent, now retired bishop in the Methodist Church, and by Lewis Miller of Akron, O. Within four years there developed a complete system of popular education, the main features of which have survived to the present day.

The activities of the institution center primarily about a summer assembly conducted on the Institution ground for eight weeks from late June to late August. At this assembly two main educational features are carried on side by side. A series of summer schools has been evolved which divides itself into two main groups: the first—the academic courses or schools—including the English language and literature, modern languages, classical languages, mathematics and science, psychology and pedagogy, and religious teaching. The second—the professional schools—includes library training, domestic science, music, arts and crafts, expression, physical education, and practical arts. The work in these schools is carried on for six weeks (July-August) and is conducted by a faculty of some ninety instructors from universities, colleges, and normal schools from the Atlantic Coast to the Middle West and the Far South. The second systematic scheme for general education is promoted by means of a popular programme which includes during the season over three hundred lectures, readings, concerts, and entertainments.

Besides the two divisions of the summer schools and public programme, Chautauqua Institution shows its sense of responsibility toward visitors through an established series of clubs which makes place for Chautauquans of all ages from the kindergarten child to the members of the men's and women's clubs. Of these different organizations, five—the Kindergarten, the Girls' Club, the Boys' Club, the Athletic Club, and the Men's Club—now have their own well-equipped and centrally located buildings.

The work of the Institution, however, does not cease with the close of the summer assembly, for through the Chautauqua Literary and Scientific Circle large numbers of people are reached throughout the year by means of a regular series of university extension readings. Four books are prepared yearly for the course and *The Chautauquan*, a monthly magazine, supplements the lines of thought developed in the text-books. The activity of the Reading Circle is directed and systematized by the adoption of a succession of years—the American Year, English-Russian Year, Franco-German Year, and Classical Year; by reading for four years a person passes through the series and qualifies himself for the certificate of completion of the course. During 1905–07 registration in the summer schools averaged 2,465, the total attendance at the assembly each summer was somewhat over 50,000, and the total membership for the Reading Circle from the beginning to 1907 approximated 270,000.

The plan of Chautauqua Institution is extensive, but constantly developing. On the tract of nearly three hundred acres a town with some five hundred cottages has sprung up. An amphitheater seating five thousand, a hall of philosophy with a capacity of eight hundred, and a dozen smaller halls and class buildings provide amply for the various classes and audiences. The Institution holds a charter from the State of New York whereby no element of private profit is permitted. It owns its own lighting and water plants and its own printing establishment, and performs all the functions of an ordinary town although upon a system of government which is entirely unique. The Extension Department circulates each year over a million pieces of matter, and the number of assemblies more or less similar in nature which all owe their stimulus to the original Chautauqua aggregates nearly three hundred. P. H. BOYNTON.

BIBLIOGRAPHY: J. H. Vincent, *The Chautauqua Movement*, Boston, 1886; C. A. Teal, *Counting the Cost; or, a Summer at Chautauqua*, New York, 1889; F. C. Bray, *Reading Journey through Chautauqua*, Chautauqua, 1905 (on the system of instruction).

CHAVASSE, shă"vās', **FRANCIS JAMES:** Anglican bishop of Liverpool; b. at Edgbaston (a suburb of Birmingham) Sept. 27, 1846. He studied at Christ Church, Oxford (B.A., 1869), and was curate of St. Paul's, Preston (1870–73), vicar of St. Paul's, Upper Holloway (1873–78), and rector of St. Peter-le-Bailey, Oxford (1878–89). He was then principal of Wycliffe Hall, Oxford, in 1889–1900, and in the latter year was consecrated bishop of Liverpool. He was select preacher at Oxford in 1888–1889 and 1901–02, and at Cambridge in 1893 and 1902, and was also lecturer in pastoral theology in the latter university in 1898.

CHEDORLAOMER. See BABYLONIA (vol. i., p. 407, foot-note); ISRAEL, HISTORY OF, I.

CHEETHAM, SAMUEL: Anglican archdeacon and canon of Rochester; b. at Hambleton (20 m. n.e. of Leicester), Rutlandshire, Mar. 3, 1827; d. at Rochester July 19, 1908. He was educated at Christ's College, Cambridge (B.A., 1850), became deacon in 1851, and priest in 1852. He was vice-principal of the Collegiate Institute, Liverpool, in 1851–53, and from 1853 to 1858 was assistant tutor of Christ's College, where he was also fellow from 1850 to 1866. He was curate of Hitchin, Herts, in 1858–61, vice-principal of the Theological College, Chichester, and curate of St. Bartholomew's in the same city in 1861–63, and professor of pastoral theology in King's College, London, from 1863 to 1882. He was also chaplain of Dulwich College from 1866 to 1884 and archdeacon of Southwark from 1879 to 1882. In the latter year he was made archdeacon of Rochester, and has also been canon of the same cathedral since 1883, as well as examining chaplain to the bishop of Rochester from 1878 to 1897. He was Hulsean lecturer at Cambridge in 1896. In theology he is a Broad-churchman. In addition to numerous minor contributions, he has written *The Law of the Land and the Law of the Mind* (London, 1866); *Colleges and Tests* (1871); *A History of the Christian Church during the First Six Centuries* (1894); same, *Since the Reformation* (1908); *The Mysteries, Pagan and Christian* (Hulsean Lectures for 1896, 1897); *Mediæval Greek History* (1899). He likewise edited the *Dictionary of Christian Antiquities* (2 vols., London, 1875–80) with Sir William Smith, and contributed a large number of articles to it.

CHEKE, SIR JOHN: English scholar; b. at Cambridge June 16, 1514; d. in London Sept. 13, 1557. He studied at St. John's, Cambridge, and adopted the Reformation doctrines there; became one of the first Greek scholars in England, and in 1540 regius professor at Cambridge; in 1544 was made tutor to Prince Edward, and when the latter succeeded to the throne, in 1547, received honor and wealth. He espoused the cause of Lady Jane Grey, was her secretary of state, and was committed to the Tower by Mary in 1553; released the next year, he went abroad and settled at Strasburg. In 1556 he visited Belgium, was arrested there by order of Philip II., and taken to England; through fear of dying at the stake he renounced the Protestant religion, and his death is said to have been hastened by shame and regret for his weakness. He made an English translation of the Gospel of Matthew (all but the last ten verses) and of the first twenty verses of the first chapter of Mark, with notes (ed., with seven of his letters, James Goodwin, London, 1843), to illustrate a notion he had about "reform" in English spelling and to show that it was possible to use only Saxon words; he edited and translated into Latin some of the homilies of Chrysostom; also Cranmer's treatise upon the Eucharist (1553) and wrote some other tracts; of special interest is *The Hurt of Sedition, how grievous it is to a Commonwealth* (1549).

Bibliography: J. Strype, *Life of the Learned Sir John Cheke*, Oxford, 1821 (contains a transl. of Cheke's "Treatise of Superstition"); an account of the *Life* is also added to G. Langbaine's ed. of *The True Subject to the Rebell*, Oxford, 1641. For his Gospel transl. consult J. I. Mombert, *English Versions of the Bible*, pp. 234–237, London, new ed., 1908.

CHEMNITZ (KEMNITZ), MARTIN.

Pretheological Activity (§ 1).
Work as a Theologian (§ 2).
Share in the Formula of Concord (§ 3).
Part in the Adiaphorist Controversy (§ 4).
Polemics against the Roman Catholics (§ 5).
Evaluation of Chemnitz (§ 6).

German theologian and controversialist of the Reformation period; b. at Treuenbrietzen (35 m. s.w. of Berlin), Brunswick, Nov. 9, 1522; d. at Brunswick Apr. 8, 1586. The death of his father when he was a boy made attainment of education difficult; he was at the Magdeburg school from 1539 to 1542, and then earned money enough by teaching to go to the University of Frankfort-on-the-Oder for a time, and in 1545 to that of Wittenberg. Here he came into contact with Melanchthon, on whose advice he took up mathematics, which led him to astrology. These studies consumed so much time that he paid little heed to Luther's teaching, though he heard him. The outbreak of war took him away from Wittenberg; in 1547 he settled at Königsberg and supported himself by teaching some young Polish noblemen, becoming later rector of the school at Kneiphof.

1. Pretheological Activity.

He still pursued his astrological studies, until on a visit to Wittenberg he was advised by Melanchthon to turn his attention to theology. The plague put an end to his school work, and he accompanied Melanchthon's son-in-law Sabinus to Salfeld, where he laid the foundation of his theological learning. In 1550 he returned to Königsberg, where the duke, who esteemed him as an astrologer, made him his librarian. He was now convinced of the insecure foundations of astrology, and devoted himself systematically to theology, studying the Bible in the original, the Fathers, and the controversial writers of the time. The disturbances stirred up by Osiander's controversy on justification made him uncomfortable at Königsberg, and in 1553 he returned to Wittenberg, where he lectured for a time; but in the following year went to Brunswick to settle permanently, as coadjutor to the superintendent, becoming superintendent himself in 1567 and holding the post until 1584, when he resigned on account of his health.

2. Work as a Theologian.

He was not noted as a preacher, but he was a diligent and methodical pastor. The continuance of his studies, however, made him known rather as one of the first theologians of his time, and he was called upon to take part in every controversy. In 1567 he went with his superior Mörlin to Prussia to reorganize the Church there, distracted by the divisions over Osiander's teaching, and the *Corpus doctrinæ Prutenicum* was the result. He rendered still more important services in the principality of Brunswick-Wolfenbüttel, where, in 1568, Duke Julius summoned him, with Andreä, to assist in establishing Protestantism. The documentary results of his work here, and at Lüneburg with Duke William, remain in the *Corpus doctrinæ Julium* and the *Corpus Wilhelminum*. He also gave the impulse to the founding of the Julian University at Helmstädt in 1576. The later years of his life were largely taken up by work connected with the Formula of Concord (q.v.). Its final acceptance, in spite of all difficulties, was largely due to the untiring work of Chemnitz. Before this, however, he had the misfortune to fall out with Duke Julius, whom he rebuked sharply for having his son consecrated bishop of Halberstadt with all the rites of the old Church.

3. Share in the Formula of Concord.

The Protestant princes who were working for the adoption of the Formula omitted on this account to invite the duke to their conferences at Jüterbock, and he declined to have anything further to do with their undertaking. Thus the Formula was not definitely accepted in Brunswick, and the *Corpus Julium* remained the standard there, as at the University of Helmstädt, which thus assumed an isolated position ultimately favorable to the growth of the doctrines of a Calixtus. Chemnitz wrote a defense of the Formula against its critics, which was published at Magdeburg in 1582. This the Helmstädt theologians attacked, especially on the ground of its containing the doctrine of ubiquity, and a conference was called at Quedlinburg by the three electors and Duke Julius to reconcile the differences. Chemnitz made his last important public appearance at this meeting, but could not prevail. His death was felt as a public calamity by all Protestant Germany.

His first participation in the disputes of the time was occasioned by the Adiaphorist controversy (see ADIAPHORA), at the instance of Mörlin, who was a steadfast Lutheran. He was next moved to utterance on the question of the Lord's Supper by the fact that Zwinglianism had found an entrance into Brunswick. He was not present at the conference held there in 1561 by Mörlin against Hardenberg, the principal representative of this doctrine in northern Germany, but sent a treatise which contributed to Hardenberg's condemnation. In the same year he published a more complete and systematic *Repetitio sanæ doctrinæ de vera præsentia*, in which, avoiding dogmatic subtleties, he rests his belief in the real presence on the plain sense of the words of institution. In 1570 he went on to treat directly of the Incarnation, which then (exactly contrary to the logical sequence of the early Church) was treated as dependent on the eucharistic controversy, in his *De duabus naturis in Christo*, etc. Soon afterward he declared against Crypto-Calvinism (see PHILIPPISTS) in two forcible expressions of opinion on the Wittenberg Catechism, which influenced the action of the authorities in Brunswick and Lower Saxony.

4. Part in the Adiaphorist Controversy.

But he was even better known through his polemics against the Roman Catholic Church and the Jesuits. The latter in 1560 had published in Cologne, where they were strong, a criticism of a Protestant catechism. This was the first literary onslaught of theirs to attract general attention in Germany, and Chemnitz was the first to take it up and warn people of the danger from the Order. His counterblast was entitled *Theologiæ Jesuitarum præcipua capita* (1572). Payva d'Andrada (q.v.), a Portuguese Jesuit and member of the Council of Trent, published two works in rejoinder (1564), the first of which came into Chemnitz's hands together with the decrees of the Council, to which it appealed. This seemed to him to open the way for a more thoroughgoing work, and gave him the idea of his famous *Examen concilii Tridentini* (1565–73), than which no book of the period was more damaging to the Roman claims. It ran through numerous editions, and was translated into German and French; a modern edition was brought out by Preuss (Berlin, 1861). His dogmatic standpoint is indicated not only in these polemical works, but in the *Loci theologici*, commenting on Melanchthon's *Loci*, which, left uncompleted by him, his successor Leyser and his son published in 1591. Here, without directly contradicting Melanchthon, he interprets him in a tone of moderate Lutheran orthodoxy, attempting to work out a consistent integral body of doctrine, and to show its relation to the Christian life. Leyser also edited and published his incomplete exegetical works, the *Harmonia evangelica* and the *Postilla oder Auslegung der Evangelien*, in 1593.

5. Polemics Against the Roman Catholics.

Chemnitz's mind was not of the creative order; but it was just what was needed for his time, following upon an age of productivity, when systematization and confirmation were the great requirements. He took a middle course among the parties of the age; strongly influenced as he had been by Melanchthon, his doctrine leaned more to strict Lutheranism, and the Philippists (q.v.) upbraided him as an apostate. Sober discretion characterized both his writings and his practical work. He was suspicious of innovations, exhorting his readers to "hold fast the form of sound words," and never going to the extremes of the younger Lutheran school. His practical cast of mind shows itself in his theology, which is never merely speculative, but occupied rather with laying down serviceable and unquestionable formulas. His life, taken as a whole, must certainly be pronounced a blessing to the Church he served so long. (JOHANNES KUNZE.)

6. Evaluation of Chemnitz.

BIBLIOGRAPHY: The best source for a life is J. Rehtmeyer, *Der berühmten Stadt Braunschweig Kirchenhistorie*, iii. 273 sqq., Brunswick, 1710. Other sources are the letters of Chemnitz in the library of the University of Göttingen, and J. Gasner, *Oratio de vita, studiis et obitu M. Chemnitii* [Brunswick], 1588. Other accounts are: T. Pressel, *Martin Chemnitz*, Elberfeld, 1862; C. G. H. Lentz, *Dr. Martin Chemnitz*, Gotha, 1866 (uses MSS. sources); H. Hachfeld, *Martin Chemnitz*, Leipsic, 1867 (also based partly on unprinted sources); R. Mumm, *Die Polemik des M. Chemnitz gegen das Konzil von Trent*, Leipsic, 1905; Schaff, *Christian Church*, vii. 601.

CHEMOSH: The national god of the Moabites according to the Old Testament, confirmed by the Moabite Stone (q.v.); by the Moabitish names *Kamūsunadbi* (i.e., Chemoshnadab, cf. the Hebr. Jehonadab), mentioned as a king of Moab in an inscription of Sennacherib ("Taylor Cylinder," ii. 53; H. Zimmern, in Schrader, *KAT*, p. 472), *Chemoshmelek* (or *Chemoshgad*), the father of Mesha (Moabite Stone, 1), and *Chemoshyehi*, upon a gem with Phenician inscription found at Beirut and probably Moabitish (E. Renan, *Mission de Phénicie*, Paris, 1864, pp. 351–352; De Vogüé, *Mélanges d'archéologie orientale*, Paris, 1868, p. 89). The name may possibly be found also in one or two other inscriptions (W. Gesenius, in *Scripturæ linguæque Phœniciæ monumenta*, Leipsic, 1837, p. 159; P. Le Bas and W. H. Waddington, *Inscriptions grecques et latines recueillies en Grèce et en Asie Mineure*, iii. 1, Paris, 1870, n. 2220). In Judges xi. 24 Chemosh is spoken of apparently as god of the Ammonites; but elsewhere in the Old Testament the Ammonitish god is called Milcom (related to Molech) (I Kings xi. 5, 7, 33; II Kings xxiii. 13), and there is reason to believe that the passage Judges xi. 12–28 is an interpolation and originally referred to the Moabites (cf. the commentaries on Judges). The etymology of Chemosh is uncertain. Concerning the character of the god and his worship not much is known. His priests are mentioned, and an image of him (which was to be carried away as a trophy by enemies) is implied in Jer. xlviii. 7 (cf.

verse 13); the expression "Chemosh said to me" (Moabite Stone, 14, 32) indicates prophets or an oracle; he was worshiped at a "high place" (I Kings xi. 7; Isa. xvi. 12; II Kings xxiii. 13; Moabite Stone, 3) and, at least in extreme cases, his cult included human sacrifice (II Kings iii. 27; cf. Moabite Stone, 14–17). The expression "Ashtar Chemosh" (Moabite Stone, 17) probably indicates that a female deity was associated with Chemosh; it is thought by some, however, that Ashtar is another name for Chemosh and that the compound "Ashtar Chemosh" is formed like Yahweh Elohim (cf. E. Meyer, in *ZDMG*, vol. xxxi., 1877, p. 733; F. Baethgen, *Beiträge zur semitischen Religionsgeschichte*, Berlin, 1888, pp. 13 sqq.; G. A. Barton, *A Sketch of Semitic Origins*, New York, 1902, pp. 141–144). Chemosh was worshiped by the idolatrous Israelites (I Kings xi. 7, 33; II Kings xxiii. 13). The similarity of the language applied to Chemosh, both in the Old Testament and in the Moabite Stone, to that used of Yahweh is very striking. The Moabites are the "people of Chemosh," his sons and daughters he "gives into captivity" (Num. xxi. 29; cf. Jer. xlviii. 46); Chemosh gives possessions (Judges xi. 24). In the Moabite Stone Chemosh is the lord and protector of Moab; he commanded Mesha to go to war (14, 32) and gave the victory (4, 19); the slaughter of his enemies was a "pleasing spectacle for Chemosh" (11–12); because he was "angry with his land" Chemosh allowed Omri to oppress Moab (5). See Moab, and for the inscription, Moabite Stone.

Bibliography: Besides the works already mentioned and those referred to in the article Moabite Stone, consult: D. Hackmann, *De Chemoscho Moabitarum idolo*, Bremen, 1730; F. C. Movers, *Die Phönizier*, i. 334–337, Bonn, 1841; P. Scholz, *Götzendienst und Zauberwesen bei den alten Hebräern*, pp. 176–182, Regensburg, 1877, and the literature under Moab.

CHENEY, CHARLES EDWARD: Reformed Episcopal bishop; b. at Canandaigua, N. Y., Feb. 12, 1836. He was educated at Hobart College (B.A., 1857) and at the Protestant Episcopal Theological Seminary, Alexandria, Va., from which he was graduated in 1859. He was ordered deacon in 1858 and ordained priest two years later. After being curate of St. Luke's, Rochester, N. Y. (1858–1859), and of St. Paul's, Havana, N. Y. (1859–60), he became rector of Christ Church, Chicago, in 1860. His pronounced evangelicalism, however, caused him to be tried by Bishop Whitehouse, although the verdict was overruled by the civil courts. His church, nevertheless, seceded from the Protestant Episcopal communion, and in 1873, on the organization of the Reformed Episcopal Church, he was elected first bishop, still retaining his rectorate, which he has since held continuously. His jurisdiction was changed in 1878 from the Northwest to the Synod of Chicago, and in 1905 he was president of the Synod of Reformed Episcopal Churches of the Central States. While in the Protestant Episcopal Church he was, naturally, an adherent of the pronounced Low-church party, and now describes himself as "believing heartily in the great fundamental principles held by all *evangelical* Christians," and as "totally opposed to all that leans toward any compromise with Romanism, and equally opposed to the radicalism involved in the destructive criticism of God's Word." He has written: *Twenty-Eight Sermons* (Chicago, 1880); *A Word to Old-Fashioned Episcopalians* (Philadelphia, 1884); *What is the Reformed Episcopal Church?* (1885); *What do Reformed Episcopalians Believe?* (1888); *The Enlistment of the Christian Soldier* (Chicago, 1893); *A King of France unnamed in History* (1903); and *The Second Norman Conquest of England* (1907).

CHERBURY, EDWARD HERBERT, LORD. See Deism, I., § 1.

CHERETHITES, ker′e-thaits, **AND PELETHITES,** pel′e-thaits (Heb. *hakkerethi wehappelethi*): The designation of the royal body-guard of King David, commanded by Benaiah (II Sam. viii. 18, xv. 18, xx. 7, 23; I Kings i. 38, 44; I Chron. xviii. 17; called *sōmatophylakes* by Josephus, *Ant.*, VII. v. 4). The interpretations "executioners and runners" (Gesenius and others) and "bowmen and slingers" (Targum Jonathan, Peshitto) are not supported by etymological proof, and are inadmissible because the Hebrew forms are unquestionably gentilic nouns. The name "Cherethite" in the above passages is to be taken as in I Sam. xxx. 14 (cf. Zeph. ii. 5; Ezek. xxv. 16), where the reference is to the Philistine population, or at least to a part of the same. The connection of this people with the island of Crete is less certain, though it is easily possible that they were Cretans (see Caphtor). The word *Pelethi* ("Pelethites") seems to be an abbreviation of *Pelishti* ("Philistines"), intended to rime with *Kerethi*, and the two words taken together allude in a general way to the various elements of the Philistine population. There is nothing improbable in David's having a standing body-guard wholly or chiefly of Philistines, subject to himself alone and reliable in times of civil strife. His attitude toward Ittai and his countrymen from Gath (II Sam. xv. 18–22, xviii. 2) shows that such relations with foreigners (even uncircumcised) were not found offensive, either from a national or a theocratic point of view. This body-guard is not to be confused with the "mighty men" who constituted the native *corps d'élite* (cf. II Sam. xx. 7).

Probably the royal body-guard was popularly known as the "Cherethites and Pelethites" until long after David's time, though the appellation must soon have become inapplicable to the nationality of the guardsmen. In the time of Athaliah mention is made of the "captains and the guard" (II Kings xi. 4, 19; Heb. *hakkari weharaṣim*, evidently formed after analogy with the old double name). The "guard" are the footmen and the accompanying halberdiers who ran before the king's chariot (II Sam. xv. 1; cf. I Sam. xxii. 17 and elsewhere). The "captains," however, are more correctly the "Carites" (cf. R.V.) or "Carians," and the passage shows that in a later period this adventurous people, who were often employed as mercenaries (cf. Herodotus, ii. 152, v. 111; Livy, xxxvii. 40) had come to occupy in Jerusalem the place of the old Philistines. The Hebrew text (*kethibh*) of II Sam. xx. 23 has *kari* (both English versions follow the *keri* in translating "Cherethites"), perhaps by confusion with the later passage. The Great Cylinder Inscription of Sennacherib seems to indicate that Hezekiah had an Arabian body-guard (cf. Sayce, *Higher Criticism and the Monuments*, pp. 431, 433, London, 1894).

C. von Orelli.

Bibliography: The dissertations of Carpsov and Opitz, still valuable, are in Ugolini, *Thesaurus antiquitatum sacrorum*, xxvii. 423 sqq., 451 sqq., 34 vols., Venice, 1744-1769. Consult also C. Iken, *Dissertationes philologico-theologicæ*, pp. 111-132, Leyden, 1727; B. Behrend, *Die Kreti und Pleti*, Krotoschin, 1868; S. R. Driver, *Notes on the Hebr. Text of Samuel*, London, 1890; R. Kittel, *History of the Hebrews*, ii. 153, 164, ib. 1896; *DB*, i. 376-377; *EB*, i. 739-740; Smith, *OTJC*, p. 262.

CHERUB. See Angel.

CHESHIRE, JOSEPH BLOUNT, JR.: Protestant Episcopal bishop of North Carolina; b. at Tarborough, N. C., Mar. 27, 1850. He was graduated at Trinity College, Hartford, Conn., in 1869, and after teaching for two years, studied law and was admitted to the North Carolina bar in 1872. He practised for six years, and then, having studied theology privately, was ordered deacon in 1878, and priested two years later. He was curate at Chapel Hill, N. C., 1878-81, and was rector of St. Peter's, Charlotte, N. C., 1881-93. In the latter year he was consecrated bishop coadjutor of North Carolina, and within the year, on the death of Bishop Lyman, he became bishop of the diocese.

Bibliography: W. S. Perry, *The Episcopate in America*, p. 361, New York, 1895.

CHEYNE, chē'ni', THOMAS KELLY: Church of England; b. at London Sept. 18, 1841. He was educated at Worcester College, Oxford (B.A., 1862), and also studied at the University of Göttingen. He was ordered deacon in 1864, and ordained priest in the following year, and from 1868 to 1882 was fellow of Balliol College, Oxford, in addition to being a college lecturer on Hebrew and divinity in the same college from 1870 to 1871. He became rector of Tendring, Essex, from 1880 to 1885; was Oriel professor of the interpretation of Scripture, Oxford 1885-1908; became canon of Rochester 1885. He became a member of the Old Testament Revision Company in 1884, was Bampton Lecturer in 1889, and American Lecturer on the History of Religions in 1897-98. He is one of the leaders of the "higher criticism" of the Bible in the English-speaking world, and in this spirit edited the *Encyclopædia Biblica* in collaboration with J. S. Black (4 vols., London, 1899-1903). His independent works include, in addition to numerous contributions to standard works of reference, as well as to theological periodicals, *Notes and Criticisms on the Hebrew Text of Isaiah* (London, 1868); *The Book of Isaiah Chronologically Arranged* (1870, in collaboration with S. R. Driver); *The Prophecies of Isaiah* (2 vols., 1880-81); *Micah* (1882) and *Hosea* (1884) in *The Cambridge Bible*, *Jeremiah* in *The Pulpit Commentary* (1883-84); *The Book of Psalms, a New Translation* (1884); *Job and Solomon* (1887); *Jeremiah, his Life and Times* (1888); *The Origin and Religious Contents of the Psalter* (1891; the Bampton Lectures for 1889); *Aids to the Devout Study of Criticism* (1892); *Founders of Old Testament Criticism* (1893); *Introduction to the Book of Isaiah* (1895); *Book of Isaiah* (critical text and translation) in the Polychrome Bible (2 vols., 1898-99); *Jewish Religious Life after the Exile* (New York, 1898; American Lectures on the history of religions for 1897-98); *The Christian Use of the Psalms* (London, 1899); *Critica Biblica* (1904); *Bible Problems and the New Materials for their Solution* (1904); and *Traditions and Beliefs of Ancient Israel* (1907).

CHEYNELL, FRANCIS: Puritan; b. in Oxford 1608; d. at Preston, near Brighton, Sussex, 1665. He studied at Merton College, Oxford, and became fellow; took orders and held a curacy near Oxford and a living near Banbury; on the outbreak of the civil war he became an active partizan of the parliamentary side, and, as a reward for his services, was given the living of Petworth, Sussex, in 1643. He was a member of the Westminster Assembly the same year. In 1646 parliament determined to "reform" the University of Oxford and appointed Cheynell one of a commission to "prepare the way," and the next year made him one of the visitors; he is said to have been "the most detested as well as the most active and meddlesome of all." In 1648 he took forcible possession of the Lady Margaret professorship of divinity and the presidency of St. John's College, but either resigned or was removed in 1650. He was deprived of his living some time before the general ejection of non-conforming ministers in 1662. He attended William Chillingworth (q.v.) in his last illness, showing himself "as charitable and compassionate as his rigid orthodoxy would permit him to be" (Des Maizeaux, *Life of Chillingworth*, p. 314): he refused to officiate at the burial, but attended the ceremony with Chillingworth's book in his hand, and in the course of a bitter harangue threw it into the grave, exclaiming, "Get thee gone, thou cursed book, . . . rot with thy author and see corruption." To justify his conduct he published *Chillingworthi novissima, or the sickness, heresy, death, and burial of W. Chillingworth* (London, 1664); he also published *The Rise, Growth, and Danger of Socinianism* (1643) and other works.

Bibliography: A. à Wood, *Athenæ Oxonienses*, ed. P. Bliss, vol. ii., 4 vols., London, 1813-20; D. Neal, *Hist. of the Puritans*, vol. iv., ib. 1738; *DNB*, x. 222-224.

CHICAGO-LAMBETH ARTICLES. See Fundamental Doctrines of Christianity, § 4; Lambeth Conference.

CHIEMSEE, ki''em-sê', BISHOPRIC OF: A bishopric of the modern Bavaria. Before the middle of the eighth century, a monastery was founded, probably from Salzburg, on an island in the Chiemsee, the largest lake of Bavaria. In 788 it was given by Charlemagne to the church of Metz, which retained possession of it till 891, when King Arnulf exchanged it for Luxeuil and presented it to Salzburg. The foundation of the bishopric was due to Archbishop Eberhard of that see (1200-46), and was confirmed by the Lateran Council in 1215 and by Innocent III. shortly after The extent of its jurisdiction was only about eight miles by four, comprising the valleys of the Prien and the Achen with their tributaries. The see was suppressed in 1807, in the process of reorganization of the Bavarian Church. (A. HAUCK.)

BIBLIOGRAPHY: J. E. von Koch-Sternfeld, *Beyträge zur teutschen Länder- . . . und Staaten-Kunde*, ii. 269–314, 3 vols., Munich, 1825–33; Rettberg, *KD*, ii. 243; Hauck, *KD*, ii. 432, iv. 655, 924; *KL*, iii. 134–137.

CHILDREN'S BIBLES. See BIBLES FOR CHILDREN.

CHILDREN'S COMMUNION. See LORD'S SUPPER, V.

CHILDREN'S DAY, CHILDREN'S SERVICES. See SUNDAY-SCHOOLS AND CHILDREN'S SERVICES.

CHILE: A republic of South America, bounded on the north by Peru, on the east by Bolivia and Argentina, on the south and west by the Pacific Ocean; area, 307,620 square miles; population, 2,712,150 by census of 1895, estimated in 1903 at 3,205,992. The Indians number about 50,000.

The predominant religion is Roman Catholic. An active missionary propaganda, in which Franciscans and Jesuits were especially zealous, began immediately after the Spanish conquest under Valdivia in 1539–41, from the town of Santiago (founded 1541) as a base. The heroic resistance of the Araucanians, the ruling native people, prevented extensive results till late in the seventeenth century. The period of separation from Spain began in 1810 and ended in 1827, when the Spanish garrisons were finally withdrawn. The present ecclesiastical organization includes the archdiocese of Santiago of Chile (founded 1561, raised to archiepiscopal rank in 1840) and the dioceses of Concepcion (1563), Ancud (1840), and La Serena (1840). The vicariates apostolic of Antofagasta (for Chile and Bolivia) and Tarapacá (for Chile and Peru), and the prefecture of Araucania have been established in recent years. There is an apostolic delegate and envoy extraordinary.

The Roman Catholic religion is legally recognized as "protected" (*protetta*) by the State, and the Church receives an annual subsidy of about one million pesos. Freedom of religious confession, however, is granted. Plans of the curia concerning the relations between the Church and non-Catholics and educational affairs led to a difference with the government in 1883; nevertheless President Balmaceda maintained the provisions respecting complete tolerance of Protestant worship, and state promotion of higher instruction. One consequence was the founding of a Catholic University at Santiago in 1889; beside which the State University (founded by the Jesuits, 1743) with five faculties is still active.

Primary instruction is not uniform, and school attendance is not compulsory; private, parochial, and public schools exist side by side for both white children and Indians; approximately 1,960 schools are maintained by public funds as against somewhat over 500 by other arrangements. The State also provides for several normal schools. There is evidence of a noteworthy expansion of secondary schools for boys and girls, and the management and equipment are good; a state pedagogical institute for this branch of education is in operation at Santiago. Higher education is served, apart from the university, by an Academy of Art, a Conservatory, and an Institute for Agriculture and Mining.

Immigration has given rise to a number of considerable congregations of the Anglican Church and of the Presbyterian confession, and a German Evangelical Church "of the country." The former are found especially in Valparaiso, Santiago, Concepcion, Iquique. The fourteen German Evangelical congregations are not yet completely coordinated by synodical union, but they have everywhere an assuring support in the way of German schools, even though most of these are not strictly associated with the Church. The German total is estimated at 12,000; that of English-speaking Protestants at 7,000.

WILHELM GOETZ.

BIBLIOGRAPHY: Mrs. M. R. Wright, *Republic of Chile*, Philadelphia, 1905; J. T. Medina, *Los Aborigines de Chile*, Santiago, 1882; C. Ochsenius, *Chile, Land und Leute*, Leipsic, 1885; H. Kunz, *Chile und die deutschen Kolonien*, Leipsic, 1891; A. U. Hancock, *A Hist. of Chile*, Chicago, 1893.

CHILIASM, kil'i-azm. See MILLENNIUM, MILLENARIANISM.

CHILLINGWORTH, WILLIAM: Church of England; b. at Oxford Oct., 1602; d. at Chichester Jan. 30, 1644. He became a scholar of Trinity College, Oxford, 1618 (B.A., 1620; M.A., 1623; fellow, 1628). He entered heartily into the theological controversies of the time, and, undertaking to argue against a Jesuit at Oxford (John Percy, but known as John Fisher), became himself a convert to Romanism and went to Douai in 1630; here he attempted to write out the reasons for his change of faith with the result that he wavered, returned to Oxford in 1631, and in 1634 declared himself again a Protestant. He seems to have been influenced by a longing for authority and certainty; the apparently firmer foundation offered by the Church of Rome proved delusive; and then he settled upon Scripture interpreted by reason. Some of the claims of the Church of England seemed to him unreasonable, and he declined to take orders. His great work was called forth by a controversy between a Jesuit, Matthias Wilson (alias Edward Knott), and Dr. Christopher Potter, provost of Queen's College, Oxford, as to whether Protestants could be saved. Three books had already appeared when Chillingworth entered the contest (*Charity Mistaken*, 1630, and *Mercy and Truth*, 1634, by the Jesuit; *Want of Charity Justly Charged*, 1633, by Dr. Potter). His work, after being examined and approved by the vice-chancellor of Oxford and two divinity professors, appeared at Oxford in 1638 with the title *The Religion of Protestants a Safe Way to Salvation: or an Answer to a Book entitled Mercy and Truth.* A second edition was necessary within five months, and a host of answers and criticisms was called forth, from Puritans as well as Roman Catholics. It is a defense of Protestantism, which, he says, he understands to be not "the doctrine of Luther, or Calvin, or Melanchthon; nor the confession of Augusta [Augsburg], or

Geneva; nor the catechism of Heidelberg, nor the articles of the Church of England; no, nor the harmony of Protestant confessions; but that wherein they all agree, and which they all subscribe with a greater harmony as a perfect rule of their faith and actions, that is, the BIBLE. The BIBLE, I say, the BIBLE only is the religion of Protestants" (part i., chap. vi., sec. 56). He argues strongly for free inquiry, and denies that any church is infallible. Concerning the Church of England he declares that he believes its doctrine "so pure and orthodox that whosoever believes it, and lives according to it, undoubtedly he shall be saved; and that there is no error in it which may necessitate or warrant any man to disturb the peace or renounce the communion of it. This, in my opinion, is all intended by subscription" (preface, sec. 40). This being acceptable to the bishops, in 1638 Chillingworth was made chancellor of Salisbury with the prebend of Brixworth in Northamptonshire annexed. He took the royalist side in the contest between king and parliament, and wrote against "rebels"; became chaplain in the royal army and was taken prisoner at Arundel Castle in Dec., 1643; being ill at the time, he was taken to Chichester, where his death was hastened, as was believed by his friends, by the injudicious efforts of the Puritan Francis Cheynell (q.v.) to convert him.

BIBLIOGRAPHY: Chillingworth's minor writings were published in 1687 under the title *Additional Discourses;* the best edition of his *Works* is that of Oxford, 1838, 3 vols.; a *Historical and Critical Account of the Life and Writings of William Chillingworth* by P. Des Maiseaux appeared in London, 1725; and his *Life* by Thomas Birch was prefixed to the tenth folio edition of his *Works* (1742), reprinted in the edition of 1838. Cf. *DNB*, x. 252-257.

CHIMERE. SEE VESTMENTS AND INSIGNIA, ECCLESIASTICAL.

CHINA.

China forms the southeastern part of the Chinese empire, is from 1,300,000 to 1,500,000 square miles in extent, and has a population of perhaps 375,000,000. Its capital is Peking. The name "China" is often loosely used for the entire empire, which includes, besides China proper, Manchuria, Mongolia, East Turkestan, and Tibet. The governmental authority in large districts is purely nominal, and for this reason and owing to the encroachments of European powers, the boundaries and area are uncertain and fluctuating. The extent is given as about 4,200,000 square miles, and a late estimate of the population (admittedly very uncertain) is 425,000,000.

I. Native Religions: In speaking of the "religions" of the Chinese it is always necessary to point out that not only does the Chinese language contain no such word as "religion" in the sense of a relation between God and man, but there has never been any equivalent to this idea in the minds of the Chinese people. The teaching of the Sages, which are ethical as distinguished from religious, are grouped under the term "instruction." To "worship the gods" means also to pay one's respects.

1. Confucianism: Confucius (q.v.) was a teacher and a philosopher who wished to reform his native state by a return to the past. At the age of fifty-five he became an official, but his morals were too pure and his aims too lofty to make him successful and he retired in disgust to private life. His great work was the instruction of his pupils, who are said to have numbered 3,000, seventy-two of whom are enrolled among the Sages of the empire. They gathered up his sayings in a kind of Memorabilia which for ages has been a text-book in every Chinese school. Confucius edited the books already reckoned as classical, but added comparatively little of his own, his most important work being a bald compendium of Chinese history covering about 240 years, including his own lifetime. Through the use of them as text-books his comments on the Book of Rites, the Book of Poetry, the Book of History, and the Book of Changes, together with the Memorabilia, have probably exerted more influence upon a greater number of human beings than any other writings in the history of mankind. The Book of History should be especially mentioned, which, as Dr. Williams remarks, "contains the seeds of all things that are valuable in the estimation of the Chinese—it is at once the foundation of their political system, their history, and their religious rites, the basis of their tactics, music, and astronomy."

1. Confucius.

Although while he lived his precepts were neglected, Confucius began to be appreciated after he was dead, and has long been regarded by the Chinese as a perfect Sage (otherwise called "Holy Man"), to whom there is a temple in every city, where there are annual offerings of animals and of silk. The ornamental portals inform the passer-by that his "Virtue Equaled Heaven and Earth," which is tantamount to his deification. In the words of Dr. Legge: "The homage which is offered to the Master could not be more complete were he Shang Ti himself." In striking contrast with this universal estimate of the Chinese people is that of Confucius himself in such modest sentences as the following: "The Sage and the man of perfect virtue—how dare I rank myself with them? It may simply be said of me that I strive to become such without satiety, and to teach others without weariness. In letters I am perhaps equal to other men; but the character of the Superior Man, carrying out in his conduct what he professes, is what I have not attained to. The leaving virtue without proper cultivation; the not thoroughly discussing what is learned; not being able to move toward righteousness of which knowledge is gained; and not being able to change what is not good—these are the things which occasion me solicitude. I am not one who was born in possession of knowledge; I am one who is fond of antiquity, and earnest in seeking it. A transmitter, and not a maker, believing in and loving the ancients." This latter trait of the Master has been perpetuated in the Chinese people, whose face has for more than two millenniums continued to be turned to the past. Aside from the voluminous works which constitute the Chinese classics, a view of what is for convenience comprehensively termed Confucianism must take account of the standard interpretation of these works by Chu Hsi, a highly distinguished scholar of the Sung dynasty (1130–1200 A.D.), whose commentaries on the classical works have for centuries formed the recognized standard of orthodoxy.

Like all other complex systems of human thought, Confucianism is many-sided. But its essence is expressed in the "Five Constant Virtues" of Benevolence, Righteousness, Propriety, Wisdom, and Sincerity, as well as in enforcing the duties of the "five relations" of Prince and Minister, Husband and Wife, Father and Son, Brother to Brother, and Friend to Friend.

2. The Teaching of Confucius.

Confucius taught the duty of keeping aloof from spirits, while at the same time treating them respectfully. "We have not performed our duties to men," he says; "how then can we perform our duties to spirits?" "Not knowing life, how can we know about death?" The laws of nature, and of the spiritual world as well, lie beyond the comprehension of all men except those endowed by nature with the spirit of wisdom. "He who has sinned against Heaven has no place for prayer." It has been claimed that there are six essential elements in Confucianism, five of which differentiate it from any other system of non-Christian thought. These are: (1) The direct responsibility of the sovereign to Heaven, Shang Ti, or God. (2) The greater importance of the people than the sovereign. (3) The discrimination of the five social relations, with their appropriate duties. (4) Insistence on the virtues just mentioned, with the doctrine that the wise and the able should rule, the object of the ancient civil service examination being to ascertain who the wise and the able are. (5) The presentation of an ideal, or Princely Man, as a model upon which every Confucianist should form his character. The influence of this upon the unnumbered millions of Chinese must have been measureless. (6) Filial piety, which involves not merely suitable treatment of the living, but the worship of ancestors, the real religion of the Chinese people, and perhaps the most potent among several causes which have perpetuated the race through all the millenniums of Chinese history.

Confucianism is mixed with and debased by an intricate system of nature-worship, including worship of heaven and earth, the sun and the moon, the clouds, the rain, thunder, the five great mountains, the north pole, the spirits of dead worthies, and much else, combining in one ritual gods, ghosts, flags, and cannon. It embodies much of ideal excellence for an ideal world, but it is deficient in the chief of the relations, for it has no knowledge of God, its account of men is inadequate, it has no elucidation of the fact of sin, and no remedy for it, nor any explanation of the relation between man and God. Confucius used the term Heaven instead of Shang Ti. As Dr. Legge says: "He was unreligious rather than irreligious; yet by the coldness of his temperament and intellect in this matter his influence is unfavorable to the development of true religious feeling among the Chinese people generally, and he prepared the way for the speculations of the literati of medieval and modern times which have exposed them to the charge of atheism."

3. Its Defects.

Confucianism is a wonderful product of human development, with a unique grip on its adherents. Its strength lies in the inherent rectitude of its injunctions, which, if followed, would make the world a very different one from that which we see. But it has the fatal defect of altogether failing to recognize the inherent weakness and inability of human nature to fulfil these high behests, and for this inability Confucianism has neither explanation nor remedy. In its adoration of Confucius and other worthies, its face is ever toward the past. Its worship of ancestors has no ethical value,* and is quite destitute of any directive or restraining power. While Confucianism has unified and consolidated the Chinese people, it has not, as the Great Learning enjoins, *renovated* them, and it never can do so. It can do no more for China than it has already accomplished, and it is now a spent force.

2. Taoism: The Chinese character Tao signifies a "road, reason, doctrine." The indigenous religion called by this name owes its reputed origin to Lao-tsze ("Old Master," as distinguished from Confucius *the* Master; see LAO-TSZE), who is supposed to have been half a century older than Confucius, and to whom is generally attributed the work called "Canons of Reason and Virtue," a treatise remarkable alike for its brevity and its profundity.

1. Origin and Characteristics.

Historically next to nothing is known of Lao-tsze, and the authenticity of the treatise passing under his name is much disputed. Taoists are linked to Confucianists by a common regard for the Book of Changes, of which great use is made by them. The Taoism of the present day has nothing to do either with the Canon of Reason just mentioned or with its alleged author, whose philosophy is now only a historical curiosity. Modern Taoism occupies itself with a quest for the elixir of immortality, the conquest

* [This statement will not be accepted by all students of Chinese religion. Many of them look upon ancestor-worship as the apotheosis of the family, and point out that the practise of laying before the ancestral tablet as a worthy offering the article or document which evidences that the individual had done something which reflected credit on the family must affect the offerer and his descendants. The contemplation of distinguished or even respectable ancestors has stirred many among us to nobler living. Yet it is true that the evangelising of China is hindered by the practise.—ED.]

of the passions, and especially with the exorcising of demons. It is extensively mixed with Buddhist ideas, having borrowed from that system the notion of a trinity of Pure Ones. A being having the same title as the Shang Ti of the Confucianists is worshiped, but his functions are practically delegated to a divinity called Pearly Emperor Supreme Ruler, who is regarded as an apotheosis of a man named Chang who lived in the Han dynasty (189 B.C.), and whose supposed successors, into each of whom the soul of the founder transmigrates, lives on the Dragon-Tiger mountain in Kiangsi, and is by foreigners termed "the Taoist Pope." Eight "Immortals," each of great capacity, some of them objects of worship, figure largely in popular Taoism. In almost all villages there is a temple to the local god (or god of the soil) who is regarded as a constable reporting deaths, etc., to the city god (Ch'eng Huang) in whose temple are represented by images the most horrible tortures of the future life, visited upon the wicked. A Sea Dragon King rules the waters, and is often worshiped in the form of water (or even land) snakes. Taoism boasts an immense literature, but with the exception of the classic named it is of little value, and is not reducible to a system. It descends into animal worship of the "Five Great Families," viz., the Fox, the Rat, the Weasel, the Snake, and the Hedgehog, each of which is spoken of in terms of the highest respect, and considered to be endowed with supernatural powers.

2. Superstition of the Chinese. The dense ignorance of the Chinese regarding the uniformity of nature, and the apparent absence of any intuition of cause and effect, make the popular mind a fertile seed-bed for the cultivation of superstitious germs of every sort. Every few years a wave of fanaticism seems to be propagated throughout the empire, issuing in tales of cue-cutting without visible agency, kidnaping of children, and the like. The whole Boxer movement in China was stimulated by beliefs which negative and defy the laws of nature.

Men who are confident that no sword that was ever forged can cut them, that no rifle-bullet can penetrate their charmed bodies, that no artillery can destroy them are dangerous elements in any civilized land, and China is full of such men. It is difficult to find in Taoism at the present day a single redeeming feature. Its assumptions are wholly false, its bald materialism inevitably and hopelessly debasing.

3. Buddhism: This Indian religion is supposed to have been introduced into China in the Han dynasty, by the Emperor Ming Ti, in consequence of a dream. At different periods it encountered great opposition both from the agnostic Confucianists and the materialistic Taoists. The essential doctrines of Buddhism (q.v.) are the vanity of all material things, the supreme importance of charity, and the certainty of rewards and punishment by means of the transmigration of souls. The Five Precepts of Buddhism forbid the taking of life, stealing, lust, improper speech, and the use of wine.

The Buddhist habit of renouncing one's family and becoming priests or nuns is in theory totally opposed to Confucian teaching and instincts, yet like the belief in the transmigration of souls, and the bliss of attaining to be a Buddha, it is commended to the Chinese by long custom. The poverty of thousands of Chinese makes their children available for service in the temples, though Confucianism has never assented to it. Yet whatever their theoretical views, Chinese of all ranks call in Buddhist or Taoist priests, or both, upon due provocation, especially at funerals. The unlimited utterance of the name of Omito Fo (Amita Buddha) will bring great felicity, and its incessant enunciation is one of the principal industries of the Mongols. The power of Buddhism has arisen from the fatal weakness of Confucianism, which has nothing to say of the hereafter. The literature of Buddhism, like that of Taoism, is appallingly extensive, embracing both translations from the Sanskrit (which embodies the northern form of Buddhism as the Pali language does the southern), and also attempts to write Sanskrit texts in Chinese characters. Although Buddhist tenets are deeply enshrined in the hearts of the Chinese people, Chinese scholars, even when adopting Buddhism, have always affected to despise it. It has rendered the Chinese more compassionate to the brute creation than they would otherwise have been, and it has introduced the graceful but costly pagoda, as well as the dagoba, or memorial tope. While often displaying the negative activity arising from the cohesive power of ancient, vested interests, Buddhism in China has long since lost the virility which it attained through persecution, and has passed into a hopeless and senile decay.

4. Mohammedanism: Mohammedans are scattered throughout China, particularly in the cities, being strongest in the southwestern provinces, their total number being estimated at twenty millions. They reached China in the T'ang dynasty, over a thousand years ago. Their mosques are especially in evidence in such great centers as Peking, Tien-Tsin, Canton, etc. The Mohammedans are much more lax in their practises than their coreligionists in India. They do not intermarry with the Chinese, but sometimes adopt Chinese children. They do nothing to propagate their faith, and apparently have never done so. The Chinese consider them as more violent in temper and more cruel in disposition than themselves, but the days of their early persecution have long since passed away. With the exception of their monotheism there is often very little distinction between the followers of the Prophet and the Chinese.

5. Chinese Sects: China is honeycombed with many varieties of secret societies, nearly all of which profess to "practise virtue" as an end. Many of them are, however, semipolitical, and all of them are tabooed by the government. Their manuals are copied by hand, and are practically inaccessible, and their tenets are compounded of fragments of Confucianism, Taoism, and Buddhism brewed in a common kettle. Their practises have unquestionably had their origin in Indian sources, the Chinese intellect not being sufficiently metaphysical to originate, or even to comprehend, subtleties of this sort. Some use a species of planchette for obtaining adumbrations of fate, some keep ledger accounts of merits and demerits, while others strive after the (Taoist) "pill of immortality." The I Ho Ch'üan (or "Boxers") in 1899 adopted the name of an organization much more than a century old. Whenever any society is vigorously repressed, it invariably reappears under a new name. The existence of these countless sects is a conspicuous witness to the radical insufficiency of each of the standard "religions" of China to satisfy the wants of the human soul.

II. Christian Missions.—1. Nestorian Missions: According to ancient tradition Christianity was carried to India and perhaps even to China by the apostle Thomas. While it is not impossible that a knowledge of the new faith may have penetrated so far in the early centuries, no certain evidence of it is now to be obtained. The Nestorians, however, sent missionaries to China at the beginning of the sixth century, as is proved by the black marble tablet discovered near the present Si Ngan Fu, the western capital of China, in 1625, recording the establishment of the "Illustrious Doctrine." The date of this justly famous monument of the past is 781 A.D., and its authenticity, once hotly disputed, is now irrefragably established. Judging by the allusions in Marco Polo's narrative, in the thirteenth century Nestorian churches must have been numerous. The followers of this faith were no doubt bitterly antagonized by the aggressive Mohammedans, who came to China somewhat later than they, the Nestorians in turn persecuting the early Roman Catholic missionaries. Nestorianism seems to have survived for almost a thousand years, traces of it being mentioned by travelers as late as the fourteenth century. But not a building which the Nestorians erected, not a page which they wrote has been preserved, and after more than twelve centuries they are remembered only by a stone tablet [In Nov., 1907, probably on account of the increasing number of European vandals in the province, the governor of Shen-Si removed the Nestorian Tablet from its ancient position in an open field near Si Ngan Fu and placed it in the Peilin Temple, inside the walls of the city.]

2. Roman Catholic Missions: The efforts of the Roman Catholic Church to establish itself in China are divisible into several well-marked periods, of which the first began with the arrival of John of Monte Corvino (q.v.), who reached China in 1292, during the Yuan, or Mongol dynasty. This zealous priest labored alone for eleven years, being later reenforced by seven assistants and himself made archbishop. His letters speak of translating the Psalms and the New Testament into Mongol, and of some 30,000 "infidels" converted. But with the advent of the native Ming dynasty and the expulsion of the Mongols in 1368, so completely were the traces of the past effaced that it was long forgotten that Christianity had ever entered the Celestial empire at all.

1. The Earliest Period.

The second period of Roman Catholic missions is separated from the first by more than two centuries of silence. The great missionary Francis Xavier (q.v.) died on the island of St. John in 1552, after heroic but unavailing efforts to enter China. In 1582 two Jesuit priests succeeded by a stratagem in getting a foothold in the province of Kwangtung. One of these was Michele Ruggieri (Roger), and the other the celebrated Matteo Ricci (q.v.), a man of great natural abilities, of a genial diplomatic temperament, and gifted with an unwearying patience. After nearly twenty years of romantic adventures he at last accomplished his great purpose, reaching Peking in Jan., 1601, where his labors were most indefatigable, and at his death in 1610 at the early age of fifty-five, they appeared to be crowned with success, especially in winning the literati. Ricci's Chinese writings remain to this day as an evidence of his unique achievements. His most famous convert was a Han Lin named Hsü, who took the name of Paul, and whose daughter (baptized as Candida) was a foster-mother to the infant Church. The family estate near Shanghai (locally called Sikawei—"home of the Hsü family") is now perhaps the most important center of Roman Catholic influence in China. Ricci nominated Longobardi (Lombard) as his successor, who after careful investigation felt obliged to reverse the policy of concession to Chinese customs in regard to the worship of ancestors, and in the use of the characters Shang Ti as the designation for God. These divisive and perversive questions were the rock upon which Roman Catholic missions in China ultimately split. The talents of Adam Schaal, one of his successors, like those of Ricci himself, were various and imposing, his labors ranging from astronomical erudition, exhibited in the reform of the Imperial calendar, to the composition of works of theology, and of metal for the casting of cannon. His success was provocative of jealousy, so that he was undermined by intrigues, and died of grief and mortification at the age of seventy-eight, having been thirty-seven years in the employ of five monarchs. The achievements and honors of his successor, Ferdinand Verbiest, were if possible even greater, continuing for a period of thirty years to 1688. This trio of men of extraordinary abilities and devotion not perhaps equaled in missions in any other part of the world might have been expected to insure the success of the Church to which they gave themselves.

2. The Second Period.

But meantime the seeds of dissension which ultimately proved the ruin not only of the Jesuit labors in China but also of those of the Franciscans and Dominicans who followed them were yielding their harvest of ill. Ricci had endeavored in everything to regard Chinese prejudices that he might win the literati. Upon the representations of Lombard, Pope Innocent X. (1645) forbade the worship of Heaven, and the rites to the dead, but the Jesuits succeeded in getting a bull from Alexander VII. (1656) practically (although not in form) reversing the decision. A third bull maintained the validity of each of the former, the rites being forbidden to those who thought them idolatrous, but lawful to those who considered them as merely civil and not religious. In 1699 the Jesuits with signal imprudence appealed the question to the Emperor K'ang Hsi, whose decision in their favor was flatly contradicted by a bull of Clement XI. (1704) absolutely forbidding the rites, and the use of the terms "Heaven" and "Shang Ti" for God. The Emperor K'ang Hsi was not the man to divide his rule with an Italian gentleman, and the result was that while missions were still patronized at court for scientific purposes, they were persecuted in the provinces with the connivance of the emperor. On the accession of his successor, Yung Cheng (1723–35), by various decrees the missionaries were banished and the Church extinguished. It is said that "more than 300 churches were destroyed or suppressed, and 300,000 Christians abandoned to the fury of the heathen."

2. The Modern Period.

Thus at the end of a century and a half of great prosperity the work of the past appeared to be again wholly undone; but the fortitude under bitter persecutions and the constancy of the Roman Catholic Christians during the succeeding century and a quarter till the practical toleration of the Treaty of Whampoa, and the fuller liberty of the treaties of 1858, afford the most convincing proof of the genuineness of their religion. During the last half-century the expansion of the Roman Catholic Church in all parts of the empire has been marked, but as it does not publish statistics, only estimates are possible. In a recent work by the vicar apostolic of the province of Chehkiang there are said to be twenty-seven bishops, and the number of Christians is estimated at three-quarters of a million, although figures twice as large are often met with. From the Protestant standpoint it is a capital defect of the Roman Catholic policy that practically no use is made of street chapel preaching, and that the Bible as a whole is not translated for the converts. The standard of admission to the Church is not high, and great harm is done to the cause by the too ready acceptance of many applicants whose obvious motive is the prosecution of lawsuits, and revenge.* It should be said that in many cases the Roman Catholic converts showed the greatest firmness under the persecution of the Boxer period, unknown numbers enduring martyrdom for their faith.

3. Protestant Missions: Protestant missions to China owe their origin to a general revival of spiritual life at the end of the eighteenth century, which was naturally manifested in greatly increased activity both at home and abroad.

1. The First Period, to 1842.

These missions in China are naturally divisible into four distinct periods, each terminated by a foreign war. In this vast field the London Missionary Society had the honor of being the pioneer, in the face of difficulties which can now be but imperfectly comprehended. Robert Morrison (q. v.) reached Canton by way of New York Sept. 7, 1807. The East India Company would not allow him passage on its ships, but later was glad to employ him as its interpreter, when it was evidently for its interest to command the services of so thorough a Chinese scholar. His labors were unintermittent and immense. He completed the translation of the entire Bible into Chinese in 1818, partly in collaboration with his associate, William Milne. In 1823 his great Chinese Dictionary was published by the East India Company at an expense of twelve thousand pounds sterling. Dr. Morrison died in 1834, when the relations between Great Britain and China were becoming every year more strained, the missionary outlook being then almost as unpromising as when he began his work. The impossibility of getting a foothold on Chinese soil led to the establishment of an Anglo-Chinese College at Malacca (subsequently transferred to the newly ceded island of Hongkong) in which Mr. Milne labored with diligence in teaching, and in preparing and printing Christian books. Walter Henry Medhurst, who came as a printer, spent many years at Batavia. The next society to begin work in China was the American Board, which sent out Rev. Elijah Coleman Bridgman, who reached Canton in Feb., 1830, together with Rev. David Abeel (q.v.), who soon after joined the mission. Three years later, Mr. Samuel Wells Williams, then a mere youth, went out as a printer. In the ensuing decade, before the opening of the war with Great Britain, three other American societies entered the field, the Protestant Episcopal, 1835, the Baptist Missionary Union, 1836, and the Presbyterians (North), 1838. Medical work in this period was begun in 1834 by Dr. Peter Parker, who opened a hospital in Canton Oct., 1835, where the successful treatments, especially in eye and surgical cases, were phenomenal and most influential in diminishing prejudice. Dr. Thomas Richardson Colledge, of the East India Company, opened a dispensary at his own expense in 1827.

* On March 15, 1899, the Chinese government was induced to issue this decree, which is thus translated in President Hawks Pott's *The Outbreak in China*, pp. 107 sq. (New York, 1900): "Churches of the Catholic religion, the propagation of which has been long since authorised by the Imperial Government, having been built at this time in all the provinces of China, we long to see the Christians and the people live in peace, and, in order to make their protection more easy, it has been agreed that local authorities shall exchange visits with missionaries under the conditions indicated in the following articles: 1. In the different degrees of the ecclesiastical hierarchy, bishops being in rank and dignity the equals of viceroys and governors, it is agreed to authorise them to demand to see viceroys and governors. . . . Vicars-general and archdeacons will be authorised to demand to see provincial treasurers and judges, and taotais. Other priests will be authorised to see prefects of the first and second class, independent prefects, subprefects, and other functionaries. 2. When a mission affair, grave or important, shall come up unexpectedly in any province, the bishops and the missionaries of the place should ask for the intervention of the minister or consuls of the power to which the pope has confided the protection of religion. These last will regulate or finish the matter, either with the Tsungli Yamên or the local authorities. In order to avoid protracted proceedings, the bishop and the missionaries have equal right to address themselves at once to the local authorities, with whom they may negotiate the matter and finish it." President Pott adds: "The missions of the Anglican Communion and other Protestant Churches have unanimously refused to ask for any similar privileges, foreseeing clearly that, although the possession of such would vastly increase their power, yet this assumption would be attended with the gravest dangers, and could but make their cause unpopular in the eyes of the Chinese."—S. M. J.

Dr. Benjamin Hobson, of the London Mission, also conducted a hospital in Canton, Macao, and Hongkong, from 1839 to 1843. The war with Great Britain was terminated by the Treaty of Nanking in 1842, as a result of which the ports of Canton, Amoy, Fuchau, Ning-po, and Shanghai were definitely opened to trade.

From the close of the war to the settlement at the end of the next one is to be reckoned as the second period of Protestant missions to China, characterized by an activity on the part of the British, American, and German missionary societies fully equal to that of the agents of commerce.

2. The Second Period, 1842-60.

The various missions to the Chinese in Java, Siam, and the Straits of Malacca were now transferred to the Chinese empire itself. Among them were those of the American Baptist Missionary Union, removed from Bangkok to Hongkong in 1842, and thence to Swatow in 1860; the American Presbyterian Mission from Singapore to Canton, with work opened later at Amoy and Ning-po, the Southern Baptists likewise beginning in Hongkong in 1842, and in Canton in 1845. During this period of renewed energy the American (Dutch) Reformed, the Church Missionary Society, the English Baptist Society, the American Methodist Episcopal (both North and South), the Berlin and Basel Mission, the English Presbyterian, the American Seventh-day Baptists, the Wesleyan Mission, and the Methodist New Connexion were first seen in China (discrepancy in the dates of the opening of some of these missions is often due to the fact that in some instances the preliminary work was discontinued). The difficulties inherent in the initial stages of missions among the self-centered, suspicious, and practically hostile people like the Chinese were greatly aggravated by the rise and rapid growth of the T'ai P'ing rebellion, which devastated nearly all the provinces of the empire, lasting from 1850 to 1864, when Nanking was captured, and in its sequelæ for three years more. The last four years of this period witnessed another war with Great Britain—the effects of the defeat half a generation before having worn off—the Taku Forts were taken, and Peking was entered by the British and French in Oct., 1860. At the close of the war of 1840–42 the number of living Chinese converts might have been counted on the fingers of one hand. After eighteen years more of sapping, mining, and laying of foundations, there were in 1860 at the most but a few score, but important beginnings had everywhere been made in evangelistic, medical, educational, and literary work.

All the open ports of China were at this time centers of intense and unwearied activity, confined within these limited areas like waters behind a closed lock. By the Treaty of Tien-Tsin many new ports were opened, and Christianity in each of its forms was explicitly tolerated. More than a hundred missionaries had been penned up in Shanghai awaiting the expected opening of inland China. Tien-Tsin was first reached by Henry Blodget (American Board) in company with British troops, and Peking by Mr. Joseph Edkins (London Mission), while Mr. Griffith John, of the same society, settled at Hankow, from which strategic point missions were opened in Hupeh and later in Szechuen and Hunan. Similar expansion took place from each of the other ports.

3. The Third Period, 1860-95.

This period of missions is full of important political events so intimately related to all foreign interests that the one can not be considered without the other, and they must therefore be briefly mentioned. Among them are the suppression of the T'ai P'ing rebellion (1864), the reception by the emperor of the foreign ministers in audience (1873), the murder of Mr. Augustus Raymond Margary (1875), with the resultant Chefu Convention (1876), by which greater security was given to foreigners in China, and in connection with which more new ports were opened. A great steamship company was organized under Chinese management, and a network of telegraph lines began to overspread the empire.

The most important single step in the evangelization of China was the development (rather than the organization) of the China Inland Mission (1865), founded on a combination of faith and works, which within a single generation has covered China with a chain of mission stations. Each of the older societies endeavored to expand into the illimitable regions beyond, and many new missions were begun. At the first general conference of missionaries in Shanghai in May, 1877, attended by 126 representatives, the total number of Protestant workers was 473, of whom 228 were connected with thirteen British societies, 212 with ten American societies, and two of German origin. The number of Christians in ninety-one stations with 312 organized churches was about 13,000. Thirteen years later a second conference was held, in May, 1890, when the societies had increased to forty, male missionaries to 589, married women to 391, and the unmarried to 316, a total of 1,296. There were 522 churches, and the Christians were nearly three times as numerous as in 1877, numbering 37,287. More than sixty hospitals and forty-four dispensaries treated in 1889 348,000 patients. By the end of the century, however, this work had vastly expanded, so that 128 hospitals and 245 dispensaries, conducted by 162 male and 79 lady physicians, treated in one year 685,047 patients. The influence of this branch of missionary work in a country like China is immeasurable. Other opportunities for philanthropy arose in connection with the great famine of 1877–78, which overspread all northern China. The loss of life among the Chinese was estimated at between nine and a half and thirteen millions. Famine relief proved a golden key to unlock many closed doors. Similar relief has been afforded upon a large scale at other times in connection with other famines, floods, and pestilence, not without visible effect. The terrible massacre at Tien-Tsin in June, 1870, was one of a long series, the most numerous outbreaks taking place in 1891–93, apparently as a direct result of the blasphemous Hunan tracts, the whole Yang-tzu valley being ablaze with excitement. Another atrocity took place at Ku Ch'eng, Fukien province, in 1895, when Mr. Robert Warren Stewart and most of his family were murdered. The great province of Szechuen became a hotbed of violence, foreigners were temporarily expelled, and 50,000 Christians (largely Roman Catholics) suffered, many being killed. These events were directly connected with China's ignominious defeat by Japan (1894–95), for which all foreigners were supposed to be in some way responsible. These continual outrages occurred in every part of the empire, and often without warning, in spite of imperial edicts and official proclamations, but in no instance had they any permanent effect in restraining mission work.

4. The Fourth Period, from 1895. For a long time the bitter but wholesome lessons of the war with Japan seemed to be forgotten or ignored. But in 1898 the emperor began a series of reform measures which soon brought on a crisis, and he was set aside by his aunt, the empress dowager, who reversed all his measures. The effect of this reaction was instantly felt throughout the empire. The cumulative force of the loss of Chinese territory by foreign aggression, of commercial intrusion, of railways, and the opening of mines, added to the chronic prejudice against foreign religions, led to the fanatical I Ho Ch'üan crusade of 1899–1900, with its spectacular consequences of the flight of the court and the occupation of Peking by foreign armies, which, however, within a few months retired. The native Christians had now established their right to exist, and often afforded striking object-lessons of fidelity. Although practically all mission property (except at protected ports) had been destroyed from the Yellow River to the Amur, within two years almost everything was replaced with a far better plant than would otherwise have been possible. The fidelity of the Chinese Christians, while not uniform nor universal, won praise from every quarter, many thousands of them losing their lives, as well as 135 Protestant missionaries, and fifty-three children, thirty-five Roman Catholic fathers, and nine sisters.

5. General Features. Christian Literature. It will be convenient to combine in a brief and summary view some features of missionary work which have been slowly developing during the sixty and more years since the Treaty of Nanking. Bible translation, one of the great labors of the first missionary, has ever since been prosecuted with untiring zeal, and is still in progress. It is impossible to go into details, but in general it may be said that the word of God has been put into the literary style (adapted for universal circulation among scholars), into mandarin colloquial, supposed to be spoken in some form by 75 per cent of China's four hundred millions, and into the patois of special districts, the last-named both in Chinese characters and in an increasing degree by the use of Roman letters. The three great Bible societies, the British and Foreign, the American, and the Scotch, have been indefatigable in their work of distribution, largely by sales, which were never on so extensive a scale as at present. Numerous societies, especially the Chinese and the Central China Tract societies, have put into circulation uncounted millions of sheets, booklets, and books, so that at times it has been impossible to keep pace with the demand. Great mission presses, notably for nearly sixty years that of the American Presbyterian Mission, and more recently those of the United Methodist Missions in Shanghai and Fuchau, are kept constantly busy. Influential religious journals and magazines are issued in nearly all the principal mission centers, especially at Shanghai, penetrating not only all parts of the empire, but every part of the world where Chinese are to be found. One of the most important agencies for influencing Chinese thought is the Society for the Diffusion of Christian and General Knowledge Among the Chinese, founded by Dr. Alexander Williamson, and now under the leadership of Dr. Timothy Richard. Its *Review of the Times*, conducted by Dr. Y. J. Allen, has long reached a large circle of officials in every province, and previously to the reform plans of 1898 it was especially procured by the emperor himself for his study. Great quantities of Christian and useful literature are distributed to scholars at the civil-service examinations in the provincial capitals, tending to dissipate prejudice in influential quarters.

6. Various Forms of Work. The distinction between the Roman Catholic and the Protestant form of Christianity has now become well understood both by officials and people. Woman's work for woman has been expanded in every direction, in evangelizing, medical, and educational lines, the first Woman's Medical College being opened in Canton Dec., 1902, with an immediate success, foretokening speedy imitation elsewhere. The Educational Association of China is a most important unifying and developing force for every agency connected with teaching, especially in the preparation of text-books. At the St. Louis Exposition of 1904 this association made an important exhibit of education in China in all its aspects. The Young Men's Christian Association has established an energetic work in Shanghai, Tien-Tsin, Peking, and other centers, which promises great results in the future. Christian Endeavor societies (and Epworth leagues) have taken firm root in China, and an experienced missionary has been chosen to act as a traveling secretary in the interests of this effective agency. Student Volunteer conferences have been repeatedly held, at which influential and representative men have been gathered in large numbers. An antifoot-binding reform movement, distinct from that of missionary origin but allied to it and in sympathy with it, has spread widely over China, promoted by some of its highest statesmen, and favored by the empress dowager. Special work for the insane has been begun at Canton, for the deaf at Chefu, and for the blind at Peking. The hostile and bitterly antiforeign province of Hunan has been entered and is now occupied by thirteen societies with a force comprising at present about eighty-seven missionaries. As an incidental result of the cataclysm of 1900 three leading societies, the London Mission, the American Board, and the American Presbyterian, have formed an important union in educational work in the Chili province, looking toward a union university. In Shangtung there is a similar partnership between the American Presbyterian and the English Baptist Missions.

The relations between officials and all missionaries since 1900 have been much improved. Although occasional outbreaks still occur, earnest efforts are now made to prevent them on account of their possible consequences. It can not be doubted that the result of the war between Japan and Russia will exert an important influence upon Christian work throughout the Chinese Empire.

7. Statistics. In Beach's *Geography and Atlas of Protestant Missions* (New York, 1903), 68 Protestant societies are reported as working in China (33 American, 22 British, 12 Continental, and 1 international), with a total of 2,785 workers, of whom 610 were ordained men, 578 unordained, 772 wives, and 825 other missionary women, living in 653 stations, and working 2,476 outstations. There were 162 male physicians and 79 women physicians, with 259 hospitals and dispensaries treating more than 691,000 patients annually. H. O. Dwight's *Blue Book of Missions for 1907* indicates that the number of workers was rapidly increasing, as it gives from the reports of 59 societies an aggregate of 3,146 missionaries. The aggregate of native workers is 8,243, and the total number of Christians 249,878. Fukien, at the beginning the most difficult province, has the largest number of converts, with continuous accessions. There were 1,819 day-schools with 35,412 pupils, and 170 higher institutions instructing 5,150 students. According to tables published in Shanghai in 1904 by Dr. Richard, there were in 1901 4,126 Roman Catholic churches and chapels in China, 904 European missionaries, 471 native priests, 3,584 schools, 60 colleges, and 720,540 Christians. Considering the brevity of a century in comparison with the age-long periods of Chinese history, the exceptional difficulties to be overcome, the ignorance, the conservatism, and the contempt of the Chinese race for everything from abroad, the results of a hundred years of Protestant missions are in every way remarkable as a prophecy and a promise of what is yet in the future. ARTHUR H. SMITH.

BIBLIOGRAPHY: For history: S. W. Williams, *The Middle Kingdom*, New York, 1899 (comprehensive and standard); A. H. Smith, *Chinese Characteristics*, New York, 1900. On geography: H. P. Beach, *Geography and Atlas of Protestant Missions*, New York, 1903; E. L. Oxenham, *Historical Atlas of the Chinese Empire*, London, 1898.

On the language and literature: W. A. P. Martin, *The Lore of Cathay*, New York, 1901 (best); R. K. Douglass, *Language and Literature of China*, London, 1875; T. Walters, *Essays on the Chinese Language*, Shanghai, 1889.

On the religious sources: For Confucianism, *SBE*, iii., xvi., xxvii., xxviii.; J. Legge, *Chinese Classics*, 7 vols., London, 1861–87. For Taoism: Lao-Tsze, *The Canon of Reason and Virtue*, by P. Carus, Chicago, 1903; W. G. Old, *The Classics of Confucius, Shu King*, London, 1906. For Buddhism: *SBE*, xix.; S. Beal, *Buddhist Literature in China*, London, 1882, and *Catena of Buddhist Scriptures*, London, 1871, also *Dhammapada; Texts from the Buddhist Canon*, London, 1878; E. Chavannes, *Les Inscriptions chinoises de Bodh-Gaya*, Paris, 1896. On the religions in general: P. D. Chantepie de la Saussaye, *Lehrbuch der Religionsgeschichte*, i. 57-114, Tübingen, 1905; S. Johnson, *Oriental Religions . . . China*, Boston, 1877 (full, but discursive); J. H. Plath, *Die Religion und der Cultus der alten Chinesen*, Munich, 1862; R. K. Douglas, *Confucianism and Taoism*, London, 1879; J. Legge, *Religions of China, Confucianism and Taoism*, London, 1881; A. Reville, *La Religion chinoise*, Paris, 1889; C. de Harlez, *Les Religions de la Chine*, Paris, 1891; E. H. Parker, *China and Religion*, London, 1905. On Confucianism: H. A. Giles, *Confucianism*, in *Religious Systems of the World*, London, 1901; idem, *Religions of Ancient China*, ib. 1906; E. Faber, *Digest of the Doctrines of Confucius*, Hongkong, 1875, and *Mind of Mencius*, Shanghai, 1882. On Taoism: A. de Pouvoirville, *Le Taoisme et les sociétés secrètes chinoises*, Paris, 1897; I. W. Heysinger, *Lao Tsze, the Light of China*, Philadelphia, 1903; E. H. Parker, *China and Religion*, London, 1905. On Chinese Buddhism: E. Lamairesse, *Le Bouddhisme en Chine . . .*, Paris, 1893; J. Edkins, *Chinese Buddhism*, London, 1880; S. Beal, *Buddhism in China*, in *Non-Christian Religious Systems*, London, 1884 (Beal is the authority on Buddhism in China); E. J. Eitel, *Handbook . . . of Chinese Buddhism*, London, 1888; J. J. M. de Groot, *Religious System of China*, vols. i.–v., Leyden, 1892–1907 (still in progress); *Tai-shang kan-ying pien: Treatise of the Exalted one on Response and Retribution, from the Chinese by Teitaro Suzuki and Paul Carus*, Chicago, 1906; J. D. Ball, *The Celestial and his Religions; or, the Religious Aspect in China*, ib. 1906.

On missions: Statistical: J. S. Dennis, *Centennial Survey of Foreign Missions*, New York, 1902. General: *Memorials of Protestant Missionaries to the Chinese*, Shanghai, 1867; *Conferences on Missions*, at Shanghai, 1877 and 1890, at Shantung 1893 and 1897 (*Reports* published at Shanghai); J. Gilmour, *Among the Mongols*, London, 1884; W. Campbell, *Missionary Success in . . . Formosa*, London, 1889; *Church Work in North China*, London, 1893 (on Anglican missions); M. G. Guinness, *Story of the China Inland Mission*, 2 vols., London, 1893; *China Mission Handbook*, Shanghai, 1896; G. L. Mackay, *From Far Formosa, . . . Island, People and Missions*, New York, 1896; R. Lovett, *Hist. of London Missionary Society*, chaps. xix.-xxvi., London, 1899; J. C. Gibson, *Mission Problems and Mission Methods in South China*, London, 1901; L. Miner, *China's Book of Martyrs*, Boston, 1903; J. Ross, *Methods of Mission Work in Manchuria*, London, 1903; M. Broomhall, *Pioneer Work in Hunan*, ib. 1906; W. A. P. Martin, *Awakening of China*, New York, 1907; W. E. Soothill, *A Typical Mission in China*, New York, 1907.

For the Boxer troubles: A. H. Smith, *China in Convulsion*, New York, 1901; M. Broomhall, *Martyred Missionaries of the China Inland Mission*, London, 1901; E. H. Edwards, *Fire and Sword in Shansi*, London, 1903; R. C. Forsyth, *China Martyrs of 1900*, London, 1904.

On Roman Catholic missions: F. Prandi, *Memoirs of Father Ripa*, London, 1844; Abbé Huc, *Christianity in China, Tartary and Thibet*, best ed., 3 vols., London, 1857; T. Chaney, *La Colonie du Sacré-Cœur dans les Cévennes de la Chine au xviii. siècle*, Paris, 1889; Abbé Pierre, *La Chine chrétienne. La Vie et les œuvres de H. A. Languillat*, 2 vols., Paris, 1893.

CHINIQUY, shî″nî″kî′ *or* chin″i-kwî′, **CHARLES PASCHAL TELESPHORE**: Presbyterian: b. of Roman Catholic parents at Kamouraska, Quebec, Canada, July 30, 1809; d. in Montreal Jan. 16, 1899. He studied at the college of Nicolet, Canada, 1822–29, and was professor of belles-lettres there till 1833; was ordained a Roman Catholic priest 1833; vicar and curate in the province of Quebec till 1846; he established the first temperance society there and won the title "Apostle of Temperance of Canada." In 1851 he was called by Bishop Vandevelde, of Chicago, to direct the tide of Roman Catholic emigration toward the prairies of Illinois; in 1858, with his congregation at St. Anne, Kankakee County, Ill., he left the Church of Rome, and joined the Canadian Presbyterian Church. He lectured in England 1860, 1874, and 1882, and in Australia 1878–80, and published a number of books and tracts upon temperance, and others bitterly hostile to the Roman Catholic

Church, which have passed through many editions and been translated into different languages.

BIBLIOGRAPHY: His autobiography, *Forty Years in the Church of Rome*, appeared Chicago, 1900.

CHIUN, coi'un. See REMPHAN.

CHOIR: 1. In the older churches, especially the Gothic, that part which contains the high altar and in which the services are sung. It is usually separated from the nave by a railing or rood-screen, and in monastic churches only members of the order sit within it. See ARCHITECTURE, ECCLESIASTICAL, I., §§ 15, 18. 2. A body of singers appointed to lead the music in public worship.

CHOISY, shwā"zī', **JACQUES EUGÈNE:** Swiss Protestant; b. at Geneva, Switzerland, Feb. 26, 1866. He was educated at the college and university of his native city, from which he was graduated in 1885, the theological faculty of Montauban, from which he was graduated in 1888, and the University of Berlin. Since 1898 he has been pastor of the parish of Plainpalais, Geneva, and was also moderator of the Compagnie des Pasteurs from 1904 to 1905. In 1898 he received from the faculty of arts of the University of Geneva the Théodore Claparède prize, and three years later was awarded the Daniel Colladan prize by the consistory of the National Protestant Church of Geneva. He has been a member of the Société des sciences théologiques of Geneva since 1890 and was its president in 1903–05, and has also been a member of the Geneva Société d'histoire et d'archéologie since 1893 and president of the Société du musée historique de la réformation in the same city since its foundation in 1897. In theology he terms himself a "broad Evangelical, much indebted to higher criticism for a more accurate and trustworthy understanding of God's revelation in the Bible." In addition to a translation of A. Harnack's *Grundriss der Dogmengeschichte* (Paris, 1893), he has written *Paschase Radbert, étude historique sur le neuvième siècle et sur le dogme de la Cène* (Geneva, 1888); *La Théocratie à Genève au temps de Calvin* (1897); and *L'État chrétien calviniste à Genève au temps de Théodore de Bèze* (1903).

CHORAL. See MUSIC, SACRED.

CHORENTÆ, co-ren'tī *or* -tē. See MESSALIANS.

CHOREPISCOPUS, cō"re-pis'co-pus (Gk. *chōrepiskopos*, "country bishop"): The name given to a class of assistants to the bishops in the administration of their dioceses from the third to the eleventh century. As the name implies, they rendered this service principally in the country districts. In the fourth century they attended councils like the bishops (Ancyra, 314; Neocæsarea, between 313 and 325; Antioch, 341) and had some at least of the episcopal prerogatives, though the question whether they received episcopal consecration is disputed. A tendency showed itself in the same century to restrict their powers and make them altogether dependent on the diocesan bishops. The Councils of Sardica and Laodicea attempted to suppress them entirely, forbidding the installation of bishops in country places and providing for the needs of such districts by itinerant visitors of a merely priestly character. These efforts were only partially successful, and the institution continued in partial use in the East as late as the sixth century, though now in entire subordination to the diocesan bishops and with no further claim to the strictly episcopal character. In the West chorepiscopi are heard of only from the eighth century, as assistants or deputies of missionary bishops in the new dioceses, or as administrators of vacant sees. There is no demonstrable connection with the Eastern usage. In the ninth century they are also found in the see cities as assistants to bishops who were much occupied with affairs of state. The reforming legislation of this period, appealing to the Eastern canons, emphasized their dependence on the diocesan bishops, and toward the middle of the century undertook to suppress them altogether. They disappeared in the first half of the tenth century in France, but in the extensive German dioceses, supported by Rabanus Maurus, they maintained their existence to the middle of this century, and were found in Ireland as late as the thirteenth. Their place was to a great extent taken by the archdeacons (see ARCHDEACON AND ARCHPRIEST).

(P. HINSCHIUS†.)

BIBLIOGRAPHY: Hefele, *Conciliengeschichte*, ii. 290, iii. 478, 603, 665, 745, Eng. transl., ii. 69, 321, iii. 158; J. L. von Mosheim, *Institutes of Eccl. Hist.*, ed. W. Stubbs, i. 63, 239 sqq., London, 1863; Bingham, *Origines*, book ii., chap. xiv., § 12; Schaff, *Christian Church*, iii. 269–270; *KL*, iii. 188–191.

CHRISM: The specially prepared mixture used for anointing in the Eastern and Roman Catholic Churches, except in the case of Extreme Unction (q.v.) when olive-oil mixed with water is used. That employed in the administration of baptism, confirmation, and holy orders, and in the consecration of churches and altars, is composed according to Roman usage of oil and balsam, to which other odorous spices are added by the Greeks. It early received a special benediction, as is shown by Tertullian, *De baptismo*, vii.; Cyprian, *Epist.*, lxx. 2; *Apostolic Constitutions*, VII. xxvii. 1. From the end of the fourth century the right to consecrate it was reserved to the bishops—in the East later to the patriarchs. From the fifth century Maundy Thursday was the day appointed for the blessing.

(A. HAUCK.)

CHRISMAL: A word used in the same senses as "chrisom" (q.v.); also a cloth for covering relics.

CHRISOM: The white cloth with which the Roman priest covers the head of an infant after the administration of baptism or, in the early Church, the white garment put upon the newly baptized as a symbol of purity; also the vessel in which the chrism is preserved.

CHRIST, BRETHREN IN. See RIVER BRETHREN.

CHRIST, DISCIPLES OF, CHRISTIANS. See DISCIPLES OF CHRIST.

CHRIST, ORDER OF: The Knights of Jesus Christ, an order founded by King Dionysius of

Portugal in 1317, like the Spanish orders of Alcantara and Calatrava (qq.v.) under Cistercian rule and to fight against the Moors. It was endowed with property of the Templars, who had been suppressed in 1312. Papal confirmation was received from John XXII. in 1319, the grand master being made subordinate to the abbot of the Cistercian monastery of Alcobaça. The knights gained important victories and became rich and powerful. At their chief seat, Thomar (75 m. n.e. of Lisbon) in Estremadura, and at Batalha, twenty miles farther west, they erected magnificent buildings in pointed style, imitating the churches of the Templars in Cyprus and the Mosque of Omar in Jerusalem (cf. the Viscount de Condeixa, *O mosteiro da Batalha*, with French transl., Lisbon and Paris, 1892; J. Dernjac, *Thomar und Batalha*, in the *Zeitschrift für bildende Kunst*, new series, vi [1895], 98–106). About 1500 Pope Alexander VI. released the order from the vow of poverty. It had then 450 commanderies and an enormous income. A reform was effected in 1550 by the Hieronymite abbot Anton of Lisbon, and confirmed by Pope Julius III. At the same time the grandmastership was formally attached to the crown, as it had been actually from the time of King Emmanuel (1495–1521). Pius V. in 1567 removed the jurisdiction of the abbot of Alcobaça, and Gregory XIII. in 1576 granted the king supreme power over both knights and monks. The order was secularized in 1797 and its property confiscated in 1834. It is now merely an order of merit. A less important Italian *Ordine di Christo* was founded by Pope John XXII. about 1320. It also became an order of merit. (O. Zöckler†.)

Bibliography: Helyot, *Ordres monastiques*, vi. 72 76, Paris, 1718; G. Giucci, *Iconografia storica degli ordini religiosi e cavallereschi*, i. 34–36, Rome, 1836; G. Moroni, *Dizionario di erudizione storico-ecclesiastica*, xviii. 210–219, Venice, 1843; Heimbucher, *Orden und Kongregationen*, i. 227; Currier, *Religious Orders*, p. 217.

CHRIST, crist, PAUL: Swiss Protestant; b. at Zurich Oct. 25, 1836; d. there Jan. 14, 1908. He was educated at the universities of Tübingen and Basel, and after being a pastor successively in the canton of Grisons (1858–62) and at Chur, the capital of the same canton (1862–65), he was a professor in the cantonal school of Chur from 1865 to 1870. He was then pastor at Lichtensteig (1871–75) and Rheineck (1875–80), both in the canton of St. Gall, and after four years of retirement on account of impaired health (1880–84) was municipal archivist at Chur (1884–87) and again professor in the cantonal school of the same city (1887–89). Since 1889 he has been professor of systematic and practical theology at the University of Zurich. In theology he represents the speculative and liberal school. He has written *Christliche Religionslehre* (Zurich, 1875); *Bilder aus der Geschichte der christlichen Kirche und Sitte* (St. Gall, 1876); *Religiöse Betrachtungen* (1881); *Der Pessimismus und die Sittenlehre* (Haarlem, 1882); *Die Lehre vom Gebet nach dem Neuen Testament* (Leyden, 1886); *Die sittliche Weltordnung* (1894); and *Grundriss der Ethik* (Berlin, 1905).

CHRISTADELPHIANS: A small sect which originated in the United States about 1850. They call themselves Christadelphians because of the belief that all that are in Christ are his brethren, and designate their congregations as "ecclesias" to "distinguish them from the so-called churches of the apostasy." John Thomas, the founder, a physician, born in England, came to America in 1844 and joined the Disciples of Christ. In a short time, however, he established a separate denomination, because he believed that, though the Disciples were the most "apostolic and spiritually enlightened religious organization in America," the religious teaching of the day was contrary to the teaching of the Bible.

Christadelphians reject the Trinity. They believe in one supreme God, who dwells in unapproachable light; in Jesus Christ, in whom was manifest the eternal spirit of God, and who died for the offenses of sinners, and rose for the justification of believing men and women; in one baptism only—immersion, the "burial with Christ in water into death to sin," which is essential to salvation; in immortality only in Christ; in eternal punishment of the wicked, but not in eternal torment; in hell, not as a place of torment, but as the grave; in the resurrection of the just and unjust; in the utter annihilation of the wicked, and in the non-resurrection of those who have never heard the Gospel, lack in intelligence (as infants), or are sunk in ignorance or brutality; in a second coming of Christ to establish his kingdom on earth, which is to be fitted for the everlasting abode of the saints; in the proximity of this second coming; in Satan as a Scriptural personification of sin; in the millennial reign of Christ on earth over the nations, during which sin and death will continue in a milder degree, and after which Christ will surrender his position of supremacy, and God will reveal himself, and become Father and Governor of a complete family; in salvation only for those who can understand the faith as taught by the Christadelphians, and become obedient to it. They have no ordained ministers. There are about sixty "ecclesias" in the United States, and a few in England, where most of their literature is published. H. K. Carroll.

Bibliography: Sources of doctrine are the works of the founder, generally published in pamphlet form in Birmingham and London. The principal are: *Eureka*, 1869; *The Revealed Mystery*, 1869; *Who are the Christadelphians?* 1869; *The Book Unsealed*, 1870; *Phanerosis*, 1870; *Anastasis*, 1871; *Clerical Theology Unscriptural*, 1877, and *Elpis Israel*, West Hoboken, 1871. Also the following works by Robert Roberts: *A Defence of the Faith Proclaimed in Ancient Times, . . . Revived in the Christadelphians*, Birmingham, 1868; *Everlasting Punishment not "Eternal Torments,"* ib. 1871; *Meaning of the Christadelphian Movement*, London, 1872; *Thirteen Lectures on the Things Revealed in . . . "Revelation,"* Birmingham, 1880; *The Good Confession*, ib. 1881; *Dr. Thomas, his Life and Work*, ib. 1884. Their organ is *The Christadelphian*, published at Birmingham, Eng. Consult H. K. Carroll, *Religious Forces of the U. S.*, pp. 89–90, 454, New York, 1896.

CHRISTENTUMSGESELLSCHAFT, DIE DEUTSCHE ("The German Society for Christendom"): A society which had a wide influence at the end of the eighteenth and beginning of the nineteenth centuries. In that period of deep depression and discouragement for the Evangelical

Church of Germany, it brought believing, earnest Christians together by personal intercourse and by correspondence, and helped them to successful cooperation. Its special object was to oppose the bold depreciation and mockery of the Word of God then so common, as well as the tendency represented by Nikolai's *Zeitschrift* in Berlin and the *Gothaer Zeitung*. Its founder was Dr. Johann August Urlsperger (q.v.), of Augsburg, who belonged to the old school of simple Scriptural faith and piety. He thought that the friends of the Gospel should stand together and strengthen one another as did its enemies. In 1777 he wrote to a number of German, Dutch, Danish, and English theologians without getting much response, and in 1779 and 1780 traveled widely in the hope of effecting more by personal contact. But the result was still the same, and he came home much discouraged. In Basel, the last place he had planned to visit, he found a response. Here since 1756, stirred up by D'Annone, the zealous pastor of Muttenz, a number of like-minded men had already been organized, who listened with delight to Urlsperger's ideas; and the society was able to hold its first formal meeting on Aug. 30, 1780. The beginning once made, the thing spread; branches were formed at Nuremberg the next year, then at Stuttgart, Frankfort, Berlin, Magdeburg, etc. As the numbers grew, and correspondence came in even from America, a more formal organization was required. Basel was made the headquarters at the end of 1782, and a manifold activity radiated from it, embracing all that is meant nowadays by home and foreign missions. Selections from the vast mass of correspondence were sent to all the branches, in printed form after 1783. Urlsperger had originally wished to write and circulate good theological treatises, but the central body turned its efforts in a more practical direction, wishing indeed to uphold the true faith, but not to renew the old controversies. The name, too, was changed from the original *Deutsche Gesellschaft zur Beförderung christlicher Wahrheit und Gottseligkeit* ("German Society for the Promotion of Christian Truth and Piety") to the present title. In 1801 Steinkopf, who had been the general secretary, was called to the Savoy Chapel in London, and formed a link between Germany and England, where the mighty revival of spiritual life set a standard for emulation. The Basel Bible Society was founded in 1804 as the first result; and the second was the mission house, also at Basel, planned as early as 1805 by C. F. Spittler on the model of the Berlin mission school (founded in 1800 by Jänicke, a member of the society), and realized in 1815 with the help of C. G. Blumhardt (q.v.). A number of other foundations and special organizations marked the succeeding years. Among them were the training-school and orphanage at Beuggen (1820); the Society of the Friends of Israel (1831); the Society for the Spread of Christian Literature (1833); the deaf and dumb asylum at Riehen (1838); and the deaconess home in the same place (1852). The original association fulfilled its task in giving the impulse to so many and varied good works; it still exists, however, under the direction of a central committee in Basel, where the *Sammlungen fur Liebhaber christlicher Wahrheit und Gottseligkeit* is still published periodically, after an existence of more than a century. (R. ANSTEIN†.)

BIBLIOGRAPHY: C. J. Riggenbach, I. Stockmeyer, and H. Prätorius, *Zur hundertjährigen Gedächtnissfeier der deutschen Christentumsgesellschaft*, Basel, 1881; A. Ostertag, *Entstehungsgeschichte der evangelischen Missionsgesellschaft zu Basel*, ib. 1865.

CHRISTIAN: The term *Christianos*, "of the party of Christ," occurs in the New Testament only in Acts xi. 26, xxvi. 28; I Pet. iv. 16. The first passage states that it originated at Antioch, which accords with the fact that the termination *-anos* was recognized and employed especially in Grecian Asia. The date implied by the passage is 40–44 A.D. None of the New Testament passages requires an invidious meaning, though it is suggested in the second and third. There is no historical foundation for the statement often made that it was a "nickname." Tertullian says that non-Christians pronounced it Chrestianos, the word commonly associated with the Greek word *chrestos*, "serviceable," and the *Codex Sinaiticus* reads *Chrestianos* in all New Testament passages. Its earliest use by Christians, apart from the New Testament, is found in the Apologists, Justin Martyr, Athenagoras, Theophilus, etc., after whose time it was generally appropriated by Christians. That it originated outside of Christian and Jewish circles is most likely because (1) Christians spoke of one another as "the brethren," "the saints," "the disciples," "the faithful," etc.; (2) the Jews used the term "Nazarene." Its convenience would justify its use; while the frequency with which the term "Christ" occurred in the Christocentric preaching of the early apostolic age would justify its application to the disciples.

GEO. W. GILMORE.

BIBLIOGRAPHY: R. A. Lipsius, *Ueber den Ursprung und . . . Gebrauch des Christennamens*, in *Gratulationsprogramm der theologischen Facultät Jena für Hase*, 1873, pp. 6–10; *DB*, i. 384–386; *EB*, i. 752–763; *DCG*, i. 316–318.

CHRISTIAN BROTHERS (BROTHERS OF THE CHRISTIAN SCHOOLS): The most noted and influential of the Roman Catholic educational brotherhoods, founded by Jean Baptiste de la Salle (b. at Reims Apr. 30, 1651; d. at Rouen Apr. 7, 1719), who was canonized May 24, 1900. Placed in charge of a congregation of Sisters of Jesus in Reims in 1680, De la Salle soon added to his duties the direction of a number of schools for boys, whose teachers he bound to a life of renunciation and union. The brothers were required, in addition to the three simple vows, to give instruction invariably without compensation, and to wear a special habit. In 1688 their founder was appointed their first superior-general and removed to Vaugirard near Paris, in 1696 to Saint Yon, a house of novices at Rouen, which remained the center of the congregation until 1770. The Christian Brothers spread rapidly throughout France, and in 1724 were recognized by Benedict XIII. The antimonastic decree of the National Assembly of Feb. 13, 1790, dissolved the congregation, which then had 121 houses in France, but it still retained its organization in Italy, and was reestablished in

France under Napoleon in 1804. By 1822 the houses of the Christian Brothers numbered 180 in France, and since that time the congregation has spread over the greater part of the Roman Catholic world (especially Belgium, Spain, Italy, and Austria), and is represented in Turkey, India, Egypt, Australia, and America. With about 1,300 houses, over 2,000 schools, and 14,000 members, the Christian Brothers are now the strongest Roman Catholic male order.

Although without official connection with the Jesuits, the Christian Brothers, who are also called Ignorantins because of their law which forbids them to admit to their number priests with a theological education, have many points in common with the older order. When the Jesuits were expelled from France in 1764, the Christian Brothers aided materially in maintaining sympathy for the exiles among the people and preparing the way for their return. Much of their organization and discipline also recalls the Jesuit system, especially the assistants charged with the supervision of the acts of the superior-general, the frequent visitations, the rules for confession and prayer, and the training of their members, which consists of a novitiate and a course of practical teaching of one year each. (O. Zöckler†.)

Bibliography: Heimbucher, *Orden und Kongregationen*, ii. 280–285; *Die christliche Schulbrüder*, 2 vols., Augsburg, 1844; J. A. Krebs, *Leben des . . . J. B. de la Salle, nebst Anhang über Geschichte . . . seines Ordens*, Regensburg, 1858; F. J. Knecht, *J. B. de la Salle und das Institut der christlichen Schulbrüder*, Freiburg, 1879; Mrs. M. Wilson, *The Christian Brothers, their Origin and Work*, London, 1883; J. B. Blain, *La Vie du . . . J.-B. de la Salle*, Versailles, 1887; P. Helyot, *Ordres monastiques*, viii. 233 sqq.; Currier, *Religious Orders*, pp. 456–457.

CHRISTIAN CATHOLIC APOSTOLIC CHURCH IN ZION: A religious society, the formal organization of which was effected by John Alexander Dowie (q.v.) in Chicago, 1896. The growth of the movement dates back to the founder's discovery of his alleged power to obtain cure of disease through prayer, on account of which he retired from the Congregational ministry in Melbourne and established a church and tabernacle for "divine healing." His emigration to the United States in 1888 was followed by the establishment of "missions of healing" on the Pacific Coast. After his settlement at Evanston, Ill., in 1890 he conducted work on the same lines there and in Chicago, with missions in Canada, Minnesota, Pennsylvania, and Maryland. The success of his efforts in Chicago decided him in 1893 to make that his center of operations, and a tabernacle and "divine healing rooms" were erected. His following was so large that organization was determined upon. In 1900 a large tract of land was bought on Lake Michigan, 42 m. n. of Chicago, and "Zion City" was planned, where were to be erected schools, a college to train the ministry and propagandists, various business establishments and factories (for which large sums have been solicited and received from believers), and residences for the adherents of the Church. The branches already established in the West and elsewhere were brought into connection with the central organization, in which a theocratic element was claimed.

In the organization of the Church Dowie was "general overseer," and claimed to be Elijah III., John the Baptist being Elijah II. Other officers are overseers, elders, evangelists, deaconesses, and conductors of gatherings. The propaganda is carried on by bands of "Zion Seventies" who in twos act as tract-distributors. Missionaries are sent in all directions, and branches are established in different countries in Europe, eastern Asia, and South America. The basis of church-membership is belief in the Scriptures as the rule of faith and practise, in the necessity of repentance for sin and of trust in Christ for salvation, and belief in the witness of the Spirit.

In 1905 Mr. Dowie was compulsorily retired, and Wilbur Glenn Voliva elected in his place, though the former objected that the election violated the theocratic constitution. No statistics are obtainable as to membership or ministry. The receiver appointed for the affairs of Zion City reported in Sept., 1906, total assets of $2,528,581 and liabilities of $6,125,018. W. H. Larrabee.

Bibliography: R. Harlan, *John Alexander Dowie and the Christian Catholic Apostolic Church in Zion*, Evansville, Wis., 1906; *J. A. Dowie and his Zions*, in *Independent*, liii (1901), 1786; *Dowie Movement in Chicago*, in *Outlook*, lxviii (1901), 429; J. M. Buckley, *John Alexander Dowie, Analyzed and Classified*, in *Century Magazine*, xlii (1902), 928–982; J. Swain, *The Prophet and his Profits*, ib., pp. 122 sqq.; J. J. Halsey, *Genesis of a Modern Prophet*, in *American Journal of Sociology*, ix (1903), 310; J. K. Friedman, in *Everybody's Magazine*, ix (1903), 567; J. H. Shepstone, *Dowie and his City of Zion*, in the London *Sunday Magazine*, xxxiii (1904), 553.

The Church periodical is *Leaves of Healing*, a weekly published at Zion City.

CHRISTIAN COMMISSION, THE UNITED STATES: An organization to care for the religious needs of the soldiers in the field during the Civil War, first proposed by Vincent Colyer, of New York, in 1861. The idea was taken up by the Young Men's Christian Association, and at a convention held in New York in Nov., 1861, a commission of twelve was organized to take charge of the work. Bibles, hymnals, tracts, religious books, and newspapers were distributed through the armies, and personal religious work was done. Two special works were undertaken: The Commission aimed to be a medium of speedy and reliable communication between the soldiers and sailors and their friends at home, and it circulated loan-libraries of general literature. The total value of money contributed and other gifts was officially estimated at $6,291,107.68. The final meeting of the Commission was held in Washington Feb. 11, 1866. The leading men in the movement were the president, George H. Stuart, of Philadelphia, and Nathan Bishop (q.v.), of New York.

Bibliography: Lemuel Moss, *Annals of the United States Christian Commission*, Philadelphia, 1868.

CHRISTIAN CONNECTION. See Christians.

CHRISTIAN DOCTRINE, SOCIETY OF: The name of several religious associations of which the most important are. (1) The Society of Christian Doctrine (*Società della dottrina cristiana*), founded at Rome in 1562 by Marco de Sadis Cusani, of Milan (d. 1595), to instruct the people in Christian teachings. It consisted of priests and laymen, and spread in Upper Italy, Germany, and Austria. In 1586 the Roman branch was made a spiritual congregation with its seat at the church of St. Agatha in Trastevere (whence they are sometimes called Agathists). The others constituted a brotherhood under secular presidents, connected with the clerical congregation by a common directing body (*definitorium*). They founded schools and undertook general as well as religious instruction, taught in the churches, and strove to lead the young to a religious life. The number of clerical members had fallen to fifty-four in 1747, for which reason Benedict XIV. in that year united them with a French congregation of like name, (2) the Fathers of Christian Doctrine (*Pères de la doctrine chrétienne*), founded in 1592 by César de Bus (b. at Cavaillon 1544; d. 1607), with the help of a former Calvinist, J. B. Romillon, canon of Isle, and a canon of Avignon, named Pinelli. The object was to instruct in Roman doctrine and to check the spread of Calvinism. Clement VIII. confirmed the constitution in 1597. Most of the members were united with the Somaschians (q.v.), while a minority joined the Oratorians of Berulle in 1616. In 1647, however, Innocent X. again made the *Pères doctrinaires* an independent body, and Alexander VII. in 1659 allowed them to take the simple vows. At the outbreak of the French Revolution they had twenty-eight houses in France; in 1900 they had one in France (at Cavaillon, diocese of Avignon) and six in Italy. Cardinal Bellarmine wrote his *Dottrina cristiana* and *Dichiaratione più copiosa della dottrina cristiana* for the use of the Italian congregation, and De Bus composed a popular exposition of the catechism for the French congregation (published at Paris, 1666). The only scholar of the congregation worthy of note was the general superior Pierre Annat (d. 1715), author of an *Apparatus methodicus ad positivam theologiam* (Paris, 1700, and often).

(O. Zöckler†.)

Bibliography: Helyot, *Ordres monastiques*, iv. 232–252; Heimbucher, *Orden und Kongregationen*, ii. 338–341; Currier, *Religious Orders*, pp. 436–438; P. du Mas, *La Vie du vénérable César de Bus*, Paris, 1703; J. J. Chamoux, *Vie du vénérable César de Bus*, Paris, 1864.

CHRISTIAN ENDEAVOR SOCIETY. See Young People's Societies.

CHRISTIAN LOVE, BROTHERS OF. See Hippolytus, Saint, Brothers of.

CHRISTIAN AND MISSIONARY ALLIANCE: An organization to promote a deeper spiritual life among Christians of all denominations, and a more aggressive missionary work in neglected fields at home and abroad. The work was begun during a convention at Old Orchard, Me., in 1887 by a number of Christian men and women, connected with various Evangelical denominations in the United States and Canada. It is not a sectarian body, but a fraternal union of Christians. It is incorporated under the laws of the State of New York, and is managed by a board of fifteen directors, elected for a term of three years at the annual meeting of the society. It has about 200 branches in the United States and Canada, and 100 mission stations in foreign countries. There are about 200 official workers in the home land, and 600 foreign laborers in the mission fields abroad, of whom one-half are natives and the others American and Canadian missionaries. There are about 4,000 communicants in the various native churches. The fields include western India, southern, central, and western China, Japan, the Kongo and the Sudan in West Africa, Palestine, the West Indies, Venezuela, Chile, Bolivia, Ecuador, and Argentina.

The special object in beginning the foreign mission work was to endeavor to reach neglected fields, where other missions had not been established. Tibet was the first objective point of the society, and for many years a successful mission has been established on its borders. In other countries the most destitute fields have always been chosen, and the society endeavors to avoid duplicating the work of other societies. Another object was to employ a class of laborers for whom an open door was not easily found under other organizations. Many of the missionaries of the Alliance are laymen specially trained for this work, and also unmarried women. A large and successful Bible Institute is maintained at South Nyack, N. Y., for the preparation of the laborers, from which over 3,000 students have gone out in the past twenty years. The attendance in the classes of 1906–07 was over 300.

The work of the society is sustained by voluntary contributions. During the past twenty years about $3,000,000 have been contributed in this way, and the annual income at the present time is about a quarter of a million dollars. One aim of the society is to cultivate a spirit of rigid economy and great simplicity and self-denial in the methods of work. The missionaries voluntarily receive no fixed salary, but a sufficient amount to meet their actual expenses on the field, gladly giving their lives in disinterested service and simple faith in God to take care of them through the friends at home. There are no expensive buildings, and most of the home workers and officials receive no salary and give their services freely for Christ's sake. In this way the maximum service is secured at the smallest expense, and the self-denial of those who give finds its response in the self-sacrifice of those who go.

A. B. Simpson.

CHRISTIAN MISSIONARY ASSOCIATION: A loose confederation of churches in Kentucky, in which each church was independent and claimed to be unsectarian. The churches were bound together by no creed or ecclesiastical tie, but the general system of doctrine was Evangelical, and baptism by immersion was preferred. The confederation, now extinct, reported in 1895 thirteen organizations and 754 communicants.

Bibliography: H. K. Carroll, *Religious Forces of the United States*, p. 95, New York, 1896.

CHRISTIAN REFORMED CHURCH. See Reformed Church, Christian.

CHRISTIAN SCIENCE. See Science, Christian.

CHRISTIAN SOCIALISM.

I. Definition and Principles: The term "Christian Socialism" was first used in 1848 by J. F. D. Maurice (q.v.). He wished to express the idea that socialism is a development and outcome of Christianity; and that, if it is to be effective, it must have a definite Christian basis. To this view later Christian Socialists have always adhered, although the term has been used to express a number of other ideas, especially in Europe. It is frequently employed there loosely to indicate any application of Christian principles to social life. Both Protestants and Roman Catholics have so applied the phrase, perhaps in order to show that the Church was not antagonistic to socialism when subjoined to the leadership of the Church. The term should, however, be restricted in use to the idea which Maurice desired to express; although this restriction does not imply adherence to the economic views held by early Christian Socialists. Circumstances have changed and social thought has developed. Christian Socialists may, and do, hold various views on economics; but they must believe in socialism as a development and outcome of Christianity if they would be counted among the followers of Maurice and Charles Kingsley.

1. The Term.

The definition of Christian Socialism as given by Maurice can be understood only on the basis of his ethical and religious principles. The most important of these is that there are two forces which came into prominence in the nineteenth century, although they had had a prior existence—science, and man as an end in himself. The Church was compelled to adopt some attitude in regard to both, since both seemed hostile—science as threatening the entire structure of theology, and the new theory of man as giving rise to the labor movement with socialism as an attendant, emphasizing the material advantages of civilization. Christian Socialists maintained an attitude of hospitality toward both of these forces. They claimed an essential agreement between the ascertained results of science and the fundamental teachings of the Bible, and argued that, since God was ruler both in the spiritual and the secular spheres of life, there could be no discrepancy between revealed religion and science when both were rightly and fully understood. Both were inspired by God, although in different degrees and for different purposes. With respect to the endeavor of the masses to obtain recognition as individuals, Christian Socialists maintained that the essence of Christianity was brotherhood, and that its aim was the acquirement of dignity by every man as a child of God. They contended that the system of privileged classes was foreign to the spirit of Christianity, and a parasitic growth upon the body politic. The fundamental principle of their philosophy may be summarized in the statement that the world is created by God; the Christian religion is revealed by him. The principle has, however, other corollaries: (1) Since God has created the world, he has also redeemed it—the whole of it, each human being in it, and all human relations—because the incarnation was a universal redemption. (2) Since all men are, at least potentially, the children of God, they are brothers in all relations. (3) Since God has created men individuals, each with a special endowment, every man must do some useful work and develop his God-given faculties; he should, moreover, have the opportunity so to do.

2. Relations to Science and Religion.

From the vantage-point of this principle Christian Socialists began to wage war upon their contemporaries. They fought the Calvinistic doctrine of a partial redemption through election; Roman Catholicism, because as an organization that Church depreciates family life more or less by its teaching of asceticism and by making reward in heaven dependent upon "good works," in this way putting a premium on wealth and requiring the continuation of a system whereby the few are able to reap rewards from the labor of the many. Against communists, socialists, and anarchists it was urged that they denied the *raison d'être* of nationality, and thus violated a fundamental law of human nature, since the development of the individual could take place only on the basis of nationalism, and not on that of cosmopolitanism. They inveighed against the *laissez-faire* doctrine as a perversion of Christian doctrine and of sound economic principles. They berated the rich who paid wages merely sufficient to keep their workmen alive and thus used human beings as a means to selfish ends. They questioned the ability of socialism to remedy present evils merely by changing the system of economic production and distribution, and pointed out that only by the infusion of the spirit of Christian brotherhood and by the conversion of every individual could the individual be induced to work for all, and all for one, since the best work in the world had not been done from economic motives, but from an unselfish desire to help others.

3. Attitude to Various Forces and Theories.

II. History.—1. England: The year 1848 was a dark one for English workingmen. Conditions combined to bring their wrongs and sufferings to a head. Chartism had, moreover, stirred up considerable discussion and caused much political unrest. On April 10 there was an immense mass-meeting at Kennington Common, London; 100,000 men proposed to march to Parliament and force it to accept the so-called six points; viz., universal suffrage, abolition of property qualifications for members of Parliament, annual parliaments, equal representation, payment of representatives, and vote by ballot. This programme seemed revolutionary; the Gov-

1. Initiation of the Movement.

ernment put Wellington in charge of London, and 150,000 householders were sworn in as special constables. But the assemblage was a mere rabble, since sober workingmen stayed away, and O'Connor, the Irish agitator, absented himself. A heavy downpour of rain cowed the crowd completely, so that the meeting dispersed in confusion.

But the danger was not yet passed. In order to prevent the recurrence of similar or more dangerous meetings, three men, Frederick Denison Maurice, Charles Kingsley, and John M. Ludlow, decided after consultation to write and publish *Politics for the People* (May 6, 1848). Only seventeen weekly numbers appeared, but these succeeded in turning the impending revolution into a peaceful social evolution. The writers declared their sympathy with the workingmen, warned them against violence, appealed to the justice and charity of the rich, and expounded their principles with skill and zeal. Others joined them, and numerous meetings were held, both for the instruction of workingmen and for mutual encouragement. Henry Mayhew had contributed a series of articles to the *Morning Chronicle* of London during 1849 on the sweating system, and these called forth in 1850 Kingsley's tract *Cheap Clothes and Nasty*. In the same year the little group of friends decided to issue *Tracts on Christian Socialism*, with the keyword: Association, i.e., Cooperation versus Competition. In order to alleviate at least the direct poverty among the laboring classes, the Christian Socialists started in 1850 the Society for the Promotion of Workingmen's Associations. Since cooperative societies were not legal at that time, Ludlow exerted all his influence to have the Industrial and Provident Societies' Act passed in 1852. Maurice and his friends immediately used this opportunity to establish a number of cooperative concerns. The principles underlying them, adopted at Manchester May 15, 1853, were: (1) human society is a body consisting of many members, not a collection of warring atoms; (2) true workers must be fellow workers, not rivals; (3) the principle of justice, not of selfishness, must govern exchanges.

These societies thus established have prospered to a remarkable degree. In 1906 the turnover of the Cooperative Wholesale Society, with more than 2,000 local branches, was $500,000,000, with a surplus of over $12,000,000. In 1876 the Guild of St.

2. Results. Matthew was formed for the purpose of drawing the Church and the workingmen closer together, and to close as far as possible the social chasm between the rich and the poor. It was absorbed in 1880 by the Christian Social Union, under the leadership of Canon Scott Holland, although it still maintains an individual existence within the larger body, and has a spokesman in the *Church Reformer*. The Union consists of men of all classes who are willing to work for the following purposes: (1) to claim for the Christian law the ultimate authority in social practise; (2) to study how the truths and principles of Christianity may be applied to the social and economic difficulties of the present time; and (3) to present Christ as the living king and master, the enemy of wrong and of selfishness, and the power of love and righteousness. The earlier Christian Socialists also worked in other fields, such as village improvement societies, drew up a programme for the National Health League, founded the Workingmen's College in London, and secured the passage by Parliament of a number of laws for the benefit of workingmen. They encountered much bitter opposition both in and out of the Anglican Church. Some of them suffered persecution, as when Maurice was removed from his professorship at King's College in 1853, although he was later (1866) appointed to one at Cambridge. Nevertheless, their fearless and sincere conduct and self-sacrifice made many friends for them. While the movement as a separate organization has died, it has been the seed of many reforms throughout England in every sphere of life, while the United Kingdom itself has been greatly improved socially and morally by the lives and teachings of these men. The conference of 194 Anglican bishops assembled in 1897 practically adopted as its principles the platform of Maurice and of the Christian Social Union (see LAMBETH CONFERENCE). The non-conformists have also caught the spirit, and the Rev. John Clifford and many others are members of the Christian Socialist League.

2. Continental Europe: Analogous Continental movements can not properly be called Christian Socialism. They were always Christian, but never socialistic. They were started largely with the purpose of undermining secular socialism. But the principal

1. Basal Principles. objection to applying the term to the Continental movements is that they never formulated a philosophy of life and of the State such as Maurice and Kingsley gave to England. As a result they were unable to present a world-view as systematic, far-reaching, and comprehensive as that offered to English workingmen. This difference may explain why in Great Britain the socialist party and other extremists did not develop great strength after the appearance of the Christian Socialists. The English workingman has been taught to look at the economic problem as only one among many, whereas German and French laborers came to consider that of supreme, if not of sole, importance. Marx simply systematized that view in his *Kapital*. The Christian workers of France and Germany had nothing to put into the hands of workingmen which could compare with that book. There is another difference of prime importance between the two schools. The Continentals always leaned on the arm of the Church, of the State, or of both; whereas Englishmen were not afraid to attack either or both whenever necessary. Continental laboring-men regarded these leaders as hirelings of the State or emissaries of the hierarchy, while in fact they were defenders of society on Church and State principles, and sought to ally the altar and the crown.

For these reasons the Continental movement was doomed to failure. The laboring class has kept aloof, and adopted Marxism. The leaders were, nevertheless, in earnest, and began work along other lines. The Roman Catholics founded numerous societies under the leadership of Baron von Ketteler (q.v.), archbishop of Mainz, who exerted a great influence. The object of these societies was partly ecclesiastical, partly political—the people were to be guarded from the infidelity of the socialists, and were to be used because of their possession of the ballot. The Roman Catholic Church has in Germany succeeded so well in this that it has been able through the votes of artisans, laborers, and peasants to secure a large number of seats in the Reichstag. There has been no hesitation at times to form an alliance with the socialists, when the Church's purposes were served, and the State has been several times compelled to capitulate before the union thus effected. But along with this political and ecclesiastical activity an immense amount of valuable practical Christian work has been done—a description of which would be foreign to this article.

The Protestant Church in Germany began practical Christian work in the early part of the nineteenth century, which made rapid headway after 1850. Hardly any Church in Christendom does so much valuable work as the Lutheran, but—it is all done under the auspices or in alliance with the State, and is, therefore, discredited among the socialists who showed their opposition by withdrawal *en masse* from the Church. Men of influence like Drs. Stöcker and Kögel failed after earnest endeavors to organize an independent political or Christian party, while they have been eminently successful in uniting various charitable and philanthropic movements in the Innere Mission (q.v.). In France, Belgium, Switzerland, Austria, Denmark, and elsewhere no distinctively Christian Socialist movements have developed. The Christians of eminence in these countries, such as the Comte de Mun in France, Laveleye in Belgium, and Prince von Lichtenstein in Austria, who might have led in this direction, were either dependent on the Roman Catholic Church for the expression of their views, or did not imitate a distinctive independent Christian Socialism. They simply contributed to literature or founded charitable and philanthropic institutions.

2. Results.

3. The United States: The seed which was sent out from England found a much more favorable soil in the United States. This country had been the camping-ground of numerous communistic and other societies (see COMMUNISM), and the experimental station for such idealistic organizations as Brook Farm near Boston. No hostility was manifested by either State or Church to independent movements along Christian Socialist lines, nor was the attitude of the people unfavorable. Nevertheless, no movement of any national importance has been inaugurated. A number of men prominent in the Church and in business became interested in the work of Maurice and Kingsley. A paper, the *Equity*, was published in 1874–75 in Boston. An organization was formed in that city April 15, 1889, largely under the leadership of W. D. P. Bliss, called the Society of Christian Socialists. The constitution emphasized the stewardship of all gifts and of property, the fatherhood of God, and the brotherhood of man, it deprecated the present industrial and commercial systems as individualistic, unjust, and contrary to the law of God; recommended socialism (without defining it) as the necessary outcome of Christian teachings; and invited all Christians and Churches to join the new movement. But the ideas did not take root, and the movement to-day is a mere sentiment which finds a channel for its activities in charity and philanthropy. Some journals, such as the *Outlook*, the *Kingdom*, the *Christian Statesman*, advocate Christian Socialism to a limited extent, but as a whole the movement has taken the shape of practical reform. See SOCIALISM.

RUDOLPH M. BINDER.

BIBLIOGRAPHY: Besides the publications mentioned in the text, the sources are contained in *Tracts on Christian Socialism*, London, 1850 sqq.; the *Christian Socialist*, a journal issued from Nov. 2, 1850, to June 28, 1851; Charles Kingsley's two novels, *Yeast*, London, 1848, and *Alton Locke*, ib. 1850; F. D. Maurice, *Moral and Metaphysical Philosophy*, 2 vols., ib. 1871–72; and other writings of these two leaders. Further light is to be gained from the biographies of these two men. For different phases of the subject consult: A. V. Woodworth, *Christian Socialism in England*, London, 1903 (contains a full bibliography); E. R. A. Seligman, *Owen and the Christian Socialists*, in *Political Science Quarterly*, June, 1886; B. F. Westcott, *Social Aspects of Christianity*, London, 1887; idem, *The Incarnation and Common Life*, ib. 1893; M. Kaufmann, *Christian Socialism*, ib. 1888; W. D. P. Bliss, *What Christian Socialism Is*, and *The Social Faith of the Catholic Church* (tracts), New York, 1894; G. D. Herron, *The New Redemption and the New Society*, Boston, 1894; F. S. Nitti, *Catholic Socialism*, London, 1895; W. D. P. Bliss, et alia, *Encyclopedia Social Reform*, New York, 1908.

CHRISTIAN UNION, THE: A religious organization of the United States, founded by James F. Given in the first year of the Civil War. Mr. Given (d. 1869) was a graduate of Marietta College and an ordained minister of the Methodist Episcopal Church. In 1860, when political excitement and prejudice were high and bitter, he found himself out of sympathy with his Church. He began the publication of a religious paper, the *Christian Witness* (Columbus, O.), and called a meeting of others who shared his views to organize an antipolitical and antisectarian brotherhood. Ministers and laymen of several denominations, chiefly from Ohio, met in Columbus in 1861, where they chose the name "The Christian Union," declared the Bible the only rule of faith and practise, and adopted strict congregational government for each local church. The first general council, held in Terre Haute, Ind., in 1863, adopted the following principles: (1) Christ the only head of the Church; (2) the Holy Bible the only rule of faith and practise; (3) good fruits the only test of fellowship; (4) each local church to be self-governed; (5) the union of all Christians to be worked for; (6) political preaching discountenanced. The *Christian Witness* was made the organ of the society.

The membership of the Union is found chiefly in the country and small villages, there being no city churches. It stands for Evangelical Christianity and pleads for the union of all Christians on the basis of the Bible. At first its numbers increased rapidly, but in recent years losses and gains have been about equal. There are now about 250 ministers, 300 churches, and 20,000 members, of whom more than two-thirds are in Ohio and Missouri, with churches also in Indiana, Illinois, Iowa, Kansas, Kentucky, Oklahoma, and Tennessee. Two or three schools have been established, but have failed to receive adequate support, and at present there are no denominational schools or colleges. The *Christian Union Messenger* (Greencastle, Ind.) and the *Witness Herald* (Excelsior Springs, Mo.) are papers published by clergymen of the Union. H. J. DUCKWORTH.

CHRISTIANI, ARNOLD: German theologian; b. at Johannenhof Dec. 14, 1807; d. at Riga Mar. 16, 1886. In 1838 he became pastor of Ringen; in 1849 dean of the district of Werro; in 1852 professor of practical theology at Dorpat and preacher to the university. From 1865 to 1882, when he retired, he was general superintendent of Livonia. Besides a volume of sermons (Dorpat, 1852), he published three books on the Apocalypse (Riga, 1861-75), in which he followed the Erlangen school. (A. HAUCK.)

CHRISTIANS: As a denominational designation, a name given to two religious bodies of America.

1. A Church dating from the early part of the nineteenth century, also known as the Disciples of Christ (q.v.).

2. A denomination sometimes called the Christian Connection for purposes of identification—a phrase which they admit usually refers to them. The name which they use themselves was formerly sometimes incorrectly pronounced Christ-ians. The denomination resulted from three independent movements, two of which partook of the nature of secession. In 1793, in North Carolina and Virginia, twenty or thirty ministers, influenced chiefly by Rev. James O'Kelly (q.v.), withdrew from the Methodist Episcopal Church on account of objections to the government of bishops and the use of creeds and disciplines. They were followed by about 1,000 members. At first they were called Republican Methodists; but in 1794 on motion of Rev. Rice Haggard the name Christian was unanimously adopted, and since that time they have accepted no other name. The second movement was in Vermont, in 1800, among the Baptists, Abner Jones, a physician, and Rev. Elias Smith being prominent in it. The third movement, in 1800 and 1801, was in Kentucky chiefly, among the Presbyterians; prominent here were David Purviance, John Thomson, Robert Marshall, John Dunlavy, William Kinkade, Richard McNemar, Nathan Worley, and Barton W. Stone (q.v.). The three movements were severally unknown to each other until a number of years had passed, when they came together without negotiation or formal organic action.

Origin.

They all accepted the Bible as the only creed, Christian as the only name, and Christian character as the only test of fellowship. Generally they baptize by immersion, but some ministers sprinkle. They are universally open communionists, as their test of fellowship compels. Sometimes they are called trinitarian, and sometimes antitrinitarian; but almost universally they hold to the divinity of Christ. They themselves refuse to pronounce on these dogmas, which are disputed among Christian people. They are congregational in government; but there seems to have been no pressure on this point organically since the O'Kelly movement in the South. They have annual district conferences and quadrennial general conventions.

In 1854, at the general convention at Cincinnati, resolutions were passed condemning human slavery. The Southern brethren of the denomination withdrew, and perfected a separate organization. The division lasted till long after the Civil War; but at the convention at Haverhill, Mass., in 1894, under uncontested ruling of a brother temporarily called to the chair by the president, that the Southern brethren "only called themselves Christians, took the Bible for their only creed, and granted full fellowship to all Christians, and therefore were entitled to membership in the convention on the same basis of representation as others," they took their seats in the convention and have been working with the general body ever since, greatly increasing its organic effectiveness.

History.

The question of the "union" of denominations has several times proved injurious to the Christians. A third of a century after their rise, Barton W. Stone, one of their prominent ministers, made a "union" with Alexander Campbell, the founder of the Disciples of Christ (q.v.), which really proved a surrender by Stone. Somewhat more than fifty churches were in this way lost to the Christians. This element in the Disciple denomination clung to the name "Christian"; so that there has been some confusion, many supposing that the Disciples are the original body. But the Disciples differ from the Christians in giving fellowship exclusively to the immersed; while the Christians make Christian character their only test of fellowship or membership. In 1885 and 1886 there was agitation for union with the Free Baptists, whose genius is more like that of the Christians; and in some sections it was actually voted and supposed to be effected. But the churches did not follow the leaders, and the movement was abandoned. From 1893 to 1898 organic union with the Congregationalists was talked of, making some denominational friction, which led to the cessation of the agitation.

The membership of the Christians is almost wholly in the United States and Canada, numbering about 120,000. Former estimates were too large. They have few churches west of Kansas, or south of North Carolina. The following institutions of learning belong to them or are affiliated with them: Union Christian College, at Merom, Ind.; Christian Biblical Institute (a theological seminary), at Stanfordville, N. Y.; Elon College, at Elon College, N. C.; Starkey Seminary, at Lakemont, N. Y.; Defiance College, at Defiance, O.; Palmer College, at Le Grand, Ia.; Kansas Christian College, at Lincoln,

Numbers and Educational Institutions.

Kan.; and Franklinton Christian College (for negroes), at Franklinton, N. C. Their quadrennial convention of Oct., 1850, held at Marion, N. Y., directed the founding of a college giving equal privileges to the sexes; and they established Antioch College at Yellow Springs, O., and made Hon. Horace Mann its first president; but they later lost the institution to the Unitarians. It was the first college to give fully equal honors to both sexes in "coeducation." Union Christian College, their next college, may be considered the effect of the abortive attempt at Antioch. [In Canada the Christians pay the salary of one of their members as professor in McMaster University, a Baptist institution, and encourage their young people to study there.—A. H. N.]

The Christians were also the first in modern times as a denomination to authorize the ordination of a woman to the Gospel ministry; but they were not the first to ordain; this being done irregularly before their action. The foreign mission work of the Christians is only twenty years old; it is carried on now in Japan and Porto Rico, and there is agitation to begin work in India.

In 1808 the Rev. Elias Smith established the first religious newspaper, the *Herald of Gospel Liberty*, at Portsmouth, N. H. After various vicissitudes, it is now the property of the general body and is published by the Christian Publishing Association, a denominational corporation at Dayton, O. Other periodicals to be mentioned are: the *Christian Sun*, weekly, property of the Southern Christian Convention, Elon College, N. C.; the *Christian Vanguard*, semimonthly, property of the Ontario Christian Conference, Toronto and Newmarket, Ontario; the *Young People's Worker*, monthly, Raleigh, N. C.; various Sunday-school periodicals, issued by the Christian Publishing Association, Dayton, O., quarterlies and weeklies, and the *Christian Missionary*, monthly, property of the American Christian Convention, Dayton, O.; the *Afro-Christian Messenger*, monthly, Franklinton, N. C.

J. J. Summerbell.

Bibliography: *Smith's Works*, by Elias Smith, Exeter, N. H., 1805; John Dunlavy, *Manifesto*, Pleasant Hill, Ky., 1818; John Rogers, *Biography of Barton Warren Stone*, Cincinnati, 1847; D. Purviance, *Biography of D. Purviance*, Dayton, O., 1848; J. R. Freese, *Christian Church History*, Philadelphia, 1852; N. Summerbell, *History of the Christians*, Cincinnati, 1871; E. W. Humphreys, *Memoirs of Deceased Christian Ministers*, Dayton, 1880; J. F. Burnett, *Origin and Principles of the Christians*, Dayton, 1903; J. J. Summerbell, *Scripture Doctrine*, Dayton, 1904; idem, *The Christians and the Disciples*, Dayton, 1906.

CHRISTIANS OF ST. JOHN. See Mandæans.

CHRISTIANS OF ST. THOMAS. See Nestorians.

CHRISTIE, FRANCIS ALBERT: Unitarian; b. at Lowell, Mass., Dec. 3, 1858. He was educated at Amherst College (B.A., 1881), and studied philology at Johns Hopkins (1884–86) and theology at the universities of Berlin, Heidelberg, and Marburg (1889–93). He taught in the Roxbury Latin School, Roxbury, Mass., in 1881–84 and was classical master at Lawrenceville School, Lawrenceville, N. J., in 1887–89. He was subsequently an instructor in the Harvard Divinity School (1891–92), and since 1893 has been professor of church history in Meadville Theological School, Meadville, Pa.

CHRISTLIEB, THEODOR: A voluminous theological author; b. at Birkenfeld (27 m. w.n.w. of Stuttgart), Württemberg, Mar. 7, 1833; d. at Bonn Aug. 15, 1889. His education was received mainly at Tübingen, where he studied theology under Tobias Beck and F. C. Baur. He was ordained in 1856 as assistant to his father, and soon took charge of a church at Ruith near Stuttgart. A Lutheran by education and conviction, he laid more stress on honest faith and real conversion than on dogmatic subtleties; the narrow exclusiveness of many Lutherans repelled him, and he had close associations with numbers of the Reformed, coming later to be among the supporters of definite union. His pastoral duties left him time for literary work, out of which grew his *Leben und Lehre des Johann Scotus Erigena* (Gotha, 1860). From 1858 to 1865 he was in London as pastor of the Lutheran German church of Islington. He was recalled by the king of Württemberg to be pastor at Friedrichshafen. While there he delivered lectures at St. Gall and Winterthur, afterward enlarged into his second important work, *Moderne Zweifel am christlichen Glauben* (Bonn, 1868; Eng. transl., Edinburgh, 1874). In a moderate and conciliatory tone, yet not paying sufficient attention to the results of Biblical science, he attempted to meet some of the principal modern objections to Christianity, dealing especially with materialism, pantheism, and deism, and going on to develop a Christian theism, paying particular attention to the doctrine of the Trinity and the possibility of miracles, and vigorously opposing the rationalistic conceptions of Strauss, Renan, and Baur. In 1868 he was called to Bonn as professor of practical theology and preacher to the university, and here he remained until his death. The purpose of his lectures was rather the formation of earnest and devout pastors than the display of scientific learning. Similarly, his preaching, which had a wide influence, was characterized rather by warm, earnest pressing home of the great truths of Christianity than by a seeking after oratorical effect. His work extended far beyond the bounds of the university. In England he had learned to know and to esteem members of other churches than his own, and he worked constantly for unity of spirit between them, without wasting time in fruitless efforts for external unity. He took part in the work of the Evangelical Alliance, and attended its conferences in Basel, Copenhagen, and New York, where he read a paper on *The Best Methods of Counteracting Modern Infidelity* (New York, 1873), dealing with unbelief as it shows itself in the individual, in scientific investigations, and in the practise of social life. In order to stir up the German churches to more zealous activity, he delivered a lecture at Copenhagen in 1884 on the best means of counteracting religious indifference, in which, while deprecating sensational methods such as those of the Salvation Army, he suggested the appointment, especially in large places, of evangelists who should carry the Gospel to the people outside the church building, working in harmony with the pastor. To carry this idea into effect, he founded the German Evangelistic Union, in conjunction with Bernstorff and Pückler. He purchased in Bonn a disused Presbyterian chapel with a large house attached, and turned it into a training-school for evangelists. After his death the institution was transferred to Barmen, where there was thought to be a wider field for its work. He was also an enthusiastic advocate of foreign missions, and in 1874, with Warneck, founded the *Allgemeine Missionszeitschrift*, in which most of his writings on missionary topics first appeared. The best known of these is *Der gegenwärtige Stand der evangelischen Heidenmission* (Gütersloh, 1879; Eng. transl., London, 1880). Another of his numerous works which was translated into English was his sharp arraignment of England for permitting and even encouraging the opium traffic, *Der indobritische Opiumhandel und seine Wirkungen* (1878; Eng. transl., London, 1879). (E. Sachsse.)

Bibliography: *Zum Gedächtniss Theodor Christliebs*, Bonn, 1889; Mrs. T. Christlieb, *Theodor Christlieb of Bonn*, London, 1892 (by his widow).

CHRISTMAS: The supposed anniversary of the birth of Jesus Christ, occurring on Dec. 25. No sufficient data, however, exist, for the determination of the month or the day of the event. Efforts to reach a fixed date for Zacharias's ministration and to combine this with the "sixth month" mentioned in connection with the annunciation to Mary (Luke i. 26) have given no assured result. Hippolytus seems to have been the first to fix upon Dec. 25. He had reached the conviction that Jesus's life from conception to crucifixion was precisely thirty-three years and that both events occurred on Mar. 25. By calculating nine months from the annunciation or conception he arrived at Dec. 25 as the day of Christ's birth. The uncertainty of all the data discredits the computation. There is no historical evidence that our Lord's birthday was celebrated during the apostolic or early postapostolic times. The uncertainty that existed at the beginning of the third century in the minds of Hippolytus and others—Hippolytus earlier favored Jan. 2, Clement of Alexandria (*Strom.*, i. 21) "the 25th day of Pachon" (=May 20), while others, according to Clement, fixed upon Apr. 18 or 19 and Mar. 28—proves that no Christmas festival had been established much before the middle of the century. Jan. 6 was earlier fixed upon as the date of the baptism or spiritual birth of Christ, and the feast of Epiphany (q.v.) was celebrated by the Basilidian Gnostics in the second century (cf. Clement of Alexandria, ut sup.) and by catholic Christians by about the beginning of the fourth century.

The Day of Christ's Birth not Known.

The earliest record of the recognition of Dec. 25 as a church festival is in the Philocalian Calendar (copied 354 but representing Roman practise in 336; cf. Ruinart, *Acta Martyrum*, p. 617; *MPL*, xiii.; Lightfoot, *The Liberian Calendar*, in his *Clement of Rome*, vol. i., p. 246). In the East the celebration of Jan. 6 as the physical as well as the spiritual birthday of the Lord prevailed generally as early as the first half of the fourth century. Chrysostom (in 386) states that the celebration of the birth of Christ "according to the flesh" was not inaugurated at Antioch until ten years before that date. He intimates that this festival, approved by himself, was opposed by many. An Armenian writer of the eleventh century states that the Christmas festival, invented in Rome by a heretic, Artemon, was first celebrated in Constantinople in 373. In Egypt the Western birthday festival was opposed during the early years of the fifth century, but was celebrated in Alexandria as early as 432. The Jerusalem church was celebrating birth and baptism on the same day (Jan. 6) about the middle of the fourth century, the former at Bethlehem, the latter at the Jordan, although the twenty-mile journey between involved great inconveniences (supposed letter of Bishop Cyril of Jerusalem to Bishop Julius of Rome, preserved in Combefis, *Historia hæresis monothelitarum*). The Jerusalem bishop asks the Roman bishop to ascertain the real date of Christ's birth in order that, if possible, the practical difficulty may be overcome. Julius is represented as sending to Cyril a calculation in favor of Dec. 25, based upon the supposition (derived from Josephus) that Zacharias's vision took place at the Feast of Tabernacles. The Jerusalem church, however, persisted till 549 or later in celebrating birth and baptism on Jan. 6 (Cosmas Indicopleustes). The Christmas festival has never been adopted by the Armenians, the physical and spiritual birthdays being still celebrated conjointly on Jan. 6.

Earliest Traces of the Church Festival.

The wide-spread conviction during the early centuries that the baptism of Jesus was the occasion of his spiritual birth, or his adoption as Son of God and his exaltation to divine rank and power, tended to magnify the anniversary of his baptism and to cause comparative indifference as regards the precise date of his birth according to the flesh. In two Latin homilies, ascribed by some to Ambrose of Milan (4th cent.) and by others to Maximus of Turin (5th cent.), Jan. 6 is declared to be the birthday of the Lord Jesus, "whether he was born of the Virgin on that day or was born again in baptism." It is his "natal feast," his "nativity both of flesh and of spirit." As thirty years before he "was given forth through the Virgin," so on the same day he was "regenerated" and "sanctified" "through the mystery." The writer, or an interpolator, virtually contradicts the statement about Christ's regeneration by explaining that "Christ is baptized, not in order that he may be sanctified by the waters, but that he may himself sanctify the waters."

Relation to the Epiphany.

The naive adoptionism that was so widely prevalent till the end of the second century in Syria, Asia Minor, Italy, northern Africa, and elsewhere, and for centuries later in Armenia, Spain, etc., was gradually displaced by the formulation and general acceptance of a christology (based upon the prologue of John's Gospel and the Epistles of Paul) which laid stress upon the preexistence of Christ as the eternal divine Logos and of the absolute deity of Jesus Christ from the time of his conception. The physical birth assumed more and more importance in the Christian consciousness. The celebration of Christmas as a special Christian festival spread rapidly from the middle of the fourth century onward in sympathy with the triumph of the orthodox christology.

Relation to the Roman Saturnalia.

How much the calculation of Hippolytus had to do with the fixing of the festival on Dec. 25, and how much the date of the festival depended upon the pagan Brumalia (Dec. 25), following the Saturnalia (Dec. 17–24) and celebrating the shortest day in the year and the "new sun" or the beginning of the lengthening of days, can not be accurately determined. The pagan Saturnalia and Brumalia were too deeply entrenched in popular custom to be set aside by Christian influence. The recognition of Sunday (the day of Phœbus and Mithras as well as the Lord's Day) by the emperor Constantine as a legal holiday, along with the influence of Manicheism, which identified the Son of God with the physical sun, may have led Christians of the fourth century to feel the appropriateness of making the birthday of the Son of God coincide with that of the physical sun. The pagan festival with its riot and merrymaking was so popular that Christians were glad of an excuse to continue its celebration with little change in spirit or in manner. Christian preachers of the West and the Nearer East protested against the unseemly frivolity with which Christ's birthday was celebrated, while Christians of Mesopotamia accused their Western brethren of idolatry and sun-worship for adopting as Christian this pagan festival. Yet the festival rapidly gained acceptance and became at last so firmly established that even the Protestant revolution of the sixteenth century was not able to dislodge it and Evangelical Christians even of the more radical types, who reject or ignore nearly all of the ecclesiastical festivals, have never been able wholly to ignore it.

The religious significance of Christmas has been too commonly minimized among Christians, the day among adults being degraded into one merely for the exchange of presents, often neither given nor received in any affection, but out of a sense of obligation or as barter. In too many homes the children, whose day it more particularly is, are not taught to link their merrymaking on Christmas with the gift of God to the world in the person of his Son Jesus Christ. Although some of our denominations hold service on that day, the vast majority of Protestants do not attend, and most of our denominations keep their churches closed. But as it is unquestioned that the Christian Church was founded by Jesus Christ, it will be well to celebrate the event of his birth, if not on Christmas day, then on some other day. The old gospel story of the Nativity was formerly taken literally and has inspired many beautiful hymns and been the suggestion of many legends and elaborate festivities. By design, on Christmas many important events have taken place, as the crowning of Charlemagne as Holy Roman Emperor (800), and William as King of England (1066). A. H. NEWMAN.

BIBLIOGRAPHY: E. Martène, *De antiquis ecclesiæ ritibus*, iii. 31 sqq., Venice, 1783; A. J. Binterim, *Denkwürdigkeiten*, v. 1, pp. 528 sqq., Mainz, 1829; J. C. W. Augusti, *Handbuch der christlichen Archäologie*, 3 vols., Leipsic, 1836–1837; J. P. Thompson, *Christmas and the Saturnalia*, in *Bibliotheca Sacra*, xii (1855), 144 sqq.; P. Cassel, *Weihnachten; Ursprünge, Bräuche und Aberglauben*, Berlin, 1862; J. Marbach, *Die heilige Weihnachtsfeier*, Frankfort, 1865; A. H. Grant, *The Church Seasons*, New York, 1881; J. H. Hobart, *Festivals and Feasts*, London, 1887; T. K. Hervey, *The Book of Christmas; descriptive of the Customs, Ceremonies, Traditions, Superstitions, Fun, Feeling, Festivities of the Christmas Season*, London, 1841, New York, 1888; H. Usener, *Religionsgeschichtliche Untersuchungen*, vol. i., Bonn, 1889; P. de Lagarde, *Mittheilungen*, iv. 241–323, Göttingen, 1891; F. C. Conybeare, *Hist. of Christmas*, in *AJT*, iii (1899), 1–21; idem, *The Key of Truth*, Introduction, Oxford, 1898; H. Thurston, in *American Ecclesiastical Review*, Dec., 1898; A. Tille, *Yule and Christmas*, London, 1899; H. Anz, *Die lateinischen Magierspiel. Untersuchungen und Texte zur Vorgeschichte des . . . Weihnachtsspiels*, Leipsic, 1907; R. H. Schauffler, *Christmas, its Origin, Celebration and Significance*, New York, 1907; Bingham, *Origines*, XX. iv. (investigation of sources); *DCA*, i. 357–364; *DCG*, i. 261–262.

CHRISTO SACRUM ("Sacred to Christ"): The name of a religious society organized in 1792, at Delft in Holland, by certain well-educated young men belonging to the Walloon deacons' confraternity. Its purpose was the defense of the Christian faith against deistic and Voltairean tendencies, and the promotion of universal Christian love, independent of ecclesiastical affiliations. Though it disregarded separate creeds, it had a creed of its own, expressing its own minimum of belief; it recognized as brothers "all who honestly believe that all men are sinful and corrupt; that God requires the punishment of sin; that Jesus Christ came as a mediator to take this punishment upon himself, which he alone, being both God and man, could do; that those who believe in him and in his satisfaction, and penitently invoke his intercession, are immediately saved; and that through his ascension the Holy Spirit operates faith and conversion in them." The society grew by the accession of members of various churches, until a special meeting-place was needed, which was dedicated by Canzius, one of the principal founders, in 1802. The services were more like Lutheran or Anglican worship than Reformed, and everything was done to enhance the solemnity of the Lord's Supper. The original intention was to have the members retain their former church connections; but when the society was condemned by the Walloon and Reformed authorities, it gradually took shape as a separate sect. It numbered as many as 117 members under Canzius, but when in 1810 he removed to Leyden it gradually fell off, maintaining a precarious existence until 1836, when the building was closed. (J. A. GERTH VAN WIJK.)

BIBLIOGRAPHY: *Kalender voor de Protestanten in Nederland*, vii (1862), 195–256; H. Grégoire, *Histoire des sectes religieuses*, v. 331, 6 vols., Paris, 1828–45; B. Glasius, *Geschiedenis der christelijke kerk en godsdienst in Nederland*, iii. 376–380, Amsterdam, 1844; J. Reitsma, *Geschiedenis der Hervorming en hervormde kerk in Nederland*, p. 347, Groningen, 1893.

CHRISTOLOGY.

I. The Biblical Christology.
1. The Old Testament Christology.
2. The New Testament Christology.
Christ the Ideal Man (§ 1).
Yet also God (§ 2).
II. The Ante-Nicene Christology.
1. The Early Simple Faith.
Heresies (§ 1).
The Church Doctrine (§ 2).
The Divinity of Christ Consistently Held (§ 3).
2. Theological Speculations.
Justin Martyr (§ 1).
Clement of Alexandria (§ 2).
Origen (§ 3).
Irenæus (§ 4).
Tertullian (§ 5).
Dionysius of Rome (§ 6).
III. The Nicene Christology.
IV. The Chalcedonian Christology.
An Answer to Heresies (§ 1).
The Chalcedonian Statement (§ 2).
V. The Post-Chalcedonian Christology.
Monophysitism (§ 1).
Monothelitism (§ 2).
Adoptionism (§ 3).
The Medieval Church (§ 4).
VI. The Ecumenical Christology.
1. Its Leading Ideas.
2. Criticism.
Favorable Opinions (§ 1).
Objections and Criticisms (§ 2).
Real Value (§ 3).
VII. The Orthodox Protestant Christology.
VIII. The Scholastic Lutheran Christology.
1. The Communicatio Idiomatum.
2. The Doctrine of the Twofold State of Christ.
3. The Threefold Office of Christ.
IX. The Kenosis Controversy Between Giessen and Tübingen.
X. Modern Christologies.
1. The Humanitarian or Unitarian Christology.
2. The Pantheistic Christology.
3. The Christology of Schleiermacher and His School.
Schleiermacher (§ 1).
Ullmann (§ 2).
Rothe (§ 3).
Horace Bushnell (§ 4).
4. The Modern Kenotic Theory.
General Outline (§ 1).
Gess (§ 2).
Martensen (§ 3).
Kahnis and Lange (§ 4).
Julius Müller (§ 5).
Goodwin and Crosby (§ 6).
Criticism (§ 7).
5. The Ritschlian Theory.
The Theory Stated (§ 1).
Its Merit and Limitation (§ 2).
6. The Theory of a Gradual or Progressive Incarnation.
The Theory (§ 1).
Its Merits (§ 2).
7. Conclusion.
Elements of Truth in All Theories (§ 1).
The Mystery of Christ (§ 2).
Limits of This Article (§ 3).
XI. Additional Note.
Preexistence (§ 1).
Incarnation (§ 2).

Christology is a word derived from the Greek after the analogy of "theology" (q.v.). It embraces the doctrine of Christ's person; while soteriology is the doctrine of Christ's work (the doctrine of salvation). The word was used by the English theologians in the seventeenth century,* and during the nineteenth was reintroduced from Germany. Christology is based upon the life and testimony of Christ, as represented historically in the Gospels, and as reflected doctrinally and experimentally in the Acts and Epistles. It treats of the mystery of the incarnation as a problem of personality, viz., (1) the humanity, (2) the divinity of our Lord, and (3) their relation to each other in his one person. This divine-human personality forms the basis of his work, which is the redemption, reconciliation, and reunion of man with God. It is the central doctrine of Christianity, was the one article of St. Peter's creed (Matt. xvi. 16), and forms the heart of the Apostles' Creed. The leading evangelical theologians of Europe and America have come to agree more and more in this estimate of its importance; and the ever-increasing number of lives of Christ and works on his incarnation and work strengthens the christocentric character of modern theology. Yet care must be taken not to emphasize the incarnation at the expense of the equally important doctrines of atonement by Christ's death, and regeneration by the Holy Spirit (see ATONEMENT; REGENERATION).

* Dr. Thomas Jackson (1595–1640) defined it correctly as "that part of divinity which displays the great mystery of godliness—God manifested in the human flesh." John Owen used the term in his *Χριστολογία, or a Declaration of the Glorious Mystery of the Person of Christ, God and Man* (London, 1679), and Robert Fleming, jun., a Scotch divine (d. 1716), wrote a *Christology* (3 vols., London, 1705–1708). Some French writers also use it. Lichtenberger (*Encyclopédie*, iii. 129) defines it correctly: "On comprend sous ce nom" [Christologie] "l'ensemble des doctrines touchant la personne de Jésus-Christ dans ses rapports avec Dieu et avec l'humanité, telles qu'elles sont contenues dans le *Nouveau Testament* et telles qu'elles ont été développées dans le cours des siècles, au sein de l'Église chrétienne."

I. The Biblical Christology: This embraces (1) the Messianic prophecies of the Old Testament; and (2) the christology of the New Testament, which includes (a) the testimony of Christ in the Gospels; and (b) the christology of the apostles—James, Peter, Paul (including the christology of the Epistle to the Hebrews), and John (including the Apocalypse). Christ is the heart of the Scriptures and the key to their spiritual understanding.

1. The Old Testament Christology: The Old Testament is the preparation for the New. The soul of the Old Testament is the promise of the Messiah, which began in Paradise with the protevangelium of the serpent-bruiser, and culminated in the testimony of John the Baptist, pointing to Jesus of Nazareth as the Lamb of God, which taketh away the sin of the world. See MESSIAH, MESSIANISM.

2. The New Testament Christology: It is the unanimous teaching of the New Testament writings that Christ combines in a most real though mysterious way the double character of a unique divine sonship and a unique sinless manhood in one harmonious personality; and that by this very constitution of his person he is qualified to be the Lord and Savior of the human race, and the only Mediator between God and man. He represents at once the nearest approach which God can make to man, and the nearest approach which man can make to God. The orthodox christology, handed down from the early Church, is an attempt to formulate this "mystery of godliness" in definite statements and to guard it against error; but every age must grapple anew with this problem of problems, and make it alive and fruitful for its own intellectual and spiritual benefit.

Christ strongly asserts his humanity, and calls himself about eighty times in the Gospels "the Son of Man" (q.v.); not a son of man among other descendants of Adam, but the Son of Man emphatically as the representative of the whole race. He is thus interpreted by the apostles to be the second Adam, descended from heaven (cf. Rom. v. and

I Cor. xv.); the ideal, the perfect, the absolute man, the head of a new race, the king of Jews and Gentiles, the model man for universal imitation. While putting himself on a *par* with us as man, he claims at the same time, as the Son of Man, superiority over all, and freedom from sin, and thus stands solitary and alone as the one and only spotless human being in the midst of a fallen race, as an oasis of living water and fresh verdure, surrounded by a barren desert. He nowhere confesses sin, betrays a consciousness of sin, or asks pardon for sin; and this was not because he did not feel the evil of sin, for he pardoned sin and condemned sins in the severest terms. He alone needed no repentance, no conversion, no regeneration, no pardon. This sinlessness of Christ is the great moral miracle of history which underlies all his miraculous works, and explains them as natural manifestations of his miraculous person.

1. Christ the Ideal Man.

On the other hand, Christ as emphatically asserts his divinity, and calls himself not simply a son of God among other children of God by adoption, but "the Son of God" (q.v.) above all others, in a peculiar sense; the Son by nature; the Son from eternity; the Son who alone knows the Father, who reveals the Father to us, who calls him, not "our" Father (as we are directed to pray), but "my" Father. He is, as his favorite disciple calls him, the "only-begotten Son" (according to some of the oldest manuscripts, "the only-begotten God," Gk. *theos*); or, as the Nicene theology expresses it, "eternally begotten of the essence (Gk. *ousia*) of the Father." He is thus represented by himself; and the representation which he makes of himself was affirmed by the apostles. Paul never calls him "the son of man," but frequently "the son of God" ("God's own son," Rom. viii. 3, 32, etc.). To the apostles Christ was a divine-human being, truly God and truly man in one person; and his words and acts and sufferings have a corresponding character and effect. Hence he puts forth claims which in the mouth of every other man, no matter how wise and how good, would sound like blasphemy or lunacy, but which from his lips appear as natural as the rays of light emanating from the sun. He represents himself constantly as being sent from God, or as having come directly from God, to teach this world what he had not learned from any school or book. He calls himself the Light of the World, the Way, the Truth, and the Life; he invites all men to come to him, that they may find rest and peace; he claims the power to forgive sins, and to raise the dead; he says, "I am the Resurrection and the Life," and he promises eternal life to every one that believeth in him. Even in the moment of his deepest humiliation, he proclaimed himself the King of truth, and the Ruler and Judge of mankind. His kingdom is to be coextensive with the race, and everlasting as eternity itself. And with this consciousness he sent forth his disciples to proclaim the gospel of salvation to every creature, forewarning them of persecution and pledging them his presence to the end of the world, and a crown of glory in heaven. He coordinates himself in the baptismal formula with the Eternal Father and the Eternal Spirit, and allows himself to be worshiped by the skeptical Thomas as his "Lord" and his "God."

2. Yet also God.

This central truth of Christ's divine-human person and work is set forth in the New Testament writings, not as a logically formulated dogma, but as a living fact and glorious truth, as an object of faith, a source of comfort, and a stimulus to a holy life, in humble imitation of his perfect example. The simple narrative of the Gospels is far more powerful for the general benefit of mankind than all the systems of theology. But the mind of the Church must meditate, and try to grasp this truth; and the New Testament itself furnishes ever new impulse and food for theological speculation. The formulated statement of christology begins as early as Paul and John.

II. The Ante-Nicene Christology, from 100 A.D. to the Council of Nicæa, 325.—**1. The Early Simple Faith:** The ecclesiastical development of the fundamental dogma started from Peter's confession of the Messiahship of Jesus (Matt. xvi. 16), and from John's doctrine of the incarnate Logos (John i. 14). It was stimulated by two opposite heresies—Ebionism and Gnosticism; the one essentially Jewish, the other essentially heathen; the one affirming the humanity of Christ to the exclusion of his divinity, the other running into the opposite error by resolving his humanity into a delusive show (Gk. *dokēsis*, *phantasma*; see DOCETISM); both agreeing in the denial of the incarnation, or the real and abiding union of the divine and human in the person of our Lord. There also arose in the second and third centuries two forms of Unitarianism or Monarchianism: (1) The Rationalistic or Dynamic Unitarianism—represented by the Alogi, Theodotus, Artemon, and Paul of Samosata—which either denied the divinity of Christ altogether, or resolved it into a mere power (Gk. *dynamis*), although its representatives generally admitted his supernatural generation by the Holy Spirit. (2) The Patripassian and Sabellian Unitarianism, which maintained the divinity of Christ, but merged it into the essence of the Father, and so denied the independent, preexistent personality of Christ. So Praxeas, Noëtus, Callistus (Pope Calixtus I.), Beryllus of Bostra, and Sabellius. See the articles on the heresies named and their representatives.

1. Heresies.

In antagonism to these heresies, the Church taught the full divinity of Christ (against Ebionism and rationalistic Monarchianism), his full humanity (against Gnosticism and Manicheism), and his independent personality (against Patripassianism and Sabellianism). The dogma was developed in close connection with the dogma of the Trinity, which resulted, by logical necessity, from the deity of Christ and the deity of the Holy Spirit on the basis of the fundamental truth of Monotheism.

2. The Church Doctrine.

The ante-Nicene christology passed through many obstructions, loose statements, uncertain conjectures and speculations; but the instinct and main current of the Church was steadily toward the Nicene and Chalcedonian creed-statements, especially if the worship and devotional life as well as the theological literature be considered. Christ was the object of worship, prayer, and praise from the very beginning, as must be inferred from such passages of the New Testament as John xx. 28; Acts vii. 59, 60, ix. 14, 21; I Cor. i. 2; Phil. ii. 10; Heb. i. 6; I John v. 13–15; Rev. v. 6–13; from the heathen testimony of Pliny the Younger concerning the singing of hymns to Christ as God ("*Carmen Christo quasi Deo dicere*," *Epist.*, x. 97); from the "Gloria in Excelsis," which was the daily morning hymn of the Eastern Church as early as the second century; from the "Tersanctus"; from the Hymn of Clement of Alexandria to the divine Logos (*Pædagogus*, iii. 12); from the statements of Origen (*Contra Celsum*, viii. 67) and Eusebius (*Hist. eccl.*, v. 28); and from many other testimonies. Christ was believed to be divine, and adored as divine, before he was clearly taught to be divine. The ante-Nicene rules of faith as they are found in the writings of Irenæus, Origen, Tertullian, Cyprian, etc., are in essential agreement among themselves and with the Apostles' Creed, as it appears, first in the fourth century, especially at Rome and Aquileia. (Cf. Rufinus, *De symbolo*.) They all confess the divine-human character of Christ as the chief object of the Christian faith, but in the form of facts, and in simple, popular style, not in the form of doctrinal or logical statement. The Nicene Creed is much more explicit and dogmatic in consequence of the preceding contest with heresy; but the substance of the faith is the same in the Nicene and Apostles' Creeds. (For these Ante-Nicene Rules of Faith, cf. Schaff, *Creeds*, ii. 11–45.)

3. The Divinity of Christ Consistently Held.

2. Theological Speculations: In the apostolic Fathers only simple practical, Biblical statements are found, with reminiscences of apostolic preaching for the purposes of edification. Ignatius of Antioch calls Christ God without qualification (*Ad Ephes.*, vii. 18; cf. *Ad Rom.*, vi.). Polycarp calls him "the eternal Son of God" (*Ad Phil.*, ii. 8), and associates him in his last prayer with the Father and the Spirit (*Martyrium Polycarpi*, xiv.). The theological speculation on the person of Christ began with Justin Martyr, and was carried on by Clement of Alexandria and Origen, in the East; by Irenæus, Hippolytus, and Tertullian, in the West.

1. Justin Martyr.

Justin Martyr (d. 166) takes up the Johannean Logos idea, which proved a very fruitful germ of theological speculation. It was prepared by the Old Testament personification of the word and wisdom of God, assumed an idealistic shape in Philo of Alexandria, and reached a realistic completion in St. John, although it is not likely that John's had anything more in common with Philo's idea than the name "Logos." Following the suggestion of the double meaning of the Greek *logos* (*ratio* and *oratio*), Justin distinguishes in the Logos two elements—the immanent and the transitive; the revelation of God *ad intra*, and the revelation *ad extra*. He teaches the procession of the Logos from the free will (not the essence) of God by generation, without division or diminution of the divine substance. This begotten Logos he conceives as a hypostatical being, a person distinct from the Father, and subordinate to him. He coordinates God, the Son, and the prophetic Spirit, as objects of Christian worship (*Apol.*, i. 6). Peculiar is his doctrine of the *logos spermatikos*, the "seminal Logos," or the Word disseminated among men, i.e., Christ before the incarnation, who scattered elements of truth and virtue among the heathen philosophers and poets, although they did not know it.

2. Clement of Alexandria.

Clement of Alexandria (d. 220) sees in the Logos the ultimate principle of all existence (without beginning, and timeless), the revealer of the Father, the sum of all intelligence and wisdom, the personal truth, the author of the world, the source of light and life, the educator of the race, who at last became man to make us partakers of his divine nature. Like some other ante-Nicene Fathers (Justin Martyr, Tertullian, and Origen), he conceived the outward appearance of Christ's humanity in the state of humiliation to have been literally without form or comeliness (Isa. liii. 2, 3); but he had made a distinction between two kinds of beauty—the outward beauty of the flesh, which soon fades away; and the moral beauty of the soul, which is permanent, and shone even through the servant form of our Lord (*Pædagogus*, iii. 1).

3. Origen.

Origen (d. 254) felt the whole weight of the christological problem, but obscured it by foreign speculations, and prepared the way both for the Arian heresy and the Athanasian orthodoxy, though more fully for the latter. On the one hand he closely approaches the Nicene *homoousion* by bringing the Son into union with the essence of the Father, and ascribing to him the attribute of eternity. He is, properly, the author of the Nicene doctrine of eternal generation of the Son from the essence of the Father (though he usually represents the generation as an act of the will of the Father). But, on the other hand, he teaches subordinationism by calling the Son simply "God," and "a second God," but not "the God" (*ho theos* or *autos theos*). In his views on the humanity of Christ, he approached the semi-Gnostic Docetism, and ascribed to the glorified body of Christ ubiquity (in which he was followed by Gregory of Nyssa). His enemies charged him with teaching a double Christ (answering to the lower Jesus, and the higher *Sotēr* of the Gnostics), and a merely temporary validity of the body of the Redeemer. As to the relation of the two natures in Christ, he was the first to use the term "God-man" and to apply the favorite illustration of fire heating and penetrating the iron, without altering its character.

The Western Church was not so fruitful in speculation, but, upon the whole, sounder and more self-consistent. The key-note was struck by Irenæus (d. 202), who, though of Eastern origin, spent his active life in the south of France. He carries special weight as a pupil of Polycarp of

Smyrna, and through him a grand-pupil of St. John, the inspired master. He likewise uses the terms "Logos" and "Son of God" interchangeably, and concedes the distinction, made also by the Valentinians, between the inward and the uttered word, in reference to man; but contests the application of it to God, who is above all antitheses, absolutely simple and unchangeable, and in whom before and after, thinking and speaking, coincide. He repudiates also speculative or *a priori* attempts to explain the derivation of the Son from the Father. This he holds to be an incomprehensible mystery. He is content to define the actual distinction between Father and Son by saying that the former is God revealing himself; the latter, God revealed. The one is the ground of revelation; the other is the actual, appearing revelation itself. Hence he calls the Father "the invisible of the Son"; and the Son, "the visible of the Father." He discriminates most rigidly the conceptions of generation and of creation. The Son, though begotten of the Father, is still, like him, distinguished from the created world as increate—without beginning, and eternal; all plainly showing that Irenæus is much nearer the Nicene dogma of the essential identity of the Son with the Father than Justin Martyr and the Alexandrians. When, as he does in several passages, he still subordinates the Son to the Father, he is certainly inconsistent, and that for want of an accurate distinction between the eternal Logos and the incarnate Christ. Expressions like "My Father is greater than I," which apply only to the Christ of history, in the state of humiliation, he refers also, like Justin and Origen, to the eternal Logos. On the other hand, he is charged with leaning in the opposite direction—toward the Sabellian and Patripassian views—but unjustly. Apart from his frequent want of precision in expression, he steers in general, with sure Biblical and churchly tact, equally clear of both extremes, and asserts alike the essential unity and the eternal personal distinction of the Father and the Son. He vindicates at length the true and full humanity of Christ against the Docetism of the Gnostic schools. Christ must be man, like us in body, soul, and spirit, though without sin if he would redeem us from sin, and make us perfect. He is the second Adam, the absolute, universal man, the prototype and summing up of the whole race. He also teaches a close union of the divinity and humanity in Christ, in which the former is the active principle, and the seat of personality, the latter the passive and receptive principle.

4. Irenæus.

Tertullian (about 220) can not escape the charge of subordinationism. He bluntly calls the Father the whole divine substance, and the Son a part of it, illustrating their relation by the figures of the fountain and the stream, the sun and the beam. He would not have two suns, he says; but he might call Christ God, as Paul does in Rom. ix. 5. The sunbeam, too, in itself considered, may be called sun, but not the sun a beam. Sun and beam are two distinct things (*species*) in one essence (*substantia*), as God and the World, as the Father and the Son. But figurative language must not be taken too strictly, and it must be remembered that Tertullian was especially interested to distinguish the Son from the Father, in opposition to the Patripassian Praxeas. In other respects he did the Church christology material service. He propounds a threefold hypostatical existence of the Son (*filiatio*): (1) The preexistent, eternal immanence of the Son in the Father, they being as inseparable as reason and word in man, who was created in the image of God, and hence in a measure reflects his being; (2) the coming forth of the Son with the Father for the purpose of the creation; (3) the manifestation of the Son in the world by the incarnation. He advocates the entire yet sinless humanity of Christ, against both the Docetistic Gnostics (*Adv. Marcionem* and *De carne Christi*) and the Patripassians (*Adv. Praxeam*). He accuses the former of making Christ, who is all truth, a half lie, and, by the denial of his flesh, resolving all his work in the flesh into an empty show. He urges against the latter that God the Father is incapable of suffering and change. Professor Warfield (see bibliography) lays much stress upon the definition which Tertullian gives of the Trinity, and regards Tertullian rather than Origen as the real father of the Christian doctrine of the Trinity.

5. Tertullian.

Dionysius, bishop of Rome (262), came nearest the Nicene view. He maintained distinctly, in the controversy with Dionysius of Alexandria, the unity of essence and the threefold personal distinction of Father, Son, and Spirit, in opposition to Sabellianism, tritheism, and subordinationism. His view is embodied in a fragment preserved by Athanasius (*De sententiis Dionysii*, iv., and Routh, *Reliquiæ sacræ*, iii., Oxford, 1846, p. 384).

6. Dionysius of Rome.

III. The Nicene Christology, from 325 to 381: This is the result of the struggle with Arianism and semi-Arianism, which agitated the Eastern Church for more than half a century. The Arian heresy denied the strict deity of Christ (his coequality with the Father), and taught that he is a subordinate divinity, different in essence from God (Gk. *hetero-ousios*), preexisting before the world, yet not eternal ("there was a time when he was not"), himself a creature of the will of God out of nothing (Gk. *ktisma ex ouk ontōn*), who created this present world, and became incarnate for our salvation. Semi-Arianism held an untenable middle ground between the Arian *hetero-ousia* and the orthodox *homo-ousia*, or coequality of the Son with the Father, and asserted the *homoi-ousia*, or *similarity* of essence, which was a very elastic term, and might be contracted into an Arian, or stretched into an orthodox, sense, according to the general spirit and tendency of the men who held it.

In opposition to these heresies, Athanasius of Alexandria ("the father of orthodoxy") and the three Cappadocian bishops—Basil, Gregory of Nazianzus, and Gregory of Nyssa—maintained and defended with superior ability, vigor, and perseverance, the *homo-ousia*, i.e., the essential oneness of the Son with the Father, or his eternal divinity, as the corner-stone of the whole Christian system. This doctrine triumphed in the councils of Nicæa (325) and Constantinople (381), and is expressed in the Nicæno-Constantinopolitan Creed, which has stood ever since like an immovable rock:

"(We believe) . . . in one Lord Jesus Christ, the only-begotten Son of God, begotten of the Father before all worlds [God of God], Light of Light, Very God of Very God, Begotten, not made, being of one substance with the Father; by whom all things were made; who for us men and for our salvation came down from heaven, and was incarnate by the Holy Ghost of the Virgin Mary," etc.

See ARIANISM; ATHANASIUS; CONSTANTINOPOLITAN CREED; NICÆA, COUNCILS OF.

IV. The Chalcedonian Christology: This finds its normal expression in the Chalcedonian statement of 451 (see below, § 2). It was the answer of the orthodox Church to the heresies relating to the proper constitution of Christ's divine-human person, of which the chief were three, viz., (1) Apollinarianism, a partial denial of the humanity of Christ. Apollinaris (the Younger) of Laodicea (q.v.; d. 390), on the basis of the Platonic trichotomy, ascribed to Christ a human body (Gk. *sōma*) and animal soul (*psychē alogos*), but not a human spirit or reason (*psychē logikē, nous, pneuma*); he put the divine Logos in the place of the rational soul, and thus substituted a *theos sarkophoros* for a real *theanthrōpos*—a mixed middle being for a divine-human person. From this error it follows, either that the rational soul of man was not redeemed, or that it needed no redemption. (2) Nestorianism (from Nestorius, patriarch of Constantinople, d. in exile 440; see NESTORIUS) admitted the full deity and the full humanity of Christ, but put them into loose mechanical conjunction, or affinity (Gk. *synapheia*), rather than a vital and personal union (*henōsis*); and hence it objected to the unscriptural term "mother of God" (Gk. *theotokos*, Lat. *Deipara*), as applied to the Virgin Mary, while willing to call her "mother of Christ" (*Christotokos*). (3) Eutychianism (from Eutyches, presbyter at Constantinople, d. after 451; see EUTYCHIANISM) is the very opposite of Nestorianism, and sacrificed the distinction of the two natures in Christ to the unity of the person to such an extent as to make the incarnation an absorption of the human nature by the divine, or a deification of human nature, even of the body: hence the Eutychians thought it proper to use the phrases "God is born," "God suffered," "God was crucified," "God died."

1. An Answer to Heresies.

The third and fourth ecumenical councils (Ephesus, 431, and Chalcedon, 451) settled the question of the precise relation of the two natures in Christ's person. The decree of the Council of Ephesus, under the lead of the violent Cyril of Alexandria, was merely negative, a condemnation of the error of Nestorius, and leaned a little toward the opposite error of Eutyches. Nestorianism triumphed temporarily in the "Robber Synod" of Ephesus, in 449, under the lead of Dioscurus of Alexandria, who inherited all the bad, and none of the good, qualities of his predecessor, Cyril. But Dyophysitism reasserted itself; and Dioscurus and Eutyches were condemned by the Council of Chalcedon. This council gave a clear and full statement of the orthodox christology as follows (for Greek and Latin text and notes, cf. Schaff, *Creeds*, ii. 62–65):

2. The Chalcedonian Statement.

"Following the holy Fathers, we all with one consent teach men to confess one and the same Son, our Lord Jesus Christ, the same perfect in Godhead and also perfect in Manhood; truly God and truly man, of a reasonable [rational] soul and body; consubstantial [coequal] with the Father according to the Godhead, and consubstantial with us according to the Manhood; in all things like unto us, without sin, begotten before all ages of the Father according to the Godhead, and in these latter days, for us and for our salvation, born of the Virgin Mary, the Mother of God, according to the Manhood; one and the same Christ, Son, Lord, Only-begotten, to be acknowledged in two natures, *inconfusedly, unchangeably, indivisibly, inseparably;* the distinction of natures being by no means taken away by the union, but rather the property of each nature being preserved, and concurring in one Person and one Subsistence, not parted or divided into two Persons, but one and the same Son, and only-begotten, God the Word, the Lord Jesus Christ; as the prophets from the beginning [have declared] concerning him, and the Lord Jesus Christ himself has taught us, and the Creed of the holy Fathers has handed down to us."

The same doctrine is set forth in a more condensed form in the second part of the *Symbolum Quicunque*, or the so-called Athanasian Creed (for text and transl., with notes, cf. Schaff, *Creeds*, ii. 66–71; see ATHANASIAN CREED).

V. The Post-Chalcedonian Christology: The Chalcedonian decision did not stop the controversy, and called for a supplementary statement concerning the two wills of Christ, corresponding to the two natures. Eutychianism revived in the form of Monophysitism (see MONOPHYSITES), or the doctrine that Christ had but one composite nature (Gk. *mia physis synthetos* or *mia physis ditte*). It makes the humanity of Christ a mere accident of the immutable divine substance. The liturgical shibboleth of the Monophysites was "God has been crucified," and they even introduced the idea into the Trisagion (q.v.); hence they are also called Theopaschites (from *theos*, "God," and *paschein*, "to suffer"). The tedious Monophysite controversies convulsed the Eastern Church for more than a hundred years, weakened its power, and facilitated the conquest of Mohammedanism. The fifth ecumenical council (553) made a partial concession to the Monophysites, but did not reconcile them. They separated, like the Nestorians, from the orthodox Greek Church, and continue to this day under various names and organizations—the Jacobites in Syria, the Copts in Egypt, the Abyssinians, and the Armenians.

1. Monophysitism.

Closely connected with Monophysitism was Monothelitism (see MONOTHELITES), or the doctrine that Christ had but one will, as he had but one person. The orthodox maintained that will is an attribute of nature, rather than of person, and consequently that Christ had two wills—a human will and a divine will—both working in harmony. The Monothelite controversy lasted from 633 to 680. The Emperor Heraclius proposed a compromise formula—one divine-human energy (*mia theandrikē energeia*); but it was opposed in the West. The sixth ecumenical council condemned

2. Monothelitism.

the Monothelite heresy, and repeated the Chalcedonian Creed, with the following supplement concerning the two wills (cf. Schaff, *Creeds*, ii. 72–73):

"And we likewise preach *two natural wills* in him [Jesus Christ], and *two natural operations* undivided, inconvertible, inseparable, unmixed, according to the doctrine of the holy Fathers; and the two natural wills [are] not contrary (far from it), as the impious heretics assert, but his human will follows the divine will, and is not resisting or reluctant, but rather subject to his divine and omnipotent will. For it was proper that the will of the flesh should be moved, but be subjected to the divine will, according to the wise Athanasius."

The same council condemned Pope Honorius I. (625–638) as a Monothelite heretic, and his successors confirmed its decision. Monothelitism continued among the Maronites on Mount Lebanon, who, however, afterward submitted to the Roman Church, as well as among the Monophysites, who are all Monothelites.

With the sixth ecumenical council closes the development of the ancient Catholic christology.

3. Adoptionism. The Adoption controversy (see ADOPTIONISM), which arose in Spain and France toward the close of the eighth century, turned upon the question whether Christ as man was the Son of God by nature (*naturaliter*), or simply by adoption (*nuncupative*). The Adoptionists maintained the latter, and shifted the whole idea of sonship from the person to whom it belongs to the nature. Their theory was a modification of the Nestorian error, and was condemned in a synod at Frankfort, 794; but it did not result in a positive addition to the creed statements.

4. The Medieval Church. The scholastic theology of the Middle Ages made no progress in christology, and confined itself to a dialectical analysis and defense of the Chalcedonian dogma, with a one-sided reference to the divine nature of Christ. John of Damascus in the East, and Thomas Aquinas in the West, were the ablest exponents of the Chalcedonian dogma. The medieval Church almost forgot, over the glorious divinity of our Lord, his real humanity (except his passion), and substituted for it virtually the worship of the Virgin Mary, who seemed to appeal more tenderly and effectively to all the human sensibilities and sympathies of the heart than the exalted Savior.

VI. The Ecumenical Christology (i.e., the christology taught in common by the doctrinal standards of the Greek, Latin, and Evangelical Protestant Churches).

1. Its Leading Ideas: These may be stated as follows: (1) A true incarnation of the Logos, i.e., the second person in the Godhead (Gk. *enanthrōpēsis theou, ensarkōsis tou logou*, Lat. *incarnatio verbi*). This is an actual assumption of the whole human nature—body, soul, and spirit—into an abiding union with the divine personality of the eternal Logos, so that they constitute, from the moment of the supernatural conception, one undivided life. The incarnation is neither a conversion or transmutation of the divine nature into the human nature, nor a conversion of man into God, and consequent absorption of the one, nor a confusion (Gk. *krasis, synchysis*) of the two. On the other hand, it is not a mere indwelling (Gk. *enoikēsis*, Lat. *inhabitatio*) of the one in the other, nor an outward, transitory connection (Gk. *synapheia*, Lat. *conjunctio*) of the two factors. (2) The distinction between nature and person. Nature or substance (essence, Gk. *ousia*) denotes the totality of powers and qualities which constitute a being; while person (Gk. *hypostasis, prosōpon*) is the ego, the self-conscious, self-asserting, and acting subject. The Logos assumed, not a human person (else we should have two persons—a divine and a human), but human nature, which is common to us all. (3) The God-man (Gk. *theanthrōpos*) as the result of the incarnation. Christ is not a (Nestorian) double being, with two persons, nor a compound (Apollinarian or Monophysite) middle being, a *tertium quid*, partly divine and partly human; but he is one person, at once wholly divine and wholly human. (4) The duality of the natures. The orthodox doctrine maintains, against Eutychianism, the distinction of natures, even after the act of incarnation, without confusion or conversion (Gk. *asynchytōs* and *atreptōs*, Lat. *inconfuse* and *immutabiliter*), yet, on the other hand, without division or separation (Gk. *adiairetōs* and *achōristōs*, Lat. *indivise* and *inseparabiliter*); so that the divine will ever remain divine, and the human ever human; and yet the two have continually one common life, and interpenetrate each other, like the persons of the Trinity (Gk. *perichōrēsis*). According to a familiar figure, the divine nature pervades the human as the fire pervades the iron. Christ has all the properties which the Father has, except the property of being unbegotten; and he has all the properties which the first Adam had before the fall; he has, therefore (according to John of Damascus), two consciousnesses and two physical wills, or faculties of self-determination (Gk. *autexousia*). This is the extreme border to which the doctrine of two natures can be carried, without an assertion of two full personalities; and it is almost impossible to draw the line. (5) The unity of the person (Gk. *henōsis kath' hypostasin, henōsis hypostatikē*, Lat. *unio hypostatica* or *unio personalis*). The union of the divine and human nature in Christ is a permanent state, resulting from the incarnation, and is a real, supernatural, personal, and inseparable union, in distinction from an essential absorption or confusion, or from a mere moral union, or from a mystical union, such as holds between the believer and Christ. The two natures constitute but one personal life, and yet remain distinct. "The same who is true God," says Pope Leo I. in his famous Epistle, which anticipated the decision of Chalcedon, "is also true man; and in this unity there is no deceit, for in it the lowliness of man and the majesty of God perfectly pervade one another. . . . Because the two natures make only one person, we read, on the one hand, 'The Son of man came down from heaven' (John iii. 13), while yet the Son of God took flesh from the Virgin; and, on the other hand, 'The Son of God was crucified and buried,' while yet he suffered, not in his Godhead, as coeternal and consubstantial with the Father, but in the weakness of human nature." (6) The whole work of Christ is to be attributed to his person, and not to the one or the other nature exclusively. The person is the acting subject; the nature, the organ or medium. It is the one divine-human person of Christ that wrought miracles by virtue of his divine nature, and that suffered through the sensorium of his human nature. The superhuman effect and infinite merit of the Redeemer's work must be ascribed to his person, because of his divinity; while it is his humanity alone that made him capable of, and liable to, temptation, suffering, and death, and renders him an example for our imitation. (7) The *Anhypostasia*, or, more accurately, the *Enhypostasia* (Impersonality), of the human nature of Christ. The meaning is that Christ's human nature had no independent personality of its own, and that the divine nature is the root and basis of his personality. His humanity was enhypostatized through union with the Logos, or incorporated into his personality. The Synod of Chalcedon says nothing of this feature; it was an afterthought developed by John of Damascus. It seems inconsistent with the dyotheletic theory; for a being with consciousness and will has the two essential elements of personality, while an impersonal will seems to be a mere animal instinct. Ritschl (*Justification and Reconciliation*, New York, 1900, p. 437) says: "That the divine revealing Word constitutes the form, and the human individual the substance, of the person of Christ . . . is what in the end the doctrine of the Greek Church comes to. For the theory of the anhypostasis of the human nature in Christ . . . is intelligible only if the Divine Logos is the form in which this human individual exists, outside of which he has no real existence at all. For the form is the basis of reality."

2. Criticism: The Chalcedonian christology is regarded by the Greek and Roman, and by the majority of the orthodox English and American theologians, as the highest christological knowledge attainable in this world.

1. Favorable Opinions. Dr. Shedd (*History of Christian Doctrine*, i., New York, 1863, p. 408) thinks it probable that "the human mind is unable to go beyond it in the endeavor to unfold the mystery of Christ's complex person." Dr. Hodge (*Systematic Theology*, ii., New York, 1872, pp. 397 sqq.) notices and criticizes several of the more recent "erroneous and heretical doctrines," but holds to the Chalcedonian statement as adopted by the scholastic Calvinists of the seventeenth century.

On the other hand, the Chalcedonian christology has been subjected to a rigorous criticism in Germany by Evangelical as well as rationalistic divines—by Schleiermacher, Baur, Dorner, Rothe, and the modern Kenoticists, also by Ritschl and his followers, and by Professor Paine in America. It is charged with a defective psychology, and now with dualism, now with docetism, according as its distinction of two natures or the personal unity is made its most prominent feature. It is said to oscillate between two extremes, without truly reconciling them; as the orthodox doctrine of the Trinity stands between tritheism and modalism, now leaning to the one, now to the other, when either the tri-personality or the union is emphasized. It assumes two natures in one person; while the dogma of the Trinity assumes three persons in one nature. Professor Paine (*Critical History of the Evolution of Trinitarianism*, Boston, 1900, p. 279) marvels "how such a bald antinomy, Christ wholly God and wholly man, could have been adopted by theologians who were adepts in the Aristotelian and Platonic philosophies." Again he speaks of the Chalcedonian christology as "an unhistorical and unscientific violation of logical and psychological laws." The Chalcedonian definition, it is further

2. Objections and Criticisms. objected, teaches a complete human nature with reason and will, and yet denies it personality. It does not do justice to the genuine humanity of Christ in the Gospels, and to all those passages which assert its real growth. It overshadows the human by the divine. It puts the final result at the beginning, and ignores the intervening process. If we read the Gospel history, we find that Christ was a helpless infant on his mother's breast—and therefore not omnipotent till after the resurrection, when "all authority in heaven and on earth" was given unto him (Matt. xxviii. 18); he grew in wisdom, and learned obedience (Luke ii. 40; Heb. v. 8), and was ignorant of the day of judgment (Mark xiii. 32), therefore not omniscient; he moved from place to place, and was therefore not omnipresent before his ascension to heaven; he was destitute of his divine glory, which he was to regain after his death (John xvii. 5). To confine these limitations and imperfections to his human nature, while in his divine nature he was, at one and the same time, omnipotent, omniscient, and omnipresent, even in the manger and on the cross, is to destroy the personal unity of life, and to make two Christs. How can ignorance and omniscience simultaneously coexist in one and the same mind? How can one and the same individual pervade and rule the universe in the same moment in which he exclaims, "My God, my God, why hast thou forsaken me?" Christ speaks and acts throughout as one undivided ego. We must, therefore, so reconstruct or improve the Chalcedonian christology as to conform it to the historical realness of his humanity, to the full meaning of his own sayings concerning himself, and to all the facts of his life. This is generally felt among the Evangelical theologians in Germany, where christological speculation has been most active since the Reformation, and by not a few in other countries. If anything has resulted from the multitude of lives of Christ, written by learned and able men in the nineteenth century, it is the fact of the perfect and unique divine-human personality of Jesus of Nazareth (cf. some good remarks on this subject by Dr. J. O. Dykes, in the *Expository Times*, Jan., 1906, pp. 151 sqq.).

At the same time the Chalcedonian dogma is the ripest fruit of the christological speculations and controversies of the ancient Church, and can never be lost. It gave the clearest expression to the faith in the incarnation for ages to come. It saves the full idea of the God-man as to the essential elements, however imperfect the form in which it is cast. It defines with sound religious judgment the boundary-line which separates christological truth from christological error. It guards against two opposite dangers—the Scylla of Nestorian dualism, and the Charybdis of Eutychian Monophysitism, or against an abstract separation of the divine and human, and an absorption of the human by the divine. It excludes also every kind of mixture of the two natures which would result in a being which is neither divine nor human. With these safeguards, theological speculation may boldly and hopefully move on, and penetrate, if possible, deeper and deeper into the central truth of Christianity.

3. Real Value.

VII. The Orthodox Protestant Christology: The churches of the Reformation (Lutheran, Anglican, and Calvinistic) adopted in their confessions of faith, either in form or in substance, the three ecumenical creeds, and with them the ancient Catholic doctrines of the Trinity and of Christ's divine-human character and work. They condemned the old and new Antitrinitarians, and the peculiar doctrine of the Socinians—that Christ was raised by his own merit to a participation in the divine honor and dignity. The Unitarians, like the Anabaptists, were everywhere (except in Poland and Transylvania) imprisoned, exiled, or executed; and the unfortunate Servetus was burned as a heretic under the eyes of Calvin and with the approval of the mild Bullinger and Melanchthon. The following are the relevant passages from the principal Protestant confessions.

The *Augsburg Confession* of the Lutheran Church (1530), Art. iii. (*De Filio Dei*):

"The Word, that is, the Son of God, took unto him man's nature in the womb of the blessed Virgin Mary, so that there are two natures, the divine and the human, inseparably joined together in unity of person; one Christ, true God and true man: who was born of the Virgin Mary, truly suffered, was crucified, dead, and buried."

The *Second Helvetic Confession*, by Bullinger (1566), chap. xi.:

"There are in one and the same Jesus Christ our Lord, two natures, the divine and the human nature; and we say that these two are so conjoined or united that they are not swallowed up, confounded, or mingled together, but rather united or joined together in one person, the properties of each nature being safe and remaining still: so that we do worship one Christ our Lord, and not two; I say, one, true, God and man; as touching his divine nature, of the same substance with the Father, and as touching his human nature, of the same substance with us, and 'like unto us in all things, sin only excepted.'"

The *Thirty-nine Articles* of the Church of England, Art. ii.:

"The Son, which is the Word of the Father, begotten from everlasting of the Father, the very and eternal God, and of one substance with the Father, took man's nature in the womb of the blessed Virgin, of her substance; so that two whole and perfect natures, that is to say, the Godhead and Manhood, were joined together in one person, never to be divided, whereof is one Christ, very God and very man; who truly suffered, was crucified, dead, and buried."

The *Westminster Confession*, chap. viii., § 2:

"The Son of God, the second person in the Trinity being very and eternal God, of one substance and equal with the Father, did when the fulness of time was come, take upon him man's nature with all the essential properties and common infirmities thereof, yet without sin, being conceived by the Holy Ghost in the womb of the Virgin Mary, of her substance: so that two whole, perfect, and distinct natures, the Godhead and the Manhood, were inseparably joined together in one person, without conversion, composition, or confusion. Which person is very God and very man, yet one Christ, the only Mediator between God and men."

The *Westminster Shorter Catechism*, which is famous for clear and terse definitions, says (Qu. xxi.):

"The only Redeemer of God's elect is the Lord Jesus Christ, who being the eternal Son of God, became man, and so was, and continueth to be, God and man, in two distinct natures, and one person forever."

VIII. The Scholastic Lutheran Christology: On the general basis of the Chalcedonian christology, and following the indications of the Scriptures as the only rule of faith, the Protestant, especially the Lutheran, scholastics, at the close of the sixteenth, and during the seventeenth, century, built some additional features, and developed new aspects of Christ's person. The propelling cause was the Lutheran doctrine of the real presence or omnipresence of Christ's body in the Lord's Supper, and the controversies growing out of it with the Zwinglians and Calvinists, and among the Lutherans themselves (see LORD'S SUPPER; LUTHER; ZWINGLI; BRENZ; CHEMNITZ; etc.). These new features relate to the communion of the two natures, and to the states and the offices of Christ. The first was the production of the Lutheran Church, and was never adopted, but partly rejected, by the Reformed; the second and third were the joint doctrines of both, but with a very material difference in the understanding of the second.

1. The Communicatio Idiomatum: The communication of attributes or properties (Gk. *idiōmata*, Lat. *proprietates*) of one nature to the other, or to the whole person. It is derived from the *unio personalis* and the *communio naturarum*. The Lutheran divines distinguish three kinds or genera: (1) The *genus idiomaticum* (or *idiopoiētikon*), whereby the properties of one nature are transferred and applied to the whole person, for which are quoted such passages as Rom. i. 3; I Pet. iii. 18, iv. 1. (2) The *genus apotelesmaticum* (*koinopoiētikon*), whereby the redemptory functions and actions which belong to the whole person (the *apotelesmata*) are predicated only of one or the other nature (I Tim. ii. 5–6; Heb. i. 2–3). (3) The *genus auchematicum*, or *majestaticum*, whereby the human nature is clothed with and magnified by the attributes of the divine nature (John iii. 13, v. 27; Matt. xxviii. 18, 20; Rom. ix. 5; Phil. ii. 10). Under this head the Lutheran Church claims a certain ubiquity or omnipresence for the body of Christ, on the ground of the personal union of the two natures; but as to the extent of this omnipresence there were two distinct schools which are both represented in the *Formula of Concord* (1577). Brenz and the Swabian Lutherans maintained an absolute ubiquity of Christ's humanity from his very infancy, thus making the incarnation not only an assumption of the human nature, but also a deification of it, although the divine attributes were admitted to have been concealed during the state of humiliation. Chemnitz and the Saxon divines called this view a monstrosity, and taught only a relative ubiquity, depending on Christ's will (hence called *volipræsentia*, or *multivolipræsentia*), who may be present with his whole person wherever he pleases to be or has promised to be. (4) A fourth kind would be the *genus kenoticum* (from *kenōsis*), or *tapeinoticum* (from *tapeinōsis*), Phil. ii. 7, 8; i.e., a communication of the properties of the human nature to the divine nature. But this is decidedly rejected by the old Lutherans as inconsistent with the unchangeableness of the divine nature, and as a "horrible and blasphemous" doctrine (*Formula of Concord*, p. 612), but is asserted by the modern Kenoticists (see below, IX.).

The Reformed divines never committed themselves to the *communicatio idiomatum* as a whole (although they might approve the first two kinds, at least by way of what Zwingli termed *allaiōsis*, or a rhetorical exchange of one part for another); and they decidedly rejected the third kind, because omnipresence, whether absolute or relative, is inconsistent with the necessary limitation of a human body, as well as with the Scripture facts of Christ's ascension to heaven, and promised return. The third genus can never be fully carried out, unless the humanity of Christ is also eternalized. The attributes, moreover, are not an outside appendix, but inherent qualities of the substance to which they belong, and inseparable from it. Hence a communication of attributes would imply a communication or mixture of natures. The divine and human natures can indeed hold free and intimate intercourse with each other; but the divine nature can never be transformed into the human, nor the human nature into the divine. Christ possessed all the attributes of both natures; but the natures, nevertheless, remain separate and distinct. See COMMUNICATIO IDIOMATUM.

2. The Doctrine of the Twofold State of Christ: This is the state of humiliation and the state of exaltation. This doctrine is based upon Phil. ii. 5–9, and is substantially true. The state of humiliation embraces the supernatural conception, birth, circumcision, education, earthly life, passion, death, and burial of Christ; the state of exaltation includes the resurrection, ascension, and the sitting at the right hand of God.

But here, again, the two confessions differ very considerably. First as to the descent into Hades. The Lutherans regarded it as a triumph over hell, and made it the first stage of exaltation; while the Reformed divines viewed it as the last stage of the state of humiliation. It is properly the turning-point from the one state to the other, and thus belongs to both (see DESCENT OF CHRIST INTO HELL). Secondly, the Lutheran Creed refers the two states only to the human nature of Christ, regarding the divine as not susceptible of any humiliation or exaltation. The Reformed divines refer them to both natures; so that Christ's human nature was in a state of humiliation as compared with its future exaltation, and his divine nature was in the state of humiliation as to its external manifestation (*ratione occultationis*). With them the incarnation itself is the beginning of the state of humiliation, while the Lutheran symbols exclude the incarnation from the humiliation. Finally, the Lutherans regard the humiliation only as a partial concealment of the actual use (Gk. *krypsis chrēseōs*) of the divine attributes by the incarnate Logos.

The proper exegesis of the classical passage, Phil. ii. 7 sqq., decides here in favor of the Reformed, and against the Lutheran theory. The *kenōsis*, or self-humiliation, can not refer to the incarnate Logos, who never was "in the form of God," but must refer to the preexistent Logos (the *Logos asarkos*). This is admitted by the Greek Fathers, and by the best modern commentators, Lutheran as well as Reformed. (Cf. quotations in Schaff, *Creeds*, i. 328–329, and see JESUS CHRIST, TWOFOLD STATE OF.)

3. The Threefold Office of Christ: (a) The prophetical office (*munus*, or *officium propheticum*) includes teaching and the miracles of Christ. (b) The priestly office (*munus sacerdotale*) consists of the satisfaction made for the sins of the world by the death on the cross, and in the continued intercession of the exalted Savior for his people (*redemptio et intercessio sacerdotalis*). (c) The kingly office (*munus regium*), whereby Christ founded his kingdom, defends his Church against all enemies, and rules all things in heaven and on earth. The old divines distinguish between the reign of nature (*regnum naturæ sive potentiæ*), which embraces all things; the reign of grace (*regnum gratiæ*), which relates to the Church militant on earth; and the reign of glory (*regnum gloriæ*), which belongs to the Church triumphant in heaven. The threefold office or function of Christ was first presented by Eusebius of Cæsarea. The theologians who followed Luther and Melanchthon down to the middle of the seventeenth century treat Christ's saving work under the two heads of king and priest. Calvin, in the first edition of his "Institutes" (1536), did the same, and it was not till the third edition (1559) and the Genevan Catechism that he fully presented the three offices. This convenient threefold division of the office of Christ was used by the theologians of both confessions during the seventeenth century. Ernesti opposed it, but Schleiermacher restored it. See JESUS CHRIST, THREEFOLD OFFICE OF.

IX. The Kenosis Controversy Between Giessen and Tübingen: This is the last chapter in the development of the orthodox Lutheran christology on the basis of the Formula of Concord. It arose in the early part of the seventeenth century, between the Lutheran divines of the universities of Giessen and Tübingen over the *Kenōsis* and *Krypsis*; that is, over the question whether Christ, in the state of humiliation, entirely abstained from the use of his divine attributes (*kenōsis, abstinentia ab usu*, Phil. ii. 7), or whether he used them secretly (*krypsis*). The divines of Giessen (Balthasar Mentzer, his son-in-law Feuerborn, and Winkelmann) defended the Kenotic; those of Tübingen (Thumm, Hafenreffer, Osiander, Nicolai), the cryptic view. Both schools were agreed as to the possession of the divine attributes by Christ, including omnipotence, omniscience, and omnipresence, during all the stages of his humiliation, and differed only as to the use (*chrēsis*) of them—whether it was a *krypsis chrēseōs* (a concealed use), or a *kenōsis chrēseōs* (a non-use). The cryptic view of Tübingen is logically (i.e., from Lutheran premises) more consistent, but carries the theory of the *communicatio idiomatum* to the very verge of Gnostic Docetism, which resolves the human life of Christ on earth into a magical illusion. The Kenotic view of Giessen is more in accordance with the facts of Christ's life, but agrees with the other in principle, and admits, after all, an exceptional use in the performance of miracles. The controversy was waged with violence, and threatened to weaken the Protestant cause at a very critical period. The Lutheran princes interfered. In their name, Hoe von Hoenegg (q.v.), court preacher at Dresden, issued a *Solida decisio* (1624), essentially favoring the cause of the Giessen Kenoticists; but the Tübingen theologians defended their position till the controversy was lost in the disastrous events of the Thirty Years' War, without leading to any positive result. The Kenotic controversy was renewed recently, but in a modified form, and on a new basis (see below, X., 4; see also KENOSIS).

X. Modern Christologies: The orthodox christology emphasized the divinity of Christ, and left his humanity more or less out of sight and, in the last stage of its Lutheran development, arrived at the brink of Gnostic Docetism. Rationalism arose, toward the close of the eighteenth century, as a reaction against symbolical and scholastic orthodoxy, and ran into the opposite extreme; it ignored the divine nature, and fell back upon a purely human, or Ebionitic, Christ. Its worth, as well as its weakness, consists in the examination of the human element in Christ and in the Bible.

With the revival of Evangelical faith in Germany, the divine element of Christ was again duly appreciated by theologians. Hegel and Schleiermacher mark a new epoch in christological speculation, with two tendencies—the one pantheistic, the other humanistic; and these, again, were followed by original reconstructions and modifications of the Catholic doctrine of the God-man. The pantheistic tendency of Hegel is more congenial to the maxim of the Lutheran Confession, that the finite is capable of the infinite; the humanistic of Schleiermacher to the tendency of the Reformed Confession, which guards the genuine humanity of Christ against confusion with the divine. The former starts from the divine, the latter, from the human element; but both may unite, and often do unite when they proceed from naturalistic premises. Both Hegel and Schleiermacher gave impulse to orthodox as well as negative and destructive tendencies. To most of his pupils Schleiermacher was a sort of John the Baptist, who led them to Christ.

1. The Humanitarian or Unitarian Christology makes Christ a mere man, though the wisest and best of men, and a model for imitation. It is held in various forms, from the communicated semi-divinity of the old Socinians down to the pure humanity of modern Unitarians and Humanitarians. Professor Bruce (*Humiliation of Christ*, Edinburgh, 1881, lecture v., p. 193) distinguishes five classes of Humanitarians. Kant may be said to have inaugurated the modern Humanitarian view. He regarded Christ as the representative of the moral ideal, but made a distinction between the ideal Christ and the historical Jesus. The conservative Unitarians admit the sinless perfection of Christ. William Ellery Channing (q.v.) was, at least in his earlier period, a firm believer in the preexistence of Christ, and is sometimes called an Arian by his nephew and biographer. He certainly rose above the mere Humanitarianism of Priestley. He saw in Christ the perfect manifestation of God to man, and the highest ideal of humanity, and paid one of the noblest and most eloquent tributes to Christ's character and inspiring example. With this school must be reckoned Prof. Levi L. Payne, who dissociates christology, or the person of Christ, from theology, or the doctrine of God, and joins it to anthropology. Christ is a man and to be judged as a man. It was "not necessary that his moral consciousness should be divinized." He is separated by no miraculous act from the beings he came to save, and yet his moral consciousness has surpassed that of all other men (*Critical History of the Evolution of Trinitarianism*, Boston, 1900, pp. 199, 281).

2. The Pantheistic Christology, suggested by Schelling and Hegel, and best represented by Daub, Marheincke, and Göschel (of the right, or conservative, wing of Hegelianism), and by Baur, Strauss, and Biedermann (of the left, or radical, wing), starts from the idea of the essential unity of the divine and human, and teaches a continuous incarnation of God in the human race as a whole, but denies, for this very reason, the specific dignity of Christ as the one and only God-man. This, at least, is the theory of the "left," or radical and negative, wing of the Hegelian School, although Hegel himself had no sympathy with rationalism, but despised it. "The infinite," says Strauss, "can not pour out its fulness into a single individual." The peculiar position of Christ, however, is that he first awoke to a consciousness of this unity, and that he represents it in its purest and strongest form. Under this view Biedermann (*Christliche Dogmatik*, Zurich, 1869) places Christ highest in the scale of humanity, not only in the past, but for all time to come. Even Strauss was at one time willing to go so far; but he destroyed nearly the whole historic foundation of his life, and ended in the philosophical bankruptcy of materialism.

3. The Christology of Schleiermacher (d. 1834) and his School represents the highest form of Humanitarianism with an important admission of the supernatural or divine element. He regards Christ as a perfect man, in whom, and in whom alone, the ideal of humanity (the *Urbild*) has been fully realized. At the same time he rises above Humanitarianism by emphatically asserting Christ's essential sinlessness and absolute perfection ("*wesentliche Unsündlichkeit*" and "*schlechthinige Vollkommenheit*"), and a peculiar and abiding indwelling of the Godhead in him (*"ein eigentliches Sein Gottes in ihm"*), by which he differs from all men.

1. Schleiermacher. He admits him to be "a moral miracle," which means a great deal for a theologian of the boldest and keenest criticism in matters of history. He was willing to surrender almost every miracle of action in order to save the miracle of the person of him whom he adored and loved as his Lord and Savior. He adopts the Sabellian view of the Trinity as a threefold manifestation of God in creation (in the world), redemption (in Christ), and sanctification (in the Church). Christ is God as Redeemer, and originated an incessant flow of a new spiritual life, with all its pure and holy emotions and aspirations, which must be traced to that source. Sabellian as he was, Schleiermacher did not hold an eternal personal preexistence of the Logos which would correspond to the historical indwelling of God in Christ. His conception of the abstract unity and simplicity of the Godhead excluded an immanent Trinity. (For his christology, cf. his *Der christliche Glaube*, §§ 92–99, vol. ii., Berlin, 1830, pp. 26–93; cf. also the sharp criticism of Strauss, in *Die christliche Glaubenslehre*, ii., Tübingen, 1841, pp. 175 sqq.)

2. Ullmann. Ullmann (d. 1865), originally a pupil of Schleiermacher, but more orthodox, wrote the best book on the important topic of the sinlessness of Christ, which has an abiding doctrinal and apologetic value, independently of all speculative theories (*Die Sündlosigkeit Jesu*, 7th ed., Gotha, 1863, Eng. transl., Edinburgh, 1870).

3. Rothe. Somewhat similar is the christology of Richard Rothe (d. 1866), one of the greatest speculative theologians of the nineteenth century. He wrought out an original system of ethics of the highest order. He abandons the orthodox dogma of the Trinity and the Chalcedonian dyophysitism (which he thinks goes far beyond the simplicity of Biblical teaching, and makes the union physical rather than moral), but fully admits the divine-human character of the one personality of Christ, and lays great stress on the ethical feature in the development of Christ, by which alone he can become our redeemer and example. God, by a creative act, calls the second Adam into existence in the bosom of the old natural humanity. Christ is born of a woman, yet not begotten by man, but created by God (as to his humanity), hence is free from all sinful bias, as well as actual sin. His development is a real, but normal and harmonious, religious moral growth, with a correspondingly increasing indwelling of God in him. There was not a single moment in his conscious life in which he stood not in personal union with God; but the absolute union took place with the completion of the personal development of the second Adam. This completion coincided with his perfect self-sacrifice in death. Henceforth he was wholly and absolutely God (*ganz und schlechthin Gott*), since his being is extensively and intensively filled with the true God; but it can not be said, *vice versa*, that God is wholly the second Adam; for God is not limited by an individual person. The death of Christ on earth was at the same time his ascension to heaven and his elevation above all the limitations of material existence into the divine mode of existence (a return to the *morphē theou*), which, however, implies also his perpetual presence with his Church on earth (Matt. xxviii. 20).

4. Horace Bushnell. Here is the place also for the theory of Horace Bushnell (q.v.; d. 1876), which strongly resembles those of Schleiermacher and Rothe, but differs from them by adhering to the eternal preexistence of Christ (though only in a Sabellian sense). It was first announced in his *Concio ad Clerum*, at the annual commencement of Yale College, New Haven, Aug. 15, 1848, and gave rise to his trial for heresy. Bushnell, one of the most independent and vigorous American thinkers, read Schleiermacher's essay on Sabellius as translated by Professor Moses Stuart in the *Biblical Repository*, and said that "the general view of the Trinity given in that article coincides" with his own view, and confirmed him in the results of his own private struggles (*God in Christ*, New York, 1877, pp. 111–112). He maintains the full divinity of Christ on the Sabellian basis. He rejects the theory of "three metaphysical or essential persons in the being of God," with three distinct consciousnesses, wills, and understandings; and he substitutes for it simply a trinity of revelation, or what he calls (p. 175) an "instrumental trinity," or three impersonations, in which the one divine being presents himself to our human capacities and wants, and which are necessary to produce mutuality, or terms of conversableness, between us and him, and to pour his love most effectually into our feeling (p. 137). "God may act," he says (p. 152), "as a human personality, without being measured by it." The real divinity came into the finite, and was subject to human conditions. There are not two distinct subsistences in the person of Christ, one infinite and the other finite; but it is the one infinite God who expresses himself in Christ, and brings himself down to the level of our humanity, without any loss of his greatness or reduction of his majesty. At the same time, Bushnell holds to the full yet sinless humanity of Christ; and the tenth chapter of his work on *Nature and the Supernatural* is one of the ablest and most eloquent tributes to the sinless perfection of the moral character of Christ.

4. The Modern Kenotic Theory (see KENOSIS) differs from the theories just noticed by its orthodox premises and conclusions as far as the dogma of the Trinity and of the eternal Deity of Christ is concerned; but it likewise departs from the Chalcedonian dyophysitism, by holding to one divine-human Christ, with one consciousness and one will. It is chiefly based on the famous passage Phil. ii. 6–8 (Gk. *heauton ekenosen*, verse 7, "he emptied himself," A. V., "made himself of no reputation," the subject of the Kenosis being the preexistent, not the incarnate, Logos), and also on II Cor. viii. 9; John i. 14 (Gk. *egeneto*, "became"); Heb. ii. 17, 18, v. 8, 9; and on the general impression which the gospel history makes of Christ, as a truly human yet divinely human being, speaking of himself always as a unit. It was suggested by Zinzendorf in the form of devout sentimentalism that brought the divine Christ down to the closest intimacy with men; it was scientifically developed, though with various modifications, by a number of eminent German divines of the Lutheran Confession (Thomasius, Liebner, Gess, Von Hofmann, Kahnis, Delitzsch, Schöberlein, Kübel), and several Reformed divines (Lange, Ebrard, Godet, Pressensé, in Europe, Henry M. Goodwin and Howard Crosby in America). It is hardly just to call it (with Dorner) a revival of Apollinarianism and Patripassianism; for, while it resembles both in some features, it differs from them by assuming a truly humanized Logos dwelling in a human body. It carries the Kenosis much farther than the Giessen Lutherans, and makes it consist, not in a concealment merely (*krypsis*), but in an actual abandonment of the divine attributes of omnipotence, omniscience, and omnipresence, during the whole period of humiliation from the incarnation to the resurrection; the differences between the advocates of this theory referring to the degree of the Kenosis. It substitutes a *genus kenoticum*, or *tapeinoticum*, for the *genus majesticum* of the Lutheran Creed: in other words, a communication of the properties of humanity to the divinity for a communication of the properties of the divine nature to the human. Instead of raising the finite to the infinite, the Kenotic theory lowers the infinite to the finite. It teaches a temporary self-exinanition or depotentiation of the preexistent Logos. In becoming incarnate, the second Person of the holy Trinity reduced himself to the limitations of humanity. He literally emptied himself, not only of his divine glory, but also of his divine mode of existence (the *morphē theou*), and assumed the human mode of existence (the *morphē doulou*), subject to the limits of space and time and the laws of development and growth. The incarnation is not only an assumption by the Son of God of human nature, but also a self-limitation of the divine Logos; and both constitute one divine-human personality. Otherwise the infinite consciousness of the Logos could not coincide with the human consciousness of the historical Christ: it would transcend and outreach it, and the result would be a double personality. The self-limitation is to be conceived as an act of will, an act of God's love, which is the motive of the incarnation; and his love is absolutely powerful, even to the extent of the utmost self-surrender. This was the view of Thomasius, a Bavarian Lutheran. He and Liebner held, first, that the Logos actually became a rational human soul; but afterward they assumed a truly human soul along with the Kenosis of the Logos, and thereby they lost the chief benefit of the Kenosis theory.

1. General Outline.

Gess, a Swabian divine brought up under the influence of the school of Bengel, Oetinger, and Beck, and starting from a theosophic Biblical realism, carried the Kenosis to the extent of a suspension of self-consciousness and will. He identified it with the outgoing of the Son from the Father, or his descent from heaven, which resulted in a temporary suspension of the influx of the eternal life of the Father into the Son, and a transition from a state of equality with God into a state of dependence and need. Gess and Ebrard assume an actual transformation of the Logos into a human soul, i.e., he assumed a human body from the flesh of the Virgin, but became a rational human soul so that he had no need of assuming another soul. Consequently the soul of Christ was not derived from Mary: it was the result of a voluntary Kenosis, while an ordinary human soul derives its existence from a creative act of God. It is very questionable whether such a soul, which is the result of a transformation which begins with divinity and ends with divinity, can be called a truly human soul any more than the Apollinarian Logos, who, remaining unchanged, occupied the place and exercised the functions of the human soul.

2. Gess.

Martensen, the Danish theologian, more cautiously taught only a relative, though real, Kenosis. The eternal Logos continues in God and in his general revelation to the world as the author of all reason; while at the same time he enters into the bosom of humanity as a holy seed, that he may arise within the human race as a mediator and redeemer. He would, however, have become man even without sin, though not as redeemer. Martensen taught, with several of the Fathers and modern German theologians, that the incarnation was necessary for the highest revelation of God, and was only modified, not conditioned, by the fall.

3. Martensen.

Kahnis and Lange limited the Kenosis substantially to an abandonment of the use, rather than the possession, of the attributes. Lange's christology abounds in fruitful and original hints for further and clearer development.

4. Kahnis and Lange.

Julius Müller, one of the profoundest theologians, taught likewise in his lectures a moderate Kenosis theory. Paul contrasts the earthly and preearthly existence of the Son of God as poverty and riches (II Cor. viii. 9), and represents the incarnation as an emptying himself of the full possession of the divine mode of existence (Phil. ii. 6). This implies more than a mere assumption of human nature into union with the Son of God: the incarnation is a real self-exinanition (*Selbstentäusserung*), and a renunciation, not only of the use, but also of the possession, of the divine attributes and powers. . . . The Church is undoubtedly right in teaching a real union of the divine and human nature in Christ. But in the state of humiliation this union was first only potential and concealed; and the unfolded reality belongs to the state of exaltation. Only with the assumption of a self-exinanition can we fully appreciate the act of the self-denying condescension of divine love; while in the orthodox dogma God gives nothing in the incarnation, but simply receives and unites something with his person.

5. Julius Müller.

Goodwin differed from the German Kenoticists by assuming that the Logos is the human element in God which preexisted in him from eternity, and became incarnate by taking flesh, and occupying the place of the soul. No incarnation is possible without a humanization of the divine; and this implies a self-limitation, and true development from ignorance to knowledge and wisdom. The incarnation is not a synthesis or union of opposite natures, but a development of the divine in the form of the human. The Word did not assume flesh or human nature, but it became flesh. As the true idea of God includes humanity, so the true idea of man includes God. The divine and human differ only as the ideal differs from the actual, or the prototype from the copy. This essential unity is the basis of the possibility of the incarnation as a Kenosis. Howard Crosby held that, according to the Scripture, the Son of God reduced himself to the dimensions of humanity, to a state of "dormancy." His Godhead, therefore, was in a state of quiescence during his humiliation and awoke with the resurrection, after which the divine overshadowed the human.

6. Goodwin and Crosby.

A theory advocated by so many learned and pious theologians can not be altogether false. The Kenotic theory has the merit of bringing out the truth of the classical passage in Phil. ii. more forcibly than ever before. But it carries the idea of the self-limitation of the Logos to the extent of a metaphysical impossibility: it contradicts the essential unchangeableness of God. The humiliation of the Logos is an abandonment of the divine *doxa* and its enjoyment, but not of the divine being. The true Kenosis is a renunciation of the use (*chrēsis*), but not of the possession (*ktēsis*), of divine attributes. The former is possible, the latter impossible. God can do nothing that is contrary to his rational and moral nature. It is admitted by the Kenoticists that the Logos can not, in the incarnation, limit or suspend his moral attributes of love and holiness, but reveals them most fully in the state of humiliation. But his metaphysical and intellectual attributes belong just as much to the essence and nature of God as his moral attributes, and all are inseparable from his nature; so that God can not give up any of his attributes without mutilating and so far destroying his own being. He can not commit suicide, nor can he go to sleep. He can not reduce himself to the unconscious existence of an embryo, without ceasing to be God, and without destroying the life of the world, which without him can not exist a single moment. The illustration borrowed from sleep proves nothing; for man's identity continues undisturbed in sleep, and he awakes with the full exercise of all the faculties. Moreover, we can not conceive of such a self-reduction of the Logos without suspending the intertrinitarian process, and also the Trinity of revelation. It would stop for thirty-three years, as Gess frankly admits, the eternal generation of the Son, the procession of the Spirit from the Father and the Son, and the government of the world through the Logos. To say that the Logos remained unchanged in the Trinity, while at the same time he went out of the Trinity and became man, is virtually to establish two distinct Logoi, which is no better than the orthodox theory of two parallel natures, one infinite, the other finite. The Father and the Son have but one essence; how, then, could the divinity of the Son be suspended, or almost annihilated for a time, without suspending the divinity of the Father? It may be said, with Thomas Aquinas, that it was not the nature, but the person, of the Logos that became man. True, but a person without a nature is an impossible abstraction. If the Logos surrendered his divine self-consciousness, his omnipotence, and omniscience, how did he regain them? Was it by a recollection of his preexistent state? Or by a reflection on the Old Testament Scriptures? Or by a revelation from the Father? Or by the development of a native instinct? These and similar questions can not be satisfactorily answered by the consistent Kenoticists. Professor Paine (*Critical History of the Evolution of Trinitarianism*, Boston, 1900, p. 281) pronounces the Kenosis theory "only a metaphysical makeshift to cover the real contradiction which in the Chalcedonian theology stands visible to every intelligent eye."

7. Criticism.

5. The Ritschlian Theory is the product of Albrecht Ritschl (q.v.), the founder of the theological school which goes by his name. It is set forth adequately in his *Christliche Lehre von der Rechtfertigung und der Versöhnung* (3 vols., Bonn, 1870–74; 3d ed., 1888–89; Eng. transl., Edinburgh, vol. i., 1872, vol. iii., 1900), chap. vi., "The Doctrine of Christ's Person and Work" (iii. 385–484 of Eng. ed.). The theory is an appreciation of Christ's ethical and religious unity with the Father and a denial of man's ability to find out the "physical origin" of the Person of Christ. Christ is "unique in his own order," that is, regarded as the revealer and bearer of religious and ethical truth. In this sense he is the Son of God; and his "apprehension of himself as the Son of God is ever attained through his adoration of God as his Father." It is folly to attempt to explain the physical origin of the Person of Christ. Ritschl's theory is in accord with his discarding of the metaphysical element and his assertion only of that which is truly religious. In other words, all is to be set aside from the discussion of Christ's Person which can not be and has not been tested by the Church, or "the Christian community," in its experience. Ritschl says that the three offices of Christ—prophet, priest, and king—are a step toward grasping the significance of Christ for the Church, but they afford only a defective conception of him. Jesus was conscious of a new and previously unknown relation to God, as he testified to his disciples (p. 386). He esteemed himself more than a mere human being. He regarded his life as an instrument of God's complete revelation of himself. The theology of the Reformers adopted, it is true, the ethical mode of looking at Christ (p. 440); but all the older theologies in their doctrine of Christ failed to consider his religious activities, namely his habit of prayer and

1. The Theory Stated.

his submission to the dispensations of God. Christ as the Word of God realizes in himself, that is in a human person, his vocation, which is the establishment of the universal ethical kingdom of God. This kingdom is the supreme self-end of God in the world, so that the complete revelation of God is present in Christ, "in whom the word of God is a human person" (p. 451). The origin of the Person of Christ is not a proper subject of inquiry, for the problem transcends all investigation (p. 451). What ecclesiastical tradition offers in this respect is obscure in itself and is not fitted to make anything clear. Christ, as the instrument of the perfect revelation, is given that we may believe on him, and believing on him we find him to be the revealer of God. But the determination of the personal relation of Christ to God the Father is not a matter of scientific inquiry. Straining after explanations will prove fruitless. It will result only in obscuring the recognition of Christ as the perfect revelation of God (p. 452). The specific and complete revelation of God in Christ is "the grace and truth" which dwelt in him. These are his divinity, and divinity does not reside in the will (p. 467). In the discharge of his vocation the essential will of God is revealed, which is love (p. 454). The only tests of the revelation of God in a human personality are "grace and truth." In Christ the divine attributes of omniscience, omnipotence, and omnipresence are not to be sought. To be sure, to Christ is ascribed power over the world (Matt. xi. 27; etc.), but this power manifests itself chiefly as patience under suffering (p. 460). Christ's divinity is in his world-conquering power, in his own patience, and in the Christian community. It rests not in his physical origin, which has never yet been reconciled with his historic appearance and never can be (p. 467). In virtue of the love which inspired him and in view of the lordship which in his own estimate of himself and by his patience he exercised over the world, he is equal with God (p. 483).

2. Its Merit and Limitation. It is Ritschl's merit that he emphasized the ethical element of Christianity and insisted upon human experience as a test of the great principles of the Gospel. He can preserve the terms "equality with the Father" and "preexistence" by exalting the love which moved Christ and by exalting Christ's vocation, which was to advance the universal kingdom of God. In doing this he can not avoid metaphysical subtlety and he must leave out, or explain away, utterances of Christ which on their face refer to what he calls "his physical origin" and which he says the older theologies in vain attempted to solve. Theology will not be satisfied with formulas bearing on the ethical and religious relationship of Christ and God while so much is said in the New Testament about the "physical (essential) relationship," especially as this "physical relationship" seems to be the basis of the ethical and religious unity of the Son of God and the Father.

6. The Theory of a Gradual or Progressive Incarnation is the last to be mentioned as promoting a solution of the problem. It carried the divine Kenosis, or the motion of God's love to men, through the whole earthly life of Christ, instead of confining it to an instantaneous act when the Holy Spirit overshadowed the Blessed Virgin. When John says that the "Logos became flesh," he spoke as one of those who "beheld his glory, the glory of the only-begotten of the Father," as it manifested itself in his whole public life. The impossible idea of an essential self-limitation of

1. The Theory. the Logos is discarded, and in its place is assumed the rational idea of a limitation of the self-communication of the Logos to humanity. There are various degrees in this self-communication. The being and actuality of the Logos remained metaphysically and morally unchanged; but Jesus of Nazareth possessed the Logos merely so far as was compatible with the truth of human growth and the capacity of his expanding consciousness. In other words, the eternal personality of the divine Logos entered into the humanity of Jesus, measure by measure as it grew, and became capable and worthy of receiving it. There were two corresponding movements in the life of Christ—a descent of the divine consciousness, and an ascent of the human consciousness. There was a progressive self-communication of the divine Logos to Jesus, and a moral growth of Jesus in holiness keeping step with the former. The process of union began with the supernatural conception, and was completed with the ascension. The first act of the incarnation of the Logos was the beginning of the man Jesus, and both constituted one undivided personality. There was a personal unity and identity throughout the whole period, the same life of the divine-human personality, but in actual growth and development from germ to full organization, from infancy to ripe manhood. Christ became conscious of his Godhead as he became conscious of his manhood; but the divine life always was the basis of his human life. The twelfth year of Jesus in the temple, and the baptism in the Jordan, mark two important epochs in the development of this divine-human consciousness. There was in connection with the gradual incorporation of the divine Logos into the humanity of Jesus an actual elevation of his humanity into personal union with the Godhead, as he grew in moral perfection: hence his exaltation is spoken of by Paul as a reward for his humiliation and obedience (Phil. ii. 9; cf. Heb. v. 7–10).

2. Its Merits. This theory escapes the difficulties of the Kenotic theory, and is even better reconcilable with the orthodox christology of the creeds, as far as the result is concerned. Nearly all christologists admit now the genuine growth and development of Christ's humanity, to which the Kenoticists add the impossible growth of the divine Logos from unconsciousness and impotence to omniscience and omnipotence. This view teaches the former without the latter, and saves the continued integrity of the Logos. There still remains the speculative problem perceived by the Reformed divines—how the infinite consciousness of the eternal Logos can ever become absolutely coincident with the limited consciousness of the man Jesus; but this difficulty attaches to every theory which holds fast to the strict divinity of our Lord

7. Conclusion: In reviewing these various theories we can readily accept the elements of truth which they variously express. Christ is the ideal man realized, the head of the redeemed race, the perfect model for universal imitation. So far, even the Humanitarian theory is correct; only it does not go far enough, and it becomes a serious error when it denies the higher truth beyond. For Christ is also the eternal Son of God, who in infinite love renounced his glory and majesty, and lowered himself to a fallen race, entering into all its wants, trials, and temptations, yet without sin, and humbled himself, even to the death on the cross, in order to emancipate men from the guilt and power of sin, and to reconcile them to God. He is the one undivided God-man, who, as man, calls out all our sympathies and trust, and, as God, is the object of true worship. In this respect we accept fully the faith of the Church in all ages, and consider the divinity of our Lord as the corner-stone of Christianity. We hold, with Ritschl and Paine, to the moral nature of the God-manhood of Christ, but without sacrificing his eternal divinity. We would go as far with the Kenosis theory as the unchangeable nature of God permits, and as the unbounded love of God demands. We dissent from the dyophysitic and dualistic psychology of Chalcedon, and hold to the inseparable personal unity of the life, and at the same time to the genuine growth of Christ, without asserting, with the Kenoticists, a growth of the divine Logos, who is unchangeable in his nature; but we substitute for this impossible idea a gradual communication of the divinity to the God-man.

1. Elements of Truth in All Theories.

This is, in substance, the Christ of the Catholic creeds and the Protestant confessions of faith. He is a mystery indeed to our intellectual and philosophical comprehension, but a mystery made manifest as the most glorious fact in history—the blessed mystery of godliness, the inexhaustible theme of meditation and praise for all generations. How the whole fulness of uncreated divinity can be poured out into a human being passes our understanding, but not more, perhaps, than the familiar fact that an immaterial and immortal soul made in God's image, and capable of endless perfectibility, inhabits and interpenetrates a material and mortal body. And deeper and grander than both mysteries is the infinite love of God which lies back of them in the very depths of eternity, and which prompted the incarnation and the death of his only-begotten Son for the salvation of a sinful world. Yet this love of God in Christ, whose "breadth and length and height and depth passeth knowledge" (Eph. iii. 18, 19), is more certain and constant than the light of the sun in heaven and the voice of conscience in man.

2. The Mystery of Christ.

It has been thought best not to discuss in this article the bearing of the denial of the virgin-birth of our Lord upon the problems of christology. Origen and other early Fathers, whose names have a prominent place in the development of christology, emphasized the virgin-birth as an integral element of Christ's divinity. The purely human origin of Christ from a human father and mother favors strongly, if it does not necessitate, the view that Christ was only a man and precludes the view that he was either preexistent or essentially divine. Nor has it seemed necessary to take into consideration the view of the contemporary school of historical critics, Pfleiderer, Wernle, and others, who make a sharp distinction between Paul's theology and the much simpler claims Christ made for himself, and who regard Paul as the inventor of the deity of Christ and other doctrines which the Church has always held. This article assumes the integrity of the four Gospels, and that the Pauline epistles interpreted but did not originate the doctrines concerning Christ's person.

3. Limits of This Article.

(PHILIP SCHAFF†) D. S. SCHAFF.

XI. Additional Note: Certain questions which have come up in the recent dogmatic consideration of the person of Christ require an additional statement. That this problem engaged the early attention of the church is evident by the birth-stories of Matthew and Luke, the stories of the baptism, the Logos-doctrine of the Fourth Gospel and the Epistle to the Hebrews, and Paul's conception of preexistence. In addition to the orthodox theory of the Logos, or the second person of the Trinity, who assumed human nature in Jesus Christ, and the speculations of those who have advocated the several Kenotic theories (see KENOSIS), various attempts have been made to do justice to the New Testament teaching concerning preexistence. (1) The preexistence is ideal. According to a form of expression common in the time of Jesus, things of exceeding worth, as the ark of the covenant, the temple, Jerusalem, are conceived as already existing in heaven with God before they are manifested on earth. Thus the transcendent ground of the person of Christ was within God's eternal knowledge, so that in the divine idea and purpose of redemption Jesus had eternal existence (cf. Harnack, *Dogma*, vol. i., Appendix I.). Or, the meaning of preexistence is that Christ in human form is the revelation of the eternal cosmic principle through which in creation and redemption God is disclosing himself (W. A. Brown, *Christian Theology in Outline*, pp. 179–180, 347, New York, 1906). (2) The "heavenly man" preexisting in the image of God (I Cor. xv. 47, cf. Col. i. 15–17; II Cor. viii. 9) does not assume human nature, but becomes incarnate in Jesus Christ. This interpretation, originating in Paul's antithesis of flesh and spirit, found a congenial soil in the religious ideas of the time—a logical deduction backward drawn from belief in the risen Christ (cf. O. Pfleiderer, *Paulinism*, part I., chap. iii., London). Or, the "heavenly man" had a preexistent life, and this life was divine not in the absolute sense, but as conferred upon him by God, thus identical in principle with the glorified life (C. H. von Weizsäcker, *Apostolic Age*, book II.,

1. Preexistence.

chap. ii., §§ 10–11, New York, 1894). Or, again, in one aspect the Logos is to be regarded as the eternal Humanity in God, the "Archetype of the not yet created Man," which became incarnate in Jesus Christ (T. C. Edwards, *The God-Man*, London, 1896). (3) W. Herrmann holds that the preexistence was not ideal, but personal—a contradiction indeed, to be removed only when the riddle of time in which we now conceive reality had been solved for us (*Die Religion im Verhältniss zum Welterkennen und zur Sittlichkeit*, p. 438, Halle, 1879).

2. Incarnation.

As to theories of incarnation several tendencies are evident. (1) The ethical aspect of the incarnation is increasingly emphasized. The traditional christology has been based on the essential disparity of the divine and human natures. This was held to be necessary in order to safeguard the integrity of the two natures. But however carefully the statement of the doctrine was protected, it did not escape the force of the criticism in the preceding text (see VI., 2, § 2). To meet this difficulty, therefore, attention has been directed away from the two-nature doctrine on its purely metaphysical side to the ethical and religious aspects of the incarnation. As in the traditional view, God and man are here affirmed in all the integrity of their spiritual being, but the point of view is changed. It is not so much a question of nature and essence and hypostasis as of psychological experience and character, of inner development and historical influence, i.e., of the moral and spiritual consciousness of Jesus Christ in which the purpose of God is revealed and realized, and the unity of God and man are disclosed. Accordingly, the proof of the incarnation is found in Jesus's consciousness of his vocation, in his grace and truth, his dominion over the world, and his success in establishing his community with attributes analogous to his own. This ethical estimate of Jesus results in a religious valuation of him. We call Christ God because he has for us the religious worth of God (Ritschl). (2) The incarnation is conceived of as an immanent necessity in the love of God to self-expression. Again, if man was created in the image of God, and his perfection was possible only in union with God, then an incarnation of one who should enable man to consummate this union was necessary apart from sin. Thus, incarnation for the sake of redemption, instead of being an afterthought of God, an accidental expedient in behalf of man, was involved in the essential ethical relation of God to the creation (B. F. Westcott, "Gospel of the Creation," in *Commentary on the Epistles of St. John*, London, 1885). (3) The proof of the divinity of Christ is becoming less external and dogmatic than internal and ethical. If in the earlier arguments the greater stress was on the application to Christ of Old Testament terms referring to God, the ascription to him of names, attributes, and works of God, the New Testament designation of him as Son of God in a metaphysical sense, and the fact that he was an object of religious worship, in more recent thought the principal emphasis is laid on the uniqueness of his moral character, the might of his moral appeal to the conscience and the will, the transformation in experience which follows obedience to his leadership; in a word, in him is a revelation of that which is most real in God and most ideal in man—love. This ethical impulse to the interpretation of Christ, which among many recent attempts of the same kind was disclosed in Bushnell's incomparable tenth chapter of *Nature and the Supernatural*—"The Character of Jesus Forbids His Possible Classification with Men"—has by no means lost its force, and every modern treatment of the person of Jesus pays tribute to this demand. (4) The incarnation is increasingly regarded in an essential relation to the redemptive work of Christ. Not, then, the atonement irrespective of the life of Jesus, but—a truth which was deeply voiced by Athanasius in *The Incarnation of the Word*—God comes to man both to reveal and to realize the ideal oneness of God and man. Thus the incarnation is the atonement (cf. J. M. Wilson, *The Gospel of the Atonement*, London, 1899). (5) Further, the cosmic relations of the incarnation are receiving renewed attention. Here several currents meet and mingle: the Pauline conception of the universal significance of Christ (Col. i. 15–17), the federal, based on the natural, headship of Christ, the pantheistic trend which discerns in the particular the essence of the universal, and evolution which finds the goal and crown of the creation in the ethical and religious consciousness. Christ is, accordingly, the supreme expression and consummation of the Logos of God in which the whole creation finds its interpretative principle and end. C. A. B.

Bibliography: I. For O. T. Christology consult the works cited under Messiah. For N. T. Christology consult the works on N. T. Theology, especially: W. Beyschlag, *N. T. Theology*, 2 vols., Edinburgh, 1896; E. Reuss, *La Théologie chrétienne au siècle apostolique*, 2 vols., Strasburg, 1864; J. J. Van Oosterzee, *Theology of N. T.*, London, 1879; B. Weiss, *Biblische Theologie des N. T.*, Stuttgart, 1903, Eng. transl., 2 vols., Edinburgh, 1882–83; H. H. Wendt, *Lehre Jesu*, 2 vols., Göttingen, 1886–90, Eng. transl., London, 1892; G. B. Stevens, *Theology of N. T.*, New York, 1899; E. P. Gould, *Biblical Theology of N. T.*, ib. 1900. Consult further: C. F. Nösgen, *Christus der Menschen- und Gottessohn*, Gotha, 1869; W. F. Gess, *Christi Person und Werk*, 3 vols., Basel, 1870–78; H. Bushnell, *God in Christ*, New York, 1877; I. A. Dorner, *Christliche Glaubenslehre*, ii. 257 sqq., Berlin, 1880; P. Schaff, *Person of Christ*, New York, 1882; A. B. Bruce, *Kingdom of God*, Edinburgh, 1889; J. A. Beet, *Through Christ to God*, pp. 215–301, London, 1892; J. Stalker, *Christology of Jesus*, ib. 1899; A. M. Fairbairn, *Philosophy of the Christian Religion*, pp. 356–379, ib. 1902; N. Schmidt, *Prophet of Nazareth*, New York, 1905.

II.–III. The best detailed account of the development of doctrine with its environment is still Neander, *Christian Church*, i. 575–608, 630–640, ii. 405–406, 478–504. Especially valuable are the histories of doctrine, particularly: Harnack, *Dogma*, vols. i.–iii.; I. A. Dorner, *History of the Development of the Doctrine of the Person of Christ*, Edinburgh, 1859; F. Nietzsche, *Dogmengeschichte*, Berlin, 1870; A. Reville, *Histoire du dogme de la divinité de Jésus Christ*, 3d. ed., Paris, 1904, Eng. transl., *Hist. of the Doctrine of the Deity of Jesus Christ*, London, 1870; K. R. Hagenbach, *Hist. of Doctrine*, vol. i., Edinburgh, 1880; F. Loofs, *Dogmengeschichte*, Halle, 1893; R. Seeberg, *Lehrbuch der Dogmengeschichte*, 2 vols., Erlangen, 1895–98; G. P. Fisher, *Hist. of Christian Doctrine*, New York, 1896; Hefele, *Conciliengeschichte*, vol. i., Eng. transl., vols. i.–ii. Consult also: D. Petavius, *De theologicis dogmatibus*, 5 vols., Paris, 1644–50 (collects ante-Nicene and Nicene testimonies); G. Bull, *Defensio fidei Nicænæ*, Oxford, 1685 (a standard); E. Burton, *Testimonies of Ante-Nicene Fathers to the Divinity of*

Christ, Oxford, 1829 (also a classic); F. C. Baur, *Die christliche Lehre von der Dreieinigkeit und Menschwerdung Gottes*, 3 vols. Tübingen, 1841–43; H. Voigt, *Die Lehre des Athanasius*, Bremen, 1861; W. Mackintosh, *Study of the Doctrine of Jesus as Developed from Judaism and Converted into Dogma*, Glasgow, 1894; O. Pfleiderer, *Early Christian Conception of Christ*, London, 1905; B. B. Warfield, in *Princeton Theological Review*, 1905, pp. 529–557, 1906, pp. 1–37, 145–168; Schaff, *Christian Church*, ii. 544–560, iii. 705–740.

IV.–VII. Consult, besides the works on the history of doctrine cited above (especially Harnack, *Dogma*, vols. iii.–iv.): Schaff, *Christian Church*, vol. iv.; W. A. Arendt, *Leo der Grosse*, Mainz, 1835; J. Fulton, *The Chalcedonian Decree*, New York, 1892; L. L. Paine, *Critical History of the Evolution of Trinitarianism*, Boston, 1900; J. O. Dykes, in *Expository Times*, Oct., 1905–Jan., 1906; Hefele, *Conciliengeschichte*, vols. iii.–iv., Eng. transl., vols. iii.–v.

VIII. Original documents are, Lutheran: *Formula Concordiæ* (convenient in Jacob's edition, vol. i., Philadelphia, 1893); J. Brenz, *De personale unione duarum naturarum in Christo*, 1560; idem, *De majestate domini nostri*, 1562; M. Chemnitz, *De duabus naturis in Christo*, Frankfort, 1578. Reformed: *Admonitio Neostadiensis*, 1577; L. Danæus, *De duabus naturis a Chemnitio*, Geneva, 1581; H. Zanchi, *De incarnatione filii Dei*, Heidelberg, 1593; the christological writings of T. Beza and Z. Ursinus. For specific discussions consult, Lutheran: F. H. R. Frank, *Theologie der Concordienformel*, iii. 165–396, Erlangen, 1865; C. P. Krauth, *Conservative Reformation and its Theology*, pp. 456 sqq., Philadelphia, 1872; H. E. Jacobs, *Book of Concord*, vol. ii., ib. 1893. Reformed: H. L. J. Heppe, *Reformirte Dogmatik*, pp. 351 sqq., Elberfeld, 1861; Schaff, *Creeds*, i. 285 sqq., 317 sqq. Critical: M. Schneckenburger, *Zur kirchlichen Christologie*, Pforzheim, 1861; idem, *Vergleichende Darstellung des lutherischen und reformirten Lehrbegriffs*, Stuttgart, 1855. General works are those already cited of Dorner, Reville, Nietzsche, Seeberg, and Baur; R. A. Lipsius, *Dogmatik*, pp. 441–483, Brunswick, 1893. Consult also H. Schultz, *Die Lehre von der Gottheit Christi, Communicatio idiomatum*, Gotha, 1881; A. Ritschl, *Christian Doctrine of Justification and Reconciliation*, pp. 416 sqq., Edinburgh, 1872.

IX. On the Giessen side, the Saxon *Solida decisio*, Leipsic, 1624; J. Feuerborn, *Sciagraphia de divino Jesu Christo . . .*, 1621; idem, *Κενωσιγραφία χριστολογική*, Marburg, 1627; B. Mentzer, *Necessaria et justa defensio*, Giessen, 1624. On the Tübingen side: L. Osiander, *De omnipræsentia Christi hominis*, Tübingen, 1620; T. Thumm, *Majestatis Jesu Christi θεανθρώπου*, ib. 1621; idem, *Ταπεινωσιγραφία sacra*, ib. 1623; *Acta Mentzeriana*, ib. 1625. On the Roman Catholic side: *Bellum ubiquisticum vetus et novum*, Dillingen, 1627; *Alter und neuer lutherischer Katzenkrieg von der Ubiquität*, Ingolstadt, 1629. Historical and critical: J. F. Cotta, *Historia doctrinæ de duplice statu Christi*, in his ed. of Gerhard's *Loci theologici*, iv. 60 sqq., Tübingen, 1762–88; J. E. I. Walch, *Einleitung in die Religionstreitigkeiten*, i. 206, Jena, 1733; F. C. Baur, ut sup., ii. 450; G. Thomasius, *Christi Person und Werk*, ii. 391–450, Erlangen, 1857; I. A. Dorner, ut sup., ii. 788–800; R. Rocholl, *Realpräsenz*, pp. 198 sqq., Gütersloh, 1875.

X. 1. For the *Racovian Catechism* (Eng. transl. by T. Rees, London, 1818) see SOCINUS; J. Priestley, *Early Opinions concerning Jesus Christ*, Birmingham, 1786; I. Kant, *Religion innerhalb der Grenzen der blossen Vernunft*, Königsberg, 1793, Eng. transl., *Religion within the Boundary of Pure Reason*, Edinburgh, 1838; W. E. Channing, *Works*, 6 vols., Boston, 1874; T. Parker, *Discourse of Matters Pertaining to Religion*, ib. 1847; A. Coquerel, *Christologie*, 2 vols., Paris, 1858; J. Martineau, *Studies of Christianity*, London, 1858; idem, *Essays Philosophical and Theological*, 2 vols., New York, 1879; idem, *Religion as Affected by Modern Materialism*, London, 1874; idem, *Seat of Authority in Religion*, ib. 1890; F. H. Hedge, *Reason in Religion*, Boston, 1875; M. J. Savage, *Out of Nazareth*, ib. 1904.

2. D. F. Strauss, *Die christliche Glaubenslehre in ihrer geschichtlichen Entwicklung und im Kampfe mit der modernen Wissenschaft*, ii. 193 sqq., Tübingen, 1841 (a work as destructive of Christian dogmatics as his *Leben Jesu* is of the evangelical history); A. E. Biedermann, *Christliche Dogmatik*, Zurich, 1869 (more serious, but almost equally revolutionary in its results); E. Marius, *Die Persönlichkeit Jesu Christi. Mit besonderer Rücksicht auf die Mythologien und Mysterien der alten Völker*, Leipsic, 1881 (a strange compound of the mythical views of Strauss and the mystical interpretation of Swedenborg).

4. On the Kenotic theory: J. L. König, *Die Menschwerdung Gottes*, Mainz, 1844; G. Thomasius, *Beiträge zur kirchlichen Christologie*, Erlangen, 1845; idem, *Christi Person und Werk*, ib. 1856; T. A. Liebner, *Die christliche Dogmatik*, Göttingen, 1849; J. H. A. Ebrard, *Christliche Dogmatik*, Königsberg, 1851–52; J. P. Lange, *Positive Dogmatik*, pp. 595–782, Heidelberg, 1851; W. F. Gess, ut sup.; H. L. Martensen, *Christliche Dogmatik*, Berlin, 1853, Eng. transl., Edinburgh, 1866; F. Delitzsch, *System der biblischen Psychologie*, pp. 325 sqq., Leipsic, 1861, Eng. transl., Edinburgh, 1865; J. Bodemeyer, *Die Lehre von der Kenosis*, Göttingen, 1860; K. F. A. Kahnis, *Die lutherische Dogmatik*, iii. 343, Leipsic, 1868; L. Schöberlein, *Die Geheimnisse des Glaubens*, Heidelberg, 1872; R. Kübel, *Christliches Lehrsystem*, Stuttgart, 1873; J. J. van Oosterzee, *Christian Dogmatics*, London, 1878 (moderately and cautiously Kenotic); F. Godet, in *Studies on the New Testament*, Edinburgh, 1876; idem, *Commentary on . . . John*, ib. 1881; E. de Pressensé, *Jésus Christ*, Paris, 1866, Eng. transl., London, 1866; idem, *La Divinité de Jésus Christ*, in *Revue chrétienne*, iii. 641 sqq.; H. M. Goodwin, *Christ and Humanity*, New York, 1875; H. Crosby, *The True Humanity of Christ*, ib. 1881; F. J. Hall, *The Kenotic Theory*, London, 1898; J. Kunze, *Die ewige Gottheit Jesu Christi*, Leipsic, 1904; W. Lütgert, *Gottes Sohn und Gottes Geist*, ib. 1904.

For adverse criticism of the Kenosis theory consult: I. A. Dorner, ut sup., Eng. transl., II. iii., pp. 100 sqq.; idem, in *Jahrbücher für deutsche Theologie*, 1856, 1858; idem, *Christliche Glaubenslehre*, ii. 367 sqq., Berlin, 1880, Eng. transl., Edinburgh, 1880–82. The fullest account in Eng. is in A. B. Bruce, *Humiliation of Christ*, Lect. iv., Edinburgh, 1881. Dr. Hodge, *Systematic Theology*, ii. 439, New York, 1871, notices the Kenotic theories of Thomasius, Ebrard, and Gess, and condemns them.

In general, I. A. Dorner, ut sup. The following English works deserve notice, though mostly confined to an exposition and defense of the Chalcedonian dogma: R. J. Wilberforce, *The Doctrine of the Incarnation of our Lord*, London, 1852; H. P. Liddon, *The Divinity of our Lord and Saviour Jesus Christ*, ib. 1868. The ablest discussion of Christ's person and work is A. M. Fairbairn, *Place of Christ in Modern Theology*, London, 1893. Consult further: C. Gore, *Incarnation of the Son of God*, ib. 1891; J. Denney, *Studies in Theology*, chaps. ii.–iii., New York, 1895; "Christologie" in Hauck-Herzog, *RE*, iv. 4–56; M. Brückner, *Die Entstehung der paulinischen Christologie*, Strasburg, 1903; G. Krüger, *Das Dogma von der Dreieinigkeit und Gott Menschheit*, Tübingen, 1905 (dedicated to Harnack, written from the Unitarian standpoint); S. Faut, *Die Christologie seit Schleiermacher, ihre Geschichte und ihre Begründung*, Tübingen, 1907.

CHRISTOPHER, SAINT: A saint highly honored from very early times both in the Greek and Latin churches. According to the martyrologies of Ado, Usuard, Notker, and others, as well as the *Martyrologium Romanum*, he lived at Samos in Lycia, converted many to Christianity, and died a martyr under the emperor Decius, or, according to some accounts, under an emperor (or king) called Dagnus. No Samos in Lycia, however, is known, and Dagnus is otherwise unheard of; the name may be a corruption of Daza, the original name of the emperor Maximin II. (305–314). The later forms of the Christopher legend are in the highest degree fantastic. For example, a manuscript of Fulda describes him as of gigantic stature, with the head of a dog, and decks out his life and death with most silly wonders. Somewhat more attractive and credible is another version, containing apparently elements of old Germanic mythology, according to which the giant Christopher at first served the devil, then in order to know Christ, one said to be stronger than the devil, undertook the duties of a ferryman. Finally a child, whom he was carrying across the river on his shoulders, disclosed himself as the Savior, forced the giant beneath the waves by his ever increasing weight and so baptized him, giving him the name of Christopher ("Christ-bearer"). The veneration of Christopher was general in the East, in Italy, Spain, France, Germany, and other lands. Mention of his wonder-working relics is frequent, as of his head, said to have been carried from Constantinople to France after the capture of the city in 1204, and of his leg, said to have been kept in Constantinople till 1453. He was an attractive figure to medieval art and poetry, and is represented as a huge fellow wading through waters, carrying a child on his shoulders, and with a green staff in his hand. His picture is frequent in the vestibules of churches as a sort of guard. Brotherhoods of St. Christopher, especially for the care of travelers, are mentioned up to the Reformation. His day in the Greek Church is May 9, and in the Latin July 25. (O. Zöckler†.)

Bibliography: The older *Vitæ* are to be found in *ASB*, July, vi. 125–149; in B. Pez, *Thesaurus anecdotorum novissimus*, II. iii. 27–122, Augsburg, 1721; and in *Analecta Bollandiana*, ed. C. de Smedt and others, i. 121–148, x. 393–405, Paris, 1882, 1891. All the different elements of the legend are combined by Jacobus de Varagine (q.v.) in the *Golden Legend*. Consult: J. Grimm, *Deutsche Mythologie*, pp. 496–509, Göttingen, 1844; H. P. Huot, *Vie de S. Christophe*, Soissons, 1861; A. Sinemus, *Die Legende vom heiligen Christoph und die Plastik und Malerei*, Hanover, 1868; *Le Grand S. Christophe de Palestine, son histoire authentique et sa popularité dans les deux mondes, par des Lorrains bibliophiles*, Nantes, 1890; A. Mussafia, *Zur Christoph-Legende*, Vienna, 1893; K. Richter, *Der deutsche Christoph*, Berlin, 1896.

CHRISTOPHER, DUKE OF WUERTTEMBERG, AND THE REFORMATION IN WUERTTEMBERG: Christopher, duke of Württemberg, 1550–68, was born at Urach (22 m. s.e. of Stuttgart) May 12, 1515; d. at Stuttgart Dec. 28, 1568. When he was six months old, his mother, Sabina of Bavaria, fled to her native land, and in 1519 his father, Ulric, was driven from his country. The boy came into the hands of Charles V. and his brother Ferdinand, but was well educated by Michael Tiffernus. At the court of Charles V., from which he fled in 1532, and in France, where he spent eight years, he grew up a statesman and soldier. His father, who in 1534 regained his country and reformed it, made him governor at Mömpelgard, and in 1544 brought about his marriage with Anna Maria, daughter of the margrave George of Brandenburg-Ansbach. The reading of the Bible and the writings of the Reformers gave Christopher a firm and clear Evangelical faith, which he proved in filial reverence and love toward the often severe father and obstinate mother and in restless activity for his people and the Evangelical Church.

On Nov. 6, 1550, he succeeded his father as duke and soon obtained a leading position among the Evangelical princes. He presented the *Confessio Wirtembergica*, prepared by Brenz, to the Council at Trent, and sent Brenz and other theologians to defend it, but they were not heard. He then prohibited the mass in the parish-churches, abolished the Interim, removed the images, altars, field-chapels, and all remains of the former religious service, turned the male monasteries into schools with Evangelical abbots, but allowed the nuns to die in their monasteries; those, however, who left were provided for. He gave a new discipline to the Evangelical Church of Württemberg, introduced poor-boxes in 1552, and appointed four district-physicians for the care of the sick. The marriage-law was regulated by act of Jan. 1, 1553; the activity of the higher church-authorities by the visitation act. The religious service, in the simplicity given to it by Blaurer and Schnepff (qq.v.), and the catechetical instruction of the youth were regulated by the *Kleine Kirchenordnung* of 1553, which was superseded by the *Grosse Kirchenordnung* of May 15, 1559, including also school, sanitary, and poor regulations. The duke treated the church-property of the Evangelical Church with perfect disinterestedness, divided the large parishes for the better care of the congregation, established new parishes in the Black Forest, cared for the repair of the churches, and enacted in 1559 that church-registers should be kept. He insisted that the teaching of the *Confessio Wirtembergica* should be maintained, and issued harsh injunctions against Schwenckfeld and all "sectaries." His harshness was felt especially by the Baptists and by Bartholomäus Hagen, preacher at Dettigen, who was suspected of Calvinism but was convinced of his error at the Stuttgart Synod in Dec., 1559. The university received new regulations in 1557. The scholarship founded by his father was applied to the education of theologians who had received a humanistic preparation in the monastic schools. Students of other faculties, who were prepared in the pedagogical schools at Stuttgart and Tübingen, were assisted from the funds of the church-property. By the school-regulation of 1559 popular education was promoted; the sacristan now acted also as teacher.

The Reformation in Württemberg.

Christopher was anxious for the reunion of the different religious parties, proposed in 1552 a national council, and avoided all malicious fault-finding. Calvinism he disliked much, especially as it made its inroad into the Palatinate, but he respected the religious courage of the elector Frederick of the Palatinate and did not favor his exclusion from the religious peace. He promoted Protestantism in Austria by supporting the Slavic press at Urach under the former imperial captain Hans Ungnad. He offered a refuge at Tübingen to the former papal nuncio Petrus Paulus Vergerius. In 1557 he solicited the king of France for the oppressed Waldensians, in 1559 for the Protestants; in 1561 he sent Beurlin (q.v.) and Andreä to Paris, and even went in 1562 with Brenz to Zabern to attend a colloquy with the Guises to win France over to Protestantism, but saw himself at last shamefully deceived, though Catherine de Medici offered him the office of a supreme viceroy. In the interest of Protestantism his active mind was long busy with matrimonial plans for the daughters of Renata of Ferrara and for Queen Elizabeth of England. He aided the Reformation by his advice and by sending theo-

Christopher's Influence Abroad.

logians to the Palatinate, in the margravate Baden-Pforzheim, in the domain of Count Helfenstein, in the country of Oettingen, in the free-towns of Rothenburg, on the Tauber, and Hagenau, also in the remote duchies of Jülich-Cleves and Brunswick-Wolfenbüttel, whose Duke Julius, his cousin, followed him implicitly. The ecclesiastical reservation carried through by Ferdinand at the Religious Peace of Augsburg (q.v.) Christopher opposed as an impediment to Protestantism and a denial of the principle of religious liberty. His hopes, however, in Maximilian II., the son and successor of Ferdinand, his friend, who had been influenced by the spirit of the Reformation, were not realized. He helped exiled Englishmen in 1554-55, the Waldensians in 1557, and in a quiet manner, not to excite the wrath of the emperor, in 1568 William of Orange in the war of liberation in the Netherlands. For his people and the Evangelical Church of Germany Christopher's death came too soon. His efforts for his people's welfare, his zeal for the Church and Protestantism, his pure intentions mark him as one of the ablest princes of Germany. His reign and that of his son Louis (1569–93) form the golden age of Württemberg. G. BOSSERT.

BIBLIOGRAPHY: J. C. Pfister, *Herzog Christoph von Württemberg*, 2 vols., Tübingen, 1819–20; B. Kugler, *Christoph, Herzog von Württemberg*, 2 vols., Stuttgart, 1868–70; C. F. Stälin, *Württembergische Geschichte*, vol. iv., Stuttgart, 1873; E. Schneider, *Württembergische Reformationsgeschichte*, Stuttgart, 1887; *Württembergische Kirchengeschichte*, Stuttgart, 1893; E. Schneider, *Württembergische Geschichte*, Stuttgart, 1896; V. Ernst, *Briefwechsel des Herzogs Christoph*, 3 vols., Stuttgart, 1899-1902.

CHRISTOPHORUS: Pope 903–904. In the autumn of 903 he overthrew Leo V. and seized the papal throne; but a few months later he met the same fate at the hands of Sergius III. According to Herimannus, he became a monk; Vulgarius, on the other hand, says that he was murdered in prison. (A. HAUCK.)

BIBLIOGRAPHY: Jaffé, *Regesta*, i. 443–444; Bower, *Popes*, ii. 306.

CHRO'DE-GANG (Hrodegandus, Ruotgang, Ruggandus): Frankish bishop; b. in Hasbania (*ex pago Hasbaniensi*, in the Belgian province of Limburg) early in the eighth century; d. at Metz Mar. 6, 766. He was the son of Sigramnus and Landrada, who belonged to one of the noblest families of the Ripuarian Franks, was set aside for the Church, admitted into the clergy of the court, and was raised by Charles Martel to the post of referendarius, a position influential in secular as well as in spiritual affairs. In 742 he was made bishop of Metz by Pepin, and became the means of reestablishing the long-interrupted intercourse of his country with Rome. When Stephen II. was hard pressed by the Lombards, Chrodegang received from Pepin in 733 the commission to go to Italy and to accompany the pope to Gaul, which he accomplished successfully; for this he was rewarded by the pope with the dignity of archbishop, the use of the pallium, the privilege of having the cross borne before him, and of consecrating bishops, although Metz was not an archbishopric. His property he gave to the needy, for the founding of church-establishments, particularly of monasteries (among which Gorze and the reestablished Lorsch were notable), and for the beautifying and renovating of churches. In 764 he journeyed to Rome in quest of relics, but his chief claim to be remembered is found in his exertions in behalf of ecclesiastical discipline and morals, which were in a sad plight in the Gallic Church. This task Boniface had in part accomplished. Chrodegang considered that the most proper means of accomplishing this end would be to carry over the discipline and mode of life of the regular clergy into that of the secular clergy. He enforced strictly the rule of Benedict of Nursia, strengthened the work begun by Eusebius of Vercelli, Augustine, and his predecessors among the Franks, and drew up a rule of thirty-four chapters. This was in great part a verbal repetition of Benedict's rule (cf. Hauck, ii. 60), retaining even the term *claustrum* for his new institution, though exchanging *episcopus* and *archidiaconus* for *abbas* and *præpositus*, and *canonici* for *monachi*. The *vita canonica*, the keeping of the *horæ canonicæ*, and so on, are mainly the same, differing however in two places, necessarily so, since the complete identification of the secular clergy with the regulars seemed hardly profitable. These differences were (1) the distinction between major and minor orders, with their interrelations, and (2) the vow of poverty, which was not required of the canonicals. The rule in its first form (cf. Mansi, *Concilia*, xiv. 313–314) is intended only for the cathedral of Metz. Later it was enlarged to eighty-six chapters and has now a more common form, in which it found a place in the *Regula Aquisgranensis*, 817 A.D. That Chrodegang thus helped to diffuse Roman customs through Germany was noted by Paul Warnefried, who tells us also that Chrodegang was bishop of Metz for twenty-three years, five months, and five days. He lies buried in the monastery of Gorze, and his epitaph is to be found in Mabillon, *Vetera Analecta*, Paris, 1723, 377. (E. FRIEDBERG.)

BIBLIOGRAPHY: Sources for a history are in Paulus Warnefridus, *Liber de episcopis Mettensibus*, ed. G. H. Pertz, in *MGH*, *Script.*, ii (1829), 267; the *Epitaphium*, ed. E. Dümmler, in *MGH*, *Poetæ latini ævi Carolini*, i (1881), 108–109; and the *Vita* by John of Gorze, ed. Pertz, in *MGH*, *Script.*, x (1852), 552–572, and in *ASB*, March, i. 352 sqq. (cf. G. H. Pertz, *Ueber die Vita Chrodegangi*, Berlin, 1852). Consult: Rettberg, *KD*, i., §§ 87–88; Hauck, *KD*, ii. 48 sqq.

CHROMATIUS, crō-mê'shius: Bishop of Aquileia from 387 or 389; d. 406 or a little later. He was a highly respected and much revered contemporary of Ambrose, Rufinus, and Jerome, who owed to him many encouragements in scientific endeavors. In the dogmatic controversies of the time he was a bold defender of orthodoxy. The destruction of Arianism in Aquileia was his work. To the emperor Honorius he presented an opinion on Chrysostom, who was suspected at the Byzantine court, and Honorius officially transmitted it to his brother Arcadius. His exegetical writings include a treatise on the Gospel of Matthew, seventeen short writings, and an excellent popular homily on the beatitudes. The best edition of his works is that by P. Braida (Udine, 1816), reprinted in *MPL*, xx. 247–368, where the literature is also given. G. KRÜGER.

CHRONICLES, BOOKS OF.

I. Name.
II. Range and Divisions.
III. Place in the Canon.
IV. The Text.
The Aramaic Targum (§ 1).
The Syriac Translation of the London Polyglot (§ 2).
The Septuagint (§ 3).
The Latin Translation of Jerome (§ 4).
The Masoretic Text (§ 5).
V. Contents and Purpose.
VI. The Author and His Sources.

I. Name: The Hebrew title, *Dibhre hayamim*, of the two historical books standing, in the English Bible, between II Kings and Ezra may be translated "the occurrences of the times"; for the first word expresses the content (history), the second the form (chronological). As this refers to time, the content can be only the sum of deeds or fortunes of men. But this meaningless general title can be but the practical abbreviation of a longer one, which either added the subject referred to (as in I Chron. xxvii. 24, "of King David"), or named a particular period within the whole time. In view of the greater part of the subject-matter, the (lost) explanatory clause could be only "of the Kings of Judah." Indeed, the Syriac gives the name "The Book of the Reign of the Days of the Kings of Judah, which Bears the Name *Sepher D'baryamin*"; the Arabic title is similar; and the Septuagint reads in *Codex Alexandrinus* and elsewhere "Deeds (?) of the Kings of Judah." Strangely enough, the Arabic, after translating the title adds, "the Hebrew is *dibra hayyamim*"; in the Syriac the title is followed by the Hebrew name in the Syriacized form *D'baryamin*. The title "Chronicles" dates back to a comment by Jerome in his "Preface to the Books of Samuel and Kings" (translated in *NPNF*, 2d series, vi. 490).

II. Range and Divisions: The Masoretic notes at the end of Chronicles reckon 1,656 divisions, evidently meaning verses separated by a colon; actual count in the editions of Opitz and Michaelis gives the number as 1,764. Computations based upon smaller "commata" are as follows: the Talmud gives 5,880 (cf. H. L. Strack, *Prolegomena critica in Vetus Testamentum Hebraicum*, Leipsic, 1873, p. 11), the Syriac 5,603, Nicephorus 5,500, codices of the Septuagint and Synopsis (cf. E. Klostermann, *Analekta zu Septuaginta, Hexapla und Patristik*, Leipsic, 1895, pp. 45, 81) 5,000, the Canon Mommsen only 4,140. The division into two books is comparatively modern, unknown to the Masora and the canon-catalogues. Origen (cf. Eusebius, *Hist. eccl.*, VI. xxv. 2), Epiphanius, Synod of Laodicea, Athanasius, and Rufinus state expressly that Chronicles, given by the Septuagint as two books, is to be looked upon as one. The Septuagint divides it after the death of David, a principle adopted by the Syriac and Arabic; the former has, however, another division after II. v. The *codex Amiatinus* of the Vulgate has blank spaces after I. ix. and I. xxix., and writes I. x. 1 and II. i. 1 in red ink, suggestive of early division at those points.

III. Place in the Canon: Tradition has two places for Chronicles among the Kethubhim (see Canon of Scripture, I.). The order followed by the German manuscripts and by the printed Hebrew Bibles is: Ps., Prov., Job, the five Rolls (arranged according to the Jewish church-calendar), Dan., Ezra–Neh., Chron. The position of Chronicles, following Ezra, suggests to the memory the remark of the Mishnah: "Chronicles is given only for investigation"; Daniel and Ezra were edifying to the congregation, whereas Chronicles was rather scholastic in character. More likely, however, is it that Daniel and Ezra–Nehemiah seem to belong together, as on the one hand, a statement of the divine programme and the story of its partial fulfilment, and, on the other hand, as possessing literary kinship, since both belonged to the time of Cyrus, and both were largely transmitted in Aramaic. The Talmudic order is similar: Ruth, Ps., Job, three Rolls, Dan., Esther, Ezra–Neh., Chron. The other arrangement is the totally different one of the Masora: Chron., Ps., Job, Prov., the Rolls, Dan., Ezra–Neh.; as though Chronicles together with Ezra, ranging from Adam to Jaddua, furnished the historical setting for the rest of the Kethubhim (cf. Augustine, *Christian Doctrine*, II. viii. 13, in *NPNF*, 1st series, ii. 541). According to a Masoretic *codex Tschufutc* (13 *'Adath dibburim*, cf. H. Strack, in G. A. Kohut, *Semitic Studies*, London, 1897, p. 570) this order is that of the Land of Israel, and is the only correct one, to be adopted ultimately by all scribes; whereas the other, in which Chronicles or Esther stand at the end, is called a corruption by the people of the Land of Sinear. Among the old translations of the Christian Church is the fanciful order given by Junilius and by Epiphanius. The other transmitted catalogues either join Chronicles to Ezra, to Kings, or separate them. That gives four arrangements: (1) Kings, Chron., Ezra (so Origen, Cyril of Jerusalem, Canon of the Apostles, Apostolic Constitutions, Council of Laodicea, Gregory Nazianzen, Amphilochius, Athanasius in his "Easter Letter," Vulgate, Rufinus, Ethiopic Bible); (2) Kings, Chron., . . . Ezra (Melito, Augustine, *Codex Alexandrinus*, *Codex Amiatinus*, Canon of Hippo, *Decreta Gelasii*, Canon of Mommsen, the *Second Order* of Cassiodorus); (3) Kings, . . . Chron., Ezra (*First Order* of Cassiodorus, Jerome in "Preface to the Books of Samuel and Kings"); (4) Kings, . . . Ezra, Chron. (Rescript of Innocent I.). In general, it seems that where Jewish scholasticism did not influence the Christian Church the latter's arrangement was ruled by the conviction that Ezra–Nehemiah was intended to be the continuation of Chronicles, which latter in its relation to Kings bore in the Septuagint correctly the name "Deeds (?) of the Kings of Judah."

IV. The Text: For the verification of the Masoretic text there are excellent means in the translations from the early Hebrew. The Aramaic Targum is a translation which shows, on the one hand, a close following of the letter of the text and an endeavor to reproduce it correctly; and, on the other hand, an attempt to satisfy the spiritual hunger which mere names and brief statements must create in the hearers

1. The Aramaic Targum.

anxious for edification and entertainment. This could be brought about by etymological interpretation (as in I Chron. viii. 33: "He was called Ner because he lighted the lamp, Hebr. *Ner*, in the synagogue"); or by an interpretation of the text more in harmony with the spiritual vision of later Judaism, to which the war-heroes of old had become doctors of the Law. The zeal of late Judaism for interpretation recognizes no limits; it knows how to harmonize, to combine, to do away with differences and contradictions. The spirit which beguiled the prophets of Ahab is Naboth's (II Chron. xviii. 20); the Syrian archer (II Chron. xviii. 33) is Naaman; Jabez is identified with Othniel (I Chron. iv. 9); Ner's original name is said to have been Abiel (I Chron. viii. 33). On II Chron. xxviii. 3 it comments that Hezekiah's life was saved from the fire by divine intervention. But the Midrash-additions do not hinder in most cases from recognizing the text which lay before the authors of the Targum. Hence it is worth while for the textual critic to consult this earliest translation in restoring the text.

2. The Syriac Translation of the London Polyglot.

A Syriac translation, not found in the Peshito, with a translator other than he who rendered Ezra, is found in the London Polyglot alongside of its Arabic translation. This latter is an excellent help in correcting the many textual mistakes of the Syriac; but where both have the same omission, it is difficult to determine whether the omission is purposed by the translator (as perhaps in I Chron. xxvii., xxvi. 13–32; II Chron. xvi. 12) or whether it is due to a corrupt Syriac text, or to a shorter Hebrew text (II Chron. xxvii. 8, also wanting in *Codex Vaticanus*, cf. II Chron. x. 2). The numerous agreements of the Syriac with the Targum show a thorough acquaintance with Jewish traditional interpretation. While the translator tries to apply the lesson of history to his time, makes blunders on account of his deficiency in historical knowledge, and takes delight now and then in etymological dallying, he supplies few of the Midrashic excursuses so characteristic of the Aramaic. The additions to the text are either helps to a correct understanding (as in II Chron. xviii. 6, xvi. 10), do away with apparent contradictions (so in II Chron. xxi. 6, xxii. 3), are based upon scholastic theories (as in I Chron. viii. 33, 34, 39, 40, ix. 2), or attempt to give to the story a greater definiteness and completeness, using for that purpose not legend but Biblical lore (II Chron. xxi. 11, xxxii. 1, 9, xxxiii. 20; I Chron. vi. 13, xix. 16). The longest addition is found in II Chron. xi. where vv. 4–17 are taken from I Kings xii. and xiv. For the rest, the translator followed very closely his Hebrew copy and was very anxious to give the idiom of the Hebrew, but here the sparseness of tradition as to the meaning of technical expressions led him into many queer errors (as in I Chron. xv. 16, xx. 3, xxix. 19; II Chron. viii. 5, ix. 27, xxx. 3, etc.). Many of his odd mistakes are due to a misreading of the Hebrew text (I Chron. xi. 8[a]; II Chron. xxiv. 4, xxv. 13, 16). But because he permits himself to be influenced by the Hebrew letter his translation deserves to be considered wherever it differs from the Hebrew.

3. The Septuagint.

Of the Greek translations, since remarkably few variants of Aquila, Symmachus, and Theodotion have come down (Field, in his Hexapla, *Origenis Hexaplorum quæ supersunt*, London, 1867, gives also those of Lucian), only the Septuagint requires attention. It is a most important witness, since it has no other object in view than to render the Hebrew text into Greek, which it generally does in such a way that the Greek can with certainty be reconverted into the original. Seldom is there an un-Hebraic sentence (like II Chron. xxxvi. 13). There is abundant proof that Chronicles had a translator different from Kings (cf. A. Klostermann, *Die Bücher Samuelis und der Könige*, Munich, 1887, on II Kings xxiii. 7). Unfortunately, with the mass of names appearing barbaric to the copyists such a confusion has been imported into the genealogical tables that, as Origen and Jerome complain, it is difficult to decide how the original read. Moreover, the many recensions underlying the codices used by Swete differ so much that the exegete, in spite of the many editions of the Septuagint, is still obliged to reconstruct for himself its original readings by comparing the different recensions. In parallel passages that reading is preferable which in the context gives the better sense while differing most from the Hebrew, since the Greek has often been brought by Jews into harmony with the text of their times. Consequently where there is an excess or a deficiency in the text, the one which has it is to be considered nearer the original than the one which agrees more closely with the Hebrew. But it does not follow that the Hebrew should always be corrected by the Septuagint, though it may be that the aberration can be detected through the Greek as due to purpose or mishap on the part of the Hebrew. As already noted, it was the habit of the scribes to search for parallels in other Biblical books, and to write any addition either in the margin or in the text; in such cases, the recension which has the shorter text is to be preferred if the Hebrew text contains the longer text. Again, it may happen that the inferior Septuagint text which has the shorter reading is still to be preferred to the better Septuagint text with the longer reading, if this reading can be shown to have its parallel elsewhere.

4. The Latin Translation of Jerome.

In his preface to Chromatius Jerome asserts that it was his purpose in his Latin translation to correct the many variations in the Septuagint by means of the Hebrew; in the preface to Domnio and Rogatianus he makes evident that he used the old Latin translation of the Septuagint. To be absolutely sure in the use of his Hebrew authority he had the help of a Jewish rabbi of Tiberias, with whom he went over the entire book. In using Jerome's translation one has therefore to bear in mind, in the first place, that his endeavor was to give an intelligent Latin translation, and, secondly, that in spite of his own higher culture and better taste he permitted himself to be influenced by the Jewish interpretations of his teacher. He has the good sense to follow Lucian's Septuagint in I Chron. iv. 22 rather than the Jewish fiction of the Targum. But when, contrary to his custom, he translated in the same verse the proper names Jokim, Kozeba, Joash, and Saraf, his action can be explained only as due to the influence of his Hebrew teacher.

When one tries, with the help of the versions, to solve the many riddles found in the Masoretic text, the latter proves to be a descendant of an older type which has come to its present condition through omissions or additions, misreadings or scribal errors, corrections or interpretations. But even this older type is not the text written by the author. It bears like marks of change, but for want of older witnesses it is less frequently possible to bring proof of the fact. For example, I Chron. i. 11–16, 17ᵇ–23 according to the Septuagint are very likely additions; similarly I Chron. i. 4–10, 30–34ᵃ, 35–54; I Chron. ii. 3ᵇ are transferred from Genesis; I Chron. xi. 10–41ᵇ from II Sam. xxiii. (cf. A. Klostermann, *Geschichte Israels*, Munich, 1896, p. 157). Against such designed augmentation exists another kind due to scribal errors, as when, owing to the identity of I Chron. viii. 28ᵇ and ix. 34ᵇ, the copyist repeats viii. 29–38 in ix. 35–44. It is natural that to such additions correspond omissions, as when a scribe having copied out of the wrong column, noticing his mistake, skips as much of the right as he copied from the wrong. For it is certain I Chron. x. 1 is the continuation of a story which had begun a new book, the beginning of which was lost and thus the story became unintelligible. How much confusion may be created by the omission of a single word may be seen in I Chron. iv. 7–10, where the student is at a loss what to make of *Ḳoẓ* (verse 8) and *Ja'bẹẓ* (verse 9) until he adds with the Targum *weḳoẓ* at the end of verse 7. Similarly the Lucianic codices still retain in I Chron. ix. 18 the two words which were lost in the Hebrew. In these cases the claim of antiquity is with the versions. In other cases the right reading exists alongside of the wrong one, as when in I Chron. vii. 5 one copyist wrote a meaningless word, and another put the correct reading in the margin, whence it found its way again into the text, where both stand to-day. These few examples suffice to show that the original text of Chronicles was written in a more careless orthography than that of the books generally used in the community. For that reason it was misunderstood and misinterpreted by punctuators and translators. In very early times it had already undergone correction and variation, had been extended by interpretations and quotations of parallel passages, and had lost its original form through additions and omissions. The consequence is that it, more than any other Biblical book, needs a thorough revision before it may be used as a witness or its claims denied.

5. The Masoretic Text.

V. Contents and Purpose: To understand these, use must be made of Ezra–Nehemiah, which constitutes the second half of Chronicles. Examination of Ezra i. 1–3ᵃ (=II Chron. xxxvi. 22–23) proves the unity of Chronicles–Ezra–Nehemiah. For the meaning of the repetition is (cf. Nestle, *TSK*, 1879, p. 517) that the author thereby indicates that the story of Chronicles is continued in Ezra–Nehemiah. Just as Ezra–Neh. falls into three sections (cf. A. Klostermann, *Geschichte Israels*, Munich, 1896, pp. 215–216) so with Chronicles, as follows: (1) I Chron. i.–ix., the Book of Genealogies, gives the place of Israel in the Adamic family of nations, a tabular ramification of its tribes, mostly of Judah and the Davidic family, of the Benjamites of Saul's family and of Jerusalem, of Levi and Aaron, and of a few families of Josephites. (2) The second section, I Chron. x.–II Chron. v., ends (as the Syriac correctly surmises) not with the death of David (I Chron. xxix.) but with the dedication of Solomon's temple. It describes how David became Israel's sole king, how he prepared the way for the temple, selected its site in Jerusalem, and collected the means for its construction; how the personnel of its service was organized and how Solomon became the divine means for the accomplishment of David's purpose. (3) The third section, II Chron. vi. to the end, narrates the history of the temple till its destruction, tells of good days and evil, of pious and godless kings, of faithful and neglected temple-service, of obedience and disobedience of prophetic teaching, and ends with the edict of Cyrus. It was evidently the purpose of the historian to bring before the little, politically dependent congregation of the insignificant second temple, which had been built by self-sacrificing religious zeal in obedience to the prophetic word, the ideal of ancient Israel as the adopted congregation of the living God, revealing in its history both a stimulus and a warning.

VI. The Author and His Sources: The Talmud says (*Baba Bathra* i. 14–15), "Ezra wrote his book (Ezra–Nehemiah) and the genealogies in Chronicles." Modern critics conclude from doubtful indications that the author wrote in the beginning of the Greek period and, from his full description of cult and clergy, that he was a priest or a Levite. Certain it is that he wrote at a time when the memorabilia of Ezra and Nehemiah were consulted for the understanding of their time. Of high importance are the questions, what the author accomplished, and how he obtained and handled his material. From the second half of his work (Ezra–Nehemiah), where he contents himself (cf. A. Klostermann, *Geschichte Israels*, pp. 216–217) with giving extracts from the autobiographies of Ezra and Nehemiah and from other official documents, the student may conclude that he used a similar method elsewhere. For I Chron. i.–ix. there was a multitude of genealogies valued the more highly the more the Dispersion and the little colony at home attempted to figure as the continuation of classic Israel. From the Lucian Codex (I Chron. v. 17) one receives the impression that the genealogies existed in the Book of Kings; so in I Chron. ix. 1, according to the Syriac. The same is true of the other two sections. The author knew the Book of Isaiah (II Chron. xxxii. 32), in which at this time stood already chapters xxxvi. and xxxix., also Samuel and Kings (II Chron. xx. 34, xxiv. 7, 23, xxv. 26, etc.), and the hymns of David and his chief musician. To appreciate our author rightly it is important to have a clear conception of this extensive Book of Kings. It is certain that it was finished only in the days of the Restoration, that it treated in the same manner as the canonical Books of Kings the history of both kingdoms. From this one may infer that Chronicles was intended to be a revised, enlarged edition of Kings, for the use and benefit of the new congregation, to pave the way to a theodicy. As the new Israel renewed its life around the new temple and wished to know of the past and of its organization, there were written books about the first years and the last years of David, one about Solomon, one about the Judaic kings, and one about the Israelitic kings. The last three still existed in 560 B.C. Besides these there was a collection of Judaic prophetic narratives. Then grew up the traditional interpretations of the schools, vitalising dead names, and finally the traditions of priests and Levites and important families. While it is true that imagination has here a wide field, and that not all epochs received equally careful attention, nevertheless both author and editor acted in good faith, for the latter only arranged the matter which he extracted from the former, where he employed new material, cited his sources, and his statements could be verified. The picture of the beginning of the cult which the chronicler and his forerunner carried in their soul may be totally different from that of modern critics, but the material which underlies that picture they neither invented nor did they purposely change its meaning. The historical books of the Bible, including Chronicles, were written for the practical need of the community, and the test by which they are to be judged is whether they satisfied it or not. Just here lie the limits of their value to the modern historian who would like to reproduce out of authentic documents a picture of persons and events as the immediate eye-witnesses had it. Like all historical books, even more so, because of its origin, Chronicles demands an able and cautious examination, if one would not sin against the Biblical book, nor against the science of impartial historical investigation. (A. KLOSTERMANN.)

BIBLIOGRAPHY: The best editions of the Hebrew text are by S. Baer and F. Delitzsch, *Liber Chronicorum*, Leipsic, 1888, and by R. Kittel, in *SBOT*, New York, 1895. Critical discussions are by. A. Kuenen, *Historisch-kritisch Onderzoek . . . des ouden Verbonds*, i. 433–520, Leyden, 1887 (very thorough); K. H. Graf, *Die geschichtlichen Bücher des Alten Testaments*, pp. 114–247, Leipsic, 1866 (important); J. Wellhausen, *De gentibus et familiis Judæis quæ in I Chron. ii.–iv. enumerantur*, Göttingen, 1870; idem, *Prolegomena*, pp. 176–237, Berlin, 1883, Eng. transl., pp. 171–227, London, 1885; G. T. Ladd, *Doctrine of Sacred Scripture*, vol. i. passim, New York, 1883; W. E. Barnes, *Religious Standpoint of the Chronicler*, in *American Journal of Semitic Languages*, Oct., 1896; G. B. Gray, *Studies in Hebrew Proper Names*, chap. iii., London, 1896; W. Sanday, *Biblical Inspiration*, ib. 1896; books on Introduction, notably Driver, *Introduction*, chap. xii., and C. H. Cornill, *Einleitung*, pp. 268–276, Freiburg, 1891. Among the best of the commentaries are. C. F. Keil, Leipsic, 1870; S. Oettli, in *Kurzgefasster Kommentar*, Munich, 1889; and W. H. Bennett, in the *Expositor's Bible*, London, 1894. Very thorough discussions are in *EB*, i. 763–772, and *DB*, i. 389–397. The Germ. transl. in Kautzsch's *Die heilige Schrift des Alten Testaments*, pp. 937–1012, Leipsic, 1896, is very useful for its paragraphing and indication of sources of the text.

CHRONICON PASCHALE, cren'i-con pas-cā'le ("Easter Chronicle," also called *Chronicon Alexandrinum*, or *Constantinopolitanum*): A chronological work, probably composed by a cleric who belonged to the entourage of Sergius, patriarch of Constantinople, 610–638. It extended from the creation of Adam to the year 629, but the beginning and end are lost, and, as preserved, it stops in 627. The name "Easter Chronicle" is derived from the computation of the Easter canon, which forms the basis of Christian chronology. The author, except for his own time, confined himself to copying the sources (Eusebius, John Malalas, and others). The so-called Byzantine or Roman era is used for the first time as basis of the chronology. The Chronicon paschale was edited by L. Dindorf in the *Corpus Scriptorum historicorum Byzantinorum* (2 vols., Bonn, 1832), reprinted in *MPG*, xcii. 69–1028.

G. KRÜGER.

BIBLIOGRAPHY: H. Gelzer, *Sextus Julius Africanus und die byzantinische Chronographie*, ii. 1, Leipsic, 1885; K. Krumbacher, *Geschichte der byzantinischen Literatur*, Munich, 1897 (where the literature is given).

CHRONOLOGY. See TIME, RECKONING OF.

CHRYSANTHOS, cri-san'thos, **NOTARAS**, nō-tā'ras: Patriarch of Jerusalem; b. in the second half of the seventeenth century; d. at Jerusalem 1731. He was the nephew of the celebrated Dositheos (q.v.), patriarch of Jerusalem; having completed his studies at Padua and Paris, in the year 1700 he was created bishop of Cæsarea in Palestine by his uncle, whom he succeeded in the patriarchate in the year 1707. He was a man of scientific culture and also a strong, energetic churchman. With force and success he applied himself to church reform in Palestine, by which he made bitter enemies of the Roman Catholics while doing much for his own monasteries. He encouraged theological science, to which he contributed by his own writings, such as the "History and Description of the Holy Land" (Venice, 1728) and "On the Mysteries of the Great Church" (last ed. Venice, 1778). For the Greek Church he did great service through his edition of the "History of the Patriarchs of Jerusalem" by Dositheos. Le Quien in his *Oriens Christianus* has borrowed liberally from Chrysanthos. (PHILIPP MEYER.)

BIBLIOGRAPHY: J. A. Fabricius, *Bibliotheca Græca*, xi. 792, xiii. 479 sqq., 14 vols., Hamburg, 1718–54.

CHRYSOLOGUS, cris"o-lō'gus, **PETRUS**, pē'trus ("Peter the Golden-worded"): Archbishop of Ravenna; b. at Imola (22 m. e.s.e. from Bologna) 406 (?); d. at Ravenna 449 or 450. He was a contemporary of Leo the Great, and stood at the head of the Church at Ravenna at the time when that city was the capital of the Western Empire. As a patron of art he is still remembered (cf. V. Schultze, *Archaeologie der altchristlichen Kunst*, p. 85, Munich, 1895). He is still more famous as an orator: his sermons betray everywhere that they dealt with a select and pampered public, which listened leisurely and "delighted in being startled," and they show a continuous striving for the sensational and the unusual. They are better written than most sermons of those times, bear witness to religious experience and moral earnestness, and at times carry one away with their pathos and the energy of their condensed diction. But finally the sententious unrest, the compression, the avoidance of the simple, and the presence of much that is obscure or grotesque induce tedium in the reader. Yet throughout a great talent is recognizable, and much which would otherwise be repulsive is useful to the historian. In his sermons, gathered by Felix, archbishop of Ravenna (d. Nov. 25, 724), his by-name does not appear; it is found first in Agnellus (chap. 47), and seems to have been given him in order that the Western Church also might have its Chrysostom. What Agnellus knows of his life is taken partly from local tradition; how uncertain this had become in 400 years is proven by the mass of chronological errors and the confusion among the Peters, the bishops of Ravenna. That modern biographers know as much of Chrysologus is due to the fact that they take the Roman Breviary (Dec. 4) as a reliable source. The year of his birth and that of his death are equally uncertain (by Oct. 24, 458, Neo, bishop of Ravenna, appears). He was named Peter by his parents in anticipation of future greatness (cf. *MPL*, lii. 497), but that he was educated in a monastery can not be inferred from sermon 107. Agnellus says that Sixtus III. (432–440) made him bishop contrary to the wishes of Ravenna. It is doubtful whether all the sermons in the edition by Felix are genuine. The title "*s. Joannis episcopi*" which some of them bear in various manuscripts is strange, and may have been due to the copyist's confounding Chrysologus with Chrysostom, and a help to the confusion is the fact that the former used the latter's sermons liberally. Sermon 149 is undoubtedly a translation of the speech of Severianus of Gabala delivered in the year 401 (cf. *MPL*, lii. 599a, with Neander, *Chrysostomus*, ii., 3d edition, Berlin, 1848, p. 114). How much of this absorption of foreign matter into his sermons is due to Chrysologus himself is impossible to determine; but the principal matter is undoubtedly authentic. As a dogmatician, Chrysologus wrestled with the problem of a theodicy (sermon 101); in spite of his letter to Eutyches, he leaned strongly toward Monophysitism, attacked Pelagianism, was dependent upon Augustine (sermons 11 and 30), sympathized with Paulinism (sermons 108–116), "and at the feasts of the Saints preached more of faithful endurance than of works" (sermon 128). In his polemics he never named his adversary, but combated Arians, Pelagians, Nestorians, Novatians, and Manicheans. Sermon 6 was highly prized by the ancients, sermon 35 seems to have been used by Fulgentius, sermons 50, 142, 143 found a place in the Roman Breviary, while sermons 67–72 are valuable for the history of catechetics. In sermon 34 (*MPL*, lii. 299a) Chrysologus combated the conditional immortality of the Stoics from the text I Cor. xv. 52; in sermon 61 he touched upon the same subject, and the conclusion of sermon 62 asserted that the resurrection has the character of eternity because it is accomplished through the eternal Christ, which is better rhetoric than logic.

(F. Arnold.)

Bibliography: The *Sermons*, together with the authoritative life by Agnellus, were published Venice, 1750, reprinted in *MPL*, lii.; German select transl. by M. Held, Kempten, 1874. The life is also in *MGH*, *Script. rer. Langob.*, 1878, pp. 307–375. New material is gathered by F. Liverani, in *Spicilegium Liberianum*, pp. 125–203, Florence, 1863. Consult: H. Dapper, *Der heilige Petrus Chrysologus*, Cologne, 1867; the biographical sketch by Held is in his transl., ut sup.; L. S. Tillemont, *Mémoires . . . ecclésiastiques*, xv. 184–195, 864–867; Ceillier, *Auteurs sacrés*, x. 6–16; J. Fessler, *Institutiones patrologiæ*, ed. B. Jungmann, ii. 2, pp. 240–256, Innsbruck, 1896; *DCB*, i. 517–518; *KL*, ix. 1898–1900.

CHRYSOSTOM, cris'es-tem.

1. Life to 398.

John Chrysostom (*Joannes Chrysostomos*, "John the Golden-mouthed"), patriarch of Constantinople, was born at Antioch, probably c. 345 or 347; d. near Comana, in Pontus, Sept. 14, 407. The name "Chrysostom," borrowed from Dion of Prusa, was given to him soon after his death. He came of a rich patrician family, and his father, Secundus, died soon after his son's birth; the boy was brought up by his mother Anthusa. At twenty he was among the pupils of the rhetorician Libanius at Antioch, and attended the lectures of the philosopher Andragathius. He intended at first to follow the law, but the details of the life displeased him, and he decided to leave the world entirely, finding a companion in his fellow student Basil, of whom nothing more is known. He busied himself now with the Scriptures, and prepared for baptism, which he received three years later from Meletius, bishop of Antioch (c. 368, certainly before 370, in which year Meletius left Antioch). Almost immediately after, he seems to have been ordained as a reader. His teachers in this period were Diodorus of Tarsus and a certain Karterius, of whom nothing more is known; his friends were Maximus, later bishop of Seleucia, and Theodore, bishop of Mopsuestia. He himself tells of the strictness of the ascetic life which he now led in his mother's house. Declining a bishopric about 373, on his mother's death a year or two later he betook himself to a mountain solitude near Antioch, where he spent four years in ascetic exercises with an old Syrian monk, and two more alone in a cave, until need of medical treatment brought him back to Antioch about 380. Probably in the early part of the next year, he was ordained deacon by Meletius, and priest by his successor Flavian at the beginning of 386. In this capacity he labored in Antioch for twelve years, laying the foundations of his fame as a preacher and teacher and distinguishing himself by the holiness of his life.

When Nectarius, the successor of Gregory Nazianzen in the episcopal see of Constantinople, died on Sept. 27, 397, intrigue was busy with the new choice. The weak emperor Arcadius was entirely in the hands of his chamberlain Eutropius, for whom the choice was interesting only as subserving his political plans. Theophilus, patriarch of Alexandria, more diplomat than bishop, endeavored to fill the place with one of his creatures, Isidore by name; but Eutropius, pursuing the policy inaugurated by Theodosius the Great in 381, was not disposed to support the Alexandrian influence in this manner, and gave Theophilus his choice between consenting to the elevation of John or facing serious charges. He chose the former course, and John was consecrated on Feb. 26, 398.

2. Patriarch of Constantinople, 398.

He threw himself with energy into the task of reforming manifold abuses, especially among the clergy. He drove out the "spiritual sisters," with whom many of them were living in a nominally spiritual marriage, and checked the parasitic habits of others who were mere hangers-on to the rich; he cut down the ecclesiastical expenses, and applied the saving to hospitals. Naturally his reforms made enemies for him, but they were powerless as long as the court was on his side. Before long, however, he came into conflict with the all-powerful favorite, whose shameful conduct he fearlessly rebuked; but before Eutropius could avenge himself, he fell from power (399), and was obliged to take refuge in the very church where he had himself violated the right of asylum to others a few years earlier. Chrysostom protected him from the soldiers who rushed in to seize him.

Meantime the number of the devoted prelate's enemies was growing. Among them are named various ecclesiastics who were dissatisfied with his strict rule, and a number of rich and worldly women whose lives he had rebuked. He made fresh enemies at a council held at Ephesus in 400, where he deposed six bishops who had obtained their office by simony. The empress, however, who now held the reins of government, still upheld him, and when a male heir to the throne was born (401), he seems to have officiated at the child's baptism.

3. His Opponents and Controversies.

His position was none the less insecure, as was shown in the course of his conflict with Severianus (q.v.) of Gabala who had gained a footing in Constantinople and was pushing his ambitious plans there. Chrysostom forbade him to preach; Severianus yielded and retired to Chalcedon, but Eudocia forced Chrysostom to recall him. A more dangerous foe was Theophilus of Alexandria, who had by no means given up his designs for the aggrandizement of his see. He found a new occasion to press his claim that the bishopric of Constantinople belonged to his patriarchal jurisdiction. In the Origenistic controversy which then agitated the Egyptian Church, Theophilus found many of the monks of the desert recalcitrant and unwilling to give up their beloved teacher Origen. Four among them of special influence, the "long brothers" Dioscorus, Ammonius, Eusebius, and Euthymius, were banished by Theophilus, and went first to Palestine; pursued thither by the enmity of Theophilus, they went on to Constantinople. Chrysostom behaved guardedly and sought to effect a reconciliation. Theophilus at first did not answer, and then adopted a haughty tone. When it appeared that Eudocia took the side of the monks, he bent all his energies to their destruction and that of Chrysostom, who, he thought, stood behind them. He did not go himself to Constantinople, but sent Epiphanius of Salamis, whose narrow zeal was easily enlisted, to carry on the campaign against the alleged Origenism of Chrysostom. Epiphanius departed in ill humor without accomplishing anything, and died on the way home.

Chrysostom now ruined himself with the empress by preaching vehemently against the luxury of women's dress, in a way which she and others thought was aimed directly at her. Theophilus came to Constantinople at her summons, and found the train laid. He had assembled the bishops on whom he could count in a church in a suburb of Chalcedon, on the imperial estate called "The Oak" (whence the gathering is known by the Latin name, *Synodus ad Quercum*), in the autumn of 403, and began his synod when all was ready. There were thirty-six present, of whom twenty-nine were from Egypt (Photius, who has preserved a part of their proceedings, says forty-five, but perhaps some signed afterward).

4. The Synod ad Quercum.

The charges brought against Chrysostom, by some of his own clergy, were for the most part of no importance, and showed nothing but the enmity of the accusers. Yet he felt, as he sat with forty friendly bishops in his palace in Constantinople, that the situation was a very dangerous one. Summoned to appear before the hostile synod, he made the condition that those who had expressed their intention to destroy him—Theophilus, Acacius, Severianus, and Antiochus—should be excluded. Meantime application had been made to the emperor to compel his attendance in case of hesitation; when he still delayed, he was condemned in his absence and deprived of his bishopric. The emperor was notified and requested to enforce the sentence. Although it was obviously illegal, Chrysostom yielded to force and, when the emperor had confirmed the deposition, went into exile at Prænetus (or Pronectus), in Bithynia (28 m. n.w. of Nicæa), after he had sought to calm the excited people in a wonderful sermon. The next night something alarming happened in the imperial palace—Theodoret speaks of an earthquake, but neither Socrates nor Sozomen give this—and it was put down to his banishment. The temper of the people, too, was threatening. Theophilus thought it best to depart in haste, and a few days later an imperial messenger was sent to recall Chrysostom.

The peace, however, was not of long duration. Two months later the strife broke out afresh, on a fresh affront to the empress's vanity. The prefect Simplicius had erected a silver statue of her on the south side of the great church, which was dedicated with loud rejoicings; and Chrysostom complained, in a sermon, of noisy popular festivities which disturbed the devotions of the faithful. Again he was accused of intending to insult the empress, and once more she set herself to effect his downfall. A synod assembled in Constantinople, instructed by the absent Theophilus, and the pliant bishops, with but few exceptions, followed the imperial will. The method to be employed gave rise to lengthy discussions, until shortly before Easter, 404, the emperor ordered Chrysostom to leave his church since he had been condemned by two synods. The bishop said he would yield only to force; and force was employed on Thursday in Holy Week, the adherents of Chrysostom being driven out of the church by a violent onslaught. He himself remained in the suburbs, strengthening his party, until on June 10 his enemies moved the emperor to further measures, and on the 20th, after an affecting farewell, he took ship for Asia Minor, the country indicated for his banishment. The same night a fire broke out in the cathedral church, for which his adherents were blamed, and they were severely repressed. A feeble old man named Arsacius, the brother of his predecessor, was put in his place on June 26.

5. Chrysostom Banished.

But while Chrysostom was on his way to Cucusus in Armenia, his friends were not idle. Four bishops went to Rome with a letter from him, to move Innocent I. in his favor. The acts of the synod which had first condemned Chrysostom were sent to Innocent shortly after by the opposite party, and he saw that the sentence had been illegal. He wrote to Theophilus that the affair should be brought up before a general council, and exhorted Chrysostom and his adherents to steadfastness. Honorius, the Western emperor and brother of Arcadius, also wrote to the latter in favor of the banished bishop, but without success. The outcome was a breach of communion between Old and New Rome. After the death of Arsacius (Nov. 11, 405), Atticus became bishop in the following spring, and persecuted the "Johannites" with renewed severity. Chrysostom himself was ordered transferred from Cucusus to Pityus, a still more desolate place; but the hardships of the journey were too much for him, and he died near Comana, the modern Tokat, in Sivas, Asia Minor. Thirty years later his remains were solemnly translated to Constantinople and buried with honor in the church of the Apostles, Theodosius II. thus atoning for the deeds of his parents.

The writings of Chrysostom may be divided, according to his biographer Palladius, into "homilies, treatises, and letters." The list known as the *Catalogus Augustanus* (from a lost Augsburg MS.) numbers 102 separate titles, including none which is not genuine. His sermons cover practically the whole Bible, including, for example, seventy-six on Genesis, ninety on Matthew, eighty-eight on John, fifty-five on Acts, and 242 on the Pauline epistles, without counting those on Galatians, which are preserved only in the form of a connected commentary worked up from the sermons.

6. Writings. There are also discourses for all the principal festivals, and a large number on various saints, of which the most notable are the seven on Paul. The "treatises" are partly apologetic and partly practical, the latter being the more numerous. The earliest we have are two letters to Theodore, afterward bishop of Mopsuestia, who, on account of a love-affair, was thinking of returning to the world. To justify his declination of a bishopric, about 373, he addressed to his friend Basil the six books "On the Priesthood"; according to Socrates, the composition of this work falls in the period after his ordination as deacon, i.e., after 381. To this period probably belong also the two books "On Penance," and the three against the enemies of the monastic life. The superiority of the single life is dealt with in a work on virginity, written about 380, and two smaller works of about the same period, "To a Young Widow" and "Against a Second Marriage." With these may be classed the two pastoral letters of his early Constantinople days, directed against the abuses in clerical life already referred to. His letters, about 245 in number, are almost all from the period of his second exile, and give an interesting picture of his life and his cares. Of works improperly attributed to him there is no lack. The liturgy bearing his name is not his, though its relation to that of Antioch deserves a closer investigation than it has yet received—as does the "Synopsis of the Old and New Testaments." The "Incomplete Work on Matthew," consisting of fifty-four sermons, is a Latin original composed by an Arian toward the end of the sixth century.

The significance of Chrysostom's work does not lie in the domain of scientific theology, on the development of which he had but little influence. He was preeminently a practical man, and it was through practical teaching that he left his mark. A disciple of the school of Antioch (q.v.), he displayed throughout his life the characteristics of that school. The pupil of Diodorus of Tarsus is easily to be recognized in his sober exegesis, occupied with determining the literal sense of his text. Constantly bearing in mind the needs of his flock, he naturally did not carry the exegetical principles of his school to the extreme which is found in the commentaries of Theodore of Mopsuestia; but he was a master of the art of developing practical truths for every-day life from the Scripture. Thus his sermons surpass Origen's in practical value as far as they are inferior to them in speculative insight. His was not, in any case, a systematic mind; the logical development of dogma from point to point he left to others. Where the Church had decided, the question was settled for him. He took his stand on the Nicene theology, and was ready to defend it against all comers. In order fully to understand and respect this position, one must remember the difficulties in which the church teachers of Antioch were placed—how they had to contend not only against pagans and Jews, but against Christian sects of every description, the various kinds of Gnostics, Novatians, Arians, Manicheans, and many others.

7. His Significance and Doctrine. In his anthropology and soteriology Chrysostom faithfully represents the teaching of Diodorus. Man, consisting of body and soul, is disposed both to good and to evil, and thus there is no room for Manichean dualism. For the development of the first man, as he was created perfect and immortal by God, the possession of free will proved fatal. Not knowing how to use his freedom, man rebelled against God and brought on himself all the corruption of mortality. Thus sin spread from our first parents to the whole race. He expressly controverts the view, however, that sin is an integral part of our nature. Then death followed as a consequence of sin. From this position man attains the good by means of his free will, which can turn away from evil; but this is only possible by means of divine grace. Yet the operation of grace does not impair our free will; our own decision must come first, and then God begins to do his part. That the East took so little interest in the controversy about grace is due largely to the position assumed by the school of Antioch and especially by Chrysostom. His ascetic inclination is shown not only in his early writings, but in many passages of his sermons. His Eucharistic doctrine is specially noteworthy; he asserts emphatically the identity of the bread and wine with the body and blood of Christ, going so far as to say that Christ drank of his own blood at the Institution. The change is caused by the words of institution repeated by the priest; their operation is analogous to that of the words of creation spoken by God. The consequence of this view for his conception of his office is obvious, and in this point his influence on succeeding ages is important. It should be added that he never had an opportunity to develop his thoughts carefully; they were uttered in sermons of which only a small part probably was prepared beforehand, and perhaps received no very thorough revision after they had been taken down in shorthand. What made his preaching so powerful was not only the native rhetorical force which he undoubtedly possessed, but his skill in illuminating the questions of daily life from the Scriptures, in guiding men in their path through the world. He could venture to preach in his own way, "and not as the scribes." He boldly rebuked the rich, to such an extent that he was sometimes blamed for it, and no fear of the displeasure of the powerful ever restrained him from declaring the truth of God. (Erwin Preuschen.)

Bibliography: The *Opera* were published in 13 vols., Paris, 1718–38, and Venice, 1734–41. Selections are translated in *NPNF*, 1. ser., vols. ix.–xiv. The best account of the life and activities is in L. S. Tillemont, *Mémoires . . . ecclésiastiques*, xi. 1–405, 547–626, Paris, 1706. In English the best single work is W. R. W. Stephens, *St. Chrysostom, his Life and Times*, London, 1883. On the life consult further: A. Neander, *Der heilige Chrysostomus*, 2 vols., Berlin, 1848, Eng. transl., London, 1845; E. Martin, *S. Jean Chrysostome*, 3 vols., Montpellier, 1860; R. W. Bush, *Life and Times of Chrysostom*, London, 1885; F. H. Chase, *Chrysostom, a Study in the Hist. of Interpretation*, Cambridge, 1887; A. Puech, *S. Jean Chrysostome*, Paris, 1891; Schaff, *Christian Church*, iii. 933–941 et passim; idem, *St. Chrysostom and St. Augustine*, New York. 1891; *DCB*, i. 518–535; J. H. Willey, *Chrysostom the Orator*, Cincinnati, 1906. On special subjects connected with Chrysostom consult: F. Ludwig, *Johannes Chrysostomus in seinem Verhältnis zum byzantinischen Hof*, Braunsberg, 1883; C. Molines, *Chrysostome orateur*, Montauban, 1886; L. Ackermann, *Die Beredsamkeit des . . . Johannes Chrysostomus*, Würsburg, 1889; S. Haidacher, *Die Lehre des . . . Johannes Chrysostomus über die Schriftinspiration*, Salzburg, 1897; G. Marchal, *St. Jean Chrysostome*, Paris, 1898.

CHUBB, THOMAS: English Deist; b. at East Harnham, near Salisbury, Sept. 29, 1679; d. in Salisbury Feb. 8, 1747. He was a tallow-chandler's assistant all his life, and had only a most elementary education. After Whiston published his *Primitive Christianity Revived* (1710) Chubb wrote for his own amusement a defense of the idea of the supremacy of the One God and Father expressed in the preface; the manuscript was shown to Whiston, who corrected it and had it published under the title *The Supremacy of the Father Asserted* (London, 1715). This brought Chubb into notice, he obtained patrons, and wrote many tracts which were much read and talked about, and Jonathan Edwards noticed and criticized his doctrine of free will; lack of knowledge and training, however, impair the value of his work. His principal writings were *A Discourse concerning Reason* (London, 1731), in which he undertook to show that reason is a sufficient guide in matters of religion; *The True Gospel of Jesus Christ Vindicated* (1739), in which he advocates the pregnant idea that Christianity is not doctrine, but life; and *The Author's Farewell to his Readers*, published in *Posthumous Works* (2 vols., 1748), which is the most complete summary of his opinions. He denied special providence, miracles, literal inspiration, and apparently the resurrection of Jesus. He was a man of exemplary life, attended church faithfully, and considered himself a Christian. See Deism, I., § 6.

Bibliography: L. Stephen, *Hist. of English Thought in the 18th Century*, i. 163, London, 1880; J. Cairns, *Unbelief in the 18th Century*, ib. 1881; *DNB*, x. 297–298.

CHUR, BISHOPRIC OF: A bishopric named from the capital of the Swiss canton of Grisons. The valley of the upper Rhine was incorporated with the Roman Empire in 15 B.C., after the subjection of the Rhætii. Communication with Italy was provided by two great roads, one over the Septimer, the other over the Splügen. Where the Rhine bends to the north, a *castellum* was erected for their defense, and this was the origin of the town of Chur. When Christianity penetrated this region is uncertain. The oldest information shows a Christian community already fully organized. In 452 Bishop Abundantius of Como signs the decrees of a Milanese synod for himself and for the bishop of Chur, who is absent. The only notice going further back is the fantastic legend of the British king Lucius (see Eleutherus), who is said to have labored as a missionary under Marcus Aurelius, at first in Germany and finally in the vicinity of Chur; but this is mere legend, though relics of a certain Lucius are mentioned in a petition of Victor II. of Chur to Louis the Pious in 822. The Roman bishopric of Chur seems never to have gone out of existence; its continuance in the sixth century is attested by an inscription (of later date, it is true) in the monastery of St. Lucius, commemorating Bishop Valentinian, who died in 548; and in the seventh by the signature of Bishop Victor at the Council of Paris, 614. This is explicable by the fact that the Roman population was never exterminated. The Alamanni settled in eastern Switzerland, but Theodoric maintained peaceful relations with them, and the old institutions were not disturbed. The connection with Milan still continued in 842, but was dissolved not long afterward, and Chur was incorporated with the ecclesiastical province of Mainz. In the Frankish period the diocese was practically coterminous with the present canton of Grisons. Under Louis the Pious the diocese had more than 230 churches. The principal monasteries were Disentis, first mentioned in 736, and Pfeffers, founded about 731. The diocese was maintained through the Reformation changes, though most of its inhabitants became Protestants. At present its jurisdiction embraces the Roman Catholics in the cantons of Grisons, Zurich, Glarus, Schwyz, Uri, and the principality of Liechtenstein. (A. Hauck.)

Bibliography: T. von Mohr, *Codex Diplomaticus, Sammlung der Urkunden zur Geschichte Cur-Rätiens*, 3 vols., Chur, 1848–61; Rettberg, *KD*, i. 216, ii. 132; P. C. Planta, *Das alte Rätien*, Berlin, 1872.

CHURCH ARMY: An organization of laity inside the Church of England for aggressive mission efforts, founded by Rev. Wilson Carlile (q.v.) in 1882. It is the resultant of four similar movements started simultaneously and independently at Kensington, London, by Mr. Carlile ("The Church Militant Mission"), at Richmond, London, by Rev. Evan Hopkins ("The Church Gospel Army"), at Oxford by Rev. Francis Scott Webster ("The Church Salvation Army"), and at Bristol by Rev. Charles Isaac Atherton, canon of Exeter ("The Church Mission Army"). The present headquarters are at 55 Bryanston Street, Marble Arch, London, W. In 1883 the first army organ, *The Battleaxe*, was begun, and the first army training home was opened at Oxford, which in 1885 was moved to London. In 1885 the first conference of officers and workers was held, at which the report was made that whereas in Jan., 1884, the Army had only fifteen lay officers, then it had forty-five, and that its income was £2,500 in regular subscriptions and £4,000 in working people's pence. The Church Army Blue Book for 1906 shows that at the end of 1905 the Army had 318 evangelistic officers, eighty-four men's labor home managers and assistants, forty-six associate evangelists, 285 mission-nurses, and twenty-three associate mission-nurses.

The great object of the Army is to reach the unchurched and submerged masses with all agencies which tend to uplift soul and body. It differs from some similar movements in that it works inside the Anglican Church. It never begins operations in a parish without being invited by the vicar, works under his direction, and stays as long as he thinks it desirable. Its converts, therefore, help to increase the number and efficiency of the church agencies. At first there was prejudice against its name and its utterly unconventional methods for gathering a crowd, its out-of-door preaching and testifying, and to its employment of laity, both men and women, generally of very little or no culture and often of past lives of vice and crime, to speak on Christian themes and win new hearers and professed Christians to a deeper religious experience. There was also considerable disorderly conduct on the part of its audiences. But now the Army is accepted both by the Church, whose errant children it recalls, and by the classes benefited as an accredited helper and friend. It has now much to do with the body, having "labor homes, work test shelters, labor relief depots for men, women, and youths who are unemployed, criminal, inebriate, unfortunate, outcast; coffee taverns, lodging homes, boarding homes, employment agencies, fresh air homes, old clothes department; test farms for emigrants and others"; and undertakes to send emigrants to Canada. But spiritual work, after all, commands the first place, and "the Church Army works in town and country parishes by trained evangelists and mission-nurses working under the clergy; in country places by vans continually itinerating; in crowded slums by pioneer tent evangelists; in workhouses and reformatories by special missions; in convict establishments and local prisons by special services, personal interviews, and aid to discharged prisoners." Its lay workers are largely recruited from the working class, but they are carefully trained and under strict discipline. The Church Army is a limited liability company; each member of the executive is responsible up to £100, and each patron or president up to ten shillings, in the event of the winding up of the Society.

Bibliography: E. Rowan, *Wilson Carlile and the Church Army*, London, 1905; *The Church Army Blue Book* (annual).

CHURCH BUILDING, TAXATION FOR: Originally (see Taxation, Ecclesiastical) all the property of each diocese was vested in the bishop, who had, accordingly, to provide for all necessities, including church-building. The Roman decrees of Simplicius (475) and Gelasius (494) prescribe a division of this property into four parts, one to serve for the *Fabrica ecclesiæ* (q.v.), i.e., both building and the maintenance of public worship. Similarly, in Spain one-third was set apart for this purpose (Synod of Tarragona, 516). A different principle came up in the Teutonic law, by which, since the church in a sense belonged to the landowner, he was required to provide for keeping it—unless, indeed, he chose to let it fall into decay. The church authorities strove against this conception; e.g., the Synod of Frankfort (794) conceded this kind of ownership only on condition that the church should not be allowed to fall into decay. Nevertheless, the later ecclesiastical principles are really founded on Frankish law. After the development of the system of benefices (see Benefice), the holders of benefices were required to contribute for this purpose from what they had over their necessary living (*congrua*). And in case of necessity the parishioners were obliged, as had been the case in the Frankish law, to bear their part of the burden. There is evidence that this provision was sometimes enforced in the Middle Ages, though the wealth of the Church and the generosity of benefactors made it seldom necessary. There was great local diversity in the laws on this whole subject; and the Council of Trent, which settled the standard of modern Roman Catholic practise, failed to unify them, leaving plenty of room for local traditional customs and laws. According to its decree (Sess. xxi. 7, *de reformatione*), a distinction is made between patronal and other churches. In the case of the latter, the burden falls primarily on the building-fund, though usually the capital is not to be touched, nor even the income entirely exhausted. Appeal is rather to be made to the classes who are bound to contribute by local law or custom; to all who receive income from the church, the holders of the benefice and tithes in particular, in a proportion to be judicially determined; if there are not enough of these, to the parishioners, including non-resident landowners, in case the tax is real and not personal —and only in this last case is the exaction independent of the taxpayer's personal belief. In patronal churches the patron is included among those who share this obligation; but only (by the present interpretation) when he receives a portion of the "fruits" of the benefice. In cathedrals the burden rests first on the building-fund, if there is one; if not, upon the bishop and chapter, then upon the cathedral clergy, and finally upon the diocesan clergy. In some places, as in Prussia, a certain percentage of the fees in each church is levied for the support of the cathedral. In the Protestant churches of Germany, the obligation comes primarily upon the building-fund and next upon the congregation, and is frequently a land-tax.

(E. Friedberg.)

CHURCH CHEST (Ger. *Kirchenkasten*, Lat. *Arca ecclesiæ*): Properly a receptacle for church funds, but applied also to the funds themselves. Then it signifies the portion of the revenues appropriated for the expenses of divine service and for the maintenance of the church building (see Fabrica Ecclesiæ). In a narrower sense it is a box (Lat. *truncus*, Fr. *tronc*) put in a church to receive offerings of money, which seems to have originated in connection with the Crusades. Innocent III. (1198–1216) ordered that one should be put in every church, and, in spite of opposition and mocking jibes, the custom persisted.

CHURCH, THE CHRISTIAN.

I. Meaning and Use of the Word: The word "church" (from Greek *kyriakon*, "the Lord's," i.e., "house" or "body") meant in original Christian usage either the universal body of Christian believers or a local congregation of believers. In the Romance languages the idea is expressed by a word from another root (Fr. *église*, Ital. *chiesa*, from Greek *ekklēsia* "the [body] called together" or "called out"). The Old Testament had two words to express the idea, *'edhah* and *ḳahal* (Lev. iv. 13, 14), both meaning "assembly," the latter implying a distinctly religious object. In modern usage the term is employed to denote also the building in which a body of Christians meets for worship. An extension has taken place in recognized usage in accordance with which men speak of the Buddhist or the Jewish Church, meaning the whole body of believers in Buddhist or Jewish teaching.

II. The Church in the New Testament: It has been disputed whether Jesus intended to found a church, i.e., a particular, organized association of his disciples, differing specifically from the existing national unity of Israel. He proclaimed the nearness of the kingdom of God, and then announced that it was already present. His discourses dealt with this kingdom, with the conditions for membership in it, and with the blessings to be enjoyed within it. The question is whether there is a connection between the foundation of such an organized body of believers as has been mentioned and the heavenly kingdom which is to be set up in the world by divine power. The statements and parables in the Gospels do not, with the exception of Matt. xvi. 18, 19, bear on this question. In the parables, for example, of the sower, of the wheat and the tares, of the net, there is no word of any binding connection among those who enter the kingdom. In that of the leaven there is indeed the idea of the spread of the kingdom as a body with an objective unity; but we are not told how or to what extent an organic form is destined for it, nor how far it is to be distinguished from the organic association of Israel.

1. The Intentions of Jesus.

But in truth the disciples were actually, by the very fact of their adherence to Jesus, connected with each other. They formed the flock of the Good Shepherd (Luke xii. 32; John x. 1–16). They were associated by the fact that they and they alone were the children of the kingdom which had already made its appearance in the world. The opposition and hatred which they, as well as their Master, were to find on the part of the Jewish people and the world plainly made it necessary that they should exhibit an external unity, and herein dissociate themselves from their former fellows in nationality and religion.

There is thus nothing surprising in the fact that Jesus speaks in two places of a community of his own which he is to found; it is surprising only that there are no more definite or detailed statements on the subject. It is significant that the first time that he spoke of this was when he had just received the first clear, divinely inspired confession of faith in him, and when he was beginning to prepare his disciples for his death. In that place (Matt. xvi.

18) he spoke of that community in a general way; but in the other (Matt. xviii. 17 sqq.) he referred more definitely to the association of his followers as met together to deal with events and needs affecting their inner life. According to the former passage, he intended to build his church upon the rock Peter, who just before had taken the lead among the disciples with his confession. The word and its historical fulfilment must be construed by the context. It will not do to interpret the rock as faith in Christ. Peter is not the foundation in the sense in which Christ applies the term to himself (Matt. xxi. 42). But the church was originally built, as the Acts testify, upon the preaching and work of this "rock-man," though other apostles were joined with him (Eph. ii. 20; Rev. xxi. 14; Gal. ii. 9). Whether the promise in regard to the foundation had anything to do with a continuous government of the church, or with a line of successors to Peter, is one of the fundamental points of controversy between Protestants and Roman Catholics.

2. The Rock Apostle.

The twelve apostles were indeed designated for a position of prominence in the future organization by the status which they acquired in relation to Jesus during his earthly ministry, as witnesses of his deeds and the bearers of his words (John xv. 27; Acts i. 21, 22). But no definite difference in authority was provided between them and other disciples; and their work seems to consist not in the internal direction of the churches, but rather, as soon as these were once established, in further dissemination of the message. Christ spoke of sending "prophets and wise men and scribes" to give this message (Matt. xxiii. 34); but nowhere did he sum up such activities as are thus indicated into the terms of a fixed and limited office, or prescribe the manner in which any persons were to be appointed to discharge them. The names here used recall the pre-Christian dispensation, when such limits and external ordinances did not exist. To the preaching of the gospel of the kingdom and the cultivation of a religious and moral life in the power of that gospel, baptism (q.v.) was added by Christ's own ordinance, as would be known even without the gospel record by the way in which the rite at once took its place and in which it is spoken of by Paul as an essential element of Christianity. The act of baptism in itself had, as the baptism of John shows, no necessary connection with entrance into an organized society; but as soon as there was a society of Christians, it undoubtedly belonged to that. Finally, the Lord's Supper (q.v.), as he had instituted it for his disciples, was celebrated by them as a main element in their corporate edification. Evidently, therefore, the foundations already discussed were laid not only for a wider extension of the kingdom of God and for the development of the new life in its individual members, but for a corporate connection between them. Yet so far no reason has appeared for the negation of a theory upon which the new Christian community, spreading throughout Palestine and thence among the heathen, might still live under the external institutions of the old covenant, until the great revelation of the kingdom which was expected at the return of its Lord. The working out of the truth expressed in the saying about putting new wine into old bottles was left to the increasing knowledge of the disciples, as conditioned by their wider experience.

3. Relations of the Twelve.

The existence and development of the church is inextricably interwoven with the realization of the kingdom of God in the world. It would be wrong to press such differences as appear between the two conceptions as though the kingdom were the inner or ideal, and the church the external or real. The kingdom has a real existence in its subjects and their actual relations; it accomplishes its destiny by means of the external preaching of the word, and announces itself by external fruits. The church, on the other hand, although like other associations of men it is an external union, is what it is only by virtue of its inner connection with Christ, who remains in the midst of it. There is nothing of an external nature which (if the words of Jesus are the only criterion) is necessary to the existence of the church which does not also belong to the realization of the kingdom. It is commonly said that the church was definitely founded with the descent of the Holy Ghost on the day of Pentecost, and in fact it did on that day enter upon its career with full powers. But it must not be forgotten that the gathering was composed of the disciples who had already formed a coherent body in the name of Christ; to whom he had already said "Receive ye the Holy Ghost" (John xx. 22); and from whose number, by a corporate act, the number of the apostles had been filled out after the fall of Judas. It had thus already been living and working, at first as an association within the larger one of Israel, though with its own meetings for worship and its own officers. The name *ekklēsia* was undoubtedly applied to it very early, before the beginning of Paul's ministry, since he uses it as the universally current title for both Jewish and Gentile associations. It is commonly applied to the separate local bodies of which he spoke, but he used it in the same way for the whole body of Christians whenever he had occasion to mention it, in the older epistles (Gal. i. 13; I Cor. x. 32, xii. 28, xv. 9) as well as in that to the Ephesians, which some have tried to separate in this particular from the others; and it is so used in Acts ix. 31.

4. The Kingdom and the Church.

Whether general or local, the church consisted of those who were "sanctified in Christ Jesus" (I Cor. i. 2) or "called to be saints" (Rom. i. 7), with a possible allusion to the etymological connection between *klētoi*, "called," and *ekklēsia*. Paul's conception was characterized by a deep sense of the unity constituted by the possession of "one Lord, one faith, one baptism" (Eph. iv. 5); and elsewhere the entrance into this united fellowship, both with Christ and with each other, was attached to baptism (Gal. iii. 27; I Cor. xii. 13). If the question is asked whether the church as an

5. Membership of the Church.

institution stands outside and above those who compose it, or simply consists of them, the answer must be that in the apostolic use of the word it is regarded as having its existence wholly in those who are called, not as though it had come to them from without but as though they were, by their calling and reception of the message of salvation and baptism, united with each other and with Christ into one body. Paul indeed spoke once of a "Jerusalem which is above" (Gal. iv. 26) as the mother of Christians, and therefore as preexistent; but this is not the same thing as the earthly church. He had in mind a common Jewish and apostolic conception, difficult now to realize, of a reality preexistent in heaven which was the prototype of the Old Testament theocracy, which had for its offspring the members of the church on earth, who were born from above, which, finally, was one day to descend in its completeness when the full revelation of the kingdom takes place (Heb. xii. 22; Phil. iii. 20; Rev. xxi. 2). The name "church" was applied solely to the earthly fellowship, not to the company of the departed saints (as in the later conception of "church triumphant")—though in a sense to them, as to the heavenly Jerusalem, the faithful on earth "are come" already. The various vital functions and activities of the church relate to mutual edification in God, whose word is to "dwell in them richly" (Col. iii. 16); to the promotion of the moral and religious life in the individual members by loving admonition, encouragement, and care. All the members of the church were regarded as having (just as under the old covenant, Ex. xix. 6) a priestly position before God (I Pet. ii. 5, 9; Rev. i. 6, v. 10); they were to offer to him themselves, their bodies, their acts of praise, thanksgiving, and brotherly love as a sacrifice (Rom. xii. 1; Heb. xiii. 15, 16). Each member had his own part in the common work of edification; but the special gifts which enable him to perform it varied (see CHARISMATA).

This leads to the question of offices in the apostolic church. The word *diakoniai*, "ministries," in I Cor. xii. 5, denotes special functions incumbent upon definite members of the body in the service of the whole. While the word "office" is generally applied more strictly to functions committed to a particular man, whether by church or state, the New Testament has no word for offices in this sense. The functions coming under this head would naturally cover the external direction of the church, in so far as this required definite institutions and formally appointed and recognized officers. So the elders, or *episcopoi*, stood at the head of the churches, and deacons were charged with the care of material needs and especially of the poor. Formal appointments or election and formal installation occurred; but the New Testament nowhere gives a law prescribing this course. The needs of the church determined the arrangement. Thus the apostles, originally appointed by Christ to the headship of all his disciples, were obliged to abandon first the detailed care of the poor, and then, under the pressure of their wider tasks and frequent absence from Jerusalem, the regular direction of the internal affairs of the church there. Besides the offices mentioned, prophecy was allowed to work freely under the impulse of the Holy Spirit. For the exercise of the function of teaching or admonition, the possession of the necessary *charisma* was held to suffice. The elders naturally took a prominent part in the instruction and exhortation that found place in the gatherings (I Tim. iii. 2, v. 17), but participation in it was by no means confined to them. The office of the apostles was unique, resting upon its special institution by the Lord, concerned with the establishment of his kingdom and the original spread of the Gospel, and thus incapable of transmission to others.

6. Church Offices Determined by Church Needs.

There was a notable difference between the churches of Jewish and those of Gentile origin, the former desiring to give the latter only such a position in the church of God as the proselytes of the gate held under the old dispensation, while Paul, on the contrary, regarded both classes alike as saints and members of the body of Christ. The association of the various local communities into one church was not expressed by any formal constitution, but by the free communion of fraternal love. At the close of the apostolic period, the epistles of John, while insisting strongly on the necessity of this loving union, laid down no rules governing external unity and said nothing of ecclesiastical forms. Nor is there any warrant [according to the views of some modern scholars] for seeing in the "angel" of Rev. ii., iii. the early stage of an episcopal office; they are not the heads and rulers of the seven churches, but rather represent in each case the characteristic spirit of the particular church. See ORGANIZATION OF THE EARLY CHURCH.

III. The Church in Traditional Christianity.— 1. In Primitive Catholicism: Out of the *ekklēsia* of the apostles, and principally on the territory covered by Jewish Christianity, grew up a post-apostolic development which is called the Catholic Church. From the Evangelical standpoint we can but recognize in its conception of the way of salvation and the nature of the church a notable declension from the original principles, which continued progressively down to the Reformation. Christianity maintained itself, indeed, as an organic whole against the assaults of persecution on one side and heresy on the other; it set up as a permanent standard for its religious belief the New Testament writings admitted to be apostolic, together with the canon of the Old Testament; and it undertook on the basis of these to formulate a summary of the common faith in its Rule of Faith (q.v.). But even in the subapostolic period there is evident a general weakening of the original spirit, a lack of vital comprehension of the plan of salvation as at first revealed, and a tendency toward a legalistic conception and regulation of Christian life, as well as to a conception of the church which found its essence in external ordinances. And these ordinances, especially as pertaining to the government of the church and the priesthood, continued to develop until they ended in what is known as Roman Catholic Christianity. The

1. Tendency toward Legalism.

explanation of this early development is not to be found, as the Tübingen school attempted to show, in a fusion of Jewish and Pauline Christianity. It is rather to be sought in the fact that with the decay of the apostolic spirit and the wide expansion of Christianity the forces prevalent among men before Christ's coming, which had been for a while held in check, resumed their sway as primitive fervor decayed. The postapostolic church needed, in view of its position in the world, a more definite external organization; it is in the meaning and form given to this that a perversion of primitive Christianity is discerned. In the first stage of this development there was a diversity of tendencies in regard to the doctrine concerning the church. Clement of Rome, admonishing the Corinthians to unity and subjection to those who are over them, drew a parallel between the organization of the ruling office in the church (i.e., of an episcopate as yet identical with the presbytery) and the divinely appointed ordinances of the old law; between the gifts which the presbyters brought to God in prayer and the sacrifices of the Jewish priests. Somewhat later, however, a free prophetic voice was heard in the Shepherd of Hermas, which ventured to rebuke and warn the officers of the church. Its main subject was the purification of the church by repentance. The high place which the church had taken in the minds of Christians is shown by the idea that (recalling Paul's "Jerusalem which is above") it existed before the world, and that the world had been created for it.

Presently, in Ignatius and in the Muratorian Fragment, a "catholic church" appears. The original significance of this phrase has been much discussed, and is still uncertain. Even at the date of these passages, it had already developed more than one sense. The church was called catholic when it was spoken of as constituting a united whole made up of different parts; and these parts were both local churches and single members. Ignatius compared the relation of the local church to its bishop with that of the catholic church to Christ; and similarly the Muratorian Fragment speaks of a catholic church whose edification the writers of the epistles had in mind even when addressing local churches or individuals. But the idea of a universal church comes out most strongly in contrast with the heretics who by their personal beliefs and practises separated themselves from the great body of Christians. With this catholicity was connected the idea that this church alone had the necessary character of embracing all true believers, the love that holds fast to unity, and the primitive Christian truth. The epithet "catholic" designates here not its extension throughout the whole world, but the inclusion within it of all Christians, wheresoever they dwell. As yet the definite sense applied to the term by Roman Catholicism was not expressed by it. This is met first in the question of what constituted valid membership in this church; and according to the Catholic conception there was required the recognition of a definite external organization, ordained by God, and the acceptance of a confession of faith sanctioned by the church.

2. Significance of "Catholic Church."

The idea of the episcopate comes out with remarkable definiteness and dignity in the Ignatian epistles. Each local church was subject to its bishop, who stood in the place of Christ, with his presbyters about him like the apostles. Ignatius left unanswered the questions how the bishops as a class reached this position, how individual bishops were raised to it, how far they were endowed with special spiritual gifts and the churches assured against error on their part. The extent to which the elevation of the episcopate to such a position met a felt want of the times is shown by the calmness with which it was accepted universally, with no record preserved of any discussion on the subject. [This circumstance is naturally urged by Roman Catholic apologists, together with other arguments, as proving the apostolic and consequently divine origin of the episcopal office.] In the general view (cf. especially Irenæus and Tertullian), the bishops stood in the place of the apostles, whose teaching office they continued, and thus guaranteed the preservation of the truth. Their succession from the apostles involved a second "note" of the church—apostolicity. From the idea of a specially guaranteed possession of the truth by the bishops in virtue of their historical connection with the apostles grew the belief in a particular *charisma* attached to their office. From Tertullian can be seen how the priestly title was attributed to the rulers of the church, and especially to the bishops, although the mediatorial functions later attributed to them were of gradual development. The church thus possessed a sacerdotal order, and the bishop stood out as high priest, *pontifex maximus* (Tertullian, Hippolytus, Apostolic Constitutions). The Alexandrian theology, as in Clement and Origen, did nothing to check this development. It did, indeed, insist on the inner and spiritual side of the church, and claim independently to recognize, in its Christian *gnōsis*, the truth of the doctrines handed down by the apostles. But it had no word against the authority of the episcopal office, in which it recognized the inheritance of the apostolic pastoral function. Its philosophic and aristocratic *gnōsis* was not fitted to contend for the spiritual character of true Christianity in the New Testament sense. A vigorous reaction did set in with the rise of Montanism, which attempted to purify the church by casting out such members as were stained with mortal sin and holding those who remained to a high standard, in virtue of a spirit from above which was not subject to these external offices. Thus Tertullian said, "The church is essentially and chiefly spirit," and contrasts this "church as spirit" with the "church as the body of the episcopate." But the spirit of Montanism was not that of the New Testament; and it could not alter the course of the Catholic Church, which was then hard at work building up in the world its well-organized kingdom.

3. The Ignatian Episcopate.

A powerful representative of the progress of the latter is found in Cyprian, for whom the bishops are now essentially and without distinction the rulers of the church, endued with divine authority. The government of the whole church belonged to the episcopate as a whole. Such strong statements appear as "the bishop is in the church and the church in the bishop," "the church is a people united with the priest," "he can not have God as father who has not the church as mother." The last was uttered against Novatianism, to whose members Cyprian denied the possibility of salvation on the ground of their schism, and the validity of whose baptism he refused to admit.

4. The Cyprianic Episcopate.

In regard to the conception of priesthood, which for him was centered in the bishop, it is observed that in the Lord's Supper the priest stood in the place of Christ, did what Christ did, offered the body of Christ (see MASS). Even if all his expressions, like those of Augustine, can not be taken in the sense in which the later Catholic Church would understand them, they still lead up to the highest function attributed by the latter to its priests.

But Catholicism owes to Augustine the most and the deepest of the statements which express its mind on the subject of the church. Their occasion was a new separatist movement in favor of enforced sanctity, that of the Donatists. Augustine had a deep and vivid conception of the inner, spiritual being of the church, of the operation of the Spirit of God in it and in its members, of Christ living in it and them, of all-pervading and all-uniting love. Consequently it was not a mere controversial argument against the Donatists when he distinguished in his doctrine of the church as the body of Christ between "the true body of the Lord" and a "confused" or "pretended" one, a distinction misinterpreted by his opponents as though he believed in two churches. According to his view of grace, it is entirely a matter of the free grace of God who among the members of the visible church is a member of the true body; and those who are predestined, even though they are outside the visible unity, yet belong to the invisible church. Still, it is the will of God to bring these into external communion, and participation in the blessings of salvation and real Christian love are possible only within this. He did not lay as much stress as Cyprian upon the divine right of the episcopate; but this was admitted by his opponents and by himself, and against the Manicheans he did appeal to the "succession of bishops" in the apostolic sees. The question then arose which of the two organizations, both provided with sacraments, priesthood, and episcopate, and both appealing to apostolic tradition, was the true Catholic Church. Augustine answered it by saying that the church had spread, according to the purpose of Christ, throughout the whole earth; and thus only that communion from which the Donatists had severed themselves could claim the title of Catholic—assuredly not their small sect, confined to a few districts in Africa. He made the belief of the individual Christian depend upon the authority of the church as catholic in this sense of the word, God having confirmed it "partly by miracles, partly by the multitude of adherents"; indeed, he went so far as to say "I could not believe in the Gospel if the authority of the church catholic had not forced me." How the authoritative judgment of this Catholic Church upon questions of doctrine and the Christian life was to be expressed Augustine did not definitely state; he regarded the Church as represented in its episcopate, but did not name any constituted organ for a declaration of the truth by this episcopate as a unit.

5. Views of Augustine.

Besides Augustine's statements, there is another important definition in the *Commonitorium* of Vincent of Lerins, which is in substantial agreement with them. According to him, there is a "test of universal understanding," by which we are bound to believe *quod semper, quod ubique, quod ab omnibus creditum est.* Here, instead of an authority of the Church as one whole, an overwhelming majority must suffice, which comes more definitely to a majority of the "sacerdotal orders" and "rulers." Vincent contemplated further definition of the traditional doctrine; and this led to the questions how such a consensus is to be attained in order to assure people of the truth of such later definitions, and how far what is supposed to have been contained implicitly in the original deposit may be elevated to the rank of an article of faith. The Church as itself an object of faith requiring formal recognition was made a part of the formula of the African baptismal confession, and directly introduced into the Constantinopolitan supplement to the Nicene Creed (381), "in one Holy, Catholic, and Apostolic Church," and into the Apostles' Creed.

2. Later (or Roman) Catholicism in East and West: The foregoing has traced the development of the idea of one. holy, catholic, and apostolic church, with its priesthood and episcopate, which was common to both Eastern and Western Christianity. But the East laid much less stress upon the sacerdotal and episcopal office as a system of government analogous to the legal discipline of the state; and it is noteworthy that both the schisms which arose out of questions relating to such organization (Novatianism and Donatism) were of Western origin. The Greek Church dwelt more on the idea of communion with the Incarnate Savior in devout contemplation and knowledge, and upon the representation of the work of redemption in the rich mysteries of the liturgy. Thus the priestly and episcopal organization never attained an established external unity for the whole church; and, without objection from the East, the "one Catholic Church" developed there into a number of communities belonging to various states or countries and closely allied in their supreme government with the secular polity. To the Roman claims it opposed the idea of Christ as the sole head of the Church; and it developed no infallible organ for the decision of questions of faith. The possibility of development of the original sacred deposit, as maintained by Vincent of Lerins, was no longer strongly affirmed, and ultimately stagnation overtook any attempt at dogmatic inquiry.

1. Eastern Church Mystical.

In the West, on the other hand, the definite organization of the church at large took shape in the papal monarchy; the further history of Catholicism and its idea of the church is really a history of the Roman primacy (see POPE, PAPACY, AND PAPAL SYSTEM). Irenæus had placed the Roman church, as founded by Peter and Paul, in the forefront of his appeal to apostolic succession and tradition, finding in it the preeminent survival of primitive leadership, and on this ground requiring from the other churches agreement with it. This purely historical basis for deference to Rome developed into dogmatic insistence on the supremacy and infallibility of the church founded by Peter; just as Cyprian's view of the unity of the church as represented by and summed up in Peter and the authority given to him grew into the assumption and the dogma that this unity must have its permanent visible representatives in the successors of Peter, each of whom becomes the visible head of the church, the representative of Christ. Pope Leo I. claimed for his see the "cure of the church universal," making it the head of the body from which the other members can not be separated and live. Though he thought of discipline and polity, not of the communication of grace or of the establishment of doctrine, his statements are strong enough to afford a basis for all the later claims of the papacy. It found powerful support in the recognition of its primacy by the emperors (cf. especially an edict of Valentinian in 445), and in the political position of Rome, while the German emperors in their day built up their whole ecclesiastical fabric on the assumption of subordination to one central authority. The process was a logical continuation of the impulse which had early endeavored to bring Christianity to expression and to a firm position in the world by a solid constitutional organization. Moreover, the medieval nations, both Latin and Teutonic, had a marked craving for a representation of the divine and the heavenly by visible and tangible things—of the one heavenly Lord by the one Roman vicegerent, the crucified Savior by the host in the mass, the blessings of salvation by the sacraments. In its way the papacy did indeed, in its greatest representatives, a Gregory VII. or an Innocent III., accomplish much to fulfil this ideal. They held the church together amid all the wild tumults of the life of their day; they protected true moral and religious interests against the invasion of the world, and they stood for the maintenance of ethical discipline—though it is also true that they identified these interests with their own claims, that human ambition and avarice was not always excluded from their acts, and that finally the eternal commandments of God were subordinated to human decisions.

2. Western Church Governmental.

The high papal conception of the church's constitution was not yet, however, a dogma sanctioned by a formal decision on the part of the church. Against its prevalence were not only the secular power (which endeavored to reverse the process and subject the church to itself) and the national spirit on which that power could rely (as in France against Boniface VIII.), but also the consciousness on the part of the bishops of the meaning of their office and a recollection of the earlier history of the church; while the inequalities of papal character and the great schism tended to stir up a spirit of protest and rebellion. Thus the so-called "episcopal system" (see EPISCOPACY) was worked out mainly by French theologians, such as Gerson and D'Ailly, and represented in the great councils, where the theory was heard of a "universal catholic church" distinct from the Roman. The latter, consisting of pope, cardinals, bishops, and clergy, might err, and was subject to the authority of general councils, which represented not only the classes named, but also all true members of the body of Christ, and in which Christian princes and delegates of the universities were to have a voice.

3. "Papal" and "Episcopal" Systems.

But the papal theory raised its head once more when the councils had succeeded in restoring unity, and dominated the Lateran Council under Leo X. The Thomist Sylvester Prierias (q.v.) maintained against Luther the proposition "The Church universal is essentially the assembly of all believers, practically the Roman Church and the pope; representatively the Roman Church is the college of cardinals, practically it is the pope." Of this view the Jesuits were the principal upholders. Bellarmine maintained against the Protestants the definition of the church as "the company of men bound together by confession of the same Christian faith under the rule of legitimate pastors and especially of the one vicar of Christ on earth." The Council of Trent did not venture to make an outspoken decision between the papal and episcopal theories; and such a decision was expressed only after the latter had repeatedly tried to enforce its claims (see GALLICANISM; EMS, CONGRESS OF; JANSENIST CHURCH), in the Vatican Council of 1870.

IV. Protestant Doctrine of the Church: The first medieval Christian body which, while holding fast to the general Christian faith, abandoned that doctrine of the church sketched above was the Waldenses. They considered themselves members of the church of Christ and partakers of his salvation, in spite of their exclusion from organized Christendom, recognizing at the same time a "church of Christ" within the organization whose heads were hostile to them. There is not, however, in their teaching any clear definition of the nature of the church or any new principle in reference to it. The first theologian to bring forward a conception of the church radically opposed to that which had been developing was Wyclif; and Huss followed him in it. According to him the church is the "totality of the predestinated"; there, as in his doctrine of grace, he followed Augustine, but took a standpoint contrary as well to Augustine's as to that of later Catholicism in his account of the institutions and means of grace by which God communicates the blessings of salvation to the predestined, excluding from them the polity of priest, bishop, and pope. He denied the divine institution both of papal primacy and of the episcopate as distinct from the presbyterate, and attributed infallible authority to the Scriptures alone.

1. Wyclif's Teaching.

The idea of both Wyclif and Huss was thus not of an actually existing body of united associates, but merely the total of predestined Christians who at any time are living holy lives, scattered among those who are not predestined, together with those who are predestined but not yet converted, and the faithful who have passed away.

Luther defended Wyclif's definition at the Leipsic Disputation of 1519, in spite of its condemnation by the Council of Constance. But his own idea was that the real nature of the church was defined by the words following its mention in the creed—"the communion of saints," taking the word "saints" in its Pauline sense. These (although sin may still cling to them) are sanctified by God through his word and sacraments—sacraments not depending upon an organized, episcopally ordained clergy, but committed to the church as a whole; it is their faith, called forth by the word of God, which makes them righteous and accepted members of Christ and heirs of eternal life. Thus the Lutheran and, in general, the Calvinist conception of the church depended from the first upon the doctrine of justification by faith. In harmony with Luther's teaching, the Augsburg Confession defines the church as "the congregation of saints in which the Gospel is rightly taught and the sacraments are rightly administered." In one sense the church is invisible, since the earthly eye can not tell who has true faith and in this sense is a "saint," but in another it is visible, since it has its being here in outward and visible vital forms, ordained by God, in which those who are only "saints" in appearance have an external share. The church, too, always has need of some sort of external forms, of human ordinances, in which to clothe the administration of the means of grace, the preaching of the word, and public worship; but these must not claim divine sanction or unconditional obligation. There was, however, one thing on which Luther insisted as essential—that the public administration of the means of grace entrusted to the church by God should be performed only by persons duly called to that function, who were to feed the flock with the word of God. His conclusion of its necessity is drawn not from any divine revelation or law, but from the nature of the case and the need of a settled order. The division of offices, the placing of superintendents or bishops over the pastors of the local churches, was considered a matter of variable human arrangement. While Luther rejected the papal claim to condition salvation by its forms and ordinances, declaring them anti-Christian and opposed to God's will, he recognized the possibility of sanctified believers and true members of the body of Christ living within the Roman Church, because even there, in spite of all corruption, the power of the word and sacraments was still working. Here is a difference between the Reformation view and other postapostolic conceptions of the church. For the first time there were two bodies with opposite religious principles, each accusing the other of grievous error, and yet one of them admitting a communion in grace with the other, and indeed with all Christians of whatever name who cling to the fundamental elements in the message of salvation. It was in this sense that the Reformers taught one catholic church, spread throughout the Christendom of all times and places, the unity of which lacked external organization, but was sufficiently established by its possession of one invisible head, one faith, one baptism. Its holiness is shown by the fact that Christ is its head, and that the sanctifying grace of God works within it; its apostolicity, by its original foundation at the hands of the apostles and its continued resting upon their word.

2. Luther's Teaching.

The view here set forth left unsettled a number of questions which then came up for the first time and influenced later theological movements. To what extent the pure preaching of the Gospel and due administration of the sacraments was necessary; how far the name of a church of Christ might be given to a particular church which was lacking in these requisites; how far an effort should be made to attain a pure expression of Evangelical truth in the shape of creed and dogma—these were some of the questions. The last led to the distinction between essentials and non-essentials, and to that between the Gospel, or the simple preaching of the word of God as a source of life and grace, and theological dogma. Another question was the external government of the church. If it was not regarded as a matter of divine institution, who was to establish and exercise it? Who was to organize the churches that were springing up outside the ancient or traditional Christendom? Luther seems to have contemplated originally a free organization by these true believers themselves into a church with simple, Evangelical worship and discipline; but historical circumstances led to this function, as well as the continued direction of the church, being left largely to secular princes and magistrates, as charged by God with the maintenance of morality and order among Christian people and with the enforcement of the first as well as the second table of the decalogue. This result was brought about partly by the fact that for years a hope was cherished of a reunion with the old episcopate, and such institutions as were set up were regarded as to some extent provisional. So by degrees the organ of the supreme direction of the Lutheran Church came to be in the hands of consistories appointed by the local secular government, and the share of the other members of the church was reduced to an assumed tacit consent to legislation. Melanchthon's later teaching differed somewhat from Luther's. He was influenced by a fear of spiritualistic fanaticism and a desire to see the Evangelical religion firmly and practically established. He considered the Christian church visible on the ground of its self-expression in the preaching of the word and administration of the sacraments; and he emphasized its institutional character much more than Luther. He clung as long as possible to the desire for reunion with the great, firmly established traditional church. Among Lutheran theologians it was not till after Chemnitz that the doctrine appeared and prevailed which

3. Questions Left Unsettled by the Reformers.

distinguished between the visible church as the "assembly of the called" and the invisible church existing within this, as the sum of all the really faithful or sanctified or regenerate. This distinction belonged originally to the Calvinists (see below); though, unlike them and Wyclif, the Lutheran theologians had in mind not the predestined, but all who were within the real, existing inner body. The idea of the objective and external use of the means of grace is thus no longer connected, as by Luther, with the idea of a church which is still proclaimed invisible, but with that of a visible church within which the saints also partake of those means of grace. The Lutheran Church is thus in its essence an institution existing for the communication of grace by these means, in relation to which the individual members assume a receptive attitude.

The Reformed leaders also designated the church as the congregation of believers or saints, and made the preaching of the pure word of God a condition of its existence. But they laid stress on the distinction between the visible and the invisible church, taking their conception of the latter from Wyclif and Huss. Zwingli not only allowed the significance of the sacraments to drop out, but even minimized that of the revealed word, outside of the sphere of influence of which he believed that there were elect among the heathen. Of this last belief Calvin knew nothing, though he, too, considered the church as the invisible fellowship of the predestined; and he emphasized much more than Zwingli the necessity of the word and sacraments, laying besides a peculiar stress on the exercise of government and discipline, through teachers, pastors, and elders. The definite Calvinistic conception found expression more or less in the various confessions.

4. Calvinistic Doctrine of the Church.

Thus the Heidelberg Catechism defines the church generally as "a company elected to life," assembled by God through his Spirit and his word. That of Geneva has the phrase "body of the faithful whom God predestinated to eternal life"; but besides this church, which is recognized by faith alone, it speaks of a visible church with definite signs. The Westminster Confession mentions both visible and invisible side by side. The great difference between Lutheran and Calvinist views lay in their attitude toward the means of grace. The church could not be to the Calvinist an institution for conveying grace, on account of his idea of the absolute sovereignty of God and the operation of the Spirit as entirely independent of created means. Again, the energetic effort to sanctify God's people for his service led to a sort of new legalism in both corporate and individual life among the Calvinists; while Lutheranism tended either to a Quietism in which the church contented itself with offering the means of grace and the individual with receiving them, or to a worldly spirit which abused the liberty of the children of God.

As to the question of external organization and government, Zwingli wished discipline to be exercised not by special ecclesiastical organs, but by those who stood in general at the head of the Christian people, thus leading to Erastianism (see ERASTUS). The theory of necessary independence of the state was a later growth. As for organization, different theories were held. Presbyterianism developed its teaching and ruling elders, and its general synodal constitution based on the local presbyteries; the Independents or Congregationalists erected no general organization, identified the functions of pastor and elder, and put discipline and the decision of questions affecting the church into the hands of the local churches; Quakerism denied that any such forms or laws were permissible, appealing to Scripture in support of its contention. The position of the Church of England is a peculiar one. While the doctrine of its Articles on the Lord's Supper is distinctly Calvinistic, it defined the church, under the influence of Melanchthon's later teaching, is "a visible congregation of faithful men" with the pure word of God and due administration of the sacraments. With its episcopal organization, it preserved more the character of official Christianity than any other Protestant body; but the doctrine of the necessity of the apostolic succession supposed to be there preserved was not stated in the Articles, and did not become influential until a later period.

5. Post-Reformation Doctrines of the Church.

After the dominion of Protestant orthodoxy, which marked the period with both its strength and its weakness, followed another in which the newly aroused subjective piety departed more or less from the rigid forms of corporate church life. The tendency of Pietism was rather to erect "little churches" for the satisfying of spiritual needs; and the devotion which thus found expression took on a narrow, legalistic, and rather Calvinistic character. Then came rationalism, with its religious indifferentism and lack of belief in the importance of the church, as that importance had been understood in both early and Reformation times. To it the church was merely an association on a par with other human and earthly societies, and it asserted with great positiveness that Christ himself had no intention of founding a church in the received sense of the word. But it would require far too much space to trace in detail all the later variations of local or individual attitude toward the complicated questions which have been here discussed. It may, however, be remarked that the tendency to form churches wholly independent of the state and receiving no support from it is characteristic especially of the Reformed bodies, though, as we have seen, it can not be traced back to Zwingli or to Calvin. Connection of any kind with the state was felt to be prejudicial to the liberty of self-expression claimed for the Christian Spirit. The "free church" movement manifested itself first and most forcibly in Scotland, in the Secession Church of 1733, the Church of Relief of 1752, the union of both under the name of United Presbyterian Church in 1847, and particularly the Free Church of 1843, the two last having effected a further union in 1900. See CHURCH AND STATE.

6. Pietistic and Rationalistic Doctrines.

(J. KÖSTLIN†.)

BIBLIOGRAPHY: On the early church and its constitution the best book is E. Hatch, *The Growth of Church Institutions*, London, 1887. Consult further: W. Sclater, *Original Draught of the Primitive Church*, Oxford, 1840; S. Davidson, *Ecclesiastical Polity of the N. T.*, London, 1850; L. Coleman, *Ancient Christianity Exemplified*, Philadelphia, 1852; T. Witherow, *The Form of the Christian Church . . . the Constitution of the N. T. Church*, Edinburgh, 1888; C. J. Vaughan, *The Church of the First Days*, London, 1890; J. Hammond, *What does the Bible say about the Church*, ib. 1894; O. Pfleiderer, *Christian Origins*, New York, 1906; J. C. V. Durell, *The Historic Church. An Essay on the Conception of the Christian Church . . . in the sub-Apostolic Age*, Cambridge, 1906; K. Adam, *Der Kirchenbegriff Tertullians*, Paderborn, 1907; *DCG*, i. 324-330.

On the idea of the church: K. Hackenschmidt, *Anfänge des katholischen Kirchenbegriffs*, Strasburg, 1874; R. Seeberg, *Studien zur Geschichte des Begriffs der Kirche*, Erlangen, 1885; W. Palmer, *Treatise on the Church of Christ*, 2 vols., London, 1842; W. G. Ward, *Ideal of a Christian Church*, ib. 1844; E. Schérer, *Esquisse d'une théorie de l'église chrétienne*, Paris, 1845; J. J. White, *Exposition of the Church and its Doctrine*, Philadelphia, 1855; R. Whately, *Kingdom of Christ Delineated*, London, 1860; J. Bannermann, *The Church of Christ, . . . Nature, Powers, Discipline, and Government*, 2 vols., Edinburgh, 1868; idem, *Scripture Doctrine of the Church*, ib. 1868; *Ecce Ecclesia, . . . the Essential Unity of the Church in all Ages*, New York, 1868; H. R. Reynolds, *Ecclesia, Church Problems*, London, 1870; S. S. Schmucker, *Unity of Christ's Church*, New York, 1870; J. J. McElhinney, *Doctrine of the Church*, Philadelphia, 1871 (with bibliography); J. Köstlin, *Das Wesen der Kirche nach Lehre und Geschichte des N. T.'s*, Gotha, 1872; E. M. Goulburn, *The . . . Church; its divine Ideals, Ministry and Institutions*, London, 1875; A. de Gasparin, *L'Église selon l'évangile*, 2 vols., Paris, 1878-79; H. Schmidt, *Die Kirche*, Leipsic, 1884; E. D. Morris, *Ecclesiology*, New York, 1885; W. Bornemann, *Kirchenideale und Kirchenreformen*, Leipsic, 1887; H. J. Van Dyke, *The Church, her Ministry and Sacraments*, New York, 1890; F. A. Milne, *Ecclesiology*, Boston, 1894; A. Westphal, *Qu'est-ce qu'une église*, Paris, 1896; J. B. Johnson, *The Church and the Sacraments*, London, 1898; E. A. Litton, *Church of Christ in its Idea, Attributes and Ministry*, ib. 1898; P. F. Jalaguier, *De l'église*, Paris, 1899; C. Gove, *The Church and the Ministry*, London, 1900; G. D. Boardman, *The Church (ecclesia)*, New York, 1901; J. Ireland, *Church and Modern Society*, 2 vols., ib. 1903-04; H. Gallwitz, *Die Grundlagen der Kirche*, Leipsic, 1904; G. Vos, *Teaching of Jesus concerning the . . . Church*, New York, 1904; A. H. Charteris, *Church of Christ, its Life and Work*, London, 1905; E. C. Dargan, *Ecclesiology*, Louisville, 1905; J. W. Legge, *Ecclesiological Essays*, London, 1906; J. A. Kern, *The Idea of the Church*, Nashville, 1907.

On the constitution of the church: R. Parkinson, *The Constitution of the Visible Church*, London, 1839; F. D. Maurice, *The Kingdom of Christ: . . . Principles, Constitution and Ordinances of the Catholic Church*, 2 vols., ib. 1842; F. Brandes, *Die Verfassung der Kirche nach evangelischen Grundsätzen*, 2 vols., Elberfeld, 1867; G. A. Jacob, *Ecclesiastical Polity in the New Testament*, New York, 1874; J. Cunningham, *The Growth of the Church in its Organizations and Institutions*, London, 1886; J. H. Rigg, *Comparative View of Church Organizations, Primitive and Protestant*, ib. 1887; W. D. Killen, *Framework of the Church*, Edinburgh, 1890; J. Jebb, *Divine Economy of the Church*, Philadelphia, n.d.

On the aim and mission of the church: J. Harris, *The Great Commission*, London, 1852; J. Sanford, *Mission and Extension of the Church*, ib. 1862; W. H. Fremantle, *The World as the Subject of Redemption, . . . the Functions of the Church*, ib. 1885; J. M. Lang, *The Church and its Social Mission*, New York, 1902.

CHURCH COUNCIL (*concilium ecclesiæ, Kirchenrat*): A meeting of the authorities of the Church to take counsel and make decisions in regard to church affairs. Councils may be ecumenical, of the whole Church, or of the Church of a single country, or of a province, or even of a single church, in which case it is a committee chosen from a congregation to represent it (see COUNCILS AND SYNODS). In the Roman Catholic Church originally the laity had no share in the councils, but in the course of time assistants had to be found among them for the clergy, especially in financial matters. These assistants were at first chosen by the church authorities; only in the nineteenth century have the laity had a right to take part in the selection. In regard to councils in the Evangelical churches, see CONGREGATIONALISTS, IV.; and POLITY.

(F. H. JACOBSON†.)

CHURCH DIET, GERMAN EVANGELICAL (DEUTSCHER EVANGELISCHER KIRCHENTAG): A convention of delegates from the Evangelical churches of Germany—the Lutheran and Reformed, the churches of the Union, and the Moravians. Originating in 1848, its chief aims were: (1) to unite the German Evangelical churches; (2) make provision for the Church in case of a separation of Church and State; (3) to oppose the unbelief of the time; and (4) to ameliorate the miserable condition of the people. The real conductor of the whole undertaking was Von Bethmann-Hollweg, professor of law at Bonn, who presided over the first session and was the leader until the last meeting. In 1848 he published a treatise, *Vorschlag einer evangelischen Kirchenversammlung im laufenden Jahre 1848*, in which he advocated a call to all Evangelical Christians of the German nation. Simultaneously and independently, the idea occurred to Philipp Wackernagel (q.v.), of Wiesbaden, and two of his friends, P. Heller, pastor of Kleinheubach-on-the-Main in Bavaria, and Dr. Haupt, then pastor of Rimhorn in the Hessian Odenwald. Their ideas found ready acceptance at a conference of ministers from Frankfort and the neighboring states, Nassau, Hesse, and a part of Bavaria; and a commission was appointed to "discuss and prepare the convocation of a general ecclesiastical convention of Evangelical Germany."

The first general convention was held Sept. 21, 1848, at Wittenberg. Five hundred participated in it, the leaders being such prominent men as Von Bethmann-Hollweg, Stahl, Wackernagel, Schmieder, Dorner, Nitzsch, Müller, and Krummacher. Of the resolutions adopted the following are the most important: (1) The Evangelical communities of Germany meet for the purpose of forming a church alliance. (2) The Evangelical Church Alliance is not a union which obliterates the confessional churches, but a confederation of churches. (3) The Evangelical Church Alliance comprises all ecclesiastical communities which stand upon the basis of the Reformed confessions, especially the Lutheran, the Reformed, the Union, and the congregations of Brethren. (4) Each community which joins the Alliance retains its relations to the State and its independence in matters of teaching, service, and constitution. (5) The aim of the Evangelical Church Alliance is the care and advancement of all common interests of the church communities belonging to it. The Eisenach Conference (q.v.), which was called into life in 1851, did not come up fully to the idea of the church alliance, but the Congress for Home Missions was an immediate result of the efforts for a church alliance. The Church Diet was at first held every year, later every second year. In 1872 the last Diet was held at Halle. Although it did not bring about church alliance, it was for a quarter of a century a rallying-point of living church forces.

(Wilhelm Baur†.)

CHURCH DISCIPLINE.

Church discipline is a means of securing and maintaining the spiritual purity of the Christian Church. This exercise arises from the fact that the Church is a human institution, the members of which are subject to the limitations and weaknesses of humanity. The Christian congregation, therefore, like every other community, needs a means of self-protection in order to suppress or eliminate whatever might impair or destroy its life. But, from the constitution of the Church, the character of its discipline is purely spiritual. Therefore the only means which can properly be employed is exclusion, partial or total, of those whose acts jeopardize it.

I. In the Apostolic and Postapostolic Periods: The center of the Scriptural doctrine of ecclesiastical discipline is Matt. xviii. 15–18; and its practical application in the apostolical church is learned from I Cor. v. and II Cor. ii. 4–8. A member of the Corinthian congregation had married his stepmother, and the congregation had suffered the deed. Paul then wrote to the Corinthians that the offender should be excommunicated, and "delivered unto Satan." His words produced such an impression, not only on the congregation, but also on the offender, that, when he wrote again to the Corinthians, Paul could recommend mercy. It is, however, not only for such flagrant offenses as the above that Paul demands punishment, but also for minor failings by which a man is made a burden to his fellow men (II Thess. iii. 6); and he warns the congregations against heresy, for it eats like a canker (II Tim. ii. 17). A heretic, after admonishing him once or twice in vain, avoid (Tit. iii. 10); do not even bid him Godspeed (II John 10, 11). The punishment, however, must never be administered in a spirit of retaliation. Church discipline, though necessary for the self-protection of the church, has as its aim the reclamation and reconciliation of the offender; hence in the spirit of love it must dictate its punishments (II Cor. ii. 6–8). That the discipline is exercised by the Church is indicated in all the passages cited except that from Titus, where the direction is given for personal guidance alone (cf. verse 9). The apostolical institutions of Excommunication (q.v.) and reconciliation lived on in the postapostolic church, and during the period of persecution became even more peremptory. Under Decius, whose goal seems to have been the total destruction of Christianity, there occurred, by the side of the most admirable examples of faithfulness, so frequent instances of defection that a special regulation for the reconciliation of the lapsed became a necessity. This regulation, which continued valid down to the fifth century, established a course of penance which ran through various stages, and comprised a period of several years; but its severity naturally called forth devices of evasion and subterfuge, such as the libelli of the confessors (see Lapsed), and church discipline became somewhat lax. A reaction toward greater severity followed, and the Montanists declared that the excommunicated ought to remain for their whole life in a state of penance, while the Novatians affirmed that the Church had no right at all to forgive the lapsed, though the Lord might be willing to do so. Meanwhile the developing organization of the Church had reached the department of discipline, and the penitents, who had been excommunicated and desired to be received back into fellowship, were divided into four classes and compelled to pass through as many stages of penance (see Excommunication).

II. In the Roman Catholic Church: The union of Church and State led to developments in discipline, the most important of which was the imposition of civil penalties for spiritual offenses. This was carried to the extreme of capital punishment, inflicted for heresy in the case of the Spanish bishop Priscillian and six companions, 385 A.D. The many sentences of deposition from office accompanied with exile during the controversial period attest the alliance of Church and State in the infliction of church discipline. Penitential discipline in its four grades was continued from the earlier period and was sanctioned by the councils of the fourth century. Yet the alliance of Church and State and the controversial activities produced a concentration of disciplinary attention upon heresy which allowed grave offenses against morals to go unpunished. A noteworthy exception to this was the refusal of Ambrose of Milan to administer the communion to Theodosius I. because of a massacre by the latter's soldiers in Thessalonica. In the early Middle Ages the extension of the Church among the barbaric races brought about further systematization. Discipline was administered by the bishops through synodical courts. The Penitential Books (q.v.), particularly the *Liber pœnitentialis* of Halitgarius of Cambrai, were written for the guidance of confessors. Besides excommunication, the penalties of the Anathema and the Interdict (qq.v.) were developed. Penance (see Penance, Repentance), including auricular confession (see Confession of Sins) and priestly absolution, became a sacrament, and the system of Indulgences (q.v.) was originated which later became so great a scandal and was one of the primary causes of the Reformation. Geo. W. Gilmore.

III. In the Lutheran Churches: According to

the Evangelical Lutheran conception, exclusion from the sacraments forms the core and center of church discipline. The employment of this discipline (the power of the keys) is a part of the practical duties of the pastor. The pastor who administers the sacrament dare not knowingly admit an unworthy person, since to do so is to participate in the sin. But on the basis of Matt. xviii. and I Cor. v. the congregation has a right to cooperate in church discipline since it may not tolerate offense in its midst. The ban, even if uttered by the pastor, always proceeds in the name of the congregation; but participation by the congregation in church discipline is little developed in Lutheran state churches in consequence of the peculiar organization of the congregations. Instead of the congregations, the consistories received authority to assist the pastor in this exercise. The early practise was that a member of the congregation, charged with public sins, was at first admonished by the pastor as his confessor, and if he did not change his conduct, he was excluded from the Lord's Supper; this was called the small ban. If the sinner remained stubborn, he was excluded from churchly communion altogether, was put under the so-called great ban. If he were in any way compromised before the congregation, the permission of the consistory had to be obtained, and the so-called great ban could be pronounced by the consistory or the state only after investigation. The whole procedure was looked upon not as a real punishment, but as a means of discipline. The ban could be nullified when the sinner showed repentance. He was readmitted on condition of publicly asking the forgiveness of the congregation. This procedure was called church penance, which is consequently not an act of punishment, but of reconciliation. If the sinner died without church penance, he was buried in a separate place without the services of the minister and the congregation. Church discipline so conducted was doomed to failure because it was not rooted in the consciousness of the congregation. During the seventeenth century, from an act of reconciliation church penance degenerated into an act of punishment which at first was imposed by the consistories and then by secular courts. Attempts were made by men like Johann Valentin Andreä and Spener to restore the old church discipline, but without success. Pietism produced no changes in this exercise, and rationalism completed its destruction. In most states church discipline was expressly abolished, and to-day there are only sporadic instances of it.

1. Methods and Results.

With the reawakening of churchly life a desire for the reintroduction of church discipline made itself felt. Schleiermacher's draft of a church constitution contained propositions to this effect; during 1840–60 the question was earnestly discussed because of the reproach which the lack of discipline caused the churches and sects, also because of the social element which crept into the old church constitutions. Since the introduction of civil marriage and the abolition of compulsory baptism there has been felt anew the need of measures against such as despise ecclesiastical marriage and baptism. The state does not oppose the imposition of church discipline as long as it is of a purely religious nature and is not public.

2. Modern Requirements.

(G. Uhlhorn.†)

IV. In the Reformed Churches: The Reformed Church has always emphasized that faith without moral submission to the law of God is inconceivable, but it was only Calvinism that laid the responsibility for the regulation and discipline of the moral life of the members upon the church. According to the common Evangelical view, the power of the keys was exercised by the preaching of the Word, but Calvinism found it expressed chiefly in Christian penitential discipline as divinely ordered.

The German-Swiss Reformation brought about not only religious knowledge, but an immediate ethical renovation of popular life. There existed, however, as yet no churchly discipline. Zwingli tried to preserve it from the medieval Church in so far as it did not conflict with the new doctrines, but the secular authorities were much more successful in influencing the moral education of the people. An authoritative position in regard to matrimonial matters only was assumed apart from the civil authority in 1525. A tribunal was created consisting of two secular priests, two members of the larger council, and two members of the smaller council; but this institution was still far removed from an organization of the ecclesiastical congregation, it simply reported its findings to the secular authority. Although there existed a desire for an independent church discipline also in the sphere of the German-Swiss Reformation, Zwingli was satisfied with the discipline carried through by the Christian secular authorities, as he deemed the discipline itself of more importance than the method by which it was attained. The sermon, he thought, gave the idea, while the civil authority was the executing organ in the union of State and Church.

1. The Zwinglian System.

In strong contrast with this surrender of ecclesiastical independence, there reappeared in Geneva under the guidance of Calvin the original type of strict moral discipline, based entirely upon the church. Calvin laid down his dogmatic views concerning ecclesiastical organization and discipline in his *Institutio*, especially after 1543, in great detail, and they form the basis of his practical efforts. The normal form of the church must be shaped according to Scripture. The body of Christ ("Institutes," IV. iii. 2) must be governed according to that political order and form which Scripture prescribes (IV. vi. 9; cf. x. 1, i. 15, iv. 1; "Gallican Confession," 29). Thus discipline or government becomes the third constituting function of the right church (*Opera*, xiii. 283; "Belgic Confession," 29). But apart from dependence upon Biblical forms, Calvin had the conviction that the church could not exercise her educational function without a corresponding organization. Discipline aims primarily to prevent desecration of Christ's congregation and his holy sacrament, the betterment of the individual is considered second-

2. Calvin's Basal Principles.

ary. If the interest of Calvin had been confined to individual discipline, he would have been satisfied, like Zwingli, with the moral surveillance which was zealously and often rigorously exercised by the magistrate. But as the honor of Christ seemed to him to demand the independent exercise of ecclesiastical functions, he could not tolerate the refusal of a parochial organization. The church can solve her ethical problem only if she forms herself according to her own principles. Calvin realized his plan only after his expulsion from Geneva, in his independent congregation at Strasburg, and thence brought it back to Geneva.

Immediately after his return in 1541, the *Ordonnances ecclésiastiques* were drawn up and approved by the two councils and the assembly of citizens. The church order establishes as a basis the four offices (*pasteurs, docteurs, anciens, diacres*) which the Lord instituted for the government of his church. It is the task of the people to create a congregation that enjoys the blessings of God in a becoming manner and with a mature consciousness, especially in the sacraments. For the regular supervision over the congregation, the college of elders is instituted (officially called *Consistoire*), consisting of the clergymen and twelve members of the different colleges of council. The lay elders are elected by the smaller council on the initiative of the pastor. Their discipline covers matters of faith and morals. Smaller offenses were adjusted by the personal admonition of an elder; obstinate sinners were summoned before the college which met every week. If they remained in their rebellious disposition, they were excluded from the Lord's Supper or the congregation of believers. Obstinate opposition against the religion of the state and its institutions was reported to the secular authorities, who inflicted their own penalties. There resulted an intolerable confusion of ecclesiastical and secular power; these conditions, however, were due not so much to the peculiar ecclesiastical theories of Calvin as to the spirit of the time, which could not conceive the possibility of different religions existing side by side in one single State. It is rather due to Calvin that, in spite of this general view, the Church was not absorbed altogether in the State.

3. Genevan Ecclesiastical Tribunals.

The spirit of the ordinances of Geneva rules in all later Reformed church orders. In the French Protestant Church the purely ecclesiastical character of discipline found a clearer expression, owing to the fact that this church had to be built up independently of the State and even in opposition to it. It is the difference between theocracy and free churchism. The degrees of discipline were the same as in Geneva. The discipline of the Church extends not only over gross vices, but strives after honesty and modesty in the whole conduct of life. It was also earnestly intent upon the preservation of the right confession.

4. In France.

The church order of Lasco in London dates from 1550. It shares the view of Calvin that the Church, according to the word of God, needs a special government and discipline with a presbyterial constitution, but it embodies a freer democratic spirit. Puritanism in England received its characteristic stamp from Scotland. The congregation of strangers, formed by John Knox in Geneva, followed closely in the wake of Calvin, and their *Book of Common Order* (1558) took whole pages from the "Institutes," but after their removal to Scotland the fear of hierarchism led them into the paths of Lasco. Under its king Christ and according to his word in Matt. xvi. and xviii., the congregation rules itself by its officers: ministers, or teaching elders; ruling elders, including the pastor, for the supervision of morals in the congregation; and deacons. Presbyterial Puritanism found its completion in the Westminster Standards of 1647, the discipline of which exerted great influence upon the whole non-episcopal English-American Protestantism.

5. In Great Britain.

Another group is formed by Holland, East Frisia, and the German Lower Rhine, the ecclesiastical discipline of which was based upon the orders of the Wesel Convention (1568) and the Emden Synod (1571). Here the chief stress is laid upon the moral and social organization. The Lord's Supper belongs only to members of a constituted church. Each elder possesses his own district, and his duty is chiefly pastoral. The elders are to visit the members of the congregation regularly, together with their pastor. Upon this solid substructure the different degrees of discipline were built up. In the other German territories which received their Calvinism from their rulers, efforts to introduce church discipline were made, but in many cases they were obstructed by unfavorable conditions. Hesse-Cassel derived its order of discipline from the time when it was Lutheran, but the Palatinate furnished the example for other territories. Here it was only in 1750 that the congregations received presbyteries, and not till a century later was a presbyterial order thoroughly worked out and put into operation at the time when in other territories the Reformed Church was reconstructed, after the Thirty Years' War. The organization of the college of elders and the degrees of discipline correspond exactly to the French church order, but the whole is put into the frame of the State, the presbyteries being dependent upon the secular authorities.

6. In Holland and Germany.

Modern times have greatly modified or in part abolished the old orders of discipline, not only in Germany, but also in France and Switzerland. The principle of alliance superseded the order of individual congregations. The Dutch Church has preserved considerable remnants of the old discipline, but the firmest connection with their historical origin has been maintained by the Presbyterian churches—their strict order of church-membership forms still a solid basis of discipline. The Scottish Free Church returned even consciously to the old traditions. In Germany the old remnants of Reformed discipline are being met with the beginnings of a general Evangelical reorganization. (E. F. Karl Müller.)

7. Modern Modifications.

V. In the United States: In the Episcopal Church the discipline is laid down in the *canons*. It relates mainly to the clergy; but laymen can be kept from the sacrament of the Lord's Supper on conviction of serious offenses.

In the Presbyterian Church discipline is in the hands of the session, or the governing board of each local church, consisting of the pastor and elders; but, if the party feels aggrieved, an appeal can be made to the next higher court, the presbytery, thence to the synod, and thence to the general assembly. The method of trial in all such cases is minutely laid down in book ii. of the *Form of Government*. In the Northern Presbyterian Church, reference to the highest court can only be made when the points involved are doctrinal or constitutional. Discipline is defined to be "the exercise of that authority, and the application of that system of laws which the Lord Jesus Christ has appointed in his church." The subjects of discipline are "all baptized persons." The offense must be public, or such as demands the cognizance of the church judicatory; but private exhortation must first be employed.

Similar in definition and practise of discipline are the Dutch Reformed and German Reformed churches. Cf. *The Constitution of the Reformed Church in America*, articles xi.–xiv., and *Constitution of the Reformed Church in the United States*, part iii.

In churches holding the Congregational polity discipline is a matter for the local congregation, which may be advised by a council composed of ministers and delegates from other congregations, though the recommendations of the council are not obligatory upon the local church. Cf. H. M. Dexter, *Congregationalism*, pp. 188–195, Boston, 1876.

In the Methodist Church "an accused member shall be brought to trial before a committee of not less than five, who shall not be members of the quarterly conference (and, if the preacher judge it necessary, he may select the committee from any part of the district), in the presence of the preacher-in-charge, who shall preside at the trial, and cause exact minutes of the evidence and proceedings in the case to be taken. In the selection of the committee the parties may challenge for cause." The various causes of such action are stated. "The accused shall have the right to call to his assistance as counsel any member in good and regular standing in the Methodist Episcopal Church." If the pastor-in-charge dissent from the finding of the committee, he may appeal to the ensuing quarterly conference. Expulsion is the penalty for unworthy conduct on the part of accused members. Cf. *The Doctrines and Discipline of the Methodist-Episcopal Church*, 1880, pp. 144–151.

For further discussion see DEGRADATION; DEPOSITION; CHURCH GOVERNMENT; JURISDICTION, ECCLESIASTICAL; and INQUISITION.

BIBLIOGRAPHY: The history of discipline may be traced in Schaff, *Christian Church*, i. 501–503, ii. 187–192, iii. 356–359, iv. 371 sqq., and Neander, *Christian Church*, i. 217–221, ii. 213–216, iii. 137 sqq., 45[illegible] sqq., iv. 347 sqq. Consult also: *DCA*, i. 566 sqq.; *KL*, ii. 1561–90. For the history of discipline in the early Church the sources are the *Didache*, the works of Tertullian (especially *De pœnitentia*), Hippolytus, Cyprian (especially *De lapsis*), the Apostolical Constitutions, and the Canons of the early councils. Consult: N. Marshall, *Penitential Discipline of the Primitive Church*, reprinted in the *Library of Anglo-Catholic Theology*, Oxford, 1844; J. Kaye, *External Government and Discipline of the Church of . . . the First Three Centuries*, London, 1855; G. N. Bonwetsch, *Die Geschichte des Montanismus*, pp. 108–118, Erlangen, 1881; Hefele, *Conciliengeschichte*, i. 225 sqq., 246.

For the Catholic Church consult: F. W. H. Wasserschleben, *Bussordnungen der abendländischen Kirche*, Halle, 1851; F. Frank, *Die Bussdisciplin der Kirche*, Mainz, 1868; T. L. Green, *Indulgences, Sacramental Absolutions, and the Tax Tables of the Roman Penitentiary*, London, 1872 (Roman Catholic apologetic); R. Gibbings, *The Taxes of the Apostolic Penitentiary; or the Prices of Sins in the Church of Rome*, Dublin, 1872 (Protestant polemic); F. Probst, *Sacramentale und Sacramentalien*, Tübingen, 1872; Vacandard, *The Inquisition*, London, 1908; and literature under INQUISITION.

For the Lutheran Church consult: O. Goeschen, *Doctrina de disciplina eccl. . . .*, Halle, 1859; A. L. Richter, *Geschichte der evangelischen Kirchenverfassung in Deutschland*, Leipsic, 1851; idem, *Kirchenrecht*, ed. Kahl, § 227, ib. 1886; F. A. Tholuck, *Vorgeschichte des Rationalismus*, II. i., pp. 190 sqq., Halle, 1859–62; O. K. E. F. Fabri, *Ueber Kirchenzucht*, Stuttgart, 1854; O. Mejer, *Kirchenzucht*, Rostock, 1854; idem, *Lehrbuch des deutschen Kirchenrechts*, Göttingen, 1869; C. I. Nitzsch, *Praktische Theologie*, i. 221 sqq., Bonn, 1859; Schaff, *Creeds* (for the standards); H. E. Jacobs, *Book of Concord*, 2 vols., Philadelphia, 1893.

For the Reformed Churches consult on the general question, besides the works of Goeschen and Richter above: A. L. Richter, *Die evangelischen Kirchenordnungen des 16. Jahrhunderts*, Weimar, 1846; S. Miller, *Manual of Presbytery*, ed. J. G. Lorimer, Edinburgh, 1842; G. V. Lechler, *Geschichte der Presbyterial- und Synodalverfassung*, Leyden, 1854; C. B. Hundeshagen, *Beiträge zur Kirchenverfassungsgeschichte*, Wiesbaden, 1864; G. Galli, *Die lutherischen und calvinischen Kirchenstrafen*, Breslau, 1879; K. Rieker, *Grundsätze reformirter Kirchenverfassung;* R. Staehelin, *H. Zwingli*, i. 445 sqq., ii. 137 sqq., 440 sqq., Basel, 1895–97; E. Egli, *Analecta reformatoria*, i. 99 sqq., Zurich, 1899; F. W. Kampfschulte, *Joh. Calvin*, i. 385 sqq., ii. 354 sqq., Leipsic, 1899; *La Discipline ecclésiastique des églises réformées de France*, ed. D'Huisseau, Charenton, 1667; J. Aymon, *Tous les synodes nationaux des églises réformées de France*, The Hague, 1710; [W. Dunlop], *A Collection of Confessions of Faith, Catechisms, Directories, Books of Discipline . . .*, Edinburgh, 1722; J. Bannermann, *The Church of Christ*, ib. 1868; J. Cook, *Styles of Writs, Forms of Procedure and Practice of the Church Courts of Scotland*, ib. 1870; W. Pierce, *Ecclesiastical Principles . . . of the Wesleyan Methodists*, London, 1873; T. B. Hardern, *Church Discipline, its Hist. and Present Aspect*, Cambridge, 1892; Raitsma en van Veen, *Acta . . . en particuliere synoden*, Groningen, 1892–99.

For the United States, besides the works mentioned in the text, consult: T. C. Upham, *Ratio disciplinæ*, Portland, 1844; F. Wayland, *Principles and Practice of Baptist Churches*, New York, 1857; R. Emory, *Hist. of the Discipline of the Methodist Episcopal Church*, ib. 1864; R. H. Tyler, *American Ecclesiastical Law*, Albany, 1866; T. B. McFalls and B. Sunderland, *Manual of Presbyterian Law and Usage*, Washington, 1873; A. T. McGill, *Church Government*, Philadelphia, 1890; J. Fulton, *Index canonum*, New York, 1892; J. Andrews, *Church Law*, ib., n.d. Vol. iii. of Schaff's *Creeds* contains the texts of the principal standards.

CHURCH OF ENGLAND. See ENGLAND, CHURCH OF.

CHURCH EXTENSION SOCIETY: A society founded in Chicago in 1905 for the purpose of assisting Roman Catholic home missionary work in the United States. The movement was inaugurated and organized by Rev. Francis C. Kelley, then pastor at Lapeer, Mich. The object of the society is to raise funds for the erection and maintenance of churches and chapels in those numerous Western and Southern districts where the Catholic population is so small and scattered that self-supporting parishes are either an impossibility or, at least, can subsist only in distressing conditions. The means adopted to this end is a systematized contribution of two cents per week from all Catholics in the United States. The movement soon became popular, and at present it counts among its governing officers many of the most prominent bishops and archbishops of the country. A monthly paper, *Extension*, the official organ of the society, is published in Chicago under the direction of Father Kelley. JAMES F. DRISCOLL.

CHURCH FATHERS: A title of honor applied to the early writers of the Christian Church. It was originally given to the bishops; when appeal was made to their testimony as representatives of the teaching office of the Church, it was an easy transition to the inclusion with them of venerated writers of an earlier period, even though they had not held the episcopal office. Thus by the fifth century the term "Fathers" is found used in very much its modern sense. Antiquity alone, however, is not held sufficient to confer this title, as Vincent of Lerins clearly states (*Commonitorium*, ii. 24); Hilary of Poitiers (on Matt. v.) says that Tertullian "by his subsequent error destroyed the authority of his approved writings." Accordingly modern Roman Catholic theologians, among whom the title is most strictly used, are accustomed to require four qualifications—orthodoxy of doctrine, sanctity of life, the approbation of the Church, and antiquity. For the Latin Church the line of the Fathers closes with Pope Gregory I. (d. 604); for the Greek Church with John of Damascus (d. 754). See APOSTOLIC FATHERS; DOCTOR; PATRISTICS.

BIBLIOGRAPHY: G. R. Crooks and J. F. Hurst, *Theological Encyclopædia and Methodology*, pp. 396-399, New York, 1894.

CHURCH FEDERATION.

The term "church federation" has come into use in recent years to designate the spirit and methods of cooperation and unity that in varied ways are bringing Protestant Churches and Christian bodies into organized affiliation and united action in matters of common interest and service. As a movement it is for the most part confined to the fellowship of the Churches that hold to historical and Evangelical Christianity. As a practical working force it has found expression especially in the United States and Great Britain and in countries where foreign missionary work is carried on by societies supported by these nations.

I. The United States: Historically the federation movement in the United States is linked with the development of the spirit of unity which found expression in the nineteenth century through the American branch of the Evangelical Alliance (q.v.). A conference held in New York, Dec. 3, 1899, took steps which resulted in the organization of the National Federation of Churches and Christian Workers. A letter was then prepared and sent out by the Executive Committee expressing the hope that it might be the forerunner of a "National Federation of all our Protestant Christian denominations, through their official action." At the annual meeting held in Washington, Feb., 1903, action was taken requesting "the highest ecclesiastical or advisory bodies of the Evangelical Churches to appoint representative delegates to a National Conference." Thirty denominational bodies having an aggregate membership of over seventeen million members responded and were represented by nearly five hundred delegates in the great Interchurch Conference on Federation held in New York, Nov. 15-21, 1905.[1] By a substantially unanimous vote a Plan of Federation was adopted and recommended "to the Christian bodies represented in the Conference for their approval." This plan created a "Federal Council of the Churches of Christ in America" and became operative when approved by two-thirds of the constituent bodies. Such approval having been received, the council was organized and its first meeting was held in Dec., 1908.

1. The National Federation of Churches.

The preamble to this Plan of Federation expresses the conviction that "in the providence of God, the time has come when it seems fitting more fully to manifest the essential oneness of the Christian Churches of America, in Jesus Christ as their Divine Lord and Savior, and to promote the spirit of fellowship, service, and cooperation among them." The object of the Federal Council is stated in the Constitution to be: "(1) To express the fellowship and catholic unity of the Christian Church. (2) To bring the Christian bodies of America into united service for Christ and the world. (3) To encourage devotional fellowship and mutual counsel concerning the spiritual life and religious activities of the Churches. (4) To secure a larger combined influence for the Churches of Christ in all matters affecting the moral and social conditions of the people, so as to promote the application

2. Its Aims and Achievements.

[1] The following is the list of Churches represented: the Baptist Churches of the United States; the Free Baptist General Conference; the Christians (Christian Connection); the Congregational Churches; the Disciples of Christ; the Evangelical Association; the Evangelical Synod of North America; the Friends; the Evangelical Lutheran Church, General Synod; the Methodist Episcopal Church; the Methodist Episcopal Church, South; the Primitive Methodist Church; the Colored Methodist Episcopal Church in America; the Methodist Protestant Church; the African Methodist Episcopal Church; the African Methodist Episcopal Zion Church; the General Conference of the Mennonite Church of North America; the Moravian Church; the Presbyterian Church in the United States of America; the Cumberland Presbyterian Church; the Welsh Calvinistic Methodist or Presbyterian Church; the Reformed Presbyterian Church; the United Presbyterian Church; the Protestant Episcopal Church; the Reformed Church in America; the Reformed Church in the United States of America; the Reformed Episcopal Church; the Seventh-day Baptist Churches; the United Brethren in Christ; the United Evangelical Church.

of the law of Christ in every relation of human life. (5) To assist in the organization of local branches of the Federal Council to promote its aims in their communities." The difference between federated union and organic church union is clearly defined in the stipulation that "this Federal Council shall have no authority over the constituent bodies adhering to it: but its province shall be limited to the expression of its counsel and the recommending of a course of action in matters of common interest to the Churches, local councils, and individual Christians." The Council "has no authority to draw up a common creed or form of government or of worship, or in any way to limit the full autonomy of the Christian bodies adhering to it."

Historically this national movement "for the prosecution of work that can be better done in union than in separation" has found initiative and encouragement through federated activities, State and local. The Interdenominational Commission of Maine was organized in 1892, and is composed of members appointed by official State bodies representing the Baptist, Free Baptist, Christian, Congregational, and Methodist Churches. The principles under which this Commission acts seek to secure practical reciprocity among these denominations, both in the planting of new churches and in the readjustment of forces when through overmultiplication of churches or decrease in population conditions exist that demand consolidation through union and comity of action. The plans of the Commission aim not to organize so-called "union churches," but to consolidate religious forces, still leaving them within the limits of denominational fellowship. The secretary of the Commission, who has held this position since its work began in 1905, bears testimony "that in thirty-seven of the fifty-one cases entered on the records of the Commission consultation respecting the clash of interests has sufficed to relieve the strain: mere friendly conference has led to an adjustment of the difficulties. Many other cases, without such mention as would justify entrance on the records, have been adjusted by the same friendly means, and in a great many other instances still an effective influence has been exerted in ways that have maintained an ideal of fraternal cooperation which has tended to elevate very much of the church work of the State from the low level of partizan and sectarian strife." Commissions similar to that in Maine exist in other States, but their work as yet has not been as effective in its results. In the aggregate, however, consultation and comity are increasingly taking the place of competitive action in home mission and church extension work. The State Federations organized in Massachusetts, Rhode Island, Wisconsin, and other commonwealths have already proved the need and effectiveness of united effort. In their purposes they have a common aim, but in methods they are working along lines suggested by local environment and limited by executive resources.

II. Great Britain and Other Lands: Church federation in England and Great Britain is largely a movement unifying the activities of Nonconformist Churches in matters of common interest. Its organizing center is the National Council of the Evangelical Free Churches which was founded in 1894. Membership in this Council comes through local Councils. "The Churches constituting the local Councils are the Congregational, the Baptist Churches, the Methodist Churches, the Presbyterian Church of England, the Free Episcopal Churches, the Society of Friends, and such other Evangelical Churches as the National Council may at any time admit." The total number of Councils in 1906 was 807 with more than fifty District Federations. The latest report says: "The aim of our Movement has from the beginning been preeminently spiritual, and the main work of the local Councils in all parts of the country has been United Missions." The relation in which the Free Churches stand to the Established Church of England has been a powerful factor in drawing them into close and effective fellowship. The work of the local Councils includes activities not only evangelistic, but social and philanthropic.

In other lands church federation is already a potent factor in the unifying of Christian forces represented through missionary organizations. The Standing Committee of Cooperating Christian Missions in Japan is made up of representatives from nearly all the different missions. Since its organization in 1902 it has exerted a notable influence in advancing plans of comity and cooperation. At the great China Centenary Missionary Conference held at Shanghai in May, 1907, steps were taken to federate all of the Christian forces in the empire. In India the missionary workers are laboring not only to federate their activities, but achieve definite plans of organic church union. This spirit of unity and desire for closer fellowship is illustrated in action that is being taken in every part of the world by those having in charge the missionary work of Protestant Churches.

The indications multiply that church federation stands for a movement of profound significance in its relation to the present and future history of Christianity in its institutional life and fellowship.

E. B. Sanford.

Bibliography: E. B. Sanford, *Church Federation*, New York, 1905 (contains reports of the Interchurch Conference on Federation); *Federation* (the quarterly published in New York by the Federation of Churches in New York City); the *Annual Reports* of the National Federation of Churches, of the Committee of Cooperating Missions (Japan), and of the National Council of Free Churches (England).

CHURCH (CHURCHES) OF GOD: The name of several religious bodies in America.

1. The Church of God in North America, popularly known as **Winebrennarians,** is a Baptist denomination founded by John Winebrenner in 1830. The founder was born at Glade Valley, Frederick County, Md., Mar. 25, 1797; d. at Harrisburg, Pa., Sept. 12, 1860. He studied at Dickinson College, Carlisle, Pa., and learned theology under Dr. Samuel Helfenstein. Called to the pastorate of the German Reformed Church at Harrisburg, Pa., he was ordained at Hagerstown, Md., Sept. 24, 1820. His earnest preaching resulted in a revival, in which he opposed theaters, dancing, gambling, lotteries, and racing, thus causing opposition which resulted in official charges against him. He severed his relations with his charge and with the Reformed Church in 1825, but continued his ministry in and around Harrisburg, extensive revivals of religion following. His theological views gradually changed as the result of his study of the Bible. Congregations were formed at a number of points, and several ministers were ordained. In Oct., 1830, six of these ministers met in Harrisburg and agreed to form a body to be called the General Eldership of the Church of God, the term "general eldership" being used to distinguish this body from the eldership of the local church.

In doctrine the Church is prevailingly Arminian and orthodox. It is largely premillenarian, and practises three ordinances: baptism, by immersion; the Lord's Supper, observed in the evening; and washing of feet. The local church polity is presbyterial, each church having its own board of elders and deacons. The churches within a given district are associated together for cooperation in general work. The pastors and other ordained ministers within a district, together with an equal number of lay elders, constitute an annual eldership which appoints the ministers to the various charges. These annual elderships elect an equal number of ministerial and lay delegates, who constitute the general eldership, changed in 1905 from a triennial to a quadrennial body, the highest judicatory of the denomination.

The Church now reports two annual elderships in Pennsylvania, two in West Virginia, two in Oklahoma, and one each in Maryland, Ohio, Indiana, Michigan, Illinois, Iowa, Nebraska, Missouri, Kansas, Arkansas, and Oregon. A general eldership, composed of delegates from the annual elderships, was organized in 1845, and the General Eldership of the Church of God organized in 1830 became the East Pennsylvania eldership. In 1866 the title of the general eldership, as also those of the annual elderships, was changed to the form, The General Eldership of the Churches of God. The total membership is estimated to be about 40,000, with 500 ministers. The general eldership controls the institutions of learning, of which there are three (Findlay College, Findlay, O.; Fort Scott Collegiate Institute, Fort Scott, Kan.; and Barkeyville Academy, Barkeyville, Pa.), and the publishing house and book store at Harrisburg, Pa. Each annual eldership is engaged in missionary work in its own territory, and frontier mission work is carried on by the general eldership in Missouri, Kansas, Nebraska, Colorado, Oklahoma, Arkansas, Oregon, and Washington. There is a Woman's General Missionary Society, which, through the Board of Missions of the general eldership, supports four American missionaries, ten or twelve native workers, and a number of Bible readers in Ulubaria and Bogra Districts, Bengal Province, India.

C. H. Forney.

Bibliography: J. Winebrenner, *Brief Views of the Church of God*, Harrisburg, 1840; idem, *A Treatise on Regeneration*, ib. 1844; idem, *Practical and Doctrinal Sermons*, ib. 1860. The church paper is the *Church Advocate*, Harrisburg, Pa.

2. The Church of God and Saints of Christ (the "Black Jews") are chiefly negroes who claim to be the descendants and representatives of the true Jews; it is held that the latter were originally a black people and that the descendants of the lost tribes have changed color through mixture with the Gentiles. The Church was founded at Topeka, Kan., in 1897 by William S. Crowdy, who claimed to be called "to be a prophet of God sent to the whole world." The Saints respect both Jewish and Christian law and ritual, and interpret the Scriptures literally. Their system of doctrine is presented in Crowdy's manual, *The Bible Story Revealed* (Philadelphia, 1902). Among the principal points of belief are: repentance the first step to the kingdom; the seventh day the Sabbath; abstinence from wine and strong drink; foot-washing; prayer in the words of Jesus; the holy kiss; religion the exercise of love, charity, and hospitality; the law of Moses completed, supplemented, or abolished by the law of God in Christ. The ministry consists of the Prophet Crowdy, two bishops (one in Africa), evangelists (whose functions are those of visitation), and elders or pastors of churches. The polity is presbyterial, with an annual "Board Meeting," and a quadrennial General Assembly. There is also an annual celebration of the Passover with mingled Hebrew and Christian rites. The organization reports about one hundred churches (seven in Africa) and 8,000 to 9,000 members. The largest church and the denominational headquarters are in Philadelphia. Business enterprises are conducted in connection with many of the churches, a farm colony is located at Belleville, Va., and the establishment of a widows' and orphans' home and a training-school there is contemplated.

W. H. Larrabee.

Bibliography: The organ of the denomination is the *Weekly Prophet*, Philadelphia.

3. The Adventist Church of God, a branch of the Seventh-day Adventists. See Adventists, 5.

4. The Churches of God in Christ Jesus, popularly known as the Age-to-come Adventists. See Adventists, 6.

5. The Mennonite Church of God in Christ. See Mennonites.

CHURCH GOVERNMENT.

[The following article is a condensation of the article *Kirchenregiment* in the Hauck-Herzog *RE*; for more general discussion of the subject see Polity.]

Church government in the speech of to-day denotes that particular conduct of the ecclesiastical community which is not effected by means of the spiritual administration of word and sacraments, but by means which on occasion may be of civil constitution. Prior to the Reformation the pastor was called *rector*, and *regere ecclesiam* ("to govern the Church") indicated his spiritual care over the congregation through the word and sacraments. Church government is thus, originally, the pastoral, though logically also the episcopal, and, in the last resort, the papal cure of souls; because the bishop is properly the pastor of his diocese, and the pope—at all events according to the doctrine of the curia—*parochus mundi* (see CURE OF SOULS). However, the divinely given authority for the spiritual control (*potestas ecclesiastica;* see AUTHORITY, ECCLESIASTICAL) embraces, according to the theory then in vogue, every regulative function, whether in a proper sense spiritual or not; that is, certain functions not within the direct sphere of word and sacrament, provided only the same appear expedient to the bishop or pope, as the case may be, with relation to the cure of souls. Hence prior to the Reformation church government was regarded as part and parcel of the episcopal, or ultimately papal, cure of souls. It was only after the establishment of the Reformers' principle, that this theory conflicts with Scripture, and that the ecclesiastical authority which is to be exercised by the spiritual office in virtue of divine commission comprises rather the sole administration of word and sacraments, and not, in addition, external control, that the institution of church government as a power by itself could become developed and was actually developed. The idea of church government in this sense is Protestant; the Roman Catholic Church, in so far as it has continued upon the pre-Reformation basis, still construes the matter as falling within the spiritual province of ecclesiastical authority.

1. Meaning of the Expression.

Of the two Protestant Church bodies in which, upon the basis of the aforesaid Reformation doctrine, a scheme of church government has taken shape distinct from the spiritual economy it is pertinent to consider first the Reformed Church; and in fact its Calvinistic branch is of exceptional interest in this connection. The task of organizing the Protestant Church in France was complicated at the outset by the hostility of the government. In the face of this enmity, the Church had to organize as an independent association. Starting with Calvin's tenets that the church organization described in the Acts of the Apostles and the pastoral epistles is ordained by God to be directed by a college of elders, and that this Church is an example or article of faith for every particular congregation, it developed this assumption, following Calvin's interpretation of Eph. iv. 11 sqq., Rom. xii. 7, and I Cor. xii. 28, into the doctrine that in accordance with the aforesaid divine arrangement there are two kinds of elders; namely, not only bearers of the teaching office—who, in agreement with the Lutheran Church, were held to be restricted to teaching and the administration of the sacraments—but also "ruling" elders, who were regarded as filling the spiritual, but not the teaching office (Calvin's "Institutes," IV., chaps. i.–v., xi., xii.). Pastor and ruling elders together constituted the governing body of the congregation (Fr. *consistoire*, cf. K. Rieker, *Grundsätze reformirter Kirchenverfassung*, Leipsic, 1899, pp. 102 sqq., 141 sqq.). Then there came together from the congregations, comprising a definite group, certain delegates of the *consistoires*, both teaching and ruling officers, to form committees ("synods"), through whose agency the corresponding church circuit was governed, the same as the congregation by the agency of the *consistoire*. Further, the French Evangelical Church as a whole is governed by a general synod (cf. G. von Polenz, *Geschichte des französischen Calvinismus*, 4 vols., Gotha, 1857; G. V. Lechler, *Geschichte der Presbyterial- und Synodalverfassung*, Leyden, 1854, pp. 64 sqq.). The essential basis of the [Reformed] church government is thus clearly apparent in the main, even though now and then its lines of distinction coalesce. It rests upon divine authority just as in the pre-Reformation Church; save that this commissioned authority is not imparted to the teaching elders, but only to the ruling ones. Yet the former take part, and indeed as weighty personages, in the sessions of the governing bodies, though this is only because they administer the order of salvation, and because all church government, in the nature of the case, has no other object than to render possible and make sure the order of salvation; hence the teaching presbyters enjoy their influence upon church government not as retainers of a divine commission to rule, but as expert representatives of their divine commission to teach; so much so, for instance, that in questions of doctrine the non-spiritual members of synods have no voice. These fundamental ideas of the French constitution of presbyterial-synodal church government have undergone, in the course of time and in connection with their development in German territories, various alterations an account of which properly belongs to church history.

2. The Reformed Church Government.

Two fundamental points differentiate the Lutheran theory of church government both from the pre-Reformation and Roman Catholic theory and from the Calvinistic-Reformed theory. In the first place, the Lutheran Church does not assume that there is any form of church government ordained by divine commission, coincidently with the institution of the Church, but rather esteems every form of government admissible by whose operation sufficient provision is made for the rightful administration of word and sacraments. Hence there is no Lutheran dogmatic basis of church government; and Lutherans accord to the claim of the Reformed that there is no such higher dignity than that of a theological opinion. The second point is the fact that the Lutheran Church, when, in accordance with the imperial decree of 1526 at Speyer, it developed the State Church polity, virtually from the very start placed church government in the State sovereign's hand. In consequence of these two differences the question of Lutheran church government is much more complicated than that of the pre-Reformation Church, or of the Roman Catholic or of the Reformed Churches.

3. Fundamental Differences of Lutheran View.

It has been asserted that the Reformers' ideals

were inconsistent with state government of the Church; and some (notably so F. J. Stahl, in *Kirchenverfassung nach Lehre und Recht der Protestanten*, Erlangen, 1840, 2d ed., 1862; *Lutherische Kirche und Union*, Berlin, 1859) have interpreted these ideals as tending in the direction of the pre-Reformation conception; others (as A. L. Richter, in the *Zeitschrift für deutsches Recht und die Rechtswissenschaft*, iv., 1840, pp. 1 sqq.; *Lehrbuch des Kirchenrechts*, Leipsic, 1841 sqq.; *Geschichte der evangelischen Kirchenverfassung in Deutschland*, 1851) think that they sympathize with the presbyterial-synodal organization. This difference of opinion shows how slight is the foundation for either side. Both views have arisen from the rational desire to obtain historic support and Reformation authority for party strivings—the product and expression of modern times—and the contentions of both Stahl and Richter are inadmissible. The chief argument against Stahl's theory is the attitude of the Reformers with reference to the actual institution and organization of church government by the territorial sovereigns: it is incompatible with a conception of polity fundamentally contrary. Richter, on his side, to demonstrate his proposition of presbyterial-synodal ideals of organization on the part of the Reformers, assumes that their views underwent a change somewhere about 1525; before that time their ideals were presbyterial-synodal, but, owing to their experiences with Anabaptism and the Peasants' War, the said ideals were crowded out, and the Reformers were obliged to admit the actual necessity of church government under territorial sovereignty. Richter submits this contention without more particular evidence, which would be hard to find. He forgets, for one thing, that the principles from which the territorial sovereignty form of church polity is deduced theologically were extant even prior to 1525, and were declared by the Reformers; on another side, that not until after that year did the Reformation begin its ecclesiastical organization, so that only the ideas realized by the Reformers after that year are in question; it was not in the spirit of that age to project and formulate ideal systems of organization without practical conditions to uphold them.

4. German Reformers not Opposed to State Government.

5. State Government Accepted in Luther's Time.

R. Sohm in his *Kirchenrecht* (Leipsic, 1892) has defended the thesis that the territorial sovereignty form of church government came about in opposition to Luther's doctrine and after his death, and that it was a product of the pusillanimous faith of Luther's contemporaries and successors, being closely related to the reaction, especially on Melanchthon's part, to Roman theories and to the consistorial fabric which grew out of their influence, and the reenforcement of these consistories with temporal means of coercion. This thesis is untenable. If historical evolution be taken just as it stands, and the literature of the sixteenth century be considered as a whole, there can be no doubt that the government of the Church by the sovereigns of the State was in harmony with the Reformers' theory; provided in this connection is understood by church government not the Reformers' "ecclesiastical authority" (see AUTHORITY, ECCLESIASTICAL), but all that is involved in a legal direction of the church organism. The theory in question is not in any way taught by Melanchthon exclusively, as had been occasionally affirmed before Sohm; but in its main outlines it is apparent as early as Luther's tract *An den Adel deutscher Nation* (cf. O. Mejer, *Die Grundlagen des lutherischen Kirchenregiments*, Rostock, 1864, pp. 26 sqq.), and it is elsewhere taught by Luther and others. It is clearly implied in the Lutheran confessional writings (Augs. Con., art. xxviii.; Art. Schmal., *de potestate papæ*, pp. 354–355; Larger and Smaller Catechisms, pp. 361, 363, 446, and elsewhere; most plainly in *Augs. Con. variata*, article on marriage of priests, in Hase, *Libri symbolici*, p. L.). Its theological basic thoughts come to light in a long array of liturgies and other kinds of promulgations on the part of the Reformatory territorial sovereigns.

6. Actual Views of Luther and his Contemporaries.

The Church as a corporate unity separated from the State is a thoroughly modern idea, to Luther thoroughly unknown (cf. Schenkel, *TSK*, 1850, p. 1; Hundeshagen, *ZKR*, i., pp. 451 sqq.; W. Kahl, *Verschiedenheit der katholischen und evangelischen Anschauung über das Verhältnis von Staat und Kirche*, Leipsic, 1886; O. Mejer, *Rechtsleben der deutschen evangelischen Landeskirchen*, Hanover, 1899, pp. 28 sqq.; K. Rieker, ut sup., pp. 55 sqq.). In this unity two powers work side by side, the two swords of the Middle Ages; but this indicates merely a "division of the administrative organization of the single body"; the well-known and so often misunderstood utterances of Luther as to the relation of the temporal to the spiritual power are not intended to mean that the temporal power has nothing at all to do in the Church, but rather that within the one body two members, each in its office, have to cooperate for the weal of the whole organism, only neither is to encroach upon the other within its rightful sphere. The spiritual commission of the teaching order thus appears to be confined to the word and administration of the sacraments (that is, ecclesiastical power in Luther's sense of the term); the authority of the governing order appears to be directed toward rightfully upholding the laws of God as expressed in the Ten Commandments, especially according to the first table of the same, to the end that no unlawful form of divine service be endured in the land. From these premises everything essential to the state control of church government proceeds with logical finality. Nor is this conclusion impaired by the fact that the Reformers themselves accounted the government's position not so much a source of rights as a sum of obligations the government was to fulfil, a responsible office which called into play all those prerogatives which moderns are wont to designate as corollaries to a "government."

To be sure, alongside these lines of thought are

also to be found certain documentary indications of the germs of a second and divergent theory; not one, however, that reaches backward toward the pastoral form of church government, but one out of which, in favoring circumstances, a presbyterial-synodal polity might have grown. There is here in mind, above all, that fundamental principle of Protestantism, the common priesthood. For even though it be true that this principle was conceived by the Reformers only as a religious principle (so that things were carried too far when in earlier times it was attempted to derive from this basis independent administration and congregational tenets, and set these up as express doctrines of the Reformation), it is none the less an overshooting of the mark on another side when modern writers like Sohm (ut sup., p. 510) and Rieker (ut sup., p. 79) profess to credit this thought with no influence at all upon the constitution of the Evangelical Church (cf. E. Sehling, in *ZKR*, 1894, p. 229, and *Kirchengesetzgebung unter Moriz von Sachsen*, Leipsic, 1898, pp. 3 sqq.). If, conformably to the well-known doctrine of the Lutheran confessional writings (cf. the same collected with the pertinent citations in O. Mejer, *Lehrbuch des Kirchenrechts*, Göttingen, 1869), the congregation of believers is bound by the obligations of faith to see to it that sufficient provision is made at all times for the rightful administration of word and sacraments, and if, furthermore, this congregation is charged with responsibility before God in this matter (*Apol.*, p. 292, and elsewhere), it follows that the congregation as a congregation must see to it that this divine commission is properly exercised by those whom it appoints to this end. Upon such bases a presbyterial-synodal church government might very well be constructed. But these ideas were not developed, because, as above set forth, they were thrust aside and suppressed by the system of territorial sovereignty that governed the Church. Or, slightly changed, they were introduced into the territorial system by the teaching that since each member of the congregation is bound to contribute according to the measure of his ability toward the maintenance of a rightful and adequate administration of the word and sacraments, and since the territorial sovereign possesses an especially high measure of such ability (in virtue whereof he is designated as *membrum ecclesiæ præcipuum*), he must accordingly apply all his power entrusted to him by God toward the satisfaction of that obligation. By this process the government of the Church might practically fall into the hands of the territorial sovereign alone; because the means at his disposal are so vastly superior to those of all other church-members that these, in comparison, find nothing further to do (Luther's *Bedenken von 1530*. Erlangen ed., liv., p. 179; Art. Schmal., p. 350; Mejer, ut sup., pp. 109 sqq., cf. 27, 36, 46). The idea of *membrum ecclesiæ præcipuum*, to be sure, is again and again obscured by subsequent absurd usage; but it always carries the assumption that the territorial sovereign has the power to apply his governing rights to the furtherance of ecclesiastical ends. This was the case in the Reformation period and in general so long as his rights were regarded and exercised as operative private rights. According to the civil law of to-day, however, the governing rights of the territorial sovereign are in the nature of public powers, which reach no further than their corresponding official obligations. The doctrine of *membrum ecclesiæ præcipuum* is therefore antiquated, and has no significance in present praxis. On the other hand, conjointly with the *custodia prioris tabulæ*, it constituted, down to the middle, or thereabout, of the nineteenth century, the principal foundation upon which the territorial sovereignty rule of the Church was declared to be a part of the territorial governing office, and as such was regarded as an adjunct of state supremacy.

7. Influence of the Idea of the Common Priesthood.

Meanwhile, after some beginnings of changing views that were even earlier apparent, since the middle of the eighteenth century the point of view according to which church government is administered by the State has changed more and more. In place of the purpose to uphold the first table of the Ten Commandments, there intervened, as Territorialism (q.v.) came into power, the humanitarian-political aim to make the State religiously a unity, to the end that quiet and peace, the supreme ends of the State, be achieved; and when a subsequent further evolution of things brought the tolerance principle into play, for this aim was substituted one deriving from freedom of conscience, which determines state activity on this side to-day. The theory of the Church was next changed by the natural right school; the Church is not an institution founded by God, but a society, an association within the State. But several equally legitimate churches standing side by side in the State can be treated by the state government only as church associations which govern themselves; and if among them there is a Lutheran Church, its status does not differ from that of any other, and the right of the State in its government becomes a mere *Kirchenhoheit* (*jus circa sacra*), which is essentially the police control of associations. This appears the more equitable since the new constitutional progress has brought matters to such a pass that the popular representatives have acquired directly or indirectly a determining influence in legislation and certain other specific rights of government, indeed the entire sphere of operation; since, further, all representatives in the Diet have equal voice—the Reformed, the Roman Catholic, and the non-Christian members the same as the Lutherans—and this equality of influence on the part of non-adherents of the Lutheran Church is inconsistent with its constitutional parity. Accordingly there are projects on every side in the direction of a logical transformation of the territorial sovereignty form of church polity into corporate self-government. It has been previously remarked that the Reformers' theology opened the way to progress in this direction; and that the example of the Calvinistic Reformed Church was not far removed, even though the latter's dogmatic tenets were not here to the purpose. And in fact it is true that

8. Modern Development of German Church Government.

as soon as the collegialistic and constitutional State theories gained force and were here earlier, there later, here more, there less, carried into execution, likewise in the Lutheran Church the congregations have employed presbyterial church committees; synods have been constituted of representatives of these committees for districts; and finally a general synod for the land, or, where several Lutheran denominations exist, a synod of the denominations has been brought together as the general representative body of the church. So the Lutheran Church is acquiring the organization of a corporate Church, in virtue whereof it governs itself.

E. SEHLING.

CHURCH HISTORY.

I. Nature and Aim: Church history embraces, in the widest sense, the whole religious development from the creation to the present time, and is continually growing in bulk. In a narrower sense, it is confined to a history of Christianity and the Christian Church from the birth of Christ and the Day of Pentecost, when Christianity made its first appearance in an organized form as distinct from the Jewish religion. The historian has to trace the origin, growth, and fortunes of the Church, and to reproduce its life in the different ages. The value of his work depends upon the degree of its truthfulness, or exact correspondence with the facts. Church history is not a heap of dry bones, but life and power: it is the Church itself in constant motion and progress from land to land, and from age to age, until the whole world shall be filled with the knowledge of Christ. It is the most interesting part of the world's history, as religion is the deepest and most important concern of man, the bond that unites him to God. It embraces the external expansion and contraction of Christianity, or the history of missions and persecutions, the visible organization of church polity and discipline, the development of doctrine and theology, the worship, with its various rites and ceremonies, liturgies, sacred poetry and music, the manifestations of practical piety, Christian morality, and benevolent institutions; in one word, all that belongs to the inner and outer life of Christianity in the world. It is a panorama of God's dealings with the human race, and man's relations to God under all aspects. It shows the gradual unfolding of the plan of redemption—a plan of infinite wisdom and goodness, in constant conflict with the Satanic powers and influences which are struggling for the ascendency, but are doomed to ultimate defeat, and to be overruled for good. It is the greatest triumph of God's wisdom to bring good out of evil, and to overrule the wrath of man for his own glory and for the progress of truth and righteousness. Church history is a book of life, full of warning and precept, of hope and encouragement.

II. Church History and Secular History: These differ as Church and State, as Christianity and humanity, as the order of grace and the order of nature; yet they are inseparably connected, and the one can not be understood without the other. Among the Jews the spiritual and secular history together form the one history of theocracy. Both currents intermingle in the Byzantine Empire, in the European States and the Latin Church during the Middle Ages, in the period of the Reformation, during the colonial period of America, and in all countries where Church and State are united. Gibbon's *History of the Decline and Fall of the Roman Empire* is in great part also a history of the rise and progress of Christianity, which survived the fall of Old and New Rome, and went forth to conquer the barbarian conquerors by Christianizing and civilizing them. Every history of the papacy is also a history of the German Roman Empire, and *vice versa*. No history of the sixteenth century can be written without constant reference to the Protestant Reformation and Roman Catholic reaction. The Franciscan, Dominican, and Jesuit missions along the St. Lawrence, down the Mississippi, and in Mexico, Florida, and the islands of the Caribbean Sea, and the Puritan settlements of New England are the beginning, alike of the ecclesiastical and secular history of North America. In modern times the tendency is more and more toward a separation of the spiritual and temporal powers; nevertheless, the Church will always be influenced by the surrounding state of civil society, and must adapt itself to the wants of the age, and progress of events; while, on the other hand, the world will always feel the moral influence, the restraining, stimulating, and sanctifying power of Christianity, which works like a leaven from within upon the ramifications of society.

III. Sources: These are mostly written, though in part unwritten. The written sources include (1) The official documents of ecclesiastical and civil authorities, such as acts of councils, creeds, liturgies, hymn-books, church-laws, papal bulls and encyclicals. (2) The writings of the personal actors in the history, and contemporary observers and reporters, such as the Fathers for ancient Christianity, the Schoolmen for medieval, the Reformers and their opponents for the Reformation period. (3) Inscriptions on walls, pictures, churches, tombstones, and other monuments. The history of the Hebrew religion has derived much light from modern discoveries of monumental remains in Egypt, Babylonia, and Assyria (qq.v.), the deciphering of the hieroglyphic and cuneiform inscriptions, the Moabite Stone, and the code of Hammurabi. See INSCRIPTIONS; MOABITE STONE; and HAMMURABI AND HIS CODE.

1. Written Sources.

The unwritten sources are works of Christian art, such as churches, chapels, pictures, sculptures, crosses, crucifixes, relics, and other monuments which symbolize and embody Christian ideas. The Roman catacombs, with their vast extent, their solemn darkness, their labyrinthine mystery, their rude epitaphs and sculptures, their symbols of faith, and their relics of martyrdom, give a lifelike idea of the Church in the period of persecution, its trials and sufferings, its faith and hope, its simple worship and devoted piety. "He who is thoroughly steeped in the imagery of the catacombs will be nearer to the thoughts of the early Church than he who has learned by heart the most elaborate treatises of Tertullian or Origen." The basilicas are characteristic of the Nicene period; the Byzantine churches, of the Byzantine age and the Eastern and Russian Church; the Gothic cathedrals, of the palmy days of medieval Catholicism; the Renaissance style, of the revival of letters. Even now, most churches and sects can be best appreciated in the localities, and in view of the monuments and the people, where they originated, or have their center of life and action.

2. Unwritten Sources.

IV. Duty of the Historian: The historian must master the sources in the original languages in which they were written (Greek, Latin, Syriac, Coptic, and the modern languages of Europe); separating the genuine from the spurious, the original from corruptions and interpolations, sifting the truth from falsehood, the facts from fiction and partizan judgment, comparing the accounts of all actors, friend and foe, narrator, eulogist, advocate, and antagonist, whether orthodox or heretic, whether Christian, Jew, or Gentile, aiming in all this laborious investigation at "the truth, the whole truth, and nothing but the truth."

1. Investigation.

He must, then, reproduce the clearly ascertained facts and results of his investigation in a faithful and lifelike narrative, so as to present the objective course of history itself, as it were, in a photograph, or rather in an artistic painting; for a photograph gives a dull view of the momentary look of a person, while the portrait of the artist combines the changing moods and various aspects of his subject into a living whole. The genuine writer of history differs as much from the dry chronicler of isolated facts and dates as from the novelist. He must represent both thoughts and facts. He must particularize and generalize, descend into minute details and take a comprehensive bird's-eye view of whole ages and periods. He must have a judicial mind, which deals impartially with all persons and events coming before his tribunal. He must be free from partizan and sectarian bias, and aim at justice and truth. It is the exclusive privilege of the divine mind to view all things *sub specie æternitatis*, and to see the end from the beginning. Man can know things only consecutively and in fragments. But history is its own best interpreter; and the farther it advances the more one is able to understand and appreciate the past. Historians differ in gifts and vocation. Some are miners, who bring out the raw material from the sources (Flacius, Baronius, Tillemont, Gieseler, Denifle, Harnack, Pastor); others are manufacturers, who work up the material for the use of scholars (Bossuet, Mosheim, Gibbon, Döllinger, Milman, Neander). Some are wholesale merchants, some retailers. Some are bold critics, who open new avenues of thought (Ewald, Baur, Renan); others popularize the results of laborious researches for the general benefit (Hagenbach, Merle, Hase, Pressensé, Fisher).

2. Presentation of Results.

V. Periods and Epochs: These represent the different stages in the religious development of the race. They must not be made arbitrarily, according to a mechanical scheme (such as the centurial division, introduced by Flacius in the "Magdeburg Centuries," and followed by Mosheim), but taken from the actual stops or starting-points (which is the real meaning of "epoch," from Gk. *epochē*, "to stop," "to pause") and circuits (Gk. *peridoi*) of the history itself. The following are the natural divisions:

1. Sacred or Biblical History: The history of divine revelation, from the creation to the close of the apostolic age, running parallel with the Scriptures, from Genesis to Revelation. Here distinction must be made between the dispensation of the Law and the dispensation of the Gospel, or the history of the Old Covenant religion and that of the New Covenant religion.

2. Christian History or Ecclesiastical History proper, from the beginning of the apostolic age to modern times. Subdivisions:

(a) History of **Ancient Christianity,** embracing the first six centuries to Gregory I. (590): Greco-Latin, Patristic, Catholic, the common stock from which the Greek, the Roman, and the Protestant churches have sprung. Subdivisions: (1) The life of Christ and the apostolic age. (2) The age of persecution, to Constantine the Great and the Council of Nicæa (325). (3) The age of the union of Church and State, of the formulation of Christian doctrine, and ecumenical councils (to 590). Some historians carry ancient Christianity down to Charlemagne (800) and the beginning of the Holy Roman Empire and the temporal power of the papacy. In this case there is a fourth subdivision, from Gregory I. to Charlemagne (590 to 800). But Charlemagne belongs to the Middle Ages and the Germanic phase of Christianity.

(b) History of **Medieval Christianity,** from the close of the sixth to the beginning of the sixteenth century, or from Gregory the Great (590), the first medieval pope, to Luther (1517). The Greek and Roman churches, divided since the controversy of Photius and Pope Nicholas I., pursue their independent course. The papacy receives its full development, the Holy Roman Empire is the dominant power, religious thought gradually moves toward the Reformation, and Western Europe comes more and more into prominence. Subdivisions: (1) The missionary period, Gregory I. to Gregory VII. (590–1050); the Church spreads among the Celtic, Slavonic, and Teutonic races of Northern and Western Europe, Mohammedanism originates and grows, the Great Schism occurs between the East and the West. (2) The absolute papacy, Gregory VII. to Boniface VIII. (1050–1294)—the period of the Crusades, the rise of the mendicant orders, scholasticism, the rise of the universities and Gothic architecture, the development of heretical sects, and the Inquisition. (3) The decline of the papacy and signs of the Reformation, Boniface VIII. to Luther's theses (1294–1517)—the "exile" of the popes at Avignon, the papal schism, the reforming councils of Pisa, Constance, and Basel, Wyclif, Huss, Savonarola, Wessel, the German mystics, Eckhart and Tauler, the Renaissance, the discovery of printing and the New World.

(c) History of **Modern Christianity**, from the Reformation (1517) to the present time. Protestantism and Romanism; founding of the various Evangelical Churches (the Lutheran, Calvinistic, Anglican, etc.); restoration and revival of Romanism; the Council of Trent; Jesuitism; Jansenism; the Puritan conflict in England; the Westminster Assembly; the restoration of the Episcopal Church under Charles II.; the expulsion of the Stuarts; the Edict of Toleration; the organization of the dissenting denominations (Presbyterians, Independents, Baptists, Quakers); the settlement of North America; Pietism and the Moravians in Germany; the rise of rationalism in Germany, deism in England; the Methodist revival in England and the Colonies; the French Revolution and spread of infidelity; organization of philanthropic agencies, the Sunday-school, and modern missions; progress and triumph of ultramontane Romanism, culminating in the Vatican Council (1870); conflict of faith with rationalism and infidelity; growth of the churches in the United States on the basis of the voluntary principle; unionistic movement among English-speaking Protestants; the new criticism, based on the historic study of the Scriptures and early church history, shaking traditional views of the Old Testament and the person and mission of Christ. Subdivisions: (1) The age of the Protestant Reformation and the Roman Catholic Counterreformation or reaction (1517–1648). (2) The age of scholastic and polemic confessionalism, in conflict with non-conformity and subjective piety (1650–1750). (3) The age of rationalism and religious revival and church union (1750–1900).

VI. Value: The study of history enables one to understand the present, which is the fruit of the past and the germ of the future. It is the richest storehouse of wisdom and experience. It is the best commentary of Christianity. It is full of comfort and encouragement. It verifies on every page the promise of the Savior to be with his people always, and to build his Church on an indestructible rock. It exhibits his life in all its forms and phases, and the triumphant march of his kingdom from land to land and generation to generation. Earthly empires, systems of philosophy, have their day, human institutions decay, all things of this world bloom and fade away, like the grass of the field; but the Christian religion has the dew of perennial youth, survives all changes, makes steady progress from age to age, overcomes all persecution from without, and corruption from within, is now stronger and more widely spread than ever before, directs the course of civilization, and bears the hopes of the human race. The history of the world is governed in the interest, and for the ultimate triumph, of Christianity. The experience of the past is a sure guaranty of the future.

VII. Literature: Only works on general church history will be mentioned here.

1. Ancient Historians: Eusebius (d. 340)—"Church History" from the birth of Christ to Constantine the Great, 324—and his successors in the Greek Church, Socrates, Sozomen, Theodoret. The Latin Church (e.g., Rufinus) contented itself with translations and extracts from Eusebius and his continuators. The Middle Ages produced most valuable material for history (chronicles, papal bulls, theological treatises, etc.), but no great general church history; the Reformation first called forth the spirit of critical inquiry.

2. Historians from 1500 to 1800: Matthias Flacius (d. 1575) and other Lutheran divines of Germany wrote the "Magdeburg Centuries" (Latin, Basel, 1559–74), covering thirteen Christian centuries in as many volumes—the first history from a Protestant point of view, in opposition to the claims of Romanism (see MAGDEBURG CENTURIES). In defense of Romanism, and in refutation of Flacius, Cæsar Baronius (d. 1607) wrote in Latin "Ecclesiastical Annals," in 12 folio vols. (Rome, 1588 sqq.; new ed., by A. Theiner, Bar-le-Duc, 1868 sqq.), continued by Raynaldus, Spondanus, Theiner, and others—a work of extraordinary learning and industry, but to be used with caution. Tillemont (d. 1698), in his invaluable *Mémoires* (16 vols., Paris, 1693–1712), wrote the history of the first six centuries from the sources, in bibliographical style and in the spirit of the more liberal Gallican Catholicism. Gottfried Arnold (d. 1714), of the Pietistic school of Spener, in his *Unparteiische Kirchen- und Ketzerhistorie* (4 vols. folio, Frankfort, 1699 sqq.; to 1688 A.D.), advocated the interests of practical piety, and the claims of heretics and schismatics, and all those who suffered persecution from an intolerant hierarchy and orthodoxy. J. L. Mosheim (d. 1755) wrote his "Institutes of Ecclesiastical History" (in Latin, Helmstädt, 1755, and often since in several translations) in the spirit of a moderate Lutheran orthodoxy, with solid learning and impartiality, in clear style, after the centurial arrangement of Flacius, and furnished a convenient text-book, which (in the translation of Murdock, with valuable supplements) has continued in use in England and America much longer than in Germany. J. M. Schroeckh's *Christliche Kirchengeschichte* (35 vols., Leipsic, 1768–1803), continued by *Kirchengeschichte seit der Reformation* (10 vols., 1804–12), is far more extensive and far less readable, but invaluable for reference, and full of information from the sources. It forsakes the mechanical centurial division, and substitutes for it the periodic arrangement. H. P. K. Henke (d. 1809) followed with a thoroughly rationalistic work (6 vols., Brunswick, 1795–1806; continued by J. S. Vater, 3 vols., 1818–20).

3. Historians from 1800 to 1900: August Neander, a converted Israelite, professor of church history in Berlin (d. 1850), marks an epoch in this branch of theological literature; and by his truly Christian, conscientious, impartial, truth-loving, just, and liberal, and, withal, thoroughly learned and profound spirit and method, he earned the title of "Father of Church History." His *Allgemeine Geschichte der christlichen Religion und Kirche* (6 vols., Hamburg, 1825–52), though incomplete (it stops with the Council of Basel, 1430), and somewhat diffuse and monotonous in style, is an immortal monument of genius and learning. It pays special attention to the development of Christian life and doctrine, and is edifying as well as instructive. It has been naturalized in England and America by the translation of Professor Torrey (5 vols., Boston, 1847–52; 12th ed., 1872; new ed., with a complete index, 6 vols., 1881), and will long be studied with profit, although in some respects superseded by more recent researches in the first three centuries. Equally valuable, though of an altogether different plan and spirit, is the *Kirchengeschichte* of J. K. L. Gieseler (5 vols., Bonn, 1824–56), translated first by Cunningham in Philadelphia (1846), then by Davidson and Hull in England, and revised and completed by H. B. Smith of New York (5 vols., 1857–80). The text is a meager skeleton of facts and dates; but the body of the work consists of carefully selected extracts and proof-texts from the sources which furnish the data for an independent judgment. F. C. Baur's work on church history, partly published after his death (5 vols., Tübingen, 1853 sqq.), is distinguished for philosophic grasp, critical combinations, and bold conjectures, especially in the treatment of the apostolic and postapostolic ages, and the ancient heresies and systems of doctrine. K. R. Hagenbach's *Kirchengeschichte* (7 vols., Leipsic, 1869 sqq.; revised ed., by Nippold, 1885 sqq.) is a popular digest for the educated lay reader. Philip Schaff's *History of the Christian Church* (3 vols., New York, 1859 sqq.; Germ. ed. of the 1st three vols., Leipsic, 1868, revised ed. of same in English, New York, 1882–1907) is written from the Anglo-German and Anglo-American standpoint. H. C. Sheldon's *History of the Christian Church* (5 vols., New York, 1894) is by an American Methodist. England has produced greater works in special departments than in general church history —e.g., Gibbon's *Decline and Fall of the Roman Empire*, Milman's *Latin Christianity*, Stanley's *Jewish Church* and *Eastern Church*, Farrar's *Life of Christ*, *The Apostle Paul*, and *Early Days of Christianity*, J. B. Lightfoot's *Apostolic Fathers*, Trench's *Lectures on the Mediæval Church*, the *Texts and Studies* ed. J. A. Robinson. George Waddington presents the general history to the Reformation inclusive (6 vols., London, 1833 sqq.); his work is superseded by J. C. Robertson's *History of the Christian Church to the Reformation* (3 vols., London, 1854 sqq.; new ed., 8 small vols., 1875). The older work of Milner (d. 1797) is written in popular style for edification. The most valuable contributions of modern English scholarship to ancient church history are found in Smith and Cheetham's *Dictionary of Christian Antiquities* (2 vols., London, 1875–80) and Smith and Wace's *Dictionary of Christian Biography* (4 vols., 1877–87). The largest Roman Catholic church history of recent times is Abbé Rohrbacher's *Histoire universelle de l'église catholique* (25 vols., Paris, 1842 sqq.).

4. Manuals of Church History in One or More Volumes: (a) Roman Catholic: J. J. I. von Döllinger (Vienna, 1836, unfinished; Eng. transl., 4 vols., London, 1840–42); J. A. Möhler (posthumous, ed. P. B. Gams, 3 vols., Regensburg, 1867–70); J. B. Alzog (10th ed., by F. X. Kraus, 2 vols., Mainz, 1882; Eng. transl., 4 vols., London, 1879–82; 3 vols., Cincinnati, 1876); F. X. Kraus (3 parts, Treves, 1872–75; 4th ed., 1896); J. Hergenröther (4th ed., ed. J. P. Kirsch, 3 vols., Freiburg, 1902 sqq.); F. X. Funk (4th ed., Paderborn, 1902); C. J. von Hefele (4th ed., by A. Knöpfler, 1905). (b) Protestant: K. A. Hase (11th ed., Leipsic, 1886; a masterly miniature picture; Eng. transl., New York, 1855); C. W. Niedner (2d ed., Berlin, 1866; very learned and very heavy); J. H. Kurtz (14th ed., by N. Bonwetsch and P. Tschackert, 2 vols., Leipsic, 1906; Eng. transl., 3 vols., New York, 1888–89); A. Ebrard (4 vols., Erlangen, 1865–67; polemically Reformed); J. J. Herzog (3 vols., Erlangen, 1880–82; moderately Reformed); E. Chastel (French, 4 vols., Paris, 1859–74; new ed., 1881 sqq.); H. Schmid (2 vols., Erlangen, 1881); K. A. Hase, *Vorlesungen* (4 vols., Leipsic, 1885 sqq.); R. Sohm (9th ed., Leipsic, 1894; Eng. transl., London, 1895); W. Möller (3 vols., Freiburg, 1889–94; 2d ed., by H. von Schubert and G. Kawerau, 1897–1902; Eng. transl., London, 1892–1900); Karl Müller (2 vols., Tübingen, 1892–1902); F. Loofs (Halle, 1901); H. von Schubert (2d ed., Tübingen, 1904). By American and English scholars are G. P. Fisher, *History of the Christian Church* (New York, 1887); J. F. Hurst, *History of the Christian Church* (2 vols., New York, 1897–1900); A. H. Newman, *Manual of Church History* (2 vols., Philadelphia, 1900–03); Cheetham and Hardwick, *Church History* (4 vols., London, 1908).

5. Histories of Doctrine: G. Münscher (4 vols., Marburg, 1797–1809); F. C. Baur, *Lehrbuch der Dogmengeschichte* (Tübingen, 1847; 3d ed., 1867); idem, *Vorlesungen*, ed. by his son (3 vols., Leipsic, 1865–67); A. Neander (ed. J. L. Jacobi, Berlin, 1857; Eng. transl., 2 vols., London, 1858); K. R. Hagenbach (5th ed., Leipsic, 1867; Eng. transl., 2 vols., Edinburgh, 1880); W. G. T. Shedd (2 vols., New York, 1863); G. Thomasius (2 vols., Erlangen, 1874–76); F. D. Nitzsch (Berlin, 1870; unfinished); A. Harnack, *Lehrbuch der Dogmengeschichte* (3d ed., 3 vols., Freiburg, 1894–97; Eng. transl., 7 vols., London and Boston, 1895–1900); idem, *Grundriss der Dogmengeschichte* (4th ed., Freiburg, 1905; Eng. transl., New York, 1893); F. Loofs (3d ed., Halle, 1893); R. Seeberg (2 vols., Leipsic, 1895–98); G. P. Fisher (International Theological Library, 1896); H. C. Sheldon (4th ed., 2 vols., New York, 1906). See DOGMA, DOGMATICS.

6. Chronological Tables: H. B. Smith, *History of the Church of Christ in Sixteen Chronological Tables* (New York, 1860); F. X. Kraus, *Synchronistische Tabellen zur Kirchengeschichte* (Treves,

1876); idem, *Synchronistische Tabellen zur christlichen Kunstgeschichte* (Freiburg, 1880); H. Weingarten, *Zeittafeln und Ueberblicke zur Kirchengeschichte* (6th ed., by C. F. Arnold, Leipsic, 1905).

7. Atlases: K. Heussi and H. Mulert, *Atlas zur Kirchengeschichte*, 66 maps with 18 pages of introduction and index (Tübingen, 1905). The general historical atlases of R. H. Labberton (14th ed., Boston, 1889), F. W. Putzger (24th ed., Bielefeld, 1900), and E. A. Freeman (accompanying his *Historical Geography of Europe*, 3d ed., London, 1903) are also useful for church history.

The main activity in recent times in historical investigation and treatment has been devoted to the first three Christian centuries, including the work of Harnack, Funk, Kattenbusch, Lightfoot, Robinson, McGiffert, and many others. The Middle Ages are receiving an increasing amount of attention; names worthy of mention in this field are Döllinger, Ehrle, Denifle, Schwane, Kirsch, and Finke among Roman Catholics, and Karl Müller, Hauck, Mirbt, Sabatier, Creighton, Stubbs, Lea, and others among Protestants.

(PHILIP SCHAFF†) D. S. SCHAFF.

BIBLIOGRAPHY: For fuller information cf. Philip Schaff, *History of the Christian Church*, i. 1–53, New York, 1882; and introductions to other general works on church history. Further, Schaff, *What is Church History?* Philadelphia, 1846; W. G. T. Shedd, *The Philosophy of History*, Andover, 1861; H. B. Smith, *The Nature and Worth of the Science of Church History*, in his volume of essays, *Faith and Philosophy*, pp. 49–87, New York, 1877; J. De Witt, *Church History as a Science*, in the *Bibliotheca Sacra*, 1883; E. A. Freeman, *The Method of Historical Study*, London, 1886; A. C. McGiffert, *The Study of Church History*, in the *Bibliotheca Sacra*, 1893; W. Bright, *The Study of History*, in *Waymarks of Church History*, London, 1894; Lord Acton, *The Study of History*, London, 1895; A. Harnack, *Das Christentum und die Geschichte*, Leipsic, 1895; K. Lamprecht, *What Is History?* transl. from the Germ. by E. A. Andrews, New York, 1905.

CHURCH ORDER (Ger. *Kirchenordnung*): The general ecclesiastical constitution of a State. The early Evangelical Church attached less importance to ecclesiastical ritual than the pre-Reformation Church had done. As early as 1526 Luther observes in *Deutsche Messe und Ordnung des Gottesdienst*: "In sum, this and all other forms are so to be used that where they give rise to a misuse they should be forthwith set aside, and a new form be made ready; since outward forms are intended to serve to the advancement of faith and love, and not to the detriment of faith. Where this they cease to do, they are already dead and void, and are of no more value; just as when a good coin is debased and retired on account of its abuse, and issued anew; or when every-day shoes wax old and rub, they are not longer worn, but thrown away and new ones bought. Form is an external thing, be it ever so good, and thus it may lapse into misuse; but then it is no longer an orderly form, but a disorder; so that no external order stands and avails at all of itself, as hitherto the papal forms are judged to have done, but all forms have their life, worth, strength, and virtues in proper use; or else they are of no avail and value whatever" (*Werke*, Weimar ed., xix. 72 sqq.). According to Lutheran ecclesiastical teaching (Formula of Concord, II.; *Solida declaratio*, x.; Apology, xiv.; Melanchthon's *Loci*, 2d redaction in *CR*, xxi. 555–556; the Saxon *Visitationsbuch* of 1528; etc.) a uniform liturgy is requisite only in so far as it is indispensable to uphold proper doctrine and the administration of the sacraments; whereas in general the rightful appointment of the external functions of church officers and their sphere in the congregations is committed to the church governing board of the state authorities. The spontaneous development of church law, and especially the regulation of divine service, the sacraments, and discipline, as Luther ideally conceived it, proved impracticable, and gave place, though not invariably so, to definition on the part of temporal sovereigns. All these regulations, especially those of governments and cities, by means of which the canonical church forms that had previously prevailed in the land were modified in a reformatory direction, while the newly developing church system became progressively established, are called "Church Orders." Those of the sixteenth century are the most important (cf. E. Sehling, in *ZKR*, xxix., 1897, pp. 328 sqq., and introduction to his edition of the Church Orders, i., Leipsic, 1902).

A Church Order usually begins with a dogmatic part in which the agreement of the State Church with the general Lutheran confessions is set forth with more or less of detail (*Credenda*); then follow regulations concerning liturgy, the appointment of church officers, organization of church government, discipline, marriage, schools, the pay of church and school officials, the administration of church property, care of the poor, etc. (*Agenda*, q.v.). A systematic topical arrangement is by no means always adhered to. As a rule, later compilations have made use of earlier forms, and thus the Orders are grouped in families.

E. SEHLING.

BIBLIOGRAPHY: H. C. König, *Bibliotheca agendorum*, Zellerfeld, 1726; J. J. Moser, *Corpus juris evangeliorum ecclesiastici*, 2 vols., Züllichau, 1737–38; A. L. Richter, *Die evangelischen Kirchenordnungen des 16. Jahrhunderts*, 2 vols., Weimar, 1846.

CHURCH PATRON SAINT (*patronus sanctus*): The particular saint to whom a church is dedicated, and under whose protection it stands. The early Church in a great variety of ways put guardian saints in the place of the tutelary deities (*dei titulares*) known to the pagan religions in connection with specific objects and relationships. In primitive times church patrons were taken especially from the number of the martyrs, who were esteemed to be influential mediators with God. Then when the worship of saints had developed from the veneration of martyrs, the guardian patrons were selected from among the saints not only for separate churches, but also for countries, dioceses, orders, cloisters, cities, congregations, gilds, brotherhoods, etc. The possession of relics of a saint in a certain church often determined his choice as patron. When subsequently the custom arose of naming churches after some Christian mystery—as, for instance, the Holy Trinity, the Holy Ghost, the Sacred Heart of Jesus—it came about that a church might be commended to the protection of a saint without bearing his name, thus creating the distinction between a protective and a titular patron. In accordance with its teaching as to the saints and veneration of relics, the Roman Catholic Church has developed a special doctrine concerning veneration, election, alteration, etc., of church patron saints (cf. the decree confirmed by Urban VIII., Mar. 23, 1630, in L. Ferraris, *Bibliotheca prompta canonica*, 11 vols., Venice, 1782-94, s.v. *patroni sancti*).

The Reformers and Protestants generally have retained the old custom of designating churches after saints and Christian mysteries for the purpose of thus bestowing upon them a definite, distinguishing name. In the choice of it, more or less deference is shown to the preferences of the congregation and the founder. E. Sehling.

Bibliography: M. E. C. Walcott, *Sacred Archæology*, s.v. "Patron," London, 1868.

CHURCH REGISTERS.

Early Church Books (§ 1).
Medieval Registers (§ 2).
The Beginnings of Modern Registers (§ 3).
Contents and Character (§ 4).
Value for Other than Church Uses (§ 5).
Ecclesiastical and Civil Registers (§ 6).
Collections of Church Registers (§ 7).

The German word *Kirchenbuch* has different meanings. It refers to church books in the sense of "service-books," and to parish books which recorded inventories, rents, income, ecclesiastical celebrations, and other matters referring to worship; but in modern times the word has generally taken the meaning of registers of sacramental acts, such as baptism, marriage ceremonies, confessions, and funerals.

An especially old and remarkable example of a "church book" in the older sense is that of Oldesloe, which begins before 1371 and contains a table for determining Quinquagesima Sunday, the pastoral epistle of Bertram, bishop of Lübeck (1376), lists of pastors, also of tithes, income of pastors, donations, etc. Church books of another kind, but differing from modern church registers, are the cartularies of bishops in England, as, for instance, the Register of John Pontissara (1282-1304) and the Registers of John de Sandale and Rigaud de Asserio, bishops of Winchester, 1316-23 (London and Winchester, 1897). These books contain everything relating to the government of bishops.

1. Early Church Books. The church book in the sense of a register of ecclesiastical celebrations is important for the history of modern registers, since in the sixteenth and seventeenth centuries it was transformed into the church register of baptisms, marriages, etc., for instance in Mecklenburg and Holstein. Land-registers and registers of taxation go back much farther in Germany into the fifteenth century, in England, France, Italy into the fourteenth or thirteenth, even earlier. Another source for the date of personal records are the church bills found in the older parish registers. A more thorough knowledge of the history, nature, and importance of church registers began only when efforts were made to collect and test existing material. Church registers, or at least compilations corresponding to them, are traceable to the civilized nations of the earliest times, for instance the Egyptians. The Hebrews had also their records of birth and genealogical tables. In the Roman empire registers of births may be traced back to the time of the kings; from the time of Augustus are found registers of marriages. As Christianity took its rise in the Roman empire, it accepted to a certain extent the existing elements of culture. The diptyches (see Liber Vitæ; Sculpture, Christian) were adopted from the Romans, and adapted to Christian usages, the members of the congregation being registered not for military reasons or for the levying of taxes, but as citizens of the kingdom of God. Besides the dates of birth, there were also recorded dates of marriage and of death. These "sacred books and tablets" were important preeminently from a historical standpoint, as they contained the names of bishops, martyrs, and benefactors.

The diptyches did not develop into church registers of the modern kind, nor were they of any importance for the modern Church, owing chiefly to the degeneration of culture after the destruction of the Roman empire, and to a perverted tendency of the medieval Church. Instead of the diptyches of the deceased and living,

2. Medieval Registers. churches and monasteries adopted necrologies and morilogies, in which were entered especially the names of donors and benefactors. They were usually called "books of life" (see Liber Vitæ). Besides these, there were in existence church books in the older sense, that is, registers of taxes, inventories, etc. On account of the lack of personal registers, princes and lords had their own family books, while the age of other people had to be determined, even as late as the sixteenth century, by the testimony of living persons. At the close of the Middle Ages the census in the modern sense was instituted in flourishing cities like Augsburg and Breslau.

The Renaissance had a wholesome effect upon the development of church registers, in France and Italy as early as the beginning of the fourteenth century. A register of baptisms from Cabrières near Vaucluse dates from 1308, fragments of a register of marriages and deaths in Middle France from 1335 and 1336. In Italy the use of such registers may be traced to the fourteenth century. In Spain the famous cardinal Ximenez in 1497 at the Synod of Toledo ordered the introduction of baptismal and matrimonial registers; soon afterward similar orders were issued in Portugal. In

3. The Beginnings of Modern Registers. Switzerland and Germany church registers go back to the time of the Reformation. Earlier attempts had not been successful. The first baptismal register in Zurich dates from 1525, the register of marriages in Strasburg from the same time. Church registers in Constance began in 1531, and in Frankfort, Thuringia, Saxony, and Bohemia about the same time. In the imperial city of Nuremberg they existed from 1524, in Silesia from 1534, under the influence of the Silesian Reformer Hess; the other territories followed soon afterward, in the early sixties of the sixteenth century. The number of these registers, since the enormous losses resulting from the Thirty Years' War, especially in Electoral Saxony, can be estimated only approximately. There is reliable information of the existence of more than 150 registers dated 1522–63. The earlier introduction of church registers in Italy and France must be ascribed to the independent influence of the classical renaissance, which became of importance in Germany only after its union with the religious efforts of Luther. In the Netherlands the Reformation was for a long time suppressed and its confessors were exiled, but a synod in 1574 changed these conditions, and church registers were soon generally introduced; but there are extant fragments of earlier date. From Germany the use of church registers penetrated the Scandinavian kingdoms at a comparatively late date. In Denmark they were introduced by royal order in 1646, in Norway in 1685, in Sweden in 1686. As in Germany, so in England, the general introduction of church registers followed separation from the Papal Church, by order of King Henry VIII. in 1538. In spite of this unevangelical origin, the introduction of church registers in England was accompanied by immediate success. There have been preserved not less than 812 church registers from the year 1538, 1,822 from 1528 to 1558, and 2,448 from 1558 to 1600. From 1551 date the first evidences of church registers in Scotland; in Ireland their general introduction took place only in the nineteenth century. In transoceanic countries personal registers were used from settlement there by the civilized peoples of Europe. The earliest church register is that of the Dutch in Reciff, Brazil, 1633. The East India House in London preserves church registers from Bombay from 1703, from Bengal dated 1713, from Madras dated 1743. Of Roman Catholic church registers there are only sporadic cases in Germany at the time of the Reformation. Their general introduction followed the decrees of the Council of Trent in 1563. These decrees referred only to registers of baptisms and marriages; records of funerals were introduced in 1614 by the *Rituale Romanum*. During the Thirty Years' War church registers were sometimes taken away from the Evangelicals and continued by the Catholics, so that the supposed antiquity of some Catholic registers has no basis in fact.

4. Contents and Character.

The church registers did not consist solely of lists of baptisms, marriages, and funerals; a church register at Lehrbach in Hesse contains not less than twelve columns. The registers, especially those of the seventeenth century, are frequently a rich source for the history of church discipline. The registers of the catechumens and confirmed form a part of the church record which is very important for the history of Christian worship. They may be traced back to the first period of the Reformation. The most curious church records are found among the so-called family books. There the members of the congregations are arranged alphabetically according to families, and their residences, with the religious acts performed on them, are given. In this way there originated chronicles of whole villages; so, for instance, the village of Dankerode in the Hartz mountains. Another noteworthy class is found in the so-called ministerial books which were introduced after 1686 in Sweden. They consist of six different parts: Register (1) of births and baptisms; (2) of deaths and funerals; (3) of marriages; (4) of catechetical examinations at home; (5) of newly admitted members; (6) of members who had moved to other parishes. The most interesting part is the fourth, which contained records of religious instruction, of examinations, and of attendance at the Lord's Supper, and notes on conduct and discipline before and after marriage.

5. Value for Other than Church Uses.

After the church registers had become known and been generally introduced in all civilized states of Europe, about the end of the seventeenth and beginning of the eighteenth century, their value and importance began to be appreciated from other points of view, and they were used as sociological sources, first in England after the seventeenth century. After *Natural and Political Annotations upon the Bills of Mortality*, by John Graunt (London, 1666 and 1676), there followed a rich literature of similar character in England, France, Germany, Holland, Italy, and Sweden. It is true, many of these productions were merely sociological, but some of them included the theological side, as, for instance, William Derham's *Physical Theology* (London, 1713). This work formed the model for *Die göttliche Ordnung in den Veränderungen des menschlichen Geschlechts*, by Johann Peter Süssmilch (1741, 3 vols., 1776), and Möhsen, a physician, published in his work on vaccination for the first time a history of church registers of baptisms and deaths. Thus, a powerful influence was exerted upon them by the rapid growth of sociology and statistics, and the attention of large circles was called to them. After the end of the seventeenth century extracts from church registers were ordered to be made by the pastors and superintendents of Brandenburg-Prussia and sent to the government offices in Berlin for purposes of vital statistics. The keeping of church registers became dependent upon the orders of civil authorities; this led to their general adoption and to stricter enforcement of rules, but at the same time the registers lost much of their churchly character as they were used chiefly in court and for purposes of taxation and for military purposes. In conformity with the general law of Prussia, every pastor had to make one copy of his church register and send it to the local court. Electoral Saxony and Austria issued similar orders. In the course of time personal records were separated altogether from the Church and entrusted to the municipal authorities, civil lists taking the place of church registers. This was due in France in part to the Revolution, in part to the peculiar development of the royal authority. King Francis I. issued as early as 1539 an order making church registers subject to the supervision of the municipal courts. Under Louis XIV. the keeping of church registers was altogether due to himself and the secular government, according to a decree of 1667. Further decrees were issued in France in 1736 and 1792. They were received into the civil code of Napoleon, and with the Napoleonic conquests were carried over to Belgium in 1796, then to Holland and to several states of Germany. In Germany, the entire separation of civil affairs from connection with the Church was brought about especially by the revolutionary movement of 1848. The Prussian constitution of 1850 provided for the introduction of provisions like those of the French in regard to records of persons. This provision was made a law in Prussia in 1874; accordingly, special civil registry-offices were introduced, and from that time church registers lost their importance in public affairs. In 1875 these same decisions were applied to the whole German empire. Clergymen are not eligible as registry officers. In 1895 civil registers were introduced also in Austria-Hungary. But with the enactment of those laws church registers did not disappear in Germany; on the contrary, they regained their original significance and were given back to the Church. In place of the secular authorities, the ecclesiastical leaders, in Prussia the members of the consistories and of the Evangelical Superior Church Council, assumed the supervision of the church registers. The kingdom of God and the civil order of the State are two different spheres with their own special aims and purposes. Registration of baptisms and of admission into the congregation, of marriages and funerals, of attendance at confessions and the Lord's Supper, and of spiritual discipline are facts for the church registers, while data concerning physical births and deaths, matrimony from the civil point of view, together with all facts concerning the physical and natural being of man, are a matter of the civil registry.

6. Ecclesiastical and Civil Registers.

In modern times collections of church registers have been undertaken; there is a genealogico-statistical center in Denmark, in the academy of Sweden, and in state archives in Mecklenburg and Oldenburg. But in case of such collections duplicate copies should always be made, because it is essential that at least one copy of the church register remain with the local church. The collections should be under the supervision of church authorities and be deposited in church archives, not in state archives or other secular institutions. As a result of the French Revolution and subsequent wars, the church records of Alsace-Lorraine, the Netherlands, the Rhine Palatinate, the Lower Rhine, and the duchy of Berg are in state archives or in superior district courts. In Prussia and German Austria-Hungary the church registers were left with the churches, in spite of the introduction of civil registry-offices. Recently attempts have been made in Germany, Denmark, Sweden, Austria, England, and Belgium to consolidate the different collections of church registers for statistical purposes. In Belgium a general index for all old church registers was prepared in 1865. In Austria a statistical central commission was instituted in 1882 for a similar purpose. In England an enormous amount of material has been collected in the Record Office, on the basis of the Parish Register Act of 1882.

7. Collections of Church Registers.

(E. Jacobs.)

Bibliography: J. C. W. Augusti, *Handbuch der christlichen Archäologie*, iii. 690–730, Leipsic, 1837; J. S. Burn, *Hist. of Parish Registers, also of the Registers of Scotland, Ireland* . . . , London, 1862; J. Jastrow, *Die Volkszahl deutscher Städte*, Berlin, 1876; R. E. C. Waters, *Parish Registers in England*, London, 1883; H. Trusen, *Das preussische Kirchenrecht im Bereiche der evangelischen Landeskirche*, Berlin, 1894; E. Friedberg, *Lehrbuch des evangelischen und katholischen Kirchenrechts*, Leipsic, 1895; *Episcopal Registers of the Diocese of Winchester*, London, 1897; J. Gmelin, in *Deutsche Geschichtsblätter*, i (1900), 155–170; Krieg, in *Korrespondenzblatt des Gesamtvereins der deutschen Geschichts- und Altertumsvereine*, 1907, no. 25, pp. 192–195.

CHURCH AND SCHOOL.

Public Schools not Originally Maintained by the Church (§ 1).
Influence of the Reformation (§ 2).
Pietism (§ 3).
Compulsory Education (§ 4).
Religion and Coercion Exclusive (§ 5).
Compulsory Religious Instruction not Desirable (§ 6).
Position and Attitude of Teachers (§ 7).
Denominational and Undenominational Schools (§ 8).
Clerical Control of Schools (§ 9).

The question of the relation of Church and School did not become a burning one until after the Reformation, when the modern State began to recognise its duty to provide public elementary schools for its subjects and make school-attendance obligatory. Since compulsory attendance was the necessary condition for the success of public elementary schools, the Church, from its very nature prevented from employing coercion, could not compete with the State in this field. It was necessary, therefore, for Church and State to come to an understanding, particularly as the latter never organized its school-system *de novo*, but took over and developed the educational organization of the Church.

1. Public Schools not Originally Maintained by the Church.

The proposition that the School is the daughter of the Church is not confirmed by the history of the early Church. Religious education was considered the business of the family and the community; and education in any other sense was a private matter. During the Middle Ages the Church maintained schools for future clerics and a few noblemen, and prepared children for confirmation. It was Charlemagne who gave the first great impetus to popular education. Even at the close of the Middle Ages the writing-schools in Germany were maintained either by the cities or by private individuals, not by the Church.

2. Influence of the Reformation.

With the Reformation, the Church assumes a different attitude toward popular education. Luther insists on the establishment of schools; and Melanchthon declares that the union of Church and School is necessary. Popular education is demanded for religious reasons; but the right to provide for the same is recognized as belonging to the State. The existing elementary schools in the towns were reorganized; and the introduction of religious instruction gave them the character of public schools. Similar schools were founded in the country villages. All these schools were quite elementary in character, religion, reading, and writing forming practically the only subjects of instruction; but for more than two centuries they offered the only educational opportunity to the great majority of the population.

Even such schools could exist only under favorable circumstances. Before the Thirty Years' War there were not many of them left; and after the war, when the ideas of Ratke and Comenius began to be effective, the tendency was to try something new, rather than to reestablish the old system.

3. Pietism.

In this movement the Pietists took the lead. The public school, as revived by them in the interest of religious education, was introduced by various German states, but first by Prussia in 1763. The State recognized the service of the Church, and even entrusted the supervision of these schools to the clergy, who were regarded as officials of the State.

4. Compulsory Education.

The example of Prussia was followed by Bavaria (1802), Denmark (1814), Austria (1869), and France (1882), with the enforcement of school-attendance. Holland, England, and the United States have attained all that is necessary by less incisive measures. In Italy and Spain education is compulsory only from the sixth to the ninth year, and wretched conditions prevail even to-day in the Roman Catholic states of South America. In Russia attendance at an elementary school shortens the period of military service.

Ever since the State took charge of elementary education and made it compulsory there has been a movement in progress toward the emancipation of the schools from the clergy; and for over a hundred years three questions have been in dispute: (1) Is compulsory school-attendance consistent with religious instruction? (2) Ought the school to be denominational or undenominational? (3) Does the control of the school belong to the clergy or to trained schoolmen?

In principle, religion and coercion exclude each other. This is a matter about which Protestantism is now becoming more sensitive, and it is possible that the present protest against compulsory religious instruction may develop into a general protest against all enforced culture. Of course, no similar protest is heard from Rome. The Roman Church, accustomed to the maxim "compel them to come in," is striving for power, and, for this reason, seeks control of the schools.

5. Religion and Coercion Exclusive.

It is willing for the State to enforce education, so long as the Church is benefited thereby. It has no feeling for the inner conflict between compulsory education and freedom of conscience, regarding coercion as necessary in view of present social and religious conditions. So much the stronger, however, is this feeling in Protestantism. To be sure, in the training of children a certain amount of coercion is necessary, since the pathway of education leads through obedience to freedom. Particularly in religious instruction, though, is it desirable to keep the end in view and gradually diminish coercion as freedom is approached. The custom of the early Church to leave religious instruction to the family justified itself. Even if it is evident that the religious instruction of the family needs to be supplemented, still it is clear that the school can not replace the family, since the teacher always represents the law, while religion requires freedom. There have been many school-teachers of large religious nature who have touched the hearts and consciences of their pupils without employing coercion; but still the fact remains that the prevalence of religion is not due to the religious instruction given in the public schools.

As regards the parents, even in modern states they can be compelled to send their children to schools where religious instruction is given. This is justified on the ground that the children are minors; and that whatever arbitrary control over the children the parents may lose is more than made up for by the mental growth of the children. But while the State can enforce education, the Church is prevented from doing this and must, therefore, protest when its services are thrust upon those who do not want them.

6. Compulsory Religious Instruction not Desirable.

An effort has been made to conceal the nature of this religious coercion by insisting that instruction in the Bible has to do with historical information only. While such an argument might be applied to mere church history, it is inapplicable here. It involves a misunderstanding of the most important part of the subject. Two methods have been employed to escape this difficulty. Either religious instruction has been banished from the school entirely; or an effort has been made to modify it to meet the needs of dissenters, which is impossible if they are atheists. If the Church is to exercise educational activity, provision must be made for it. For instance, one whole school-day may be set apart each week for the instruction of youth in religious subjects, as is the case in France. Also in Italy, Holland, England, and some states of the United States the state schools are non-religious in principle. No cogent argument can be brought against such a system, for religious instruction is certainly not the business of the State. After all, the interests of Christianity are furthered by it. By assuming the responsibility of instruction in the usual school branches, the State makes it possible for the Church to concentrate its efforts in the religious field. It is not so much the mere separation of Church and State that seems objectionable as the severing of an old historical union that has richly justified its existence by its works.

This solution of the old problem would relieve the teacher of the embarrassment of teaching things that are possibly not an expression of his own inmost convictions—a difficulty often experienced by ministers.

7. Position and Attitude of Teachers.

The teacher should either be allowed to teach religious subjects in his own way, or else be relieved of the duty entirely. It must be added, however, that this separation of Church and State, in the manner in which it has been accomplished in Holland, France, England, and the United States, has aroused opposition in the ranks of the teachers. Conscious of their high calling as educators, rather than as mere instructors, they are unwilling to see religion banished from the schools, however much they may be opposed to the domination of the schools by the Church.

Through modern emigration the various religious sects have been mixed together, especially in the cities. Practical considerations make it necessary

8. Denominational and Undenominational Schools.

that the children of a community where a number of confessions are represented shall all attend one school; and thus originated the undenominational school. This arrangement gives children of a confession that is in the minority the advantage of a larger and better equipped school than they could attend otherwise. Further, such schools are favored by the spirit of tolerance and liberalism now prevailing in religious matters, and by the non-religious character of the modern State. Against undenominationalism it is urged that the public school, as an educational institution, can least of all dispense with religious instruction, which forms the basis of all instruction; that religion, which carries with it the literary and historical studies, can not be separated from all other subjects and made an independent study; that the personality of the teacher will of necessity make such schools either Protestant or Catholic; and that spies of the opposite confession will then undermine the confidence between the children and the teacher. The force of these objections can not be denied. It is clear that a school that educates must have harmony among its pupils; but in this view denominationalism in the school becomes a postulate of pedagogy, not of the Church. There is no question as to the importance of the Church for education. The question is whether practical theology or pedagogy is the better qualified to dictate the method to be employed in using the educative material contributed by the Church. It is plain that theology needs pedagogy as badly as pedagogy needs theology.

Among the reasons that have decided teachers against the denominational school one remains to be mentioned: the usual [in Germany], but not necessary, supervision by the clergy.

9. Clerical Control of Schools.

Reasons alleged in favor of clerical control are: the splendid pedagogical services rendered by the Church through such men as Comenius, Francke, Niemeyer, and Schleiermacher; the fine background of religious life which the clergy bring to the school, and their unselfishness in the work; the confidence expressed in the clergy by the State in turning over to them the public schools after the Reformation; and, not least, the high culture of the clergy. Against such control it is argued that the public school is only following the higher institutions of learning in emancipating itself from clerical guardianship; that the uneducated teachers of the clerical régime have been replaced with teachers trained scientifically in the theory and practise of pedagogy; that the clergy have not kept abreast of the growing science of education, and are, therefore, unprepared for the work; that this work is prejudicial to their high calling as ministers of the Gospel; and, finally, that clerical control benefits chiefly the ultramontanes. The clergy themselves are becoming less prejudiced in the matter and are beginning to admit the force of these arguments; and, on the other hand, their more prudent opponents recognize that it is the duty of the Church, not of the State, to keep a lookout over the religious and moral welfare of the public schools.

C. Geyer.

Bibliography: On the theory of education in relation to Church and State consult: C. Diekmann, *Der biblische Geschichtsunterricht in der Volksschule*, Leipsic, 1878; G. A. L. Baur, *Grundzüge der Erziehungslehre*, Giessen, 1887; R. H. Quick, *Remarks About Moral and Religious Education*, in his *Essays*, London, 1887; G. A. Coe, *Education in Religion and Morals*, New York, 1884.

On the history of education consult: K. Schmidt, *Geschichte der Pädagogik*, Köthen, 1889; W. C. Grasby, *Teaching in Three Continents*, London, 1891; J. Payne, *History of Education*, ib. 1892; J. Böhm, *Geschichte der Pädagogik*, Nuremberg, 1893; S. G. Williams, *History of Modern Education . . . from the Revival of Learning to the Present*, Syracuse, 1896; T. Davidson, *History of Education*, New York, 1900; E. G. Dexter, *History of Education in the U. S.*, New York, 1904.

On the question of religious instruction in various countries consult in Germany: E. Sachsse, *Die Lehre von der kirchlichen Erziehung*, Berlin, 1897; J. Beyhl, *Die Befreiung der Volksschullehrer aus der geistlichen Herrschaft*, Berlin, 1903; F. Naumann, *Der Streit der Konfessionen um die Schule*, Berlin, 1904. In France: L. Duchesne, *Autonomies ecclésiastiques. Églises séparées*, Paris, 1905. In England: Of the Education Acts, 1870–91, there are discussions by A. E. Steinthal, London, 1891; C. W. A. Brooke, ib. 1897. Of those from 1870 to 1902, by Sir H. Owen, and by W. A. Casson and G. C. Whiteley, both London, 1903. On the Act of 1902 consult: C. E. Benham, H. H. Hanson, H. Mothersole, E. C. Rawlings, all London, 1903; also: W. H. Carnegie, *Church and the Schools; Churchman's View of the Education Controversy*, ib. 1905. In the U. S.: S. T. Spear, *Religion and the State*, New York, 1876; J. Conway, *Respective Rights and Duties of Family, State and Church in Regard to Education*, ib. 1890; J. H. Crooker, *Religious Freedom in American Education*, Boston, 1903.

CHURCH AND STATE.

I. General Treatment: Since the Christian community presents itself outwardly as a part of the social order, for the regulation of which the State exists, the question arises, What shall be the relation between Church and State? From the point of view of the different confessions this question might be variously answered. However,

1. Scope of Subject.

disregarding minor distinctions, three answers are possible: The State may rule the Church and administer ecclesiastical affairs for its own purposes; the Church may rule the State and use the temporal authority to further the interests of the Church; or Church and State may be completely separated, each confining itself to its own sphere, and neither exercising any authority over the other. As a matter of history, however, Church and State have seldom been completely independent of each other, the one occupying itself solely with things spiritual, the other restricting itself to things temporal. The Roman Catholic Church still insists on having a voice in the control of temporal affairs, and the Protestant states of Europe usually claim a considerable share in ecclesiastical affairs. The difficulty of coordinating the ecclesiastical and the political authority as two distinct systems, or, indeed, of effecting any great innovation where the Church is concerned, is to be accounted for on historical grounds. The fundamental legal ordinances involved here are not made by act of will, but are passed along from one period to the next, from one community to another. Laws and rights are inherited; and in no field is this so true as in that where religion is concerned. Even where new forces have effected the most complete changes, the effort is made to prove that each form links itself back on the old. The time of King Josiah, which saw the reconstruction of the Israelitic tradition in the spirit of the new law; the Pseudo-Isidor, who represents the asserted increase in the power of the hierarchy as an old right; even the Reformation itself, which claimed so frequently to restore the primitive Church—all bear witness to the statement.

2. Ancient Rome and the Eastern Empire.

From the very beginning the relation between religious worship and temporal authority was a most intimate one. The chief of the tribe, as likewise the king of the first community that could be called a state, united in himself the functions of judge, military leader, and priest. He represented his people in their relations toward one another, toward their enemies, and toward God. Religion was an affair of the State. In the later development the ruler might transfer his priestly duties to a special class of priests, but the close relation between religion and rule remained. At the advent of Christianity into the world's history the Roman emperor, as *pontifex maximus*, stood at the head of the religious system in the Roman Empire. It was not his object, however, to suppress the foreign gods worshiped in Roman possessions in the interest of the Roman deities whose high priest he was. In so far as these foreign gods had their states over which they ruled, all, including Yahweh, were regarded juristically as free and equal, though Yahweh was deposed after the destruction of Jerusalem. The God of Christianity, on the other hand, having no visible kingdom, was not a deity in the Roman sense of the word. Hence the persecution of the Christians as atheists. With the advent of the Christian emperor the organization of the Church and its relation to the State was definitely determined for centuries to come. The position of *pontifex maximus* which Constantine united with his arbitrary authority had not been depreciated by the decay of the old Roman faith. He was the absolute head of the Church. Even after the title of *pontifex maximus* had been dropped, toward the end of the fourth century, the office remained. The designation *episcopus universalis* is only a Christian translation of the heathen expression. To be sure, the emperor no longer performed the functions of a priest, but he united in himself all ecclesiastical authority. He appointed and disciplined the priests and exercised a protectorate over the *leges regiæ*, those duties toward God which were required of every one. Laws and rights were created by the dictum of the emperor. Thus the Church became an institution of the State, and at the same time a compulsory institution. The very persecution which, in the name of religion, had formerly been directed against Christianity was now employed to uproot heathenism, as well as to put down dissent within the Church. To be a citizen of the empire one had to be an orthodox Christian. This system, which was most consistently developed in the Eastern Empire, after its separation from Rome, became the heritage of the Russian autocracy. Though Russia has had its Holy Synod since the time of Peter the Great, the Czar remains the only source of authority in the Church, and uses the ecclesiastical organization to strengthen the State. Consequently withdrawal from the state church is not permitted.

3. Rise of Papal Temporal Power.

The second characteristic relation of Church to State was developed in the Western Empire. While the temporal power in the West gradually waned after the division of the empire, the ecclesiastical organization remained intact; and, when the ancient State disappeared, the pope virtually succeeded the emperor as *pontifex maximus* and appropriated as much temporal authority as was consistent with his priestly character. This transition of authority may be said to have begun in the year 445, when Valentinian III. promulgated a law requiring obedience to the ordinances of the pope. Thus the religious dream of a *civitas dei* was fused with the Roman tradition of an *imperium mundi*. Over against this papal State stood the Germanic tribes. Their conversion had been accomplished without difficulty, but for this very reason it had not been profound. Their indifference toward the Roman Church is explained by their relation to Arianism. Goths, Burgundians, and Vandals had their own churches, which were separate from those of the provincials. The bishops were representatives of the king, and the subjected Roman provincials were treated just as the Phanariots are treated by the Turks. Even the conversion of the Franks did not greatly improve the position of the Roman Church. The Frankish king suffered no foreign interference in ecclesiastical affairs, not even from the pope himself. Here material interests take precedence, and the Church assumes importance chiefly as a large property-holder. In fact, it was the Franks who discovered the process of secularization. With the restoration of the Western Empire by Charlemagne Byzantine ideas came into play. The Roman idea of a papal *imperium mundi* was apparently dormant. When, therefore, Germany became the center of gravity of European history it was quite natural that the bishops should be advanced to the position of temporal princes, in the interest of the State. Otto the Great completed this innovation by taking under his protection the spiritual head of these princes, the pope himself. Thus the functions of the bishop were largely secularized. Investiture with property constituted his title, and his chief duty was to aid in carrying on the business of the empire. Without any premonition of the danger ahead of them, the Germanic people entered upon this fatal course.

It remained for Gregory VII. to lift the veil and show the Church in its character of a ruling power. With him begins the period of the so-called spiritual universal state, which lasted for several centuries. Just as formerly the State had ruled the Church, so now the Church, to a large extent, ruled the State. The officials of the Church were brought under the authority of Rome, and such public interests as education, charity, care of the sick, and even legislation and the administration of justice, were made affairs of the Church. As against the powerful Roman hierarchy the State, crude, undeveloped, and split by dissensions, was practically helpless. It should be added, however, that not infrequently the State rebelled against having to take a subordinate position; and toward the close of this period it developed such legal institutions as *placetum regium* and *recursus ab abusu* to curtail ecclesiastical authority. In view of this fact, the spiritual universal state must be regarded as theory, rather than reality, and the relation of Church to State during this period as one of legal coordination, but with the preponderance of competency on the side of the Church.

4. Subordination of Church to State.

The Renaissance brought a revival of the ancient idea of the State, and with this a transformation of the relation of Church to State. The new state made it its chief function to advance the welfare, or happiness, of its subjects, but, since preparation for eternity was seen to be essential to human welfare, the State now extended its activities into the ecclesiastical field. In short, to a greater or less extent, it took over the organization of the Church and assumed responsibility for the intellectual and spiritual well-being of the people. The famous sentence *Dux Cliviæ est papa in suis terris*, the reform-program of the Bavarian grand dukes, of George of Saxony, of Louis XIV., of Joseph II., and finally the *Constitution civile du clergé* of 1790—all these give proof of the characteristic relation between Church and State which had its origin in the Renaissance. It was the fate of the Reformation to fall in the midst of this political development. It was necessary that the new Christian community should have an outward organization; but whence was this to come? Considered juristically, that was a grave question. For Luther, however, it presented no difficulties. It was sufficient that means of grace be provided, and immaterial how this might be accomplished. In the end, it was found that the simplest arrangement was to entrust the care of the Church to the existing authorities. Thus arose the German state churches, as the mature product of the state of the sixteenth century. The Reformation did not recognize the necessity for an ecclesiastical organization distinct from that of the State. The Church was a homogeneous mass, and each temporal prince fostered that particular section which was conterminous with his temporal domain. With the appearance of dissent and the rise of other confessions, the inadequacy of this simple arrangement became manifest. The solution of the difficulty was offered by the theory of natural right, which was expounded by Hobbes (q.v.) and Rousseau. This is the view that the State is based upon an original agreement among the people, who delegate to the sovereign whatever authority he has. Every church, just as the State, is a community; but the State remains the supreme community, in which these other communities take their place. Thus the State again becomes secular in character. To be sure, the temporal prince retains his authority over the churches. This he no longer claims on Christian grounds, but by right of *jus territoriale*. In this way the territorial system was developed (see TERRITORIALISM). It should not be forgotten that this was the form in which tolerance first asserted itself. The next step in the development was Collegialism (q.v.), which is only a palliated territorialism. The ruling prince remains the highest authority in the Church. The only result was that now a sharper distinction was drawn between *jura circa sacra*, rights which are naturally incident to the position of a sovereign, and *jura in sacra*, rights which are deduced from the Church. The fact that these rights are exercised through two sets of officials is merely incidental, being due to considerations of convenience. Prussia affords the classic example of this kind of relation between Church and State.

5. The Modern State.

Whatever may be characteristic of the present position of the Church in its relations to the State has not been brought about by any essential change in the Church, but by the wonderful development of the modern State and the rapid growth of constitutional government. The State, as the political organization, holds the supreme authority, which can not be modified or limited, except by the State itself. Such a self-limitation, however, is the striking characteristic of the modern constitutional State. The people have been given a voice in the government. In sharp contrast to the police-state, which absorbed everything, has been the fostering care exercised by the government over private organizations for the conduct of affairs of public interest. This new position taken by the State has been particularly favorable to the manifestations of religious life. Religious liberty is now generally secured to all by state constitutions. At the head of the various societies, or organizations, which now enjoy a certain independence under the law, stand those great religious communities called churches. Legally they occupy a very high position; and the reason for this is clear. Their functions are not merely of a private nature; from time immemorial the interests of the Church have been regarded as national and ethically coequal with the affairs of the State itself. In a word, religion is a matter of public interest, and is recognized as such by the State. To be sure, the Church is subject to the State; otherwise the sovereignty of the State would be a fiction. On the other hand, the modern German state waives its right to take the Church so closely under its control as did the old police-state. In fact, the constitutional state regards it as essential that the independence of the Church be maintained. This principle has been often proclaimed, e.g., in the Frankfort *Grundrechte* and in the Prussian Constitution. Thus the Church is quite properly given the position of a separate community, existing under the State and working for the public weal. The legal terminology employed to characterize this relation of Church to State recognizes self-government as the essential feature. The French law, which has become typical, speaks of *cultes reconnus*, not as a juristic person, but as a part of the public authority, and calls the local organizations *établissements publiques*, analogous to political communities. Hence the protection and aid rendered to the Church by the civil government.

6. Relations with Rome.

While theoretically the State may subordinate the Church completely to itself, in practise it does not do it. The degree of authority exercised varies, as does also the degree of independence enjoyed by the Church. In view of the fundamental conception of the State, the Roman Catholic Church is given too much latitude in Germany and the Protestant Church too little. In reality, the Roman Catholic Church is not simply a self-governing state church, holding itself subject to the State. It remains that same remarkable world-power which in the Middle Ages shared with the State the functions of government. If the power of Rome has been greatly diminished in the modern State, this has been accomplished only by force. In principle, the Roman Church has yielded nothing. The manner in which the present organization of the Roman Catholic Church in Germany came into being is characteristic. The German states entered into agreements with the Holy See just as they would make treaties among themselves regarding secular things (see CONCORDATS AND DELIMITING BULLS). France led the way in the Napoleonic Concordat. The necessity of restoring the lost equilibrium at once manifested itself, and, too, in a curious manner. All the states, on their own initiative, proceeded to supplement the treaty with Rome by promulgating laws to give them a certain supervision over the Roman Catholic Church. Here the *articles organiques* furnished the model. Of course, such restrictions have never been recognized by the pope; and the fact that they are directed against him only serves to emphasize his position as a temporal ruler. In following such a course, the State puts itself in the position it occupied during the Middle Ages, when it sought to assert its authority against Rome by means of the now obsolete *placetum regium*, *recursus ab abusu*, *nominatio regia*, and by the exclusion of *personæ minus gratæ* (see PLACET; NOMINATIO REGIA). That the State is unable to substitute for these ancient institutions something more in accord with present political ideals and conditions can be due only to a lack of confidence in its own sovereignty. The inner contradiction between the theory and practise of the State in the matter of exercising its authority toward the Roman Catholic Church is strikingly shown in cases where the pope is actually invoked to curb some Romanist official who is attacking state institutions. Thus, through the force of tradition, the modern German state has been placed in this false and extremely objectionable attitude toward Rome.

7. The Evangelical State Church.

Quite different in this regard is the position of the Evangelical Church. In contrast to the Roman Catholic Church, which claims such a large interest in the control of external affairs, the Protestant body, whose interests are spiritual rather than temporal, would be satisfied to occupy the modest position of a self-governing body within the State. As a matter of fact, however, the Evangelical Church in Germany has never attained to that measure of freedom and independence which the constitutional state recognizes to be its right. Despite all the assurances on the side of the government, the old territorial system, the administration of church affairs by the State, continues to thrive. It is futile to assert that it is not the State, but the sovereign in person, who rules the Church; for, in public affairs, the person of the ruler can not be separated from the State. In Germany it seems to be taken as a matter of course that the Evangelical Church ought to be, and must be, ruled by the State. Of course, the Church enjoys a certain academic freedom; also the provision is maintained that the State shall exercise its rule here through separate authorities. It was a further step in this direction when the present synodal system was introduced in the last century. The local parishes have their administrative boards, and send their representatives, clergy and laymen, to the Synod. The General Synod, the highest representative body, cooperates with the sovereign in the matter of ecclesiastical legislation. The logical outcome of this process of development should have been complete self-government for the Church; but such has not been the case. Indeed, this entire movement is only a phase of that more general movement whose object has been to develop and strengthen the State. The Church is organized along parallel lines with the State, and church administration remains state administration. Just as in things temporal the sovereign remains supreme, despite local self-government and popular representation, so in things ecclesiastical.

The present relation between the State and the Roman Catholic Church is recognized as unsatisfactory, and on both sides there has been a tendency to change it. To be mentioned particularly is that significant modern movement on the part of the State whose object has been the complete separation of Church and State. In this new departure the United States took the lead. Since then, strange to say, this essentially Calvinistic idea has been carried out by such Roman Catholic countries as Mexico, Brazil, Cuba, and most recently by France. One might almost say that the separation of the Church from the State is recognized by a republican government as an obligation. Such separation is due to hostility toward the Church, and its object is the subordination of the Church. The Protestant sees nothing objectionable in this. In his view the fact that the State claims a certain surveillance over the outward organization of the Church has no significance for the inner life of faith. The Roman Catholic, on the other hand, who carries his religious sentiment into these external things, strenuously opposes any influence of the State in this direction. The *Toleranzantrag* of the Center, which was introduced in the German Reichstag in 1900, is suggestive. Under the guise of demanding freedom for the Church in general, it embodies the complaints of the Roman Catholics. It demands, among other things, complete freedom for the cure of souls throughout the empire, for the erection of church buildings and the holding of religious worship, and also demands the removal of the *placetum* and of all restrictions placed by the State upon religious societies and associations. It is this last point, the question of religious orders, that is not so easily conceded. Here economic interests come into consideration; and it is unlikely that the existing laws limiting the acquisition of property by mortmain will be changed in the interest of religious orders. This *Toleranzantrag* makes no mention of ministerial education. The State now provides for the education of ministers, but whether it will be able to nationalize the clergy, and thus remove present religious dissensions, is doubtful. The Evangelical Church gives the State no occasion to resort to radical measures; but naturally a separation of the Roman Catholic Church from the State carries with it a similar separation as regards the Evangelical Church. This is illustrated by recent events in France.

8. Tendency Toward Separation.

While the old territorial state rendered a magnificent service in rescuing the Gospel, the close embrace of the State now threatens the Church with suffocation. The Evangelical Church in Germany has completely lost the support of the masses. For them it is an institution of the State, or of the aristocracy, and part of the system which they oppose. It is regarded as *une partie du gouvernement*, just as was the Roman Catholic Church in France in the eighteenth century. But how is any other condition possible under a church regiment whose fundamental principle is that the Church must subserve the political interests of the State? As the Prussian state law puts it, the Church must show "gentleness and tolerance in doctrine and behavior," and it "must abstain from all interference in private and family affairs." It must maintain "quiet and order," "quiet and peace"; and that is the main consideration for the State. This program is carried out by German officials with perfect fidelity to duty, and with as much love to the Church as the Church, in its present depressed condition, is able to inspire in them. Naturally, the legal pastor must fit into this *régime*. The result is that in any great religious movement, for instance against Rome, the ecclesiastical organization may leave a Protestant people completely in the lurch. Political interests predominate; but such interests, which come and go with ministries, do not coincide with those of the Evangelical Church, whose chief interest is to extend the Kingdom of Jesus Christ.

9. Decadence of Protestantism in Germany.

While it would be a mistake for the Evangelical Church in Germany to aim at immediate separation from the State, the remedy for existing evils lies in that direction. There is no doubt that complete separation is only a question of time; but for the present what the Protestant Church needs is that measure of independence which, in theory, the modern State accords to it. The attainment of self-government is the serious task that the Church now confronts. But those who uphold the old territorial system ask if this is practicable. Here the only thing worthy of earnest consideration is the question of the continued existence of the state church. It has been argued that independence for the Church would bring with it a dissolution of the religious body into innumerable sects, thus destroying the national character of the Church. Although the small religious society offers advantages in the way of individual freedom, it must be admitted that the large community best provides for the service of the Master. The fear, however, that the Church would disintegrate if released from the grasp of the State is ungrounded. The removal of the antiquated territorial system does not mean necessarily that henceforth there would be no relation whatsoever between Church and State. Between the territorial system and the French system of sheer separation there is a mean. Self-government for the Church constitutes this mean. Under such a system the Church would be freed from the stifling domination of the State, without being reduced to the position of a mere company, or association. Such a relationship for the Church would not be inconsistent with its popular character. In France the two branches of the Evangelical Church have been placed in the position of secular organizations; but even in such a guise they continue to flourish as national churches. The various branches of the Protestant Church in the United States are also popular in character, the general impression to the contrary notwithstanding. In each case the Church is something more than the aggregate of local organizations. Over and above the local society stands the denomination, the Church, to which others than the members of such organizations belong. It is a spiritual body; but as such it is formally organized. It is provided with a constitution, and is recognized by law.

10. Self-Government for Church the Remedy.

From a juristic point of view the relations between Church and State resulting from self-government on the part of the Church offer no difficulty. From a practical point of view the question might be raised: Has the Evangelical Church in Germany the strength and vitality to maintain itself without the support of the strong arm of the State? It should be remembered, however, that it has been just this antiquated system of state government for the Church that has made such a question possible. A people is educated by its institutions; and in this respect the Evangelical population of Germany has been badly educated. If the Evangelical Church is now without confidence in itself this condition of affairs is due to centuries of state domination over the Church. It may be admitted that independence for the Church would involve a difficult period of transition, but it is assumed that the State would continue to aid the Church until the Church had become self-supporting. For the relations between Church and State in different countries see the articles upon the countries and states. See also the numerous related articles, such as CHURCH, THE CHRISTIAN; CHURCH GOVERNMENT; JURISDICTION, ECCLESIASTICAL; POLITY; and RELIGIOUS CORPORATIONS. (OTTO MAYER.)

II. The United States: The relations of the religious and political institutions in the United States differ radically from those found elsewhere in Christendom, and need to be considered separately. The American people are without an ecclesiastical establishment provided by organic law. The popular description of this condition is that there is "a complete separation of Church and State in the United States." While this phrase holds the kernel of a truth, it does not fairly express that truth. The fact of the political separation is unduly emphasized, while the real connection between the two institutions is overlooked.

1. Philosophical Background.

At the time of the settlement of this country it was universally regarded as a normal function of the civil power to see to it that all subjects, in theory at least, sustained some definite ecclesiastical relation; and the aggregate of such relations as had the sanction and support of the civil power constituted an ecclesiastical establishment. American political philosophy as it developed through the colonial and early national periods preserved the concept that the civil power is charged with a duty in respect to the religious affairs of the people, that it has an ecclesiastical function to perform; and it developed this concept to the effect that it is a normal function of the civil powers to make it politically possible and legally convenient for all the people to sustain voluntary ecclesiastical relations, or to sustain none at all. Under the American political system all ecclesiastical relations must be voluntary, must be without political penalty, and must be legal; but the demand upon the civil government as the physically dominant institution of society to realize these conditions is as great as it ever was to protect a state church. This obligation of American civil governments is now confirmed by a public opinion which has been gaining strength through four generations and is now generally accepted without controversy. It is now expressed in a series of guaranties and limitations contained in the organic law of the several commonwealths, in a well-developed system of statute legislation providing definite legal procedure covering many ecclesiastical relations, and in a body of notable judicial decisions rendered by the civil courts of last resort defining under ever changing circumstances what shall be the relation of Church and State.

2. Colonial Period.

Historically, this development has been as follows: At the outbreak of the American Revolution the colonies were divided ecclesiastically into three groups. In one group, consisting of New York, New Jersey, Delaware, Maryland, Virginia, North Carolina, South Carolina, and Georgia, the direct establishment of the communion of the Church of England, without, however, a resident episcopacy, was more or less complete in law. In a second group, consisting of Massachusetts, New Hampshire, and Connecticut, the congregational form of ecclesiastical organization on the basis of the territorial parish was established in law and in fact. In a third group, consisting of Rhode Island and Pennsylvania, no ecclesiastical establishment had been developed either in law or in fact. Wherever there was an establishment, what may be described as the civil church law was largely political and administrative in its character. As a result of political revolution the direct establishments by royal authority were nullified in law and degraded in popular estimation. The indirect establishments in the New England commonwealths, inasmuch as they were based upon provincial legislation and local administration, remained undisturbed for some years. There remained, however, as survivals of the direct establishments a number of incorporated parishes in New York and Virginia and a few in other states. As the remains of a still earlier establishment in New York, there were several incorporated Reformed Dutch churches which had received special protection by the terms of the Treaty of Breda (1664). During all the colonial period dissent had resisted the legal church establishments, especially the system of taxation for their support; and after the overthrow of British sovereignty a demand developed for a divorcement of political and ecclesiastical affairs. An illustration of the sentiment prevailing at the close of the Revolution is to be found in an act of the Assembly of Virginia of the year 1785, the preamble of which declares that "to suffer this civil magistrate to intrude his powers into the field of opinion, and to restrain the profession or propagation of principles on the supposition of their ill tendency, is a dangerous fallacy which at once destroys all religious liberty," and that "it is time enough for the rightful purposes of civil government for its officials to interfere when principles break out into overt acts against peace and good order."

At the formation of the Federal government religious liberty was secured to the people of the United States, as far as the action of Congress was concerned, by provision of the Constitution (art. iv., chap. 3, and the first amendment). It will be seen that both of these provisions are limitations upon the powers of Congress only. That body might pass no law in order to establish a state religion, neither could it provide any religious test as a qualification for holding office under the Federal government. The framers of the Constitution did not undertake to protect the religious liberty of the people against the action of their respective state governments. Religious affairs were declared to be within the sphere of domestic relations, and therefore reserved to the control of the states. The development of the local peculiarities in the ecclesiastical institutions of the several sections of the country continued without interruption. The colonial legislatures had granted a few charters of incorporation to local churches, and this practise was continued for a few years by the state legislatures. It was, however, soon abandoned because of the popular sympathy with the complaint that such particular charters of incorporation constituted special legislation secured through political influence. After the Revolution there arose a demand in the middle states for a uniform procedure by which the local organizations of all religious denominations might receive a corporate form. To meet the needs of the time legislation was enacted which introduced the second stage in the development of American ecclesiastical policy, viz., the era of the general statute. The first general statute that could serve the churches of all denominations became law in New York on April 6, 1784. An act of similar intent and like provisions was passed in 1793 by the state of New Jersey, and these two statutes with their subsequent revisions became the models for similar statutes in many of the northern states. These early statutes resulted from the necessity of providing legal trustees with a standing in court, in whom might rest the title to property devoted to religious purposes. They were enacted at a time of little religious interest and of bare toleration of religious bodies by legislators. The powers conferred upon religious corporations that might come into being under these general statutes were very limited; and in no state were such corporations allowed to be self-perpetuating. Partiality to religious denominations on the part of the state legislatures was dreaded, and there was also a very real fear among the lawmakers themselves lest something might be done toward recreating an ecclesiastical establishment. The method of providing for the incorporation of religious societies by means of a general statute has developed unequally in different sections of the country, and it has not yet been adopted by all the states. As late as 1866, the states of Rhode Island, Virginia, and South Carolina had no such statute; and in 1896 a general statute of incorporation was still forbidden by constitution in the states of Virginia and West Virginia.

3. Conditions after the Revolution.

A third stage in the development of American civil church law has come as the result of specializing legislation with reference to religious organizations in two directions. In one direction increased discrimination has been made between ecclesiastical bodies proper, and other social, educational, and philanthropic organizations. The second form of specialization, however, is of far more importance than the first. In the states having the most highly developed legislation the general provisions of the statutes have, from time to time, been supplemented by special optional provisions affecting convocations of particular religious denominations. The demand for this class of legislation has in nearly every case come from the churches themselves. As the denominations have grown in strength and their members have developed a more intelligent interest in their own special features of polity, many of them have made efforts to find legal expression for the essential features of their respective polities. Through these supplemental provisions, there has been wrought into the statute law of many of the states the recognition of purely ecclesiastical functionaries. It can not now be said to be the intention of the legislatures to keep the control of the temporal affairs of the churches in the hands of corporations, "independent of priest, bishop, presbytery, or synod or other ecclesiastical judicatory." There has developed in recent years a marked legislative cordiality toward the churches. While at the beginning of the nineteenth century the avowed policy in American legislation was to treat all religious interests alike by doing as little as possible for any of them and forcing all to conform to one procedure, at the beginning of the twentieth century the policy seems to be to treat all interests alike by giving to each all that is asked.

4. Special Legislation.

The early concept of religious organization in American law was very naturally that of a simple and completely autonomous local society. To denominations whose types of polity correspond to this concept the legislation of the general statute era has been satisfactory. The special optional provisions referred to, have, therefore, been enacted for the benefit of churches having polities by which the local bodies sustain a definite relation to some more general authority. It has been those denominations which have an administrative or episcopal type of organization that have shown the greatest energy in securing denominational legislation of the kind mentioned. At the present time twenty-five distinct religious denominations have thus been specially legislated for. The statutes of sixteen states now contain special provisions for the incorporation and regulation of Protestant Episcopal churches. Eight states make similar provision for Roman Catholic churches, and seven states for Methodist Episcopal churches. The privilege that is being accorded to religious bodies of having such legislation enacted as best developed their respective polities is resulting in what may be defined as a legal crystallization of ecclesiastical polity. Presbyteries, conferences, synods, classes, conventions, superintendents, overseers, presiding elders, vicars general, bishops, and archbishops, have come to have a legal status by virtue of their ecclesiastical status and legal powers incidental to their spiritual jurisdiction. Such features of ecclesiastical organization as secure recognition in the civil law are thereby less liable to alteration than the non-legal features, and more capable of resisting the influences of social environment.

The fundamental principles of political philosophy which were to regulate the relations of Church and State among the American people had been well defined and generally accepted while the nation was still confined to the original states along the Atlantic coast; and successive expansions of the national domain have not resulted in any radical changes of policy. The same principles have been applied by the Federal government in Alaska, the Hawaiian Islands, Porto Rico, and the Philippine Islands. Nowhere has the civil power failed in its function of affording legal protection and procedure for religious organizations, and nowhere have the churches exceeded these legal powers and infringed upon civil rights. The alien peoples who have come under American political training give evidence of appreciating the altered relation of Church and State. After more than one hundred years of test under all conditions, it is now as true as at the beginning of American national life that the full and free right to entertain any religious belief, to practise any religious principle, and to teach any religious doctrine which does not violate the laws of morality, and which does not infringe personal rights, is conceded to all. The law knows no heresy, is committed to the support of no dogma and to the establishment of no sect. GEORGE JAMES BAYLES.

BIBLIOGRAPHY: W. E. Gladstone, *The State in its Relations with the Church*, 2 vols., London, 1841; S. T. Coleridge, *On the Constitution of Church and State*, ib. 1852; T. R. Birks, *Church and State*, ib. 1869; J. W. Joyce, *The Civil Power in its Relation to the Church*, ib. 1869; E. de Pressensé, *Church and French Revolution*, ib. 1869; J. Rüttiman, *Kirche und Staat in Nordamerika*, Basel, 1871; E. Friedberg, *Die Grenzen zwischen Staat und Kirche und die Garantien gegen deren Verletzung*, Tübingen, 1872; J. P. Thompson, *Church and State in the United States*, Boston, 1873; J. S. Mill, *State Interference with Church Property*, in his *Dissertations*, 4 vols., London, 1873–75; J. Hergenröther, *The Catholic Church and the Christian State*, London, 1876; H. Geffcken, *Church and State, their Relations historically Considered*, 2 vols., London, 1877; M. Minghetti, *Staat und Kirche*, Gotha, 1881; F. Nippold, *Die Theorie der Trennung von Kirche und Staat*, Bern, 1881; P. Hinschius, *Allgemeine Darstellung der Verhältnisse von Staat und Kirche*, Freiburg, 1883; A. P. Stanley, *Essays chiefly on Questions of Church and State*, London, 1884; De Gabriac, *L'Église et l'état*, Paris, 1886; W. Armitage, *Sketches of Church and State in the First Eight Centuries*, London, 1888; P. Schaff, *Church and State in the United States*, New York, 1888; U. Balzani, *The Popes and the Hohenstaufen*, New York, 1889; A. T. Jones, *Church and State*, Edinburgh, 1890; C. Benoist, *L'État et l'église*, Paris, 1892; P. E. Lauer, *Church and State in New England*, Baltimore, 1892 (Johns Hopkins University Studies, 10 ser., nos. 2–3); K. Rieker, *Die rechtliche Stellung der evangelischen Kirche Deutschlands in ihrer geschichtlichen Entwicklung*, Leipsic, 1893; W. Kahl, *Lehrsystem des Kirchenrechts und der Kirchenpolitik*, i. 246 sqq., Freiburg, 1894; D. A. Wirgmann, *The Church and the Civil Power*, London, 1894; F. Satolli, *Loyalty to Church and State*, Baltimore, 1895; W. D. and J. H. Johnston, *Relations between Church and State*, Ann Arbor, 1896–97; T. Mommsen, *Römisches Strafrecht*, Leipsic, 1899; T. Kaftan, *Vier Kapitel von der Landeskirche*, Sleswick, 1903; W. D. Abraham, *Church and State in England*, London, 1905; M. Lecomte, *Rapport au sénat sur le projet de loi concernant la séparation des églises et de l'état*, Paris, 1905; E. Troeltsch, in P. Hinneberg, *Die Kultur der Gegenwart*, I. iv., Leipsic, 1905; P. Sabatier, *À propos de la séparation des églises et de l'état*, Paris, 1906, Eng. transl., *Disestablishment in France*, New York, 1906; W. Birney, *France and the Pope; the Separation of the Churches and the French Republic*, New York, 1907; A. Eitel, *Der Kirchenstaat unter Klemens V.*, Berlin, 1907.

CHURCH TRIUMPHANT: 1. A church founded by a Mrs. Beekman (d. 1883), who claimed to be the "spiritual mother of Christ in the second coming" and declared George Jacob Schweinfurth the "Messiah of the New Dispensation." Mr. Schweinfurth left the ministry of the Methodist Episcopal Church, became a follower of Mrs. Beekman, and subsequently the leader of her followers. Headquarters of the body were established at the Weldon Farm, six miles from Rockford, Ill. The Church accepted the Bible as the word of God, but denied the essential divinity of Christ, holding that he received the spirit of God, became free from sin and its curse and so divine. Schweinfurth claimed equality with Jesus in this respect and was accepted as the "Christ of the second coming." The Church is now extinct, and when most flourishing numbered only twelve congregations with 384 communicants.

BIBLIOGRAPHY: H. K. Carroll, *Religious Forces of the United States*, pp. 105–106, New York, 1896.

2. A religious and communistic society, having headquarters at Estero, Fla., founded by Cyrus F. Teed, and also known as the Koreshan Ecclesia. See COMMUNISM, II., 4.

CHURCH VISITATIONS: A method of ecclesiastical supervision of churches and church work. This institution has for its purpose the oversight of church government, and is a means of securing insight into, and of promoting, church life. As early as the fourth century it was the custom of the Eastern Church for the bishops or their deputies to visit the churches of the diocese. In the West also this visitation by the bishop dates from an early time. This institution was especially cultivated in the Frankish Church. There visitations took place when the bishop traversed his diocese to perform the rite of confirmation. Under Charlemagne the bishop was aided and controlled by the count or his mayor. They jointly held the synodal court (*Sendgericht*), punishing not only ecclesiastical offenses, but also sins like theft, perjury, sorcery, etc. The decay of visitations in the following period was due to two causes: (1) the bishops were more and more estranged from their spiritual calling by becoming secular princes; (2) the custom of redemption—that is, exemption from penalties on payment of a sum of money—was introduced into the synodal courts, making them an important source of revenue. The Council of Trent ameliorated these conditions, and made it the duty of the bishops to visit their diocese either every year or every second year, according to its size.

Early Practise and Its Decay.

Visitations became important again at the time of the Reformation. They were the means of carrying out the Reformation in individual territories. That in electoral Saxony became the model and basis of the others. The first impulse in this direction came not from Luther, but from Jacob Strauss in Eisenach (1525) and from Nicolaus

Hausmann, preacher at Zwickau. Both showed the necessity of such oversight. Induced by the fanatics and the Peasants' War, Luther strongly urged the elector to order a thorough visitation. It was immediately begun, and, although at first only sporadic, it soon revealed its necessity. In 1526 Luther proposed a general church- and school-visitation, which was carried out by a commission of clergy and laymen in 1527–29. The Saxon book of visitation, composed by Melanchthon, *Unterricht der Visitatoren an die Pfarhern ym Kurfürstenthum zu Sachssen* (1528), was generally adopted as the model. There the principle of church government by the state found its first expression. The visitation included in its scope the official conduct of the pastors, the order of church service, confession, and church discipline. The whole constitution of the Lutheran Church has its basis and model in this institution. Because of their historical value the proceedings of the visitations were published, either as a whole or in part, those of the Wittenberg district by Winter (1862), those of the district of Jüterbogk by Götze, those of Magdeburg by Danneil (1864). Burkhardt planned a comprehensive history of the German church- and school-visitations in this period, but only the Saxon visitations appeared (1879). Nebe published in 1880 (in abstract only) the proceedings of the visitations of the bishopric of Halberstadt from 1564 to 1589; the complete visitations in the Guelphic states from 1542 to 1544 were published in 1897 by Kayser. While the first visitations were extraordinary measures, they were soon made a stated order. The Prussian articles of 1540 order one annually, and most of the later church orders contain ordinances for periodical repetition.

Revival During the Reformation.

After the Thirty Years' War these functions attained again their former importance and contributed greatly to the restoration of order and church life. In the eighteenth century they degenerated, but were reinstituted in their old form in the German state churches in the nineteenth century, largely through their advocacy at the Eisenach conference of 1852–53. They recur regularly, two to six years apart. The superintendent or general superintendent is the visitor, often in cooperation with an officer of the state; or a commission is instituted with the superintendent as leader. The visitations are usually held on Sunday and consist of a sermon by the pastor, an address by the visitor, an examination of the conditions of religious instruction, discussion with the ministers and teachers, the vestry or the house fathers, revision of administrative affairs, of church registers and buildings, of the cemetery, etc. The question has been discussed whether in these visitations the element of devotion and churchly revival should predominate, or whether they should be conducted merely for the purpose of obtaining information. In this respect there is no uniformity in the different German state churches, nor do they agree on the question whether part should be taken by synodical representatives. (G. Uhlhorn†.)

Modern Practise.

Bibliography: On the early and the Lutheran visitations: J. Auerbach, *De visitationum ecclesiæ progressu a primis temporibus*, Frankfort, 1862; A. L. Richter, *Geschichte der evangelischen Kirchenverfassung in Deutschland*, pp. 43 sqq., Leipsic, 1851; C. A. H. Burkhardt, *Geschichte der sächsischen Kirchen- und Schul-Visitationen, 1524–45*, ib. 1879; K. Kayser, *Die reformatorischen Kirchenvisitationen in den welfischen Landen, 1542–44*, Göttingen, 1897. On Roman Catholic rules concerning visitations consult L. Thomassinus, *Vetus ac nova ecclesiæ . . . instructio exposita*, 3 vols., Lucca, 1728; P. Melchers, *De canonica diocesium visitatione*, Cologne, 1803; Bingham, *Origines*, books V., IX., XVII.; *KL*, s.v. "Visitationen."

CHURCHWARDENS: Two lay officers in each parish of the Anglican communion, whose duty is to have charge, with the vestry, of the temporalities of the church, and to see that provision is made for the maintenance and orderly celebration of public worship. In England one is usually nominated by the incumbent and the other elected by the parishioners; in the Protestant Episcopal Church both (called "senior" and "junior" wardens) are elected by the congregation annually in Easter-week.

CHURCHYARD: Conformably to the contemporary Greek and Roman custom, the primitive Christian burial-places lay outside the community. There was no difference in this respect between corporate cemeteries and private grounds, between the subterranean and those on the surface. East and West, this actual condition is the same. It appears that this custom was broken for the first time within the pale of Christendom through the circumstance that Constantine the Great was entombed in the Church of the Apostles at Constantinople—a decisive precedent for the future. For that matter, during antiquity in general there was provision for urban burial as a mark of special honor (*virtutis causa*)—Augustus and Trajan, for instance, at Rome; and, without exception, the Vestals. Under a flexible construction there also soon followed eminent ecclesiastics (e.g., Ambrose) and persons of worldly distinction, but first and foremost the martyrs and saints, whose bodies were exalted and lodged in the neighborhood churches. During the fourth century it was even customary in Egypt to preserve mummified bodies of saints in their homes. In fact, what was originally the exception began to be the general rule toward the end of the fourth century, so that secular and spiritual authorities were obliged to forbid the multiplication of burials in churches. Finally a compromise was arranged whereby burial inside the church was granted in exceptional cases by episcopal authorization; whereas to the congregation as such was made over the ground enclosing the church (*atrium ecclesiæ*: "churchyard"). This ground, it is true, did not attain to the high esteem of the church interior; but still it availed, being consecrated, as holy ground; while the vicinity of the sacrificial mass and of the sanctuary prayer contributed also, in a degree, to enhance its favor. See Cemeteries.

The medieval Church exercised unrestricted authority over the churchyard, which it regarded as an adjunct of God's house. The same right of asylum protected them both (cf. German *Friedhof*, in the sense "safeguard"). By consecration a particular seal was imparted to the churchyard; and a dedication of the church demanded likewise a new consecration of the churchyard, though not *vice versa*. The execution of a bloody sentence on this ground involved excommunication. The not infrequent custom of fortifying the churchyard, together with the church, for the protection of the church was ecclesiastically contested, indeed, but not annulled. On the other hand, it is required that the graveyard be well fenced in or hedged. Special plots are reserved for the priests. The graves of children who die without baptism are located in a place distinct from the rest of the cemetery. No one who has not departed this life in peace with the church may be laid to rest in consecrated ground.

A tall cross must be set up in the middle of the cemetery. Another necessary requirement is a charnel-house (*ossuarium*), into which the disinterred bones are gathered. There belongs lastly to the structural completeness of the cemetery the lantern of the dead, a round or polygonal tower with a top-piece for the reception of a perpetual light. Its origin inheres, perhaps, in the symbolism of light; but popular credulity saw in this light a means of defense against evil spirits. Artistic decoration of the graveyard appears to have been the exception in medieval times. Such an exception is the renowned Campo Santo in Pisa, begun in 1278, and further embellished in the fourteenth and fifteenth centuries. The Church of Rome has retained the observances and canonical regulations of medieval usage, but only in isolated instances—as with reference to tombstone inscriptions and the maintenance of cemeteries adjoining the church—have the same been supplemented with new regulations.

Cemetery development in the Greek Church generally parallels that in the West. The Greek Church likewise classes the graveyard with consecrated things, provides for it official dedication, and reckons with the possibility of desecration.

The Reformation consistently broke with the medieval conception of the cemetery as *locus religiosus*, and at the same time did away with the specific Roman Catholic burial rites. With all this, however, the duty by no means lapsed of showing a pious regard for the resting-place of the dead. The church ordinances dwell on the matter frequently. Modern legislation has revised former customs and legal usages. Interment in the churches, with exceptions of princes and bishops, has been forbidden. And alongside the confessional cemetery for believers, there has grown up the municipal cemetery for non-confessors.

VICTOR SCHULTZE.

BIBLIOGRAPHY: Lists of works germane to the subject will be found under BURIAL and CEMETERIES.

CHURCH YEAR: The comprehensive term given to the regular succession of seasons, feasts, and fasts in the calendar of the Christian Church, independent of the civil calendar although to some extent making use of it for convenience of reckoning. The simplest basis of division is that denoted by the week of seven days, which was in use among the Jews from early times, and had been introduced into Roman usage shortly before the beginning of the Christian era, replacing the period of eight days (*internundinum*). Both Jewish and Gentile Christians, accordingly, were prepared to accept this division, although they rejected the pagan names for the days of the week, and preferred to call Sunday the Lord's Day (*dies dominica, hēmera kuriakē*), numbering the others in order as *feria secunda, tertia*, etc. With this for a basis, and Sunday, the commemoration of the resurrection of Christ, as the earliest approach to a recurrent festival (see SUNDAY), the entire sequence of festivals and seasons gradually grew up (see FEASTS AND FESTIVALS, II., and the articles on the separate days thus distinguished).

In the Western Churches which have adopted such a chronological scheme the ecclesiastical year begins with the first Sunday in Advent, which is always "the nearest Sunday to the feast of St. Andrew" (Nov. 30), whether before or after (i.e., the first Sunday after Nov. 26). There are four Sundays in this season of preparation for Christians. In the Roman Catholic and Anglican Churches one or two "Sundays after Christmas" follow as the case may be to the feast of the Epiphany (Jan. 6). In the German Lutheran Churches Dec. 26 is the "second Christmas," a Sunday from Dec. 27 to Dec. 31 is the "Sunday after Christmas," and a Sunday from Jan. 2 to Jan. 5 is the "Sunday after New Year" (which is also observed as a church day). Sundays after Epiphany are numbered in order, there being from one to six of them according to the date of Easter. Then three Sundays, named Septuagesima, Sexagesima, and Quinquagesima from the approximate distance to Easter, lead up to the forty days (forty week-days, the Sundays not being included as fasting-days) of lent beginning with Ash Wednesday and terminating in the festival of Easter. The next five Lord's days are known as Sundays after Easter, and the whole period of fifty days following Easter, with the feast of the Ascension occurring on the fortieth, is a time of the highest spiritual joyfulness. The paschal season terminates with the festival of Pentecost (Whitsunday), which falls on the seventh Sunday after Easter (the sixth Sunday after Easter being the "Sunday after Ascension-day"). The succeeding Sundays to the end of the church year are designated in the Roman Catholic Church Sundays after Pentecost, in the Anglican and Lutheran after Trinity, the Feast of the Holy Trinity falling in all these bodies on the octave of Pentecost. There may be from twenty-three to twenty-eight Sundays after Trinity, twenty-four to twenty-nine after Pentecost.

In the Eastern Church the year is divided into three parts without reference to the date on which it begins (Sept. 1); the part preparatory to Easter, called *triōdion* after the book containing the liturgical forms used during the season, begins with the "Sunday of the Pharisee and the Publican" (so called from the Gospel for the day), which corresponds to the last Sunday after Epiphany in the Western reckoning; the paschal season (*pentēkostarion*) extends to and includes the first Sunday after Pentecost (the Greek feast of All Saints) and the remaining period (*oktoēchos*) has its Sundays designated, according to the evangelical lections, either as "Matthew Sundays" (second to fourteenth after Pentecost) or as "Luke Sundays" (fifteenth after Pentecost to the Western second in Advent and those after Epiphany). See CALENDAR, THE CHRISTIAN.

The following are the earliest and latest dates on which the various church days named can fall:

First Sunday in Advent, Nov. 27-Dec. 3.
Septuagesima Sunday, Jan. 18-Feb. 22.
Ash Wednesday, Feb. 4-Mar. 11.
Easter, Mar. 22-Apr. 25.
Ascension Day, Apr. 30-June 3.
Whitsunday, May 10-June 13.
Trinity Sunday, May 17-June 20.

BIBLIOGRAPHY: Consult the literature cited under FEASTS AND FESTIVALS, especially the works of Augusti, Bingham, Binterim, and Cruser: J. C. W. Augusti, *Die Feste der alten Christen*, Leipsic, 1817-20; F. H. Rheinwald, *Die kirchliche Archäologie*, pp. 154-257, Berlin, 1830; H. Alt, *Der christliche Cultus*, part 2, *das Kirchenjahr*, ib. 1860; W. I. Kip, *The Hist., Object and Proper Observance of Lent*, New York, 1875; S. Butcher, *The Ecclesiastical Calendar*, London, 1877; A. H. Grant, *Church Seasons, Historical and Poetical*, New York, 1881; *Handbuch der theologischen Wissenschaften*, ed. O. Zöckler, iv. 361 sqq., Nördlingen, 1885; A. Tait, *High Days of the Christian Year*, London, 1890; *DCA*, ii. 2054-59 (gives list of the celebrations and their names in the different calendars); the literature under CALENDAR; COMMON PRAYER, BOOK OF.

CHURCH, ALFRED JOHN: Church of England classical scholar; b. in London Jan. 29, 1829. He was educated at Lincoln College, Oxford (B.A., 1851), and was curate of Westport St. Mary's, Gloucester, 1853-56; of St. Peter's Chapel, St. Marylebone, London, 1861-68; rector of Ashley, Tilbury, Gloucestershire, 1892-97; professor of Latin in University College, London, 1880-87. In theology he is an orthodox liberal Anglican, with a distinct appreciation of the value of higher criticism. His reputation rests upon his many pleasing tales from the Latin and Greek classics and from church history, those from the latter being such as *The Story of Jerusalem* (London, 1880); "*To the Lions*" (1889); *The Crusaders* (1904).

CHURCH, RICHARD WILLIAM: Dean of St. Paul's; b. in Lisbon Apr. 25, 1815; d. in Dover Dec. 9, 1890. He entered Wadham College, Oxford, 1833 (B.A., 1836; M.A., 1839; hon. D.C.L., 1875); was fellow of Oriel 1838-52; tutor 1839-42; junior proctor 1844-45; rector of Whatley, Somerset, from 1852 to 1871, when he became dean of St. Paul's. He was select preacher at Oxford 1868, 1876-78, 1881-82. The religious influences to which he was subjected at Redlands, near Bristol, where he attended school 1828-33, were narrowly evangelical; at Oxford, however, he was drawn into the Tractarian movement and he became an intimate friend of Newman. A striking incident of his career was the veto by the proctors in convocation at Oxford, Feb., 1845, of the proposition to condemn Newman's *Tract 90*, in connection with the degradation of William George Ward (q.v.). The veto was pronounced by the senior proctor, Henry Peter Guillemard, but it was inspired by the junior proctor, Church. As dean he restored St. Paul's Cathedral, readjusted its revenues, and reorganized its staff; he was faithful and zealous, but unostentatious. He translated *The Catechetical Lectures of St. Cyril of Jerusalem* (London, 1838) for Pusey and Newman's *Library of the Fathers*, wrote *The Beginnings of the Middle Ages* (1877) for the *Epochs of Modern History* series, and, with Canon Paget, revised Keble's edition of Hooker's *Ecclesiastical Polity* (Oxford, 1888). He published a critical study of *St. Anselm* (London, 1870); an essay on *Dante* (first printed in the *Christian Remembrancer*, 1850; reprinted with a translation of Dante's *De monarchia* by his son, F. J. Church, 1878); *Spenser* (1879) and *Bacon* (1884) in the *English Men of Letters* series. His last work was *The Oxford Movement* (1891).

BIBLIOGRAPHY: Mary C. Church, *Life and Letters of Dean Church*, London, 1894 (by his daughter); A. B. Donaldson, *Richard William Church*, ib. 1905; *DNB*, supplement, ii. 6-9.

CHURCHES OF GOD IN CHRIST JESUS. See ADVENTISTS, 6.

CHURCHING OF WOMEN: According to the prescriptions of Lev. xii., women were regarded as ceremonially unclean after childbirth (see DEFILEMENT AND PURIFICATION, CEREMONIAL, I., 1, § 2; II., 1, § 1), and, especially since Mary submitted herself to the ordinance of purification (Luke ii. 22), the idea found entrance into the Church. Dionysius of Alexandria, in his epistle to Basilides (*MPG*, x. 1281), treats it as a matter of course that pious mothers will not approach the Lord's table until ceremonially clean, and Zonaras and Balsamon gave it canonical force. According to the ritual laid down for the first visit to the church (Goar, *Euchologion*, p. 267), the mother was to present herself on the fortieth day after delivery with her child and its sponsor; the priest offered a prayer for her complete purification, and another for the child, accompanied with the sign of the cross; then, carrying the child, he led the mother within the church with an appropriate formula. In an Ethiopian ritual mother and child were anointed on the forehead with holy oil. The Western Church took a different view. Gregory the Great wrote in answer to a question of Augustine of Canterbury that recent mothers might indeed abstain for a time from communion out of reverence, but that they were not to be condemned if they received it soon after childbirth; and this decision passed into the canon law (*Decreta Gregorii*, iii. 47). The Western custom, however, was to bring the mother formally to church, with the child, usually on the fortieth day, and the conception of purification still maintained itself, symbolized by the aspersion with holy water at the church door. An office for the "benediction of women after childbirth" is contained in the *Rituale Romanum* as edited by Paul V. in 1614. The priest, wearing a white stole, meets the woman at the door, and after the recitation of Ps. xxiv. holds out one end of his stole to her and conducts her into the church; she kneels before the altar while certain prayers are said, ending with a blessing. The Reformation in Germany, for the most part, abolished the ceremony as giving rise to misconceptions and abuses, though some churches retained it, giving an evangelical character to the rite, and the duty of thanksgiving after safe delivery was frequently insisted on. In the rationalistic period the practise of giving a special blessing to the mother was usually dropped, though to this day it is usual to ask the prayers of the congregation for her and for the child at her first appearance in church; and several of the most recent Lutheran service-books contain an office for her benediction at the altar after the public service. [Such an office is also contained in the Book of Common Prayer . . . of the Church of England. Its title in the first book of Edward VI. was "The Order of the Purification of Women," but this was altered in the second to "The Thanksgiving of Women after Child-birth, commonly called the Churching of Women."] (Georg Rietschel.)

Bibliography: A. J. Stephens, *Book of Common Prayer with Notes*, iii. 1751–63, London, 1853.

CHYTRÆUS, kai-trî'us (**KOCHHAFE**), **DAVID**: The last of the "Fathers of the Lutheran Church"; b. at Ingelfingen (43 m. n.n.e. of Stuttgart), Württemberg, Feb. 26, 1531; d. at Rostock June 25, 1600. As a pupil of Melanchthon he belonged to the mediating theologians. He was no original genius, but owing to his disposition and power of work he was a scholar of almost encyclopedic knowledge, but without the gift of preaching. His organizing and academical activity was effective. He was the center of the University of Rostock, a pure personality, filled with love of peace, not willingly harsh, but rather timid, and inclined to avoid conflicts. He studied at Tübingen and at Wittenberg, where he lived in Melanchthon's house, and attended Luther's lectures on Genesis, those of Paul Eber, and others. After a brief return to Tübingen (1547), he lectured at Wittenberg on Melanchthon's *Loci*, on rhetoric, and on astronomy. He accompanied his friend Johannes Aurifaber to Rostock, whither he was called after a visit to Italy, in 1550. His work was to introduce beginners into the doctrine of salvation, expound the classics, and deliver encyclopedic and exegetical lectures on the Old and New Testaments. Rostock was thenceforth his home. He enjoyed in a high degree the favor of the duke, to which he responded by a mixture of frankness and sometimes rather nauseating servility. After the division of the country (1555), Chytræus entreated the dukes to build up the university, which was slowly effected in spite of personal, political, financial, and physical difficulties. The office of university-superintendent he declined, but he was looked upon as the pillar of the institution. He was also busy with ecclesiastical regulations, opposed the Flacian adversaries of the Formula of Concord who had been driven from the duchy, and looked upon the plan of some princes to call a general synod of all Evangelicals as hopeless. Another field of labor opened for him in Austria. Emperor Maximilian II., who sympathized with Melanchthon, granted to the Lutheran estates of Lower and Upper Austria in 1568 the free exercise of religion on the basis of the Augsburg Confession, with the condition that they first agree upon a church-discipline. The estates elected a commission for that purpose, and Chytræus, known for his moderation, was invited to assist. In the beginning of 1569 he arrived in Austria. Of the fourfold work—the preparation of a liturgy, an order for superintendents and consistories, an exposition of the Augsburg Confession, and an *examen ordinandorum*—the first two were speedily prepared. The third was beset with difficulties on account of the Flacian ministers, not to speak of delays from other causes. Finally the free exercise of religion was obtained, and Chytræus, praised by the emperor, returned home, underrating the depth of the antagonistic principles. The publication of the liturgy caused a bitter controversy, which the emperor terminated by force. By his work in Austria the estates of Styria had their attention drawn to Chytræus, and he was invited to rearrange church matters there, after the religious compromise had been confirmed by Archduke Charles. He arrived at Graz Jan. 2, 1574. Despite difficulties, the church-discipline was completed in May, 1574. With a vote of thanks he returned home and took up his relations with the Scandinavian kingdoms. Being attacked by Antonio Possevino for his activity in Austria and his influence in Sweden, he wrote a rejoinder (Wittenberg, 1584), and he replied to a request from Antwerp to give his opinion on a catechism, in 1581.

His works include: (1) Exegetical: glossatory, dogmatizing commentaries of slight importance. (2) Dogmatic: a *Catechesis* (Wittenberg, 1555, and often) imitating Melanchthon's *Loci*, a short, comprehensive, and able work, used for almost a century in universities, gymnasia, and public schools, and recommended even in agenda; *De studio theologiæ recte inchoando* (1562; enlarged, Rostock, 1572), belonging also to the Melanchthonian type, and following closely the Augsburg Confession, the Apology, the Wittenberg Concordia, and the Schmalkald Articles; *De morte et vita æterna* (Wittenberg, 1581), the first attempt at a complete eschatology in the Melanchthonian spirit; it even gave occasion for a charge of crypto-Calvinism; the colorless *Regulæ vitæ* (1555), following the decalogue, were originally composed by Melanchthon. In treating of single doctrinal points a more Lutheran tendency is perceptible, consistent with his participation in the work of the Concordia; but Chytræus found the forms of the true doctrines "mediocriter constituta" in the Formula of Concord, and deplored the damnation of the excluded (Reformed) churches. (3) Polemical: the rejoinder to Possevino and a controversial letter against the provost Georg Cœlestinus concerning the "history of the Augsburg Confession." (4) Of his philosophical, or rather methodological, writings the *Regulæ studiorum* (best ed., Leipsic, 1595) had a far-reaching influence; the rich contents of the *Præcepta rhetoricæ inventionis* (Wittenberg, 1558) suffer by its fragmentary character. (5) In his historical works, written with care and freshness, Chytræus appears to better advantage than in his theological writings; the proper scientific treatment, however, is lacking. The very popular *Onomasticon theologicum* (1557) was an attempt to combine a theological encyclopedia and a Hebrew dictionary; it displays the knowledge of church history possessed at the time. *De lectione historiarum recte instituenda* (Rostock, 1563) shows little criticism, but is important for the history of historiography. The *Historia der Augspurgischen Confession* (Rostock, 1571; Latin, Frankfort, 1578) was the first special work on a part of this period based upon original sources. The *Chronicon Saxoniæ* (Wittenberg, 1585; Leipsic, 1593), written in the manner of annals from a religious point of view, was appreciated in all Europe. In his very carefully prepared genealogical labors Chytræus was encouraged by Duke Ulrich, and in general his historical writings bear, so to speak, the official stamp of the duchy of Mecklenburg, as, following the custom of his time, he preferred to give the result of his researches in academical lectures. Chytræus's publications include also the works of others edited by him and several volumes of a public character; his "Orations" were many and interesting—a collection of thirty-six was published posthumously by his son David (Hanover, 1614). GEORG LOESCHE.

BIBLIOGRAPHY: The early source is O. F. Schütz, *De vita Davidis Chytræi* . . . , 3 vols., Hamburg, 1720–28. Consult: T. Pressel, *David Chytræus*, Elberfeld, 1862; O. Krabbe, *David Chytræus*, Rostock, 1870.

CIARAN, kī'ār-an (**KIERAN**), **SAINT, OF CLONMACNOISE**, "the son of the carpenter": Irish saint of the first half of the sixth century. He studied under Finnian at Clonard, where he had Columba and Brendan among his fellows, and under Enda at Aran. He founded the monastery at Clonmacnoise (in King's County, 8 m. s.w. of Athlone) after 540, and died at the age of thirty-three. The accounts of his life contain much of the miraculous. Clonmacnoise became the most national of the Irish monasteries and more than half of them, it is said, followed its rule. The site is still a place of pilgrimage on St. Ciaran's day (Sept. 9).

BIBLIOGRAPHY: Lanigan, *Eccl. Hist.*, i. 31, 468, ii. 50–61; A. P. Forbes, *Kalendars of Scottish Saints*, pp. 435–436, Edinburgh, 1872; C. de Smedt and J. de Backer, *Acta sanctorum Hibernica*, pp. 155–160, Edinburgh, 1888; A. Stokes, *Lives of Saints from the Book of Lismore*, pp. 117–134, 262–280, 355–359, Oxford, 1890; J. Healy, *Insula sanctorum et doctorum*, pp. 258 sqq., 550 565, Dublin, 1890.

CIARAN (KIERAN), SAINT, OF SAIGIR: Bishop of Ossory, one of the "twelve apostles of Ireland." His "Lives" say that he was born while Ireland was still heathen, that he studied for twenty years at Rome and was ordained bishop there, and that while returning home he met Patrick, who prophesied of a future meeting in Ireland; he is also said to have been a contemporary of Finnian of Clonard and of Ciaran of Clonmacnoise, and to reconcile these statements his life is lengthened to three hundred or more years. He established himself as a hermit at Saigir (4 m. e. of Birr, or Parsonstown, King's County), where others joined him, and in time the great monastery of Seirkieran arose, a center for the preaching of the Gospel and a large industrial community noted for its wealth. Some identify him with a saint who is said to have passed over to Cornwall and labored and died there under the name of Piran.

BIBLIOGRAPHY: Lanigan, *Eccl. Hist.*, i. 29–33, ii. 7–9, 98, 101; C. de Smedt and J. de Backer, *Acta sanctorum Hibernica*, pp. 805–818, Edinburgh, 1888; J. O'Hanlon, *Lives of the Irish Saints*, iii. 115, Dublin [1875].

CIBORIUM, si-bō'ri-um: Originally the canopy which, borne by four columns, surmounted the altar, but afterward specially applied to the vessel in which the host was kept. See BALDACHIN; VESSELS, SACRED, § 3.

CILICIUM, si-lis'i-um (**CILICE**): A garment of coarse goat's hair, such as was worn in ancient times by soldiers, sailors, and peasants; made principally in Cilicia, whence the name. It was worn by penitents on Maundy Thursday at their reconciliation in the church. The same name was applied from about the end of the fourth century to the hair shirt worn by monks and other ascetics next to the skin as a measure of self-discipline. Cassian knows of the practise, but disapproves it as an innovation, and as tending to vainglory, besides hindering the monk in his daily task. The custom, however, spread widely, and became a normal characteristic of the ascetic. The hair shirt was worn either constantly or at certain times. Sometimes it was replaced by a girdle of the same material, worn about the legs or arms, or (after the sixteenth century) by one made of wire, sometimes with sharp points turned inward. (A. HAUCK.)

CIRCUMCELLIONES, ser"cum-sel"i-ō'nīz: North African fanatics who appear in the Donatist controversy about 340. That they were of pagan origin (Thümmel, pp. 85–86) can not be proved, nor did Donatist schism call them into being—they had already sprung up from both ecclesiastical and social conditions. They seem to have called themselves *agonistici* (with reference to II Tim. iv. 7) and designated their leaders, Axido and Fasir, as leaders of the saints. The Donatist Tichonius characterizes them as "superstitious" because of their unnecessary religious observances including things not regularly instituted, and as seekers after martyrdom; he says they overrun whole provinces because they can not live in peace with others anywhere. That they were socialistic appears from attacks upon property, the use of threatening letters and violence to prevent the execution of properly imposed sentences, and their interference between masters and slaves. Donatus of Bagæ, a Donatist bishop, endeavored to make use of them against the orthodox party, and this led to an outbreak of persecution in North Africa. See DONATISM.

BIBLIOGRAPHY: W. Thümmel, *Zur Beurtheilung des Donatismus*, Halle, 1893; and literature under DONATISM.

CIRCUMCISION: Strictly and properly, the removal of the foreskin (or a portion of it), accomplished by drawing the part forward and cutting transversely—whence the name, from *circumcidere*, "to cut around." The word is loosely used, however, and often does not have this precise signification. Mutilations of the sexual organs of both male and female are common as general national or tribal customs of peoples in the barbarous or semicivilized state. The first of such mutilations to become known to modern Europe was circumcision as practised by Jews and Mohammedans (true circumcision as defined above), by whom the custom has been carried on to the higher stages of culture. When wider knowledge of the earth and its inhabitants brought to light other more or less similar customs, it was natural to give to each the name already known. So it has come about that practises differing widely in operative method and results, if not in significance and origin, are all alike called "circumcision," and the term, in actual usage, is almost synonymous with mutilation of the sexual organs. A complete and satisfactory study of circumcision has not yet been published. When it is, the first endeavor will necessarily be to clear up the confusion of thought manifest in this vague use of the term and resulting from it. Preliminary to a fruitful investigation, the various mutilations must be precisely defined and named, their relations must be determined, and such as may not properly be classed and considered with circumcision must be set aside. Incidentally this introductory study will probably modify somewhat—perhaps very considerably—the statements now common concerning the wide extent of circumcision, ascribing it as an indigenous practise to Africa, Asia, North and South America, Australia, and the islands of the Pacific.

Meaning and Use of the Term.

In the search for significance and origin practically no help is to be obtained directly from any people who circumcise. The explanation uniformly given and considered quite sufficient by the givers is "We follow the custom of the fathers." Indirectly, however—by noting and comparing details of the operation, and acts and remarks connected with it or with the circumcised and uncircumcised states—significance may be discovered. Circumcision serves as a national or tribal sign (Hebrews, Jews, and certain African tribes), or a mark of distinction for classes or individuals (ancient Egypt [?], cf. Josephus, *Apion*, ii. 14; Clement of Alexandria, *Strom.*, i. 15; Origen on Rom. ii. 13; negroes of the Niger delta, cf. *Journal of the Anthropological Institute*, xxix., new ser., ii., 1899, p. 56). It passes as a bodily adornment (cf. the peculiar Masai mutilation, best described in *Verhandlungen der Berliner Gesellschaft für Anthropologie*, Apr. 27, 1895, pp. [302]-[303]; cf. H. H. Johnston, *The Kilima-njaro Expedition*, London, 1886, p. 412, note). It is regarded as a hygienic precaution or grounded in reasons of physiology (for cleanliness, to moderate sexual desire, to prevent venereal diseases, to secure offspring, to remove an abnormal development, etc.). The operation marks the entrance to maturity, being closely connected with the so-called initiation ceremonies, and sometimes a severe test of courage and endurance (cf. C. Niebuhr, *Beschreibung von Arabien*, Copenhagen, 1772, p. 269; R. F. Burton, *Personal Narrative of a Pilgrimage to El-Medinah and Meccah*, vol. iii., London, 1856, p. 80, note;* David Livingstone, *Missionary Travels and Researches in South Africa*, New York, 1858, pp. 164–165; *Zeitschrift für Ethnologie*, vi., 1874, pp. 37–38; C. M. Doughty, *Travels in Arabia Deserta*, vol. i., Cambridge, 1888, pp. 128–129; accounts for South America, collected by Ploss, see below); the circumcised state is necessary to the full enjoyment of the rights and privileges of manhood (cf. references already cited and *Zeitschrift für allgemeine Erdkunde, neue Folge*, iv., 1858, p. 357, for the island of Rook, east of New Guinea; J. Sibree, *The Great African Island* [Madagascar], London, 1880, p. 217). Such explanations may account for the retention of the practise in later times; but they are speculations of a more advanced culture and do not indicate the origin, which must be consistent with primitive knowledge and thought. Nor is the origin found by naming circumcision a rite of religion. It remains to explain why and how this peculiar mutilation became a religious rite, and the attempts to do so (making it a development of phallic worship, or of human sacrifice as a substitutionary act, or symbolic) are, like the explanations already referred to, products of later times and too conjectural to be convincing. As a matter of fact, in most cases religious significance is not apparent. It has been asserted among the ancient Mexicans; but a careful examination of the early accounts offers little support for the statement that they either circumcised or practised any distinctly sexual mutilation. It is found among Hebrews and Mohammedans. The case of the former will be considered below. The latter have adopted it as a part of their religion because the first Mohammedans observed it, and with them it was already the "custom of the fathers." The more intelligent seem to have regarded it as one of the requirements of common decency (it is not commanded in the Koran, but taken for granted—cf. the fact that there is no mention of circumcision in the decalogue or the older laws of the Pentateuch. The commentators class it as one of the usages of *fitrah*, "natural religion"; cf. J. Wellhausen, *Reste arabischen Heidentums*, Berlin, 1897, pp. 167 sqq.). The Bedouin women of Medain Salih may be allowed to speak for the more ignorant and primitive (cf. Doughty, ut sup., vol. i., p. 410). And some connection with the sexual life is the significance most frequent, most prominent, and most primitive, so far as information goes (cf. references already cited and *Zeitschrift für Ethnologie*, x., 1878, p. 399; *Edinburgh Medical Journal*, x., 1864–65, p. 222; *Revue d'Anthropologie*, 2d ser., iv., 1881, p. 292; *Verhandlungen der Berliner Gesellschaft für Anthropologie*, Apr. 28, 1877, p. [180]; *Zeitschrift für Ethnologie*, x., 1878, p. 18; A. Bastian, *Die deutsche Expedition an der Loango-Küste*, Jena, 1874, p. 177; Riedel and Valentijn for Dutch East Indies, quoted in Ploss, *Knabenbeschneidung*, pp. 21, 22, 24). To conclude that the primary significance is indicated herein is consistent with the knowledge and conditions of the time when circumcision must

Significance and Origin.

* The note is omitted in later editions of Burton. It is copied by Julius Wellhausen in the first edition of his *Reste arabischen Heidentums* (Berlin, 1887), p. 215, and omitted in the second edition.

have arisen; it is easier to explain the other significances as secondary to this than to explain it as secondary to any of them; and the conclusion is confirmed by the fact and phenomena of "female circumcision" (improperly so called), i.e., the cutting off of the internal labia, which is almost, if not quite, as common as the male mutilation and as a rule accompanies it—a fact which has generally been ignored and its significance strangely overlooked.

Hebrew and Jewish Circumcision.

In the circumcision of Hebrews and Jews three things are noteworthy: (1) Its marked religious significance; (2) the early age at which the operation is performed; (3) the absence of all trace of a female mutilation. Evidence is not at hand to prove indisputably whether these features are original or secondary. The Biblical data are scanty, and when they were committed to writing primitive practises were already followed because they were "the custom of the fathers." Circumcision is stated to be "a token of the covenant" and the covenant itself, and its institution is attributed to the Almighty (Gen. xvii. 10—11). It was regarded as the indispensable requisite to the right relation with God, participation in his worship, and a share in his favor being exacted of "strangers" and slaves (Gen. xvii. 12–14; Ex. xii. 43–48)—in later times of proselytes. The popular mind went a step further and looked upon circumcision as the guaranty of the divine favor, a conception strenuously combated by the prophets (Jer. iv. 4, vi. 10, ix. 25–26; Ezek. xliv. 9; cf. Deut. x. 16, xxx. 6). These ideas appear in the New Testament (Acts vii. 8, 51, xv. 1; Rom. ii. 28–29, iv. 11). Indications are not lacking, however, that in its origin and early significance Hebrew circumcision did not differ from that of other peoples.* If the statement that "Ishmael was thirteen years old when he was circumcised" (Gen. xvii. 25) preserves an old and true tradition, it indicates that the age in early times was the usual one of maturing manhood. The account of a general circumcising at Gilgal in the time of Joshua (Josh. v. 2–9) has still more the mark of an old tradition, which the scribe who wrote it down thought necessary to explain in the light of the custom of his own time (verses 4–7 being generally considered an interpolation); if so, it evidences that the Hebrews originally circumcised at the same age as other peoples, and the circumcision of a number at one time, with the hint of a special place of circumcision, is in accord with custom frequently found (cf. B. Stade, in *ZATW*, vi., 1886, pp. 132–142). The use of flint knives (cf. Ex. iv. 25) is also noteworthy, being a circumstance not uncommon, even after better cutting tools have been obtained, and indicating, perhaps, the antiquity of the practise. The Dinah story (Gen. xxxiv.) makes circumcision a prerequisite to marriage. The passage Ex. iv. 24–26, commonly called (with slight reason) J's account of the origin of circumcision, is evidently a mutilated and incomplete fragment of a longer narrative, and the text of what is preserved is uncertain. Its meaning is well-nigh unintelligible and it affords no secure basis for inference. Yet, if anything is clear from it, it is a connection between circumcision and marriage or the sexual life (for an interesting discussion of this passage, tracing parallels with the use made of the severed foreskin by various tribes, cf. H. P. Smith, in *JBL*, xxv., 1906, pp. 14–24).

CHARLES C. SHERMAN.

*Cf. Stade, quoted in Ploss, *Knabenbeschneidung*, p. 12: "In preexilic time circumcision in Israel was solely a tribal sign; only in the Exile did it acquire the significance of a religious symbol (Heb. *oth*)."

BIBLIOGRAPHY: The literature is enormous, but much of it may be dismissed as "freakish," the subject being one which has naturally proved attractive to erratic minds; almost all of the more serious treatises consider the practise too exclusively from the Biblical or Jewish point of view. The best treatment in existence is that of H. Ploss, in *Das Kind in Brauch und Sitte der Völker*, 2d ed., Leipsic, 1884, vol. i., pp. 342–394, with which should be compared the chapter on *Der Abschluss der Kinderjahre*, vol. ii., pp. 411–446. The same author's *Geschichtliches und Ethnologisches über Knabenbeschneidung*, Leipsic, 1885 (reprinted from *Archiv für Geschichte der Medicin und medicinische Geographie*, viii., 1885), is a partial repetition of what is contained in the earlier work with not much that is new. An article, *Die Beschneidung*, by R. Andree, in *Archiv für Anthropologie*, xiii (1880), pp. 53–78, is worth consulting with Ploss, who by no means exhausted all the material available when he wrote. Since then a large amount of valuable matter has accumulated in the pages of anthropological and ethnographical journals, the works of special investigators, and books of travel. The studies of the natives of Australia by Baldwin Spencer, F. J. Gillen, A. W. Howitt, and others may be specially mentioned. *Die Beschneidung in ihrer geschichtlichen, ethnographischen, religiösen und medicinischen Bedeutung*, ed. A. Glassberg, Berlin, 1896, is a sane treatment of various phases of the subject. The works on the Mosaic law, Old Testament theology, Hebrew archeology, and the Biblical commentaries may be consulted for the conventional treatment; and for Jewish conceptions and practises, *JE*, iv. 92–102.

CIRCUMCISION OF CHRIST, FESTIVAL OF. See NEW-YEAR'S FESTIVAL.

CISTERCIANS, sis-ter′shians.

1. Origin and Character of the Order.

A certain Robert (d. 1108; life in *ASB*, Apr., iii. 662–678) retired from his position as prior at Montier la Celle to become head of a company of anchorites in the forest of Molême, northwest of Dijon. The monks objected to his strict rule, however, and in 1098 with twenty followers he withdrew and founded a monastery at Cîteaux (Lat. *Cistercium*, 20 m. s.e. of Dijon) in Burgundy. A papal command required him to return to Molême (1099), and he was succeeded as abbot at Cîteaux by Alberic, who composed the *Instituta monachorum Cisterciensium de Molismo venientium*. Alberic was succeeded by the able and pious Englishman Harding (or Stephen; see HARDING), who came near seeing the end of the monastery for want of novices. But the entrance of the young Bernard (see BERNARD OF CLAIRVAUX) and thirty of his friends brought a change. From this time on the number of monks increased and daughter monasteries were established—at La Ferté, 1113; Pontigny, 1114; Morimud and Clairvaux, 1115. Bernard became abbot of the last. To these establishments others were added by Citeaux and the daughter foundations. It soon appeared necessary to regulate the relation of the monasteries to one another, and this was done in a manner which formed a new stage in the development of monasticism; for the first time a union of monasteries was effected by a formal constitution. The *Charta charitatis*, the result of the deliberations of the abbots, formed the basis, which was further expanded by resolutions of subsequent general chapters.

The characteristic peculiarities of the order may be comprised in the following points: (1) A strict observance of the letter of the rule of Benedict. (2) The greatest simplicity, even poverty, in the mode of life; the very churches should be devoid of all show and adornment. (3) The subsistence of the monasteries to be derived exclusively from agriculture and cattle-raising—an arrangement from which sprang the importance that the order obtained in the cultivation of the land and colonization. (4) Besides the monks, lay brothers (*conversi, laici, barbati*) are also to be received; as the monk, in accordance with the regulations, while not freed entirely from labor, has mostly to devote himself to devotion and choir-service, so the lay brother is chiefly occupied with manual labor; the example of Mary and Martha is often quoted; there were also laborers (*mercenarii*, afterward called *familiares*) mentioned as early as the statutes of Alberic, who were free men serving for pay (since the possession of serfs was precluded on principle). (5) As concerns the relation of parent and daughter monasteries, each monastery has a certain authority over its filiations. At the head stands Citeaux, but the four oldest under-monasteries also enjoy an exceptional position: their abbots visit the mother monastery once every year, and with Citeaux, one of them stands at the head of each of the five divisions (*lineæ*) of the order. But all these authorities are subject to the general chapter, which meets annually at Citeaux, in which all abbots have a voice, and which has not only the highest legislative power, but also the decision in all cases of questions which may arise. (6) It was considered highly important at the beginning that there should be no loosening of diocesan bonds. The foremost representative of this idea is Bernard (cf. *De moribus et officiis*, ix. 33–37, in *MPL*, clxxxii. 830–834; *De Consid.*, III. iv. 4–18). Afterward, however, this principle was greatly neglected. In almost all these regulations can be perceived a contrast to those of the Cluniacensians, and this contrast was intentional, for the latter were considered as having apostatized from the true nature of monasticism. Bernard also at first was severe and bitter against them (*Epist.*, i.), but later he was much more lenient (*Apol. ad Guill.*). Peter the Venerable of Cluny was still more friendly (cf., e.g., his *Epist.*, i. 28, in *MPL*, clxxxix. 112–159; iv. 17=ccxxix. of the letters of Bernard, *MPL*, clxxxii. 398–417). Thus the tension was relaxed, but did not disappear altogether. Devotion to the Virgin Mary, the tendency of the time, was not only accepted by the Cistercians, but their fervency heightened it. Mary is the patroness of the order; the general chapter of 1134 declares that all churches of the order shall be dedicated to her, and it devoted to her a special liturgical office on Saturday.

2. Golden Age of the Order. The golden age of the order extends to the second half of the thirteenth century. Different causes contributed to a powerful growth of the order: besides the monastic tendency of the age, there were especially the personality and the labor of Bernard, who is considered as the real saint of the order, and from him the Cistercians are frequently called Bernardines. Pious contemplation was coupled with activity in agriculture and strictly regulated authoritative relations and government, in which all took part. At the death of Bernard the number of convents was 288, and in vain did the general chapter try to stop their increase; at the end of the century there were 529 abbeys, to which were added yet 142 in the thirteenth century until about 1270. Then began a standstill. During the fourteenth century forty-one were added, in the fifteenth century twenty-six, so that the whole number was 738 during the medieval period. In the mean time some foundations were discontinued: to the *linea Claraevallis* belong 353 (half of the entire number). From France to Hungary, Poland, and Livonia; from Sweden to Portugal; from Scotland to Sicily, Cistercian monasteries were found. During the period of prosperity the connection with Citeaux and the other mother monasteries was maintained. In the outward construction of the monasteries as well as in the mode of life of the monks, especially in the regulation of religious worship, a conformity existed which united the Cistercians of the different countries among themselves and separated them from all other communities. In the Spanish peninsula the knightly orders of Alcantara, Calatrava, and Truxillo (qq.v.); in Portugal the order of Aviz (q.v.) were connected with the Cistercians. In northeastern Germany and further to the east the Cistercians rendered great service to civilization by their colonizing activity. Marshes were drained and forests were cleared; orchards and vineyards were planted on a gigantic scale; and cattle and sheep were raised. The improvement of its property was the principal aim of each monastery. This period has been lucidly described by Winter (cf., however, Hauck, *KD*, iv., Leipsic, 1903). During the twelfth century and into the middle of the thirteenth the Cistercians occupied an important position in the government of the Church. Not a few of them were made cardinals. Arnold of Citeaux under Innocent III. undertook the crusade against the Albigenses. Innocent III. charged them with so many things that the chapter of 1211 asked for moderation. Honorius III. and Innocent IV. overwhelmed them with privileges.

In the task of influencing spiritually the masses the mendicant friars took precedence of the Cistercians. The great facility with which they went from place to place made them at the same time more efficient instruments for the popes.

3. Gradual Decay of the Order.

Tension between the two orders is evident in the exclusion of the mendicant friars from the studies of the Cistercians, and in the rule that no member of the order should go to confession to a priest of another order. Yet the decay of the order was due mainly and essentially to inner causes. The riches accumulated through industry and economy gradually exercised a detrimental influence on the life of the brothers. The remark of Cæsarius of Heisterbach (q.v.) on the ancient monasteries, "Religion brought forth riches, riches destroyed religion," proved true also with regard to the Cistercians. To this must be added the impossibility of further colonization. Deprived of its strongest outward incentive, the order rapidly declined in inner zeal and energy. The life became lax. General chapters sought to stem the tide, and popes also tried to interfere (as Clement IV. in 1265 and Benedict XII. in 1335). The fourteenth century and later witnessed the financial decay of many monasteries. Under the laxity of discipline and the increasing demoralization the former industry and strict economy suffered. While it proved impossible to reform the entire order, two new congregations were organized in the fifteenth century, the *Congregatio regularis observantiæ regnorum Hispanicorum* in Spain (1425) and the *Congregatio Italica S. Bernardi*, definitively confirmed by Julius II. in 1511 in Lombardy and Tuscany, which separated almost entirely from the order and observed greater strictness. It must also be mentioned that, under the incitement of the mendicant friars, the Cistercians cultivated scientific pursuits to a certain degree and founded *studia generalia*, of which the college of St. Bernard at Paris was the most important. These measures, however, were not sufficient to induce scientific productiveness on a large scale, and services rendered by the Cistercians in that line are insignificant compared with those of the Dominicans and Franciscans.

4. History Since the Reformation.

Through the Reformation the order lost all its possessions in England and Scotland, Denmark, Sweden and Norway, and the greater part in Germany. It retained them in France, but after the concordat of 1516 it suffered under the appointment of abbots *in commendam* by the royal power. Even the Counter-reformation did not help the order much. It had no more any important practical tasks, and the large body of the order proved incapable of returning to the austerity of ancient monasticism. Nevertheless, efforts of this kind were not wanting and led in part to the formation of new branches, such as the *Congregatio Lusitana*, confirmed in 1567 by Pius V., the Feuillants after 1506, who spread in France and Italy, and others in the sixteenth and seventeenth centuries. The reform, surpassing in austerity even the Carthusians, which was introduced by Abbot Rancé in the monastery of La Trappe did not attain to much importance until after the French Revolution. From these branches must be distinguished the congregations, improperly so called, which united after the fashion of provinces, when the *lineæ* and the relation of filiation had lost much of their importance, such as the Polish or Pelpline and the Upper German, with the monastery Salem (Salmansweiler) as center. Many interesting details concerning conditions in the seventeenth century are learned from notes of a monk of Raittenhaslach (*Drey Raisen nach Cistertz*, *Cistercienser-Chronik*, iv., 1892, 45 sqq.) in 1605, 1609, and 1615, and in Joseph Meglinger's *Iter Cisterciense von 1667* (*MPL*, clxxxv. 1565–1622), and from the journey of Abbot Laurentius Scipio of Ossegg to the general chapter in the year 1667 (*Cistercienser-Chronik*, viii., 1896, 289). In spite of all losses, the number of Cistercian monasteries was still great in the last quarter of the eighteenth century. From that time on the order received blows which left only a few scanty remains of this once powerful community. In Austria Joseph II. confiscated a large number of the monasteries; the French Revolution dissolved the order in its mother country; its most venerable places, Cîteaux and Clairvaux, have since then been partly destroyed. New losses were caused by the decree of 1803 passed by the imperial deputation and by the secularization in Prussia in 1810. In 1834 the abbeys in Portugal and in 1835 those in Spain were abolished, and the like fate befell the Polish under Nicholas I. On the other hand, a restoration of the former abbey Senanque in the Vaucluse took place in 1854, which was followed by the founding of some others.

At present the order consists of: I. The *Observantia communis*, comprising (1) the *Congregatio S. Bernardi in Italia*; (2) the vicariate in Belgium; (3) the Austro-Hungarian province of the order; (4) the Swiss-German province. II. The *Observantia media*, to which belong (1) the congregation of Senanque; (2) the *Trappenses mitigati* of Casamari. III. The *Observantia stricta* (Trappists), who, however, were entirely separated in 1892 from the jurisdiction of the general abbot chosen by the *Observantia communis*. More particulars concerning the present organization and rules of the different congregations are given in the article *Ueber die Observanzen der Cistercienser* in the *Cistercienser-Chronik*, vii (1895), 117 sqq.

S. M. Deutsch.

Bibliography: The only reliable source for the early history of Cîteaux is the *Exordium ordinis Cisterciensis* (the so-called *Exordium parvum*), by Stephen Harding, in *MPL*, clxvi. 1501–10. Of a partly legendary character is the *Exordium magnum O. C.*, *MPL*, clxxxv. 995–1198. For the time from 1115 to 1153 Bernard of Clairvaux and the older biographies of him must be consulted. An important source for the history of the order are the resolutions of the general chapters, of which the most copious collection is in Martène and Durand, *Thesaurus novus*, iv. 1243–1646, Paris, 1717. The basis of all later works on the order is L. Janauschek, *Originum Cisterciensium*, vol. i., Vienna, 1877, containing the first trustworthy list of all Cistercian abbeys. Collections of the regulations of the order are contained in P. Guignard, *Les Monuments primitifs de la règle Cistercienne*, Dijon, 1878; *Nomasticon seu antiquiores O. C. constitutiones a Juliano Paris, Fulcardimontis abbate collectæ*, Paris, 1664, *editio nova . . . usque ad nostra tempora deducta a R. P. Hug. Séjalon*, Solesmes, 1892. Consult further: C. de Visch, *Bibliotheca scriptorum sacri O. C.*, Douai, 1649, Cologne, 1656; B. Tissier, *Bibliotheca patrum Cisterciensium*, 2 vols., Bonofonte, 1660–69; Angelus Manrique, *Cisterciensium . . . annalium tomi iv*, Lyons, 1642–59 (reaching to the year 1236; very important, yet to be used with critical care); D'Arbois de Jubainville, *Études sur l'état intérieur des abbayes Cisterciennes au 12. et au 13. siècles*, Paris, 1850; Franz Winter, *Die Cistercienser des nordöstlichen Deutschlands bis zum Auftreten der Bettelorden*, 3 vols., Gotha, 1868–71 (an excellent work). Many contributions are found in *Studien und Mitteilungen aus dem Benediktiner und Cistercienserorden*, Würzburg, 1879 sqq., and in the *Cistercienserchronik*, Bregenz, 1889 sqq. The literature on the different monasteries is found in Janauschek, ut sup. Additional material may be found in J. L. von Mosheim, *Institutes of Eccl. Hist.*, ii. 44, London, 1863; R. C. Trench, *Lectures on Medieval Church Hist.*, pp. 110 sqq., New York, 1878; H. C. Sheldon, *Hist. of the Christian Church; the Mediæval Church*, pp. 271–287, ib. 1894; W. W. Capes, *Eng. Church in 14th and 15th Centuries*, passim, ib. 1900; W. R. W. Stephens, *Eng. Church, 1066–1272*, pp. 213, 255–263, ib. 1901; *Cistercian Order, its Object, its Rule. By a secular Priest*, Cambridge, U. S., 1905; W. A. P. Mason, *Beginnings of the Cistercian Order*, in *Transactions of the Royal Historical Society*, xiv (1905); Schaff, *Christian Church*, v. i., pp. 337 sqq.

CITIES IN PALESTINE.

1. Origin. The Israelitic cities west of the Jordan in most cases were of Canaanite origin. An astonishing number of fortified places is named in the Amarna letters and in the Egyptian lists. These walled cities were ruled by petty princes, whose authority extended to the neighboring villages. Examples of such strongholds are Jerusalem, Gezer, Lachish, Megiddo, etc. The Old Testament narrators were well aware that these cities were conquered by the Israelites only at a relatively late period (cf., e.g., the case of Jerusalem, II Sam. v. 6–9). There were, however, cities of Israelitic origin. Many settlements of the invading tribes must have grown gradually into villages and cities, which were later walled in (Josh. xix. 50; I Kings xii. 25). In the Greek period the founding of cities was quite usual; in many cases, however, some older city was merely enlarged and renamed. Herod the Great was especially devoted to building (see HEROD AND HIS FAMILY). Cæsarea, Phasælis, and Herodeion, Alexandreion, Hyrcania, and other strongholds were built during his reign.

2. Cities and Villages. City and village are always distinguished in the Old Testament; a city is a walled stronghold (*'ir ḥomah*, Lev. xxv. 30), in contrast to the unprotected villages and the scattered hamlets (*ḥaṣerim*, Lev. xxv. 31; *kepharim*, I Chron. xxvii. 25). Further, in the cities, the seats of the princes and the lords of the land, civilization made more rapid progress than in the open country. At times this distinction was unusually marked, for, in the various migrations which overran the land, the invaders first occupied the open country, while the cities remained for a long time in the hands of the original inhabitants. Among both the Canaanites and the Israelites the unprotected villages were under the jurisdiction of the cities (cf. the expression "mother in Israel," applied to a city, II Sam. xx. 19, and "a city and the villages thereof," Num. xxi. 25, 32, xxxii. 42). In the Greek period the distinction was that the cities (*poleis*) had a constitution and privileges different from those of the villages (*kōmai*; cf. *kōmopoleis* in Mark i. 38).

3. Sites and Names. The choice of a site for a settlement was largely determined by the presence of a supply of water, though Jerusalem is a noteworthy exception. Numerous places are named after their fountains—En-gedi ("Fountain of the Kid"), En-shemesh ("Fountain of the Sun"), and others. Another consideration was that the site should afford a certain protection; elevations were therefore preferred. All larger fortified cities were built upon hills or mountain slopes. It is generally difficult to explain the names of towns; except where the common appellations are used (*'ayin*, "fountain"; *beth*, "house"; *'ir*, "city"; etc.). The common attempts at etymological explanation may generally be rejected, for the names usually belong to the ancient pre-Israelitic language, and have often changed greatly in the course of centuries. In the explanations given in the Old Testament the name has often evidently given rise to the legend (e.g., Gilgal, which is explained to signify the rolling off of a reproach, Josh. v. 9). It may be remarked that many places bore the name of the divinity who was worshiped there (Beth-el, "the Seat of El"; Beth-shemesh, "the House of the Sun"; etc.). It is unlikely that two names were in use for the same place in the earliest period. Most of such cases found in the Old Testament seem either to have arisen from misunderstanding, or else to have been adapted for harmonistic purposes. For example Jebus-Jerusalem is a name freely invented from the tribal name of the Jebusites. Only in the Greek period did a change of names become the fashion (Samaria to Sebaste, etc.).

4. Features and Characteristics. Aided by the excavations at Megiddo Taanach, Gezer, Lachish, and elsewhere, the picture of an ancient city can be reconstructed to a certain extent. Confined to a small space, with thick walls made of clay bricks or of medium-sized rough-hewn stones, these cities may be compared in many respects to those found to-day in Palestine. The streets were narrow and tortuous; the houses (see HOUSE) were small; and the gate or gates, close to which was the only open square (Gen. xxiii. 10; Ruth iv. 1; II Sam. xv. 2; II Kings vii. 1, etc.), were built in an angle of the wall. The houses usually had the natural rock for their rear wall; indeed, they were little more than enlarged caves built up in front. The roofs of the lower houses formed the street in front of those built higher up; paved streets are first found in the time of the Herods (Josephus, *Ant.*, XX. ix. 7). A regular police is not employed even now, but night watchmen are mentioned in the Old Testament (Ps. cxxvii. 1; Cant. iii. 3, v. 7; Isa. xxi. 11). The work of cleaning the streets was left to the dogs (Isa. v. 25; see DOGS). Trades and shops of the same kind were grouped together in particular streets (see COMMERCE AMONG THE ANCIENT ISRAELITES; HANDICRAFTS, HEBREW). Every walled city must have been well supplied with cisterns in the rocks, for it was rarely possible to introduce water from outside within the circuit of the walls; uncovered pools were common (see JERUSALEM; WATER SUPPLY IN PALESTINE).

I. BENZINGER.

BIBLIOGRAPHY: A. Billerbeck, *Der Festungsbau im alten Orient*, Leipsic, 1903; the publications of the *PEF*, particularly the *Survey of Western Palestine*, 7 vols., and of *Eastern Palestine*, 1 vol.; C. R. Conder, *Tent Work in Palestine*, 1880; idem, *Heth and Moab*, 1883; G. Schumacher, *Across the Jordan*, 1886; idem, *The Jaulan*, 1888; G. Armstrong, *Names and Places in the O. and N. T. and Apocrypha*, 1887; F. Petrie, *Tel el Hesy, Lachish*, 1891; F. J. Bliss, *A Mound of Many Cities*, 1894; and the *Quarterly Statements*. Consult also the literature under PALESTINE and under the articles discussing the several cities.

CITY MISSIONS.

I. In Germany.
II. In the United States.
The New York City Mission (§ 1).

I. In Germany: City missions constitute one form of home mission work, necessitated by the peculiar conditions of life in large cities and because the needs and moral shortcomings caused by these conditions can be supplied and corrected most usefully and effectively by a union of existing activities and by a uniform plan of action. A city mission was organized in Glasgow in 1826 by David Nasmiths (q.v.), who as secretary of twenty-three Christian societies saw the necessity of uniting them more closely and employing a number of faithful workers in missionary service without connection with an individual congregation. His suggestion was followed by the city of London in 1835, under the vigorous cooperation of Lord Shaftesbury (q.v.). In Germany it was J. H. Wichern (q.v.) who, after his return from the Wittenberg Church Diet of 1848, suggested among the friends of the *Rauhes Haus* in Hamburg the organization of the "Hamburg Society for the Inner Mission," calling attention to the London City Mission. His association had the twofold task of bringing about a closer union of existing agencies and practising missionary activity in Hamburg after the model of London, with due regard, however, to specifically German conditions, by organizing special committees for the visitation of the poor, for the care of needy artisans, for journeymen and apprentices, for the circulation of good literature, for the union of young merchants, and for the suppression of public immorality. In course of time these separate committees were replaced by local district societies which were in close connection with their respective parishes and became the basis for similar societies in other cities. The first suggestion for similar efforts in Berlin proceeded also from Wichern. But real success was not attained here until 1874, when Dr. B. B. Brückner, general superintendent of Berlin, devoted his energies to this work. His efforts were continued in 1877 by Court Preacher Adolf Stöcker and Privy Councilor J. R. Bosse, the latter minister of public worship and instruction. They were assisted by two theological inspectors and thirteen city missionaries. In Apr., 1906, there were six theological inspectors and sixty-two city missionaries, including eight women. During 1905, 95,000 visits were made, including 4,677 because of unbaptized children, 3,539 because of couples who had discarded the marriage ceremony, and 959 because of children brought into the criminal courts. Thirty-three hundred children were enrolled in sixty-nine Sunday-schools and religious services were held in twenty-four places. Other organizations which serve missionary purposes in Berlin are the "Young Men's Christian Association" (since 1882); "St. Michael's Christian Association" (since 1883); an association called "Service for the Unemployed" (since 1882); and especially the "City Committee (now called "Main Association") for the Inner Mission" (since 1899). According to statistics of 1899, seventy other cities of Germany had followed the example of Hamburg and Berlin. There is a distinction made between assistants of the congregations (*Gemeindehelfer*) and city missionaries in the more restricted sense of the word. The former confine themselves to the work of deacons, while the duties of city missionaries are of an evangelizing nature. The latter, therefore, aim to serve classes who are compelled to work on Sundays, and those who have no permanent home such as fishermen, seamen, the unemployed, and prisoners. They also combat drunkenness and immorality, circulate Christian tracts, and lecture to reconcile social distinctions. In 1888, under the influence of the present emperor and empress, there was called into existence the "Evangelical Church Aid Society" to support all efforts for the suppression of irreligious and immoral conditions in Berlin and other large cities and in the industrial districts of Prussia. A select committee of this association supports the existing city missions and tries to call others into life. (H. RAHLENBECK.)

II. In the United States: City mission work is done in most of the larger cities of the United States, the call for such work being specially urgent here because so large a part of the enormous emigration from all over the world finds its permanent home in our cities. Many of these people who leave their church homes on the other side of the ocean would drift into utter godlessness were it not for the effort of the city missionary, who seeks them out and brings them into vital connection with some existing church organization. Furthermore, the inevitable tendency toward the separation of the well-to-do classes from the very poor leaves whole sections of some of our cities with only those whose incomes hardly suffice to maintain church services. Unless they are to be wholly abandoned, some outside means must be provided for their religious upbuilding—a legitimate field for city mission activity.

There are three ways in which city mission work is carried on in the United States. Individual churches establish missions, which the mother church supports, and for which it furnishes both volunteer and paid workers. Such missions are often organized as churches, having the ordinances, but dependent on the mother church both for the necessary means of support and for ecclesiastical government. In other cases a denomination organizes a city mission society, appealing to the denomination for the needed financial support, and directing the work along denominational lines. In New York City, for example, there are such societies managed by the Methodist, the Baptist, and the Protestant Episcopal denominations. The third method is that of undenominational work. The different denominations unite their forces, and put missionaries into the field, who are not supposed to teach the distinctive tenets of the denominations, but work directly and exclusively for the moral and spiritual regeneration of those to whom they are sent.

Taking the New York City Mission and Tract Society, as the largest and oldest of such organizations, as a norm, the following may serve as an illustration of the methods of work.

1. The New York City Mission. This society began over eighty years ago, and at first was purely volunteer in its corps of visitors. The aim was to visit the churchless population, and invite them to the house of God, at the same time leaving at each dwelling some religious literature. In 1833 the first paid agent was employed, as the work had grown beyond the ability of the volunteers to accomplish all that was needed. At present there are between sixty and seventy paid workers, the majority of them being women, since women can do much work among the tenement house population that men can not accomplish. In 1866 the society was incorporated so as to be able to hold property.

As churches followed their members to more favored portions of the city, large sections were left without church accommodations, making it necessary for the visiting missionaries to establish tenement house prayer-meetings and Sunday-schools. Some of those who were thus influenced for good asked to have the ordinances administered to them, which necessitated the erection of suitable structures for worship, and the carrying on of proper church activities. The first of these churches was built by the City Mission in 1867 in a crowded part of the city. Because of the cosmopolitan nature of the population, preaching and teaching is carried on in English, German, Italian, Yiddish, Arabic, Greek, Japanese, and in English among the Chinese. In New York City overcrowding has gone on to an extent unknown elsewhere in the world. Many a block measuring only seven hundred feet by two hundred contains a population of 2,500 people. In certain districts whole blocks are filled with Israelites, while in others only Italians are to be found, and in yet others only Bohemians or negroes—a condition which increases both the need and the difficulties of city mission work.

In course of time the New York City Mission found it necessary to employ regularly trained nurses for those who for various good reasons could not go to a hospital. Furthermore, as time passed and experience grew it was found that many other things besides the preaching of the Word and the instruction of Sunday-school scholars was called for. The result was the establishment of what are called in modern parlance "institutional churches," aiming to minister to the threefold nature of man—to his body, his mind, and his spirit. This necessitates kindergarten work, library and gymnasium facilities with appropriate attendants, fresh-air work in the summer, and clubs of various kinds both for boys and girls.

Regularly ordained men administer the ordinances, and the women missionaries aid in the work of house-to-house visitation. Since trained workers can do the best work, the City Mission years ago established a regular training-school. A building was purchased and fitted up where those in training live together under the care of a superintendent. The course is one year, and includes lectures and practical work. The total cost for each student is only $125.00 a year.

At present the City Mission owns property to the amount of about $600,000 free of encumbrance. This includes three costly and well-equipped church buildings, a Christian workers' home where the women missionaries live, a training-school, and a sort of settlement house on the lower west side of the city, which has already in it an organized Italian Church. The annual expenditure is about $65,000 a year, which comes from purely voluntary sources. The doctrinal basis of the churches formed under the care of the society is the Apostles' Creed. The churches, of which there are two German, two Italian, and two English, govern themselves in all matters spiritual, though the directors of the City Mission hold the veto right over any action that the churches may take. This right has never been exercised. The property is held by the society, but the churches have the use of it without payment other than the usual offertory taken for actual expenses. This does not suffice for the defraying of all outlay by any means, and the City Mission provides the balance. Since its establishment the City Mission has received about $375,000 in legacies besides large gifts for the erection of its church edifices.

A. F. Schauffler.

Bibliography: On I. consult: E. G. Lehmann, *Die Stadtmission*, Leipsic, 1875; E. Kayser, *Die evangelische Stadtmission*, Gotha, 1890; E. Evers, *Die Berliner Stadtmission*, Berlin, 1902; T. Schäfer, *Leitfaden der inneren Mission*, Hamburg, 1903, and the periodical *Fliegende Blätter aus dem Rauhen Hause*, 1849–1907. On II. consult: S. L. Loomis, *Modern Cities and the Religious Problems*, New York, 1887; W. S. Ufford, *Fresh Air Charity in the United States*, ib. 1897; E. Judson, *The Institutional Church*, ib. 1899; J. Strong, *Religious Movements for Social Betterment*, ib. 1900; W. H. Tollman, *The Better New York*, ib. 1904. The best sources of information are afforded by the reports of the various societies, annual and in some cases monthly, e.g., of the New York City Mission and Tract Society, The Brooklyn City Mission and Tract Society, The City Mission Society of Boston, The Albany City Tract and Mission Society; also the *Circulars of Information of the Armour Mission* in Chicago. For London consult: J. M. Weylland, *These Fifty Years*, London, 1884 (deals with the London City Mission); C. Booth, *Life and Labour*, 14 vols., ib. 1903 (in three series; one of these deals with the religious forces working upon city problems).

CIUDAD, JUAN (JOHN OF GOD). See Charity, Brothers of.

CLAIRVAUX. See Bernard of Clairvaux; Cistercians.

CLAP, THOMAS: Fifth president of Yale College; b. at Scituate, Mass., June 26, 1703; d. in New Haven Jan. 7, 1767. He was graduated at Harvard 1722; was minister of Windham, Conn., from 1725 till his induction as president of Yale,

1740. He was already noted for stringency of discipline and pronounced Calvinism, and as president his course was somewhat arbitrary and autocratic, but nevertheless was marked by regard for sound scholarship and propriety. The college funds were increased in legitimate ways and two new buildings were added; the college church was organized and the professorship of divinity was established. He sympathized with the "Old Lights" in the disputes stirred up by Whitefield and the revival preaching of his time. He resigned the presidency in 1766, a few months before his death. Besides many controversial pamphlets he wrote *An Essay on the Nature and Foundation of Moral Virtue and Obligation*, intended for a textbook (New Haven, 1765), and *The Annals or History of Yale College* (1766).

BIBLIOGRAPHY: F. B. Dexter, in the *Papers of the New Haven Colony Historical Society*, v. 247-274, New Haven, 1894.

CLARE (CLARA), SAINT, AND THE POOR CLARES: The founder of an order of women parallel to the Franciscans, and the order itself. Clara Scefi was born at Assisi, of a noble family, July 16, 1194. At the age of eighteen she was expecting to be married, when a sermon of St. Francis showed her the vanity of earthly things. Under his direction she put on sackcloth and went out to beg for the poor. On Palm Sunday (Mar. 18, 1212), she took the three vows, and went to reside provisionally in the Benedictine convent of St. Paul. Soon she was joined by her younger sister Agnes, and Francis made a little cloister for them near the church of St. Damian. Others, including her mother and youngest sister, joined her here; and she acted as head of the community until her death, Aug. 11, 1253. She was canonized by Alexander IV. in 1255.

The growth of her order was rapid; and it was not long before all the larger towns to which the Franciscans came had also a convent of Poor Clares. At the end of the sixteenth century, even after the Reformation had diminished the number, there were still 900 houses, with some 25,000 sisters, under the immediate direction of the general of the Franciscans, and a scarcely smaller number under the diocesan bishops.

Until 1219 Clare and her associates had nothing but the oral counsels of Francis to follow. In 1219 Cardinal Ugolino gave them the rule of St. Benedict, with some additions in the direction of severity. Later, Francis and Ugolino drew up for them a rule in twelve chapters, analogous to that of the Friars Minor. It prescribed the strictest poverty, confinement to the enclosure of the convent, fasting and abstinence, and prohibited the holding of any property, even by the convents. This rule was formally confirmed by Innocent IV. in 1246, and accepted by the majority of the convents. By degrees, however, varieties of observance grew up, and in 1264 Pope Urban IV. attempted to enforce a revised rule, with certain mitigations in the matter of fasting and income for their support. This was accepted in most countries; but there were (and are still) some convents in Italy and Spain which adhered to the primitive rigor, and claimed the exclusive right to the name Clarisses, while the others were known as Urbanists. At the beginning of the fifteenth century the strict reform of St. Coleta, based upon the original rule of Francis and Ugolino, was introduced in all the convents over which she had influence. Upon the representation of the Franciscan John Capistran to Eugenius IV. that the rule contained more than a hundred precepts binding under pain of grievous sin, the pope ruled in 1447 that the only precepts binding under pain of mortal sin should be those relating to the three vows, the enclosure, and the election or deposition of an abbess. This is still the case. The Capuchin Sisters, originating in Naples, 1538, and the Alcantarines, 1631, taking their name from the reform of St. Peter of Alcantara, are simply Clarisses of the strict observance. The Poor Clares have houses in England and Ireland. They established themselves in the United States in 1875, where they have (1907) five houses.

BIBLIOGRAPHY: *ASB*, August, ii. 739-768; *Life of St. Claire*, Dublin, 1854; F. de More, *Vie de S. Claire d'Assise*, Paris, 1856; P. Jouhanneaud, *Vie de S. Claire d'Assise*, Limoges, 1873; Joseph de Madrid, *Vie de S. Claire d'Assise*, Paris, 1880; E. Wauer, *Entstehung und Ausbreitung des Klarissenordens*, Leipsic, 1906. The *Regula* was published in Italian at Barcelona, 1644, and in French at Laval, 1651. On the order consult: E. Lempp, in *ZKG*, xiii (1892), 181-245; Currier, *Religious Orders*, pp. 249-252.

CLARENDON, CONSTITUTIONS OF. See BECKET, THOMAS.

CLARENI (CLARENINI). See FRANCIS, SAINT, OF ASSISI, AND THE FRANCISCAN ORDER, III., § 7.

CLARK, FRANCIS EDWARD: Congregationalist, founder of the United Society of Christian Endeavor; b. at Aylmer, Quebec, Sept. 12, 1851. He was graduated at Dartmouth in 1873 and Andover Theological Seminary in 1876, after which he was pastor of Williston Church, Portland, Me. (1876-83), and of Phillips Church, South Boston (1883-87). In 1881 he founded the Society of Christian Endeavor, and in 1887 resigned his pastorate to devote his entire energies to its promotion. Since that year he has been president of the United Society of Christian Endeavor, and is also president of the World's Christian Endeavor Union and editor of *The Christian Endeavor World*, the official organ of the society. In the interest of the society he has traveled over the world. Among his publications may be mentioned *Young People's Prayer Meetings* (New York, 1887); *Our Journey around the World* (1894); *World-Wide Endeavor* (Boston, 1897); and *A New Way around an Old World* (New York, 1900).

CLARK, GEORGE WHITFIELD: Baptist; b. at South Orange, N. J., Feb. 15, 1831. He was graduated at Amherst in 1853 and Rochester Theological Seminary in 1855, and was pastor at New Market, N. J. (1855-59), Elizabeth, N. J. (1859-68), Balston Spa, N. Y. (1868-73), and Somerville, N. J. (1873-77). He retired from the active ministry in 1877 on account of ill health, and since 1880 has been engaged in missionary, financial, and literary work for the American Baptist Publication Society. Besides a *History* *of the First Baptist Church of Elizabeth, N. J.* (Newark, 1863) and a *Gospel Harmony in English* (New York, 1870), he has written a *Commentary on the New Testament* (9 vols., Philadelphia, 1870–1907).

CLARK, THOMAS MARCH: Second Protestant Episcopal bishop of Rhode Island; b. at Newburyport, Mass., July 4, 1812; d. at Middletown, Conn., Sept. 7, 1903. He was graduated at Yale 1831; studied in Princeton Theological Seminary 1833–35 and was licensed as a Presbyterian at Newburyport 1835; was ordained priest in the Protestant Episcopal Church 1836; became rector of Grace Church, Boston, 1836; of St. Andrew's, Philadelphia, 1843; assistant at Trinity, Boston, 1847; rector of Christ Church, Hartford, 1851; was consecrated bishop of Rhode Island, 1854. His books include *Lectures to Young Men on the Formation of Character* (Hartford, 1852); *The Primary Truths of Religion* (New York, 1869); *Readings and Prayers for Aid in Private Devotion* (1888); *Reminiscences* (1895).

CLARK, WILLIAM ROBINSON: Church of England; b. at Inverurie (13 m. n.w. of Aberdeen), Aberdeenshire, Scotland, Mar. 26, 1829. He studied at King's College, Aberdeen, and Hertford College, Oxford (B.A., 1864), and was ordered deacon in 1857 and ordained priest in the following year. He was curate of St. Matthias', Birmingham (1857–58) and of St. Mary Magdalene, Taunton, in 1858, where he was vicar 1859–80. From 1870 to 1882 he was prebendary of Wells, and since 1883 has been professor of philosophy in Trinity College, Toronto. He was lecturer of St. George, Toronto, 1882–85, and lecturer in history in Trinity College, Toronto, 1883–91, as well as Baldwin lecturer in the University of Michigan in 1887, and Slocum lecturer in the same university in 1899. In 1900 he was elected president of the Royal Society of Canada. He translated Hagenbach's *History of Doctrines* (3 vols., Edinburgh, 1880–81) and the major portion of Hefele's *History of the Councils* (to 787, 4 vols., 1871–96), and has written, besides other works, *Witnesses to Christ* (Baldwin Lectures; London, 1888); *Savonarola: his Life and Times* (1892); *The Anglican Reformation* (1896); *The Paraclete* (Slocum Lectures, 1900); and *Pascal and Port Royal* (1902).

CLARKE, ADAM: Wesleyan preacher, commentator, and theologian; b. at Moybeg (near Kilcronaghan, 2 m. e. of Draperstown), County Londonderry, Ireland, c. 1762; d. in London Aug. 26, 1832. He became a Methodist in 1778, and was in a succession an exhorter, local preacher, and regular preacher. His first circuit was that of Bradford, Wiltshire, to which he was appointed in 1782. He served in various places and traveled throughout Great Britain, achieving fame as a preacher, and being president of the British Conference in 1806, 1814, and 1822. After 1805 he held an appointment in London, where he was a member of the committee of the British and Foreign Bible Society for several years, and one of the advisers of its Oriental publications, in addition to editing certain ancient documents of state in continuation of the *Fœdera* of Thomas Rymer. He resigned from this task in 1819, having retired four years previously, in view of his impaired health, to Millbrook, Lancashire, where he resided until his return to the vicinity of London in 1823. He was also active in the service of the Wesleyan Missionary Society from its inception in 1814, making two missionary journeys in 1826 and 1828 to the Shetland Islands, where he established Methodism. The most important of his numerous works was his commentary on the Bible (8 vols., Liverpool, 1810–26), which long had an extensive circulation. He also published a *Biographical Dictionary* (6 vols., London, 1802) and its supplement, *The Biographical Miscellany* (2 vols., 1806). His *Miscellaneous Works* were edited in thirteen volumes by J. Everett (London, 1836–37).

Bibliography: *An Account of the Infancy, Religious and Literary Life of Adam Clarke*, 3 vols., London, 1833 (vol. i. is autobiographical, vols. ii., iii. by his daughter, M. A. Smith, with an *Appendix* by his son, J. B. B. Clarke). Consult lives by J. Everett, London, 1843; J. W. Etheridge, ib. 1858; S. Dunn, ib. 1863; and *DNB*, x. 413–414.

CLARKE, JAMES FREEMAN: Unitarian; b. in Hanover, N. H., Apr. 4, 1810; d. in Boston June 8, 1888. He was graduated at Harvard 1829, and at the Cambridge Divinity School 1833; was pastor in Louisville, Ky., 1833–40; became pastor of the newly organized Church of the Disciples, Boston, 1841, and remained there till his death, with the exception of an interval between 1850 and 1853 when the church was temporarily disbanded. He was a director of the Unitarian Association from 1845, was chosen its secretary in 1859, and helped to form the National Conference of Unitarian Churches in 1865. He was a leader of the anti-slavery movement, and an efficient member of the Sanitary Commission during the Civil War; at a later period he advocated civil service reform. He was prominent in educational work in Boston, an overseer of Harvard, and a trustee of the public library. In 1867 he was made professor in the Harvard Divinity School and gave lectures on comparative theology, Christian doctrine, and other subjects, from which his important books, *Steps of Belief* (Boston, 1870) and *Ten Great Religions* (2 parts, 1871–83) were developed. The Church of the Disciples was founded expressly to allow its members entire freedom of individual belief, and he prepared a *Service and Hymn Book* (1844) for its use, combining the features of ritualistic and non-ritualistic worship. Of his other original works mention may be made of the *History of the Campaign of 1812 and Defence of Gen. William Hull* [his grandfather] *for the Surrender of Detroit* (1848); *The Christian Doctrine of Forgiveness of Sin* (1852); *The Christian Doctrine of Prayer* (1854); *Orthodoxy, its Truths and its Errors* (1866); *Common Sense in Religion*, essays (1874); *Essentials and Non-essentials in Religion* (1878); *Events and Epochs in Religious History* (1881); *Legend of Thomas Didymus, the Jewish skeptic* (1881; re-issued as *The Life and Times of Jesus, as Related by Thomas Didymus*, 1887); *Anti-Slavery Days* (New York, 1883); *The Ideas of the Apostle Paul Translated into their Modern Equivalents* (Boston, 1884);

Manual of Unitarian Belief (1884); *Every Day Religion* (1886); *Vexed Questions in Theology* (1886); *The Problem of the Fourth Gospel* (1886). He edited *The Western Messenger* at Louisville 1836–39 and printed in it the first poems of Emerson; with W. H. Channing and R. W. Emerson he prepared the *Memoirs of Margaret Fuller Ossoli* (3 vols., 1852); and published many magazine articles, addresses, sermons, and pamphlets.

BIBLIOGRAPHY: *J. F. Clarke, Autobiography, Diary, and Correspondence*, ed. Edward Everett Hale, Boston, 1891.

CLARKE, JOHN: Early American Baptist, with Roger Williams founder of Rhode Island; b. probably in Suffolk, England, Oct. 8, 1609; d. in Newport, R. I., Apr., 1676. He was a highly educated physician who left England as a persecuted separatist and arrived at Boston Nov., 1637, just as drastic measures were being taken by the Massachusetts government against Anne Hutchinson and John Wheelwright (see ANTINOMIANISM AND ANTINOMIAN CONTROVERSIES, II., 2). Whether from sympathy with Mrs. Hutchinson's views or from his aversion toward intolerance, he cast in his lot with the banished party and became a leader in the search for a home where liberty of conscience could be enjoyed. The climate of New Hampshire having been found too severe, the party led by Clarke and William Coddington secured, through the good offices of Roger Williams, the right to settle on Rhode Island; and in March, 1638, the nineteen male members entered into a covenant to subject their persons, lives, and possessions to the Lord Jesus Christ, and to do his will as revealed in Holy Scripture. Yet they guarded jealously the principle of liberty of conscience by providing that " none be accounted a delinquent for doctrine provided it be not directly repugnant to the government of laws established." In 1641 the law establishing liberty of conscience was reiterated and fortified. Clarke had much to do with the uniting of the Rhode Island settlements with Providence under a charter procured by Williams, and is thought to have drafted the law-book, which provides for democracy and liberty of conscience. If not an antipedobaptist before he left England, he became such probably as early as 1641, certainly by 1644, when Mark Lukar, an antipedobaptist, became associated with him in a church at Newport, of which Clarke had been pastor from about 1641. While visiting Lynn, Mass., in 1651, Clarke and two fellow workers were arrested and fined, and one of them was whipped. Thereupon Clarke published *Ill Newes from New England* (London, 1652), in which he vindicated the principles of liberty of conscience and believers' baptism. The next twelve years he resided in England as representative of his colony. In 1663 he secured from Charles II. a charter which provided for complete civil and religious liberty. To the Newport church many Baptist churches owe their origin.

ALBERT H. NEWMAN.

BIBLIOGRAPHY: *Records of the Colony of Rhode Island and Providence Plantations in New England*, vol. i., Providence, 1856; J. Callender, *An Historical Discourse on the Civil and Religious Affairs of the Colony of Rhode Island and Providence Plantations*, Boston, 1739; S. G. Arnold, *Hist. of the State of Rhode Island*, vol. i., New York, 1859; I. Backus, *Hist. of New England, with particular Reference to the Denomination of Christians called Baptists*, Newton, Mass., 1871; H. S. Burrage, *Hist. of the Baptists in New England*, ib. 1894; A. H. Newman, *Hist. of the Baptist Churches in the U. S.*, ib. 1898; *DNB*, x. 432.

CLARKE, SAMUEL: The name of four prominent English theologians.

1. English non-conformist; b. at Wolston (22 m. s.w. of Leicester), Warwickshire, Oct. 10, 1599; d. at Isleworth (11 m. s.w. of London), Middlesex, Dec. 25, 1683. He was educated at Coventry and Emmanuel College, Cambridge, was ordained about 1622, and held charges at Knowle, Warwickshire, Thornton-le-Moors and Shotwick, Cheshire, but his Puritan tendencies soon exposed him to the rebuke of his ecclesiastical superiors. He held a lectureship at Coventry, but was inhibited by the bishop from preaching, only to give offense by a similar course at Warwick. In 1633 he was presented to the parish of Alcester, Warwickshire, whence he went, seven years later, to protest to the king against the *et cetera* oath. In 1642 he went to London and was chosen curate of St. Bennet Fink. There he was a governor and twice president of Sion College, and was also a member of the committee of ordainers in 1643. He was one of those who protested against the execution of the king, and opposed the lay-preaching permitted by the Independents. After the Restoration he took part with his close friend Richard Baxter in the Savoy Conference, and was ejected from his living in 1662. He removed to Hammersmith in 1666 and later went to Isleworth, where he spent the remainder of his life. Among his numerous works, valuable on account of the sources used, which are now frequently almost inaccessible, special mention may be made of the following biographical collections: *The Saints Nosegay* (London, 1642); *A Mirror or Looking-Glass both for Saints and Sinners* (1646); *The Marrow of Ecclesiastical History* (2 vols., 1649–50); *General Martyrology* (1651); *English Martyrology* (1652); and *Lives of Sundry Eminent Persons in the Later Age* (1683). He also published, among other works, *England's Remembrancer* (London, 1657); *A Discourse against Toleration* (1660); and *Book of Apothegms* (1681).

BIBLIOGRAPHY: His autobiography was prefixed to the *Lives of Sundry Eminent Persons*, 1683; a *Memoir* by G. T. Clarke, a descendant, was prefixed to the reprint of the *Saints Nosegay*, London, 1881; *DNB*, x. 441–442.

2. Orientalist; b. at Brackley (16 m. s.w. of Northampton), Northamptonshire, 1625; d. at Oxford Dec. 27, 1669. He entered Merton College, Oxford, in 1640, but left the university during its occupation by the royal troops. After the surrender he returned (M.A., 1648). In 1649 he was appointed the first architypographus of the university and was also upper bedell of the civil law. In 1650 he was master of a school at Islington, where he assisted Brian Walton in his Polyglot Bible, his attention being directed chiefly to the Hebrew text, the Aramaic paraphrase, and the Latin translation of the Persian version of the Gospels. He returned to Oxford in 1658 and was reelected to both his former positions. In addition to his work for

Walton, he wrote *Scientiæ metrica et rhythmica, seu tractatus de prosodia Arabica* (Oxford, 1661), while the *Massereth Beracoth Titulus Talmudicus* (1667) is also ascribed to him.

BIBLIOGRAPHY: A. à Wood, *Athenæ Oxonienses*, ed. P. Bliss, iii. 882–886, 4 vols., London, 1813–20; *DNB*, x. 440–441.

3. Biblical commentator, eldest son of Samuel Clarke the non-conformist; b. at Shotwick (6 m. n.w. of Chester), Cheshire, Nov. 12, 1626; d. at High Wycombe (24 m. s.e. of Oxford), Bucks, Feb. 27, 1701. He received his education at Pembroke Hall, Cambridge, and was appointed fellow in 1644, but was deprived of his fellowship seven years later for refusing to take the oath of allegiance to the Commonwealth. At the Restoration he held the rectory of Grendon Underwood, Bucks, but was ejected for non-conformity in 1662. He then settled at High Wycombe. In theology he was Baxterian, and extended divine inspiration to the verse-divisions of the Bible. His chief work was his *Old and New Testaments with Annotations and Parallel Scriptures* (London, 1690), beside which mention may be made of his *Survey of the Bible* (1694), designed to supplement his earlier work, and *The Divine Authority of the Scriptures* (1699).

BIBLIOGRAPHY: *DNB*, x. 442–443, where further literature is given.

4. Philosopher; b. at Norwich Oct. 11, 1675; d. in London May 17, 1729. He was educated in his native city and at Caius College, Cambridge (B.A., 1695). There, in 1697, he prepared a Latin translation of the *Traité de physique* by Jean Rohault, to which he added notes based on Newton's *Principia*. The work was long the standard text-book of its subject at Cambridge and went through repeated editions. In 1698 Clarke became chaplain to John Moore, bishop of Norwich, and held this post for twelve years, in addition to the rectory of Drayton near Norwich and a small living in the city. In 1704–05 he delivered the Boyle Lectures on *The Being and Attributes of God, the Obligations of Natural Religion, and the Truth and Certainty of the Christian Revelation* (2 vols., London, 1705–06). These addresses won him the reputation of the leading English metaphysician for the next quarter of a century, but his rationalism exposed him to the criticisms of the ultraconservatives on the one hand, while his orthodoxy brought upon him the attacks of the deists on the other. In 1706 he assailed the doctrine maintained by the nonjuror Henry Dodwell that the soul receives immortality only through baptism, and in the same year was presented to the rectory of St. Benet's, London, holding this until 1709, when Queen Anne made him rector of St. James's, Westminster. There, however, he gave offense in 1712 by his *Scripture Doctrine of the Trinity*, which exposed him to the charge of Arianism. A prolonged controversy ensued, and the matter was finally taken up by the House of Convocation, the lower house being especially hostile. The upper house practically dropped the case, and Clarke refrained from giving further offense, although he does not seem to have altered his views. About 1718 he was appointed master of Wigston's Hospital, Leicester, but the remainder of his life was devoted to philosophy rather than theology. He became involved in a controversy with Leibnitz, Clarke declaring that time and space have a real existence, and the correspondence was published at London in 1717. He had many adherents among the Latitudinarians and metaphysicians, including Bishop Berkeley, Arthur Collier, Francis Hutcheson, Bishop Butler, William Whiston, Sir Isaac Newton, and Bishop Hoadly. The High-church party, on the other hand, was hostile to him. Clarke's writings included, in addition to those already mentioned, sermons, a Latin translation of Newton's *Optics* (London, 1706), and editions of Cæsar (1712) and the *Iliad* (1729). They were collected and edited by Bishop Benjamin Hoadly in four volumes (London, 1738).

BIBLIOGRAPHY: W. Whiston, *Historical Memoirs of . . . Dr. Samuel Clarke*, London, 1741 (contains A. A. Syke's *Elogium* of Samuel Clarke, and T. Emlyn's *Memoirs of . . . Dr. Samuel Clarke*); the Life, by B. Hoadly, was prefixed to his *Works*, ib. 1738; *DNB*, x. 443–446.

CLARKE, WILLIAM NEWTON: Baptist; b. at Cazenovia, N. Y., Dec. 2, 1841. He was graduated at Madison (now Colgate) University (B.A., 1861) and Hamilton Theological Seminary, Hamilton, N. Y. (1863). He held Baptist pastorates at Keene, N. H. (1863–69), Newton Centre, Mass. (1869–80), and Montreal, Canada (1880–83). He was professor of New Testament interpretation in the Toronto Baptist College 1883–87, and pastor at Hamilton, N. Y., 1887–90. Since 1890 he has been professor of Christian theology in Colgate University. His theological position "is intended to present the substance of the Scriptural teaching, interpreted by Christian thought, in the light of modern knowledge." He has written a *Commentary on the Gospel of Mark* (Philadelphia, 1882); *Outline of Christian Theology* (New York, 1898); *What Shall We Think of Christianity?* (1899); *Can I Believe in God the Father?* (1899); *A Study of Christian Missions* (1900); and *The Use of the Scriptures in Theology* (1905).

CLARKSON, THOMAS: Antislavery agitator; b. at Wisbeach (35 m. n. of Cambridge), Cambridgeshire, England, Mar. 28, 1760; d. at Playford Hall, near Ipswich, Sept. 26, 1846. He studied at St. John's College, Cambridge (B.A., 1783). In 1785 he won a prize for a Latin essay upon the negative side of the question "whether involuntary servitude is justifiable" (Eng. transl., London, 1786; enlarged, 1788). Thenceforth the story of his life is the history of the anti-slavery struggle. He labored with indefatigable perseverance in collecting and disseminating information, and spent most of his modest fortune upon this cause. His labors were crowned with success under the lead of William Wilberforce (q.v.). Of his many writings concerning slavery the most important is *The History of the . . . Abolition of the African Slave Trade by the British Parliament* (2 vols., London, 1808; new ed., 1839). He also wrote *A Portraiture of Quakerism* (3 vols., 1806); *Memoirs of . . . William Penn* (2 vols., 1813); *An Essay on the Doctrine and Practice of the Early Christians as they Relate to War* (1817); *Researches, Antediluvian, Patriarchal, and Historical concerning* *the Way in which Men first Acquired their Knowledge of God and Religion* (1836); *Essay on Baptism* (1843); *The Grievances of our Mercantile Seamen* (1845).

BIBLIOGRAPHY: T. Taylor, *Biographical Sketch of Thomas Clarkson*, London, 1839; J. Elmes, *Thomas Clarkson, a Monograph*, ib. 1854; *DNB*, x. 454–456.

CLASS-MEETING: A part of the discipline of the Methodist Churches, whereby the members of a congregation are divided into sections or classes, over each of which is a class-leader, appointed by the pastor, whose duty it is (according to the *Book of Discipline* of the Methodist Episcopal Church, pt. i., chap. ii., § 1): "I. To see each person in his class once a week at least; in order (1) To inquire how their souls prosper. (2) To advise, reprove, comfort, or exhort, as occasion may require. (3) To receive what they are willing to give toward the relief of the preachers, church, and poor. II. To meet the ministers and the stewards of the society once a week; in order (1) To inform the minister of any that are sick, or of any that walk disorderly, and will not be reproved. (2) To pay the stewards what they have received of their several classes in the week preceding." The class-meeting is said to have arisen accidentally in 1742 in connection with a plan to pay off the church debt contracted by building the edifice at Bristol. The members were divided into sections of twelve, and one of each section was appointed to call regularly every week upon the others of his section to receive their contributions. They soon began to report delinquencies in conduct on the part of those whom they visited, and the possibilities of the plan in providing a means of discipline for the congregations was at once apparent to Wesley. He introduced the plan in London, and it became a distinctive feature of Methodism. At first the leaders called personally upon each member at his own house; but this was found inconvenient and a common meeting-place was appointed. The leader began and ended each meeting with singing and prayer, and about an hour was spent in conversation.

BIBLIOGRAPHY: L. Tyerman, *Life of John Wesley*, vol. i., pp. 377-380, London, 1876.

CLAUDE, JEAN: A French Calvinist preacher and controversialist; b. at Sauvetat-du-Dropt, in the department of Lot-et-Garonne, 1619; d. at The Hague Jan. 13, 1687. He studied theology at Montauban, and was ordained in 1645. He held charges at La Treisse and St. Affrique, but became pastor at Nîmes in 1654. Here he lectured before the Academy in 1656 on homiletics and practical exegesis. In 1661 he presided over the provincial synod held at Nîmes, and opposed so vehemently a project of reunion with the Roman Catholic Church brought forward by the Prince de Conti, governor of Languedoc, that he was inhibited from preaching in the province. In October, 1661, he went to Paris, called by Countess Turenne, in order to refute a treatise by Nicole who sought to show that transubstantiation had always been held in the Church. In 1662 he was appointed professor and pastor at Montauban. When the government forbade his preaching here also, he returned to Paris, and was in 1666 called as pastor of the Protestants to the capital by the consistory of Charenton. In 1668 and 1669 he took part in the celebrated controversy with the Jesuit Nouet and the Jansenist Arnauld on the mass; and in 1678, on the invitation of Mlle. de Duras, he had a discussion with Bossuet in her presence, which, however, resulted in her conversion to Bossuet's faith. On the revocation of the Edict of Nantes he retired to The Hague. He was an eloquent preacher and one of the most profound thinkers of his day. Among his works are: *Réponse aux deux traités de Nicole, sur la perpétuité de la foi* (Charenton, 1665); *Relation succincte de l'état où sont maintenant les églises réformées de France* (1666); *Traité de l'Eucharistie* (Amsterdam, 1668); *Réponse au livre de M. Arnauld "De la perpétuité de la foi"* (Quevilly, 1670); *La défense de la Réformation contre le livre intitulé "Préjugés légitimes contre les Calvinistes"* (Quevilly, 1673; Eng. transl., by J. Townsend, *A Defence of the Reformation*, 2 vols., London, 1815); *Traité de la lecture des Pères et la justification* (Amsterdam, 1685); *Les plaintes des Protestants cruellement opprimés dans le royaume de France* (Cologne, 1686; Eng. transl., *An Account of the Persecutions . . . of the Protestants in France*, London, 1686). Certain posthumous writings were published at Amsterdam in 1688 and 1689, and selections were translated into English; some have proved very popular, e.g., *On the Composition of a Sermon* (latest ed., London, 1853).

G. BONET-MAURY.

BIBLIOGRAPHY: [Devèse, A. R. de la], *Abrégé de la vie de M. Claude*, Amsterdam, 1687; E. and É. Haag, *La France protestante*, ed. H. L. Bordier, Paris, 1877–88; Lichtenberger, *ESR*, iii. 195–199, Paris, 1878.

CLAUDIANUS MAMERTUS: Viennese philosopher and theologian; b. at or near Lyons c. 425; d. at Vienna between 470 and 474. His brother Mamertus, before 462 bishop of Vienna, called him there as a presbyter. He devoted himself to church music and appears to have compiled a lectionary. Apollinaris Sidonius celebrated the industry of the two brothers (in *Epistolæ*, iv. 11). The hymns ascribed to him are by other authors. His letter to Sapaudus (Engelbrecht, *Untersuchungen über die Sprache des Claudianus Mamertus*, p. 203, Vienna, 1885), in which he laments the decay of the sciences, has historical value. About 470 he wrote his main work, *De statu animæ*, in which he showed acquaintance with Jerome and dependence upon Augustine. Of the Greek Fathers he cites only Gregory Nazianzen; he was unacquainted with the work of Nemisius of Emesa, "On the Nature of Man." Plato was to him king of philosophers, though Plotinus's Enneads influenced him greatly; in the use of the categories of Aristotle, he was a forerunner of the Schoolmen. His work is used by Cassiodorus (*MPL*, lxx. 1279). Berengar of Tours studied and valued it (*MPL*, clxxviii. 1869), and Nicolas, secretary to Bernard of Clairvaux, gave him and it the highest praise (*MPL*, ccii. 499 C.). He was one of the most consistent and positive champions of the dualism of soul and body, against the naturalistic conception of the soul as a mere product or "harmony" of the body, held by such men as Tertullian, Hilary of Poitiers, Cassian, and Faustus of Riez. His arguments for a spiritual substance have reappeared substantially in works of Thomas Aquinas and Descartes. (F. ARNOLD.)

BIBLIOGRAPHY: The *Epistola ad Sidonium* is in *MGH, Auct. ant.*, viii (1887), 53–54. Consult: Tillemont, *Mémoires*, xvi. 119–126, 741, cf. *Histoire littéraire de la France*, ii. 442–446; M. Schultze, *Claudianus Mamertus über das Wesen der Seele*, Dresden, 1883; F. Ueberweg, *Geschichte der Philosophie*, ii. 121, Berlin, 1886, Eng. transl., i. 352–354, New York, 1872; De la Broise, *Mamerti Claudiani vita ejusque doctrina de anima hominis*, Paris, 1890; C. F. Arnold, *Cæsarius von Arelate und die gallische Kirche seiner Zeit*, pp. 89, 131, 325–326, Leipsic, 1894.

CLAUDIUS (Tiberius Claudius Germanicus): Roman emperor 41–54 A.D. His name comes into connection with the history of primitive Christianity through the steps taken by him against the Jews in Rome. Soon after his accession, in opposition to the policy of his predecessor, Caligula, he had restored to them religious liberty. As time went on, he saw himself obliged, at least as concerned the Roman Jews, to return to a policy of repression. It is to this that Suetonius alludes (*Claudius*, xxv.). This measure affected the Jewish couple Aquila and Priscilla, who were then residents of Rome (Acts xviii. 2). The reference of Suetonius to "Chrestus" has given rise to a long-standing controversy whether he means to imply that the disturbances were caused by the preaching of Christianity (about which Suetonius evidently knew little, if he represents Christ as living in Rome), or whether he refers to a later, otherwise unknown, Jewish agitator named Chrestus. The possibility of the former hypothesis is confirmed by other events in the Apostolic Age (Acts xvii. 5 sqq., xxi. 27 sqq.); but it is unlikely that such a gross mistake was made by Suetonius, who must have known from Tacitus, with whom he was acquainted, that Christ had already been put to death at Jerusalem in the time of Tiberius. Considering, moreover, the active intercourse between the Roman Jews and Palestine, it is hard to believe that the Messianic controversies should have taken fifteen or twenty years to reach an acute stage in Rome, and that, on the other hand, the Christian community there should have already attained sufficient importance for their relations with orthodox Judaism to cause disturbances of so serious a nature as to necessitate such severe measures on the part of a government in general friendly to the Jews. The exact date of the expulsion is unknown. Orosius (*Hist.*, VII. vi. 15) assigns it to the ninth year of Claudius (49 A.D.). Josephus is silent on the point. The vague term "lately" of Acts xviii. 2 offers no objection to this date. Dio Cassius (lx. 6) apparently refers to a different procedure; it is impossible to harmonise the two accounts. VICTOR SCHULTZE.

BIBLIOGRAPHY: H. Lehmann, *Claudius und Nero und ihre Zeit*, vol. i., Gotha, 1858; H. Vogelstein and P. Rieger, *Geschichte der Juden in Rom*, i. 18 sqq., Berlin, 1869; K. Schmidt, *Anfänge des Christentums in der Stadt Rom*, Heidelberg, 1879; T. Keim, *Rom und das Christentum*, Berlin, 1881; J. Kneucker, *Anfänge des römischen Christentums*, Carlsruhe, 1881; Schürer, *Geschichte*, i. 502–503, iii. 31–33, 74, Eng. transl., I. ii. 99, II. ii. 236–237, 266; Moeller, *Christian Church*, i. 75–76.

CLAUDIUS, MATTHIAS: German author; b. at Reinfeld (10 m. w. of Lübeck) Aug. 15, 1740; d. at Hamburg Jan. 21, 1815. He studied law at Jena, and spent the most of his life at Wandsbeck, as auditor of the Bank of Sleswick-Holstein at Altona, and as private citizen. His writings are poems and articles published over the signature "Asmus" in the *Wandsbecker Bote* and other periodicals. He issued the first collection of these contributions at Hamburg in 1775, and the last in 1812 (8 vols., 13th ed., 2 vols., Gotha, 1902), entitling his work *Asmus omnia sua secum portans, oder sämtliche Werke des Wandsbecker Boten.* Claudius was not a theologian, nor were his essays homiletic or devotional, while his poems are never used as hymns in the churches. His leading characteristics were practical Christianity, expressed in the language of the people, and earnestness, thinly veiled by irony and humor. In tendency he was decidedly opposed to the rationalism of his time, even though he ridiculed the pedantry of an antiquated orthodoxy. He became involved in a controversy with Friedrich Jacobi, in which he based his own position on the Biblical proof of redemption through Christ, and his general view was that philosophy and human reason are subordinate in credibility to revelation.

BIBLIOGRAPHY: The *Werke* were edited by C. Redlich, 2 vols., Gotha, 1882; selections are in Meyer's *Volksbücher*, Nos. 681–683, Leipsic, 1889. His life was written by C. Monckeberg, Hamburg, 1869; W. Herbst, Gotha, 1878; K. Stockmeyer, Basel, 1895. Consult also C. Redlich, *Die poetischen Beiträge zum Wandsbecker Boten gesammelt*, Hamburg, 1871.

CLAUDIUS OF TURIN: Bishop of Turin, an example of the type of statesman-bishop under Charlemagne and Louis the Pious; b. in Spain in the latter half of the eighth century; d. in Turin before 832. Although a pupil of Felix of Urgel, the leader of the Adoptionists (see ADOPTIONISM), he did not share his heretical views. He is next found at the court of the king of Aquitaine as a priest, instructing his fellow clergy in Scriptural learning. Immediately after his accession, Louis the Pious sent Claudius to Turin as bishop to instruct the ignorant population in the Holy Scriptures, and to cope with the piratical Mohammedans in the maritime Alps. Charlemagne had acquired large territories in northwestern Italy by his defeat of the Lombards, and used some of these lands to endow the church there, which had been plundered by the Arian Lombards. Feudal service in the field was required of the prelates in return. Claudius himself relates that he rendered such service against the Moors, taking his literary work with him to the campaign. He produced commentaries in the form of catenæ on Genesis (811), Exodus (821), and Leviticus (825), also on Matthew (815), Galatians (816), and Ephesians (817). His works were read throughout Gaul. At the request of the abbot Theodemir, he wrote a work on the books of Kings, which is mostly a compilation from Augustine, Gregory, Isidore, Bede, and Rabanus. Some expressions in it brought him under suspicion of Nestorianism; and Theodemir laid his commentary on I Corinthians before the bishops and dignitaries at court for judgment. Claudius wrote a defense, of which a copy was seen in the monastery of Bobbio in 1461, but it has since been lost, and is only known by the rejoinders of Dungalus and Jonas. He gave offense also by his attitude toward the veneration of images, which among the half-civilized people of his diocese amounted to idolatry. He accepted Augustine's views on predestination, but overlooked that side of his teaching which sets forth the Church as the abiding means of communication between God and man. He disapproved of the increasing honor paid to the bishop of Rome, and did not favor pilgrimages to Rome. He denied that Peter had received power to bind and loose, and spoke of a double primacy among the apostles, one given to Peter for the Jewish mission, and one to Paul for the heathen. These and other expressions, together with the fact that he removed not only images, but even the crosses from his churches, gave rise to deep suspicion, and Theodemir wrote to him that it was reported he had founded a new sect *contra regulam fidei catholicæ*. There is no evidence to support the view that he was the real founder of the Waldensians; though he may, in a sense, be numbered among the precursors of the Reformation. (R. Foss†.)

Bibliography: The best collection of the works is in *MPL*, civ., cvi. Consult: T. Förster, *Drei Erzbischöfe vor 1000 Jahren (Claudius von Turin, . . .)*, Gütersloh, 1874; H. F. Reuter, *Geschichte der religiösen Aufklärung im Mittelalter*, i. 16–24, Berlin, 1875; A. Ebert, *Geschichte der Literatur des Mittelalters*, ii. 222–224, Leipsic, 1880; Wattenbach, *DGQ*, 6th ed., i. 155, 205, 207; *KL*, iii. 434–437.

CLEANNESS AND UNCLEANNESS. See Defilement and Purification, Ceremonial.

CLÉMANGES, clē"mānzh' (**CLAMANGES**), **NICHOLAS POILLEVILLAIN**, pwāl"le-vil"lañ', **OF**: A French theological author and ecclesiastical statesman; b. at Clamanges near Châlons-sur-Marne, 90 m. n. by e. of Paris, c. 1367; d. at Paris in 1437. Like Gerson, his teacher, he was educated at the college of Navarre in Paris where, by his studies in the classics, he attained a degree of excellence in rhetoric that his contemporaries thought almost Ciceronian. The influence of ancient literature revealed itself only in his style, however, as his interests in life were entirely churchly and theological. At an early age he entered the arena of ecclesiastical politics, devoting himself with great earnestness to furthering the movement for the healing of the Great Schism (see Schism). In 1397 he became papal secretary to Benedict XIII. In 1405 he accompanied Benedict on a journey to Genoa, and remained there on the latter's return to Avignon in the fall of the following year. There was, however, no formal separation; and when Benedict in 1408 threatened the royal house of France with excommunication, the odium aroused fell in full measure upon the head of Nicholas, the supposed author of the obnoxious bull. Partly out of fear of possible consequences, partly in obedience to a long cherished desire, he abandoned his canonicate at Langres and retired to a Cistercian cloister, first at Valprofonds, and then at Fontaine-du-bosc. There he gave himself up to serious Biblical study, which, he said, he had hitherto neglected. Aside from letters addressed to such friends as Gerson and D'Ailly, he composed a number of treatises dealing with the errors and corruptions that he saw in the Church of his time. *De fructu eremi* and *De fructu rerum adversarium* deal with the beneficent influence which solitude and misfortune may exercise on the inner life. *De novis festivitatibus non instituendis* protests against the harmful multiplication of holy days, and *De studio theologico* extols the life of the active parish priest above that of the student. In his *Oratio ad Galliarum Principes* (c. 1411) he pleaded for a cessation of the civil strife that was sapping the life of France. He threw himself with energy into the movement that culminated in the Council of Constance, depicting with power and feeling the degenerate state of the Church in his *De ruina ecclesiæ*, or *De corrupto ecclesiæ statu* (1401). His authorship of this work has been denied by some. He was displeased at the action of the Council of Constance in decreeing the deposition of the three rival popes, believing that the recognition of Benedict would have brought harmony to the Church. He was more fortunate than his friend Gerson in retaining the favor of the men in power in France. He sided with Philip of Burgundy against the Dauphin; and when in 1425 their reconciliation seemed at hand, he returned to his earliest occupation as lecturer on rhetoric and theology at the college of Navarre. He holds a high place in the history of the early French renaissance, and as a precursor of the "humanistic reformation." His ecclesiastical ideals, which the brain of a Wyclif converted into revolutionary principles, allowed the humanist scholar to remain a faithful son of the Church. (B. Bess.)

Bibliography: An incomplete ed. of the *Opera* was put out by J. M. Lydius, 2 vols., Leyden, 1613. The best account of Clémanges is by G. Voigt, *Die Wiederbelebung des klassischen Alterthums*, ii. 349–356, Berlin, 1881; A. Müntz, *Nicholas de Clémanges, sa vie et ses écrits*, Strassburg, 1846; G. Schuberth, *Nikolaus von Clémanges als Verfasser*, Grossenhain, 1888; Hefele, *Conciliengeschichte*, vol. vi.; *KL*, ix. 298–306; Creighton, *Papacy*, i. 151, 221, 301–303, 375.

CLEMEN, CARL CHRISTIAN: German Protestant; b. at Sommerfeld (a suburb of Leipsic) Mar. 30, 1865. He studied in Tübingen, Halle, Berlin, and Leipsic (Ph.D., 1889), and after being an assistant pastor in London 1889–90, became privat-docent at Halle in 1892. In 1903 he accepted a call to Bonn as titular professor of New Testament exegesis and systematic and practical theology, and was also an assistant in the university library 1903–05. In 1899–1903 he was general secretary of the *Evangelischer Bund*, and since 1902 has been convener of the international committee for the promotion of the Evangelical Church among the Czechs. His theological position is scientific. He has written *Die Chronologie der paulinischen Briefe* (Halle, 1893); *Die Einheitlichkeit der paulinischen Briefe* (Göttingen, 1894); *Niedergefahren zu den Toten* (Giessen, 1900); *Paulus, sein Leben und Wirken* (2 vols., 1904); *Schleiermachers Glaubenslehre* (1905); *Die Apostelgeschichte im Lichte der neueren text-, quellen- und historisch-kritischen Forschungen* (1905); *Die Entstehung des Neuen*

Testaments (Leipsic, 1906); and *Predigt und biblischer Text* (Giessen, 1906).

CLEMENT: The name of fourteen popes and three antipopes.

Clement I. See CLEMENT OF ROME.

Clement II. (Suidger): Pope 1046–47. After the abdication of the simoniacal pope Gregory VI., Henry III., the German king, then all-powerful in Rome, nominated Bishop Suidger of Bamberg in a synod held in St. Peter's, Dec. 24, 1046. He took the title of Clement II., and crowned Henry and his consort on the following day. In January he held a synod with Henry to condemn simony, though allowing those ordained by simoniacs to retain their clerical position. He died Oct. 9, 1047. (A. HAUCK.)

BIBLIOGRAPHY: The *Epistolæ et privilegia* are in *MPL*, cxlii.; Jaffé, *Regesta*, i. 525; F. Gregorovius, *Hist. of the City of Rome*, iv. 57–69, London, 1896; J. Langen, *Geschichte der römischen Kirche*, iii. 436, Bonn, 1892; Hauck, *KD*, iii. 589 sqq.; Bower, *Popes*, ii. 342; Milman, *Latin Christianity*, iii. 237–238; Neander, *Christian Church*, iii. 378.

Clement III. Antipope 1080–1100. See GUIBERT OF RAVENNA.

Clement III. (Paolo Scolari): Pope 1187–91. A Roman by birth, he became cardinal bishop of Palestrina and was elected pope at Pisa Dec. 19, 1187. In the following February he was able to enter Rome, which his two predecessors had never visited, and by the end of May the differences between the papacy and the senate were composed. Continuing the policy of Gregory VIII., he also brought about peace with the empire, agreeing to crown the young Henry VI. and terminating the strife between papal and imperial claimants of the archbishopric of Treves, and demanding in return the restoration of the States of the Church to their extent under Lucius III. By these mutual concessions peace was restored in Apr., 1189. Clement's principal motive for this attitude was the condition of affairs in the East, where Saladin had defeated the Christian forces at Hattin on July 4 and 5, 1187, and Jerusalem had fallen on Oct. 2. This news had aroused a zeal in Christendom which exceeded even that of the first crusade. Clement used every means in his power to forward the undertaking. The maritime cities of Italy made great preparations; peace was restored between Venice and the king of Hungary, who claimed Dalmatia; the aged emperor Ferderick I. took the cross (Mar., 1188); and the legate Henry of Albano prevailed upon the kings of England and France to lay aside their differences and support the crusade. The death of the emperor on June 10, 1190, was a heavy blow to Clement's hopes; and he did not live to see the end of the crusade. The conflict with the king of Scotland over the possession of the bishopric of St. Andrews, inherited from his predecessors, was terminated by him in 1188, not altogether in favor of the Roman See. The final settlement declared Scotland immediately subject to the pope, and freed it from the legatine authority which the archbishops of York had claimed over it. Fresh difficulties arose in another quarter on the death of William II. of Sicily (Nov. 18, 1189). Clement claimed the rights of a suzerain over the kingdom, and invested with it the illegitimate Tancred, whom a faction of the Norman barons had set up as king. This brought on a new struggle with the Hohenstaufen dynasty, and Henry VI. was marching on Rome when Clement died, Mar. 13, 1191. (A. HAUCK.)

BIBLIOGRAPHY: Jaffé, *Regesta*, ii. 535; J. M. Watterich, *Romanorum pontificum . . . vitæ*, ii. 693, Leipsic, 1862; F. Gregorovius, *Hist. of the City of Rome*, iv. 617–625, London, 1896; J. Langen, *Geschichte der römischen Kirche*, iv. 575, Bonn, 1893; W. von Giesebrecht, *Geschichte der deutschen Kaiserzeit*, vol. vi., Brunswick, 1895; Hefele, *Conciliengeschichte*, v. 737 sqq.; Bower, *Popes*, ii. 529–531; Milman, *Latin Christianity*, iv. 446; Neander, *Christian Church*, iv. 118–129.

Clement IV. (Guido Le Gros): Pope 1265–68. He was born at St. Gilles on the Rhone, of a noble Provençal family, studied law, and practised it with distinction at the court of Louis IX. On the death of his wife he took orders and received rapid promotion, becoming bishop of Puy in 1256 or 1257, archbishop of Narbonne in 1259, and cardinal in 1262. After a four months' interregnum, the French party among the cardinals elected him pope Feb. 5, 1265. In the distracted state of Italy he could only approach Rome with great precaution, reaching Perugia through the Ghibelline towns in the disguise of a mendicant friar. Here he held his court for some time, and after Apr., 1266, mostly at Viterbo. The principal question of his pontificate was that of Sicily, in which he followed the policy of Innocent IV. in opposition to the Hohenstaufen. On Feb. 26, 1265, he invested Charles of Anjou with the kingdom, in return for certain money payments and a promise to abolish the institutions of Frederick II. as far as they affected the Church. Clement, however, soon became dissatisfied with Charles's conduct, and was thinking of negotiating with Manfred when news came of the battle of Benevento and Manfred's death (Feb. 26, 1266). He rebuked Charles still more strongly for his bloodthirstiness and avarice, but was obliged by the difficulties of his position and the traditional policy of the Curia to maintain his alliance. When the young Conradin appeared in Italy, Clement excommunicated him after unheeded warnings, and remained undaunted even after Conradin's victory on the Arno, the brilliancy of which was soon obscured by the fatal defeat of Tagliacozzo. That he contributed to or approved of Conradin's execution is improbable. Charles of Anjou went on in his own way more high-handedly than ever, and Clement had every reason to fear that the Hohenstaufen would be the only ones to make war upon the Church when, just a month after the last of them, he died on Nov. 29, 1268, leaving the reputation of a just and noble-minded ruler. (A. HAUCK.)

BIBLIOGRAPHY: A. Potthast, *Regesta pontificum Romanorum*, ii. 1542, Berlin, 1875; E. Jordan, *Les Régistres de Clément IV*, Paris, 1893 sqq.; *MGH*, *Epist. pont.*, iii (1894), 627 sqq.; F. Gregorovius, *Hist. of the City of Rome*, iv. 359, London, 1896; Muratori, *Scriptores*, III. i. 594, ii. 421; Hefele, *Conciliengeschichte*, vi. 26 sqq.; Bower, *Popes*, iii. 9–15; Milman, *Latin Christianity*, vi. 87–117; Neander, *Christian Church*, iv. 289 et passim.

Clement V. (Bertrand de Goth): Pope 1305–14. The son of a nobleman of Aquitaine, he was made archbishop of Bordeaux by Boniface VIII., and elected pope at Perugia June 5, 1305, after the conclave had lasted eleven months. His coronation took place in Lyons. Under Philip the Fair's influence he remained in France, residing first at Bordeaux, Poitiers, and elsewhere, and fixing his seat at Avignon in the spring of 1309. He is accused by Villani of avarice, nepotism, and simony; he certainly surrounded himself with the pomp of a worldly sovereign, and was suspected of a criminal attachment to the beautiful countess of Périgord. Another fault was the weakness of character which made him a slave of the cold and unscrupulous king, and to the suppression of the Templars (q.v.). At the same time another process was begun against Boniface VIII., which Philip pressed for personal reasons, refusing, however, to push it to extremes and contenting himself with the bull of April 27, 1311, in which Clement declared that Philip was innocent of Nogaret's deeds of violence and of the plundering of the papal treasure (see BONIFACE VIII.), and annulled Boniface's excommunications and interdicts, especially the bull *Unam sanctam*. In the affairs of the Empire Clement pursued a vacillating course; he had recommended the election of Philip's brother Charles of Valois, but willingly recognized Henry VII., and crowned him in the Lateran, June 29, 1312. When Henry, however, fell out with Robert of Naples, Clement took the latter's side, threatening the emperor with excommunication. On Henry's death (Aug. 24, 1313) he named Robert imperial vicar for Italy, claiming the supreme exercise of the imperial power during the vacancy for himself. His own death followed a few months later (Apr. 20, 1314). His collection of decretals, which he meant to form a seventh book in the great collection, though first formally confirmed by his successor John XXII., is known under the name of *Clementina* (see CANON LAW, II., 6, § 3).

(A. HAUCK.)

BIBLIOGRAPHY: *Regestum*, edited by the Benedictines, Rome, 9 vols. and appendix, 1885-92; his *Tractatus cum Heinrico VII.*, ed. J. Schwalm, is in *MGH, Const. imper.*, iv. 1, pp. 338 sqq.; J. Schwalm, *Neue Aktenstücke zur Geschichte . . . Clemens V.*, Rome, 1904, i., pp. 492-496. The old *Vitæ* are collected in É. Baluze, *Vitæ paparum Avenionensium*, i. 1-62, 85-152, Paris, 1693. Consult: Muratori, *Scriptores*, III. i. 673, ii. 441; L. König, *Die päpstliche Kammer unter Clemens V.*, Vienna, 1894; E. Berchon, *Hist. du pape Clément V.*, Paris, 1896; F. Lacoste, *Nouvelles études sur Clément V.*, Bordeaux, 1896; Hefele, *Conciliengeschichte*, vi. 394 sqq.; Pastor, *Popes*, i. 58-61, 63-64 et passim; Bower, *Popes*, iii. 58-72; Milman, *Latin Christianity*, vi. 373-531; Neander, *Christian Church*, v. 70, 341, notes 2-23.

Clement VI. (Pierre Roger): Pope 1342-52. Originally a member of the Benedictine order, councilor and keeper of the seals to Philip the Fair, then archbishop of Rouen, he was elected pope at Avignon May 7, 1342. A talented man and a brilliant orator, he was wholly devoted to the French policy, and refused the pressing invitation of a Roman deputation, which included Petrarch, to return to Rome. He vigorously carried on the struggle with Louis the Bavarian, favored by the divisions in the electoral college and by the emperor's weakness. Louis showed his readiness to submit to any humiliations, but Clement was obdurate. In the spring of 1346 he pronounced the emperor's excommunication and deposition. At his bidding Charles of Luxemburg was informally chosen as Charles IV. by the three archbishops, John of Bohemia, and Rudolph of Saxony (July 11, 1346). Louis died Oct. 11, 1347. The failure of the attempt to set up another claimant in his place justified Clement's assertion of the necessity of papal confirmation. Fortune seemed to favor him. The republican rising in Rome under Cola di Rienzo (May-Dec., 1347) fell to pieces of itself. Queen Joanna of Sicily, suspected of the murder of her husband, appeared before him and was acquitted and allowed to retain her crown. Needing money, she sold the county of Avignon to the pope for 80,000 florins, Charles IV. renouncing his claims to it. To please the Romans and to fill his treasure, Clement reduced the period between jubilees from a hundred to fifty years. In connection with the jubilee of 1350, the scholastic doctrine of the superabundant merits of Christ was extended to include those of the saints, and the right to distribute the indulgences based upon it was formally claimed for the successors of Peter. Clement died Dec. 6, 1352.

(A. HAUCK.)

BIBLIOGRAPHY: The *Epistola ad archiepiscopum Trevirensem* is in J. P. Schunk, *Beiträge zur mainzischen Geschichte*, ii. 474, Mainz, 1789; the *Sermo adv. Heinricum*, ib. ii. 332 sqq. The older *Vitæ* are collected in É. Baluze, *Vitæ paparum Avenionensium*, i. 243-322, Paris, 1693. Consult: M. Freyberg, *Die Stellung der deutschen Geistlichkeit zur Wahl Karls IV.*, Halle, 1880; C. Müller, *Der Kampf Ludwigs . . . mit der römischen Kurie*, ii. 163 sqq., Tübingen, 1880; F. Gregorovius, *Hist. of the City of Rome*, London, 1899; Hefele, *Conciliengeschichte*, vi. 663; Pastor, *Popes*, vi. 6 et passim; Bower, *Popes*, iii. 93-104; Milman, *Latin Christianity*, vii. 135-196; Neander, *Christian Church*, v. 41-43.

Clement VII. (Robert, Count of Geneva): Antipope 1378-94. He was a canon in Paris, bishop of Thérouanne, and finally cardinal. The French cardinals who deserted Urban VI. chose him pope at Fondi. He soon lost hope of maintaining himself in Italy, and returned to Avignon. The struggle between the rival claimants is narrated under Urban VI. Its course was unfavorable to Clement, in spite of his attempts by seductive promises to stir up Louis of Anjou and Charles VI., and he died, no nearer the goal of his ambition, Sept. 16, 1394.

(A. HAUCK.)

BIBLIOGRAPHY: N. Valois, *La France et le grand schisme*, vol. ii., Paris, 1896; idem, in *Römische Quartalschrift*, 1893, pp. 170 sqq.; J. Fraikin, *Nonciatures de Clément VII*, vol. i., Paris, 1906; Bower, *Popes*, iii. 141; Pastor, *Popes*, i. passim; Creighton, *Papacy*, i. 72-144.

Clement VIII. (Egidio Muñoz): Antipope 1425-1429. He was canon of Barcelona when three cardinals of the party of Benedict XIII. (q.v.) elected him to succeed the latter. He was recognized by Alfonso V. of Aragon, but never attained any importance and resigned his claims July 26, 1429.

(A. HAUCK.)

BIBLIOGRAPHY: Hefele, *Conciliengeschichte*, vii. 396, 417; Bower, *Popes*, iii. 212; Pastor, *Popes*, i. 274-277.

Clement VII. (Giulio de' Medici): Pope 1523-1534. He was born May 26, 1478, the illegitimate son of the Giuliano who was murdered in the conspiracy of the Pazzi. He joined the Knights of St. John, and was prior of Capua when his cousin ascended the papal throne as Leo X. Gaining from him a dispensation from the impediment of illegitimacy, and then a declaration that he was not illegitimate after all, since his parents had been secretly married, he became archbishop of Florence and cardinal, occupying a position of great influence at Rome. On Nov. 18, 1523, he was elected to succeed Adrian VI. His position was extremely difficult, between the conflicting powers of the Empire and France, which he endeavored to play off against each other in order to increase the temporal dominions of the papacy and the power of his family.

Policy Toward France and Germany.

Charles V. expected him to continue the alliance of his predecessor with the Empire; but he first assumed a neutral position, and then entered into close relations with Francis I. After the battle of Pavia (Feb. 24, 1525), he saw himself obliged to conciliate the emperor, and made an alliance with him. Charles's power seemed, however, so threatening to Italy that Clement entered (May 22, 1526) the league composed of France, Venice, Florence, and Milan. After an interchange of diplomatic communications, in which Charles spoke his mind very clearly as to the pope's course and appealed to a general council, hostilities broke out in the summer. The league came to a sudden and humiliating end, and on May 6, 1527, Rome was taken and plundered by the German *Landsknechts* under the Constable of Bourbon. The temporal power of the papacy was threatened with annihilation; but Charles was unwilling to go so far, and in November, on Clement's promise of neutrality, restored him his liberty and his states. Clement now aimed at restoring to his family the dominion of Florence, which he attained at the peace of Barcelona (June 29, 1529). On Feb. 24, 1530, he crowned Charles at Bologna; the emperor kissed his feet according to custom, but was more powerful in Italy than his predecessors had been for many a day, and Italian independence was lost.

Clement still hoped at least to see his authority upheld in Germany by the imperial power. Neither he nor the Curia understood the position there; Campeggio's action as legate at the Diet of Nuremberg (1524) proved entirely unsuccessful, and the foundation of the League of Regensburg in the same year had not much better results, since it led to the formal organization of the Protestant party in the Empire. After the treaty of Barcelona and that of Cambrai (Aug. 5, 1529), pope and emperor seemed likely to work together for the suppression of Protestantism;

Events in Germany.

but when Campeggio appeared at the Diet of Augsburg in 1530 to propose confiscation, fire and sword, and the Inquisition, Charles was not inclined to go with him until after much further investigation, and renewed his request for a council to be summoned within six and held within eighteen months. Clement, disinclined as he was, did not dare openly to reject the proposal, but he threw all manner of obstacles in the way of its fulfilment. Time went by without anything being done, even after a fresh personal interview with Charles at Bologna; and Clement began gradually to draw closer to Francis I. again. He had discussed the marriage of his niece Catherine with Francis' second son Henry as early as the middle of 1531; and this union, consummated Oct. 27, 1533, only set the seal to the alliance which was practically resolved upon in two meetings between pope and king at Marseilles about the same time. Francis had all along opposed the idea of a council, and the pope's unwillingness was only increased by the new association. To be fair, one must admit that it was out of the question for him to call such a council as the Protestants wanted, while such a gathering as he might have approved would have done no good. The council idea was really only a stick which Charles kept to beat the pope with, in the hope of furthering his own political and ecclesiastical plans.

The worst reproach that can be brought against Clement's policy is its utter fruitlessness and purely negative character. During his pontificate the new doctrines made giant strides in Germany, Scandinavia, and Switzerland, acquired considerable power in France and England, and threatened even Italy and Spain.

His Policy Fruitless and Futile.

Clement's policy, intended to strengthen himself and his family as temporal powers, really helped his ecclesiastical opponents. The loss of England was a consequence of this policy (see CRANMER, THOMAS). This, the perpetual insistence of Charles upon a council, the discord of his Florentine relatives, and the general failure of his plans so preyed upon Clement as to hasten his end, which came Sept. 25, 1534, leaving the papacy notably poorer in both temporal and spiritual power for his rule. (A. HAUCK.)

BIBLIOGRAPHY: *Bullarium Romanum*, vi. 26, Turin, 1860; P. Balan, *Monumenta sæculi xvi.*, Innsbruck, 1885; idem, *La Politica di Clemente VII*, Rome, 1884; W. Hellwig, *Die politische Beziehungen Clements VII. zu Karl V.*, Leipsic, 1889; S. Ehses, *Römische Dokumente zur Geschichte der Ehescheidung Heinrichs VIII.*, Paderborn, 1893; idem, in *Römische Quartalschrift*, 1891, p. 292, 1892, p. 220; Hefele, *Conciliengeschichte*, ix. 325 sqq.; Ranke, *Popes*, i. 74–98, iii. 28–96; Bower, *Popes*, iii. 302–310; Creighton, *Papacy*, vi. 275 sqq.; Milman, *Latin Christianity*, vii. 220–273; Neander, *Christian Church*, vii. 47–49, 52, 55–58.

Clement VIII. (Ippolito Aldobrandini): Pope 1592–1605. He was elected in a short but stormy conclave (Jan. 10–30), as the candidate of the "cardinals' party," which aimed at vindicating the independence of the Curia against Spanish influence. This was the task of his pontificate; he accomplished it slowly but surely. In French politics he took the side of the League against Henry of Navarre, and proceeded with great caution toward his reception into the Church, giving him solemn absolution on Dec. 17, 1595. His good understanding with Henry IV. helped to free the papacy from the power of Spain and to restore French influence in Italy. Henry's support made it possible for Clement in 1598, on the extinction of the direct line of the house of Este, to resume possession of the duchy of Ferrara as an ancient papal fief; and in return the pope allowed the toleration of the Huguenots by the Edict of Nantes.

Other important events of his reign are the diplomatic decision of the controversy between the Jesuits and the Dominicans on the question of grace, and the burning of Giordano Bruno (q.v.) for heresy in Rome (Feb. 17, 1600). He enlarged and defined the rules for the censorship of books, and revised the breviary by the bull *Cum in ecclesia* (1602); for his work in revising the Vulgate see BIBLE VERSIONS, A, II., 2, § 5.

(A. HAUCK.)

BIBLIOGRAPHY: *Bullarium Romanum*, ix. 518, Turin, 1865; A. Degert, *Le Cardinal d'Ossat, . . . sa vie, ses négociations à Rome*, Paris, 1894; Ranke, *Popes*, ii. 39 sqq., iii. 272–274; Bower, *Popes*, iii. 326.

Clement IX. (Giulio Rospigliosi): Pope 1667–1669. He was born at Pistoia Jan. 28, 1600, made cardinal in 1657, and chosen pope June 20, 1667, as the candidate of the French party. In order to oppose a united Christendom to the Turks, he urged Louis XIV. to the peace of Aix-la-Chapelle (1668). Acting in harmony with Louis, he attempted to reconcile the warring factions in the church of France by the *Pax Clementina* (see JANSEN, CORNELIUS, JANSENISM), though a fresh outburst of strife was destined to follow his death on Dec. 9, 1669. (A. HAUCK.)

BIBLIOGRAPHY: *Bullarium Romanum*, xvii. 512, Turin, 1869; Bower, *Popes*, iii. 332; Ranke, *Popes*, ii. 330 sqq.; De Bildt, *Christine de Suède et le conclave de Clément IX. (1669–1670)*, Paris, 1906.

Clement X. (Emilio Altieri): Pope 1670–76. After a five months' conclave, he was elected on Apr. 29, 1670, as a compromise candidate, because he was eighty years old. He left political questions mainly to Cardinal Paluzzi, who was adopted by him and took the name of Altieri. Paluzzi was to blame for the outbreak of the conflict with Louis XIV. over the *droit de régale* (see REGALE). Another international question was stirred up by the unsuccessful attempt to withdraw the privilege of extraterritorial immunity from the foreign ambassadors in Rome. Clement died July 22, 1676.

(A. HAUCK.)

BIBLIOGRAPHY: *Bullarium Romanum*, vol. xviii., Turin, 1869; Ranke, *Popes*, ii. 417 sqq., iii. 445–453; Bower, *Popes*, iii. 332.

Clement XI. (Giovanni Francesco Albani): Pope 1700–21. He was born at Urbino, and was elected pope when comparatively young, only fifty-one, on Nov. 23, 1700. Though he had not been formally the French candidate, he maintained close relations with France. His learning and his political acumen are indisputable; but his foreign policy was unlucky. At the beginning of his reign, his protest against the assumption of the kingly title by Frederick I. of Prussia showed the traditional incapacity of the Curia to understand the circumstances of Protestant countries. In the war of the Spanish Succession, while maintaining an appearance of neutrality, he secretly favored the Bourbon side. As this came more and more to light, his relations with the emperor were increasingly strained—so far that he even threatened him with excommunication. The entry of imperial troops into the Papal States compelled him to make peace with Joseph I. (Jan. 15, 1709), acknowledging Charles III. as king of Spain and promising to invest him with the crown of Naples. This embittered Louis XIV. and Philip of Anjou against him. Another trouble was the conflict over ecclesiastical jurisdiction in Naples, which lasted even beyond the peace of Utrecht. In the controversy between the Dominicans and the Jesuits over the advisability of allowing the Chinese converts to retain certain pagan customs, he decided in favor of the former; the Jesuits apparently submitted, but the conflict continued. In the Jansenist controversy, on the other hand, he strongly supported the Jesuits (see JANSEN, CORNELIUS, JANSENISM; QUESNEL). He achieved considerable results as a reformer of the internal administration of his states and of the Roman clergy, supported learning and art, and was a liberal benefactor of the poor. In 1713 he issued the famous bull *Unigenitus* against Jansenism. He died March 19, 1721.

(A. HAUCK.)

BIBLIOGRAPHY: *Epistolæ et brevia selecta*, 2 vols., Rome, 1724; *Bullarium Romanum*, vol. xxi., Turin, 1871; Ranke, *Popes*, ii. 428 sqq., iii. 463–466, 471–473; Bower, *Popes*, iii. 335–338. The bull *Unigenitus* is given in Reich, *Documents*, pp. 386–389.

Clement XII. (Lorenzo Corsini): Pope 1730–40. He was born April 7, 1652, and rose in life as a protégé of the Albani family, taking Clement XI. for his model as pope, though without his gifts. He did not attempt to mingle in the wider politics of Europe, but made unsuccessful attempts to assert ancient feudal claims to Parma and Piacenza (1731) and to incorporate with the Papal States the small but ancient republic of San Marino (1739). The power of the Church was limited by Charles III. and his minister Tanucci in Naples, and by Philip V. in Spain; and in France the literary and scientific opposition to the papacy grew more pronounced. His services to foreign missions were considerable, and his domestic policy creditably followed that of Clement XI. He died Feb. 6, 1740. (A. HAUCK.)

BIBLIOGRAPHY: *Bullarium Romanum*, vols. xxiii., xxiv., Turin; Pastor, *Popes*, i. 360; Ranke, *Popes*, ii. 431; Bower, *Popes*, iii. 340.

Clement XIII. (Carlo Rezzonico): Pope 1758–69. He was born in Venice March 7, 1693, made cardinal in 1757, and on July 6 of the next year elected pope. It is impossible to decide whether he was a convinced friend of the Jesuits or simply their tool, either directly or indirectly through the influence of Cardinal Torreggiani. Though the order had been suppressed in Portugal, France, Spain, Naples, and Sicily, he solemnly confirmed and approved it by the bull *Apostolicum pascendi munus* (Jan. 7, 1765), and in that beginning *Animarum saluti* declared under an interdict the countries which had expelled the Jesuits, allowing them alone to say mass and administer the sacraments there during it. The bull called out vehement opposition, and the popular outburst in favor of the society on which he had counted did not occur. Some of the cardinals implored him to moderate his support of it, but without effect. As a blow at the Bourbon courts, he took notice of some reforming measures adopted by the duke of Parma, an unimportant member of the family. A sharp and threatening brief (*Aliud ad apostolatus*, Jan. 30, 1768) was addressed to him; it rebuked him as a contumacious vassal, pronounced null and void the measures which limited ecclesiastical freedom, and menaced him with excommunication. The duke, inspired by his grandfather Louis XV., replied by arresting and then expelling all the Jesuits in his dominions. The Bourbon kings all protested against the brief and the use which it made of the bull *In cœna Domini*, and insisted on its withdrawal and the suppression of the Society of Jesus. Clement was stubborn, and the sovereigns proceeded to use force, Louis XV. occupying Avignon and the Comtat Venaissin, and the king of Sicily taking possession of Benevento and Ponte Corvo and preparing to go farther. Clement had called a secret consistory for Feb. 3, 1769, to discuss the situation; but in the preceding night he died of apoplexy, a natural result of such heavy cares in a man of his age. (A. HAUCK.)

BIBLIOGRAPHY: A. von Reumont, *Geschichte der Stadt Rom*, III. ii. 658, Berlin, 1870; Ranke, *Popes*, ii. 443–448; Bower, *Popes*, iii. 347–359.

Clement XIV. (Lorenzo Ganganelli): Pope 1769–1774. He was the son of a physician, b. at Arcangelo, in the Papal States, Oct. 31, 1705; he entered the Franciscan Order, became a consultor of the Inquisition, and was made cardinal in 1759. He had been an advocate of reconciliation with the Bourbon courts, and it has been often asserted that he promised before his election to suppress the Jesuits. He was chosen only after a three months' conclave, marked by incessant intrigue. He disappointed those who looked for a speedy decision of the burning question by adopting a cautious and temporizing policy. He gave the Jesuits new privileges, and declared to Louis XV. that he could neither censure nor suppress an institute confirmed by nineteen of his predecessors; but, on the other hand, he refused to see the general of the Order, and closed his eyes to the fact that laws which infringed on ecclesiastical prerogatives had been passed in Portugal, Naples, Venice, the electoral provinces of Bavaria and Mainz, and even in the Empire under Maria Theresa. The brief directed against Parma was recalled, and the bull *In cœna Domini* (q.v.) no longer solemnly read. Conciliation, in fact, was offered to all the estranged powers: an understanding was reached with Portugal; and the nunciature at Lisbon was reestablished. But the ambassadors of France, Spain, and Naples insisted pertinaciously on the suppression of the Jesuits. France and Naples held ecclesiastical territory, as it were a pledge for the granting of their demands; there was talk in all three kingdoms of a formal renunciation of papal authority and the establishment of an independent patriarch. The pope now resolved to suppress the Order. It was important, however, that the step would content the Roman Catholic powers, and not rather give the signal for fresh attacks. Clement seems to have first assured himself cautiously of this. The devout Maria Theresa was so attached to the Order that he had to use his authority to detach her from it. Then he took the first definite steps, as sovereign of the Papal States; on Oct. 17, 1772, the Jesuits were removed from the Collegio Romano and the Roman seminary on a pretext, and then their houses in the Papal States were closed, generally after a visitation. The support previously given to the exiled Portuguese Jesuits was withdrawn. Finally, on July 21, 1773, Clement signed the brief *Dominus ac Redemptor noster*, entirely suppressing the Order. It was signed only after it had been submitted to the Catholic powers, and not published until Aug. 16. In this document he gave as the ground for his action that the Order was no longer bringing forth the rich fruits for which it was designed, and cited other instances of the suppression of regular orders. He explained his long hesitation as due to the need of diligent investigation and mature deliberation. Not a word implied the abandonment of any claim made by the Church or its head; his censures of the Order were not based on the popular charges. The decree was at once put into execution in Rome. Several of the fathers who were proved to have concealed or misappropriated money, property, or documents belonging to the Order were imprisoned, and Ricci, the general, was put under strict surveillance. The news gave great satisfaction in many quarters; France and Naples restored the papal territories in Apr., 1774. Only in the non-papal countries of Prussia and Russia were the Jesuits allowed openly to continue their ministrations. Much obscurity hangs over the close of Clement's life. The assertions that he repented of his action and declared it had been wrung from him by force, and that he was poisoned by the Jesuits, have been often made and as often denied. He died Sept. 22, 1774, leaving in the Museum Pio-Clementinum a monument to his uncontested devotion to art and learning, though the most diverse views have been and will always be held as to his general character.

(A. HAUCK.)

BIBLIOGRAPHY: *Lettere, bolle e discorsi di Ganganelli*, Florence, 1845; *Clementis XIV. epistolæ ac brevia*, ed. a Theiner, Paris, 1852. Consult: A. von Reumont, *Ganganelli, Papst Clement XIV.*, Berlin, 1847; J. Crétineau-Joly, *Clément XIV. et les Jésuites*, Paris, 1847; A. Theiner, *Geschichte des Pontificats Clemens' XIV.*, 2 vols., Paris, 1853; G. X. D. Ravignan, *Clément XIII. et Clément XIV.*, Paris, 1855; Bower, *Popes*, iii. 359–389; Ranke, *Popes*, ii. 449–451.

CLEMENT: A missionary bishop of the Celtic or old British Church in the Eastern parts of the Frankish domains who, like Adalbert (q.v.) in Neustria, stood in the way of the Romanizing innovations of Boniface in the first half of the eighth century (see BONIFACE, SAINT). We know of him only from the accounts of his opponents, who stigmatize him as a "heretic, misleader of the people, disseminator of error, servant of the devil, and false priest." He was married and had two sons. Justifying himself by the Mosaic law, he rejected the canonical prohibition of marriage with the widow of a deceased brother. He had views of his own on predestination and election, and seems to have held to some sort of universalism. He disputed the authority of the Fathers, Augustine and Jerome, and did not acknowledge the supremacy of the pope. At the instigation of Boniface a Frankish synod in 745 condemned him to imprisonment; a Roman synod added the anathema of the Church. Nevertheless Clement held fast to the opinions and practises of his fatherland. His ultimate fate is not known. A. WERNER.

BIBLIOGRAPHY: Rettberg, *KD*, i. 324–325; H. Hahn, *Jahrbücher des fränkischen Reichs*, pp. 67–82, Berlin, 1863; P. Jaffé, *Bibliotheca rerum Germanicarum*, iii. 133, 136–149, Berlin, 1866; J. H. A. Ebrard, *Die iroschottische Missionskirche*, Gütersloh, 1874; A. Werner, *Bonifatius*, pp. 113, 273, Leipsic, 1875; Hauck, *KD*, i. 511.

CLEMENT OF ALEXANDRIA.

Clement of Alexandria (Titus Flavius Clemens), one of the most distinguished teachers of the Church of Alexandria, was born about the middle of the second century, and died between 211 and 216. He was certainly not born in Egypt (*Strom.*, i. 1). The indication of Athens as his birthplace by Epiphanius is supported by the classical quality of his Greek. His parents seem to have been pagans, of the well-to-do class. The thoroughness of his education is attested by his constant quotation of the Greek poets and philosophers. In quest of the best instruction, he traveled in Greece, Italy, Palestine, and finally Egypt. He became the colleague of Pantænus, the head of the catechetical school of Alexandria, and finally succeeded him in the direction of the school. During the persecution of Septimius Severus (202 or 203) he sought refuge with Alexander, then bishop [possibly of Flaviada] in Cappadocia, afterward of Jerusalem, from whom he brought a letter to Antioch in 211.

1. His Life.

The trilogy into which Clement's principal remains are connected by their purpose and mode of treatment is composed of the *Protrepticus* ("*Exhortation*"), the *Pædagogus* ("*Instructor*"), and the *Stromata* ("*Miscellanies*"). Overbeck calls it the boldest literary undertaking in the history of the Church, since in it Clement for the first time attempted to set forth Christianity for the faithful in the traditional forms of profane literature. The *Protrepticus* forms an introduction inviting the reader to listen, not to the mythical legends of the heathen gods, but to the "new song" of the Logos, the beginning of all things and creator of the world. He demonstrates the folly of idolatry and the pagan mysteries, the horrors of pagan sacrifice, and shows that the Greek philosophers and poets only guessed at the truth, while the prophets set forth a direct way to salvation; and now the divine Logos speaks in his own person, to awaken all that is good in the soul of man and to lead it to immortality. Having thus laid a foundation in the knowledge of divine truth, he goes on in the *Pædagogus* to develop a Christian ethic. His design does not prevent him from taking a large part of his material from the Stoic Musonius, the master of Epictetus; but for Clement the real instructor is the incarnate Logos. The first book deals with the religious basis of Christian morality, the second and third with the individual cases of conduct. As with Epictetus, true virtue shows itself with him in its external evidences by a natural, simple, and moderate way of living. The *Stromata* goes further and aims at the perfection of the Christian life by initiation into complete knowledge. The first of these works is addressed to the unconverted, the second to the new Christian, and the third appeals to the mature believer. It attempts, on the basis of Scripture and tradition, to give such an account of the Christian faith as shall answer all the demands of learned men, and conduct the student into the innermost realities of his belief. Clement entitled this work *Strōmateis*, "patchwork," because it dealt with such a variety of matters. He intended to make but one book of this; at least seven grew out of it, without his having treated all the subjects proposed. The absence of certain things definitely promised has led scholars to ask whether he wrote an eighth book, as would appear from Eusebius (VI. xiii. 1) and the Florilegia, and various attempts have been made to identify with it short or fragmentary treatises appearing among his remains. In any case the "excerpts" and "selections" which, with part of a treatise on logical method, are designated as the eighth book in the single (11th century) manuscript of the *Stromata*, are not parts of the *Hypotyposes* which Clement is known to have written. This work was a brief commentary on selected passages covering the whole Bible, as is shown in the fragments preserved by Œcumenius and in the Latin version of the commentary on the Catholic Epistles made at the instance of Cassiodorus. Besides the great trilogy, the only complete work preserved is the treatise "Who is the Rich Man that Shall Be Saved?" based on Mark x. 17–31, and laying down the principle that not the possession of riches but their misuse is to be condemned. There are extant a few fragments of the treatise on the Passover, against the Quartodeciman position of Melito, and only a single passage from the "Ecclesiastical Canon" against the Judaizers. Several other works are only known by their titles.

2. His Literary Work.

The significance of Clement in the history of the development of doctrine is, according to Harnack, that he knew how to replace the apologetic method by the constructive or systematic, to turn the simple church tradition into a scientific dogmatic theology. It is a marked characteristic of his that he sees only superficial and transient disagreement where others find a fundamental opposition. He is able to reconcile, or even to fuse, differing views to an extent which makes it almost impossible to attribute to him a definite individual system. He is admittedly an eclectic (*Strom.*, i. 37). This attitude determines especially his treatment of non-Christian philosophy. Although the theory of a diabolical origin for it is not unknown to him, and although he shows exhaustively that the philosophers owe a large part of their knowledge to the writings of the Old Testament, yet he seems to express his own personal conviction when he describes philosophy as a direct operation of the divine Logos, working through it as well as through the law and his direct revelation in the Gospel to communicate the truth to men. It is

3. His Significance for the Church.

true that the knowledge of the philosophers was elementary, fragmentary, and incapable of imparting true righteousness; and it was far surpassed by the revelation given through the law and the prophets, as that again was still further surpassed by the direct revelation of the incarnate Logos; but this idea of relative inferiority does not prevent him from showing that his whole mental attitude is determined and dominated by the philosophical tradition. Thus he emphasizes the permanent importance of philosophy for the fulness of Christian knowledge, explains with special predilection the relation between knowledge and faith, and sharply criticizes those who are unwilling to make any use of philosophy. He pronounces definitely against the sophists and against the hedonism of the school of Epicurus.

4. His Eclecticism.

Although he generally expresses himself unfavorably in regard to the Stoic philosophy, he really pays marked deference to that mixture of Stoicism and Platonism which characterized the religious and ethical thought of the educated classes in his day. This explains the value set by Clement on gnosis. To be sure, he constantly opposes the heretical gnosis. Faith is the foundation of all gnosis, and both are given by Christ. As faith involves a comprehensive knowledge of the essentials, knowledge allows the believer to penetrate deeply into the understanding of what he believes; and this is the making perfect, the completion, of faith. In order to attain this kind of faith, the "faith of knowledge," which is so much higher than the mere "faith of conjecture," or simple reception of a truth on authority, philosophy is permanently necessary. In fact, Christianity is the true philosophy, and the perfect Christian the true Gnostic—but again only the "Gnostic according to the canon of the Church" has this distinction. Also, he rejects the Gnostic distinction of "psychic" and "pneumatic" men; all are alike destined to perfection if they will embrace it.

From philosophy he takes his conception of the Logos, the principle of Christian gnosis, through whom alone God's relation to the world and his revelation is maintained. God he considers transcendentally as unqualified Being, who can not be defined in too abstract a way.

5. His Dependence Upon Philosophy.

Though his goodness operated in the creation of the world, yet immutability, self-sufficiency, incapability of suffering are the characteristic notes of the divine essence. Though the Logos is most closely one with the Father, whose powers he resumes in himself, yet to Clement both the Son and the Spirit are "first-born powers and first created"; they form the highest stages in the scale of intelligent beings, and Clement distinguishes the Son-Logos from the Logos who is immutably immanent in God, and thus gives a foundation to the charge of Photius that he "degraded the Son to the rank of a creature." Separate from the world as the principle of creation, he is yet in it as its guiding principle. Thus a natural life is a life according to the will of the Logos. The Incarnation, in spite of Clement's rejection of the Gnostic Docetism, has with him a decidedly Docetic character. The body of Christ was not subject to human needs. He is the good Physician; the medicine which he offers is the communication of saving gnosis, leading men from heathenism to faith and from faith to the higher state of knowledge. This true philosophy includes within itself the freedom from sin and the attainment of virtue. As all sin has its root in ignorance, so the knowledge of God and of goodness is followed by well-doing. Against the Gnostics Clement emphasizes the freedom of all to do good.

Clement lays great stress on the fulfilment of moral obligations. In his ethical expressions he is influenced strongly by Plato and the Stoics, from whom he borrows much of his terminology. He praises Plato for setting forth the greatest possible likeness to God as the aim of life;

6. His Relation to Ethics.

and his portrait of the perfect Gnostic closely resembles that of the wise man as drawn by the Stoics. Hence he counsels his readers to shake off the chains of the flesh as far as possible, to live already as if out of the body, and thus to rise above earthly things. He is a true Greek in the value which he sets on moderation; but his highest ideal of conduct remains the mortification of all affections which may in any way disturb the soul in its career. As Harnack says, the lofty ethical-religious ideal of the attainment of man's perfection in union with God, which Greek philosophy from Plato down had worked out, and to which it had subordinated all scientific worldly knowledge, is taken over by Clement, deepened in meaning, and connected not only with Christ, but with ecclesiastical tradition.

The way, however, to this union with God is for Clement only the Church's way. The communication of the gnosis is bound up with holy orders, which give the divine light and life. The simple faith of the baptized Christian contains all the essentials of the highest knowledge; by the Eucharist the believer is united with the Logos and the Spirit, and made partaker of incorruptibility. Though he lays down at starting a purely spiritual conception of the Church, later the exigencies of his controversy with the Gnostics make him lay more stress on the visible church.

7. And to Scripture and the Church.

As to his use of Scripture, the extraordinary breadth of his reading and manifold variety of his quotations from the most diverse authors make it very difficult to determine exactly what was received as canonical by the Alexandrian Church of that period. Though he uses the Apocryphal Gospels, our four alone have supreme authority for him. For the other New Testament writings he seems not to have had as definite a line of demarcation; but whatever he recognized as of apostolic origin had for him an authority distinct from, and higher than, that of all other ecclesiastical tradition. (N. Bonwetsch.)

Bibliography: The best text of Clement is in course of publication by O. Stählin, to be in 3 vols., vols. i.–ii., Leipsic, 1905–06; that by J. Potter, 2 vols., Oxford, 1715, is reproduced in *MPG*, viii.–ix. T. Zahn has given a *Supplementum Clementinum* in his *Forschungen*, iii. 1–176, 319–321, Erlangen, 1884. The best Eng. transl. is in *ANF*,

ii. 171–604. An exhaustive bibliography to 1886 is in *ANF*, Bibliography, pp. 38–42; a list of later works is given in Harnack, *Litteratur*, ii. 1, pp. 4–5. On the criticism of the text consult: C. C. J. Bunsen, *Analecta Ante-Nicæna*, i. 157–340, London, 1854; T. B. Mayor, in *Classical Review*, ix (1894), 385–391; O. Stählin, *Beiträge zur Kenntniss der MSS. des Clemens Alex.*, Nuremberg, 1895; W. Christ, *Philologische Studien zu Clemens Alexandrinus*, Munich, 1900.

General discussions are: C. E. Freppel, *Clément d'Alexandrie*, Paris, 1873; B. F. Westcott, *General Hist. of N. T. Canon*, pp. 339–340, 350–354, London, 1875; C. Bigg, *Christian Platonists of Alexandria*, pp. 36–114, Oxford, 1886; Krüger, *History*, pp. 162–173; Schaff, *Christian Church*, ii. 781–785 et passim; Harnack, *Litteratur*, i. 296–327, 836–841, ii. 1, pp. 1 sqq.; O. Stählin, *TU*, new series, vol. v., 1901; *DCB*, i. 559–567; *KL*, iii. 508–517; O. Bardenhewer, *Geschichte der altkirchlichen Litteratur*, vol. ii., Freiburg, 1903.

On the teaching of Clement consult: F. J. Winter, *Die Ethik des Clement von Alexandrien*, Leipsic, 1882; J. H. Müller, *Idées dogmatiques de Clément d'Alexandrie*, Strasburg, 1861; J. Kaye, *Some Account of the Writings and Opinions of Clement of Alexandria*, London, 1835; J. Cognat, *Clément d'Alexandrie, sa doctrine et sa polémique*, Paris, 1859; W. Scherer, *Klemens von Alexandrien und seine Erkenntnissprinzipien*, Munich, 1907.

On his relation to earlier teaching consult: C. Merk, *Clemens Alex. in seiner Abhängigkeit von der griechischen Philosophie*, Leipsic, 1879; E. Hiller, in *Hermes*, xxi (1886), 126–133; E. Kutter, *Clemens Alex. und das N. T.*, Giessen, 1897; E. de Faye, *Clément d'Alexandrie*, Paris, 1898.

On Clement as a hymnist consult Julian, *Hymnology*.

CLEMENT OF ROME.

Discordant Traditions (§ 1).
Relationship to the Flavians (§ 2).
The First Epistle (§ 3).
Questions Unsettled (§ 4).
Second Epistle and Other Writings (§ 5).

1. Discordant Traditions.

According to tradition Clement was an early bishop of Rome and a distinguished Christian author. But of the writings attributed to him most are certainly not his and not one is undisputed, and the facts of his life are no better authenticated. He is mentioned in all the lists of the early bishops of Rome, though there is no agreement about the place of his name. Irenæus (*Hær.*, III. iii. 3), representing the Roman tradition of c. 180, gives Peter, Linus, Anencletus, Clement; with this agree Eusebius (*Hist eccl.* and *Chron.*), Epiphanius (*Hær.*, xxvii. 6), and Jerome (*De vir. ill.*, xv.), though the last-named is aware that some of the Latins give a different order, and he, as well as Epiphanius, gives the form Cletus for Anencletus. A different order occurs first in the "Chronicle" of Hippolytus, where Clement takes third place, before Cletus; this order recurs in the *Catalogus Liberianus*, and is accepted by Augustine, Optatus, and others. In the Apostolic Constitutions also (vii. 46), Clement immediately follows Linus, the variant name now giving two distinct persons, Cletus and Anencletus. The catalogue of the time of Sylvester reverts to the older order, while the *Liber Felicianus*, fusing this and the Liberian, gives Peter, Linus, Cletus, Clement, Anencletus. According to the epistle to James attributed to Clement (preceding the Clementine Homilies), Peter designated Clement as his successor, and himself installed him. This view probably originated with the purpose of bringing Clement into closer relation with Peter; and the lists which put Clement third, between Linus and Cletus or Anencletus, are very likely attempting a compromise between it and the other tradition. It is safe to say that Clement does not belong to the epoch immediately following the apostles, but that two men came between him and Peter. He was not bishop of Rome in the strict sense, as the first epistle shows that there was no bishop there in his time. The developed episcopal idea of a later age was carried back in the attempt to trace the succession to the apostles; and the earliest authorities justify no more than the assertion that he was one of the leading presbyters, or perhaps the first of them.

Irenæus (ut sup.) makes Clement a disciple of the apostles. Origen (on John i. 29), Eusebius, Epiphanius, and Jerome identify him with the Clement mentioned by Paul in Phil. iv. 3, and Chrysostom (on I Tim.) even makes him a companion of Paul on all his journeys; while the Jewish-Christian Clementina place him in the closest relations to Peter. Various attempts were made to combine these conflicting views. The Apostolic Constitutions regard Linus as appointed by Paul, Clement by Peter. Rufinus regards Linus and Cletus as having performed episcopal functions in Peter's lifetime, and Clement as appointed by the apostle when both were dead. Epiphanius explains that Clement was appointed by Peter indeed, but laid down his office for a time, during which Linus and Cletus held it. Modern scholars have usually doubted his being a disciple of the apostles, even when they admit his authorship of the first epistle to the Corinthians. The identification with the Clement of Phil. iv. 3 is abandoned by most of these scholars.

2. Relationship to the Flavians.

Another mooted question concerns the assertion of the Homilies and Recognitions that Clement was a connection of the imperial house. It is in any case necessary to substitute Domitian for Tiberius, whom the Clementina name in order to secure greater antiquity. Assuming that not only the Flavia Domitilla mentioned by Eusebius, but also the consul Flavius Clemens whom Domitian put to death, belonged to the Christian community, we should have two prominent Christians of the name of Clement in Rome at the same time. The pseudo-Clementine literature identified them as one person. Von Gebhardt and Harnack leave the question undecided, while Lightfoot is inclined to regard them as two persons. Really nothing is known of Clement's life except what the first epistle tells us. It is even uncertain whether he was of Jewish or pagan descent, though both views have found convinced advocates.

Among the numerous writings which bear the name of Clement, decidedly the most important are the two epistles to the Corinthians. Until 1875 only one manuscript of these was known, an imperfect copy forming part of the famous *Codex Alexandrinus*, from which Junius published them with a Latin translation (Oxford, 1633); new editions were made from the manuscript by Wotton (Cambridge, 1718), Jacobson (Oxford, 1834), Tischendorf (Leipsic, 1863, 1873), Lightfoot (London, 1869), and Von Gebhardt and Harnack (Leipsic, 1875), besides facsimile reproductions in 1856 and 1879. In 1875, however, appeared the first complete edition, based upon a new manuscript discovered in Constantinople. Von Gebhardt still considered the Alexandrine manuscript the more authoritative, and there are reasons for holding this view, even since further light has been thrown on the question by the discovery of a Syriac and a Latin version, the latter only of the first epistle.

This first epistle is an official communication from the Church of Rome to that of Corinth, which was then divided by controversies apparently relating to the position and authority of the presbyters. In order to put an end to the strife, the Roman Church intervenes, apparently unsolicited, and sends a deputation to Corinth, "to be witnesses between you and us." The official character of the letter comes out more clearly now that it exists complete, and new light is thrown on the relation of the Roman Church to the others.

3. The First Epistle.

It is true there is no question of a constitutionally established primacy, but the Roman Church, as the most mature and firmly settled, keeps a watchful eye on the concerns of the others. The Clementine authorship is attested by Dionysius, bishop of Corinth (cf. Eusebius, *Hist. eccl.*, iv. 23), Irenæus (*Hær.*, III. iii. 3), Clement of Alexandria, and Origen. In the East the letter was read in public worship as Scripture. Attempts made by Calovius (1673) and others to deny its authenticity were revived with Semler, Ammon, and later with Baur and Schwegler; but the arguments of such critics have not been found decisive. The majority of scholars now hold that it was written in the first century, though many of them leave the question of authorship unanswered. Doubts have been expressed in recent years about the prayer in chap. 59, but Lightfoot and others have rendered improbable the theory of a later addition; the question is still unsettled whether this prayer is an official formula of the Roman Church or the composition of Clement.

The attempt to determine the date of the epistle depends, first, on the question whether the persecution at Rome mentioned at the outset was that under Nero or that under Domitian. The earlier critics preferred the former, which gives 64–68 as the date. Scarcely any modern scholars, except Hefele and Wieseler, adhere to this view. On the other hand, sufficient reasons forbid placing the date as late as the second century. According to xliv. 3 there are still some presbyters in office who were instituted by the apostles, and similarly v. 3 seems to assert that members of the Church contemporary with Peter and Paul are living; there is no trace of Gnostic heresies; the

4. Questions Unsettled.

constitution of the Church, in both Rome and Corinth, is not the episcopal, but the presbyterial. Most authorities, accordingly date the epistle between 93 and 97; Lightfoot would come down as far as the reign of Nerva, and Harnack's latest opinion is in favor of the end of Domitian's (93–95), which is supported by Hegesippus (in Eusebius, *Hist. eccl.*, iii. 16). Diverse views, again, have been held as to the doctrinal standpoint of the epistle. Schwegler, followed by Reusch, considered it a compromise between Jewish Christianity and Paulinism. Lemme's view that the author was a fanatical Jewish Christian is disproved by the way in which he speaks of Paul and uses the Pauline epistles and Hebrews. However, Paul's propositions appear here as little more than mere formulas. His great doctrine of justification through faith is indeed strongly expressed (xxxii. 4); but the obligation of doing good works is derived only from the will and example of God, without the mention of any relation between justifying faith and moral power.

The second epistle, completely known only since 1875, is regarded by most scholars as a homily, rather than a letter. The question remains in what church and by whom it was delivered. Harnack's theory that it is of Roman origin, perhaps written by another Clement, the one mentioned by Hermas in his *Shepherd*, is scarcely tenable. Lightfoot thinks it originated in Corinth, which is likely. Its date is shown to be in the second century by its attitude toward the New Testament canon and toward Gnosticism. Be-

5. Second Epistle and Other Writings.

tween 130 and 140 is the most probable time. Its teaching contains some peculiar points, which can not be pressed to show that the author belonged to a separate sect, but mean only that he lived in a time of little exact dogmatic formulation. Of the numerous other writings which have borne the name of Clement, it may safely be said that the Homilies and Recognitions, in the various forms comprised under the name *Clementina* (q.v.), are not by him; nor are the Apostolic Constitutions (q.v.). The two "Letters to the Virgins" are worth notice. They exist only in a Syriac version in a codex belonging to the Remonstrant seminary at Amsterdam, and were first printed by Wetstein in 1752, then more carefully by Beelen (Loewen, 1856, with a Latin rendering, which Funk improved and appended to his *Opera patrum apostolicorum*, vol. i., Tubingen, 1887). The theories of their origin range between two impossible extremes—one medieval, that of Cotterill; the other Clementine, that of Villecourt (who edited the epistles for *MPG*) and Beelen (ut sup.). The form they presuppose for ecclesiastical customs and ascetic practise belongs to a later time, possibly that of Cyprian—but not too much later, since they were probably known by Epiphanius (*Hær.*, xxx. 12), and certainly by Jerome (*Ad Jovin.*, i. 12). They must have been originally one book, and were perhaps divided into two (as Harnack suggests) to take the place of the two epistles of Clement, which were contained in the older Syria manuscripts of the New Testament. This would account for their ascription to Clement, as nothing else does.

(G. Uhlhorn†.)

Bibliography: The best text and discussion is in J. B. Lightfoot, *The Apostolic Fathers*, part i., *S. Clement of Rome, a Revised Text with Introductions*, 2 vols., London, 1890; text alone in idem, *The Apostolic Fathers* . . . , ed. J. R. Harmer, ib. 1891. Translation is in *ANF*, ix. 229-

256, and in *Christian Classic Series*, vol. vii., London, 1892. Next to Lightfoot's the best discussion is R. A. Lipsius, *De Clementis Romani epistola*, Leipsic, 1855; idem, *Chronologie der römischen Bischöfe*, Kiel, 1869. Consult further: M. J. Wocher, *Die Briefe des . . . Clemens und Polycarpus*, Tübingen, 1830; C. J. von Hefele, *Patrum apostolicorum opera*, ib. 1842; E. W. E. Reuss, *Histoire de la théologie chrétienne*, ii. 609 sqq., Paris, 1852; A. R. M. Dressel, *Patrum apostolicorum opera*, Leipsic, 1857; J. Donaldson, *History of Christian Literature*, i. 90-153, London, 1864-66; idem, *Apostolic Fathers*, pp. 113-190, ib. 1874; F. C. Baur, *Lehrbuch der Dogmengeschichte*, i. 155, 249 et passim, Leipsic, 1865; T. Zahn, *Hirt des Hermas*, Gotha, 1868; A. Hilgenfeld, *Die apostolischen Väter*, Halle, 1853; idem, *Clementis Romani epistolæ*, Leipsic, 1876; J. M. Cotterill, *Peregrinus Proteus*, Edinburgh, 1879; idem, *Modern Criticism and Clement's Epistles to Virgins*, ib. 1884; F. X. Funk, in *TQ*, 1879, pp. 539 sqq.; idem, *Opera patrum apostolicorum*, vol. ii., Tübingen, 1881; S. Maistre, *Clément de Rome, son histoire*, 2 vols., Paris, 1883-84; C. H. Hoole, *Apostolic Fathers . . . transl. into English, with introductory Notes*, London, 1885; Harnack, in *TU*, v (1886), 82-84; idem, *Litteratur*, i. 780 et passim, II. i. 251 sqq., 442, 438 sqq., II. ii. 298, 304 sqq.; E. Burton, *Apostolic Fathers*, part i., *Epistles of Clement, with Introduction*, London, 1888; W. Wrede, *Untersuchungen zum ersten Clemensbriefe*, Göttingen, 1891; C. T. Cruttwell, *Literary History of Early Christianity*, 2 vols., London, 1893; Krüger, *History*, pp. 21-25, 62-63; Schaff, *Christian Church*, ii. 636-651; *DCB*, i. 554-559; *KL*, iii. 449-458.

CLEMENTINA.

The "Clementina" discussed in this article are a very remarkable and still in many points mysterious group of early Christian writings, closely related in their contents and evidently coming from a single source, of which three are still extant—the Clementine Homilies, Recognitions, and Epitome. For the collection of decretals made by Pope Clement V. and intended by him to form a seventh book in the great collection, also known as "Clementina," see CANON LAW, II., 6, § 3.

Turrianus was the first, in his *Pro canonibus apostolorum* (1573), to give information about the Homilies, using a manuscript which has apparently disappeared. They were published in 1672 by Cotelerius from a manuscript in the library of Paris, which, however, stopped with the nineteenth homily, and offered a very corrupt text. The first complete editon was that of Dressel (1853), from a newly discovered manuscript in the Ottobonian library at Rome. Lagarde made the first attempt to give a critically accurate text in 1865. The book consists of two letters to the apostle James and twenty "homilies" also addressed to him. The first letter purports to be from Peter, asking James to keep secret the special doctrines he has transmitted to him. The second is supposed to be from Clement, announcing that Peter has appointed him his successor in Rome, and charged him to send James an account of their long association. Clement, having sought truth in vain in the philosophical schools, hearing something of Jesus, decides to go to Judea for an answer to his questions. In Alexandria he meets Barnabas, who conducts him to Peter at Cæsarea Stratonis. Peter instructs him in Christianity, and invites him to be present at the disputation with Simon Magus which is soon to take place. It lasts three days. At the end Simon, defeated, takes flight; Peter remains a while, founds a local church, and sets apart Zacchæus as its bishop. Before himself following Simon, he sends Clement, with Niceta and Aquila, to bring back news of him. They do not find him in Tyre, but meet some of his friends, with one of whom, Appion the Alexandrian grammarian, Clement disputes till Peter arrives. Together they continue their journey, Peter preaching to the heathen and founding churches. On the way Clement narrates his own life—how his parents and two brothers have mysteriously disappeared long before. Niceta and Aquila turn out to be his brothers. Discourses and dialogues are interspersed with these events. Simon arrives here, and the principal disputation follows, lasting four days, on divine revelations in visions, on the most high God, and on evil. Simon is defeated and retires, but presently, by his magic arts, changes the appearance of Clement's brother Faustus into his own likeness. In this form Peter sends him to Antioch, where the real Simon has many adherents, to make a recantation of all his teaching. Peter having organized a church in Laodicea, departs for Antioch.

1. The Homilies.

This romantic narrative, however, is only a framework for doctrinal development. The doctrine has two sides, a metaphysical and an ethical, which allows irreconcilable views to be stated side by side. The aim of human life is the attainment of the highest good, only possible through a true knowledge of God and of all things, which sin prevents man from gaining without revelation. God revealed himself first in creation, and then, this being obscured by sin, through the "true Prophet." He is to be recognized through prophecy, and, once known, must be followed implicitly. He has appeared not in one single person, but under divers forms and names. Eight persons have had a special relation to this revelation—Adam, Enoch, Noah, Abraham, Isaac, Jacob, Moses, and Christ; Adam, Moses, and Christ stand above the others, Christ being the highest. The primeval revelation in Adam, the Mosaic teaching, and Christianity are essentially identical. Christianity is purified Mosaism, with the addition, however, of preaching to the heathen and baptism. The death of Christ does not mean salvation to the author, and he is silent on the Resurrection. The fundamental doctrine of the one God, the Creator, develops in two different directions—one decidedly pantheistic, and another which leads not less strongly, by an ethical road, to a totally opposite view of the universe. Here God is still one, but personal, and described in the most anthropomorphic terms. Man, made in his image, is free, and hence comes sin. The devil is always seducing men, and the "true Prophet" teaching them again how to serve God. If evil comes out of freedom, there can be only one end to it, eternal punishment. The author has evidently tried to reconcile these two conflicting tendencies, especially in his teaching on evil. All property is sin; the eating of flesh is

2. Doctrinal Teachings.

forbidden; marriage, though considered a defilement, is allowed, and even praised; frequent ablutions are recommended or commanded. The episcopate appears as a living institution; the bishop sums up in himself, as the representative of Christ, the local church, and James, the bishop of Jerusalem, the whole Church.

The Recognitions are extant only in the translation of Rufinus. The name is taken from the technical language of the drama, and refers to the reuniting of Clement's family. The Latin version exists in numerous manuscripts, without as yet an adequate modern edition. The arrangement of the material corresponds on the whole to that of the main body of the Homilies. Barnabas, however, comes to Rome instead of Clement to Alexandria. A report is given of all three days of the first disputation with Simon, varying considerably from that in the Homilies. Instead of the second disputation with Simon, there is a three days' discussion on fate between Peter, Clement, and his father and brothers. The end is much the same, but it goes further to narrate the foundation of a church in Antioch and the baptism of Clement's father. In doctrine it shows fewer peculiarities than do the Homilies and it gives the impression of a revision to suit a certain class of readers.

3. The Recognitions.

The Epitome, first published by Turnebus (Paris, 1555), then by Cotelerius in his *Patres Apostolici*, is an extract from the Homilies, with the addition of a portion of Clement's letter to James, another from the account of his martyrdom by Simeon Metaphrastes, and a conclusion from the narrative of a miracle performed by him which is attributed to Ephraim, bishop of Cherson. Dressel published an edition based on a new collation of manuscripts (Leipsic, 1859), with a variant copy which differs from the first only by taking in more of the Homilies. These extracts have no important bearing on the main questions at issue. Great hopes were based on the appearance of Lagarde's edition of a Syriac version (1861), but this throws no new light on the origin and history of the group. The narrative matter continued to interest long after the original significance of the books was forgotten. It was taken into the body of medieval legend, and has been thought to have influenced the development of the Faust-story.

4. The Epitome.

The scientific discussion of the whole question really began with Neander, who in the appendix to his *Genetische Entwicklung der gnostischen Systeme* (1818) gave an exposition of the doctrinal content, and Baur, who drew a good deal of evidence for his conception of the primitive Church from the Homilies. He considered the book, originating in the Roman Church, to be an evidence of the prevalence of Judaism there, and the ecclesiastical constitution shown in it to be the basis of the Catholic system. In opposition to him appeared the thorough work of Schliemann. He was the first to argue the priority of the Homilies and the dependence of the Recognitions. Schwegler accepted this view, and considered the Homilies to show the turning-point from Ebionitism to fusion, while the Recognitions marked the conclusion of this process, the stage of neutrality and peace.

5. Discussion of the Clementine Problem.

Up to this point the literary question of the relation of the two books and their origin from older writings had been neglected. Hilgenfeld's epoch-making work took this up. He saw the original in the Recognitions and a recasting in the Homilies. On the basis of minute investigation, he evolved the theory of an earlier "Preaching of Peter," written at Rome not long before the destruction of Jerusalem, in the interest of Jewish Christianity. On the indications of polemical attitude, he traced a series of recastings; he thought it likely that the opponent of Peter in the original work was not Simon Magus but Paul, then becoming successively the representative of Basilidian, Valentinian, and Marcionite Gnosticism, the last in the Homilies, which he believed to have been recast from the Recognitions at Rome under Anicetus (151–161). Against Hilgenfeld, Uhlhorn undertook to defend the priority of the Homilies once more, contending that a fragment of the nucleus was to be found not, as Hilgenfeld had thought, in Recogn. i. 27–72, but in Hom. xvi.–xxix., and that the birthplace of the whole group was neither Rome nor Asia Minor, but eastern Syria. This he considered to be proven by the composite nature of the doctrinal system, most closely related to that of the Elkesaites, though influenced by Hellenic culture and showing distinct Stoic elements. His theory was that the original work was composed there about 150, and the Homilies adapted from it about 170, with a view to a propaganda in the pagan world, especially at Rome. For this purpose Clement was introduced and Roman local color added. The Recognitions would then be a further adaptation made in Rome not long after 170, more acceptable because of its nearer approach to orthodox Christianity.

6. Relation of the Recognitions to the Homilies.

The next important contribution to the discussion was Lehmann's, who took a middle course between Hilgenfeld's and Uhlhorn's, separating the Recognitions into two parts of different authorship (i.–iii. and iv.–x.), of which the first is earlier and the second later than the Homilies. This treatment was carried further by Lipsius, who found the nucleus in a hypothetical *Acta Petri* of strongly anti-Pauline tendency written some time before 150; traces of this work are found in the extant *Acta Petri et Pauli* (in Tischendorf, *Acta apostolorum apocrypha*, Leipsic, 1851), but revised in an orthodox sense. A fragment of this was worked up in an anti-Gnostic sense about 140–145, the result again expanded by the addition of the Clement romance, and further adapted into an early form of the Recognitions, of which two later forms exist, one strongly anti-Marcionite in the Homilies, the other in the present Recognitions, in which the dogmatic interest is subordinated to the ethical, and the specifically Ebionite matter is eliminated. Langen took quite a different view, presupposing a "Preaching of Peter" composed in Rome after 135, with the purpose of claiming for Rome the primacy of

Jewish Christendom lost by Jerusalem. This was revised at Cæsarea shortly before 200 in a strongly Jewish-Christian sense, to support the claim of Cæsarea to the primacy, and gave us the Homilies, while the Recognitions are a fresh version made in favor of Antioch early in the third century.

None of these views has obtained universal acceptance. It is impossible to assert the absolute priority of either the Homilies or the Recognitions, or to regard one as a working-over of the other. Opinions as to date of composition differ more widely than ever. Where there used to be practical unanimity in referring the works to the second century, 170 or 180 at latest, Harnack has said that they can not go further back than the first half of the third. The importance of the Clementina for early church history, asserted by Baur and Schwegler, is now abandoned. (G. UHLHORN†.)

BIBLIOGRAPHY: A bibliography to 1886 is in *ANF*, Bibliography, pp. 92–95; cf. Krüger, *History*, p. 371, and Harnack, *Litteratur*, ii. 2, pp. 518–519. Eng. transl. is in *ANF*, viii. 77–211, 215–346. Consult: Krüger, *History*, pp. 371–377; A. Neander, *Die pseudoclementinischen Homilien*, Berlin, 1818; F. C. A. Schwegler, *Das nachapostolische Zeitalter*, i. 386–406, 481–490, Tübingen, 1846; A. Hilgenfeld, *Die clementinischen Recognitionen und Homilien*, Jena, 1848; J. Lehmann, *Die clementinischen Schriften*, Gotha, 1869; R. A. Lipsius, *Die Quellen der römischen Petrus-Sage*, Kiel, 1872; A. B. Lutterbeck, *Die Clementinen*, Giessen, 1872; [W. R. Cassels], *Supernatural Religion*, ii. 1–37, 336–354, London, 1879; Harnack, *Dogma*, i. 311 sqq.; idem, *Litteratur*, i. 144, 212–213, 322 sqq., ii., part 1, 701; C. Bigg, in *Studia Biblica*, ii. 157–193, Oxford, 1890; J. Langen, *Die Klemensromane*, Gotha, 1890; *DCB*, i. 567–578; Schaff, *Christian Church*, ii. 435–442.

CLERGY.

The clergy constitute the entire body of public servants or ministers in the Christian Church, duly set apart for their office by Consecration or Ordination (qq.v.); the remainder of the Christian community, in contradistinction to the clergy, constitute the Laity (q.v.).

I. The Name: The English word "clergy" (and the French *clergé, clergie*) is from ecclesiastical Latin (*clericus* = "clergyman, priest, clerk"; see CLERK) and is more remotely connected with the Greek *klēros*, "lot," which was applied to the clergy "either because they are the lot of the Lord, or else because the Lord himself is their lot and portion" (Jerome, *Epist.*, lii., *ANF*, vi. 91; cf. Acts i. 26; Num. xviii. 20; Deut. x. 9, xviii. 2, LXX.). Another term of ecclesiastical Latin is *spirituales*. Paul had designated as "spiritual" certain Christians in whom the spirit of Christ manifested itself with special power (I Cor. xiv. 37; Gal. vi. 1; cf. Irenæus on I Cor. ii. 6, *Hær.*, V. vi. 1; Theodoret on I Cor. ii. 15). The priest, according to Chrysostom ("On the Priesthood," iii. 4; *NPNF*, 1st ser., ix. 46), has a vocation instituted neither by "man, nor angel, nor archangel, nor any other created power, but the Paraclete himself." According to Peter Lombard (*Sent.*, iv., dist. 4), the office is a *munus spirituale*; all the seven grades of holy orders are *spirituales*; the *ordo* is "something sacred by which the power of the Spirit is imparted to the ordained." In consequence of this point of view the designation "*spirituales*" and its German equivalent "*Geistliche*" were transferred to the incumbents of the office.

II. The Doctrine of the Clerical Office: Christ promised and sent the Holy Spirit to his congregation here below, and instituted the sacraments. According to Roman Catholic and Anglican belief he also instituted a special status within his congregation, which in distinction from the rest of the congregation should be furnished with the prerogatives of the spiritual profession. Thus he called the Twelve, made them his companions and representatives, and in Matt. xviii. 18 he gives his disciples the assurance that whatever dispositions they shall adopt as his disciples, in his name, and for the continuation of his work shall be effectual as of divine, not human ordination. Protestant bodies other than the Anglican reject these claims. In the farewell addresses, John xiii.–xvii., the assembled disciples are considered in a twofold relation: on one side as the founders appointed by Jesus himself for his congregation, on another side as the congregation itself, left behind by Jesus on earth; but not as an ordained estate of administrators with a commission over the rest of the congregation. In John xx. 21–23 the risen Christ reveals to those present the transformation which his resurrection has effected in their relation to his person, and in their attitude toward the world; but what he says does not apply to them and their contingent successors in distinction from the rest of the congregation. In II Cor. iii. 3–10 Paul treats of the glory of the New Testament ministration, but not of its particular institution; in Eph. iv. 11 the emphasis rests on the "he" (Gk. *autos*): by him, the exalted Christ, are they all given who labor for the congregation, but the passage knows naught of a special act of institution by Jesus when living in the flesh. Again it is stated in Acts xx. 28–29 that the Holy Spirit has appointed the persons addressed as "overseers," but not that this was done by means of a special ecclesiastical act. In reality there confront us in the New Testament all kinds of designations with respect to such as were active in the instruction and administration of the congregations: "elders" (Gk. *presbyteroi*; Acts xv. 2, xx. 17; I Tim. v. 17; Titus i. 5; James v. 14); "those over you" (*proistamenoi*; I Thess. v. 12); "those which have the rule over you" (*hēgoumenoi*; Heb. xiii. 7); "overseers" or "bishops" (*episkopoi*; Acts xx. 28; Phil. i. 1; I Tim. iii. 2); "deacons" (*diakonoi*; Phil. i. 1; I Tim. iii. 8, 12); "pastors" (*poimenes*; Eph. iv. 11); "angels" (*anggeloi*; Rev. i. 20); "evangelists" and "teachers" (*euanggelistai, didaskaloi*; Eph. iv. 11). The most evident inference from any of these names is the special activity of those mentioned; there can be no question

1. Not Instituted by Christ as a Distinct Office.

of a hierarchy, or an organism continuing unchanged in its main features. And the most that can be said is that at that early period the New Testament congregations were not wanting in defined personalities, active in their charges; in this respect the Corinthian congregation constituted no exception.

2. But Necessary and Indispensable.

But the clerical profession is indispensable though it is not the immediate institution of Christ. For the means of grace by word and sacrament conferred by Jesus on the congregation must be administered; the powers which are present in the congregation through the Spirit of Christ must be organized and directed. To this end there is need of definite personalities who belong to the congregation and are no less dependent, as individuals, upon the means of grace and powers bestowed on the congregation than the congregation as a whole, but who still assume a position of leadership within the congregation; which leadership is authoritative for the congregation in so far as the holders of this office administer these gifts and powers in the name and according to the will of the Lord. To this extent there is a clerical or spiritual profession and a spiritual office, and there must be both of these so long as Christ's congregation lives on earth separated from its Lord by the confines of the visible, and associated with the unchristian world.

3. View of Roman and Greek Churches.

Historical evolution parted into two conceptions of the clerical office, of which one has found its expression in the Roman *sacerdotium*, the other in the Protestant *ministerium ecclesiasticum*. As early as the postapostolic age, the celebration of the Lord's Supper was accounted valid only when conducted or authorized by the bishop (Ignatius, *Ad Smyr.*, viii.). The right to baptize devolves principally on the bishop; on the presbyters and deacons "not without the authority of the bishop," Tertullian, *De bapt.*, xvii.; on the priest, *Apostolic Constitutions*, VI. xv. 1. The bishops and other priests have been entrusted by the apostles with the charge of doctrine (*Apostolic Constitutions*, VI. xviii. 5); they must be heard, for through them the Lord speaks (Augustine, *Serm.*, class ii. 20). In the celebration of the sacrament the priest accomplishes a sacrifice which far surpasses the act of Elijah on Carmel; the priest excels rulers, for his authority extends to heaven. From this doctrine developed the Roman theory of the priest's profession, a mediation between God and men (cf. the Roman catechism, part ii., chap. 7; see PRIEST). The view of the Greek Church of to-day is substantially the same. The consecration of priests is a sacrament wherein the Holy Spirit, through a bishop, ordains duly elected candidates to the office of administering the sacraments and feeding Christ's flock.

Luther rejected the theory that the clerical dignity depends upon any ecclesiastical consecration. "Were there not in us a higher consecration than the pope or bishop gives, there would nevermore a priest be made by pope or bishop's consecration; neither could he celebrate masses or preach or absolve" (*An den christlichen Adel*). But at the same time he was convinced of the necessity of a special profession.

4. The Lutheran Doctrine.

"The Church requires the word of God, baptism, the sacrament of the altar, the use of the keys, and, lastly, we know the Church outwardly by the fact that it consecrates or calls church ministers, or has offices to be administered. For one must have bishops, pastors, or preachers who shall publicly and expressly dispense, administer, and exercise the aforesaid four articles of salvation on account and in the name of the Church, and also—much rather, indeed—by reason of Christ's institution" (*Von den Conciliis und Kirchen*, part iii.). He holds that the clerical profession is not rendered unnecessary by the universal priesthood. "Although we are all priests, yet we can not, nor should we, all preach and teach and rule: one must then certainly, from the entire body, separate and elect some to whom such duties shall be committed; and he that wields the same is not a priest on account of the office (as all the others are), but a servant of all the others" (Exposition of Psalm cx.). To hold that the spiritual profession is instituted by God is not inconsistent with these views of Luther, since the work it must carry forward is instituted by God; hence the Lutheran confessions and dogmaticians without hesitation designate the profession as of divine institution. From this theory there deviates a new doctrine, represented principally by Kliefoth and Vilmar, according to which the clerical profession is instituted immediately by Christ, being entrusted with the fulfilment of the means of grace, not as trustee on the part of the congregation, but as exclusively empowered thereto by the Lord; and that the same has been perpetuated throughout the centuries by the imposition of hands. This doctrine, which is not substantiated by Scripture, has been contested especially by Höfling, Hofmann, and Harless.

5. The Reformed and Anglican Doctrine.

The Calvinists likewise reject the Roman idea of priesthood, though they strongly emphasize the divine institution, authorization, and organization of ministers (Confession of Basel, xv.–xx.; Gallican Confession, xxix.; Geneva Catechism, *De verbo Dei*; Second Helvetic Confession, xviii.). Divine election is confirmed through the appointment to office (Confession of Basel, xvii.). The Anglican Church makes membership in the clerical profession dependent upon reception by act of the privileged estate itself (cf. the Latin text of the Thirty-nine Articles, art. xxiii., and the forms of the Book of Common Prayer on the "Making, Ordaining, and Consecrating of Bishops, Priests, and Deacons").

III. The Call (*Vocatio*): The cooperation of the congregation in the calling of its clergy is very old. The circumstance that Paul makes no mention of this cooperation in Titus i. 5, in connection with the commission to appoint presbyters, is not a convincing argument to the contrary, since exceptional conditions in Crete may have compelled Titus to disregard the cooperation of the congregation; or, what is just as possible, he may have executed the commission in conference with the congregation. In favor of the cooperation of the congregation are found more or less distinct references (*Didache*, xv. 1; Cyprian, *Epist.*, xxxviii., lxvii. 4; Chrysostom, "On the Priesthood," iii. 15; *Apostolic Constitutions*, vii. 31; Leo the Great, *Epist.*, x. 6; Synod of Orléans, ii. 7, iii. 3; *Missale Francorum, allocutio in ordinatione presbyteri*). That, as a matter of fact, this right of the congregation was often enough greatly encroached upon is not to be disputed. But the Council of Trent did not revoke the right in principle, merely pronouncing the opposite procedure to be just as valid (Session xxiii., chap. 4).

Luther distinguished two kinds of calling. The first proceeds from God alone, without any medium; and this calling must have external signs and witness. The other calling needs no signs; it comes about through men and is previously confirmed by the command of God on Mount Sinai: Love God, and thy neighbor as thyself. From this view of Luther's has been evolved the Lutheran doctrine of the *vocatio immediata* and *mediata*. With reference to the latter the Augsburg Confession requires that he who holds a clerical office must be "duly called." Lutheran dogmaticians generally recognize the cooperation of the congregation. It is to be observed that this vocation is always understood as to a definitely circumscribed sphere of operation.

According to Calvin ("Institutes," IV. iii. 17) the *vocatio* must come about "with the consent and approval of the people; but other pastors ought to preside at the election." According to the Geneva ordinances the clergy do the electing and the laity voices its consent (Second Helvetic Confession, xviii.). A detailed description of the election as conducted by the whole congregation is found at the close of the *Liturgia in ecclesia peregrinorum* at Frankfort-on-the-Main, 1554. W. CASPARI.

IV. Legal Status of the Clergy: In the United States, there being no ecclesiastical establishment, the clergy, with the exception of chaplains in the Army and Navy and those attached to legislative bodies, have no governmental connection. The clerical profession is, however, recognized in the statute law of all the States and Territories. In law a clergyman, priest, or minister is one who has been regularly authorized to preach the Gospel and administer the ordinances of religion, according to the rules of the religious body to which he is attached. The legal status of the clergy remains so long as this clerical office is recognized by the body to which they belong. The law grants them exemption from military duty and from service in petit juries. In the case of grand juries this exemption is sometimes optional. The law also grants the clergy the right to solemnize marriage, which right is shared by a number of civil officials, and is purely statutory. Under some State laws providing for the incorporation of religious bodies the minister in charge may be elected a trustee and thus a member of the corporation. The profession of pastor or minister in any general religious body does not in law develop any contract for his support, while he is bound by the laws of the body as to his official and personal conduct so long as his office is recognized; but no ecclesiastical connection can impair his civil and property rights. A minister is under no legal obligation to mantain his ecclesiastical connection. The law reads into a contract of a minister for employment by a local church all the rules of the denomination that recognizes his standing as a minister as though such rules had been inserted in the call. Where the religious society is an independent organization, the salary is generally fixed by the qualified electors of the society, and certified by the trustees having control of the temporalities of the Church. For salary is a lien upon all the church property other than that held in trust. See ORDINATION; BENEFIT OF CLERGY; BISHOP; EPISCOPACY; DEACON; PRESBYTER; PRIEST; ORDERS, HOLY; etc.

GEO. J. BAYLES.

BIBLIOGRAPHY: For the Roman Catholic doctrine consult: *KL*, iii. 537-547; De Marca, *De discrimine clericorum et laicorum*, ed. Baluze, pp. 84-93, Venice, 1770; H. Rump, *Das allgemeine Priesterthum der Christen*, Münster, 1860; W. Schens, *Das Laien- und das himmlische Priesterthum*, Freiburg, 1873; H. Hurter, *Theologiæ dogmaticæ compendium*, vol. iii., chap. "*De ordine*," Innsbruck, 1893.

For the Lutheran: K. Ullmann, preface to *TSK* for 1849; G. C. A. von Harless, *Kirche und Amt*, Stuttgart, 1853; J. W. F. Höfling, *Grundsätze evangelisch-lutherischer Kirchenverfassung*, Erlangen, 1853; K. Lechler, *Die neutestamentliche Lehre vom heiligen Amte*, Stuttgart, 1857; W. Preger, *Geschichte vom geistlichen Amte*, Nördlingen, 1857; A. F. C. Vilmar, *Die Lehre vom geistlichen Amte*, Marburg, 1870.

For the Reformed and Anglican sides consult: Bingham, *Origines*, books iv., vi.; Calvin, *Institutes*, I. iv. 3; J. B. Lightfoot, *The Christian Ministry*, new ed., New York, 1894; E. A. Litton, *The Church of Christ, in its Idea, Attributes and Ministry*, London, 1851; C. Wordsworth, *Outlines of the Christian Ministry*, ib. 1872; C. Gore, *Ministry of the Christian Church*, ib. 1889; H. J. Van Dyke, *The Church, her Ministry and Sacraments*, New York, 1890; W. Lefroy, *The Christian Ministry*, London, 1891. The subject is treated in works on the Encyclopedia of Theology (q.v.) and on Practical Theology. See the literature under ORDINATION.

CLERICUS, JOHANNES (JEAN LE CLERC): Reformed theologian; b. at Geneva Mar. 19, 1657; d. at Amsterdam Jan. 8, 1736. He studied at Geneva under Turretin and Mestrezat, and later went to Grenoble, Saumur, Paris, and London, where for some months he preached to the Reformed fugitives from Savoy and published his *Epistolæ theologicæ* under the name of Liberius de Sancto Amore. By studying the works of Étienne de Courcelles and Episcopius he was drawn over to the Dutch Remonstrants, went to Amsterdam, and was appointed there professor of literature and philosophy in the Remonstrant Seminary. Here he developed a great activity in all branches of science. He published much and corresponded with many scholars. In his *Entretiens* (Amsterdam, 1684) he maintained that reason is an infallible guide in judging of all that man needs to know for salvation, but in other writings he declared his belief in revelation and defended himself against the charge of Socinianism. As a theologian his chief service was his contribution to a better understanding of the Bible, free from dogmatic prejudices.

H. C. ROGGE†.

BIBLIOGRAPHY: An anonymous life in Latin was published Amsterdam, 1711; A. des Amorie van der Hoeven, *De Joanne Clerico*, ib. 1843.

CLERK: The name originally used, in its Latin form *clericus*, to designate all ordained persons, or members of the "clergy" (q.v.). From the fact that during the Middle Ages they were the most frequent possessors of a higher education, the name came to be loosely applied to educated men. In English post-Reformation usage the name of clerk was applied to a lay official of parish churches whose duty it was to assist the minister, especially by leading the responses of the congregation.

CLERMONT, SYNODS OF: Of synods held at the town of Clermont (Clermont-Ferrand, *Arvernum*, capital of the present department of Puy-de-Dome, 250 m. s.s.e. of Paris) the most important was that convoked by Urban II. in 1095, in which the crusades originated (see URBAN II.). Two earlier synods belong to the Merovingian time, the first on Nov. 8, 535, under Theudebert I., the acts of which have some importance for knowledge of conditions at the beginning of the Frankish period, and the second between 584 and 591 under Childebert II. to consider a question of discipline. For the alleged second synod in 549 cf. F. Maassen, *Geschichte der Quellen des kanonischen Rechts*, i (Graz, 1871), 209-210. Other synods have no general interest. (A. HAUCK.)

CLETUS. See ANACLETUS; CLEMENT OF ROME.

CLEVERNESS: A term applied to mental as opposed to spiritual ability. It is related to, but not identical with wisdom, is often connected with it (cf. Jas. iii. 13), but generally with the distinction that cleverness is referred to the worldly side of knowledge and ability, wisdom to the spiritual side. Frequently it has an ironical undertone, implying the reverse of simplicity and humility.

The Jewish nation owns cleverness as an inheritance from Jacob. Its most brilliant representative in the Old Testament is Solomon. In the New Testament the word expressing the idea is *phronimos*, the principal passage is Matt. x. 16. The disciple of Christ must have a discerning mind and eyes open to the things of this world in order to discern the dangers threatening him and the means he may employ against them. Cleverness, a natural gift of God, is not objectionable in itself, but it should be controlled and raised to the quality of a moral virtue. Attaching to it is the temptation of self-conceit (cf. Rom. xii. 16; I Cor. iv. 10; II Cor. xi. 19). The world uses cleverness to serve self-interest (Luke xvi. 1-9). The "wisdom of the just" (Luke i. 17) must have the foundation given Matt. vii. 24, and must be controlled so as to keep an unsullied conscience (Jas. iii. 13) in order to attain a blissful issue of earthly life (Ps. xc. 12). Worldly cleverness is entirely in the service of eudemonism. While the vocation of a minister calls for cleverness, the clergyman must look for it in the sense of Jas. i. 5. KARL BURGER†.

CLIFFORD, JOHN: English Baptist; b. at Sawley (7 m. s.e. of Derby), Derbyshire, England, Oct. 16, 1836. He studied at Midland Baptist College, Leicester, and University College, London (B.A., 1861). Since 1858 he has been minister of Praed Street and Westbourne Park Church, Paddington, London. He was president of the General Baptist Association in 1872, and from 1876 to 1878 was secretary of the London Baptist Association, becoming president in 1879. He was also president of the Baptist Union of Great Britain and Ireland in 1888 and 1899, as well as of the National Council of Free Evangelical Churches in 1898-99 and of the British Chautauqua in 1899-1900. He edited *The General Baptist Magazine* 1870-83 and was coeditor of *The Review of the Churches* 1891-94 and of *The Baptist Union Magazine* 1892-95. Of his publications may be mentioned *George Mostyn* (London, 1874); *Daily Strength for Daily Living: Expositions of Old Testament Themes* (1885); *The Inspiration and Authority of the Bible* (1892); *Typical Christian Leaders* (1898); *God's Greater Britain* (1899); *The Ultimate Problems of Christianity* (Angus lectures for 1906).

BIBLIOGRAPHY: C. T. Bateman, *Life of John Clifford*, London, 1908.

CLIFTON (CLYFTON), RICHARD: English Separatist; d. at Amsterdam May 20, 1616. He was pastor of the congregation which met at the house of William Brewster (q.v.) in Scrooby and had John Robinson as his assistant; emigrated to Amsterdam in Aug., 1608, joined the church of Francis Johnson there, and became its "teacher." He wrote *A Plea for Infants and Elder People concerning their Baptism* (Amsterdam, 1610) against the views of John Smyth (q.v.), and *An Advertisement concerning a Book Lately Published by Christopher Lawne and Others against the Exiled English Church at Amsterdam* (1612), which called forth an *Animadversion* from Henry Ainsworth (1613). He is said to have been the most effective writer among the Separatists.

CLINICAL BAPTISM: The name of *clinici* was applied, from the third century, to those who were baptized at home in illness by sprinkling, not immersion. Cyprian, the first in whom the word is found, disapproves of it (*Epist.*, lxix.) but asserts the full validity of such baptism. On the other hand, Pope Cornelius, referring to the case of Novatian, who was thus baptized, apparently expressed a doubt (Eusebius, *Hist. eccl.*, VI. xliii. 14, 17). This doubt or prejudice so far maintained itself that the fourth century Council of Neocæsarea (canon xii.) forbade the ordination of such persons. Since the traditional but not essential accompanying ceremonies were of necessity omitted in these baptisms, it appears from the letter of Cornelius that it was customary, if not enjoined, to supply them later. [The same rule is found to-day in the *Rituale Romanum* (ii. 15); and the Anglican Prayer-book provides for the bringing to church of those who have been privately baptized, and their formal reception into the Church. (A. HAUCK.)

CLOWES, WILLIAM. See METHODISTS, I., 4.

CLUNY, ABBEY AND CONGREGATION OF.

The abbey of Cluny was the seat, and its congregation the result of an early and far-reaching reform of the Benedictine order. At the beginning

1. Foundation, 910.

of the tenth century, after Frankish civilization and religious institutions had suffered from the incursions of the Normans and Saracens, a general movement of monastic reform began, which is associated with the abbey of Cluny in the diocese of Mâcon and the present department of Saône-et-Loire. This was founded by Duke William the Pious of Aquitaine in 910, and Berno, a Burgundian of noble family, who had already distinguished himself by the reform of two other abbeys, was placed at its head. The act of foundation placed it under the special protection of the apostles Peter and Paul, and of the pope, which meant exemption from all other jurisdiction, temporal or spiritual. This relation, while it protected the abbey from the exactions and ambitions of local magnates, committed it to a constant interest in the development of the papal power.

The Benedictine rule formed the basis of the new institutions, with the addition of the capitularies of Aix-la-Chapelle of 817 and the reforms of Benedict of Aniane. Special stress was laid upon the renunciation of private property and the abstinence from the flesh of quadrupeds, and silence was enjoined. The recitation of the psalms and reading of Holy Scripture were enforced, and unconditional obedience to the strict monarchical government of the abbot required.

2. Odo, Second Abbot, 927–941.

On Berno's death in 927 his disciple Odo succeeded him. The new abbot, a man of singular spiritual and intellectual power, undertook a wide reform of monastic life, on the strength of a privilege of John XI. (931) which permitted him to assume the oversight of more than one monastery and to receive at Cluny monks from those houses which had not been reformed. He succeeded in bringing back a number to primitive strictness, though most of them remained independent of Cluny. With the support of Leo VII. and Alberic, the secular ruler of the city, he reformed several abbeys in Rome itself, as well as other Italian monasteries, including Subiaco and Monte Cassino. When he died in 941 at Tours the reform had spread throughout all France, and as far south as Palermo. His sermons and other writings with a life by an Italian monk are in *MPL*, cxxxiii.

Under Berno's successor Aymard there were 160 monks at Cluny, but as yet only five of the larger abbeys were directly under the jurisdiction of its abbot. Majolus, its next head, was highly esteemed and favored by the emperor, Otto I., who was credited with a design to place all the monasteries in his German and Italian dominions under Cluny. Majolus died in 994, and was succeeded by Odilo,

3. Odilo, Fifth Abbot, 994–1049.

a typical eleventh century abbot in his combination of rigorous asceticism and mystical piety with wise and skilful management. Under him the reform spread into Spain, and through the influence of Cluny the native rule of Isidore was generally replaced by that of Benedict. From Odilo's time dates the definite beginning of a "congregation," the reformed or newly founded monasteries being placed in permanent dependence upon the mother house. He had a great influence upon the youthful Otto III., though not equal to that of the Italian reformers, with whose work the French is now for the first time demonstrably connected (see CAMALDOLITES). Poppo carried the movement into Germany, becoming abbot of Stablo in the diocese of Liége and of St. Maximin in that of Treves, and wielding a powerful influence under Henry II. and Conrad II., the latter of whom entrusted to him a number of great imperial abbeys, including St. Gall.

By degrees the reform movement widened to embrace social life outside the monastery walls. The efforts of Odilo to enforce the "Truce of God," a notable blessing to agriculture and commerce, are universally recognized as important.

4. Reforming Influence.

The reformers attacked the problems of general church life, combating simony, clerical marriage, and the uncanonical marriages of the laity. A definite program, however, was first laid down by Abbo of Fleury and the reformers of Lorraine, in the full enforcement of the canon law. Henry III. found powerful support in the leaders of the movement, especially Odilo and Petrus Damianus, for his efforts to improve the condition of the Church; and when the papacy, now raised from its degradation, took the lead in the general effort for betterment, it found its main allies in the monks of Cluny. They were not, however, at first decidedly on the side of the pope as against the emperor, and in the conflict between Henry IV. and Gregory VII. the successor of Odilo, Hugo I. (1049–1109), remained practically neutral. His influence was especially great under Urban II., the first Cluniac pope. In 1089 he began the building of the great basilica, the largest church in the world after St. Peter's at Rome. The first Cluniac house was established in England with the help of William the Conqueror, and, though there were not many direct colonies in Germany, the spirit of Cluny spread there through the cognate reforms of St. Blasien and at Hirschau.

The first symptoms of decline appeared under Abbot Pontius, who in 1114 mediated between Paschal II. and Henry V. and four years later offered an asylum to Gelasius II. fleeing from the emperor, as Anselm of Canterbury had found one there in 1097. The deposition of Gelasius and the election of his successor Calixtus II. took place in the abbey.

5. Peter the Venerable, Abbot 1122–55.

Under Peter the Venerable the *Consuetudines Cluniacenses* were drawn up. In contrast with the aristocratic constitution of the Cistercians, they emphasize the monarchical and centralized system of Cluny. Without the permission of its abbot no novice might be received into the congregation, and each must present himself at the mother house within three years from his reception for the abbot's benediction. Peter arrested the process of decline, and the congregation had 314 houses at his death. But the predominant position of Cluny began to be taken by the Premonstratensians, and then still more by the Cistercians. The declaration of Hugo III. for the imperial claimant of the papacy in

1159 damaged the position of Cluny still more, and neither the reforms of his successors nor the attempt of Ivo II. in 1269 to establish a seat of learning in Paris, the College of Cluny, had permanent effects.

6. Decline.

The independent position of the abbey was partially abandoned by Ivo I. in 1258 when it was placed under the protection of Louis IX., which led later to subjection to the French crown. First the Avignon popes claimed the right to name the abbot—John XXII. and Clement VI. put in their own relations—and from 1456, when Charles VII. of France appointed John of Bourbon, an illegitimate member of his house, the kings dominated it. From 1528 to 1622 it was held *in commendam* by the family of Guise. At the Reformation, with the suppression of the English, German, and Swiss houses and the attainment of independence by the Spanish and Italian, the congregation lost its international character. During the Guise period the abbey suffered severely in the wars of religion; in 1562 the Huguenots destroyed a great part of the fine buildings and dispersed the library. Cardinal Richelieu held it in succession to the last regular abbot, and attempted in 1634 to combine the congregation with that of St. Maur, an act which was reversed ten years later by his successor Armand, prince of Conti. The next abbots were Cardinal Mazarin (1654–61) and Cardinal Rinaldo d'Este, brother of the duke of Modena and protector of France at Rome (1662–72). After him followed an interregnum of eleven years, and then it was held from 1683 to 1710 by the Cardinal de Bouillon. In 1790 it was suppressed by the Constituent Assembly, which sold the magnificent church to the commune for 100,000 francs, and thus brought about its almost complete destruction. The Musée de Cluny in Paris, originally built (1334) as the Parisian headquarters of the abbot, preserves a splendid collection of antiquities, a large part of which came from the abbey. (G. GRÜTZMACHER.)

BIBLIOGRAPHY: Parts of the records, ed. A. Bernard and A. Bruel, *Recueil des chartes de l'Abbaye de Cluny 802–1300*, 5 vols., Paris, 1876–94; and G. F. Duckett, *Record Evidence among the Archives of Cluny*, 4 vols., Lewes, 1886–88. The early account is M. Marrier and A. Queretanus, *Bibliotheca Cluniacensis*, Paris, 1614. Consult: L. Niepce, *Les Stalles de Cluny, les chartes et la bibliothèque*, Lyons, 1882; E. Sackur, *Die Cluniacenser bis zur Mitte des 11. Jahrhunderts*, 2 vols., Halle, 1892–94; *Visitations and Chapters-General of the Order of Cluni, 1269–1529*, London, 1893; *Cluny: luminare sacri monasterii Cluniacensis*, Paris, 1898; Helyot, *Ordres monastiques*, vol. v.; Heimbucher, *Orden und Kongregationen*, i. 116 sqq.; Neander, *Christian Church*, iii. 381, 417–419; Hauck, *KD*, vol. iii.; *KL*, iii. 554–561; Schaff, *Christian Church*, v. 1, pp. 330 sqq.

COADJUTOR: An assistant to a cleric who is partly or wholly incapacitated; appointed either temporarily or permanently, and in the latter case with or without the right of succession. By the canon law a parish priest thus incapacitated may obtain an assistant or *vicarius* from his superiors; but this appointment is temporary and revocable, and the Council of Trent expressly forbids the right of succession to be given—though this has not been held to prevent the pope from making exceptions. The title coadjutor is regularly applied to such an assistant given to a bishop. By ancient law no successor to a bishop could be chosen in his lifetime, and the duties of an incapacitated bishop were performed either by neighboring prelates or by a specially designated *interventor* (*dispensator*, *intercessor*). Such arrangements were usually made by the provincial council; sometimes the pope was consulted, and this *causa episcopalis* was gradually reserved to him. The ancient principle, laid down by the Council of Nicæa, that there should not be two bishops in one city was respected at least formally by the designation of the coadjutor from the title of some other see (see BISHOP, TITULAR). According to the Council of Trent, coadjutors may be appointed only in case of urgent necessity, and not with right of succession unless the pope, after full investigation, approves the necessity and the person chosen. The diocesan bishop may make the request, with the assent of his chapter; or the chapter may take the initiative in case of the incapacity or refusal of the bishop, in which case the decision rests with the pope. A coadjutor with right of succession enters on the full jurisdiction immediately upon the decease of his principal, without further formality. (O. MEJER†.)

BIBLIOGRAPHY: G. Grunau, *De coadjutoribus episcoporum*, Breslau, 1894; Held, *Das Recht zur Aufstellung eines Koadjutors*, Munich, 1848; A. L. Richter, *Lehrbuch des . . . Kirchenrechts*, Leipsic, 1886; E. Friedberg, *Lehrbuch des . . . Kirchenrechts*, p. 172, Leipsic, 1895; Bingham, *Origines*, books iv.–vi.

COAN, TITUS: Missionary; b. at Killingworth, Conn., Feb. 1, 1801; d. at Hilo, Hawaii, Dec. 1, 1882. He was a cousin of Asahel Nettleton (q.v.), by whom he was influenced as also by Charles G. Finney; he studied at Auburn Theological Seminary 1831–33; spent several months in Patagonia examining the country for the American Board 1833–34; sailed for Hawaii late in 1834, in July, 1835, took up his residence at Hilo, and spent the rest of his life there, with the exception of a brief visit to America in 1870–71. He was a man of great physical strength, endowed with tact and evangelistic gifts. "In three months from the time he first set foot on the shores of Hawaii he began to preach in the native tongue. Before his first year closed the audiences drawn to hear the Word by his peculiar power reached many hundreds. And in six years from his arrival three-fourths of the adult population of his parish, to the number of more than seven thousand, were gathered into the bonds of Christian fellowship." He was an authority concerning the Hawaiian volcanoes. He published *Adventures in Patagonia* (New York, 1881); *Life in Hawaii, an Autobiographic Sketch, 1835–81* (1882).

BIBLIOGRAPHY: Besides the autobiography, consult: Mrs. L. B. Coan, *Titus Coan, a Memorial*, Chicago, 1885.

COBB, HENRY NITCHIE: Reformed (Dutch); b. in New York Nov. 15, 1834. He was graduated at Yale in 1855 and studied at Union Theological Seminary 1856–57. He was a Presbyterian missionary to Persia under the auspices of the American Board of Commissioners for Foreign Missions in 1860–62; pastor of the Reformed Church at Millbrook, N. Y., 1866–81, and since 1882 has been corresponding secretary of the Board of Foreign Missions of the Reformed Church in America. He was chairman of the executive committee of the Ecumenical Conference on Foreign Missions held in New York in 1900 and was a deputy to the Missions of the Reformed Church from Oct., 1904, to May, 1905. He has written *Far Hence: a Budget of Letters from Our Mission Fields in Asia* (New York, 1893).

COBB, SANFORD HOADLEY: Presbyterian; b. in New York Feb. 4, 1838. He was graduated at Yale in 1858 and Princeton Theological Seminary in 1862, was pastor of Reformed churches at Schoharie, N. Y. (1864–71), and Saugerties, N. Y. (1871–83), the Westminster Presbyterian Church, Grand Rapids, Mich. (1885-94), and the Presbyterian Church of Greenwich, Conn. (1900–1901). He made a tour of the world in 1883–84, visiting the various mission fields, and has written *The Story of the Palatines* (New York, 1897) and *The Rise of Religious Liberty in America* (1902).

COBB, SYLVANUS: Universalist; b. at Norway, Me., July 17, 1798; d. in East Boston, Mass., Oct. 31, 1866. His early life was that of a New England farmer's son of the time. He became a Universalist before reaching his majority, began to preach in 1820, was ordained in 1821, and settled in Waterville, Me., where he organized the first Universalist church in the State in 1826. He was pastor at Malden, Mass., 1828–37, removed to Waltham in 1838, and to East Boston in 1841. Much of his time was given to evangelizing tours which made him widely known as preacher and lecturer. He was a member of the Maine and Massachusetts legislatures. In 1839 he began the publication of *The Christian Freeman and Family Visitor*, a weekly paper devoted to Universalism and the antislavery and temperance causes, and continued it till 1862, when it was united with *The Trumpet*, Mr. Cobb remaining as editor till 1864. In 1858–59 he carried on discussions in *The Freeman* with the Rev. Nehemiah Adams on the subject of endless punishment, and with the Rev. C. F. Hudson upon annihilationism, which were afterward published in book form. He wrote *A Compend of Christian Divinity* (Boston, 1845) and *The New Testament with Explanatory Notes and Practical Observations* (1864).

BIBLIOGRAPHY: S. Cobb, *Autobiography, with Memoir by* S. Cobb, Jr., Boston, 1867 (the *Autobiography* goes to his forty-first year and is continued in the *Memoir*).

COBLENZ ARTICLES. See EMS, CONGRESS OF.

COCCEIUS, JOHANNES, AND HIS SCHOOL.

I. Johannes Cocceius: Dutch theologian; b. at Bremen Aug. 9, 1603; d. at Leyden Nov. 4, 1669. He was the son of the municipal secretary Timann Koch. Early in life he showed extraordinary ability in the ancient languages, and his knowledge of Greek was deepened through his association with Metrophanes Kritopulos, who for a time lived at Bremen. Among his theological teachers was Ludwig Crocius. In 1625 he went to Hamburg to continue his Hebrew and rabbinic studies under a learned Jew. In the year 1629, to complete his theological education and "to escape the dissolute life of the German universities," Coch (so he wrote his name until that year) went to Franeker, Holland. He had as teacher there, besides Maccovius and Amesius [William Ames], the great Orientalist Sixtinus Amana, at whose suggestion he published Talmudic studies which brought him the recognition of Grotius.

1. Life and Character. After a short visit to other Dutch universities he returned to Bremen and accepted in 1630 the professorship of Biblical philology at the Gymnasium Illustre. The University of Franeker called him in 1636 to the chair of Hebrew. His commentaries on passages about Antichrist and his "Introduction to Ephesians" brought him a theological professorship in 1643. As successor to Fr. Spanheim the elder in 1650, he moved to Leyden. His peaceful character, which even opponents such as the worthy Voetius duly acknowledged, made an agreeable impression in that age of unmeasured wrangling. Though full of pure piety, he withdrew from the common life of the church, for as a German he never felt at home in the precision of strict Dutch Calvinism.

As an author he was extremely productive. The "Collected Works" of Cocceius, completed later, appeared in eight volumes, Amsterdam, 1673–75; a 2d ed., revised and corrected, Frankfort, 1689, repr., 1702; inferior ed., 10 vols., Amsterdam, 1701, and 2 vols., *Opera anecdota*, 1706, principally letters. Previously unprinted letters appear in the Thesaurus of Hottinger, xvi. 34. His works may be arranged as follows: (1) Commentaries, which treat of the principal books of the Bible, viz., Job, Ps., Eccles., Cant., Jer., Mal., John, Rom.,

2. Literary Works. Gal.-Col., Tim.-Titus, Heb., Jude, Rev. (2) Works on Biblical Theology; *Summa doctrina de fœdere et testamento Dei*, Leyden, 1648, enlarged ed., 1654; *Summa theologiæ ex Sacris Scripturis repetita*, Leyden, 1662, reprinted, Amsterdam and Geneva, 1665; vol. vi. of his "Collected Works," Amsterdam ed., contains his *Aphorismi per universam theologiam*; finally his last work, *Explicatio catecheseos Heydelbergensis*, setting forth his system of doctrine. (3) Dogmatics and Ethics; *Disputationes . . . de via salutis*; *Brevis repetitio quorundam illustrium locorum Veteris et Novi Testamenti qui de Antichristo agunt*; an anti-Socinian polemic in justification of an edict of Sept. 19, 1653, *Equitis Poloni* (Jonas Schliting?) *Apologia . . . examinata*; several tracts directed against the Jesuits Walenburg and Masenius, *Sacræ Scripturæ potentia demonstrata*, *Jac. Macenii factata probatio Scripturaria*, *Admonitio de principio fidei ecclesiæ reformatæ*, *De ecclesia et Babylone disquisitio*, and a number of tracts on the Sabbath. (4) Academical Lectures, the most important of which are inaugural addresses given when taking his positions as professor or as rector in the different universities where he labored. (5) Philological Works; among which may be mentioned *Duo tituli thalmudici sanhedrin et maccoth*; *Defensio altera auctoritatis verbi divini Veteris Testamenti*; the great *Lexicon et commentarius* *sermonis Hebraici et Chaldaici*, Amsterdam, 1669 and often.

Cocceius based his theory of life upon the Bible, and in this lies his significance. In contradistinction to devotion to church and orthodoxy, he recommends a life in and through the Scriptures. Against Hoornbeek's "Authority of the Church" he put that of the Bible only, which was to him a wonderful expression of the deeds and words of God. Consequently all his theological concepts received a Biblical coloring; and his peculiarity was not scholastic but Biblical in origin. Concordant with this was the essentially practical bent of his theology, in which lived a mild type of the German-Reformed spirit, deviating not in doctrine, but in disposition from later Calvinism. To be sure, Biblical theology does not operate through mere uniform exposition. Cocceius unlocked its treasure by means of the central idea of the covenant of God. Not that he originated "Federal Theology," the roots of which lay in the Reformation, while its outline had through Calvin's influence long passed current in Holland by means of the activities of Hyperius, Olevian, and Bullinger. Perhaps Cocceius received the idea from Raph. Eglin's *De fœdere gratiæ* (Marburg, 1613). What was new was the dynamic force of his Biblical theology, on the lines of which he carried out the conception, and the richness of knowledge of Biblical history with which he enriched it. His main work, *De fœdere et testamento Dei*, portrays in bold and clear outline the whole Scriptural teaching on salvation. The relation between God and man is represented as a covenant at first existing as a divine order, then as a compact between God and man. Then came the covenant of works, under which developed the first step in sin, followed by the proclamation of the "covenant of grace." Though faith then took the place of works, this faith was no new law and Christ no new lawgiver. The power of the "Covenant of Grace" consists in this, that in contradistinction to the "covenant of works" it develops into a "Testament." This method runs through Cocceius's exegetical works; everywhere in the Old Testament he finds Jesus Christ. Though differing in the mode of interpretation, he nowhere departs from the doctrine of his Church. It is his merit to have turned from the abstract deductions of orthodoxy to the position of Calvin. In his doctrine of the Church, by keeping the sacraments in the background and by understanding law spiritually, he greatly assisted Pietism. Though he found a place in the covenant of grace for the decalogue, the New Testament idea of a sanctified life and disbelief in the necessity to keep special days led to the dispute upon the Sabbath question. It was through this that the Church became aware of the peculiarities of his doctrine; the polemical Maresius and the worthy puritanic Voetius entered the fray.

3. Doctrines.

II. His School: Meanwhile Cocceius died, but the battle continued with renewed fury. A schism in the Church was narrowly averted; on the Sabbath question the pupils outdid the prudent, practical master, the affray involved the laity whom the Biblical sermons of Cocceius had made theologians, from there it entered politics, the "Voetians" being the Central party, and the Cocceians the Remonstrants. A change in the prayer-book was widely resented, and such Cocceians as Heidanus, W. Momma, and J. van der Waeyen were expelled from the universities. The neighboring synods urged peace "in the name of the communion of the saints," and the consistory of Amsterdam observed strict impartiality; none the less in 1694 it was necessary for the Court to curb the parties. The practise was adopted, and continued until last century, of appointing a Voetian for the chair of systematic theology, a Cocceian for the chair of exegesis, and a Lampean for the chair of practical theology. The last-named school was founded by the moderate Cocceian Fr. A. Lampe (q.v.), who did much to heal the breach of the parties. A complete change for the better was brought about in the Cocceian system through Fr. Burmann's *Synopsis Theologiæ*, the text-book of later "Federalists." Among the friends and pupils of Cocceius were the Burmanns, father and son, Heidanus (d. 1760), J. Braun, and the great exegete Campegius Vitringa.

(E. F. Karl Müller.)

Bibliography: His autobiography, completed by his son, J. H. Cocceius, is prefixed to the "Collected Works," ed. of 1673-75. His life is also given in Nicéron, *Mémoires*, viii. 193 sqq., and in A. J. van der Aa, *Biographisch Woordenboek der Nederlanden*, iii. 518 sqq., Haarlem, 1852. Consult: F. A. Tholuck, *Das akademische Leben des 17ten Jahrhunderts*, ii. 226 sqq., Halle, 1853; G. Frank, *Geschichte der protestantischen Theologie*, ii. 240 sqq., Leipsic, 1865; H. L. J. Heppe, *Geschichte des Pietismus und der Mystik in der reformirten Kirche*, pp. 216 sqq., Leyden, 1879; A. Ritschl, *Geschichte des Pietismus in der reformirten Kirche*, pp. 130 sqq., Bonn, 1880.

COCHLÆUS (DOBNECK, WENDELSTINUS), JOHANNES: Roman Catholic controversialist; b. at Wendelstein (near Schwabach, 9 m. s.s.w. of Nuremberg), in Middle Franconia, Jan. 10, 1479; d. at Breslau Jan. 10, 1552. He was the son of a peasant, and began his studies comparatively late. He first studied in Nuremberg, where Heinrich Grieninger, a humanist, was teacher of poetics. In 1504 he entered the University of Cologne where Count Hermann von Neuenar, Ulrich von Hutten, and other humanists were his associates. He also was on intimate terms with Carl von Miltitz who later became papal chamberlain. From 1510 till 1515 he taught at St. Sebald in Nuremberg and edited several of his manuals, which were highly esteemed. During the years 1515–19 he traveled in Italy as tutor to three nephews of Willibald Pirkheimer. Here the laxity of morals and lack of religious zeal confirmed a dislike already formed for Italian and Roman affairs. Although repelled by scholastic theology, he studied with great zeal the Bible, Origen, Chrysostom, and Augustine, and, in 1517, acquired the degree of doctor of theology at Ferrara. At Rome he was consecrated priest and appointed deacon of the Church of Our Beloved Lady at Frankfort-on-the-Main. On his return to Germany he was inclined to side with Luther, but changed his mind to retain good relations with the episcopal court of Mainz and with Hieronymus Aleander of Worms, who applied to him personally for the purpose of a discussion on the best means of opposing Luther. From this time he employed his pen for the cause of Romanism.

His one ambition was to meet Luther in a public disputation, and with the aid of Aleander he succeeded in being admitted to private negotiations with Luther. His polemical attacks and invectives overshot the mark so that even the Roman Catholics disapproved of his actions. Though without friends or money, his zeal increased the more, and he never tired of finding ways to obstruct the cause of Luther.

Controversy with Luther.

He even recommended the suppression of the University of Wittenberg. In 1521 he offered his services to the pope, but nobody cared for him at Rome. It was not till 1522 that his first treatise against Luther appeared—*De gratia sacramentorum liber unus Joannis Cochlæi adversus assertionem M. Lutheri* (Strasburg). Luther replied with his *Adversus armatum virum Cocleum*, which again was answered by Cochlæus in *Adversus cucullatum minotaurum Wittenbergensem. . . . De sacrorum gratia, iterum* (1523).

In the autumn of 1523 he went to Rome as he did not feel himself safe at Frankfort, but returned early in 1524. Meanwhile his patrons and friends at Frankfort had joined the opposing party. Cochlæus accompanied Campeggi, the papal nuncio, to the Convention of Regensburg as interpreter and member of the commission which discussed the reform of the clergy. His position at Frankfort becoming untenable, he fled to Cologne in 1525, and in 1526 received a canonry at St. Victor's in Mainz. He attended the Diet of Speyer in 1526, but his hope of holding a disputation with Luther was not fulfilled. Although Luther had ignored him after replying to his first treatise, Cochlæus was indefatigable in writing polemical tracts against Luther and the Reformation.

Disappointments of his Later Life.

After the death of Hieronymus Emser in 1528 he went to Dresden as adviser and assistant of Duke George of Saxony in his literary feuds with Luther. He followed the duke to the Diet of Augsburg, and was one of the Roman theologians commissioned to refute the Augsburg Confession. His attacks found little favor with the Romanists, and Johann Eck became the chief author of the *Confutatio*. Cochlæus's hope of receiving financial support from Rome proved illusory, and it became more and more difficult for him to get his numerous unsalable pamphlets printed. In 1534 or 1535 George of Saxony secured for him a canonry at Meissen. Subsequently he was provost of St. Severus at Erfurt until 1539. The death of George was a severe blow for him, and for the cause of Romanism. As the progress of the Reformation in Saxony made it impossible for him to retain his ecclesiastical offices, he accepted in 1539 a canonry from the cathedral chapter in Breslau. King Ferdinand called him to the diets of Hagenau, Worms, and Regensburg, but here again he was ignored. He followed with zeal the preparations for the Council of Trent without being able to take part in it. He remained the same zealous champion of Roman Catholicism to the end, although he found little recognition, and, to complete his tragic fate, Pope Paul IV. put his name on the Index.

Cochlæus's *Historiæ Hussitarum libri xii.* (Mainz, 1549) is still valuable, but the work which has made his name popular to the present is his history of Luther,

His Most Important Works.

Commentaria de actis et scriptis Martini Lutheri Saxonis chronographice ex ordine ab anno Domini 1517 usque ad annum 1546 inclusive fideliter conscripta (Mainz, 1549). The book became the model and source for many later polemical productions, and the view expounded in it that the whole Reformation was nothing but an incidental jealousy between the Dominican and Augustinian orders was believed even by intelligent men. (T. Kolde.)

Bibliography: U. de Weldige Cremer, *De Joannis Cochlæi vita et scriptis*, Münster, 1865; K. Otto, *Johannes Cochlæus der Humanist*, Breslau, 1874; F. Gess, *Johannes Cochlæus der Gegner Luthers*, Leipsic, 1886; M. Spahn, *Johannes Cochlæus, Lebensbild*, Berlin, 1898; J. Köstlin, *Martin Luther*, passim, 2 vols., ib. 1903.

CODMAN, ROBERT: Protestant Episcopal bishop of Maine; b. in Boston, Mass., Dec. 30, 1859. He was educated at Harvard (B.A., 1882) and at the Harvard Law School, from which he was graduated in 1885. After practising a few years, however, he determined to take orders, and accordingly studied at the General Theological Seminary, from which he was graduated in 1894. After his ordination to the priesthood, he was rector of St. John's, Roxbury, Mass., until 1900, when he was consecrated third bishop of the diocese of Maine.

COE, GEORGE ALBERT: American philosopher; b. at Mendon, N. Y., Mar. 26, 1862. He was graduated at Rochester University (B.A., 1884) and Boston University (Ph.D., 1891), and as traveling fellow of the latter institution spent the year 1890–91 at the University of Berlin. He was professor of philosophy in the University of Southern California 1889–90 and acting professor of philosophy in Northwestern University, Evanston, Ill., 1891–93. Since the latter year he has been John Evans professor of philosophy in the same institution. He was lecturer on the psychology of religion in Boston University in 1900. He has written *The Spiritual Life: Studies in the Science of Religion* (New York, 1900); *The Religion of a Mature Mind* (Chicago, 1902); and *Education in Religion and Morals* (1904).

COELDE, DIETRICH (Dietrich of Münster). See Francis, Saint, of Assisi, and the Franciscan Order.

CŒLE-SYRIA ("Hollow Syria"): The early name for the valley which separates the parallel ranges of Lebanon and Anti-Lebanon. In later times the name came to have a wider application and to include the whole of southern Syria except Phenicia (cf. Josephus, *Ant.*, XIV. iv. 5). It therefore contained nearly all the cities of Decapolis within its limits. Though the name does not occur in the Bible, it is frequently mentioned in the Apocrypha (I Esd. ii. 24, 27, iv. 48, vi. 29; I Macc. x. 69; II Macc. viii. 8, x. 11) and by Josephus (*Ant.*, XIII. iv. 2, XIV. ix. 5, xi. 4) and other writers. It has a legendary history of its own, attested by curious monuments. At Kerak Nûh is shown the grave of Noah, one hundred and thirty-two feet long; and on the opposite side of the plain is the tomb of the prophet Seth; while the temples at Baalbek (q.v.) have astonished the world for many centuries. Long before "Toi, King of Hamath," sent presents to David (II Sam. viii. 9–11), the Hittites of that region were sufficiently powerful to contend there for supremacy with the Pharaohs of Egypt.

This remarkable valley, now called el-Bûkâ'a, "the cleft," extends to the northeast, from Jubb Jenin, under Hermon, for about one hundred miles, having an average width of seven miles. Its surface as seen from above seems to be quite level; but this appearance is deceptive. It is, in fact, an elevated plateau rising gradually northward, until, at the northeast end, it is nearly four thousand feet above the level of the sea, a cold, rugged, and barren region. The northern end is drained by the Orontes, called el'Asy, "the rebellious," because its course is northward, contrary to the other rivers of Syria. Its most southern source is at Lebweh, the Libo of the ancients. The main source is the copious fountain that flows out from under the cliffs of Lebanon, near Mughârat al-Râhib. Passing below Kamû'a Hûrmul, a unique monument with hunting scenes carved upon its four sides, the Orontes irrigates the extensive plains of the Biblical Riblah (II Kings xxv. 6) and the equally fertile region around the small lake of Kedes. The shapeless ruins near Tell Neby Mindau may mark the site of the chief city of the Hittite kingdom. Issuing from the artificial lake of Kedes, six miles south of Huma, the river pursues its winding course through the land of Hamath, past the extensive ruins of Apamea, and along the eastern foot-hills of the Nusairiyeh Mountains, where it turns westward, and, passing by Antioch, it enters the sea near the base of Mount Casius. The central and southern portions of the Bukâ'a are comparatively level, and their fertility and beauty are entirely due to the abundance of water. Perennial streams descend from the mountains on either side, and copious fountains rise in the plain itself, in such positions that the water can be conducted to all parts of its surface. The center and south of the Bukâ'a is drained by the Lîtâny, the ancient Leontes, one of the longest and largest rivers of Syria. It rises at 'Ain al-Sultân, above Baalbek, and is joined, as it flows southward, by many tributaries, among them el Berdûny, which descends from snow-crowned Lebanon, and the large remitting fountain near 'Anjar, that flows out from the very roots of Anti-Lebanon, near the site of the ancient Chalcis. Below Jub Jenin the Lîtâny enters a profound gorge, along which it has worn its way through southern Lebanon to the sea, near Tyre. For the history see SYRIA.

BIBLIOGRAPHY: G. A. Smith, *Historical Geography of the Holy Land*, pp. 538–539, 553, London, 1897; W. Smith, *Dictionary of Greek and Roman Geography*, p. 1071, London, 1878, and the literature under SYRIA.

CŒLICOLÆ, sî-lĭ'-cō'lî ("Heaven Worshipers"): A name applied to a Christian sect extant in northern Africa in the time of Augustine (cf. *Epist.*, xliv., *NPNF*, i. 289). They doubtless owe their name to controversial polemics. They seem to have laid special stress on adoration of the deity without images, and to have been closely related to the Eastern Hypsistarians (q.v.). An edict of the emperors Honorius and Theodosius II., 408 (*Cod. Theodos.*, XVI. v. 43), awarded the houses of worship of the Cœlicolæ to the Catholic Church; and in the year following (409) it was further decreed that the Cœlicolæ must either adopt the Christian faith within a year or incur, in the contrary case, the penalty imposed upon heresy (*Cod. Theodos.*, XVI. viii. 19). G. KRÜGER.

BIBLIOGRAPHY: E. Schürer, in *Sitzungsberichte der Berliner Akademie*, 1897, pp. 200–225; J. M. Schröckh, *Christliche Kirchengeschichte*, vii. 442–444, Leipsic, 1780.

COELLN, cöln, **DANIEL GEORG KONRAD VON**: German theologian; b. at Oerlinghausen, Lippe-Detmold, Dec. 21, 1788; d. at Breslau Feb. 17, 1833. He was educated at Marburg, Tübingen, and Göttingen, and became privat-docent at Marburg 1811, associate professor of theology 1816, and professor of theology at Breslau 1818. In a spirit of moderate rationalism he wrote *Historische Beiträge zur Erläuterung und Berichtigung der Begriffe Pietismus, Mysticismus und Fanatismus* (Halberstadt, 1830). His zeal for the union of the two leading Protestant denominations of Germany was shown by his *Ideen über den inneren Zusammenhang der Glaubenseinigung und Glaubensreinigung* (Leipsic, 1823). The celebration of the jubilee of the Augsburg Confession caused him and his friend David Schulz to publish their *Ueber theologische Lehrfreiheit auf den evangelischen Universitäten und deren Beschränkung durch symbolische Bücher* (Breslau, 1830), in which they condemned the Confession as antiquated and advocated the preparation of a new creed. Their position was attacked by Schleiermacher, and they replied in their *Zwei Antwortschreiben an Herrn D. Friedr. Schleiermacher* (Leipsic, 1831), the controversy ending in a practical defeat for the older theologian. In addition to numerous contributions to periodicals and to his academic writings, Coelln edited the first volume and a half of the third edition of Wilhelm Münscher's *Lehrbuch der christlichen Dogmengeschichte* (Cassel, 1832–34), but his chief work was the *Biblische Theologie* (ed. D. Schulz, 2 vols., Leipsic, 1836), which was long the standard on its subject, especially for the Old Testament.

(G. FRANK†.)

BIBLIOGRAPHY: A memoir by D. Schulz was prefixed to the *Biblische Theologie*. Consult *ADB*, iv. 391.

CŒMGEN, kem'gen (**KEVIN**), **SAINT, OF GLENDALOUGH**: A very popular Irish hermit saint of the fifth century, whose story is given here as typical of those of his kind.* He is said to have

* With regard to the alleged histories of the early Irish saints the Bollandists remark (June, iii. 331, *com. hist.* to life of S. Molingus or Dayrgellus): "To such a degree are the same things related of all Irish saints that it is difficult to believe them. For example, baptism is received from an angel, future sanctity is foretold in boyhood, the hermit life is followed in a hollow tree, a forward woman showing her preference too boldly is flogged, and there is a wonderful power over the animal world."

died June 3, 618, at the age of 120 years. His parents were Christians and had their son educated by Petroc, a pious Briton, and by holy men in Ireland. When a young girl showed a liking for Cœmgen he flogged her with nettles. Finding a lonely valley with a lake overshadowed by mountains (Glendalough, County Wicklow, 8 m. n.w. of Rathdrum), he settled there, living in a hollow tree, and subsisting on herbs and water. Afterward he was admitted to the priesthood, and returned to Glendalough, where he founded a monastery. Then he withdrew some little distance, giving orders that no one should come to him, and spent four years in his new retreat in fasting and prayer. For a time he was prevailed upon to leave his hermit life and rejoin the monks in his monastery, but he soon returned to solitude. The birds and beasts were his familiar companions, "the branches and leaves of the trees sang sweet songs to him," and he received celestial visitors. Then he was seized with the desire of wandering, visited holy men in various parts of Ireland, and had in mind a longer journey, but gave it up on the advice of a hermit, who told him that "it was more becoming for him to fix himself in one place than to ramble here and there in his old age, as he could not but know that no bird could hatch her eggs while flying." So he went back to his hermitage. When the king of Ireland invaded Leinster Cœmgen advised the local king to fight for his country; and the invader was utterly defeated and slain. Remains of Cœmgen's monastery still exist in Glendalough and a cave is shown as "St. Cœmgen's Bed."

Bibliography: *ASB*, June, i. 303-313; Lanigan, *Eccl. Hist.*, ii. 43-50; G. Petrie, *The Ecclesiastical Architecture of Ireland*, pp. 170-174, 247-267, Dublin, 1845; J. Healy, *Insula sanctorum*, pp. 414 sqq., Dublin, 1890.

CŒNOBITES. See Monasticism.

COIT, STANTON: Ethical culturist; b. at Columbus, O., Aug. 11, 1857. He was graduated at Amherst in 1879, studied at Columbia and the University of Berlin (Ph.D., 1885), and after acting as pastor of the South Place Chapel, London, E. C., in 1888–91, withdrew from the ministry, and in 1892–93 was head of the University Settlement in New York. Since 1897 he has been chairman of the Moral Instruction League, London, and was also lecturer for the West London Ethical Society in 1892 and 1906. In theology he denies the need of a belief in immortality or in supernatural beings, and would transform churches into ethical societies. He is editor of the weekly *Ethical Review*, and has written *Neighbourhood Guilds* (London, 1890) and *Die ethischen Bewegungen in der Religion* (Leipsic, 1890).

COKE, THOMAS: First Methodist bishop; b. at Brecon, Wales, Sept. 9, 1747; d. at sea on a voyage to Ceylon May 3, 1814. He studied at Jesus College, Oxford (B.A., 1768; M.A., 1770; D.C.L., 1775); took orders in the English Church and became curate at South Petherton, Somerset; fell under Methodist influences and in 1777 openly joined that body and attended the conference at Bristol. He gave much help to Wesley, who styled him "his right hand"; in 1782 he became first president of the Irish conference; in 1784 he was set apart by Wesley at Bristol as "superintendent" for America. Wesley did not approve of the title bishop, which the American conference adopted in 1787 at Coke's instigation. The latter, with two elders, arrived in America, Nov., 1784, and proceeded to the famous Christmas conference at Baltimore, at which he ordained Francis Asbury as superintendent. With Asbury he drew up the *Doctrines and Discipline* for the Methodist Church in America. He made nine voyages to America (the last in 1803) and fulfilled his duties there energetically and well. He was a leader in England after Wesley's death (1791), and was indefatigable in the cause of missions. In 1813 he wished an appointment from the government as bishop of India and offered to return to the Established Church; when the proposal was rejected he furnished funds himself to establish a Methodist mission there, sailed with a band of helpers, but died on the voyage. His numerous publications include *Extracts of the Journals of the Rev. Dr. Coke's Five Visits to America* (London, 1793); a life of John Wesley (1792), prepared in collaboration with Henry Moore (see Wesley, John); *A Commentary on the Old and New Testaments* (6 vols., 1801–03); *A History of the West Indies* (3 vols., Liverpool, 1808–11).

Bibliography: Lives were published by: S. Drew, New York, 1837, and J. W. Etheridge, London, 1860; cf. L. Tyerman, *Life and Times of John Wesley*, vol. iii., ib. 1871; W. Moister, *The Father of our Missions*, ib. 1871; *DNB*, xi. 247-249.

COLANI, cō''lā''nī', TIMOTHÉE: French theologian; b. at Lemé, near Sains (190 m. n.e. of Paris), department of Aisne, Jan. 29, 1824; d. at Grindelwald, Switzerland, Sept. 2, 1888. He was a son of the Reformed minister at Lemé, and a zealous adherent of the *Réveil*, who brought him up in a narrow dogmatism which was enhanced by influences at Neuchâtel and by the Moravians of the Kornthal. At the age of sixteen he went to Strasburg to study theology. Influenced by Reuss, he devoted himself to the study of the New Testament, and also studied philosophy, history, and literature. In 1845 he finished his academical studies and published a dissertation on Kant's religious philosophy. Two years later he obtained a theological licentiate by a treatise on the idea of the absolute. He was also a contributor to *La Réformation au 19ème siècle*, edited by Edmond Scherer at Geneva, which represented the individualistic ideas of Vinet.

He now considered it his duty to contribute to the regeneration of theological science in France. An impulse had already been given by the Strasburg faculty, but without lasting effect; and the orthodoxy of a Grandpierre and Adolphe Monod had full sway. In 1849 Edmond Scherer, till then professor at the independent theological school in Geneva, published his two letters on criticism and faith, in which he pointed out a revision of church dogmas and the return to the original ideas of the Gospel as the task of modern theology. Colani soon joined him and together they founded the

Revue de théologie et de philosophie chrétienne, which under Colani's direction became the organ of the "Strasburg School." From 1856 Colani preached often, and in vol. xiv. of the *Revue* he developed his ideas on the sermon. The attacks upon his manner of preaching induced him to publish first some of his discourses (*L'Individualisme chrétien*, *Le Sacerdoce universel*, *L'Éducation protestante*), and afterward three collections, *Sermons prêchés à Strasbourg* (Strasburg, 1857), *Nouveaux sermons* (1860), and *Quatre sermons prêchés à Nîmes* (1861).

The fame which Colani had acquired seemed to point him out for one of the first places in church or school; but the authorities were afraid to sanction officially his ideas. For this reason he had to support himself for years as private tutor. His appointment in 1861 as lecturer on French literature at the Protestant Seminary in Strasburg raised a storm of protest. Still greater and louder was the protest when, a few months later (May 15, 1862), he was appointed pastor of the French congregation of St. Nicolas, and two years later professor of homiletics in the theological faculty and professor of philosophy at the Protestant seminary. In 1864 he was made doctor of theology after publishing his noteworthy work *Jésus-Christ et les croyances messianiques de son temps* (Strasburg, 1864). Toward the end of that year he commenced his lectures on homiletics, catechetics, and liturgics in the theological faculty, and on philosophy at the Protestant seminary. His lectures, distinguished by scientific depth, keen judgment, and elegant form, attracted a large audience. In 1866 he resigned the pastorate to devote himself wholly to his two professorships. The war of 1870, however, compelled him to leave Strasburg; he joined Gambetta at Bordeaux and devoted himself to politics. He now renounced theology, but took part as a lay delegate in the deliberations at the synod of the Reformed Church of France in 1872, and with great eloquence advocated Protestant liberty. For a time interested in an industrial undertaking at Royon, Colani founded in 1876 a literary journal, *Le Courrier littéraire*, published at Paris. He afterward became sublibrarian of the Sorbonne, editor of the Gambettistic journal *La République française*, and contributor to *La Nouvelle Revue*. He was chosen as editor of *Le Temps* in 1888, but his death intervened. Over against the rationalistic and orthodox intellectualism Colani emphasized again the mystical and ethical element in Christianity; and against the principle of authority, the right of historical and inner criticism. He brought about a change of the Protestant theology of France in a strictly scientific sense. T. Gerold.

Bibliography: A biographical notice may be found in *Progrès religieux*, Strasburg, 1888, nos. 40 sqq., and another by J. Reinach in a posthumous volume of *Essais*, Paris, 1895.

COLARBASUS, COLARBASIANS. See Valentinus and his School.

COLEMAN, LEIGHTON: Protestant Episcopal bishop of Delaware; b. at Philadelphia May 3, 1837; d. at Wilmington, Del., Dec. 14, 1907. He was educated at the Protestant Episcopal Academy in his native city and the General Theological Seminary, New York City, from which he was graduated in 1861. He was rector of St. Luke's, Bustleton, Pa. (1861–63), St. John's, Wilmington, Del. (1863–66), St. Mark's, Mauch Chunk, Pa. (1866–74), and Trinity Church, Toledo, O. (1874–79). From 1879 to 1887 he resided in England, and on his return to the United States was rector of the Church of the Redeemer, Sayre, Pa., in 1887–88. In the latter year he was consecrated bishop of Delaware. He was chairman of the American Church Temperance Society 1900–06 and frequently member of important ecclesiastical committees. In theology he was a Catholic Churchman, and as such energetically maintained the cardinal doctrines of the Church and Christianity. He published: *History of the Lehigh Valley* (Philadelphia, 1868); *History of the American Church* (London, 1895); and *Popular History of the American Church* (1905).

COLEMAN, LYMAN: Congregationalist; b. at Middlefield, Mass., June 14, 1796; d. at Easton, Pa., Mar. 16, 1882. He was graduated at Yale 1817; was principal of the Latin Grammar School at Hartford 1817–20; tutor in Yale 1820–25; student of theology, and for seven years pastor of the Belchertown (Mass.) Congregational Church. He resigned, spent two years in foreign travel, held various positions, until in 1862 he became professor of Latin in Lafayette College. He published: *Antiquities of the Christian Church* (Philadelphia, 1841), a translation and compilation from Augusti's *Christliche Archäologie* and other German works; *Ancient Christianity Exemplified* (1852); *Historical Text-book and Atlas of Biblical Geography* (1854); and *Prelacy and Ritualism* (1869).

COLENSO, JOHN WILLIAM: Bishop of Natal; b. at St. Austell (13 m. n.n.e. of Truro), Cornwall, Jan. 24, 1814; d. at Durban, Natal, June 20, 1883. After taking his degree at Cambridge (St. John's College) in 1836, he was an assistant master at Harrow (1839–42), and then returned to St. John's, of which he had been a fellow since 1837, as tutor for four years. From 1846 to 1853 he was vicar of Forncett St. Mary in Norfolk, and in 1853 became the first bishop of the new see of Natal in South Africa. He worked zealously for the conversion of the natives, for whom he wrote manuals of instruction both sacred and secular in the Zulu language, as well as a Zulu grammar and dictionary. Suspicion as to his orthodoxy was aroused by his commentary on the Epistle to the Romans (1861); and when his *Pentateuch and Book of Joshua Critically Examined* (7 parts, London, 1862–79) began to appear, its line of thought (originally suggested to him by the questions of his simple Zulu converts) and especially his calling in question the historical accuracy and traditional authorship of these books, wherein he anticipated many of the ideas of later scholarship, aroused a perfect storm of opposition. His metropolitan, Bishop Gray of Cape Town, put him on trial and deposed him at the end of 1863, while his book was condemned in the following year by both houses of the Convocation of Canterbury. Denying Bishop Gray's jurisdiction, Colenso appealed to the Crown, and the judicial committee of the Privy Council pronounced his deposition null and void. A state of schism ensued, Colenso maintaining himself as still lawfully bishop of Natal, while out of communion with the rest of the Anglican body in South Africa, which set up the bishopric of Maritzburg to take the place of Natal.

Bishop Colenso was a warm friend of the Zulus, and in the later part of his life alienated many of his English adherents in South Africa by his advocacy of their cause. In 1875 he visited England to obtain justice for a native chief against the local authorities, and in the war with Cetywayo in 1879 and following years he stood boldly for right treatment of the king and his people regardless of the fears and selfish interests of the colonists. Besides the works already mentioned, he published two volumes of *Natal Sermons* (London, 1866–68) and *The New Bible Commentary by Bishops and Other Clergy of the Anglican Church* [i.e., the "Speaker's Commentary," ed. F. C. Cook, which was gotten up largely to answer his views] *Critically Examined* (6 parts, London, 1871–74).

Bibliography: For list of writings by and on Bishop Colenso, consult: G. C. Boase and W. D. Courtney, *Bibliotheca Cornubiensis*, i. 76–79, iii. 1125–27, London, 1874–81; *Life* is by G. W. Cox, 2 vols., ib. 1888; *DNB*, xi. 290–293.

COLERIDGE, SAMUEL TAYLOR: A famous English poet, philosopher, and critic; b. at Ottery St. Mary (12 m. e. of Exeter) Oct. 21, 1772; d. in London July 25, 1834. After gaining a thorough knowledge of the classics, and of Shakespeare and Milton, at the "Bluecoat School" in London, he was sent in 1791 to Jesus College, Cambridge. He suddenly left the university without a degree in 1793, and enlisted in a regiment of dragoons, from which, however, his friends procured his discharge not long afterward. He decided now to devote himself to a literary career, and joined Southey at Bristol, forming part of a group of enthusiastic young men who hailed the French Revolution as the beginning of a new order of things. They dreamed of founding a sort of communistic colony, to which they gave the high-sounding name of Pantisocracy, on the banks of the Susquehanna. Southey soon saw the futility of the undertaking, and withdrew from it; and Coleridge settled for a while at Nether Stowey, near Bridgewater, in Somersetshire, whither presently Wordsworth also came. The two friends, during their long walks and talks, felt the need of applying their principles of freedom to literature, and especially to poetry. They broke altogether with the stiff, artificial style which had been the rule of the eighteenth century, and boldly proclaimed their intention of going straight to nature for both subject and manner of treatment. Their first appearance in print after this decision was taken—anonymous, so little confidence had they in its reception—was with the epoch-making book *Lyrical Ballads* (1798), which is usually considered as marking the formal beginning of the English romantic movement. Coleridge's contributions to the book were only four in number, of which "The Ancient Mariner" was the most important. In fact, there is probably no poet in the whole range of English literature to whom so high a rank has been universally conceded on the basis of so small a body of first-rate poetry, including, besides the poem mentioned, especially "Christabel," "Kubla Khan," and "Genevieve." Coleridge made a trip to Germany in the company of Wordsworth and his sister Dorothy, spent some time at Göttingen, and became absorbed in the philosophy of Kant, which he was the first to introduce to his countrymen. Indeed, the main purpose of his later life was the interpretation and enforcement of its principles. With the exception of a year in Malta and Rome, he spent most of the time until 1810 with his friends in the Lake District, after which he went to London, and for the last nineteen years of his life was an inmate of the house of Dr. Gillman at Highgate Hill. Gillman's influence and care finally succeeded in weaning him from the opium habit, to which, at first under the stress of physical suffering, he had become enslaved. He planned many books, and partly executed a few; but he exerted more power in wonderful conversations with his friends, including a large number of younger men who, as his reputation for transcendental wisdom increased, resorted to him as an oracle. The combination of manifold gifts which he possessed was, in a way, a hindrance to achievement. He was too much of a poet to be a strict philosopher, and too much of a philosopher, at least in his later life, to give free play to his marvelous poetic faculty. Moreover, with all his learning, he was lacking in the energy necessary to fuse into one whole, according to a definite plan, the scattered material of which his mind was full. He was a very great critic; in fact the decided opinion of so competent a judge as Mr. Saintsbury (*History of Criticism*, iii. 230, London, 1904) is that he deserves in this capacity the third rank, surpassed only by Aristotle and Longinus. Not the least of the services which he rendered as a critic was the restoration of Shakespeare to his rightful position, after the oblivion into which the eighteenth century had cast him.

Life.

Coleridge had especially what is called a "seminal" mind; there was probably no one in his generation who sowed the seeds of so many ideas which were destined later to bring forth much fruit. Even more than in poetry, he was the originator of new tendencies in religious thought. On account of the desultory and fragmentary way in which he left his reflections, it is not easy to bring his views into a clear and definite system. While some have seen in him a convinced defender of revealed religion against deism and pantheism, others have thought that he was a pantheist himself, or at least a thorough Neoplatonist. There is no doubt that he passed through successive phases of belief, from the empirical philosophy through pantheism to Christian theism.

His Religion and Philosophy.

In his youthful ambition for freedom, he cut loose from the dogmas of the Church of England and threw in his lot with the Unitarian movement. Of his German masters he followed Kant most closely, though he went a good deal beyond him in a positive direction. At the same time he adopted not a few Neoplatonist ideas, and so finally by this eclectic process built up the fabric of belief which is found in his *Biographia literaria* (1816), still more in his *Aids to Reflection* (1825), and also in his essay *On the Constitution of Church and State* (1820).

Coleridge recognizes the equality of the claims of belief and knowledge; but as he wishes to hold the entire content of revelation, especially the specifically Christian doctrines, he is anxious to show the reasonable nature of revelation. The Christian faith is a perfect completion of human reason; but the less this truth is generally recognized the more necessary it is to clear away misunderstandings which lead to false conclusions. At the beginning of his intellectual process man must know himself, in order to rise to the knowledge of God, in whose likeness he is created. Now man finds in himself a spiritual element, which is his will. This will, however, is limited on one side by the law of conscience, on the other by the existence of evil. In accordance with this foundation, religion is essentially ethical—its aim a practical one, the moral and intellectual elevation of mankind. Questions of Christian doctrine must thus be decided by the practical reason rather than by the intellect. Speculative thought has no place in religion but the formal and negative one of showing that the Christian doctrines do not contradict human reason. This practical reason, the source of our religious knowledge, is the gift of God, who is himself the highest Reason and in whose light we see light. It is an intuitive power, and the ideas perceived by it are of a true reality. In regard to the relation of this practical reason to Holy Scripture, Coleridge says that the Gospel must be taken at its own valuation—not as a theological system of theoretical propositions designed to enlarge our knowledge, whether ethical or metaphysical, but as a historical narrative recounting or explaining certain facts which, though they are doctrinal truths, are none the less facts. The Bible is inspired only so far as it brings the voice of God to the heart.

Everything must be considered in the light of the significance it has for the moral life of mankind. The ethical character of Coleridge thus comes out especially in his doctrine of sin, regeneration, and justification. Sin has its source in the will, which inclines to evil and thus loses its freedom and power for good; but it can liberate itself once more, by renewed subjection to the light of God in the conscience, to become again a rational will. This is regeneration, by which man recovers the possibility of vital intercourse with the divine spirit. Redemption is thus an ethical act of the subject, and there is no room in this scheme for an objective redemption. Salvation is indeed said to proceed from Christ; but his person as well as his work remains a mystery, since the capacity of suffering is inconsistent with his divine attributes, and a vicarious sacrifice with ethical conceptions. In the attempt to include the whole content of revelation, Coleridge admits the possibility of believing doctrines which transcend human reason. Some of these, like that of the Trinity, he does not consider objects of the practical reason, although he says that the true idea of God includes such a notion. His understanding of it is based on Neoplatonism. The Logos, the divine light, is immanent in humanity. He has revealed himself in history, in religion, as well as in philosophy and poetry—most perfectly in Christ and Christianity, but Socrates and Plato have a place beside Paul and John. The Logos leads mankind to ever higher moral and intellectual development, not only in this life but also in the next; and thus the restoration of all things is made possible.

It is not surprising that the attempt to widen Christianity into a religion embracing all that is true, good, and beautiful in the world should have met with strong opposition and equally strong approval. Coleridge's modest earnestness, the pacific tone of his argument, the mystical element in the intuitive reason, the emphasis laid upon the ethical side of Christianity, the reconciliation of faith and knowledge, the recognition of good in any form, and the wide freedom given to individual conceptions were characteristics which appealed to many minds in that period more than any other form of Christian belief. Those who were influenced by this teaching, though they did not go so far as to found a new church, took up some element or elements of it and developed them further along the same lines; and it is not too much to say that Coleridge was the originator of the Broad-church or liberal movement in the Church of England which was so striking a feature of the nineteenth century.

BIBLIOGRAPHY: Materials for a life are found in his own *Biographia literaria*, ed. with notes by his nephew, H. N. Coleridge, for *Bohn's Library*, 1866; in the *Table Talk* and *Omniana*, ed. for the same series by T. Ashe, 1888, republished by Bell, 1905; and in his *Miscellanies*, ed. Ashe, 1888. Various *Letters* appear in Sir H. Davy's *Fragmentary Remains*, London, 1858; in C. K. Paul's *W. Godwin*, ib. 1876; in *Fraser's Magazine*, July, 1878; *Westminster Review*, April and July, 1870; and in E. V. Lucas's *Charles Lamb and the Lloyds*, New York, 1898. Coleridge *Bibliographies* are provided by R. H. Shepherd, London, 1901, and by J. L. Haney, ib. 1904. Lives are by: J. D. Campbell, ib. 1894 (a critical study of the life, not going into the literary work); A. Brandl, Berlin, 1886, Eng. transl., London, 1887; H. Caine, ib. 1887; W. Pater, in *Appreciations*, ib. 1889; H. D. Traill, in *English Men of Letters Series*, ib. 1890; cf. L. Stephen, *Hours in a Library*, ib. 1892; W. Watson, in *Excursions in Criticism*, ib. 1893. Consult further the essays by W. G. T. Shedd and J. Marsh in the *Complete Works* of Coleridge, i. 9–64, 67–110, New York, 1856; J. Tulloch, *Movement of Religious Thought in Britain*, pp. 1–40, ib. 1886.

COLET, JOHN: One of the "reformers before the Reformation"; b., probably in London, 1466 or 1467; d. there Sept. 16, 1519. He studied at Oxford and on the Continent. In 1497 he began to give lectures on the New Testament at Oxford. Rejecting the allegorical interpretation and the scholastic method, he aimed to get at the sense, and he showed independence by suggesting that the first chapters of Genesis were poetry. At Oxford he met Erasmus and became his intimate friend. In 1504 he was made dean of St. Paul's and took the degree of D.D.; he introduced expository preaching and a perpetual divinity lecture on three days in each week. In 1505 he inherited a fortune from his father, the greater part of which he shortly after applied to the foundation of St. Paul's School. In 1509 he prepared in English a little treatise on Latin accidence for the boys in St. Paul's School, to which William Lilly, head master of the school, furnished a syntax; it was probably printed about 1510, and has been reprinted many times since, even as late as 1836. *A Right Fruitful Admonition concerning the Order of a Good Christian Man's Life Made by the Famous Dr. Colet* was first printed in 1534; later it came to be known as *Daily Devotions, or the Christian's morning and evening sacrifice*, and to include matter not by Colet.

BIBLIOGRAPHY: His manuscripts have been published with transl. and notes, 5 vols., London, 1867–74, by J. H. Lupton, who edited and translated Erasmus's life of Colet, ib. 1883, and wrote *A Life of Dean Colet*, ib. 1887 (the best modern life). Consult: F. Seebohm, *Three Oxford Reformers, Colet, Erasmus, More*, ib. 1887; A. J. Mason, *Lectures on Colet, Fisher, and More*, ib. 1895; *DNB*, xi. 321–328.

COLIGNY, cō″lī″nyī′, **GASPARD DE**: French statesman and Huguenot leader; b. at Châtillon-sur-Loing (80 m. s.e. of Paris) Feb. 16, 1516; assassinated at Paris Aug. 24, 1572. He was the second son of Gaspard de Châtillon, marshal of France (d. 1522), and Louise de Montmorency, a sister of the famous constable of France, but became the head of the family in 1533. He had thorough military and diplomatic training, and at the same time a character of singular purity. He fought with great distinction against Charles V. (1542–44), and in 1547 was made commander of the French infantry. In 1552 he was made admiral of France, and in 1555 governor of Picardy. As such he signed the armistice of Vancelles Feb. 5, 1156; but when Henry II. broke it he fought valiantly, despite his disapproval of the act, and after the defeat of the constable at St. Quentin, Aug. 10, 1557, he actually saved Paris by holding the city of St. Quentin for seventeen days, thus enabling the French to reorganize their army. On its surrender he was carried a prisoner into the Netherlands, where he was confined first at Sluis and then at Ghent, until ransomed at enormous expense after the peace of Château-Cambrésis (Apr. 3, 1559). But from the prisons of Philip II. he returned a Protestant. He was not entirely a stranger to the Reformation. His mother was familiar with the "new ideas," and had refused to allow a priest to attend her at death. His tutor, Nicolas Bérauld, was a friend of Erasmus. His wife, Charlotte de Laval, was strongly attracted by the movement; his brother Odet later joined the Reformed, and his other brother Andelot had openly embraced Protestantism. In his long imprisonment Coligny had leisure to read Calvinistic writings sent him by Andelot. His resolve to break with the established faith was strengthened by a letter from Calvin, dated Sept. 4, 1558.

1. Life to 1559. Conversion to Protestantism.

Through the sudden death of Henry II. (1559), and the accession of Francis II., the Guises gained full control, whereupon Coligny retired from court and resigned the governorship of Picardy (1560), though he retained his post as admiral. He did not openly acknowledge his belief until July, 1559, being fully aware that his step might be fatal to his family. Meanwhile the public discontent at the usurpation of the Guises reached a climax. The conspiracy of Amboise in 1560 amply shows the state of popular opinion in France. At the Convention of the Notables at Fontainebleau (Aug. 21–26, 1559) Coligny made brave but inefficient attempts to gain more freedom of worship for the Protestants, but the sudden death of Francis II. (Dec. 5, 1560) changed the whole aspect of affairs. Catherine de' Medici became regent for her son Charles IX., then ten years of age, and adopted a policy of accommodation which furthered the spread of Protestantism throughout France, so that when Coligny again pleaded for his coreligionists at the assembly of the States-General at Orléans (Dec. 13, 1560) his words were not ignored. Persecution ceased, toleration was shown on both sides, and there were fair prospects of ending the conflict with a peaceable settlement. But on Mar. 1, 1562, the massacre of Vassy took place, and a month later the first religious war began with the occupation of Orléans by Andelot. On one side were the Roman Catholics, the Guises, and Anthony of Navarre; on the other, the Protestants, Coligny, the Prince of Condé, and Henry of Navarre; and between the two parties, the court, the king, and Catherine de' Medici. The war actually ended with the assassination of Francis of Guise by Jean Poltrot de Merey, in the camp before Orléans, Feb. 24, 1563; and on Mar. 19 peace was concluded at Amboise, by which freedom of conscience, and, within certain limits, liberty of worship were granted to the Protestants. But the hatred of the house of Guise for Coligny was only deepened by the events. Poltrot declared that he had been encouraged to murder Francis of Guise by Coligny, Beza, and others, but Coligny was acquitted by the Assembly of Notables at Moulins (Jan. 29, 1566).

2. 1560–66.

Four years of peace followed. But in the mean time the development of affairs in the Netherlands, the imprisonment of Egmont and Horn (Sept. 9, 1567), and rumors of a plan to capture the prince of Condé and execute Coligny so aroused the Protestants that they incited the second religious war. The scheme of seizing the king at Monceaux, near Meaux, failed (Sept. 27, 1567), but the victory at St. Denis (Nov. 10, 1567) led to the brief peace of Longjumeau (Mar. 23, 1568), by which the agreement of Amboise was renewed. Within the year, however, the third religious war began. It ended with the peace of St. Germain (Aug. 2, 1570), after the battles of Jarnac, Moncontour, and Arnay le Duc, and gave the Protestants freedom of conscience and worship together with three cities of safety. Meanwhile Charles IX. had become averse to the Spanish direction which French politics had lately shown. Coligny was called to Blois Sept. 12, 1571; and the king seemed to listen to him with confidence. The negotiations for a marriage between Margaret of Valois, the sister of the king, and Henry of Navarre finally succeeded, and were regarded as favorable to the Protestant cause. The wedding

3. 1566–72. The Massacre of St. Bartholomew.

ceremony was celebrated Aug. 18. But Aug. 22, when Coligny returned from the Louvre to his house (the present No. 144 Rue de Rivoli) he was fired upon twice and slightly wounded by an assassin. The next day the king and queen dowager visited him. On the way back to the Louvre the king confessed to his mother that Coligny had urged him to retain the royal power in his own hands. The queen mother, already an avowed enemy of Coligny, now resolved to destroy both him and his adherents. All arrangements having been quickly completed, the massacre of the Huguenots (q.v.) was begun at four o'clock on Sunday, Aug. 24, St. Bartholomew's Day. The first object of attack was Coligny, who was slain, thrown from the window, his head cut off, and his body dragged through the streets and hanged on the gallows of Montfaucon. After a few days his corpse was taken down and buried by Marshal Montmorency, and after many vicissitudes it was reinterred in a fragment of the wall of his ancestral castle (which was destroyed during the French Revolution) on Sept. 7, 1851. From Paris the massacre spread throughout France, sparing neither sex, age, rank, nor learning. The estimated number of Huguenots killed varies between 10,000 and 100,000, but may most probably be reckoned at 5,000 in the capital and somewhat over 20,000 in the rest of France. At the command of the king the Parliament declared Coligny guilty of high treason and pronounced his children infamous (Oct. 27, 1572), although this decision was reversed by another of the same body on June 10, 1599. A solemn *Te Deum* was sung at the Vatican by Gregory XIII., who also had Vasari paint three frescos representing the wounding of Coligny, the conference concerning the massacre, and its execution. On July 17, 1889, a marble statue was erected in honor of Coligny by Protestant subscriptions and in disregard of Roman Catholic protests, in the Rue de Rivoli near the place where he was wounded.

The literary work of Coligny was scanty. His account of the siege of St. Quentin, written in admirable style, was first printed under the title *Mémoires de l'amiral de Coligny* (Paris, 1623; Eng. transl. by D. D. Scott, Edinburgh, 1844), while a number of briefer works and letters are scattered in various journals, and his military regulations have been edited by M. L. Cimber and F. Danjou (*Archives curieuses de l'histoire de France*, series i., vol. viii.). (THEODOR SCHOTT†.)

BIBLIOGRAPHY: The first life was written at the request of the family by F. Hotmann, *Gasparis Colonii . . . vita*, Leyden, 1575, Eng. transl., London, 1596, Fr. transl., Paris, 1576. An excellent account is by E. Bersier, *Coligny avant les guerres de religion*, Paris, 1884, Eng. transl., *The Earlier Life of Coligny*, London, 1885 (comes down to 1560). A still more elaborate life was begun by E. Marcks, *Gaspard von Coligny. Sein Leben und das Frankreich seiner Zeit*, vol. i., part 1, Stuttgart, 1892 (comes down to 1562). Consult further: J. Delaborde, *Gaspard de Coligny*, Paris, 1879–83; A. Meylau, *Vie de Gaspard de Coligny*, ib. 1862; W. M. Blackburn, *Admiral Coligny and the Rise of the Huguenots*, Philadelphia, 1869; C. Buet, *L'Amiral de Coligny et les guerres de religion*, Paris, 1884; W. Besant, *Gaspard de Coligny*, London, 1894; *Cambridge Modern History*, vol. iii., chaps. i., vii., viii., New York, 1905.

On the Massacre of St. Bartholomew consult: W. Soldan, *Geschichte des Protestantismus in Frankreich*, Leipsic, 1855 (still the best); H. White, *Massacre of St. Bartholomew*, New York, 1868; H. M. Baird, *Rise of the Huguenots*, ib. 1879; H. Baumgarten, *Vor der Bartholomäusnacht*, Strasburg, 1882.

COLIGNY, ODET DE: Cardinal of Châtillon, brother of Gaspard de Coligny; b. at the castle of Châtillon-sur-Loing (75 m. s.e. of Paris), department of Loiret, July 10, 1517; d. at Canterbury, England, Mar. 22, 1571. He received a cardinal's hat from Clement VII. in 1533, and in 1534 went to Rome for the election of a new pope; and, although he had not yet been ordained priest, he was made archbishop of Toulouse, and, in 1535, bishop count of Cambrai, which raised him to the rank of a nobleman of France. In 1560 Pius IV. named him grand inquisitor of France, but the opposition to the institution on the part of the Parliament of Paris relieved him from the odious duties of the position. During the reign of Henry II. (d. 1559) he was apparently indifferent to the religious dissensions, but in April, 1561, he publicly accepted the Reformed faith. He now took active part with his brother in the religious quarrels and mediated between the Huguenots and Catherine de' Medici. In 1562 he was declared heretical by the Inquisition. He fled to Lyons, relinquished his title of cardinal, calling himself the count of Beauvais, and served in the field in the religious wars. In 1568 he went to London, where Queen Elizabeth showed many marks of favor to him and his wife ("Mme. la Cardinale"). While preparing to join his brother at La Rochelle, he was poisoned, as it was rumored, by his valet at the instigation of Catherine de' Medici. He wrote *Les Constitutions synodales* (Paris, 1554), and a number of unpublished letters are in the Bibliothèque Nationale in Paris and the Record Office in London. He is buried in the Canterbury cathedral.

G. BONET-MAURY.

BIBLIOGRAPHY: Bouchet, *Preuves de l'histoire généalogique de la maison de Coligny*, Paris, 1662; G. Bonet-Maury, *Les origines de la réforme à Beauvais*, ib. 1874; Becquerel, *Souvenirs historiques sur l'Amiral Coligny, sa famille et sa seigneurie*, Paris, 1876; L. Marlet, *Le Cardinal de Châtillon*, ib. 1883; idem, *Correspondance d'Odet de Coligny*, ib. 1885; E. G. Atkinson, *The Cardinal of Châtillon in England, 1568–71*, London, 1890.

COLLECT: A short prayer which forms a normal part of the mass and breviary offices in the Roman Catholic Church, as of the communion service and morning and evening prayer in the Anglican communion. Like the epistle and gospel which follow it in the altar service, it changes with the day or season, and on festivals has reference to the event or person commemorated. It is usually concise, and its normal structure embraces an invocation, a reason for the petition, the petition itself, the benefit hoped for from its granting, and the conclusion pleading the merits of Christ, since most collects (especially the ancient) are addressed to God the Father. Many of the collects now in use can be traced back to the sacramentaries of Gelasius and Gregory the Great, if not farther.

BIBLIOGRAPHY: W. Bright, *Ancient Collects*, London, 1861; *DCA*, i. 403–404; *KL*, iii. 603–605; McClintock and Strong, *Cyclopædia*, ii. 409–410 (valuable).

Origin and Early History.

COLLEGIA NATIONALIA (PONTIFICIA): The name of several training-schools in Rome for missionaries destined to labor in Christian but not Roman Catholic countries. Their original foundation was due to Ignatius Loyola, who established the first of them for Germany in 1552. The later ones are all modeled after this, the Collegium Germanicum. After a short period of prosperity, it declined and was in a poor condition when Gregory XIII. restored it in 1573, following up this action by the foundation of Greek (1577), English (1579), Hungarian (united in 1584 with the German), Maronite (1584), and Thracian-Illyrian colleges, as well as three similar institutions at Vienna, Prague, and Fulda. The system received two notable additions on the foundation of the English College. Candidates for admission were to be received only after several months' probation and the taking of a vow never to abandon the clerical state and to be always ready to return to their native country and work there at the bidding of their superiors. Five special privileges, moreover, considerably facilitating ordination, were conceded to those who were thus received. These two points, with their analogy to monastic conditions, made the colleges almost monastic congregations, whose superiors were the cardinal protectors assigned to them. The revised statutes, however, given to the German College in 1584 forbade the reception of those who had already taken the vows of an order, or the taking of such vows by a member of the college, as this would have been inconsistent with their lifelong dedication to their special work.

Later Development.

Some of Gregory's foundations, including those at Prague, Vienna, and Fulda, lapsed in course of time. The German-Hungarian, Greek, English, and Maronite went on, and Clement VIII. added a Scottish College in 1600. On the establishment in 1622 of the Congregation de Propaganda Fide the oversight of the colleges gradually passed into its hands in all essential points. Under its auspices the Collegium Urbanum de Propaganda Fide was founded by Gregory XV. in 1627, and the Irish College a year later. Other new or revived foundations outside of Rome with similar aims were those of Vienna, Prague and Loreto (1627), Fulda (1628), the archiepiscopal seminary of Prague (1638), the Greek seminary at San Benedetto in Ullano (1732), and the Chinese at Naples (1736). By the middle of the nineteenth century the Maronite College had been united with the Urbanum, and a number of others founded, including a Greek seminary at Palermo; a Swiss at Milan; the great Séminaire des Missions Étrangères for China and the neighboring regions and the Séminaire du Saint-Esprit for the French colonies, both in Paris; an Irish college there and at Douai, and four colleges in Ireland itself, at Dublin, Youghall, Thurles, and Carlow, the last destined for foreign missionaries.

Present Status.

Of the national colleges erected in Rome the German, Greco-Ruthenian, English, Scottish, and Irish are still in operation. These all train their students for work in a definite geographical area; even the general Collegium Urbanum educates each student for his own native country, and as a rule sends him back there. The constitutions of all these colleges follow more or less closely that of the German College. The students, drawn as far as possible from the country in which they are to work, are under the direction of some order, usually the Jesuits. They remain in a permanent relation of intercourse with the rector of their college, who in his turn is subject to the Propaganda. There are a number of other more or less similar institutions in Rome which must not be confounded with the national colleges. These serve for their respective countries (North and South America, Belgium, Poland, Bohemia, Switzerland, France) as homes for the students coming thence to attend the lectures of the Collegium Romanum; only the North American and the Polish have the status of collegia pontificia, i.e., under the immediate supervision of the pope. (See CURIA.)

(E. FRIEDBERG.)

BIBLIOGRAPHY: O. Mejer, *Die Propaganda*, Göttingen, i. 73-91, 225-245, Göttingen, 1852; A. Bellesheim, *William Cardinal Allen und die englischen Seminare auf dem Festlande*, Mainz, 1885; *KL*, iii. 610-646 (very extended treatment). On the German College: *Das deutsche Collegium in Rom*, Leipsic, 1843; A. Steinhuber, *Geschichte des Collegium germanicum-hungaricum in Rom*, 2 vols., Freiburg, 1894.

COLLEGIAL OR COLLEGIATE CHURCHES: In the Roman Catholic Church, churches served by a body of canons, regular or secular, living together in *collegia;* and in the Anglican Church, by a dean and a number of canons, while the cathedral churches are always served by a bishop. In New York City the term "Collegiate Church" is best known as applied to a corporation in the Reformed (Dutch) Church which owns considerable property, out of whose rental the deficit in the support of four churches with their clergy and chapels is met.

COLLEGIALISM: [A term denoting a conception of the relation between Church and State which developed in Germany in the seventeenth and eighteenth centuries. The name, first used by J. H. Böhmer of Halle (d. 1749), was derived from the Roman law, which, before Constantine, considered the Christian congregations as *collegia illicita* ("illegal associations").]

The school of natural rights, which has been running its triumphant course since the middle of the seventeenth century, teaches as follows: the State is not a divine foundation and institution, but a corporate unity, founded by means of a social compact of free men (*pactum unionis*); under this bond the "powers that be" have arisen by virtue of an additional compact, or *pactum subjectionis*. Furthermore, neither is the Church any longer a divine institution, but a *collegium* which has grown up in the State through a social compact. According to these doctrines, the medieval idea of the unity of Church and State, of *unum corpus christianum*, is given up. The State has no longer in common with the Church the object of promoting the spiritual welfare of men, but the object of the State is the prosperity of its subjects: the State is an object in itself. Several religious associations are conceivable side by side; and, intrinsically regarded, all these associations stand on a perfectly equal footing: there is no internal warrant given for any difference of treatment among them on the side of the State. Still again, if the Church is only one association within the State, it is of course but logical that the Church governs itself and administers its affairs independently, and that the sovereign State authority exercises over this association, the same as over other associations, merely a right of surveillance.

On the basis of this doctrine of natural right, territorialism (q.v.) had maintained, in theory, the independence of the Church; but it was collegialism, an elaboration of territorialism, that carried that doctrine to its logical conclusion. The first and foremost exponent of collegialism is conceded to be Christoph Matthäus Pfaff (q.v.). Its adherents include Mosheim, G. L. Böhmer (whose views are embodied in the Prussian common law, his *Principia juris canonici speciatim juris ecclesiastici*, Göttingen, 1762, having been used in the revision of the ecclesiastical law), Georg Wiese, Schleiermacher, Puchta, and others. It may be summarized as follows: The Church as a voluntary association has only two classes of members, teachers and hearers—not the three estates of nobility, clergy, and people (Germ. *Wehr-, Lehr- und Nährstände*)—and these two classes stand side by side with equal rights, the teachers having no sovereign authority over the hearers.

In this way the rights of the third estate become still more sharply emphasized than was the case under territorialism. As free associations the churches are self-governing (*jura sacrorum collegialia*); the State has only the same rights, as affecting them, that it has in relation to any other associations existing in the State; that is, only the right of supervision, the *jura sacrorum majestatica*. And these latter are restricted by the exponents of collegialism to actual rights of supervision; so that the power inherent in association is guaranteed the character of a real government. At the same time, this power of association may be made over by an act of transfer to the State ruler; and the exponents of collegialism teach that this was the case in Germany by virtue of a tacit transfer. The rights of the State sovereign over the Church are therefore not identical with the State's rights (as in territorialism), but they are the power of association as conveyed *per pactum*, which is to be distinguished from the sovereign's inherent rights in the way of State surveillance. Although this system has been able to change practically nothing in actual conditions, nevertheless, by defining more sharply than did territorialism the division between Church and State, between power of association and State sovereignty, it has prepared the way toward the modern comprehension of things and the modern construction of the constitution of the Church. See CHURCH AND STATE. E. SEHLING.

BIBLIOGRAPHY: F. J. Stahl, *Kirchenverfassung nach Lehre und Recht der Protestanten*, Erlangen, 1840; A. L. Richter, *Geschichte der evangelischen Kirchenverfassung in Deutschland*, Leipsic, 1851; O. Mejer, *Grundlagen des lutherischen Kirchenregiments*, Rostock, 1864; K. Rieker, *Rechtliche Stellung der evangelischen Kirche Deutschlands*, Leipsic, 1893.

COLLEGIANTS (RHYNSBURGERS): A branch of the Remonstrants in Holland (see REMONSTRANTS). In 1619 the Remonstrant minister Christopher Sopingius was dismissed at Warmond, whereupon Gysbert van der Kodde proposed that the congregation hold services without the ministrations of a clergyman. Such *exercitia* or *colloquia prophetica* were common in the time of the Reformation. One prayed and read and any one who felt inclined addressed the congregation. At first meetings were held every month, afterward every week. After the death of Prince Maurice (1625) the Remonstrant ministers were allowed to return, but Van der Kodde opposed the settlement of a minister at Warmond and, with a number of followers, removed to the neighboring village of Rhynsburg (3 m. n. of Leyden), where they continued their services.

The example of Rhynsburg was followed and *collegia* were formed in various places, one of which (at Rotterdam) lasted till 1787. Delegates met annually at Rhynsburg, where the Lord's Supper was celebrated and adults were baptized. A result of Spinoza's residence at Rhynsburg (1661–64) was that many Collegiants accepted his ideas and rejected prophecy and miracles. This caused a split, and for years two parties met separately until a reconciliation was effected at the beginning of the seventeenth century.

The Collegiants believed that Christianity had sadly degenerated through the influence of the sects. They claimed freedom of speech for all and mutual toleration. They did not desire to establish a new Church and admitted all Christians to their meetings. They were noted for benevolence, especially for caring for the poor and for orphans. They did not seek public offices and they had a horror of war. Their significance lies in the fact that they defended the principle of the Reformation—the right of the individual in matters of religion—against those who wished to limit this right. H. C. ROGGE†.

The influence of Polish Socinianism is discerned in two particulars, in the liberal type of doctrine and in the practise of immersion. The Collegiants drew largely from the Mennonites, who had no adequate educational facilities and were attracted by the able exegesis of the Bible in the Collegiant meetings. The last meeting seems to have been held May 27, 1787. A. H. N.

BIBLIOGRAPHY: J. C. van Slee, *De Rijnsburger Collegianten*, Haarlem, 1895 (best); J. M. Schröck, *Kirchengeschichte*, v. 330–331, 10 vols., Leipsic, 1804–12; H. Grégoire, *Histoire des sectes religieuses*, v. 328 sqq., 6 vols., Paris, 1828–45; J. L. von Mosheim, *Church History*, cent. xvii., book iv., chap. viii., London, 1863; *KL*, iii. 607–608.

COLLENBUSCH, SAMUEL: German mystic; b. at Wicklinghausen (a suburb of Barmen) Sept. 1, 1724; d. at Barmen Sept. 1, 1803. He studied medicine at Duisburg and Strasburg, in the latter place becoming interested in mysticism through the large collection of works on that subject and on alchemy found there. For a time he engaged in experiments in alchemy, but after repeated failure returned to Duisburg and took up the practise of medicine. In 1784 he removed to Barmen.

His reading included Leibnitz's *Théodicée* and the writings of Anton, Oetinger, and Bengel, by which his tendency toward a mystic piety was strengthened. In Duisburg he had won a place in the circle in which J. G. Hasencamp was leader, and in Barmen he was brought into relations with a similar circle, the characteristic of which was a deep and earnest piety. He became interested in problems of dogmatics, particularly in soteriology and eschatology.

His system is to be understood from the standpoint of the new learning. To the question, Why has God sent his Son into the world? the answer was given in the words of Rom. viii. 4: That the ordinance of the law might be fulfilled in us. Christ as the antithesis of Adam, who brought death on man, offers life, and this has come about through the love of God, which induces faith. But in his doctrine of the Christ he held a thoroughgoing Kenosis (q.v.) as best expressing the self-humiliation through which Christ achieved salvation. Going with this was a strong opposition to the doctrine of predestination. For him revelation was history, and Biblical history the story of redemption, finally accomplished on the cross. The force of his exposition gained him large influence, and his teaching, extended by the labors of his disciples Krafft, of Erlangen, and G. Menken, had a formative bearing upon the newer theology as represented by Thomasius and Hofmann. His outlook upon this life gave a practical turn to the activities of his followers which is expressed in the Missionary Society and Mission House of Barmen. (H. Cremer†.)

Bibliography: For his doctrines consult: *Erklärung biblischer Wahrheiten*, 2 vols., Elberfeld, 1807–16; *Goldene Aepfel in silbernen Schalen*, Barmen, 1854; F. W. Krug, *Die Lehre des Dr. Collenbusch*, Elberfeld, 1846. For his life consult: *Mittheilungen aus dem Leben und Wirken S. Collenbusch in Barmen*, Barmen, 1853; K. C. E. Ehmann, *F. C. Oetinger's Leben und Briefe*, pp. 778–798, Stuttgart, 1859.

COLLIER, JEREMY: Nonjuring English clergyman; b. at Stowe Qui or Quire (5 m. n.e. of Cambridge), Cambridgeshire, Sept. 23, 1650; d. in London Apr. 26, 1726. He studied at Caius College, Cambridge (B.A., 1673; M.A., 1676), took orders, and was rector at Ampton, Suffolk, 1679–85, then resided in London. After the Revolution he wrote a number of bitter political pamphlets on the Jacobite side, and made himself offensive to the government by his conduct; he was twice imprisoned (1688 and 1692), but was treated leniently on the whole; was made bishop by the nonjurors in 1713. He led a life of great literary activity; his *Short View of the Immorality and Profaneness of the English Stage* (London, 1698) was a vigorous attack and was vigorously resisted; it is hypercritical and too vehement, nevertheless it marks the beginning of a better day for the English drama. His *Essays* (complete collected edition, 1722) are interesting and not without historical value. His work of most permanent value was *An Ecclesiastical History of Great Britain to the End of the Reign of Charles II.* (2 vols., 1708–14; ed. with life by T. Lathbury, 9 vols., 1852). He published also *The Great Historical, Geographical, Genealogical, and Poetical Dictionary* (4 vols., 1701–21), a translation and continuation of Moreri's *Dictionnaire historique*, and translated the *Meditations* of Marcus Aurelius (1701).

Bibliography: There is an extended notice in *DNB*, xi. 341–347, with references to literature.

COLLINS, ANTHONY: Deist; b. at Isleworth (2 m. s.w. of Brentford, a s.w. suburb of London) or at Heston (3 m. w. of Brentford) June 21, 1676; d. in London Dec. 13, 1729. He studied at Eton and King's College, Cambridge, and in the Temple, London, but never practised law. He was a man of means, possessed of no slight ability in practical affairs, amiable and blameless in private life. Locke was his intimate friend, and during visits to Holland in 1711 and 1713 he became acquainted with Le Clerc and other scholars there. After 1715 he lived in Essex and was justice of the peace, deputy lieutenant, and treasurer of the county. His works are noteworthy more for the commotion they occasioned than for their intrinsic merit. The best known is *A Discourse of Free-Thinking* (London, 1713), in which he asserts that sound belief must rest on free inquiry, and hints that the adoption of rational principles would exclude a belief in supernaturalism. Richard Bentley made a reply (*Remarks . . . by Phileleutherus Lipsiensis*, 1713), in which he showed many defects in Collins' scholarship; Swift also entered the lists with *Mr. Collins's Discourse of Freethinking Put into Plain English by Way of Abstract for the Use of the Poor* (1713). Earlier works were *An Essay Concerning the Use of Reason* (1707), *Priestcraft in Perfection* (1709), and *A Vindication of the Divine Attributes* (1710); in the last-named he maintains that we can have a true, even if limited, knowledge of the divine attributes. In 1715 he published *A Philosophical Inquiry Concerning Human Liberty*, a defense of determinism. *A Historical and Critical Essay on the Thirty-nine Articles* (1724) elaborates an argument of *Priestcraft in Perfection* that the twentieth of the Thirty-nine Articles is fraudulent. In *A Discourse on the Grounds and Reasons of the Christian Religion* (1724) he assumes that the fulfilment of prophecy is the only valid proof of Christianity, and, since such fulfilment can be found only by taking unwarranted liberties with the text, he argues that Christianity has no valid proof. A reply to this work by Edward Chandler (q.v.) called forth *The Scheme of Literal Prophecy Considered* (1726). Collins's works were published anonymously, but their authorship was really no secret. See Deism, I., § 5.

Bibliography: L. Stephen, *History of English Thought*, 2 vols., London, 1881; J. Cairns, *Unbelief in the Eighteenth Century*, pp. 37–78, ib. 1881; *DNB*, xi. 363–364.

COLLINS, WILLIAM RUSSELL: Reformed Episcopalian; b. in New York City Dec. 14, 1862. He was graduated from the Reformed Episcopal Theological Seminary at Philadelphia in 1888, and was minister and rector of Emanuel Church, Baltimore (1887–91); assistant rector of St. Paul's, Philadelphia (1891–93); and rector of Christ Church, Cumberland, Md. (1893–97); Trinity, Ashtabula, O. (1897–1900); Church of the Reconciliation, Brooklyn (1900–02); and St. Paul's, Woodlawn Heights, New York City (since 1903). Since 1903 he has also been professor of liturgiology

III.—11

and ecclesiology and of the literary study of the English Bible in the Reformed Episcopal Seminary, Philadelphia. In theology he is an adherent of moderate Calvinism, being likewise opposed to ritualism and to the higher criticism.

COLLYER, ROBERT: Unitarian; b. at Keighley (31 m. n.e. of Manchester), Yorkshire, England, Dec. 8, 1823. He was a mill-hand from 1832 to 1838, and a blacksmith in England and America from 1838 to 1859, being also a local Methodist Episcopal preacher during the latter ten years of this period. He emigrated to the United States in 1850, and nine years later, becoming a convert to Unitarianism, went to Chicago as pastor of Unity Church, where he remained until 1879. He then accepted a call to the Church of the Messiah, New York City, holding this charge until 1903, when he became pastor emeritus. He has published several volumes of discourses and addresses, a biography of A. H. Conant (Boston, 1868), and collaborated with J. H. Turner in the *History of the Town and Parish of Ilkley* (London, 1886).

COLLYRIDIANS: A sect of women, mentioned by Epiphanius (*Hær.*, lxxviii.-lxxix.), who came from Thrace to Arabia, and seem to have espoused a peculiar form of devotion to the Virgin, offering to Mary, on appointed days, a cake or loaf (Gk. *kollyris*). While there are not wanting religious and historic analogies to this custom, they nevertheless come short of certain application. According to Jer. xliv. 19, the Jewish women in Egypt prepared cakes for the queen of heaven (cf. Rösch, *Astarte und Maria*, in *TSK*, lxi. 265 sqq.). Ceremonial pastry was likewise a feature of the Thesmophoric rites in Athens (cf. Mommsen, *Feste der Stadt Athen im Altertum*, Leipsic, 1898). There is possible, also, some misconception of a Christmas custom (cf. Möller, *Kirchengeschichte*, i. 535, Freiburg, 1889). Indeed, to this day in modern Greece the word *kolloura* is used for a kind of cake, and in certain of the Ionian Islands such a *kolloura* is consecrated and consumed on Christmas eve in the family circle with all sorts of ceremonies (cf. B. Schmidt, *Das Volksleben der Neugriechen und das hellenische Altertum*, i. 62 sqq., Leipsic, 1871).

G. Krüger.

Bibliography: C. W. F. Walch, *Historie der Ketzereien*, iii. 625-634, Leipsic, 1766; J. L. von Mosheim, *Institutes of Eccl. Hist.*, ed. W. Stubbs, i. 317, London, 1863; Neander, *Christian Church*, ii. 376.

COLMAN, SAINT: Third abbot and bishop of Lindisfarne; d. on the island of Inishbofin, off the coast of County Galway, Ireland, Aug. 8, 676. He was a monk of Iona, and succeeded Finan (q.v.) at Lindisfarne in 661. The dispute between the Roman and Irish parties in England came to a crisis shortly thereafter. Colman was the leader of the latter at the Synod of Whitby (q.v.) in 664, and when he was defeated, with the Irish monks and about thirty of the English, he left the country, taking with him the bones of Aidan (q.v.). They went first to Iona, and, after four years there, to Inishbofin. Dissensions arising between the Irish and English, Colman founded a new monastery for the latter on the mainland, but himself remained on the island.

Bibliography: Bede, *Hist. eccl.*, iii. 25-27, iv. 1, 4, 24; W. Bright, *Early English Church History*, pp. 221-232, Oxford, 1897.

COLOGNE, ARCHBISHOPRIC OF: The rise of the city of Cologne is connected with the transplantation by Augustus of the Germanic tribe of the Ubii to the left bank of the Rhine. Their capital was Oppidum Ubiorum, in the year 50 made a Roman veterans' colony (Colonia Agrippina). It became the political and military headquarters of the province of Lower Germany, and soon the most populous town on the lower Rhine. If the remark of Irenæus (I. x. 2) about Christian communities in the Germanic provinces is to be taken literally, it would indicate an antiquity for the church of Cologne extending into the second century. The first certain datum is reached with the participation of Bishop Maternus in the Synod of Arles (mentioned by Eusebius and Optatus), and with some fourth-century inscriptions given by Kraus. The small number of the latter shows that Cologne was a less important Christian center than the neighboring Treves; with which agrees the mention of the church there as a *conventiculum* by the pagan writer Ammianus Marcellinus in 355. The list of bishops goes no farther back than Maternus, and the attribution of the same name to the legendary founder indicates that tradition knew of no earlier bishop. His successor, Euphrates, is mentioned as a participant in the Synod of Sardica by Athanasius; his name does not occur in the lists, and was probably erased in consequence of a later (Frankish) legend which stigmatized him as an Arian, and asserted that he was deposed by a synod at Cologne in 346. The mention by Venantius Fortunatus of Carentius, who does not occur in the lists, shows that they are not to be depended on; and the same conclusion follows from the fact that only four names are given for the first three centuries. It is probable, though not certain, that the church of Cologne lasted through the downfall of the Roman power and the Frankish conquest, in the first years of which it is possible that the bishops gained or claimed metropolitan rank; but the metropolitan system soon lost its importance in the Frankish kingdom, and the occupants of the see appear as simple bishops in the eighth century. The elevation of Cologne to a metropolitan see did not take place until the consecration of Hildebold about 795; the suffragan sees were at first the Frankish Liége, the Friesian Utrecht, and later the Saxon Münster, Osnabrück, Minden, and Bremen. The actual diocese of Cologne was a very large one. Under the rule of Philip of Heinsberg (1168-91) its previous possessions were enlarged and consolidated by purchase and exchange, and after the downfall of Henry the Lion the duchy of Westphalia and Engern (*Angraria*) was added (1180). From this time on the archbishops were the most powerful princes in northwestern Germany.

(A. Hauck.)

The archbishops of Cologne were prominent in the conflicts of the Hohenstaufens with their enemies, and Engelbert I., count of Berg (1216-25), was the leading magnate of Germany and the administrator of the empire during the absence of Frederick II. in Sicily. A position of equal importance was held by Conrad of Hostaden (1238–61) for a time after Frederick's deposition, when he was papal legate for Germany, anointed William of Holland at Aachen, and, according to the traditional prerogative of his see, crowned Richard of Cornwall as his successor. The history of the next two centuries is largely a record of strife arising out of contested imperial, papal, and archiepiscopal elections, until the rule of the sixty-sixth incumbent of the see, Herman IV. of Hesse, called the Peacemaker (1480–1508), brought about many reforms. Herman V., count of Wied (see HERMAN OF WIED), became a favorer of the Reformation in the last five years of his rule, and was deposed and excommunicated in 1546, and the same was the case with Gebhard II., Truchsess of Waldburg (1577–83; see GEBHARD II.), while the young Ernest, prince of Bavaria (1583–1612), set no very creditable example to his flock. His nephew Ferdinand (1612–50) followed him, and did much to repair the damage already wrought to the Roman Catholic cause; and his nephew, again, Maximilian Henry ruled the great archdiocese from 1650 to 1688 with such a lack of political wisdom that it was laid waste by contending armies, and French influence became predominant. Under another Bavarian prince, Joseph Clement (1688–1723), the external history of Cologne was bound up with that of the general European conflicts. His secular interests so preoccupied him in the earlier part of his reign that he did not even take up his spiritual functions until 1707, when he was consecrated at Lille by Fénelon, and thereafter devoted himself zealously to the promotion of religion. The last archbishop of the Bavarian house was Clement August I. (1723–61), brother of the Elector Max Emmanuel; but the house of Austria supplied an archduke, brother of the Emperor Joseph II., Maximilian Francis (1784–1801), who was driven out by the French and spent his last days in Vienna. The diocese was divided by Napoleon, and the ecclesiastical conditions were full of confusion until 1821, when the archbishopric was reconstituted with a diminished territory, and with Treves, Münster, and Paderborn for suffragans. The most notable of the nineteenth-century archbishops was Clement August II., Baron Droste-Vischering (1835–45), whose episcopate was marked by a vigorous conflict with Hermesianism and with the Prussian government over the question of mixed marriages (see DROSTE-VISCHERING).

BIBLIOGRAPHY: Sources are: T. J. Lacomblet, *Urkundenbuch für die Geschichte des Niederrheins*, 4 vols., Düsseldorf, 1840–58; *MGH*, *Script.*, xiii (1881), 282 sqq., xvii (1861), 723 sqq., xxiv (1879), 332 sqq. Consult: E. Podlech, *Geschichte der Erzdiöcese Köln*, Mainz, 1879; C. A. Ley, *Kölnische Kirchengeschichte*, Cologne, 1882; F. Lau, *Die erzbischöflichen Beamten in der Stadt Köln*, Lübeck, 1891; A. J. Binterim and J. H. Mooren, *Die Erzdiöcese Köln*, Düsseldorf, 1892; Rettberg, *KD*, vol. i.; Friedrich, *KD;* Hauck, *KD*, vols. i.–iii.

COLOMBIA: A republic of northwestern South America, bounded on the north by the Caribbean Sea and Venezuela, on the east by Venezuela and Brazil, on the south by Brazil and Ecuador, on the west by the Pacific Ocean. No exact figures are available for either the area or the population, but an estimate of the former is 473,000 square miles and of the latter 4,000,000 souls, including 500,000 whites and 1,500,000 or more half-breeds.

The constitution of 1886 declares the Roman Catholic religion the religion of the nation, but that the Catholic Church shall not be a State Church, and grants religious toleration. Ecclesiastics are excluded from public office, though Catholic priests may be employed in public instruction and charity. The buildings of the Catholic worship and clergy are exempt from taxation. A concordat was made between Pope Leo XIII. and the republic, Dec. 31, 1887 (see CONCORDATS AND DELIMITING BULLS, VI., 6). The church organization is as follows: Archdiocese of Bogotá (founded 1563), with the suffragan dioceses of Ibagué (1900), Nueva Pamplona (1835), Socorro (1895), and Tunja (1880); archdiocese of Cartagena in the Indies (diocese, 1534; archdiocese, 1900), with the suffragan dioceses of Santa Marta (1534) and Panama (1534); archdiocese of Medellin (diocese, 1868; archdiocese, 1902), with the suffragan dioceses of Antioquia (1873) and Manizales (1900); archdiocese of Popayan (diocese, 1546; archdiocese, 1900), with the suffragan dioceses of Garzón (1900) and Pasto (1859). There are also two vicariates apostolic, Casanare (1893) and Goajira (1905), and three prefectures apostolic, Caquetá (1904), the East (1903), and San Martin (1904). A delegate apostolic and envoy extraordinary of the pope resides in Bogotá.

Protestants are represented by the few foreigners resident in the country. There is a Presbyterian mission in Bogotá. Elementary education is free, but not compulsory. Public education is organized and administered in harmony with the Roman Catholic religion; all education is largely in the hands of congregations. WILHELM GOETZ.

BIBLIOGRAPHY: R. S. Pereira, *Les États-Unis de Colombia*, Paris, 1883; R. Nuñez and H. Jalbay, *La République de Colombie*, ib. 1898; W. L. Scruggs, *Colombian and Venezuelan Republics*, Boston, 1905.

COLONNA, EGIDIO. See ÆGIDIUS DE COLUMNA.

COLORED METHODIST EPISCOPAL CHURCH. See METHODISTS, IV., 8.

COLORS IN THE BIBLE.

I. Color-Perception and Color-Nomenclature.
II. Coloring-Materials.
  Purple (§ 1).
  Scarlet (§ 2).
III. Symbolical Significance.
  White (§ 1).
  Scarlet, Purple, and Blue (§ 2).

I. Color-Perception and Color-Nomenclature: A Midrash story (*Bamidhbar Rabbah* xii.) indicates that red, blue, purple, and white fire were collectively a symbolic representation of the being of God. In the old Semitic scale of colors green and blue were not distinguished, so that sea, grass, and sky appeared of the same tint. The Semite has as yet no distinct word for the blue of heaven. People remaining in primitive conditions paint themselves either red or yellow. But among the

Semites there is no word for "yellow," and that color plays no part in the cultus. The same word in the Old Testament applies to the green of the leaf, the yellow of the grain, and the paleness of the countenance; another word is used for the blood-red or brown skin-color of men, the brown of the horse or the cow, and the yellow-brown of the lentil; still another stands for the raven-blackness of the hair, for the color of the skin [when tanned by exposure], and for the gray of the morning twilight.

II. Coloring-Materials: At the head of coloring-material in the Bible stands purple. For this the Old Testament had no appellative; it had only special words for the purple-red, to which as a dye it gave a name, and for purple-violet, to which it applied the name of the shell-fish. The Septuagint and Latin translations render the latter by *hyacinthus* and use the word for both the blue stone and a blue flower. Purple was an early monopoly of the artistic Phenicians of the Mediterranean coast.

1. Purple. The mussel which produced it was afterward found on other coasts (Ezek. xxvii. 7, where "Elisha" probably means the Lacedæmonian coast). Thyatira was later celebrated for its purple (cf. Acts xvi. 14), though Tyre was the place where it was first made. The mounds near the latter place prove what the shell-fish was from which the dye was obtained. There are a number of varieties of fish which furnish a red or violet liquid, but their product fades on exposure to light and air. The varieties which furnished the old purple dye were the *Murex trunculus* and the *Murex brandaris*. The dye is not the blood, but a slimy secretion. At first this is not purple or red, but whitish, changing through yellowish and greenish tints to purple and making an unfading dye. Pliny says (*Hist. nat.*, ix. 62) that the purple of Tyre was best when it was like coagulated blood and when looked at from above ran into black while from the side it reflected the light. Of the purple-blue he said that it was a cold color, like the angry sea.

Scarlet is a red which has more of yellow or brown in it than has the purple. It was obtained from an insect (*coccus ilicis*) which fed on oaks and shrubs, supposed to be a product of the tree, hence called *coccus*, "berry," and the oak on which it was found was called the "berry-bearing oak." The Pentateuch recognizes the insect and names it the "shining worm." The Persian name *kirm* found its way into late Hebrew (II Chron. ii. 6, 13; iii. 14); and the word scarlet, since the Middle Ages the name of the coloring obtained from this insect, is a loan-word from the Turkish.

2. Scarlet. This was among Greeks and Romans the color of the outer garments of soldiers, hence according to Matt. xxvii. 28 the soldiers put a scarlet cloak on Jesus (Mark xv. 17; John xix. 2 makes it purple). The *coccus ilicis* is still a source for this coloring-matter, though less extensively used than the *coccus cacti* of Mexico and Peru. Another red coloring-matter, "vermilion," is mentioned as a material for painting walls and images (Jer. xxii. 14; Ezek. xxiii. 14). This is a mineral red, in the Septuagint *miltos*, elsewhere meaning "crayon," also "oxid of lead" and "minium." These four mineral reds were used by the ancients, who did not always discriminate in their employment of the names. The henna used in the East as a means of beautifying the person is not mentioned in the Old Testament. The Talmud and Targum wrongly find in Isa. iii. 16 a hint at painting the eyes with a red or yellow-red powder, though kohl, used to darken eyelids and eyebrows, was a favorite cosmetic among the Hebrews (Ezek. xxiii. 40; II Kings ix. 30). When it is said that the Lord will make the foundations of the New Jerusalem of sapphires, the pinnacles of rubies, and the gates with carbuncles the question arises why sapphire-blue is appropriated to the foundation and fiery-red to the battlements and walls, and it also leads to the problem of the symbolism of Biblical representations and to that of the cultus founded upon the Pentateuch. The Babylonians divided the various colors among the "seven lights of earth," and (Herodotus, i. 98) the seven concentric walls of Ecbatana had each its own color.

III. Symbolical Significance: Purple, blue, scarlet, and white are the four colors of the Mosaic cultus. Philo and Josephus associate these colors with the four elements, the sea (purple), the fire (scarlet), the air (blue), the earth (white), combinations which are purely arbitrary. The four colors were used in the outer curtains, the veil, the entrance-curtain, and the gate of the court, as also in the ephod, girdle, and breastplate of the high priest. The first three were used in the pomegranates about the hem of the robe of the high priest. Exclusively blue were the robe of the high priest, the lace of the high priest's breastplate, the lace on his miter, and the fifty loops of the curtains. Exclusively white were the breeches and miter of the high priest. The cloths for wrapping the sacred vessels were blue, scarlet, or purple. White were also the clothes of the lower priests. Add to this the blue ribbon and the fringe of the Hebrew dress, and there is seen at once the use and application of the colors employed in the Hebrew service. The red is used only once (Ex. xxvi. 14); the sealskins which covered the tabernacle were dyed that color. Black is excluded everywhere, as well as yellow and green. That purple, blue, scarlet, and white only were used is not accidental, but the outgrowth of the consciousness of their significance. The reason for the use of the white to the total exclusion of the black is easy to perceive. Black, as it absorbs all colors and thus buries the light, is the symbol of death. But activity, life, light, holiness, and joy, on the one hand, and cessation, death, darkness, malice, and sorrow, on the other hand, are Biblical contrasts, of which white and black are the representatives of this twofold series of opposites. White, however, reflects the light; hence it symbolizes purity and victory. While the third rider of the Apocalypse sits on a black horse, bringing with him famine and death (Rev. vi. 5), the Persian horses in the

1. White. eighth vision of Zechariah are white, because no worldly power had ever shown a more noble disposition toward Israel than the dynasty of the Achæmenidæ, which set the exiles free and promoted the building of the temple. The first of the four apocalyptic riders has a white horse (Rev. vi. 2); for he went forth to conquer. The "Ancient of Days," i.e., the Ever-living (Dan. vii. 9), appears in a garment white as snow; even the hair of his head is like the pure wool. And thus, likewise, the glorified Christ (Rev. i. 14). Even the throne of God which Ezekiel saw was white. White denotes the victory of the light; hence it is clear why the garments of the priests were white. Even the high priest wore the so-called golden robes over the white ones; and in the temple which Ezekiel saw in his vision the priests wore white garments only. The robes of the priests are, according to their natural color, white, as the angels and blessed appeared to the seers, and as the garments of Jesus became white "like the light" on the mount of transfiguration. God is light, and gives light, or he is holy, i.e., holy love. The colors in the garments of the priests have reference to their office; viz., to act as the medium between God and his congregation, it is their duty to go before the people in holiness and purity.

The three other colors are not inherently symbolic as is white. Strictly speaking, white is not a color. No color is inherently symbolic, but gains symbolic value by its associations. It is true that the colors produce psychological effects, and that in proportion to their relation to the yellow-red; bright-red is disquieting, while blue is soothing. But this does not create symbolism. Thus green is the color of hope because associated with plant-growth, with the period to which people look forward in winter. Connected with white is its opposite, scarlet, as the emblem of fire. The dark-red horses in the first vision of Zechariah bring about bloody war; and the yellow-red, a consuming fire. But light and fire are opposites according to the ethical idea of Holy Writ; viz., the light is the symbol of communicating love, the fire, that of consuming anger. When Isaiah describes the sins of his people he speaks of them as being red like scarlet, not like purple. The scarlet along with the white in the high priest's garment means, therefore, to say that he is not only the servant of the God of love, but also of the God of anger (Ex. xx. 5). As to the purple and blue, which are always connected, be it along with white and scarlet, or between,

2. Scarlet, Purple, and Blue.

as they are only two kinds of one and the same purple color, which again is not a natural but an artificial color, consisting of red and violet, they refer to a twofold attribute of the royal King—the purple to the majesty of God in his glory, and the blue to God's majesty in his condescension. The purple of the garments of the high priest denotes, therefore, that he is a servant of that God of whom the song at the Red Sea says, "The Lord will reign forever and ever" (Ex. xv. 18); and the song of Moses, "And he was king in Jeshurun" (Deut. xxxiii. 5). The red color of the red heifer, whose ashes, mixed with water, were to be used in purification of the unclean, had also a symbolical signification. Red is the color of blood, which, again, is the life. The animal intended as antidote against uncleanness through contact with a dead body was to be without blemish, and upon which never came yoke, and thus represented in its color a picture of fresh and vigorous life. It may be that the colors of the twelve precious stones which were on the breastplate of the high priest had a symbolical significance as to their relation to the twelve tribes whose names were engraved on them (Ex. xxviii. 17–21). This at least may be derived from Jewish tradition.

(W. Lotz.)

Bibliography: F. Delitzsch, *Iris. Farbenstudien und Blumenstücke*, Leipsic, 1888; G. Perrot and C. Chipiez, *Hist. of Art in Sardinia, Judæa, Syria and Asia Minor*, i. 109–370, London, 1890; Benzinger, *Archäologie*, pp. 269–270; Nowack, *Archäologie*, pp. 263 sqq.; E. C. A. Riehm, *Handwörterbuch des biblischen Altertums*, pp. 436 sqq., Bielefeld, 1893–94; *EB*, i. 869–877; *DB*, i. 457–458; *JE*, iv. 174–178.

COLOSSIANS, EPISTLE TO THE. See Paul the Apostle.

COLUMBA, SAINT (in Ireland and the western isles known as *Colum-cille*, "Columba of the church"): The apostle of the Picts; b. at Gartan (25 m. w. of Londonderry), County Donegal, Ireland, Dec. 7, most probably in the year 521; d. on the island of Iona June 9, 597. He was of royal blood on both his father's and his mother's side and akin to many powerful families. His studies were begun under Finnian of Moville and

In Ireland.

continued with Gemman, an aged bard of Leinster, with Finnian of Clonard, and with Mobhi, the head of a monastery at the present Glasnevin, near Dublin. About 546 he founded his first monastery, at Derry (Londonderry), and during the next fifteen years added about forty others, the most famous being at Durrow (about 50 m. w. of Dublin), his most important establishment in Ireland, founded in 553, and at Kells (35 m. n.w. of Dublin), founded at an uncertain date.

In 563 he left his native land, actuated doubtless by the love of wandering, and, possibly, other motives. A bloody battle took place in 561 between Columba's clansmen and the followers of the king, and the Irish accounts state that Columba instigated it because the king had violated the right of sanctuary at one of his monasteries, and had also given what he considered an unjust decision against him concerning the ownership of a book (see Finnian, Saint, of Moville). Adamnan tells of an attempt to excommunicate him at a synod at Teltown in Meath; it is not known when it was held or what was the charge, but presumably it was an effort of the king to retaliate. According to an Irish legend Columba's conscience troubled him for his part in inciting strife and bloodshed, and, on the advice of a friend, he decided to go into exile as penance, to win as many souls for Christ as lives had been lost in the battle, and never to look upon his native land again. If this be true he modified his determination, for he

In Scotland.

returned to Ireland more than once and continued prominent in Irish affairs. Missionary zeal is indicated by his choice of a refuge. With twelve associates he established himself on the island of Iona (q.v.), off the west coast of Scotland, on the border between the territories of the Picts and the Scots (Irish) of British Dalriada, whose king, Conall, was his kinsman. It was an admirable center for missionary work. At first he labored chiefly among his countrymen, whose Christian faith was sorely tried by their heathen neighbors. Then he proceeded through Pictland to the court of King Brude, near Inverness. He converted the king (565), and the people followed as a matter of course. During the following years he visited in person nearly all of modern Scotland. Everywhere he founded churches and monasteries, adding their charge to those already under his rule in Ireland. When Conall died (574) his successor, Aidan, sought and obtained inauguration at Columba's hand. In 575 he attended a convention at Drumceatt in northern Ireland. It was proposed there to abolish the order of bards; but Columba, who not improbably belonged to the order himself, succeeded in having measures adopted looking toward reformation rather than annihilation. He also secured a more independent position for Aidan and his kingdom.

Columba was fond of fine manuscripts, and during his last years spent much time in transcribing. On the day before his death he was at work upon the Psalter and reached the end of a page with the words: "They that seek the Lord shall not want any good thing" (Ps. xxxiv. 10). "Here," he said, "I must stop; let Baithene [his cousin and successor as abbot] do the rest." When the monks entered the church for matins the next morning they found him lying before the altar, and, with a feeble effort to give his blessing, he passed away. Columba was impulsive and at times, perhaps, failed to curb an imperious temper. But his faults were those of his race, and were lightly regarded in his time.

His Character.

He was emphatically a man of action, born to lead and also to win. Adamnan describes him as "like an angel in countenance, of polished speech, holy in work, of most excellent disposition, great in counsel, through thirty-four years living as an island soldier [of Christ]. Not a single hour would he allow to pass without devoting himself to prayer, or reading, or writing, or at least to some manual labor. Day and night, without any intermission, he was so occupied in unwearied exercises of fasts and vigils that the special burden of any one labor might seem beyond human possibility. And meanwhile he was dear to all, always showing a cheerful, holy face, and was gladdened in his inmost heart by the joy of the Holy Spirit." Three Latin hymns are attributed to Columba and several Irish poems of more or less doubtful genuineness. The *Rule of St. Columba* is a collection of maxims for a solitary living near a monastery rather than a monastic rule properly so called.

Bibliography: For the hymns consult J. H. Todd. *The Book of Hymns of the Ancient Church of Ireland*, ii. 201-263, Dublin, 1869; *The Altus of St. Columba*, ed. by the Marquess of Bute, Edinburgh, 1882; Bernard and Atkinson, *The Irish Liber Hymnorum*, for the Henry Bradshaw Society, xiii (1898), i. 62-89, ii. 23-28, 140-172; for the Irish poems, W. Reeves, *Life of St. Columba*, pp. lxxviii.-lxxix., 264-277, 285-289. Dublin, 1857; for the rule, Haddan and Stubbs, *Councils*, ii. 119-121; W. F. Skene, *Celtic Scotland*, ii. 508-509, Edinburgh, 1877. The standard life is by Adamnan [679-704], edited with notes and dissertations by W. Reeves, Dublin, 1857, new ed., with Eng. transl. and an unfortunate rearrangement of the notes by W. F. Skene, Edinburgh, 1874. A useful edition of Adamnan's work is by J. T. Fowler, Oxford, 1894, transl. 1895; it is newly translated by W. Huyshe, London, 1906, and is in *MPL*, lxxxviii. For other lives, etc., consult *ASB*, June, ii. 180-236; J. Colgan, *Trias thaumaturga*, pp. 317-514, Louvain, 1647; Lanigan, *Eccl. Hist.*, ii. 106-181, 236-259; C. F. R. de Montalembert, *Les Moines d'occident*, iii. 99-331, Paris, 1866, Eng. transl. printed separately as *St. Columba, Apostle of Caledonia*, London, 1868; W. D. Killen, *Ecclesiastical History of Ireland*, i. 30-39, London, 1875; W. F. Skene, *Celtic Scotland*, ii. 52-55, 79-84, 85 sqq., 467-507, Edinburgh, 1877; A. Bellesheim, *Geschichte der katholischen Kirche in Schottland*, i. 27-65, Mainz, 1883; J. Healy, *Insula sanctorum*, pp. 291-331, Dublin, 1890; G. F. Maclear, *Apostles of Mediæval Europe*, pp. 41-56, London, 1888; E. A. Cooke, *St. Columba, his Life and Work*, Edinburgh, 1893.

COLUMBAN, SAINT (called also the "Younger Columba"): Abbot of Luxeuil and of Bobbio; b. in Leinster, Ireland, c. 550; d. in Bobbio (37 m. n.e. of Genoa) Nov. 23, 615. Like his older namesake and so many of his countrymen, impelled by the love of wandering and the longing for the ascetic life, influenced also by the admonition of an aged female recluse, he left parents and home. For many years he was a member of Comgall's monastery at Bangor on Belfast Lough. Then with twelve companions he went by way of Britain to Gaul (c. 590). Christian life on the Continent was then suffering from the irruption of the barbarians, which had destroyed the old civilization and settled large bodies of heathen in many places. Columban and his company were well received at the court of Guntram, king of Burgundy (d. 593), and established themselves in the wilderness of the Vosges, at the site of a ruined fortress, Anagrates (Anegray), in the present department of Haute-Saône (590-591). As the number of monks increased he founded another monastery eight miles distant, amid the ruins of Luxuvium (Luxeuil, 72 m. n. e. of Dijon), once famous for its warm baths. The little band brought with them their Irish teachings and customs and comported themselves to a large extent independent of the diocesan bishop. Nevertheless, they suffered little interference. Their date for Easter gave most offense, and Columban saw fit to send letters defending his practises to Pope Gregory the Great, to a synod of Gallican bishops (603), and to a later pope, probably Sabinian. In 610 all Irish monks were expelled from Burgundy, not, however, because of religious differences, but in consequence of the boldness with which Columban rebuked the vices of the king, Theodoric, and of the court. It was intended to send them back to Ireland, but at Nantes they were allowed to go at will. After spending some time with Clothair II., king of Neustria, at Soissons, Columban went to Theodebert, king of Austrasia, at Metz, and at the king's request undertook missionary work among the heathen Alemanni and Suevi. He settled at Bregenz, at the east end of Lake Constance, but in 612 his old enemy, Theodoric, defeated Theodebert and seized his dominions. Columban then crossed the Alps, tarried for a while at Milan with Agilulf, the Lombard king, and wrote there a treatise against the Arians, which is not preserved. In 614 he established himself at Bobbio, restoring an old basilica for a monastery and building a new church to the Virgin. For many years this monastery remained a center of learning and study, while Luxeuil became the most famous house in Gaul with affiliated foundations extending from Lake Geneva to the North Sea. Columban was a man of strong convictions, unwavering, and courageous, but also headstrong and stubborn. His writings in many passages breathe the true spirit of the Gospel, but in others show a tendency to formalism and legality. He counseled moderation in ascetic practises, but was himself overrigorous. He addressed the pope with all respect and acknowledged Rome as the metropolis of the Church. His learning was genuine and he is eminent among the writers of the Merovingian time. He shows an acquaintance with Vergil, Horace, and Seneca, perhaps also with Ovid and Juvenal; he had some knowledge of Greek, and was well read in Christian Latin literature. The most important of his extant works are his letters and his monastic rule, which consisted originally of two parts, the first commonly known as the *Regula S. Columbani*, containing ten chapters giving general rules for the monastic life in a spirit of moderation and Christian freedom; the second, the so-called *Regula cœnobialis fratrum Hibernensium*, gives punishments for offenses of monks and imposes rigorous penalties for trivial faults. In its existing form it has been added to from old Irish sources, which doubtless were also used originally by Columban. There are frequent indications that he used the Basilian rule, as well as reminiscences of Cassian and Pachomius (cf. O. Seebass, *Ueber Columban von Luxeuils Klosterregel und Bussbuch*, Dresden, 1883).

OTTO SEEBASS.

BIBLIOGRAPHY: Columban's works, excepting a commentary on the Psalms (found in *Il codice irlandese dell'Ambrosiana*, ed. G. I. Ascoli, 2 vols., Rome, 1878–79), are in *MPL*, lxxx. The letters, ed. W. Grundlach, are in *MGH*, *Epist.*, iii (1891), 154–190. All the other works have been published by O. Seebass in *ZKG*, xiv (1894), 76–92, 430–448, xv (1895), 366–386, xvii (1897), 215–234. Columban's life by Jonas, a contemporary monk of Bobbio, is in *MPL*, lxxxvii., Eng. transl. by D. C. Munro in *Translations and Reprints* published by the Univ. of Pa., ii. 7, Philadelphia, 1895; also, ed. Krusch, in *Mitteilungen des Instituts für österreichische Geschichtsforschung*, xiv. 385 sqq., Innsbruck, 1893. Consult Lanigan, *Eccl. Hist.*, ii. 260–299, iv. 348 sqq.; G. F. Maclear, *Apostles of Mediæval Europe*, pp. 57–76, London, 1888; J. Healy, *Insula sanctorum*, pp. 370–381, Dublin, 1890; T. Olden, *The Church of Ireland*, pp. 91–98, London, 1892; Hauck, *KD*, i. 240–276.

COMBA, EMILIO: Waldensian; b. at San Germano, Waldensian Valleys, Italy, Aug. 31, 1839; d. at Guttannen, 9 m. s.e. of Meiringen, Switzerland, Sept. 3, 1904. He studied at Torre-Pellice and at Geneva (under Merle d'Aubigné), was ordained in 1863, and until 1872 was an evangelist, chiefly in Venice. In Sept., 1872, he became professor of historical theology and homiletics in the Waldensian college, Florence. He was also for many years pastor of a Waldensian church in Florence, and after 1873 the editor of the monthly *Rivista Cristiana* which he had founded. He defended with learning and success the proposition that the original Waldensians date from Peter Waldo in the twelfth century and not from the days of the apostles, also that they had much to learn from the Protestant Reformers of the sixteenth century. His publications are very numerous. Besides reprinting in his *Biblioteca della Riforma Italiana Sec. XVI.* works of Vergerio (1883), Vermigli (1883), Valdes (1884), Ochino (1884), Parravicino (1886), and Virginio (1886), he wrote *Francesco Spiera* (Florence, 1872), *Enrico Arnaud* (1889, also in French, *Henri Arnaud*, La Tour, 1889), and *I nostri protestanti*, 2 vols., Florence, 1895–97; but his life-work was upon the history of his own people, drawn from the sources, which he told best in the *Histoire des Vaudois* (Paris, 1901); unfortunately he brought out only the first part, *De Valdo à la réforme*. The English reader has these researches in their earlier form in the *History of the Waldenses of Italy, from Their Origin to the Reformation* (London, 1889).

COMBEFIS, cōn"be"fī', **FRANÇOIS**: Patristic scholar; b. at Marmande (30 m. s.e. of Bordeaux), France, Nov., 1605; d. in Paris Mar. 23, 1679. He studied with the Jesuits in Bordeaux, and joined the Dominicans in 1624; taught philosophy and theology in various houses of his order, and in 1640 was sent to Paris; here he soon retired from teaching and devoted himself to the preparation of texts, translations, etc., of the works of the Fathers. His publications include *Novum auctarium Græcolatinæ bibliothecæ patrum* (2 vols., Paris, 1648), a work which was not well received at Rome because of certain statements about the Monothelite controversy; *Bibliotheca patrum concionatoria* (8 vols., 1662; reprinted 1747); a complete edition of the works of Basil the Great (2 vols., 1679); the works and fragments of Amphilochus, Methodius, Andrew of Crete, Maximus, and others.

COMBER, THOMAS JAMES: Baptist pioneer missionary to the Kongo; b. in Clarendon street, Camberwell, London, Nov. 7, 1852; d. at Loango, French Kongoland, June 27, 1887. He studied at Regent's Park College, was sent in 1876 by the Baptist Missionary Society to western Africa, labored in Victoria and the Kamerun, and the next year was sent into the Kongo. After a brief visit to England in 1878–79 he returned to his post. In 1882 he reached Stanley Pool and conducted missionary operations. In 1885 he paid another visit to England, but before that year closed was again at work in the Upper Kongo. There sickness overtook him and he hastened to the coast, only to die. His work was in new fields of difficulty and danger.

BIBLIOGRAPHY: J. B. Myers, *T. J. Comber, Missionary Pioneer to the Congo*, London, 1888.

COMENIUS, co-mé'ni-us, **JOHANNES AMOS** (Latinized from **Komenski**, ko-men'ski): Moravian bishop; b. at Niwnitz (near Ungarisch-Brod, 48 m. e. of Brünn), in Moravia, July 28, 1592; d. at Amsterdam Nov. 15, 1670. In his sixteenth year he entered the Latin school, and in 1611 was able to enter Herborn University, where he came under the influence of the encyclopedist Alsted. After an educational journey as far as Holland, he completed his studies in Heidelberg under the care of Pareus. Returning to his home in 1614, he took charge of the high school at Prerau. He was, in 1616, ordained in the church of the United Brethren, becoming pastor at Fulnek, 1618. The misfortunes which, during the Thirty Years' War, came upon the Evangelicals in Bohemia and Moravia visited him. In 1621 the Spaniards burned Fulnek, and the plague robbed Comenius of wife and child. From 1624, when the Evangelical ministers were driven from their pulpits, until 1627, when all Evangelicals were banished, he traveled among his scattered comrades and lived in the mountain castles of the nobility, ministering to his brethren in the faith. He then accompanied some of them to Poland, where others had preceded them, and in the border city Lissa, under the protection of Count Leszczynski, there sprang up a flourishing Protestant population whose gymnasium under Comenius grew into great fame. His text-books, practical works, and reform of educational methods brought him into contact with other states. In 1641 he went to England and Sweden, and in 1650 to Transylvania. From 1632 he had been senior bishop, and from 1648 the only bishop of the Brethren's Church. Returning to Lissa shortly before the Swedish-Polish War, he and the Protestants were banished by the Poles in revenge for the victory of Charles X. He fled to Amsterdam, where he lived in high honor and busied himself in literary labor, in the care of his scattered brethren, and in the training of youth.

He was a man of varied talents. To his church he gave in 1626 the Psalter in ancient verse-form and in 1659 a new edition of the hymnal; he was also its foremost preacher; his two books "The Labyrinth of the World and the Paradise of the Heart" (1623) and "One Thing Necessary" (in the latter of which the man of seventy-seven years gives the harvest of a rich and tireless life) will live among the classics of Christian teaching. He was no less great in his activity as bishop. But the different forms of government, and the current confessionalism with its emphasis on "central dogmas," seemed to him only to confuse the common man. Peaceful by nature, he tried to combine excellences and develop good qualities wherever he found them. His claim to world-fame rests upon his work as pedagogue. Here he owed much to his church and its catechetical system. The "Door to Language Opened," translated within a few years into fifteen languages, and the "World Portrayed" (Eng. transl., by C. Hoole, reprint, Syracuse, N. Y., 1887) were the most famous of his works. In this labor also it was his religious nature which controlled him. Here he developed what later made the names of Rousseau and Pestalozzi famous. The child should grow into knowledge by assimilation, should not be forced but should be assisted to know, to think, and to speak. But the object should ever be to understand all that is worth knowing of God, the world, and oneself. The end of his pedagogical labor is "universal knowledge," the striving for universal education, the founding of scientific academies, the translation of the Bible into all languages, the creation of a universal language, and the establishment of congresses of religion. When he had been almost forgotten Herder rediscovered him by bringing to light one of the most beautiful of his works. In 1890, at the third centenary of his birth, the Comenius Society was founded to perpetuate his name and labor.

(P. Kleinert.)

Bibliography: The important literature is found in the *Comenius-Studien*, 6 parts, Znaim, 1892–93, and in the publications of the Comenius-Gesellschaft, Berlin, 1892 sqq. Consult: H. F. von Criegern, *J. A. Comenius als Theolog*, Leipsic, 1881; J. Beeger and E. Zoubek, *Comenius nach seinem Leben und Schriften*, ib. 1883; L. W. Seyffarth, *Comenius nach seinem Leben und pädagogischer Bedeutung*, ib. 1883; R. H. Quick, in *Essays on Educational Reformers*, privately printed, 1887; J. Kvacsala, *J. A. Comenius; sein Leben und seine Schriften*, Leipsic, 1892; S. S. Laurie, *J. A. Comenius, . . . his Life and Educational Works*, Cambridge, 1885, Syracuse, 1893. Consult also J. A. Comenius, *The Great Didactic, now for the First Time Englished, with Introduction by M. W. Keatinge*, London, 1896 (gives a bibliography).

COMES. See Pericope.

COMGALL, SAINT, OF BANGOR: Founder of a famous Irish monastery at Bangor on the southern shore of Belfast Lough. He flourished in the latter half of the sixth century and was a friend and associate of Columba, Brendan, and other monastic founders. He established many monasteries, that at Bangor in 554 or 558, and is said at one time to have had 3,000 monks under him there and in affiliated houses. A so-called rule of Comgall is extant, consisting of thirty-six quatrains written in Irish; it is of great age and may possibly have formed the basis of Columban's discipline at Luxeuil and Bobbio, and of that at St. Gall. The "Antiphonary of Bangor," a book of anthems compiled for the congregation at Bangor, written, it is supposed, soon after 680, preserved at Milan, contains an alphabetical hymn in Comgall's honor.

Bibliography: *ASB*, May, ii. 577–587; Lanigan, *Eccl. Hist.*, ii. 61–69; W. Reeves, *Ecclesiastical Antiquities of Down, Connor, and Dromore*, pp. 93 et passim, Dublin, 1847; J. O'Hanlon, *Lives of the Irish Saints*, v. 152–185, Dublin, n.d.; J. Healy, *Insula sanctorum*, pp. 364 sqq., Dublin, 1890; The *Antiphonary of Bangor*, ed. F. E. Warren for the Henry Bradshaw Society, 2 vols., London, 1893–95.

COMMANDMENTS OF THE CHURCH (*præcepta* or *mandata ecclesiæ*): The title of a section of the catechism of the Roman Catholic Church. The Church of the Middle Ages was not familiar with it. The Council of Trent (session vi., canon xxii.; session xxii., passim) uses the phrase for regulations which the Church sets forth authoritatively for the guidance of the faithful, especially in the province of devout morality; such commandments complement the commands of God (*præcepta Dei*), as learned from the Bible. The Jesuit Petrus Canisius (q.v.) made the doctrine of these commandments a part of the catechism. He prepared a brief summary of those devotional precepts of the Church which he regarded as the most important for the life of the people, five in number, and since his time it has been usual in the Roman Church to speak of "Ten Commandments of God and five chief commandments of the Church." The latter commandments, as Canisius selected them, are as follows: (1) Thou shalt observe the appointed feasts of the Church. (2) Thou shalt hear mass and the sermon every Sunday. (3) Thou shalt observe the fasting seasons. (4) Thou shalt confess thy sins at least once every year, and this to thy regular parish priest. (5) Thou shalt seek the communion at least every year at Easter. These commandments were adopted in almost all catechisms after Canisius. In countries where the Roman Church is not supported by the State, an additional sixth commandment has been widely introduced into the catechism: Thou shalt provide according to thy means toward the support of the Church and the priests. Pius X. formulates these commandments more strictly and detailed as follows: (1) Thou shalt attend holy mass on all Sundays and festivals of obligation. (2) Thou shalt observe the lenten fast, the four ember-days, and the vigils of obligation; thou shalt eat no meat on prohibited days. (3) Thou shalt confess at least once every year, and at Easter communicate in the parish church proper. (4) Thou shalt pay the bounden or customary dues to the Church. (5) Thou shalt not wed in forbidden seasons; namely, from the first Advent Sunday till Epiphany and from the first Sunday in Lent until the octave after Easter.

In the Greek Church the following commandments are in force: (1) Every one shall be present at the principal hours and the liturgy on all Sundays and festivals. (2) Observe the four great fasts. (3) Reverence the clergy, and especially the father confessor. (4) Confess regularly four times a year, in particular at Easter. (5) Beware of heretical books and intercourse with heretics. (6) Make intercessions for every estate, especially the clergy, the government, and benefactors of the Church. (7) Keep not aloof from any specially prescribed fasts and processions. (8) See to it that the Church does not suffer in her incomes. (9) Take no part in stage performances and adopt no strange manners. It is probable that Petrus Mogilas was indirectly influenced by Canisius in the matter of minutely specifying the chief commandments set forth by the Church beside the commandments of God.

F. KATTENBUSCH.

BIBLIOGRAPHY: Roman Catholic: P. Canisius, *Summa doctrinæ christianæ* in three editions, the "larger," 1555; "smallest," 1556; "small," 1558; *Compendio della dottrina christiana* (the catechism of Pius IX.), Rome, 1905 (also in three forms); O. Braunsberger, *Entstehung und erste Entwickelung der Katechismen des . . . P. Canisius*, Freiburg, 1893; F. Loofs, *Symbolik*, i. 307 sqq., Freiburg, 1902; *KL*, v. 161 sqq., vii. 288 sqq.

Greek: *Confessio orthodoxa des Petrus Mogilas*, part 1, questions 87-95, in *Monumenta fidei ecclesiæ orientalis*, ed. E. J. Kimmel, vol. i., Jena, 1850; W. Gass, *Symbolik der griechischen Kirche*, pp. 379 sqq., Berlin, 1872; F. Kattenbusch, *Confessionskunde*, i. 510 sqq., Freiburg, 1891; F. Loofs, ut sup., i. 162 sqq.

COMMENDA: A technical term for the administration of an ecclesiastical office, especially of the temporalities connected with it, committed to a person who has no actual right to the office. Normally, according to canon law, *commendæ* are granted only in order to provide for the administration of the office in the case of a vacancy or of the incapacity of the holder; only to a qualified person who already holds an ecclesiastical office; and to him merely as administrator. The custom gave rise, however, to great abuses. The Avignon popes especially used this means to bestow the incomes of benefices upon persons whom the prohibition of pluralities prevented from holding the benefices themselves; they were granted for life, and without any obligation to the discharge of the duties of the office. Thus abbeys were frequently granted *in commendam* to secular clergy. This latter practise was so deeply rooted that the Council of Trent, which attempted to extend to the whole system of irregular *commendæ* the law against pluralities, was not able to do more than regulate it. Temporal rulers often in like manner "commended" monasteries and churches, with their property, to laymen, in order to reward their services by the enjoyment of the temporalities, on a pretext of protection. (C. T. G. v. SCHEURL†.)

BIBLIOGRAPHY: L. Thomassin, *Vetus et nova ecclesiæ disciplina*, P. I. 1, iii., chaps. 10-21, Lucca, 1728; Richter, *Kirchenrecht*, p. 1323; Friedberg, *Kirchenrecht*, p. 325.

COMMENDATORY LETTERS (LITERÆ FORMATÆ): Letters of introduction and recommendation (called also *literæ canonicæ*) given in the early Church to Christians traveling from one place to another. The use of such letters is extremely ancient, dating from the time of the New Testament (Acts xviii. 27; Rom. xvi. 1, 2; II Cor. iii. 1), and is readily explicable from the close mutual relations of the communities and their generous hospitality. On the other hand, II John 10 forbade the reception of one who was unsound in doctrine, and it accordingly became necessary for a traveler to be able to prove his orthodoxy (cf. Didache xii. 1), this usually being done by a letter of commendation written by the head of the congregation. These letters must be distinguished from the official communications of the congregations with each other, of which an entire series antedating Irenæus is either extant or known by title. Another category, which may be traced to the third century, is formed by the "letters of peace" readmitting excommunicated members of the Church. Later, however, "letters of peace" connoted the certificates given those who intended to visit the emperor or high dignitaries of the Church and showing that the recipient of the letter was making his journey with the approval of the writer. After the fourth century these letters were distinguished, in their turn, from the "letters of introduction," which were given only to persons of rank. As early as the end of the second or the beginning of the third century the bishops seem to have announced their elections by letters and to have exchanged letters of recommendation, while in the same manner they reported their celebration of festivals, especially of Easter. There were also general encyclicals, and special regulations have been preserved regarding all problems connected with letters of commendation and introduction.

Letters of both these types were forged at a very early date, as is clear from the complaint of Dionysius of Corinth during the reign of Marcus Aurelius, and by the time of the great councils from the fourth to the seventh century these forgeries had increased to such an extent that letters were required to have a definite prescribed form, and were accordingly termed *formatæ* or *canonicæ*. It is uncertain whether the designation *formata* refers to the fact that they were modeled on public documents, or whether it is derived from *forma* in the sense of "seal," or whether the rigid phraseology gave rise to the epithet. (A. Harnack.)

Bibliography: Bingham, *Origines*, XVII. iii. 6–8, cf. II. iv. 5, and references given there to earlier literature; *DCA*, i. 407–408.

COMMENTARIES. See Exegesis or Hermeneutics, IV., § 2, and bibliography; see also the articles on the different books of the Bible for commentaries on particular books.

COMMERCE AMONG THE ANCIENT ISRAELITES.

Palestine lay on the chief commercial highways of the ancient world, being traversed by the roads which connected Babylon and Egypt, and by the routes which united the more distant East with the Mediterranean. From Egypt the great military road ran along the coast to Beirut and then inland to Assyria, while south of Mount Carmel a branch traversed the plain of Jezreel, and crossed the Jordan on its way to Damascus and the Euphrates. Gaza was the terminus of the road connecting Akabah and southern Arabia with the Mediterranean, while the second great road out of Arabia ran along the eastern edge of the east-Jordan district northward to Damascus. Active commerce early developed along these routes. As early as 3000 B.C. Sargon I. and Gudea of Lagash obtained cedars from the Amanus as well as stone and timber from Phenicia. The Egyptian trade with Syria developed but little later. This interchange became important even at this early period inasmuch as each region lacked some of the products of the other. Egypt obtained its silver from Asia, while Babylon needed gold from Nubia; Amanus and the Lebanon were the sources of timber; Arabia produced perfumes and spices. The middlemen were, in the main, in the oldest time the Phenicians, who by virtue of their geographical position were well qualified to perform such a function. By 1500 B.C. Phenicia controlled trade with Egypt, while for the East the Arameans, somewhat later, assumed a similar position. In the South the trade with Arabia and India passed through the hands of the Minæans, who had centers for trade with Damascus in their North Arabian province of Muṣri, as well as on the coast, their warehouses being at Gaza.

1. Trade Routes Through Palestine.

Through their settlement in Canaan the Israelites became interested in this system of commerce, although it was not until they had assimilated the culture of the region that they could take part in trade. Nor did they, at first, need commerce, since the native productions were sufficient for them. Trade accordingly pursued its old course undisturbed, and Canaanite and Phenician retailers traversed the land with their wares, so that "Canaanite" long remained a synonym for "merchant" (Job xli. 6; Isa. xxiii. 8; Hos. xii. 7). Within Palestine salt was an article which could be obtained only by trade from the Dead Sea. When, however, in the reign of Solomon, Israel was secure against foreign aggression and had assimilated the Canaanites, it sought its share in international commerce. Trade with Phenicia increased as the development of culture created needs not met by native products and workmanship. Solomon imported from Tyre timber and artisans (II Sam. v. 11; I Kings v. 13–18). The establishment of the northern kingdom by the house of Omri had a powerful influence on trade and the development of Phenician industries. Purple, products of the loom, and works of art in brass, silver, gold, and the like found ready purchasers among the Israelites, who gave in return the surplus of their oil, wheat, honey, and similar exports (I Kings v. 11; Ezek. xxvii. 16 sqq.). There was also an active trade in slaves (Amos i. 9), and the tribes of Zebulun and Issachar, settled near the Phenicians and along the trade routes through the plain of Jezreel, were the chief middlemen (Deut. xxxiii. 18–19).

2. The Beginnings of Hebrew Commerce.

Solomon cooperated with the Phenicians in voyages from Ezion-geber on the Red Sea to Ophir, the land of gold, which apparently lay on the southern coast of Arabia (see Ophir). In their "ships of Tarshish," as the vessels were later called when Tarshish became their port of destination, the crews of Hiram of Tyre sailed with the officials of Solomon, returning with gold, silver, ivory, apes, and peacocks (I Kings ix. 26–28; cf. x. 22 and Benzinger's commentary ad loc.). The account of the queen of Sheba seems to show that trade was carried on with the Minæans, who were succeeded by the Sabeans, and Minæan Midianites are described as merchants and leaders of caravans (Gen. xxxvii. 28, 36). At a later time Ezion-geber and the road leading to it came under the sway of the Edomites, but the attempt of Jehoshaphat to resume control of the Red Sea ended in failure (I Kings xxii. 48–49), and there is no record of further really successful undertakings of a similar character.

3. Solomon.

It is obvious that trade with Egypt was active in the reign of Solomon, especially as he was connected by marriage with the Pharaoh. After the division of the kingdoms, Israel traded with Phenicia and Syria rather than with Egypt, while Judah dealt with its southern neighbor, although in all other respects it was cut off from international commerce, since the trade routes ran through the northern kingdom. Commerce was likewise carried on in the north with the Arameans. Solomon obtained horses from Muṣri in northern Syria and from Kuë (Cilicia) through the Arameans and Hittites (I Kings x. 28–29, according to the correct reading). Later, when Israel came under the political domination of the Arameans, commerce increased correspondingly, and Israelitic merchants in Damascus had at one time their bazaars in the markets just as Damascus traders had theirs in Samaria (I Kings xx. 34), although what the articles of commerce were is unknown.

4. The Two Kingdoms.

Previous to the exile, however, Israel was not a

commercial people, nor was trade the occupation of a large portion of the population. Neither the earlier legislation nor the Deuteronomist took commerce into consideration or regulated it. The captivity, on the contrary, altered the entire condition of affairs. In Babylonia commerce was highly developed, and many of the exiles had no alternative but to take part in it. In Palestine, on the other hand, the Israelites were at first too poor to engage in trade, which was still in the hands of Phenicians, Edomites, and other foreigners (cf. Neh. x. 31, xiii. 15–22). Not until the Greek period did the Jews again become merchants; but during this epoch there were colonies of Jews engaged in traffic in Alexandria, Antioch, Asia Minor, and Greece, and even in Rome. For the means of transportation see ASS; CAMEL; HORSE; MULE.

5. After the Exile.

I. BENZINGER.

BIBLIOGRAPHY: L. Herzfeld, *Handelsgeschichte der Juden des Altertums*, Brunswick, 1879 (the one book); F. Buhl, *Die socialen Verhältnisse der Israeliten*, pp. 76–83, Berlin, 1899; Schürer, *Geschichte*, Index, s.v. "Handel." Eng. transl., Index, s.v. "Trade"; *DB*, iv. 802–806; *JE*, iv. 186–188; *EB*, iv. 5145–99 (exhaustive).

COMMINATION SERVICE: An addition to the usual service on Ash Wednesday in the Prayer-book of the Church of England, designed by the Reformers to take the place of the ceremony of sprinkling ashes on the congregation in token of penitence. It consists of the recitation of the curses pronounced by God against impenitent sinners in the Old Testament (whence its name, commination—"threatening"), and of Ps. li. and other penitential prayers. In the revised Prayer-book of the American Episcopal Church is a modified form called "A Penitential office for Ash-Wednesday."

COMMODIANUS, com-mo-di-ē'nus: Early Christian poet of the middle of the third century. His birthplace is unknown, but his close contact with Cyprian makes it likely that he spent at least his manhood in North Africa. By birth a heathen, after groping from one superstition to another, he was converted by becoming acquainted with the Scriptures. A manuscript calls him bishop. He is the oldest known Christian poet writing in Latin, and seems to have written for the common people. His form of verse, though externally hexameter, deviates from the strict principle of quantity in favor of accent, and his verse must have been painful to the educated. For that reason, no doubt, he is ignored by the Fathers, though heretical views might have had much influence, for he was a Patripassian and a Chiliast. Hence his writings are designated in the decree of Gelasius as "apocryphal" (*MPL*, lix. 163); nevertheless, this very disapproval shows that he still had his readers. The *Instructiones* and the *Carmen Apologeticum* are all that have survived. The former (of 1,259 lines, divided into two books of forty-one and thirty-nine [thirty-eight] separate poems, mostly acrostic in form) treats in book i. of the heathen, contrasting their religion with the Christian faith; at the same time Christians are reprimanded for being too intimate with their heathen neighbors; the conclusion is a polemic against the Jews. The second book has sober exhortations for all classes of Christians. Between the two parts are instructions which treat of Antichrist, of the resurrection, and the final judgment. The *Carmen Apologeticum* (of about 1,060 lines) begins likewise with the heathen and continues with a dogmatic-historical review of the Christian faith; in the second part is a description of the end of the world, containing among other things references to the invasion of the Goths (249 A.D.?) and the appearance of two Antichrists among the heathen and the Jews (though the *Instructiones* knew only of one). From his writings Commodianus appears to have been a Christian of strong principles and robust nature; he is never extreme and does not commend the aspiration for a bloody martyrdom; his diction is faulty, but his thoughts often border on the sublime, and at times he is successful in satire. Surprising are his aversion to the Roman government (cf. *Carmen*, line 887) and his leaning toward the Goths, as though he were aware of the coming union of Christianity and the German world.

(B. DOMBART †.)

BIBLIOGRAPHY: The works are in *MPL*, v., and (best) ed. Dombart in *CSEL*, xv., 1887. Eng. transl. is in *ANF*, iv. 203–218. Consult: W. S. Teuffel, *Geschichte der römischen Litteratur*, p. 972, Leipsic, 1890; Harnack, *Litteratur*, i. 731, ii. 2, pp. 433–449; Krüger, *History*, pp. 317–320; *KL*, iii. 701–704; *DCB*, i. 610–611.

COM'MO-DUS (MARCUS AURELIUS COMMODUS ANTONINUS): Roman emperor 180–192. The son of Marcus Aurelius and Faustina, he inherited far more his mother's than his father's character, and spent his time in games and dissipation, leaving the government in the hands of his favorites. Utterly indifferent to religious questions, he left his Christian subjects in peace. At the beginning of his reign the effects of his father's policy were still felt; but before long persecution ceased throughout the empire, to which Eusebius (*Hist. eccl.*, V. xxi. 1) attributes the accession of large numbers of converts. According to Irenæus (IV. xxx. 1) some of these were found even in the imperial household. Among these was Marcia Aurelia Cejonia Demetrias, who seems to have been responsible for the tolerant attitude of the government. She was the daughter of a freedman, but brought up by Hyacinthus, a Christian. Hippolytus, her contemporary, calls her (*Philos.*, ix. 12) "the pious concubine (παλλακή) of Commodus," and mentions important services rendered by her to Christian exiles in Sardinia. Dio Cassius also speaks of her benevolence toward the Christians and her intercession for them with Commodus, "with whom she could do anything" (lxxii. 4). In these days she was probably a catechumen; neither Christian nor pagan authors speak of her absolutely as a Christian. The difficulty of understanding her relations to the Roman Church in connection with that in which she stood to the dissolute emperor are lessened by recalling the fact that the regular concubinage in which she lived with Commodus at this time was not forbidden by either secular or ecclesiastical law, and that there is no evidence of her taking any personal part in the corrupt practises by which she was surrounded. After the assassination of Commodus, she married the freedman Eclectus and remained at the court of Pertinax. When he in turn, together with Eclectus, had been murdered by the pretorian guards, the new Emperor Didius Julianus, yielding to their demands, ordered Marcia's execution.

VICTOR SCHULTZE.

BIBLIOGRAPHY: B. Aube, *Les Chrétiens dans l'empire Romain*, pp. 1 sqq., Paris, 1881; T. Keim, *Rom und das Christentum*, pp. 634 sqq., Berlin, 1881; H. Schiller, *Geschichte der römischen Kaiserzeit*, I. ii. 660 sqq., Gotha, 1883; Neander, *Christian Church*, vol. i. passim; Moeller, *Christian Church*, i. 166; Schaff, *Christian Church*, ii. 56; *DCB*, i. 611.

COMMON LIFE, BRETHREN OF THE.

Geert Groote. The First Community (§ 1).
Busch's Account Inaccurate (§ 2).
The Life of the Brethren an Active One (§ 3).
Prejudice and Opposition (§ 4).
Characteristic Features (§ 5).
The Various Houses (§ 6).
The Houses for Women (§ 7).
Different Names (§ 8).
Dress (§ 9).
Organization and Discipline (§ 10).
The "Modern Devotion" (§ 11).
Daily Life (§ 12).
Tendency to Asceticism (§ 13).
The Copying of Manuscripts (§ 14).
Their Influence and Importance (§ 15).
Their Limitations (§ 16).
Their Influence on Education, Literature, and Art (§ 17).

The Brethren of the Common Life (*Fratres communis vitæ*) were a religious association of a semimonastic nature which flourished in the transition period between the Middle Ages and the Reformation. It dates from the second half of the fourteenth century, when the northern Netherlands were the scene of constant conflicts of the nobility among themselves, with their vassals, and with the towns, which had notably increased in wealth and power since the Crusades. This increase in power had given rise to a lively interest in political, social, and ecclesiastical questions, and the growing love of liberty had shown itself in a wide-spread antagonism to the clergy, which was fostered by the development of scientific study, and still more by the mysticism which was then so popular, in contrast with the hard and unbending scholasticism of an earlier period. Two men especially represented this warmer and more earnest religious feeling—Jan van Ruysbroeck (q.v.), a priest of Brabant, and Geert Groote (q.v.), a citizen of Deventer, who was the founder not only of the influential congregation of Windesheim (q.v.) and the monastic reform that proceeded from it, but also of the Brethren of the Common Life.

1. Geert Groote. The First Community.

Groote makes his appearance in the time of the great Western Schism (see SCHISM) and of the "Babylonish exile" of the popes (see AVIGNON). By the counsel of Ruysbroeck, then eighty-four years old, and with the bishop's license, he began to preach repentance throughout the diocese of Utrecht. Crowds flocked to hear him from all classes, at Deventer, Zwolle, Leyden, Delft, Gouda, and Amsterdam. But when he attacked the sins of the clergy and the lazy beggary of the monks the bishop forbade his preaching after four years, and he retired to his native town of Deventer. Here he matured his plan, already conceived, for enabling those who had been converted to a pious Christian life to carry out practically their desire for perfection. He gathered a few friends around him, who regarded him as their head until his death, after which the leadership was taken up by Florentius Radewyns (q.v.). It was not originally a quasimonastic community separated from the world, with a definite system of common life and work. This is evident from the fact that several of Groote's friends, such as Jan Brinckerinck (q.v.), belonged to the circle without deserting their own monastic associations. It was only after the founder's death that the community was shaped by Florentius in a direction that promised greater stability and growth.

This view, as put forth and justified by Gerretsen in his biography of Florentius (Nymwegen, 1891), differs in not a few important particulars from that previously held by such writers as Acquoy, Hirsche, and Grube. According to their view, which rests mainly on the *Liber de origine devotionis modernæ* by Jan Busch (q.v.), Groote sought to create a better type of clergy by educational influence upon the young, and supported many poor students at the cathedral school of Deventer by giving them manuscripts to copy for his library. After a while he handed over the care, both temporal and spiritual, of these youths to his younger friend Florentius, who took them into his own house and had them work under his direction. Then one day, according to Busch's account, Florentius suggested that it would be more economical, as times were hard, if they should all combine their resources and live in common. Groote at first feared that the jealousy of the mendicant orders would be aroused, but finally bade him go on in the name of the Lord.

2. Busch's Account Inaccurate.

Busch, however, reads into the earliest history the practise of later times, which even then was casual and not of primary importance. It is true that Groote, and still more Florentius, cared for poor scholars; but these were not a part of the brotherhood, and left when their education was completed. There are other inaccuracies in Busch's account. Relating that Groote on his death-bed answered the question of his adherents by saying that Florentius should be their head, he understands this of the Deventer house and brothers, while it is clear that Groote meant the movement as a whole. The final choice of a head for the Deventer house was long delayed; the deed for its purchase in 1391 indicates a joint rule by Florentius, Brinckerinck, and Gronde, and Florentius was not made sole head until later—probably between 1391 and 1396, by which time a more definite organization had been rendered necessary not only by the growth of the brotherhood and the foundation of new houses, but as a means of protection against external attacks. As long as Groote lived his influence was a sufficient shield for his converts; but soon after his death so great hostility showed itself among the citizens that the Brethren scarcely dared to appear in the streets, and a municipal official converted by Groote was obliged to interpose. Yet Florentius succeeded in carrying on the work—at first in his own presbytery, and when that grew too small in a rented house near-by, exchanged in 1391 for another which had been inhabited by a community of pious women.

But even after the organization had crystallized still further there remained a fundamental difference between it and the Windesheim congregation. Both institutions sprang from the same spirit of "modern devotion"; but while some thought they could preserve this spirit only in the monasteries where they knew it to prevail, the Brethren of the Common Life felt called to help on the spread of that spirit by preaching to the people, by caring for the education of the young and especially those who were to be priests, and by the mighty influence of a godly life lived in the world.

3. The Life of the Brethren an Active One.

The associations of serious pious men which thus began to spring up in various places, followed by the foundation of houses for the community life of women, had features of novelty which excited attention and not infrequently disapproval. As a loose and informal association, the Brethren were classed by many with the Beghards and Beguines (see BEGHARDS), and thus fell under suspicion of heresy;

4. Prejudice and Opposition.

as communities somewhat resembling the monastic orders, they incurred the jealousy of the latter, especially of the mendicants by the very difference that they did not beg but worked for their living; as communities of workingmen, again, they were regarded as competitors by the ordinary workingmen and women. It was some time, therefore, before they could secure general permission for the formation of their communities and the acquisition of land. Formal opinions as to the lawfulness of their position were frequently sought from the authorities, both by their friends and by their enemies. The most important of these opinions is the unprejudiced and favorable one pronounced in 1393 by Abbot Arnold of the Benedictine abbey of Dickeninge, in the province of Drenthe (Holland), and now extant in the Royal Library of The Hague. With this may be classed another procured by the Brethren from the law faculty of the new University of Cologne, when the first was not accepted by their opponent Matthias Grabow, who had asked for it. According to both the following seem to have been regarded as the characteristic features of the new organization: (1) They wished to live a common life *extra religionem*; that is, without taking the ordinary monastic vows. (2)

5. Characteristic Features.

They lived by their work, rejecting mendicancy. (3) They lived *in communi*, men and women separately and thus without marriage, sharing freely with each other, so as to gain the advantage of mutual influence and brotherly exhortations. (4) They rendered voluntary obedience, not conditioned by a vow, to a leader chosen from their brotherhood. (5) They edified each other and people outside by the reading of the Scriptures in the vernacular. Of these points, what principally struck people in general was their living in common, whence their name; but their living thus without monastic vows was what seemed to the older religious communities dangerous, and was the chief ground of the attacks upon them up to the Council of Constance. But if they differed from the monks in feeling it unnecessary to leave the world and bind themselves by solemn vows, they had many of the characteristics of the monastic life—obedience, absolute while it lasted though not irrevocable, celibacy, poverty in the sense of common ownership; and they only seemed to stand in contrast with it because so many monasteries had fallen away from their original principles.

Nor had either founders or followers any idea of departing from the teaching of the Church. What they strove for was an ever-increasing reformation in life—the life of the Church and the life of the world. The statutes of their houses show plainly enough what was the main thing in their minds. Those of the community at Herford may be quoted: "For the promotion of our souls' salvation, as well as for the edification of our neighbor in the purity of the true Christian faith and the unity of our Mother the holy Christian Church, we will and intend to live a pure life, in harmony and community, by the work of our own hands, in true Christian religion and the service of God. We purpose to live a life of moderation, without beggary; to render obedience with reverence to our superiors; to wear a humble and simple habit; diligently to observe the canons of the holy Fathers, in so far as they are of profit; diligently to apply ourselves to the virtues and other holy exercises and studies; and not alone to live a blameless life, but to give a good pattern and example to other men."

The mother house of Deventer has an interesting history, extending to 1574; here Erasmus was a student for several years, and learned Greek from the distinguished scholar Synthis (Sinder). The next in age and importance, that of Zwolle, also founded by Groote himself, was governed with wisdom and energy from 1407 to 1456 by Diderik van Herxen, a writer of note, who made it a center of colonization. It held together until 1590.

6. The Various Houses.

Thomas à Kempis and Jan Busch both probably taught in the school here, and were certainly inmates of the house, as was Wessel, the most significant precursor of the Reformation. Hoorn (1385) and Ammersfoort (1395) were the only other foundations in the lifetime of Florentius. Of importance for the history of the movement in the northern provinces where it originated are Delft (1403), Hulsbergen (1407), Gouda, Hertogenbosch, and Doesburg (1425), Utrecht (1474), and Nymwegen (1592). In the southern Netherlands Liége was the first town to receive a colony of the Brethren, and was followed by Louvain, Ghent, Brussels, probably Antwerp, Mechlin, and Cambrai. The earliest settlements in Germany were due to the labors of Heinrich von Ahaus (q.v.), who founded the three most famous German houses, those of Münster, Cologne, and Wesel, of which the second lasted on until its secularization by the French in 1802, and has an interesting connection with the early history of printing. Others were early founded at Osnabrück, Emmerich, Treves,

Herford, Hildesheim, Cassel, Butzbach, Marburg, Königstein, Rostock, and Culm (1473, the farthest point reached to the eastward). The Herford community, which (see below, § 16) went over bodily to the Reformation, remained in existence as a Lutheran brotherhood until 1841.

7. The Houses for Women.

Even before the foundation of the first house for the brothers, Groote had presented (1374) to the burgomaster of Deventer a dwelling owned by him, to serve as a home for poor women, either unmarried or widows and without any monastic ties. The house did not seem at first to prosper, either under Groote or under his successor Jan van Gronde, who was an able preacher, but lacked the special gifts required. The sixteen women lived much as they pleased, and did little work, so that poverty pressed them and the outlook was discouraging, when in 1393 Brinckerinck took charge of the house and put new life into it, with constant spiritual care and strict discipline. As in the case of the brothers, new houses were soon founded, which offered a striking contrast to many of the nunneries, in the degenerate condition in which the latter too often were. The rapid spread of these houses affords a proof of the strength which the spirit of free devotion possessed in its earliest days. In the first half of the fifteenth century, at least eighty-seven of these communities sprang up, nearly all in the Netherlands. Usually there was only one in a town, though Zutphen had three, Deventer five, and Zwolle six. Many of them, however, transferred themselves before long to the Third Order of Saint Francis or adopted the rule of the Windesheim nuns, though such a change does not seem to have involved the total severance of relations with the brothers and sisters of Groote's society. The sisters were very commonly known, not only in Deventer but elsewhere, as Beguines—the name frequently given in those days to the tertiaries of the mendicant orders and other non-cloistered associations of women. The rule which governed them is known from the extant statutes of more than one house; it does not differ essentially from that of the tertiaries under the charge of the Utrecht chapter. Their dress was gray in color, rather old-fashioned in cut, so that they were frequently objects of ridicule. Their food was as simple as their dress. There seems to have been no definite age-limit for reception; at Deventer girls of nine and women of fifty were admitted. Each house was ruled by a mistress, and had other officials corresponding, *mutatis mutandis*, to those of the brothers. They occupied themselves in all kinds of women's work, as it was then understood; occasionally in nursing, teaching girls, and copying manuscripts. Outside of the Netherlands their extension was greatest in Germany, where they seem to have reached a considerable number in the middle of the fifteenth century.

8. Different Names.

Besides the names most usually employed by themselves (*fratres vitæ communis* or *bonæ voluntatis*), the Brethren had a variety of popular appellations in different places. Thus they were called, from their manner of delivering not formal sermons but plain talks, *fratres collationum* or *collationarii*; because they imitated the apostles in their manner of living, "apostolic brothers"; from their diligence in copying manuscripts, "brothers of the pen"; where they had schools, "school brothers"; "cowled brothers" or "blue brothers," from their habit; and various other names taken from the saints to whom they were specially devoted as patrons or examples, Gregory, Jerome, Michael, George, Martin, and Mark. The names of "Lollards" or "Nollards" seem also to have been applied to them by their enemies.

Since they made no vows on entrance, each brother could leave at any time without incurring ecclesiastical penalty. For this reason, as well as because they considered it possible to combine the interior life with mingling in the world, the title of *religiosi* was frequently denied to them.

9. Dress. Their clothing consisted in a uniform, simple, but dignified outer garment of black or gray linen, confined at the waist by a black woolen girdle; for clerics it reached to the feet, for novices and lay brothers only to the knees. Beneath this was worn a rough shirt, to be washed once a month in summer, every other month in winter, and drawers of the same material. The cloak was a bluish-gray, and a black hood or cowl covered the head.

10. Organization and Discipline.

The inmates of the houses were divided into three classes—priests and clerics, laymen, and probationary candidates. The first class performed all spiritual and ecclesiastical functions, the second the domestic tasks of house and garden; but all were brothers. The time of probation ranged from two or three months to a year. Each new brother was free to dispose of his property as he chose; but if he gave it to the house he could not reclaim it on leaving. Every house had a head called the rector, not as among the Windesheim communities, the prior; there was an effort to avoid imitating monastic usage in such details. In the sisters' houses the confessor was also called rector. The rector was chosen with the greatest care; later, the choice was not left wholly to the individual house, and if no suitable person were among the community, one was sent from another house. All the members were pledged to obey him; without his permission none could leave the house or go anywhere except to church. In the rector's absence one of the clerical brothers in his place decided all questions that did not admit of postponement. If there were any complaints against the rector, it was the duty of the priests to consider them. Next to the rector's, the office of procurator was of importance; he had charge of the external relations of the house, of the buildings, of receipts and purchases. In the larger houses a cellarer was also required. One of the most important officials was always the librarian, who not only was custodian of the books, but supervised the copying industry and provided the materials for it. Other officials mentioned are a novice-master, a precentor, a sacristan, an infirmarian, a cook, a gardener, etc. For purposes of discipline a chapter of faults (as distinguished from the occasional particular chapter for the discussion of the affairs of the community) was to be held at least once a week. First the youngest brother was to kneel in the midst and accuse himself of any breaches of the statutes or customs of the house; but (with the sober common sense which characterized all the regulations) he was not to presume to go beyond two. Having asked pardon for his faults, accepted the penalty imposed by the rector, and promised amendment, he returned to his place and the next in order followed. If the penalty of expulsion were inflicted, in case of a grave offense, such as heresy, immorality, or theft, the rector decided how much the offender might take with him in addition to his clothes, which were always allowed. Besides these domestic gatherings, there were yearly meetings of representatives of a group of related houses. These, with the visitations, formed a means of keeping up an essentially united spirit in the ever-increasing circle of communities; they were instituted soon after the death of Florentius, and took place on Low Sunday, first at Zwolle and then in different places, such as Groningen, Hertogenbosch, and Emmerich.

At the very foundation of the whole life lay the *moderna devotio*, daily progress in communion with God, out of a spirit of love and a pure heart. The means to this were the knowledge of self, the continual struggle to conquer the baser desires, to abase pride, to despise temporal things, to break down self-will. To this end were directed all their spiritual exercises, their early rising and their hard work, their speech and their silence, their submissive obedience. The man who asked to be received into the brotherhood could not but know that he "desired a good work." That was the purpose of the care shown in admitting new members, the time of probation, the oversight of the novice-master, before they could be added to the list of the "perpetual" or "canonical" brothers.

11. The "Modern Devotion."

The life of each day was strictly organized. The bell rang at three each morning, and at half-past three all must be ready to rise and offer the first-fruits of the day to God in prayer and meditation. From that hour until nine at night, when the brothers went to bed, every hour (with the exception of the periods for meals and recreation) was divided between work and spiritual exercises. The work was varied; the educated clerics spent a good deal of time in copying manuscripts, and many of the laymen learned the art from them, but there were all kinds of other tasks. Humility was especially insisted upon; it was common for the Brethren to confess their sins not only to a priest but to each other, a custom which gave rise among outsiders to a suspicion of their orthodoxy. The spirit of submission in which they were taught to accept reproof and chastisement from superiors was shown also in the patient bearing of sickness or suffering. A regular feature of the life was the *collationes* or conferences—edifying discourses, frequently diversified by question and answer, or taking the form of a dialogue for a longer time. These were of two classes, one destined for outsiders to whom on Sundays and holidays the doors of the house were open, and always in the vernacular, the other taking place daily among the inmates of the house at the time of their midday or evening meal (the name probably coming from the use of the word *collatio* in the sense of a common meal).

12. Daily Life.

The life of the Brethren could never, as has been seen, have been a luxurious one; but its ordinary limitations did not suffice the devotion of some, who attempted to strengthen themselves still further against temptation and increase their power of despising temporal things by accustoming themselves to specially poor and distasteful food, or by wearing a torturing hair-shirt. If they found their health was being injured by these austerities, they thought of some other way to practise mortification and abandoned what had proved excessive—though this exercise of common sense, in the spirit of the time and especially of the religious life of the time, was frequently justified by an appeal to some vision or revelation. The spiritual life of the Brethren was largely nourished on Holy Scripture, to the study of which a special section is devoted both in the Herford statutes and in the *Reformatorium vitæ clericorum*. The quiet morning hours were consecrated to this, and all unnecessary running about was accordingly forbidden. Systematic meditation on spiritual things was another feature; each day had its special subject—Sunday the kingdom of heaven, Monday death, Tuesday the mercies of God, Wednesday the last judgment, Thursday the pains of hell, Friday the sufferings of Christ (which they were also to contemplate during mass), and Saturday their sins. From this practise arose many little books of written meditations, some of which, like the various *Specula* (*monachorum, Bernardi, peccatorum*), enjoyed wide popularity.

13. Tendency to Asceticism.

Among the great variety of trades and occupations by which the Brethren sought to provide for their own subsistence, and at the same time to have enough left over for works of charity, that of copying manuscripts held an important place. Florentius had specially commended it to his immediate associates, who were principally clerics, as the most becoming for them; and the increasing practise of it became a permanent blessing to the Christian world. A large number of manuscripts are still extant, in private and public collections of Holland and Belgium especially, which were written in the houses of the Brethren. Those most frequently selected were liturgical books, the Vulgate, the Fathers, and works of spiritual edification. They had the custom also of compiling collections of the most striking passages from the books they read or copied, sometimes with the addition of reflections by the compiler. These anthologies (*rapiaria*) are not always written throughout by the same hand. Perhaps the work was taken up by another after the death of the first compiler, or several small collections were fused into one. The most diverse authors are met with

14. The Copying of Manuscripts.

in them: some classical, especially Seneca; some patristic, most frequently Augustine, Bernard, and Johannes Climacus, to whom Gerson may be added; and some from their own circle, like Thomas à Kempis or David of Augsburg, the author of the *Speculum monachorum* particularly cherished and commended by Florentius.

Such a life as has been described was the best defense of the Brethren against all attacks which could be made upon them. Even if there are some things in their system which seem to our minds exaggerated or objectionable, it is impossible to deny their importance to the Church's history. In attempting to sum up this importance, it is necessary to say at once that, with our fuller knowledge, they can no longer be described, in the way once customary, as precursors of the Reformation. None the less, their influence, both personal and corporate, was an inspiring and a purifying one. They took different ground from the already existing "religious" communities when they showed that free-will offerings made in a spirit of devotion might serve God and one's neighbor

15. Their Influence and Importance.

acceptably, from both the ethical and the social standpoints; that a life of piety was possible in the midst of daily labor and intercourse with the world in its lower and earthly as well as its higher spiritual tasks. Such separation from the world as they practised was not a flight in the false and one-sided conception of devotion and the service of God, but was intended to render positive service to human society. Their ideal of true inner piety, springing from the love of the heart, had a powerful influence on many who were merely externally members of the Church, especially such priests and monks as were performing their service in a mere formal spirit. To say nothing of their direct influence on the clergy by education of young candidates for orders, they stirred up many a secular priest to a more faithful care of souls, a greater diligence in imparting spiritual gifts by preaching and teaching. The "conferences," offering religious instruction to the plain man in his mother tongue, had an effect that extended far beyond the walls of the houses; and the same is true of the close adherence to Scripture and its application to the practical details of every-day life.

But the best preaching is that of example; and this spoke so eloquently to the people that everywhere, except where hostility was stirred up against them by the jealousy of bad priests or monks, their life was revered. Municipal authorities, private citizens, parochial clergy were forward to help them in their work. After the Church had pronounced a formal approval of their work at the Council of Constance, bishops, cardinals, and popes were desirous to assist it in every way, as by the granting of many privileges, even including special indulgences.

The "modern devotion" which has been described, with its insistence on conversion and real sanctification, has been compared not altogether unjustly by Acquoy with Methodism, and by Ritschl with Pietism; but both comparisons are only true up to a certain point. The system of the Brethren was far more ecclesiastical than either of the others; the Word by which alone new life can be planted and nourished takes a less prominent place with them. Instead of it, they have their self-chosen exercises and meditations. This is only natural, in view of the traditional church teaching which, with their Semi-Pelagian scheme of salvation requiring absolutely their own cooperation, they fully shared. In their meditations

16. Their Limitations.

the life and sufferings of Christ counted more as an example and encouragement for their own trials than as the sacrifice for their sins and the sins of the whole world. Justifying faith, as the source of the new life called into existence by the grace of God, as the synthesis of religion and ethics, meant less to them than the process of sanctification. They lacked both the deep consciousness of sin and the certainty of faith in the healing grace that blots out sin. Thus they emphasized, indeed, the freedom of the will, but not that which makes it free, the operation of the Holy Ghost through the Word; they stood out as a free association compared with the monasteries, but not free with the perfect liberty of the children of God. Attempts at reformation of Christian life in those days, whether of individuals, monastic communities, or the whole Church, thus remained restricted to the region of externals; they did not touch the heart of the matter. The long-desired reformation could not be brought about in the way offered by the Brethren of the Common Life. When Luther's call to repentance and his preaching of faith penetrated into their houses some of them thought they had all that was required in the inward reality of their devotion, not knowing the true freedom; others closed their ears to the proposal of what seemed innovations; others, again, were influenced by the intellectual power of the humanist forces that took the side of the Reformation; and some few, like the brothers of Herford, gave themselves up to the gospel of free grace, winning Luther's word of praise that he could gladly suffer such houses, and wished there were more of them. But nearly all the communities began to decay from this time; and as the old ones were dissolved new ones did not arise to take their place. Their organization had not, on the one hand (as the Windesheim monks had always said), the security of vows and complete renunciation of the world; nor, on the other, was it adapted to fulfilling the high demands of the spiritual life, on the plane on which the Reformation, following the Word of God, had set it; the old bottles could not be filled with the new wine.

A word remains to be said of their more specifically educational and intellectual influence, which was considerable and excellent, although it has been often misunderstood. The old view, represented by Cramer, Von Raumer, and Kämmel, ascribed to them a very far-reaching effect upon the school system and upon the improvement of the curriculum and the methods of teaching. But careful recent investigation shows that this was much exaggerated. There were not many places where the schools belonged to the Brethren or were under their direction. Most of the houses educated only young candidates for orders; they seldom supplied teachers to the public schools except in special cases.

17. Their Influence on Education, Literature, and Art.

Nor did they possess a particular educational method of their own, outside of the general principles followed in their houses. Their influence, in fact, was mainly that of their sincere Christian piety, which had its effect on all who came within their sphere. In this way, beginning with Groote himself and his relation with Petrarch, as well as his own humanistic studies, a friendship sprang up between them and the leading German humanists which had notable results. Men like Cela, Hegius, Sinthis, and Arsenius at Rostock imbibed from the Brethren a simple Christian piety which was one of the great causes of the difference between the tendency of German and Italian humanism. In this sense both the Reformation and the liberation of the sciences which proceeded from it were indebted to the Brethren. They were not hostile to art; their churches were adorned to the best of their power, and in miniature-painting they have left some creditable results. From the literary standpoint, their own productions, whether original or compiled, are mainly in the department of ascetics. Poetry occasionally found a home among them; and Heinrich of Alkmar, the author of *Reineke Vos*, came from the Zwolle house. Of special importance to popular culture is the fact that they showed a strong tendency to write in the vernacular or to make translations into it. Besides the Scriptures and other spiritual works (e.g., a German verse translation of the "Imitation" made at Cologne), they circulated numerous books in the vernacular of a historical or otherwise educational nature; in the earlier period they engaged not only in the copying of manuscripts, but also in the work of adorning them with miniatures and illustrations, and even of preparing the parchment for them, and of arranging libraries; and with the invention of typography, not a few houses set up presses and sold printed books, thus contributing in a new way to the general spread of learning.

L. SCHULZE.

BIBLIOGRAPHY: For the founders the sources are in the "Life" by Thomas à Kempis in his *Chronicon monasterii S. Agnetis*, ed. Rosweyde, Antwerp, 1615, 1622, Eng. transl. by J. C. Arthur, London, 1905. Consult: G. Bonet-Maury, *Gerard de Groote d'après des documents inédits*, Paris, 1878; K. Grube, *Gerard Groot und seine Stiftungen*, Cologne, 1883; *KL*, v. 1286.

For the brotherhood the sources, besides Thomas à Kempis, are *Scriptum Rudolphi Dier de Muden de Magistro G. Grote*, in G. Dumbar, *Analecta*, pp. 88–244, Deventer, 1719-22; J. Buschius, *Chronicon Windeshemense*, ed. K. Grube, pp. 1–375, Halle, 1886. Consult: C. H. M. Delprat, *Over de Broederschap van Geert Groot*, Arnhem, 1856, J. G. R. Acquoy, *Het Klooster te Windesheim en zijn invloed*, 3 vols., Leyden, 1875–80; S. Kettlewell, *Thomas à Kempis and the Brothers of the Common Life*, 2 vols., London, 1882–84; E. Möbius, *Characteristik der Brüder des gemeinsamen Lebens*, 1887; G. Bonet-Maury, *De opera scholastica fratrum communis vitæ*, Paris, 1889; G. Höning, *Die Brüder des gemeinsamen Lebens und ihre Bedeutung für ihre Zeit*, Gütersloh, 1884; Döbner, *Brüder des gemeinsamen Lebens in Hildesheim*, Leipsic, 1903; S. H. Gem, *Hidden Saints, a Study of the Brothers of the Common Life*, New York, 1907; Heimbucher, *Orden und Kongregationen*, i. 396, 403, 409-410, ii. 326 sqq., 335; Pastor, *Popes*, i. 147-148, 150; *KL*, iv. 1924 sqq.

COMMON PRAYER, BOOK OF.

The Book of Common Prayer is the only official service-book used in the Church of England and its affiliated bodies. Although the service-books of the English Church before the Reformation were mostly in Latin, English primers, originating, probably, in still simpler manuals of great antiquity, were in use at the beginning of the fifteenth century. The *Portiforium secundum usum Sarum*, or "Primer of the Salisbury Use" (c. 1400), is clearly the basis of the Book of Common Prayer, and contains in English: (1) Matins and Hours of our Lady; (2) Evensong and Compline; (3) The seven penitential psalms; (4) The fifteen gradual psalms; (5) The Litany; (6) Placebo; (7) Dirige; (8) The psalms of commendation; (9) Pater noster; (10) Ave Maria; (11) Creed; (12) The ten commandments; (13) The seven deadly sins.

1. Early Forms.

Marshall's *Prymer* (ante 1530 and 1535) and Hilsey's *Prymer* (1539), set forth at the command of Cromwell, led the way, with others, for *The Prymer Set Forth by the King's Majesty* (1545), which omits Nos. 4, 6, 10, and 13 of the aforesaid contents, but makes several additions as of the Calendar and "certain godly prayers." The *Litany* contains petitions requesting the prayers of angels, saints, and martyrs, and to be delivered from the tyranny of the Church of Rome; and the Dirige has prayers for the dead. The former was compiled by Cranmer from the old litanies and the litany prepared by Melanchthon and Butzer in 1543 for Herman (q.v.) of Wied, archbishop of Cologne. Before the *Prymer* of 1545, convocation had authorised, in 1537, *The Godly and Pious Institution of a Chrysten Man*, containing the Lord's Prayer, Hail Mary, Creed, decalogue, the seven sacraments, etc., and in 1543 the same, corrected and altered, entitled *A Necessary Doctrine and Erudition for any Chrysten Man*. The former was called "The Bishops' Book"; the latter, "The King's Book"; and both, with the *Articles* of 1536, contain the authoritative opinions of the Church of England during Henry VIII.'s reign, and exhibit, on the whole, a retrogression in matters of doctrine. A commission, appointed in 1547 to revise the church-service, published March 8, 1548, as a first instalment, *The Order of the Communion*, framed in its new portions on Herman's *Consultation*, from which the Exhortation, the Confession, and the Comfortable Words are derived. It was a tremendous step in the direction of reform; for it ordered the communion to be solemnised in English, and restored the cup to the laity.

The First Prayer-book of Edward VI., published June 9, 1549, differed from the Prayer-book now in use as follows: *Matins* and *Evensong* began with the Lord's Prayer, and omitted all prayers after the third collect. The *Litany* contained a petition for deliverance from the tyranny of the bishop of Rome, while it omitted the invocations formerly addressed to the Virgin and other saints. The *Communion Office* began with an introit, and omitted the Decalogue; the Virgin was mentioned by name in the praise given for the saints; the sign of the cross was used twice in the consecration of the elements, and the formula of administration contained only the first clause of that now in use; water was mixed with the wine. In the *Baptismal Office* forms for exorcism, anointing, and trine immersion were provided. In the offices for *Confirmation*, *Matrimony*, and the *Visitation of the Sick* the sign of the cross was retained; in the first, the candidate made no promise, in the second, money was given to the bride, and, in the third, the sick might be anointed; the *Burial-Service* contained a prayer for the person deceased and a special service for communion. The Collects, Epistles, and Gospels were almost identical with those in the Sarum Missal; much of the new matter introduced was taken from Herman's *Consultation*. The ordinal, entitled *The Forme and Manner of Makyng and Consecrating of Archbishoppes, Bishoppes, Priestes, and Deacons* (1549), was published separately, and differed from the present office in requiring the chalice and paten, as well as the Bible, to be placed in the priests' hands, and the pastoral staff to be committed to bishops before the words, "Be to the flock of Christ a shepherd."

2. First Prayer-book of Edward VI.

The **Second Prayer-book of Edward VI.**, published in 1552, went much farther in the Protestant direction. It introduced: (1) the sentences, exhortation, confession, and absolution at the opening of the service; (2) the Decalogue in the communion office; (3) the use of the Litany on Sundays. It omitted: (1) in the Communion-Service: the Introit, the name of the Virgin in the thanksgiving for the Saints, the sign of the cross in consecration, the invocation of the Word and the Holy Spirit, the admixture of water with wine, and the first clause of the present form at the delivery of the elements; (2) in Baptism, the form of exorcism, the anointing, and the trine immersion; (3) in Confirmation, the sign of the cross; (4) in Matrimony, the sign of the cross and the giving of money; (5) in the Visitation of the Sick, the allusion to Tobias and Sarah, the anointing, and the directions about private confession; (6) in the Burial-Service, the prayers for the dead and the Eucharist. The most important change referred to the presence of Christ in the consecrated elements as not differing from his presence to the prayers of believers. As the influence of Luther's Service of 1533 colored the first Liturgy of 1549, so that of Butzer, Peter Martyr, Valerandus Pollanus, and John à Lasco may be traced in the second Liturgy of 1552.

3. Second Prayer-book of Edward VI.

The **Liturgy of Elizabeth** (1560) agreed substantially with the book of 1552, except "with one alteration, or addition of certain Lessons to be used on every Sunday in the year, and the form of the Litany altered and corrected, and two sentences only added in the delivery of the Sacrament to the communicants, and none other or otherwise"; and "that such ornaments of the Church and of the ministers thereof shall be retained and be in use as was in this Church of England, by authority of Parliament, in the second year of King Edward VI., until other order shall be therein taken, etc." (1 Eliz. c. 2, April 28, 1559). The prayers for the queen, and for the clergy and people, and the collect, "O God, whose nature," etc., were introduced, but placed at the end of the litany; and one of two collects for the time of death was omitted. Some further changes were made early in the reign of James I., including the addition of forms of thanksgiving on various occasions and of questions and answers on the sacraments in the catechism (see HAMPTON COURT CONFERENCE).

4. Liturgy of Elizabeth.

In 1645 (Jan. 3) Parliament took away the Book of Common Prayer, and established the Directory, which rejected the Apocrypha, discontinued private baptism, sponsors, the sign of the cross, the wedding-ring, and private communion, removed the communion-table into the body of the church, abolished saints' days and vestments, the burial-service, and the public recitation of the Decalogue and of the creeds, though the Decalogue and the Apostles' Creed were subsequently supplied.

The last revision of the English Prayer-book was made in 1662. Among the important changes were, (1) the extracts from the Bible—except the Psalter (which is Coverdale's text of 1539), the Decalogue, and the sentences in the communion-service—give the text of the Authorized Version; (2) the separate printing of the Order for Morning and Evening Prayer, with the introduction of the last five prayers from the Litany, and of the Occasional Prayers, augmented by a second prayer for fair weather, the two prayers for the ember weeks, the prayers for Parliament and All Conditions of Men, as well as the General Thanksgiving, and a thanksgiving for restoring public peace at home; (3) some new collects, epistles, and gospels were supplied, and verbal changes made, such as "church" for "congregation," and "bishops, priests, and deacons," for "bishops, pastors, and ministers"; (4) the exhortations in the communion-service were altered; the rubrics relating to the offertory, the placing of the bread and wine on the table, and their disposition, directing the form of consecrating additional bread and wine, and the covering of the elements, were added; the last clause respecting departed saints was added to the Prayer for the Church Militant; and in the Order in Council (1552), at the end of the office, the phrase "corporal presence" was substituted for "real and essential presence"; (5) among the more important *additions* in the rest of the book are the Office for the Baptism of those of Riper Years, the Form of Prayer to be used at Sea, new psalms in the Churching Service, and the last five prayers in the Visitation of the Sick.

5. Last Revision.

The Prayer-book of 1549 was used first in Ireland on Easter-day, 1551; and the Irish Act of Uniformity authorized a Latin version. The book of 1552 not having been ordered for observance, the Irish

Parliament, in January, 1560, passed an Act of Uniformity, authorizing the Prayer-book set forth in England, and the Latin version

6. Irish and Scotch Prayer-books.

(made by Haddon) for the benefit of ministers unable to use English, and because there was no Irish printing-press, and few could read Irish. The use of the Book of 1662, approved by the Irish Convocation (August–November, 1562), was enjoined by the Irish Parliament in 1666. Since the disestablishment of the Irish Church in 1870, a revision of the Prayer-book has been made, strongly "evangelical" in tendency. In Scotland the Prayer-book had been in general use in the time of Elizabeth (between 1557 and 1564); but the Scottish bishops being averse to the adoption of the English Book, urged by James I., in the next reign framed a book of their own on the English model, with certain variations, which, though sanctioned by royal authority and printed, never came into general use. The English Book, except the Communion Office (framed upon the Book of 1549), is now used by most of the ministers of the Episcopal Church in Scotland; but the Scottish Communion Office is still preferred in many places.

The American Prayer-book is framed closely upon the model of the English book, and was the work of three successive General Conventions (1785, 1786, 1789). It was adopted substantially in its present form by the General Convention of 1789, with many variations from the English book, of which the following are the most

7. American Prayer-book.

important: it entirely *omits* the Athanasian Creed, the Absolution in the Visitation Office, the *Magnificat* and the *Nunc dimittis*, the Commination, and the versicles after the Creed; it leaves *optional* the use of the cross in baptism, of the words "He descended into hell" in the Creed, of the *Gloria Patri* between the Psalms, and altogether considerably enlarges the discretionary power of the minister. It *adds* to the number of the Occasional Prayers also a form of prayers for the Visitation of Prisoners, a form of prayer, etc., for the Fruits of the Earth, a form of Family Prayers. A form for Consecrating Churches (resembling that published by Bishop Andrewes) was provided in 1795, and an Office of Institution in 1804. The change of "Absolution" into "Declaration of Absolution," of "verily and indeed taken" into "spiritually taken" (Catechism), and the permission of using an alternative formula instead of "Receive the Holy Ghost," etc. (Ordinal), are as significant as the introduction of the prayers of invocation and oblation in the Communion Office, which was insisted on, as rendering the liturgy more in accordance with primitive models, by the Scottish bishops in the Concordat drawn up prior to their consecration of Bishop Seabury. The changes rendered necessary by political and local causes need not be mentioned: in the Thirty-nine Articles, the eighth does not mention the Athanasian Creed, the twenty-first is omitted, and the thirty-fifth printed with a proviso.

A strong desire arose in the latter part of the nineteenth century for a revision in the direction of liturgical enrichment and increased flexibility, which resulted, after careful consideration at three General Conventions, in the final adoption in 1892 of a considerable number of changes, many of which, as the restoration of the *Magnificat* and *Nunc Dimittis*, brought the book into closer harmony both with the English and with the earlier models. See Liturgics; Liturgical Formulas; and Thirty-nine Articles.

J. I. Mombert.

Bibliography: Reprints or facsimile reproductions which are noteworthy are: *Book of Common Prayer from the original MS. attached to the Act of Uniformity of 1662*, London, 1892; *Book of Common Prayer of 1549*, facsimile, ib. 1896; *Prayer Book of Queen Elizabeth, . . . from Originals*, ib. 1898; *First Prayer Book of Edward VI.*, ib. 1903, 1905; *Second Prayer Book of King Edward VI.*, ib. 1905. Consult: J. H. Blunt, *Annotated Book of Common Prayer*, ib. 1890; E. Cardwell, *The Two Books of Common Prayer set forth . . . in the Reign of Edward VI.*, ib. 1852; C. E. Hammond, *Liturgies Eastern and Western*, ib. 1878; W. M. Campion and W. J. Beaumont, *Prayer Book Interleaved*, ib. 1880; W. Maskell, *Ancient Liturgy of the Church of England*, ib. 1882; A. T. Wirgmann, *The English Reformation and the Book of Common Prayer, 1531–1662*, Milwaukee, 1887; F. A. Gasquet, *Eward VI. and the Book of Common Prayer*, London, 1891; J. Cornford, *Book of Common Prayer with Explanatory Notes*, ib. 1897; J. C. Jones, *Concordance to the Book of Common Prayer*, Philadelphia, 1896; J. Dowden, *Workmanship of the Prayer Book*, London, 1899; L. Pullan, *Hist. of the Book of Common Prayer*, ib. 1900; E. Daniel, *Prayer-Book; its History, Language and Contents*, ib. 1901; H. Gee, *Elizabethan Prayer Book and Ornaments*, ib. 1902; F. Procter and W. H. Frere, *New Hist. of the Book of Common Prayer*, ib. 1905; A. R. Fausset, *Guide to the Study of the Book of Common Prayer*, ib. 1904; M. McColl, *The Royal Commission and the Ornaments Rubric*, ib. 1906.

On the American Prayer-book consult: C. M. Butler, *Hist. of Book of Common Prayer*, New York, 1880; J. H. Garrison, *The American Prayer Book, its Principles and the Law of its Use*, Philadelphia, 1887; C. E. Stevens, *Genesis of the American Prayer Book*, New York, 1893; W. R. Huntington, *Short History of the Book of Common Prayer*, ib. 1898.

COMMUNICATIO IDIOMATUM.

Doctrine before the Reformation (§ 1).
Luther (§ 2).
Brenz, Chemnitz, and their Followers (§ 3).
The Formula of Concord (§ 4).
Later Lutheran Theology (§ 5).

In Lutheran dogmatics Communicatio Idiomatum ("communication of the attributes or properties") is a term referring to the relation between the divine and the human nature as united in the one person of Christ. The thought which it expresses aims to establish the connection between the *unio personalis* and the *communio naturarum*. Having for its purpose to illustrate the undivided personal life and work of the God-man on the basis of the twofold nature united in him, it stands in the closest connection with the historical appearance of Jesus, since it undertakes to give the final dogmatic declaration concerning the person of Christ.

The doctrine starts with the assertion that by virtue of the incarnation of the Son of God as the second person of the Divine Trinity there exists an undivided subject of the God-man by virtue of the initiative of the Logos assuming the human nature so that both natures, the divine and the human, are indissolubly and perfectly connected with one another in personal unity. The dogmatic formulation of the ancient Church limited itself to fixing the fact of the incarnation—*one* divine-human person (Gk. *hen prosōpon* or *mia hypostasis*) of perfect and like essence with God according to the divine nature, of perfect and like essence with man according to the human nature, vindicating the integrity of both natures in the union and within the personal unity and retaining its plainly indissoluble connection (Chalcedonian Statement of 451). When the question as to the natures of the God-man turned into that concerning the will and volition in the Monothelitic controversy, it was natural that the statement of the integrity and absolute connection already made concerning the natures should also be extended to the *thelēmata* and *energeia*, as adhering to the natures, constituting their essence (Constantinopolitan Creed of 680–681; cf. R. Seeberg, *Dogmengeschichte*, i., Leipsic, 1895, pp. 221–222, 230). John of Damascus tried to define more clearly the communication of the properties. By virtue of the "penetration" (Gk. *perichōrēsis*) of both natures in the personal unity each communicates to the other of its own, and it may therefore be said: "the Lord of glory was crucified," and on the other hand: "this man is uncreated" (*De fide orthodoxa*, iii. 3–4). The penetration proceeds indeed from the deity (iii. 7, end), but after the divine nature has once penetrated the flesh it allows also the flesh to penetrate it. The penetration is so far mutual; the human, without abrogating its essence, becomes divine, the human knowledge of Christ is enriched with all wisdom, the human will becomes almighty by means of the permeating divine will, the flesh making alive. An advance in this direction in medieval scholasticism was the less possible as the notion of God became more and more opposed to everything changeable, creature-like, human, and as the disinclination grew to revise the foundations on which rests the doctrine of the *communicatio idiomatum*.

1. Doctrine before the Reformation.

2. Luther.

It was with no theological scientific interest, but to help faith, that Luther from the very start emphasized the fact that the Son of God had assumed so much of our flesh and blood that we have now become one flesh with him. To this end he emphasized the truly human being and human development of Christ, without limiting thereby the divine essence of the Logos; everything that Christ does or suffers he refers back as being done and suffered by God, but without an equal extension to both natures. Starting with the unity of the God-man, he went so far in the assertion of the union of natures and the communication of the properties that he supposed that the divine nature gives its property to the human, and again the humanity also to the divine nature. Influenced especially by the controversy over the Lord's Supper, he gave the human nature of Christ a share in the illocal existence of the Logos, and this since the unity of persons on which this communication rests exists from the moment of the incarnation.

3. Brenz, Chemnitz, and their Followers.

The Württemberg theologians, headed by Johann Brenz, took up Luther's conception most decidedly and carried it to its logical conclusion, viz., that by means of the personal union of both natures in the incarnation the humanity of Christ is also everywhere where the divinity is, so that all communication of the natures and their properties actually existed with this accomplished unity; and that for the subsequent exaltation of Christ there remained only the emerging and manifestation of what actually existed. Hereby the truth of the human nature and development was the less obscured, since they retained not only the statement "God has suffered and died," but also advanced to the assertion that even the divine nature has in its way taken part in the suffering of Christ. "The properties and acts of these natures have their condition, that one communicates its properties or acts to the other, which is called the '*communicatio idiomatum*'" (Brenz, *De libello Bullingeri*, p. 105). The Lower Saxon theologians, headed by Martin Chemnitz, shrank from this logical carrying out of the unity of person with reference to the communion of the natures and their properties, and endeavored to maintain in spite of the unity of the person the lasting difference of the natures as well as that of the two states of Christ. But this does not mean that an essential difference existed between the Saxon and Swabian doctrine with reference to the suppositions and foundations themselves. For Chemnitz himself expressly denied that the hypostatic union or the personal indwelling of the entire fulness of the deity in the assumed human nature had become "in the course of years, progressively greater, closer, fuller, and more perfect," and rather asserted this indwelling "from the first moment of the hypostatic union" (*De duabus naturis*, p. 216), and most decidedly declared against the assumption that God can be placed somewhere without placing there also the humanity assumed by him (p. 203).

4. The Formula of Concord.

The statement of the doctrine of the *communicatio idiomatum* as developed in the Formula of Concord is thus plainly unintelligible in all points, if detached from the immediate interest of faith. Starting therefore with the so-called *propositiones personales* (God is man, man is God) concerning which, according to the statement, no difference existed between the Philippistic and the Swiss theologians, they proceeded to the statement of the *communicatio idiomatum* based upon the generally acknowledged personal union of the natures and to be interpreted by it. They asserted first the *genus idiomaticum*, that kind of communication of properties whereby the common properties are to be ascribed to the person of the God-man with distinction of the natures. For example, the son of God was born according to the human nature, the son of man is almighty according to the divine nature. Here, too, there was agreement with their opponents, but the difference of the meaning which was discerned in the expression results from this, that on the part of the Reformed this *communicatio* was only considered as a *dialectica prædicatio*, not as a *realis communicatio*.

It is evident that in the confession of the Lutheran

Church the question was not decided, whether and in what respect all divine attributes of the divine nature were communicated to the human, but that the attempt was made merely to point out those properties whose communication was immediately connected with the reality of the work of redemption and the functions of Christ based thereon (*Solida Declaratio*, viii. 55). Concerning the manner of the communication they were satisfied to assert that it really took place, but without fusion and equalization of the natures, after the manner of personal union (viii. 63–64). The immediate interests of faith at the time, according to which the statement must be interpreted, were thus satisfied, and they were satisfied also by knowing that the divine omnipotence, power, majesty, and glory showed themselves in, with, and through the assumed human nature, "when and how it seemed good to Christ," namely where his office "as mediator, head, king, and high priest" required it (cf. viii. 78). And this irrespective of the general statement that wherever the person of Christ is it is as God and man (viii. 82); for this statement also is not meant to be conceived of as an abstract one, but as one of Christian faith, for which the God-man is just this, since otherwise it would not consider him as being able to save (cf. F. H. R. Frank, *Die Theologie der Konkordienformel*, iii., Erlangen, 1862).

5. Later Lutheran Theology.

The Lutheran theology which followed the Formula of Concord has contributed little toward advancing the doctrine of the *communicatio idiomatum* (cf. H. Schmid, *Die Dogmatik der evangelischen lutherischen Kirche*, Gütersloh, 1893, pp. 226 sqq., 234 sqq.). Wherever in modern theology the original position of the Church has been abolished—which necessarily led to the question pertaining to the *communicatio idiomatum*—that the second person of the Trinity, hypostatically conceived of, in the act of incarnation assumed the human nature for a personal, from that time lasting and existing union, the question can be no more of further advancing that doctrine of the communication of the properties in the old ecclesiastical sense. Modern Lutheran theology which participates in that old ecclesiastical suggestion has abided mostly either by the statement of the confession and the corresponding doctrine of the theology of the seventeenth century, or has endeavored to bring about the dogmatically necessary advance by revising and recasting more minutely the foundations on which rests the doctrine of the communication of the properties, especially by assuming a self-limitation, a kenosis of the Logos at the incarnation, without, however, a general agreement or adoption within the Lutheran Church. See CHRISTOLOGY, VIII.

R. SEEBERG.

BIBLIOGRAPHY: Consult besides the works cited under CHRISTOLOGY by Baur, Dorner, Thomasius, Liebner, Kahnis, Frank, Nitzsch, Lipsius, Gess, Brens, Danæus, Heppe, Schneckenburger, and Hodge; J. Wigand, *De communicatione idiomatum*, Basel, 1568; H. E. Jacobs, *Book of Concord*, i. 519, 630, 632–633, 641, Philadelphia, 1893; H. Schmid, *Doctrinal Theology of the Evangelical Lutheran Church*, Eng. transl., ib. 1889; Neander, *Christian Church*, ii. 469, 501–502, iii. 159–162, 183, iii. 340.

COMMUNION. See LORD'S SUPPER.

COMMUNION OF THE DEAD: In the ancient church the custom existed of putting a piece of the eucharistic bread as *viaticum* into the mouth of Christians who by sudden death had been prevented from communing. The practise was prohibited by the synods of Hippo (393), third of Carthage (397), Auxerre (578), and the second Trullan (692). Balsamon states that bishops were given the Eucharist after their death, to protect them from demons while on their way to heaven. This idea was at the bottom of the custom. Later, a piece of the consecrated bread, instead of being put in the mouth of the corpse, was simply laid upon the breast, and buried with it. Gregory the Great tells (*Dialogi*, book ii.) how Benedict of Nursia did this in the case of a young monk who had left his monastery and gone home without permission, lest the earth should refuse to harbor his dead body. The monk Yso relates in the ninth century that when the body of Othmar, abbot of St. Gall, was moved, under his head and upon his breast were found round pieces of bread. Yso was ignorant of the object of the bread—showing how entirely the early custom had vanished even from memory.

BIBLIOGRAPHY: F. X. Kraus, *Real-Encyklopädie der christlichen Alterthümer*, ii. 885, Freiburg, 1886; Bingham, *Origines*, book xv.; Hefele, *Conciliengeschichte*, ii. 56; H. M. Luckock, *Eucharistic Sacrifice and Intercession for the Departed*, London, 1907; *DCA*, i. 535.

COMMUNION OF SAINTS: A dogmatic term, found in the Apostles' Creed, though not in the doctrinal formulas of the Eastern Church. The time and motive of its insertion in the ancient baptismal symbol and the meaning originally attached to it are still matters of controversy among theologians. The earliest certain evidence for the inclusion of the words *sanctorum communionem* in the creed is furnished by Faustus, bishop of Riez in the south of France, in the second half of the fifth century, from whose use it may be inferred that the clause was received as of unquestioned antiquity in the wide region represented by Faustus, and that he knew no form of the creed without it.

Early Testimonies to the Formula.

He understands it specifically in the catholic sense of the word "saint," already pretty definitely established in his time, and refers it to the saints in their state of perfection in the other world. Not much later are the pseudo-Augustinian sermons ccxli. and ccxlii., which quote the words as part of the creed, and interpret them as meaning communion "with the saints who have died in the faith which we have received." A still older, though not so well authenticated witness is that of the *Explanatio symboli*, composed, according to Gennadius, by Bishop Nicetas—probably not Nicetas of Aquileia, but one who lived at Remesiana in Dalmatia as a missionary bishop about 400, and was a friend of Paulinus of Nola. His words have evident reference to the baptismal formula, and are important as showing a wider reception of the clause than could have been argued from Faustus alone. Here it seems to adopt the same interpretation as that borne by the words of Faustus. This amounts to saying that in the earlier period at which we know of the clause the only meaning assigned to it is a different one from that which it bears in modern Protestant theology—though this is not to say that it was introduced for the purpose of sanctioning the cultus of the saints and defending it against attack. The question is whether this meaning was borne by it at the time of its origin, which must have preceded the date already mentioned by a sufficient interval to allow it to attain the wide recognition already seen. The words were certainly not used, before they became part of the creed, with reference only to the perfected saints in heaven, but rather to the fellowship here below of those who are sanctified in Christ, just as the Church on earth is called holy. The controversy between Augustine and the Donatists turned on the question whether the existence of the *ecclesia sancta* depended on the expulsion of all those whose character gave them no right to belong to it. And so Nicetas calls the existing Church, whose members are only later to attain the fulness of the *communio sanctorum*, a *congregatio sanctorum*. It is at least a plausible theory that the clause was originally put into the creed to express in the widest sense the fellowship of all the saints, existing already here and to be perfected hereafter; and that the narrower interpretation came in under the influence of the increasing cultus of those whom we now call the saints. This view would bring the clause into connection with the Donatist controversy; while the sectaries boasted of their "communion of saints," the catholic Church desired solemnly to testify to its belief in that same blessing, and its confidence of possessing it. But the theory is weakened by the fact that the North African Church recited the creed without this clause. The theory that *communio sanctorum* is a rendering of the Greek *koinōnia tōn hagiōn*, "holy things" in the neuter sense, as in the versicle of the liturgy *ta hagia tois hagiois*, may be dismissed.

Meaning.

It is worth remarking that the Roman Catholic Church, strongly as it presses the veneration of the saints in the narrower sense, has never confined itself to this meaning in its interpretation of the clause, but is rather inclined (as in the *Catechismus Romanus*) to expound it as an expansion or complement of the preceding "Holy Catholic Church." To this communion belong the members of the Church on earth (the Church militant), those in purgatory (the Church patient), and the saints in heaven (the Church Triumphant). The communion is emphasized by the prayers which the last-named offer for their brethren on earth and in purgatory, and by the doctrine of the treasure of the merits both of Christ and the saints which are available for the Church on earth. In a somewhat similar manner Luther explains the clause under discussion as an alternative expression for "Holy Catholic Church," translating it rather as "the fellowship of the saints"; he understands, however, different terms for the sharing of the blessings, and knows nothing of saints in the narrow sense. The older Lutheran theologians followed this view; and the Calvinist confessions do not differ widely from it, explaining that those who are sanctified in Christ's fellowship are bound to a mutual sharing of all the benefits they receive from God. (J. Köstlin†.)

Roman Catholic Interpretation.

Bibliography: H. B. Wilson, *The Communion of Saints*, Oxford, 1851; W. Rede, *The Communion of Saints*, London, 1893. Discussions will generally be found in treatises on the creeds, such as: C. P. Caspari, *Quellen zur Geschichte des Taufsymbols*, Leipsic, 1866–75; H. Cremer, *Zum Kampf um das Apostolicum*, Berlin, 1893; T. Zahn, *Das apostolische Symbol*, Nuremberg, 1893; O. Zöckler, *Zum Apostolikumstreit*, Munich, 1893; F. Kattenbusch, *Das apostolische Symbol*, Leipsic, 1894–1900; A. Hahn, *Symbole und Glaubensregeln der alten Kirche*, Breslau, 1897; A. Harnack, *The Apostles' Creed*, London, 1901; A. C. McGiffert, *Apostles Creed*, New York, 1902; *KL*, v. 1621–22.

COMMUNION OF THE SICK. See Lord's Supper, V., § 2.

COMMUNISM.

I. Theory, History, and Criticism: The words communism and socialism are often used synonymously; but this usage leads to confusion. As the opposite of individualism, socialism is merely the general view that, in the organization of society, the welfare of the whole shall take precedence of the rights of individuals. It is not something absolute, but admits of degrees, according to the extent to which it recognizes individualism. Communism, or collectivism, on the other hand, is a definite system. It is a theory as to the distribution of property in the interest of humanity and morality, and forms a definite social and economic system. It demands the abolishment of private property and the ownership of all industries and utilities by the State. Property is divided into two classes: one of things intended for consumption—food, clothing, and the like; the other of things serving for production—land, machines, factories, etc. According to communism, the interests of society are best served when all productive property belongs to the community. The individual then is an employee of the State, and has a right only to those commodities that are apportioned out to him from the common

1. The Communist Theory.

storehouse in remuneration for his contribution to the common work. The communist maintains that many of the existing economic evils would be removed by such a system. Production, he believes, would regulate itself automatically; there would be no more crises caused by overproduction; and there would be no more strikes. Besides, by concentrating the industries the work-day would be shortened, thereby allowing more time for intellectual enjoyments. Poverty would disappear, and also the kindred evil, wealth. The source of all evil passions and crime, private property, would be removed. Jealousy, selfishness, egoism would be meaningless. The whole social and economic world would be unified; there would be only one government, and that by the people. The whole of humanity would form one happy family. Since the basis of this system is the equal enjoyment of this world's goods, it is evident that the kind of communism here described is thoroughly materialistic. It is to be distinguished from ascetic communism, in which it is contempt for things earthly that leads to renunciation of private property.

2. History. History shows that the higher the civilization of a country the more highly developed have been the forms of private property. Among Slavic peoples the land surrounding the village is still held in common. The Germanic peoples early divided the arable land; but in modern Germany forests have remained common property to a great extent, and likewise pasture-land till near the end of the nineteenth century. Communism as a theoretical system first appeared among the Greeks, the most famous example being furnished by Plato's "Republic." Aristotle recognized its impracticability, but believed that the use of private property ought to be regulated by law in the interest of the public. Similar reactions against the division of society into rich and poor are found in the Orient, where disdain of riches leads to renunciation of property; the Buddhist monks are particularly noteworthy. Christianity pointed a new way. True, Christ taught that earthly treasures are unimportant compared with things eternal (Matt. xvi. 26); but for this very reason both poverty and riches are of like import to the Christian. Both were considered only from the standpoint of the moral dangers they bring with them. So far from commending renunciation of earthly goods, Paul declared work and remunerative work fundamental for every Christian (Eph. iv. 28; II Thess. iii. 10); and Jesus emphasized the duty of faithfulness where private possessions are concerned (Luke xvi. 11). The New Testament teaches complete self-denial, but not communism; and to conceive of the first congregation in Jerusalem as communistic is to misunderstand both the passage describing it (Acts ii.–v.) and Christianity (cf. O. Holtzmann, in *ZKG*, xiv., 1893, p. 327; Nathusius, *Mitarbeit*, p. 402; W. Roscher, *Grundlagen der Nationalökonomie*, Stuttgart, 1892, p. 199). The later communistic interpretation of Christianity was due to two causes: the taking up into Christian thought of the heathen contempt for matter as such, and the substitution of the Law for the Gospel. In its Christian garb communism has been based upon asceticism, or upon greed disguised as asceticism, as with the Circumcelliones (q.v.) of the Donatist controversy (see DONATISM). The idea that communism is ethically a higher form of possession than individualism was common in the Church throughout the Middle Ages. This made it easy for the Church to move the people to surrender their property.

3. Historical Examples. [Strong communistic tendencies appeared among the medieval Waldenses, Apostolic Brethren, Beghards, and Lollards. But the most important medieval communistic experiment was that of the Taborites (q.v.), the radical Bohemian party in the Hussite wars. Among the articles set forth by them in 1420 were the following: "In these days there shall be no king, ruler, or subject on the earth, and all imposts and taxes shall cease; no one shall force another to do anything, for all shall be equal brethren and sisters. As in the town of Tabor there is no mine or thine, but all is held in common, so shall everything be common to all, and no one own anything for himself alone. Whoever does so commits a deadly sin." All were required to deposit their possessions in a common treasury. Later each carried on his own industry, but brought all the surplus product for common use. The more radical of the Taborites insisted upon community even in wives (see ADAMITES, 3; and NICOLAITANS). At first the Bohemian Brethren (q.v.) required all who would enter their fellowship to renounce property and rank, and schism occurred (1491) when the dominant elements decided to relax the conditions of membership in the body, in favor of nobles and gentry. In the early Reformation time Thomas Münzer (q.v.), influenced by Nicholas Storch (see ZWICKAU PROPHETS), made a determined and enthusiastic effort to overthrow the existing order with its injustice and oppression, and to establish a kingdom of Christ on earth, conceived of as communistic or semicommunistic. The revolutionary peasants (see PEASANTS' WAR) did not demand absolute community of goods; but the forests for timber, fuel, and game, the streams for fish, exemption from oppressive taxes, rents, and imposts, and a free enjoyment of the products of labor by the laborer were earnestly insisted upon. All of the Anabaptists recognized the obligation of contributing freely of their means for the supplying of the needs of brethren, and many of them taught and practised a thoroughgoing communism. This is true especially of the Moravian Anabaptists, who established larger households, in which thousands lived in a communistic way under a general superintendent. (Consult on medieval and sixteenth century communism: K. Kautsky, *Communism in Central Europe in the Time of the Reformation*, London, 1897, and J. Loserth, *Der Communismus der Mährischen Wiedertäufer*, Vienna, 1894.)

A. H. N.]

In the sixteenth century the propaganda for communism assumed the form of fiction. The most important work of this character was the *Utopia* (1516) of Sir Thomas More (q.v.). Communism in its present form may be said to have begun in the party of the Mountain in the French Revolution, when Marat maintained that equality of rights leads to equality in enjoyment. Thus communism was robbed of its religious guise and placed upon its present materialistic basis. However, the real father of modern communism was Saint-Simon (q.v.). His ideas were taken up by Fourier (d. 1837); Enfantin (d. 1864), who advocated community of women; and others, including Cabet (d. 1856), who founded communistic colonies in America (see below, II., 6). Later Karl Marx (d. 1883) attempted to reduce the more or less obscure and idealistic thoughts of Saint-Simon to a cold logical system by deducing common ownership from the nature of property. The position of the radical social party in Germany to-day is founded upon the theories of Marx. A product of the latter-day communistic thought was Edward Bellamy's *Looking Backward* (1888). The philanthropic aims of the later communism have attracted certain of the clergy, as they did earlier the contemporary of Saint-Simon, Robert Owen (q.v.); but the result is a new mixture of the ideas of Christian asceticism, based on a misunderstanding of the Gospel, with the materialistic desires of the multitude. A like tendency, with the same confusion of thought and result, appears in the Roman Catholic Church in Lamennais (q.v.) and other Frenchmen. The theories of Henry George (d. 1896) differ from communism in essential points and are only allied to the latter.

4. Criticism. Like many other things, communism is beautiful in theory; but it does not work in practise. The successful control by the government of isolated utilities forms no argument for the common ownership of everything. Granting that the entire industrial world could be organized under a single management, on what principle would the fruits of the common work be divided among the individual members of society? According to the needs of the individual, or the amount of his production? according to the number of hours employed, or according to the quality of his work, physical or intellectual? Such practical considerations show that thoroughgoing communism is only a theory. We are neither machines nor slaves; yet such a system would, in effect, condemn the whole of humanity to penal servitude. There would be no longer any individual endeavor; for all articles of use, whether pig iron, potted ham, or poetry, would be forthcoming at the command of some general committee. Even a philosopher would be prohibited from spending his leisure hours in pleasant meditation; for in a communistic society all philosophical problems would have been solved, and further speculation must be considered dangerous to the existing social organization. Such an offense would constitute a sort of lese-majesty. Arguments for communism are superficial and can be met by a simple appeal to the nature of man as a full moral agent. Communism based upon an equal enjoyment of this world's goods is unchristian and is not supported by revelation. God makes men to differ from one another, and this fact is recognized in the Bible. The institution of private property is supported by every passage in the Bible where property is mentioned; and, in fact, it is a postulate of Christian ethics. Is it not through accumulating that the Christian is to make himself a useful member of society?

(M. von Nathusius†.)

II. Communism in America: **Type and Character of American Communism.** [Almost from its discovery America seemed marked out as the home of communistic experiments. The Jamestown charter (1606) included a provision for a common storehouse, and the Pilgrims for a time maintained some features of communism. More direct and systematic attempts to embody the idea in practise were the Labadist community in Maryland (1680; see Labadie, Jean de, Labadists) and the community of the "Woman in the Wilderness" in Pennsylvania (1694). It is significant of the hopes which were entertained concerning America that such communistic bodies as the Shakers, Harmonists, Separatists, Amana Society, and Icarians (see below) were growths transplanted from other lands. The teachings of Owenism, Fourierism, and Cabetism were tested here, as well as in later times those of Marx and his school. In many of these the religious principle was central. Other efforts disregarded the religious basis and were either purely social or a mingling of the social and economic. Some of those which started as religious movements became purely economic. Of early foundations only the Oneida Community, the Amana Society, and the Shakers are now in existence. Where the basis was the thought of a single mind emphasizing personal idiosyncrasy, and where the essay was made in ignorance of vital and economic laws success could be only temporary. Division and dissension soon wrought the ruin of the experiment. Some of these essays at a communal life left their impress upon both life and literature. Such a one was Brook Farm, which figures in the works of Hawthorne, Alcott, and the New England writers of their time. The tendency of the last two decades has been away from a strictly communistic and toward a cooperative type of society. The life of these experiments is not yet sufficiently extended to afford basis for judgment as to the permanence they will attain. The more important of them are the following.]

1. The Adonai Shomo ("the Lord is there"): A religious society holding the doctrines of the Second Advent, which existed in Massachusetts 1861–96. Its founder, Frederick I. Howland, a Quaker of New Bedford, was converted to the Second Advent doctrine under the preaching of William Miller (q.v.) in 1843. Believing that he had received the gift of inspiration in 1855, he formed an association in 1861 with other like-minded persons, who settled in Athol and afterward in Petersham, Mass. The fundamental principles of the society as given by one of its presidents were: "The Jesus, the Mystery of Christ, and belief in times of restitution of all things, of which God hath spoken by the mouth of all his holy prophets since the world began; and that the elect, by grace through said faith, will attain to the Melchisidek priesthood, which is after the power of an endless life." All possessions were held in common; the seventh day was observed as the Sabbath, and the Lord's Prayer was presented as the offering of the morning and evening sacrifice. Howland held also that the true followers of Christ had already begun the eternal life. The Adonai Shomo never had more than twenty-five or thirty members. It possessed 840 acres of land and a dwelling. It was chartered in 1876. In 1896, only one of its members surviving, the charter was annulled by the State Supreme Court; and in the following year the property was sold.

W. H. Larrabee.

Bibliography: H. F. Hager, in *American Socialist*, 1877; W. A. Hinds, *American Communities*, pp. 403-407, Chicago, 1908.

2. The Altruist Community: A society occupying a small estate at Sulphur Springs, on the Mississippi River, 23 m. s. by w. of St. Louis, Mo. It was founded by Alcander Longley, who had been a member of the North American Phalanx (one of the most successful of the American communities based upon Fourieristic principles) and of the Icaria Community (see below, 7) and also a member and director in several cooperative stores and colonies. It allows equal rights and privileges to all its members, both men and women, in all the business affairs; and it makes no interference with the marriage or family affairs of its members, or with their religious, political, or other opinions. It carries on a poultry and gardening business. It has few members, but additional ones will be received as fast as they can be profitably employed. The society has also headquarters at St. Louis, with a printing establishment where its monthly journal, books, and tracts are published.

W. H. Larrabee.

Bibliography: W. A. Hinds, *American Communities*, pp. 486, 487, Chicago, 1908; *The Altruist*, St. Louis (a monthly); A. Longley, *What is Communism?* St. Louis.

3. The Amana Society: Located at Amana, Iowa. The origins of the society go back to the revived communities of the "inspired" in Germany in the first quarter of the eighteenth century (see Inspired, The). The annoyances which the members of these revivified congregations suffered at home because they separated from the State Church, refused to send their children to the public schools, declined to bear arms, serve in war, take oaths, and the like, led to their emigration to America. Under the lead of Christian Metz, Barbara Heinemann (see Inspired, The), Councilor G. A. Weber of Lich, and a manufacturer of Ronneburg named Mörschel, they bought a tract of land near Buffalo, N. Y., where they built six villages, besides two in Canada. About 800 persons came during the years 1843-46. They gave their settlement the name Ebenezer, and engaged in agriculture and cloth manufacture. In 1854 a tract was bought on the Iowa River, on which seven villages were laid out, and the colony removed thither during the ensuing ten years. The community was incorporated in 1859 as the Amana Society, under a constitution providing that all property should be held in common, that agriculture, manufacturing, and trade should furnish the means of sustenance, and that the surplus should be applied to communal improvements and educational and benevolent purposes. Metz was the head till his death in 1867, when he was succeeded by Barbara Heinemann (who had married Georg Landmann). Since her death (1884) no member has received the gift of prophecy.

The fundamental doctrine of the Amana Society is that "God can now as well as of old inspire men to declare his word and will, and thus act as messengers of divine teaching to the world." This gift is not continuous, but is supposed to fall upon special persons. The utterances of all the society's prophets have been recorded and are read at the meetings along with the Scriptures. The doctrines of the Trinity, justification by faith, the resurrection of the dead, and the final judgment are inculcated in the catechism. The Lord's Supper is celebrated whenever inspired direction is given to do so, and then with peculiar observances; baptism is not practised.

The basis of the communistic system is wholly religious. Persons joining the society surrender all their property and all claim to wages, and are promised in return board and dwelling, support in old age, sickness, and infirmity, and an annual allowance for clothing and other expenses. If they withdraw, they receive back what they originally contributed to the common fund. Marriage is permitted; but those who marry lose their standing for a time. Membership is of three orders, of which the first includes the youth and probationers. A thorough inquisitorial examination of the spiritual condition of the whole community is held every year. The temporal government of the society is vested in a board of thirteen trustees, who are chosen annually by the male members. A suit brought for the dissolution of the Amana Corporation on the ground of its carrying on a secular business was decided by the District Court in Iowa in 1905 in favor of the society. The society reports (1906) a membership of 1,770, and property aggregating in value $1,750,000.

W. H. Larrabee.

Bibliography: The society has issued *A Brief History of the Amana Society* (Amana, Ia., 1900). Consult W. A. Hinds, *American Communities*, pp. 301-326, Chicago, 1908; C. Nordhoff, *Communistic Societies of the United States*, New York, 1875; A. Shaw, *Life in the Amana Colony*, in *The Chautauquan*, viii (1888), pp. 300 sqq.; K. Knortz, *Die wahre Inspirationsgemeinde in Iowa*, Leipsic, 1896; R. Ely, *Amana; A Study of Religious Communism*, in *Harper's Magazine*, cv (1902), pp. 659 sqq. See the bibliography of Inspired, The.

4. The Church Triumphant, Koreshanity: A religious society at Estero, Lee County, Fla., whither its headquarters were removed from Chicago in 1903. It was founded in Chicago in 1886 by Dr. Cyrus R. Teed, who claimed to have experienced a spiritual illumination in 1870, with a revelation of the system which he denominated Koreshanity (from *Koresh*, the Hebrew equivalent of his own name, Cyrus), while a practising physician of Utica, N. Y. The system is based on the Koreshan Cosmogony, which holds that the universe is a hollow sphere, whose physical body is the earth, and that men live in the inside of the cell. The sun, moon, planets, and stars are all within the globe. The earth is supposed to be eternal, a great battery continually renewing itself. Alchemy, rather than chemistry, is held to be true, matter and spirit to be interchangeable and interdependent. God is a personal being, invested with a trinity of specific attributes; Jesus Christ was God Almighty, and the Holy Spirit was the product of his transmutation or of the burning of his body. The coming of the Messiah is the fruition of an evolution through a succession of reincarnations. The divine seed was sown 1,800 years ago, and the first fruit is another Messianic personality, who is affirmed to be now in the world, declaiming his scientific gospel. Reincarnation is the central law of life and identical with resurrection, which is reached through a succession of reembodiments. The origin and destiny of man are found in God. The standard of Koreshan purity is the virgin life of Jesus. The Bible is accepted as the best written expression of the divine mind, and its truth is demonstrated by Koreshanity. The Koreshan government has as its principal divisions the Church Triumphant, the College of Life, and the Society Arch-Triumphant. There are also three general orders: the investigative court, the marital order, and the communistic and celibate order, the last being the highest and most central of the three. The following of Koreshanity is estimated at about 5,000, and the property at $250,000. The town of Estero includes an area of 110 square miles. W. H. LARRABEE.

BIBLIOGRAPHY: The literature of the society comprises: C. R. Teed's *Koresh*. *The Immortal Manhood;* L. Page Borden, *The Logos or Word Book;* C. R. Teed and U. G. Morrow, *The Cellular Cosmology*, a series of pamphlets explaining the principles of the society, all published at Estero, and *The Flaming Sword*, the periodical of the community. Consult also W. A. Hinds, *American Communities*, pp. 471–485, Chicago, 1908.

5. The Ephrata Community: A society founded in Lancaster County, Pa., in 1732 by John Conrad Beissel (b. at Eberbach, 12 m. e. of Heidelberg, Germany, 1690; d. at Ephrata July 6, 1768). He is said to have been converted in 1715, to have come under Pietistic influence, and especially to have been affected by the ideas of Gottfried Arnold (q.v.). In 1720 he emigrated to America, intending to join the community of the "Woman in the Wilderness," on the banks of the Wissahickon; but finding that society no longer in existence, he joined the Dunkers (q.v.) in 1724. Later he became convinced of the duty of celebrating the seventh day as Sabbath and published *Das Büchlein vom Sabbath* (Philadelphia, 1728). He then withdrew from the Dunkers and adopted a solitary life in a cabin on the Cocalico Creek, where he was joined by three men and two women. About this nucleus a community was formed, composed mainly of Dunkers, and in 1733 a conventual mode of life was formally adopted; buildings for the accommodation of the members were erected, of which those constructed in 1746–47 are still standing (near the borough limits of the present town of Ephrata, 19 m. s.w. of Reading). They were made entirely of wood, and the use of iron was long avoided in the entire life of the community. The sister house shows the method of construction, being divided into some fifty cells, each about six feet long by five wide, containing a window eighteen inches by fourteen and a door sixty inches by twenty, while under the window was a bench about eighteen inches wide upon which the occupant slept with a block for a pillow. The halls were so narrow that they permitted the passage of only one person at a time. The walls of the Saal, another early building, are still hung with charts, illustrated texts, and drawings made by the inmates in the early days, all done with the quill pen; and in the library are preserved manuscript hymn- and tune-books done not later than 1750.

1. John Conrad Beissel. The Buildings.

The community was organized upon a basis of voluntary celibacy, those who were married living apart. In the neighborhood gradually gathered a number of persons who accepted the religious principles of the community except those of celibacy and communism. Within the community the members assumed monastic names, and the founder was known as Friedsam and Gottrecht. A small tract of land was acquired, all the work on which was done by the members. In 1740 the holding of property by individual members was declared sinful, and all who joined the community were required to surrender all they had to the common fund; in 1786 this regulation was abolished. The religious mysticism which underlay the society assumed that true Christianity could be attained only by overcoming the bonds of the flesh, and true wisdom was to be sought by union with the celestial *Sophia*. Man originally combined in one perfect being the male and the female elements, which condition, lost at the Fall, is to be regained in the body of Christ. To the attainment of perfect happiness there is necessary right living, purity of life, renunciation of self and of human love and marriage, meditation, and praise of Christ, all of which lead to the mental state where the celestial male and female elements shall be united. The New Testament was accepted as the bond of faith, trine baptism was practised with the laying on of hands while the candidate knelt in the water, the Lord's Supper was celebrated on the evening of the Sabbath together with washing of feet, and love-feasts and night services were held as occasion demanded. The community was opposed to the taking of oaths and to bearing arms, though the buildings were opened as a refuge after fights on the frontier, and after the battle of Brandywine the place served as a hospital with the members of the community as nurses. Compensation from the British government and from the State of Pennsylvania for these services was refused on the ground that it would be a temptation to worldliness.

2. Organization and Doctrines.

By 1740 thirty-six men and thirty-five women had united with the society. Its largest membership is given as 300. While the society regarded agriculture as its principal business, it possessed the second printing-press set up in the State, had a paper mill, and also saw mills, grist mills, and other like enterprises. It furnished the paper, and is believed to have printed and bound a part of the edition of Christopher Sower's Bible, published at Germantown, 1743 (see SOWER, CHRISTOPHER). The school maintained by the brethren enjoyed a high reputation, and drew students from Philadelphia and Baltimore. The community was celebrated also as a musical center, and the founder was a prolific writer of hymns and music. His *Göttliche Liebe* and *Lobesgetöne*, printed by Benjamin Franklin in 1730, are believed to be the earliest books of German poetry printed as native productions in America.

3. Growth and Decline.

After the death of Beissel in 1768 the society declined; and in 1814 the remaining members became incorporated as the Seventh-day Baptists, German, receiving authority to hold the land and buildings in trust for religious and educational purposes. Their principles and practises are substantially those of the Ephrata Community, with the elimination of the communistic and celibate principles. They have congregations in the counties of Bedford, Franklin, Lancaster, and Somerset, Pennsylvania, a bishop emeritus, six active and two retired ministers, and about 250 members. They possess an estate of 110 acres, and the total value of all property is about $100,000. The numbers are not increasing, and in 1907 one of the churches united with the Seventh-day Baptist General Conference. W. H. LARRABEE.

BIBLIOGRAPHY: *Chronicon Ephratense: a Hist. of the Community of Seventh Day Baptists at Ephrata*, finished in 1786, translated by J. M. Hark, Lancaster, Pa., 1889 (carries the reader to the death of the founder); C. Nordhoff, *Communistic Societies*, pp. 133–134, New York, 1875; O. Seidensticker, in *The Century Magazine*, vol. i., no. 1, 1881; S. G. Fisher, *The Making of Pennsylvania*, Philadelphia, 1896; J. F. Sachse, *The German Sectarians of Pennsylvania. Critical and Legendary Hist. of the Ephrata Cloister and the Dunkers*, Philadelphia, 1900; W. A. Hinds, *American Communities*, pp. 16–24, Chicago, 1908; A. H. Lewis, in *The Sabbath Recorder*, Plainfield, N. J., May and June, 1906.

6. The Harmony Society: Founded in Pennsylvania and Indiana by Georg Rapp (q.v.), who came to America with a number of followers from Württemberg in 1803. Five thousand acres of land were bought in Butler County, Pa., as a site for a settlement, to which the name Harmony was given. Other followers of Rapp came the next year and the organization of the community was completed in 1805. The members placed their property in a common fund, covenanted to labor for the good of the community, and promised to make no demand, in case of withdrawal from the society, for compensation for their labor or that of their children. In 1807 they gave up marriage; in 1818 they renounced the right of receiving back their original contributions in case of withdrawal, and the records of these contributions were burned.

The site of the colony proving unsuitable in some respects, 30,000 acres of land were bought in Posey County, Ind., in 1814 and a new settlement was founded. Agricultural and manufacturing enterprises were undertaken on a liberal scale, and a considerable trade was built up. But unpleasant conditions developed, and the property was sold in 1824 to Robert Owen (q.v.), who established another community upon it. Rapp and his associates returned to Pennsylvania, and settled at Economy, on the Ohio River (17 m. n.w. of Pittsburg), which remained the home of the community during the rest of its existence. In 1832 the society suffered severe loss by the withdrawal of 250 members following a disaffected leader, whose claims it was deemed expedient to satisfy by the payment of upward of $100,000.

While they were without any religious organization separate from their community and had no written creed except the Bible, the Harmonists made the salvation of their souls their supreme object. They believed that Adam was created in the likeness of God, androgynous; that he became discontented when God separated the female part from him, and this was the fall of man; that the celibate state is the more pleasing to God; that in the renewed world man will be restored to the dual Godlike and Adamic condition; that Jesus was born in the likeness of the Father, a dual being, and taught and commanded a community of goods. A cardinal point of their doctrine was that the coming of Christ and the regeneration of the world were near at hand; and one of their aims was to be in readiness for the event. All who sought admission to the society were required to make a complete confession of sins to one of the elders.

The society declined rapidly during the later years of the nineteenth century. In 1890 the United States Census gave the number of members as 250; in 1900 there were nine. After a period of financial strain, of lawsuits brought by seceding members, which were decided in the society's favor in the Supreme Court of the United States, their property was sold in Apr., 1903.

W. H. LARRABEE.

BIBLIOGRAPHY: W. A. Hinds, *American Communities*, pp. 69–98, Chicago, 1908; A. Williams, *The Harmony Society at Economy, Pa.*, Pittsburg, 1866; C. Nordhoff, *Communistic Societies*, New York, 1875; G. B. Lockwood, *New Harmony Communities*, Marion, Ind., 1902; W. G. Davis, *The Passing of the Rappists*, in *Gunton's Magazine*, xxv (1903), 20 sqq.; J. A. Bole, *The Harmony Society*, Philadelphia, 1904; F. Podmore, *Robert Owen; a Biography*, 2 vols., New York, 1907.

7. Icaria and New Icaria: A society formed in 1848 by French immigrants who settled in Texas under the leadership of Étienne Cabet, a French revolutionary agitator connected with the society of the Carbonari, author of several historical and socialistic works, and a member of the French Assembly of 1831. His radical utterance against the French king and ministry led to his expulsion from France, but, in 1840, he returned and gained many thousand adherents to his socialistic theories through his fanciful descriptions in *Le Voyage en Icarie* (Paris, 1842) of an ideal society in which all class distinctions were abolished and equality prevailed, and through their promulgation in the journal *Le Populaire*. In 1848 he purchased land in Texas for the purposes of a colony. The country being wild and practically inaccessible, it proved unfit for the purpose. Homes were procured for the baffled and disappointed immigrants, several hundred in number, who had suffered great hardships in fruitless efforts to establish themselves on this site, in Nauvoo, Ill., then recently abandoned by the Mormons (q.v.). The society was afflicted with dissensions that resulted in several secessions and the founding of new colonies, which had only short lives.

The community at Nauvoo removed to Iowa in 1860, and was again involved in a controversy in which legal measures were employed. By a settlement in 1879, one of the parties remained on the site and retained the name, Icaria; while the other formed a new settlement, named New Icaria, on the Nodaway River. The older colony lived only a short time; while the community of New Icaria existed till 1895, when it was dissolved by the unanimous vote of the twenty-three remaining members.

The Icarian Community was organized without any religious basis. Complete tolerance was given to individual opinion in matters of religion so long as its expression did not provoke dissension. The society was a pure democracy, in which a complete community of goods was contemplated. Direction was vested in a general assembly of all the members, whose decisions were carried into effect through officers elected annually. Transgressions of the principles, laws, and regulations of the community were punished by public censure, deprivation of civil rights, or exclusion of the transgressor, according to the gravity of the offense.

W. H. Larrabee.

Bibliography: W. A. Hinds, *American Communities*, pp. 361-396, Chicago, 1908; C. Nordhoff, *Communistic Societies*, New York, 1875; A. Shaw, *Icaria. A Chapter in the Hist. of Communism*, ib. 1884; J. Prudhommeaux, *Icarie et son fondateur Étienne Cabet*, Paris, 1907 (a large volume of more than 700 pages).

8. The Perfectionists or Oneida Community: Founded in 1845 by John Humphrey Noyes (b. at Brattleboro, Vt., Sept. 6, 1811; d. at Niagara Falls, Canada, Apr. 13, 1886). He was graduated at Dartmouth College in 1830, studied theology at Andover and Yale, and was licensed as a Congregationalist minister about 1833. Avowing a belief that the second coming of Christ had occurred within a generation and professing the doctrine of Perfectionism (q.v.), he withdrew from the ministry and retired to his home in Putney, Vt. There he established a Bible class, which grew into an association of Perfectionists and was organized in 1845 into the Putney Corporation. Adverse public opinion gradually developed especially against its views respecting marriage. In Nov., 1847, Noyes and other members withdrew and with new recruits settled in Central New York, where, in Sept., 1848, a new community was formed, "for the establishment of the kingdom on the principles of heavenly association," of which the renunciation of any claim to private property was one. The remainder of the Putney community joined them in June, 1849. Besides the main community at Oneida, N. Y., six branch societies were maintained for a time, but all these were eventually given up except one at Wallingford, Conn. Agricultural and small manufacturing industries were carried on, and the products of the community acquired a wide reputation for excellence.

The Perfectionists had a peculiar theory of the sexual relations which they called complex marriage, and the marriage contract was regarded as an affair of the community. Couples were united temporarily according to their preferences under the supervision of the society, but a permanent exclusive attachment of one person to another was regarded as wrong. Children who had reached an age to bear separation from the mother were put into the children's house to be cared for by nurses during the day and returned to their mothers at night; later they were passed to a second department, and the mother resumed her place in the household. A unique feature of the society was a system of mutual criticism to which all were subject, and in which all might take part. This constituted the principal means of discipline and government.

The pressure of public opinion against the doctrines and practises of the Oneida Community became so strong that the community yielded and gave up the system of complex marriage in 1880. Finally, Jan. 1, 1881, the community organization was dissolved and the society was converted into a joint stock company. The Oneida Community was exceptionally well managed and enjoyed a prosperity and harmony seldom found in such enterprises. At the time of dissolution there were 306 members at Oneida and Wallingford and the new company started with a paid up capital of $600,000. The present capital stock is $1,200,000 held by about 250 stockholders, of whom not far from 120 are connected with the factories or offices of the company. Employment is given to some 800 people in addition to the resident stockholders.

W. H. Larrabee.

Bibliography: For history consult W. A. Hinds, *American Communities*, pp. 181-231, Chicago, 1908; C. Nordhoff, *Communistic Societies*, New York, 1875; J. H. Noyes, *Hist. of American Socialisms*, Philadelphia, 1870; A. Estlake, *The Oneida Community*, London, 1900; H. Dixon, *New America*, London, 1867 (a criticism to which Mr. Noyes replied in *Dixon and his Copyists*, Oneida, 1871); J. H. Noyes, *Handbook of the Oneida Community*, Oneida, 1871. The doctrines of the community appear in the writings of Noyes—*The Perfectionist*, Putney, Vt., 1843-1846; *The Berean*, ib. 1847; *Religious Experiences*, 1850; *On Scientific Propagation*, 1873. From 1854 to 1874 the organ of the community was *The Circular*.

9. The Separatists: A society of German origin, which settled in Zoar, Tuscarawas County, O., 1817-19. The movement gathered first in Württemberg around Barbara Grubermann, a Swiss refugee to Germany, whom those who separated from the German State Church (whence the name) accepted as their leader. On her death Joseph Baumeler (Bimeler; d. 1853) became the head of the movement, and, securing the aid of some English Quakers in the persecution which followed, led the emigration of his followers to the United States. The first intention was not to adopt the communistic principles, but the diversity of station among the members and the great inequality of means seemed to make this necessary. Marriage was discouraged in the beginning, but was adopted a few years later. The society reached its largest membership about 1832 through immigration from Germany, when it numbered about 500 persons. The original enthusiasm continually declined and the society was finally dissolved. On Sept. 13, 1898, the property was allotted to the remaining members, 222 in number.

The articles of faith of the Separatists embraced belief in the Trinity, the fall of man, return through Christ to God the Father, and recognition of the Holy Scriptures as the ultimate authority. All ceremonies were rejected, all ecclesiastical connections and constitutions were repudiated, and such signs of respect as uncovering the head, bending the knee, and the distinctions of courtesy in forms of address were refused as according to mortals honors which were due to God. Members were of two classes. Minors and those who had not signed the covenant constituted the first class, and were eligible to full membership on coming of age or after a year's delay following application. The candidate for the second class or full membership signed a covenant giving up all his property, his present and prospective rights, titles, and possessions, to the society forever, and obligated himself to give obedience to the trustees. In the early period of the society the children were under the care of the trustees; but later they were left with their parents. The government of the community was vested in a standing committee of five members, under whom a board of three trustees directed business affairs. W. H. Larrabee.

Bibliography: E. O. Randall, *Hist. of the Zoar Society*, Columbus, O., 1899; C. Nordhoff, *Communistic Societies*, New York, 1875; W. A. Hinds, *American Communities*, pp. 99–131, Chicago, 1908. The society issued Baumeler's Works in three volumes, regarded as inspired, and also collections of hymns by Barbara Grubermann and Baumeler.

10. The Shakers or the Millennial Church: A body of believers living in communistic celibacy, who hold their founder, Ann Lee (q.v.), to have been a prophetess inspired by God, and the doctrines which she taught to be divine revelations. Their origin is connected with a revival that followed the demonstrations of the so-called French Prophets in England (see French Prophets), who exhibited under religious excitement marked physical manifestations. Some members of the Society of Friends in Manchester, England, of whom James and Jane Wardley were the most prominent, came under the influence of the revival, and were joined by Ann Lee and her parents. From their movements under religious excitement these people were called "Shaking Quakers" or "Shakers." They were subjected to persecution, and the leader and some of the members were imprisoned. On Jan. 5, 1762, Ann Lee married Abraham Standerin, a blacksmith, and became the mother of four children who died in infancy. She then learned that celibacy was the holy state, for proclaiming which doctrine she was sent to jail, where, in 1770, she experienced a vision of Jesus Christ, in which she claimed to have received a revelation "of Christ's kingdom and glory, of man's loss, and the way of redemption." From that time she was acknowledged as a mother in Christ and called "Mother Ann." In obedience to one of these revelations, she came to America in 1774, with a few other members of the society. The band supported themselves by labor for two years, and then settled in Niskeyuna, now Watervliet, N. Y. They attracted much attention, and prejudices were aroused against them, under the influence of which they were imprisoned, but were released by Governor George Clinton. A revival in the Baptist Churches of the vicinity brought additions to their number. Through numerous visitors from New York and the New England States to the settlement knowledge of Shaker doctrine was widely spread. Mother Ann, with five other members of the society, made a journey through New England of more than two years' duration, preaching and prophesying, but not without many trials and sufferings. After her death in 1784 she was succeeded by James Whittaker, under whom the first Shaker meeting-house was built, at Mt. Lebanon, N. Y.; and he in 1787 by Joseph Meacham, followed by Lucy Wright (d. 1821), who were all active in founding other societies in New England, New York, and the West. These new communities were generally the fruits of revivals, upon which the Shakers laid great stress. They were actively interested in the great revival in Kentucky at the beginning of the nineteenth century. James Meacham with two companions set out on a missionary journey from Mt. Lebanon Jan. 8, 1805, and traveled on foot to Lebanon, O.; thence into Indiana and Kentucky, where several societies were formed.

1. Origin and Early History.

According to one of its books, the Shaker Church rests upon the principles of virginal purity, Christian communism, and separation from the world. It holds that God is a duality, male and female; that Adam was dual, having been created in God's image; that all spirits are also dualities, male and female; and that Christ is the highest of spirits, appearing first in the person of Jesus, representing the male, and later in the person of Ann Lee, representing the female element of God. It teaches that the religious history of mankind is divided into four cycles, which are also represented in the spirit-world, each of which has its appropriate heaven and hell. The first cycle included the antediluvians; the second, the Jews up to the coming of Jesus; the third, those who lived up to the appearance of Ann Lee; and the fourth and last is the present dispensation, the heaven of which is in process of formation and will supersede all other heavens. The Shaker Church is, therefore, the Church of the last dispensation, and its establishment marks the dawn of the day of judgment, or the beginning of Christ's kingdom on earth. It is held, further, that the Pentecostal Church was established on right principles, that the Christian Churches rapidly and fatally fell away from it, and that the Shakers have returned to this perfect doctrine and practise. The Shakers reject the doctrines of the Trinity, of the resurrection of the body, and of the atonement. They consider Jesus and Ann Lee elders of the Church, to be respected and loved, but not objects of worship. They are spiritualists, believing fully in the reality of spiritualistic communications.

2. Doctrines.

3. Organization and Government. There are three orders of membership. The first, the novitiate or outer order, consists of those who receive the faith, but choose to live in their own families. The second or junior order is composed of those who, being under no charges or bonds to prevent their living in community, choose to enjoy the benefits of that situation without entering into full membership. They retain the title to their property, though they may give the use of it for the time to the family. The third order is made up of those who become full members and dedicate themselves permanently to the society. Should such members afterward withdraw, they take nothing away as a matter of right, but in practise "no person who withdraws peaceably is sent away empty." The government of the community is vested in a ministry composed of four elders, two of each sex. Of the several ministries, that of Mt. Lebanon, N. Y., is recognized as the central executive of all the societies. Subordinate to the ministry are two male and two female elders in every fully organized community or family in each society, having charge of its spiritual affairs, and two deacons and two deaconesses subordinate to the elders and having charge of the temporal concerns. A Shaker village usually includes two or more families of thirty or forty persons each, living in unitary houses, having their own households, and being independent in domestic affairs.

4. Religious Services. Present Status. The religious service includes addresses, singing of hymns and anthems, and a characteristic rhythmical marching, accompanied by other movements, in which all take part. These exercises are supposed to be a survival of movements characteristic of the founders of the society. The Shakers had at one time eighteen societies. The present number is fifteen, with about twenty-five families and about 1,000 members. No exact evaluation of their property has ever been made, but it is believed to be worth between $3,000,000 and $5,000,000.

W. H. LARRABEE.

BIBLIOGRAPHY: For list of Shaker literature consult J. P. MacLean, *A Bibliography of Shaker Literature*, Columbus, O., 1905. For the history consult: H. Elkins, *Fifteen Years in the Senior Order of Shakers*, Hanover, N. H., 1853; F. W. Evans, *Compendium of the Origin, History, Principles, . . . of the United Society of Believers in Christ's Second Appearing*, New York, 1853; C. E. Robinson, *Concise Hist. of the . . . Shakers*, E. Canterbury, N. H., 1893; W. A. Hinds, *American Communities*, pp. 32–68, Chicago, 1908; Anna White and Leila S. Taylor, *Shakerism, its Meaning and Message*, Columbus, O., 1904. For the doctrines and practises consult: F. W. Evans, ut sup.; idem, *Second Appearing of Christ*, Boston, 1853; idem, *Tests of Divine Inspiration*, New Lebanon, 1853; idem, *Celibacy from the Shaker Standpoint*, New Lebanon, 1866; idem, *Shaker Communism*, London, 1871; *Testimony of Christ's Second Appearing*, 4th ed., Albany, 1856; H. L. Eads, *Shaker Sermons* [Lebanon, N. Y.], 1879.

BIBLIOGRAPHY of the general subject: Besides the works of Nordhoff, J. H. Noyes, and W. A. Hinds, mentioned under the societies above, all of which deal more or less with general features, consult: H. A. James, *Communism in America*, New York, 1879; V. Steccanella, *Del Comunismo*, Rome, 1882; L. Felix, *Entwickelungsgeschichte des Eigentums*, Leipsic, 1883; M. Kaufmann, *Socialism and Communism*, London, 1883; E. de Laveleye, *Le Socialisme contemporain*, Paris, 1888; D. Bergström, *Kommunism och Socialism*, Stockholm, 1890; A. Hauck, *Der Kommunismus im christlichen Gewande*, Leipsic, 1891; B. Malon, *Le Socialisme intégral*, Paris, 1893; R. Pohlmann, *Geschichte des antiken Kommunismus und Socialismus*, 2 vols., Munich, 1893–1901; K. Kautsky, *Communism in Central Europe at the Time of the Reformation*, London, 1897; M. von Nathusius, *Die Mitarbeit der Kirche an der Lösung der sozialen Frage*, Leipsic, 1897. Phases of the subject are treated under CHRISTIAN SOCIALISM and SOCIALISM.

COMPARATIVE RELIGION.

I. Definition and Names: Scientifically considered, "Comparative Religion" is the second of three stages of study—the History, Comparison, and Philosophy of Religion; but because of the newness of the discipline and because the collection of data is still in progress, the term as popularly employed includes all three stages, and this usage is, for the time at least, justified by the state of the science. Other phrases have indeed been proposed as substitutes, among which the most fitting is "The Science of Religion"—a name against which three objections are urged: (1) the other term is now in possession, and popular usage in language is conservative; (2) rigid scientists affirm that for the present stage the term "science" is too ambitious; (3) religionists shrink from admitting that the rigorous methods of investigation implied by "science" may be applied in the sacred sphere of religion. To these objections the reply may be made that "science" does not imply knowledge completed, but only knowledge verified and systematized so far as the state of learning permits. To the third objection it must be opposed that science admits no bar to its investigation. It claims all spheres as rightly its own and is not deterred by the charge of irreverence: indeed, its only reverence is for verified fact, before which alone it bows. Hence the time is near when the expression "Science of Religion" may be admitted, and when the entry of the scientific method into religious inquiry will be not only permitted, but privileged. The term "Comparative Religion" is employed in this article as best expressing the common conception of what is here to be discussed.

II. History of the Discipline: This discipline is comparatively new. Max Müller remarked just before his death that within his own recollection the "History of Religion" (*Religionsgeschichte*) embraced only Christianity and Judaism (*Littell's Living Age*, Dec. 31, 1898). The religions of Greece and Rome were classed as "superstition" or "mythology," and other religions were practically unknown. For centuries, up to the Elizabethan era, the only other faith within the ken of Christians was Mohammedanism, and candid or sympathetic examination of the faith of the other by the adherents of either was precluded by the antagonism engendered by centuries of warfare.

1. Reasons for its Recent Origin.

Before Comparative Religion could come into being, two things were necessary: the existence of many faiths had to become known, and recognized as religion. For the first, the age of travel and discovery begun by the fifteenth century was necessary; for the second, a process of education in candor and a grounding in the historical method were essential. Lack of information and prejudice were the two barriers against the new science, and the second was the more difficult to surmount. Three centuries were occupied in the collection of data the importance of which was of course at the time unrecognized; even the direction in which it bore was unnoted. For the discovery of the pertinence of this body of facts to religious inquiry further illumination was needed which came only in the nineteenth century in the discovery of some of the ethnic sacred books and in the growth of the science of anthropology.

To discern the nature and difficulty of the obstacle interposed by prejudice is not easy in this more tolerant age. It is easy to forget that the native attitude of religion is exclusive and intolerant. When some Christians could declare of others that the latter were "unregenerate" and could do no good thing, and that, if they could, it could not be pleasing to deity, other faiths could scarcely be judged on their merits. This attitude of Christianity toward other religions may be illustrated by two examples: (1) by the naive explanation given by Roman Catholic missionaries of monasticism, the mass, the rosary, and like parallels of Catholic practise found in non-Christian lands—they were the mocking devices of the devil; (2) by the curt censure administered by Franke to the pioneer missionary Ziegenbalg, who had sent home a book on the Hindu faiths: "You were not sent to India to study Hinduism, but to preach the Gospel." Further, this attitude of contempt and scorn was changed into something like hate when it was discovered that many of the claims put forward for Christianity were duplicated by "blasphemous" claims for the other faiths. Thus each of the "book religions" claims inspiration for its scriptures. It then seemed that such claims must either be unqualifiedly denied or the inspiration of the Christian Bible be given up. The unscriptural dogma that the voice of God was heard for only a few centuries and only in a limited area closed the ear and the eye of Christianity to testimony that he had spoken to others than the chosen people in lands other than the "Holy Land." Hence the view concerning other religions entertained by Christians is well expressed in the title of more than one book or chapter on religion—"The True Religion and the False Religions."

2. Prejudice Peculiarly Potent.

Comparative Religion in its original phase is an outcome of Comparative Linguistics. Two events precipitated the formation of the discipline: first, the opening of India with the learning of Sanskrit and the discovery of the Vedas and other literature of the country; second, the (somewhat earlier) finding of the Zend-Avesta, resulting in the discovery that Hindus, Persians, Greeks, Romans, Teutons, Slavs, and Celts spoke languages which were akin. This led to the knowledge that these peoples had gods who were related and had inspired faiths which were not unlike. Comparative Linguistics led to Comparative Mythology, and the step to Comparative Religion then became easy and short. The man to whom more than to any other the praise is due for leading the way to this result is the famous Oxford professor already mentioned, F. Max Müller.

In thus giving the chief meed of praise to the celebrated Sanskritist, no injustice is intended or done to those who preceded him. All great discoveries have their adumbrations. The gestation of the science of religion was a long one. *The Religions of the World* (London, 1653), by Alexander Ross, was a prophecy of coming interest in the non-Christian faiths, though to the author they were still "false" religions. B. Picart and J. F. Bernard (*Cérémonies et coutumes de tous les peuples du monde*, 9 vols., Amsterdam, 1723–43, partly translated in *Ceremonies and Religious Customs of the . . . World*, 6 vols., London, 1733–34) discovered in other religions the degenerate descendants of a pure primitive faith—the comparative method began here. J. G. von Herder (*Ideen zur Philosophie der Geschichte*, 4 parts, Leipsic, 1784–91) laid a broader basis in a sort of anthropology which was to concatenate mankind and his faiths. C. Meiners (*Grundriss der Geschichte aller Religionen*, Lemgo, 1785, and *Allgemeine kritische Geschichte der Religionen*, 2 vols., Hanover, 1806–07) proved that the historical spirit as against the dogmatic had entered the sphere of religious investigation. Charles Dupuis (*Origine de*

3. Preparatory Work.

tous les cultes, Paris, 1795) anticipated Herbert Spencer and Mr. Tylor in attempting to derive all religion from some one root, in his case the worship of the great powers of nature. G. W. von Hegel (*Philosophie der Religion*, Berlin, 1832) anticipated still another line of modern research, investigation of savage or primitive belief and practise.

4. Max Müller and Recent Developments.

But undue emphasis has often been laid upon the work of these and other forerunners, such as the Deists in England. They were prophets rather than achievers, their methods speculative rather than historical. The real start was made by Max Müller. Despite the criticism by Mr. Jordan (*Comparative Religion*, pp. 150 sqq., 521 sqq., New York, 1905), no one did so much as Professor Müller to establish the new science. No series of works, hardly any collection of other volumes which could be made, has so stimulated the study as the *Sacred Books of the East*. Since Max Müller's first approach to the study in the *Rig Veda Sanhita* (6 vols., London, 1849–1874) the development has been rapid. To mention only the great names, C. P. Tiele and C. de la Saussaye in Holland, Réville, father and son, in France, Herbert Spencer, E. B. Tylor, J. G. Frazer, S. Hartland, and Andrew Lang in England, D. G. Brinton and James Freeman Clarke in America, have uncovered a wealth of material long buried and have shown how it is to be intelligently employed. In this development two schools have grown up. The first, of which the Oxford professor was the leader, was the linguistic school, which sought by investigating purely linguistic material, the roots and changes of words and the structure of language, to determine the development of religious ideas. The result was often a forced method of explanation which was obviously inadequate. A school developed in the second half of the nineteenth century to which the name of the anthropological school has been given, the fundamental method of which is historical, which examines data gathered from all regions and times, and upon the basis of comparative psychology and anthropology explains the resemblances and differences in religious beliefs and practises and their origins. In the hands of this second class, which of course does not discard linguistic data, the science has rapidly taken form, materials fall easily into their appropriate setting, and the law of evolution is revealed as operating in the field of religion with a distinctness which is almost beauty.

III. Aim and Scope: The aim of the study includes the collection, collation, and explanation of religious phenomena in order to discover the nature, genesis, development, and laws of religion. From what has already been said of the preconceptions with which early investigations were conducted, it is evident that so comprehensive a purpose was not originally in view. Early studies were polemic as against ethnic faith and practise, apologetic as concerned Christian faith and practise. But the progress of the study has already compelled a modification of earlier estimates of other religions and an increasing gentleness in discussing them. The statement can no longer be made without challenge even from Christians that the world outside Christendom is an "immense welter of errors" (Calvin). In living non-Christian religions (Mohammedanism Buddhism, Confucianism, Parseeism), as in those that have fallen (the religions of Egypt and Babylonia), are recognized mighty truths, and the claim to the exclusive possession of these by Christian dogmatists is no longer made, or if made is disallowed. There results (1) an increasing appreciation of the discovery that religion is one, in different stages of growth, and (2) a growing willingness to grant to all religious faiths impartial examination and candid recognition of whatever excellencies they may possess. The endeavor is made to discover whether there be a common basis for all forms of religion, and if so, what it is, and to set forth the nature, origin, growth, and laws of religion in general.

The scope of the science is involved in the foregoing. No place, time, or people from which evidence or testimony can be gathered is exempted from its examination. Evidence from neolithic graves in the shape of vessels or implements (which bespeak belief in the continued existence of the defunct), or from modern savage life, involving belief in obligations to powers superhuman, is no less pertinent than are the injunctions of Zoroaster, Confucius, the Buddha, or the Christ. Neither the religion of Jesus nor the mysteries of the Australian Bushman may be excluded from the inquiry. Moreover, facts and practises once thought purely social or merely utilitarian are now seen to be informed with the religious spirit. The area of religion has been immensely widened during the progress of the investigation. It has been no uncommon thing for a book to assert of some tribe that it had no religion, though the volume contained accounts of whole series of acts which were only and all religious. Such mistakes arose in the author's too narrow conception of what religion is. A further discovery is that the very comprehensiveness of the influence of the supernatural in the life of the savage makes it necessary to ask of his every act whether or not it be religious or at least have religion as an element. Hence the examination covers not only the "great" religions, but also primitive faith and all the gradations which lie between.

IV. The Methods Employed: Comparative Religion is an inductive science. Its operation is threefold: (1) collection and verification of facts (the historical method); (2) collocation of these verified data to ascertain their relations and interrelations (the comparative method); (3) explanation of the results reached by the other two methods upon a psychological basis, referring local features to ascertained mental habits of the tribes, groups, or peoples where those features are manifested, and universal features to general characteristics of the human mind (the psychological method). A fair illustration of the combined operation of these methods, uniting the extreme past with the present and with world-wide belief, is presented in the following case, which is but one out of many which might be chosen. The skulls of neolithic man sometimes bear unmistakable traces of trepanning during life—an operation which must have been excruciating torture in times when the only instruments were flints and there were probably no anesthetics, and an explanation was long sought in vain. It has recently been discovered, however, that in cases of epilepsy modern Kabyles trepan the patient and then conjure forth the obsessing spirit which they believe to be seated in the brain, causing the affection. Alongside these two facts is put a third, viz., wide induction has proved that primitive peoples of diverse race and habitat attribute diseases, especially mental affections, to obsession by spirits. The neolithic fact receives a most probable explanation from the modern Kabyle practise, while the psychological habit is made clear from a wide circle of induction.

V. The Auxiliary Sciences: Comparative Religion is necessarily dependent upon a number of auxiliary sciences. Its most intimate associations are with the science of history in its modern form. To this a twofold debt is due, first for the historico-critical method. The phenomena under investigation are by nature elusive, and the observer is liable to error because his point of view differs from that of the people whose actions and beliefs he studies. The motives a Christian imputes to worshipers belonging to another religion may be quite other than the real motives. Moreover, the phenomena lie in a realm where voluntary testimony is seldom given, because primitive peoples believe that between them and their deities exists a confidential relation which would be endangered by reporting to a stranger in what that relationship consists. So there is necessitated in this kind of investigation relentless criticism of alleged facts, which have to be pursued to their very lair and dragged out naked of falsehood and stripped of misconstruction.

1. The Method of History.

A second debt is incurred by the access given to the great body of facts presented by history. This storehouse, new treasures from which are constantly coming into use, is being worked over and over as more accurate knowledge illumines both the items and the *tout ensemble*. An example of the way in which this is being accomplished is furnished by the history of Greek religion. A half century ago Greek religion was regarded as thoroughly known. It had been for two millenniums the source of literary allusion and flavor; nearly all Western literature is seasoned with Attic salt. Yet in the light of phenomena, some of which had been on record all the time (as in Pausanias and Herodotus), and others which have been gained by modern research like the investigations at Mycenæ and in Crete and Cyprus, the entire history of Greek religion is being rewritten, the Olympic pantheon is traced to its elements, and the construction and growth of a national faith is revealed to the modern observer. Still another department, that of travel, is proving rich treasure trove. Sailors and merchants, travelers, and trained observers whose business it is to discover what is done and thought by other peoples, officers in government service who by long residence have come to know thoroughly the tribes among which they lived, and faithful missionaries furnish material which only the trained investigator can appreciate. The very detachment from each other of the reports made by these observers proves of the greatest value; for example the use of the swastika as a symbol with religious significance is proved for practically all quarters of the world in remote antiquity and in the living present, and the "bull-roarer" is discovered to be nearly ubiquitous as a sign of the performance of the mysteries of primitive tribes. Other departments of history, such as art and architecture, have their pregnant lessons and indispensable use. The subdepartment of ceramics has contributed to the history of Greek religion some of its most convincing material. On the value of the history of architecture there is no need to dilate; the mere mention of it suggests reverence and worshipful toil as represented in structures from the reed booth of the fetish-worshiper to the peerless Parthenon.

2. The Facts of History.

Newer and younger offshoots of the historic spirit are Comparative Mythology and Folk-lore. The key to appreciation is understanding, and the world had largely forgotten its infancy. Upon the recovery of his memory depended man's understanding of nearly the whole of primitive religion. When the practises of modern primitive tribes stand out as the parallels of the practises of the Greeks and Romans, what once seemed foolish or inexplicable in the latter and "curious" in the former received explanation as performances of the childhood of the race. How could human beings trace their descent from animals or plants on the one side, or from deities on the other? These things were done and were accepted as facts. As the doings of the childhood of humanity they have their perfect explanation. Thus Comparative Mythology and Folk-lore by recovering the methods of thought of the race in its childhood have contributed much to the understanding of such "oddities."

3. Comparative Mythology and Folk-lore.

No slight debt also is due to the mental sciences, particularly to psychology, though in this department a part of the obligation is repaid by return contributions. Psychology has exposed the method of operation of the mind of savage and epileptic, of individuals and of the crowd. In turn, epidemics like that of the dancing mania of the Middle Ages, communication of prophetic frenzy like that of Saul, the mental operations of an Elisha and a Mohammed, and the working of revivals are explained upon sound principles and reveal the methods by which religious acts began, became customary and authoritative. It may seem out of place to claim as an ally of Comparative Religion the sciences of geology and paleontology. Yet a moment's consideration of the example of the neolithic trepanning referred to above will show that the dating of the early subject of the operation must depend upon the pronouncements of geology upon the environment in which the relics were

4. Other Allies.

III.—13

found. Similarly, paleontology has no little to say as to the relative height of man in the scale of being in the age to which the trepanned is referred. Many other facts, all significant in settling the question of the age of man on the earth—an important factor for the evolution of religion—might be adduced to show the dependence of Comparative Religion on the one side, and the helpfulness of geology and paleontology on the other in the quest for the origin and authority of religious ideas.

VI. The Results: What are the accomplishments of a branch of study thus defined, thus born and developed, with such an aim and scope, using such materials, and with such auxiliaries? It has discovered and oriented the whole realm of primitive religion, has discovered the conditions under which were originated what may be called the organized religions and has established their part and value in the uplift of the race, and has discovered a genetic relationship between the two varieties; it shows that all religion is one in various stages of development, that religion is a development, and that man is one in acknowledging by action in all times and places of which there is record an impulse to worship a being or beings whom he deems greater than himself.

1. In Primitive Religion: The distinction between "primitive" and "organized" religions is difficult to make. Mr. Frazer (*Golden Bough*, i. 348, ed. of 1890) gives as the marks of primitive religion the following: (1) no special class is set apart to perform rites; (2) no special place is designated for this purpose—there are no temples; (3) spirits, not gods, are recognized; (4) the rites are magical, rather than propitiatory. But no one of these marks can be held everywhere to delimit the two spheres. The shaman shades into the priest. A temple is not necessarily a structure, and in primitive religion localities are the residence of spirits where they are worshiped. Moreover, gods have been found among some of the tribes lowest in the scale of being, and magic versus prayer is an insecure test. It is proved in some cases that primitive religion passed by degrees from this stage to that of organized religion, notably so in the cases of Greece and India. While then Mr. Frazer's tests individually break down, it may yet be held that the total effect of his distinctions make a practical line of demarcation.

a. Primitive Religion in the Psychological Sphere: Animism is usually but loosely defined as "the doctrine of souls and spirits." A more lucid statement is that animism means that stage in human development in which man believes in the parity of all existences so far as their possession of sentient life is concerned. Men in that stage may hold that a stone, a tree, a mountain, a stream, a wild animal, a heavenly body, a wind, indeed any object within the realm of real or fancied experience, possesses just such a "soul" as he conceives himself to have, and that it is animated by desires and moved by emotions parallel to those he perceives in himself.

1. Animism Defined.

The question how man came to possess the idea of soul has been answered in two ways, both of which reproduce reasons given under primitive conditions for asserting the existence of a non-corporeal yet intracorporeal entity. The phenomena leading to such a conception are (1) those of dream life, (2) the difference between the waking and the sleeping state, or between life and death. If in a company of primitive hunters one sleeps in his companions' presence and in that sleep has a dream which upon waking he relates, stating that he has been upon the chase, he and his companions make and accept the explanation that some part of him not his body has been away, and no reasoning could convince him that the dream experience was unreal. In this way in part the conception that man is a duality manifested itself. But the fact that nothing had been seen to go and return invested the fugitive part with a character expressed in many languages by the equivalent of "spirit" (Lat. *spiritus*, "breath"), and this spirit was regarded as an intangible but very real entity. The second line of experience corroborated and strengthened this impression. The superficial difference between a living and a dead body is the absence from the latter of the breathing function. The last act observable in the dying is the expulsion of the final breath. It is no wonder then that man in his primitive philosophy began the habit of speaking of his second part as the "spirit" or breath. And that the phenomenon of sleep is also explained by absence of the spirit from the body, is proved by the fact that existent tribes do not permit a sleeper to be waked suddenly lest his spirit have not time to return and he die. To these two lines of what had the force of convincing evidence to early man a third must be added, viz.: the appearance in dreams of those who had died. Such visions were accepted as realities in advanced stages of civilization (cf. Augustine, *De civitate dei*, xviii. 18), confirmed the belief already accepted of a dual existence of man, and had other momentous results. They opened up the entire region of a future existence, as well as other beliefs which still survive as "superstitions."

2. Idea of Soul, how Obtained.

A fact which had great influence on man's early conceptions was that many of the events which he witnessed were traceable to visible causes. In the infancy of the race death was probably in a large proportion of cases due to external causes. Death was not always "the inevitable."* And since man himself caused death and knew himself the agent of that change, when death resulted from visible causes he attributed to the material agent conscious and determined action. Even when death came from what are now termed natural causes, he would seek and find causes of the same sort. So that both disease and death were regarded as consciously brought about, if not by visible means,

* For cases where death is even yet regarded as an abnormal event, consult: E. Crawley, *Mystic Rose*, pp. 26–27, 60, 67, 68, 69, 85, 95, New York, 1902; L. Decle, *Three Years in Africa*, pp. 75, 512, London, 1898; C. B. Kloss, *In the Andamans*, p. 123, London, 1903; B. Spencer and F. J. Gillen, *Native Tribes of Central Australia*, p. 476, London, 1899; J. Macdonald, in *Folklore*, iii. 344.

then by beings mysterious in their nature and mode of working.

3. Anthropomorphic Conception of Causation.

Thus to practically all objects he attributed life, power, emotions, and determinative acts such as those he felt or committed. So he came to apply his experience (supposed or real) to all existence; all events were effects, though he could not detect the causes. If the spirit could go unperceived from the sleeping or moribund and participate in the hunt or leave the forsaken one dead, if the dead could reappear in the dream, were there not other spirits which interfered with human action, helped or thwarted human effort, inflicted disease and death? Thus man was furnished with a primitive philosophy which answered his queries in a way that seemed conclusive and satisfied his desire for explanation. With this may be compared the habit of calling a pestilence a "visitation of God" instead of considering it the inevitable consequence either of ignorance or of disregard of natural law. Objects which to modern man are inanimate to early man had both life and soul; they had power which they employed determinatively. Into animal, plant, and inorganic substance were read the nature and qualities of humanity. In accord with this belief modern savages talk to the beasts they slay, smoke the pipe of peace with the dead bear, and attempt to deceive the trapped tiger so that its kin or its ghost may not exact vengeance. And beside these tangible things there were imagined innumerable spirits until the world swarmed with them, and forest and field, glen, hill, and stream were peopled with spirits having power and purpose to work weal or wo to humans.

But it would not be long before man came to the conclusion that the results of his own efforts were not always commensurate with what he seemed to have the right to expect. That the spirits about him interfered either for good or ill was a natural conclusion.

4. Incipient Dualism.

Spirits were roughly divided into the well-disposed and the spiteful and malicious. This is the belief constantly encountered among primitive peoples, some of whom dare not move during the night, so great is their fear of the ghosts which lie in wait. And when such belief is established, a demonology is created out of which develops the whole hierarchy of evil; while out of the conception of good spirits come angelology and theism of various sorts (see DEMON).

But man would carry this process further. He knew himself subject to menace and blandishment, to tricky bluff or actual force, he was conciliated by gift or persuasion and made hostile by assault or trespass. To the spirits he attributed the same qualities. So that threats and bluffs were used against the spirits (even against the gods), magic was employed to overpower them, gifts and persuasion were tried to render them complaisant. Out of this developed the cults and the practise of magic and witchcraft in all their varieties.

In magic particularly lies a result of this reasoning. Magic may for convenience be divided into natural and sympathetic. The former is the use of anthropomorphic devices to gain one's end from the spirits. Chinese sailors carry paper junks to throw overboard in a hurricane so that when the mimic bark sinks in the waves the storm spirits may suppose that the real ship has sunk and be satisfied. Gongs are beaten to frighten away unwelcome spirits. A herb which is supposed to have qualities obnoxious to a spirit is burned that the smoke may keep off the undesired. In these and other ways natural magic works.

5. Magic—Natural, Mimetic, Sympathetic.

Sympathetic magic in one of its varieties depends upon the supposed fact that like affects like, any effect may be produced by an imitation of it. Rain may be caused by scattering of water, a thunder-storm by imitation of the sound and by scattering sparks to imitate the lightning, a yam field may be made fruitful by burying in it a stone shaped like a yam, or the yield of a palm is increased by hanging on the trunk or laying at the root a stone or other natural object which looks like the date or the coconut. An enemy is made to suffer by performing operations upon a wax image which represents him. Another variety depends upon the supposed sympathy between a man and his belongings. His hair, nail-parings, any article of clothing, even his shadow or his name, may be used against him. His footprint on the sand is sufficient, if one knows how, to work him ill. And that some men claimed, perhaps honestly, to be expert in these practises and that the claim was allowed is a matter of history. Thus the witch and shaman and medicine man had their careers prepared, ready to practise on spirits and men, and with all the terrible consequences known to history.

An interesting group of results from the conceptions of the animistic stage is that which centers about metempsychosis in its various forms. Metamorphosis, transmigration, lycanthropy, are but variant shapes of the same idea. If man, animals, and plants (and eventually spirits and gods) are on the same plane of existence, exchange of form and being might be brought about either purposely or by accident. So in the 550 births of the Buddha he passed through every grade of being—vegetable, animal, human, and divine. That a man should be transformed into an animal seemed not strange, and Circe's miracles were not only credible but reasonable to Homer's hearers.

6. Metempsychosis.

Further, these exchanges were not confined to the lower order of beings. Why should not a spirit take possession of a human body, or why should not a god become incarnate? With spirits good and bad all about, eager to exercise their power, the virgin birth of a god (a common thesis in religion) and obsession of a human by evil spirits are but opposite consequences of the theory of equality of being. Moreover, if the soul is so loosely attached to its tenement that in sleep it goes forth to adventures, the idea of a wandering soul consciously put forth in the interest of its owner or of some one who has power over him becomes possible and apparently actual. The lineage of the mahatma idea of modern theosophy is thus revealed. But if the soul or life could be thus isolated, it might perhaps be laid aside or deposited in some safe place, thus rendering its possessor immune in the midst of some deadly encounter. This motif rules in many folk-lore cycles and even invaded the Old Testament.

7. Myth Defined. A final psychological effect is discovered in Mythology (Gk. *mythos*, "narrative"). In modern usage the word has two meanings: (1) the branch of investigation which deals with the narratives about gods and demigods, heroes, creation, origins, and the like; (2) the narratives themselves. A myth is a story, on a subject kindred to those just mentioned, now admitted to be untrue and often irrational, but to its first hearers and their immediate descendants self-evident. It shows primitive reason working according to primitive logic, seeking to explain a real or a supposed fact.* Magic is primitive science, myth is primitive philosophy. Thus the sacred stone at Delphi, a fact, was accounted for by the myth that it was the stone by which Chronos was deceived when Zeus was born, which he disgorged some time later. The Crayfish Clan of the Choctaws explained their name and origin by the myth that the first of the clan were crayfish which were coaxed from their shells, taught to stand up and use their claws, finally becoming ancestors of the Crayfish Clan. Gen. vi. 1–4 is a myth accounting for the reputed giants as the product of a union between spirits and women.

8. Explanations of Myth. When larger experience and growing mentality discredited these tales, various attempts were made to account for them. Xenophanes (sixth century B.C.) and Porphyry (d. 303 A.D.) regarded them as inventions to inculcate moral truth. Theagenes (c. 520 B.C.) and Empedocles (c. 444 B.C.) regarded them as allegorical expressions of physical philosophy. Aristotle looked on them as intended to inculcate respect for legal and social institutions ("Metaphysics," XI. viii. 19). Euhemerus (c. 300 B.C.) accounted them the imaginative rendering of history—e.g., the gods were deified men. Of modern theories Herbert Spencer's revives Euhemerism. Max Müller and the philological school attributed myth to a "disease of language" by which events narrated of one object were attributed to another bearing the same or a similar name. The anthropological school accounts for myth by making it a "disease of thought" taking its rise in animism. Thus later Egyptians were perplexed by the animal forms of their deities and accounted for the supposed fact by the story that the gods took refuge from their enemies in the animal bodies. To modern man both the supposed fact and the explanation are irrational; to the Egyptians the fact was real and the explanation all-sufficient under the hypothetical parity of being. The distinction between myth, religion, and theology should be clearly made. Theology is man's belief about the gods, myth is the tale he tells to account for his belief in them, religion expresses his practical attitude toward them (cf. A. Lang, *Custom and Myth*, pp. 45 sqq., New York, 1885)

b. Primitive Religion in the Social Sphere:

1. Kinship. The institution of totemism can be understood only by recognizing that kinship as reckoned by civilized society is very different from kinship under primitive conditions. To the civilized, kinship is a matter of degree. Under the totemistic régime it is absolute and reckoned not by family but by the clan or totem gens. It is not even solely a matter of birth, but may be acquired (see below, Blood-Brotherhood). The absoluteness of this tie is shown by W. R. Smith, *Rel. of Sem.*, pp. 272–273, 277: "In a case of homicide Arabian tribesmen do not say 'the blood of M or N has been spilt,' they say, 'our blood has been spilt.'" The clan-brethren are all of one blood, no others are of their blood. And the contrariety of this form of relationship to that current in civilized communities is sharply expressed by the statement that under it husband and wife are not kin, that in most cases father and children are not kin, but that mother and children are. Totemism is then an affair of the community. But since all community matters are under primitive conditions religious, the interest of comparative religion in the subject becomes evident.

2. Totemism Defined. Totemism "is the name for the custom by which a stock (scattered through many tribes) claims descent from and kindred with some plant, animal, or other natural object. It is a state of society and cult . . . in which sets of persons, believing themselves to be akin by blood, call each other by the name of some plant, beast, or other object in nature" (A. Lang, *Custom and Myth*, p. 260). Jevons shows another phase when he says that it is "the alliance of a clan with an animal (or plant or other natural object) species" (*Introduction to Hist. of Religion*, p. 120). W. R. Smith makes the proofs of the existence of totemism in any one place to depend upon "(1) the existence of stocks named after plants and animals; (2) the . . . conception that the members of the stock are of the blood of the eponym animal or are sprung from a plant of the species chosen as totem; (3) the ascription to the totem of a sacred character" (*Kinship*, p. 188).

3. Marks of Totemism. Because the matter has been confused (e.g., by Mr. Frazer, *Encyclopædia Britannica*, "Totemism," and in his *Totemism*, London, 1885, and others), it must be noted (1) that totemism is a community affair, and individual only as the individual is a part of the community; (2) the totem is always a species, never an individual, except in the (rare) case of the heavenly bodies; (3) it involves both sexes, never one alone; (4) the solidarity of the human clan is treated as absolute, as is that of the animal species. Thus is to be corrected Mr. Fraser's statement that there are three kinds of

* Prof. N. S. Shaler has, without intending it, given a good description of the mythological process: "The commonest misuse of the reason and the imagination is to support an irrational motive which is strong enough to be mastering, yet is felt to need explanation" (*The Neighbor*, p. 268, Boston, 1904).

totems, "the sex-, individual-, and clan-totem." There is but one, the clan-totem; the "sex- and individual-totem" belong in a totally different realm, do not affect kinship or descent or society, and have but one thing in common with clan-totem, viz.: that neither is eaten. The totem tie is like the family name: a man becomes a Brown, Jones, or Robinson by being born into the family; similarly, a man is born into the wolf, bear, or beaver clan. But whether a particular Brown shall be named William or Clarence or some other "Christian" name is fortuitous; similarly whether the "individual-totem" shall be wolf or oak depends on what the individual sees in his puberty watch or chooses under advice. The two things are discrete. With these fundamental characteristics go certain vital accompaniments. First, relationship is usually traced through the mother; second, marriage is prohibited between members of the same totem gens. Husband and wife are of different blood and are not made kin by marriage. The totem bond overrides what is now blood-relationship; half-brother and sister not of uterine relationship may marry, they are of different gens (cf. II Sam. xiii. 13 and Gen. xii. 13, xx. 2, Abraham and Sarah were probably half-brother and sister). And, finally, to all members of any totem gens the corresponding animal species is sacrosanct.

Totemism is a human institution, subject therefore to the changes of advancing civilization. In one place it may appear in its bloom, in another only the vestiges may remain. Thus in North America and in Australia it appears complete, only its vestiges are discernible among the ancient Egyptians, Greeks, Romans, and Hindus. It passes through several stages, each of which reveals a relationship to the institution in its prime. The salient evidences of the former existence of totemism in any place are: (1) the tradition of the sacredness of an animal species, (2) a clan name the same as that of an animal or plant species, (3) a place name derived from a clan name, (4) an animal epithet given locally to a deity, (5) images of an animal associated with a deity, (6) an animal used as a badge or mark, (7) myths accounting for the place of the animal in the cult.

The origin of totemism can be only conjectured; but granted the truth of the hypothesis put forward to explain the origin, every subsequent stage can be fully accounted for on the basis of known laws. The accepted explanation is that the institution arose under animistic conceptions of existence. In the struggle for life man sought allies. The supposedly superior quality of some animals or plants made them seem desirable in that relationship and the pact was made. In later stages the notion of kinship and then of descent entered as explanations of the fact once imagined as real. Meanwhile the living and the dead animal were treated as was the living or dead human; in Egypt corpses of both were mummified, in Greece they were buried or burned. But from sacredness to godship was but a stage, the individual became deity—so with the cat, bull, crocodile, etc., in Egypt, and in Greece the horse, mouse, snake, ram, even the lobster. But thought grew more anthropomorphic, and the animal head was placed on a human body (so in Greece and Egypt). Next the animal came to represent deity, and finally was simply sacred to him. The relationship of totemism to religion is thus in part revealed, though there are other connections. That out of this came in part zoolatry, idolatry, and even polytheism is demonstrable.

4. Its Supposed Origin.

Totemism had a ritual which affected the crises of life. As an infant born a Christian must be baptized, perhaps confirmed, before the fulness of his birthright is his, and as at marriage and death the Church has its functions, so with totemism. At birth the totem mark is tattooed or painted on the infant or the totem formula is repeated. Before being admitted to rank as a brave the neophyte undergoes ordeals, while even at marriage appropriate rites occur and at death the member may be laid in a grave shaped like the totem. Of all these ceremonies the most important is the initiation in the "mysteries" of the tribe, a fact only recently discovered. Evident in many cases is the connection of these mysteries with the power of reproduction, in itself no less a mystery to civilized man than to the savage. The use of the phallic emblems is proved in many cases. The initiation takes place at puberty. Each sex has its ceremonial from which the other is barred. The initiations take place in secluded spots, often at night, and a well-understood signal is displayed or the "bull-roarer" is employed to warn away the profane. The neophyte is instructed in the privileges and duties of adulthood and submits to severe ordeals. The dance, having religious purport, is among the accompaniments, and not seldom there is a mimic death, burial, and resurrection, implying ethical or eschatological reference.

5. Its Ritual; the Mysteries.

The usual method of entrance into a totem clan is then by birth and initiation. But since the conception of the tie was that of a common blood flowing in the veins of the clan, it was conceived that this fact could be artificially produced. To make a man not a brother take that relationship it was necessary that the blood of each should flow in the other's veins. Accordingly, if an individual wished to become a member of another clan, blood was drawn from his veins and transferred to the body of one or more of the clan, while he absorbed blood from some member of the same. This was done by making incisions, often in the arms, and putting the bleeding parts together; transfusion was supposed to take place. Or each sucked blood from the other's wound, or the blood of both was mingled with a medium and both partook of the mixture; or a sacrificial animal was slain and both partook of the blood, a common fluid thus flowing in the veins of both.

6. Blood-Brotherhood.

c. Primitive Religion in the Ethical Sphere: Taboo (Polynesian, "strongly marked") denotes whatever is prohibited under severe (supernatural) penalties. In primitive life it controls the entire life of the adult. It governs "his food and drink, his marriage and social relations, the disposition of property and the choice of his wives. An infraction of its laws . . . means exile or death" (D. G. Brinton, *Religions of Primitive Peoples*, p. 38, New York, 1897). "In the earliest phases of religion the law is essentially prohibitory. It is in the form of the negative 'thou shalt not.' . . . The taboo extends its veto into every department of primitive life. It forbids the use of certain articles of food or raiment; it hallows the sacred areas; it lays restrictions on marriage; . . . it denounces various actions, often the most trivial and innocent, and thus lays the foundation for the ceremonial law" (idem, p. 108).

1. Things Taboo.

The character of the institution is seen in the things it prohibits. (1) The sanctuary, with all its furnishings, vestments and the like, is taboo. Intrusion renders the intruder, man or beast, the property of the god. (2) Persons are taboo. A chief may not be touched nor any of his possessions, while what he touches becomes his—he represents or is deity. Similarly, priests, shamans, attendants are sacred persons. The sick are often taboo and are removed that they may not "infect" the house. Especially taboo is the woman in childbirth (see DEFILEMENT AND PURIFICATION, CEREMONIAL). A corpse is taboo, and infects all who come into contact with it. (3) Blood is of all things taboo. Sacrificial blood was caught in vessels that it might not infect the ground. Its sacredness in covenants is a matter of history and survives in Christian theology. It was not eaten by sacrificers, but was sacred to deity. By association of ideas things red are taboo. In Africa red earth may not be trodden or red berries eaten. In Japan entrances to holy places and bridges reserved for the Mikado's use are red. (4) A name may be taboo, that of God or of the chief or of the dead. Even the syllables which composed a name may not be used, and new ones have to be employed in their place. Thus the quadriliteral name of God was not used by the later Jews, and out of a device to avoid it arose the name Jehovah (see YAHWEH). (5) The hair and the beard may be taboo. The Naziritic vow of the Hebrews (see NAZIRITE) is in point, and the sacrifice of the hair is a frequent fact. (6) The totem animal species is taboo to all of the clan. (7) Time may be taboo. This is the origin of the Sabbath, derived from pre-Semitic Babylonians. (8) Whole groups of things may be taboo, as food, or the use of food for a period may be taboo. (9) The paraphernalia of the mysteries are taboo.

2. Characteristics of Taboo.

A characteristic of taboo is its transmissibility. An article which has become taboo communicates this quality to whatever comes into contact with it, this second to a third, and so on. The same is true of persons (cf. Isa. lxv. 5, which should read "which say, keep by thyself, come not near to me; for else shall I sanctify thee," i.e., make thee taboo). Contact of a person ceremonially unclean with sacred vessels was forbidden (cf. Vergil, *Æneid*, ii. 717–720 for a fine illustration). Taboo might be communicated in several ways—by touch, as in the preceding cases; or by a look, as when the African king may not look at a river; or through the ear, as when a man who hears of a death in his family becomes unclean; or through speech, as when a man pronounces the name of a chief. The duration of a taboo varies. It may be perpetual, as of a sanctuary and its appurtenances; or of a chief or other sacred person, during his lifetime. Or it may be temporary, depending upon purgation by ceremonial, or by expiration after a conventional period (as in mourning). Similarly, a taboo may be natural (after a fashion), like that of the sanctuary or chief; or arbitrary, like the taboo of food for a day by Saul (I Sam. xiv. 24 sqq.). The explanation of taboo is that it was connected with the supernatural. Fear of offense of the potent powers which were supposed to exist and of consequent evil to self or kin or possessions seems to be the bottom fact. That a tree in a sacred domain is taboo is easily explained. But it has not been so clear why a newborn babe, a woman in childbirth, a corpse should be taboo. The reason is that under primitive conditions whatever deals with the mysteries of the beginning or end of life has the aspect of awe. Man stands in awe of the mystery of life and death. Taboo involves therefore (1) caution against things holy (for the things' sake) and things unclean (for the person's sake); (2) purification from the contact with holy things so as not mediately to convey holiness to other things (as when the priest washed after exercising his office before putting on his ordinary apparel); (3) purification from contact with the unclean to restore a lost condition of purity.

3. Penalties of Breach of Taboo.

Some taboos are from their nature fatal. The murder of a clansman or the killing of a totem animal involved either the execution of the culprit or (which amounted to the same thing) his exile from the clan. In the latter case he was in the position of the masterless man of feudal times, whosoever found him could kill him without fear of the blood feud (cf. Gen. iv. 14). An absolute taboo, breach of which was death, is given I Sam. xiv. 24, 44. The basis of this was a rude social utilitarian ethics. Were the offender not punished, the offended spirit might avenge himself on the tribe (cf. I Sam. xxi. 1). But all breaches were not so serious; even primitive man has a sense of proportion. Means of purification were hit upon in accordance with primitive philosophy. The principal agents were water and fire, often accompanied by gifts. In Madagascar a babe is kept in the presence of fire and lifted over or through it when first taken from the house. Many tribes use water or a decoction, some applying it by aspersion. Christian baptism, whether by aspersion or immersion, has a long ancestry. Other means were the touch of a sacred person, as of a chief, a priest, or a child.

The effect of taboo on ethics is profound and far-reaching, beyond what has been adduced. So with totemism, especially in inducing fidelity and educing gratitude. On the other hand, suggestion (a subject only just becoming understood) had tremendous power ethically, working along all the lines already suggested. The thought that the supernatural interferes to secure justice and right, always powerful in the primitive realm, still works in civilized society, as may be seen in the oath and the otherwise meaningless ceremony of kissing the Bible in court, which is the last vestige of the primitive, ancient, and medieval ordeal. The influence of the transmigration upon ethics may be seen in the written records of religious peoples, and heard in the naive explanations of tribes yet without writing, as they tell why this one became a snake and that one a noble animal. Distinctions between modes of existence are made by savages and attributed to ethical or non-ethical behavior in this life. To this contributed belief in the return of the dead. A crude heaven and hell is found among savages as a cardinal doctrine of belief, in which existence hereafter is conditioned by conduct in this life; reward and retribution are the salient ideas.

d. Primitive Religion in the Sphere of Cult: The most characteristic and illuminative facts in this region are connected with sacrifice (Lat. *sacrificium*, Gk. *hierourgia*, "action within the sphere of things sacred"). In modern usage the word implies painful or costly self-denial. In this it follows the later developments of the institution, in the earlier phases such a sense was entirely lacking. The motive of sacrifice is to initiate or maintain friendly relationship with the supernatural, or to recover it if lost, the end being the blessing of mankind. That it had its origin as far back as the animistic stage is clear both from the forms and the conceptions attached to the rite and from the anthropopathic views of the supernatural powers with which sacrificial communion was had. Sacrifice as seen in history may be treated as communal, honorific, and piacular.

1. Communal Sacrifice.

A full definition of communal sacrifice embraces the following. It is in its primitive form a festal meal, with the god and his worshipers as participants, a meal equally necessary to both parties to it, the essential part of which was a slain victim; the title to participation was vested in kinship as then conceived; the meal was both a pledge of the tie of kinship and a means of its continuance; the celebration was a community affair, and the entire consumption of the victim was a necessity. The unfolding of the definition requires the remark that sacrifice antedated the idea of property (cf. Jevons, pp. 385, 390, and the authorities cited there). The leading idea was not a gift to the god, but a meal in which god and worshipers partook in common of a victim (Smith, *Rel. of Sem.*, p. 226). The notion of the kinship of gods and men is an old one of which the "Our Father" of the Lord's Prayer and the line of Aratus quoted by Paul (Acts xvii. 28) are late expressions. It is animistic in origin, arising in the conceived parity of all existence. The god was of the same stock as his worshipers, and commensality implied all that these mutual relations involved. The meal was festal. Observers have often remarked that the earlier stages of religion seem less afflicted with awe than the later. Instances as wide apart as the Vedic religion compared with the Brahmanic, and the celebrations of the period of the Judges and the Priestly sacrifice of the Hebrews confirm this. The normal spirit was that of music, dancing, and mirth. Of this meal the god was a partaker, not the only recipient. That the deity should eat was a notion not at all abnormal, and is illustrated by the fact that the dead were supposed to need nourishment and were supplied, often by channels opening into the grave. Advancing culture modified this idea, and to gods was given the blood or the fat or both, and later the food was suited to the spiritual nature of deity, being etherealized by fire. But for long the gods were supposed to require nourishment. In Egypt records exist of the threat that were not the gods complacent the magic word of power would be uttered which would blot out the worlds and starve the gods out of existence. Anthropopathism was carried to its logical limits (cf. Judges ix. 13). Inasmuch as kinship was a matter of blood, as a part of the feast a slain victim was required; without blood there was no sacrifice (Smith, *Rel. of Sem.*, pp. 280, 376). The mystic sacrifice of totemism and the camel sacrifice cited from Nilus when a camel was torn in pieces alive and eaten on the spot (cf. G. Allen, *Idea of God*, pp. 323–324, London, 1897; J. E. Harrison, *Prolegomena*, p. 482, ib. 1903; J. M. Robinson, *Pagan Christs*, pp. 110 sqq., ib. 1903; J. G. Frazer, *Golden Bough*, iii. 134 sqq., ib. 1900; Réville, "Hibbert Lectures," pp. 89 sqq., ib. 1884) may as a survival point to the time when the victim was eaten raw and in the blood. The totem as a mystic sacrifice appears as the only case in which the animal was eaten by its human kin, except in case of dire necessity. The explanation of this mystic rite is that it was an actual eating of the god to renew the kinship and to obtain some share of his qualities, as a savage devours the heart of his slain enemy that he may absorb the courage and skill of that enemy. The explanation of the law of consuming the entire animal is not easy. It may have been that nothing might be left to cause a breach of taboo, or it might have been a desire to obtain as much of the feast as possible. The Jewish Passover is but one case out of many that may be adduced for the custom.

2. Honorific Sacrifice.

The origin of honorific sacrifice was likewise anthropopathic. Man's conception of deity led him to attribute to the gods the same pleasure in gifts as he himself felt, so that honorific sacrifice in perhaps three varieties developed out of varying experience, viz.: emergential, implying special communion when a favor was desired; periodical (a form which the communal came to take), having the idea of tribute; and piacular, which became the general type when the idea of sin (by no means a primitive idea) came into experience. Honorific sacrifice was the effect of transferring to deity the position, attributes, and qualities of a ruler. As the chief was pleased with gifts and kindly disposed to those who made them, and in emergencies would grant his favor to a donor, and as he demanded them as tribute, deity was regarded as governed by the same motives. Out of this grew the gifts and libations at the beginning of an enterprise of whatever sort, the thank-offerings for the like when successfully accomplished, the periodical precative offerings at seed-time and the thank-offerings of harvest.

That piacular sacrifice in its earliest phases involved no more than that the deity was temporarily estranged is the conclusion of W. R. Smith and most anthropologists. But the seriousness of the estrangement grew in the mind and came to dominate the whole conception of sacrifice.

3. Piacular Sacrifice. It became necessary for community and individual to take note of actual and putative transgression which required purgation at stated intervals, that the relationship of god and people might be reestablished. While honorific sacrifice continued and the old feast-sacrifice tried to hold its own, the type which expressed atonement came to be regarded as sacrifice proper. The idea of an angry god to be propitiated became regnant in theology, the atoning sacrifice, devoted to the deity, became dominant in cult.

The question of human sacrifice is difficult. That it was primeval is improbable, that it was primitive is certain. The cases of foundation sacrifice, of human victims offered to rivers, and particularly the redemption of the first-born are decisive. That after savagery was left behind it was an extreme measure appears from II Kings iii. 27. In times of famine the German tribes offered sacrifices of increasing worth, the last and noblest the life of the chief, if the gods did not take pity.

4. Human Sacrifice. Yet that at an earlier period the sacrifice of a guilty tribesman was required is proved not only by such narratives as Josh. vii. 25, but by the primitive law of blood-revenge, a life for a life. Substitution came in time in both spheres, divine and human; but the redemption of the first-born, man and beast, common to many nations, speaks for the absolute surrender of that first-born in the primitive age. Substitution in divine affairs is anthropopathic. An offended clan with a blood-feud would compound for a lesser victim or a money consideration, so would the deity. This was carried so far that among some peoples, as in Mexico, the mimicry of sacrifice of the human was performed upon a puppet of dough, or, as in Egypt, the maiden sacrificed to Father Nile was an image of mud formed on the bank of the river. But this mimicry is no less decisive of the former fact of human sacrifice than is the play of the rape of the virgin of the earlier marriage by capture.

2. In National and Universal Religions.—a. Dependence on Tribal Religion: It is but asserting the evolution of religion to declare that the verdict of historical investigation is that the great religions developed out of preexisting religion. This is true both of the "personal" religions which owed their origin in each case to a great teacher and of those faiths which can be traced to no single founder. The indebtedness of Zoroaster to the Indo-Persian "Urreligion" is made out; the rise of Brahmanism out of Vedism and the evidences of animistic and fetishistic belief in the hymns of the Rik carry the ancestry of the great religions of India back to its roots in primitive faith and practise; recent study in the religions of Greece and Rome (Harrison's *Prolegomena* and Granger's *Worship of the Romans*) is leading to similar animistic paternity in the faiths of Homer and Vergil; Moses built on old Semitic foundations and Jesus on Mosaism; Mohammed combined elements from Judaism, Christianity, and the earlier Arabic religion. In the Chinese Book of Rites there is embedded evidence of the old magical régime against the repeated assertion of an original monotheism against which every detail of history cries out. An element of proof in this direction consists of survivals or "superstitions." This last word etymologically explains itself and the argument. It tells of something *superstans*, "remaining over" (from a former condition of things). And it is the discovery by modern investigators of the fact of survivals in religion and of the other fact that psychological law is constant in the mass which has brought the roots of religion to light. The one example of the "harvest-maiden" may be adduced, a practise still followed in many parts of Europe which leads in direct recession back to the worship of Core or the earth-maiden, and thence to the corn-spirit of each plot of land, and thence into sheer animism (Frazer, *Golden Bough*).

b. Common Features: The great religions all show two conflicting methods in their psychological operations. One is the enunciation of crystallized dogma, the formulation of regulations which, once expressed, are expected to govern permanently the life of man. This mode of thought defines God, man, the relations of each

1. Psychological. to the other and to the universe, and endeavors so to express duty that that expression shall wholly ensphere man's entire life of thought and act. It creates an orthodoxy to repudiate which involves the charge of heterodoxy, not seldom of atheism. The other method notes the freedom of thought, the elusiveness of the idea of the supernatural, the indefinableness of the spiritual, and claims the right of the individual soul to achieve in its own way right relationship with God, man, and the universe. These two roads to right relationship, the dogmatic and the mystic, opposed in the main though they are, show often a curious effort to come together. The dogmatician loses himself in metaphysical vagueness, while the mystic, turning aside to lonely contemplation, finds himself at the head of a community and formulates rules of guidance for his followers.

A second psychological tendency is that which envelops as with a halo the founder of the religion, if a founder there be, and conceives him as in a special sense divine. Even Mohammed, who disclaimed miracle, was by his own generation reported to have performed miraculous deeds. The habit of forming legend concerning a religious leader is the operation in the religious sphere of that which works in all spheres. Æsculapius became a god, Lycurgus was thought impeccable, Frederick the Great and Washington might have been as religiously sinless as they are politically, had their activities been in the religious sphere.

The extent to which use of religious legend runs is governed largely by the need created by dogmatic assertion, by the necessities of the system developed. Operating in another region, each religion sees in its own scriptures the very word of God, and from this word the dogmatician draws his proof texts for his closely cut definitions, while the mystic seeks from the same source justification for his wildest imaginings and even for his antinomian practise. Common psychological action is observable in the religions which perceive in the physical something by nature so opposed to good that conquest over the body, even to its destruction, becomes a religious necessity. And this conquest is sought by the same two methods; either by an asceticism which starves and so vanquishes the material, or gives it free rein and destroys it by extreme license. The development in so many regions, in India, China, Arabia, Greece, Rome, Peru, and Mexico, with features which repeat or caricature Christian monasticism, is one of the facts of history.

2. Social. Socially, it is rarely that religion becomes the controlling factor in advanced stages of civilization. Mohammedanism was unique in that it welded together the Arab tribes into a whole in which intense tribalism was merged into fanatical religious fervor. Society and religion interact. Religion responds to the change made by the transformation of pastoral into agricultural and commercial life, and modifies its idea of God and of the service due him. Yet there is always a conservative element opposed to these transformations in life of which the Rechabites (q.v.) in Israel are fairly representative. The factors which are influential in the development of society and of culture are, however, in early stages the care of religion. The first tribunals are the sanctuaries, where the god pronounces judgment. Physical ills are first treated by the priests learned both in simples and in the magic spells which condition their correct use. Astronomy develops in the priestly schools; mythology gives way to philosophy in priestly speculation; music is often the development of the service at the shrine; architecture and art make their noblest flights in the erection and adornment of the sanctuary. Yet these arts and sciences emancipate themselves from the thraldom of the priesthood, become independent and even opposing forces, and the interaction of these forces, no longer one but many, contribute to the diversity and so to the development of society.

3. Ethical. It is the natural result of the early dominance of religion in the life of man that religion sought to control ethics. Yet the moral sense and the religious have interacted throughout history. Ethics itself has a history, a development. No absolute standard of ethics is yet attained, nor is it likely that the highest standard of conduct now ideally possible will not have to give way to one still higher. That is the law of history. It is asserted, and with reason, that religion has offended against the ethics of a later age, sometimes of its own age. Samuel hewed Agag in pieces "before the Lord"; Servetus was burned as a heretic; the Quakers were persecuted for righteousness' sake in godly Massachusetts; and it was the moral sense which did away with that religious but immoral institution, the Inquisition. Religion, in primitive stages the arbiter of conduct, in the organized religions has had to submit to the dicta of moral consciousness. The relations of the family and the intercourse of man in society have had much to do with the advancement of morals; but religion gives its sanction to the development and elevates the standard by introducing consideration of the divine. And it is memorable that in most regions the most powerful incentive to right living has come through the religious teaching upon eschatology. The concept that happiness in the future life is contingent upon right conduct in this life constitutes an appeal to that powerful and ever-present motive, desire for one's welfare. A powerful adjunct to the forces developing morality are the codes put forth from the heart of the sanctuary.

4. Cultic. When the organized religions came into existence the sense of the holiness of God and of the sinfulness of man produced the idea of a chasm between deity and humanity. The bridge of that chasm was the cultic institution of the sacrifice, the mediator between god and man being the sacrificer. So sacrifice, which in the earlier stages of religion had been the sign of the community of god and man, became an at-one-ment, the means of reintroducing a harmony which had been lost. But the right method of offering this appeasing gift had come to be almost as important as the gift itself, so that a ritual developed which fell into the hands of a class claiming the knowledge and therefore the right exclusively to perform the sacred office. Hence the universal factors in religion in the cultic sphere are the sacrifice and the priest. Worship may be multiform and diverse, but these factors remain, though disguised more or less skilfully. Originally as accompaniments of the sacrifice, later in part divorced from them, prayer and praise became so universal that the Psalms of the Hebrew temple have their analogues in all the worship of man.

c. Modifications Due to Ethnic or Local Differences: Why different religions exist can no more be answered than why races are brown, yellow, white, or black. Each people has its favorite notions, in religion as elsewhere. Hence each developed religion has something of its own upon which it places emphasis. Egypt was dominated by the idea of the effect of conduct here upon the life beyond; China taught the apotheosis of the family and emphasized the fifth commandment; India laid special stress upon the immanence of God in his world; Persia was concerned with the absolute holiness of God; Mohammedanism is absorbed with the oneness of deity; Greece laid stress on the divine in the human; Rome emphasized the supremacy of law and the fixity of ritual. That these separate specialties were the expression of national peculiarities is as far as one may go, the wherefore is inexplicable.

d. Parallel Lines of Development: The organized religions often follow parallel lines of development. (1) In the primitive stage spirits are innumerable, "they swarm." No limits can be placed on the number of objects possessed by them as their home, and countless hordes besides roam homeless in earth and sea and air. But as man's mentality grows, he compares and generalizes and groups. To take one example: whereas each plot of ground once had its corn-spirit whose gift the crop of that field was, comparison gave rise to the idea of an earth-goddess, a Demeter or Ceres or Core, by whose beneficence came all the gifts earth made to man in growing crops. The corn-spirits of a district coalesced and then became a national deity to whom finally all increase of the earth was attributed. The history of Zeus among the Greeks also illustrates this principle. Nearly 200 names are known for this deity, only about one-third of which are poetic or descriptive. Nearly all the rest are referred to local or elemental deities whom he absorbed or displaced, assuming their functions and their cults, the latter of which are in several cases discordant with his normal worship and alien to his nature as a sky-god. The explanation is that as Zeus became the great national deity through the leadership of the tribes whose principal god he was, he took over the being, attributes, offices, shrines, and worship of older gods whose memory lingered solely in the names added to his as expressive of some special phase. So was it everywhere. The number of the gods was ever diminishing. Pantheons replaced the hordes of worshipful spirits, and in these the principal god obscured the lesser who tended to vanish from cult and recognition. Thus in Assyria Asshur became almost the only god aside from Ishtar, and in Israel, where according to the first commandment the gods of the nations were recognized as real existences, by the time of the exile Yahweh had come to be regarded as the only god of all the earth. Sometimes in this process gods were associated in triads or trinities, as in Egypt, Babylonia, and India, in the last case paralleling every phase of the Christian doctrine of the Trinity. Thus the tendency is toward monotheism, a result achieved only in Judaism, Christianity, Mohammedanism, and possibly in Zoroastrianism. (2) Another general tendency is that toward crystallization in ritual and creed. At the rise of a religion observances and conceptions are spontaneous, free, individualistic. But as the community grows exhortation hardens into doctrine, confession into creed, observance into ritual, acceptance of which and conformity to which mark the true believer. Thus orthodoxy and heterodoxy take their rise and become integral parts of religious thinking and terminology. (3) There is also a general tendency toward sectarianism. Against the disposition to define correct modes of teaching, of belief, and of worship arises the individualistic and diversified mentality of mankind, protesting against the limitations placed upon conceptions of God and on ways of serving him. Groups of individuals find themselves agreeing together in disagreeing with the standards erected. The result is that sect arises wherever attempt is made at uniformity. As an example, what is perhaps the most rigid and unyielding religious platform yet made, the teaching of Mohammed, is obliged to accommodate Sunni and Shiah with their almost untellable variety of subdivisions. Judging from the universal tendency of religion to develop sect, if history forecasts the future, oneness of belief will never be attained. And if the apparent demands of human nature be taken into the reckoning, such a result is not desirable. The Calvinistic mind must be left to its adoration of the mathematical precision of definite and exact foreordination, while the Arminian mind rejoices in the absolute responsibility of the individual for his own salvation or destruction.

GEO. W. GILMORE.

BIBLIOGRAPHY: I.-V.: The indispensable book here is M. Jastrow, *The Study of Religion*, New York, 1901 (thorough, profound, and sound). Consult also: J. E. Carpenter, *Place of Hist. of Religion in Theological Study*, London, 1891; Chabin, *La Science de la Religion*, Paris, 1898; L. H. Jordan, *Comparative Religion, Its Genesis and Growth*, New York, 1905 (very useful for bibliography, but uneven and not always sound in judgment); P. D. Chantepie de la Saussaye, *Lehrbuch der Religionsgeschichte*, i. 1-16, Tübingen, 1905; E. Crawley, *The Tree of Life. A Study of Religion*, London, 1905 (rationalistic but suggestive); S. von Czobel, *Die Entwickelung der Religionsbegriffe*, 2 vols., Leipsic, 1907; O. Pfleiderer, *Religion and Historic Faiths*, New York, 1907; C. Schnarschmidt, *Die Religion. Einführung in ihre Entwicklungsgeschichte*, Leipsic, 1907.

VI.: On primitive religion the literature is immense. On the whole field the following four books are indispensable and supplement each other: E. B. Tylor, *Primitive Culture*, London, 1903 (the classic on Animism); D. G. Brinton, *Religions of Primitive Peoples*, New York, 1897 (by the highest American authority); J. G. Fraser, *Golden Bough*, 3 vols., London, 1900 (primarily concerned with Magic, it covers the whole field of primitive religious conceptions); F. B. Jevons, *Introduction to Hist. of Religion*, London, 1896 (valuable, but handicapped by presuppositions; cf. the keen criticism in J. M. Robertson, *Pagan Christs*, ib. 1903).

For Animism and primitive psychology consult: W. Mannhardt, *Antike Wald- und Feld-Kulte*, 2 vols., Berlin, 1875-77; F. Granger, *Worship of the Romans*, London, 1895; Marian R. Cox, *Introduction to Folklore*, ib. 1897 (valuable as a "first book"); Mrs. J. H. Philpot, *The Sacred Tree*, ib. 1897; A. S. Geden, *Studies in Comparative Religion*, ib. 1898 (clear, excellent); A. Borchart, *Der Animismus*, Freiburg, 1900; F. Schultze, *Psychologie der Naturvölker*, book iii., Leipsic, 1900; A. E. Crawley, *Mystic Rose*, New York, 1902 (suggestive, though erratic); F. H. Cushing, *Zuni Tales*, New York, 1902 (should be read by all students of primitive notions); R. H. Nassau, *Fetichism in West Africa*, ib. 1904 ("Fetichism" is equivalent here to "religion"); E. Clodd, *Animism*, London, 1905 (low-priced, should be in every library); *Anthropological Essays Presented to E. B. Tylor in Honour of his 75th Birthday*, Oxford, 1907 (treats many of the more recondite matters touched on in the text).

On Magic, besides the general works mentioned above, consult: A. C. Haddon, *Magic and Fetishism*, London, 1906 (one of the "good little books"); F. Lenormant, *Chaldæan Magic*, London, 1877; L. W. King, *Babylonian Magic*, ib. 1896; T. W. Davies, *Magic, Divination, and Demonology*, ib. 1898; E. A. T. Budge, *Egyptian Magic*, ib. 1899; W. W. Skeat, *Malay Magic*, ib. 1900; A. Lang, *Magic and Religion*, ib. 1901.

On Mythology consult: F. Max Müller, *Contributions to the Science of Mythology*, 2 vols., London, 1897 (his completed statement, cf. his *Natural Religion*, Lect. xvi., 1889, and *Science of Language*, Lect. ix., 1880); A. Lang, *Custom and Myth*, London, 1884; idem, *Myth, Ritual and Religion*, ib. 1899 (Mr. Lang is the leading exponent of the anthropological school); J. Fiske, *Myths and Mythmakers*, Boston, 1872; D. G. Brinton, *Myths of the New World*, Philadelphia, 1896; Jevons, ut sup., chap. xix.

On Totemism consult: A. Lang, *Secret of the Totem*, London, 1905 (with which may be compared his *Custom and Myth* and his *Myth, Ritual and Religion*); J. McLennan, *Studies in Ancient History*, 2 series, ib. 1876–96; W. R. Smith, in *Journal of Philology*, ix (1880), 79 sqq., and in his *Rel. of Sem.* and *Kinship* (Smith and McLennan are the highest authorities); J. Köhler, *Zur Urgeschichte der Ehe, Totemismus . . .*, Stuttgart, 1897; Mrs. K. Langloh Parker, *The Euahlayi Tribe*, ib. 1905 (with Mrs. Parker's books should be read B. Spencer and F. J. Gillen, *Native Tribes of Central Australia*, ib. 1899, and *Northern Tribes of Central Australia*, ib. 1904); H. Webster, *Primitive Secret Societies*, New York, 1908. The subject is illustrated also by H. C. Trumbull, *Blood Covenant*, New York, 1885; idem, *Threshold Covenant*, ib. 1896.

On Taboo consult: Smith, *Rel. of Sem.*, 151 sqq., 446 sqq., 479 sqq.; idem, *Kinship*, passim; A. Lang, *Custom and Myth*, pp. 64–86; Granger, ut sup., pp. 200–219; S. Hartland, *Legend of Perseus*, ii., chaps. ix.–xiii., London, 1897; Crawley, *Mystic Rose*, pp. 10–80.

On Sacrifice consult: A. Lang, *Custom and Myth*, pp. 105–120; idem, *Modern Mythology*, pp. 70–91; H. Spencer, *Principles of Sociology*, part i., chap. xix., London, 1889; G. Allen, *Evolution of Idea of God*, chaps. v.–vii., xvi., ib. 1897; F. B. Jevons, ut sup., chaps. xi.–xii.; W. R. Smith, *Rel. of Sem.*, pp. 213–end; idem, *Kinship*, pp. 308 sqq.; Fraser, ut sup., chap. iii.; S. Hartland, ut sup., chap. xviii.

Consult further: J. F. C. Hecker, *Dancing Mania of the Middle Ages*, New York, 1888; B. Sidis, *Psychology of Suggestion*, ib. 1898; R. N. Cust, *Common Features which appear in all Religions*, London, 1895.

COMPLINE: The concluding part of the day's office in the breviary (q.v.), normally recited just before bedtime and corresponding in some ways to prime, though even more than the latter office it has a general and invariable character all through the year. It begins with a short lesson (I Pet. v. 8), followed by the confession and absolution, four psalms, the hymn, another short lesson with responsory, the *Nunc dimittis* or Song of Simeon (Luke ii. 29–32), and certain prayers. See VESPERS.

COMPOSTELLA: Properly Santiago de Compostella, a city of Galicia, northwestern Spain (33 m. s. by w. of Corunna), reputed burial-place of the apostle James the Greater and for several centuries the most frequented place of pilgrimage in Western Europe. Although the book of Acts (xii. 2) states that James was put to death in Jerusalem (44 A.D.), Spanish tradition declares that he went to Spain and suffered martyrdom there. For a long time his burial-place was unknown, but it was miraculously discovered early in the ninth century. A chapel—which in time gave way to a cathedral—was built on the spot, and a town grew up there, called *Ad sanctum Jacobum apostolum* or *Giacomo postolo*, whence Compostella (?). The story is first found in the ninth century (Walafried Strabo, *Poema de xii. apostolis*, and others), and is generally rejected by Protestants. Most Roman Catholic scholars also do not accept the alleged visit of James to Spain, but incline to believe the tradition concerning his burial-place. Santiago is now a town of about 25,000 inhabitants, the seat of an archbishop and of a university. For the Order of Compostella see JAMES, SAINT, OF COMPOSTELLA, ORDER OF. (O. ZÖCKLER†.)

BIBLIOGRAPHY: H. Flores, *España sagrada*, iii., app. x., pp. 414–435, Madrid, 1754; Natalis Alexander, *Historia ecclesiastica*, sec. i., dissert., prop. i., vol. iii. 161 sqq., Venice, 1778; P. B. Gams, *Die Kirchengeschichte Spaniens*, ii. 1, pp. 285–299, ii. 2, pp. 361–396, Regensburg, 1864; *KL*, iii. 774–777.

COMPSTON, HERBERT FULLER BRIGHT: Church of England; b. at Barnsley (21 m. n. of Sheffield), Yorkshire, England, Oct. 17, 1866. He studied at Exeter College, Oxford (B.A., 1891), and was curate of Totnes (1893–94), Holy Trinity, Bournemouth (1895–97), and St. Saviour's, Brixton Hill (1898–1903). In 1900 he was appointed lecturer in Latin at King's College, London, and lecturer in Hebrew three years later. He is also a member of the faculty of theology in the University of London and has been curate of St. Mark's, North Audley Street, London, W., since 1903. In theology he is a liberal Churchman.

COMPTON, HENRY: Bishop of London; b. at Compton Wynyates (25 m. n.n.w. of Oxford), Warwickshire, 1632, youngest son of the Earl of Northampton; d. at Fulham, near London, July 7, 1713. He studied at Queen's College, Oxford, 1649–52, went abroad and did not return to England until the Restoration, when he received a commission in the army; decided to enter the Church and was admitted M.A. at Cambridge 1661; entered Christ Church, Oxford, 1666 (B.D. and D.D., 1669); was consecrated bishop of Oxford 1674, translated to London 1675. He was privy councilor, and was entrusted with the religious education of the king's nieces, Mary and Anne, each of whom afterward became queen of England. In 1686, under James II., he was suspended from his bishopric for having refused to suspend at the king's command Dr. John Sharp, dean of Norwich, who had preached against popery. He actively espoused the cause of William and Mary, crowned them king and queen in 1689, and was reinstated in his old positions and given new honors and responsibilities. The close of his life was embittered by disappointment at not receiving the primacy. He was conciliatory toward dissenters, but his efforts to unite them to the Church met with little appreciation from either churchmen or non-conformists. He gave liberally to all in need and for building churches and hospitals, and died poor in consequence. He was a good botanist and in his grounds at Fulham had "a greater variety of curious exotic plants and trees than had at the time been collected in any garden in England." Besides episcopal letters (republished as *Episcopalia* with Memoir by S. W. Cornish, Oxford, 1842) and charges, he published *The Life of Donna Olimpia Maldachini* (1667), translated from the Italian; *The Jesuits' Intrigues* (1669) and *A Treatise of the Holy Communion* (1677), translated from the French.

COMTE, cōnt, ISIDORE AUGUSTE MARIE FRANÇOIS XAVIER (usually simply **AUGUSTE**): The founder of the positive school of philosophy (see POSITIVISM); b. at Montpellier (76 m. w.n.w. of Marseilles) Jan. 19, 1798; d. in Paris Sept. 5, 1857. He was educated mainly at the École Polytechnique in Paris. In 1817 he came under the influence of Saint-Simon, who helped to determine the future course of his mental activity. In 1826 he began a course of lectures covering the whole range of science as conceived by him, which was terminated by an attack of brain fever, resulting in such cerebral disturbance as to necessitate his confinement in an asylum and to cause several attempts at suicide. In 1828 he took up the course again, and the next year definitely began the construction of his *Cours de philosophie positive* (6 vols., 1830–42). Some minor educational appointments assured him a modest income, until in 1842, when he lost the post of examiner for admission to the École Polytechnique, and with it the half of his revenue. Through the efforts of John Stuart Mill, some of his English admirers made up the deficiency for a time, and from 1848 Littré and other French friends did the same. After the completion of the *Philosophie positive*, he proceeded to apply its principles to the reconstruction of society in the *Système de politique positive* (4 vols., 1851–1854). He gave practical expression to his views by founding in 1848 the "Positive Society," and by giving courses of free lectures, which were suppressed by the government in 1851. The *Politique positive* is much less coldly intellectual than his first great work, and is marked by an enthusiasm for the welfare of humanity which he exalted into a religion. The book, however, with certain small later works, the *Catéchisme positiviste* (1853), *Appel aux conservateurs* (1855), and *Synthèse subjective* (1856), did not meet with the approval of a section of his followers, of whom Littré was the most important. In his later years Comte was less the founder of a philosophical system than the high priest of a new religion of humanity.

Bibliography: Among the many translations of Comte's works the following may be mentioned: *The Philosophy of Mathematics*, by W. M. Gillespie, New York, 1851; *The Positive Philosophy*, by Harriet Martineau, 4 vols., London, 1853, 2 vols., 1875, republished by Bohn, 3 vols., ib. 1896; *The Catechism of Positive Religion*, ib. 1858; *A General View of Positivism*, ib. 1865; *System of Positive Polity*, by J. H. Bridges, F. Harrison, and others, 4 vols., ib. 1875–79; *The Eight Circulars*, by S. Lobb and others, ib. 1882; *Religion of Humanity*, by R. Congreve, ib. 1891. For discussion of the philosophy of Comte see Positivism and the literature there. For the life and work consult: his *Correspondance inédite*, 2 vols., Paris, 1903; J. S. Mill, *Auguste Comte and Positivism*, London, 1865, new ed., 1882 (answered by M. P. E. Littré, *Auguste Comte et Stuart Mill*, Paris, 1866, and J. H. Bridges, *The Unity of Comte's Life and Doctrines*, London, 1866); E. Caird, *The Social Philosophy and Religion of Comte*, Glasgow, 1885, H. Gruber, *Auguste Comte . . . Leben und Lehre*, Freiburg, 1889 (translated into Fr. and Ital.); J. F. E. Robinet, *L'Œuvre et la vie d'Auguste Comte*, Paris, 1891; G. Audeffrent, *Auguste Comte . . . sa vie et sa doctrine*, ib. 1894; A. Schaefer, *Die Moralphilosophie A. Comtes*, Basel, 1906.

CONANT, THOMAS JEFFERSON: Baptist; b. at Brandon, Vt., Dec. 13, 1802; d. in Brooklyn Apr. 30, 1891. He was graduated at Middlebury College, Vt., 1823; was professor of languages at Waterville College (Colby University), Me., 1827–1833; professor of languages and Biblical literature Hamilton Theological Institution (Colgate University), N. Y., 1835–51, professor of Hebrew and Biblical exegesis Rochester Theological Seminary 1851–57. From 1857 to 1875 he was in the service of the American Bible Union (see Bible Societies) and edited their revision of the New Testament (1871) and portions of the Old. He also published *The Meaning and Use of Baptizein philologically and historically investigated for the American Bible Union* (New York, 1860), translated the eleventh edition of Gesenius's *Hebrew Grammar* (Boston, 1839), contributed a new version and philological notes to the volume on the Psalms in the Schaff-Lange commentary (New York, 1872), and with Lyman Abbott edited a *Dictionary of Religious Knowledge* (1875). He was a member of the American Old Testament Revision Company.

CONATY, THOMAS JAMES: Roman Catholic bishop of Monterey and Los Angeles; b. at Kilnaleck (57 m. n.w. of Dublin), County Cavan, Ireland, Aug. 1, 1847. He studied at Montreal College (1863–67), College of the Holy Cross, Worcester, Mass. (B.A., 1869), and Montreal Theological School (1872). He was assistant rector of St. John's Church, Worcester, Mass. (1873–80), and rector of the Church of the Sacred Heart in the same city (1880–97). On nomination of the Roman Catholic bishops of the United States he was appointed rector of the Catholic University of America, Washington, by Pope Leo XIII. in 1896. In 1897 he was designated domestic prelate to the pope with the title of Right Reverend Monsignor, and in 1901 he was appointed titular bishop of Samos. In 1903 he was consecrated bishop of Monterey and Los Angeles. He was founder and editor of the monthly *Catholic School and Home Magazine* 1892–96, and has written *Bible Studies for Schools* (New York, 1897).

CONCEPTION, THE IMMACULATE. See Immaculate Conception.

CONCEPTION OF OUR LADY, NUNS OF THE ORDER OF THE: A religious order founded by Beatrix de Silva, sister of James, first count of Poralego, Portugal, in 1484; confirmed by Innocent VIII. 1489; given the rule of St. Clare by Cardinal Ximenes, but by Julius II. given a separate rule in 1511.

CONCEPTUALISM. See Scholasticism.

CONCLAVE. See Pope, Papacy, and Papal System.

CONCOMITANCE: An expression originating with Alexander of Hales and made by Thomas Aquinas a regular part of scholastic theology, sanctioned later by the Council of Trent, to designate the doctrine that as the living Christ is received in the Eucharist, and thus his body and blood can not be separated, both, together with his divinity, must inevitably be received under the species either of bread or of wine. It is in accordance with this doctrine that the Roman Catholic Church justifies the giving of communion in one kind, asserting that "the whole Christ" is thus received, though under the form of bread alone. See Transubstantiation.

CONCORD, BOOK OF; FORMULA OF. See Formula of Concord.

CONCORDANCES.

The name concordance is applied to books listing the words of the Bible in alphabetical or other classified order. Every great book needs a table of contents. The lists for the Bible are called concordances, perhaps because of the unison of the one word that stands out in each reference, or perhaps because the chief reason in old times for comparing passages was the attempt to make them agree with each other. Verbal concordances are usually arranged according to the single words of the text and either add to each the simple chapter and verse where the word occurs, or give besides the words of the passage. Subject concordances or topical indexes aim rather at the matter than at the words, and often contain a brief explanation of the subject. In this article the verbal concordances are chiefly in view.

I. The First Concordances: The first concordance seems to have been in Latin and to have been made by the Burgundian Hugo of St. Cher (*Hugo Carensis*, d. 1263 or 1264), the first Dominican cardinal; it is fabled that he set five hundred Dominicans at work on it. He finished it about 1230 in the monastery of St. James at Paris, whence the name *Concordantiæ S. Jacobi*, also called *Concordantiæ breves* because without the wording of the passages. About the year 1250 three Englishmen in the same monastery, John of Darlington, Richard of Stavenesby, and Hugh of Croydon, added the full wording in the *Concordantiæ S. Jacobi, Anglicanæ* or *Maximæ*, so named because of the complete passages. Arlot (Arlotto) of Prato, a Tuscan, in 1285 appointed minister general of the Franciscans, improved Hugo's concordance. Conrad of Deutschland or of Halberstadt (flourished about 1290), rewrought and abbreviated Hugo's book and added, according to Sixtus Senensis, the indeclinable words (on Hugo, Arlot, and Conrad cf. Sixtus Senensis, *Bibliotheca sancta . . . a Joanne Hayo . . . illustrata*, pp. 249, 250, 201, 220, the last also falsely printed 201, Lyons, 1593). In connection with the Council of Basel in 1433, 1435–40, because of the discussions with the Bohemians about *nisi*, John vi. 54, and with the Greeks about *ex* and *per*, John Stoikowitz (also called John of Ragusa) is said to have been especially distressed at the lack of a concordance of the particles and directed his Scotch chaplain, Walter Jonas, to make one. Jonas began to prepare a volume with the particles arranged according to the books of the Bible, which he nearly finished in three years. Then two others took it up and completed it, and they probably introduced the alphabetical arrangement. John of Socubia or Segovia, archdeacon of Villaviciesa in the diocese of Oviedo, wrote the preface. Some have thought that the *Concordantiæ maximæ* were so named not, as stated above, because they gave the full passages instead of merely chapter and verse, but because they contained also the indeclinable words.

II. Hebrew Concordances: Rabbi Isaac Mordecai (on the name cf. Buxtorf's preface, leaf 4a) ben Nathan made a Hebrew concordance 1438–1448: מאיר נתיב הנקרא קונקורדאנשייש. He arranged the roots alphabetically, save that the quadrilaterals stood at the end; derivatives stood under the roots. It was published by Daniel Bomberg Venice, 1524, in folio, and again in 1564 under the Doge Arnald Ferrer, superintended by Meir ben Jacob Franconi an. published by Lorenzo Bragadini, printed by Maggio Parentini. Ambrose Froben republished it in Basel, 1580, under the title: ספר יאיר נתיב הנקרא בלעז קונקורדאנסייאש (in the *editio prima* of 1524 this was the second title, after the sheet with the preface, but closing with יייש), in fifty sheets beside the sheet in front (at least in the Leipsic copy); the columns often agree with the columns of 1524; at the end is Aaron Pesaro's list of the passages explained in the

1. 1524–1878. Babylonian Talmud. Anton Reuchlin, professor of Hebrew at Strasburg, published an edition at Basel, 1556, in which Rabbi Nathan's explanation of the words was given in Latin, but badly; Johann Brenz wrote the preface; it appeared again, Basel, 1569. Solomon Mandelkern saw in the royal library at Munich the manuscript of a concordance that Elias Levita Bachur wrote in 1516–21: ספר הזכרונות. Another manuscript revised by Elias Levita and provided with a German translation is in the National Library at Paris (cf. Mandelkern's preface). Conrad Kircher of Augsburg, pastor at Donauwörth, published a Hebrew concordance; unfortunately, because he had given the wording of the passages from the Greek text of the Septuagint he called the book incorrectly: *Concordantiæ V. T. Græcæ, Ebræis vocibus respondentes*, πολύχρηστοι . . . , 2 vols. Frankfort, 1607 (4 leaves), 2,271, 2,310 cols. (1 leaf), 290 pp., quarto. The second volume gives the Greek words with references to the places in which they occur in the first volume and with the passages from the Apocrypha. Le Long mentions (p. 456) a manuscript summary from Kircher made by Arnold Bootius and called it *Bibliotheca Sequeriana pag. 37* and a manuscript Greek-Danish concordance to the Apocrypha by Frants Michael Vogel. Martin Troost treated the Chaldee sections by themselves: *Concordantiæ Chaldaicæ et Syriacæ ex Danielis et Esræ capitibus Chaldaice scriptis*, Wittenberg, 1617, quarto. Marius de Calasio, a Franciscan (d. 1620), made an edition published in Rome, 1621–22, by Michael Angelo of St. Romulus: *Concordantiæ sacrorum bibliorum Hebraicorum . . .*, published again,

Cologne, 1646; London, 1648; Rome, 1657; and by William Romaine, London, 1747–49, in 4 vols. (15 leaves), 1,366, 1,234, 1,326, 852, 184 cols. (43 leaves), folio. John Buxtorf's concordance was published by his son: *Concordantiæ bibliorum Hebraicæ, nova et artificiosa methodo dispositæ in locis innumeris depravatis emendatæ. . . . Accesserunt novæ concord. Chaldaicæ . . . per Johannem Buxtorf fil.*, Basel, 1632 (10 leaves), and sheets A–Yyyyy. The preface tells of the earlier concordances. Buxtorf left the particles out (cf. Glauch, *De usu concordantiarum biblicarum schediasma*, Leipsic, 1668, p. 24). In Le Long, *Bibliotheca sacra*, Paris, 1723, there is found under Christopher Crinesius: "*Conc. Hebr.*, Wittenberg, 1627, quarto." Jöcher has ספר זכרון *seu analysis Novi Ti. per 27 tabulas*. (Is that the same book?) Andreas Sennert published at Wittenberg, 1653, 12 leaves to announce a book that he would like to publish if some one would bear the cost: מראה מקום הקטן. *sive manuale concordantiarum Ebræo-Biblicarum cl. J. Buxtorfii*. Christian Raue abbreviated Buxtorf: *Conc. Hebr. et Chald. I. Buxtorfii epitome*, Berlin and Frankfort, 1677. Christian Nolde gave the particles: *Concor. particularum Ebr.-Chald.*, Copenhagen, 1679; Sim. Bened. Tympe added to it Joh. Michaelis's and Christian Koerber's particles: Nolde, *Conc. partic. . . . S. Gottfr. Tympius summa cura recensuit . . . inseruit concordantias pronominum separatorum Ebr. et Chald. nunc primum congestas a Simeone Benedicto Tympio denique appendicis loco subjunxit lexica particularum Ebraicarum Joh. Michaelis* [*cum præfatione Aug. Pfeifferi*; cf. Bindseil, xxxv., note 1] *et Christiani Koerberi*, Jena, 1734. Le Long names William Robertson, *Thesaurus ling. sanct. seu conc. lexicon Ebr.-Lat.-bibl.*, London, 1680, and Antony Laymann, *Concordantiæ Hebræo-sacræ iuxta seriem cuiusque constructionis syntacticæ*, n.p., 1681. (Is that really a concordance?) John Taylor made a very good Hebrew concordance adapted to the English text, 1764, 2 vols. Isaac ben Tsebi from Soldin in Prussia summarized Buxtorf: . . . שרש ישע והוא קיצור הספר מאיר נתיב הנקרא קונקורדאנציא, Frankfort-on-the-Oder, 1768. Julius Fürst's great work: אוצר לשון הקדש, Leipsic, 1840, is still much used; editions by B. Baer, Stettin, 1847 and 1861. G. V. Wigram aided by S. P. Tregelles and B. Davidson published the *Englishman's Hebrew and Chaldee Concordance*, London, 1843, 3d ed., 1866; Davidson, revised by Joseph Hughes, London, 1876. Strack refers to concordances of proper names by Gid. Brecher, Frankfort-on-Main, 1876, and by L. M. Schusslowitz, ספר אצור השמות, Wilna, 1878.

In the year 1884 Solomon Mandelkern announced a new concordance: *Die neubearbeitete Hebräisch-chaldäische Bibel-Concordanz . . . nebst Gutachten von Fachgelehrten*, and published 15 pp. quarto; later an approving word of H. L. Fleischer's was added on a separate leaf. Finally the book appeared: *Solomon Mandelkern Veteris Testamenti concordantiæ Hebraicæ et Chaldaicæ* . . . (and a Hebrew title), 2 vols., Leipsic, 1896, xv., 1,532 pp. folio. Later Mandelkern made a small edition without the wording of the passages, Leipsic, n.d., viii. (1), 1,010 (1) pp. quarto. This work had been long preparing and was published at Leipsic where there are good compositors and good proof-readers in every branch; it should therefore have been careful and accurate, but it is not at all well done. Consequently it is desirable that scholars in this department should collect their contributions to the correction of the errors and send in the lists of mistakes found, so that the publishers can issue a supplement, which they are willing to do. The best way would be to divide the book up between a large number of men, so that nothing could escape detection. Some of the contributions are already made: Carl Siegfried, *Stellenfehler in Mandelkern's V. T. conc. Hebr.*, in *ZWT*, 1897, 465–467; Rudolf Kittel, *Ein kurzes Wort über die beiden Mandelkernschen Concordanzen*, in *ZATW*, 1898, 165–167; B. Jakob, Georg Beer, Gustaf Dalman, Bernhard Stade, *ZATW*, 1898, 348–351; Herman L. Strack, *TLZ*, 1898, no. 13, 358–359; (Mandelkern, . . . *Pro domo*, *ZATW*, 1899, 183–186); A. Büchler, B. Jakob, K. Ludwig, E. König, A. von Gall, *ZATW*, 1899, 187–191, 350; (I. I. Kahan, *ZATW*, 1899, 353–356; Mandelkern, *ZATW*, 1900, 173–176; Kahan, *ZATW*, 1900, 338–344); E. Rosenwasser, *ZATW*, 1902, 320; A. Zillessen, *ZATW*, 1903, 94–95; Von Gall, ib. 95–96; Mayer Lambert, ib. 352–354; Von Gall and E. Nestle, ib. 354; Rosenwasser, *ZATW*, 1904, 146, 326; M. Brann, in *Monatsschrift für Geschichte und Wissenschaft des Judentums*, 1898, 529–537; Badt, in *Monatsschrift für Geschichte und Wissenschaft des Judentums*, 1899, 523, 524; J. Göttsberger, *Biblische Zeitschrift*, ii., 1904, 259; Sven Herner, in *ZDMG*, lxi (1907), 7–17. Doubtless other scholars have further corrections. Professor Kautzsch in Halle has given the following:

2. Mandelkern's Concordance.

p. 34 ולי חומיכם read Hos. 2, 3, instead of 2, 2.
p. 251 read ותנולתי instead of התנולתי.
p. 315 read הַיִירָם, but Job 6, 21, הַיִיתם.
p. 371 חֲרָך Ct 3, 4 should be put by itself as stat. constr.
p. 479 Why has Mandelk. I Chr. 3, 5, נולדו? Ed. Mant., Baer, Ginsb. have here also נולדו).
p. 488 תוֹסְףְ Prov. 30, 6 is wanting.
p. 503 at least I Ki. 18, 3 does not belong under the perfect ירא, but under the *adj. verbale*, and probably also I Ki. 1, 51; 18, 12; Prov. 14, 16; Job. 1, 9.
p. 729 instead of הינחה ed. Mant., Baer הינחה.
p. 733 read וַיִּן (= וַיִּיִן) instead of וַיִּן and וַיִּן.
p. 771 נִשְׂאֹת (infin. absol. Niph.?) II Sam. 19, 43 is wanting.
p. 1005 וַיֵּצֶר Gen. 32, 8, instead of 32, 7.

He expressed the wish that some one would make a concordance of the words arranged according to the end of the words, so that a scholar could work rapidly with fragments of the inscriptions and of manuscripts; cf. Friedrich Zimmer's Greek termination-concordance.

III. Greek Concordances: Sixtus Senensis relates that about 1300 a Basilian monk, Euthalius of Rhodes, made a Greek concordance of the whole Bible, following Hugo of St. Cher's example in the Latin Bible. This is said to have been seen in manuscript at Rome, but is unknown. Another Greek, George Sugdures, who studied at Rome toward the end of the seventeenth century and afterward taught at Constantinople, is said to have worked thirty years on a Greek concordance of the whole Bible, but not to have published it; cf. Le Long, 456a, and Jöcher.

1. The Old Testament: Trommius (Abraham van der Trommen), *Concordantiæ Græcæ versionis vulgo dictæ LXX interpretum . . . Leguntur hic præterea voces Græcæ pro Hebraicis redditæ ab antiquis omnibus Veteris Testamenti interpretibus . . . Aquila, Symmacho, Theodotione, . . .* Amsterdam and Utrecht, 1718, was until lately the only concordance for the Greek Old Testament. At the end are given a Hebrew-Chaldee dictionary, a Greek dictionary to Origen's Hexapla from Montfaucon, prepared by Lambert Bos, and Bos's comparison of the chapters and verses in the Sixtino-Vatican edition of the Septuagint with those in the Frankfort edition of 1597, which both Kircher and Trommen used. Trommen wrote in 1718 a defense of his book against Gagnier, who defended Kircher. A second edition of Trommen appeared at Amsterdam, 1742. Bagster published: *A Handy Concordance* of the Septuagint, London, 1887. Now there exists the great work of Edwin Hatch and Henry A. Redpath, *A Concordance to the Septuagint . . .*, Oxford (1892, 1897, 1900), with a supplement giving the proper names (all should have been in one list).

2. The New Testament: Sixtus Birken of Augsburg made a concordance for the New Testament: Xystus Betulejus, *Συμφωνία ἡ σύλλεξις τῆς διαθήκης τῆς Ni. Ti. concord.*, Basel, 1546. Henri Estienne finished his father's (d. 1559) concordance: *Concordantiæ Gr.-Lat. Testam. novi*, Paris, 1594; 2d ed., Geneva, 1624. Erasmus Schmid of Wittenberg made a concordance, *Ni. Ti. . . . TAMEION*, Wittenberg, 1638, repeated by Ernst Salomon Cyprian, Gotha and Leipsic, 1717, often reprinted, e.g., by John Williams, London, 1767; without name, 2 vols., Glasgow, 1819; by William Greenfield, London, 1830; in the most convenient form by the London publisher Bagster. Ethelbert W. Bullinger issued *A Critical Lexicon and Concordance to the English and Greek New Testament*, London, 1877, 5th ed., 1908. The chief work at present is Karl Hermann Bruder's, Leipsic, 1842, 4th ed., 1888, but it will be surpassed by Paul Wilhelm Schmiedel's, now preparing. George V. Wigram (see above) also prepared: *The Englishman's Greek Concordance*, London, 1839 and later. Otto Schmeller, *TAMEION*, London, 1869. In America Hosea L. Hastings had an excellent concordance prepared by Charles F. Hudson and revised by Ezra Abbot: *A Critical Greek and English Concordance*, Boston, 1870, 3d ed., 1875. Especial attention must be called to Friedrich Zimmer's *Concordantiæ supplementariæ omnium vocum Novi Testamenti Græci et classibus secundum terminationes distributarum et derivatarum cum nativis verbis collocatarum compositæ a F. Z.*, Gotha, 1882, and to W. F. Moulton and A. S. Geden, *A Concordance to the Greek Testament according to the Texts of Westcott and Hort, Tischendorf, and the English Revisers*, Edinburgh, 1897; 2d ed., 1899.

IV. Latin Concordances: The Latin concordances were the earliest and are now very complete. They have an interesting history, closely bound up with the development of academic life in Western Europe. A few manuscripts are noted here as an incitement for one who can give himself to the history of these books, also a few out of the many printed concordances of the Latin Bible. The Bibliothèque Nationale at Paris contains ten manuscripts of concordances all of which are dated from the fourteenth century. These are the

1. Manuscripts. MSS. Lat. 513, 514, 515, 516, 517, (all five from Colbert's library); 518 and 519 (from the Carmelite Monastery); 520, 601 (belonged formerly to Baluze: *in quinque libros distributæ*); 602 (once Tellier's: *concordantia ordine alphabetico digesta*); 603, 606 scarcely seem to contain concordances. The city library at Bordeaux owns a MS. of the "larger concordance," MS. 15, fourteenth century, parchment, 470 leaves, 3 cols. on a page: *bibliorum concordantiæ maiores*; the beginning is: *Cuilibet volenti requirere concordancias in hoc libro, unum est primo attendendum*, and the end is: *Ge. XXX. b. sentiens lya quod parere desiisset, Zelfam ancillam marito tradidit. Expliciunt magnæ concordantie.* MS. no. 6 in the monastery Heiligenkreuz (-Neukloster) in Vienna seems to begin and end in the same way. The university library at Leipsic has three manuscripts which seem to be of the same kind as those at Bordeaux and Vienna; they are ascribed to Conrad of Germany; these are MS. Lat. 99, perhaps of the 14th century, MS. Lat. 100, of about the 15th century, and MS. Lat. 101, of about the 15th century.

Conrad of Alemannia's *Concordantiæ bibliorum* is said to have appeared at Strasburg, 1470. At Leipsic there is one (Hain, 5620, says by J. Mentelin, Strasburg, c. 1475) dated 1474 by the rubricator, who probably knew the precise date. It appeared again at Bologna, 1479, 1486; Basel, 1480, *studio Joan. Nivicellensis*. The first edition of the *Concordantiæ Anglicanæ* is supposed to be Nuremberg, 1485, as *Concord. magnæ*; again 1487.

2. 1470–1533. Sebastian Brant published Conrad's concordance as *Conc. S. Jacobi*, and John of Segovia's at Froben's in Basel, 1496, in two parts, repeated by Froben 1506; *Concordantiæ maiores biblie tam dictionum declinabilium quam indeclinabilium de novo summa diligentia cum textu vise ac secundum veram orthographiam emendatissime excuse*, with preface by Conradus Leontorius Mulbrunnensis, dated May 12, 1506, *Ex Artavalle ultro Birsam Basileanam;* the colophon says that the work was printed *opera et impensis Johannini Amerbachii, Petri de Langendorff, et Froben de Hammelburg iam denuo in urbe Basileorum.* The first part contains sheets a–z, A–Z, Aa–Ff, folio; the second part is entitled *Concordantie partium sive dictionum indeclinabilium totius biblie*, and the preface of John of Segovia tells something of the way in which preparations for it were made. A further title, over the first word, says that John of Segovia published the book at the Council of Basel in 1430; this is probably intended as a general date for the council and not for the book, for according to John's preface the book was not done before 1440 at the earliest; repeated Basel, 1516, 1521, 1523, 1525, 1526; Strasburg, 1526, 1530; Lyons, 1526, 1528, 1540,

1545; ed. Johannes Gaste from Breisach, Basel, 1552. In 1533 Joannes Steels, an Antwerp bookseller, published a handy little volume *Index utriusque Testamenti*, the first convenient rival of the large concordances.

In Paris, 1555, Robert Estienne's improved concordance came out: *Concordantiæ bibliorum utriusque Testamenti, V. et Ni., novæ et integræ. Quas revera maiores appellare possis*, for which Estienne divided the New Testament into verses. At Basel Joh. Hervage published, 1561 and again 1568, a concordance by his father. Jean Benoit made an edition (Paris?), 1562, George Bullock one in Antwerp, 1572, Leyden, 1586, 1603, 1615. From the Clementine Vulgate of 1592, Antwerp, 1599; (Frankfort), 1600; again 1618 (Hanover?); Cologne, 1611; Geneva, 1611; with notes by Franz Lukas from Bruges, Antwerp, 1606, 1612; Venice, 1612; Orléans, 1612; Lyons, 1612, 1615 (confused with Leyden, 1615?); Antwerp and Venice, 1618; Geneva, 1620, 1624; Geneva and Frankfort, 1625; Rome, 1627, by Gaspard de Zamora, S. J.; Paris, 1635, 1638, 1646; Cologne, 1628 (1629?), 1661, 1663; Bamberg, 1721. Hubert Phalesius corrected in 1642 Franz Lukas's edition of 1617, printed Lyons, 1649, 1652, 1667, 1687, 1700; Paris, 1656; Cologne, 1684; Mainz, 1685; and at other times and places, for example, Vienna, 1825.

3. 1555–1685.

The Benedictine monks in Wessobrunn published: *Concordantiæ nova methodo ornatæ*, Augsburg, 1751, with whole verses or at least sentences. F. F. Dutripon's *Vulgatæ editionis bibliorum sacrorum concordantiæ*, Paris, 1838, has reached at least a 7th ed., Paris, 1880, Regensburg, 1886. Tonimi revised it, Prado, 1861. H. de Raze, Ed. de Lechaux, and J. B. Flandrin, all S. J., published a *Concordantium s. s. manuale*, Lyons, 1852, 13th ed., Paris, 1895. De Raze's arrangement of words according to cases or tenses is also used by Peultier, Étienne, Gantois, in their *Concordantium . . . thesaurus* (in R. Cornely, J. Knabenbauer, Fr. von Hummelauer's *Cursus sacr. script. Pars. III. Textus V.*), Brussels [1897]. Add here: V. P. Robert, *Aurifodina sacra scientiarum divinarum ex fontibus aureis utriusque Testamenti, ordine alphabetico digesta*, Turin, 1873; M. Bechi's *Concord. præter alphab. ordinem in grammaticalem redactæ*, Turin, 1887; C. Legrand, Bruges, 1889; V. Cornært, *Concordantiæ* for preachers in choosing texts, Paris and Bruges, 1892.

4. 1751–1892.

V. German Concordances: Several small books appeared with only a selection of passages, first of all Johannes Schroeter's *Konkordantz des Newen Testaments zu teutsch*, Strasburg, 1524, according to Luther's translation. Leonhard Brunner, pastor in Worms, extended this to the whole Bible, Strasburg, 1546. Michael Müling published a little *Conkordanz-Bibel*, Leipsic, 1602, and finally Lucas Stöckle, *H. Göttlicher Schrift Schatzkammer: oder Teutsche Biblische Concordantzen*, Herborn in the county Nassaw Catzenelnbogen, 1606.

The first large work came from the Nuremberg printer Conrad Bawr (Latinized Agricola), with a preface of July 5th, 1609: *Concordantiæ bibliorum, d. i. bibl. Concordantz und Verzeichniss der Fürnembsten Wörter . . . auf Mart. Luther's Ao. 1545 am letzten revidirte Bibel gerichtet*, Frankfort-on-Main, 1610, 1621, 1632, 1640. In 1612 he added an appendix. Christian Zeise, pastor in Oeltzschau near Leipsic, improved Bawr's work, Frankfort-on-Main (1657), 1658, 1674; a supplement in 1664. Le Long mentions concordances by Johannes Fischer, Herborn, 1610; Johannes Faber, Ingolstadt, 1615; Paul Orell, Frankfort, 1627; Daniel Fessel, Frankfort, 1662; Johannes Janus, *Scripturæ oder Stella cælorum*, Frankfort, 1650; Martin Gumbrecht, Dresden, 1654.

1. 1609–50.

Friedrich Lanckisch, a Leipsic bookseller, prepared an enormous work, but died in 1669 before he could print it. Volume i. came out in the shape the author had intended: *Concordantiæ bibliorum Germanico-Hebraico-Græcæ*, Leipsic, 1677, new ed., 1688; 3d ed., 1696, 4th ed., 1705, enlarged by Christian Reineccius, 1718, second part, 1742. The Hebrew or the Greek word was placed beside each German word. Volumes ii. and iii. were then abbreviated and published as follows: *Concordantiæ bibliorum Hebræo- et Græco-Germanicæ, duabus partibus absolutæ, quarum prior voces Hebraicas et Chaldaicas V. Ti., posterior voces omnes Græcas [N. Ti., Apocr. et LXX. interpp.] . . . cum significatibus Germanicis e versione Lutheri ordine alphabet. recenset. Magni concordantiarum operis a F. Lanckisch conscripti epitome*, 2 parts, Leipsic and Frankfort, 1680. This is a Hebrew-Latin-German and Greek-Latin-German dictionary without any note of the passages.

2. Lanckisch's Concordance.

Georg Michaelis's *Kleine Concordantz* of 1686 appeared in a sixth edition of the first part, Leipsic, 1707, and in a second edition of the second part, Leipsic and Jena, 1718; with preface by F. A. Hallbauer, Jena, 1733; *G. Michaelis vollständige Real- und Verbal-Concordanz . . . vermehret von M. Adam Lebrecht Müller. Mit einer Vorrede Joh. Georg Walchs*, Jena, 1767. *Wohleingerichtete Anweisung zur Biblischen Concordanz vermittelst einem Biblischen Spruch Register . . .*, Lemgo (1720?), 1725; *Biblisches Spruchregister*, 5th ed., Lemgo, 1736, enlarged, Basel, 1746. Avenarius issued *Biblisches Spruchregister*, Gotha, 1713. Niederwerfer's *Biblischer Kern und Stern oder Hand-concordantz* appeared Leipsic, 1814. Johannes Kamprads made a Biblical *Sprachregister*, published with preface by Siegfried Becker, the Leipsic superintendent, Dresden and Leipsic, 1727. Gottfried Büchner made: *Verbal Hand-Concordanz oder exegetisch-homiletisches Lexikon*, Jena, 1740, 3d enlarged ed., Jena, 1756; 6th ed., enlarged by Heinrich Leonhard Heubner, Halle, 1840, 23d ed., Berlin, 1899; with supplement of 12,000 Bible passages by Lutz and Riehm, Basel, 1890; Philip Schaff prepared a reprint of the Heubner ed. by Büchner, Philadelphia, 1871, in which A. Späth added 8,060 passages. Büchner first issued his *Grosse Bibl. Real und Verbal-Concordanzien*, Jena, 1750, 3d ed., 1765. Others are: Jacob Christof Beck, *Vollständiges Biblisches Wörterbuch, oder*

3. 1707–1893.

Real- und Verbal-Concordanz, Basel, 1770; Gottfried Joachim Wichmann, *Biblische Handconcordanz. Nebst Vorrede von Christian Wilhelm Franz Walch*, Dessau and Leipsic, 1782; 2d ed., thoroughly wrought over, Leipsic, 1796; new unchanged ed., with preface by Kindervater, Leipsic, 1806; Heinrich Schott, *Biblische Handconcordanz*, Leipsic, 1827; *Biblische Hand-Concordanz*, 1841, 2d much enlarged ed., Leipsic, 1847; Frank Julius Bernhard, pastor at Magdeborn near Leipsic, *Biblische Concordanz oder dreifaches Register über Sprüche im Allgemeinen, über Textstellen für besondere Fälle und über Sachen, Namen und Worte der von Dr. Luther übersetzten heiligen Schrift*, Leipsic, 1850, 1851; 2d thoroughly revised ed., 1857; 7th reprint, Dresden, 1888; *Calwer Bibelkonkordanz oder vollständiges biblisches Wortregister. Nach der revidirten Luther Uebersetzung*, Calw and Stuttgart, 1893.

VI. English Concordances (cf. M. C. Hazard, in Walker's *Concordance*): *The Concordance of the New Testament*, apparently by John Day helped by the printer Thomas Gybson, came out undated, but before 1540. John Marbeck published: *A Concordance* for the whole Bible, London, 1550. Walter Lynne translated Conrad Pellican's *Index Librorum* [Zurich, 1537]; *A brief and a compendious Table, in the Manner of a Concordance*, London, 1550. Robert F. Herrey made *Two Right Profitable and Fruitfull Concordances*, London, 1578, and his printer, Christopher Barker, published *A Concordance by J. W.*, London, 1579. Clement Cotton prepared a larger work, London (1618 sqq.?), 1625, from the Geneva New Testament; 1627, from the Old Testament; 1631, from the whole Bible. John Downame made a summary of this at Cotton's wish, London, 1635, again 1689. Richard Bernard made a *Thesaurus biblicus*, London (?), 1644, and Robert Wickens, *A Compleat and Perfect Concordance*, Oxford, 1647; 1655. Samuel Newman, who went to New England in 1636 or 1638, published: *A Large and Complete Concordance*, on the basis of Cotton, London, 1643; 2d ed., 1650; 3d ed., 1658 (in this the Apocrypha); then 1662, only with Newman's initials S. N.; and finally as the *Cambridge Concordance*, 1720, without Newman's name. Mulbing issued one, London, 1666. John Jackson wrote a short concordance (Cambridge), 1668; John Owen, London, 1673; and Samuel Clark, 1696. Cruden's *Concordance* came out in 1737 and has often been republished in various forms, for example, by John Butterworth, Philadelphia, 1867; John Brown, London, 1816; C. S. Carey, London, 1867; John Eadie, with preface by David King, New York, 1850; with preface by Joel Hawes, Hartford, 1867; Cole; Hawker; David King, Boston, 1845; Alfred Jones, London, about 1855; Smith, Youngman, and Thomas Taylor, Brooklyn, 1809. Robert Young's *Analytical Concordance*, Edinburgh, 1873, also 1881, added the Hebrew and Greek original words. James Bradford Richmond Walker's *Comprehensive Concordance with an Introduction by Marshall Custiss Hazard*, leaves unimportant matter out, yet contains 50,000 more passages than Cruden; it appeared Boston and Chicago, 1894; James Strong, *Exhaustive Concordance of the Bible; also brief dictionaries of the Hebrew and Greek words of the original, with reference to the English words*, New York, 1894 (takes in every word).

VII. French Concordances: Only Protestant ones are given. *Concordance de la Bible*, Geneva, 1566; Marc Wilks, *Concordances des Saintes Écritures*, Paris, 1840; W. B. Mackensie, *Concordance* for the Osterwald translation, Paris, 1867, again 1874; *Dictionnaire des concordances des Saintes Écritures d'après la version du Dr. Segond*, Lausanne, 1886.

VIII. Dutch Concordances: Peder Jans Twisck, a Mennonite, published a concordance to the Flemish Luther-Bible, Hoorn, 1615; then Sebastian Dranck, Haarlem, 1618, and again 1648. Jan Martin (van Dantzig? from Danzig?) began a Flemish concordance, and Abraham van der Trommen finished it before his Greek one: *Nederlandsche Concordantie des Bijbels*, Groningen, 1685–92; Leeuwarden, 1754. H. Valse issued *Kleyne concordantie*, The Hague, 1704.

IX. Danish Concordances: E. Ewald, Copenhagen, 1748, 1749; E. Levinsen, *Verbal-Concordans eller Bibel-Ordbog til det Nye Testamente*, Copenhagen, 1856.

X. Swedish Concordances: According to Le Long, Achaz Rahamb translated a German concordance, of which the letter A was published in Stockholm about 1709. Lorenz Holenius (Halenius?), *Svensk-Hebraisk og Svensk-Grekisk concordans over G. og N. Testam.*, Stockholm, 1734, 1742.

XI. Syriac Concordances: Carl Schaaf, *Lexicon Syriacum concordantiale omnes Ni. Ti. Syriaci voces . . . complectens*, Leyden, 1709.

XII. Topical Indexes: Cf. C. Mangenot, in Vigouroux's *Dictionnaire de la bible*, ii. 892–905, Paris, 1899. Many of the concordances named above were at the same time more or less topical, the concordance of the words being the best concordance of the subjects. The topical indexes go back to the work of Antony of Padua (1195–1231), whose *Concordantiæ morales ss. bibliæ* seem to be contained in the library of the University of Leipsic, MS. Lat. 102, leaf 1–123r, with possibly a fragment in MS. Lat. 543 (5). It was often printed, as for example, Venice, 1575; Rome, 1621, again 1623 (?); by De la Haye, Paris, 1641; Cologne, 1647. Franz Lukas Wading (cf. Mangenot) added to Antony a sermon-prompter by an Irish monk of the thirteenth century, and something similar was printed at Paris, 1497. A great many indexes could be added to this book of Antony's, for example Conrad Pellican's, Zurich, 1537; Peter Patiens, in Landau, Frankfort, 1571; Jan Harlems, in the *Antwerp Polyglotte*, viii., Antwerp, 1572; Anton Broickwy von Koninsteyn, Cologne, 1550; Paris, 1551 and 1554; William Allot, Antwerp, 1581, 2d ed., 1585; Anton von Balinghem, Douai, 1621; Cologne, 1659; Trevoux, 1705; Lyons, 1711; Eulard, Antwerp, 1625; Philip Paul Merz after Allot, Augsburg, 1731, 1738, 1751, 1791; Venice, 1758, 1818; Paris, 1822, 1825, 1883; Johannes Jakob Ohm, *Biblische Spruchconcordanz* by Chr. Liebeyott Simon, Leipsic, 1812; Joh. Michael Otto, *Biblisches Spruchregister*, ed. J. G. Rübner,

Sulzbach, 1823; C. G. Haupt, *Biblische Real- und Verbal-Encyclopädie*, Quedlinburg, 1823–27; J. G. Hauff, *Biblische Real- und Verbalkonkordanz*, Stuttgart, 1828–34; Matalène, Paris, 1837, again 1864; A. J. James, Paris, 1835; Lueg, *Biblische Realconcordanz*, 2d ed. by Heim, Regensburg, 1855; C. Mazeron, Paris, 1869. CASPAR RENÉ GREGORY.

BIBLIOGRAPHY: C. Kircher, *De concordantiæ biblicæ . . usu*, Wittenberg, 1622 (a polemic against Romanism); J. Buxtorf, preface to his *Concordantiæ*, Basel 1632; A. Glauch, *De concordantiarum biblicarum usu*, Leipsic, 1668; W. Frantz, *Tractatus theologicus de interpretatione sacrarum Scripturarium*, pp. 52–70, Wittenberg, 1708; J. Le Long, *Biblicum sacrum*, i. 454a–459b, Paris, 1723; H. E. Bindseil, *Concordantiarum . . . specimen . . .*, Halle, 1867; Vigouroux, *Dictionnaire de la bible*, ii. 892–905, Paris, 1899.

CONCORDATS AND DELIMITING BULLS.

The term concordat was used in a much broader sense in past centuries than to-day. Concordats are now usually understood to be treaties between the sovereign of a state and the pope of Rome, whereby the affairs of the Roman Catholic Church in the country concerned receive general regulation. Agreements between a state sovereign and the pope with respect to particular questions are not designated as concordats; for instance, the so-called *bullæ circumscriptionis*, by which the bounds of a diocese are determined. Nor is an understanding between a state sovereign and the bishops of a country so named, or an agreement between the State and a Protestant church. In former centuries the conclusion of such agreements was despatched in very diversified forms; in modern times it has been customary to comprehend the result of the transactions effected by plenipotentiaries of both sides in a document which is duly published as state law upon ratification by the State and as canon law when accepted by the Church.

1. Legal Theories of Concordats.

The legal nature of concordats is disputed; but essentially three theories obtain: (1) *The Privilege Theory:* If the State be the servant of the Church, it is obliged to fulfil the offices undertaken by it in the concordat; hence all concessions of Church to State are privileges. Every concordat therefore consists of two elements, which legally are not coordinate; viz., the acknowledgment of obligations on the part of the State which were already incumbent on the State, and the grant of an indult on the part of the Church. The former is permanent; the latter, in the nature of the case, revocable. The evolution of the modern State has removed the foundation of a practical realization of these elementary principles; but the privilege theory itself has not been surrendered on the Roman side, and Pius IX. in a brief of June 19, 1872, referred to the concordats as *pacta seu indulta*. (2) *The Treaty Theory:* Concordats are treaties equally binding on both sides, of the nature of international or public law. The fulfilment of these treaties inheres in the fact that each of the two parties promulgates a law conformably to the text of the treaty, and makes no alteration in the status thus determined without the consent of the other party; it being, however, understood that in the event of changed circumstances each party retains the right of withdrawal. This construction of concordats was prevalent at the beginning of the nineteenth century, but it is not satisfactory, since it assumes a coordination of Church and State that can not be reconciled with the State's pretention to ecclesiastical supremacy; and since there is wanting a common legal basis for Church and State, such as must obtain for the conclusion of legal treaties. There is consequently reason to prefer (3) *The Legal Theory:* The agreement expressed in the concordat is not legally obligatory, but is merely a preliminary step to the state law that is to be promulgated subsequently, for which the agreement collects and arranges the material. The substance of the concordat becomes civil and canon law only when the civil and canonical enactments to that effect have been decreed on the basis of the concordat. The State, however, is not bound by such law any more than by any other law by it enacted; that is to say, it can modify the same by process of new legislation the same as any other act of state legislation.

I. Early Concordats: The so-called Concordat of Worms, dated Sept. 23, 1122 (text and bibliography in Mirbt, *Quellen*, pp. 115–116; cf. also D. Schäfer, *Zur Beurteilung des Wormser Konkordats*, in the *Abhandlungen der Berliner Akademie*, 1905), and terminating the German investiture dispute (see INVESTITURE), is usually accounted the oldest concordat. The emperor Henry V. at this time renounced the investiture with ring and staff, as practised by him till then; conceded that in the churches of his realm the election and consecration of bishops should be free; promised the restoration of all church possessions; and agreed to give temporal aid to the Church whenever it was demanded. Pope Calixtus II., on his part, conceded to the emperor that the German elections should be held in his presence; and that the dignitary elect should receive his regalia from the emperor in feudal tenure, in Germany before, in other parts of the empire (Italy and Burgundy) after, his consecration.

Besides the Concordat of Worms, the following agreements lay claim to the name of concordats during the twelfth, thirteenth, and fourteenth centuries: (1) The treaty between Adrian IV. and King William of Sicily at Benevento in 1156. (2) The treaty between Celestine III. (1191–98) and King Tancred. (3) Between Innocent III. and Queen Constance of Sicily (1198). (4) Clement IV. and Charles I. of Anjou (1265), referring entirely to Sicily. (5) Gregory XI. and Queen Eleanor of Aragon (1372). (6) The understanding between the bishops of Portugal and King Dionysius, approved by Nicholas IV. (1288–92).

II. Concordats Resulting from the Council of Constance: The shattering of the ecclesiastical preponderance which prevailed in the prime of the Middle Ages created new conditions for the conclusion of concordats in the fifteenth century. The councils of Pisa (1409) and Constance (1414–18), contrary to the Curia's intention, divided themselves into "nations," each consisting of the bishops, abbots, and prelates of the national Church, the delegates from the princes, and the doctors in theology and canon law, and each constituting an independent college with defined spheres of activity officially recognized as representative of the ecclesiastical and civil interests of its respective people. There was thus a German, an English, a French, an Italian, and finally also a Spanish nation (cf. B. Hübler, *Die Konstanzer Reformation und die Konkordate von 1418*, Leipsic, 1867; see Constance, Council of).

The German nation did not succeed in pushing through at Constance its demand for the reformation of the Church before the election of a new pope, and, on Nov. 11, 1417, the council elected Cardinal Colonna as Pope Martin V. Little was thereby gained toward solving the council's major task; but in view of the impossibility of bringing about a general reform in the Church, it was still an essential advance that some expedient was found in the way of particular laws for the churches of the several countries, for removing their most serious distresses. The first impulse along these lines was furnished by the German nation by means of a memorial presented in the opening days of the year 1418 (cf. Hermann von der Hardt, *Magnum œcumenicum Constantiense concilium*, i. 999–1011, Frankfort and Leipsic, 1700). Like steps were also taken by the other nations. As they were unable to agree in regard to the pope's answer, Martin V. proffered separate treaties with each nation; and in this way concordats were concluded, on the basis of the papal proposals, with the German, English, French, Italian, and Spanish nations.

The German (Von der Hardt, ut sup., i. 1055 sqq.) and the French concordat (Von der Hardt, iv. 1566 sqq.), of nearly equivalent import, were published May 2, 1418. The English concordat (Von der Hardt, i. 1079 sqq.; Wilkens, *Concilia Magnæ Brittaniæ*, iii., London, 1737, 391 sqq.) is dated July 21, 1418. The Spanish concordat is dated May 13, 1418 (Tejada, *Coleccion completa de concordatos españoles*, Madrid, 1862, pp. 9 sqq.; B. Fromme, *Die spanische Nation und das Konstanzer Konzil*, Münster, 1896). Probably a separate Italian concordat was also concluded.

With reference to the contents of these concordats, chap. i. restricts the number of the cardinals, and defines their qualifications and the manner of their nomination; chap. ii. restricts the papal reservations; chap. iii. treats of the so-called annates or taxes; chap. iv. explains what grievances are to be carried to Rome and what not; chap. v. circumscribes the right *in commendam*; chap. vi. declares against simony; chap. vii. declares that excommunicated persons need not be avoided before the express publication of the ban; chap. viii. circumscribes the dispensations of the Curia; chap. ix. treats of the income of the Curia; chap. x. limits the bestowal of indulgences in Germany; chap. xi. makes the qualification for Germany and France that all this is merely a provisional status to be binding for five years only; the English agreement was permanent.

The concordat was accepted in France notwithstanding opposition on the part of the Parliament of Paris; the history of its experience in Spain and Italy still continues obscure; and the same is true of the English concordat. The German concordat took effect at once, but being of a provisional tenor, like the French concordat, it proved of no lasting significance, and served simply as foundation for subsequent transactions, for which an occasion was furnished by the Council of Basel.

III. Concordats after the Council of Basel.—1. Germany: The great contest between the Council of Basel (1431–47) and Pope Eugenius IV divided Western Christendom into two hostile camps for many years; but when Germany and France reached an understanding with Eugenius the victory of the papacy over "councilism" was decided. In Germany the electors, assembled after the death of Emperor Sigismund for the election of King Albert V., declared themselves against pope and council Mar. 18, 1438, and proclaimed their neutrality. On Mar. 24, 1439, an imperial diet at Mainz adopted the reform decrees of Basel, though with some alterations, and excluding the resolutions which centered upon the contest with Eugenius IV. (cf. C. Koch, *Sanctio pragmatica Germanorum illustrata*, Strasburg, 1789, pp. 105–171). King Albert, too, approved this "acceptation." In the same year the Council of Basel took the final step, deposing Eugenius IV. on July 25, 1439, and electing for his successor Felix V. Nov. 5. The development of the Church question in Germany was greatly affected by the sudden death of King Albert Oct. 27, 1439. He was succeeded on Feb. 2, 1440, by his cousin, Frederick III.; and in the course of a few years the latter sided entirely with Eugenius IV. Decisive understandings ensued in Sept., 1445, at Vienna, Frederick demanding and obtaining large concessions as to the declaration of obedience.

Eugenius IV. by this time felt himself strong enough to proceed against his most considerable opponents in Germany with aggressive measures. Through the bull *Ad comprimendam quorundam*, Jan. 29, 1446, he deposed the archbishops of Cologne and Treves, and forthwith replaced them with new appointments. But those whom he attacked found succor with their peers. The electors of Mainz, Cologne, Treves, and the Palatinate met at Frankfort, and on Mar. 21, 1446, they concluded a treaty for the common vindication of their rights; which on Apr. 23 was also subscribed by Saxony and Brandenburg. The electors addressed four demands to the pope and proffered him obedience on condition of their being granted; in the event of refusal, a rapprochement with the Council of Basel was contemplated. King Frederick III., when besought to intervene, sent his secretary, Æneas Sylvius Piccolomini, to Rome. But the negotiations carried on at Rome in July were without positive result, although an understanding was reached at last in connection with the Imperial Diet convened at Frankfort in September of the same year. Still, shortly before his death, Eugenius IV. complied with the desires of the German princes, in the so-called Princes' Concordats; and thus brought it about that they and with them the German Empire accorded their submission.

1. The Princes' Concordats, 1446.

There are four principal documents (Koch, ut sup., pp. 181 sqq.): (1) The brief *Ad ea ex debito*, to King Frederick, Feb. 5, 1447, promises to convoke a new general council in a German city within fifteen months, and to open the same within eighteen months. (2) The bull *Ad tranquillitatem*, Feb. 15, 1447, is concerned with the decrees of Basel accepted at Mainz, and also with the indemnity awarded to the Roman See. (3) In the bull *Ad ea quæ*, Feb. 5, 1447, Eugenius promises the reinstatement of the deposed archbishops of Mainz and Treves. (4) The bull *Inter cætera desideria*, Feb. 7, 1447, recognizes all the changes effected in the German Church during the so-called "neutrality" period.

Eugenius IV. believed he had made great concessions with all these grants. To guard against going too far he prepared a fifth bull, *Decet Romani pontificis prudentiam* (Raynaldus, *Annales ecclesiastici*, no. 7), Feb. 8, 1447, in which he explains that he had not intended to concede anything "that might be contrary to the doctrine of the Holy Fathers or that should tend to the prejudice of this Holy Apostolic See." After the promulgation of these bulls, the embassy formally accorded him obedience.

Eugenius IV. died Feb. 23, 1447. His successor, Nicholas V., forthwith confirmed his predecessor's constitutions. He recognized the assemblage of German princes convoked at Aschaffenburg on July 13, 1447, by King Frederick III. Moreover, the still recalcitrant electors of Cologne, Treves, and the Palatinate acknowledged obedience to Nicholas V.; so that there was now concluded a treaty between the emperor in the name of the German nation and the cardinal legates, Feb. 14, 1448, which is known as the Concordat of Aschaffenburg, though it might be more correctly designated as Concordat of Vienna (Mirbt, *Quellen*, pp. 165–169). Its import has reference only to the constitution *Ad tranquillitatem* of 1447, mentioned above, whose concessions are confirmed while the indemnity previously promised to the See of Rome is fulfilled by surrender of the Basel decrees as accepted at Mainz and provisionally ratified by Eugenius IV.; also by recurring in part almost literally to the second and third chapters of the Concordat of Constance in 1418. Through the text of the bull *Ad sacram Petri sedem*, Mar. 19, 1448, Nicholas V. promulgated this Vienna treaty as law of the Church. The concordat was opposed at the start by various territorial sovereigns, but as these were promptly won over by favorable rulings, it soon gained such recognition that the Princes' Concordats were quite forgotten.

2. The Concordat of Aschaffenburg or of Vienna, 1448.

3. France: King Charles VII. of France managed to secure for his country the reformatory decrees published at Basel in 1438 with the modifications demanded by French interests, by means of the so-called Pragmatic Sanction of Bourges, July 7, 1438 (*Ordonnances des rois de France de la troisième race*, vol. xiii., ed. Vilevault and Bréquigny, Paris, 1782, p. 267; Mirbt, *Quellen*, pp. 160–161; see PRAGMATIC SANCTION). The Curia never recognized it, and repeatedly pronounced it null and void (Eugenius IV., 1439; Pius II., 1459; Sixtus IV., 1471). Charles nevertheless remained firm, and appealed in particular against the declaration of 1459 to a general council in the year following. His successor, Louis XI. (1461–83), repealed the Pragmatic Sanction in 1461; but when he found that his political ends were not advanced to the degree desired by this means, he did not maintain his decision against the opposition of Parliament. Between this acceptance and non-acceptance of the Pragmatic Sanction there naturally ensued a vacillating practise. At the council convened by Pope Julius II. (1512) and continued as the Fifth Lateran Council by Leo X. the Sanction was again declared null and void (Mirbt, *Quellen*, p. 178). Hereupon, after a personal conference at Bologna, Dec. 11, 1515, and after prolonged negotiations extending into Aug., 1516, a concordat was concluded between King Francis I. and Pope Leo X. It was signed by Francis on Aug. 18, 1516, and was adopted by the Lateran Council on Dec. 19 of the same year. Notwithstanding opposition of the Parliament and the University of Paris, the king carried this concordat through as law of the land. It is mainly identical with the German concordats of 1447 and 1448, including the subsequent concessions to German territorial sovereigns (Nussi, pp. 20 sqq.).

For the concordat of Nicholas V. with Savoy, 1451, cf. Hefele, *Konziliengeschichte*, vii. 846 sqq.

For the agreements of Emperor Charles V. with Popes Adrian VI. and Clement VII., 1523 and 1529, see below, VII.

IV. The Seventeenth Century: As belonging to the seventeenth century, Nussi (pp. 39–40) sets forth a treaty between Ferdinand II. and Urban VIII., in 1630, wherein the pope cedes to the emperor as king of Bohemia all ecclesiastical rights that were alienated there in the bygone "heretical times," and any church estates that still rested in private hands, in return for the concession of a tax on salt to be paid to the Church.

For the Spanish concordat of 1640 see below, VII.

V. The Eighteenth Century: In the eighteenth century not a few concordats were concluded, consistently with the evolution of the absolute State and the alterations thence resulting with respect to the relations of Church and State. The contracts thus brought about fell to the several countries as follows:

Sardinia: The treaties between Pope Benedict XIII. and King Victor Amadeus, Mar. 24 and May 29, 1727 (Nussi, pp. 48 sqq.; 54 sqq.). The treaties between Pope Benedict XIV. and King Charles Emmanuel III., 1741 (Nussi, pp. 69 sqq.), 1742 (Nussi, pp. 98 sqq.), 1750 (Nussi, pp. 117 sqq.), and 1770 (Nussi, pp. 132 sqq.).

Sicily: Convention between Pope Benedict XIV. and King Charles III., 1741 (Nussi, pp. 72 sqq.; secret articles to this convention, pp. 377 sqq.).

Milan: Concordat between Pope Benedict XIV. and Empress Maria Theresa with reference to the duchy of Milan, 1757 (Nussi, pp. 128 sqq.); between Pope Pius VI. and Emperor Joseph II. as duke of Milan and Mantua, 1784 (Nussi, pp. 138 sqq.).

Poland: Convention between Cardinal Paulutius, in the name of the Apostolic See, and King Augustus and the Commonwealth of Poland, 1736, confirmed by Pope Clement XII. (Nussi, pp. 64 sqq.).

Portugal: Concordat between Pope Pius VI. and Queen Maria of Portugal, 1778 (Nussi, pp. 136 sqq.).

For Spanish concordats of the eighteenth century see below, VII.

VI. The Nineteenth Century.—1. France: First and foremost among the concordats of the nineteenth century—which is preeminently the time of concordats—stands the French concordat of 1801. It evokes peculiar interest both on account of its antecedent history and by reason of its influence upon the conclusion of concordats in Germany during the following decades. Like most of its successors, it was called forth by the perturbations which the French Revolution had occasioned in relation to the Church, and was intended, as far as possible, to surmount them. Napoleon had become First Consul on Dec. 25, 1799. Pius VII. was chosen pope on Mar. 14, 1800, was enthroned on Mar. 24, and on July 3 was able to enter Rome. On June 19 Napoleon opened negotiations with the pope through Cardinal Martiniana, bishop of Vercelli, with reference to restoring the status of the Church in France. After an ex-

1. The Concordat of 1801.

plicit answer from Pius VII. on July 10, the negotiations proceeded, and from Nov., 1800, they were conducted in Paris between the papal delegate, Monsignor Spina, and the Abbé Bernier. Napoleon demanded a reduction of the number of bishoprics from 158 to 60; resignation of all existent French bishops; right of episcopal nominations for the First Consul; remuneration of the clergy out of the state exchequer, and express pledge of obedience to the state government; relinquishment of claims to church property that had been sold; pardon for the priests who during the Revolution had married; and transfer of the police inspection of public worship to the Council of State. Spina in turn demanded that with the repeal of all adverse laws the Roman Catholic religion should be declared as that of the State, and the consuls be bound to that confession. The proceedings dragged along, and when Napoleon had despatched to Rome a draft elaborated by Spina and Bernier and accepted by Talleyrand, but found it subjected there to procrastinating explanations, he demanded, on May 13, 1801, either an immediate, unconditional acceptance or the rupture of diplomatic relations. Cacault, who shortly before had been sent to Rome for the resumption of diplomatic intercourse, was, in fact, recalled. At his suggestion, however, the papal secretary of state, Consalvi, went straightway in person with large and full powers to Paris, where he arrived on June 20; and after an arduous conference on July 15, 1801, with the imperial commissioners, Bernier and Joseph Bonaparte, he concluded the concordat, which then was ratified on both sides, though not without demurrings.

The concordat (Mirbt, *Quellen*, pp. 334–336) is drawn up in French: it contains seventeen articles, and is entitled, *Convention entre le gouvernement français et sa Sainteté Pie VII*. By way of preamble it declares: "The government of the French Republic recognises the fact that the Catholic, Apostolic, and Roman religion is the religion of the great majority of French citizens. His Holiness likewise recognises the fact that this same religion has derived, and still anticipates at this time, the best and greatest advantage from the establishment of the Catholic worship in France; and from the particular profession thereof on the part of the consuls of the Republic." Art. i. reads: "The Catholic, Apostolic, and Roman religion shall be freely exercised in France; its acts of worship shall be public, and in accord with such civil regulations as the Government shall judge necessary in behalf of public tranquillity." Art. ii. promises a reduction of the bishoprics. Art. iii. regulates the dismissal of former bishops, and provision is then made in arts. iv.–vi. for future episcopal appointments. The Church relinquishes legal claims to ecclesiastical property sold during the Revolution (art. xiii.), but the State guarantees a competent maintenance for the bishops and parochial clergy (art. xiv.), and allows foundations beneficial to the Church (art. xv.). The same rights and prerogatives are conceded to the First Consul as the former government had enjoyed in relation to the Apostolic See (art. xvi.). The first articles proved the most troublesome, because the Church was unwilling to yield the point that Roman Catholicism was a state religion in France; and the State hesitated to waive the point that the Church must comply with all and sundry state police provisions, instead of simply with those of a general scope.

The ratification on the pope's side ensued, as in the case of preceding concordats, by his embodying the entire Latin text in the bull *Ecclesia Christi*, dated Aug. 13, 1801. On Sept. 10 (*23 Fructidor an IX.*) the ratifications were interchanged at Paris; upon which the publication for France took place as follows. A state law was passed on Apr. 8, 1802 (*Loi relative à l'organisation du culte du 18 Germinal an X.*), by which the concordat (not the papal bull) was promulgated with statutory force, together with two separate appertaining "organic articles" (Mirbt, *Quellen*, pp. 336–338) relating to Catholic and Protestant worship. These "organic articles" aimed to institute an introductory status, but they start from premises about the State's influence in ecclesiastical affairs that were not acknowledged by the Church. At the same time the powers of the papal representative at Paris, Cardinal Caprara, were recognised, and on the following day he published the papal bull of ratification of Aug. 13; a brief of Nov. 29, 1801, which gave him authority to institute new bishoprics; the promised delimiting bull for France (*Qui Christi Dominis vices*); and an indult reducing the number of festivals, all of the same date. The government expressed a qualified acquiescence on Apr. 19.

The original documents relating to the concordat are found complete in J. Desenne, *Code général français contenant les lois et actes du gouvernement publiés depuis le 5 mai, 1789, jusqu'au 8 juillet, 1815*, Paris, 1818 sqq., vol. x., pp. 438–493. Material for the history of the concordat was gathered by J. E. M. Portalis in *Discours, rapports et travaux inédits sur le concordat de 1801, les Articles organiques etc.*, Paris, 1845, and has been lately augmented by Boulay de la Meurthe, *Documents sur la négociation du concordat et les autres rapports de la France avec le Saint-Siège en 1800 et 1801*, 5 vols., Paris, 1891–99. Consult also *Mémoires du Cardinal Consalvi etc., avec une introduction et des notes par J. Crétineau-Joly*, 2 vols., Paris, 1864; Comte d'Haussonville, *L'Église romaine et le premier Empire, 1800–1814*, 5 vols., Paris, 1868 sqq.; A. Theiner, *Histoire des deux concordats de la république française et de la république cisalpine etc.*, 2 vols., Paris, 1869; O. Mejer, *Zur Geschichte der römisch-deutschen Frage*, part i., Rostock, 1871, pp. 152–200; L. Séché, *Les Origines du concordat*, 2 vols., Paris, 1894; A. Debidour, *Histoire des rapports de l'Église et de l'État en France de 1789 à 1870*, Paris, 1898; Wirtz, *Das französische Konkordat von 1801*, in *AKR*, vol. lxxxv. 85 sqq., 209 sqq. For the concordat in Alsace-Lorraine cf. *AKR*, vol. lxxiv., p. 306; vol. xlv., p. 302.

This concordat regulated the relations between Church and State in France for more than a hundred years. Tension between France and the Papal See, due to various causes, occasioned the rupture of their diplomatic relations in 1904, and it was then proposed, after the fall of Minister Combes and under the ministry of Rouvier, to disestablish the Church. The repeal of the concordat was decreed by the legislative bodies. The law respecting the separation of State and Church came before the Chamber of Deputies on Mar. 21, 1905, and was adopted on July 3 by 341 votes to 233. The Senate began to deliberate the measure on Nov. 9, and on Dec. 6 approved the bill by 179 votes to 103. See FRANCE.

The concordat of 1801 and the new circumscription became operative within the boundaries of France as determined by the peace negotiations of Lunéville and Amiens; hence they applied also to Belgium, the left bank of the Rhine, and the parts which France had acquired of Switzerland and Savoy. For the Italian Republic, Pius VII. concluded a special concordat with Napoleon as its president, on Sept. 16, 1803; it was approved by the State Council at Milan, Sept. 27, and ratified by the pope on Oct. 29, by Napoleon on Nov. 2 of the same year. It is a recasting of the French concordat, whose arts. iv., vi., vii., x., xiii. it contains literally, while others are of a more favorable construction for the Church. It also contains rulings upon points that were not touched in the Concordat of 1801, but were first agitated on occasion of the strife which even then broke out on account of the "organic articles" (*Bullarium Romanum*, ed. Barberi, vol. xii., pp. 59 sqq.). It continued in force also for the Kingdom of Italy that was erected in the year 1805, superseding the Italian Republic.

2. French Dependencies.

The so-called Concordat of Fontainebleau, or second concordat of Napoleon, dated Jan. 25, 1813, which he negotiated and concluded personally with the pope; which he published, contrary to the pope's will, as imperial law on Feb. 13, and on Mar. 25 provided with the necessary executive provisions for France and the Kingdom of Italy (cf. Desenne, ut sup., pp. 581, 583; Debidour, ut sup., pp. 693 sqq.), was never recognised by Pius VII. as a concordat, but was always declared to be only a preliminary outline, and even as such was revoked by him on Mar. 24, 1813. It refers mainly to the official confirmation of the bishops. The treaty never actually went into effect, inasmuch as the Napoleonic rule ceased.

3. The Concordat of Fontainebleau, 1813.

The concordat of 1817 between Pope Pius VII. and King Louis XVIII. of France never attained to the force of law. An attempt was made after the Restoration to repeal the concordat of 1801 and the "organic articles," and negotiate a new concordat, more acceptable to the Curia; extensive proceedings to that end took place at Rome between the French envoy, Count Blacas d'Aulps, and the cardinal secretary of state, Consalvi. The result was the treaty of June 11, 1817, which restored the concordat of 1516 in place of the concordat of 1801 and the "organic articles," and promised to rehabilitate the episcopal sees abrogated by the bull of Nov. 29, 1801, and coordinate them with the existing dioceses by endowing both alike with landed estates and public revenues. Moreover, the king declared in art. x. of his agreement with the pope that he purposed to employ all the means at his command "to abate as soon as possible the disorders and obstructions which interfere with the weal of religion and the execution of the laws of the Church." As the Protestants likewise would lose their legal protection by repeal of the "organic articles," it is obvious that this step contemplated some redress for them also. The French government being too shrewd to mistake the dangers of this agreement, submitted the concordat to the legislative chambers in modified form, safeguarding the State's position; but as it encountered vehement opposition both inside and outside the chambers, it was withdrawn by the government and never again introduced (*Bullarium Romanum*, xv., pp. 365 sqq.; Debidour, ut sup., pp. 696 sqq.; Nussi, pp. 153 sqq.).

4. The Concordat of 1817.

2. Germany and Austria: The status set up by the Princes' Concordats and by the Concordat of Vienna was modified in Germany by the Reformation, the Religious Peace of Augsburg in 1555, and the Peace of Osnabrück in 1648, but not overturned. Not until the secularization of church property in the German Empire by the decree of the imperial deputation, Feb. 25, 1803 (Mirbt, *Quellen*, pp. 338–339), did the ancient Roman Catholic Church of Germany collapse. At the outset Pius VII. had hoped to be able to reconstruct the Roman Catholic Church in Germany by means of a concordat with the empire, and in this he had counted upon Napoleon's assistance. But when he saw that he was deceived therein, and when furthermore the Peace of Pressburg (Dec. 26, 1805), the conclusion of the Rhenish Confederation (July, 1806), and the abdication of the German imperial crown by Emperor Francis II. (Aug. 6, 1806) precluded the prospect of an alliance with the empire as such, he entered into negotiations through an extraordinary nuncio, Cardinal della Genga (subsequently Pope Leo XII.), with various individual German states. From July, 1806, till Sept., 1807, he negotiated fruitlessly with Bavaria (cf. H. von Sicherer, *Staat und Kirche in Bayern vom Regierungsantritt des Kurfürsten Max Josephs IV. bis zur Erklärung von Tegernsee, 1799–1821*, Munich, 1874, pp. 112–113), and he proceeded with Württemberg and Baden from Sept. 8, 1807, till the close of October. Owing to the intervention of Napoleon, however, all negotiations came to nothing; and the Roman Church in Germany still found itself in the same status in 1813 and 1815 as in 1803. At the time of the Congress of Vienna (Sept., 1814–June, 1815) only five incumbents of German episcopal sees were still alive; and four of these were past seventy years. The Curia proposed no new arrangement, but as far as possible the restoration of the old. It asked for restitution of the *status quo ante bellum*, and in Germany especially the relinquishment of ecclesiastical property and revenues that had been lost to the Church since 1801 and 1803; also the rehabilitation of the spiritual principalities, and of the Holy Roman Empire of the German Nation with its old legal temporal and ecclesiastical relations with the papacy. When the Curia failed to obtain its demands at the Congress it reserved all of its rights in the form of a solemn protest on the part of the papal legate, on July 14, 1815; and Pius VII. confirmed his action in an allocution of Sept. 4 of the same year. At the same time he expressed the hope of a salutary—in the Roman view—understanding with the German Confederation, an idea which was entertained at Rome till 1816.

1. Inconclusive Negotiations of the Napoleonic Era.

Meanwhile, as early as February of the year in question, the Curia made known its disposition to institute separate negotiations, at all events with Bavaria. The Bavarian government had cherished the thought of a separate concordat ever since the Peace of Lunéville and the decree of the imperial deputation in 1803. It had resumed diplomatic intercourse with the pope in the summer of 1815, for this purpose, and instructed its envoy Häffelin to further the business. The upshot was the conclusion of a concordat at the beginning of Oct., 1817, though it is dated June 5. King Maximilian ratified it on Oct. 24; the pope, in an allocution of Nov. 15, published the bull which confirmed the same.

2. Concordat with Bavaria, 1817.

The "convention" is worded in Latin, and its form is patterned after the French agreement (*Bullarium Romanum*, xiv., pp. 314 sqq.; Nussi, pp. 146 sqq.; Mirbt, *Quellen*, p. 344). A tacit reservation of the State found expression when the concordat was published as state law. This was accomplished first by an "Edict concerning the External Legal Relations of the Kingdom to Religion and Ecclesiastical Organisations" (the so-called "Religious Edict") of May 26, 1818. Herein the provisions of the concordat were treated not as applying to the kingdom, but merely to the Catholics of the kingdom, and that only with respect to the internal affairs of their communion. These "organic articles" could not have been a surprise to the Curia, but some appearance was made of regarding them in that light; and in connection with them there arose a dispute similar to the one in France, not even yet quite settled, between the Bavarian government and the papal court as to the actual signification of the concordat. Not until a declaration of the religious edict was assured by King Maximilian Joseph of Bavaria did Pius VII. publish the delimiting bull of Apr. 1, 1818, *Dei ac domini nostri Jesu Christi* (*Bullarium Romanum*, xv. 17 sqq.), on Sept. 8, 1821. The history of the Bavarian Concordat is thoroughly treated on the basis of the archives in Von Sicherer's *Staat und Kirche*, mentioned above; cf. also N. von Lerchenfeld, *Zur Geschichte des bayrischen Konkordats*, Nördlingen, 1882; H. Brück, *Geschichte der katholischen Kirche*, ii., Mainz, 1889, pp. 12 sqq.; M. von Seydel, *Bayrisches Staatsrecht*, vi., Freiburg, 1893.

With the Protestant states of Germany the Curia desired to conclude concordats in order to secure in them the rights of the Roman Church in a legal form that should bind the State as closely as possible. At the outset, too, the Protestant states were disposed to the conclusion of concordats.

3. Delimiting Bull for Prussia, 1821. Prussia, like Bavaria, had entertained the thought of an understanding with Rome since the summer of 1814—a matter that seemed indispensable, indeed, on account of the disorganization of the Prussian dioceses. With reference to the kind of stipulation to be concluded, great differences of opinion prevailed in Berlin. The final result of negotiations conducted by Niebuhr was the bull *De salute animarum*, of July 16, 1821, which, having been sanctioned according to its essential substance and incorporated into the legal code, was published in Prussia by a cabinet order, August 23, albeit with reservation of all sovereign rights.

For the bull consult the *Bullarium Romanum*, xv. 403 sqq.; Nussi, pp. 188 sqq.; Mirbt, *Quellen*, pp. 347–349; for the negotiations consult Mejer, ut sup., vol. ii., part 2, pp. 3–116, 265 sqq., 300, vol. iii., part 1, pp. 88–184; E. A. T. Laspeyres, *Geschichte und heutige Verfassung der katholischen Kirche Preussens*, part i., Halle, 1840; Brück, ut sup., ii. 38 sqq.; C. Mirbt, *Die preussische Gesandtschaft am Hofe des Papstes*, Leipsic, 1899, pp. 13 sqq.

Negotiations for a concordat with Hanover were opened in the summer of 1817, and continued with long intermissions until about the middle of 1820. The Hanoverian government conditioned its consent to the concordat upon the concession of four

4. Delimiting Bull for Hanover, 1824. provisos: absolute right of rejecting the clergy that might be appointed; oversight of church property; reservation of certain prerogatives; and the dependence of the legal status of new foundations upon government confirmation. The Curia just as definitely refused these concessions. In Mar., 1822, following the example of Prussia, the Hanoverian government announced through its envoy that, instead of a concordat, it likewise desired merely a delimiting bull. A draft of agreement was therefore prepared, which, being substantially accepted by the Hanoverian government, was approved by Pope Pius VII. a few days before his death, in a note dated Aug. 13, 1823. The ratification by Hanover took place early in 1824, and the bull *Impensa Romanorum pontificum* was issued by Pope Leo XII. on Mar. 26, 1824, authorizing the organization of the episcopal sees of Hildesheim and Osnabrück (Nussi, pp. 222 sqq.). Their constitution is similar to the Prussian, and their confirmation by King George IV. took effect under date of May 20, 1824 (cf. Mejer, ut sup., vol. ii., part 2, pp. 117–164, 241–264, vol. iii., part 1, pp. 62–87; Brück, ut sup., vol. ii., pp. 75 sqq.).

At the initiative of Württemberg, delegates of Württemberg, Baden, both the Hessian states, Nassau, the Saxon duchies, Mecklenburg-Schwerin, Oldenburg, Lübeck, and Bremen, assembled at Frankfort-on-the-Main, Mar. 24, 1818, to deliberate concerning the conclusion of a common concordat with Rome. Afterward Frankfort, Lippe, Waldeck, and both Hohenzollerns took part in the deliberations. It is true that the interest of all these states in the conference was not the same, and some of them shortly withdrew. The delegates finally agreed to formulate a

5. The States of the Ecclesiastical Province of the Upper Rhine. state law concerning the affairs of the Catholic Church in their districts in terms of a declaration and submit the same to the pope. The declaration was in shape by July, 1818, and at the same time there were outlined certain "Fundamental Provisions for an Organic Church Law of the State," resembling in the main the French "organic articles"—together with instructions for an embassy that was to carry the declaration to Rome. The states represented at Frankfort accepted these documents as the basis of transactions with the Curia by a formal agreement, Oct. 7, 1818. In Feb., 1819, Baron von Türckheim (Protestant) and Schmitz-Grollenburg (Catholic) went to Rome as envoys of the federated states. After long waiting for enlightenment in regard to the pope's real attitude, on Aug. 10, 1819, Consalvi issued the explicit note entitled "Exposition of the Views of His Holiness concerning the Declaration of the United Protestant Princes and States of the German Federation." In this note certain modifications of the declaration are proposed, which would have completely changed its tenor; and finally the proposition was made of merely a new delimitation of the bishoprics. The several governments voted, in Mar., 1821, to accept the delimitation, still expecting further negotiations in relation to its details, and they were surprised when the bull (*Provida sollersque*; Nussi, pp. 229 sqq.) actually appeared, dated Aug. 16, 1821, constituting the present ecclesiastical province of the Upper Rhine. The conference reassembled at Frankfort in Oct., 1821, and its acceptance of the bull was communicated to the Roman Court at the close of November. All parts of the declaration of 1818 which were not touched upon in the bull had been meanwhile embodied in the contemplated statute, and with the same had been made into a so-called "Church Pragmatic," which it was intended to publish in all the states at the same time with the bull. This evoked energetic opposition from the Roman See, but the federated governments refused to yield and added a new compact, Feb. 8, 1822, to that of Oct. 7, 1818. On June 13, 1823, the pope refused to substantiate propositions in regard to the episcopal appointments, he demanded the total retraction of the "Church Pragmatic," and then issued, on June 16, 1825, an ultimatum which gave occasion to the reopening of the Frankfort Conference (Jan., 1826). The net result of all the negotiations was that on Apr. 11, 1827, Leo XII. issued the bull *Ad dominici gregis custodiam*, which in its first four articles gave directions for the election of the bishops and chapters; but then in articles v. and vi., agreeably to the ultimatum and without regarding the rejoinder of the governments, prescribed that in every diocese there should be a seminary conformably to the decrees of Trent, and that the bishops and archbishops should enjoy free communication with the pope, and all the rights of jurisdiction which accrued to them according to the canon law as previously in force and consistently with the vital discipline of the Church. Upon the statutory confirmations and publications of both bulls, which took place at last after the signature, on Oct. 8, 1827, of an amendment to their state compact of 1818 and 1822 (in Nassau, Oct. 9, 1827; in Baden, Oct. 16; in Württemberg, Oct. 24; in Electoral Hesse, Aug. 31; in the Grand Duchy of Hesse, Oct. 16, 1829), the bull *Ad dominici*, with the omission, in part, of its last two articles, and with express insistence upon sovereignty rights of the State, etc., was incorporated into the states' legislative acts. But, besides this, there was issued in all these states, Jan. 30, 1830, a similarly worded regulation with respect to the protection of state sovereignty and supervisory rights over the Roman Catholic Church; the "Church Pragmatic" was literally repeated in all essential points, insomuch that Pius VIII., esteeming this edict contrary to agreement, protested against it in a brief of June 30, 1830, addressed to all the bishops of the Ecclesiastical Province of the Upper Rhine, rejected the regulation, and admonished the bishops to guard the rights of the Church.

The documents are in Münch, ut sup., ii. 309–417; Nussi, pp. 209 sqq., 239 sqq.; for the history consult Mejer, ut sup., vol. ii., part 2, pp. 165–240, vol. iii., part 1, pp. 7–61, 186–229; H. Brück, *Die oberrheinische Kirchenprovinz von ihrer Gründung bis zur Gegenwart*, Mainz, 1868; E. Friedberg, *Der Staat und die Bischofswahlen in Deutschland*, Leipsic, 1874, part i., pp. 125 sqq., part ii., pp. 114 sqq.; C. Mirbt, *Die katholisch-theologische Fakultät zu Marburg*, Marburg, 1905, pp. 15–44, 75–130.

The governments which had taken part in the Frankfort Conference and were not directly affected by the delimitation of the bull *Provida sollersque* attached themselves subsequently in part to the Prussian, in part to the Upper Rhenish diocesan circuits, save that Brunswick joined the circuit of Hanover (cf. Mejer, *Die Propaganda, ihre Provinzen und ihr Recht*, ii., Göttingen, 1853, pp. 500 sqq.).

6. Concordat with Austria, 1855.

In Austria the territorialism of Emperor Joseph II. was abandoned even at the time of the German-Austrian constitution of Apr. 25, 1848, and afterward in the constitution of Mar. 5, 1849, and in an imperial patent of the same date the social freedom of the Church was set forth in the formula then in vogue deriving from the Frankfort "Fundamental Rights," to the effect that the Church should "independently regulate and administer" its affairs. As early as 1848, all sorts of memorials from Austrian bishops relating to particular ecclesiastical demands had appeared, and in the following year they were summoned by the government to a convention at Vienna to formulate their demands. The detailed and extensive petitions which were there drawn up were approved by the pope on July 9 (cf. M. Brühl, *Acta ecclesiastica*, Mainz, 1853). The government answered with the decrees of Apr. 18 and 23, 1850, and the patent of Dec. 31, 1851, which, however, were to have only a temporary effect, pending the result of negotiations with Rome for a concordat. The negotiations were begun in Vienna in 1853, and were completed at Rome on Aug. 18, 1855. The concordat was published as law in the bull *Deus humanæ salutis auctor*, Nov. 3, 1855, and by the imperial patent of Nov. 5, 1855. See Austria.

The concordat begins with the assurance of the Bavarian concordat, namely, that the Roman Catholic religion in Austria shall have "all powers and prerogatives" which belong to it "according to divine dispensation and the canonical ordinances"; the restriction which was subjoined in Bavaria by the religious edict was not appended. In other respects also, the Church in Austria was established on a much more favorable basis. In the closing articles (34, 35), all and sundry state laws of Austria which are contrary to the concordat, or to the doctrine of the Church, or to its present practise as approved by the Holy See, are repealed; in articles 5 sqq., 10 sqq., the Church is charged with education, the surveillance of literature, the regulation of marriage; and, furthermore, it is expressly guaranteed all freedom of action with repeal of *placet* and the right of appeal. In fact, this concordat concedes to the Church the full sovereignty demanded by the Ultramontanes, together with the subordination of State to Church, in all essential relationships.

For the text of the concordat consult Nussi, pp. 310 sqq.; *AKR*, i., pp. iv. sqq., xiv., 93 sqq.; xviii. 449 sqq.; *Coll. Lacensis*, v. 1321 sqq.; secret articles in Mirbt, *Quellen*, pp. 363–365. Consult further: *AKR*, i. 180 sqq., 218 sqq., 365 sqq.; vi. 176 sqq., 190 sqq.; viii. 292 sqq. E. Friedberg, *Die Grenzen zwischen Staat und Kirche*, Tübingen, 1872, pp. 403 sqq.

7. Agreements with Hesse-Darmstadt, Württemberg, and Baden, 1856–59.

After the demands for "church freedom" had repeatedly been expressed in the so-called popular demands of 1848, though the Frankfort national assembly adhered to the practise of describing the churches as societies subordinated to the laws of the State, the German episcopate assembled at Würzburg in October of that year for common conference. The bishops here united in a plea to the state governments, which was afterward voiced in a series of memorials issued by all the separate sees, to the end that the governments should recognize the independence of the church corporation. By "independence" the bishops understood that in all its affairs which the Church interpreted as church business it should be subjected to no kind of restrictions or surveillance by the State. As no German government consented to the demands of these petitions, the leaders of the movement next pursued the contest in Baden, where a majority of Roman Catholic subjects happened to be governed by a Protestant line of princes. They gradually stirred up conditions which led the neighboring governments of Hesse-Darmstadt and Württemberg, and at last also that of Baden, to seek relief from the Church itself. By means of agreements in the nature of concordats, they recognized, much as Austria had done, the non-competency of the State in the domain of canonical legislation, so far as to request of the Curia the institution of the regulations they deemed necessary. On the other hand, they granted "church freedom." Such promises as those of the first article of the Bavarian and the Austrian concordats, could not, indeed, be adopted by Protestant governments, but at least they guaranteed to protect the full development of the episcopal jurisdiction according to canonical definition, without qualification for the Protestants and without express reservation of sovereignty rights over the Church. This was, however, distinctly assumed.

It is evident in not a few passages that they also followed the outlines of the Austrian concordat in drawing up the paper. The Hessian agreement of Aug. 23, 1854 (cf. A. Schmidt, *Kirchenrechtsquellen des Grossherzogtums Hessen*, Giessen, 1891, pp. 57 sqq.), did not satisfy the Curia, and was supplemented in 1856 by the desired amendments. The Württemberg agreement was concluded directly with the Curia on Apr. 8, 1857 (Nussi, pp. 321 sqq.; cf. Friedberg, *Grenzen*, ut sup., pp. 440–471; L. Golther, *Der Staat und die katholische Kirche im Königreich Württemberg*, Stuttgart, 1874; *AKR*, ii. 688 sqq.; iii. 444 sqq., 577 sqq.; iv. 307 sqq.; v. 202; vi. 398 sqq.). It was published by the pope in the bull *Cum in sublimi*, June 22; by King William I., Dec. 21, 1857, subject to the maintenance of state sovereignty rights, and with reservation of legislative approval for the points wherein the State's laws were affected. The Baden agreement was concluded with the same clauses, June 28, 1859, and published by the pope on Sept. 22 in the bull *Æterni patris vicaria* (Nussi, pp. 330 sqq.; cf. H. Maas, *Geschichte der katholischen Kirche im Grossherzogtum Baden*, Freiburg, 1891, pp. 229 sqq.). The agreement was published by the government on Dec. 5, 1859. In Baden, and then in Württemberg, the legislative bodies refused their approbation. Both governments thus found themselves obliged to announce to the Curia that they were not in a position to carry out their agreements, but must suffer them to lapse; whereupon, first in Baden, under several laws dated Oct. 9, 1860, then also in Württemberg, under laws of Dec. 31, 1861, Jan. 23 and 30, 1862, the relation of the Roman Catholic Church to the State was regulated in a one-sided way. The same thing subsequently took place in Hesse-Darmstadt.

8. Modification and Repeal of the Austrian Concordat, 1867–70.

Austria, too, had promptly learned that the concessions of the concordat could not be maintained, and consequently made efforts as early as 1860, and again in 1863, to have it modified, but in vain. Owing to the outcome of the Diet of Princes at Frankfort in 1863, and to the result of the war of 1866, Austria's plans in relation to Germany were frustrated, and the government applied itself to the reorganization of internal affairs. In the laws of Dec. 21, 1867, "Concerning the Common Rights of Citizens" (§ xv.) it declared that "every legally recognized church and religious association should independently regulate and administer its internal affairs"; but "every association is to be subordinated to the State's laws as a whole." Herein it diverged from the concordat, and there followed a marriage law, a law respecting schools, and a law touching interconfessional relations, all three dated May 25, 1868; there were several subsequent decrees of like nature (*AKR*, xix 459 sqq.). The pope forthwith protested against these laws through his Vienna nuncio, Falcinelli, and in an allocution of June 22, 1868, pronounced the entire array of Austrian constitutional laws as issued without the requisite competency, and "abhorrent" (*leges abominales*; Mirbt, *Quellen*, p. 371). After the Vatican Council the Austrian government formally retracted the concordat, on July 30, 1870 (*AKR*, xxiv. 284 sqq.), declaring in the accompanying despatch that the government had found itself constrained "to return to its perfect freedom of action, in order to be equipped against the eventual institution of the ecclesiastical power, such as it was to be construed by the terms of the decrees of the Vatican Council."

3. Italy: For the concordat of Sept. 16, 1803, between Napoleon and Pius VII., see above, VI., 1, § 3. Other concordats with Italian states in the nineteenth century were made as follows: (1) Between Pius VII. and King Victor Emmanuel I. of Sardinia in the bull *Beati Petrum apostolorum*, July 17, 1817 (*Bullarium Romanum*, xiv. 344 sqq.; Nussi, pp. 155 sqq.). (2) Between Gregory XVI. and King Charles Albert of Sardinia, Aug. 23, 1836, and Mar. 27, 1841 (Nussi, pp. 245 sqq., 266 sqq.). (3) Between Pius VII. and King Ferdinand I. of Naples for the kingdom of the two Sicilies, concluded Feb. 16, 1818, published by the bull *In supremo apostolicæ*, Mar. 5, and by law of Mar. 21, 1818 (*Bullarium Romanum*, xv. 7 sqq.; Nussi, pp. 178 sqq.). (4) Between Pius VII. and King Ferdinand II. of Naples, Apr. 16, 1834 (Nussi, pp. 254 sqq.). (5) Between Pius IX. and Leopold II., grand duke of Tuscany, Apr. 25, 1851 (Nussi, pp. 278 sqq.).

4. Other European States: For concordats with Spain in the nineteenth century see below, VII.

A concordat was concluded between Pedro V., king of Portugal, and Pius IX. in 1857 respecting Indian episcopal appointments (Nussi, pp. 318 sqq., 390–391). It was superseded under Leo XIII. by a concordat of June 23, 1886 (*AKR*, lviii. 3 sqq.).

Gregory XVI. made a convention with Czar Nicholas I. of Russia, Aug. 3, 1847, with reference to Catholics of the Latin rite (Nussi, pp. 273 sqq.; *AKR*, vi. 170 sqq.). It was not carried out, and the same is true of a later concordat, Dec. 23, 1882 (*AKR*, xlix. 323 sqq.; l. 352 sqq.; liii. 144).

A concordat was concluded with Montenegro, Oct. 18, 1886 (*AKR*, lviii. 26 sqq.).

Leo XII. made a concordat with William I., king of Belgium, June 18, 1827 (Nussi, pp. 232 sqq.).

There was an understanding of Mar. 26, 1828, between Leo XII. and the Swiss cantons of Bern, Lucerne, Soleure, and Zug concerning the foundation of the bishopric of Basel (Nussi, pp. 242 sqq. for the history; cf. F. Fleiner, *Staat und Bischofswahl im Bistum Basel*, Leipsic, 1897). The understanding reached between Gregory XVI. and the Council of the canton of Saint Gall with reference to the founding of that diocese is dated Nov. 7, 1845 (Nussi, pp. 269 sqq.; cf. C. Gareis and P. Zorn, *Staat und Kirche in der Schweiz*, 2 vols., Zurich, 1877–78).

5. Central America: The ecclesiastical affairs of the Central American republics were regulated after their emancipation from the Spanish dominion by concordats modeled after the Spanish concordat of 1851 (see below, VII.). These concordats are substantially the same in contents (cf. F. Sentis, *Die Konkordate des römischen Stuhles mit den Republiken Centralamerikas*, in *AKR*, xii. 225–234), and were concluded with Pius IX. as follows: with Costa Rica under President Mora, Oct. 7, 1852, confirmed by the pope May 15, 1853 (Nussi, pp. 297–303); with Guatemala under General Carrera, Oct. 7, 1852, confirmed Aug. 3, 1853 (Nussi, pp. 303–310); with Nicaragua, Nov. 2, 1861, confirmed May 25, 1862 (Nussi, pp. 361–367); with San Salvador, Apr. 22, 1862, confirmed June 1, 1863 (Nussi, pp. 367–372); with Honduras, Apr. 22, 1862 (Nussi, p. 349).

6. South America: Agreements were made between Pius IX. and the president of Venezuela, July 26, 1862 (Nussi, pp. 356 sqq.); between the same pope and the president of Ecuador, Sept. 26, 1862, repealed 1878 (Nussi, pp. 349 sqq.; Mirbt, *Quellen*, pp. 365–366; *AKR*, xl. 321); between Leo XIII. and Colombia, Dec. 31, 1887 (*AKR*, lxii., pp. 113–114).

A concordat was concluded between Pius IX. and the president of Haiti, Mar. 28, 1860 (Nussi, pp. 346 sqq.).

VII. Spanish Concordats: The compact of Pope Adrian VI. with Emperor Charles V., Sept. 6, 1523, accorded the latter a limited right of appointment to the archiepiscopal and episcopal churches of the realm; by terms of an agreement with Clement VII., Dec. 14, 1529, he was allowed a perfectly free hand. The *Concordia Facheneti*, of Oct. 8, 1640, named after the nuncio of that time at Madrid, Cesare Facheneti, archbishop of Damiate, endeavored to rectify grievances which King Philip IV. (1621–65) had set forth to the Curia in a memorial of Dec. 18, 1634, on the subject of ecclesiastical disorders; and especially concerning the nuncio's official conduct. When early in the eighteenth century, on account of the pope's attitude in the war of the Spanish Succession, things had come to a complete rupture between King Philip V. (1700–46) and Clement XI., the difficulties of bringing about a reconciliation proved extraordinarily serious. The concordat concluded on June 17, 1717, continued unfulfilled notwithstanding ratification on both sides; nor did the bull of Innocent XIII., *Apostolici ministerii*, dated Mar. 13, 1723, prove a satisfactory substitute, though this bull, being acknowledged by royal decree and statutory legislation, and renewed by Benedict XIII., is classed among the Spanish concordats. The complete restoration of harmony with Rome did not ensue prior to the concordat of Sept. 26, 1737, which all in all was very favorable to the See of Rome. In sharp contrast herewith stands the concordat concluded between Pope Benedict XIV. and King Ferdinand VI. of Spain, on Jan. 11, 1753 (Nussi, pp. 120 sqq.; P. A. Kirsch, *Das durch Papst Benedict XIV. im Jahre 1578 mit Spanien abgeschlossene Konkordat*, in *AKR*, lxxx. 313–322), whereby the pope was compelled, against an indemnity of 1,300,000 *scudi* (about 6,500,000 francs), to grant royal patronage *in toto*, and be satisfied with the fact that he was allowed the bestowal of fifty-two benefices. This concordat remained in force until the conflicts which broke out after the death of Ferdinand VII., Sept. 29, 1833. When with a view to newly ordering the affairs of the Church a compact had been concluded on Apr. 27, 1845, French statecraft brought it about that the royal ratification was withheld. The proceedings led to no positive result before 1851. The concordat of Mar. 16, of that year, between Pius IX. and Queen Isabella II. comprises forty-six articles (*Acta Pii IX.*, Rome, 1858, part i., 293–341; Nussi, pp. 281–297; Mirbt, *Quellen*, p. 361). The good understanding between the papacy and the Spanish kingdom was again disturbed not many years later, but an agreement was concluded at Rome, on Aug. 25, 1859, between Cardinal Antonelli and the Spanish envoy (*AKR*, vii. 391–399; Nussi, pp. 341–345), which assumes the operation of the concordat of 1851, and seeks to supplement it in the matter of the endowment of public worship and the clergy. After the Cortes had approved on Nov. 7, 1859, there followed on the part of the queen and the pope the ratification of the concordat, Nov. 7 and 24 respectively, and its publication as law of the State Apr. 4, 1860. Pope Pius X. concluded a concordat with King Alphonso XIII. concerning the religious orders, on June 19, 1904, which was legally confirmed by the Spanish Cortes June 23, 1904 (*AKR*, lxxxv. 319 sqq.).

The concordats with Spain are treated comprehensively by Hergenröther, *Spaniens Verhandlungen mit dem römischen Stuhle*, in *AKR*, x. 1–45, 185–214; xi. 252–263, 367–401; xii. 46–60, 385–430; xiii. 91–106, 393–444; xv. 170–215. There is an anonymous *Coleccion de los concordatos y demas convenios celebrados despues del Concilio Tridentino entre los reyes de España y la Santa Sede*, Madrid, 1848.

CARL MIRBT.

BIBLIOGRAPHY: References for particular concordats and special points have been given in the article. The work cited as "Nussi" is Vincentio Nussi, *Conventiones de rebus ecclesiasticis inter sanctam sedem et civilem potestatem variis formis initæ ex collectione Romana* (i.e., the *Bullarium Romanum*), Mainz, 1870; "Mirbt, *Quellen*" is Carl Mirbt, *Quellen zur Geschichte des Papsttums und des römischen Katholicismus*, Tübingen, 1901; the edition of the *Bullarium Romanum* cited is that of A. Barberi, 19 vols., Rome, 1835–57; *AKR*, vol. i., Innsbruck, 1857, vol. lxxxvii., Mainz, 1907. An additional collection of concordats is E. Münch, *Vollständige Sammlung aller älteren und neueren Konkordate, nebst einer Geschichte ihrer Entstehung und ihrer Schicksale*, 2 parts, Leipsic, 1830–31. For general presentations cf. T. Balvy, *Kirche und Staat in ihren Vereinbarungen auf dem Grunde des Kirchenrechts, Staatsrechts und Völkerrechts*, Regensburg, 1881; B. Huebler, *Zur Revision der Lehre von der rechtlichen Natur der Konkordate*, in *Zeitschrift für Kirchenrecht*, iii (1864), iv (1864). The subject is treated by: N. P. S. Wiseman, *Four Advent Lectures on Concordats*, London, 1855; R. J. Phillimore, *Commentaries on International Law*, 4 vols., ib. 1879–89. Also by J. L. von Mosheim, *Institutes of Eccl. Hist.*, ed. W. Stubbs, ii. 225, 331, 376, iii. 536, 545, ib. 1863. Consult also Reich, *Documents*, pp. 162–163, 240, 448–452; the Concordat of Worms is translated in Thatcher and McNeal, *Documents*, pp. 164–166.

CONCUBINAGE (Lat. *concubinatus*): A legal and durable union between two persons of opposite sex, differing from marriage in that it did not include the *affectio maritalis*. It resembled marriage *de facto*, but not *de jure*, as the woman was not the man's coequal companion for life. It could be entered into only with a freed woman or freeborn woman of the lowest class; whereas a *honesta femina* could become a concubine only by the process of express *testatio*, without which the union came under the head of *stuprum*. Not until the ninth century was concubinage prohibited in the Eastern Empire, by Emperor Leo VI. (cf. P. Meyer, *Der römische Koncubinat nach den Rechtsquellen und den Inschriften*, Leipsic, 1895). The Germanic peoples also admitted, collaterally with marriage, a valid union of distinguished men with free women of inferior estate, or even with bondwomen.

Down to the fifth century the state of concubinage was not contested on the side of the Church. Since that time, however, the Church has disallowed concubinage, having qualified marriage as the sole morally justified sexual union, although not forbidding concubinage altogether. Accordingly it persisted, especially in the Roman and the Germanic empires, and even the national council of Mainz in 851 merely repeated certain moderate restrictions of the fifth century. Though concubinage was interdicted in the case of certain of the clergy, ecclesiastical legislation down to the sixteenth century conveyed no threat of actual penalties against the practise on the part of laymen. In the Evangelical Church the moral opprobrium of concubinage has never been doubtful; so little, indeed, that it is liable to church discipline.

Concubinage is not recognized by the civil law, being rather treated as other extramarital sexual intercourse, and in particular as touching the claims of concubines on account of illicit pregnancy, and the rights of a concubine's children to support and inheritance against him who maintained her.

For concubinage among the Hebrews see FAMILY AND MARRIAGE RELATIONS, HEBREW.

E. SEHLING.

BIBLIOGRAPHY: G. E. Howard, *Hist. of Matrimonial Institutions*, 3 vols., Chicago, 1904; H. Klee, *Die Ehe, eine dogmatisch-archäologische Abhandlung*, Mainz, 1833; J. J. I. Döllinger, *Hippolytus and Callistus*, pp. 147 sqq., Edinburgh, 1876; H. C. Lea, *Sacerdotal Celibacy*, chap. xii., New York, 1907; Hefele, *Conciliengeschichte*, v. 380 et passim.

CONCURSUS DIVINUS: The divine activity in its relation to the agency of finite creatures and potencies, or in its relation to the development of the world in so far as this is conditioned by finite "efficient causes." This relation to cosmic evolution through "final causes" is termed "governance." Both *concursus* and "governance" accordingly involve the problem of the relation of the divine activity to the free will of man. In the Bible both concepts are represented.

Biblical and Scholastic Doctrines.

The earth brings forth verdure, and man and animals multiply (Gen. i. 11 sqq.), while "thine hands have made me and fashioned me altogether round about" (Job x. 8); so that, on the one hand, man acts from the impulses of his own heart, and, on the other, in God alone "we live, and move, and have our being" (Acts xvii. 28). The relation of the two theses involves not only dogmatics, but also philosophy. The chief hypotheses on the *concursus divinus* were developed by the schoolmen, and the view current in Roman Catholic and early Protestant dogmatics was best elaborated by Thomas Aquinas. He teaches (*Summa*, i., *quæstio* 105): "God works in every work," not only as the end of all and as prime mover and preserver of the forms and powers of all things, but also because "he directs the forms and powers of all things to act"; no creature can "proceed in action unless it is moved by God" (*quæstio* 109). This view was opposed by Durand of St. Pourçain (q.v.), who contended that God need not cooperate immediately in that which takes place through finite or intermediate causes, but only mediately; and a third opinion was advanced by Gabriel Biel (q.v.) that creatures themselves do not act, that God himself is the sole factor, though his operations are conditioned by the existence of creatures. The Thomistic conception is also expressed in the Roman catechism, and has become the prevailing view in the Roman Catholic Church.

Among the Reformers the conviction that only God's pure, free grace can save from the misery of sin was combined from the very beginning with the deepest sense of the universal dependence of the creatures on their creator, and on the most vital relation of their creator to them. This consciousness shows itself in the works of the old Lutheran dogmaticians.

Protestant Doctrine.

J. Gerhard (*Loci*, VII. vii.–viii.) did not advance to the stage of a general definition of the *concursus*, since he treated only of the relation of God to the evil acts of the creatures. After him sharply defined metaphysical utterances on this subject are found in A. Calovius (*Systema locorum theologicorum*, iii., *De providentia*, ii.), A. Quenstedt (*Theologia didactico-polemica*, xiii.), D. Hollaz (*Examen theologicum*, I. vi. 14, 16 sqq.), and others who followed Thomas in theory. Whereas Gerhard stated merely that God preserves unto his creatures the power of actual and free activity and assists them in their work, his successors argued that God influences the individual act and activity of the creature so that the act is the work both of God and of the creature, thus postulating a teaching midway between Durand and Biel. Unlike the doctrines of Thomas Aquinas, however, the divine act is regarded by these theologians as excluding an "initial motion" of the creature, and as merely cooperating with the creature. In the main, Lutheran dogmaticians agree with the theories of Roman Catholics. The specifically Protestant doctrine commences only with the question of the limitation of the human will, especially by original sin rather than by the cooperation of God. On account of this limitation an anticipatory as well as a cooperative activity on the part of God becomes necessary to raise man from his sin, and this divine agency is found in the activity of the Holy Spirit. Man being thus morally transformed, a "cooperation" of grace commences, which must be distinguished from the general cooperation of God with the natural agencies. In Reformed dogmatics the *concursus* is treated by some as a special part beside the "conservation" (the divine activity considered as a first cause) and governance; by others it is subsumed with the rest (cf. H. L. J. Heppe, *Dogmatik der evangelisch-reformirten Kirche*, Gotha, 1861, p. 190). Here the *concursus* is regarded not merely as simultaneous, but as anticipatory (J. H. Heidegger, *Medulla theologiæ Christianæ*, Zurich, 1697, loc. vii. 14), and it is also taught that God works according to the individuality of the creatures. It is likewise held both in the Protestant and the Roman Catholic doctrine that God, who in such orderly manner cooperates with the natural agencies, has nevertheless the power to stop their activity or to work without them, or, in other words, can do miracles. Thus God, by whose *concursus* the fire burns, can withdraw his *concursus* and the fire burns no more, as in the case of the three men in the fiery furnace.

The question has been treated by such moderns as A. D. G. Twesten, F. A Philippi, K. F. A. Kahnis, J. Müller, F. A. B. Nitzsch, and R. A. Lipsius. The problem belongs to philosophy, rather than to dogmatics. Divine control of events and things is inconceivable without the assumption that God works in them; his activity can not be referred to an initial point, as if he directed them then, but were now inactive, and it is equally impossible to declare his activity to be merely preservative in character, for in contradistinction to a truly effective activity it would then appear as something negative or not admitting of destruction. On the other hand, the ethico-religious consciousness itself concedes to the world a real existence, just as man is conscious of existing in it as a relatively independent creature, with a sphere and material for his work, and just as the word is perceived to be a true revelation of God and a practical proof of divine love. For these reasons it must always be acknowledged that finite events are produced by the will of a personal God, already above nature and the world, and working in such a way as to preserve the world and lead it to his purposes. The term *concursus* is awkward, as suggesting that one activity runs parallel with another. (J. Köstlin†.)

CONDER, CLAUDE REIGNIER: English soldier and archeologist; b. at Cheltenham (90 m. w.n.w. of London), Gloucestershire, Dec. 29, 1842. He studied at University College, London, but did not graduate, and was in command of the survey of Western Palestine in 1872–78 and 1881–82. He was in the army till 1906. He has written *Tent Work in Palestine* (2 vols., London, 1878); *Judas Maccabæus* (1879); *Handbook to the Bible* (in collaboration with F. R. Conder, 1879); *Memoirs of the Survey of Western Palestine* (4 vols., in collaboration with H. H. Kitchener, 1881–83); *Heth and Moab* (1883); *Primer of Bible Geography* (1884); *Altaic Hieroglyphs and Hittite Inscriptions* (1887); *The Survey of Eastern Palestine* (1889); *Palestine* (1889); *Tell Amarna Tablets* (1893); *The Bible and the East* (1896); *The Latin Kingdom of Jerusalem* (1897); *The Hittites and their Language* (1898); *The Hebrew Tragedy* (1900); *The First Bible* (1903); and *The Rise of Man* (1908).

CONDIGNITY AND CONGRUITY, or *meritum de condigno* and *meritum de congruo:* Terms used by the schoolmen after Thomas Aquinas in their attempts to reduce the doctrines of grace to one harmonious system. In a general way, *meritum* in the concrete signifies a supernatural work worthy of a recompense. If the work be such that the reward is due *ex justitia*, or rather in virtue of the divine promise, it is called *de condigno*, and chief among the conditions required for its existence is that the agent be in the state of grace. If, however, he be not yet justified, and perform under the influence of actual graces certain good works conducive to justification, such are reckoned as merit only in an imperfect sense, *meritum de congruo*. The Catholic doctrine of merit is based on those New Testament texts (e.g., II Tim. iv. 7; I Cor. ix. 24–25; Matt. v. 12, etc.) which represent eternal life as a reward, for though it is a gift of divine grace, God has willed to give it the character of a recompense. Protestants generally deny the existence of merit, but the controversy is not so much one of principle as of definition of terms.

CONDITIONALISM, CONDITIONAL IMMORTALITY. See ANNIHILATIONISM; and IMMORTALITY.

CONE, ORELLO: Universalist; b. at Lincklaen, N. Y., Nov. 16, 1835; d. at Canton, N. Y., June 23, 1905. He was educated at Cazenovia Seminary, Cazenovia, N. Y., and after teaching in the public schools for several years was an instructor in St. Paul's College, Palmyra, Mo. (1858–61). He was pastor of the Universalist Church at Little Falls, N. Y., 1863–65; professor of Biblical language and literature in St. Lawrence University, Canton, N. Y., 1865–80; president of Buchtel College, Akron, O., 1880–96; resided in Boston and Berlin 1896–98; professor in St. Lawrence University, 1899 till his death. He wrote *Gospel Criticism and Historical Christianity* (New York, 1891); *The Gospel and Its Earliest Interpretations* (1893); *Paul, the Man, the Missionary, and the Teacher* (1898); and *Rich and Poor in the New Testament* (1902). He also edited the *International Handbooks to the New Testament* to which he himself contributed *Epistles to the Hebrews, Colossians, Ephesians, Philemon, the Pastoral Epistles, James, Peter*, and *Jude* (1901).

CONFERENCE: A word of various meanings in religious usage. In the Roman Catholic Church it signifies (1) a homiletic address, aiming at instruction, in conversational manner. The so-called "higher conferences" are defined as "instructive addresses for educated hearers on religious or religio-social truths in freer form than a sermon," and less frequently given in a church. They were employed, especially by the clergy of Paris in the late eighteenth and early nineteenth centuries, to refute the alleged attacks of science on religion, and have been given elsewhere to meet local or passing conditions. (2) Conferences of the clergy appear in the ninth century because of the great size of the diocesan synods, which made it impossible for all the clergy to meet together. Accordingly district meetings were summoned by the archpriest, archdeacon, or dean, on the first of each month (hence called *Calendæ*, also *Collationes, Consistoria, Synodi*, etc.). The aim was general consultation and mutual edification. They considered cases of conscience and the like, and sometimes investigated crimes and announced the penalties. The last of such conferences recorded is said to have been held in London in 1237. In 1565 Cardinal Carlo Borromeo instituted clerical conferences and issued directions for their organization and guidance with a view to the better instruction of the clergy. The example was followed widely, but toward the end of the eighteenth century such conferences fell into disuse. Since then they have been revived in many places.

In the Lutheran Churches of Germany there are diocesan clerical conferences, at which the superintendents preside. See also CONFERENCE, FREE ECCLESIASTICAL-SOCIAL; and EISENACH CONFERENCE. For the Lutheran Synodical Conference in the United States see LUTHERANS. For the Conferences of the Methodist Episcopal Church see METHODISTS. The Wesleyans of England and Ireland have annual conferences attended by all the ministers. The Free-will Baptists and other minor bodies call their annual meeting by this term.

CONFERENCE, FREE ECCLESIASTICAL-SOCIAL: An organization in Germany which aims to popularize Christianity by bringing it to bear upon social problems. It was organized at Cassel Apr. 27–28, 1897, as an offshoot of the Evangelical-Social Congress (q.v.). A second general conference was held at Barmen the following November; and since then conferences have been convened annually, usually in April or May. The membership has grown from 100 in 1897 to 3,251 in 1906. There are seven standing committees for various phases of

Christian-social work, viz.: (1) confession, church law, and church policy; (2) popular evangelization; (3) social problems; (4) the press, art, and literature; (5) apologetics; (6) education; (7) the woman-question. The conference seeks particularly to overcome the enmity toward the Church common among the laboring classes, and to Christianize Social Democracy. Its purpose was outlined in resolutions adopted at the third general meeting held in Berlin Apr. 19–20, 1898, and its chief work has been to organize Evangelical unions among working people, both men and women. There are branches of the organization in most of the German states. Dr. Adolf Stöcker, court preacher in Berlin, is president. The official organs are: *Kirchlich-sociale Blätter* (Berlin, 1901 sqq.), a weekly, and *Hefte der freien kirchlich-socialen Konferenz* (Berlin, 1900 sqq.), in which are printed the papers read at the various conferences. (R. Mumm.)

Bibliography: The gist of the proceedings is contained in *Hefte der freien kirchlich-socialen Konferenz*, Berlin, 1890 sqq. Statistical material is contained in the current *Deutsch-evangelisches Jahrbuch*, Berlin; and in J. Schneider, *Kirchliches Jahrbuch*, Gütersloh, 1907.

CONFESSION OF FAITH. See Symbolics.

CONFESSION OF SINS.

Confession of sins is an acknowledgment of sin, which may be made by a Christian either to God alone, to a fellow Christian, or to one who holds an ecclesiastical office. Confession as an act prescribed or recommended by the Church is made in accordance with the free decision of the individual (voluntary private confession), in compliance with special rules of church training and discipline (confession of catechumens and penitents), and in conformity with general regulations binding on all (a prescribed confession, either of individuals or the congregation as a whole). The present article is confined to the last-named form; its end is to attain absolution.

1. Confession not General in the Early Church. The New Testament knows nothing of confession as a formal institution, Jas. v. 16 referring to the close association with the brethren, although the words of Jesus in Luke v. 20, vii. 48 may be compared to ecclesiastical absolution. Individual confession as a part of ecclesiastical discipline was, of course, customary in ancient times, and also served as a voluntary act of a distressed sinner. The confession of sin and proclamation of pardon were likewise customary in the service of the ancient Church. But that confession existed in the earliest time as an established ecclesiastical institution is not proved by such isolated instances as are occasionally met with.

The authorities desired and recommended confession, but the laity opposed it. It was thus first enforced upon the monks and clergy, and afterward upon the laity as well. The Irish Columban, abbot of Luxeuil, endeavored to introduce the confession which existed in his country both for clergy and laity into the Frankish Church. This could not be accomplished at once, but by degrees the people were moved through the exhortations of the priests to adopt it. The general mode of procedure was as follows: the priest humbled himself in prayer before God, asked the penitent concerning his faith, his readiness to forgive others, and his sins, and gave him absolution in the form of a wish or prayer.

2. Its Earliest Forms. Since the priest spoke with the penitents in the vernacular, the formularies were translated. Connected with absolution was the obligation of Penance (q.v.). But as the penitents could be treated neither arbitrarily nor uniformly as to penance, the duration of the period of penitence was fixed according to individual sins, while the payment of a certain sum of money instead of doing penance was allowed at an early period.

After the laity had become accustomed to make confession at certain times, to specify gross offenses, and to be questioned by the confessor, the Lateran Council of 1215 made regular confession an absolute law of the Church: "The faithful of both sexes, after arriving at years of discretion, shall confess at least once annually to their own priests, reverently receiving the sacrament of the Eucharist at least at Easter, and faithfully acknowledging in private all their sins." The form of absolution was now changed to the judicial: "I absolve thee." The penitent was assured of the secrecy of the priest, who was to be unfrocked and imprisoned for life in a monastery if he violated the seal of the confessional.

3. Made a Law of the Church, 1215. A second kind of confession, a general confession, gained ground in the Middle Ages. During the service a confession was read in the vernacular and the congregation received absolution in the precatory form. This general confession existed in Italy, France, and Germany (see General Confession).

As early as 1519 Luther wrote: "There is nothing in the Church which needs reform so much as confession and penance," and in addition to occasional expressions he spoke of this reform of the confessional system in special writings: *Kurze Unterweisung, wie man beichten soll*, 1519; *Von der Beichte*, 1521; *Sermon von der Beichte und dem Sakrament*, 1524; *Kurze Vermahnung zur Beichte*, 1529 (at the end of the Larger Catechism).

4. Attitude of Luther. Luther controverted the existing confessional system because it had become a source of pecuniary gain, because he disapproved the torture of the conscience in mentioning individual sins, and because the unworthy demeanor of the medieval friars who largely controlled the confessional system was offensive to him. He did not, however, reject confession itself, but, on the contrary, recognized no one as a Christian who withdrew from confession, though he sometimes takes it in the wider sense of confession of one's sins to God and prayer for mercy.

Luther also advocated confession to the brethren. The main thing with him was absolution. This might be received without ecclesiastical confession, and took place also in baptism and in the communion.

The Reformers wished, moreover, to avail themselves of the custom of the laity to go to confession at regular intervals, since they were thus enabled to gain a knowledge of their lives, examine their conversation, instruct them, and influence them. The old order that the laity should go to confession before the communion was maintained. The penitent went to church, either without special reason or a day or two before the celebration of the communion; the confessor arranged an examination in the catechism, which might, however, be omitted, if he had confidence in the penitent; the latter was asked to name a sin which especially troubled him, and was examined concerning some special sins.

5. Confession as Retained by Lutherans and Reformed.

If there was no impediment, he was absolved. Luther's formula of absolution was the collative: "I forgive thee," while the Brandenburg-Nuremberg ritual has the declarative formula: "I pronounce to thee." But the difference is not a matter of principle, because this same ritual has the parallel formulas: "God forgiveth thee" and "I absolve thee." Luther preferred the collative form because of its clearness. The power to forgive sins, he says, belongs alone to God, but he exercises it through the outward office of the forgiveness of sins. If absolution is to be right and effective, it must proceed from the command of Christ in John xx. 21–23 and read thus: "I absolve thee from thy sins in the name of Christ and by virtue of his command, so that it is not I, but he, who through my mouth forgives thee thy sin, and this thou must accept and firmly believe as if thou hadst heard it from the lips of Christ the Lord." Private or individual absolution was best in keeping with this concept of absolution. When, therefore, the Nuremberg congregation would not give up the public confession and general absolution, the Wittenbergers expressed their acceptance of private and individual confession in harmony with ancient custom, so long as both parties would exhort their people to private confession. In the first half of the Reformation-period the Lutherans of Württemberg had become content with a general exhortation and the offer to hear a private confession. Among the Reformed private confession was mostly dropped, but a service preparatory to the communion was retained, as well as the general confession of sin. Compare also the Book of Common Prayer with its general confession at the communion and its confession of sin in morning and evening prayer.

Among the Lutherans the carrying out of the private confession met with great difficulties. In large communions the clergy were obliged to perform it in an unsatisfactory manner, and the moral harm of these mechanical confessions was justly regarded as a ground of complaint. The collative or exhibitive formula of absolution roused opposition. Spener declared that the collative and declarative formulas were, on the whole, the same, and that he would not hesitate to use the absolute formula, where it was prescribed.

6. Opposition to Private Confession among Lutherans.

But the spirit of antagonism remained and has remained to this day. The confessional fees, moreover, debased the existing practise of the Lutherans. Although Luther had repudiated these fees, they remained, since many ministers could then not very well get along without them, especially as they were regarded as justified and not as extorted by compulsion. But they soon gave rise to scandal, and it was felt that both the dignity of the office and the proper cooperation of colleagues suffered by the system. In some congregations the fees were not customary. Here and there they were voluntarily changed into New Year's gifts, while some ministers declared that they would take no fees at all on account of the abuses of the custom.

Most of these abuses concerned the general confession just as much as the private confession, but popular disapproval was directed against the latter. The general confession existed as early as the sixteenth century among the Lutherans of Württemberg while in the electorate of Saxony it became general after 1657. In 1697 J. K. Schade convened his communicants in a general confession and absolved them as a whole.

7. Its Place Taken by a General Confession.

His colleagues disapproved of his procedure, which had also provoked dissatisfaction among the citizens, but the elector dispensed with private confession in 1698, appealing to many Lutheran churches in Sweden and Denmark, in Upper Germany, and to all the Lutheran churches in Holland and neighborhood, where neither a confessional nor private confession is to be found. The older national churches followed this example, except in Mecklenburg, where, according to Kliefoth, private confession and absolution have never been abolished. On the other hand, the rule was observed that each communicant had to confess before the communion and thus take part in the general confession. With private confession private absolution ceased; and though here and there the penitents are individually absolved by laying on of hands, it is only a special application of the general absolution. In place of hearing the individual the confessionary sermon was introduced. The privilege of making a private confession to the confessor was not abrogated by this arrangement, but was seldom claimed.

With the cessation of the private confession a very useful instrument was taken from special pastoral care, and a revival has taken place during the nineteenth century.

8. Private Confession Revived in the Nineteenth Century.

This is not intended as a mere restoration, however, for the same abuses which were felt in times past would again return in an increased degree. An ecclesiastical body which would make private confession an obligatory preliminary to communion would not only injure the celebration of the communion, but such a law would be unjustifiable. Private confession can be only voluntary, and the penitent must be convinced that the seal of the confessional remains secure. This was the duty of the confessor in former times, but even this obligation had its exceptions. Aside from the theoretical question whether the Protestant churches have or can have a seal of the confessional which must be kept absolutely, their relation to the government and to public weal must also be taken into consideration. This point, moreover, can scarcely be of practical importance, for things which would sometimes compel the confessor to ignore the seal of the confessional would seldom be confessed in a voluntary private confession.

9. Usage of Different Churches. Among the Moravians, after the communion has been announced, an examination of the families is arranged with the minister, and at the communion a penitential prayer with absolution is used, which the communicants answer with "Amen" and a song of praise. The Catholic Apostolic Church commences the Eucharist with confession and absolution; the Methodists, after the invitation to receive the communion has been made, have a general confession which closes with a prayer for forgiveness. The Anglican liturgy has a confession and a precative absolution at the communion, and contemplates private confession with judicial absolution in the visitation of the sick. The preparation for the communion among the Reformed is like confession among the Lutherans. The Greek churches, the Russian as well as that under the patriarch of Constantinpole, demand confession as an act of preparation for the communion. Whenever the communion of the laity takes place in the Roman Church, during or outside of the mass an assistant pronounces the *Confiteor* and the priest the *Misereatur* and *Indulgentiam*. W. CASPARI.

BIBLIOGRAPHY: H. C. Lea, *A Hist. of Auricular Confession*, 3 vols., Philadelphia, 1896; W. Elwin, *Confession and Absolution in the Bible*, ib. 1883; J. Ferret, *La Confession*, Paris, 1883; H. J. Schmitz, *Die Bussbücher und die Bussdisciplin der Kirche*, pp. 864, Mainz, 1883; C. P. Reichel, *History and Claims of the Confessional*, London, 1884; G. Pell, *Das Dogma von der Sünde und Erlösung*, Regensburg, 1886; C. H. Davis, *Apostolical and Ministerial Absolution*, London, 1887; L. Desanctis, *The Confessional*, ib. 1887; K. E. Schieler, *Die Verwaltung des Bussesakraments*, Paderborn, 1894, Eng. transl., *Theory and Practice of the Confessional*, New York, 1905; E. C. Achelis, *Lehrbuch der praktischen Theologie*, i. 389 sqq., Leipsic, 1898; T. W. Drury, *Confession and Absolution*, London, 1904; J. Reuter, *Der Beichtvater in der Verwaltung seines Amtes*, Regensburg, 1901; C. M. Roberts, *The Hist. of Confession until it developed into Auricular Confession*, London, 1901; *Fulham Palace Conference; Confession and Absolution*, ib. 1902; H. H. Henson, *Moral Discipline in the Christian Church*, ib. 1905; A. G. Mortimer, *Confession and Absolution*, New York, 1906.

CONFIRMATION.

Confirmation is a rite which in the Roman Catholic and Greek churches is considered a sacrament conveying strength for the Christian warfare and completing the gift of the Holy Ghost bestowed in baptism, and by which in the Anglican and Lutheran churches baptized persons are received into full communion. At an early period in the primitive Church baptism was accompanied with unction (Tertullian, *De baptismo*, vii.; Cyril, "Mystagogic Lectures," iii. 2-6), with which theologians associated communication of the Spirit. A second

1. In the Early Church. rite connected with baptism was the laying on of hands (Acts viii. 17, xix. 6). Unction and laying on of hands became later separate ceremonies, performed by the bishop; but since baptism remained associated with unction, there were two anointings, one at baptism and a second performed by the bishop. From the latter ceremony developed confirmation. According to medieval doctrine this took the place of the laying on of hands (Decrees of the Council of Florence, 1439). The historical development of the rite culminates in the bull *Exultate* of Eugenius IV. (1431-47); the material is an unguent of oil and balsam; the formula, "I seal thee with the sign of the cross and confirm thee with the oil of salvation in the name of the Father, Son, and Holy Ghost" [the form employed in the Greek Church is: "the seal of the gift of the Holy Spirit" (is imparted to thee)]; the ordinary minister is the bishop; the effect is the giving of the Holy Ghost with strength boldly to confess Christ. The *alapa*, i.e., the practise of giving the candidate a blow on the cheek is not mentioned in this bull, though already customary (William Durand, *Rationale divinorum officiorum*, vi. 84).

In the Middle Ages opposition to confirmation had been aroused by Wyclif and the Bohemians, and the latter replaced it by a rite which is to be regarded as the prototype of Evangelical confirmation (W. Caspari, *Konfirmation*, Leipsic, 1890, pp. 168-171). The Reformers also decisively pronounced against it. The fact that infant baptism was retained; the consequent Anabaptist objections that

2. Medieval and Later Developments. in this way, contrary to the baptismal command of the Lord, baptism became anterior to teaching; the ignorance of the congregations in the main articles of Christianity; the fear that on this account the Eucharist might be received by the unworthy; and, above all, solicitude for the flock imposed on the Reformers the duty of promoting Christian instruction through catechizing. Admission to communion was made contingent upon an examination in the chief truths of the Christian religion. As early as 1534 Butzer (in *Ad monasterienses*) taught that baptized children after antecedent Christian instruction might make public profession, and that the ancient usage from which confirmation had arisen might be renewed, namely, that the bishops should lay hands on the baptized and thereby "literally" impart to them the Holy Ghost. The section "Confirmatio" of the Wittenberg *Reformation* of 1545 (*CR*, v. 579) expressed itself in similar terms.

Meanwhile in certain districts in Hesse and Strasburg a rite had been introduced, instituted by Butzer, who was acquainted with the Moravian laying on of hands (the *Kirchenordnung* of Cassel, 1539). The same liturgical manual contains the formula still in use: "Receive the Holy Ghost, safeguard and shelter against all malice, strength and help toward all good, from the gracious hand of God the Father."

3. Practise of the Reformers. But this rite gained ground in only a few districts of the Lutheran jurisdiction, since during the transitional negotiations this modified *confirmatio* fell under suspicion of being an unjustified concession to the Church of Rome, and was on that account rejected by the opposers of the Interim. Hence for a long time the rite was not instituted in some of the Lutheran districts, though it readily gained admission with the Calvinists. Among the Lutherans it was customary to observe only the so-called private confirmation; the catechumen, in his later boyhood, was brought by his sponsors before the qualified minister, by him examined, and thereupon, if found competent, admitted to communion. The general adoption of public confirmation was expedited by the desire to enhance the effect of catechetical instruction by a ceremonial conclusion; by the endeavor to counteract the inroads of the Roman propaganda, and by the effort to implant religion in the child's receptive nature. Since, however, the introduction of public confirmation coincided in part with a time when the existing liturgies were no longer binding, the rite was frequently shaped according to the preference of individual ministers.

Now that confirmation has become in the Lutheran churches a generally solemnized ecclesiastical rite, and also a church rite which even the outer world notices with deference to family ties and friendship, theologians have naturally attempted to account for its nature and meaning. It has been

4. Modern Lutheran Teachings. regarded as supplementary to baptism (Schleiermacher), or as an act of reception into the confessional church (Wegschneider, Bretschneider); as a testimonial of majority in the case of those baptized as children (Nitzsch, Dorner); as reception into the congregation of adults; as a means of constituting a more limited congregation upon which devolves the direction of the life of the Church, but which also alone enjoys the privilege of communion (J. C. C. von Hofmann); as a consummation of the state of a baptized catechumen and as a renewal of the baptismal bond on the subjective side; as a lay ordination and reception into the communing congregation (Zezschwitz); as a charismal communication of the Spirit through the laying on of hands (Vilmar). To all these explanations there are weighty objections. The theory of modern times, that confirmation in so far as it bestows the right to communion should be deferred, is subject to the objection that a potential participation in the Eucharist is compatible with such penitent and faithful reception as may be presupposed in the case of baptized and instructed children. So it is best to bestow the right to commune upon baptized and instructed children, by solemn confirmation or laying on of hands before the assembled congregation.

W. Caspari.

In the Anglican Church there has been a widespread popular tendency to look upon the rite in the light of a formal admission to communion, the rubric in the Prayer-book reading: "And there shall none be admitted to the Holy Communion until

5. The Anglican and Roman Catholic Churches. such time as he be confirmed, or be ready and desirous to be confirmed." But the latter alternative shows that no essential connection exists between the two; and, as a matter of fact, there is no practical difference between the teaching of at least the High-church party and that of the Roman Catholic Church on this subject. The definition in Article XXV., which includes confirmation as among "those five commonly called sacraments," but "not to be counted for sacraments of the Gospel," seems to place it with the things which "have grown of the corrupt following of the Apostles"—as regards, that is, the medieval form. Omitting the chrism, and emphasizing the laying on of hands, the Anglican Church goes back to the New Testament record; but it is contended by Roman Catholic theologians that the contact with the bishop's hand in the act of unction, to say nothing of the blow upon the cheek (intended to symbolize the conferring of the character of a soldier of Christ, who must be ready to "endure hardness"), is quite sufficient to cover this point.

Bibliography: Bingham, *Origines*, book xii.; E. Martène, *De antiquis ecclesiæ ritibus*, vol. i., chap. i., Antwerp, 1736; J. F. Bachmann, *Die Confirmation der Catechumenen*, 3 vols., Berlin, 1852; F. X. Kraus, *Realencyklopädie*, article "Salbung," Freiburg, 1882–86; H. Hurter, *Theologiæ dogmaticæ compendium*, vol. iii., Innsbruck, 1893; *KL*, iv. 1506–14; *DCA*, i. 424–425.

CONFITEOR: The name applied, from its first word in Latin, to the formula used for public confession in the Roman Catholic missal and breviary, and also usually employed to begin a private confession. It consists of an acknowledgment of sin primarily to God, and then also to the Virgin Mary and other saints and to the priest or congregation present, as all injured in some degree by the sins acknowledged (I Cor. xii. 26); and of a request addressed to the same persons to pray God for the sinner. The oldest sacramentaries and *Ordines Romani* do not contain this formula; the first trace of it appears with Egbert, archbishop of York (735), and Chrodegang, bishop of Metz (d. 743), as an introduction to sacramental confession. Thereafter it appears in various forms and uses, until the revised missal of Pius V. finally introduced uniformity.

CONFLICT OF DUTIES: A term which usually covers a larger ground than that strictly and

Origin. logically falling under it. It actually means the coincidence of ethical demands which exclude each other and thus excite a conflict in the person whose actions they claim. Under the influence of classical antiquity, especially of Cicero, the doctrine of virtue, combined with the doctrine of duties, became the fundamental basis of ethics, and the conflict of duties became a favorite theme. Where ethics was developed essentially in the form of a doctrine of duties the question became inevitable how various demands could exist side by side and what should be done if they should clash with each other. Since Cicero gave the word *officium* the signification of a universal ethical conception, there originated in actual practise the possibility of a collision between the universal idea of moral obligation and the individual concrete action. This difficulty finds its illustration in the ethics of Kant and Schleiermacher. With Kant, the conception of duty loses its concrete content by changing itself into the law of free will, obedience to the consciousness of duty which is not bound by any moral law. It is evident that no conflict of duties can here be spoken of, "since duty and obligation are conceptions which express the objective practical necessity of a certain action, and two rules that oppose each other can not present themselves at the same time." According to Schleiermacher, "man's highest good is the totality of all actions in conformity with duty. If these were in conflict, some parts of the highest good of man would be in conflict, which is impossible. Thus there can be no conflict between duties." Kant and Schleiermacher were followed by ethical teachers who did not share their presuppositions—Reinhard, Baumgarten-Crusius, Daub, Marheineke, Rothe, Schwarz, Heppe, Luthardt, and others.

Three Kinds of Conflict.

Conflicts of duties may be arranged under three heads. There may be (1) a conflict between duty and personal inclination. In this case, strictly speaking, there is no conflict of duties; but still there are cases in which sinful habits take on the form of an objective claim of duty, as in the conception of honor prevalent among Germans and other peoples. A Christian officer of the army may wish to discard dueling in conformity with the law and his own conviction; but when he has to choose between participation in a duel and relinquishment of his calling, there originates a real conflict of duties. Moreover, inclination and duty are often hard to distinguish; since the choice of a calling should correspond closely to one's gifts, there may originate a conflict between the inclination to such choice and the duty toward the family. Also many matrimonial unions create not only conflicts, but real collisions. Or, (2) concrete duty may conflict with the general moral obligation. An officer of the State, in executing his official duty, may be compelled to commit actions the injustice of which he recognizes, and to omit others which according to his moral conviction are just. A judge may be compelled by the laws in force to acquit in cases where clear insight and moral consciousness condemn, and to condemn where reason and morality acquit. There are also cases in which the concrete duties of one's official calling or to his family claim his whole attention and activity in such a way that faith in the practise of love toward one's neighbor is considerably impaired. Again (3) a conflict of duties exists when concrete duty is opposed to concrete duty. Thus duty toward the State and duty toward the family may conflict; also duty toward the Church and duty toward the State; duty toward the Church and duty toward the family. Even specific duties of one sphere may conflict with each other; duty toward children and duty toward wife or husband, duty toward one's calling and duty of obedience to the authorities. Only one whose vision has been obscured by abstract theories can think that such conflicts are only apparent and imaginary, or due to defective moral development. On the contrary, moral character intensifies them.

Biblical Illustrations.

The cases of Abraham (Gen. xxii.), Jephthah (Judg. xi. 34–40), David (II Sam. xxiv. 12–14), and others present conflicts of duties in the Old Testament; in the New Testament there are conflicts in Matt. viii. 22, xvii. 24 sqq. In conflict between faithfulness to confession and obedience to the secular authorities (Matt. x. 17 sqq.; John xvi. 2) the Lord exhorted to a strength which, even in martyrdom, would maintain the freedom of religion (Acts iv. 19, v. 29); but he foresaw that not all would find this strength (cf. Luke xiv. 18 sqq.). Paul also felt the conflict between his duty to attack Judaism and the love for his people (Rom. ix. 1 sqq.).

Solution.

According to the old casuistry, there ought to be a solution of every conflict. The most important and correct rule that has been laid down is that the duty of right precedes the duty of love. Apart from such rules, the solution is often expected from the perfect development of Christian character. This view might be correct if conflicts originated inwardly; but their peculiarity consists in the pressure of external demands upon the moral consciousness, and thus they may be rather intensified by the development of Christian character (Matt. x. 34). There is, however, a deep-rooted conviction in the consciousness of redemption possessed by God's children that such conflicts can not disturb the peace and joy of the state of grace (John xiv. 27, xv. 11, xvii. 13) since the attainment of the highest good is independent of our actions. When a Christian father of a family, for instance, finds himself forced to neglect the duty of educating his children, on account of his duty to support his family, there is after all no solution of the conflict in the inevitable choice of the latter duty before the former; the conflict rather becomes continuous. In many cases self-renunciation must take the place of an actual solution. Conflicts of duty may be looked upon not only from the personal, but also from the social point of view. Public reforms and progress often make their way through conflicts of duty. Where consciences sleep there are no conflicts; but where men with living conscience take hold of duties and earnestly desire their fulfilment there will grow from the conflicts of duties energetic efforts for their redress. In all conflicts the believing Christian ought to remember not only the words of Luke xvii. 10, but also of I John iii. 19–21. See CASUISTRY; CONSCIENCE; DUTY; and ETHICS.

(L. LEMME.)

BIBLIOGRAPHY: J. E. Erdmann, *Ueber Kollision der Pflichten*, Berlin, 1853; G. Schulze, *Ueber den Widerstreit der Pflichten*, Halle, 1878; H. L. Martensen, *Christian Ethics*, § 139, 5 vols., Edinburgh, 1865–82; F. H. R. Frank, *System der christlichen Sittlichkeit*, i., § 22, pp. 7 sqq., Erlangen, 1884; and in general treatises on ethics and casuistry.

CONFRATERNITIES, RELIGIOUS.

Origin and Development (§ 1).
The Modern System (§ 2).
In the Nineteenth Century (§ 3).

By this term are now usually understood organizations of men and women in the Roman Catholic Church which are formed under ecclesiastical sanction, often with a definite rule of life, for the purpose of devotion to some special good work, doctrine, or saint, or merely of obtaining a special grace.

1. Origin and Development. They seem to have derived their initial impulse (under a form which has no historical continuity with the present) from England, where, it appears, there were as early as the beginning of the eighth century associations for mutual intercession among the members of one monastic community, or of two or more together, sometimes including outsiders. St. Boniface introduced this custom on the Continent. A variant of it appears in the undertaking of the bishops and abbots at national and provincial synods to unite their chapters and monasteries for this purpose; the first documentary evidence of this is from the Synod of Attigny in 762, though the custom is doubtless earlier. It was not long before the laity sought to have a share in the spiritual advantages of these systematic intercessions, those of the monks being especially valued. The reception of laymen into these confraternities was the return for notable gifts or services. The names of members were inscribed in what was often called the "book of life" (see LIBER VITÆ), which took in a manner the place of the ancient diptychs as lists of the living or dead Christians for whom the Holy Sacrifice was offered. The system spread throughout the whole Western Church, and seems to have attained its greatest strength under the influence of the Cistercian order. As the number of members of a confraternity increased into the thousands, the advantages of special prayer for the individual (whether in life or after death) decreased in proportion; and the old confraternities, though in some cases they maintained their existence, gradually lost their importance for the religious life.

The modern brotherhood system dates from the period of the rise of the cities and their industries—

2. The Modern System. the trade gilds, though serving an economic purpose, were usually under the patronage of some saint—and of the almost simultaneous development of the mendicant orders. Bonaventura is said to have founded (1267) the Confraternity of the Gonfalonieri in Paris, for the purpose of ransoming Christians held in captivity among the Mohammedans. Others attribute it to St. Dominic; but the establishment of the Confraternity of the Rosary is wrongly ascribed to the latter, and the most that can be said with certainty is that the first real development of the more modern confraternities took place under the influence of the mendicant orders. Their special aim was the union of people living in the world for some definite spiritual purpose not already of universal obligation. It is possible that the Carmelites were the first to crystallize this general tendency, by forming those who wished to unite with them in devotion to the Virgin Mary and to receive the scapular supposed to have been revealed in a vision to St. Simon Stock (at Cambridge, 1251) into the Confraternity of the Scapular of our Lady of Mount Carmel. Tradition names the Servites as the next to follow this pattern, with their Confraternity of the Seven Sorrows of Mary. Similar confraternities attached to numbers of houses of mendicants were soon striving, under the leadership of the friars, to attain greater holiness, and were attracted by the expectation of many graces in accordance with the papal indulgences. How widely they had extended by the second half of the fourteenth century is shown by Wyclif's sharp attacks on them; he scourges the hypocrisy, the self-seeking, the commercial spirit of expecting a *quid pro quo* from heaven, which had already crept into them. They had their real popular development in the fifteenth century, when nearly every mendicant house had its special association, with a special altar in the church, before which the members assembled at least once a month, often once a week. In return for their prayers and alms, they were entitled to rich indulgences and to a share in the prayers and good works of the friars; in case of death masses were said for them, and the brotherhood followed them to the grave, sometimes paying the expenses of the funeral. The particular feasts of the confraternity were celebrated with much pomp, and as an additional attraction a social meal was held, which in places led to great disorders before the close of the century. The services of the saints were now for the first time specialized, as patrons in various kinds of danger or necessity; and nothing helped so much to make a new saint popular as the foundation of a brotherhood in his honor. The entrance fee—to say nothing of other payments—ranged from one to twenty florins in Germany for example, or at the present value of money say from four to eighty dollars; from which it may be seen both how highly the people valued these religious privileges and what vast sums must have passed through the hands of the directors. Luther sternly rebuked their abuses, and pointed men to the real confraternity of Christ's Church in their place; and in a short time they disappeared from all places which were conquered by the Reformation, except a few which were recast in a Protestant shape or served secular purposes. Even in the Roman Catholic countries their influence decayed. The Jesuits recognizing the service they could render to the Counterreformation, infused fresh life into them. The confusion of the seventeenth century was unfavorable to the growth of brotherhoods, though the great League of the Sacred Heart arose toward the end of it, and in the rationalizing eighteenth they seem to have had but a precarious existence. Still, Vienna had in the year 1779 no less than 116 confraternities, with property valued at nearly 700,000 florins. In the early part of the nineteenth century, partly through the recovered power of the Jesuits, they took a fresh start, and ultimately reached a height never before attained. They have learned some things from Protestant polemics; whereas in the Middle Ages the chief duty of the members was to pay dues, and the devotional exercises were almost incidental, now little or no money contributions are required, the essence of membership consisting in pious works, exercises of devotion, and fidelity to the pope.

3. In the Nineteenth Century.

The associations which are strictly called confraternities (as distinguished from "pious unions") must be established by competent ecclesiastical authority, and attached to a definite church. What are called arch-confraternities are sometimes established by the pope, in cases where the aim is very important or corresponds to a universal need of the Church; these have power to affiliate to themselves other confraternities of like aim and name, imparting to them the privileges already granted to the arch-confraternity. These are frequently limited to a definite country; as a rule, only the Roman arch-confraternities have the power of unlimited aggregation, though there are exceptions, such as that of the Immaculate Heart of Mary in Paris. The tendency of the period has given the greatest extension to those which are dedicated to the Virgin Mary, especially the Marian sodalities. The first was founded at the Collegio Romano by the scholastic John Leon of Liége in 1563, and confirmed as an arch-confraternity by Gregory XIII. in 1584. It was originally intended for young students, and the Jesuits found it a powerful auxiliary to their work in educational institutions. In 1586 Sixtus V. extended its operation to all the faithful of the male sex; it was not the Jesuits' wish to include women, as their idea was to form a body of active public workers; but from the middle of the eighteenth century branches for women and girls have been affiliated. According to their own description, the Jesuits aim through these societies at promoting Christian perfection, according to each member's state of life, and so ultimately reforming each class, and thus the world. Since the conversion of heretics has always been one of the works principally encouraged, it is easy to see what importance these societies assumed in the Counterreformation, especially in Austria and Bavaria. Each "congregation" has a priest, normally a Jesuit, as "moderator." A president, to be approved by the moderator, is chosen by the members. A number of other officers assist him, thus enabling as many as possible to be specially interested in the work. The applicant for membership must pass through a period of probation, under strict supervision, after which he is received with impressive ceremonies. He takes a solemn obligation of special devotion to the Virgin, makes the Tridentine profession of faith, including an obligation to maintain and spread it among all those who are in any way under his charge, and receives a blessed medal as a badge of membership and a protection against harm; this may be taken from him in case of misconduct, so that a system of discipline and of supervision comes into existence. The regulations prescribe the frequency of attendance at mass, of communion, and of meetings, besides the making each year of the spiritual exercises of St. Ignatius, and a number of devotional practises; in return for which an abundance of plenary and partial indulgences is at the disposal of members. This system has been described at length because it has served in general as a model for the modern confraternities.

Next in antiquity and in importance come the tertiaries (q.v.) of the Franciscan order, who, although they have the form of a confraternity, in one sense are reckoned as members of the order. Nowadays the most approved and undoubtedly the most wide-spread of these organizations is the League of the Sacred Heart or Apostleship of Prayer (see SACRED HEART OF JESUS, DEVOTION TO), which has a membership of many millions, as has also the cognate arch-confraternity of the Immaculate Heart of Mary for the Conversion of Sinners, founded in Paris, 1856. Among the obligations of members of the latter is "the offering of all one's good works, in union with the sacred heart of Mary, for the conversion of sinners," and assisting at the special masses said for that intention. Of the numerous others that have arisen in late years may be mentioned the following: the arch-confraternity of the Assumption, for the aid of the souls in purgatory; the Brotherhood of St. Michael, founded at Vienna, 1860, and the Leonine Society, both devoted to the defense of the pope, and the latter especially of the temporal power; the arch-confraternity of St. Joseph, founded 1860, confirmed 1862; the arch-confraternity of St. Peter's Chains, whose members wear a small representation of the alleged original chains of St. Peter, as preserved in Rome, in token of their loyalty to the (captive) pope; and the Confraternity of "Our Lady of Compassion," established by Leo XIII. in 1897 for the conversion of England to the Catholic faith. Besides those which are strictly to be called confraternities, there are a large number of pious unions, which differ from them principally in being more free and elastic. Among them may be mentioned the association founded in 1862 by Julie von Massow, and a similar one dating from 1868, with the title *Ut omnes unum* ("that they all may be one," John xvii. 21)—both having for their purpose the promotion of the reunion of Christendom, and both connected with the arch-confraternity of Our Lady of Sorrows (founded 1450), in which, since the Reformation, prayer for reunion has been a regular practise. Their members use the white "reunion rosary," for whose daily recitation Leo XIII. offered large indulgences in 1888.

(T. KOLDE.)

Organizations called "brotherhoods" have been formed in the Protestant churches which, while having some resemblance to the confraternities of the Roman Catholic Church, necessarily differ in form and in purpose. There may be named here the interdenominational Brotherhood of Andrew and Philip (see ANDREW AND PHILIP, BROTHERHOOD OF), the Brotherhood of St. Andrew (see PROTESTANT EPISCOPAL CHURCH), and the Brotherhood of St. Paul (see METHODISTS).

BIBLIOGRAPHY: F. Falk, *Die Confraternitäten des Mittelalters*, in *Der Katholik*, xlviii. 1 (1868), 548 sqq.; T. Kolde, *Die kirchlichen Bruderschaften . . . im modernen Katholicismus*, Erlangen, 1895; Bouvier, *Der Ablass, die Bruderschaften und das Jubiläum*, Regensburg, 1859; M. V. Sattler, *Geschichte der marianischen Kongregationen in*

Bayern, Munich, 1864; L. Delplace, *Histoire des congrégations de la S. Vierge*, Lille, 1884; P. Löffler, in *Stimmen aus Maria Laach*, xxvii (1884), 230 sqq., 343 sqq.; A. Ebner, *Die klösterlichen Gebetsvereinigungen bis zum Ausgange des karolingischen Zeitalters*, Regensburg, 1890; F. Beringer, *Die Ablässe, ihr Wesen und Gebrauch*, pp. 996 sqq., Paderborn, 1895.

CONFUCIUS, con-fū'shi-us.

The name of this Chinese sage is the Latinized form of *Kung fu-tsze*, i.e., the "Master Kung"; he was born in the district of Tsow, in the feudal kingdom of Lu, now the southern part of Shantung, in the year 551 B.C.; d. in Lu 478 B.C. His father was governor of the district at the time—a man honored by his country, who died at the age of seventy-three, when his son was three years old. His mother carefully cherished his love of learning, but information concerning his early training is scanty and legendary. His grave demeanor and precocious mind early attracted attention, and he was led to study carefully the ancient laws and records. At nineteen he married. The following year he became a keeper of granaries and overseer of public fields, and the reforms he instituted gained him the favor of his sovereign. Induced by the disregard for law among his countrymen to examine more closely the ancient writings, and satisfied of the ability of their teachings to check existing evils, he began to gather pupils. Although only twenty-two, his reputation attracted many young men to his house; and their numbers increased as the value of his instructions was recognized. The death of his mother when he was twenty-four afforded him opportunity to offer a tribute to her memory and to revive an old custom of retiring from office in order to mourn three years. His example has been followed to the present day. With the exception of a visit to the court of the Duke of Lu, he devoted the next ten years to further study and instruction of his disciples, all the while rising in influence as a public teacher and learned man, qualified to rule and advise in affairs of the state. This course of life he continued till he was thirty-four years old, when his wish to enter public service was gratified. One of the chief ministers of Lu on his death-bed (517 B.C.) advised his son to join the school of Confucius to learn the nature of ceremonial observances, in order better to perform his official duties. He and a near relative did so; and they gave new *éclat* to the master, who was, at their representation, sent by Duke Chao to the imperial court at Loh-yang to study the rites then in use, so as to introduce them into Lu. He went as a private man, to see and learn, and returned home the same year.

1. Early Life.

Soon after, Duke Chao was obliged to fly to the adjoining state of Tsi to save his life, and Confucius followed as a loyal subject. Not approving his position there, the sage returned home. He was now known as a great teacher. Lu was distracted by civil strife, from which he kept aloof during the next fifteen years. In the year 500 Duke Chao's brother, Ting, came into power in Lu, and the rival factions were put down. Confucius when fifty years old was appointed magistrate of the town of Chung-tu. The influence of his virtue and the wisdom of his administration wrought a speedy revolution in the condition of the place. The next year he was raised to be minister of crime, in which position he introduced many reforms to simplify and enforce the administration of justice. These reforms excited the envy of neighboring lords, whose efforts finally succeeded in inducing the ruler of Lu to remove the sage from office (496 B.C.). During the next thirteen years he wandered from state to state, at one time honored, at another in danger of his life, but always surrounded by a band of faithful disciples. When sixty-six years old he returned to Lu, and employed his remaining years in completing his literary works. His wife and only son, Kung Li, had died before him; but he was honored and mourned by many attached followers. His tomb at Kiuh-fau in Shantung is surrounded by an extensive collection of temples, halls, and courts, and has been well described by Rev. A. Williamson in his *Journeys in North China*, i., chap. xiii. His descendants still live in that region, and the head of the family is known as the Sacred Duke Kung. Though discouraged and neglected at the end of his career, Confucius, through his literary works, was destined to compel such homage from his fellow men as few others have had. In every city of China, down to those of the third order, there is a temple to him, and in every college and school he is venerated and adored.

2. Later Life and Posthumous Honors.

The ideal of Confucius, to the attainment of which all his efforts and teachings were directed, was a condition of happy tranquillity throughout the empire. He considered that this could be accomplished by maintaining the sacredness of the five obligations of human society; viz., those between sovereign and minister, father and son, husband and wife, elder and younger brother, and between friends, all persons faithfully performing the reciprocal duties arising from each relationship. He claimed an almost unlimited authority for the sovereign over the minister, father over the son, husband over the wife, elder brother over younger; and enjoined kind and upright dealings among friends, thus inculcating as his leading tenets subordination to superiors, and virtuous conduct. In harmony with the practical character of his system, he laid special stress upon the care and education of the young, which he regarded as the foundation of the welfare of the state. His teachings in regard to political and social morality are based essentially upon the same grounds. His idea of government was a paternal despotism. But on the other hand, ascribing great importance to the power of example, he insisted upon personal rectitude and good government as the pledges and arguments for a ruler's maintenance in power. The general tendency of the philosophy of Confucius is good; and, compared with that of Greece and Rome, it takes

3. His Ideals and Teaching.

precedence by the purity of its teachings and the attention paid to the rules governing the common intercourse of life, but is inferior to them in profundity. Throughout his teaching Confucius seldom referred to the great problems of human condition and destiny. To his practical mind the consideration of theology and metaphysics seemed uncertain; and be evaded, if he did not rebuke, his disciples when they pried into things beyond their depth. "To give one's self earnestly," said he, "to the duties due to men, and, while respecting spiritual beings, to keep aloof from them, may be called wisdom." This is his teaching in regard to the ancient creed of China. While he enjoined respect for its worship and religious observances, enforcing command by example, he crushed out every spiritual tendency by discountenancing speculation upon higher things.

4. His Influence.

For twenty-three centuries Confucius has held sway over the minds of nearly a third of the human race. The source of this influence may be ascribed to the use of the Four Books and the Five Classics as text-books (see CHINA, I., 1, § 1). In adopting them as the text-books at the national examinations, the rulers of China took the best moral guides their literature afforded, and trained their rising youth in the best principles of government they possessed. Not only does every scholar learn at the lap of Confucius, but civil offices are reached only after going through the competitive examinations in those nine classics. His doctrines are thus deeply impressed upon the Chinese mind. But, however great his influence has been in the past, it is destined to wane in the near future. His system is not capable of being expanded proportionately with the progress of the nation, for it lacks the high sanctions and the vital force of Christianity.

S. WELLS WILLIAMS†.

The attitude of Confucius to the Golden Rule is often discussed. The facts are these: He was asked what one word would serve as a rule of practise for all of life, and replied with the word *shu*, which Williams translates "reciprocity," and added: "What you do not want done to yourself do not to others" (*Analects*, xv. 23). Again some one asked: "What say you of the principle that injury should be recompensed with kindness?" The Master said: "With what then will you recompense kindness? Recompense injury with justice, and kindness with kindness" (*Analects*, xiv. 36). Thus it appears that though Confucius specifically rejected the doctrine later embodied by Christ in the teaching "love your enemies," that doctrine was discussed in China 500 years before its utterance by Christ in Palestine—a most interesting fact. See CHINA, I., 1.

G. W. G.

BIBLIOGRAPHY: J. Legge, *Chinese Classics*, i. 56–129, London, 1861 (contains all that is trustworthy); A. Loomis, *Confucius and the Chinese Classics*, San Francisco, 1867; J. H. Plath, *Confucius und seine Schüler: Leben und Lehren*, 4 parts, Munich, 1869–74; A. H. Smith, *Chinese Characteristics*, New York, 1900 (exhibits the profound influence of the sage on Chinese life). Consult also the books mentioned under CHINA.

CONGREGATION: [A word variously employed in religious and ecclesiastical usage. In the English Old Testament it represents several Hebrew words, especially *mo'edh*, *'edhah*, and *kahal*. The first (from *ya'adh*, "to appoint") means an appointed meeting, then the place or time of such meeting; it occurs especially in the phrase *ohel mo'edh*, rendered "tabernacle of the congregation" in the A. V., but better "tent of meeting" in the R. V. The second (from the same root) denotes the theocratic assembly of Israel, thought of as meeting by appointment with Yahweh. *Kahal* (from *kahal*, "to assemble") denotes any assembly, and the gathering of Israel in particular. The commonest Septuagint renderings of these words were *synagōgē* and *ekklēsia*, and these passed into the New Testament (see CHURCH, THE CHRISTIAN; cf. Hebrew dictionaries and dictionaries of New Testament Greek under the words named and the Bible dictionaries, articles "Assembly" and "Congregation").

Various Usages.

In Roman Catholic usage congregation denotes: (1) One of the standing committees of cardinals charged with some particular branch of ecclesiastical administration (see CURIA). (2) An association of men or women, usually of modern origin, living under a quasimonastic rule, but not strictly included among the monastic orders and not bound by the solemn and irrevocable vows of the latter; e.g., the Christian Brothers, English Ladies, Redemptorists, and many others (see the separate articles). (3) A congregation may also be an association of houses within a certain order, united in some special manner, as the congregations of Cluny and St. Maur (qq.v.). (4) At the Council of Constance (1414–18) the name "congregation" was given to the separate sessions of the different nations (see CONSTANCE, COUNCIL OF), and since then has designated meetings in which only a portion of the members take part—practically committees appointed to prepare and facilitate the business of the council, like the committees of modern legislative bodies. In modern Protestant usage "congregation" means an assembly for religious purposes, in more restricted sense a local church or the lay members of a local church as distinguished from the minister and authorities, sometimes where a distinction is made between professed "members" and mere attendants, the latter as distinguished from the former. The condensation of the article *Gemeinde, kirchliche*, in the Hauck-Herzog *RE* follows.]

The ecclesiastical congregation (Germ. *kirchliche Gemeinde*; Lat. *ecclesia*, *congregatio fidelium*) in the widest sense is the association (*Gemeinschaft*) of all faithful Christians; in a narrower sense, the members of a particular Church—confessional, national, provincial, etc.—or of a local church. In the following article the word is understood in the last-named sense.

After the development of the conception of the mass as a sacrifice, of the priesthood as a necessary medium of salvation, and of the consequent essential difference between clergy and laity which made the latter merely the passive object of clerical activity, there remained for the layman no independent share in the life of the congregation. In accordance with the fundamental principles of the pre-Reformation ecclesiastical system, as developed from the time of Gregory VII., the pope, as vicar of Christ, is pastor of the world; he appoints bishops as his representatives, one for each geographical district (diocese); every bishop appoints priests as his representatives, one for every subdistrict (parish; see CHURCH GOVERNMENT, § 1; CURE OF SOULS). The Christian population of such a parochial district, ecclesiastically united because placed under the care of a pastor and regularly dependent on him alone for its spiritual needs, forms the parochial congregation. The latter is naturally interested in having the funds of the local church, from which the expenses of the pastor and his helpers as well as of the religious services are defrayed, administered faithfully and properly. This interest was recognized in pre-Reformation canon law by allowing the so-called "church-fathers" and "patrons" (*patrini*), who were chosen from the members of the parish, to share in the administration; but they can scarcely be called representatives of the congregation, as they were generally chosen by the clergy. Only in consequence of privileges and old customs did a few churches here and there have any degree of independence, e.g., the right to choose their own pastor. As a rule, the congregation was merely a "flock united to the shepherd," and its position is expressed in the *Corpus juris canonici*, when it says: "We have decreed that laymen should not presume to transact ecclesiastical affairs" (2, X., *de judiciis* [ii. 1]); "we forbid any layman to be allowed to dispute concerning the Catholic faith" (2, § 1, *de hæreticis*, and VI. [v. 2]); "laymen must obey, not exercise authority" (12, X., *de rebus ecclesiasticis non aliendis* [iii. 13]).

The Pre-Reformation Idea.

The Churches of the Reformation, both Lutheran and Reformed, placed the congregations on a different basis. Rejecting the mediatory position of the priesthood and its consequences, and emphasizing the responsibility of the individual, they make it the religious duty of the layman to see that word and sacraments are rightly administered; accordingly, they teach that the congregations have a divine commission to turn away from false doctrine and to provide for a right ministry in case the ecclesiastical authorities do not do so. The Lutheran Church asserts the right of members of the congregation to representation and a voice in synods and church courts, so far as they are qualified to serve in such capacities, and of admonishing or lodging complaint against preachers offensive in doctrine or conduct. It allows the congregation at least the right of veto in the choice of pastor and a share in the administration of the local funds. The congregation must be consulted by the authorities before constitutional changes can be made, and the right to a share in church discipline, so far as allowed by Scripture, is granted. The Reformers themselves and the Rostock theologians, Johan Quistorp and Theophilus Grossgebauer in the seventeenth century, recognized the need of church committees and boards of elders to make these congregational rights effective. But in the evolution of the German national Church boards of elders had no proper place and therefore, like the congregational rights themselves, did not flourish. The modern development, however, has everywhere asserted the principle of self-government in individual Lutheran congregations, though in varying degree in different churches (see CHURCH GOVERNMENT, §§ 3–8).

The Lutheran Churches.

The Reformed Churches gave the congregations a more important development. That of Zwingli, to be sure, followed essentially the same principles as the Lutherans, and certain modifications resulted only from the fact that it grew on republican soil and the Swiss churches already enjoyed privileges in the choice of a pastor. Calvin, however, taught separation of Church and State and independent church government as divinely instituted. According to his view there must be a board (*consistoire*, session) at the head of each church, consisting of two kinds of elders, ruling and teaching. The care of the poor is entrusted to deacons. These ideas came to full realization in France, and extended thence to the Spanish Netherlands, and to Germany when Reformed congregations settled there to escape persecution. [See CHURCH GOVERNMENT, §§ 2–3; BAPTISTS, I., 3, § 1; and CONGREGATIONALISTS, IV. These and other denominations, including many of the minor ones, have embodied in their church polity the principle of democracy more fully than the parties mentioned in the text.] E. SEHLING.

The Reformed Churches.

BIBLIOGRAPHY: For the Biblical conception consult: G. F. Moore, *Commentary on Judges*, on Judges xx. 1, New York, 1895; W. M. Ramsay, in *Expositor*, 5th ser., iii. 137 sqq.; Schürer, *Geschichte*, ii. 427 sqq., Eng. transl., II., ii. 59 sqq. For the early Christian congregation consult: F. J. A. Hort, *Christian Ecclesia*, London, 1897. For Lutheran and Reformed Churches: A. L. Richter, *Geschichte der evangelischen Kirchenverfassung*, Leipsic, 1851; O. Mejer, *Grundlagen des lutherischen Kirchenregiments*, Rostock, 1864; idem, *Kirchenrecht*, pp. 156 sqq., Göttingen, 1869; R. Sohm, *Kirchenrecht*, i. 460 sqq., Leipsic, 1892.

CONGREGATIONAL METHODISTS: See METHODISTS, IV., 9.

CONGREGATIONAL UNION LECTURES: A lectureship under the auspices of the Congregational Union of Great Britain. It was established in 1831, and the first series was delivered in 1833 by Ralph Wardlaw on Christian ethics (published in London, 1833). The aim is "to illustrate the evidence . . . of the great doctrines of Revelation, to exhibit the . . . principles of philology in their application to such doctrines, to prove the accordance . . . of genuine philosophy with . . . Scripture, to trace to their sources the . . . corruptions which have existed in the Christian Church, and to point out the methods of refutation and counteraction." The lectureship is not endowed, the funds coming from the sales of volumes of lectures already delivered; consequently the lectures are given at irregular intervals. The last series was delivered in 1897 by John Brown on *Apostolical Succession in the Light of History and of Fact* (London, 1898). A full list of lectures and their subjects is given in L. H. Jordan, *Comparative Religion*, pp. 564–565, New York, 1905.

CONGREGATIONALISTS.

Congregationalism is a form of ecclesiastical polity rather than of doctrinal belief. Its distinctive features are two: (1) the absolute independence of each local church; (2) the privilege and duty of cooperative fellowship among the churches. It is believed that the apostolic churches were Congregational and remained such until after the middle of the second century.

I. History.—1. The English Congregationalists: Modern Congregationalism can be traced back to the third quarter of the sixteenth century. Some assert that a small church in London, in 1570, of which Richard Fytz was pastor, was Congregational, but this claim is doubtful. The earliest demonstrable Congregational church of that era was formed by Robert Browne (q.v.) at Norwich, apparently in 1580. The Anglican Church was characterised by worldliness and even corruption, and it retained many Roman Catholic practises. These defects its more enlightened and devout adherents deplored but failed to correct. Consequently, many of its members—especially those who had fled to the Continent in the time of Mary, and had become acquainted there with the principles and leaders of the Reformation—had learned to favor Presbyterianism and sought to introduce it at home after their return. They were Puritans. But the proposed reform seemed to some insufficient. It waited for the civil rulers to inaugurate and direct it. It indorsed the old theory of a State Church, including every citizen of whatever character. To Browne it did not appear radical enough. He sought for immediate reform and the purity of the Church. About 1578 he was called to a parish in Cambridge. But in his view the church, not the bishop, should have invited him, and, although he served six months, he refused to be regularly inducted into office. Then he went to Norwich, and, conferring with Robert Harrison (q.v.), gathered an independent church.

1. Robert Browne.

He declared that all true Christians should withdraw from the Anglican Church, as it then was, and form new churches including only sincerely religious persons; that any company of such believers, united by a public covenant with each other and with God, is a true and, so far as concerns organization, a perfect church; that ecclesiastical authority rests only in Christ's supremacy over such local churches, whose members are to interpret the teachings of the Bible and the suggestions of divine providence under the promised guidance of the Holy Spirit; that each such church should have for officers—choosing them itself, each member having equal rights with every other—a pastor, a teacher, one or more elders, one or more deacons, and one or more deaconesses; that all members of such a church should exercise constant mutual watchfulness and correct each other's faults; and that all such churches should claim the privilege and fulfil the duty of mutual fellowship and cooperation. This system—called Brownism by its opponents and by many since, although its early adherents generally did not accept the title—was substantial Congregationalism and offered immediate and adequate remedy for existing evils.

2. His Views.

Persecution soon drove Browne's church from Norwich, at least in part. Some members either maintained it there or revived it after a few years, for its existence is mentioned as late as 1598 (G. Johnson, *Discourse, etc.*, Amsterdam, 1603, p. 205). Yet, practically as a body, it emigrated in 1581 to Middelburg in Zealand. But after about two years it was dissolved, largely because of ill-judged applications of its rule as to mutual criticism, and Browne, returning to England, abandoned the work of reform and reentered the State Church. Six books by him survived, five continuing, so far as they were accessible, the work which he gave up, and their conceded importance is proved by a royal proclamation against them. But the sixth defended the State Church. (See Browne, Robert.)

It was not long before another, although less self-consistent, type of Congregationalism appeared, since, known as Barrowism. Henry Barrowe (q.v.) a lawyer of Gray's Inn, London, was arrested in 1586, and he and his friend John Greenwood (q.v.) were imprisoned together during most of the time until their martyrdom in 1593. But even in jail they managed to become voluminous authors. They promulgated a new theory of ecclesiastical government, for which Barrowe seems to have been chiefly responsible. They accepted Browne's fundamental principle of the independence of each local church. But they distrusted his teaching of the equality of all church-members in managing church affairs, and advocated the

3. Barrowe and Greenwood.

Presbyterian theory of Thomas Cartwright (q.v.), that such control should be vested in a board of elders. Browne's plan had included elders among church officers, but only meaning that such men, representing the "most forwarde in gifte," should do substantially the work of the church (or standing) committee in modern Congregationalism, without dominating the church. Upon the Barrowist theory the elders were to rule. It offered a compromise, of which the Congregationalism was to promote reform of belief and life, while the Presbyterianism was to prevent such errors as that which had ruined Browne's church at Middelburg. But the danger that the elders might assume excessive authority was overlooked. This Barrowist system met with some approval.

There are proofs of the existence of a Barrowist church in London in 1592, which had existed informally since 1589, or even 1587, of which Francis Johnson (q.v.) became pastor in 1592. John Greenwood—probably at large on bail at his election—was chosen its "teacher." This, too, was persecuted sharply and part of it escaped to Holland during that year. The remainder, including the pastor, remained imprisoned in London until 1597, but then the church was re-united at Amsterdam, Henry Ainsworth (q.v.) succeeding Greenwood as "teacher." Although at first harmonious, later it was rent by divisions, of which the gravest was due to the determination of the pastor and one or two elders to exalt the elders in authority above the other members. Practically it became a Presbyterian church, and of an exaggerated type. By 1618, when Johnson died, it was nearly extinct. In 1610 many members, under Ainsworth, withdrew, were given the church property by the courts, and thenceforth continued as a separate church and practised a more modest theory of the eldership, although still magnifying it, until Ainsworth's death in 1622 or 1623.

4. Johnson and Ainsworth.

In 1602 a Congregational church was formed at Gainsborough, England. It was identified with John Smyth (q.v.), who became its pastor in 1606. He agreed with Browne rather than Barrowe, although emphasizing the fellowship of the churches less than Browne. This church also underwent persecution almost at once, and in 1608 it emigrated under Smyth's leadership to Amsterdam. But it had included members from a distance, some of whom did not accompany it. Of these a number lived in, or near, the village of Scrooby, Nottinghamshire, and they formed there, in 1606, the church which later became that of the Mayflower and of the Plymouth Colony in America. At that date one of them, William Brewster (q.v.), was bailiff of the archbishop of York and a royal postmaster, and occupied the Scrooby Palace, or Manor-house, which belonged to the see of York. Doubtless the church was formed in the chapel of the palace, and the manner of its organization is recorded (J. Murton, *Description, etc.*, London ?, 1620, p. 169). Probably its original pastor was Richard Clifton (q.v.), formerly rector of Babworth (7 m. s.e.), and the famous John Robinson (q.v.) apparently was its "teacher," and certainly was its pastor afterward. Another member was William Bradford, who became the governor of the Plymouth Colony for many years and its first historian. His graphic narrative portrays touchingly the oppression of the church by the government and its flight to Amsterdam in 1608.

5. The Scrooby Congregation.

Thus there were then three professedly Congregational churches in Amsterdam. The first was Francis Johnson's, called the Ancient Church because the oldest, which became practically Presbyterian. The second was Smyth's, which, because of his personal peculiarities, repeatedly dissolved and reorganized itself and soon disappeared. Neither afforded an example of true Congregationalism. The third was the Pilgrim church, under Robinson. This lived harmoniously but, after a year, in order to avoid involvement in the troubles of the others, it removed to Leyden. There it remained eleven years. It was distinctly Congregational. Although it retained the eldership, its elders were merely leaders among equals, and had little authority, excepting that of high character and ability. The church was not precisely like a modern Congregational church, but the differences were slight and did not relate to essentials.

6. The Pilgrim Church in Holland.

Ecclesiastically it was peaceful and prosperous, but its members suffered severely from the inevitable hardships of their life in a foreign land. Finally, appreciating the impossibility of attracting other English people in sufficient numbers and fearing absorption into the Dutch community, hoping for greater material prosperity elsewhere, distrusting the influence of Dutch example upon its young people, dreading the renewal of the Dutch war with Spain, and animated by an earnest missionary spirit, the Pilgrim church resolved to emigrate again, and this time to America. In the end a part, including Robinson, remained, intending to follow as soon as possible. The others, including Brewster and Bradford, sailed from Delfshaven on July 22 (Aug. 1), 1620, and after various detentions left Plymouth, England, on Sept. 6 (16) and reached Cape Cod, Mass., on Nov. 11 (21) and the site of the future Plymouth on Dec. 11 (21).

7. The Emigration to America.

In 1616 Henry Jacob organized in Southwark, London, the earliest of the surviving English churches (see BAPTISTS, I., 2, § 1), and in 1621, also in Southwark, another church was formed by a Mr. Hubbard. Allusions also occur in the corporation records of Yarmouth in 1630 to a Brownist church there, consisting chiefly of persons recently returned from Holland. But Congregationalism made no noteworthy progress in England for another ten years. Then history repeated itself. In the days of Laud many Puritans had exiled themselves to the Continent because of the popish ceremonies in the State Church, the silencing and suspension of devout ministers, and the persecution of all who disputed the demands of the ecclesiastical

8. Congregationalists in England to 1660.

authorities. They had fled, as they said, "to enjoy the liberty of their conscience in God's worship, and to free themselves from human inventions." Returning about 1640, a number of them, including William Bridge, Jeremiah Burroughs, Thomas Goodwin, Philip Nye, and Sidrach Simpson, became members of the Westminster Assembly (q.v.). They tried to secure a new national ecclesiastical organization, or, at any rate, fully tolerated Congregational churches. The rigid Presbyterians opposed them, but under Cromwell Congregational churches were founded widely. Other leaders among them were Joseph Caryl, Stephen Charnock, Theophilus Gale, and John Howe.

But theories of religious freedom were still vague and sometimes contradictory. Many Congregationalists then advocated a liberty including only Christians, and Congregationalism was not regarded as inconsistent with a State Church. Some of its churches were formed independently of territorial boundaries. Others were parochial, i.e., limited to a given parish and supported by tithes. This attempt to be independent Congregationalists within a State Church enabled their ministers to be maintained more easily; but it led to serious difficulties. In some cases non-professors of religion, residing in a parish, demanded on the ground of such residence that the sacraments be administered to them. At this time Congregationalism had gained no footing in Scotland, but had made some progress in Ireland.

After the restoration of Charles II. (1660) the State Church regained supremacy and resumed its attitude of severity toward dissenters. On Aug. 24, 1662, all clergymen refusing the new Act of Uniformity (q.v.) were ejected. They numbered over two thousand. Most were Presbyterians, but many were Congregationalists. Congregationalism then was severed from the State Church finally and remained under the ban for a quarter-century. But after the revolution of 1688 the Act of Toleration (q.v.) allowed the revival of both Congregationalism and Presbyterianism. As the latter then had no presbyteries, they resembled each other considerably, excepting that in the Presbyterian churches the elders had greater power. In 1691 an unsuccessful effort was made to combine them as the United Brethren. Yet the more general statements of the proposed heads of agreement supplanted the stricter provisions of the Savoy Declaration (see below, III., § 1), to which Congregationalists had conformed, and have prevailed ever since. After the death of William III. it was attempted again to deprive dissenters of their partial liberty, but since that of Queen Anne that liberty gradually has been increased and now is practically complete.

9. Since 1660.

During the nineteenth century English Congregational churches increased rapidly in number and their importance became conspicuous. They still hold firmly to their independence and often are called the Independent Churches. But they recognize increasingly the value of fellowship and cooperation. In 1831 they formed the Congregational Union of England and Wales. Although organized only for purposes of deliberation and advice and guarded carefully against assuming authority over the churches, it is a uniting, stimulating force of great importance. Most English Congregational churches agree to its Declaration of Faith (see below, III., § 1), although this is not binding. The Congregational Union of Scotland dates from 1812, and that of Ireland from 1829. At present a tendency is apparent to approve some method of closer cooperation among the churches which shall render the denominational activities more fruitful. A national Council has just been formed, intended to be a legislative, administrative body, but without involving any appreciable sacrifice of individual liberty. Only within the last half-century have associations and local councils of churches found much favor. But the needs of the feebler churches and of missions have caused them to become better appreciated, although councils are not yet common.

10. At the Present Time.

Foreign missionary work was undertaken as early as 1760. The London Missionary Society was organized in 1795. At first several denominations united in its support, but for some time it has been sustained mainly by Congregationalists. It began work in the South Sea Islands in 1797, in India and South Africa in 1798, in China in 1807, in the West Indies in 1818, and in Madagascar in 1861. The Colonial Missionary Society was formed in 1836, and the two cooperate. The Congregational Church Aid and Home Missionary Society was founded in 1878, and the Irish Evangelical Society and Congregational Home Missionary Society in 1814. The work of these societies now is being transferred to the charge of the national Council.

11. Missionary Work.

2. Congregationalists in the British Colonies: Congregational churches in the various British colonies are numerous. The earliest church in Canada was formed in 1760, in British Guiana in 1808, in South Africa (colored) in 1811 and (white) in 1820, in Tasmania and in New South Wales in 1833, in Jamaica in 1834, in South Australia in 1837, in Victoria in 1838, in New Zealand in 1842, in West Australia in 1846, and in Queensland in 1853. The Canadian churches maintain cordial relations with those of the United States, but are counted as British rather than American.

3. Congregationalists on the Continent of Europe: Details of Congregationalism on the Continent of Europe are not abundant. In France the McAll Missions are practically Congregational, and, apart from missions, a few churches exist in Germany, Hungary, Poland, Norway, Switzerland, and Portugal. In Holland the Band van Vrije Christelijke Gemeenten numbers sixteen churches, and in Sweden there are more than a thousand free churches with more than 100,000 members.

4. Congregationalists in America: The Plymouth colonists brought an organized Congregational Church, that formed in 1606 at Scrooby. Not all of them belonged to it, although nearly all who came from Leyden must have been members. As part of this church was to emigrate and part to remain, it was agreed that each part should be considered a complete church, and that, if any members of either should rejoin the other, they should be recognized as already members. The Congregationalism of this Pilgrim church was essentially like that of the present. But it did not blend the offices of pastor and teacher and it retained the eldership, to which attached for some time rather more of authority than to the diaconate, which gradually absorbed the eldership. In Leyden it had been trained to a liberality which permitted communion with the Reformed churches, and in the Plymouth Colony no man was interfered with for his religion unless he antagonized the Congregational churches actively. But such was its high conception of the ministry that, as it had no ordained pastor until 1629, when it secured Rev. Ralph Smith, it had no administration of the Lord's Supper until then. Elder Brewster, however, served efficiently as its preacher and religious leader.

1. The Pilgrim Church at Plymouth.

The Massachusetts Bay colonists, in 1628–30, were Puritans rather than Congregationalists. Although repelled by many of its features, they did not mean to separate from the Anglican Church. Moreover, although animated strongly by a religious motive, theirs was primarily a commercial colony. But Congregationalism, as illustrated at Plymouth, seemed so peculiarly adapted to their new conditions that they adopted it at once, organizing a church at Salem in Aug. 1629, the Plymouth church being represented. Other similar churches soon were formed, as well as in the neighboring New England colonies, and until 1700 there were hardly any others than Congregational churches, although a policy of entire ecclesiastical freedom was adopted in 1691. But soon the original simplicity of their Congregationalism was modified. The Massachusetts Bay and Connecticut colonies limited political suffrage to church-members, although the former abandoned this practise in 1693 and the latter as early as 1664. Moreover, and this continued until well into the nineteenth century, Congregational churches and ministers were supported by public taxation, a plain violation of the principle of a free Church in a free State. But for some time before its abandonment taxpayers were allowed to select the church which they preferred to help maintain.

2. Massachusetts and Other Colonies.

An important feature in Congregational history during that century was the Half-way Covenant. It was the early rule to baptize infants one of whose parents was a church-member. When such baptized persons grew up and married but failed to join the Church, the question arose whether their children should be baptized, and it became customary to allow such baptized but non-communicant parents to "own the covenant." They publicly accepted the fundamental truths of the Gospel and promised to maintain a general fellowship with the Church, and then, although they could not receive the communion or vote in church matters, they could have their children baptized. This compromise, although strongly opposed, became common, but led to laxity in admitting members to the churches and was practically abandoned about 1800 (cf. Walker, *Creeds*, 238–339).

3. The Half-way Covenant.

In Vermont the first church was established at Brattleboro in 1762, and by 1800 there were seventy-four and they had formed a general convention. New York had been occupied by the Dutch, but it contained a few Congregational churches. In New England churches continued to multiply rapidly, most, and in many localities all, being Congregational. But the specially noteworthy feature of the Congregationalism of that century was its theological and religious development. In 1700 a serious spiritual decline had become general. Carelessness in requiring evidence of piety before admission to the Church, the influence of the deism then prevalent in Europe, increased absorption in the pursuit of material prosperity, and the diversion of public attention from religion due to the excitements of the Revolution had combined to diminish the vividness of personal religious belief and experience. Partly to counteract this tendency, Yale College had been founded at Saybrook, Conn., in 1701, and the synod at Saybrook, Sept. 9, 1708, instituted by the General Court of Connecticut to prepare a form of ecclesiastical discipline, had recommended as a doctrinal statement the Savoy Declaration, which Massachusetts had adopted in 1680, and had drawn up the Saybrook Platform, which remained civil law until 1784 (see below, III., § 1). But the chief cause of the spiritual change which followed was the Great Awakening, a wide-spread religious revival, which began in 1734–35 and continued intermittently for about seven years (see REVIVALS OF RELIGION).

4. Growth and Development after 1700.

Out of the inevitable theological discussions accompanying it grew up two schools of belief. The more conservative was that of the New England Theology (q.v.), or the New Divinity. The more advanced was called the Arminian, or Liberal. The former adhered to the traditional Calvinism, with minor modifications. The latter rejected it in respect to certain prominent doctrines, e.g., sin, Christ's deity, and the atonement, and exalted rectitude of life rather than the work of Christ as the means of salvation. A long and earnest controversy resulted which produced a considerable literature. On the conservative side the elder and the younger Edwards, President Timothy Dwight of Yale, Joseph Bellamy, Samuel Hopkins, and Stephen West were eminent, and among the Arminians Lemuel Briant, Charles Chauncy, Experience and Jonathan Mayhew, and Samuel Webster.

5. Theological Controversy.

But this controversy caused no open rupture and political affairs soon overshadowed ecclesiastical. Congregationalism had so aided in developing the democratic spirit, alike in Church and State, that it was an influential cause of the Revolution, and its ministers and other leaders, with few exceptions, were active in promoting the colonial success. The earliest written code of Massachusetts, The Body of Liberties, published in 1641, had been the work of a Congregational minister, Rev. Nathaniel Ward, of Ipswich, and the earliest written constitution in human history which led to a civil government—excepting the famous Mayflower compact—that of Connecticut, had been largely drawn up by Rev. Thomas Hooker (q.v.), of Hartford, in 1639.

6. Attempted Change of Polity.

Contemporaneously with the efforts for spiritual reform in the earlier years of the century occurred a modification of Congregationalism in practise. Probably the prevalent religious indifference caused within the churches some consciousness of inefficiency, and an external, rather than the more necessary internal, remedy was sought. Associations of ministers had been distrusted as inclining their members to assume excessive authority over the churches. There had been a Ministers' Convention in Massachusetts, but it was feeble. At this time it was revived, new local associations were formed, and it was proposed to "consociate" the churches into formal unions and to establish standing councils. In Massachusetts this policy was attempted in 1705, but, although adopted, it became a dead letter. But in Connecticut, where it was adopted somewhat later than in Massachusetts, it prevailed generally, and, although of little significance, it never has been abandoned wholly. The Mathers were chiefly responsible for it, and that it accomplished so little was due principally to Rev. John Wise (q.v.), of Ipswich, Mass. Its tendency was to destroy the independence of the churches, but practically it has had scanty results of any sort.

7. Growth in the West and South.

During the nineteenth century Congregationalism made rapid progress, in spite of hindrance outside of New England by a plan of union with the Presbyterians, agreed upon in 1801, of which the unforeseen operation cost it at least 2,000 churches. In 1827 an Illinois Band was formed by a dozen recent graduates of Yale Divinity School, who accomplished large results in that State, and similar bodies afterward did notable service in other Western States. Stimulated by the needs of the native settlements in the Interior and the West, and by the enormous inflow of foreigners, Congregationalists have followed the westward movement of population indefatigably. In the Middle West the earliest church in Ohio was formed in 1796, in Michigan in 1827, in Illinois in 1831, in Indiana in 1834, in Wisconsin in 1836, in Iowa in 1838, in Minnesota in 1851, and in Kansas in 1854. On the Pacific coast the earliest in Oregon dates back to 1844, in California to 1851, and in Washington to 1865. Throughout the whole Interior and West Congregational churches have increased from hundreds to thousands within the last fifty years. They are less numerous relatively in the Middle States; and in the Southern States, although one or two were formed in 1852–53, and one even in 1832, there were very few before the Civil War. Since then they have multiplied considerably, although less rapidly than in the West. The first Congregational general assembly since the Cambridge Synod in 1646–48 was the Albany Convention in 1852, which gave a vigorous impulse to the denominational activities. Its members represented seventeen states. It abandoned the Plan of Union, indorsed the Congregational Home Missionary Societies, condemned slavery, called for $50,000 for church building in the West, and took steps resulting in the publication, in 1854, of the annual Year-Book, containing the denominational statistics, and in the organization of the American Congregational Association.

8. The Unitarian Controversy.

The theological differences of the eighteenth century became more marked during the early years of the nineteenth and developed into the Unitarian Controversy. Its special arena was eastern Massachusetts. Many ministers and churches gradually had come to deny certain doctrines believed vital, and therefore insisted upon the more strongly by others; e.g., the moral corruption of human nature, Christ's deity, the need and nature of the atonement, and eternal punishment. Friction increased steadily. Finally matters reached a climax in the election of Rev. Henry Ware (q.v.) as Hollis professor of divinity at Harvard College in 1805, a Unitarian success. Thirty-nine churches became Unitarian. Nearly a hundred others were divided, the conservatives usually being obliged to withdraw and form new churches and the Unitarians retaining what had been the common property. Among the leaders of the latter were Drs. J. S. Buckminster and W. E. Channing and President Kirkland and Prof. Andrews Norton, of Harvard. Eminent defenders of the old faith were Drs. Lyman Beecher, Nathaniel Emmons, Jedidiah Morse, Enoch Pond, Moses Stuart, Samuel West, Leonard Woods, and Samuel Worcester. The Unitarians have been zealously loyal to Independency as a polity, but the name of Congregationalists by general consent has continued to signify the Trinitarian body. A temporary result of this controversy was a revival, especially in Connecticut, of the desire for consociation, already described.

9. The Andover Controversy.

During the last twenty years of the century, another doctrinal difference caused intense feeling. Advocates of the so-called "New Theology," styling itself Christocentric, holding radical views of the nature of inspiration and the office of Biblical criticism and asserting a possible future probation for at least some of the impenitent, claimed to be true Congregationalists in doctrine, but the claim was disputed stoutly. This difference affected the settlement of pastors for some years, but was notable chiefly in connection with the choice of professors at the Andover Seminary and of candidates for foreign missionary service. It reached the courts, but indecisively. It led to no formal rupture, however, and now the teachings of the New Theology are tolerated, although not universally accepted by Congregationalists.

When the first Congregational settlers came to

America they avowed their earnest purpose to serve as Christian missionaries. The Plymouth Pilgrims made attempts in this direction, but found few natives in their vicinity. There were more near the Bay Colony, and Rev. John Eliot (q.v.) undertook work among them in 1646 and continued it until 1690 with remarkable success. The Congregational Home Missionary Society was organized in 1826, and the American Missionary Association, to do similar work among negroes, Indians, and the Chinese in this country, in 1846. The former has lately begun work in Cuba also and the latter in Porto Rico and the Sandwich Islands.

10. Home Mission Work. Other Societies. The Congregational Sunday-school and Publishing Society, founded in 1832, organizes Sunday-schools and supplies religious and general literature. The Congregational Church Building Society, formed in 1853, aids in erecting houses of worship and parsonages. These societies have established and equipped thousands of churches and Sunday-schools, and the Congregational Education Society, started in 1816, has aided thousands of young men into the ministry. The American Congregational Association, organized in 1853, has erected in Boston a fine building as the denominational headquarters, which contains the Congregational library, a large collection specially rich in denominational, colonial, and sociological literature. The world-wide Young People's Society of Christian Endeavor, although now undenominational, was founded in 1881 by Rev. F. E. Clark, then pastor of the Williston Congregation, a church in Portland, Me., and gained its first successes among Congregationalists.

Congregational foreign mission work is in charge of the American Board of Commissioners for Foreign Missions. Established in 1810, it has had successful missions among the Choctaw and Cherokee Indians in our own country and in Mexico,

11. The American Board. Spain, Austria, European and Asiatic Turkey, Persia, Ceylon, the Madura and Marathi districts of India, China, Japan, Central Africa, Zululand, the Sandwich Islands, Micronesia, and the Philippines. Some of these missions have outgrown the need of external aid. Several have been transferred to other denominations. One or two are but recently established. The Board now has ninety-six stations.

II. Educational Work: Congregationalists always have zealously promoted popular education. In the United States they have founded Harvard, Yale, Amherst, Bowdoin, Dartmouth, Middlebury, Williams, Oberlin, Illinois, Beloit, Carleton, Washburn, Colorado, Berea, Fisk, Atlanta,

1. America. and other universities or colleges, more than forty in all, as well as Mt. Holyoke, Smith, and Wellesley, among women's colleges, and many high-class preparatory schools, including the two famous Phillips Academies. But none of these institutions are sectarian. Robert College, at Constantinople, and the Doshisha University, at Kyoto, Japan, and other such educational centers are results of their missionary labors. The American Board has established seventeen in various lands. There are eight Congregational theological seminaries in the United States: Andover, Atlanta, Bangor, Chicago, Hartford, Oberlin, Pacific (Berkeley, Cal.), and Yale.

In Great Britain and its colonies there are fifteen such institutions, usually uniting the work of the college and the theological school: Bala-Bangor; Brecon Memorial; Carmarthen (Presbyterian with Congregational affiliations); Ches-

2. Great Britain and Colonies. hunt at Cambridge; the Edinburgh Theological Hall; Hackney, at Hampstead; the Lancashire Independent, at Manchester; Mansfield, at Oxford; New, at South Hampstead; the Nottingham Congregational Institute; Western, at Bristol; the Yorkshire United, at Bradford; the Montreal Congregational College; the Victoria Congregational College, in Australia; and Camden College, at Sydney, N. S. W. The London Missionary Society also has ten institutions of learning in heathen lands.

III. Theology: Congregationalists regard the Bible as the only, and sufficient, rule of faith and practise. In doctrine they agree substantially with the other Evangelical denominations. The earliest surviving Congregational creed is that of Henry Barrowe and John Greenwood in 1589 (*True Description*, 1-5), but it was only an unauthoritative expression of personal conviction.

1. Creeds and Platforms. Afterward Congregational churches generally accepted the Westminster Confession (1646) and the Savoy Declaration (1658). The former was based upon the Thirty-nine Articles of the Church of England, but was more Calvinistic. It embodies the teachings of the Reformed Churches on the Continent as well as in Great Britain. It founded the authority of the Scriptures upon internal evidence and the testimony of the Holy Spirit instead of upon the external witness of the Church; emphasized predestination and limited redemption, and the fact of two divine covenants, of works and of grace, with men; urged the Puritan view of the Sabbath; gave to presbyteries and synods large legislative and judicial authority; and conferred upon the civil magistrate power to prohibit or punish heresy, idolatry, and blasphemy. The Savoy Declaration differed little from the former, but discarded its Presbyterianism in polity and denied the authority of magistrates to interfere with ecclesiastical liberty. Modern British churches nominally adhere to the Declaration of Faith of the Congregational Union of England and Wales in 1833, which is briefer and less severely Calvinistic, but which probably would not be adopted now, partly because of changes of doctrinal emphasis and partly because such statements are increasingly believed to interfere with Christian freedom. Subsequent American utterances have been the Burial Hill Declaration (1865), adopted at Plymouth by the General Council held at Boston, which reaffirmed somewhat indefinitely the symbols of the seventeenth century, and the Creed of 1883, formulated by a committee provided for by the Triennial National Council in 1880, which set forth tersely and fairly the belief generally held by the churches then. This creed is that commonly professed at present. But the admirable statement of faith issued at Dayton, O., in Feb., 1906, by the joint committee on doctrine, in view of the proposed union of Congregationalists, Methodist Protestants, and United Brethren is likely to be adopted widely. It is sincerely Evangelical and affirms "consent to the teaching of the ancient symbols of the undivided church, and to that substance of Christian doctrine which is common to the creeds and confessions which we have inherited from the past." But it is silent as to some doctrines formerly enunciated in such utterances. No Congregational church, however, is obliged to accept any creed or declaration of faith. (For text of the documents mentioned here and further information cf. Schaff, *Creeds*, i. 820-840; iii. 707-737; W. Walker, *The Creeds and Platforms of Congregationalism*, New York, 1893; A. E. Dunning, *Congregationalists in America*, 1894; *The Congregationalist*, Feb. 17, 1906.)

2. Late Tendencies. During the last twenty-five years two tendencies have appeared. One is to put less emphasis upon certain doctrines, e.g., the fall of man, the governmental theory of the atonement, the equal and infallible inspiration of the Scriptures, and eternal punishment, and more upon certain others, e.g., the divine fatherhood, human brotherhood, and the immanence of the divine Spirit. The other is to shorten and simplify creeds. The old Calvinistic phraseology is being abandoned. Some churches adopt two creeds; one a formal declaration, like the Creed of 1883, expressing its doctrinal position fully, and another, the Apostles' Creed, or some even briefer, simpler statement of vital truths, for use in admitting children or other comparatively immature applicants for church-membership. Some churches even have discarded the creed and content themselves with a covenant.

IV. Polity and Practise: The two underlying principles of Congregationalism have been stated: (1) the independence of the local church, and (2) the fellowship of the churches. The joint committee on polity in view of the proposed union has expressed them well, viz.: "(a) The unit of our fellowship is the local church, and the character of our fellowship is that of a representative democracy. (b) Our coordinate principles are freedom and fellowship, a freedom which leaves each local church free in its separate affairs, a fellowship which unites all the churches for mutual care and cooperant action." During the Colonial period the American churches ordinarily accepted the Cambridge Platform (1649) until the Saybrook Platform (1705) superseded it in Connecticut. The framers of these accepted the Westminster and Savoy Confessions in respect to doctrine, but not as to church government. The former emphasized the independence of the local church, the fellowship of the churches, and the representative character of the ministry, fundamental principles of Congregationalism, but nevertheless gave to the civil magistrate excessive authority in matters of faith and practise alike. The latter provided for consociations of churches and associations of ministers, established by and under the authority of civil law, an abnormal system which was not abrogated formally until 1784 and which remained in more or less active use for many years longer. At present each church has entire self-control in its own ecclesiastical affairs. It may draw up its creed and covenant, formulate its order of worship, elect and install its pastor and other officers, etc. Until within about thirty years it was customary in the United States for a society, or parish, to be formed side by side with each church to attend to all its secular concerns. Ordinarily most of its members were also church-members, so that neither body antagonized the other. But differences occasionally arose. For example, as the pastor held a legal relation to the society only, the society sometimes could elect, or depose, the pastor in opposition to a majority of the church. It is now becoming common for the church itself to be incorporated, thus being enabled to manage all its affairs, whether religious or secular.

1. The Two Underlying Principles.

Most churches adopt creeds and covenants which are similar, and often identical. And in matters of common interest each church seeks the advice and cooperation of its sister churches. In the settlement or dismissal of a pastor fellowship is recognized by calling a council. Formerly no man excepting the pastor of a church was considered a minister. But within fifty years, owing largely to the need of ministers where churches had not yet been established, this conception has been broadened, and now a man ordained to serve anywhere as a pastor or evangelist is accepted as a minister.

2. Councils. Councils are temporary bodies, composed of pastors and delegates, chiefly of neighboring churches, assembled by a letter missive from some church to recognize its existence or to advise and assist it in regard to the settlement of a pastor, a case of discipline, or any other matter as to which advice is desired and in which the other churches also are interested. The membership of a council is limited strictly to the representatives of the invited churches and any individuals invited by name, and its action is limited, with equal strictness, to the matters specified in the letter missive. The result of a council is only morally binding, but usually is accepted as final. In cases of difficulty between two churches or between a church and one or more of its members, if both sides unite in calling the council, it is termed mutual. If a church refuse to join a justly aggrieved member in calling a council, he may summon one, which, if the church persist in its refusal, acts as an *ex-parte* council. A council, unless it is to be *ex parte*, always must be called by some church, excepting that one may be called by a company of persons seeking recognition as a new church. In a case affecting the welfare of the whole body of churches, and in which the church particularly involved refuses to act, a council to consider the situation in that church may be summoned by any other church. This emergency, however, occurs rarely. When controversies reach the civil courts, the courts refuse to go behind the usages of Congregationalism, as determined by councils, and merely declare what they are.

Most of the affairs of the churches in fellowship are transacted by local councils. But for sufficient reason a council of broader inclusiveness may be called. The first general council in America was that at Newtowne, now Cambridge, Mass., in 1637, to consider the Antinomian teachings of Rev. John Wheelwright and Mrs. Anne Hutchinson (see ANTINOMIANISM, and foot-note to COUNCILS AND SYNODS, § 10). The next was the Cambridge Synod in 1646–48. The third was the Albany Convention in 1852, and, to promote the better acquaintance and cooperation of all Congregational churches in the United States, a National Council was held in Boston in 1865. In 1871 the first Triennial National Council met at Oberlin, and similar gatherings have been held regularly ever since. The name of conference would be more appropriate for this body, however, as it is not strictly a council. It discusses important current topics of denominational interest and advises the churches, but has only a moral authority. In 1891 an International Council was held in London, composed of delegates from bodies of Congregational churches in all parts of the world, and a second such council met in Boston, U. S. A., in 1899. A third is to be held in Edinburgh in 1908. British and other foreign Congregational churches hitherto have made much less use of local councils than the churches of the United States, but have been zealous in promoting the International Councils.

3. Conferences and Associations.

Fellowship also is maintained by conferences of churches, local bodies, usually including the churches of a given county, or some smaller, if well populated, district, which meet semiannually for discussion of religious and kindred topics. In the United States the churches of each State also hold an annual Conference, or Association, for similar purposes. There are also Ministerial Associations, small local bodies of ministers, and until recently they have determined ministerial standing. But responsibility for this now is being transferred to the Conferences of churches.

All ministers and churches are equal, no one having any authority over others. But lately it has been urged that the Moderator of the Triennial National Council should exercise his representative function during his three years of office, giving something more than the merely nominal leadership which has been customary; and in some states also a tendency again is evident toward consociation of the churches, as in Massachusetts and Connecticut early in the eighteenth and nineteenth centuries, and it is proposed to institute some formal, permanent organization, and perhaps to revive the Standing Council. These proposals have been made only tentatively and their outcome is uncertain.

4. Worship and Practise.

In the order of public worship there is variety in minor particulars, yet a general likeness exists. Baptism customarily is administered by sprinkling, but pouring or immersion is used occasionally. The form is considered immaterial. In the colonial days it was sometimes common to install certain minor church officers formally. This practise disappeared during the eighteenth century, but lately has been revived by some churches. Apparently the early colonial churches held no mid-week meetings. But in time they established the weekly lecture, and gatherings somewhat like the modern prayer-meeting began to be held about 1740 but did not become usual until after 1800. The First and the Brattle Street churches in Boston instituted the preparatory lecture before the Communion Sunday on Mar. 4, 1720. Sunday-schools were not established until after 1800. The modern institutional church, which supplements direct spiritual efforts by promoting the physical, intellectual, and social welfare of the community, has been exemplified conspicuously among Congregationalists.

V. Statistics: The English *Year Book* for 1908 gives the following figures:

	Churches.	Ministers.	Church-members.
Great Britain..........	4,928	3,197	498,953
British Colonies and Missions	1,142	506	Not reported.
Total British	6,070	3,703	498,953 +
Continent of Europe ...	Not reported.	Not reported.	100,000 +
Total.............	6,070 +	3,703 +	598,953 +

The American *Year Book* for 1907 gives the current statistics of the denomination as follows:

	Churches.	Ministers.	Church-members.
United States..........	5,923	5,900	696,723
Dependencies (1906)...	108	94	7,827
Total.............	6,031	5,994	704,550

The world statistics for Congregationalism (1907) is given as 12,583 churches and 1,333,731 members.

MORTON DEXTER.

BIBLIOGRAPHY: On Congregational origins and English Congregationalism consult: The works of Robert Browne (q.v.); J. Smyth, *Principles and Inferences concerning the Visible Church*, Amsterdam, 1607; *Differences of the Churches of the Separation*, etc., 1608; J. Robinson, *Works*, ed. R. Ashton, 3 vols., London, 1851; R. Baxter, *Reliquiæ Baxterianæ*, ib. 1696; *Abridgement of Mr. Baxter's History of His Life, with Account of Ejected Ministers*, by E. Calamy, in S. Parker's *Nonconformist Memorial*, 2 vols., ib. 1802; D. Neal, *History of New England*, 2 vols., ib. 1720; idem, *History of Puritans*, 4 vols., ib. 1732–38, ed. J. Toulmin, 5 vols., ib. 1822; B. Brook, *Lives of Puritans*, 3 vols., ib. 1813; J. Toulmin, *Historical View of State of Protestant Dissenters in England*, Bath, 1814; T. Price, *History of Protestant Nonconformity in England*, 2 vols., London, 1836–38; B. Hanbury, *Historical Memorials Relating to the Independents*, 3 vols., ib. 1839–44; J. Fletcher, *History of Revival and Progress of Independency in England*, 4 vols., ib. 1847–49; R. Vaughan, *English Nonconformity*, 2 vols., ib. 1862; J. Stoughton, *Church and State 200 Years Ago*, ib. 1862; J. Waddington, *Congregational History*, 5 vols., ib. 1869–78; R. W. Dale, *Manual of Congregational Principles*, ib. 1884; idem, *Hist. of English Congregationalism*, ib. 1907; J. Brown, *Pilgrim Fathers of New England*, New York, 1897.

On American Congregationalism consult: W. Bradford, *History of Plimouth Plantation*, reprinted in *Collections of the Mass. Historical Society*, Boston, 1856, reproduced in facsimile, Massachusetts State edition, ib. 1898; ed. W. T. Davis, New York, 1908; idem, *Dialogue*, in A. Young, *Chronicles of Pilgrim Fathers*, ib. 1841, ed. C. Deane, ib. 1870; N. Morton, *New England's Memoriall*, Cambridge, 1669, republished, Boston, 1855; J. Winthrop, *Journal*, ed. J. Savage, ib. 1853; R. Mather, *Church Government Discussed*, London, 1643; J. Cotton, *Doctrine of the Church*, ib. 1642; idem, *Way of Congregational Churches Cleared*, ib. 1643; idem, *Way of Churches of Christ in New England*, ib. 1645; T. Hooker, *Survey of the Sum of Church Discipline*, ib. 1648; I. Mather, *First Principles of New England*, including J. Cotton's *Plan for Conferences*, Boston, 1675; idem, *Disquisition concerning Ecclesiastical Councils*, 1716, reprinted in *Congregational Quarterly*, 1870; *Platform of Church Discipline*, Cambridge, 1649 and often; C. Mather, *Magnalia Christi Americana*, London, 1702, republished, Hartford, 1855; idem, *Ratio Disciplinæ*, Boston, 1726; *Confession of Faith*, . . . *Heads of Agreement* and *Articles for the Administration of Church Discipline* (Saybrook Platform), New London, 1710; G. Punchard, *View of Congregationalism*, Salem, 1840; idem, *History of Congregationalism*, New York, 1865; idem, *Congregationalism in America*, Boston, 1880–81; J. S. Clark, *Historical Sketch of Congregational Churches in Massachusetts*, ib. 1858; H. F. Uhden, *The New England Theocracy*, ib. 1858; H. M. Dexter, *Congregationalism*, ib. 1865; idem, *Handbook of Congregationalism*, ib. 1890; idem, *Congregationalism as Seen in the Literature of the Last 300 Years*, New York, 1880; idem and M. Dexter, *The England and Holland of the Pilgrims*, Boston, 1905; L. Bacon, *Genesis of New England Churches*, New York, 1874; G. T. Ladd, *Principles of Church Polity*, New York, 1882; W. Walker, *Creeds and Platforms of Congregationalism*, New York, 1893; idem, *History of Congregational Churches in the United States*, ib. 1894; A. E. Dunning, *Congregationalists in America*, ib. 1894; G. A. Hood, *National Council of Congregational Churches*, Boston, 1901; S. L. Blake, *The Separates or Strict Congregationalists of New England*, ib. 1902; G. M. Boynton, *The Congregational Way*, ib. 1903; L. W. Bacon, *The Congregationalists*, New York, 1904; A. Anderson, *Congregational Faith and Practice*, Boston, 1906; T. P. Prudden, *Congregationalists: Who they Are*, Boston, 1906.

CONGRESS, EVANGELICAL-SOCIAL: An organization formed in Germany in 1890. The Imperial government as well as the governments of the single states turned their attention in the eighties to social questions. The empire opened, under Bismarck's leading, with insurance against illness in 1883, against accident in 1884 (both of these being further developed in 1885, 1886, and 1887), and against permanent debility and age in 1889. It was thought desirable for Christians to do something to bring the educated people and the workingman together, and to prevent the latter from supposing that religion was only a tool to keep the workmen down. At the close of 1889 or at the opening of 1890, Adolf Stöcker, then court preacher, Pastor Weber, Prof. Adolf Wagner, and Dr. Kropatschek issued an invitation to an Evangelical-Social Congress to meet at Whitsuntide in Berlin. Meanwhile Emperor Wiliam II. issued two strong social orders on Feb. 4, 1890. On May 27, 1890, a confidential conference took place, in which both Stöcker and Prof. Adolf Harnack took part, and it was agreed that all evangelical groups should be asked to share in the Congress. The first session opened at Berlin, May 29, 1890, and on Oct. 23, 1890, a committee appointed by the Congress met at Berlin and chose an executive committee. M. A. Nobbe, the director of a hail-insurance company, was made chairman of the Congress and continued to fill that position with great acceptance for twelve years, when the pressure of business compelled him to resign. In 1903 Prof. Adolf Harnack of Berlin became chairman and has shown unusual gifts for the place.

The session of 1895 at Erfurt was marked by the first public address by a woman in such meetings, delivered by Mrs. Gnauck; she spoke on the social condition of women, and Stöcker followed her in a second address. In 1896, owing to the fact that Stöcker had become the leader of a political party, it was thought by some that it would be better if he should give up his seat as second president of the Congress, although it was desired that he should remain in the committee; finally he left the Congress altogether and became one of the founders of the Ecclesiastical-Social Conference (q.v.).

The Congress has published the addresses at the yearly meetings in successive volumes of *Verhandlungen* and formerly issued "Communications" (*Mitteilungen*) in a little newspaper. This newspaper became at the thirteenth session (1904) a little magazine, under the title of *Evangelisch-Social*. Organized groups in Baden, Sleswick-Holstein, Württemberg, and Saxony are connected with the Congress. Different religious and political circles are to-day, as at the beginning, represented in the Congress. The executive committee consists of Harnack, Adolf Wagner, Prof. Gierke, Prof. Kaftan, Prof. Hans Delbrück, Pastor Friedrich Naumann, Prof. Von Soden, Pastor Kirmes, Mrs. Schmoller, Mrs. Broicher, Dr. Ludwig Keller, Pastor Schneemelcker, and the writer.

CASPAR RENÉ GREGORY.

BIBLIOGRAPHY: "Transactions" (*Verhandlungen*), "Reports" (*Berichte*), or "Communications" are published yearly, Berlin, 1890–96, Göttingen, 1897–1901, Berlin, 1892 sqq. Consult: O. Kraft, *Die Harmonie der sechs ersten evangelisch-socialen Kongresse*, Halle, 1896; M. A. Noble, *Der evangelisch-soziale Kongress und seine Gegner*, Göttingen, 1897.

CONON: Pope 686–687. After the death of John V. (Aug. 2, 686) a controversy arose between the clergy and the soldiery over the choice of his successor, the former proposing the archpriest Peter, the latter the priest Theodore. The clergy finally elected Conon, a priest, born in Thrace and educated in Sicily. He was consecrated Oct. 21, 686, but he was ill at the time and, after a pontificate of eleven months during which he accomplished nothing, died, and was buried on Sept. 22, 687.

(A. HAUCK.)

BIBLIOGRAPHY: *Liber pontificalis*, ed. T. Mommsen, in *MGH*, *Gest. pont. Rom.*, i (1898), 207–209; Jaffé, *Regesta*, i. 243; Bower, *Popes*, i. 490–491; Mann, *Popes*, I. ii. 68–76.

CONON OF TARSUS: Bishop of Tarsus in Cilicia at the beginning of the seventh century. He held certain tritheistic views which he had derived from Johannes Philoponos (q.v.; see also TRITHEISTIC CONTROVERSY). These he subsequently abandoned, and differed from his old teacher also by affirming that the substance of the human body survived death and was eternal. The sect of which he was the leader had disappeared by the end of the seventh century.

BIBLIOGRAPHY: W. Cave, *Scriptorum ecclesiasticorum historia literaria*, i, 573, London, 1688; *DCB*, i. 621; *KL*, iii, 948.

CONRAD OF GELNHAUSEN: Theologian and scholar; b. in the Electoral Palatinate 1320; d. at Heidelberg 1390. His name first appears in 1344 as member of the faculty of the University of Paris. In a document of the following year he is mentioned as provost at St. Maurice. In 1363 he was canon in Mainz and later became provost at Worms. He was procurator of the German nation in Bologna as early as 1369, and obtained the degree of doctor of canon law there. Then he returned to Paris, devoted himself to the study of theology, and finished his theological studies probably in Prague. After 1387 he was in Heidelberg, a doctor of theology and chancellor of the university. His collection of books formed the nucleus of the university library. Among them were four theological writings of his own: *Sermones; Quæstiones; Circa sententias;* and *Super librum Cantica Canticorum.*

Conrad's fame rests upon the *Epistola concordiæ* which he wrote in Paris in May, 1380, at the command of Charles V. of France, after giving this sovereign in the preceding year the same advice in a shorter form; viz., to cooperate with other princes in calling a general council without the popes. Appealing expressly to Thomas Aquinas, but in reality leaning upon Occam and developing his ideas, he argued logically from the acknowledged superiority of the Catholic Church that the exceptional circumstances of the schism exempted from the letter of the law and justified the meeting of a council without papal convocation. He did not advance beyond this step; but his work became the basis upon which Henry of Langenstein (q.v.) and the conciliar theologians continued to build.

(B. Bess.)

Bibliography: The *Epistola concordiæ* is edited in E. Martène and U. Durand, *Thesaurus novus anecdotorum*, ii. 1717, pp. 1200–26, Paris, 1717. Consult: F. J. Scheuffgen, *Beiträge zur Geschichte des grossen Schismas*, pp. 75–91, Freiburg, 1889; A. Kneer, *Die Entstehung der konziliaren Theorie*, Rome, 1893: K. Wenck, in *Historische Zeitschrift*, new series, xl., 1895.

CONRAD OF MARBURG: Inquisitor-general of Germany; killed at Marburg July 30, 1233. The year of his birth is not known, and it is not certain whether he was a Dominican or a Franciscan. He was selected by Gregory IX. for the purpose of introducing the papal inquisition into Germany (see Inquisition). He first appears probably in connection with the great auto da fé which was held at Strasburg 1212. On June 17, 1227, a bull for the extirpation of heresy (Ripoll, *Bullarium ord. præd.*, i., Rome, 1729, p. 20) gave him full power in the matter; and his powers were still further increased by Gregory's chief bull against heresy in Germany (Hartzheim, *Concilia Germaniæ*, iii. 540). When Frederick II. gave imperial confirmation to the severe papal measures against heretics (Mar., 1232), then "began the flame to get power over mortals" (*Annales Colonienses maximi, MGH, Script.*, xvii., 1861, p. 843). Conrad now proceeded, with the assistance of certain colleagues (e.g., the Dominican Droso), to utilize this unlimited power, which even dispensed him from observing ordinary forms of trial; and so led countless victims to death. The fact is confirmed especially by the report of Bishop Siegfried III. of Mainz to Gregory IX. (*MGH, Script.*, xxiii., 1874, p. 931); and in the face of its evidence, the latter-day Roman Catholic apology for Conrad (by the Jesuit Pfülf, in *KL*, vii. 951) is ineffectual. In 1233, after he had vainly endeavored to draw the German princes into a more eager persecution of heresy, Conrad brought one of their number, Count von Sayn, before the tribunal, but the count contrived to vindicate himself before a synod at Mainz. Conrad next assembled a veritable crusaders' army; but at this juncture his fate swiftly overtook him, and he was slain by certain Hessian knights, while traveling to Marburg.

A second occasion of interest in Conrad's career is his relation to the pious Landgravine Elizabeth of Thuringia. He is a typical Roman Catholic spiritual guide, to whom the confiding penitent surrenders blindly (see Elizabeth, Saint). The view that Conrad's excessive zeal in the persecution of heretics is accountable for the fact that the papal Inquisition was unable to assert itself in Germany is erroneous; after his death there still occurred (1234 and 1235) cases of the burning of heretics at the stake by papal inquisitors, and even down to the fourteenth century such cases recurred again and again. The fact is, the same Inquisition was powerfully supported in the fourteenth century by the Emperor Charles IV., and exacted numberless victims in Bohemia, Silesia, and in parts of North Germany.

K. Benrath.

Bibliography: *Gesta Treverorum, Continuatio IV.*, ed. G. Waitz, in *MGH, Script.*, xxiv (1879), 390–404; A. Hausrath, *Der Ketzermeister Konrad von Marburg*, Marburg, 1861; E. L. T. Henke, *Konrad von Marburg*, ib. 1861; L. Cuno, *Conrad von Marburg*, ib. 1877; B. Kaltner, *Konrad von Marburg und die Inquisition in Deutschland*, Prague, 1822; H. C. Lea, *Hist. of the Inquisition*, ii. 325–341, New York, 1906; K. Benrath, in *Deutsch-evangelische Blätter*, part 5, Halle, 1901.

CONRING, HERMANN (*Hermannus Conringius*): German theologian; b. at Norden (75 m. n.w. of Bremen) Nov. 9, 1606; d. at Helmstädt (21 m. e. of Brunswick) Dec. 12, 1681. He studied at Helmstädt and Leyden, was appointed professor of natural philosophy at Helmstädt in 1632, and was transferred to the medical faculty five years later. In 1650 he was made physician to the queen of Sweden, and eleven years later became privy councilor of the duke of Brunswick. He received a pension from Louis XIV. in 1664, and in 1669 was appointed councilor of state by the king of Denmark. Conring's wealth of learning, like his legal and diplomatic knowledge, was devoted to proving that the Protestant Church was entitled to exist as a part of the Church catholic. In this spirit he wrote his *De constitutione episcoporum Germaniæ* (Helmstädt, 1647), and in the same year prepared an annotated edition of the letters of Leo III. to Charlemagne. In his *De conciliis et circa ea summa potestatis auctoritate* (1650) he asserted the right of the emperor and the estates to convene, conduct, and confirm plenary councils, and also to enact ecclesiastical rulings without their aid, while in the following year his *De electione Urbani IX. et Innocentii X. pontificum* assailed the method of electing popes. The Roman Catholic propaganda which had resulted in the conversion of his close friend Baron Johann Christian von Boyneburg evoked two polemic works from his pen, the *Defensio ecclesiæ Protestantium adversum duo pontificiorum argumenta* (1654), in which he impugned the doctrine that a Church is invalid without apostolic succession, and *Fundamentorum fidei pontificiæ concussio* (1654), denying that either the pope or an ecumenical council was the infallible representative of God on earth in matters of faith and conduct. This called forth a series of refutations, to which Conring replied in the same year with vigor. He also essayed irenics, and in his posthumous *De scriptoribus sedecim post Christum natum sæculorum commentarius* (1705) discussed the Church Fathers, and in his *De Germanorum imperio Romano* (1644) considered the changed legal relations existing between emperor and pope. He likewise touched on dogmatics, exegesis, and criticism in works of minor importance

(E. Henke†.)

Bibliography: The *Opera*, ed. J. W. Goebel, incomplete, in 7 vols., appeared, Brunswick, 1730. Consult: O. Stobbe, *H. Conring*, Berlin, 1870; K. F. H. Marx, *Zur Erinnerung der ärztlichen Wirksamkeit H. Conrings*, Göttingen, 1873.

CONSALVI, ERCOLE: Italian cardinal and diplomat; b. at Rome June 8, 1757; d. there Jan. 24, 1824. He received his early education at the school of the Piarists at Urbino, which he left to enter the college founded by Cardinal Henry of York at Frascati. The youth's talents won the favor of the cardinal duke. From Frascati he went to the ecclesiastical academy at Rome. On leaving the Academy in 1783, he received a post in the papal household, and aided by the influence of his kinsman, Cardinal Negroni, moved rapidly through several grades of office, receiving in 1792 the post of auditor for Rome at the Roman Rota. He became so prominent a figure in the churchly and noble circles of Rome and Frascati that he gained the sobriquet of "Monsignore Everywhere." He was military assessor at the time of the rise of the French Directory, and when the latter compelled Pius VI. to leave Rome, Consalvi, after suffering a short term of imprisonment in the castle of St. Angelo, made his way to Venice where he was chosen secretary of the conclave that met to elect a successor to Pius VI.

Early Life and Training.

By Pius VII. he was created secretary of state Aug. 11, 1800, and at the same time was made cardinal deacon of St. Agata in Suburra. Thenceforth he appeared as the prime mover of the papal diplomacy. The first task to which he applied himself was the negotiation of a concordat with the French Republic, which was successfully accomplished July 15, 1801 (see Concordats, VI., 1, § 1). Napoleon's innovations, as Consalvi admitted, entirely annulled the results of his now laborious efforts. Napoleon knew him as his opponent and in 1806, when the French emperor submitted to the pope a plan for a defensive alliance coupled with the recognition of the pope as sovereign in Rome and of Napoleon as Holy Roman emperor, he declared that, if Consalvi refused to acquiesce in the proposition, it would be better for him to retire from his post. The proposal was rejected, and in June, 1806, Consalvi was superseded by Cardinal Casoni.

When in 1809 Pius VII. was deported from Rome Napoleon summoned the college of cardinals to assemble at Paris, partly from the desire to add the luster of their presence to the celebration of his marriage to Marie Louise, partly that he might hold them under his immediate influence in case of the death of Pius VII. Consalvi arrived at Paris in February, 1810. He was one of the thirteen "black" cardinals who refrained from attending the marriage ceremony of the emperor, thereby arousing the anger of Napoleon to the point where he threatened the ex-secretary of state with death. His property was sequestrated, with that of the other twelve, he was forbidden to display the insignia of his rank, and was ordered to take up his residence at Reims, where he composed his *Mémoires* (2 vols., Paris, 1864; 2d ed., 1866). After the conclusion of the Concordat of Fontainebleau (Jan. 25, 1813; see Concordats, VI., 1, § 3) he took up his residence with Pius VII. Upon the fall of Napoleon he was sent to Paris as representative of the papal interests in the council of the powers, and in the same capacity he visited London and attended the Congress of Vienna. There he revealed a depth of insight and suppleness of spirit which aroused the admiration of the pope and the Viennese diplomats. Thoroughly a modern, he fought zealously for the interests of the Church without deluding himself with medieval conceptions of the rights and powers of the papacy. Article 103 of the Peace of Vienna restored to the Church possession of the districts of Camerino, Beneventum, and Pontecorvo, and the legations of Ravenna, Bologna, and Ferrara, with the exception of a small strip of territory included within the last, on the left bank of the Po. "His was the boldest and keenest game played on the green table," said Talleyrand to Metternich.

Diplomatic Achievements.

Before leaving Vienna, Consalvi pledged himself to the powers to put an end to the sacerdotal régime in Rome, a promise which he found impossible to keep. For the government of the States of the Church he issued a code of laws which aimed at their reduction to a centralized and uniformly organized principality. The papal territories were divided into seventeen delegations, each under the authority of a prelate exercising functions similar to those of the prefect of a department in France. In the administration of affairs he was opposed by the zealots under Cardinal Pacca, who detested Consalvi as the representative of modern and worldly ideals. After 1815 he was engaged in the negotiation of a series of concordats by which the relations of the Church with every Catholic state but Austria were regulated anew. In the revolutionary movement of 1820 he showed himself resolutely opposed to all concession, and with the help of the Austrian troops order was maintained in the legations. Soon, however, his rela-

Failure and Retirement.

tions with the Austrian government became strained and it was the opposition of that power which destroyed his chances of being chosen successor to Pius VII., whose death occurred Aug. 20, 1823. Upon the election of Leo XII. Consalvi went into retirement. During the height of his power after the Congress of Vienna he had been a patron of the arts, Canova and Thorwaldsen being among those who enjoyed his protection.

(F. Nielsen†.)

Bibliography: *Correspondance du . . . Consalvi avec . . . Metternich, 1815–23*, ed. C. van Duerm, Louvain, 1899; N. P. S. Wiseman, *Recollections of the Last Four Popes*, London, 1859; F. Nielsen, *Geschichte des Papstthums im 19. Jahrhundert*, vol. i., Gotha, 1880, Eng. transl., New York, 1906; L. Séché, *Les Origines du concordat*, Paris, 1894; *Mémoires du Cardinal Consalvi, introduction par J. Cretineau-Joly*, new ed., published by J. E. B. Drochon, ib. 1895; E. L. Fischer, *Cardinal Consalvi, Lebens- und Charakterbild*, Mainz, 1899.

CONSCIENCE.

The English word "conscience" is derived from the Latin *conscientia*, which is parallel in derivation and meaning to the New Testament *syneidēsis* (Attic Gk. *syneidos*); but in the classical authors the word denotes originally simply consciousness, without any ethical bearing. Its use in the modern sense of "conscience," or the moral sense of the individual applied to his own conduct, occurs not infrequently in Cicero and Seneca. The latter name especially has been taken to suggest that the ethical connotation came from the Stoic anthropology and legal doctrine; but the word does not occur in this sense in any Stoic writer except Seneca, and it is more probable that it acquired its later meaning gradually in the course of the process which led the ancient world from unthinking obedience to traditional custom up to the appeal to the inner tribunal of every man's heart. This inner witness had, however, no religious connection. The *daimon* of Socrates expresses a confidence in higher guidance which has a religious coloring, the consciousness of his mission felt by the great man, but has nothing to do with the old *syneidēsis*; and the often-quoted passage (*Epist.*, xli.) in which Seneca speaks of "the holy spirit that dwells within us" is merely the expression of the Stoic, and therefore not religious, pantheism.

1. Origin of the Term.

The term is not found in the Old Testament or among the words of Jesus. It was introduced into the primitive Christian vocabulary by Paul, outside of whose letters it occurs in the New Testament only in the Acts (in Paul's mouth), in I Peter, and in Hebrews. In his work Paul comes in contact with the general human conscience (II Cor. iv. 2), and appeals to it (Rom. ii. 15; xiii. 5, 6), or corrects deviations in it proceeding from remnants of heathen ideas (I Cor. viii. 7; x. 23 sqq.). Otherwise it is the Christian conscience alone to which appeal is made (Acts xxiii. 1; II Tim. i. 3); only the author of Hebrews (ix. 9) uses the conception, by this time accepted in Christian terminology, as a short expression for the critical standpoint of the new religion toward the condition of things under the old covenant. With Paul the pre-Christian conscience stands for the divine natural order of society (Rom. xiii. 4, 5) or more generally for the moral law whose commands are felt in the heart, in substantial agreement with the Jewish revealed law, and thus in a way taking its place for the Gentiles (Rom. ii. 14, 15). It makes them morally independent by a self-judgment which penetrates to the most hidden motives (Rom. ix. 1; II Cor. i. 12), coordinate with that of the Searcher of hearts; and it is capable also of passing judgment on others (II Cor. v. 11; iv. 2). But Paul nowhere hints at a recognized theonomy through the conscience, nor yet at a distinction between the pre-Christian and the Christian conscience. Again, the imperative conscience is nowhere mentioned in the New Testament. Paul recognizes the possibility of a conscience being weak, subject to other powers than the one God (I Cor. viii. 7, 12), and erroneous in its judgment. This leads him to the recognition of the individuality of conscience, its right of independent judgment, the denial of which would destroy moral personality (I Cor. x. 29, viii. 10). By the blood of Christ the conscience is cleansed, and the Christian obtains a "good" conscience (Rom. ix. 1; II Cor. i. 12; Heb. ix. 14, x. 22); this wholly good conscience is connected (I Pet. iii. 21; Heb. x. 22) with the gift of grace in baptism. This good conscience is not the certainty of reconciliation, but the mirror of the moral condition. Hence its chief characteristic is its sincerity (II Cor. i. 12), which attests its purity (I Tim. iii. 9; II Tim. i. 3). Its opposite is a branded, defiled conscience (I Tim. iv. 2; Titus i. 15). The "faith unfeigned" stands or falls with a pure conscience (I Tim. i. 5, 19; iii. 9; iv. 1, 2).

2. Paul's Use of it.

But although Paul thus gave a definite sanction to the term, there is no evidence that it passed from him into the current speech of the early Church; it is seldom met with in the primitive literature, and then first in exegetical writings. Chrysostom, with his practical tendency, is the first to make much use of it, describing it as an independent source of moral insight and coordinating it with the created universe as a means of the knowledge of God. While he goes thus far beyond the pagan conception, Augustine and his opponent Pelagius are inclined to rest in the mere idea of a consciousness which attests and judges moral action. From Augustine the connection of conscience with the more general consciousness was handed on, sometimes, as with Abelard, in the form of the consciousness of obligation, sometimes, as with Bernard, in that of the incorruptible judgment, and served to emphasize the inner life in contrast with the externalism of ecclesiastical theology. The scholastic theology followed Alexander of Hales rather closely throughout; the classical expression of it is found in Thomas Aquinas (*Summa*, I. lxxix.; II., part ii. xciv.). The pecu-

3. The Fathers and Schoolmen.

liarity of this earliest scientific treatment of the subject is the introduction of the idea of *syntērēsis*, interpreted by the scholastics, in dependence upon the Aristotelian psychology, as the practical intellect, i.e., in their conception, the *potentia* or *habitus* of moral principles, while *conscientia* is distinguished from it as the application of these to the individual act. With this distinction came in the idea of the fallibility of the conscience; and so the door was opened to all sorts of hair-splitting judgments, exemplified in the books on casuistry. The extreme result of this tendency is seen among the Jesuits, whose moral system knows nothing of *syntērēsis*, and regards *conscientia* as a prejudice to be removed by probabilism (see ETHICS, II., § 9). The Latin mysticism, on the other hand, made a fruitful use of the scholastic doctrine when, following patristic hints, it defined (especially in Gerson) the *syntērēsis* as the power by which the soul longs and is able to come into immediate contact with God.

4. The Reformers.

The attention paid by both professional theologians and the practical system of the Church to the conscience, far as it went beyond New Testament limits, was a reason why conscience was such an important factor in the discussions of the Reformation. These, however, derive rather from Bernard and Abelard than from the schoolmen. To Luther and his fellows it was now the independent consciousness of duty, now the sorrowful consciousness of sin, the accuser not to be silenced except in the assurance of justification by faith. In whatever terms it is defined, it amounts to the relation of the moral life to God, with its judging, even its condemning, function principally emphasized; it is the organ for the relation of justice between God and man. In like manner Calvin calls it "the sense of the divine judgment and empire." Specially characteristic are the passages in which he deals with it, particularly in his doctrine of justification by faith and of Christian liberty. The eye of faith now looks out boldly and clearly from the secure watch-tower of unconditional religious obligation over the broad domain of freedom of conscience.

5. Modern Philosophers.

The way in which the orthodox theologians spoke of the Christian conscience, presupposing a relation of religious dependence upon God and obligation to obey his law, was attacked by English deism when it opposed the natural as the universal to the positive historical as the unsupported particular. Since Hutcheson it had been customary in England to replace "innate ideas" by the moral sense, understood so as to combine this moral obligation with intellectual skepticism as to a universally binding ethical law, and to deny any religious relation. The ultimate consequence of this opposition between nature and history is seen in Rousseau, whose "natural conscience" was a mere instinct leading to morality, with no content of guilt or obligation. Kant, on the other hand, emphasized and recognized an inner tribunal of incomparable dignity. Fichte defined conscience as "the immediate consciousness of specific duty," which involves the unconditional certainty of a consciousness of duty with which a practical judgment, logically deduced from recognized premises, is endowed. The exaggerated emphasis laid upon formal certainty led to the extension of the word to a judgment of taste in all practical relations, as with Herbart and with Krauss ("the innate necessity to have an ideal and to acknowledge it as a judge set over us"), and thus in the modern phrase "the artistic conscience." This is a notable declension from the former high claims; and it goes still further when Hegel, though recognizing unconditional subjective certainty from the standpoint of morality, insists that it must be measured by the idea or the objectivity of social ethics; when Schopenhauer replaces the infallible, imperative consciousness of duty by a "protocol of facts," which is a purely objective and empirical standard. Since his day there has been an increasing tendency to substitute for the self-conscious autonomy of the subject the cultural development of society, and to regard conscience, with Spencer, as a product of education, good or bad.

6. Present-Day Problems.

This, then, raises the first of the points most discussed in modern theological treatises; whether conscience is an innate, primeval thing, and then whether it is only a subjective phenomenon, the formal consciousness of duty, or has a content from without. This, with the other question of the relation of religion and morality, is a matter of great interest to those who now discuss religion from the anthropological standpoint. The solution of the problem, however, depends as a rule upon the general views held by each of the many authors who have recently treated the subject of conscience. A further question, this time rather a practical than a theoretical one, deals with freedom of conscience. This depends upon the individuality of the conscience, and is opposed to the claim that one may be morally bound by any other authority than that of God. Such a claim appears in its most obvious form when an institution like the Roman Catholic Church identifies its utterances with the divine revelation. From the Reformers' protest against such a claim have sprung first the demand for the free exercise of religion within the limits of the social order, and then that of unrestricted expression of any religious or ethical conviction; but such unqualified freedom would obviously imperil all ordered social life.

(M. KÄHLER.)

7. Intuitional and Evolutionary Views.

The moral law originates in custom and is at first identical with it, as is evident in the terms "ethics" and "morals." The outstanding, most advantageous, and necessary customs are crystallized into positive law; later, positive laws conflict with custom or with each other. This conflict may be resolved temporarily by casuistry or by making one command supreme. And the validity of the moral law may for a time rest back on punishment. Attempts to find an ultimate basis of the moral law in the nature of man have given rise to two theories of conscience, the intuitional and the evolutionary. According to the former, conscience is a clear perception of good and evil, accompanied by a feeling of unconditioned obligation and of irreversible approval or disapproval of actions—intuitive, original, universal, supernatural, "the voice of God in the soul of man." This theory has been subjected to the criticism that the conscience does not infallibly disclose what one ought to do, that the judgment of right and wrong varies in different places and is subject to change, that in the moral consciousness the judgment of good and evil may conflict, and, finally, that the ground of obligation is objective as well as subjective. Hence, the explanation of conscience is sought in evolution. The external occasion for its origination lies in social experience, registered in customs and changing laws. The earliest sense of duty is the consciousness of custom; later, the sense of obligation appears in the conflict between particular inclinations and obedience to the customary. Through experience new conditions give rise to advantageous forms of action which will in turn be antagonized by custom. The ideal principle of this newer action is, however, elevated into a controlling law, first for an individual, then for the community, resulting either in quiet and gradual readjustment of ethical relations, or in the sudden and radical beginning of a new era of ethical ideal and law. Thus the conscience is that aspect of consciousness which unifies the system of social, i.e., of moral relations with reference to individual and social development and completeness—the response in the moral consciousness of a uniform objective stimulus. Accordingly, the conscience, instead of being set free from the influence of divinity as something alien to the nature and entering it from without, discloses the immanence of the divine teleological (transcendent) action in the individual consciousness within the social order. See ETHICS; DUTY; CONFLICT OF DUTIES; and CASUISTRY.

C. A. BECKWITH.

BIBLIOGRAPHY: For the Biblical side consult the lexicons of H. Cremer and J. H. Thayer, and the works on N. T. theology; also J. T. Beck, *Umriss der biblischen Seelenlehre*, Stuttgart, 1871, Eng. transl., Edinburgh, 1877; P. Ewald, *De vocis suneidēseōs apud scriptores N. T.*, Leipsic, 1883. For the history of the subject consult: T. Ziegler, *Geschichte der Ethik*, Bonn, 1881–86; K. Köstlin, *Geschichte der Ethik*, vol. i., Tübingen, 1887; H. Sidgwick, *Hist. of Ethics*, London, 1896. For treatment of Conscience consult: E. Kant, *Critique on Practical Reason*, London, 1896; Joseph Butler, *Three Sermons on Human Nature, with Introduction and Notes by T. B. Kilpatrick*, Edinburgh, 1888; R. H. Hoffmann, *Die Lehre von dem Gewissen*, Leipsic, 1866; W. Gass, *Die Lehre vom Gewissen*, Berlin, 1869; J. F. D. Maurice, *The Conscience*, London, 1872; M. Kähler, *Das Gewissen*, Halle, 1878; W. T. Davison, *The Christian Conscience*, London, 1888; R. Seeberg, *Gewissen und Gewissenbildung*, Erlangen, 1896; N. S. Rulison, *Study of Conscience*, Philadelphia, 1901; O. Huckel, *A Modern Study of Conscience*, ib. 1907; *DB*, i. 468–475; modern works on ethics, particularly N. Smyth, *Christian Ethics*, New York, 1892, and J. Martineau, *Types of Ethical Theory*, London, 1898; and modern treatises on psychology. For the intuitional theory of the conscience consult: H. Calderwood, *Handbook of Moral Philosophy*, Edinburgh, 1888; J. Martineau, *Types of Ethical Theory*, 2 vols., London, 1886. For the evolutionary or anthropological view consult: W. K. Clifford, *Lectures and Essays*, London, 1879; S. Alexander, *Moral Order and Progress*, London, 1889; J. H. Muirhead, *Elements of Ethics*, pp. 63–88, 215–235, New York, 1892; F. Paulsen, *System of Ethics*, pp. 340–378, New York, 1899.

CONSCIENTIARII (Germ. *Gewissener*): The adherents of Matthias Knutsen, a theological candidate from Sleswick who, in Sept., 1674, came to Jena and there set on foot a propaganda for his deistic and atheistic principles. According to him, conscience was to be the sole authority, even at the cost of rejecting faith in God and immortality; but his conscience was one which could justify the most immoral relations, putting marriage on the same level as indiscriminate sexual intercourse. He boasted that he had a following of seven hundred townsmen and students in Jena and Altdorf. This brought about an investigation which showed that his claims were unfounded, and he thought it best to disappear. The University of Jena vindicated its reputation in a formal statement of the truth by Musæus, one of its professors; and the sect soon died out.

CONSECRATION: [The formal setting apart of a person or thing as sacred or devoted to God by a special religious rite. For the consecration of the elements of the Lord's Supper see EPIKLESIS; EUCHARIST, § 5. For the consecration of bishops see BISHOP; see also PRIEST. For the consecration of things (altars, bells, etc.) see BENEDICTION; SACRAMENTALS. This article will be confined to the consecration of churches.]

Churches were solemnly consecrated as early as the time of Constantine, both those which were rebuilt after destruction in times of persecution (Eusebius, *Hist. eccl.*, x. 2–5) and new buildings (Eusebius, *Vita Constantini*, xlv.). The fundamental thought was naturally the idea that the deity had obtained a new abode of visible presence (cf. Augustine, *Sermones*, clxiii.), wherewith was later associated the maxim that the sacrifice of the mass may never be performed without an altar, and, cases of necessity excepted, only in consecrated churches or public chapels. Even in comparatively early times, relics were used in connection with the consecration. In the Middle Ages the ceremonies increased; the most noteworthy, according to the *Liber sacramentorum Gregorii Magni* (after *XII. Kalendas Januarius*), was that the bishop traced with ashes the Greek and Latin alphabets (earlier also the Hebrew) diagonally across the church from corner to corner, the two lines intersecting in the form of a cross. The signification, as explained by Ivo of Chartres was "the union of both peoples [Gentiles and Jews] by the single bond of the cross." The present Roman ceremonial is found in the Pontifical, and consecration devolves upon the bishop (see SACRAMENTALS). The consecration of churches with Eastern Orthodox Christians lays great stress on relics (cf. A. Maltzew, *Bitt-, Dank- und Weihegottesdienste*, Berlin, 1897, p. xcix.). Protestant churches need neither to be cleansed of demons nor be hallowed for the administration of the sacrifice of the mass. Nevertheless, the need of some act analogous to consecration was early felt (cf. Seckendorf's description of the opening of the castle church at Torgau, in his *Historia Lutheranismi*, bk. iii., § 118, and Luther's sermon, Erlangen ed., vol. xvii.). In the later liturgies forms of consecration for separate objects—e.g., organs and bells—occur frequently.

Even as early as the fourth century the churches on Golgotha and the site of the Resurrection were thronged on occasion of the "encænia," or anniversary of the church dedication (cf. the "Pilgrimage" of Silvia of Aquitaine, Palestine Pilgrims' Text Society transl., pp. 76–77). Isidore of Seville (*De officiis*, i. 35) explains the anniversary festival as a revival of the Jewish encænia. The lessons Rev. xxi. 1–5 and Luke xix. 1–10 were transferred to the Lutheran pericopes from the medieval lectionary which was in use in Germany. Luther, however, was not partial to the church dedication festival, observing (*An den christlichen Adel*), "Church dedications ought to be abolished altogether, seeing they have become naught else than very taverns, yearly fairs, and playhouses." Nevertheless, the festival of church dedication persisted, and it may be that the attendant excesses conspired to maintain it. These excesses perhaps resulted from the fact that the day of church dedication was to be preceded by abstinence, while the day itself was to be regarded as a feast of joyousness. For Protestants the anniversary festival of church dedication can have no other significance than that of a thanksgiving feast for the blessings of a well-regulated ecclesiastical status. W. Caspari.

Bibliography: Bingham, *Origines*, book viii., chap. ix.; M. Gerbert, *Monumenta veteris liturgiæ Alemaniæ*, disquisition vi., chap. i., San Blas, 1758; E. C. Harrington, *The Object . . . of the Rite of Consecration of Churches*, London, 1844; H. A. Daniel, *Codex liturgicus*, 4 vols., Leipsic, 1847–53.

CONSILIA EVANGELICA ("Evangelical counsels"): The name given in the doctrine of the Roman Catholic Church to a class of norms of moral conduct authorized in the New Testament. The term is used in distinction from *præcepta* ("commands"; i.e., injunctions which may not be disregarded, and thus fall within the sphere of imperative duty). The distinction dates back to Tertullian, who repeats the words of I Cor. vii. 25, "I have no commandment of the Lord; yet I give my judgment," in *De exhortatione castitatis*, iv., and makes it in five other places, and it occurs in the Vulgate rendering of the passage mentioned (*præceptum domini non habeo, consilium autem do*). Two of the ideas which gave Tertullian occasion to expound the distinction came in time to have great significance: namely, "what one may disregard is advised rather than commanded;" and that a merely advised renunciation of something in itself permitted (e.g., marriage) constitutes merit. This is repeated by Cyprian (*De habitu virginum*, xxiii.), and the same doctrine had been already conveyed in the *Shepherd of Hermas* (mand. IV. iv. 2; sim. V. iii. 3). The opinion therefore seems well founded that it was Ambrose who first expressly formulated the distinction between *præcepta* and *consilia* (*De viduis*, xii.). After him it appears in Optatus, Jerome, notably in Pelagius (*ad Demetrium*, ix.–x.), and also in Augustine. With reference to the latter's doctrine, H. Reuter (*Augustinische Studien*, Gotha, 1887, pp. 399–403, 426–427, 476) has noted a conflict between two tendencies. On the one hand, the external and literal observance of the counsels (as of poverty and virginity) is commended as a higher standard of morality, procuring a higher order of merit. On the other hand, it becomes precarious to measure by this test the ultramoral, in so far as all conduct is viewed in the light of the inner moral intention.

Origin and Early Development.

Between Augustine and Aquinas the doctrine of the counsels gives ever greater and greater weight to the first tendency, upholding or exalting monasticism as the state of perfection. In St. Thomas, however, the other tendency also comes forward. According to his *Summa* (II. i., qu. 108, art. 4), the commandments are given "concerning those things which are necessary to attain the end of eternal felicity"; but the counsels, "concerning those by means of which one can attain the end aforesaid better and more quickly." Man stands between the things of this world and spiritual goods. To cleave altogether to the former is forbidden by the commandments, but it is not necessary to cast them absolutely away to reach eternal blessedness; "nevertheless one will come to it more quickly by rejecting entirely the goods of this world, and therefore the Evangelical counsels are given about this." They fall under these three general heads: poverty, chastity, and obedience; to which also the various particular specifications may all be referred. *Secunda secundæ* treats of the counsels under "the state of perfection." Query 184, art. 3, teaches that perfection consists *essentialiter* in the command of love, but *instrumentaliter* depends on the counsels. They are "so to speak, instruments for attaining to perfection"; they remove obstacles to the higher degrees of love, so long as love holds any commandments for whoever professes even the least degree of it. In the Middle Ages twelve counsels were commonly enumerated, which were found especially in the Sermon on the Mount; and after the aforesaid three general heads, which concerned the religious orders, there were recommended, for instance, the injunctions "love your enemies" (Matt. v. 44), "resist not evil" (Matt. v. 39–41), etc.

Thomistic and Medieval Teaching.

Luther contested the idea of St. Thomas that the higher degrees of love are not commanded. He condemned every infraction of the law, on the ground that it commands absolute fulfilment; inferior "perfection" is not allowed, but is a sin, which, however, God forgives on condition of faith with daily repentance and moral amendment. The Lutheran confessions oppose the Roman doctrine as to the counsels, because it sets up *merita supererogationis* (Augs. Con., xxvii. 12; Apol., xxvii. 24–25, 39); because it constructively permits private revenge (Augs. Con., xxvii. 54; Apol., xvi. 59), and casts doubt upon the civil commonwealth (Augs. Con., xxvii. 55; Apol., xvi. 56; cf. also Augs. Con., xxvii. 61; Apol., xxvii. 9). It can not, of course, be disputed that among the moral norms which concern Christendom at large there exist, side by side with "commandments of God" (I Cor. vii. 19), "commandments of the Lord" (vs. 25, 10), also the "judgments" of Paul. Paul's

Protestant Teaching.

"judgments" diverge, again, from his own "commandments" (cf. II Cor. viii. 10, 8; I Cor. xvi. 1, vii. 17, 19, 6). The essential feature of his "judgments" consists in the fact that they "cast no snare" (I Cor. vii. 35). That is to say, they do not enslave, they do not obligate all because their acceptance presupposes a gift (*charisma*) of God (vs. 7). On the basis of I Cor. vii. we may correctly distinguish between the advisory norm and the absolute force of a commandment; and indeed a similar norm occurs in Matt. xix. 11–12. But the Pauline and Lutheran doctrine as to this "counsel" is by no means identical with the Roman doctrine of the "counsels." The true general definition is: the counsels are auxiliary norms toward the discernment of those obligating commands which govern a Christian in his particular situation.

KARL THIEME.

BIBLIOGRAPHY: The works on moral theology, such as (Roman Catholic), T. H. Simar, §§ 17–18, Freiburg, 1893; and M. T. Göpfert, i., § 5, Paderborn, 1897; (Protestant), C. E. Luthardt, *Die Ethik Luthers*, pp. 72–80, 85–86, Leipsic, 1875; idem, *Kompendium der theologischen Ethik*, § 46, Leipsic, 1898; J. T. Beck, *Vorlesungen über christliche Ethik*, ii. 113–143, Gütersloh, 1883; R. Rothe, *Theologische Ethik*, iii. 856, n. 3, Bremen, 1895; K. Hase, *Handbuch der protestantischen Polemik*, Leipsic, 1900.

CONSISTORY, CONSISTORIAL ORGANIZATION.

In the Roman Catholic Church *consistorium* signifies the session of the College of Cardinals under the presidency of the pope, as well as the advisory board which assists the vicar general, the bishop's auxiliary for execution of the *jura jurisdictionis*. This latter signification affords a point of contact for the term as it is usually employed in the German Evangelical Church, the subject of this discussion. The German use first appears in a memorial addressed to the Elector John Frederick, on May 13, 1537, by a committee of the great diet of the electorate of Saxony, assembled at Torgau. The said memorial had manifestly some connection with a resolution, a few weeks previously, by the Schmalkald Convention, which had emphasized the duty of the territorial powers in cases "where the bishops rule amiss, or are negligent," in the matter of appointing ecclesiastical courts, especially in relation to matrimonial affairs; but the term "consistories" was not employed at Schmalkald. The memorial was referred to the faculty of theology and law at Wittenberg for an opinion how to put it in execution. This opinion (printed in A. L. Richter, *Geschichte der evangelischen Kirchenverfassung in Deutschland*, Leipsic, 1851, pp. 81–82), drawn up in the main by Jonas, was reported in the course of the year 1538, and it discusses the need of consistories and the powers to be assigned to them.

1. Origin of the German Consistory.

The execution of the Wittenberg opinion, especially in relation to independent executive authority and excommunication, received consideration, possibly from Luther and Brück, to whom final decision was reserved, and, at all events, from the elector; and, apparently at Brück's initiative, provision was made for the merely tentative institution of a consistory for the electorate only. This was established at Wittenberg at the beginning of Feb., 1539, but with limited competency, for it was only a matrimonial and disciplinary court; it did not consist of a single judge, but, according to the plan of the visitation committees, of a college of territorial "commissaries" composed of two theologians and two lawyers, who were selected from the younger members of the academic college of teachers. Finally it lacked executive power and specific instructions. In the absence of instructions, the consistory in difficult cases was to avail itself of the counsel of Luther "and the other theologians and jurists"; and in the autumn of 1540 it was directed to confer with Brück, and then "to formulate an orderly procedure as it may be executed, established, and written out by us." The work was done by the close of 1542, and under the title of *Constitution und Artikel des geistlichen Consistorii zu Wittenberg* it was published by Georg Buchholtzer as early as 1563 (reprint in E. Sehling, *Kirchenordnungen*, i., Leipsic, 1902, pp. 200 sqq.). Yet even this work remained a mere plan; and so long as Wittenberg belonged to the Ernestine line this consistory did not have the constitution of a formal consistory (cf. Mejer, in *ZKR*, xiii. 28–123, and in *Zum Kirchenrechte des Reformations-Jahrhunderts*, Hanover, 1891, pp. 1 sqq.).

2. The First Consistory, at Wittenberg, 1539.

Regarding Albertine Saxony, the purpose of Duke Henry at the introduction of the Reformation, of instituting a consistory at Leipsic, did not find realization (cf. E. Sehling, *Kirchenordnungen*, i. 94). Duke Maurice duly espoused the same plan, but turned aside to the project of restoring the episcopal organization. The conferences and opinions concerning the questions at issue are of great interest. At Merseburg Prince George of Anhalt took the conduct of things in hand as Evangelical bishop; and a collegiate board or consistory was given to him quite in the Roman manner. At Meissen, where the bishop persisted in the ancient doctrine, the consistory could be maintained only temporarily. The episcopal period reached its end in 1548. The Merseburg consistory was removed to Leipsic in 1550, and the consistory of Meissen was later transferred to Dresden (cf. E. Sehling, *Kirchengesetzgebung unter Moritz von Sachsen*, Leipsic, 1899, pp. 13 sqq.; *Kirchenordnungen*, i. 96 sqq.). Other bodies akin to the consistories, though the term consistory is not applied to them (cf. O. Mejer, *Die Grundlagen des lutherischen Kirchen-regiments*, Rostock, 1864, pp. 133 sqq.), belonging to the early Reformation period, turn out in every instance, upon closer examination, to be a city council or deputation of the same, reenforced by one or more clerical experts. In the year 1554 a theory of consistorial organization appeared in the book of Erasmus Sarcerius: *Von den Mitteln und Wegen, die rechte und wahre Religion, welche uns Gott in diesen letzten und gefährlichen Zeiten wiederum geoffenbaret hat, zu befördern und zu erhalten.*

3. Other Similar Attempts.

Of the subsequent history of the consistories (cf. Mejer, *Grundlagen*, pp. 144–145) only special phases need be considered here. For Prussia the subject is well treated by H. F. Jacobson, in *Evangelisches Kirchenrecht des preussischen Staates* (Halle, 1864, pp. 141 sqq.); and for Saxony by Müller, in *Beiträge zur sächsischen Kirchengeschichte*, ix. and x. (Leipsic, 1894). After the Saxon pattern, composed on collegiate lines of clerical and nonclerical members, and with superintendents as subordinate officials, the consistories became diffused through all the Lutheran churches of Germany. They took the place of the original district visitation committees. They were not mere imitations of the Saxon precedent, but spontaneous products of the operation of the theory of state church polity, which not only required officers for the protection of church property and of the outward ecclesiastical dispensation, but also theological experts for the maintenance of pure doctrine and rightful administration of the sacraments. Accordingly, with but insignificant variations, the constitution of the consistories remains always the same. Sometimes consistories were created to restrict doctrinal disputations and encroachments of clergymen upon the domain of ecclesiastical discipline; on this ground the consistory at Weimar, for instance, was called into existence in 1561 (cf. Sehling, *Kirchenordnungen*, i. 65). Where the consistories have a distinctly independent status they are said to be "*formiert*"; where they are adjuncts to temporal courts or administrative authorities they are said to be "*nichtformiert*." In smaller territories these latter were of frequent occurrence; and until the middle of the last century there was even a forestry board that was at the same time a *consistorium*. Consistories appointed by the sovereign are called immediate; those filled by authorities subordinated to civil officials are called mediate. In the Reformation period conditions of this kind arose where feudatory towns or great landed proprietors exercised certain rights of territorial supremacy, and consequently rights of church government as well; in modern times the mediate consistories were done away with by the mediatizations of 1806 and 1815.

4. The Later German Consistories.

From the very outset consistorial powers have not been everywhere the same. In not a few states they entirely took the place of episcopal jurisdiction; in others, as in case of the Wittenberg consistory of 1539, their functions were more circumscribed; so that sometimes consistories are merely church courts—the one of Mecklenburg at Rostock, for instance, was scarcely more than that; and elsewhere they have also carried with them by transfer the administrative affairs of church polity, which are ascribed to them by Sarcerius. In the former case administrative affairs devolve upon the state chancery or privy council, and the practical knowledge of spiritual affairs is furnished by affiliated court preachers or superintendents. The church-governing privileges vested in the consistories are usually called *jura vicaria*; those reserved to the personal decision of the sovereign are called *jura reservata*. The consistories are always boards of the sovereign and government; that there should also inhere in them some independent representation of the Church is a thought that first sprang up in the sixteenth century. This thought had its practical sequel in certain provisions of the Peace of Westphalia by virtue of which, even under a sovereign of different faith, consistories on a basis of confessional integrity were guaranteed. The point was overlooked, however, that in the same Westphalian peace negotiations church government was expressly characterized as an attribute of state supremacy, and that nothing more was contemplated than that the state sovereign must exercise such rights through officers of the respective confession.

5. Powers of Consistories.

According to the principle of the State's *custodia prioris tabulæ*, which obtained in government praxis far into the eighteenth century, the subjects of the State stood without exception under the church-governing surveillance of the territorial sovereignty. They were also subject as a body to the sovereign authorities with respect to the administration of this jurisdiction. Thus, not only Protestants who did not belong to the state church, but likewise Roman Catholics and even Jews were under the consistories. The consistory as modernly developed had up to that time enjoyed not only church-governing functions, but also—because no distinction was made—functions of church sovereignty; and the pioneer exponents of the tolerance principle, who likewise had not yet learned sufficiently to distinguish between the two spheres of activity, now came to attribute to church polity, in its general scope, only what were essentially church sovereignty problems; hence, too, as reacting against false theories of office, they could seriously debate the question whether the importation of theologians into the consistories were not superfluous. Nor was it the less in accord herewith that Reformed or Catholic officers were occasionally appointed to Lutheran consistories. It was a more wholesome development from the time of the absolute police régime that after the middle of the eighteenth century the civil and criminal jurisdiction over ecclesiastical persons and affairs was withdrawn more and more from the consistories, as likewise from the Roman Catholic prelatical authorities, and transferred to the ordinary courts. Even the jurisdiction in matrimonial concerns was at last taken from them, so that apart from their administrative business, they retain simply a corrective jurisdiction over official transgressions, and on occasion a denunciatory prerogative that goes with their exercise of ecclesiastical supervision. (For the law as now in force cf. E. Friedberg, *Verfassungs-Recht der evangelischen Landeskirchen*, Leipsic, 1888.) From the consistorial organization is to be distinguished the synodal, in virtue of which the Church governs itself by means of committees—synods, presbyteries, etc. (see PRESBYTER; and PRESBYTERIANS); and the so-called mixed form of church organization prevalent in Germany to-day, which combines both these theories of organization.

6. Modern Modifications.

E. SEHLING.

For the organization of the Lutheran churches in America see LUTHERANS. In the Reformed Dutch and Reformed French churches the consistory is an ecclesiastical court corresponding to the Presbyterian session in the former, and to the presbytery in the latter; in the Church of England it is a diocesan court presided over by the chancellor of the diocese.

CONSTANCE, BISHOPRIC OF: The origin of the see of Constance can not be positively determined. In the Roman period no bishopric is mentioned in northwestern Helvetia; but among the subscriptions to the Burgundian Synod of Epao (517) and the Frankish synods of Orléans (541, 549) occur the names of two bishops of Vindonissa, a name which is still preserved in that of the village of Windisch at the confluence of the Aar and the Reuss. This was the headquarters of the eleventh and twelfth legions, and it is likely that a Christian church existed there in Roman days. The last mention of such a bishopric is the signature of Grammaticus as *episcopus ecclesiæ Uindunnensis* in 549. Early in the seventh century a good authority, the *Vita Columbani*, mentions a bishop in one of the "neighbor" towns to Bregenz. The nearest episcopal sees are Augsburg, Chur, and Vindonissa; but none of these could quite be called *vicina urbs*. It is a natural supposition, therefore, that the town of Constance, founded at the end of the Roman period, was at this time an episcopal see, which probably replaced that of Vindonissa between 549 and 610. It included all the territory of the Alemanni not included in the older dioceses of Chur, Augsburg, Strasburg, and Basel, and extended from the Aar and the Rhine to the Iller, and from the middle course of the Neckar to the St. Gothard, including the Swabian highlands—thus embracing the greater part of modern Württemberg, southern Baden, central and northeastern Switzerland. No German diocese was so rich in prominent monasteries; among the best-known may be mentioned St. Gall, Reichenau, Kempten, Zurich, Lindau, Einsiedeln, St. Blasien, Petershausen, Muri, and Weingarten. (A. HAUCK.)

Originally subject to the archbishop of Besançon, Constance was placed under the jurisdiction of Mainz when the latter was raised by Boniface to the dignity of the metropolitan see of Germany. Here as elsewhere during the Middle Ages, canonical election of the bishops gave way to royal nomination, and probably all the bishops of the eleventh century owed their elevation to this source. Otto I. (1071–86) was a strong partisan of Henry IV., and, though the two bishops who covered the period from 1127 to 1165 were canonically chosen, during the struggle with Barbarossa Constance was usually on the side of the imperial claimant of the papacy. In 1220 the process of acquiring the temporal dignity of a prince of the empire for the bishop was completed, though the secular jurisdiction embraced only twenty-two square miles, only a small part of the diocese, and did not include the see city. In the fourteenth century contested papal and episcopal elections brought much unrest, until the long rule of Henry III. of Brandis, abbot of Einsiedeln (1357–83), restored order. At the Reformation most of the Swiss part of the diocese adopted the new religion, while Duke Ulrich introduced Protestantism into Württemberg in 1534. The city of Constance declared for Zwinglian tenets, and was one of the four towns which presented the Tetrapolitan Confession (q.v.) at the Diet of Augsburg in 1530. In 1526 the bishop transferred his residence to Meerstadt, where his successors preferred to remain, even after the victory of the imperial arms had crushed out both the Protestantism and the freedom of the city. But though the diocese had come through many perils without hopeless loss, it fell a victim to the changes brought about by the French Revolution. The Peace of Lunéville (1802) abolished the temporal sovereignty of the bishop, which was divided between Baden and Switzerland. The bishopric itself went down in the general upheaval, and the Swiss territory, after being administered for a time by a vicar-apostolic, was assigned to the sees of Basel, Chur, and St. Gall, that now in Württemberg to the new see of Rottenberg, and the Bavarian section to Augsburg. The last vestige of the old diocese disappeared in 1821, when the small remainder was incorporated with the diocese of Freiburg, the metropolitan see of the new province of the Upper Rhine.

BIBLIOGRAPHY: Sources are in *Wirtembergisches Urkundenbuch*, 6 vols., Stuttgart, 1849–54; *Regesta Badensia*, ed. C. G. Dümgé, Carlsruhe, 1839; *MGH*, *Script.*, xiii (1881), 324 sqq., xv (1888), 1023–24, 1284 sqq.; *Regesta episcoporum Constantiensium*, 2 vols., Innsbruck, 1894–96. Consult: Rettberg, *KD*, ii. 98 sqq.; Friedrich, *KD*, 2 vols.; Hauck, *KD*, vols. i.–iii.; E. Egli, *Kirchengeschichte der Schweiz*, Zurich, 1893.

CONSTANCE, COUNCIL OF: The second of the three "reforming councils" of the fifteenth century. It was called by Pope John XXIII. and the Emperor Sigismund, and sat from Nov. 5, 1414, to Apr. 22, 1418. Its three great objects were to heal the papal schism (see SCHISM), to examine the heresy of Wyclif and Huss and the religious disturbances thereby caused in Bohemia, and to carry through a general reform of the Church. It was attended by twenty-nine cardinals, three patriarchs, thirty-three archbishops, about one hundred and fifty bishops, more than one hundred abbots, a larger number of

General Character.

professors and doctors of theology and canon law, and more than 5,000 monks, besides princes, noblemen, ambassadors, etc. Beside an ecclesiastical assembly a general European congress was in progress. The number of strangers in Constance is put by the lowest estimate at 50,000, and among them such characters as money-lenders, strolling actors, and low women were well represented. The pope rode into the city on Oct. 28, with great magnificence, sixteen hundred horses carrying his retinue and luggage. The emperor arrived on Christmas Eve with an imposing following. The most prominent and most influential members of the council were Pierre d'Ailly and Jean Gerson, who soon became its soul.

The Council of Pisa (1409) had attempted to put an end to the schism by deposing both Gregory XII., who resided in Rome, and Benedict XIII., who resided at Avignon, and electing in their stead

Alexander V. But the result was simply that there now were three popes instead of two; and the confusion continued unabated, when, after the death of Alexander V. (1410), the leaders of the Pisan council elected John XXIII. All three popes were invited to Constance, but only John was present. He was crafty and unscrupulous, dissolute and avaricious; but he was courageous, shrewd, inexhaustible in shifts and intrigues, and equal to any emergency.

The Question of the Schism.

He hoped to control the council by means of the very great number of Italian prelates, who, mostly dependent upon him, accompanied him to Constance. But in this he failed. The order of business adopted (Feb. 7, 1415) on the proposal of the English was that of working and voting by nations; and in the plenary sessions the Italian nation, had, of course, only one vote beside the other nations—the German, French, English, and, after the deposition of Benedict XIII., the Spanish. Each nation formed an efficient organization, in which, contrary to the wishes of the pope, his chief opponents—the doctors, the lower clergy, the princes and their representatives—had voice and vote. John now endeavored to urge upon the assembly the view that the Council of Constance was nothing but a continuation of that of Pisa, which had formally condemned his two rivals, and, indirectly at least, legitimized his own election. But in this, too, he failed; and the party of Pierre d'Ailly finally succeeded in carrying a motion that the three popes should be compelled to abdicate, and a new election take place. John abdicated in the hope of being reelected; but he soon became aware of his mistake, fled in the disguise of a groom (Mar. 20, 1415), protested, was caught, and was finally brought to acquiesce in the decisions of the council. In its fifth plenary session (Apr. 6, 1415) the assembly agreed that an ecumenical council, legally convened, and fully representative of the Church, has its power directly from Christ, and that its decrees are consequently obligatory on all, even on the pope. May 29, 1415, John XXIII. was deposed; July 4 Gregory XII. voluntarily abdicated; July 26, 1417, Benedict XIII. was deposed; and Nov. 11, 1417, Cardinal Oddo Colonna was elected pope, and assumed the name of Martin V., who closed the council Apr. 22, 1418, at its forty-fifth session.

The Bohemian affairs were treated with great thoroughness; for Huss was burned July 6, 1415, and Jerome of Prague, May 30, 1416. But a final settlement was not arrived at, still less a satisfactory one (see Huss, John, Hussites). Still more conspicuously the council failed in its reform plans.

The Hussite Heresy and Question of Reform.

A *collegium reformatorium* was formed in Aug., 1415; but, characteristically enough for the whole situation, when Cardinal Zabarella read aloud to the assembly the decree of Apr. 16, 1415, he wilfully left out the passage it contained on the power of the council to undertake reforms in the Church. It was the lower clergy, the monks, the doctors, and professors, led by Pierre d'Ailly and Gerson, and supported by the emperor, who demanded reforms. But they were unable to agree among themselves, and the abuses in which reforms were necessary—such as the appeals to the pope, and the papal procedure, the administration of vacant benefices, and the giving *in commendam*, simony, dispensations, indulgences, etc.—were the sources from which the pope, the cardinals, and the huge swarm of ecclesiastical officials in Rome drew their principal revenues. In fighting against reforms, the cardinals fought for their very existence, and they proved unconquerable. In the thirty-ninth session (Oct. 9, 1417) the few articles upon which agreement was reached were approved and the decree *Frequens* was issued, providing for another council after five years, a second seven years later, and thereafter one every ten years. Eighteen specific reforms were brought forward, which the new pope should arrange with the council or "the deputies of the nations." The emperor wished the question of reform discussed and decided before the election of a new pope; but the cardinals declared that the worst ailing of the Church was its lack of a head, and when Martin V. was elected he understood how to bury the whole affair quietly and smoothly, by grave hesitations and cautious procrastinations. (B. Bess.)

Bibliography: Sources are: Ulrich von Richenthal, *Chronik des Constanzer Consils*, ed. M. R. Buck, Stuttgart, 1882; H. van der Hardt, *Magnum Constantiense concilium*, 7 vols., Frankfort and Berlin, 1698–1742; *Acta concilii Constanciensis*, ed. H. Finke, vol. i., Münster, 1896; Mansi, *Concilia*, vols. xxvi.–xxvii. Consult: J. Lenfant, *Histoire du concile de Constance*, 2 vols., Amsterdam, 1727, Eng. transl., London, 1730; F. Steinhausen, *Analecta ad historiam concilii . . . Constantiæ*, Berlin, 1862; J. Caro, *Aus der Kanzlei Kaiser Sigismunds urkundliche Beiträge zur Geschichte des Constanzer Concils*, Vienna, 1879; B. Bess, *Zur Geschichte des Konstanzer Konzils*, Marburg, 1891; B. Fromme, *Die spanische Nation und das Konstanzer Konzil*, 2 parts, Münster, 1894–96; H. Blumenthal, *Die Vorgeschichte des Constanzer Consils*, Halle, 1897; L. Salembier, *Le Grand Schisme d'Occident*, Paris, 1900; J. H. Wylie, *Council of Constance to the Death of John Hus*, London, 1900; Hefele, *Conciliengeschichte*, vols. vi.–vii.; Milman, *Latin Christianity*, vii. 426–524; Pastor, *Popes*, i. 194–207; Creighton, *Papacy*, i. 228, 307–346, ii. 26–126; also the literature cited under Huss, John.

CONSTANTINE THE GREAT AND HIS SONS.

I. Constantine the Great (Flavius Valerius Constantinus): Roman emperor 306–337; b. at Naissus, in Upper Mœsia (the present Naissa or Nish, 130 m. s.e. of Belgrade, in Servia), probably 288; d. at Achyrona, a suburb of Nicomedia, May 22, 337. A proper understanding of Constantine's early life requires a knowledge of the history and personality of his father, Flavius Valerius Constantius (the surname Chlorus comes into use only with later Byzantine writers). He belongs to the men of the third century for whom the military career paved the way to higher political station. His origin was associated with Claudius Gothicus (Claudius II., emperor 268–270). Maximianus, Augustus of the West, gave his stepdaughter Flavia Maximiana Theodora in marriage to Constantius, then prefect of the guard, after he had been obliged to separate from Constantine's mother, Helena. His elevation to the rank of Cæsar followed in 293, and with it the transfer of the Gallic, Spanish, and British provinces. In peaceful activity and warlike enterprises alike, he proved himself a man of quiet fidelity to duty and of but moderate ambition. The abdication of both Cæsars Augustus on May 1, 305, brought him the imperial dignity, but he died at Eboracum (York) in July of the following year. The question as to whether he was a Christian is open to discussion. At any rate, he did not receive baptism. On the other hand, he held his protective arm over the Christians during the persecution by Diocletian, and confined himself to a nominal obedience in the way of destroying houses of worship. The determining ground for this behavior can be sought only in his religious attitude. Belief in the gods he had renounced, and he lived in a monotheism whose Christian import is confirmed by the fact that he not only accorded complete freedom to Christianity in his environment, but also allowed Christian religious rites to be observed in his palace. One of his daughters by the second marriage bore the Christian name of Anastasia. If it is true that his coins are frequently stamped with reference to the rites of Hercules, the circumstance finds explanation in his adoptive father's preference for the worship of that hero, from whom he traced his descent and the name Herculius. In the circumstances the possibility is to be reckoned with that a sudden death cut Constantius short of obtaining baptism. That his second wife may perhaps have influenced him religiously is fairly supposable, since she, at all events, as appears from a coin which has remained heretofore unnoticed, was a Christian.

1. Constantine's Father, Constantius.

Constantine was born from a concubinal union of his father, at that time still a young officer, with Flavia Helena, a maiden of inferior station. This form of matrimonial alliance must not be understood in the modern sense of the word concubinage. According to the custom and law of that time, concubinage was a monogamous durable union with a legally recognized name, offsetting a defective capacity on the wife's part by authorizing a *justum matrimonium*. This lower form of matrimonial union was widely prevalent in the Roman empire, especially in the army. As already mentioned, Constantius was later compelled to dissolve this union, but Helena by no means vanished into obscurity; the reverence and love of her only son, who reared statues in her honor, had coins struck with her image, and called cities by her name, drew her later into publicity, and kept her thus as Augusta.

2. Constantine's Mother, Helena.

According to the division of the empire by Diocletian, Constantius had become Augustus in the West, and Galerius in the East. Their respective Cæsars were Flavius Valerius Severus and Maximinus Daza. At his father's death the army in Britain proclaimed young Constantine Augustus. Maxentius, the son of Maximianus, endeavored to secure the dignity with the aid of the pretorian guard and a discontented party in Rome. His father sided with him, Severus perished in the ensuing conflict, and Galerius found himself hard pressed in the toils of this new rebellion. Maximianus presently separated from his son, betook himself with his daughter Fausta to Constantine in Gaul, and joined them in marriage. Constantine at once assumed the title Augustus (spring, 307). Nevertheless, as the result of a conference with Diocletian at Carnuntum (Nov., 307), Valerius Licinianus Licinius was named Augustus. Maximianus soon rose in rebellion against Constantine and lost his life thereby (310). Galerius died in May of the year following. Disagreements at once set in between Maximinus Daza and Licinius touching the succession The former seeking alliance with Maxentius, Licinius was driven to side with Constantine. The betrothal of Constantine's sister with Licinius reenforced their political alliance by family bonds. Maxentius first urged on a war, which Constantine espoused by necessity. The course of the same led him to decide openly for Christianity.

3. Political Disorders, 306–311.

It is certain that Constantine had acquired from his father no doubtful inclination toward the new faith. Still his religious position was as yet obscure. The campaign in Italy brought to an end uncertainty and indecision. According to Eusebius, he beheld a cross in the clouds one day with his army; according to Lactantius, he received in a dream the command to place the monogram of Christ on the soldiers' shields. This second report undoubtedly supplements the first; and the fact of a manifestation of the Christian God appearing to the emperor in the light of a marvelous heavenly token is not to be doubted. The impression produced by this apparition found its continuation in a dream by night. It is certain from the sources that the decisive conversion of Constantine to Christianity is to be fixed at the outset of the campaign, or in the spring of 312; also that this conversion rested not upon a single experience, the apparition of the dream, but that preparatory experiences cooperated with it. Just how, religiously and psychologically, this transformation was effected, and especially whether, or to what extent, the religious motives were enhanced by political considerations can not be decided, because nothing adequate is known about Constantine's religious condition at that time. The usual analyses have therefore only a very doubtful value, even where they do not entirely vanish into the nebulous region. But undoubtedly the political side is overestimated, and it more probably played no part at all. The emperor presently conferred with spiri-

4. Constantine's Conversion. The Edict of Milan.

tual counselors and through them became more intimately instructed in regard to Christianity; the influential Hosius of Cordova (q.v.) appears among those about him, and maintained a high position of trust with him for a good while. With wonderful victories the little army, its shields adorned with the monogram of Christ, pushed on toward Rome; in a bold assault Constantine overpowered his adversary, who together with the battle lost his life, at the Pons Milvius (Oct. 28, 312); and amid the rejoicing shouts of the populace Constantine marched into Rome, where the senate reared him an arch of triumph. Constantine had his statue erected in a public square, a cross in his hand, with an inscription in praise of the victory achieved by the aid of "this salutary token." In the *labarum* (Gk. *labaron, labōron, labouron*; the derivation is quite uncertain), the sumptuous banner of the cross, whose shaft was crowned by the monogram of Christ encircled with a golden chaplet, the new symbol became an object of brilliant public exhibition. After Constantine had regulated matters in Rome, he betook himself, in Jan., 313, to Milan, where he met Licinius, and gave him in marriage his sister Constantia. At the same time they agreed upon a religious and political decree whose main outlines appeared in a rescript of Licinius from Nicomedia—the (falsely) so-called edict of Milan—and culminated in granting to Christians the free exercise of their religion.

5. Constantine's Later Life and Reign.

Maximinus Daza was soon defeated by Licinius upon the Campus Serenus in Thrace (Apr. 30, 313); and a new edict of tolerance was proclaimed, with particular application to the ecclesiastical and political situation created by Maximinus—the decree of Nicomedia, June 13, 313. The vanquished Maximinus committed suicide. The empire now had only two rulers; but the great increase of his power heightened to such a degree the insolence and the emulation of Licinius, who reckoned with Christianity only for external reasons and on the religious side had always persisted in the pagan religion and superstition, that he provoked his imperial colleague to war. After two strenuous campaigns, separated by a delusive interval of peace, Licinius was vanquished in a decisive battle at Chrysopolis, Sept. 18, 323. Thanks to the intercession of Constantia, the victor guaranteed him his life under oath and granted him Thessalonica as residence. The deposed emperor, however, sought to foment a new insurrection by secret alliances with the Danubian barbarians, consequently he was condemned to death by the senate as a public enemy and rebel, and was executed as such (325).

The great Arian controversy (see ARIANISM) had broken out during these decisive events, and when other measures had proven ineffectual Constantine convened the first general church council, at Nicæa, and opened the same in person, May 20, 325 (see NICÆA, COUNCILS OF). Yet even this led to no lasting peace. Neither was the emperor destined to see the suppression of the Danubian troubles which beset him in 313. A dark shadow upon his reign is the execution of Crispus, his eldest son. Under the tuition of Lactantius he had grown up as a youth of much promise, and in the battles with Licinius had proved himself a valiant army leader. The catastrophe wherein he and the empress perished at the beginning of 326 is not fully explained; but there was either a proved or admitted case of adultery between Fausta and her stepson. The erection of Byzantium to the dignity of imperial metropolis, under the name of Constantinople—"City of Constantine"—was a significant and more pleasing event of the time.

After the subjection of Licinius, Constantine was occupied in a military way only with insignificant border wars, particularly with the Goths. Toward the end of his life, however, the Persian force under Sapor II. advanced threateningly upon Roman jurisdiction. The emperor made hasty preparations and resolved to conduct the campaign in person. About Easter, 337, an indisposition overtook him, which soon developed into a dangerous illness. The warm baths of Helenopolis proved ineffectual; so in the certainty that his end was near he betook himself to Achyrona, a suburb of Nicomedia, and before an assembly of bishops he read aloud his resolution to receive baptism, which he would have preferred to receive in the waters of the Jordan. He was baptized by Eusebius of Nicomedia, received the Eucharist, humbled the purple in white baptismal attire, composedly and cheerfully took leave of the weeping officers, and ordered his last affairs.

The name of Constantine the Great is rightly connected with the conquest of Greek and Roman paganism by Christianity, for the bearer of the name played the leading part in this decisive crisis.

6. His Cautious and Wise Policy.

Thanks to the profound political insight that was his by nature and to his sensible course of action, he directed his religious policy to the end of consummating the transition from the old to the new era without shattering the empire. The results of persecuting the Christians, the ultimate effects of which he had witnessed, must have left no manner of doubt as to the evil character of brute force directed against religion, and so forbade every application of the like policy against heathenism; the more, too, because this still comprised the vast majority of the empire. In the army, in the government service, among the educated, in the rural population, there were merely evanescent minorities of Christians. The entire fabric of antique worship in its innumerable points of contact with life, and the powerful priesthoods, whose ramifications extended into the uppermost social circles, richly endowed with property and legal rights, were still standing intact. Even such an impassioned Christian as Constantine must have acknowledged a barrier against compulsory procedure. Though the goal of his religious policy was to free the world from heathenism and transfer it to Christianity by the utmost that the State could do, nevertheless both prudence and conscientiousness dictated the one method of procedure—to go slowly in attacking religious sensibilities and to be content with small things and details, tedious to be sure, but less dangerous, and more certain in results.

This is, in fact, the distinguishing trait of Constantine's religious policy with respect to paganism, and the fact itself is an indication of his correct estimate of the political and religious situation. There was at no time an express judicial dispossession of the antique religion as such. It is true that for every one with eyes to see, everything pointed and pressed onward to such a conclusion; but the semblance of tolerance was maintained unbroken. The masses were the more easily to be deceived in this respect inasmuch as the government never thought, and could not think, of carrying out its decrees everywhere and indiscriminately; whole districts were not affected, or but immaterially affected thereby. Even centuries later it was found necessary to make similar concessions.

The losses of paganism were augmented on another side by an increase of legal rights to the Church. As early as 313 the Church gained immunity for its clerics, exemption from all personal burdens, and the power of inheritance for itself and its individual members. The bishops were accorded a jurisdiction in the domain of private law, that gave foundation for decisions of legal validity.

7. Legal Gains of Christianity.

The influence of Christianity upon penal law comes to light in the prohibition of branding the forehead, and of condemnation to bloody games in the circus. In family law, the harsh statutes against celibacy and unfruitful marriages were repealed—probably under the influence of the ecclesiastical valuation of celibacy—concubinal marriage was driven to the background, and severe measures were devised against the customary exposure, pawning, or sale of children. If the law of slavery was generally allowed to rest in humane forms as it stood, it nevertheless received no inconsiderable modification in the direction demanded by Christianity, through the institution of *manumissio in ecclesia;* indeed even the clergy were authorized to bestow citizenship on their slaves, and this without formal process. Constantine, again, made this further concession in a legislative way, that he brought Sunday under the safeguarding care of the State.*

Constantine's religious policy is clear in its outlines, and in the main features of its progress, transparent. Any thought of equality between the two religions lay far from it; and this was of necessity

8. Constantine Opposed to Paganism from the First.

the case, because the assumption of a non-confessional State was inseparable from such thought. The idea of a non-confessional State, however, is foreign to antiquity; and it was beyond all possibility for two religions whose moral and religious content was not only different, but even sharply exclusive the one of the other, to exist harmoniously side by side in the commonwealth. The qualification that is usually subjoined to this view of the matter, to the effect that after the defeat of Licinius parity of the two religions changed to a policy favoring Christianity, makes an assumption which can not be proven. For what came to pass in the religious policy after 323–324 was only the larger fruition of thoughts and facts which began with 312–313; the difference is but one of quantity. Finally, the supposition that Constantine sought and found a deity and a religion superior to the historical religions, and destined to fuse them into one and absorb them, and that he shaped his religious policy subserviently to this drift of coalescence, just as extravagantly overestimates the religious philosopher in Constantine as it underestimates in him the practical statesman. Nothing could have been more unintelligible to his understanding than such speculations. Where in passages of Eusebius and elsewhere he speaks of the one religion and belief in one God, he means historic Christianity, and he directs not the Christians, but the pagans, to this doctrine. And in this light alone did his Christian and pagan contemporaries understand him.

The dissolution of the one religion in favor of the other made also for imperial unity. The war with Licinius again bore witness to the great political dangers of a discordant creed. Nobody could

9. Political Value of Religious Unity.

warrant that such precedents would not repeat themselves. The overthrow of paganism is therefore supplemented in the religious policy of Constantine by the rejection of all sectarian inventions which weakened the unity of the Church and set up religious discord. The emperor's attitude before and during the Council of Nicæa and through the entire course of the Arian dispute, no less than his sharp action against Donatists, Novatians, and other schismatics from the catholic ecclesiastical body, has primary significance in this direction. The undivided imperial Church was for him a valuable, even necessary support of the imperial unity. Harsh measures against the Jews, again—especially the prohibition of joining them as proselytes—were dictated not only by religious and ecclesiastical, but also by political considerations.

That the Church might have its full value in the State in this direction, a legal relationship had to be sought which allowed the State a determining influence. For that matter, the State as antiquity knew it was accustomed to take religious affairs under its inspection and on a dependent footing. Nevertheless, Constantine did not succeed in procuring this legal relationship. The transitional character of the time and the accustomed freedom of the Church explain the failure. On the other hand, his personal relations with the powers of the Church and their grateful disposition toward him were sufficient to guarantee that the legal status would not be lacking as time went on.

The question of Constantine's religious policy can not be separated from that of his personal Christianity; and there is no more doubt about the one than the other. The new religion was truly a rule of life and a force with him. As emperor he felt himself pledged to God as his sovereign Lord; and he regarded his calling as a divine commission. His manner of religion is tinged with mysticism. He

* But it was distinctly understood that it was not simply the Lord's Day, but also the day of Mithras and Apollo; hence it appealed to nearly all classes of pagans as well as Christians. A. H. N.

became willingly absorbed in Holy Scripture, and was fond of presenting his religious convictions and knowledge in oral discourse. His morality was not inferior to the better average morality common to the Church of that age. As he prosecuted unchastity in others with severe penalties, he exacted the loftiest requirements of himself in this direction. His dominating traits were strong impulse and powerful resolution. He was distinguished by a deeply rooted sense of duty to the empire; and he more than once withstood the temptation to exalt his personal interests above the common good. His education was moderate, but he sought to attain what camp life had denied him, associating gladly with scholars, even pagans; and he promoted science and art. Legislation under his rule was a very live matter; but the exchequer, owing partly to imperial lavishness, was not always without deficit. He was of handsome presence and valued imperial stateliness. He had early hardened his body in the camp, by hunting and games; and so steeled it to the fatigues of the wars that he waged with the mastery of a great campaigner and as the darling of his soldiers. In his last years his physical and intellectual vigor appears to have decreased. Nevertheless, he kept the reins of government firmly in hand to his death. See CONSTANTINOPLE; and DONATION OF CONSTANTINE.

10. Constantine's Personality.

II. Constantine's Sons: Adhering tenaciously to Diocletian's imperial régime, Constantine divided the empire before his death among his three sons, with whom was coordinated his nephew Delmatius, in 335, to complete the fourfold arrangement. The latter, however, with other members of Constantine's house, was murdered by the soldiers, who desired to have only the sons of Constantine as heirs to the empire; only Julian and his elder half-brother Gallus were spared. The brothers assumed the official dignity of Cæsar Augustus on Sept. 9, 337.

1. Constantine II. (Flavius Claudius Constantinus): Emperor 337–340; b. at Arles 317; killed near Aquileia Apr. 9, 340. He received for his imperial portion Spain, both Gauls, and Britain. A territorial dispute with his younger brother, Constans, brought on a war, and he lost his life in a battle with his brother's generals, at its outset. Athanasius, in exile, was on friendly terms with him.

2. Constantius II. (Flavius Julius Constantius): Emperor 337–361; b. Aug. 7, 317, the son of Fausta; d. at Mopsucrene, in Cilicia (12 m. n. of Tarsus), Nov. 3, 361. During his father's last sickness he was fettered in the East by a Persian war, and arrived barely in time to attend the father's funeral on its way to Constantinople. There fell to him for his imperial portion the Eastern diocese (Egypt and Asia). He survived—again in a Persian campaign—the war between his brothers; likewise the slaying of his younger brother, Constans, by the usurper Magnentius (350). Constantius straightway armed for attack, named his cousin Gallus, who till then had been kept in quasicaptivity, to the rank of Cæsar (Mar. 15, 351), and overcame his adversary in a frightful battle near Mursa in Pannonia, Sept. 28. The next years, also, he spent in the West, occupied with the changeful course of the Arian dispute, which was incessantly evoking new difficulties; also with military movements against the Germans, and with the subjugation of the usurper Claudius Silvanus in Gaul; furthermore, with prosecutions for high treason, wherein the emperor's mistrust—the fault partly of his environment—did not invariably find the right procedure. He was marching to the East when he received word of the elevation of Julian; but in his great anxiety for the weal of the empire he did not break off the campaign, but first pushed it to a provisional conclusion, and then turned against the insurgent. He died of a violent fever, however, on the military highway leading to Tarsus. The government of Constantius was burdened with extraordinary difficulties. The ecclesiastical schism crippled any thoroughly unifying force. The emperor's sympathies inclined toward the Arian side; and to this fact attaches the predominantly unfavorable estimate of him by church writers, who have been far less just to him than the pagans.

Constantius was his father's favorite son, and in fact a good part of the personality of Constantine the Great survives in him. By nature equable and benevolent, zealous for the interests of his subjects, intent on rewarding loyal services, he was mistrustful when his absolutism seemed threatened, and in that event was liable to become a ruthless tyrant. To protect the empire he created a valorous army, and maintained its efficiency by strict discipline. The sphere of justice was reconstructed by him, and administrative reforms were introduced. He had a good education and showed particular inclination to rhetoric. In his building activity, again, he was his father's true son, and his new buildings included many churches. On the other hand, his financial administration was poor; or at least the finances were in poor condition. The emperor's liberality, his blind confidence, and his wars utterly exhausted the exchequer. The bishops' practise of driving back and forth to synods by the imperial post almost destroyed it; and the continual negotiations and synods swallowed up state funds in no ordinary measure. In any summary estimate of the emperor, however, his attributes of excellence will always hold the preponderance over his failings. He lacked above all the great impulsive power of his far-seeing father; while on another side, because grown up into Christianity from the very outset, he is a more concrete, self-contained Christian type than the former; and he is strongly taken up with theology.

3. Constans (Flavius Julius Constans): Emperor 337–350; b. about 323; killed at Helena, in the Pyrenees, 350. He governed Africa, both Italies, and Pannonia; and, after the death of his brother Constantine II. (340), the entire West. He evinced force, flexibility, and loyalty to duty in governing his vast, though in its details very diversified, imperial allotment; and he succeeded in bringing about a pacific situation. His preference for the Germans was remarked and censured. Infirmity of health and evil environment subsequently weakened his energy, and suffered a demoralizing vice of extortion to come to the surface, which also debased high state offices to a mercenary footing. In Jan., 350, the chief commander of the Jovians and Herculians, the German Magnentius, made an uprising in Autun, assumed the purple, and caused the fleeing emperor to be struck down by murderers in the church of Helena. In the autumn of the next year this new dominion collapsed in the victorious battle near Mursa, and Constantius thereby became sovereign of all the empire. Destiny had spared the most valiant of the three brothers for this difficult task. As he died childless, the proper dynasty of Constantine vanishes with Constantius from the field of history. VICTOR SCHULTZE.

BIBLIOGRAPHY: Early sources are the "Life of Constantine" by Eusebius, and the *Hist. eccl.* of the two writers Socrates and Sozomen, all in Eng. transl. in *NPNF*, 2d series, vols. i.-ii. Consult: J. Burckhardt, *Die Zeit Konstantins des Grossen*, Leipsic, 1880; T. Keim, *Der Uebertritt Konstantins des Grossen zum Christentum*, Zurich, 1862; A. P. Stanley, *History of the Eastern Church*, Lecture vi., London, 1862; T. Zahn, *Konstantin der Grosse und die Kirche*, Hanover, 1876; E. L. Cutts, *Constantine*, London, 1881 (popular); V. Schultze, in *ZKG*, vii (1885), 343-371, viii (1886), 517-542; idem, *Geschichte des Unterganges des griechisch-römischen Heidentums*, vol. i.-ii., Jena, 1887; O. Seeck, *Geschichte des Unterganges der antiken Welt*, vol. i., Berlin, 1897; Gibbon, *Decline and Fall*, chaps. xiv., xvii.-xxi.; Schaff, *Christian Church*, vol. iii., chap. i.; *DCB*, i. 623-654. On the vision of Constantine consult: Abbé du Voisin, *Dissertation critique sur la vision de Constantin*, Paris, 1774; J. H. Newman, in *Two Essays on . . . Miracles*, pp. 271-286, London, 1873.

CONSTANTINE: The name of two popes.

Constantine I.: Pope 708-715. He was a Syrian by birth, consecrated Mar. 25, 708. He steadfastly adhered to the traditional papal policy toward both the Italian bishops and the Eastern emperor. Felix of Ravenna, having obtained consecration from him without furnishing the undertakings required by the emperor, was blinded by order of Justinian II. and banished to Pontus, whence he was able to return, after Justinian's death, only by assenting to the declaration required of him by Constantine, who also supported the bishop of Pavia against Benedict of Milan because he wished to enforce his own claim to jurisdiction over Pavia. The emperor commanded him to appear in Constantinople, probably to extort his assent to the Trullan canons, which had been rejected by Rome. He bore himself with discretion, and maintained the attitude of his predecessors during his two years' absence (709-711). The next emperor, Philippicus Bardanes, himself a Monothelite, attempted to impose that heresy on his subjects, but was steadily opposed by Constantine, who, by making his opposition dogmatic and not political, acquired a commanding influence among the contending factions. On the fall of Philippicus, his successor, Anastasius, hastened to send to Rome an orthodox profession, in which the patriarch John of Constantinople joined. Constantine died Apr. 9, 715, and was buried in St. Peter's.

(A. HAUCK.)

BIBLIOGRAPHY: *Liber pontificalis*, ed. T. Mommsen, in *MGH, Gest. pont. Rom.*, i (1898), 222-226; Jaffé, *Regesta*, i. 247; Paulus Diaconus, *Historia Langobardorum*, vi. 31, ed. G. Waitz, in *MGH, Script. rer. Langob.*, vi., pp. 12-187, 1878; F. Gregorovius, *History of the City of Rome*, ii. 201-202, 212, London, 1894; Bower, *Popes*, ii. 14-20; Milman, *Latin Christianity*, ii. 290-291; Mann, *Popes*, 127-140.

Constantine II.: Pope 767-768. Though a layman, he was chosen pope by the influence of a faction immediately after the death of Paul I. and was consecrated July 5, 767. He was but the creature of his ambitious brother Toto, duke of Nepi, and as soon as the opposition, headed by officials of the previous pope, could organize (July 28, 768), he was overthrown by an armed onset. Toto was killed, and Constantine sought sanctuary in a church, from which he was dragged by the soldiery. Sentence of deposition was pronounced upon him, with imprisonment in a monastery, where he was set upon and blinded, though he lived until the next year at least, when he tried in vain to make his peace with his successor Stephen III. (IV.). [By Roman Catholic writers he is not considered a strictly legitimate pope.] (A. HAUCK.)

BIBLIOGRAPHY: *Liber pontificalis*, ed. L. Duchesne, i. 468 sqq., Paris, 1886; Mansi, *Concilia*, xii. 717-718; Jaffé, *Regesta*, p. 283; F. Gregorovius, *Hist. of the City of Rome*, ii. 322-330, London, 1894; Bower, *Popes*, ii. 114-115; Milman, *Latin Christianity*, ii. 432-435; Mann, I. ii. 362 sqq.

CONSTANTINOPLE.

I. The Ancient City and the Patriarchate: The city of Byzantium, situated at the union of the Thracian Bosphorus and the Propontis (Sea of Marmora) and founded, according to tradition, by Megarian colonists in 656 B.C., attained importance at an early date as a commercial and political center. After many vicissitudes under Persian, Macedonian, Gallic, and Athenian control, it was incorporated in the Roman Empire, and, despite its destruction by Alexander Severus (192), became the second capital of the empire in the fourth century. After Constantine the Great (q.v.) had either conquered or pacified his foreign enemies, he determined to build a city which should bear his name and be equal to Rome. He chose Byzantium in

1. The City.

326, and adorned it with churches and palaces, as well as with works of art from Italy and Greece, while he forced colonists to settle there and gave vast estates to families of prominence. The first church erected by him was a magnificent structure in honor of the Apostles, and he also founded the churches of St. Michael and of St. Sophia, although the latter was rebuilt by Justinian in 538. No pagan temples were permitted in the city except during the reign of Julian, and many conversions were made among Jews and heathen.

The early history of Constantinople is given by Chrysostom. The population in his time was about 100,000, and the prevailing culture was a mixture of Greek and Roman, Christian and Gentile elements, but the predominant character was Oriental. The chief studies were medicine and law, although rhetoric and oratory were regarded with favor. The logic of Aristotle and the philosophy of Plato enjoyed wide vogue, but mathematics easily degenerated into astrology. The Byzantine mind was lacking in creative vigor, but possessed a marvelous retentive power. The art, literature, morals, and diction of the period have a close formal resemblance, and are distinguished by a curious combination of delicacy, bombast, and artificiality. The very catholicity of the Byzantines, moreover, led to such confusion that each power invaded the realm of its neighbor and sought to usurp alien functions, since the ecclesiastical and political world, sharply distinguished elsewhere, were here combined. Sometimes the monks and clergy became political despots, and again the emperors turned theologians. Yet it must not be forgotten that Constantinople protected Christian Europe against perils from the Orient, withstood papal supremacy and preserved a non-Roman catholicism, and nurtured the Greek language and learning.

In his division of the empire Constantine laid a foundation for the simultaneous development of the metropolitanate (see ARCHBISHOP) and the union of the dioceses into great hierarchic corporations. The principle that ecclesiastical organization should follow close on political gave a sudden promotion to the bishop of Constantinople, who was originally subordinate to the metropolitan of Heraclea. In 381 the second ecumenical council enacted that the bishop of Constantinople, as New Rome, should have the highest rank next to the bishop of Rome, so that the title of patriarch afterward given the metropolitans of the first class (Alexandria, Antioch, Jerusalem, and Rome) was thus assured to him. The Council of Chalcedon (451) went still further and gave the patriarch of Constantinople the same rank as the pope, while his powers were extended to comprise the dioceses of Pontus, Asia, and Thrace, the right to ordain all metropolitans subordinate to himself, to convene provincial synods, and to be the court of last appeal for ecclesiastical affairs in the East. Despite these prerogatives, certain factors combined to keep the patriarchate within bounds. The Greek Church was not amenable to centralization, so that in the Monophysite controversy the bishops of Alexandria and Antioch were able to oppose the patriarch of Constantinople without imperiling their independence, while in the Middle Ages they were subordinate to him only in so far as relations with the pope and resistance to the Latin Church were chiefly decided at the capital. The oscillating relations with Rome were also detrimental to the independence of the patriarchs. Leo I. protested against the equality of both ecclesiastical capitals decreed by the Council of Chalcedon, and it was only after his own humiliation that Anatolius succeeded in conciliating the pope. In a like spirit Pelagius II. and Gregory I. refused to allow Johannes Jejunator (587) to assume the title of ecumenical patriarch. A misunderstanding concerning the meaning of this term seems to have prevailed between Rome and Constantinople. It is scarcely probable that the patriarch ever desired to be a universal bishop, but rather a bishop of the empire, of whom there might be several. But as Flavian of Constantinople sought the aid of Leo I., and Sergius I. of Constantinople invoked the assistance of Honorius in the Monothelite controversy, there were many acts of the patriarchs which might at least be construed as appeals to Rome. The result of this alternate jealousy and recognition was a feeling of supremacy on the part of Rome which led, with such men as Photius and Cærularius (qq.v.), to a definite schism. In the following centuries the Greek Uniats showed themselves ready to admit Roman supremacy within certain limits, while the Orthodox maintained a sturdy resistance which they defended on scholarly grounds. The freedom of the patriarchs, moreover, was frequently restricted by the emperors. The patriarchs were the highest ecclesiastical vassals, but the fact that their election and deposition depended generally on the command of the emperor, that many were raised by imperial mandate almost immediately from laymen to the patriarchate, and that the emperors continually interfered in ecclesiastical and dogmatic affairs, deprived the office of much of the dignity and power which it would otherwise have possessed.

2. The Patriarchate.

The succession of the patriarchs of Constantinople is known with tolerable certainty, though a very dubious tradition carries it through the first centuries, the ostensible founder being the Apostle Andrew. Except for the early centuries, four periods may be distinguished: (1) from Constantine to the Photian controversy (861) or to the entire break with the West under Cærularius (1054); (2) to the interregnum of the Latins, which forced the patriarchs and the emperor to take refuge in Nicæa, while a Latin patriarchate existed in Constantinople (1204–61); (3) to the capture of the city by the Turks (1453); and (4) to the present time. The extent of the patriarchate was greatest in the Middle Ages, but in 1589 it suffered its first serious loss when the Russian patriarchate was created, and in the nineteenth century the development of nationalism in the Balkan peninsula produced an unnecessary number of autonomous churches, which weakened the patriarchate of Constantinople and the entire Eastern Greek Church. The first of these schisms was made by Greece; Bulgaria has been more or less independent since 1872; and Servia and Rumania have had separate churches since 1885. All these bodies, however, are more or less closely related, and the patriarch of Constantinople still possesses a certain moral authority.

The fall of Constantinople in 1453 brought an increase in power to the patriarch, who now exercised much control over the destinies of the conquered. On the other hand, he was subject, in great measure, to the caprice of the sultan and his viziers. Unfortunately, the official venality of Turkey extended even to the patriarchal throne, and no patriarch could gain the position without simony. The present legal status of the patriarchate is defined by a rescript of Feb. 18, 1856, by which the patriarch is aided, or rather restricted, by several bodies coordinated with him, of which the most important is the synod, an institution of ancient date which became obsolete, but was revived in 1593. (PHILIPP MEYER.)

II. Councils and Synods: The second, fifth, sixth, and eighth, of the general or ecumenical councils met in Constantinople as follows: (1) The First Council of Constantinople was called by Theodosius I. in 381 to confirm the Nicene faith and deal with other matters of the Arian controversy (see ARIANISM; CONSTANTINOPOLITAN CREED). Meletius of Antioch, Gregory Nazianzen, and Nectarius successively presided. Gregory Nazianzen was made patriarch, but soon resigned, and Nectarius was then put in his place. Seven canons, four doctrinal and three disciplinary, are attributed to the council and accepted by the Greek Church, but the Roman Church accepts only the first four. (2) The Second Constantinople met in 553 under Justinian, and was an episode of the Three Chapter Controversy (q.v.). (3) The Third Constantinople, Nov. 7, 680–Sept. 16, 681, was called by Constantine Pogonatus and dealt with Monothelitism. It is also known as the First Trullan Council (see MONOTHELITES; TRULLAN COUNCILS). (4) The Fourth Constantinople, Oct. 5, 869–Feb. 28, 870, was called by Emperor Basil the Macedonian and Pope Adrian II. (q.v.). It deposed and condemned Photius as patriarch (see PHOTIUS) and, of the four Eastern patriarchates, ranked Constantinople before Alexandria, Antioch, and Jerusalem (canon xxi.). Of other gatherings the most important are the Second Trullan in 692 (see TRULLAN COUNCILS), and one which met under Constantine V., Copronymus, in 754 to condemn the presence of images in the churches (see IMAGES AND IMAGE-WORSHIP, II.).

BIBLIOGRAPHY: On the city and its history consult: W. J. Brodribb and W. Besant, *Constantinople and its Sieges*, London, 1878; J. v. Tamamchef, *Der Kampf um Constantinopel*, Vienna, 1887; J. B. Bury, *History of the Later Roman Empire*, 2 vols., ib. 1889; P. Loti, *Les Capitales du monde*, Paris, 1892, Eng. transl., 2 vols., London, 1892; E. A. Grosvenor, *Constantinople*, 2 vols., ib. 1895; W. H. Hutton, *Constantinople*, ib. 1900; H. O. Dwight, *Constantinople and Its Problems*, New York, 1901; Diehl on the Hippodrome at Constantinople is in transl. in D. C. Munro and G. C. Sellery, *Mediæval Civilization*, pp. 87-113, New York, 1904.

On the patriarchate consult: Krumbacher, *Geschichte* (pp. 911–1067 contain a sketch of Byzantine history by H. Gelser, and on pp. 1068–1144 is an exhaustive bibliography); M. Le Quien, *Oriens christianus*, especially vol. i., Paris, 1740; J. Hergenröther, *Photius*, 3 vols., Regensburg, 1867; M. J. Gedeon, *Patriarchikoi Katalogoi*, ib. 1890; N. Nilles, *Kalendarium manuale utriusque ecclesiæ*, 2 vols., Innsbruck, 1896–97; E. W. Brooks, *On the Lists of the Patriarchs of Constantinople, 638–715*, Leipsic, 1896; idem, *London Catalogue of the Patriarchs of Constantinople*, ib. 1898. On the councils and synods: Hefele, *Conciliengeschichte*, ii. 1-33, 854–902, iii. 260–286, 328–344, iv. 384–434, Eng. transl., vols. i.–v.

CONSTANTINOPOLITAN CREED.

The Constantinopolitan Creed is second of the so-called ecumenical creeds of the Christian Church, and the one which has the best right to the term, being received not only by the Greek and Roman Catholic communions, but by the various heretical bodies of the East and by the great majority of Protestant churches. It is known also as the Niceno-Constantinopolitan Creed, or simply as the Nicene Creed; this name, however, connotes, not the confession of faith adopted at the First Council of Nicæa in 325 (see NICÆA, COUNCILS OF, I.), but a version professing to be a mere enlargement of it, traditionally supposed to have been adopted by the so-called ecumenical Council of Constantinople in 381 (see ARIANISM).

I. Texts: There are three principal texts of the creed. (1) The Greek text as found in the acts of the second (imperfectly), fourth, and sixth ecumenical councils and the works of the later Greek Fathers. (2) The Latin text, represented by a series of translations from the Greek in various manu-

1. The Three Principal Texts. scripts, of which the most important are the so-called interpretation of Dionysius Exiguus, the acts of the Council of Toledo (589), those of the Council of Friuli (796), and that put up by Leo III. in St. Paul's church at Rome. (3) The Greek text used in the West, as preserved in some manuscripts of the ninth and tenth centuries. Mention may also be made of certain ancient versions, such as the Syriac (Nitrian MS. of 562 in the British Museum), the Arabic-Coptic, and two Anglo-Saxon (MSS. of the eleventh and thirteenth centuries at Oxford and Cambridge). The Latin text, especially in its present form, as received by the entire West, is distinguished from the Greek, apart from small variations, by three principal peculiarities: the addition of the *Filioque*, the omission of *in* before *unam . . . ecclesiam*, and the singular form of the words used for assent, *Credo, confiteor, spero.*

The addition of *Filioque*, first met with in the acts of the Third Council of Toledo (589), occurs in several Spanish documents of the subsequent age and in some of the Carolingian State Church (796; see FILIOQUE CONTROVERSY). The

2. The Addition of "Filioque." doctrine of the double procession of the Holy Ghost was formulated by Augustine, and was prevalent in the West from the fifth to the seventh centuries. Its reception into the creed took place in Spain as a safeguard against Visigothic Arianism; thence it spread to the Carolingian empire, and was there accepted as the official version of the creed in the first decade of the ninth century. In Rome, though the Augustinian doctrine was approved, the creed was recited without the addition till the beginning of the ninth century, as is shown by the tablet of Leo III. and his reply to the Frankish envoys in 809. Soon after, however, it was introduced there also, as evidenced by the *Ordo Romanus* belonging possibly to the second half of the ninth century, and by the controversy with Photius.

The omission of *in* before *ecclesiam* was not accidental. It is coeval in the West with the first attestation of the creed. Some Latin versions restore the *in*, but they are either accurate translations by scholars, or to be referred to the fact that by the usage of that time *in* might be used merely to indicate that *ecclesiam* was the accusative.

This variant also goes back to the Augustinian theology, and ultimately to still older Western feeling, which objected to designating anything else than the Triune God as the object of religious faith in the highest sense.

3. The Omission of "in," and the Use of the Singular.

This view received formal expression in Augustine's distinction between *credere aliquid, alicui*, and *in aliquem.* The change from plural to singular in the words of acceptance, which occurs in the oldest Spanish, Roman, Frankish, and Anglo-Saxon recensions, is connected with the usage of the *traditio* and *redditio symboli*, by which the creed was used as the personal expression of the individual who recited it. The Western Greek texts largely share the peculiarities of the Latin, while that written with Roman letters in the Gelasian Sacramentary, as well as in a liturgical MS. of the Vienna library, is identical with the Eastern text.

4. Minor Texts or Forms.

There are also a number of creed-forms calling themselves Niceno-Constantinopolitan or Nicene and considered by Caspari as modifications of the Constantinopolitan. These are: (1) the revised Antiochian; (2) the Nestorian; (3) the Philadelphian; (4) the form given in the pseudo-Athanasian "Interpretation of the Creed"; (5) the second and longer creed in the *Ancoratus* of Epiphanius; (6) the Cappadocian-Armenian; (7) the exposition of the Nicene Creed ascribed to Basil; (8) one of the two creeds read at Chalcedon and there described as Nicene. In spite of the resemblance of these to the Constantinopolitan, they are (as Hort has very well shown) rather sister than daughter recensions, and are, as will be seen later, of no slight importance for the solution of the question of origin.

II. Origin:

1. Nicene Creed Proper.

The Nicene Creed proper was adopted at the Council of Nicæa in 325 as a first settlement of the Trinitarian controversy (see ARIANISM). The process which led up to the victory of the Alexandrian theology and to the reception of the creed is still obscure, and the original meaning of the crucial term *homoousios* can not be absolutely determined. But Eusebius is undoubtedly right when he says that the formula proposed by him was the basis of the new confession. The Nicene Creed differs from this formula by some omissions and slight alterations, by the insertion of the Alexandrian christological formulas, and by a thorough revision based on a comparison with the baptismal symbols of Jerusalem and Antioch. The changes made by omission are of importance as showing that the victorious Alexandrian party was bent on avoiding any ambiguity and indisposed to compromise; the omitted phrases are mostly Biblical in phraseology, but such as were on the lips of open or half-avowed opponents of the strict orthodox belief. That the Nicene Creed was intended not as a baptismal symbol but as a christological rule of faith is shown by the brevity of the third section and by the bearing of the appended anathemas. All these characteristics gave the creed a theoretical, unliturgical, and unscriptural form which was used as a justification for attacks upon it in the next period by the Arians and Eusebians, and for acceptance with reservations even by some who were in the main orthodox.

2. Inadequacy Felt Later.

The next few decades saw acute controversy rage around it, and its opponents proposed a series of alternatives for it up to 341. This controversy deepened the attachment of its defenders to its literal expression, and made them avoid even any expansion of it in an orthodox sense. Thus at the Council of Sardica (344) it was simply reaffirmed without changes, and numerous passages might be collected from both orthodox and heterodox sources between 350 and 450 to show the unique reverence paid to the Nicene formula. Difficulties arose in regard to its use as a baptismal symbol, of which there is no evidence between 325 and 361, the older provincial creeds remaining in use. Later, however, after Julian's accession and the regaining of power by the orthodox party, which strengthened its position by the great synods of 360–370 and by the labors of strong bishops in Asia Minor and Syria, the desire of expressing the pure Nicene faith in connection with the act of baptism was felt.

3. Attempts to Remedy.

This could be done in three ways: by incorporating the Nicene watchwords into the old provincial creeds, by expanding the Nicene Creed into a completeness adequate for the purpose, or by keeping it unchanged, in spite of its incompleteness and its polemical bearing, and still using it for a baptismal symbol. All these three ways were, as a matter of fact, tried in the century between the synods of Alexandria and of Chalcedon; and the origin of the creed under discussion may best be sought in the history of these experiments.

4. Traditional Account of Origin.

The traditional account, held from the sixth century and accepted in both East and West, is that the creed was drawn up at the Council of Constantinople in 381. This synod was supposed to have supplemented the Nicene Creed by an expansion of the third section, and the resulting Niceno-Constantinopolitan Creed was assumed to have been at once received into universal ecclesiastical use. The first thing that shook the common belief was the realization that the *Ancoratus* of Epiphanius (373–374) contained a creed which, apart from its being supplemented by the Nicene anathemas and from two phrases in the text, was wholly identical with the Constantinopolitan. This could only be explained in harmony with the traditional view by the theory that Epiphanius himself added it to his book after 381, as Franzelin maintains, or that it was a much later interpolation by another hand, as Vincenzi asserts. Hefele, accordingly, like Tillemont before him, took the view that the council did not actually draw up a new creed but adopted that of Epiphanius with a few slight changes, giving it the rank of an ecumenical creed. He demonstrates that it was not written by Epiphanius himself, nor in Cyprus, but rather in Syria, some years before 373. But there is no documentary evidence of a promi-

III.—17

nent part played by Epiphanius at the Council of Constantinople, to say nothing of the acceptance of a creed proposed by him.

The fact is that the tradition of the establishment of the creed by the Council of Constantinople is no longer tenable, quite apart from the view held of the creed of Epiphanius. The council was not really ecumenical; it was summoned by Theodosius from his own division of the empire, and was not completely representative even of the East. Its canons were not included in the oldest Greek collections, and the evidence goes to show that they did not find universal acceptance in

5. Its Difficulties: External.

the East until after 451. The creed is not found among the few documents which remain from the council, and when it was placed among them later, the compiler obviously knew nothing of its origin, as it appears without introduction or connection. Socrates (v. 8) tells that the council confined itself to affirming the Nicene faith after the Macedonian bishops had left; and the accounts of Sozomen (VII. vii. 9) and Theodoret (v. 8) are substantially the same. Gregory Nazianzen, who was in attendance, in his comprehensive letter on the rule of faith written soon after its close, mentions only the Nicene Creed, and is silent as to its expansion or the drawing up of a new creed, besides which he expressly remarks that the Nicene Creed is inadequate as to the Holy Ghost, which would have been quite impossible if the council had just completed it in that regard. In a word, between 381 and 451 there is no undoubted trace in East or West of the existence of the Creed of Constantinople; and during this period it was nowhere used as the Creed of Constantinople or as the official baptismal symbol, while the Nicene Creed came more and more into use for this purpose, especially in the East, and increased, if possible, in consideration. In fact, with the single exception of the Council of Chalcedon (451), which mentions the Creed of Constantinople together with the Nicene, and ascribes it to the council of 381, there is no valid evidence for it until the beginning of the sixth century, after which it is frequently mentioned. Thus the external evidence is wholly against its having been the work of the council of 381.

The internal evidence is still more unfavorable; for it can be shown that the Constantinopolitan Creed is no mere expansion of the Nicene, which disposes of the theory that the authorities who assert the simple confirmation of the Nicene by the council meant the creed under discussion; while if the council drew up a new creed or expanded the old one, its version could not possibly have been worded as this creed is. As to the first, it

6. Its Difficulties: Internal.

is to be noticed that this creed differs from the Nicene not merely by the addition to the third section, but is really different all the way through, and comes from another original source, even though it has adopted a certain number of the Nicene watchwords. To sum up the points of difference which a careful comparison of the two discloses, we find ten additions besides the long one, four omissions, and five distinct changes in order of words or sentence-structure; or, as Hort puts it, of 178 words in the Constantinopolitan Creed only thirty-three, or less than a fifth, can be positively said to be taken from the Nicene.

The creed is therefore either a new and independent one with certain Nicene insertions, or based upon some older baptismal creed, edited in a Nicene sense—probably the latter, since there is no case known of the composition of a wholly new baptismal creed in the fourth or fifth century. This hypothesis is supported by a consideration of two additions —the "before all worlds" which fol-

7. Modern Theory of Origin.

lows "begotten of his Father," and of the "according to the Scriptures" after the assertion of the resurrection. As to the former, it is well known that the Nicene Fathers carefully avoided any limitation of time for the generation of the Son by the Father, and deliberately omitted these words from the creed of Eusebius. This attitude was made even more rigid by the history of the compromise-formulas of Antioch and Sirmium; and it is impossible to suppose that these very words were with equal deliberation added by the bishops at Constantinople, when such an action would have been construed as a concession to the Semi-Arians. The whole situation at the time allows no other explanation than that these words were already contained in an ancient baptismal creed, revised in a Nicene sense (not, of course at Constantinople), and that the revisers did not see any necessity for omitting them, but were satisfied with adding the most important Nicene watchwords. The words "according to the Scriptures," again, had become so suspicious in the course of a long controversy that no adherent of Nicæa would have thought of inserting them in a creed which did not already contain them, least of all in the Nicene Creed.

These conclusions are confirmed by the third section, which is traditionally supposed to have been the especial work of the Council of Constantinople. It is certain that the Macedonians were combated at this council; that from it dates their definite exclusion from the Church; and that it showed no tendency to make the slightest compromise with them. It is equally certain that the dogmatic "tome" issued by the council (now unhappily lost) expressed the full unity of substance between the Holy Ghost and the Father and the Son. But the creed, instead of emphasizing this unity of substance, contents itself with phrases that bear, indeed, a homoousian meaning but do not clearly express it—phrases which might have sufficed against crude Arianism, but would have been quite inadequate to combat the energetic denials of the *homoousia* of the Holy Spirit about 380. The fact that the creed thus contains an evidently orthodox but not sufficiently definite expression on this point brings us again to the theory of an ancient baptismal creed which was revised in a Nicene and anti-Macedonian sense after 362 and some time before 381. Its inclusion in the *Ancoratus* of Epiphanius, which, it is now plain, can not be regarded as due to a subsequent interpolation, may help to throw light on its actual origin.

Although the words in which Epiphanius commends the creed to the church of Pamphylia are not clear and the text is possibly corrupt in at least one place, it is evident that he sets it forth as a creed substantially of apostolic and Nicene origin. Now the question as to the source from which he received it led as long ago as the days of Gerhard Voss to the comparison of its wording with that of the Jerusalem creed; and in modern times Hort has conclusively justified the statement that the creed of Constantinople is nothing but the baptismal symbol of Jerusalem increased by the addition of the most important Nicene formulas and definitions on the Holy Ghost. The whole first section and the second down to "before all worlds" is identical in both; the structure of the second section is that of Jerusalem, with the addition of the Nicene phrases and four supplementary expressions—and of these one or two may have been in the Jerusalem creed, which is only known by reconstruction from Cyril's catechetical lectures; the third reads "and in one Holy Ghost, the Comforter, who spake by the prophets," which words afford a basis for the longer statement of the Constantinopolitan Creed.

The latter would therefore be a revision of the old Jerusalem creed made between 362 and 373, under the influence, there is scarcely a doubt, of Cyril, bishop of Jerusalem from 351 to 386. Three of the creeds mentioned above as resembling but distinct from the Nicene came into being under precisely the same circumstances. The creed of Antioch was probably a revision of the old baptismal creed of that church made, in dependence on the Nicene, by Meletius about 373; the Nestorian creed still in use was a further revision of the Antiochian creed made on the basis of the Nicene about 366, and designated as Nicene in its introduction; and that laid before the Council of Ephesus by Charisius was an ancient creed of Asia Minor, revised in a thoroughly orthodox direction in the last third of the fourth century. The whole seven creeds belong to this class, in fact, may for more than one reason be attributed to the period just named, which witnessed much activity in the formulation of baptismal creeds in the East.

III. History of its Acceptance: How it came to be designated as "of Constantinople," and to enjoy ecumenical authority, is a more difficult question. The Council of Constantinople did not acquire this authority in the East until the middle of the fifth century, in the West from seventy to a hundred years later. The patriarchate of Constantinople attained supremacy in the East in 451, after which it had every reason for exalting the authority of the council held in that city in 381 as equal with the Nicene. The Monophysite churches held back for twenty years from acknowledging these claims, and they were not conceded in the West for nearly a century, not, in fact, until the dependence of the popes upon the Byzantine emperors brought about a tacit acceptance of the Council of Constantinople and its decrees. Pope Vigilius (538–555) is apparently the first to call it ecumenical; but possibly before his pontificate the creed in a Latin version was appended to the first three canons of Constantinople in the collection of Dionysius Exiguus, though he does not affirm the ecumenicity of the council. Gregory the Great, who took up the sorry inheritance of the Byzantine period, puts the four great councils, including that of Constantinople, on a level with the four Gospels. While the reverent reception of the creed in the West can not be clearly shown before the middle third of the sixth century, it increased with remarkable rapidity, once the formula was regarded as the production of a council now recognized as ecumenical, and had been raised to the rank of a baptismal creed by the Roman and Spanish churches, partly owing to the need of a strong defense against Visigothic Arianism. The addition of the word *Filioque* took place in 589—so soon after the reception of the Creed in the West that it is almost possible to defend it as, for the West, no innovation. After the creed had once taken its position as a baptismal symbol in the most important Western provinces, and the legislation of Justinian had stamped it as authoritative there also, there was little chance of any question being raised as to its origin or sanction, and it retained its place in the mass and other solemn functions as of equal validity with the Apostles', and under the name of the Nicene. The Council of Trent solemnly reaffirmed it, and the Reformers (though Calvin for a time was inclined to criticize it) accepted it as Nicene and approved its teaching.

1. Acceptance in the West.

2. Acceptance in the East.

Its reception in the West shows that soon after 500 it must have passed in at least a part of the East as a Constantinopolitan revision of the Nicene creed. The process of its enforcement as such must have begun shortly before 450 and been completed about 500. It has been maintained that its presence in the acts of the Council of Chalcedon is due to an interpolation; but there are several strong reasons against the acceptance of this view.

3. Theory as to Manner of Sanction.

It is at least plausible to suppose that Cyril, whose orthodoxy was questioned by some, presented to the council his revised Jerusalem creed as a guaranty of his soundness; that it was approved by the council, and included in their acts, just as that of Eusebius was by the Council of Nicæa, that of Charisius by the Council of Ephesus, and that of Hosius by the Council of Sardica. When, at a later period, the need was felt in Constantinople of an expansion of the Nicene Creed, and it was sought for in the acts of the council, this confession was discovered, which offered a completion of the third section capable of a homoousian construction and valuable formulas in the second section. It was comparatively easy, then, when the council began to be received as ecumenical, to give out what purported to be its ecumenical creed as a completion of the Nicene, and to secure legislative and liturgical sanction for it, though not without opposition, which finally died out only in the sixth century.

The Constantinopolitan Creed is therefore, like the Apostles' and the Nicene, in one sense of the word "apocryphal." It is both older and later than the council whose name it bears—older in its original source, later in its reception. The historical exposition of its text must rest largely upon the writings of Cyril and Athanasius, which will sometimes alter the conception of its meaning. The Fathers who received it from the second half of the fifth century as ecumenical did so because they knew how to employ its testimony against Apollinaris, Nestorius, and Eutyches. Thus also the statements as to the Holy Ghost must be accepted in the strictest homoousian sense, though their wording does not necessarily involve this; and the phrase "proceeding from the Father," historically considered, is an attempt not to answer the question as to the origin of the Spirit, but to condemn the Arian assertion that the Spirit was subordinate to and a product of the Son, by referring his origin directly to the Father, the primal *radix* of the Godhead.

4. Conclusion.

(ADOLF HARNACK.)

BIBLIOGRAPHY: For a full list of the older literature consult: E. Kollner, *Symbolik aller christlichen Confessionen*, i. 1 sqq., 28-52, Hamburg, 1837. Consult: W. W. Harney, *Hist. and Theology of the Three Creeds*, 2 vols., London, 1854; C. A. Heurtley, *Harmonia Symbolica*, Oxford, 1858; idem, *History of the Earlier Formularies of Faith*, London, 1892; A. P. Forbes, *Short Exposition of the Nicene Creed*, ib. 1866; C. A. Swainson, *Nicene and Apostles' Creeds*, ib. 1875; F. J. A. Hort, *Two Dissertations, II. on the Constantinopolitan Creed*, ib. 1876; J. R. Lumby, *Hist. of the Creeds*, ib. 1880; F. Kattenbusch, *Lehrbuch der vergleichenden Konfessionskunde*, vol. i., Freiburg, 1892; G. B. Howard, *The Canons of the Primitive Church; with the Creeds of Nicæa and Constantinople*, London, 1896; J. J. Lias, *The Nicene Creed; a Manual*, ib. 1897; Harnack, *Dogma*, iii. 209-210, iv. 95 sqq., passim, v. 302-303, vii. passim; F. Kunze, *Das nicänisch-konstantinopolitanische Symbol*, Leipsic, 1898; T. H. Bindley, *Œcumenical Documents of the Faith*, London, 1899; W. Schmidt, in *NKZ*, 1899, pp. 935 sqq.; C. Callow, *Hist. of Origin and Development of Creeds*, London, 1899; A. G. Mortimer, *The Creeds: Historical . . . Exposition of the . . . Nicene . . . Creed*, ib. 1902; Neander, *Christian Church*, ii. 415 sqq., iii. 554 sqq.; Schaff, *Creeds*, i. 12-34 (history), ii. 57-61 (text); idem, *Christian Church*, iii. 667-689. Consult also: P. Caspari, in *Zeitschrift fur lutherische Theologie*, 1857, pp. 634 sqq.; Hefele, *Conciliengeschichte*, ii. passim, Eng. transl., ii. 379 sqq., et passim.

CONSUBSTANTIATION: A technical term denoting the Lutheran view of the elements of the Lord's Supper, in contradistinction from the Roman Catholic view—transubstantiation. According to the Roman doctrine, the bread and the wine are by the consecration transformed into the flesh and blood of Christ: while, according to the Lutheran doctrine, the bread and wine remain bread and wine; though, after the consecration, the real flesh and blood of Christ coexist in and with the natural elements, just as a heated iron bar still remains an iron bar, though a new element, heat, has come to coexist in and with it—an illustration which Luther himself used in his letter to Henry VIII. Lutheran theologians repudiate the popular term "consubstantiation," in the sense of a permanent connection of the elements with the body and blood of Christ, confining this connection to the act of the communion. See TRANSUBSTANTIATION.

CONTARINI, còn"tā-rī'nī, **GASPARO:** Italian cardinal; b. at Venice Oct. 16, 1483, d. at Bologne Aug. 24, 1542. After a thorough scientific and philosophical training, he began his career in the service of his native city. In 1521 he was the Republic's ambassador to Charles V. He accompanied Charles to Spain, later, after the sack of Rome, he assisted in reconciling the emperor and Clement VII., also the emperor and the Republic of Bologna. His accomplishments, but still more his mild resoluteness and blameless character, made him everywhere respected. One of the fruits of his diplomatic activity is his *De magistratibus et republica Venetorum*. In 1535 Paul III. unexpectedly made the secular diplomat a cardinal in order to bind an able man of evangelical disposition to the Roman interests. Contarini accepted, but in his new position did not exhibit his former independence. The disposition which Ranke (*Popes*, i. 118) calls "the collected product of all his higher faculties" governed his action also in the new field. At first everything seemed to work well. In 1536 Paul III. appointed a commission to devise ways for a reformation. The evangelical movement had made such progress in Italy that something had to be done, and it seemed best that the most influential be the agents. The decision was a bold one; Paul III., however, received favorably Contarini's *Consilium de emendanda ecclesia*, but it remained a dead letter, and his successor Paul IV., once a member on the commission, in 1539 put it on the Index, a deed which still embarrasses Catholic historians. What Contarini had to do with it is shown by his letters to the pope in which he complained of the schism in the church, of simony and flattery in the papal court, but above all of papal tyranny. But he came a century too late. Contarini in a letter to his friend Cardinal Pole [dated Nov. 11, 1538] says that his hopes had been wakened anew by the pope's attitude. He and his friends thought that all would have been done when the abuses in churchly life had been put away. This was the judgment of a diplomat of noble and virtuous nature, reared on the best fruits of antiquity and refined through the Gospel, urged on by a desire for peace and unfettered by dogmatic formulas. But he was soon to see the other side. In the year 1541 he was papal delegate at the diet and religious debate at Ratisbon. There everything was unfavorable; the Catholic states were bitter, the Evangelicals were distant. Contarini's instructions though apparently free were full of papal reservations. But the papal party had gladly sent him, thinking that through him a union in doctrine could be brought about, while the interest of Rome could be attended to later. Though the princes stood aloof, the theologians and the emperor were for peace, so the main articles were put forth in a formula, Evangelical in thought and Catholic in expression. The papal legate had revised the Catholic proposal and assented to the formula agreed upon. All gave their approval, even Eck, though he later regretted it. This did little good, for the Protestants could see in it only Roman cunning; at home the cardinal fared still worse. His own position is shown in a treatise on justification, composed at Ratisbon, which in essential points is Evangelical, differing only in the omission of the negative side and in being interwoven with the teaching of Aquinas. Meanwhile the papal policy had changed, and Contarini was compelled to follow his leader. He advised the emperor, after the conference had broken up, not to renew it, but to submit everything to the pope. In a second decision he is even more ultramontane. It is not difficult to reconcile this course of action with his character, for from the beginning Luther repelled him as did the popular movement in Germany. He lived in the belief that a reformation should begin at the head, and his birth, education, and diplomatic career made him view the question rather from the point of polity than of doctrine, and consequently he was willing to mediate here. But the negative side, which had produced the schism, remained unintelligible to him, he could concede only the marriage of the clergy and communion in both elements. Meanwhile Rome had drifted further into reaction, and he died while legate at Bologna, at a time when the Inquisition had driven many of his friends and fellows in conviction into exile. He was happily spared a decision which perhaps would have been too hard for him, and so he could leave behind him the character of a man who knew the truth and willed the good.

(T. Brieger.)

Bibliography: The two earlier lives are the *Vita Contarini* by Giovanni della Casa, in *Vitæ selectorum aliquot virorum*, pp. 154–186, London, 1704, and L. Beccadilli, *Vita del Cardinale G. Contarini*, latest issue, Venice, 1827. Consult: T. Brieger, *G. Contarini und das Regensburger Concordienwerk des Jahres 1541*, Gotha, 1870; *Die Correspondenz des . . . Contarini . . . 1541*, ed. L. Pastor, Münster, 1880; F. Dittrich, *Regesten und Briefe des Contarini, 1483–1542*, Braunsberg, 1881; idem, *Gasparo Contarini, eine Monographie*, ib. 1885; Ranke, *Popes*, i. 111–128, 150, iii., no. 18.

CONVENTICLE (Lat. *conventiculum*): In the primitive church any meeting for the sake of religious worship; since the time of Charles II., applied in English only to the meetings of the dissenters from the Church of England.

CONVENTICLE ACT: An act passed by the Cavalier Parliament of Charles II. in 1664, reenacted with less severity in 1670, and repealed by the Toleration Act of 1689. By its provisions the attendance of more than five persons outside of one family at meetings for religious rites other than those of the Established Church was punished by three months' imprisonment for the first offense, six months for the second, and for the third the alternative of transportation to the American plantations for seven years, under pain of death for a return before the expiration of that period, or a fine of a hundred pounds. Elizabeth had passed a similar act in 1593; but that of 1664 was more significant and more burdensome, as part of the systematic repression of non-conformity sometimes known as the Clarendon Code, including also the Corporation, Uniformity, and Five Mile Acts (qq.v.; 1661–65), which broke forever the pretensions of Puritanism to political supremacy and confined its sphere to the middle and lower classes. These acts were administered with cruel zeal, the justices of the peace, restored Cavalier squires, being bitter foes of dissent

Bibliography: The text of the Second Conventicle Act (1670) is given in Gee and Hardy, *Documents*, pp. 623–632. Consult D. Neal, *History of the Puritans*, part iv., chaps. 7–8, Am. ed., ii. 251 sqq., New York, 1844.

CONVERSE, JAMES BOOTH: Presbyterian; b. at Philadelphia Apr. 8, 1844. He was graduated at Princeton (B.A., 1865) and Union Theological Seminary, Va. (1869), and was pastor 1869–1871 and editor of the *Christian Observer* 1872–79. He then returned to the active ministry and was an evangelist for two years, after which he held a regular charge until 1887, again becoming an evangelist in 1888, while from 1890 to 1895 he was editor of the *Christian Patriot* (Morristown, Tenn.). In theology he is a Calvinistic Presbyterian, and also holds that the teachings of the Mosaic law upon economic problems were intended and are sufficient to banish poverty from the earth. He advocates the doctrine that the authority of Christ and the Bible should be recognized by all patriots and Christians as supreme in civil affairs. He has written *A Summer Vacation Abroad* (Louisville, Ky., 1878); *The Bible and Land* (a single-tax book; Morristown, Tenn., 1889); and *Uncle Sam's Bible, or, Bible Teachings about Politics* (Chicago, 1899).

CONVERSION.

Conversion (Lat. *conversio*, Gk. *epistrophē*, the noun only in Acts xv. 3) denotes both the act in which man turns again to God and the divine activity by virtue of which this takes place. Dogmaticians differentiate the latter, as *conversio transitiva*, from the former, the *conversio intransitiva*.

1. Exegetical Basis of the Doctrine.

The New Testament terms which express the idea of conversion are *epistrephein* and *metanoein* or *metanoia* (cf. Acts iii. 19, xxvi. 20). The corresponding term in the Old Testament is *shubh* (e.g., Isa. i. 27, x. 21; Jer. iii. 12, 14, 22; II Chron. vi. 24). In New Testament usage the word *epistrephein* as a rule denotes the deed by which a person turns from idols, or evil, to God (Acts xiv. 15, cf. xv. 19, xxvi. 18, 20; I Thess. i. 9; I Sam. vii. 3); or to the Lord (Acts ix. 35; II Cor. iii. 16; cf. also I Pet. ii. 25). In the same sense the expression is used absolutely (Luke xxii. 32; Acts xxviii. 27). According to Acts the conversion is effected through the preaching of the Gospel; it consists in man's turning away from darkness and evil and toward God. If in the passages cited the word *epistrephein* is used in an intransitive sense, in Luke i. 16, James v. 19–20, it is used transitively with respect to man; whereas 1 Pet. ii. 25 is probably to be understood in a passive sense. If *epistrephein* denotes more the change of the religious tendency, *metanoein* and *metanoia* denote rather the change of the ethical disposition (Acts viii. 22). It is the giving up of the sinful disposition (Rev. ii. 21) as well as the giving up of evil conduct (Rev. ii. 5, 16, 22, iii. 3, 19, ix. 20–21, xvi. 11; Heb. vi. 1, 6; II Cor. xiii. 21; II Pet. iii. 9; Matt. xi. 20–21, xii. 41; Luke xv. 7, 10, v. 32, xvi. 30). On the other hand, the positive side of the new disposition is emphasized. The call to repentance aims at a confession of sin and a new moral life (Matt. iii. 2, 6, 8, 10; Mark

i. 15; Luke xiii. 3, 5; II Tim. ii. 25; Acts xvii. 30; Heb. xii. 17; Rev. xvi. 9), which shows itself in new moral works (Matt. iii. 8; Acts xxvi. 20) and secures for man salvation and forgiveness of sin (II Cor. vii. 10; Luke xxiv. 47; Acts viii. 22, xi. 18). The term *metanoein* when combined with *pistis* denotes the whole new life of the Christian, as in Mark i. 15; cf. Heb. vi. 1; Acts xx. 21. The *metanoia* is expected of man and is enjoined upon him (Matt. iii. 2, iv. 17; Mark vi. 12). But it is just as certain that God works repentance in man (Acts xi. 18, v. 31; Rom. ii. 4; II Tim. ii. 25).

It is here that the real problem of the conception lies. On the one hand it is required of man that he should turn toward God, and on the other hand it is said that God produces this turn. The problem is stated sharply in Phil. ii. 12–13: "Work out your own salvation with fear and trembling: for it is God that worketh in you both to will and to do." This was not in the first instance regarded as a problem by the Church; one could just as easily expect everything of the free will of man as speak of his being sunk in sin and death. The Greek Church never overcame this lack of clearness. Man begins to do good, and somehow God helps him to the goal: "For it is ours to choose and to will; but God's to complete and to bring to an end" (Chrysostom, *In Heb. hom.*, xii.; cf. R. Seeberg, *Dogmengeschichte*, i., Erlangen, 1895, 256, 238 sqq.). In the West Augustine undertook a solution in connection with his doctrines of original sin and predestination. Man dead in sin is converted to the good, provided this is predestinated. The divine *virtus* leads the human will *indeclinabiliter et insuperabiliter*, so that it becomes a new will (*De corrupt. et grat.*, xii. 38; cf. Seeberg, ut sup., 274 sqq.). In the Middle Ages man's own work was strongly emphasized. Such theories under the influence of the later Nominalism rose to Pelagianism (cf. Seeberg, ii. 186). Over against this the Reformation again emphasized the inability of man to choose the good, and redemption *sola gratia*. The Holy Spirit effects conversion. He begets in man the "new spiritual motives," the *regeneratio* and *renovatio*. The human will is only *subjectum convertendum*; "it does nothing but only suffers, it is purely passive." The conversion, however, is mediated by the "preaching and hearing of the word," that is, it is not effected without a movement on the part of the subject. Inasmuch, however, as man is man, the change can not take place in the manner in which a statue is cut out of stone or in any similar way, but the passivity that characterizes the act of reception goes over, as soon as (*quam primum*) the Holy Spirit has effectually taken hold of the heart, into the activity of a synergy, which, however, acts only by virtue of the newly received powers. The *servum arbitrium* becomes the *liberatum arbitrium*, and by virtue of this man can take hold of the good and under the continuous operation of the Spirit persevere therein. The moment in which the Holy Spirit effectually takes hold of the heart is, according to the *Formula of Concord*, the moment of conversion. But when this takes place the new life with its cooperation is also present. Even where there is a minimum of faith, prayer, longing for salvation, the *conversio* has taken place. Similarly, the old Lutheran dogmaticians: the will of man cooperates in conversion "because God first comes to us in the word and divine influence moving and impelling the will. But after this impulse has been divinely given, the human will is not purely passive, but, moved and helped by the Holy Spirit, does not resist, but assents and becomes a fellow worker with God" (Chemnitz, *Loci*, i. 199; cf. H. Schmid, *Die Dogmatik der evangelisch-lutherischen Kirche*, Gütersloh, 1893, 335–336, 340 sqq.).

2. History of the Doctrine.

3. Dogmatic Expression of the Doctrine.

According to the conception in the Scriptures and the Evangelical understanding of grace, the dogmatic conception may be framed as follows: God frees man from the old tendency through the personal operation of the Holy Spirit. When the spirit makes man feel the reality of his effectual presence and of the new aims thus brought home to man's consciousness, man is inwardly made free to let God influence him and to place his life in the service of God. But this last act can happen only when man himself experiences God and gives himself with full purpose to God. The divine influence of grace, therefore, gives man the ability to lead a new life, but this new life is not realized concretely in any other way than in acts of the soul. The *conversio transitiva* is therefore the cause of the *conversio intransitiva*. At the same time the conversion may be defined, on the one hand, as the following of the new tendency for the first time; and, on the other hand, we may use the term to designate that entire complex of inner experiences and transactions which denotes the basis of our Christian estate.

R. Seeberg.

The new study of the psychology of religion has directed attention afresh to the subject of conversion and also thrown much light on it, both as an adolescent and as an adult phenomenon. This inquiry has disclosed the following results: (1) Adolescent conversion is incidental to the flowering time of childhood and youth, during the years—between fourteen and seventeen—of greatest susceptibility and awakening, in which the soul begins to be conscious of those relations in which personality is realized. The preliminary symptoms are various, such as haunting introspection, harassing doubts, feeling of depression and of imperfection, conviction of sin, fear of death, and longing for the infinite. It is thus the awakening of the person to spiritual realities. (2) As an adult phenomenon regarded as a single act, in religious experience conversion is repudiation of sin and surrender of self to God in Christ; as an ethical fact, it is identification of self with one's individual and social ideal; as a psychical act, the hitherto more or less dissociated activities of the self are unified in an emotional experience. The two types of conversion are the volitional—one strives to become a new man—and the self-surrender type in which effort either for or against the new life gives place to an invasion from the subliminal region in which after a longer or shorter incubation one suddenly and freely identifies himself with God. Such sudden experiences are due in part to a pronounced sensibility with tendency to automatisms and suggestibility of the passive type. The change is often accompanied with a greater or less degree of emotional and physical disturbance. (3) Conversion as a gradual experience is more commonly true of those in whom the rational or volitional powers predominate: the judgment is progressively convinced, and the will is as the judgment. These various types of conversion are primarily not of religious, but of psychological significance. The essential reality is the beginning of an identification with God and with the ideal unity of personal beings. The action of the spirit of God is presupposed. The literature of the subject is growing, and the following works may be consulted: E. D. Starbuck, *Psychology of Religion*, New York, 1899; G. A. Coe, *The Spiritual Life*, ib. 1900; idem, *Education in Religion and Morals*, ib. 1904; W. James, *Varieties of Religious Experience*, pp. 189–258, ib. 1902; J. B. Pratt, *Psychology of Religious Belief*, pp. 191–261, ib. 1907; Leuba, in *American Journal of Psychology*, vii (1896), 309 sqq.; G. S. Hall, *Adolescence*, New York, 1904. C. A. B.

CONVOCATION: In the Church of England, a deliberative assembly of the bishops and clergy of each province under their respective metropolitans for the discussion of ecclesiastical affairs. In the plan devised by Edward I. for a national assembly (1283), the clerical estate was to be represented by its proctors as were the counties by their knights and the towns by their burgesses. But the clergy preferred to be an estate apart, taxing itself separately. It was brought completely under royal control by Henry VIII. in 1535, Cromwell, a layman, presiding for the king as vicar-general. The privilege of taxing itself was definitely taken from the clerical order in 1664 and settled in the House of Commons, in which clergymen were not allowed to sit, though they were in a sense represented by the bishops in the House of Lords. Convocation continued to exist until the attacks of the High-church and Tory parsons on the liberal bishops came to a head in the Bangorian controversy (see Hoadly, Benjamin), when the Convocation of Canterbury was prorogued in 1717, and the license of the crown necessary to enable it to proceed to business was no longer granted. It met from time to time as a matter of form, but its life was practically dormant until in the middle of the nineteenth century a movement was set on foot by Bishop Wilberforce and Bishop Phillpotts of Exeter for its revival. Its recovery of deliberative powers took place in 1861, since which time it has met regularly, concurrently with the sessions of Parliament, to discuss and advise on ecclesiastical affairs, though shorn of its ancient powers. It consists of two houses, the upper containing the bishops of the province, the lower the deans, archdeacons, and representatives of the cathedral and parochial clergy; the archbishop presides in the upper house, an elected prolocutor in the lower. In recent years a house of laymen has also been created, which, though not technically a part of Convocation, exercises by its debates a concurrent influence. The term convocation is applied in some dioceses of the American Episcopal Church to the annual legislative assembly, and more frequently to gatherings of clergy and laity, usually for missionary purposes.

Bibliography: J. H. Blunt, *Dictionary of Doctrinal and Historical Theology*, pp. 152–158, London, 1870 (a summary of the history); J. Overall, *The Convocation Book of 1606, commonly called Bishop Overall's Convocation Book*, in the *Library of Anglo-Catholic Theology*, Oxford, 1844; W. Kennet, *A Compleat Hist. of Convocations, 1356–1689*, London, 1730; T. H. Fellows, *Convocation: its Origin, Progress and Authority*, ib. 1852; T. Lathbury, *Hist. of the Convocation of the Church of England*, ib. 1853.

CONVULSIONISTS. See Jansen, Cornelius, Jansenism.

CONWAY, MONCURE DANIEL: Liberal; b. at Middleton Farm, Stafford Co., Va., Mar. 17, 1832; d. in Paris Nov. 15, 1907. Educated at Dickinson College, Carlisle, Pa. (B.A., 1849), and Harvard Divinity School (B.D., 1854), after having studied law (1849–50). He was first a minister of the Methodist Church in Maryland (1850–53), then of the Unitarian Church in Washington, D. C. (1854–57), the First Congregational (Unitarian) Church, Cincinnati, O. (1857–62), and the South Place Chapel, London (1863–85 and 1892–97).

Conway was active in the movement for the emancipation of the slaves, a fact which compelled him to retire from Washington, and subsequently led him to go to England to explain the attitude of the North in the Civil War. He edited the *Dial* at Cincinnati and later the Boston *Commonwealth*; while in London he was on the staff of the *Daily News* and the *Pall Mall Gazette*. He edited many works of English literature, of which the most noteworthy are *The Sacred Anthology* (New York, 1876) and *The Writings of Thomas Paine* (4 vols., 1894–95), and produced many books, of which these having religious interest may be mentioned: *Tracts for To-Day* (Cincinnati, O., 1857); *The Earthward Pilgrimage* (New York, 1870); *Idols and Ideals* (1877); *Demonology and Devil Lore* (2 vols., 1879); *The Wandering Jew* (1881); *Thomas Carlyle* (1881); *Emerson, at Home and Abroad* (Boston, 1883); *Farewell Discourses* (1884); *Life of Thomas Paine* (2 vols., 1892); *Solomon and Solomonic Literature* (Chicago, 1890); *Autobiography* (2 vols., New York, 1904); and *My Journey to the Wise Men of the East* (Boston, 1906).

CONWELL, RUSSELL HERMAN: Baptist; b. at Worthington, Mass., Feb. 15, 1842. He entered the law school at Yale in 1860, but interrupted his studies on the outbreak of the Civil War and served in the Union Army as captain of infantry, being promoted lieutenant-colonel in 1865. He then resumed his studies at Albany University (B.A., 1866), practised law in Minneapolis 1865–67, and was immigration agent of Minnesota to Germany 1867–68. He was foreign correspondent of the New York *Tribune* and the Boston *Traveler* in 1868–70, and after his return to the United States practised law in Boston until 1879. He was ordained to the Baptist ministry in 1879 and for ten years (1881–91) was pastor of Grace Baptist Church, Philadelphia, and since 1891 of the Baptist Temple there. In 1888 he founded Temple College, of which he has since been president, and two years later established the Samaritan Hospital. He has written biographies of President Hayes (1876), Bayard Taylor (1879), President Garfield (1881), Joshua Gianavello (1884), James G. Blaine (1886), Charles H. Spurgeon (1892), and other volumes.

CONYBEARE, FREDERICK CORNWALLIS: Church of England layman; b. at Kew in the year 1856. He was educated at University College, Oxford (M.A., 1883), where he became fellow and prelector in 1881. He is particularly noted for his attainments in Armenian, and is a member of the Venetian Armenian Academy. In 1903 he was elected a fellow of the British Academy. His writings embrace: *A Collation with the Ancient Armenian Versions of the Greek Texts of Aristotle's Categories*, etc. (London, 1892); *The Apology and Acts of Apollonius and Other Monuments of Early Christianity* (1894; 2d ed., *The Armenian Apology and Acts of Apollonius*, 1896); *Philo about the Contemplative Life, or, the Fourth Book of the Treatise Concerning Virtues* (Oxford, 1895); *The Key of Truth, a Manual of the Paulician Church of Armenia, the Armenian Text edited and translated* (1898); *The Story of Ahikar, from the Syriac, Arabic, Armenian, Ethiopic, Greek and Slavonic Versions* (1898); *The Dialogues of Athanasius and Zachæus and of Timothy and Aquila* (1898); *The Dreyfus Case* (London, 1898); *Roman Catholicism as a Factor in European Politics* (1901); *Rituale Armenorum* (Oxford, 1905); and *Old Armenian Texts of Revelation* (1906).

CONYBEARE, JOHN: Bishop of Bristol; b. at Pinhoe, near Exeter, Jan. 31, 1692; d. at Bath July 13, 1755. He studied at Exeter College, Oxford (fellow, 1711; B.A., 1713; proctor, 1725; B.D., 1728; D.D., 1729); became rector of Exeter 1730, dean of Christ Church 1733, and bishop of Bristol 1750. He was a popular preacher, reformed many abuses as rector of Exeter, and was an energetic dean. His most important publication was *A Defence of Revealed Religion against the Exceptions of a late Writer* (London, 1732), which was pronounced one of the four ablest books (the other three by James Foster, John Leland, and Simon Browne) written in reply to Tindal's *Christianity as Old as the Creation* (1730). Two volumes of his *Sermons* were published at London, 1757.

BIBLIOGRAPHY: J. Leland, *View of the Deistical Writers*, 3 vols., London, 1754–56; *DNB*, xii. 60–61.

CONYBEARE, WILLIAM JOHN: Church of England; b. Aug. 1, 1815, eldest son of William Daniel Conybeare; d. at Weybridge (on the Thames, 20 m. s.w. of London), Surrey, July 22, 1857. He was student and fellow of Trinity College, Cambridge (B.A., 1837; M.A., 1840); was first principal of Liverpool Collegiate Institute 1842–48; vicar of Axminster, Devonshire (succeeding his father), 1848–54. He is best known for his work upon the *Life and Epistles of St. Paul* in collaboration with J. S. Howson (2 vols., London, 1852; 2d ed., revised, 1856; many other editions); of the twenty-eight chapters of this work Mr. Conybeare contributed nine, including the speeches and letters of Paul, all of which he translated and annotated. A volume of his *Sermons Preached in the Chapel Royal, Whitehall*, appeared in 1844, and his contributions to the *Edinburgh Review* were reprinted with additions under the title *Essays, Ecclesiastical and Social* in 1855. He also published a novel, *Perversion, or the Causes and Consequences of Infidelity* (3 vols., 1856).

COOK, CHARLES: The father of Methodism in France and Switzerland; b. in London May 31, 1787; d. at Lausanne Feb. 21, 1858. He entered the Wesleyan ministry in 1817 and the next year went to France, where he was indefatigable in labor, and it was largely through his agency that there was a revival of religion among French Protestants under the Restoration. Merle d'Aubigné said of him: "The work which John Wesley did in the British kingdom, Charles Cook did upon the Continent, except that it was not so extensive." He organized numerous small societies, which either joined the Reformed Church or continued independent. A controversy with César Malan upon the doctrine of predestination led to the publication of his most important work, *L'Amour de Dieu pour tous les hommes*.

BIBLIOGRAPHY: *Vie de Charles Cook* by his son, J. P. Cook, Paris, 1862.

COOK, ÉMILE FRANCIS: French Methodist; b. at Niort (34 m. e.n.e. of La Rochelle) 1830, son of Charles Cook (q.v.); d. at Hyères (12 m. e. of Toulon) Jan. 29, 1874. He was educated in Lausanne and the Wesleyan institutions in England; ordained in 1854; and in 1866 came to Paris to be pastor of the Wesleyan Congregation there. He came to America as delegate to the General Conference of the Evangelical Alliance held in New York Oct. 2–12, 1873, and escaped shipwreck in the ill-fated *Ville du Havre* (Nov. 22, 1873), only to die shortly after on land.

BIBLIOGRAPHY: L. S. Houghton, *Faithful to the End; . . . Émile Cook's Life*, Philadelphia, 1881.

COOK, FREDERIC CHARLES: Church of England; b. at Milbrook Dec. 1, 1804; d. at Exeter June 22, 1889. He studied at St. John's College, Cambridge (B.A., 1831; M.A., 1844), and at Bonn; was ordained 1839; was inspector of schools; prebendary of St. Paul's 1856–65; preacher at Lincoln's Inn 1860–80; prebendary in Lincoln cathedral 1861–64. He became chaplain in ordinary to the Queen 1857; canon residentiary of Exeter 1864; chaplain to the bishop of London 1869; precentor of Exeter 1872. He was a learned Biblical scholar and a remarkable linguist, acquainted, it is said, with fifty-two languages. His most important work was done for *The Speaker's Commentary* (10 vols., London, 1871–82), which was planned in 1864 to refute the theories advanced by Bishop Colenso and modern critics; Canon Cook was chosen editor in chief and, in addition to his work as editor, wrote personally the introductions to Exodus, the Psalms, and the Acts, the entire commentary on Job, Habakkuk, Mark, Luke, and I Peter, and part of that on Exodus, the Psalms, and Matthew. He criticized severely the work of the New Testament revisers in *The Revised Version of the First Three Gospels Considered in its Bearings upon the Record of our Lord's Words and of Incidents in his*

Life (1882) and in *Deliver Us from Evil* (1883). His last works were *The Origins of Religion and Language* (1884) and *Letters Addressed to the Rev. H. Mace and the Rev. J. Earle* (1885), in which he argued for the unity of language and a primitive divine revelation to man.

COOK, (FLAVIUS) JOSEPH(US): Congregationalist; b. at Ticonderoga, N. Y., Jan. 26, 1838; d. there June 25, 1901. He entered Yale in 1858 but left owing to ill health in junior year; was graduated at Harvard 1865, and at Andover Theological Seminary 1868; was resident licentiate at Andover 1868–70; acting pastor of the First (Congregational) Church, Lynn, Mass., 1870–71; studied and traveled in Europe 1871–73. He was never ordained. His reputation, which was world-wide, was that of lecturer upon the relation of religion and science. His knowledge of theology was considerable, but his claim to speak for science would be disputed. From 1874 to 1895 he spoke each Monday morning during a portion of the year, for years in succession, in Tremont Temple in Boston upon his general topic, with a "prelude on current events." He also lectured elsewhere, and, indeed, during 1880 to 1883 went round the world on a lecturing tour. His conservatism was most pronounced and his dogmatism also. He was immensely popular, and really was astonishingly well informed. As a public speaker he was always vehement, but not always easily intelligible. His Monday lectures were first printed in the newspapers as stenographically reported, then revised and comprised in three volumes: *Biology* (Boston, 1877), in opposition to the "materialistic, but not the theistic theory of evolution"; *Transcendentalism* (1877) and *Orthodoxy* (1878), a discussion of the views of Theodore Parker; *Conscience* (1879); *Heredity* (1879); *Marriage* (1879); *Labor* (1880); *Socialism* (1880). To these were afterward added *Occident* (1884); *Orient* (1886); *Current Religious Perils* (1888). He established a religious monthly, *Our Day*, in 1888.

COOKE, GEORGE ALBERT: Church of England; b. in London Nov. 26, 1865, was scholar of Wadham College, Oxford (B.A., 1888); curate of Headlington, 1889–90; scholar and Hebrew lecturer of St. John's College, Oxford, 1889–92; chaplain of Magdalen College, Oxford, 1890–92; fellow of the same 1892–99; curate of St. Mary the Virgin, Oxford, 1894–96; examiner in school of Oriental languages, Oxford, 1895–99 and in 1904; rector of Beaconsfield 1896–99; rector of Dalkeith 1899–1908, when he succeeded Canon Cheyne as Oriel professor of the interpretation of Holy Scripture in Oxford. His most important book is *A Text-book of North Semitic Inscriptions*, London, 1903.

COOKE, HENRY: The champion of Orthodoxy against Arianism in the Irish Church; b. on a farm near Maghera (28 m. e.s.e. of Londonderry), County Derry, May 11, 1788; d. in Belfast Dec. 13, 1868. He studied at Glasgow College but did not graduate; was ordained assistant minister of Duneane, near Randalstown, County Antrim, 1808; settled at Donegore in the same county 1811. Here he undertook to supplement his early training by systematic study, attended two sessions at Glasgow 1815–17, and heard lectures at Trinity College, Dublin, 1817–18, acquiring a knowledge of medicine as well as of theology. In 1818 he was called to Killeleagh, County Down, and in 1829 to the May Street Church, Belfast. After 1847 he was professor of sacred rhetoric in the General Assembly's theological college at Belfast, continuing his pastoral duties at the same time. He forced the Arians in the Synod of Ulster to secede in 1829, when the Remonstrant Synod of Ulster was formed under the lead of Henry Montgomery (q.v.), and continued his opposition till Arianism was banished from the colleges, synods, and congregations of the Irish Presbyterian Church. He was also active in politics and was the founder and leader of the Protestant party in Ulster after his removal to Belfast. He was a master of all the arts of public speaking, had uncommon skill in argument, and was an unrelenting opponent. He was moderator of the General Assembly in 1841 and 1862. His statue was erected in Belfast in 1875. He wrote many pamphlets and magazine articles, but nothing of permanent value.

Bibliography: J. L. Porter, *Life and Times of Henry Cooke*, Belfast, 1875 (by his son-in-law, an able eulogy rather than a biography); *DNB*, xii. 87–90 (where a full list of sources is given).

COOKMAN, ALFRED: Methodist; b at Columbia, Pa., Jan. 4, 1828; d. in Newark, N. J., Nov. 13, 1871. He was licensed as an exhorter in Baltimore 1845; served as pastor in West Chester, Harrisburg, Pittsburg, and Philadelphia, Pa.; in New York, in Wilmington, Del., and in Newark. He warmly supported the Union cause during the Civil War and served the Christian Commission in the field. He was a leader in the movement in 1867 which led to the formation of the "National Camp-meeting Association" and was prominent at the various meetings which it held.

Bibliography: H. B. Ridgaway, *Life of Rev. Alfred Cookman, with some Account of his Father, Rev. G. C. Cookman*, New York, 1873.

COOPER, JAMES: Scotch Presbyterian; b. at Elgin (71 m. n.w. of Aberdeen), Elginshire, Scotland, Feb. 13, 1846. He studied at the University of Aberdeen (M.A., 1867), and was minister of St. Stephen's, Broughty Ferry, Fifeshire (1873–81), and the East Parish of St. Nicholas, Aberdeen (1881–1898). Since 1898 he has been professor of church history in the University of Glasgow. He is president of the Aberdeen Ecclesiological Society and edited its transactions 1886–1903, and also edited the transactions of the Scottish Ecclesiological Society, of which he was president in 1903. He edited *Cartularium Ecclesiæ Sancti Nicolai Aberdonensis* (2 vols., Aberdeen, 1888–92); and made an English translation of the Syriac *Testament of Our Lord* (London, 1902; in collaboration with A. J. Maclean).

COOPER, THOMAS: English Baptist; b. at Leicester, Eng., Mar. 20, 1805; d. at Lincoln July 15, 1892. He went to school till he was fifteen and then was apprenticed to a shoemaker. He was eager to learn, studied Greek, Latin, and Hebrew in his leisure time, and applied himself so steadily, with insufficient food, that his health failed in 1827. He then tried school-teaching at Gainsborough and Lincoln, and became also a Methodist local preacher in 1829. Differences with the Methodist superintendents, for which he does not seem to have been altogether at fault, brought him out of sympathy with religious work. He became a reporter for country newspapers and tried unsuccessfully to obtain work in London. In 1840 he joined the Chartist movement and for four years was a leader of their extreme party; served two years in Stafford jail on a charge of conspiracy and sedition. After his release he abandoned the Chartists and appeared as a lecturer on historical and political subjects before radical and freethinking audiences. In 1856 his views changed and he became an itinerant preacher, and lecturer on the evidences of natural and revealed religion. In the course of eight and one-half years he preached 1,169 times, lectured 2,204 times, visited every county of England, and many of the counties of Scotland and Wales. In 1866 his health broke down and certain of his friends presented him with an annuity of £100; he went back to his work, however, the next year. He joined the General Baptists in 1859. Besides political writings, novels, and poems (collected ed., London, 1877), he published *The Bridge of History over the Gulf of Time; a popular view of the historical evidence for the truth of Christianity* (London, 1871; 4th ed., 1889); *Plain Pulpit Talk* (1872; 2d ed., 1873); his *Life, written by himself* (1872; popular ed., 1880); *God, the Soul, and a Future State* (1873); *The Verity of Christ's Resurrection* (1875; new ed., 1884); *The Verity and Value of the Miracles of Christ* (1876); *Evolution: the stone book and the Mosaic record of creation* (1878); *The Atonement* (1880); *Thoughts at Fourscore and Earlier* (1885).

COOPERATOR: A priest appointed for an indefinite time to assist the regular incumbent, dependent upon the latter and strictly subordinate to him; the term is applied especially to an assistant in a mother church which has affiliations.

COPE. See VESTMENTS AND INSIGNIA, ECCLESIASTICAL.

COPLESTON, REGINALD STEPHEN: Anglican bishop of Calcutta and metropolitan of India; b. at Barnes (6 m. w. of London), Surrey, Dec. 26, 1845. He studied at Merton College, Oxford (B.A., 1869; M.A., 1871), was ordered deacon in 1872, and ordained priest in 1875. He became a fellow and tutor of St. John's College, Oxford, in 1869, was consecrated bishop of Colombo in 1875, and translated to the diocese of Calcutta in 1902. He has written *Æschylus* (London, 1870) and *Buddhism, Primitive and Present, in Magadha and in Ceylon* (1892).

COPPIN (COPPING), JOHN: English Separatist. He lived at Bury St. Edmunds, became an enthusiastic adherent of Robert Browne (q.v.), preached Browne's doctrines, and disseminated his books. For refusing to conform to the ecclesiastical laws and usages he was imprisoned, 1576, and kept in confinement for seven years, but was treated leniently. Persisting in his course, using violent language, and behaving offensively, in 1583, with a fellow prisoner named Elias Thacker, he was brought to trial charged with disobeying the laws and "dispersing Browne's books and Harrison's books." Both were convicted and hanged, Thacker on June 4, Coppin on June 5, 1583.

BIBLIOGRAPHY: H. M. Dexter, *Congregationalism of the Last Three Hundred Years*, pp. 208–210, New York, 1880.

COPTIC CHURCH.

The Coptic Church is the Monophysite or Jacobite Church of Egypt. The word "Coptic" is the European form of the Arabic *Kibt*, the Greek [*Ai*]*gyptos*.

I. History: The traditional apostle of Egypt is St. Mark (as early as Eusebius, *Hist. eccl.*, ii. 16), though evidences of still earlier Christianity may be seen in Acts ii. 10, viii. 26 sqq., xi. 20, xiii. 1, xviii. 24. From apostolic times to the middle of the second century little is heard beyond the names of Alexandrian teachers (see ALEXANDRIA, SCHOOL OF) and bishops. Among subsequent bishops the first to stand forth distinctly is Demetrius (d. 231), the friend and later the opponent of Origen (q.v.); of his successors, Dionysius (d. 264) and Peter (qq.v.; d. 311) are conspicuous. It is only by the heavy tribute of martyrs in the persecutions during the lives of these two, to which—under Diocletian—Peter fell a victim, that we realize something of the strength of the new religion in southern Egypt. The peace of Constantine was speedily upset by the Arian disturbance, which appears, however, to have affected mainly the Greek-speaking population of the north. In the southern districts, the real home of Egyptian Christianity, the Athanasians found steady support.

1. To the Death of Justinian, 565.

On the basis of the Nicene victory, Athanasius had raised his church to a dominant place, a position maintained for almost a century. His successors, notably Theophilus (d. 412), were ambitious of further magnifying their advantage, and, notwithstanding the rebuff at the Council of 381 (see ARIANISM), Cyril (d. 444) was eventually able, thanks to the opportunity afforded him by Nestorius (q.v.), to figure at Ephesus (431) as the champion of orthodoxy. The Coptic Church was interested in this struggle by the presence at Ephesus of Shenoute, the famous abbot of the White Monastery (Achmim), Cyril's uncompromising supporter. With Cyril's tactless and violent successor, Dioscurus, the turning-point of the Church's history is reached. Successful at the "Robber Synod" (449), he was defeated and exiled at Chalcedon (451); yet his Monophysite creed (see MONOPHYSITES), condemned by official orthodoxy, now became the national faith of Egypt, the history of whose Church is henceforth reduced to a record of the struggles between the royal ("Melkite") and Monophysite sects, each headed by its own patriarchs. The latter party always comprised the vast majority of the Egyptian population, while the royal sect consisted solely of the official class; but success or failure was not independent of the momentary attitude of the court, whose influence was exerted, now in pacification (Zeno, Anastasius), now in coercion (Justinian). The reign of Justinian (d. 565) saw the final extinction of Egyptian paganism (cf. Victor Schultze, *Geschichte des Untergangs des griechisch-römischen Heidenthums*, ii., Jena, 1892, pp. 226 sqq.), which, despite the energies of Theophilus and Cyril, still lingered in outlying districts.

In the succeeding generation the Byzantine world was occupied with the Monothelite controversy (see MONOTHELITES), and in Egypt a union with the Monophysites was enforced for the moment by the imperial patriarch, Cyrus (cf. A. J. Butler, *Arab Conquest of Egypt*, London, 1902, p. 508). The impotence of the empire had already made possible the Persian invasion (616–627); that of the Arabs in 639 finally crushed and impoverished the national Church. If the Copts looked to their new masters for relief from imperial tyranny, they were speedily undeceived. The promises of the first invaders were soon forgotten, and oppressive taxation began to cause those defections to the religion of the conquerors which characterized the subsequent history of native Christianity. The story of the Coptic Church is henceforth a mere list of oppressions due to official expediency or official greed with occasionally a consequent revolt, bloodily suppressed (cf. C. H. Becker, *Beiträge zur Geschichte Aegyptens*, Strasburg, 1902).

2. The Arab Dominion, 639–1517.

Throughout, the meager history of Severus is the sole authority; the Moslem historians, except Makrizi, pay no heed to Christian affairs. The internal war of sects continued unaffected by larger misfortunes. Dynastic changes, as from Ommiads to Abbassids (750), brought no improvement, though the new house usually found it politic to begin with promises of indulgence or relief. Extortion resulted in universal simony; all ecclesiastical offices were bought and large sums paid to the civil authorities for preferment. The rise of the Fatimites (969) saw indeed many Copts in civil employment; and ere long (996) the terrible persecution of Al-Hakim surpassed all that the Christians had hitherto suffered. A century later a succession of Armenian viziers (from 1074) lightened the burdens of their coreligionists. But indulgence provoked a renewal of Moslem animosity. Under such conditions the Church could not maintain a high code of morals or conduct. The relatively mild government of the Aiyubite Sultans (from 1169) seemed but to give freedom to the misconduct of the clergy, conspicuous among whom was the infamous patriarch Cyril III. (*Ibn Laklak*). With Cyril's death (1243) we lose even the guidance of Severus's patriarchal history, and knowledge of the subsequent medieval period is of the most threadbare nature. In 1440 one of the Coptic patriarchs is found making advances to Rome at the Council of Florence, and in the succeeding centuries various attempts were made by the popes to obtain possession of the Church.

3. Turkish and Modern Rule.

Neither the Turkish conquest (1517) nor the French (1798) had much effect upon the condition of native Christians; but Mohammed Ali (1805) gave freedom to all creeds alike and this led to the commencement of foreign missionary enterprise among the Copts and allowed a movement, initiated by Cyril IV. (1854), for their improvement in matters of church government and education. A mixed clerical and lay council was established in the hope of controlling patriarchal action, but its place was subsequently taken by a smaller committee, while the education of the clergy was provided for by the establishment of seminaries.

4. Statistics.

Statistics show a steady increase in the Coptic population since the succession of the present khedival house. Their total in 1820 was about 100,000, in 1855 about 217,000, in 1870 250,000, while the census of 1897 gave 592,374 or about one-sixteenth of the total population. The Copts are at present most numerous in the lower (northern) Said (Siut, Achmim, Girgeh), where they form, in many villages, the majority. At the time of the Arab conquest the Copts (then practically the whole population) numbered some six millions (Abu Salih, 22a); in a hundred years this number had been reduced by a million (Al Kindi, in Abu Salih, 26b), and throughout the Middle Ages they no doubt constantly diminished in numbers.

II. Constitution, Ecclesiastical Law, etc.: The bishop of the capital was doubtless not long in extending his authority over the immediately surrounding districts (Mareotis), and gradually over the rest of the Nile valley, including Nubia and (indirectly) Ethiopia to the south and Libya to the west. Originally nominated, it would seem, by presbyters (cf. Cabrol, *Dictionnaire*, 1204), the *papas* or patriarch was, in all later times, chosen by the clergy, with the concurrence of the people of Alexandria or Cairo, and eventually with that of the Moslem government. Since the eleventh century he has resided in Cairo, the remaining bishops occupying the capitals of the ancient nomes with which their sees were generally conterminous. The existence in early times of intermediate metropolitans is uncertain; at present there exist five or six. Diocesan bishops are met with under Demetrius (d. 231), and Athanasius could already count about a hundred sees. The completest list (though in recent MSS. only) gives eighty-five (cf. E. Amélineau, *La Géographie de l'Égypte à l'époque copte*, Paris, 1893, pp. 571 sqq.). Poverty and persecution, however, by degrees reduced their number, by the amalgamation of poor neighbors, until in the seventeenth century Wansleben could count but seventeen. Patriarch and bishops have been invariably chosen from the monasteries. The remaining clerical orders are: archpriest (*hēgou-*

menos, Kummus), priest, deacon, reader, and, in early times (cf. *JTS*, i. 254) the minor orders also.

The canon law whereby the Church is governed is based upon pseudoapostolic documents and conciliar and patriarchal (external as well as native) decisions, digested by medieval scholars into nomocanons or preserved independently, always in Arabic translations. Considerable judicial power still remains in the hands of the patriarch and bishops.

III. Liturgy, Church Buildings, etc.: Among the earliest sources for a knowledge of Egyptian liturgical usage are the so-called Hippolytan Canons. Those bearing the names of Basil (cf. W. Riedel, *Die Kirchenrechtsquellen des Patriarchats Alexandrien*, Leipsic, 1900, pp. 272 sqq.; *PSBA*, xxvi. 57) and Athanasius (ed. Riedel-Crum, 1904) also contain early evidence. For information from third century patristic writers cf. F. Probst, *Liturgie des vierten Jahrhunderts*, Münster, 1893, p. 106; Brightman, 504. After the schism of 451 the Egyptian Church was obliged to revise its liturgy in conformity with the dogmatic position it had adopted; hence in time arose a number of Greek, then Greco-Coptic, finally Copto-Arabic (to-day even simply Arabic) service-books, of which the Anaphoras of Basil, Gregory, and Cyril are the most conspicuous survivors. Since about the thirteenth century these and all other liturgical books have been read in the northern dialect of Coptic; but sufficient remains are extant to show that an independent series existed in the more ancient southern idiom. Besides the missal (or euchologium), there are separate books for the sacramental and paschal services, lectionaries (*kata meros*), synaxaria (lives of saints to be read in church), with several psalm and hymn-books in constant use. The church festivals are preceded by long fasts, amounting in all to seven months of the year.

1. Liturgies.

Only a few of the characteristic features of Coptic religious life can here be mentioned. The clergy communicate frequently, the laity seldom, but in both kinds; previous confession is not now demanded. Transubstantiation, the efficacy of relics, of prayers for the dead, and of the intercession of saints are accepted doctrines. Baptism is by triple immersion, boys being frequently circumcised beforehand; and confirmation follows immediately The services are generally of inordinate length, beginning often at six in the morning. Magic has always played a part in the belief of the Copts, as with their pagan ancestors, and among the less educated is still freely resorted to. Much has been written as to the relations of popular Christianity in Egypt to the foregoing heathendom (cf. Amélineau, in *RHR*, xiv., xv.; Forbes Robinson, in commentary to his *Coptic Apocryphal Gospels*, Cambridge, 1896), and it is undeniable that superficial features of the surrounding idolatry were adopted and reinterpreted by the converts to the new religion; but as yet no study of these relations has been made sufficient to warrant generalization.

2. Doctrine and Practise.

Of the earliest churches in Lower Egypt (as at Alexandria, churches of St. Mark, of Theonas, of Dionysius, of Athanasius) no undisputed traces survive. Many were destroyed in early times, or in later ages converted into mosques. In the south the sites are still visible (at Philæ, Thebes, Heracleopolis, etc., and in the Outer Oasis) of churches, set often directly within the ancient temple precincts. Pagan rock tombs also have often been utilized as chapels (Thebes, El-Amarna, Der Abu Hennis). Among the older of the churches still in use are the group in Old Cairo (Babylon). These lie to-day embedded in masses of later building and have been repeatedly restored. Their form is usually the basilican, with three parallel apsides and several cupolas. The number of churches officially recorded in Egypt in 1896 was only about 400.

3. Churches.

IV. Monasticism: A primary incentive toward the eremitic life may have been persecution; the desire for contemplative seclusion at any rate early led many in Egypt to retire into solitude, whether singly or in communities. Among the earliest of these was Anthony (c. 270) and, farther south, Pachomius (c. 315; see MONASTICISM; PACHOMIUS). Coptic monasticism since the Council of Chalcedon (451), however, has received little attention; the materials for its study are, in great part, still unpublished, while the usual authorities (Moschus, Leontius of Neapolis, Sophronius, the *Acta sanctorum*) are Catholic and ignore Monophysites. A mild form of cenobitism appears to have superseded the anchorite type. The Pachomian rule was revived and reformed by Shenoute (d. 451), the founder of the great White Monastery, near Achmim (cf. Pears, in *Archæological Journal*, June, 1904). We hear nothing of other rules, that of Anthony being a relatively late production. Yet it is by this last that Coptic monks to-day claim to live. Vows are now no longer professed, though they observe certain general precepts as to obedience, fasting, etc. For the medieval requirements cf. J. M. Wansleben, *Histoire de l'église d'Alexandrie*, Paris, 1677, 39 sqq. The *schēma* (*askim*), once the sign of superior strictness of life, is now worn by all. Inmates of the monasteries are exempt from taxation and military service—a privilege which has been fruitful of abuses. The monasteries were early liable to episcopal interference, and in the seventh century appear as under the control of two bishops. In later times the patriarch would take over the direction and so the revenues of certain houses to his own use. Monastic officials still bear the same titles as in earlier times. Those of the White Monastery in the twelfth century were: archimandrite or hegumenus (elsewhere *proestōs*), *deuterarios*, œconomus (steward), archdeacon, *didaskalos*. The property of the monastery grew by pious bequests, the number of its inmates by the "oblation" of children (at any rate in the eighth century). The abbot might sometimes dispose of the monastery by will or it might be sold, like any secular property. Of the countless monasteries and nunneries which once covered Egypt (cf. Abu Salih and Makrizi) but few have remained in use. Among these, seven are conspicuous; four of the once numerous group in the Nitrian oasis, with ten to twenty monks each; those of Anthony and Paul in the eastern desert; that of Moharrak in Middle Egypt, with some eighty monks and still considerable property.

V. Ecclesiastical Literature: A description of Coptic ecclesiastical literature is equivalent to an account of the literature of Christian Egypt generally; for of all the nations of the Christian East the Copts were the poorest in secular works. The first fruits of conversion were presumably the Bible versions, made independently in at least four dialects, at any rate by the fourth century (see BIBLE VERSIONS, A, VII., and cf. Leipoldt, in *Church Quarterly Review*, lxii. 292 sqq. Of almost equal antiquity would be the translations, on the one hand, of various Gnostic works which have reached us (*Pistis Sophia, Books of Jeu*, etc.) and, on the other, of the "apostolic fathers" (Hermas, Ignatius) and the apocryphal gospels and acts (ed. Guidi, F. Robinson, Revillout, Lacau), of which many fragments, showing varying degrees of divergence from the primitive forms, are extant. The Christian philosophy of the third century (Origen, Clement) is of course not represented; such works could find little favor with a priesthood revering Theophilus and Cyril. But from the Nicene age till the final schism of 451, the principal Greek writers are represented in translation. The vast bulk of the surviving works—and these all fragmentary—consists of homilies and *acta*, destined all to be read in the church service, and from the latter of which the synaxaria were subsequently abbreviated. The sole writer whose works we have in their original Coptic form is Shenoute (see above), the chance survival of his monastic library having preserved intact many of his writings, as well as almost all known besides of the literature of the more ancient, southern (Saidic) dialect. The northern (Bohairic) is of far less importance, though its geographical position, around the civil and ecclesiastical metropolis, insured its survival after its more interesting southern rival had been extinguished. Coptic was, it seems, written till about the fourteenth century; but before that its place had been usurped by Arabic, in which language several Christian writers have left original works (see Riedel, ut sup.) or, what is of greater value now, translations of Coptic texts, otherwise lost to us.

W. E. CRUM.

BIBLIOGRAPHY: Lists of literature are to be found in *Bessarione*, Rome, 1900–01 (by Benigni), in *Littérature chrétienne de l'Égypte*, Paris, 1899 (by P. Renaudin), in the *Archæological Reports of the Egypt-Exploration Fund* since 1893 (by W. E. Crum), and in F. Cabrol, *Dictionnaire d'archéologie chrétienne*, pt. iv. 1177–82. Accounts of Egyptian literature may be read in: E. M. Quatremère, *Recherches critiques et historiques sur la langue et la littérature de l'Égypte*, Paris, 1808; G. Zoega, *Catalogus codicum Copticorum Musei Borgiani*, Rome, 1810; E. Amélineau, *Contes et romans de l'Égypte chrétienne*, 2 vols., Paris, 1888.

Sources for history are derived from: John of Nikiou, ed. H. Zotenberg, in *Notices et extraits des MSS. de la Bibliothèque Nationale*, xxiv., part 1, pp. 125–605, Paris, 1883; Eutychius, *Annales*, Lat. transl. in *MPG*, cxi.; Abu Salih, *The Churches and Monasteries of Egypt*, ed. and transl. B. T. A. Evetts, in *Anecdota Oxoniensia*, Oxford, 1895; Makrizi, "History of the Copts," Germ. transl. by F. Wüstenfeld, Göttingen, 1845, Eng. transl. by S. C. Malan, London, 1872; Abu Dakn, "History of the Jacobites," ed. T. Marshall, Oxford, 1675, S. Haverkamp, Leyden, 1740, Eng. transl. by E. Sadleir, London, 1692; *Synaxarium*, in *Corpus scriptorum Christianorum orientalium*, xviii. 1, Leipsic, 1906 (with Germ. transl.); *Sinuthii . . . vita et opera*, ed. J. Leipoldt and W. Crum, Paris, 1906.

For more modern accounts consult: J. M. Wansleben, *Histoire de l'église d'Alexandrie*, Paris, 1677; E. Renaudot, in A. Arnauld, *La Perpétuité de la foi de l'église catholique*, vol. iv., 5 vols., Paris, 1704–13; idem, *Historia patriarcharum Alexandrinorum Jacobitarum*, ib. 1713; M. Le Quien, *Oriens christianus*, ii. 329 sqq., ib. 1740; M. Lüttke, *Aegyptens neue Zeit*, Leipsic, 1873; Kummus Feltaus, "Modern Catechism," Eng. transl. by N. Odeh, London, 1892; E. Amélineau, *Monuments pour servir à l'histoire de l'Égypte chrétienne*, Paris, 1886–89; Ellen L. Butcher, *Story of the Church of Egypt*, 2 vols., ib. 1897 (good for the modern period); *A Coptic Layman*, in *Contemporary Review*, lxxi (1897), 734 sqq. (the best account of recent times); M. Fowler, *Christian Egypt*, London, 1901 (gives statistics); S. L. Poole, *History of Egypt in the Middle Ages*, ib. 1901; K. Beth, *Die orientalische Christenheit der Mittelmeerländer*, Berlin, 1902.

On the constitution of the Church consult: W. Riedel, *Kirchenrechtsquellen des Patriarchats Alexandrien*, Leipsic, 1900; K. Lübeck, *Reichseinteilung und kirchliche Hierarchie des Orients*, Münster, 1901.

On the liturgies and church orders consult: E. Renaudot, *Liturgiarum orientalium collectio*, vol. i., Paris, 1716, Eng. transl., Dublin, 1822, partly in J. A. Giles, *Codex apocryphorum N. T.*, London, 1852; A. J. Butler, *Ancient Coptic Churches of Egypt*, 2 vols., Oxford, 1884; *Rites of the Coptic Church. Order of Baptism and . . . of Matrimony*, transl. from the Coptic by B. T. A. Evetts, ib. 1888; F. E. Brightman, *Liturgies Eastern and Western*, ib. 1896; A. Gayet, *L'Art Copte*, Paris, 1892.

On monasticism consult: E. Amélineau, Coptic Texts, in *Annales du Musée Guimet*, xvii., xxv., 1890, 1894; E. C. Butler, *Lausiac History*, in *TS*, vi (1898); M. Jullien, *L'Égypte, souvenirs bibliques et chrétiens*, Lille, 1899; W. E. Crum, *Coptic Ostraca*, London, 1902.

COQUEREL, côc"rel', ATHANASE JOSUÉ: French Protestant, son of Athanase Laurent Charles Coquerel (q.v.); b. at Amsterdam June 16, 1820; d. at Fismes (18 m. e.n.e. of Reims) July 24, 1875. He studied theology at Geneva and Strasburg; was ordained by his father at Nîmes in 1843; called to Paris in 1848. His views were even less acceptable to the orthodox party than his father's, and, after suffering much annoyance, in 1864 he was forced to relinquish his pulpit; he opened a free liberal church and became the leader of the liberal Protestants of France. He was one of the founders of the Société de l'histoire du protestantisme français in 1852, and he edited *Le Lien* from 1849 to 1870. His publications include *Des beaux-arts en Italie au point de vue religieux* (Paris, 1857; Eng. transl., London, 1859); *Jean Calas et sa famille* (1858; 2d ed., 1869); *Précis de l'histoire de l'église réformée de Paris* (1862); *Lettres inédites de Voltaire sur la tolérance* (1863); *Le Catholicisme et le protestantisme considérés dans leur origine et leur développement* (1864); *Des premières transformations historiques du Christianisme* (1866; Eng. transl., Boston, 1867); *La conscience et la foi* (1867; Eng. transl., with memoir by A. Réville, London, 1878); *Libres études, religion, critique, histoire, beaux-arts et voyages* (1868); *Histoire du Credo* (1869).

BIBLIOGRAPHY: E. Stroehlin, *Athanase Coquerel fils. Étude biographique*, 2 vols., Paris, 1886.

COQUEREL, ATHANASE LAURENT CHARLES: French Protestant; b. in Paris Aug. 27, 1795; d. there Jan. 10, 1868. He came of an old Jansenist family, and was brought up by his aunt Helen

Maria Williams (q.v.); studied theology under the Protestant faculty of Montauban 1811–16; in 1818 became pastor of the French Reformed Church at Amsterdam; was called to Paris in 1830 as assistant to Pastor Marron, and succeeded to the latter's place upon his death in 1832. He was eloquent and popular and wielded a wide influence both as preacher and as citizen. He was elected a member of the National Assembly in 1848, and of the Legislative Assembly in 1849, but after the *coup d'état* of Dec. 2, 1851, he confined himself to his pastoral duties. He was liberal in theology, rejected the doctrines of eternal punishment, and of the Atonement and the Trinity in their orthodox form, and strongly opposed the Calvinistic theory of predestination. He founded and edited three periodicals to express his views, *Le Protestant* (1831–33), *Le Libre Examen* (with M. Artaud, 1834–36), and *Le Lien* (1841–44); in the last-named he labored to unite the branches of French Protestantism. Besides many sermons (8 vols., 1819–1852), his works include: *Biographie sacrée* (4 vols., Amsterdam, 1825–26); *Histoire sainte et analyse de la Bible* (Paris, 1838); *Réponse au livre du docteur Strauss, "La vie de Jésus"* (1841; Eng. transl., 1844); *L'orthodoxie moderne* (1842); *Le Christianisme expérimental* (1847); *Christologie* (2 vols., 1858); *Observations pratiques sur la prédication* (1860); *Projet de discipline pour les églises réformées de France* (1861).

Bibliography: Lichtenberger, *ESR*, iii. 413–415; *Nouveau Larousse illustré*, iii. 265, Paris, n.d.

COQUEREL, CHARLES AUGUSTIN: French Protestant; b. at Paris Apr. 17, 1797; d. there Feb. 1, 1851. Like his brother, Athanase Laurent Charles Coquerel (q.v.), he was brought up by his aunt Helen Maria Williams (q.v.) and studied theology at Montauban. His tastes, however, were more literary and scientific and, after returning to Paris, he occupied himself as a layman in critical and exegetical studies on the history of the canon and of the Gospels, at the same time studying medicine, chemistry, mathematics, and astronomy. His chief literary work was the first *Histoire des Églises du Désert* (Paris, 1841).

CORBINIAN, cör"bi"nyän': An early Frankish missionary, one of the predecessors of Boniface, who aimed at completing the conversion of Germany, and the establishment of church authority and discipline among both clergy and laity; said to have died at Freising Sept. 8, probably 730. The only authority for his life is the biography of Aribo, bishop of Freising, written about 768. According to this, Corbinian, whose name was originally Waldekiso, was born at Chartrettes near Melun, and early adopted the life of a recluse. His renown for piety attracted the attention of Pepin of Heristal (d. 714), and brought so many disciples about him that he attempted to flee from their veneration, and went to Rome, where Gregory II. (715–731) consecrated him as bishop and sent him back. In spite of a second request to be allowed to retire into the obscurity of a monastery, he was obliged once more to retrace his steps. This time, passing through Bavaria, he was prevailed upon by the duke to remain in Freising, where he was the head of a college of priests and did much to break down heathen superstitions and enforce Christian discipline. There are numerous historical difficulties in Aribo's account; but there seems to be a more or less sound historical basis for Corbinian's Frankish birth and episcopal character conferred very likely at the request of Pepin, who favored the sending of Frankish clergy to Bavaria to spread the Frankish influence there, and his activity in Freising and southern Tyrol under Dukes Grimwald and Hugbert. (A. Hauck.)

Bibliography: The *Vita* by Aribo, ed. S. Riezler, is in *Abhandlungen der bayerischen Akademie, historische Klasse*, xviii. 219–274, Munich, 1888; and a recension of it with comment by the monk Hrotroc is in *ASB*, Sept., iii. 261–296. Consult: Rettberg, *KD*, ii. 214; Hauck, *KD*, i. 345.

CORDELIERS, cor'de-lirz *or* cor"de"lyé': A name given in France to the Franciscan monks, from the girdle of knotted cord which they wear (see Francis, Saint, of Assisi). It was also the name of a famous political club of the Revolution, which met in an old Franciscan convent.

CORDOVA: A city of Andalusia (on the Guadalquivir, 275 m. s.s.w. of Madrid), the capital of the province of Bætica in Roman times, the most important Moorish town in Spain from the eighth to the eleventh centuries, and one of the great centers of learning, art, and industry of the Middle Ages. In ecclesiastical history it is noteworthy as the episcopal seat in the fourth century of one of the foremost opponents of Arianism, the bishop Hosius (q.v.), as the gathering-place of several provincial synods, and for its university.

Synods of Cordova: The first met in 839 to suppress the "Casians," followers of a certain Casianus (Cassianus), who were then making trouble at Epagro, in the diocese of Egabra, by laxity concerning marriage, opposition to the veneration of relics, excessive rigor in fasting, and the demand that the bread of the Lord's Supper should be received not in the mouth but in the hand of the communicant. More important are synods held under Emir Abdalrahman II. (d. 852) and his successor, Mohammed. The first of these was called in 852 by Abdalrahman to try to check the fanaticism of certain Christians who sought martyrdom by reviling the prophet of the Mohammedans and in other ways giving them unnecessary offense (see Alvar of Cordova; Eulogius of Cordova). The bishops who attended, including Hostegisis of Malaga and Reccafred of Seville (or according to others of Merida), condemned the seeking of martyrdom and sanctioned a law of the State forbidding it. The acts of the synod were suppressed by the orthodox, and their content is known only from the writings of Eulogius. It is noteworthy that the majority justified their attitude toward the Mohammedans by the fact that the latter worshiped the true God and acknowledged the principles of morality and revelation. There were two later synods, in 862 and 863, both dominated by Hostegisis. At the first an abbot, Samson, a leader of the fanatics just mentioned, was condemned as a heretic for accusing Hostegisis of teaching anthropomorphic views of God, and at the second a bishop, Valentinus of Cordova, who supported Samson was deposed and a number of decrees were issued in accordance with the views and practise of the laxer party (cf. Baudissin, 177 sqq.). For the synods of 1494 and 1540 cf. Hefele, *Conciliengeschichte*, viii. 364, 796.

The **University of Cordova** was founded c. 980 by the Calif Hakim II. It is true that both theology and jurisprudence had been cultivated in Cordova before this time by famous teachers; but it was due to Hakim's energy and support that chairs were established for other branches of learning, the library was augmented, and a complete university began to flourish. That the library grew to 600,000 books may be an exaggeration, but it was certainly the best in Arab Spain. At the time of its greatest prosperity (c. 1100) Cordova had the best astronomical observatory in all Europe and was renowned as the center of the study of astronomy, mathematics, medicine, and philosophy. A little later it became the principal seat of the Arabian study of Aristotle, and thus it became the mediator between the ancient philosophy and medieval speculation. Its most famous teacher was Averroes (b. in Cordova 1126), and his most famous pupil was Maimonides (q.v.). The capture of Cordova by the Christians (1236) made an end of the university, and a Jewish school which had flourished for several centuries did not long survive the fall of the city. (O. Zöckler†.)

Bibliography: On the bishopric consult *KL*, iii. 1092-1094. On the synods: J. S. de Aguirre, *Collectio maxima conciliorum . . . Hispaniæ*, iii. 149, Rome, 1693 (also ed. G. Catalani, 6 vols., Rome, 1753-55); W. Baudissin, *Eulogius und Alvar*, pp. 70 sqq., 127-128, 177 sqq., Leipsic, 1872; W. Gams, *Kirchengeschichte Spaniens*, II. ii. 311 sqq., Regensburg, 1874; Hefele, *Conciliengeschichte*, iv. 99, 179, 260. On the university: H. Rashdall, *Universities of Europe in the Middle Ages*, 2 vols., London, 1895; V. de la Fuente, *Historia de las Universidades . . . in España*, vols. iii.-iv., Madrid, 1888-89. On the philosophy: E. Renan, *Averroès et l'averroisme*, Paris, 1861; L. Dugat, *Histoire des philosophes et des théologiens Musulmans 632-1258*, ib. 1878; A. F. Mehren, *Études sur la philosophie d'Averrhoès*, ib. 1888; *KL*, i. 1745-50; and the works on hist. of philosophy.

CORDUS, cer'dus, EURICIUS, yu-ri'shius: Humanist of the sixteenth century; b. at Simtshausen near Wetter (7 m. n.w. of Marburg), Hesse, 1486; d. at Bremen 1535. He was the son of a peasant, went to school in Marburg, and entered the University of Erfurt in 1505. Here, after teaching a while in Cassel, he became magister in 1516 and rector of St. Mary's school. In 1521 he studied medicine in Ferrara. When he returned to Erfurt the humanists were scattered as a result of civic turmoil. He, therefore, in 1523 gladly accepted a call to be a physician in Brunswick, and still more eagerly he went in 1527, on the invitation of Landgrave Philip, to the newly founded University of Marburg. But as a result of controversies with colleagues his continuance there became unpleasant, so in 1534 he accepted a position as teacher in the gymnasium at Bremen. He laid the foundations of his fame as a poet chiefly by his witty epigrams, of which more than 1,200 were collected in thirteen books; Lessing's dependence on Cordus has been demonstrated. His *Bucolicorum eclogæ* appeared at Leipsic in 1518. As a medical writer he labored to free the art of healing from superstition, and he undertook in the book *Botanologicon* (Cologne, 1534) to point out, by means of the empirical observation of nature, new paths for the investigation of the plant world. In distinction from most humanists, Cordus was not satisfied with directing his ridicule merely against the evils of church life and the faults of the clergy, but he sided energetically and permanently with the Reformation. He defended it in a poem of more than 1,500 hexameters addressed to the Emperor Charles V. and the German princes.

Carl Mirbt.

Bibliography: C. Krause, *Euricius Cordus*, Hanau, 1863; idem, *Helius Eobanus Hessus, sein Leben und seine Werke*, 2 vols., Gotha, 1879; G. Bauch, *Die Universität Erfurt im Zeitalter des Frühhumanismus*, Breslau, 1904.

CORINTH. See Greece, I.

CORINTHIANS, FIRST AND SECOND EPISTLES TO THE. See Paul the Apostle.

CORNELIUS: Pope 251-252. After the martyrdom of Fabian (Jan. 20, 250) the see was vacant for over a year, during which time the rigorist presbyter Novatian (q.v.) presided over the Church. In Apr., 251, Cornelius was chosen bishop. Of his early life little is known. Cyprian tells that he had gone through all the lower orders and that he did not seek the episcopal office, but was compelled to accept it, and characterizes him as a quiet, modest, and humble man, an excellent administrator, and a steadfast upholder of the faith. A strong man was needed at this period (that of the Decian persecution), especially as the rigorist teaching of Novatian threatened to bring about a schism in the Church. He blamed Cornelius for his conduct in the time of the persecution, and asserted that he had been a *libellaticus*, i.e., had saved himself by an equivocal written declaration made before the pagan official (see Lapsed). Novatian even had himself consecrated to the Roman See by three foreign bishops. Both he and Cornelius made efforts to have their election acknowledged by the metropolitans of Carthage, Antioch, Alexandria, Jerusalem, and Ephesus. Cyprian of Carthage delayed his decision, and sent two bishops, Caldonius and Fortunatus, to Rome to inquire into the matter. But before they returned, having in the mean time seen the legates of Cornelius, the bishops Pompeius and Stephanus, he declared against Novatian. From that time on the relations between Cyprian and Cornelius were cordial, and Cyprian earnestly and successfully endeavored to detach Novatian's followers from him and induce them to acknowledge Cornelius. On Sept. 14 or 15, 252, Cornelius suffered martyrdom with twenty-one Christians of both sexes at Centumcellæ (now Cività Vecchia). Several letters of Cornelius are extant concerning his controversy with Novatian, somewhat vehement in tone and biased in judgment. [They have been frequently appealed to by controversialists on both sides of the question of the Roman primacy, and are of interest also in regard to the question of baptism by heretics.] The death of Cornelius is placed by some authorities in June or July, 253.

K. Leimbach†.

Bibliography: The chief sources are the correspondence between Cyprian and Cornelius, in *MPL*, iii. 709–874, transl. in *ANF*, v. 319–347, cf. Mirbt, *Quellen*, pp. 21–28. Also consult: *Liber pontificalis*, ed. Duchesne, i. 150, Paris, 1886, ed. Mommsen, in *MGH*, *Gest. pont. Rom.*, i. 28–31; J. Langen, *Geschichte der römischen Kirche*, vol. i., Bonn, 1881; Bower, *Popes*, i. 25–29; Milman, *Latin Christianity*, i. 83–85.

CORNELIUS A LAPIDE (Cornelis van den Steen): A Roman Catholic Biblical commentator; b. at Borchoet, a village in the diocese of Liége, Dec. 12, 1567; d. at Rome Mar. 12, 1637. He studied philosophy at the Jesuit colleges in Maestricht and Cologne, and theology at Douai and Louvain, entering the Society of Jesus in 1597. He lectured on the Bible and on Hebrew at Louvain from 1596 to 1616, when he was appointed professor in the Roman College of the order, where he remained until his death. He was one of the most fertile exegetes of the Jesuit order, and his commentaries have retained their influence. He was an ardent advocate of Roman Catholic propaganda at a time when his society zealously devoted itself to exegesis in order to refute those heretics who appealed to the Bible. He derived much from his enemies, the influence of the *Clavis scripturæ sacræ* of Matthias Flacius being especially marked, but his chief source for historical and chronological data was Baronius. He possessed a remarkably clear sense for all that was interesting and attractive, and made profuse allusions to legends and antiquities with many apt citations. Although solving every difficulty with an affirmation of the verity of Roman Catholic dogma, he was skilled in the discovery of formulas in support of his arguments. His concept of the "literal meaning" is shown by his sixth canon in which he adopts the medieval rule of quadruple exegesis. Thus, in the account of the temptation of Joseph, Joseph allegorically represents Christ and Potiphar's wife the synagogue; symbolically Joseph represents the king and Potiphar's wife rebellion; typologically Joseph represents constancy and Potiphar's wife lust. In support of the "true meaning" he cited an abundance of legendary material, so that in his characterization of Paul, for example, he entered into a discussion of the worship of the saints. Similar digressions fill a large portion of his commentary, and much space is occupied by his classical citations, as when he prefixes to his commentary on Ecclesiastes a compendium of ancient philosophy.

His textual criticism is worthless, since he cites the Oriental versions only at second hand and regards the Vulgate as infallible. His commentaries, of which the most valued were those on the Pentateuch, the Gospels, and the Pauline epistles, appeared in Antwerp in the following order: the Pauline epistles, 1614; the Pentateuch, 1616; Jeremiah, Lamentations, Baruch, Ezekiel, Daniel, 1621; the minor prophets, 1625; Acts, the Catholic Epistles, Revelation, 1627; Ecclesiasticus, 1634; Proverbs, 1635; Ecclesiastes, Canticles, Wisdom 1638; the four Gospels, 1639; Joshua, Judges, Ruth, Samuel, Kings, Chronicles, 1642; Ezra, Nehemiah, Tobit, Judith, Esther, and Maccabees, 1645. All have been frequently reprinted (16 vols., Antwerp, 1681; 24 vols., Paris, 1859–63; 10 vols., 1874, etc.). (G. Heinrici.)

Bibliography: A translation by T. W. Mossman of the Commentaries on the O. T. is issued, 6 vols., London, 1892–93, and one of those on the N. T. is promised. Consult: Sommervogel, *Bibliothèque de la compagnie de Jésus, Bibliographie* iv., Brussels, 1893; R. Simon, *Histoire critique des principaux commentateurs*, pp. 655–665, Rotterdam, 1693; G. H. Goes, in *Vie du vénérable J. Berchmans*, pp. 507–512, Paris, 1853.

CORNILL, CARL HEINRICH: German Lutheran; b. at Heidelberg Apr. 26, 1854. He studied at Leipsic (Ph.D., 1875), Bonn, and Marburg (lic. theol., 1878), becoming lecturer at Marburg in 1877 and privat-docent in 1878, and also being first lecturer in the Seminarium Philippinum at Marburg 1877–86. In 1886 he was made associate professor, but in the same year he accepted a call to Königsberg, where he was made full professor in 1888. Since 1898 he has been professor of Old Testament exegesis at Breslau. In theology he describes himself as "scientific in matters of science and faithful in matters of faith." He has written: *Jeremia und seine Zeit* (Heidelberg, 1880); *Das Buch des Propheten Ezechiel* (Leipsic, 1886); *Einleitung in das Alte Testament* (Freiburg, 1891; Eng. transl., 2 vols., New York, 1907); *Der israelitische Prophetismus* (Strasburg, 1894; Eng. transl., Chicago, 1898); *Geschichte des Volkes Israel* (Chicago, 1898; Eng. transl., Chicago, 1898); and *Das Buch Jeremia* (Leipsic, 1905). He also edited the Hebrew text of *Jeremiah* for the *Polychrome Bible* (New York, 1895).

CORPORAL: A square linen cloth, about as wide as the altar, used in the Roman Catholic Church to place under the sacrament either before consecration in the mass or at any time of exposition. It was originally large enough to spread over the oblations, including not only the sacramental bread and wine but any other offerings brought by the faithful. In course of time, for the sake of convenience, it was divided, the smaller part now used to cover the chalice and stiffened with cardboard being called the pall. The older custom was long maintained in the Gallican Church and the Carthusian order. The Greek Church also uses a corporal, and two palls, one for the paten and one for the chalice. The corporal is supposed to symbolize the linen cloth in which the body of Jesus was wrapped before being placed in the sepulcher (Mark xv. 46). When not in use it is folded and placed with the pall in a receptacle called the burse.

CORPORATION ACT: An act passed in 1661 by the Cavalier Parliament of Charles II., the first of the series of repressive measures sometimes known as the Clarendon Code, by which the membership of the municipal bodies, who ruled the towns and usually controlled the elections of their parliamentary representatives, was confined to members of the Church of England. They were expressly required to renounce the covenant, to take the oath of nonresistance, and to receive the Lord's Supper according to the Anglican form, thus degrading a sacred rite into a political test. This provision, though suspended by temporary statutes after 1689, was not finally abolished until 1769, when a promise not to injure or weaken the Church of England was substituted.

BIBLIOGRAPHY: The text is given in Gee and Hardy, *Documents*, pp. 594–600. Titles of many pamphlets called forth by the act are given in the *British Museum Catalogue*, England, part 1, 66–68.

CORPORATIONS. See RELIGIOUS CORPORATIONS.

CORPUS CATHOLICORUM: The organization of delegates from the Roman Catholic states of the Holy Roman Empire, tacitly made in opposition to that of the Corpus Evangelicorum (q.v.). Though its formation as a definite body with a corresponding purpose is expressly asserted in the report of the Evangelical delegates in 1720, the name "Corpus Catholicorum" is never used in the Reformation period and hardly ever in the seventeenth century. This is explained by the fact that papal recognition could never be secured for it, since the recognition of a special corporation with rights and privileges would have easily led to a limitation of the papal autocracy in Germany. None the less, the body existed in fact, needing formal sanction the less because the emperor, as the protector of their Church, and the imperial councilors would naturally forward their interest. As, too, they denied the right of the Protestants to form a similar corporation, they were precluded from making open claim to such recognition. The Peace of Westphalia (1648) took cognizance of the existence of the two bodies, without mentioning the names of either. Apart from formal organization, a union of the Roman Catholic states took place earlier than of the Protestant, as their joint action at the Nuremberg Diet and the formation of the league at Regensburg (1524) shows. Jointly, again, they met the Protestants at the Diet of Speyer (1529), and concluded a peace with them at Nuremberg in 1532; and their organization appears plainly in the Holy League of 1538. The deliberations of the Corpus Catholicorum, after its action became systematized and permanent, were usually held in a monastery of the town in which the diet was sitting, sometimes in the quarters of the delegate from Mainz, which naturally, from its precedence in the empire, took the headship of the body. The dissolution of the empire itself, and of the Corpus Evangelicorum with it, in 1806, put an end tacitly to the Corpus Catholicorum as well. (E. FRIEDBERG.)

CORPUS CHRISTI, cōr'pus cris'ti ("the Body of Christ"): A festival of the Roman Catholic Church in honor of the Eucharist, celebrated on the Thursday after Trinity Sunday. As early as Augustine's time it was usual to celebrate the institution of the Holy Communion on the fifth day of the last week in Lent. In 1246 Bishop Robert of Liége, prompted by the visions of a nun (Juliana of Mont-Cornillo), inaugurated a new festival in honor of the sacrament, in a pastoral letter intended for his own diocese. The forms of its observance were quite simple: divine service, lections, antiphonal chants were the essential elements of the ceremony. Shortly afterward Pantaleon, archdeacon of Liége, became Pope Urban IV. and gave the festival its ecumenical character (see BOLSENA, MIRACLE OF). His bull of 1264 appoints the fifth day after the octave of Pentecost as the festival's calendar place, and indicates for its proper object that it shall bring Christ near in his real presence. The sumptuous exposition, together with the indulgence accorded by the pope to the participants in the festival, was designed, no doubt, to extend the same; and not less instrumental in this regard was the friendly attitude of the great schoolman Thomas Aquinas. But in this second phase also, the festival continued within modest boundaries.

III.—18

The real turning-point in the development of this festival came in the time of John XXII. (1316–34), who instituted the accompanying procession; there now took place the public exposition of the host in the monstrance. After the Council of Constance (1414–18) the popes took occasion by the amplification of indulgences to stimulate the zeal of the faithful still further. The splendid exhibition became more sumptuous, even kings and princes began to take part in the processions, and in this way there soon came about a striking mixture of ecclesiastical parade and worldly splendor. After the fifteenth century Corpus Christi plays also came into vogue, being popular presentations of sacred history. HERMANN HERING.

BIBLIOGRAPHY: J. C. W. Augusti, *Denkwürdigkeiten*, iii. 304 sqq., Leipsic, 1820; A. J. Binterim, *Denkwürdigkeiten*, v. 1, pp. 275 sqq., Mainz, 1829; A. Butler, *The Moveable Feasts, Fasts . . . of the Catholic Church*, Dublin, 1839; Bendel, in *TQS*, xxxiv (1852), 244 sqq. On the plays: W. Creizenach, *Geschichte des neueren Dramas*, i. 162 sqq., Halle, 1893. From the Protestant standpoint: P. Tschackert, *Evangelische Polemik*, pp. 81–82, 257, Gotha, 1885; C. H. H. Wright and C. Neil, *A Protestant Dictionary*, pp. 145–146, London, 1904.

CORPUS DOCTRINÆ, doc'tri-nī *or* -nê.

The name "Corpus Doctrinæ" was applied in the sixteenth century to collections of doctrinal statements composed as authorized expressions of a certain type of faith, or the belief of an individual church. The Augsburg Confession early became a standard of belief for the local Lutheran churches, and the Apology, as a commentary on it, ranked with it; appeal was likewise made to the Apostles', Nicene, and Athanasian creeds, known as *symbola*.

1. Origin of the Term. Melanchthon, however, designated the whole body of writings in which the pure faith of the Gospel is expressed *corpus doctrinæ*, and (especially after 1550) insisted strongly on the necessity of having such a recognized norm. The internal controversies of Protestantism became so threatening that a common basis for agreement was sought in 1558 in the compendium known as the Frankfort Recess (q.v.), and again, on the failure of this to find universal acceptance, at the meeting at Naumburg in Jan., 1561 (see NAUMBURG CONVENTION), but equally without success.

The so-called *Corpus doctrinæ Philippicum* or *Misnicum* met with great success among the bodies which inclined to the Philippist party. It was put out by Vögelin, the learned Leipsic publisher, as a private venture, first in German and then in Latin, in 1561. Besides the three creeds, it consisted of all the principal doctrinal writings of Melanchthon, including the Augsburg Confession, the Apology, the Saxon Confession, the *Loci theologici*, *Examen ordinandorum*, etc.

2. Corpus Misnicum and Its Rivals.

It was officially recognized in Pomerania (1561) and electoral Saxony (1566); other churches (Hesse, Nuremberg, Silesia, Anhalt, Sleswick-Holstein, and Denmark) practically though informally approved it. Representing exclusively, however, the influence of Melanchthon, it was opposed by others. In Württemberg Duke Christopher had put forth in 1559 the Württemberg Confession (drawn up originally by Brenz in 1551) as the official standard of faith; to this was added, later in the year, a special declaration on the Lord's Supper. In North Germany, the Lübeck *Formula consensus de doctrina evangelii* (1560) set forth, besides the Augsburg Confession and the Apology, the Schmalkald Articles. The Lower-Saxon gathering of Lüneburg in 1561 named besides these the Catechism "and other writings of Luther" as the true Scriptural explanation of the Augsburg Confession. At Hamburg in 1560 a collection of five declarations issued since 1549 by the clergy of that place was recognized as the *norma docendi*.

The first specifically Lutheran collection, however, to bear the title of *Corpus doctrinæ* was that of Brunswick (1563), which contained the constitution drawn up by Bugenhagen in 1528, the Augsburg Confession, the Apology, the Schmalkald Articles, and the Lüneburg Articles. The *Corpus Pomeranicum* dates from 1564; before that date Melanchthon's *Corpus* had been accepted, but its one-sided tendency was now corrected by the addition of the Schmalkald Articles, Luther's Great and Small Catechisms, and some minor treatises of his. In Prussia the final publication of a specifically Lutheran standard was brought about by the controversies originated by Osiander in 1549.

3. Lutheran Tentative Corpora.

With a view of suppressing his teaching, Duke Albert in 1567 recalled several theologians who had been exiled on account of their opposition to it, especially Mörlin, who brought Chemnitz with him from Brunswick; and as a result of their labors a *Corpus Prutenicum* was promulgated at Königsberg. The example of Brunswick was followed in 1568 by the town of Göttingen, which published its ecclesiastical constitution of 1531, the Small Catechism, and the Schmalkald Articles, with the Augsburg Confession and the Apology in the Frankfort edition of 1565 bound up with them to save expense. This *Corpus*, with the addition of the three creeds, was again recognized as the *norma docendi* in 1585; in 1600 the *Formula Concordiæ* was acknowledged for the first time, the Great Catechism added, and the Schmalkald Articles and the 1531 constitution omitted. The promulgation of a *Corpus doctrinæ* for Brunswick-Wolfenbüttel was prepared for by the constitution drawn up by Chemnitz and Andreæ and published by Duke Julius in 1569, which designated as the *Corpus doctrinæ*, not the *Misnicum*, but the Bible, the three ancient creeds, and the Augsburg Confession, as explained in the Apology, the Schmalkald Articles, the Catechism, and Luther's other writings. This ducal *Corpus* was confirmed the next year by a clerical assembly. In ducal Saxony, immediately after John William's accession, the *Corpus Thuringicum* appeared in 1570, with a preface by the duke. It contained the three creeds, the two catechisms, the Augsburg Confession and Apology, the Schmalkald Articles, the Thuringian Confession of 1549, and the Confutation of 1558. The Elector of Brandenburg, John George, followed in 1572 with the *Corpus Brandenburgicum*, prefaced by himself, and containing the Augsburg Confession, the Small Catechism, and the compilation of Luther's expository writings made in 1570 by Musculus for Joachim II. The next year saw the establishment of a *Corpus* for a part of Silesia. Duke George of Brieg declared as the valid doctrine the prophetic and apostolic writings and approved creeds, whose fundamental teaching was to be found in the Augsburg Confession and Apology, in the *Corpus Misnicum*, the Mecklenburg Agenda, the writings of Luther and others that agreed with them. The close of this process, which prepared the way for the *Formula Concordiæ*, may be seen in 1575 and 1576 in the duchies of Brunswick-Lüneburg and Brunswick-Wolfenbüttel. In the former, Duke William published in 1575 two expository treatises by Rhegius and Chemnitz, following this up in the next year with the formal *Corpus Wilhelminum*; and about the same time appeared the *Corpus Julium* of the other duchy, which contained, besides the usual formulas, the treatises of Rhegius and Chemnitz.

All these local *Corpora doctrinæ* lost their importance when the whole Lutheran Church succeeded in finding a common ground in the *Formula Concordiæ* and the *Liber Concordiæ*.

4. Formula and Liber Concordiæ.

In a considerable minority, however, of the states which had accepted the Augsburg Confession, the *Formula* was not accepted. Some of these, such as Nassau, Bremen, Anhalt, and Lower Hesse, were finally driven into Calvinism; others maintained their position as Lutherans without the *Formula*—Lutherans, that is, who were not prepared to go as far as the absolute exclusion of the Philippist party. These latter either adhered to their original *Corpus* or gradually worked out new ones. Holstein accepted the documents contained in the *Liber concordiæ* with the exception of the *Formula* itself. Brunswick-Wolfenbüttel adhered to the *Corpus Julium*; Pomerania supplemented its *Corpus* in 1593 by the addition of the sections on the Lord's Supper, the *Communicatio idiomatum*, and predestination; Hesse-Darmstadt produced a *Corpus Hassiacum* in 1617–26 by adding the Wittenberg agreement of 1536 to the Brunswick-Wolfenbüttel selection of 1569. Nuremberg took a middle course, in conjunction with Brandenburg-Ansbach, by combining writings of Luther and of Melanchthon; and much the same attitude was adopted in 1578 by the county of Hohenlohe. Among the Reformed bodies, the Geneva *Corpus et syntagma confessionum fidei* of 1612 was received in some places in the same way as the Lutheran *Corpora doctrinæ*. See FORMULA OF CONCORD.

(G. KAWERAU.)

BIBLIOGRAPHY: J. A. Schmidt, *De corporibus doctrinæ Philippico*, etc., Helmstadt, 1706; C. A. Salig, *Historie der Augsburger Confession*, i. 702 sqq., Halle, 1730; E. Köllner, *Symbolik der lutherischen Kirche*, pp. 95 sqq., Hamburg, 1837; H. Heppe, *Die konfessionelle Entwickelung der altprotestantischen Kirche Deutschlands*, pp. 179 sqq., Marburg, 1854; F. Loofs, *Leitfaden der Dogmengeschichte*, pp. 907 sqq., Halle, 1906; H. E. Jacobs, *The Book of Concord*, 2 vols., Philadelphia, 1893.

CORPUS EVANGELICORUM, ē"van-jel"i'-cōrum (also called *Corpus Sociorum Augustanæ Confessionis*): A body composed of delegates from the Evangelical states of the Holy Roman Empire and organized into what was practically an independent political assembly. Its origin is not to be sought in such temporary alliances among the German Protestants as the Leagues of Torgau and Schmalkald, nor in the repeated but always unsuccessful attempts of individual princes to unite the states with which they were in religious sympathy either by the formation of a permanent confederation or by a regular "correspondence." It grew out of the need felt by the Protestant states in the diet to treat and to protect their several interests as joint interests. The same need was felt on the other side, and so the two parties in the diet crystallized more and more into distinct corporations—the Corpus Evangelicorum and the Corpus Catholicorum (q.v.)—and came to treat with each other as such. The formal organization of the Corpus Evangelicorum as a permanent institution took place at the Diet of Regensburg, July 22, 1653, when the representatives of all the Protestant states (then thirty-nine) met for deliberation as to their action in the house of the delegate from electoral Saxony, and agreed to act permanently as a body under the leadership of that state. Though regarded with disfavor by the imperial court, it maintained its existence, took cognizance of everything which affected Evangelical interests, and corresponded quite independently with the emperor, with the several states, and with foreign sovereigns. When the Elector Frederick Augustus of Saxony became a Roman Catholic in 1677, followed later by his heir apparent, the question was hotly debated whether Saxony could still be allowed to retain the presidency. Brandenburg, Brunswick, and the Ernestine line of Saxony were anxious to take the place; but the elector gave all assurances, and the fear that his influential house might go over to the Corpus Catholicorum determined the delegates to leave the presidency where it had always been, express stipulations being made that the elector should not interfere with his representative, who was to receive directions from the privy council at Dresden. The regular meetings of the *Corpus* were held at Regensburg every fortnight. After 1770 there were two standing committees, one for the investigation of religious complaints as to which its action was requested, and one charged with the administration of the six funds belonging to it. The *Corpus Evangelicorum* existed on this basis until 1806, when it perished with the empire; but suggestions as to the usefulness of its reorganization have been since made more than once. (E. FRIEDBERG.)

CORPUS JURIS CANONICI. See CANON LAW, II., 7.

CORRECTION, HOUSES OF: Among the penalties employed by the Church, especially against delinquent clerics, was in very early times the confinement of the offender, for his own amendment, or, if he proved incorrigible, for the removal of a scandal from the eyes of the community. Special places for such imprisonment (*decanica*) are mentioned in a decree of Arcadius and Honorius in 360; other terms used for them are *decaneata*, *diaconica*, *secretaria*. Numerous synods of the sixth and seventh centuries prescribed imprisonment for delinquent and especially for deposed clerics. Monasteries and (after their erection became general) seminaries were frequently used for this purpose. The present Roman Catholic Church has institutions of this nature in some places.

(O. MEJER†.)

CORRIGAN, MICHAEL AUGUSTINE: Third Roman Catholic archbishop of New York; b. at Newark, N. J., Aug. 13, 1839; d. in New York May 5, 1902. He studied at St. Mary's College, Wilmington, Del., and at Mount St. Mary's College, Emmittsburg, Md. (B.A., 1859); was the first student from the United States to seek admission to the American College at Rome (opened 1859), and continued his studies there for four years, receiving the degree of D.D. on examination in 1864; was ordained at Rome subdeacon Mar., deacon Aug., priest Sept., 1863. He became professor of dogmatic theology and Sacred Scripture at Seton Hall Seminary, South Orange, N. J., 1864, vice-president of Seton Hall College 1865, president 1868 (resigned 1876). In Oct., 1868, he was appointed vicar-general of the diocese of Newark, bishop of Newark 1873, coadjutor to Cardinal McCloskey, archbishop of New York, with the title archbishop of Petra, 1880, and succeeded to the archbishopric 1885. He was a faithful and efficient administrator, possessed of much capacity for system and details, while his uniform courtesy and the nobility of his aims won the respect of the community. From his coming to New York in 1880 to the end of 1895, when his labor was lightened by the appointment of an auxiliary, he confirmed 104,678 persons.

BIBLIOGRAPHY: *Michael A. Corrigan, Memorial Volume*, New York, 1902.

CORRODI, HEINRICH: Rationalistic writer; b. at Zurich July 31, 1752; d. there Sept. 14, 1793. His father, a clergyman and Pietist, lived in Zurich as private tutor, and the son was brought up in Pietistic narrowness. He studied at Halle, where the influence of Semler had a decisive effect on his mind, and he followed this liberal theologian entirely. In 1781 he published anonymously an important work, *Kritische Geschichte des Chiliasmus* (2 parts, Leipsic; 2d ed., 4 vols., 1794), which has preserved his memory, being written upon the fundamental assumption of the "Enlightenment" (q.v.) that the history of dogmas is a history of human errors, and applying this assumption rigorously to each doctrine. The author discovers the essence of Christianity in the field of ethics and considers the Epistle of James as its purest expression; the writings of the apostles, he thinks, are full of Judaistic prejudices. In the same "enlightened" spirit he wrote other works to prepare the way for a rational religion. Returning to Zurich, his great learning and undoubted talent for investigation secured him an appointment there as teacher of natural law and ethics. He lived with the simplicity of Diogenes, and managed to save something every month from his meager income "for the worthy poor." PAUL TSCHACKERT.

BIBLIOGRAPHY: F. Schlichtegroll, *Nekrolog auf das Jahr 1793*, i. 283–298, Gotha, 1794; *ADB*, iv. 502–504.

CORVEY: Celebrated Benedictine abbey near the town of Höxter, at the junction of the Scheldt and the Weser (45 m. s.s.w. of Hanover). It was founded by a colony from the abbey of Corbie near Amiens, at the impulse of Abbot Adalhard and his brother Wala (see ADALHARD AND WALA). Several monks were sent about 815 with the young Saxon Theodrad to found a monastery at Hethis in the Sollinger-Wald; but the soil proved unfruitful, and the colonists were barely able to extract a living from it. Adalhard asked Louis the Pious for permission to transfer the monks to some more fertile spot, and the permanent home of the abbey was chosen. By the autumn of 822 the buildings were completed and the church was consecrated by Bishop Badurad of Paderborn under the invocation of St. Stephen, the abbey receiving the name of "New Corbie" (*Nova Corbeja*). Many rich gifts and privileges were bestowed upon it by the emperor and nobles, and it soon grew to considerable strength. Adalhard died Jan. 2, 826, and was succeeded by Warin, who ruled the community for thirty years. In the thousand years following his death sixty more abbots succeeded one another. The abbey reached its highest point of prosperity under the Saxon emperors, in whose time the convent school, founded soon after the abbey and conducted for a while by Ansgar (q.v.), attained a wide-spread fame. Literary activity distinguished the monks, among whom the best-known author is Widukind (q.v.). The collection of a library was soon begun; among its treasures was the only known manuscript (11th cent.) of the first six books of the "Annals" of Tacitus. [This is called the First Medicean MS. of Tacitus because brought to Rome to Cardinal Giovanni de' Medici (afterward Leo X.) in 1509. It is now in the Vatican Library.] Corvey had been a royal abbey from its foundation; in 1065 Adalbert of Bremen obtained a grant of it from Henry IV., but the monks, supported by Otto of Nordheim, succeeded in vindicating their independence. The administration of Wibald of Stablo (q.v.) was its last brilliant period. After his time it began to decline; discipline fell off, and internal dissensions arose. It managed, however, to sustain itself through the Reformation, only to suffer its hardest blows in the Thirty Years' War, when its library and archives were destroyed, its buildings damaged, and its property and revenues much diminished. In 1792 Pius VI. changed the abbey into a bishopric, with a jurisdiction of five square miles and 9,000 souls. Through the settlement of 1803, the territory passed to the house of Nassau-Orange, and later to the kingdom of Westphalia, finally coming under the jurisdiction of Prussia. The bishopric on its spiritual side was suppressed in 1821. (A. HAUCK.)

BIBLIOGRAPHY: The *Annales Corbejenses* are in *MGH, Script.*, iii. 1–18. Consult: P. Wigand, *Geschichte der . . . Abtey Corvey*, Höxter, 1819; idem, *Traditiones Corbeienses*, Leipsic, 1843; W. Wattenbach, *DGQ*, 5th ed., ii. 472; Neander, *Christian Church*, iii. 273–276, et passim; Hauck, *KD*, vol. ii., passim.

CORVINUS (RABE, "raven," not RAEBENER), ANTONIUS: Protestant Reformer; b. at Warburg (20 m. n.w. of Cassel) Feb. 27, 1501; d. at Hanover Apr. 5, 1553. He was educated in the Cistercian monasteries of Riddagshausen in Brunswick, and Loccum in Hanover, at the University of Leipsic, and probably also at Wittenberg. He early embraced the Reformation; in 1526 he is found at Marburg; in 1528 he went to Goslar to establish the Reformation there, and worked successfully till 1531, when persecution drove him to Witzenhausen in Hesse. There and elsewhere in the country and neighboring lands he played a prominent part and enjoyed the friendship of the landgrave. With the latter's permission he preached in Hanover and Göttingen, in Minden and Pattensen. In 1546 the duke of Göttingen-Kalenberg became a Romanist, and when Corvinus vigorously opposed the Augsburg Interim of 1548 he was thrown into prison at Kalenberg (Nov. 2, 1549) and not released till Oct. 21, 1552. He possessed considerable learning, some poetical ability, but greater organizing talents, and by devotion, patience, and self-sacrifice he won a place among the Reformers of the second rank.

BIBLIOGRAPHY: G. Uhlhorn, *Antonius Corvinus*, Hanover, 1901; P. Tschackert, *Antonius Corvinus Leben und Schriften*, ib. 1900; his *Briefwechsel*, ed. P. Tschackert, 1900; and his *Bericht vom Kolloquium zu Regensburg 1541*, ed. P. Tschackert, in *Archiv für Reformationsgeschichte*, 1903; G. Geisenhof, *Bibliotheca Corviniana*, Brunswick, 1900; J. Köstlin, *Martin Luther*, ii. 299, 311–312, Berlin, 1903.

CORWIN, EDWARD TANJORE: Reformed (Dutch); b. in New York City July 12, 1834. He was graduated at the College of the City of New York, then the Free Academy (B.A., 1853), and the New Brunswick Theological Seminary (1856), where he was a graduate student 1856–57 and instructor in Hebrew and Old Testament exegesis 1883–84. He held pastorates at Paramus, N. J. (1857–63), and Hillsborough (Millstone), N. J. (1863–88). He was then rector of Herzog Hall, New Brunswick, N. J., 1888–95, and gave instruction at various times in the Theological Seminary. After a pastorate at Greenport, N. Y., 1895–97, he was in Holland in 1897–98 as the agent of the General Synod to collect documents relating to the Amsterdam Correspondence, which passed between the classis of Amsterdam and the colonial Dutch Reformed churches of New Netherlands and the Province of New York. These papers were brought out under his editorship by the State of New York (*Ecclesiastical Records of the State of New York*, 6 vols., Albany, 1901–06). He was president of the General Synod of his denomination in 1891, and is the official historiographer of the Reformed Church in America. In theology he is a conservative. Among his numerous writings special mention may be made of his *Manual of the Reformed Protestant Dutch Church in North America* (New York, 1859, 4th ed., 1902); *History of the Reformed Church in America* (1895); and *A Digest of the Constitutional and Synodical Legislation of the Reformed Church in America* (1906). He likewise wrote a number of histories of counties and local churches, and edited *Centennial Discourses*, in collaboration with T. W. Chambers and J. Anderson (New York, 1876), and *Centennial of the Theological Seminary at New Brunswick, N. J.*, with D. D. Demarest and P. D. Van Cleef (1885).

COSIN, JOHN: Bishop of Durham; b. in Norwich Nov. 30, 1594; d. in London Jan. 15, 1672. He studied at Cambridge (Caius College); became secretary to Bishop Overall of Lichfield, and chaplain of Bishop Neile of Durham; became prebendary of Durham 1624, archdeacon of the East Riding of Yorkshire 1625, master of Peterhouse, Cambridge, 1635, vice-chancellor of the university 1639, dean of Peterborough 1640. He was a friend of Laud and a strict ritualist; also a man of strong character who made his views effective; consequently he came early into collision with the Puritans. In 1641 he was sequestered from all his benefices by vote of the House of Commons; in 1644 he was rejected from his mastership, having been concerned in sending the college plate to the royal mint. He went to Paris, where he acted as chaplain to the ladies of Queen Henrietta Maria's household belonging to the Church of England. On the Restoration he was reinstated in his benefices and made bishop of Durham (1660). His strong convictions and earnest life, his energy and administrative ability, with a thorough knowledge of the world, pleasing manners, and a commanding presence, have caused him to be characterized as "one of the greatest prelates of his own or of any age." He was severe toward Romanists and Puritans, and used his full power to rid his diocese of them; nevertheless his Puritan antagonists charged him with "popery," and some of his principles and practises were little short of Puritanical. He was a leading member of the Savoy Conference in 1661, and probably had more influence than any one else in the revision of the prayer-book made the same year. His best-known work is his *Collection of Private Devotions in the Practice of the Ancient Church Called the Hours of Prayer* (London, 1627; new ed., 1867), which was prepared by royal command for the use of the queen's maids of honor, and gave much offense to the Puritans. In France he wrote *Historia transubstantiationis papalis* (published 1675; Eng. transl., 1676; ed., with memoir, by J. S. Brewer, 1840 and 1850); *Regni Angliæ religio catholica, prisca, casta, defæcata*, a vindication of the Church of England (first published by Thomas Smith in his *Vitæ quorumdam eruditissimorum et illustrium virorum*, London, 1707; several later editions; translations into Italian, 1853, 1866, into Spanish and modern Greek, 1856, French and German, 1857, Russian, 1866, English, by F. Meyrick, 1870); and *A Scholastical History of the Canon of Holy Scripture: or the certain and indubitate books thereof as they are received in the Church of England* (1657). His *Notes on the Book of Common Prayer* (published in Nicholl's *Comment on the Book of Common Prayer*, 1710) is of interest for the history of the prayer-book. His complete works were published in the *Library of Anglo-Catholic Theology* (5 vols., Oxford, 1843–55), and his correspondence was published by the Surtees Society of Durham (2 vols., 1869–72).

Bibliography: Consult, besides the memoir in his *Historia transubstantiationis*, ut sup., *DNB*, xii. 264–271; Wright and Neil, *Protestant Dictionary*, pp. 146–148, London, 1904.

COSMAS AND DAMIAN, SAINTS: According to legend, two brothers from Arabia, Christians, who practised medicine at Ægæ, on the Bay of Issus, Cilicia, at the time of the Diocletian persecution. They took no fees, and by means of prayer and the sign of the cross accomplished wonderful cures. They refused to renounce their faith at the bidding of the governor, Lysias, endured manifold tortures, and finally were executed by the sword. Their brothers, Anthimus, Leontius, and Euprepius, suffered at the same time with like fortitude. Cosmas and Damian are the patrons of physicians and apothecaries, and are represented with the emblems of their profession. Their day is Sept. 27.

(O. Zöckler†.)

Bibliography: *ASB*, Sept., vii. 400–448; *Analecta Bollandiana*, i (1882), 586–596; J. E. Wessely, *Ikonographie Gottes und der Heiligen*, p. 135, Leipsic, 1874.

COSMAS INDICOPLEUSTES ("Cosmas the Indian navigator"): An Alexandrian merchant who, in the first half of the sixth century, visited Abyssinia, Arabia, and India; afterward he became a monk and wrote several books, of which the only one preserved is called "A Christian Topography of the World" (written in Greek, in twelve books; published, with Latin version, in *MPG*, lxxxviii. 10–475; Eng. transl., with notes and introduction by J. W. McCrindle, vol. xcviii. of the *Hakluyt Society's Publications*, London, 1897). The purpose of the writer is to set forth certain views about geography and cosmography supposed to be taught in the Bible; incidentally he has much vilification for those who drew their natural science from another source, particularly such as impiously asserted the earth to be round. To his way of thinking an exact model of the universe was furnished by the Mosaic tabernacle; there are two worlds, an upper and a lower, divided by the firmament; the table of showbread represented the earth, which consequently is a rectangular plane twice as long from east to west as broad from north to south; the candlestick typified the sun; there is another earth beyond the ocean, which was the seat of paradise and the abode of man till the deluge, when the ark floated over the intervening waters; the heavens form four walls joined to the outer edges of the earth and are vaulted overhead. Notwithstanding his fantastic science, Cosmas was a good observer, shrewd of judgment, and is considered truthful; "the nonsense of the monk was mingled with the practical knowledge of the traveler" (Gibbon, *Decline and Fall*, v. 148–149). His reports of Abyssinia, India, and China are interesting, and the fifth book has value for Biblical introduction because of statements concerning the authorship, purpose, and contents of different books.

Bibliography: R. Beazley, *The Dawn of Modern Geography*, i. 273-303 et passim, London, 1897.

COSTA, IZAAK DA. See Da Costa.

COSTA RICA. See Central America.

COTELERIUS, JOHANNES BAPTISTA (JEAN-BAPTISTE COTELIER): French classical scholar; b. at Nîmes (30 m. n.e. of Montpellier) Dec., 1627; d. at Paris Aug. 19, 1686. In 1641 he went to Paris, where he studied philosophy and theology, and became a doctor of the Sorbonne in 1648. In 1667 he was commissioned by the minister Colbert to investigate and catalogue the Greek manuscripts of the Royal Library, and in 1676 he was appointed professor of Greek at the Collège de France. He attained high fame as a church historian by his edition of the apostolic Fathers, entitled *Sanctorum Patrum qui temporibus apostolicis floruerunt, Barnabæ, Clementis, Hermæ, Ignatii, Polycarpi, opera edita et non edita* (2 vols., Paris, 1672). The most of the copies of this edition were destroyed by a fire in the Collège Montaigu, but a second and third edition was prepared by J. Leclerc (2 vols., Antwerp, 1698; Amsterdam, 1724). He also edited other documents of ecclesiastical antiquity in *Homiliæ quattuor in Psalmos et interpretatio prophetæ Danielis* (Paris, 1661), which he ascribed to Chrysostom, and in *Ecclesiæ Græcæ monumenta* (3 vols., 1677-88), of which a fourth volume appeared posthumously as *Analecta Græca* (1692).

(C. Pfender.)

Bibliography: A letter by S. Baluze, which follows the preface to vol. ii. of Leclerc's ed. of the *Patres*, ut sup.; Nicéron, *Mémoires*, iv. 243 sqq.

COTTA. See Vestments and Insignia, Ecclesiastical.

COTTA, URSULA. See Luther, Martin.

COTTERILL, THOMAS: Hymnologist; b. at Cannock (15 m. n.n.w. of Birmingham), Staffordshire, Dec. 4, 1779; d. at Sheffield Dec. 29, 1823. He was a student and fellow of St. John's, Cambridge (B.A., 1801; M.A., 1805); became curate of Tutbury and of Lane End, Staffordshire, in 1803 and 1808, respectively; perpetual curate of St. Paul's, Sheffield, 1817. He was one of the editors of *A Selection of Psalms and Hymns*, published at Uttoxeter, Staffordshire, 1805, and with the help of James Montgomery (q.v.) compiled a *Selection of Psalms and Hymns* (Sheffield, 1810; 8th and most important ed., 1819). The use of hymns in the English service was not yet established, and an attempt by Cotterill to force his book upon his congregation led to a lawsuit; the dispute was compromised by preparing a new edition (9th), London, 1820, in which the number of hymns was greatly reduced and those printed were approved by Edward Harcourt, archbishop of York. This book had great influence upon the hymnody of the Church of England and is remarkable for the freedom with which the verses of others printed in it are altered from their original form or rewritten. Cotterill also published a book of *Family Prayers* (2d ed., London, 1816).

Bibliography: S. W. Duffield, *English Hymns*, pp. 53-54, New York, 1886; Julian, *Hymnology*, pp. 263-264.

COTTON, JOHN: Puritan, early minister of Boston; b. at Derby, England, Dec. 4, 1584 (baptized at St. Alkmund's, Derby, Dec. 15, 1584); d. in Boston Dec. 23, 1652. He studied at Derby Grammar School, and Trinity and Emmanuel colleges, Cambridge (B.A., 1604 or earlier; M.A., 1606; B.D., 1613); became fellow of Emmanuel (not later than 1607), dean, and catechist, and distinguished himself as tutor, orator, and scholar. In 1612 he became vicar of St. Botolph's, Boston, Lincolnshire, and gained there a great reputation for learning and piety, as well as for Puritan inclinations, which steadily became stronger. In July, 1633, to escape from a summons to appear before the High Commission Court in London and answer to a charge of not kneeling at the Sacrament and discarding some other ritual observances, he fled to America, landing in September. In October he was ordained "teacher" of the First Church in Boston and colleague of John Wilson, and soon became the most influential person in the community.* His reputation continued great in Puritan circles in England, and in 1642 he was strongly inclined to comply with pressing entreaties to return. He engaged in controversy with Roger Williams and defended the latter's expulsion from Massachusetts. In the antinomian dispute he was at first inclined to side with his enthusiastic admirer Mrs. Hutchinson (whose son, Edward, had accompanied him on his flight to America), but ended as her opponent (see Antinomianism and Antinomian Controversies, II., 2).

John Cotton's writings were numerous and deal with a wide variety of subjects. The "bibliography" of Dr. H. M. Dexter's *Congregationalism of the Last Three Hundred Years* (New York, 1880) has 36 entries ascribed to him. For other lists consult Allen's *American Biographical Dictionary* (Boston, 1857), sub titulo; J. S. Clark, in the *Congregational Quarterly*, iii. 133-148 (Apr., 1861); and the article *John Cotton*, by Alexander Gordon, in *DNB*, supplement, vol. ii. All were published in London, and many in two or more editions. Some of the more noteworthy are: *Abstract of the Laws of New England*, a summary of Jewish laws supposed to be of perpetual obligation (1641; reprinted in the *Collections of the Massachusetts Historical Society*, ser. i., vol. v [1816], 171-192; cf. W. C. Ford, *John Cotton's Moses, his Judicialls and Abstract of the Laws of New England*, in the *Proceedings of the Massachusetts Historical Society*, Oct., 1902); *The Pouring Out of the Seven Vials, or an exposition of the 16th chapter of the Revelation, with an application of it to our times* (1642; the fifth vial is made to mean episcopal government); *The Keys of the Kingdom of Heaven and Power thereof according to the Word of God* (1644; reprinted Boston, 1852; considered one of the most authoritative expositions of Congregationalism); *Milk for Babes, Drawn out of the Breasts of both Testaments, chiefly for the spiritual nourishment of Boston babes in either England, but may be of like use for any children*, a catechism (1646; and many subsequent editions, one at Cambridge, 1656; included in the *New England Primer;* Cotton Mather calls it "peculiarly the catechism of New England," and says it will "be valued and studied and improved until New England cease to be New England"); *The Bloody Tenet Washed and Made White in the Blood of the Lamb* (1647;

*"He was the ecclesiastical leader of the Massachusetts colony, a part of about all that was done in Church and State till his death" (Walker, *Creeds and Platforms of Congregationalism*, 184, note 3). "He very quickly came to wield a power in that theocratic settlement akin to that now exercised by a political boss" (Paul Leicester Ford, *The New England Primer*, 89).

a reply to Roger Williams, who had charged him with holding a "bloody tenet of persecution"); *A Brief Exposition with Practical Observations upon the Whole Book of Ecclesiastes* (1654); *The Saints' Support and Comfort in the Time of Distress and Danger, with divers other treatises* (1658; a new edition of *God's Mercy Mixed with his Justice*, 1641). Two of his writings against Roger Williams were published by the Narragansett Club (*A Letter of John Cotton and Roger Williams's Reply*, ed. R. A. Guild, Providence, 1866; *Master John Cotton's Answer to Master Roger Williams*, ed. J. L. Diman, 1867).

Bibliography: Consult, besides the works mentioned above, Cotton Mather (his grandson), *Magnalia*, i. 252–286, Hartford ed., 1855; John Norton, *Abel Being Dead yet Speaketh, or the life and death of that deservedly famous man of God, Mr. John Cotton*, London, 1658, ed. with notes by Enoch Pond, Boston, 1834; A. W. M'Clure, *Life of John Cotton*, Boston, 1846 and 1870; P. Thompson, *The History and Antiquities of Boston* [Lincolnshire], pp. 412–424 et passim, Boston, 1856; M. C. Tyler, *History of American Literature*, i. 210–216, New York, 1878; W. Walker, *Ten New England Leaders*, pp. 49–96, New York, 1901 (where references to the sources are fully given).

COULIN, cū"lin', FRANK: Swiss Protestant; b. at Geneva Nov. 17, 1828. He was educated at the college and academy of his native city (B.A., 1844); resided in Germany 1844–47; studied in the theological faculty of Geneva until his ordination in 1851. After extensive travels he became in 1853 pastor at Genthod, a village on the shores of Lake Geneva, and there remained till 1895, when he retired from active life. He was a delegate to the conference of the Evangelical Alliance held at New York in 1873, and on his return was asked to conduct the courses in homiletics in the faculty of free theology at Geneva. He continued these lectures until 1886. He has written: *Les Œuvres chrétiennes* (Geneva, 1865); *Le Fils de l'homme* (1866; Eng. transl., by J. Sturge, London, 1869, *The Son of Man*); and *La Vocation du chrétien* (1870).

COULLIÉ, PIERRE HECTOR: Cardinal; b. at Paris Mar. 14, 1829. He was educated at the seminary of St. Nicholas-des-Champs and at St. Sulpice, and was ordained to the priesthood in 1854. He was vicar at Ste. Marguerite, St. Eustache, and Notre Dame des Victoires, and in 1876 was consecrated bishop coadjutor of Orléans with the title of bishop of Sidonia. In 1878 he succeeded to the bishopric, and in 1893 was enthroned archbishop of Lyons and Vienne. In 1897 he was created cardinal priest of Santa Francesca Romana.

COUNCILS AND SYNODS.

In the ecclesiastical sense, "councils" or "synods" are assemblies of representatives of the Church for the discussion and decision of questions of faith, points of discipline, and morals. The gathering of the apostles mentioned in Acts xv. (see Apostolic Council at Jerusalem) may be passed over as having no connection with the later development. The earliest synods deserving of mention are those held in Asia Minor in reference to the Montanist question (see Montanism), and those which in both East and West attempted to settle the quartodeciman controversy (see Easter, II., § 1).

1. Origin.

The former took place probably between 160 and 175; our information in regard to them is derived from an almost contemporary narrator whose account is utilized by Eusebius (*Hist. eccl.*, V. xvi. 10). He does not use the name "synod," and in fact his words do not necessarily imply such assemblies; but the usual interpretation of the passage is probably correct, involving gatherings of a number of local churches for the purpose of discussing the new prophecy. The term "the faithful," which he uses, of course includes bishops, but presumably is not limited to them. The method of representation is uncertain; it is possible that in some cases only the bishop appeared to speak for his church; it is also possible that a certain number of clerics accompanied him, and that prominent laymen were not absent; in some cases they may even have been more numerous than the clergy, or have constituted the only representatives of their community. The terms in which Eusebius (V. xxiii. 2) speaks of the synods held in connection with the paschal controversy give on the surface a different picture; but such knowledge as we have of his sources shows that he unconsciously approximated his account of synods at the end of the second century to those of his own day. The synods held about 195 were not gatherings of bishops exclusively; although the episcopate occupied the most prominent position, the time was still remembered when these assemblies were gatherings of all the faithful. The fact that the monarchical episcopate was fully developed by the period first alluded to (160–175), and that this constitution of synods is not altogether harmonious with it, leads to the conclusion that such gatherings had been usual, at least as early as the middle of the second century. Sohm finds their origin in the expansion of gatherings, such as are mentioned earlier, of a local church for the election of a bishop; others trace them to the analogy of the secular "provincial council," or make them a natural outgrowth of the need to discuss difficult questions.

A full understanding of their origin can not be obtained without remembering the constant intercourse by means of accredited representatives which the primitive Christian communities maintained. If a local church was distracted by discord, the neighboring churches felt bound to assist in the restoration of order (*Clementina*, I. lxiii. 3); when peace was restored after a storm of persecution, even distant churches sent envoys to express their joy (Ignatius, *Ad Philadelphenos*, x.; *ad Smyrnæos*, xi.; *ad Polycarpum*, vii.); if a bishop was to be chosen in a small church, the delegates of the larger communities round about assisted in the deliberations. Such envoys, who might be bishops or lower clergy, were chosen in a general gathering of the local church (Ignatius, *Ad Polycarpum*, vii.; *ad Smyrneos*, xi.). It is then on the surface scarcely a step further to the assembly of representatives of a number of churches for the purpose of reaching a common decision on a disputed question. But a little reflection will show that it is not the same thing. Both the discussion of a local question with the assistance of representatives from outside, and the meeting to discuss a question which affected a number of communities alike, sprang from the primitive Christian feeling of unity and from the consequent mutual intercourse; but they had different aims and significance.

The synods of the second century were loosely organized; they came together when a question happened to need decision, and represented no determinate group of churches; they had no *ex-officio* members, and no authority which could interfere with local independence.

2. Provincial Synods.

By degrees, however, the logical consequences of the monarchical episcopate and the theory of apostolic succession followed. In the third century the bishops primarily constituted the synods. It is true that in this period presbyters still universally took part with the bishops, as is evidenced in Alexandria in the first synod held by Demetrius against Origen (Photius, *MPG*, ciii. 397); in Antioch (Eusebius, *Hist. eccl.*, VII. xxx. 2, xxviii. 1); in Cappadocia (Cyprian, *Epist.*, lxxv. 4); in Rome (Eusebius, *Hist. eccl.*, VI. xliii. 2, on the basis of the letter of Cornelius to Fabius of Antioch); and in Africa (Cyprian, *Epist.*, xix. 2). But none the less the center of gravity had shifted. Though Cyprian mentions the presence of presbyters and deacons, it is evident from more than one passage that in his mind it was the bishops who decided the questions. The records of the synod of Sept., 256, note the presence of many bishops from three provinces, with presbyters and deacons and the greater part of the laity; but in the decision the votes of the bishops alone are given. Thus, too, the African synodal epistles are subscribed by the bishops only (cf. *Epist.*, lvii., lxiv., lxvii., lxx.). The presence of the lower clergy and the laity contributed to the publicity of the proceedings, not to the decision, which was now in the hands of the episcopate. The development which was complete by the middle of the second century in Africa was somewhat slower elsewhere. At Rome in 250 the *consensus* of the clergy and laity was still considered essential to a synodal decision (Cyprian, *Epist.*, xxx. 5), and a similar state of things is found in Cappadocia (Cyprian, *Epist.*, lxxv. 4). But the same tendency was everywhere in evidence. It is not, therefore, surprising that in the First Council of Nicæa and in that of Antioch (341) it should be taken for granted that only the bishops were the active members (cf. canon v. of Nicæa, xiv., xv. of Antioch). In harmony with this development was the general conception of synodal authority. The bishops, as successors of the apostles, were officially endued with the Holy Spirit; they made their decisions "under the inspiration of the Holy Ghost" (Cyprian, *Epist.*, lvii. 5) or "in the presence of the Holy Ghost and his angels" (synodal letter of the First Council of Arles, Mansi, *Concilia*, ii. 469); the decision of a synod is equivalent to a divine sentence (letter of Constantine on the dissolution of the Council of Arles, Mansi, *Concilia*, ii. 478).

The next step was to make synods ordinary institutions of the Church. Extraordinary ones continued to be held, but they were additional to the regular ones, which are assumed in the first mention of Eastern synods by a Western writer, probably between 210 and 220 (Tertullian, *De jejunio*, xiii.). Annual meetings soon became the rule, as can be evidenced in Cappadocia as early as the middle of the third century (Cyprian, *Epist.*, lxxv. 4). This regular recurrence led to the restriction of the district represented, and, probably on the analogy of secular assemblies, the bishops of each province met in its capital. The institution became legally established by the First Council of Nicæa (canon v.), which provided for two meetings in the year, one before Lent, the other in the autumn. At Antioch in 341 (canon xx.) the dates were defined as four weeks before Pentecost and Oct. 15, and the arrangement continued long in force (Council of Constantinople, 381, canon ii.; of Chalcedon, 451, canon xix.). Finally the Trullan Council of 692 (canon viii.) and the Second Nicene of 787 (canon vi.) contented themselves with requiring a single annual session. The provincial synod became the most important organ for the episcopal government of the Church. The metropolitan called it and presided over it. Its competence was practically unlimited, extending over all questions of faith and morals, public worship, and the discipline and organization of the Church. The development of provincial synods accompanied that of metropolitan jurisdiction. After the organization of the patriarchal system in the East, the idea came up of having special synods for these larger divisions, and attempts were made to carry it out; but they did not lead to regular annual meetings or to the permanency of the institution.

Ecumenical councils had come into being before the complete organization of the provincial synods. In the course of the Donatist controversy Constantine committed the decision of it first to an episcopal commission meeting in Rome, then to a larger body of bishops assembled at Arles (see DONATISM).

3. Ecumenical Councils.

These assemblies have been commonly considered as synods, and such they were in the sense of being deliberative assemblies of bishops; but it is obvious that they differed from all previous synods. Their initiative came not from the bishops but from the emperor, who determined both the membership and the place and subject of the discussion, and gave his authority to the decisions, which were to be authoritative in secular law. They were thus not, like the provincial synods, organs of free episcopal government, but assemblies for the purpose of counseling the emperor as to his decisive action in ecclesiastical questions. These, however, and not the provincial synods, were the prototypes of the ecumenical councils. Constantine acted in precisely the same manner at the convocation of the Council of Nicæa. It was his intention that the Arian question should be settled by the council, and so he took a personal part in the proceedings; the adoption of the Nicene formula was the result of his urgency, and he recognized it as binding in law, imposing penalties on those who refused to subscribe it; he himself promulgated the decision as to the Easter celebration, and imposed its observance on the bishops. Thus, though the Nicene council was theoretically a meeting of the catholic episcopate, and the authority attributed to all synods might be supposed to belong to it in a preeminent degree, it was really not an organ of the self-government of the Church, but an aid to its government by the secular ruler. The following ecumenical councils were modeled on this and bore the same character. The decision to convoke them originated at the court, and was always carried out by the secular authority. They met under the presidency, or at least in the presence, of imperial commissaries. Their decisions were submitted to the emperor before publication, as occurred in the case of the dogmatic decree of Chalcedon (Mansi, *Concilia*, vii. 117, 136). He might either confirm their decrees, as at Chalcedon (Mansi, vii. 476) and Constantinople (Mansi, xi. 697, 724), or refuse his assent, as at Ephesus (Mansi, iv. 1377). Their dependence upon the court increased, until Constantius could say with brutal frankness at the Synod of Milan, "What I will, let that be considered a canon" (Athanasius, "History of the Arians," xxxiii.). The detailed history of the several ecumenical councils will be found in other articles (see the name of the place of meeting). Roman Catholic historians number eight in this early period: Nicæa I., 325; Constantinople I., 381; Ephesus, 431; Chalcedon, 451; Constantinople II., 553; Constantinople III., 680; Nicæa II., 787; Constantinople IV., 869. But this enumeration is not historically justifiable. Apart from the facts that the Constantinopolitan council of 381 represented only the Eastern Empire [and that of 869 is rejected by the Eastern Church], those of Sardica 342, Ephesus 449, and Constantinople 754 have just as much right to the title of ecumenical, nor was confirmation lacking to the decrees of the two latter. Their omission can only be based upon the fact that later development took a direction opposite to their conclusions. The importance of the ecumenical councils lies in their legislative activity, especially in regard to doctrine, which usually furnished the reason for their convocation. They dealt also with many questions of ecclesiastical organization and private morality; but their action as a supreme judicial tribunal is comparatively unimportant. Their excommunications were always the consequences of their dogmatic decrees, which were considered infallible from the conception of the episcopate as endowed with the *charisma veritatis*.*

The synodal system underwent a new development in the Teutonic nationalities which arose on the ruins of the Roman Empire. The old division of ecclesiastical provinces had much less importance now than of old; the larger unit of church life above the diocese was not the metropolitan jurisdiction but the national Church, and the former disappeared entirely for a time in the Frankish kingdom. Moreover, at the beginning of the Middle Ages the diocese was no longer a town community governed by the bishop with a united presbytery about him, but an extended territory divided into a large number of coordinate parishes. The relation of the king, again, to the Church was important. Though not carrying such unlimited power as the emperors had possessed, it was sufficiently analogous to theirs for the provincial synod to lose much of its earlier importance, and to become a merely occasional gathering. This was especially the case in the Frankish kingdom, where in the Merovingian period only a few such synods are heard of, and the acts of only one are extant. Boniface asserted in 742 that no synod had been held for more than eighty years; but neither his efforts nor those of Charlemagne availed to alter the situation materially. The case was the same in England; the ancient provisions were not forgotten, but simply not followed.

4. Teutonic Synods of the Early Middle Ages.

Provincial synods were most frequent in Spain, as long as the Visigoths were Arian (Tarragona 516, Gerunda 517, Lerida 524, Valencia 524, Toledo 527, Barcelona 540). The place of the provincial synods was taken by national councils. The first of these in the Frankish kingdom was called by Clovis at Orléans in 511, and they never ceased to be held during the Merovingian period, either for the whole kingdom or one of its divisions. They were distinguished from provincial synods by being not regularly recurring assemblies, but meetings summoned or at least sanctioned by the king for a special purpose. Their decisions did not necessarily require royal confirmation, but the kings felt themselves at liberty to alter or abrogate them, especially when they overstepped the bounds of spiritual administration. After the middle of the seventh century they met in the presence of the king or his representative. The Burgundian kingdom also had its national synods (Epaon 517; Lyons 517). It is significant that in Spain they begin with the conversion of Recared (Toledo 589, 597, 633, 636, 638, etc.), and seem at once to have taken the place of the provincial synods. A peculiarity here was that the magnates of the kingdom and the royal officials were considered members. Only in England did the national council fail to acquire importance. This system lasted, unchanged in essentials, through the whole first half of the Middle Ages. The extension of the empire under Charle-

* The list of ecumenical councils as accepted by the Roman Catholic Church is as follows: 1. Nicæa I., 325; 2. Constantinople I., 381; 3. Ephesus, 431; 4. Chalcedon, 451; 5. Constantinople II., 553; 6. Constantinople III. (First Trullan), 680–681; 7. Nicæa II., 787; 8. Constantinople IV., 869; 9. Lateran I., 1123; 10. Lateran II., 1139; 11. Lateran III., 1179; 12. Lateran IV., 1215; 13. Lyons I., 1245; 14. Lyons II., 1274; 15. Vienne, 1311–12; 16. Constance, 1414–18; 17. Basel-Ferrara-Florence, 1431–42; 18. Lateran V., 1512–1517; 19. Trent, 1545–63; 20. Vatican, 1869–70. The first seven of these are accepted by the Greeks, the others rejected; they also accept the Second Trullan Council or Quinisextum, 692 (rejected by the West), considering it a continuation of the First Trullan or Third Constantinople. The eighth general council of the Greeks was held in Constantinople in 879 and rejected by the Latins (see PHOTIUS).

magne made these assemblies practically councils of the entire West (Regensburg 792, Frankfort 794). While adhering in essentials to the catholic doctrine and institutions, they allowed themselves a fairly wide latitude in their legislation. The new diocesan system developed synods also for each separate diocese, somewhat on the lines of the primitive *presbyterium*, presided over by the bishop and including the parish priests, abbots, and deans of the diocese. The earliest of these were the two at Auxerre, between 573 and 603 and 695, and that of Autun, between 663 and 680. The attempt was made to establish the custom of meeting annually, but apparently without much success.

5. Papal Councils of the Middle Ages. The popes did not overlook the weight which synodal decisions carried; and thus, although Italy was never a scene of much conciliar activity, more assemblies of this kind were held in Rome under papal presidency than in any other city of Christendom. The position of the popes brought about the participation in them of distant churches. Julius I. summoned one for the year 341, to which he bade the Eastern antagonists of Athanasius. They refused to appear; but more than fifty bishops attended, including some from Thrace, Cœle-syria, Phenicia, and Palestine. Gallic bishops sat with those of Italy in the synod called by Damasus in 369, and similar gatherings continued to be held. They were called by the popes not as patriarchs of the West, but as successors of St. Peter; and the papal sanction gave them high authority. The importance of the synods held by the Carolingian emperors north of the Alps somewhat diminished the preeminent authority of these Roman councils; but a change came with the pontificate of Leo IX. (1048–54), who was the first pope to raise the papal dignity once more after its prolonged humiliation. He made much use of synods, and, not content with holding them in Rome and other parts of Italy, presided in person at the imperial synods held in Germany and France. From the middle of the eleventh century the papal synods constantly increased in importance and consideration (Lateran synod of 1059 under Nicholas II.; 1063 under Alexander II.; 1074, 1075, 1076, 1078, 1079, 1080, 1083 under Gregory VII.; 1095 at Piacenza and Clermont under Urban II.; 1119 at Reims under Calixtus II.). The last of these popes summoned the Lateran council of 1123 under the name of a general council; but the placing of it on a level with the old ecumenical ones came later and gradually; that of Constance reckoned in this category only three modern councils—Lateran 1215, Lyons 1274, and Vienne 1311. Roman Catholic theologians now add to these three more Lateran synods (1123, 1139, 1179) and the first of Lyons, 1245. These had, it is true, an authority in the medieval Church answering to that of the old ecumenical councils under the Roman Empire; but they were confined to the papal obedience, called and presided over by the pope, and dependent on his sanction for the validity of their decrees, so that they were merely organs for his government of the Western Church.

6. The Reforming Councils of the Fifteenth Century. The beliefs as to the pope's position current in the thirteenth and fourteenth centuries were shaken by the Great Schism, which forced men to seek an authority powerful enough to restore unity even in spite of conflicting claimants of the papacy. This they thought they had found in the general council, on lines foreshadowed even in the fourteenth century by Marsilius of Padua and William of Occam. At the very outset of the Schism, after the election of Clement VII., the appeal to a universal council was heard (see CLEMENT VII.; URBAN VI.). Presently it was taken up by such influential theologians as Pierre d'Ailly and Gerson, and became prevalent. The attempt to end the Schism by the Council of Pisa (q.v.) was indeed a failure, but this did not affect the belief in the efficacy of this method. The Council of Constance (q.v.) boldly attempted to alter the constitution of the Western Church by the introduction of general councils as a regular factor in its government, to recur at intervals of five, seven, and ultimately ten years. But the execution of this plan, though approved by the Council of Basel (q.v.), was rendered impossible by the natural opposition of the Curia. When Eugenius IV. transferred the Council of Basel to Ferrara (see FERRARA-FLORENCE, COUNCIL OF), he took his stand on the principles accepted before Constance, and logically declared null and void, with the assent of his council, the decrees of Basel as to the superiority of the council over the pope. In the Lateran Council of 1512–1517 Leo X. struck a mortal blow at the idea in the bull *Pastor æternus*.

7. Councils and Synods: Modern Roman Catholic System. After this the Curia had an unconcealed distrust of general councils, and it was only the pressure of political powers which led to the reorganization of Catholicism after the storms of the Reformation by that of Trent (see TRENT, COUNCIL OF). It was only when the last trace of opposition to unlimited papal power disappeared in the nineteenth century that this distrust was finally lulled, so that Pius IX. could give the world the long unseen spectacle of a general council in 1870 (see VATICAN COUNCIL). The principles now accepted are that these assemblies may only be called by the pope and presided over by him or his delegates; that their membership is confined to the cardinals, bishops, vicars apostolic, generals of religious orders, and such dignitaries, to the exclusion of the laity; that the subjects discussed must be laid before them by the pope, and their decisions confirmed by him. They are thus nothing more than assemblies of advisers about the pope, with no independent power of their own. Nor have provincial synods any longer a necessary place in the polity of the Roman Catholic Church. The Council of Trent ordained, indeed, that they should be held every three years—a period which it was proposed at the Vatican Council to extend to five—but the rule is not observed in practise. Much the same may be said of the diocesan synods, which the Council of Trent required to be held annually.

8. The Synods of Protestantism. Reformed Churches.

The Reformation broke with all the medieval ideas on the subject. Luther very early repudiated the belief in the infallibility of councils, and, where Roman Catholic theology had tended to put their decisions on a par with the Written Word, was inclined rather to consider the two opposed, withdrawing the whole domain of faith, morals, and worship from their legislative jurisdiction and leaving them only the duty of guarding against departures from Scriptural faith and practise. Thus he considered them practically as judicial tribunals, in which character they were to be composed not only of bishops but also of godly secular persons. From these principles, as from the emphasis laid on the assertion that the Church needed to care only for preaching and the administration of the sacraments, there was no reason to expect that any use would be made of a Reformed synodal system in the organization of the Lutheran territorial churches; and in their later development, with a few sporadic exceptions, no such system was considered. In England the synodal system of the Middle Ages was carried over into the Established Church. But the convocations, after the Reformation as before, were exclusively clerical assemblies; and in accordance with the doctrine of royal supremacy they were not permitted to meet without the sovereign's license, nor were their decisions valid without his assent.

The home of the new synodal system was the Reformed Church, in which questions of organization were regarded as of more importance than among the Lutherans. The presbyterial organization established by Calvin at Geneva became the model for all the Reformed churches. That of France was the first to develop the synodal system for a national Church. At the first national synod (1559) it was resolved that no local church should have any precedence over any other; that general synods should meet from time to time as occasion arose, composed of the ministers and one or more elders or deacons from each church, under a president elected at the meeting; that in each province twice a year the ministers and at least one elder or deacon from each congregation should meet in synod. In 1565 the composition of the national synods was changed to either one or two elected ministers and elders from each provincial synod. These synods, of mixed clerical and lay character, were charged with the government of the Church. On the same lines proceeded the organization of the Reformed churches of Scotland, the Netherlands, and northwestern Germany. The polity was in each case built up on a national basis; the idea of completing it by an international organization seems to have been unknown, and the Synod of Dort was a mere isolated exception.

9. Adoption in the German Lutheran Churches.

The imperfection of the older Lutheran system became more and more obvious after the seventeenth century, but the first attempts at improvement dealt with the local churches. It was not until political changes gave occasion for reorganization in many of the German states that the idea of introducing the synodal element was taken up. In 1807 Schleiermacher made a proposal for a new constitution of the Protestant Church in Prussia, which included the adoption of the synodal system, and this principle has since been dominant. Since the relation of the Church to the temporal sovereigns made it impossible simply to adopt the Reformed plan, an attempt was made to combine the synodal and the consistorial systems. In 1817 presbyteries were formed in Prussia, and the first synods were constituted of ministers alone. Not much came of these attempts there, although they were followed by Bavaria in 1818 and Baden in 1821. Before half a century had passed, however, all but a few of the Lutheran churches of Germany adopted synodal constitutions, Württemberg 1854, Hanover 1864, Saxony 1868, Prussia 1873–76, etc. These German synods are not, like the old Reformed ones, charged with the government of the Church, but are rather the representatives of the Church with the government. They consist of both ministers and laymen, and are chosen for the district synods by the congregations, for the provincial and national synods by the bodies below. Owing to various causes—their restricted competence, their infrequent meetings (every four, five, or six years), their unwieldy numbers, and cumbrous parliamentary forms—they have not produced the results that were hoped from them, and can scarcely do so unless the gift of greater freedom of action makes them really organs of a self-governing Church.

The Protestant emigrants from England to America were at first mostly Independents, and it was not till after the middle of the seventeenth century that the number of Presbyterians gradually increased.* The first union of several congregations into a presbytery occurred in 1705 or 1706, and the first synod met in Philadelphia in 1717 (see PRESBYTERIANS, section on America). The system took firm root in America, and was adopted

* [The first settlers in Virginia (1607) and most of those that followed for a century or more were members of the Established English Church. Although Puritanical tendencies early appeared, episcopalian institutions long prevailed. The founders of the Plymouth colony (1620) were semi-Separatists, and soon reached a position that resembled "Independency." The founders of Salem (1622 onward) were Puritans, strongly committed from the first to non-conformist principles, and early won to essentially Congregational principles through the influence of the men of Plymouth. The Massachusetts Company (1628) were Puritans, who in leaving England professed the warmest attachment to the Church of England and so were not avowed non-conformists. They early developed a strong theocratic and presbyterial system. In August, 1637, a synod was held at Cambridge, consisting of about twenty-five ministers, "others sent by the churches," and the Massachusetts magistrates, for the suppression of the antinomian heresy. In 1648 "the elders and messengers of the churches assembled at Cambridge" agreed upon "A Platform of Church Discipline," which was afterward adopted by the churches and the General Court, in which it is declared that "Synods orderly assembled, and rightly proceeding according to the pattern, Act. 15, we acknowledge as the ordinance of Christ . . . necessary to the well-being of churches. . . . Magistrates have power to call a synod. . . . It belongeth unto synods and councils to debate and determine controversies of faith and cases of conscience," etc. For the councils of the Congregational Church see CONGREGATIONALISTS, IV., §§ 2–3. A. H. N.]

with variations not only by the Lutherans there, but also by the Episcopal Church.

10. The Synodal System in America.

The Reformed synods in America were in the main framed on the French model, except that the elders were chosen by the congregations and were considered as representatives of the congregations. As to the Lutherans, it is to be observed that they came not only from Germany, but also from the Netherlands, where the presbyterial system had been in force from the beginning, and from Sweden, which had something of a similar organization. But even among the Germans the fact that their principal organizer, H. M. Mühlenberg (q.v.), belonged to the school of Spener and organized his congregation with elders gave an impulse toward the adoption of the synodal system. The first Lutheran synod was held in Philadelphia in 1748, consisting of six pastors and a larger number of lay delegates (see LUTHERANS). After 1760 annual synods were held. The Episcopal Church, as the daughter of the Church of England, began with the same constitution; but the separation following upon the War of Independence forced it to adopt a new organization, whose principles were established in the General Conventions of Philadelphia, 1784, and Richmond, 1785, both composed of clergy and laity sitting together. The former laid down the principle "that to make canons or laws there be no other authority than that of a representative body of the clergy and laity conjointly," which has since been followed (see PROTESTANT EPISCOPAL CHURCH). See CHURCH COUNCIL. (A. HAUCK.)

BIBLIOGRAPHY: For the collections of the *Acta* of Councils by Labbé, Harduin, Mansi, and Hefele see vol. i. of this work, Preface, p. xix. The earliest collection was by J. Merlin, *Concilia generalia*, Paris, 1523, 1530, 1536, followed by that of P. Crabbe, *Concilia omnia tam generalia quam particularia*, 2 vols., Cologne, 1538. Partial collections and translations are: H. T. Bruns, *Canones apostolorum et conciliorum*, Berlin, 1839; W. Lambert, *Church Canons; the first four Councils*, London, 1871; J. Chrystal, *Authoritative Christianity; the Decisions of the six sole ecumenical Councils*, vols. i.–iii., Jersey City, 1891–1904; J. Fulton, *Index canonum; Greek text, Eng. transl., and complete Digest of the . . . Canon Law of the undivided primitive Church*, New York, 1892. A translation of the canons and decrees of the seven ecumenical councils is in *NPNF*, 2d ser., vol. xiv. The Acts of the Catholic synods since 1682 are in the *Acta et decreta sanctorum conciliorum recentiorum*, 7 vols., Freiburg, 1870 sqq.

Collections for individual lands are: J. F. Schannat and J. Hartzheim, *Concilia Germaniæ*, 11 vols., Cologne, 1749–1790; *MGH*, *Concilia*, vols. i.–ii. 1, 1893–1906; J. Sirmond, *Concilia antiqua Galliæ*, 3 vols., Paris, 1629; *Conciliorum Galliæ collectio*, Paris, 1789; D. Wilkins, *Concilia Magnæ Britanniæ et Hiberniæ*, 4 vols., London, 1737; E Gibson, *Synodus Anglicana*, ib. 1854; J. W. Joyce, *England's Sacred Synods*, ib. 1855; Haddan and Stubbs, *Councils;* J. Robertson, *Concilia Scotiæ*, Edinburgh, 1866; *Synodicon Belgicum*, ed. J. F. van de Velde and P. F. X. de Ram, 4 vols., Mechlin, 1828–59; H. Reuterdahl, *Statuta synodalia veteris ecclesiæ Sveogothicæ*, Lund, 1841; J. S. de Aguirre and J. Catalano, *Collectio maxima conciliorum omnium Hispaniæ*, Rome, 1753; C. Peterfy, *Concilia ecclesiæ Romanæ Catholicæ in regno Hungariæ*, 2 vols., Posen, 1741–42; J. Aymon, *Tous les synodes nationaux des églises réformées de France*, 2 vols., The Hague, 1710; E Hugues, *Les Synodes du désert*, 3 vols., Paris, 1885.

Discussions on the subject are: F. Salmon, *Traité de l'étude des conciles et de leurs collections*, Paris, 1724 and often; A. J. Binterim, *Geschichte der deutschen . . . Concilien*, 7 vols., Mainz, 1835–48; W. A. Hammond, *The Definitions of Faith and Canons of Discipline of the Six Œcumenical Councils*, Oxford, 1843; L. Richter, *Geschichte der evangelischen Kirchenverfassung in Deutschland*, Leipsic, 1851; G. Lechler, *Geschichte der Presbyterial- und Synodalverfassung seit der Reformation*, Leyden, 1854; J. F. von Schulte, *Die Stellung der Concilien, Päpste und Bischöfe vom historischen und canonischen Standpunkte*, Prague, 1871; E. Michaud, *Discussion sur les sept conciles œcuméniques*, Bern, 1878; E. B. Pusey, *The Councils of the Church from . . . 51 to . . . 381*, Oxford, 1878; E. Hatch, *The Growth of Church Institutions*, London, 1887; idem, *The Organization of the Early Christian Churches*, ib. 1895; H. Finke, *Konzilienstudien zur Geschichte des 13. Jahrhunderts*, Münster, 1891; W. Bright, *Notes on the Canons of the First Four General Councils*, London, 1892; E. H. Landon, *Manual of the Councils of the Holy Catholic Church*, 2 vols., ib. 1893; W. P. Du Bose, *The Ecumenical Councils*, New York, 1896; P. Guérin, *Les Conciles généraux et particuliers*, 3 vols., Paris, 1897; P. de Felice, *Les Protestants d'autrefois*, 5 vols., Paris, 1897–1902; K. von Schwartz, *Die Entstehung der Synoden*, Leipsic, 1898; H. von Hoffmann, *Das Kirchenverfassungsrecht der niederländischen Reformierten*, ib. 1902; G. B. Howard, *Stories of the First Four Councils*, London, 1906. The subject is treated in all the principal treatises on church history; the literature on the individual councils and synods will be found under the articles dealing with them. A valuable guide may be found in Ceillier, *Auteurs sacrés*, index volume under "Conciles," giving directions to a rich literature. Consult also *DCA*, i. 473–485; *KL*, iii. 779–810.

COUNTERREFORMATION: The general name for the complex of causes and results which from the middle of the sixteenth century checked the progress of the Protestant Reformation and won back to the Roman Catholic Church much of the territory and the prestige which had been apparently lost to it; in a narrower sense, the reform and revival in the Roman Church which was one of these causes. See REFORMATION; ROMAN CATHOLIC CHURCH; ITALY, THE REFORMATION IN; SPAIN, THE REFORMATION IN; also the articles upon the events, leaders, and agencies of the Counterreformation which are mentioned in these articles, as well as the articles devoted to the Counterreformation in certain lands and localities, viz.: ALBERT V. OF BAVARIA (for Bavaria); BALTHAZAR OF DERNBACH (Fulda); CYSAT, RENWARD (Switzerland); DANIEL, ELECTOR OF MAINZ (the Eichsfeld); FERDINAND II. (Austria); GEBHARD II., ELECTOR OF COLOGNE (the Lower Rhine); INNER AUSTRIA; JACOB CHRISTOPHER, BISHOP OF BASEL (Switzerland); JACOB OF ELTZ (Archbishopric of Treves); JULIUS ECHTER (Würzburg).

COURAYER, cū"rū"yê', PIERRE FRANÇOIS LE: Roman Catholic; b. at Rouen Nov. 17, 1681; d. in London Oct. 17, 1776. He became canon of St. Geneviève in Paris 1697, presbyter and professor of theology 1706, librarian of the abbey 1711. He was interested in the reunion of the Anglican with the Roman Catholic Church, and defended the validity of Anglican orders in a series of books which were fiercely attacked by Gervaise, Hardouin, Le Quien, and others, and were formally condemned by the French bishops. Encouraged and helped by Bishop Francis Atterbury, he went to England in 1728, where he spent the rest of his life. He was excommunicated in 1728; nevertheless he always professed to be a true Roman Catholic, although he rejected certain of the alleged superstitions of the Church. His works were *Dissertation sur la validité des ordinations des Anglois et sur la succession des évêques de l'église anglicane* (Brussels, 1723; Eng. transl., by D. Williams, London, 1725 and 1728; revised and corrected, with an account of the author and his works, notes, etc., Oxford, 1844); *Défense de la dissertation sur la validité des ordinations des Anglois* (2 vols., Brussels, 1726; Eng. transl., 1728); *Relation historique et apologétique des sentiments et de la conduite du P. Le Courayer* (2 vols., Amsterdam, 1729); *Supplément aux deux ouvrages faits pour la défense de la validité des ordinations anglicanes* (Amsterdam, 1732); *Examen des défauts théologiques où l'on indique les moyens de les réformer* (1744); *Déclarations de mes derniers sentiments sur les différens dogmes de la religion* (London, 1787; Eng. transl., 1787).

COURCELLES, cūr''sel' (*Curcellæus*), **ÉTIENNE DE**: Arminian; b. at Geneva May 2, 1586; d. in Amsterdam May 22, 1659. He studied theology under Calvin and Beza, and in Heidelberg, and was appointed pastor at Bois-le-Roi, near Fontainebleau, in 1614. In 1621 he became pastor at Amiens; but, having refused to subscribe the decrees of the Synod of Dort, he was deposed. He afterward gave a qualified assent, and was appointed pastor at Vitry, but gave up this position in 1634, went to Amsterdam, and became (1637) Episcopius' successor as professor of theology in the Remonstrants' College. He studied particularly the Greek text of the New Testament, and published an edition of it with many variant readings (Amsterdam, 1658). He published also a *Vindicia Arminii* (1645); *Defensio Blondelli* (1657); *Dissertationes* (1659); all of which, with others of his writings, appeared in a collected edition of his works at Amsterdam, 1675.

COURT, cūr, **ANTOINE**: 1. Reorganizer of the Reformed Church in France; b. at Villeneuve de Berg (50 m. n. of Nimes) Mar. 17, 1696; d. at Lausanne June 12, 1760. He determined at an early age to become a Protestant minister, and wandered throughout Vivarais with an itinerant preacher, delivering sermons and becoming still more firmly convinced of his calling. In 1714–15, defying the rigid laws promulgated against Protestantism by Louis XIV., he undertook his first tour, which comprised Cévennes, Languedoc, and Dauphiné. On Mar. 8, 1716, an edict of the king declared Protestantism non-existent in France, but on Aug. 21 of the same year Court convened the "first synod" in an abandoned quarry at Monoblet (Department of Gard). There certain plans of organization were drawn up, elders were chosen, the Bible was declared to be the only rule of faith and doctrine, women were forbidden to preach, and an earnest warning was made against "revelations." The resolutions were disseminated in writing, and the work of propaganda was actively carried on, while Court, who held a second synod in the following year, was unceasing in his sermons and efforts to obtain religious books forbidden by the authorities. On Nov. 21, 1718, he was ordained minister by the laying on of hands by Pierre Carrière (commonly known under the name of Corteis), and now made provision for the training of young preachers, although the administration of the sacrament and the laying on of hands were restricted to the ordained ministers. The organization thus effected was termed "the Church of the Desert" (with reference to Rev. xii. 6), and was characterised by vigorous opposition to Roman Catholicism.

Labors in Organizing Church of Desert.

The hostility manifested by Louis XIV. to the Reformed worship was continued by the regency after his death, and its observance was sternly punished. In 1719 it was rumored that the Spanish minister Alberoni intended to call the Protestants of Languedoc and Poitou to arms, and the regency, in its fear of a second Camisard revolt, entered into correspondence with Court as well as with Bénédict Pictet and Benjamin Basnage, urging them to admonish their coreligionists of their obedience. Basnage responded, but denied that the Protestants had the right to hold services publicly. He was answered by Court in his *Réponse des pasteurs du désert à l'instruction pastorale de Basnage*, but the latter's hope of securing greater leniency for the Protestants was disappointed. In 1720 he visited Geneva, where he sought to win the leaders of Swiss Protestantism to his side, and at the same time entered into correspondence with William Wake, archbishop of Canterbury. Returning in Aug., 1722, he found his church in a flourishing condition, but a decree of May 14, 1724, renewed all the restrictions placed upon Protestantism. The Reformed, however, persisted in their course, and on May 16, 1726, a general synod was held in a small valley of Vivarais. The organization prevailing in Languedoc was adopted, synods were required at regular intervals, and definite parishes were assigned the clergy. A document of the latter half of 1728 gives the number of Reformed in Languedoc and Dauphiné at 200,000 (which is probably too high). Languedoc, together with Rouergue and Vivarais, contained 120 parishes, three synods, sixteen conferences, four ministers, and eighteen candidates, and this organization was maintained in the face of the utmost difficulty and danger. Until 1729 Court shared this life of toil, acting not only as pastor but as leader of the entire movement, in addition to maintaining an enormous correspondence, instructing candidates for the ministry, convening synods, preparing memorials for the king, and collecting documents for a history of his church. In September of that year he resolved to leave France, and accordingly went to Lausanne, where for three years French students had been trained for the ministry in their native country. Under his supervision, although he occupied no fixed position in it, the seminary steadily increased in numbers and efficiency. Meanwhile a schism arose which divided the church of Languedoc into two camps, and on June 2, 1744, Court left Geneva and hastened to France. There he quickly restored harmony and was chosen general deputy in place of Duplan by the national

Court Successful Leadership.

synod of June 18, 1744. On Oct. 2 he returned to Lausanne. In that year the Reformed Church contained thirty-three pastors; Normandy had seventeen parishes, Poitou thirty, and Dauphiné sixty; and in Nîmes there were 20,000 believers. In 1756 the number of clergy was forty-eight, in addition to eighteen candidates and fifteen students; and in 1763 there were sixty-two ministers, thirty-five candidates, and fifteen students. Despite executions, imprisonments, fines, dragonades, and the reenforcement of all the old restrictions, it became evident that such measures could not overthrow the church, and a period of tacit toleration prevailed from 1754 to 1760. The final years of Court's life were passed in quiet retirement, far from this scene of struggle. Though he was a prolific writer, the library of Geneva containing 116 volumes of his manuscripts, his only published work of value was his *Histoire des troubles des Cévennes, ou de la guerre des Camisards* (Villefranche, 1760).

2. Antoine Court de Gebelin, the only son of the preceding, was born at Nîmes Jan. 25, 1725, and died at Paris May 10, 1784. After completing his education at Lausanne and Geneva, he was ordained in the former city (1754), but never held a regular charge. He acted as secretary and assistant to his father, and on the death of the latter became his informal successor. His life was devoted partly to the duties of his office and partly to scientific studies. The Calas affair in 1762, which created great excitement among the Protestants of France (see RABAUT, PAUL), inspired Court to publish his *Les Toulousaines, ou lettres historiques et apologétiques en faveur de la religion réformée* (Edinburgh, 1763), but Voltaire, who had been a leader in the agitation, disapproved of the work, and Court in anger left Lausanne. After a tour of southern France, he settled in Paris, where he soon gained great popularity and in 1765 was appointed general deputy by the Protestants. About 1780 he was made royal censor, and availed himself of his double position to ameliorate the miseries of the Protestants. His fame as a scholar was established in 1773 by the first volume of his *Le Monde primitif analysé et comparé avec le monde moderne* (9 vols., Paris, 1773–84), a learned but capricious attempt to discover the original language and alphabet, and to give an allegorical interpretation of mythology, as well as of Greek and French etymologies, and the like. He also wrote *Lettre sur le magnétisme animal* (1784) and the posthumous *Devoirs du prince et du citoyen* (1789), and collaborated on the *Affaires d'Angleterre et de l'Amérique*, a magazine edited by Benjamin Franklin and others (Antwerp, 1776 sqq.).

(THEODOR SCHOTT†.)

BIBLIOGRAPHY: E. Hugues, *Anton Court, Histoire de la restauration du protestantisme en France au xviiie. siècle*, 2 vols., Paris, 1872 (the chief work); idem, *Mémoires d'Antoine Court*, Toulouse, 1885 (autobiography); A. Coquerel, *Histoire des églises du désert*, 2 vols., Paris, 1841 (still of value); P. Rabaut, *Les lettres à A. Court*, ed. A. Picherol-Dardier and C. Dardier, ib. 1885; ib. *Les lettres à divers*, ed. C. Dardier, ib. 1891; T. Schott, *Die Kirche der Wüste*, Halle, 1893; H. M. Baird, *The Huguenots and the Revocation of the Edict of Nantes*, vol. ii., New York, 1895 (from the newest sources); E. Combe, *Anton Court et ses sermons*, Lausanne, 1896. The *Bulletin de la société de l'histoire du protestantisme français* contains many notices of Court and his times.

Concerning Corteis consult J. G. Baum, *Mémoires de Pierre Carrière dit Corteis*, Strasburg, 1871. On Roger, D. Benoit, *Un martyr du désert, Jacques Roger*, Toulouse, 1895. On Court de Gebelin consult C. Dardier, *Court de Gebelin*, Nîmes, 1896 (an acute study).

COUSIN, cū″zan′, VICTOR: Philosopher; b. in Paris Nov. 28, 1792; d. at Cannes Jan. 14, 1867. He studied at the École Normale in Paris, and began to lecture on philosophy there and at the Sorbonne 1815. In 1821 he was removed for political reasons, and during the next seven years gave himself to study, and produced the first volume of his *Fragmens philosophiques* (1826), his editions of Proclus (6 vols., 1820–27; 2d ed., 1864) and Descartes (11 vols., 1824–26), and began his translation of Plato (13 vols., 1822–40). In 1828 he was reinstated and for three years lectured to large audiences. After the Revolution of 1830 he became councilor of state, peer of France, director of the École Normale, member of the Academy, member of the council of public instruction, and minister of public instruction in the cabinet of Thiers in 1840. He was the real head of the university, and for nearly twenty years dominated the teaching of philosophy in France; he also reorganized the French primary school system. The downfall of Louis Philippe in 1848 made an end of his political career, and the remainder of his life was spent in quiet, devoted to study and the collection of a remarkable library, which he left at his death to the professors of the university.

Cousin's direct influence on Christian theology was not great, but indirectly his activity was of consequence. He changed the character of French philosophy, and led its students from the materialism of the eighteenth century to the idealism of the Scotch school. Furthermore, he made an end of the dogmatic method of the French and Scotch philosophy and introduced the dialectic method of German philosophy. He was an eclectic and did not produce a complete system, but his eclecticism was not a mere mosaic. The vigorous understanding and vivid representation of the various philosophical systems which he gives are everywhere permeated by a spirit of idealism, which, in the latter part of his life, drew him and his pupils nearer and nearer to Christianity.

His literary activity was great. His writings on philosophy appeared in many editions with extensive changes; the following works and editions are named as important for the study of his system: *Fragmens philosophiques* (4 vols., 1847–48); *L'histoire générale de la philosophie* (1861); *Du vrai, du beau et du bien* (1867); *Cours de l'histoire de la philosophie moderne* (8 vols., 1866). He edited the works of Abelard (*Ouvrages inédits d'Abélard*, 1836; *Petri Abelardi opera*, 2 vols., 1849–1859). In the latter period of his life he published several studies of the lives of women of the seventeenth century and their time (Jacqueline Pascal, 1844; Mme. de Longueville, 1853; Mme. de Hautefort, 1856; *La Société française au xvii. siècle*, 2 vols., 1858; and others), which have much historical and literary value. Certain writings concerning education, as a report upon the schools of Germany (1833) and Holland (1837), are also worthy of mention. These reports and some of his essays have been translated into English; also *The Philosophy of the Beautiful* by J. C. Daniel (London, 1848); and *Course of the History of Modern Philosophy* (2 vols.) and *Lectures on the True, the Beautiful, and the Good* by O. W. Wight (Edinburgh, 1852 and 1854).

BIBLIOGRAPHY: Sir William Hamilton ("the acutest critic of Cousin's philosophy"), *Discussions on Philosophy, Literature, Education, and University Reform*, London, 1852 (the first article is a review of Cousin); P. Janet, *Victor Cousin et son œuvre*, Paris, 1885; J. Simon, *Victor Cousin*, ib. 1887, Eng. transl., London, 1887; J. B. St. Hilaire, *Victor Cousin*, 3 vols., Paris, 1895.

COUSSIRAT, cūs″sī″rā′, **DANIEL**: Canadian Presbyterian; b. at Nérac (66 m. s.e. of Bordeaux), France, Mar. 5, 1841; d. at Montreal Jan. 8, 1907. He was graduated at Toulouse in 1859, and at the theological seminary at Montauban 1864; was stated supply to the Reformed Church at Bellocq (Basses-Pyrénées) 1864; pastor of the French Evangelical Church at Philadelphia, Pa., 1864–66; professor of divinity in Montreal, Canada, 1867–75; pastor of a Reformed church at Orthez (Basses-Pyrénées) 1875–80. After 1880 he was French professor of divinity in the Presbyterian College in Montreal, and professor of Semitic languages and literatures in McGill University after 1882. In 1885 he founded the Société musicale et littéraire de Montréal, and was an officier de l'instruction publique. Theologically his position was evangelical, and he felt no fear of either higher or lower criticism. He was one of the revisers of the French translation of the Old Testament under the auspices of the *Société Biblique de France* (Paris, 1881).

COVENANT.

The term "covenant" (Hebr. *bĕrîth*, cf. Assyrian-Babylonian *birîtu*, "bond, fetter," probably introduced into Canaan during the long Babylonian occupation of the "Westland"; Gk. *diathēkē*, "will, testament") is one of the most significant in the whole range of Biblical literature as well as in business, social, political, and religious relations.

1. Original Meaning of the Terms.

From the primary significations given above all the historical applications of the word are readily drawn. Not all, indeed not most of these, are implied in the English "covenant," which generally applies to a contract between two parties acting freely, while both the Hebrew and the Greek words may be used of anything binding upon the two parties to any transaction, whether the terms are accepted voluntarily or imposed by one of the parties or by another. The use of the Greek *diathēkē* in the sense of "covenant" in the Septuagint and New Testament is due to the usage of *bĕrîth*, as indicated above, including the disposals of the divine covenants (cf. the word "will" as suggesting the essential character of a testament from the standpoint of the testator). In classical Greek the word is very rarely employed in the sense of a contract or agreement.

The historical development of the Hebrew word which determined the usage of the Greek must be the chief guide in determining what the Bible means by "covenant."

2. Historic Development of the Meaning.

Originally the *bĕrîth* was an agreement between two clans or tribes represented by their leaders, and also between individuals for themselves. Such were the terms of peace between Isaac and Abimelech, (Gen. xxvi. 28 sqq.) or between Laban and Jacob (Gen. xxxi. 44) which also bound their respective families and dependents. Such also was the transaction, really a primitive tribal affair, between Shechem and the sons of Jacob (Gen. xxxiv.), where, however, the word for covenant is not directly used. The main object of such early agreements was the promotion of peace and safety, since the natural condition of primitive man was that of warfare. Hence the significance of the phrase "covenant of peace" (Num. xxv. 12; Isa. liv. 10) for which the word "peace" alone may be used (Jer. xvi. 5), accordingly those who were not at war with one another were supposed to be under a covenant of peace; hence breaking a covenant is equivalent to making war (I Kings xv. 19; A. V., "league"). So one could be in covenant with the beasts and with the stones of the field (Job v. 23, A.V., "league" that is, with the superhuman powers resident therein (cf. Hos. ii. 18). Covenants were made for mutual support or protection (e.g., II Sam. iii. 12–13), or for the fulfilment of common obligations to a third party (II Kings xi. 17); even submission to a superior enemy might be called making a covenant (I Sam. xi. 1), in which case also both parties were of course obligated (I Kings xx. 34). And, generally speaking, duties, obligations, or services required of his subjects or servants by a sovereign, suzerain, or feudal lord might be the subject of a covenant because they were imposed by the superior under certain conditions. This is the key to the prevailing use of the word "covenant" in the Bible, which was naturally religious, as setting forth the relations between God and his people.

There were many kinds of covenant among ancient peoples, as well as various modes of ratifying them. And, just as all covenants have the one essential condition or object of a mutual understanding and obligation, so, as seems probable, all ceremonies confirming the agreements are based upon one fundamental notion, that of

3. Covenant Ceremonies and Symbols.

a community of feeling or sentiment between the parties. This naturally implied among primitive men the conception of a community of life—the participants were for the time being members of the same community of clan or "life." Most prominent therefore among such ceremonies was the well-known ceremony of the blood-covenant (see COMPARATIVE RELIGION, VI., 1, b, § 6). As a substitute for the mixing of the blood came the natural and universal usage of animal sacrifice, which was always a most solemn method of ratifying a covenant; note how its sacredness is implied in Ps. l. 5. An elaborate symbolism in the development of this rite is shown in the custom of cutting the animal in pieces, between which, when laid out, the parties solemnly passed (Gen. xv.; cf. Jer. xxxiv. 18, 19). This ceremony is supposed by many to explain the word *bᵉrith* as being something "cut," but its obvious secondary character makes the hypothesis improbable. In another main direction the primary notion of sharing a common feeling or life is symbolized by the partaking of common food—the most convenient and frequent of all forms of covenant-making, from the "covenant of salt" to a solemn sacramental meal (see COMPARATIVE RELIGION, VI., 1, d, § 1). Both of these comprehensive types are also present in the covenant made between God and man, since in every sacrifice the blood or life of the victim was presented to God, as also at every meal a portion of the animal or vegetable partaken of was also dedicated to him. Both forms are exemplified in their deepest significance in the sacrament of the Lord's Supper.

"Religion" means literally the bond that unites man to God, and this is precisely the Biblical conception of religion which is constantly represented as the observance of a covenant with Yahweh.

4. Religion as a Covenant.

The dedication of the nation to the service of God at Sinai is figured thus: "that thou shouldst enter into the covenant of Yahweh thy God, and into his oath which Yahweh thy God maketh with thee this day" (Deut. xxix. 12; cf. Jer. ii. 2, 6, xxxi. 31). To be estranged from God and his service is to "forsake" or "forget" or "break" or "profane" or "transgress" the covenant (Gen. xvii. 14; Deut. iv. 23, 31, xxix. 25, xxxi. 20; Mal. ii. 10; Hos. viii. 1). Similar is the conception of God's own fidelity to the covenant which he has imposed (Judges ii. 1; Deut. xxxi. 16; Ps. lxxxix. 34; cf. Jer. xxxiii. 20–21). Fulfilling the duties of practical life as well as the obligation of worship is called "keeping the covenant" (Ps. ciii. 18; Isa. lvi. 4).

The provisions and sanctions of the covenant are contained or summarized in the "laws" which were at various times promulgated in Israel. This was necessarily so for two reasons. On the one hand, a covenant is not merely a theoretical

5. Provisions and Sanctions.

conception, but is concretely an actual engagement made upon explicit conditions; and these conditions as dictated by Yahweh were the obligations or rules of his service, which answer to the abstract term "covenant" as the concrete commandments or statutes answer to the abstract *torah* or "Law." On the other hand, conversely, "the covenant was the only form in which a law could be fashioned and sanctioned in Israel" (Smend). Hence the earliest legislation (Ex. xxi.–xxiii.) is called "the book of the covenant" (Ex. xxiv. 7) and the ten commandments of Ex. xxxiv. are called "the words of the covenant, the ten words" (Ex. xxxiv. 28). It is not certain that this codification and its comments were completed before the reign of Manasseh; but the idea had long been familiar, and in the Jehovistic and Elohistic writings of the ninth and eighth centuries B.C. a covenant between God and the fathers (Gen. xv. 18; cf. xxiv. 7, from J) is so taken for granted that its extension to Moses and Israel in the law of Sinai is the natural sequel.

It is through the Deuteronomistic writers that this conception of the covenant by law and precept has obtained widest currency. Although the word itself occurs only once (xvii. 2) in the legislation proper of Deuteronomy (chaps. xii.–xxvi.), it is found more often in the book as a whole than in any other of the Old Testament writings. Next in

6. Prophetic Development of the Conception.

frequency of use are the prophecy of Jeremiah, whom one might venture to call a mediator of the Old Covenant, and in the Psalms, where its hold on the thought and life of the later Israel receives practical illustration. In Deuteronomy not only are the "ten words" called "covenant," but they are said to have been written on two tablets of stone and placed in an ark (v. 2, ix. 9 sqq., x. 1 sqq.; cf. Ex. xxxii. 15–16, xxxiv. 1, probably influenced by D). Thus the covenant was incorporated into the religious life of Israel as centered in the Temple. It is in Jeremiah and his pupil Ezekiel that the prophetic conception of *bᵉrith* attains its consummation. It is still a matter of dispute whether Jeremiah was the author of the great prophecy ch. xxxi. 31–34. But all will admit that it is written in his spirit and that "the new heart" is a mere adaptation of his preaching (cf. xiii. 23, xvii. 9–10) about the essential moral bent of the human soul. In his most profound words exists in any case the germ of the "new covenant." Ezekiel, who is less set on the fundamental importance of righteousness or morality, develops on the other hand the idea of the covenant as a union between Yahweh and his people on the metaphorical basis of the marriage relation. Thus he completes and reenforces Hosea's germinal conception of the marriage-bond as a symbol of the love and fidelity which Israel owed to Yahweh as contrasted with the Baals, which the earlier prophet had not associated with the national covenant between Yahweh and Israel.

By the second Isaiah the covenant was projected from the sphere of preaching into the realm of prediction (e.g., Isa. xlii. 6, xlix. 8, lv. 4). In the course of the prophetic history the primary conception of the covenant as a body of precepts had gradually given way to its interpretation as a living

7. Later Phases of the Conception.

bond of union between Yahweh and his people and a guaranty of his faithfulness to his guardian trust. Hence the restoration of the kingdom founded by David comes to be an animating principle of religious patriotism in the closing years of the exile and the inspiration of the builders of Jerusalem during the many weary years that followed the return under Cyrus, the Messiah of Yahweh (cf. Hagg. ii. 5). Next to the practical reflections of the Psalms the latest writings on the covenant are those of the priestly narratives, which describe in detail the earliest covenants: that with Noah (Gen. ix. 9–17; cf. Isa. liv. 9) replaced by that with Abraham (Gen. xvii.) as preceding and preparing for the rise and progress of Israel as the people of Yahweh. In still later times this covenant with the fathers was most frequently in the minds of Biblical writers as the foundation-stone of the whole structure of Israel's religious history, attested as it was by the mark and sign of circumcision. So, for example, in the Psalms (e.g., cv. 6 sqq.; I Chr. xvi. 16 sqq.; Neh. ix. 8).

3. Covenant in the New Testament.

The New Testament writers in their few allusions to the ancient covenants refer in the same way to that made with Abraham. So Paul in Gal. iii. makes this fundamental and practically exclusive, the Law of Sinai, and still more the mediatorial work of Christ, being its realization and fulfilment. In the realm of his practical theology the most fruitful idea was that which saw in the propagation of the Gospel the ratification of the promise that in Abraham all the nations of the earth should be blessed. The Epistle to the Hebrews, a priestly work, while it uses the promise to Abraham incidentally as an illustration of God's covenant-faithfulness (vi. 13 sqq.), places in the foreground the shadowy figure of Melchizedek as a type of him who by his sacrifice "became the surety of a better covenant" (vii. 1–22). The author uses the word also in the later classical sense of "testament" (see § 1), combining the two meanings in the statement that Christ is "the mediator of a new covenant" according to the conditions of whose "testament," made operative only by the death of the "testator," an "external inheritance" is made sure to the beneficiaries along with "redemption for the transgressions that were under the old covenant" (ix. 15, 16; compare Acts iii. 25, vii. 8; Eph. ii. 12).

J. F. McCurdy.

Bibliography: Excellent discussions are to be found in *DB*, i. 509–515; *EB*, i. 928–937; *DCG*, i. 373–380. Consult further: H. Guthe, *De fœderis notione Jeremiana*, Leipsic, 1877; Valeton, in *ZATW*, xii (1892), 1–22, 224–260, xiii (1893), 245–279; R. Kraetzschmar, *Die Bundesvorstellung im A. T.*, Marburg, 1896; W. M. Ramsay, in *Expositor*, Nov., 1898, pp. 321–336; Smith, *Rel. of Sem.*, pp. 269 sqq., 312 sqq., 479 sqq.; idem, *Kinship*, pp. 46 sqq.; and such works on the theology of the Old and the New Testament as H. Schultz, *O. T. Theology*, ii. 1 sqq., Edinburgh, 1892; and W. Beyschlag, *N. T. Theology*, 2 vols., Edinburgh, 1896. For the modern idea consult: C. Burrage, *The Church Covenant Idea; its Origin and Development*, Philadelphia, 1907.

COVENANTERS.

1. Early Agreements to 1572.

The name "Covenanters" was given to Scotch Presbyterians, or a portion of them, in the sixteenth century, because of the solemn agreements by which they bound themselves; since then it has been applied to a small party in Scotland who have held to similar views. In the confusion of the Reformation time in Scotland, when the central authority, with little power of its own, was liable to fall under the control of temporary groups of the turbulent gentry or to be swayed by ecclesiastical dignitaries, anxious for their secular interests, the legal position of innovators and agitators was never clear. The Protestant parties therefore sought sanction and security in the various steps they took by entering into formal "covenants," which had a double character, religious and political. There is a suggestion of a "band" at a meeting of Forfarshire gentlemen in 1556; the first, however, of which there are definite details—an ancient copy is in the National Museum of Antiquities in Edinburgh—"the common band" (Knox) was drawn up in 1557 on the renewal of the Reformers' invitation to John Knox (q.v.) to return to Scotland. Three others in 1559 marked as many crises in the struggle with the queen regent, and a fourth signed in 1560 by the leading nobility was the prelude to the expulsion of the French and the triumph of the Reformation ratified in the Parliament of that year. In alarm at Mary's policy, Knox and the Ayrshire gentry signed a covenant in 1562. St. Bartholomew's massacre suggested the idea of another in 1572, but possibly this was not carried out.

2. The King's Confession and Other Agreements to 1596.

More important than these early bands directed to special emergencies was the lengthy covenant of 1580 called the King's Confession, the Second Confession of Faith, or the Negative Confession. It was drawn up by John Craig (q.v.) and subscribed by all classes from the boy king James VI. downward. The original is now in the Advocates' Library, Edinburgh. It is a strongly Protestant manifesto in which the declaration of allegiance to the crown is carefully interwoven with the declaration of the duty of the crown to maintain the constitution of the Reformed Kirk and the Protestant settlement embodied in previous acts of Parliament. It was signed again in 1587. Once more the party of the Ruthven raid in 1582 had made a "band." The Spanish Armada inspired a national "band" in 1588. Another was signed in 1589. In 1590 the King's Confession and the band of 1588 were printed and circulated, multitudes subscribing throughout Scotland. The year 1592 saw another "band" in Aberdeen against suspected treason. In 1596 a more directly religious movement was initiated by the assembly and spread downward through presbyteries to parishes. There were, if not formal signatures, at least meetings for humiliation and confession at which vows of steadfastness were renewed.

3. The National Covenant of 1638.

Court diplomacy directed to the reintroduction of episcopacy was now busy; but James' success did not much affect the local groundwork of Presbyterian practise, and Charles I. and Laud found, when they were free to turn attention to Scotland, that conformity with English episcopacy was far from being a reality. The new service-book was sent down to Edinburgh; Dean Hanney tried to read it in St. Giles' Cathedral and, according to tradition, Jenny Geddes (q.v.) threw her stool at him on July 23, 1637. The covenanting instinct of a previous generation came into play, and 1638 saw the enthusiastic and almost universal subscription to the National Covenant inaugurated in the Greyfriars' churchyard. This covenant consisted of the King's Confession of 1580 followed by a lengthy legal remonstrance and statement by Johnston, of Warriston, and a popular religious conclusion by Henderson, of Leuchars (see HENDERSON, ALEXANDER). As before, loyalty to king and religion were carefully interwound, "the true worship of God and the king's authority being so straitly joined as that they . . . did stand and fall together." The organized Presbyterians are at this time referred to in royal correspondence as "Covenanters." During two years Charles's attempts to use unwilling English forces against the Scots were thwarted by the skill of Alexander Leslie, a great ex-general of Gustavus Adolphus. Leslie avoided any vigorous invasion which would rouse English sentiment, and the peace (1641) saw the Scotch army established quietly in Northumberland and Durham and subsidized by the Long Parliament.

In 1643, in their darkest hour, the Long Parliament sought a definite alliance with the Scots. The latter suggested a religious covenant instead of the civil league favored by English Independents, and the Solemn League and Covenant was drawn up in Edinburgh by Henderson, there approved, and sent up to be adopted at Westminster by the Assembly, Lords, and Commons, the majority of the English Parliament being disposed to make trial of Presbyterianism as the only visible alternative to episcopacy. This league, which was signed throughout the length and breadth of Britain, pledged subscribers to the maintenance of the Reformed Church of Scotland and the Reformation in England and Ireland, to the extirpation of popery and prelacy, to a common endeavor after uniformity of discipline and doctrine according to the Word of God and the example of the best Reformed churches, and to loyalty to Parliament and crown. It was renewed in Scotland in 1648 and signed with the National Covenant by Charles II. in 1650 and 1651.

4. The Solemn League and Covenant, 1643.

But rigid Presbyterianism made itself impracticable in England, and the execution of Charles I. completed the alienation of the Scots. A party in Scotland signed an "engagement" with Charles with a view to his liberation, and Hamilton led an army to defeat by Cromwell at Preston in 1647. The "non-Engagers" headed by Argyll, who had protested against this treachery to the English Parliament, now came into power, and while turning against Cromwell by proclaiming Charles II., whom they kept nevertheless in strict tutelage, they passed the Act of Classes excluding "malignants," or "engagers," from all offices and from the army. Cromwell's victorious march from Dunbar made it seem expedient to a short-sighted majority to pass "resolutions" rescinding this Act, for every soldier was wanted. The stricter party protested. A remonstrance was signed in the West. The increased army availed nothing against Cromwell, who forced upon Scotland a period of profound peace and prosperity, reproaching Presbyterians with their divisions and hostility to himself and favoring the more Evangelical and zealous party of the Protesters. In these days true religion made great advances, but the strife of "Resolutioners and Protesters" continued to divide the Covenanters into bitterly opposed factions. This schism and the fact that the Resolutioners had admitted many half-hearted into place and power account for the strange facility with which Charles II. at the Restoration in 1660 was able to impose his agents on the Scotch kirk and nation.

5. Divisions Among the Covenanters.

The Resolutioners were betrayed at the outset by their chosen agent, James Sharp (q.v.), who got himself made archbishop of St. Andrews. The Court of High Commission was set up and, without effective protest, episcopacy and the machinery for enforcing it. The Solemn League and Covenant was burned in London and Linlithgow. A packed Scotch Parliament rescinded all the Acts of the preceding twenty years. One new Act commanded abjuration of the Covenant. Another voided all ministerial appointments since 1649, ordering such ministers now to request presentation from the patron and the bishop. Four hundred, chiefly in the West and South, heroically chose ejectment. The country awoke at the spectacle. Few waited on the ministrations of the new curates. Rolls of parishioners were therefore made up and soldiers sent to enforce attendance by fines. The people flocked with increasing numbers and enthusiasm to conventicles in barns or on the moors. Three successive "indulgences" to "outed" ministers being accepted by a few in spite of the compromise involved fulfilled in slight degree their aim of sowing dissension. At the same time measures against the faithful became ever harsher, and Argyll and Guthrie had been executed in 1661. Men like Graham, of Claverhouse, and Lauderdale earned immortal infamy. A long roll-call of martyrs follows during these twenty-eight years of the "killing time"—Hugh Mackail, Cargill, John Brown, of Priesthill, the two dauntless women who were slowly drowned in the rising tide at Wigtown (see WILSON, MARGARET), the preacher Renwick, nameless ones without number. Hundreds were sold into slavery in Barbados, among them many women. Others died of exposure or rotted in dungeons. Many were horribly tortured. Altogether many thousands perished. The offenses were refusals to abjure the Covenant or attend the parish kirk, and the frequenting of conventicles and "intercommuning" with those who did. It was punishable to let a child remain unbaptized by the parish curate. Fighting took place at Rullion Green, Drumclog, and Bothwell Bridge. Richard Cameron (q.v.), who proclaimed a definite rebellion at Sanquahar in 1680, was defeated and slain at Ayrsmoss. On the other hand, Sharp had been killed in 1679 by nine Covenanters. Every soldier of the government was allowed to kill, and their cruelty was directed on women and children as

6. Persecution Under Charles II. and James II.

on men. A children's covenant has survived signed in the village of Pentland by fifteen girls, the first on the list being then ten years old. The accession of James II. brought no relief. Another Argyll perished in an abortive rising in 1685. At last on James's flight in 1688 the persecution ceased.

William of Orange believed in toleration and left the Scotch Estates to settle their own religious affairs. Prelacy was at once thrown off, and the Parliament of 1690 renewed the Act of 1592 establishing Presbyterianism. As only about ninety of the ministers "outed" in 1661 now survived, the complaisant curates were allowed to stay on.

7. The Later "Covenanters."

The aggressive Presbyterian ideal of 1638 and 1643 was abandoned. Some of the obnoxious legislation since then was left unrescinded. Therefore, a stricter section calling themselves Cameronians, or the Reformed Presbyterian Church of Scotland, holding the nation still bound by the great National Covenants of the preceding generation, refused to approve the settlement and protested against the constitution of both Church and State. There was of course no more persecution, and they and their descendants maintained their testimony and their aloofness from all exercise of civil rights undisturbed. Almost all joined the Free Church in 1876, but several congregations still remain. See CAMERON, RICHARD, CAMERONIANS; also the section of PRESBYTERIANS treating of the Scotch Church.

(R. W. STEWART.) THOMAS M. LINDSAY.

BIBLIOGRAPHY: For the earlier "bands" the sources are: John Knox, *Hist. of the Reformation in Scotland*, ed. D. Laing, vols. i.–ii. of *Works*, Edinburgh, 1846–47; D. Calderwood, *Hist. of the Kirk of Scotland*, 8 vols., republished, ib. 1842–49; *A Cloud of Witnesses for the Royal Prerogatives of Jesus Christ, or the last Speeches and Testimonies of those who suffered for the Truth in Scotland since . . . 1680*, ib. 1730; J. Howie, *Scots Worthies*, ed. W. H. Carslaw, ib. 1885. Modern books are R. Simpson, *Traditions of the Covenanters*, Edinburgh, 1889; D. H. Fleming, *Story of the Scottish Covenants*, ib. 1904 (based upon earlier sources, readable, condensed). Scott's grossly unfair *Tales of My Landlord* was answered by T. McCrie in *Christian Instructor*, 1817 (reprinted with his *Sermons*), and a reply by Scott is in the *Quarterly Review*, xvi. 439–480. Other works are: J. Dodds, *Fifty Years' Struggles of the Scottish Covenanters*, London, 1871; J. K. Hewison, *Hist. of the Church in Scotland from the Reformation to the Revolution*, 2 vols., Glasgow, 1908.

COVERDALE, MILES: Bible translator; b. probably in the district known as Cover-dale, in that part of the North Riding of Yorkshire called Richmondshire, 1488; d. in London and buried in St. Bartholomew's Church Feb. 19, 1568. He studied at Cambridge (bachelor of canon law 1531), became priest at Norwich in 1514, and entered the convent of Austin friars at Cambridge, where Robert Barnes (q.v.) was prior in 1523 and probably influenced him in favor of Protestantism. When Barnes was tried for heresy in 1526 Coverdale assisted in his defense, and shortly afterward left the convent and gave himself entirely to preaching. From 1528 to 1535 he appears to have spent most of his time on the Continent, where his Bible (the first complete Bible in English) was published in 1535—at what place and by whom is disputed. In 1538 he was in Paris, superintending the printing of the "Great Bible," and the same year were published, both in London and Paris, editions of a Latin and an English New Testament, the latter being by Coverdale. He also edited "Cranmer's Bible" (1540). (For further information concerning Coverdale's Bible translations see BIBLE VERSIONS, B, IV., § 4.) He returned to England in 1539, but on the execution of Thomas Cromwell (who had been his friend and protector since 1527) in 1540 was compelled again to go into exile, lived for a time at Tübingen, and, between 1543 and 1547, was Lutheran pastor and schoolmaster at Bergzabern in the Palatinate, and very poor. In Mar., 1548, he went back to England, was well received at court and made king's chaplain and almoner to the queen dowager, Catherine Parr. In 1551 he became bishop of Exeter, but was deprived in 1553 after the succession of Mary. He went to Denmark (where his brother-in-law was chaplain to the king), then to Wesel, and finally back to Bergzabern. In 1559 he was again in England, but was not reinstated in his bishopric, perhaps because of Puritanical scruples about vestments. From 1564 to 1566 he was rector of St. Magnus's, near London Bridge. "He was pious, conscientious, laborious, generous, and a thoroughly honest and good man. He knew German and Latin well, some Greek and Hebrew, and a little French. He did little original literary work. As a translator he was faithful and harmonious. He was fairly read in theology, and became more inclined to Puritan ideas as his life wore on. All accounts agree in his remarkable popularity as a preacher. He was a leading figure during the progress of the Reformed opinions, and had a considerable share in the introduction of German spiritual culture to English readers in the second quarter of the sixteenth century."

BIBLIOGRAPHY: Coverdale's works and letters were published by the Parker Society, ed. G. Pearson, 2 vols., *Writings and Translations*, Cambridge, 1844; *Remains*, 1846. A list of his works, with information concerning his life and the sources, is given in *DNB*, xii. 364–372. Consult: *Memorials of Myles Coverdale*, London, 1838; C. Anderson, *Annals of the English Bible*, pp. 314–318, 443–440, ib. 1862; F. Fry, *The Bible by Coverdale, MDCXXXV.*, ib. 1867; J. I. Mombert, *Hand-book of the Eng. Versions of the Bible*, chap. v., New York, 1882; H. W. Hoare, *Evolution of the Eng. Bible*, chap. vi., London, 1902.

COWAN, HENRY: Church of Scotland; b. at Ayr (40 m. s.s.w. of Glasgow), Ayrshire, Scotland, Sept. 17, 1844. He studied at Edinburgh (M.A., 1864), Bonn, Halle, and Tübingen, holding from Edinburgh a Greek traveling fellowship (1865) and the Pitt theological scholarship (1866–68). In addition to being theological examiner at Edinburgh 1871–73, he held pastorates at West Parish, Aberdeen (1869–74), Rubislaw, Aberdeen (1875–1882), and New Greyfriars', Edinburgh (1882–89), and since 1889 has been professor of church history in the University of Aberdeen, as well as dean of the faculty of divinity since 1894. He has been vice-convener of the Church of Scotland Endowment Scheme since 1886, and joint-convener of the Scottish Universities' Mission Committee since 1900, and was also Baird Lecturer in 1895 and chairman of the Church of Scotland Aberdeen Normal Training College Board 1896–1906. In theological doctrine he is a broad Evangelical, and in Biblical criticism he is a moderate. In addition to briefer contributions, he has written: *Landmarks of Church History* (Edinburgh, 1894); *Influence of the Scottish Church in Christendom* (Baird lectures for 1895); and *Life of John Knox* (New York, 1905).

COWL: Primarily the hood with which the early monks, following a style of dress common among all classes in the Roman Empire, covered their heads. It increased in length after its wearing had been positively prescribed for Western monks by Benedict, until Benedict of Aniane ruled that it should be uniform in size and not reach below the knees. Thus the name came to apply not only to the hood but to the whole characteristic outer garment of a monk. The hood proper in more modern times was attached with the Franciscans and Capuchins to the habit, with the Brothers of Charity to the scapular, with canons to the *cappa* or *mozetta*; the Augustinians and Servites retained it as a separate garment. At the present time the shape varies in different orders, and the color is that of the habit. It does not as a rule form part of the dress of orders founded since the Middle Ages.

COWLES, HENRY: Commentator; b. in Norfolk, Conn., Apr. 24, 1803; d. at Janesville, Wis., Sept. 6, 1881. He was graduated at Yale 1826, studied in the Yale Divinity School 1826–28, and was from 1828 to 1835 a missionary on the Western Reserve in Ohio. From 1835 to 1848, he was professor, first of Greek and Latin, and then of ecclesiastical history and sacred literature in Oberlin College; from 1848 to 1863 he was editor of the *Oberlin Evangelist*. He published a commentary on the entire Bible (16 vols., New York, 1867–81), a *Hebrew History* (1873), and other works.

COWPER, WILLIAM: Poet and hymn-writer; b. at Great Berkhampstead (28 m. n.w. of London), Hertfordshire, Nov. 15, 1731; d. at East Dereham (15 m. w.n.w. of Norwich), Norfolk, Apr. 25, 1800. He studied law and was called to the bar in 1754, but took more interest in literature than in his profession. He was naturally inclined to morbid brooding, and suffered from an unhappy love-affair; in 1763 nervous dread of an examination for which he was preparing preliminary to entering upon a government position so wrought upon his mind that it was necessary to confine him in an asylum. After about eighteen months he was able to go free, but was subject to attacks of insanity ever afterward, and never fully recovered from the last in 1787. For thirty years he lived a retired life at Olney, Buckinghamshire, and at the neighboring village of Weston. He was tenderly cared for by his relatives and had kind friends who encouraged him to write to divert his mind; he became excessively pious and devout, was ever a prey to religious doubts and hallucinations, and often in deep depression. At Olney he was intimate with John Newton (q.v.), and helped him in his parish work as a sort of lay curate. Some of Cowper's poems are models of tender verse, and his letters have none superior in all literature. His hymns include the familiar and admirable "God moves in a mysterious way," "There is a fountain filled with blood," and "O for a closer walk with God." He joined Newton in writing the Olney Hymns (1779; see NEWTON, JOHN), and contributed sixty-eight to Newton's 280.

BIBLIOGRAPHY: The best edition of his *Works* with his life is by Robert Southey, 15 vols., London, 1836–37; reprinted in *Bohn's Standard Library*, 8 vols., ib. 1853–55; other lives are by J. Bruce, in "Aldine Edition" of his poems, 3 vols., Philadelphia, 1865; by W. Benham, in "Globe Edition" of his poems, New York, 1870; by Goldwin Smith, London, 1880; and by T. Wright, ib. 1892. Wright has also edited his *Unpublished and Uncollected Poems*, ib. 1900; and his *Correspondence*, 4 vols., ib. 1904; selections from his letters are by W. Benham, ib. 1884, and by W. T. Webb, ib. 1895.

COX, SAMUEL: English Baptist; b. in London Apr. 19, 1826; d. at Hastings Mar. 27, 1893. He was graduated at the Stepney Baptist Theological College, London, 1851, and was ordained pastor of St. Paul's Square Baptist Church, Southsea; became pastor at Ryde, Isle of Wight, 1855; resigned because of throat trouble 1859; was pastor of the General Baptist Church, Mansfield Road, Nottingham, 1863–88. He was president of the British General Baptist Association in 1873. He is best known in connection with the *Expositor*, which he founded in 1875 and edited till 1884; some of the volumes are almost entirely his work. According to his own statement, he wrote thirty independent books and edited twenty more, including *The Quest of the Chief Good: Expository Lectures on the Book Ecclesiastes, with a New Translation* (London, 1868; rewritten for the *Expositor's Bible*, 1890); *The Private Letters of St. Paul and St. John* (1867); *Salvator Mundi; or, is Christ the Saviour of all Men?* a defense of restorationism, the best known of his books (1877); *Expository Essays and Discourses* (1877); *Commentary on the Book of Job* (1880); *The Larger Hope, a sequel to Salvator Mundi* (1883); *Miracles, an Argument and a Challenge* (1884); *Expositions* (4 vols., 1885–88); and *The Hebrew Twins, a Vindication of God's Ways with Jacob and Esau* (1894) with a *Memoir* by his wife.

COX, SAMUEL HANSON: Presbyterian; b. of Quaker parentage at Rahway, N. J., Aug. 25, 1793; d. in Bronxville, N. Y., Oct. 2, 1880. He was ordained in 1817, and was pastor at Mendham, N. J., till 1820, when he settled in New York as pastor, first of the Spring Street Church (1820–25) and then of the Laight Street Church (1825–35). He was professor of sacred rhetoric and pastoral theology in Auburn Theological Seminary 1836–37, pastor of the First Presbyterian Church in Brooklyn 1837–54, was president of Ingham University 1856–63, and thenceforth lived in retirement in and near New York. He was one of the founders of the University of the City of New York and of Union Theological Seminary. He was a leader of the New School party in the disruption of 1837 and was moderator of the General Assembly in 1846. Many stories are told of his fondness for big words and peculiar expressions in public prayer. But he possessed much eloquence and learning.

COXE, ARTHUR CLEVELAND: Second bishop of western New York; b. at Mendham, N. J., May 10, 1818; d. at Clifton Springs, N. Y., July 20, 1896.

He was a son of Samuel Hanson Cox (q.v.) and himself added the "e" to his name. He was graduated at the University of the City of New York 1838, and at the General Theological Seminary, New York, 1841; became rector of St. Ann's, Morrisania, N. Y., 1841; of St. John's, Hartford, Conn., 1842; of Grace, Baltimore, 1854; of Calvary, New York, 1863; bishop of western New York 1865. In 1868 his diocese was divided and the new diocese of Central New York formed. He was provisional bishop of Haiti 1872–74. The Old Catholic movement, Père Hyacinthe, and all that concerned Gallicanism and Anglo-Catholicism had his active sympathy. He helped to form the Anglo-Continental Society (1853) and gave it its name. In 1873 he collaborated with Bishop Wilberforce in issuing a serial in defense of Anglo-Catholicism against Romanism. In his pamphlet, *An Apology for the English Bible* (New York, 1857), he gave voice to the opposition against the attempt of the American Bible Society to introduce slight changes in the text and punctuation of the Scriptures, and the plan was abandoned (see BIBLE SOCIETIES, III., 1, § 5). He also opposed the Revised Version of 1881–1885, but advocated a revision of the prayer-book. His writings include several volumes of poems, of which *Christian Ballads* (Hartford, 1840; enlarged ed., New York, 1901) is best known. Several hymns in general use ("In the silent midnight watches"; "O where are kings and empires now?" and others) are from his pen. Works upon theological topics were *Absolution and Confession* (New Haven, 1850); *Sermons on Doctrine and Duty* (Philadelphia, 1855); *Thoughts on the Services* (Baltimore, 1859; rev. ed., Philadelphia, 1900); *The Criterion*, defining his position concerning the Oxford movement (New York and Oxford, 1866); *A Letter to Pius IX.*, relating to the call for the Vatican Council (New York, 1869); *Moral Reforms* (Buffalo, 1869); *Lectures on Prophecy* (1871); *Apollos, or the Way of God* (Buffalo, 1871); *L'épiscopat de l'occident*, a defense of the Church of England (Paris, 1874); *Covenant Prayers* (1875); *The Penitential* (New York, 1882); *Institutes of Christian History*, Baldwin lectures before the University of Michigan, 1887 (Chicago, 1887); *Holy Writ and Modern Thought*, Bedell lectures at Kenyon College, 1891 (New York, 1892). He edited the American reprint of the *Ante-Nicene Fathers* (9 vols., New York, 1885–87).

BIBLIOGRAPHY: W. S. Perry, *The Episcopate in America*, pp. 159–161, New York, 1895.

COYLE, ROBERT FRANCIS: Presbyterian; b. at Roseneath, Ont., July 28, 1850. He studied at Wabash College (B.A., 1877) and Auburn Theological Seminary (B.D., 1879), and held pastorates at Fort Dodge, Ia. (1879–85), Fullerton Avenue Church, Chicago (1885–91), and the First Presbyterian Church, Oakland, Cal. (1891–1900). Since 1900 he has been pastor of the Central Presbyterian Church, Denver, Col. He was moderator of the General Assembly at Los Angeles, Cal., in 1903, and has written *Foundation Stones* (Chicago, 1887); *Workingmen and the Church* (New York, 1896); and *The Church and the Times* (1905).

CRAFTS, WILBUR FISK: Presbyterian; b. at Fryeburg, Me., Jan. 12, 1850. He studied at Wesleyan University, Middletown, Conn. (B.A., 1869), and Boston University School of Theology (B.D., 1871), and held various Methodist pastorates from 1867 to 1879. In the latter year he entered the Congregational Church, and in 1883 he became a Presbyterian. His chief pastorates were those in Stoneham, Haverville, and New Bedford, Mass., Dover, N. H., Chicago, Brooklyn, and New York. He has been active in Sunday-school work since 1871, and has written on the Sunday-school lessons for the *Sunday School Times*, *International Lesson Monthly*, *Pocket Lesson Notes*, and the *Christian Herald*. In 1889 he founded the American Sabbath Union, and for six years lectured throughout the United States chiefly on Sabbath observance. In 1895 he founded the Reform Bureau, now called the International Reform Bureau, particularly for the promotion of social purity, the defense of the Sabbath, the suppression of the liquor traffic, and the protection of children and the less civilized races. As the superintendent of this bureau he has been active both as a lecturer and in the preparation of laws to further its aims. He was chief editor of the *Christian Statesman* 1901–03, and of the *Twentieth Century Quarterly* since 1896. He also edited departments in *Our Day* (1888–91), *Ram's Horn* (1896–98), and the *Advance*, and has written, among others, the following books, several in collaboration with his wife: *Through the Eye to the Heart* (New York, 1875); *Talks to Boys and Girls About Jesus* (1881); *The Sabbath for Man* (1884); *Social Progress* (Washington, 1896); *Protection of Native Races Against Intoxicants and Opium* (Chicago, 1900); and *The March of Christ Down the Centuries* (1902).

CRAIG, crég, JAMES ALEXANDER: Layman; b. at Fitzroy Harbour, Ont., Mar. 5, 1855. He studied at McGill University, Montreal (B.A., 1880), Yale Divinity School (B.D., 1883), and the University of Leipsic (Ph.D., 1886). He was instructor and adjunct professor of Biblical languages in Lane Theological Seminary, Cincinnati, 1886–90, professor of Old Testament literature and exegesis in Oberlin Theological Seminary 1891–93; and since 1893 has been professor of Semitic languages and literatures and Hellenistic Greek in the University of Michigan. He has edited *The Semitic Series of Handbooks*, and written *The Monolith Inscription of Salmanesar II.* (Leipsic, 1888); *Hebrew Word Manual* (Cincinnati, 1890); *Assyrian and Babylonian Religious Texts* (2 vols., Leipsic, 1895–97); and *Astronomical-Astrological Texts* (1899).

CRAIG, JOHN: The name of two Scotchmen.

1. Scotch Reformer; b. about 1512; d. in Edinburgh Dec. 12, 1600. He studied at St. Andrews, and became a Dominican monk; went to England in 1536, thence to Rome, and served his order on missions in Italy and to the island of Chios, and as teacher at Bologna. He was converted to Protestantism by reading the "Institutes" of Calvin, it is said, and was in prison at Rome, condemned to the stake, when the pope, Paul IV., died (1559) and the mob opened the

prisons and he escaped. He went to Vienna, thence to England in 1560, and back to his native land; was appointed colleague to Knox in Edinburgh in 1563, and, after the death of Knox (1572), succeeded to the leadership of the Scottish Church. At first he refused to proclaim the banns between Mary and Bothwell, but yielded later, protesting that "he abhorred and detested the marriage." After 1579 he was king's chaplain and was bold enough to rebuke the king to his face, but too conciliatory to suit the extreme party led by Melville. He compiled part of the "Second Book of Discipline," wrote the "King's Confession" (see COVENANTERS, § 2) in 1580, and published *A Short Sum of the Whole Catechism* (Edinburgh, 1581; reprinted in facsimile with introduction by T. G. Law, 1883), and a shorter catechism, *A Form of Examination Before the Communion* (1590). Both catechisms are reprinted in H. Bonar's *Catechisms of the Scottish Reformation* (London, 1866).

BIBLIOGRAPHY: J. Knox, *Works*, ed. D. Laing, ii. 456, Edinburgh, 1895; T. McCrie, *Life of John Knox*, ii. 53–57, ib. 1841; *DNB*, xii. 445–447.

2. Scotch mathematician; d. in London Oct. 11, 1731. He lived in Cambridge and London, and had decided mathematical talent; from 1708 he was prebendary of Salisbury. He is mentioned here for his curious *Theologiæ Christianæ principia mathematica* (London, 1699; reprinted, with a learned preface, Leipsic, 1755), in which he endeavors "to calculate the duration of moral evidence, and the authority of historical facts." By applying the theory of probabilities he attempts to show that the proofs of the Christian religion steadily become weaker as the force of the testimony decays, and in the year 3144 Christianity will entirely disappear, "unless the second coming of Christ prevent its extinction." He also calculated "the ratio of happiness promised in another world to that obtainable in this, and proved it to be infinite."

BIBLIOGRAPHY: *DNB*, xii. 448 (gives the sources).

CRAKANTHORPE, RICHARD: Puritan; b. at or near Strickland (25 m. s.s.e. of Carlisle), Westmoreland, 1567; d. at Black Notley (35 m. n.e. of London), Essex, 1624 (buried Nov. 25). He became fellow of Queen's College, Oxford, 1598, went to Germany as chaplain to Lord Evers, ambassador extraordinary; became chaplain to the bishop of London and to the king; rector of Black Notley, and of Paglesham, Essex. His most noteworthy work was a *Defensio ecclesiæ Anglicanæ* (London, 1625; republished in the *Library of Anglo-Catholic Theology*, Oxford, 1847), a reply to the *Consilium reditus* of Marco Antonio de Dominis (q.v.). Crakanthorpe's Latin and learning are commended, but his tone is described as "savage."

CRAMER, JOHANN ANDREAS: German theologian and hymnologist; b. at Jöhstadt (7 m. s.e. of Annaberg, Saxony) Jan. 27, 1723; d. at Kiel June 12, 1788. He studied at Leipsic, and from 1748 to 1750 was pastor at Crollwitz near Merseburg, where he began the publication of a translation of sermons and minor writings of Chrysostom (10 vols., Leipsic, 1748–51). In 1750 he was appointed chief court preacher and councilor of the consistory at Quedlinburg, and four years later, at the recommendation of Klopstock, became German court preacher at Copenhagen. There his sermons and his personality gained him a position of importance, and he influenced the spiritual life of Denmark by the *Nordischer Aufseher*, which he edited (3 vols., Copenhagen, 1758–70), and which contained, in addition to reviews of important literary works, studies on ethics and esthetics. From this time date two collections of sermons and an elucidation of the Epistle to the Hebrews (2 vols., Leipsic, 1757). In 1765 he was made professor of theology at the University of Copenhagen, but was dismissed and expelled from Denmark on account of his bold opposition to Struensee. After acting for three years as superintendent at Lübeck, where he prepared a rationalistic catechism, he accepted a call to Kiel in 1774 as professor of theology and vice-chancellor of the university. There he remained fourteen years, developing a versatile activity, especially in the interests of the young theologians, and also providing for the salaries of the instructors by the establishment of a *Schulmeisterseminar*. In the Church of Sleswick-Holstein Cramer exercised great influence through the hymnal edited by him (Altona, 1780), which remained in use until 1887. Throughout his life he composed religious poems, of which 444 have been enumerated, in addition to sixty-four revisions of older hymns, and thirteen religious songs. Especially noteworthy was his *Poetische Uebersetzung der Psalmen mit Abhandlungen über dieselben* (4 vols., Leipsic, 1755–64). Some of his hymns are reminiscent of the swing of Klopstock, while others recall the measured movement of Gellert, but in too many cases quality was sacrificed to quantity.

CARL BERTHEAU.

BIBLIOGRAPHY: K. H. Jördens, *Lexikon deutscher Dichter*, i. 328–347, v. 828 sqq., Leipsic, 1806–10; E. E. Koch, *Geschichte des Kirchenlieds*, vi. 334–344, Stuttgart, 1869; S. W. Duffield, *English Hymns*, p. 589, New York, 1886; Julian, *Hymnology*, pp. 267–268; *ADB*, iv. 550.

CRAMER, SAMUEL: Dutch Mennonite; b. at Middelburg, Holland, July 3, 1842. He was educated at the Athenæum of Amsterdam and the universities of Heidelberg and Zurich, and after being a Mennonite pastor at Zijldijk (1866–70), Emden, Hanover (1870–72), Enschede (1872–85), and Zwolle (1885–90), was appointed to his present position of professor of practical theology at the Mennonite theological seminary of Amsterdam. He is a member of the editorial board of Teyler's *Theologisch Tijdschrift*, an associate editor (with F. Pijper of Leyden) of the *Bibliotheca Reformatoria Neerlandica*, and editor of the *Doopsgezinde Bijdragen*.

CRANE, LOUIS BURTON: Presbyterian; b. at Mt. Sterling, Ill., Apr. 23, 1869. He studied at Princeton University (B.A., 1891), Princeton Theological Seminary, and Berlin, Erlangen, and Giessen. He was pastor of the First Presbyterian Church, Princeton, N. J. (1896–99), and Calvary Presbyterian Church, Buffalo, N. Y. (1899–1902). In 1902–05 he was professor of New Testament literature and interpretation in Chicago Theological

Seminary, and since 1906 has been pastor of Brainerd Union Church, Easton, Pa. He has written *The Teaching of Jesus Concerning the Holy Spirit* (New York, 1905).

CRANMER, THOMAS: The first Protestant archbishop of Canterbury; b. at Aslacton (9 m. e. of Nottingham), Nottinghamshire, July 2, 1489; d. at Oxford Mar. 21, 1556. He spent eight years at Jesus College, Cambridge, where he took his B.A. in 1510 or 1511 and his M.A. in 1515, and was elected to a fellowship. About the time of the publication of Erasmus's New Testament (1516) and Luther's theses (1517), he began a systematic study of the Scriptures; he was ordained before 1520, and in that year was university preacher and examiner in theology. About 1525 he had begun "in private to pray for the abolition of the papal power in England," but did not commit himself openly.

Connection with the Royal Divorce.

In the summer of 1529, talking over the question of the divorce with the king's chief agents, Fox and Gardiner, Cranmer suggested taking the matter out of the hands of the lawyers and referring it to the theologians of the universities. Henry grasped at the suggestion, summoned Cranmer, and commissioned the preparation of a treatise on the question, making use of Cranmer's influence also in other ways, and attaching him to the embassy which left England early in 1530 to see the pope and the emperor. He brought back little definite result, but the king rewarded his services by the gift of the archdeaconry of Taunton, and early in 1532 made him ambassador to the emperor. During his sojourn in Germany he was brought much into contact with the Lutheran leader Osiander, and married his niece Margaret. In the autumn of the same year Henry determined to appoint him to the archbishopric of Canterbury, vacant by Warham's death, and he was consecrated on Mar. 30, 1533, after having drawn up a formal protest to the effect that he would consider the oath of obedience to the pope a form and not a reality, and that he did not intend to bind himself to do anything contrary to the king and commonwealth of England, or to restrain his liberty in things pertaining to the reformation of the Christian religion and the government of the Church of England. In April he asked the king's leave to proceed with the trial of Catherine's case, opened his court in May, and on the 23d pronounced sentence, declaring that the marriage of Henry and Catherine had been void from the beginning. Five days later he declared the king's marriage with Anne Boleyn valid, and on June 1 crowned her as queen.

The breach with Rome on the side of jurisdiction widened steadily; that in doctrine was somewhat behind it. In 1534 Cranmer issued a pastoral enjoining silence in regard to masses for the dead, prayers to the saints, pilgrimages, and celibacy—points on which it was hoped that an authoritative decision might be reached within a year. In 1536, though speaking with the greatest personal regard for Anne Boleyn, he was obliged officially to pronounce Henry's marriage with her also void, and on the day she was beheaded issued a license for him to marry Lady Jane Seymour.

Beginnings of the Reformation.

The revision of doctrine proceeded by degrees, and was assisted by the publication of the English version of the Scriptures, which had been a favorite project of Cranmer's for some time. He remained at his post under the reactionary system enforced by the Six Articles, but during the last years of Henry's reign was subject to continual assaults from the Roman party. Sheltered by Henry's unfailing protection, he went quietly on maturing his plans for religious reform. He worked at the preparation of English services, of which the Litany that appeared in 1545 was the first to come into use. The First Prayer-book of Edward VI. was, in the form in which it came before Parliament, to all intents and purposes the work of Cranmer, though afterward modified into the shape of a compromise between the two parties. The new ordinal, published in Mar., 1550, was also principally his work. During the reign of Edward VI. he was constantly busy with projects for completing the new order of things, including the revision of the canon law known as *Reformatio legum ecclesiasticarum*, and the Forty-two Articles, afterward reduced to thirty-nine.

The Second Prayer-book of Edward VI. represented Cranmer's furthest advance toward Continental Protestantism; but he adhered firmly to it after Mary's accession, knowing that he did so at the peril of his life. A manifesto which he wrote to define his position got into circulation before he intended it, and led to his arrest in Sept., 1553, and to his trial for treason two months later, on account of his yielding to the plan to proclaim Lady Jane Grey queen.

Fall Under Mary and Death.

He was condemned to death, but his ecclesiastical character made it impossible to carry out the sentence, as the law then stood. For months he lay a prisoner in the Tower, until the passing of the statute *De hæretico comburendo* in Jan., 1555, warned him to prepare for his end. He was taken to Oxford, and there submitted to a searching examination before a court possessing papal jurisdiction. On Nov. 25 he was pronounced contumacious by the pope for not appearing in Rome and solemnly excommunicated. Pole was appointed to the vacant archbishopric, and a commission was issued for Cranmer's degradation and delivery to the secular arm.

He appealed in vain to a general council, and in the following February Bonner and Thirlby went to Oxford to execute the sentence. Cranmer now signed the documents which have been known as his successive recantations; but the first three, at least, are not really recantations, but submissions to authority, such as his political principles always impelled him to make. His fifth, or real, recantation was signed rather under the influence of seductive hopes held out to him than under that of fear. It surrendered every point for which he had fought, anathematized the whole heresy of Luther and Zwingli, and recognized the pope as Christ's vicar and supreme head of the Church on earth. A sixth and still more humiliating confession was signed on Mar. 18. When he saw that all availed nothing, and that his death was resolved on, he braced himself to a final effort, publicly recanted his recantations and heroically met his fate, dying by fire in Broad Street, Oxford, on the same spot where Ridley and Latimer had already suffered. He was a man of simple and amiable character, a learned theologian, as well as a great patron of learning in others. Though naturally of a shrinking, sensitive temperament and a somewhat slow and hesitating mind, when once he saw his duty he showed no lack of courage; and if at the last "he tried to concede that impossible change of belief which his inquisitors required, he redeemed his fall by a heroism in the hour of death to which history can find few parallels."

Bibliography: Cranmer's *Remains* were collected by H. Jenkyns, 4 vols., Oxford, 1833; his *Works* were edited by J. E. Cox, for the Parker Society, 2 vols., London, 1844-1846; and his *Letters* in *Letters of the Martyrs of the English Church*, ib. 1883. Sources are: J. Strype, *Memorials of Cranmer*, 2 vols., Oxford, 1840 (contains appendix of documents); idem, *Ecclesiastical Memorials*, 3 vols., London, 1842; *Narratives of the Days of the Reformation . . . with Two Contemporary Biographies of Archbishop Cranmer*, ed. J. G. Nichols for Camden Society, ib. 1859. There are *Lives* by H. J. Todd, London, 1831; C. W. Le Bas, ib. 1833; W. F. Hook, in *Lives of Archbishops of Canterbury*, vols. v.-vii., 12 vols., ib. 1860-77; C. H. Collette, ib. 1887; A. J. Mason, ib. 1898; A. F. Pollard, New York, 1904. Consult also: A. D. Innes, *Cranmer and the Reformation in England*, Edinburgh, 1900; *DNB*, xiii. 19-31.

CRANSTON, EARL: Methodist Episcopal bishop; b. at Athens, O., June 27, 1840. He studied at Ohio University, Athens, O. (B.A., 1861), and served throughout the Civil War in the Ohio infantry and West Virginia cavalry, being promoted captain. He entered the Ohio Conference of the Methodist Episcopal ministry in 1867, and after holding various pastorates for fourteen years was elected publishing agent of his denomination in 1884. In 1896 he was elected bishop, and spent the years 1898-1900 in an official tour of inspection which covered China, Japan, and Korea. Since 1903 he has had special charge of the Methodist Episcopal missions in Mexico. He was one of the founders of Denver University, and has been treasurer and a member of the examining board of the Freedmen's Aid and Southern Education Society, as well as treasurer of the trustees of the Methodist Episcopal Church (at large) and a trustee of Ohio University.

CRAPSEY, ALGERNON SIDNEY: Protestant Episcopalian; b. at Fairmount, O., June 28, 1847. He was graduated at St. Stephen's College, Annandale, N. Y. (1869), and at the General Theological Seminary (1872). He was on the staff of Trinity Church, New York City, 1872-79; rector of St. Andrew's, Rochester, N. Y., 1879-1906, when he was convicted of violating his ordination vows in denying certain statements of the Apostles' Creed, particularly the Virgin Birth. In theology he holds "to the theistic conception of the universe; one God who is all in all; Jesus the son of Joseph, the manifestation of God in the ethical sphere," while to him "the catholic creeds are the interpretation of God to the Greco-Roman world," and "to love God and man is salvation." He has written: *Five Sorrowful Mysteries* (New York, 1883); *Five Joyful Mysteries* (1885); *A Voice in the Wilderness* (1897); *Life and Labors of Sarah Wisner Thorne* (1900); and *Religion and Politics* (1905).

CRATO OF CRAFFTHEIM. See Krafft, Johann.

CRAVEN, ELIJAH RICHARDSON: Presbyterian; b. at Washington, D. C., Mar. 28, 1824; d. at Philadelphia, Pa., Jan. 5, 1908. He studied at the College of New Jersey (B.A., 1842) and Princeton Theological Seminary (1848), meanwhile studying law (1842-44) and being tutor in mathematics at the College of New Jersey (1847-1849). He was pastor of the Reformed (Dutch) Church at Somerville, N. J., 1850-54, and of the Third Presbyterian Church, Newark, N. J., 1854-1887; secretary of the Presbyterian Board of Publication and Sabbath School Work 1887-1904, when he retired as secretary emeritus. He was chairman of the committee for the revision of the Book of Discipline of the Presbyterian Church 1879-82, and moderator of the General Assembly of the Presbyterian Church, North, in 1885. In theology he was an Old School Presbyterian. He edited the American edition of J. P. Lange's *Commentary on the Book of Revelation* (New York, 1874).

CRAWFORD, CLARENCE KERR: Presbyterian (Southern Church); b. at Perryville, Ky., Mar. 16, 1864. He studied at Centre College, Danville, Ky. (B.A., 1884), and Danville Theological Seminary (1889). He was tutor in Hebrew (1887-96) and professor of Old Testament exegesis (1897-1901) in the latter institution, and since its consolidation with the Louisville Theological Seminary in 1901 to form the Presbyterian Theological Seminary of Kentucky at Louisville he has been professor of Old Testament exegesis and hermeneutics in the new institution. In theological position he is a liberal conservative.

CREAGH, crēg, JOHN THOMAS: Roman Catholic; b. at Wakefield, Mass., Mar. 7, 1870. He studied at Boston College (B.A., 1891), St. John's Seminary, Brighton, Mass., and the Seminario Romano, Rome (S.T.D., 1896; J.C.D., 1897), and in 1896 was appointed professor of canon law in the Catholic University of America, Washington. He has been lecturer on Religion at Trinity College, Washington, D. C., since 1902, and has written *Remarriage After Divorce* (New York, 1905).

CREATION, BABYLONIAN ACCOUNTS: Until 1875 knowledge of the Babylonian conception of creation had come only through Berosus (a Babylonian priest of Marduk, c. 300 B.C.), whose narrative was transmitted by Alexander Polyhistor, from whose book probably it was taken by Eusebius into his *Chronicon* (book i.). This account tells of a primeval darkness in which beings combining parts of the form of man, beast, and bird inhabited a watery waste along with reptiles, fishes, and monsters, all under the rule of Thamte (Tiamat; see below). Marduk came, cut Thamte in two, of one

Account of Berosus.

half creating the heaven and of the other the earth, and destroyed or shut up the monsters whom she had ruled. This, however, left an uninhabited earth which was peopled by the device of cutting off Marduk's head (at his direction), when the blood which fell was mixed with earth by the gods, men and animals being formed from the mixture. Marduk created also the heavenly bodies.

In 1875 George Smith discovered a tablet from the library of Asshurbanipal which ran in part parallel with the account of Berosus. This he translated, in great part correctly, but made mistakes which misled many. From time to time other fragments were found and translated, **Cuneiform Accounts.** in some of which rightly and in others mistakenly parts of the creation narrative were seen. Thus the so-called "Cuthæan account" is now shown not to refer to creation but to the story of a king of Cutha. It soon became evident from the diversities that there were several accounts current in early times and that creation was attributed in different centers to different deities.

The creation account of Babylonia which finally became current, to which Mr. Smith's tablet belonged, has finally by L. W. King of the British Museum been shown to have been written on a series of seven tablets as a narrative poem in 994 lines, of which more than half are now fully recovered, and so much of the rest that three-quarters of the whole text are now in hand. The tablets carried from 138 to 146 lines each, and in some cases there are at least four copies of parts of the inscription, Mr. King's reconstruction involving the use of forty-nine separate tablets. These are of different periods, none older than the Assyrian period and some as late as the Persian, a few being the exercise studies of Babylonian students.

The epic was known to Babylonians from the opening words as the "When above" series. This account is in part at least a theogony as well as a cosmogony, this part having its closest parallel in the Japanese theogony. The primal existences are said to have been Apsu, "the deep," Mummu, "confusion" (?), and Tiamat (Hebr. **Content of the Latter.** *Tehom*), "Chaos"—watery existences which in darkness mingled their floods. No gods then existed. In the course of time appeared the primal gods Lahmu and Lahamu; then Anshar and Kishar, while Anu's name is read in a much mutilated section. After a long gap in the text it appears that in consequence of the existence of the gods an orderliness was coming into being because of which Apsu and Mummu precipitated a conflict with the gods in which Ea by his wisdom defeated the opponents of order. A second conflict was forced by Tiamat, a monster so forbidding that the gods could not stand before her until Marduk stood forth as their champion on condition that he be recognized as supreme among them. After a banquet of the gods at which the terms were accepted Marduk overcame the monster and with nets captured and imprisoned or slew her and her hosts. With the fourth tablet the narrative of creative work begins. Marduk cleft in two the body of Tiamat, and out of one half made the firmament restraining the upper waters, created heaven, and appointed to their stations Anu, Bel, and Ea. He marked out the years, months, and days, appointing for this office the heavenly bodies. Probably the fifth tablet told of the creation of trees and plants, since in the closing ode of praise Marduk is hailed as lord and giver of vegetation. The sixth tablet tells of the creation of man, caused by the plaint of the gods that there was no one to minister to them. To this end Marduk's blood was used as in the account of Berosus.

A variant is found in a tablet according to which originally there was no heaven, earth, vegetation, house, or city, only a watery waste. Marduk laid a reed on the water, poured on it dust which he created, made a habitation for the gods, and then with the help of the goddess Amaru created man and beast, then the rivers of Babylonia, and dammed out the sea and erected houses and cities. Still other texts, one in Sumerian and a parallel in Semitic, give a variant account of the creation of sun and moon.

The analysis of the principal myth pieced out by Mr. King reveals a complex narrative evidently built up after Marduk became chief deity and in his honor, the composite showing traces of diverse origin of the components in centers where other deities than Marduk were honored. The double contest, the conception of the victory by Ea in the first battle, suggestions of participation by En-lil, and the synonymity of the names of **Composite Origin.** the three primeval existences bespeak separate myths of diverse origin, which were combined into the narrative which became dominant. This conclusion is corroborated by references in isolated texts to the creative work of Ea, En-lil, Ishtar, and other deities. While none of the extant texts are earlier than the time of Asshurbanipal, the essential facts are referred to as early as the third pre-Christian millennium. The most likely time for the construction of the epic is the age of Hammurabi.

The points of contact with the Hebrew narrative have been overrated through the influence of George Smith. The Babylonian text is still too fragmentary to afford a satisfactory basis of comparison. The similarities are (1) the original watery chaos, (2) the creation of the firmament (a common ethnic notion), (3) the creation of the heavenly bodies as rulers of time, (4) the crowning of creative operations by the production of man (in one case by the blood of deity, in the other by his breath), and (5) the coincidence of *Tiamat* and *Tehom* (Gen. i. 2) and of *iṣṣimu* and *eẓem*, "bone" (Gen. ii. 23), in the two narratives.

GEO. W. GILMORE.

BIBLIOGRAPHY: The most important book is L. W. King, *Seven Tablets of Creation*, 2 vols., London, 1902. Consult: George Smith, *Chaldæan . . . Genesis*, New York, 1876 (the epoch-making work); P. Jensen, *Kosmologie der Babylonier*, Strasburg, 1890; idem, *Mythen und Epen*, Berlin, 1900; H. Gunkel, *Schöpfung und Chaos*, Göttingen, 1895 (traces relationship of Hebrew and Babylonian literature); F. Delitzsch, *Die babylonische Weltschöpfungslehre*, Leipsic, 1896; C. J. Ball, *Light from the East*, London, 1899; H. Radan, in *Monist*, xii. 604 sqq., xiv. 81-87; *Assyrian and Babylonian Literature*, ed. R. F. Harper, pp. 282-303, New York, 1901.

CREATION AND PRESERVATION OF THE WORLD.

I. The Biblical and Theological Doctrine: The idea of the origin of the universe through the creative power of God is inseparable from the fundamental conception of monotheism. If there is but one living, personal God, nothing in the world can have come into being but through his will. Nowhere is this idea more clearly expressed than in the Old and New Testaments. According to the Mosaic account, God created "the heaven and the earth," that is, the whole natural universe, "in the beginning" of all temporal being. In six working-days he called into existence all inorganic and organic beings by the simple word of power, "Let there be" this or that (Gen. i. 1–ii. 3). God is not less the absolute creator of the world to the authors of Ps. xxxiii. and civ. and Job xxxviii. With the same definiteness the deutero-canonical or apocryphal literature of pre-Christian Judaism emphasizes the monotheistic nature of the idea of creation (Ecclus. xvi. 26–xvii. 9; II Macc. vii. 28; Wisd. xi. 17 sqq.). In the New Testament the content of the Mosaic cosmogony is presupposed in numerous sayings of Christ and his apostles, as in those which mention the foundation of the world (John i. 24; Matt. xxv. 24; Luke xi. 50; Eph. i. 4; I Pet. i. 20; Heb. iv. 3), the creation of man and woman (Matt. xix. 4–6; Acts xvii. 24–26; I Tim. ii. 13), and the Sabbath, on which God rested (Heb. iv. 4; cf. John v. 17). God is repeatedly spoken of as the Lord of heaven and earth, who made both (Matt. xi. 25; Luke x. 21; Acts xvii. 24; cf. Rev. iv. 11); as the primal source, of whom are all things (I Cor. viii. 6; Rom. xi. 36; cf. Eph. iv. 6); as the everlasting Father, who through the Son made the world (John i. 3; Col. i. 15–18; Heb. i. 2); as the invisible God, who reveals his eternal power and Godhead by the works of his hands (Rom. i. 20; Acts xiv. 17). The creation of the world out of nothing is mentioned at least once in the New Testament (Heb. xi. 3).

On the basis of this Biblical teaching the dogmatic theology of the Church developed. The most important Fathers, the scholastics, and the old Protestant theologians are in essential agreement in the doctrine of a miraculous creation of the world out of nothing. The distinction is made between a first or immediate and a second or mediate creation. The former is the creation of "the heavens and the earth," i.e., of the substance of the universe both within and without this world, as well as of purely spiritual or immaterial essences. The second is the gradual development and organization of the matter immediately created out of nothing. As the operative cause of creation the entire Trinity is named, the Father creating the world by the Son in the Holy Ghost (Ps. xxxiii. 6; Gen. i. 2; John i. 3; Heb. i. 2; Col. i. 16; cf. also Rom. xi. 36; Eph. iv. 6). As the final end of creation dogmatic theology places the glorification of God or the complete revelation of his power, wisdom, and goodness—as the intermediate end the beatification of men through their union with God (cf. Gen. i. 31; Ps. viii. 5, xix. 2, cxv. 16; Is. xlv. 18; Acts xvii. 26; I Cor. xv. 46).

The variations from this doctrine which have made their appearance in the history of human speculation have related either to the creative subject or to the manner of creation, modifying either the conception of a conscious personal Creator or that of a determinate process of creation rising by a definite progression to man. On the first point, they are inclined toward changing creation into a mere cosmogony or slow development of the world; on the second, toward neglecting the element of cosmogony or well-ordered plan in creation. The former is the common error of all pagan doctrines of the origin of the universe, as well as of such pagan-pantheistic speculation as has taken place within the Church. The doctrine of later Judaism and the Judaizing supernaturalism of many of the Fathers and late Christian thinkers suffers, on the other hand, from too exclusive monotheistic emphasizing of the absolute action of God in creation.

II. The Cosmogonies of Ancient and Modern Paganism: To pagan thought, creation in its essence is a slow self-originating process, into which the theogonic element enters, if at all, only in the final stages. Its result is the universe considered as mere *thusis*, or nature, not as *ktisis*, or the creature. This is true equally of the polytheistic, dualistic, and pantheistic systems of non-Christian paganism, of modern pantheistic tendencies with Christian form, and of their logical consequence, atheistic materialism.

1. The Mythological Cosmogonies of Paganism Proper: These are all characterized by some notion of emanation; they consider the world and the substances within it as effluxes of the Godhead, and thus suggest a certain coherence of matter and the created world of spirits with God. This is true also of the dualistic religions, according to which the world originates from the joint action of the emanations from the good god of light with those from the god of darkness—either in the way of a hostile conflict of the two principles, as in the Persian legend, or in that of the parallel development of both, as in the mythologies of the Slavic, and to some extent of the Germanic, peoples. Into both the dualistic and the pantheistic systems much that is originally polytheistic has penetrated, just as scarcely any developed pagan cosmogony is without suggestion of the monotheistic conception. A complete classification of the pagan cosmogonies will not be attempted here; it will be sufficient to glance at the most characteristic ones, beginning with those most closely related to the Old Testament account.

According to the Persian myth in the *Bundahishn*, Ormuzd, with the Amshaspands, created the world in six periods by his word (see ZOROASTER, ZOROASTRIANISM). The usual order is the heavens and the light, the water, the earth, the trees, the animals, and men as descendants of the archetypal man Gayomart. The division of the process into definite periods of one thousand years is apparently later, but in both earlier and later sources an absolute creation out of nothing is affirmed. Still more definitely the traditional story of the Etruscans seems to point to an original connection with the Old Testament. The world is here said to have been created by God in six periods of one thousand years—first, heaven and earth, then the firmament, the sea and other waters, the sun, moon, and stars, the animals, and lastly men. As the earliest authority for this belief is Suidas (s.v. Τυρρηνία), it is hardly possible to avoid the conclusion of Jewish or Christian influences in the account. Much fuller of obscure mythological elements are the cosmogonies of several peoples of Western Asia. In the Old Babylonian, according to Berosus (about 300 B.C.), the primitive chaos was dominated by the sea-goddess Markaya or Homoroka, i.e., the ocean; then the supreme god Bel-Zeus split her in two and out of one half made the heavens, out of the other half the earth; then Bel had his own head cut off, and men were formed out of the blood which flowed from him, mixed with earth (see CREATION, BABYLONIAN ACCOUNTS). Some confused similarities to the Old Testament account, with a large admixture of theogonic myths, are found in the Phenician legends, as given by the somewhat doubtful authority Sanchuniathon. According to this, the spirit which, as a dark wind, brooded over the primeval chaos was in some way united with the matter of this chaos; and out of this union, which is called Desire, originated first a fertile watery slime in which lay concealed the seed of all things; then the heaven, in the shape of an egg, out of which came the sun, moon, and stars, the air and the sea, the clouds and the wind, thunder and lightning; and finally, awakened by the thunder, intellectual beings of both sexes. In the cosmogonies of the Greeks and the Egyptians, partially related to these, the gods originate together with the forming world. According to the oldest Greek legend in Hesiod, out of chaos proceeded first Gaia, Tartaros, Eros (the earth, the depths, and love); next the pair Erebos and Nyx (darkness and night), who produced Aither and Hemera (the light of heaven and the day). Gaia then brought forth at intervals other cosmic powers and the Titans from whom Zeus, the other gods of Olympus, and men were descended. A somewhat similar cosmogony, though rather more influenced by Eastern myths, is found in Aristophanes.

According to the Egyptian cosmogony, as given by Diodorus Siculus, the elements originally mixed in chaos were separated by a self-originating movement of air; the heavier ones sank and gradually separated into land and sea, under the continuous impulse of this movement. Out of the earth, while it still retained a half-fluid character, the heat of the sun generated animals. The older Egyptian mythology is more monotheistic. Amun, or Chnum, or Thoth appears as the supreme creative god, who produces the heavens, earth and its vegetation, animals, men, and gods. Here also there are several remarkable reminders of Genesis.

In the oldest religious literature of India, as in the Rig-Veda, there are also traces of monotheism. The much later book of Manu is more fantastic. According to it the universe was once a confused chaotic darkness; God, the great originator of all things, appeared and drove away the darkness by his light, creating first water, and in it the seed of light. Out of this seed developed a golden egg, in which Brahma sat a whole year in calm meditation, finally breaking it and making heaven and earth out of its halves. A similar process is described in the *Mahabharata* and generally in the later sources of Indian mythology, some of which go more into detail, as in deducing various elements from the different parts of Brahma's body. The notion of the primeval egg is found in other mythologies, such as the old Chinese, the Japanese, the Finnish (in the ancient epos *Kalewala* the formation of heaven and earth from the two halves of the egg is described just as by Manu), and even that of the South Sea Islands. Again, the story of the origin of different parts of the world from the severed limbs of a gigantic primitive man or anthropomorphic god is found also in the old Germanic and Scandinavian cosmogony.

As common traits of all these mythological cosmogonies may be mentioned the development of the process of formation from less perfect to more perfect, or from original chaos to the final creation of man; the predominance of water in the original condition of the earth; the evolution of a luminous or spiritual principle which reacts on this primeval water; and finally the emphasis laid upon the godlike origin of man, or his mediate relation to the Deity, as a ground of superiority over the animals generated from the earth by elementary forces.

2. Cosmogonic Notions in Ancient, especially Greek, Philosophy: The philosophy of both Ionians and Dorians is essentially a natural philosophy, and thus largely cosmological. The Ionian philosophers searched for the material principle of things, which they defined variously. Thales found it in water or abstract moisture; Anaximander in the *apeiron*, i.e., infinite and indefinite primeval substance; Anaximenes in the air; Heraclitus in ethereal fire; Anaxagoras in the seeds of things, once inextricably intermingled in chaos, then disentangled and formed into a well-ordered cosmos by the divine spirit, the absolutely simple, indivisible, impassible *nous;* Leucippus and Democritus in the atoms, those indivisible, infinitely small bodies which are distinguished from each other not by their qualities, but only geometrically by form, position, and arrangement, and whose sum constitutes abstract fulness in contrast with the other primeval principle of emptiness or nothingness. The Doric philosophers in Magna Græcia and Sicily directed their attention toward discovering an ideal or formal principle of things. The Pythagoreans found it in numbers, geometrical forms, and relations; the Eleatics (Xenophanes, Parmenides, Zeno, Melissus) in the conceptual unity of being. A clever attempt to combine the Ionic and Eleatic standpoints was made by Empedocles, who defined four material and two ideal elements or roots of things—the former being earth, water, air, and fire, the latter the motive powers of love and hate, to one of which the union, to the other the separation of things in the process of world-formation is attributed. See MATERIALISM.

In the main period of Greek philosophy the opposition between idealistic and realistic (or materialistic) cosmology recurs in the relation of the Platonic to the Aristotelian theory, then in that of the Stoic to the Epicurean. **Plato**, who considered ideas, and especially the highest, that of the Good, as the only eternal things, asserts the temporal nature of the world, or at most makes it to have been created by God, the absolute Good, out of matter without quality and actually unreal. First the *Anima mundi*, or soul of the world, was formed by harmonic union of indivisible and divisible substance, then the body of the world. The relation of the world-soul to the material universe corresponds, in the human microcosm, to that between the immortal soul with its seat in the head and the body with its two inferior souls. **Aristotle**, on the other hand, declared the world to be finite in space or extension, but infinite in time. According to him, the first thing to be set in motion by the "immovable mover" was the heaven of the fixed stars, as the highest of the spheres which surround the earth. The cosmology of the **Stoics**, in consequence of their generally idealistic attitude, approached more closely to the Platonic and the Eleatic than to Aristotle. They considered the world as eternal, but only in so far as it is the result or the image of the eternal power of the Godhead which works in it. This Godhead, who is in the world as an all-pervading breath, as a formative fire, as a rational soul, and includes in itself the individual rational type-forms or *logoi spermatikoi*, separates itself through a creative process into four elements, as well as into bodies formed by various combinations of them. After the expiration of a certain period things return, by a consuming conflagration, once more into the Godhead, which then creates the world anew, only to destroy it once more when the time comes. **Epicurus** and his school, going back for their physics to the realistic natural philosophers, especially Democritus, affirm the eternity of space, and in it of atoms distinguished by size, shape, and weight. These atoms, tending downward on account of their weight, generate by collision certain movements which end in the rotary motion that forms worlds, countless in number. Animals and men are mere products of the earth; the formation of the latter (whose souls are substances with the nature of air and fire, consisting of refined atoms, diffused throughout the whole body) includes a gradual evolution toward perfection.

Coming to the philosophical movements which follow the close of independent intellectual life in Greece (the last century B.C.), the **Skeptics** declared all certain knowledge on these subjects impossible, while the **Eclectics**, such as Cicero, attempted to combine various elements of the Platonic, Stoic, and Epicurean cosmology. These problems were taken up with still greater interest by the theosophic-syncretistic schools of the last century before and the first after Christ—especially the Jewish-Alexandrian school, the Neo-Pythagoreans, and the Neoplatonists. According to **Philo**, the principal representative of the first-named, in contrast with God as the absolute active principle, stands matter without form or quality as the principle of absolute passivity; the former produces first the world of ideas (the Logos or *kosmos noetos*), and then impresses the type of this ideal world on the eternal matter. The Logos, or divine ideal world, which according to this doctrine was the mediate cause of the world's existence, became in the **Neo-Pythagorean**, partially Gnostic system of Numenius of Apamea (c. 170) the demiurge, a second God beside the supreme and purely spiritual God, or *Nous*. This second God, who gains by contemplation of the transcendental archetypes the knowledge which enables him to exercise creative power on matter, constructs out of it the world as a sort of third God, or the offspring of the two higher ones. Finally, in **Neoplatonism** (q.v.), especially with Plotinus and Porphyry, the connecting principle in the formation of the universe is again the world of ideas, which is not, however, as with Plato, identified with the Godhead, but appears as an emanation or radiation from the highest Good. It generates souls in its image, together with the bodies dependent upon and governed by them, as well as the other beings perceptible by the sense or material. Matter in itself is a formless, negative substance which gains form and life first by the entrance of the higher powers, the *logoi*, which proceed from the *Nous* and its ideas.

3. The Gnostic-Manichean Cosmogonies: The ideal and abstract treatment of the question which has been seen in the speculation of these philosophers, together with much more fantastic and arbitrary solutions of the problem which come from the mythical cosmogonies of the still older period, was to a certain extent combined with Christian ideas in the **Gnostic** theories. All of them appeared as paganizing perversions of the Christian revelation. They have a more or less hostile attitude toward the Old Testament, although they usually attempt to find a place for its monotheistic teaching concerning the creation and government of the world in their practically pagan systems. For this purpose they make use of the peculiar figure of the demiurge. The demiurge of the Gnostics is not, however, a higher divine principle, like the Platonic Logos, but rather a representative of the life of the world as distinguished from God. He is generally considered from the standpoint of the natural world which is to be overcome and elevated into a higher form of existence in the spiritual kingdom of Christ. The creation accomplished by him is only an imperfect preliminary to redemption; and this he is able to bring about neither by himself nor by the psychic Messiah sent by him. For it the spiritual Christ is required, the higher eon who is revealed at his baptism in Jordan as stronger than the demiurgic Messiah, coming to execute his mission by a docetic life and death. Gnostic speculation took two distinct forms—the Western, or Greek-Egyptian, based largely upon Platonic thought, and the Eastern, or Persian-Syrian, following more the dualistic thought of the Parsees. In the former the transition from the divine being and life to the development of the world appears as an emanation or the production of a series of hypostatic effluxes from the world of light (the *Pleroma*), growing weaker and less divine the farther they go, down to the demiurge, the lowest, to whom the formation of formless or empty matter is attributed. The latter class considered the world essentially as a product of conflict between the eons of the kingdom of light and Satan and his demons, in which matter, created and dominated by Satan and thus a positive efflux of the evil principle, forms the battle-ground, and is partially wrested from him by the good eons. See GNOSTICISM.

The history of **Manicheanism**, a theory of the world whose foundation is more pagan than Christian, has been shown by recent investigation to have a special importance for the development of Christian thought on its heretical side. The roots of this remarkable syncretistic religion reach down into the primitive age of Christianity, and are connected with the Jewish-Christian and Gnostic sects of the Elkesaites and Mandæans; and the offshoots of the developed Persian Manicheanism of the third century appear throughout the latter history of medieval sects, both Eastern and Western—Priscillians, Paulicians, Euchites, Bogomiles, and Albigenses. Some of their ideas, especially those relating to the creation of the world and of man, have even had their influence on the systems of some modern Christian theosophists, such as Weigel and Jakob Böhme. Both ancient and medieval Manicheanism dispensed with the figure of the demiurge, and made the whole earthly or material creation, including mankind, both body and soul, a product of Satan and his demons as imitators of the creative activity of the Light-god. See MANICHEANS; and MANDÆANS.

4. Speculative Cosmogonies of the Modern Pantheistic-Materialistic Natural Philosophy: These are not without points of contact with the cosmological theories of the old Greek philosophers, and even with those of the Gnostic and of the old pagan mythologies. The principal difference is that modern pantheistic paganism more completely excludes the free creative and formative operation of a personal will. The most thoroughgoing in this direction is **materialism** proper or logical **sensualism**, as found in the systems of English freethinkers and deists since Hobbes, the French Encyclopedists of the eighteenth century, and the scientific atomistic theories of modern Germany, best known through Haeckel. This, excluding a personal Creator and all spirit-life, together with freedom, immortality, and all ethical principles, recognizes only abstract matter, divided into an infinite number of hypothetical atoms, infinitely small, as the operative cause and explanation of all present and past phenomena of life. This view is most logically carried out in Czolbe's *Neue Darstellung des Sensualismus* (Leipsic, 1855), according to which the world is without beginning as without end; matter exists from eternity, in its smallest atoms as well as in its organic forms; it is absolutely without beginning, coeval with the world-soul, which may be considered as the principle which holds it together and vivifies it. See ENCYCLOPEDISTS; and MATERIALISM.

In contrast with this sensualistic theory of the eternity of the world, Pantheism (q.v.) considers the universe, both in matter and form, as temporal, but regards it as the efflux or inevitable evolution of an eternal power of idea which underlies it. Where this absolute idea is considered as a primeval union of spirit and nature, or of thinking and extended substance, separating in creation, it leads to the realistic form of the pantheist theory, as represented by Spinoza and Schelling; where it is conceived as being entirely without substance, as absolute spirit, the idealistic form results, which is represented by Fichte and Hegel. For both schools the acceptance of a real creative act is impossible, since they deny any transcendence of God over nature, and consider it rather as a special form of divine existence, as a phase of development or method of manifestation of the divine principle dwelling in it and thus fully realizing itself. To all of these philosophers the world is practically an emanation of the primal divine spirit, a successive self-potentiation of the absolute idea, according to which this original nothing develops itself through the stages of ether, cosmic matter, coarse planetary matter, and organic substance up to the existence, both material and spiritual, of animal and human organisms. For the formation of space and of the earth as a body the nebular hypothesis of Kant and Laplace is taken as a basis; for the origin of the geological structure of the earth, the quietistic theory of Lyell and his school; and for the analogous development of the organic species of the vegetable and animal kingdoms, the theory of evolution as held by Darwin and Spencer.

III. The Creation Theories of the Older Judaism and the Judaizing Christianity of Many Fathers and Modern Theologians: In contrast with the systems already discussed, which emphasize the cosmogonic element at the expense of the monotheistic, these latter dwell exclusively on God's action in creation, to the neglect of what may be accomplished by the powers and laws set in motion by him.

1. In Judaism Proper: Here not only is the creation of heaven and earth out of nothing strongly emphasized, but special stress is laid on the relative nothingness or weakness of the creature in comparison with God (Wisd. xi. 23; Ps. xxiii. 6; Isa. xlviii. 13; Judith xvi. 18; Ps. xcvii. 5; Mic. i. 4; Rev. vi. 13). In harmony with the unconditional supernaturalism, nay, acosmism of such a view, it is not surprising to find the six creative days of Genesis taken in the strict literal sense, or even minimized into mere points of time in a definite prearranged sequence. The last is the case especially with Philo, who, in spite of his Platonic acceptance of the eternity of matter, regards its formation into an orderly cosmos as a work which God could, if necessary, have accomplished in a moment, and which he divided into six days merely for the sake of orderly procedure.

2. In the Patristic Period: Here the absolute nothingness out of which God created the world is sharply emphasized, as by Tertullian in opposition to the dualism of the Gnostic Hermogenes, and by later representatives of the ecclesiastical creationism, such as Ambrose, Jerome, and the scholastics from Peter Lombard. Here again occurs the assertion that God needed no more than an instant for the creation of the world. The Alexandrian school especially followed Philo's view on this point; Clement even denies that the world was created in time, since time came into existence with created things. Origen, asserting the same thing, places over against it an eternally creative activity of God, which, indeed, he confines to the production of the spiritual world. Athanasius, Basil, and Gregory of Nyssa assert the same practically instantaneous and extratemporal creation; and so also Ambrose and Augustine in the West. The underlying thought of a creation not gradual but at once concluded, and the accompanying proposition that the world was made "not in time, but with time," descended from Augustine and the schoolmen, and so to the common orthodox teaching.

3. In Modern Times: Even here a certain Judaising or abstract monotheistic treatment of the subject is to be noticed—not only among Roman Catholic theologians, but also within the boundaries of Protestantism, where the literal interpretation of the six days as six periods of twenty-four hours, generally given in orthodox dogmatics from Luther on, retained the extreme supernaturalist character, left no space for organically independent elements, and brought on an inevitable conflict with the ascertained facts of geology and astronomy. These sciences have demonstrated the origin of the heavenly bodies before the earth; the slow and gradual origin of the mountains and the strata of the earth's surface; and a long succession of many organisms, now for the most part vanished and evidenced only by fossil remains, as preliminary to those existing at present. On the other hand, it has been realized that the account in Genesis, so far from requiring a literal interpretation of the six days, lends itself readily to the explanation of indefinite periods of time—a view which is supported not only by the cosmogonic passages in Ps. civ. and Job xxxviii., but by the analogy of the old Persian and Babylonian legends of the creation, which are more or less parallel with the Scriptural narrative. Of the various hypotheses put forth by modern apologetics in order to reconcile the account in Genesis with geology and astronomy two deserve mention: one which admits the necessity of the long periods required for the formation of the earth, and conceives them as preceding the six days' work; and one which denies the great duration of the primeval epochs, and considers the geological formations, with the petrifactions contained in them, to have originated after the creative process described in Gen. i. The latter of these is supported by reference to the flood described in Gen. vi.–ix., with its accompanying cataclysms to which ancient legends testify. Its root-ideas are found as early as Tertullian and Hippolytus, and numerous modern writers have adopted the same mode of explaining the presence of petrified shells and skeletons of animals in geological formations. But while this theory has its value as a protest against the extravagant assumptions of geologists, with their formative periods of thousands or even millions of years, it is still untenable on purely scientific grounds. The other, sometimes known as the restitution theory, which places the formative period, of a length sufficient to satisfy geologists, before the six days' work, and regards this as a restoration or setting in order of the confused chaotic results of frequent cataclysms, is objectionable rather on exegetical grounds. This hypothesis, which commonly includes some traces of the partially Gnostic or Manichean idea of the interference of Satan and his demons in the process of creation, seems to have found its first expression in the Arminian theologian Episcopius; its serious scientific defense was first undertaken by J. G. Rosenmüller in his *Antiquissima telluris historia* (Ulm, 1776), while at the same time and later a number of theosophic writers used the idea of restitution in connection with the speculations of Böhme. Whatever its advantages in meeting the contentions of modern science, it is open to the obvious objection that the narrative in Genesis is clearly that of a primitive creation, not of a recreation, and in more than one of its details is irreconcilable with this theory.

IV. The Normal Via Media between Jewish and Pagan Theories: In place of the restitution theory, now usually abandoned, there has been in modern times an attempt to harmonize the conclusions of science and religion by a direct parallel between the days of creation, taken as periods of indeterminate length, and the main epochs of geological development. This was made first by some of the antideistic apologists of the latter eighteenth century, and taken up by Cuvier, the founder of modern paleontology. He was followed by a large number of both theologians and scientists, among others Hugh Miller, J. D. Dana, F. de Rougemont, G. B. Pianciani, Delitzsch, Güttler, Secchi, and Pesnel. This parallel, which is carried out in minute detail by some of its advocates, removes at least a part of the difficulties offered at the first glance by the Scriptural account. Thus the objection that light was created before the sun, which came into being after the earth, is met by the assumption that the narrative in Gen. i. 14–19 is a purely optical or phenomenological one. Certain difficulties, to be sure, still remain unsolved, such as the relation of the six days or periods in the light of their different duration, and their separation from each other, which is given variously by different harmonists. The total number of the geological epochs is considerably more than six (according to some geologists as many as twenty or thirty), so that a direct combination of them with the six days is only possible by a great reduction. In the way of a too specific harmonization stands also the fact that the Mosaic account postulates a gradual progression from vegetable to animal life, and within the latter from one class to another, while according to the geological history plants and animals must have been simultaneously present from the first. In any case, a too strict harmonizing is forbidden by the character of the Biblical narrative, which is not literally historical, but prophetically ideal; it is considered as a sort of inverse prophecy even by some of the Fathers, such as Chrysostom and Severianus. The more this view of the Mosaic narrative is accepted; the more it is realized that its author was intending not to teach the elements of geology, but to reveal the fundamental conceptions of theology; the more it is seen that his standpoint was that of religion, not of natural history, the clearer will it become that it is necessary to give up the idea of carrying out the reconciliation in every detail and to be content with establishing an ideal harmony in the main outlines. It is of no slight value to be able to include in this harmony the fundamental truths of the revealed account: (1) the priority of the inorganic elements of the earth's constitution to the creation of organisms; (2) the separate origin, in accordance with a definite plan, of the various species, orders, and classes of plants and animals; and (3) the constant rising of these representatives of the organic creation to man as the crown and dominant end of the entire process.

This view, if properly realized, leads to a deeper speculative solution of the problem which does justice also to the theological side of the whole subject, its relations to the eternal being and life of the Godhead. If the real Christian or concrete theistic idea of creation is to receive its proper development, it is of the utmost importance to conceive the act of creation as a product of the free Trinitarian self-determination of the personal God. This involves a full and exhaustive utilization of the Scriptural doctrine of the creation of all things through the Son as the absolute archetype of a universe which attains its perfection in the free intellectual life of man made in the image of God (John i. 1–3; Heb. i. 2; I Cor. viii. 6; Col. i. 16); and not less a careful speculative development of the idea of creation in the Spirit of God, or, in the Scriptural phrase, "by the breath of his mouth"—by the formative and vivifying principle from which proceed the organic disposition, differentiation, and development of the world created after the image and by the word of the Son (Ps. xxxiii. 6, civ. 30; Job xxxiii. 4; cf. Gen. i. 2). Through the conception of creation through the Son it is possible to set forth the true nature of the transcendence of God in his creative activity, while the idea of a creation in the Spirit of God brings the immanence of this activity vividly before the mind. The former doctrine serves to utilize what is true in deism for the Christian view, while the latter serves to utilize what is true in pantheism, especially the transmutation or development theory of the modern scientific pantheism. The former takes the abstract monotheistic view of Judaism, as the latter takes the polytheistic, atheistic, or pantheistic view of pagan thought, purifies them both from their one-sided or superstitious or fantastic elements and develops them into a truly Christian or concrete monotheistic belief.

V. Preservation of the World: In the form just outlined, the idea of creation by God is inseparably connected with the idea of the preservation of the world by him. God's "rest" on the seventh day is not mentioned as a contrast with his activity on the preceding six, as a transition to idle inactivity, but merely, in accordance with the radical sense of the Hebrew word, denotes the completion of the work. The New Testament leaves no doubt of this interpretation of God's rest (John v. 17; Heb. iv. 1–10, ii. 3). The doctrine of the Church gives the same view of the relation of God's activity as creator and as preserver. The scholastics designated the conservation of the world as a continuance of creation. Nor is this conservation merely negative. What is required is, in the words of Baier, "a divine action which imports a continuous influence upon created things, such as is convenient and necessary for each according to its nature, to the end that they may be able to continue in their essence and power." This influence is of fundamental importance; together with God's transcendence, his immanence must be asserted. The creation, the preservation, and the governance of the world are an inseparable group of divine activities.

The doctrine in regard to the preservation of the world attains special importance on account of its points of contact with the modern scientific doctrine of evolution. These are sufficiently numerous, since the created world nowhere presents itself to us in any other shape than as a development from lower stages and forms of life to higher and higher ones. God preserves the universe which he has created, not as a lifeless machine eternally standing still, but in a condition of progressive motion; the preservation of the world is practically equivalent to the development of the world. In this doctrine of the preservation of the universe is the point of connection for whatever elements of truth are contained in the theories of Kant and Laplace on the formation of the world and in Darwin's theory of the origin of species; and, though they may be received with caution in the province of the history of creation, freer play may and must be allowed to them in that of the preservation of the world. See Evolution. (O. Zöckler†.)

Bibliography: The most convenient book for a study of comparative cosmology is P. D. C. de la Saussaye, *Lehrbuch der Religionsgeschichte*, 2 vols., Tübingen, 1905. Consult: H. Faye, *Sur l'origine du monde. Théories cosmogoniques des anciens et des modernes*, Paris, 1885; E. B. Tylor, *Primitive Culture*, London, 1903; F. Lukas, *Grundbegriffe su den Kosmogonien der alten Völker*, Leipsic, 1893.

For special cosmogonies: A. V. W. Jackson, *Iranische Religion*, Strasburg, 1900; J. Darmesteter, *Ormuzd et Ahriman*, Paris, 1877; P. Jensen, *Kosmologie der Babylonier*, Strasburg, 1890; G. Maspéro, *Dawn of Civilization*, London, 1896; R. Pietschmann, *Geschichte der Phönicier*, Berlin, 1889; G. St. Clair, *Creation Records in Egypt*, London, 1898; H. W. Wallis, *Cosmology of the Rigveda*, London, 1887; E. H. Meyer, *Die Eddische Kosmogonie*, Freiburg, 1891; J. Curtin, *Creation Myths of*

Primitive America, Boston, 1898; D. G. Brinton, *Myths of the New World*, Philadelphia, 1896.

On the Genesis narrative and its relations to the Babylonian account the later commentaries should be consulted. One of the best single works is H. E. Ryle, *Early Narratives of Genesis*, London, 1892. Consult: W. Baudissin, *Studien zur semitischen Religionsgeschichte*, Leipsic, 1876–78; J. H. Oswald, *Die Schöpfungslehre*, Paderborn, 1885; H. Gunkel, *Schöpfung und Chaos*, Göttingen, 1895 (a remarkable book); L. T. Townsend, *Evolution or Creation, Review of the Scientific and Scriptural Theories of Creation*, New York, 1896; H. Radau, *Creation Story of Gen.* i., Chicago, 1902 (highly commended); Schrader, *KAT*.

For the classical philosophy of creation consult the works on history of philosophy by J. E. Erdman, 3 vols., London, 1893; W. Windelband, New York, 1901; P. Janet and G. Séailles, *History of the Problems of Philosophy*, 2 vols., ib. 1903. For the Gnostic and Manichean cosmologies see works cited under GNOSTICISM and MANICHEANS.

On late Jewish thought consult: A. Schmidl, *Studien über jüdische . . . Religionsphilosophie*, Vienna, 1869; J. Guttmann, *Die Scholastik des dreizehnten Jahrhunderts*, Breslau, 1902.

The following treat the subject from the scientific or philosophic standpoint: J. W. Dawson, *Origin of the World*, London, 1886; C. Wolf, *Les Hypothèses cosmogoniques*, Paris, 1886; D. Nys, *Le Problème cosmologique*, Louvain, 1888; C. Braun, *Ueber Kosmogonie vom Standpunkt christlicher Wissenschaft*, Münster, 1889; E. MacLennan, *Cosmical Evolution*, ib. 1890; E. H. P. A. Haeckel, *History of Creation*, ib. 1892; idem, *Creation or Development*, ib. 1899; *Riddle of the Universe*, New York, 1900 (all of Haeckel's works are evolutionistic); T. Mitchell, *Cosmogony*, ib. 1894; R. S. Foster, *Creation, God in Time and Space*, ib. 1895; J. Guibert, *In the Beginning*, London, 1900; J. M. E. McTaggart, *Studies in Hegelian Cosmology*, New York, 1901; F. Paulsen, *Problem of Cosmology*, ib. 1902.

From the theological standpoint: O. Zöckler, *Geschichte der Beziehungen zwischen Theologie und Naturwissenschaft*, 2 vols., Gütersloh, 1877–79; W. H. Dallinger, *The Creator and . . . Method of Creation*, London, 1881; E. de Pressensé, *Les Origines*, Paris, 1883, Eng. transl., London, 1887; A. B. Bruce, *Providential Order of the World*, ib. 1897; A. Wagenmann, *Das System der Welt*, vol. i., Cannstatt, 1905; R. Schmid, *Naturwissenschaftliches Glaubensbekenntnis eines Theologen*, Stuttgart, 1906.

On the preservation of the world: J. McCosh, *Method of Divine Government*, London, 1870; R. A. Lipsius, *Die göttliche Weltregierung*, Frankfort, 1878; W. W. Smyth, *The Government of God*, London, 1882; A. A. Hodge, *Relation of God to the World*, in *Presbyterian and Reformed Review*, 1887, pp. 1–15; W. Schmidt, *Die göttliche Vorsehung und das Selbstleben der Welt*, Berlin, 1887; F. Bettex, *Symbolik der Schöpfung und ewige Natur*, Bielefeld, 1898.

CREATIONISM. See SOUL AND SPIRIT.

CREDENCE TABLE: A small table or shelf at one side of the altar in Roman Catholic and Anglican churches, on which the bread and wine, and sometimes the sacred vessels, are placed at the beginning of the service.

CREDNER, KARL AUGUST: New Testament scholar; b. at Waltershausen (7 m. w.s.w. of Gotha), Saxe-Coburg-Gotha, Jan. 10, 1797; d. at Giessen July 16, 1857. He studied at Jena (1817) and at Breslau (1817–21). Being rejected by the Halle missionary society for service in the East Indies owing to his reluctance to bind himself to a definite creed, he went to Göttingen and studied and taught privately there from 1821 till 1825. From 1825 to 1827 he was tutor at Hanover. In 1828 he became privat-docent, in 1830 extraordinary professor at Jena, and in 1832 ordinary professor of New Testament exegesis and church history in Giessen, where his chief literary work was done. He had rationalistic tendencies, which became more marked as he grew older. Nevertheless, his labors as a Biblical critic, especially his investigations of the origin of the New Testament books and of the history of its canon, had value which is generally acknowledged, not only because of their richness of information, but also for the clearness and objectivity of presentation. His principal works were: *Beiträge zur Einleitung in die biblischen Schriften* (2 vols., Halle, 1832–38); *Einleitung in das Neue Testament* (1836), generally considered his chief work, although never finished; *Zur Geschichte des Kanons* (1847); *Geschichte des neutestamentlichen Kanons* (ed. after his death G. Volkmar, Berlin, 1860).

(O. ZÖCKLER†.)

BIBLIOGRAPHY: W. Baldensperger, *Karl August Kredner, sein Leben und seine Theologie*, Leipsic, 1897 (address on the centenary of Credner's birth); *ADB*, iv. 575 sqq.

CREEDS AND CONFESSIONS. See SYMBOLICS.

CREIGHTON, crē'tun, MANDELL: Bishop of London; b. at Carlisle July 5, 1843; d. in London Jan. 14, 1901. He studied at Merton College, Oxford (B.A., 1867; M.A., 1870), and was fellow and tutor of his college, 1866–75, during which time he devoted himself to historical work and lectured chiefly on ecclesiastical, Italian, and Byzantine history. He was ordained deacon in 1870, priest in 1873. In 1875 he became vicar of Embleton, Northumberland, and in 1884 he went to Cambridge as Dixie professor of ecclesiastical history and fellow of Emmanuel. He was appointed bishop of Peterborough in 1891, and was transferred to London in 1897. He was select preacher at Oxford 1875–77, 1883, 1886–88, at Cambridge 1887; examining chaplain to the bishop of Newcastle, 1882–1883, to the bishop of Worcester, 1886–90; was nominated canon of Worcester 1885, of Windsor 1890; honorary fellow of Merton, Oxford, 1889, of Emmanuel, Cambridge, 1891. At the time of his death he was member of the Privy Council, dean of Her Majesty's Chapels Royal, provincial dean of Canterbury, and a member of many official boards and learned societies in England and abroad. His transference to the episcopate deprived the study of church history of one of its best exponents, while it involved him in cares and anxieties which shortened his days. It is much to be regretted that his history of the papacy, which was intended to cover the entire period of the Reformation, only goes down to the sack of Rome in 1527.

Bishop Creighton was one of the greatest of modern English churchmen, an extraordinarily brilliant man, who distinguished himself in every sphere which he filled—as student at Oxford, as vicar of a country parish, as teacher at Cambridge, and as bishop. He was a man of affairs, a statesman, as well as a scholar. He was a good preacher and much in demand as speaker on social and official occasions. He represented Emmanuel College at the 250th anniversary of Harvard in 1886, and the English Church at the coronation of the Czar Nicholas II. at Moscow in 1896. As bishop of London he was confronted by serious difficulties owing to ritualistic controversies, and, although a High-churchman himself, he followed a conciliatory course, aiming to establish true liberalism. His chief books were: *A Primer of Roman History* (London, 1875); *The Age of Elizabeth, The Tudors and the Reformation*, and *Simon de Montfort* (1876); *The Shilling History of England* (1879); *A History of the Papacy during the Period of the Reformation*, his chief work, but left incomplete (5 vols., 1882–1894; 2d ed., *A History of the Papacy from the Great Schism to the Sack of Rome*, 6 vols., 1897); *Cardinal Wolsey* (1888); *Carlisle* (1889); *Persecution and Tolerance*, Hulsean lectures at Cambridge, 1893–94 (London, 1895); *The Early Renaissance in England*, Rede lecture at Cambridge, 1895 (Cambridge, 1895); *The English National Character*, Romanes lecture at Oxford, 1896 (London, 1896); *Queen Elizabeth* (1896; 2d ed., 1899); *The Heritage of the Spirit and Other Sermons* (1896); *Church and State* (1897); *The Story of Some English Shires*, papers on certain counties which he had visited on pedestrian and other tours (1897); *Lessons from the Cross, Addresses Delivered in St. Paul's Cathedral during Holy Week 1898* (1898). He was one of the founders of *The English Historical Review* and its editor 1886–91. The following volumes appeared posthumously, edited by his wife: *Church and Nation: Charges and Addresses* (1901); *Thoughts on Education: Speeches and Sermons* (1902); *Historical Essays and Reviews* (1902); *Historical Lectures and Addresses* (1903); *University and Other Sermons* (1903); *The Mind of St. Peter and Other Sermons* (1904); *Claims of the Common Life* (1905); *Counsel for the Young* (1905).

Bibliography: *Mandell Creighton, his Life and Letters, by his Wife*, London, 1904; *DNB*, supplement vol., ii. 82–88.

CRELL, JOHANN. See Socinus, Faustus, Socinians, I., § 2.

CREMER, AUGUST HERMANN: German theologian; b. at Unna (30 m. s. of Münster) Oct. 18, 1834; d. at Greifswald Oct. 4, 1903. He studied at Halle and Tübingen, and in 1859 was appointed pastor at Ostönnen, near Soest, Westphalia. Eleven years later he became professor of systematic theology at Greifswald, and pastor of St. Mary's. Cremer was a prolific writer, his principal works being as follows: *Die eschatologische Rede Jesu Christi, Matthäi 24. 25* (Stuttgart, 1860); *Ueber den biblischen Begriff der Erbauung* (Leipsic, 1863); *Ueber die Wunder im Zusammenhang der göttlichen Offenbarung* (1865); *Biblisch-theologisches Wörterbuch der neutestamentlichen Gräcität* (Gotha, 1866–67; 9th ed., 1902; Eng. transl. by W. Urwick, Edinburgh, 1872); *Vernunft, Gewissen und Offenbarung* (Gotha, 1869; Eng. transl. by D. Heagle, Boston, 1871); *Die Auferstehung der Todten* (Barmen, 1870); *Der Gott des Alten Bundes* (1872); *Ueber die Befähigung zum geistlichen Amte* (1878); *Die Bibel im Pfarrhaus und in der Gemeinde* (1878); *Ueber den Zustand nach dem Tode, nebst einigen Andeutungen über das Kindersterben und über den Spiritismus* (Gütersloh, 1883; Eng. transl. by S. T. Lowrie, *Beyond the Grave*, New York, 1885); *Zum Kampf um das Apostolikum* (7th ed., Berlin, 1893); *Glaube, Schrift und heilige Geschichte* (Gütersloh, 1896); *Die christliche Lehre von den Eigenschaften Gottes* (Gotha, 1899); *Die paulinische Rechtfertigungslehre im Zusammenhang ihrer geschichtlichen Voraussetzungen* (2d ed., Gütersloh, 1900); *Taufe, Wiedergeburt und Kindertaufe* (1900); *Weissagung und Wunder* (1900); *Bedeutung des Artikels von der Gottheit Christi für die Ethik* (1901); *Das Wesen des Christenthums* (1901; Eng. transl. by B. Pick, *Reply to Harnack, on the Essence of Christianity*, New York, 1903); and *Grundwahrheiten der christlichen Religion nach D. Seeberg* (1903).

Bibliography: *August Hermann Cremer, Gedenkblätter*, Gütersloh, 1904.

CRESPIN, crê″pan′, **JEAN:** French Protestant; b. at Arras c. 1520; d. at Geneva 1572. He studied law at Louvain. In 1540 he was in Paris, where he worked with his friend F. Baudouin under the celebrated advocate C. du Moulin, and became himself advocate at the Parliament of Paris. He became interested in the doctrine of the Reformed Church and, upon his return to his native town, his relations with the Protestants caused him to be treated as a heretic. In 1545 he went to Strasburg, where he married. In 1548 he was able to realize his dearest wish and live near his friend Calvin; with his family he settled in Geneva, where he established a printing-press. In 1555 he received citizenship. Like other printers and publishers of his time he also wrote books, viz.: *Le Livre des Martyrs* (Geneva, 1554); *Recueil de plusieurs personnes qui ont constamment enduré la mort pour le nom de N. S. J. C. depuis Jean Hus jusqu'à cette année présente 1554* (1555); *Indice et concordance des choses contenues à la Bible* (1554); *Le Marchand converti, tragédie nouvelle* (1558); *Histoire des vrays témoins de la vérité de l'Évangile depuis Jean Hus jusqu'à présent* (1570). G. Bonet-Maury.

Bibliography: E. and É. Haag, *La France protestante*, ed. H. L. Bordier, vol. iv., Paris, 1884; *Bibliographie des martyrologes protestants Néerlandais*, The Hague, 1890; Lichtenberger, *ESR*, iii. 471–474.

CRETE IN THE APOSTOLIC AGE: Crete, once the flourishing "isle of the hundred cities," was entirely devastated in the last century before Christ by continual civil wars, and for the countries of the Mediterranean it became a continuous menace on account of the pirates who swarmed there. In the Cretan war (68–67 B.C.) the proconsul Quintus Metellus subdued the island. He also began its organization as a province, which organization was completed 66 B.C. by Pompey. In the year 27 B.C. after the death of Antony its administration was united by Octavian with that of Cyrene, and the name of the province varied between Creta-Cyrene or Crete and Cyrene (Dio Cass., LIII. xii. 4; Strabo, xvii. 3, 840). It belonged to the senate and was governed by a propretor with the title proconsul. Among the cities which in the time of the Romans were connected with the government seated in Crete were the famous Gortyna, Kydonia, and Knossos; the latter was a Roman colony. When Paul on his voyage as a prisoner (Acts xxvii. 7) had come to Crete his ship passed over against Salmone. Sailing along the southern coast one comes to Fair Havens, near the city of Matala. The city of Lasea can not be located. The haven of Phœnix which the sailors wished to reach (Acts

xxvii. 12) is called by Ptolemy (III. xvii. 3) "Harbor of Phœnice"; he calls the island *Klaudos* (III. xvii. 11). The population of Crete contained a strong Semitic element. From I Macc. xv. 23 it is clear that Jews lived there (in Gortyna; cf. also Josephus, *Ant.*, XVII. xii. 1; *Wars*, II. ciii.; Philo, *Legat. ad Cajum*, § 36, ii. 587, ed. Mangey). The "Cretans" mentioned Acts ii. 11 were Cretan Jews or proselytes. The bad reputation of the population of Crete is referred to in Titus i. 12, where is given (R. V.) the translation of the well-known hexameter, "Cretans are always liars, evil beasts, idle gluttons," said by Chrysostom to have been derived from Epimenides, the priestly seer and miracle-worker, one of the seven wise men. The Greek had a verb formed from the noun which meant "to lie and deceive"; "to Crete a Cretan" meant "to outwit a knave." (JOHANNES WEISS.)

BIBLIOGRAPHY: Besides the commentaries on Acts, there may be consulted Sabatier, in Lichtenberger, *ESR*, iii. 474–475; *DB*, i. 195–520; *EB*, i. 955–956.

CRETONI, SERAFINO: Cardinal; b. at Soriano (7 m. e. of Viterbo), Italy, Sept. 4, 1833; d. at Rome Feb. 3, 1909. He was educated at Rome, became archivist of the Propaganda, secretary of the committee for Oriental affairs at the Vatican Council, and councilor at the Holy Office. In 1877 he was sent by Pius IX. to the general chapter of the Armenian Mekhitarists at Venice, but was recalled by Leo XIII. and appointed assistant secretary of state, 1879. In 1880 he returned to the Propaganda as secretary for Oriental affairs, and in 1889 became an assessor of the Holy Office. In 1893 he was consecrated titular archbishop of Damascus, and went as papal nuncio to Madrid, where he remained three years. In 1896 he was created cardinal priest of Santa Maria sopra Minerva, and in 1900 became prefect of the Congregation of Indulgences. After 1903 he was prefect of the Congregation of Rites. He was a member of the Congregations of Bishops and Regulars, the Councils, Supervision of Provincial Councils, the Propaganda, the Propaganda for the Oriental Rite, and Ceremonials, as well as of the Laurentian Congregation.

CRISP, TOBIAS: Antinomian; b. in London 1600; d. there Feb. 27, 1643. He took his first degree at Cambridge, then removed to Balliol College, Oxford (M.A., 1626; D.D., before 1642); in 1627 became rector of Brinkworth, Wiltshire; removed to London in 1642 because of persecution from royalist soldiers. At first he was a rigid Arminian, but later went to the opposite extreme, and after going to London was fiercely attacked as an Antinomian by the ministers there. Anthony Wood says (*Athenæ*, iii. 50, ed. P. Bliss, London, 1817): "He was baited by fifty-two opponents in a grand dispute concerning the freeness of the grace of God, in Jesus Christ, to poor sinners. By which encounter, which was eagerly managed on his part, he contracted a disease that brought him to his grave." His life is described as innocent and upright, "zealous and fervent of all good." He made himself popular at Brinkworth by the lavish hospitality which his private fortune enabled him to extend. His sermons were published after his death with the title *Christ Alone Exalted* (4 vols., 1643–83); they were collected by his son (London, 1690), and were republished by Dr. John Gill, with notes and brief memoir (2 vols., 1791).

CRISPIN AND CRISPINIAN, SAINTS: Two brothers of good Roman family, who, it is said, went to Gaul in the beginning of the reign of Diocletian to labor for the conversion of the pagans. They settled at Soissons, where they preached with much success by day and labored at night at their trade of shoemaking (whence they have become the patron saints of shoemakers), selling the shoes to the poor; according to a tradition they stole the leather that they might sell at a low price. They were put to death with cruel tortures by the governor in 287. Their day is Oct. 25.

BIBLIOGRAPHY: *ASB*, Oct., xi. 495–540; F. Görres, in *JPT*, xiii (1887), part 2.

CRITICI SACRI: A thesaurus of Bible antiquities and exegesis, undertaken as an appendage to Walton's Polyglot at the instigation and expense of Cornelius Bee, a London bookseller, and prepared under the direction of John Pearson, archdeacon of Surrey (afterward bishop of Chester); Anthony Scattergood, canon of Lincoln; Francis Gouldman, rector of South Ockendon, Essex; and Richard Pearson, fellow of King's College (brother of John). The full title is *Critici sacri: sive doctissimorum virorum in SS. Biblia annotationes et tractatus* (9 vols., London, 1660). The work combines the labors of many of the best English and Continental scholars of the sixteenth and seventeenth centuries.* It was reprinted twice at Frankfort, and a new edition, augmented and provided with index, appeared at Amsterdam in nine volumes, 1698. The *Thesaurus theologico-philologicus sive sylloge dissertationum elegantiorum ad selectiora et illustriora Veteris et Novi Testamenti loca, a theologis Protestantibus in Germania separatim diversis temporibus conscriptarum* (2 vols., folio, 1701–02) and the *Thesaurus novus theologico-philologicus* (2 vols., 1732), both works edited by Theodor Hase and Conrad Iken, constitute a supplement. The *Synopsis criticorum* of Matthew Poole (q.v.) is an abridgment of the original work with additional matter. For contents of the *Critici sacri* consult James Darling, *Cyclopædia Bibliographica* (London, 1854), 815–826.

CROALL LECTURES: A lectureship on a foundation created by a bequest of £5,000 by Mr. John Croall. The aim is to defend and maintain the doctrines of the Christian religion and "to increase the religious literature of Scotland." The lectures are delivered in alternate years in Edinburgh, the lecturer is by preference from one or other of the Presbyterian churches of Scotland,

* In a note from "Cornelius Bee to the reader" it is said: "If any one should be disposed to blame us either for the great size of the work or because of its price, let him know that we have aimed both to benefit him and to save him money. For here about ninety books, in their entirety, are brought together into nine, and fifty pounds more or less (you would find it hard to buy them all for less at the present time, if you could get them at all) are reduced to fifteen. So there is no good reason why any one should find fault with us; on the contrary, every one should feel much satisfaction."

though he may be a "clergyman of any Reformed Church other than Presbyterian," and may not be reappointed. The first lecturer, in 1875–76, was John Tulloch, and his subject was *The Christian Doctrine of Sin* (Edinburgh, 1877). A full list of lecturers and their subjects is given in L. H. Jordan, *Comparative Religion*, p. 568, New York, 1905.

CROCIUS, JOHANNES: Reformed theologian; b. at Laasphe (36 m. s.s.e. of Arnsberg), in the county of Wittgenstein, Germany, July 28, 1590; d. at Marburg July 1, 1659. After studying at Herborn and Marburg, he became, in 1612, court preacher to the Landgrave Maurice in Cassel and obtained the degree of doctor of theology 1613. With the permission of his prince he entered for two years the service of the elector John Sigismund of Brandenburg, who in 1617 appointed him professor of theology at the University of Marburg. In 1624 he was obliged to return to Cassel, in consequence of the closing of the university. During this period he played a great part in the Hessian Church, which had gone over to the Reformed confession, and in the time of the Thirty Years' War he wrote in support of the political demands of the Reformed party in Germany. His chief work was a polemic against Roman Catholic attacks: *Anti-Becanus i.e. controversiarum communium, quas M. Becanus . . . in manuali movit examen ex S. S. et antiquitate institutum* (Cassel, 1643). In 1631 he took part in the religious conference at Leipsic between Lutheran and Reformed theologians. At the reopening of the Reformed university in Marburg in 1653 he returned thither, and became its first rector. He had a great share in the church order published by Landgrave Louis VI. in 1657.

CARL MIRBT.

BIBLIOGRAPHY: F. C. Claus, *Johannes Crocius*, Marburg, 1857; F. W. Strieder, *Hessische Gelehrtengeschichte*, ii. 397 sqq., Göttingen, 1782; H. Heppe, *Geschichte der theologischen Fakultät zu Marburg*, Marburg, 1873.

CROMWELL, OLIVER: Lord Protector of the Commonwealth of England; b. at Huntingdon (17 m. n.w. of Cambridge), Huntingdonshire, Apr. 25, 1599; d. in London Sept. 3, 1658. He entered Cambridge University in 1616, but left it a year later to care for his mother and sisters on his father's death. In 1628 he was elected to Parliament from Huntingdon, from which town he removed to Ely in 1636. In 1640 he was again sent to the House of Commons, this time from Cambridge, and in the Long Parliament he soon took his stand in opposition to the royal prerogative. In 1642 he moved the appointment of a committee to put the kingdom in a posture of defense, and, when Essex received the commission to raise a parliamentary army, raised a troop of arquebusiers, sixty Godfearing men who fought first at Edgehill.

Defense of Religious Liberty.

Early in his career, when the modern idea of religious liberty was in its infancy, he took a decided stand in its favor, with the younger Vane but against the great majority of those who fought on his side. In defense of his Independent principles, he had to contend not only against the attempt of the Scotch to force their rigid Presbyterianism upon England, but with the English Presbyterians who had a majority in the House of Commons, and hampered and weakened the army because it was not in sympathy with their narrow views. Their action forced Cromwell into open opposition to Parliament, in favor of the liberty proclaimed in Milton's *Areopagitica* (1644) and Jeremy Taylor's *Liberty of Prophesying* (1647).

In July, 1647, Cromwell and his son-in-law Ireton submitted to the king the treaty known as the "Heads of the Proposals," which if carried into effect would have been the settlement of 1689 with a larger flavor of democracy and Puritanism, and left all forms of worship, including the Prayer-book, to the free choice of the worshipers. In all his efforts Cromwell's aim had been to strengthen toleration by intertwining it with the old constitutional pillars of king and parliament; but he found out by degrees that nothing was to be hoped for from the king, and ultimately sat as a member of the High Court of Justice which tried and executed him, contributing more than any other member to the result.

Rise to Power.

In the following August he was made lord-lieutenant and commander in chief in Ireland, and put down opposition with a strong hand. Appointed captain-general of all the forces of the Commonwealth (June 26, 1650), he marched into Scotland, and won the successive victories of Dunbar, Edinburgh, and Perth. The battle of Worcester (Sept. 3, 1651) ended the war, and Cromwell returned to London. In April, 1653, he dissolved the "Rump" Parliament and formed a council of state. After the "Little" or "Barebones" Parliament had sat from July to December, he was installed at Westminster (Dec. 16) as Lord Protector under the conditions of the "Instrument of Government" drawn up by the military power.

Policy of Protectorate.

One of the early important measures of the Protectorate was the establishment of a new scheme of church government. The minister presented to a living was to have a certificate of fitness from three persons of known godliness and integrity, one of them being a settled minister. After this had been passed by commissioners known as Triers, he became an incumbent, liable to expulsion by a local body of Ejectors for immorality, blasphemy, or atheism; but while he remained he might uphold any Puritan system he chose, and organize his congregation on the Presbyterian, Independent, or Baptist system, if they would follow him. Any who objected to the system adopted in their parish might form separate congregations at their own discretion. Later on, toward the close of 1655, the Jews, who had been exiled from England since the reign of Edward I., were allowed to return. But ultimately the position held by the Prayer-book as a symbol of attachment to royalty drove Cromwell to proscribe its use as thoroughly as that of the mass; yet the persecution along this line was sharp only for a time, and on the other hand he stood forth before all Europe as the champion of religious liberty by his espousal of the cause of the Vaudois Protestants against the duke of Savoy, and his foreign policy looked toward the establishment of an alliance which should uphold Protestantism everywhere.

Modern Estimate.

Though he was limited by the defects which make imperfect the character of the best of men, it has been generally admitted, now that old prejudices have passed away (especially since the publication of Carlyle's great work), that Cromwell was a man of sincere devotion to duty and to his ideal of what a Christian man should be. No sour fanatic, he was strict in banishing not merely vice, but the folly which leads to vice. Long reviled as a regicide, a hypocrite, and a tyrant, he is now recognized as a patriotic, wise, and just ruler.

Bibliography: A discriminating criticism of literature prior to 1887 may be found at the end of the article in the *DNB*, xiii. 155–186. The only early life of value is H. Fletcher, *The Perfect Politician . . . The Life of O. Cromwell*, London, 1660. Consult: O. Cromwell, *Memoirs of the Protector . . . and of his Sons Richard and Henry*, 2 vols., London, 1823 (by a descendant and in apologetic tone); T. Carlyle, *Oliver Cromwell's Letters and Speeches*, 3 vols., London, 1846, reprinted often, e.g., 1905 (a vindication of Cromwell, turned the current of opinion concerning the subject); D. Masson, *Life of Milton*, 6 vols., Cambridge, 1857-80 (indispensable); J. Forster, *Lives of Eminent Statesmen of the Commonwealth*, vol. i., London, 1853 (adverse); F. P. G. Guizot, *Life of Oliver Cromwell*, 9th ed., ib. 1890; J. A. Picton, *Oliver Cromwell, the Man and his Mission*, ib. 1889 (defensive); S. R. Gardiner, *Hist. of the Commonwealth and Protectorate, 1649–60*, London, 1894; idem, *Oliver Cromwell*, ib. 1903; S. H. Church, *Oliver Cromwell. Life, Extracts from Letters and Speeches*, New York and London, 4th ed., 1899; J. Morley, *Oliver Cromwell*, ib. 1904. From the view of church history: W. Clark, *Anglican Reformation*, pp. 398, 428–429, 436-440, New York, 1897; J. H. Overton, *The Church in England*, ii. 114–119, London, 1897; W. H. Hutton, *The English Church . . . 1625–1714*, ib. 1903. An interesting volume is *Menasseh Ben Israel's Mission to Oliver Cromwell. A Reprint, ed. L. Wolf*, ib. 1901.

CROOKER, JOSEPH HENRY: Unitarian; b. at Foxcroft, Me., Dec. 8, 1850. He was educated at Norway, Me. (1864-67), and Ypsilanti Union Seminary (1870), and after a Baptist ministry of five years became a convert to Unitarianism in 1877. He held charges at Madison, Wis. (1881–91), Helena, Mont. (1891–97), and Ann Arbor, Mich. (1898–1905). Since 1905 he has been minister of Roslindale Unitarian Church, Boston. He has written *Jesus Brought Back* (Boston, 1889); *Problems in American Society* (1889); *Different New Testament Views of Jesus* (1890); *The New Bible and its New Uses* (1893); *The Unitarian Church* (1901); *Religious Freedom in American Education* (1903); and *The Supremacy of Jesus* (1904).

CROOKS, GEORGE RICHARD: Methodist; b. in Philadelphia Feb. 3, 1822; d. in Madison, N. J., Feb. 20, 1897. He was graduated at Dickinson College, Carlisle, Pa., 1840; became teacher in the grammar-school of the college 1842, its principal 1843, adjunct professor of Latin and Greek in the college 1846; was pastor in Philadelphia, Wilmington, New York, and Brooklyn 1848–80; professor of historical theology in Drew Theological Seminary, Madison, N. J., 1880 till his death. In the General Conference of 1856 he led the movement which sanctioned theological seminaries in the Methodist Church, and he aimed steadily at higher ideals of culture for the ministry. From 1860 to 1875 he edited *The Methodist*. With John F. Hurst he prepared an adaptation of Hagenbach's *Encyclopædia and Methodology* (New York, 1884); independently he published an edition of Butler's *Analogy*, containing a life and completion of Emory's analysis (1852); *The Life and Letters of Rev. Dr. John McClintock* (1876); the *Sermons* (1885) and *Life* (1890) of Bishop Matthew Simpson; *The Story of the Christian Church* (1897).

CROSBY, FANNY (FRANCES JANE VAN ALSTYNE): Hymn-writer; b. at South East, N. Y., Mar. 24, 1820. She became totally blind in infancy, and was educated at the New York Institute for the Blind, where she taught English grammar and rhetoric, as well as Greek, Roman, and American history, 1847–58, when she married Alexander Van Alstyne, a blind man. She has written more than three thousand hymns, among the best known being "Safe in the arms of Jesus;" "Jesus, keep me near the Cross;" "Pass me not, O gentle Savior;" "Rescue the perishing;" and "Sweet hour of prayer." She has also written *The Blind Girl and other Poems* (New York, 1844); *Monterey and other Poems* (1849); *A Wreath of Columbia's Flowers* (1859); *Bells at Evening and other Poems, with biographical Sketch by Robert Lowry*, 1898 (5th ed., 1903); and *Memories of Eighty Years* (1907).

CROSBY, HOWARD: Presbyterian; b. in New York Feb. 27, 1826; d. there Mar. 29, 1891. He was graduated at the University of the City of New York 1844; was professor of Greek there 1851–59, at Rutgers College 1859–63; was also pastor of the First Presbyterian Church of New Brunswick 1861–1863; pastor of the Fourth Avenue Presbyterian Church, New York, 1863 till his death. From 1870 to 1881 he was chancellor of the New York University; member of the American Bible Revision Committee; moderator of the General Assembly at Baltimore 1873. He advocated Christian union, favored a restriction of wealth, and was outspoken in behalf of temperance in the proper meaning of the word (not total abstinence). He assisted in organizing the Young Men's Christian Association of New York and was its president 1852–55; he was also the chief founder of the Society for the Prevention of Crime in 1877 and its president till his death. Besides occasional pamphlets, articles, etc., he published *Lands of the Moslem*, travels (New York, 1851); an edition of the *Œdipus Tyrannus* of Sophocles (1852); *The New Testament with Brief Explanatory Notes or Scholia* (1863); *Social Hints for Young Christians*, three sermons (1866); *Bible Manual* (1870); *Jesus, his Life and Work* (1871); *The Healthy Christian, an appeal to the Church* (1871); *Thoughts on the Decalogue* (Philadelphia, 1873); *Expository Notes on the Book of Joshua* (New York, 1875); *Nehemiah* in the American Lange series (1877); *The Christian Preacher*, Yale lectures on preaching for 1879–80 (1880); *The True Humanity of Christ* (1880); *The New Testament in Both Authorized and Revised Versions Carefully Annotated* (Boston, 1885); *The Bible View of the Jewish Church* (New York, 1888); *The Good and Evil of Calvinism* (1890); *The Seven Churches of Asia, or worldliness in the Church* (1890); *Will and Providence* (1890). A volume of *Sermons* appeared in New York, 1891, and *At the Lord's Table*, 1894.

BIBLIOGRAPHY: *Howard Crosby, Memorial Papers and Reminiscences*, New York, 1892.

CROSS AND ITS USE AS A SYMBOL.

The significance and importance of the cross in Christianity are obviously due to its association with the death of Jesus. Its use as an instrument of torture and capital punishment, and the cross of Jesus are treated under the heading CRUCIFIXION. Other topics are most conveniently discussed in connection with the symbolism of the cross, to which this article will be in the main devoted. Its historical associations and its connection with the salvation of men made the cross the emblem of Christianity even from the beginning. The symbolic act known as the sign of the cross appears very early, signifying, of course, Christ's death on the cross; but inevitably importance came to be attached to the mere act and it was believed to be helpful in securing the blessing and efficacy of this holy event and of the exalted Christ. As early as about the middle of the second century a superstitious conception and application had so far developed that the popular faith of the Church, not without support from theology, sought by performing the act a powerful device against the will of demons, by whom people imagined themselves beset and threatened. The expedient was also applied in case of sickness and other perils, before battle and elsewhere. The sign was usually made on the forehead, but also on other parts of the body, which were supposed to need its protective operation. The sign is also used contemporaneously in public worship, as conferring a blessing or consecration and protection against the ungodly world. Its supposed efficacy comes to light especially in exorcism. Possibly the pagan reproach of cross-worship had some connection with this comprehensive practise.

1. The Sign of the Cross.

The medieval development occasioned in some respects a very considerable increase in the use of the sign of the cross in public worship. The Western Church exhibits the double form of the so-called Latin and the so-called German sign of the cross. The former is made by touching the forehead and breast and then the left and the right shoulder with the open right hand; using the formula: *In nomine patris et filii et spiritus sancti amen*; or: *Adjutorium nostrum in nomine domini*, or: *In nomine domini nostri Jesu Christi*. The German cross consists in touching the forehead, lips, and breast with the thumb and fingers of the right hand brought together, while the left hand rests on the breast. The accompanying words are: "In the name of God the Father, Son, and Holy Ghost. Amen." The Greeks place thumb, index finger, and middle finger of the right hand together, the two remaining fingers closed in the palm of the hand, and so touch the forehead, breast, right and left shoulders. The three extended fingers denote for them confession of the Trinity; the two closed ones express faith in the divine and human nature in Christ. Their formula runs: "Holy God, Holy Strong One, Holy Immortal, have mercy on us." The Lutheran Churches have retained the sign of the cross in particular acts of devotion (baptism, communion, and some others), and likewise the Anglican Church; whereas Reformed Protestantism rejected it strictly.

2. Its Form.

To the private and devotional appreciation of the value of the cross as a symbol correspond the extent and affluence of its representations, even in the early Christian era. The superstitious phase of the matter is exemplified in the use of the cross on amulet inscriptions; and even the amulet itself takes the form of a cross. The marking of walls, doors, and household objects with a cross may in many cases be attributed to the same motive. However, the cross occurs for the most part as a symbol and notation of Christianity. Accordingly the use of it increases with the victorious progress of the new religion through the heathen world from the time of Constantine the Great. Ornaments are marked with it, especially rings, vestments, and other dress fabrics, various utensils like lamps, combs, caskets, and boxes, as well as sarcophagi and epitaphs. Nor does the ecclesiastical use of it fall short of the private use. The cross became the outward and visible token of church edifices. Then the State had it circulated on its coins throughout its entire dominion and beyond; and it crowned the imperial globe, scepter, and diadem.

3. As an Amulet. Ecclesiastical Symbolism.

In the Middle Ages, it is true, the cross recedes in the sphere of private usage, but it gains all the more ground in the public life of the Church. It is the symbol of ecclesiastical seizin and right of possession; it is used to excess in one form or another in connection with ecclesiastical functions (altar dedication, proclamation of indulgences, processions, etc.); becomes more lavishly appropriated to devotional objects, and is the most characteristic Christian burial token. It participates in the ordeal (q.v.); admonishes, in detached situations, to religious thoughts and acts (wayside crosses, etc.), and is affixed by clerics and secular persons to their signatures. It is adopted as ground-plan of churches (both the Latin and the Greek cross). Monastic and knightly orders and civil gilds, spiritual and temporal lords, municipalities and countries adopt it as emblem. It is borne on banners and arms. Asceticism and mysticism, and religious poetry direct their thoughts to it. It is at once the simplest and most universal Christian symbol. And as far as the evidence goes, there was no distinction in this respect between Eastern and Western Christianity.

In the West a powerful reaction was occasioned by the Reformation, so far, at least, as the superstitious and generally unworthy use of the cross as a symbol was in question. But although Reformed Protestantism took radical measures in the matter, the Lutheran movement, consistently with its proper nature, confined itself to doing away with unevangelical practises.

It is doubtless true that even before Constantine's time the cross was used in plastic art and painting, and especially in the minor arts, though only infrequently. But the earliest certain representations of it extant are later than Constantine. This is explained, for one thing, by the greater wealth of monumental material preserved from the later time; but it is also due to a growing predilection which originated in Constantine's time or later; the representations become more and more frequent as time goes on. The oldest forms, probably simultaneous in origin, are the "Greek cross" (+) and the "Latin cross" (*crux immissa*, ✝). The cross was anticipated, even though not intentionally, in the Greek letter "chi" of the monogram of Christ (see JESUS CHRIST, MONOGRAM OF). It is sometimes combined with the letters "alpha" and "omega," or it is enclosed in a circle, or offset with doves or long-stemmed flowers. It is, furthermore, adorned with precious stones, and associated with the monogram in the triumphal labarum (see CONSTANTINE THE GREAT, I., § 4). As emblem of victory it soars in the starry dome, upheld by hovering angels; and in the fifth century it enters into the nimbus of Christ, imparting to the same its characteristic form down to this day. Less frequent is the "tau" form of the cross (T , "St. Anthony's" or "Egyptian cross," *crux commissa*), which originated in the symbolic reflections of church writers, and is not demonstrably extant before the fourth century. To the Middle Ages belong "St. Andrew's cross" (×, *crux decussata*), which legend reputed to be St. Andrew's implement of martyrdom (see CRUCIFIXION); the papal cross with three crossbars (‡) and the patriarchal cross with two (‡); and numerous others constructed upon the fundamental traditional outlines, and belonging distinctively to heraldry—the Maltese cross, the cross fleury, the cross patté, and others.

4. The Cross in Art. Different Forms.

Similar or equivalent pre-Christian symbols of this description have neither an intrinsic nor extraneous connection with the Christian cross, although such relationship has been and is persistently asserted. The Egyptian "handle cross" (☥, *ankh*), which has been transferred in isolated instances to Coptic art, has been merely reconstructed and transformed into the cross of Christ. The swastika (卐, *crux gamminata*, gammadion, or fylfot), a very ancient prophylactic symbol occurring among all peoples, perhaps owes its not infrequent adoption by Christians to its resemblance to the cross; at least this resemblance may have made the adoption easier; but the fylfot also stands independently beside the cross. VICTOR SCHULTZE.

5. Similar Pre-Christian Symbols.

BIBLIOGRAPHY: W. W. Seymour, *The Cross in Tradition, Hist., and Art*, New York, 1898; J. Stockbauer, *Kunstgeschichte des Kreuzes*, Schaffhausen, 1870; E. Dobbert, *Zur Entstehungsgeschichte des Kreuzes*, Berlin, 1880; G. S. Tyack, *The Cross in Ritual, Architecture and Art*, London, 1896; J. Hoppenot, *Le Crucifix dans l'histoire et dans l'art*, Paris, 1899; W. O. Stephens, *The Cross in the Life and Literature of the Anglo-Saxons*, New York, 1904; P. M. C. Kermode, *Manx Crosses . . . 5th to 13th Century*, London, 1907; E. Beresford-Cooke, *The Sign of the Cross in the Western Liturgies*, London, 1907; Schaff, *Christian Church*, vol. ii., chap. iv.; *KL*, vii. 1054-88.

On pre-Christian and non-Christian forms and usage consult: G. de Mortillet, *Le Signe de la croix avant le christianisme*, Paris, 1866; E. von Bunsen, *Das Symbol des Kreuzes bei allen Nationen, und die Entstehung des Kreuzsymbols der christlichen Kirche*, Berlin, 1876; W. W. Blake, *The Cross Ancient and Modern*, New York, 1888; Ansault, *La croix avant Jésus Christ*, Paris, 1894; J. D. Parson, *The Non-Christian Cross*, London, 1896; T. Wilson, *The Swastika*, ib. 1898.

CROSS, EXALTATION OF THE: One of the older church festivals, although, as it appears, it had no independent status to begin with, but was an addition to the festival of the Invention of the Cross (q.v.), celebrated on the following day (Sept. 14). The first mention and account of it is by the Aquitanian pilgrim Silvia, about 385. It was naturalized in Constantinople as early as the beginning of the fifth century, and in the first half of the same it is on record with respect to Syria and Egypt. Probably during the fifth century the festival spread through the entire Church of the East. The way was paved for it on every side, directly and indirectly, by the migration of alleged fragments of the cross. The recovery of the Holy Cross, which in 614 was carried off by the Persian king Chosroes II., but in 628 was brought back to Jerusalem in solemn procession by the emperor Heraclius in person, doubtless gave the festival a new impulse. It is first mentioned in the West under Pope Sergius (687-701). VICTOR SCHULTZE.

BIBLIOGRAPHY: *The Pilgrimage of S. Silvia of Aquitania*, in Palestine Pilgrims' Text Society series, vol. i., London, 1896; A. J. Binterim, *Denkwürdigkeiten*, V. i. 455 sqq., Mainz, 1829; *DCA*, i. 502-503; *ASB* and *ASM* for Sept. 14.

CROSS, INVENTION (OR FINDING) OF THE: The name of an ancient festival of the Church. In the history of the discovery of "holy sites" the finding of the cross of Jesus has its place, even prior to the middle of the fourth century. While Eusebius of Cæsarea and the Pilgrim of Bordeaux (333) have nothing to say in the matter, Cyril of Jerusalem, not long afterward (347 or 348), presupposes the existence of this cross and the wide distribution of splinters detached from it ("Catechetical Lectures," iv. 10, x. 19; "Letter to Constantine," iii.; *MPG*, xxxiii. 468, 685, 1168; *NPNF*, 2 ser., vii. 21, 63). Still in the same century, the legendary account, no doubt incited by the visit of the empress Helena (the mother of Constantine the Great) to the holy scenes, associates her directly with the event. The empress, it relates, conjointly with the bishop Macarius, instituted researches as to buried crosses on Golgotha; and thanks to the aid of a Jew, or even of a divine revelation, the three crosses were discovered. The true one was recognized by means of the attached *titulus* (Matt. xxvii. 37, and parallels) or by virtue of a miracle of healing. The reports vary in detail, but are essentially the same in substance. It is nevertheless demonstrable that this narrative has its origin in the transference to the empress Helena of a similar episode in the legend of Abgar (*Doctrina Addai*;

cf. T. Zahn, *Forschungen zur Geschichte des neutestamentlichen Kanons*, i., Erlangen, 1891, pp. 370 sqq.; Socrates, *Hist. eccl.*, i. 17, Eng. transl. in *NPNF*, 2 ser., ii. 21; Sozomen, *Hist. eccl.*, ii. 1, in *NPNF*, 2 ser., ii. 258–259. These relate the discoveries at length).

Both Greeks and Latins commemorated the occurrence in a special festival, the former combining it with the annual celebration of the dedication of Constantine's Basilica on Sept. 13, the latter appointing a particular date for it on May 3. The first traces of a Latin observance appear in Gaul at the beginning of the Middle Ages. The fusion of the Gallic and Roman ritual carried the festival to Rome about 800, whence it became gradually diffused through the Western Church.

VICTOR SCHULTZE.

BIBLIOGRAPHY: J. H. Newman, *Two essays on . . . Miracles*, pp. 287–326, London, 1873 (defends the legend); W. C. Prime, *History of the Invention, Preservation and Disappearance of the Wood known as the True Cross*, New York, 1877; *The Legendary History of the Cross, a Series of sixty-four Woodcuts from a Dutch Book . . . 1483, . . . with Preface by S. Baring-Gould*, ib. 1887; *Inventionis crucis . . . hymnus antiquus*, ed. A. Holder, Leipsic, 1889; E. Nestle, *De sancta cruce*, Berlin, 1889; J. H. Bernard, *The Churches of Constantine at Jerusalem, Being Translations from Eusebius and the early Pilgrims*, London, 1896; *DCA*, i. 503–506.

CROSS, ORDERS OF THE (*Cruciferi, Crucigeri*): A term applied to the knights of the Teutonic Order (q.v.) and also to four medieval orders in other countries.

1. The Italian Knights of the Cross traced their origin to Cyriacus, the martyr-bishop of Jerusalem, who died c. 362, or, according to another tradition of the order, to Cletus (Anacletus), one of the early bishops of Rome. Historically, however, they are not known to have existed before the middle of the twelfth century, when, c. 1160, Alexander III. granted to their mother house, a large hospital at Bologna, certain privileges which were increased by Urban III. and Innocent III. Gerhard de Rocha, the prior of the mother house under Alexander and Urban, seems to have raised the order to a position of importance in Italy by establishing daughter houses throughout the country, even if he was not actually the founder. In the time of its greatest prosperity, during the rule of Clement IV., the order possessed more than 200 houses in the five provinces of Bologna, Venice, Rome, Milan, and Naples. In the fourteenth century, however, the Knights began to degenerate through schisms and lax discipline. A general chapter held at Bologna in 1462 proved unable to check the decline by the reforms which it proposed, and the order was finally dissolved under Alexander VIII. in 1656.

2. In 1211 a canon of Liége named Theodore of Celles founded at Huy, a town in his diocese, an order which was destined to spread through Holland, France, the west and south of Germany, and, for a time, even to Ireland. The chief object of the new order was the conversion of heretics, and its Augustinian rule, modified according to Dominican principles, is said to have received the sanction of Innocent III. in 1216. These Knights of the Cross have preserved their existence until the present day, despite the losses which they suffered both at the Reformation and during the French Revolution. At present they have five houses, two in Holland, two in Belgium, and one in Germany. The indult granted them by Leo X. in 1516, by which they are permitted to bless rosaries with an indulgence of 500 days for each Pater Noster or Ave Maria, has been confirmed repeatedly by succeeding popes, most recently by Leo XIII. in 1884.

3. The Knights of the Cross with the Red Star (*Ordo militaris crucigerorum cum rubra stella*) believe that they originated as an order of knights spiritual during the Crusades, although historically they seem to have been established c. 1235 as a hospital brotherhood in a Franciscan monastery founded at Prague by the Bohemian princess Agnes. In 1252 they received their rule with their emblem of a cross within a hexagonal red star. Within the year they had assumed control of a hospital newly erected at Breslau, and Bohemia and Silesia remained the centers of their activity. The order soon became wealthy, but at the same time degenerated and many of its houses later passed to other orders, the one at Prague being controlled successively by the Jesuits (1555) and the Capuchins (1599).

4. A distinctively Polish Order of Knights of the Cross with the Red Heart was established in the monastery of St. Mark at Cracow in the second half of the thirteenth century. It was distinguished from the preceding order, which was clothed in black, by a white habit, and was primarily a penitential organization (known officially as *Ordo de pœnitentia sanctorum martyrum*). It attained its greatest prosperity about the beginning of the sixteenth century, after which it rapidly declined.

(O. ZÖCKLER†.)

BIBLIOGRAPHY: 1. B. Leoni, *Origine e fondatione dell'ordine di Crociferi*, Venice, 1598; Helyot, *Ordres monastiques*, ii. 223 sqq.; *KL*, vii. 1101–04; Currier, *Religious Orders*, p. 188. 2. C. R. Hermans, *Annales canonicorum regularium . . . ordinis S. crucis*, Bois-le-Duc, 1858, Helyot, ut sup., ii. 222–234; Heimbucher, *Orden und Kongregationen*, i. 406–408; Currier, ut sup., pp. 188–189; *KL*, vii. 1106–11. 3. F. Jachse, *Die ritterliche Orden der Kreuzherren mit dem roten Stern*, Vienna, 1882; Helyot, ut sup., ii. 236 sqq.; Heimbucher, *Orden und Kongregationen*, i. 408–409; *KL*, vii. 1111–17. 4. Helyot, ut sup., ii. 241; Heimbucher, ut sup., i. 409; *KL*, ii. 1449–1450.

CROSS, SIGN OF THE. See CROSS AND ITS USE AS A SYMBOL.

CROSTHWAITE, ROBERT JARRATT: Bishop of Beverley; b. at Wellington (7 m. s.w. of Taunton), Somersetshire, England, Oct. 13, 1837. He studied at Trinity College, Cambridge (B.A., 1860), where he was fellow 1862–67. He was successively curate of North Cave, Yorkshire (1862–66), and of Bishopthorpe, York (1866–68), private secretary and domestic chaplain to the archbishop of York (1866–69), and vicar of Wagben-Wrawne, Yorkshire (1869–74), Brayton, Yorkshire (1874–83), and St. Lawrence cum St. Nicholas, Yorkshire (1883–1885). He was also chaplain to the archbishop of York 1879–84, prebendary of Grindal in York Cathedral, and archdeacon of York since 1884, and rector of Bolton Percy, Yorkshire, since 1885. He was rural dean of Selby, Yorkshire, in 1883–85 and of Ainsty, Yorkshire, 1893–95. In 1889 he was consecrated bishop of Beverley, suffragan to the archbishop of York. He has written *The Gospels of the New Testament, their Genuineness and Authenticity* (London, 1887).

CROWTHER, SAMUEL ADJAI: Church of England missionary bishop of the Niger; b. at Oshogun Yoruba, Central Africa, 1808; d. at Lagos, West Africa, end of Oct., 1891. When twelve and a half years old he was captured by Mohammedan slave traders, sold to the Portuguese, and shipped from Lagos. The ship was captured by a British man-of-war and he was landed at Bathurst, Sierra Leone, and given his freedom. There in the Church of England mission he was educated and converted, and baptized on Dec. 11, 1825, taking the name of Samuel Crowther. He showed marked ability and learned with avidity. In 1826 he studied in the parochial school at Islington, London. In 1827 he returned to Africa and, after graduating from the Fourah Bay college at Sierra Leone, was put in charge of the school at Regents Town in 1830, in 1832 of that at Wellington, and in 1832 was professor in his alma mater. In 1841 he was sent by the Church Missionary Society to explore the Niger country. In 1842 he was ordained in England. In 1843 he resumed work at Sierra Leone. In 1844 he began the Yoruba mission. On June 29th, 1864, he was consecrated first bishop of the Niger in Canterbury Cathedral.

Bibliography: J. Page, *Samuel Crowther, Bishop of the Niger*, New York, 1889; *DNB*, supplement vol., ii. 93.

CROZIER: A tall staff, terminating in a cross, which is borne before Roman Catholic patriarchs and archbishops as a symbol of jurisdiction. That of the ordinary archbishop, which he uses only within his own province, has a single cross-piece; that of a patriarch two, and of the pope three. A cross similar to an archbishop's is also borne before cardinals in particular solemnities. The name crozier is sometimes, though less correctly, applied to the pastoral staff or crook of bishops, for which see Vestments and Insignia, Ecclesiastical.

CROZIER, JOHN BAPTIST: Bishop of Down, Connor, and Dromore; b. at Ballyhaise (65 m. s. of Londonderry), County Cavan, Ireland, Apr. 8, 1853. He studied at Trinity College, Dublin (B.A., 1872; M.A., 1875), and was curate of St. Stephen's, Belfast (1876–77), St. Anne's, Belfast (1877–80), vicar of Holywood, County Down (1880–97). He was chaplain to the bishop of Down 1885–86, chaplain to the archbishop of Armagh 1886–93, and chaplain to the lord lieutenant of Ireland 1891–07. He was also prebendary of Dunsford in Down Cathedral 1889–90, treasurer of Down Cathedral 1890–97, and prebendary of Wicklow and canon of St. Patrick's National Cathedral 1896–97 He was honorary secretary of the General Synod of the Church of Ireland in 1896–97, and select preacher to Dublin University in 1898 and 1906, and to Cambridge University in 1903. In 1897 he was consecrated to the see of Ossory, Ferns, and Leighlin, and in 1907 was translated to Down.

CRUCIFIX: A cross bearing the image of the crucified Christ. Early Christian art did not attempt to portray the crucifixion, and crucifixes do not seem to be older than the ninth century. They show the same general characteristics as artistic representations of the crucifixion in general (see Crucifixion, § 4). In the West crucifixes have been much used in the churches as objects of public devotion and also as objects of private devotion in houses, and are worn on the person by ecclesiastics and others.

CRUCIFIXION.

1. Form of the Cross.

Crucifixion ("fixing to the cross"), as a method of inflicting the death penalty, originated in the East and was practised by Medes, Persians, and Semitic peoples (except the Jews); later by the Greeks and especially by the Romans. The scanty and not always clear information extant with reference to the form of the cross used reveals two main types: the so-called *crux acuta*, a perpendicular stake or pale, sharpened at the top; and the form consisting of an upright post and a superimposed, or transverse, cross-beam (T , ✝). The so-called St. Andrew's cross, reputed to have signalized the martyrdom of the Apostle Andrew, and traditionally conceived as consisting of two arms of equal length intersecting obliquely (X), is a product of medieval legend. While the simple stake was employed for the impalement as well as for the suspension of those under sentence, the composite cross was used for the latter purpose only. The length of the main portion was ordinarily but little above human stature; the cross-piece (*patibulum*) was either bolted fast to the upright post, which stood driven into the ground; or, as oftener happened, the cross-piece was carried to the place of execution by the sentenced culprits.

2. Method of Fastening to the Cross.

There was no uniform process of fastening the delinquent on the cross. A certain latitude appears to have been allowed the executioners both in regard to the means employed and also with reference to the manner and method of suspension—a fact explicable by the circumstance that the Roman law recognized crucifixion only as punishment for slaves and people of inferior standing. Either cords alone or cords and nails were employed; and in the latter case, now only the hands, again both hands and feet were nailed fast. The "seat" (*sedile*), serving to support the body, a block or pin on which the condemned was placed astride, apparently was not used in all cases; and the same is true with respect to a wooden step for the feet (represented in the "travesty crucifixion" of the imperial palace at Rome; see Asinarii)—which, by the way, is not to be confused with the *hypopodium* or *suppedaneum* of medieval portrayals of the crucifixion, the existence of which in antiquity is not sufficiently confirmed by the testimony of Gregory of Tours. The transgressor's offense, where not made known orally by a preceding crier, was usually written on a tablet (*titulus*), which the delinquent carried himself or another carried before him. Naturally this *titulus* was attached to the cross after the act of execution (cf. Matt. xxvii. 37, and parallels).

3. The Cross and Crucifixion of Jesus.

No definite data are found in the New Testament concerning the nature of the cross on which Jesus died. It is only the Church writers after Justin Martyr who indicate the composite four-armed cross as Christ's vehicle of torture. Justin, Irenæus, Tertullian, and others mention the presence of a *sedile*. The palatine travesty cross belonging to the beginning of the third century is of the four-armed pattern, but without the *sedile* and with the wooden step. There is no valid reason for supposing that the representation of the form of the cross of Jesus given by ecclesiastical antiquity is an imaginary construction of later times. If there were witnesses of the death of Jesus, and if the words from the cross furnished the central theme of apostolic and postapostolic preaching, then a genuine tradition as to the form of the Lord's cross may well have been maintained till the time of Justin. Indeed, in the Gospel narrative itself some indications are found which confirm this conclusion. The "cross" borne by Jesus himself (John xix. 17) or by Simon of Cyrene (Matt. xxvii. 32, and parallels) can hardly have been the upright, embedded post, with or without the *patibulum*, since the strength of one man alone might scarcely have sufficed for so great a burden. If "cross," however (Gk. *stauros*), in the passages cited be interpreted as meaning the *patibulum*—which is quite possible—the narrative is in accord with custom, as already noted. Furthermore, at Jerusalem as elsewhere, posts were no doubt in readiness at the place of execution driven into the ground to serve their purpose. From the circumstance, finally, that the executionary order caused the *titulus* to be fastened at the upper end of the cross it may be deduced that the cross piece did not rest on top, but intersected the post; or, in other words, the cross was a four-armed one. A basis for estimating the height of the cross of Jesus is afforded by John xix. 29 (cf. Matt. xxvii. 48, and parallels). The length of the "[reed of] hyssop" there mentioned was probably about one yard; the height of the entire cross, therefore, was from two and a half to three yards.

Crucifixion was accounted in all antiquity the most cruel and at the same time the most infamous death penalty, and was applied almost exclusively to slaves and persons of inferior estate (*servile supplicium*), or to aliens lacking Roman citizenship; and this for both common and political transgressions. A scourging commonly preceded, conjoined with all kinds of mockery at the expense of the culprit. The disrobing which anticipated the closing act accorded with a general custom, as did also the distribution of raiment among the executioners. The corpse was ordinarily left on the cross. Nevertheless, there was no statutory obstacle to the surrender of the body. Value was attached to publicity of execution; and for this reason highways or elevated squares were selected for the place. The crucifixion of Jesus accords fully with our general knowledge of such executions, save that certain peculiar features were added owing to Jewish views and customs: for instance, the stupefying potion (cf. Prov. xxxi. 6) and the removal of the body no later than Friday evening (Deut. xxi. 22-23). The matter of nailing the feet is debatable, and a positive decision on this point is not attainable. Constantine the Great abolished the penalty of crucifixion.

4. The Crucifixion in Art.

The first picture of the crucifixion, so far as known, is the "travesty crucifixion" referred to above (§ 2), and is by a pagan hand. The religious sentiment of Christianity regarded the Savior not so much in the act of his humiliation as in his powerful exaltation; and, accordant with this feeling, Christian art for a long time made no representations of the Passion. When the first irresolute steps were taken in the way of such art, the controlling design appears to have been to soften the agony as far as possible (cf. Victor Schultze, *Archäologie der altchristlichen Kunst*, Munich, 1895, pp. 332 sqq.). The first example of a crucifixion of Christian origin is found in a relief of the timber door of Santa Sabina at Rome, dating at the earliest from about the middle of the fifth century. The background represents the walls of Jerusalem. The heroic form of the Savior is accompanied by the two malefactors, the latter being of a somewhat youthful design. Of perhaps the same age is a North Italian ivory tablet of the British Museum, grouping John and Mary with the Savior, and expressing chiefly an emotion of deep silent sorrow. In both cases Christ is represented as alive and free from suffering. How strongly, indeed, the earlier sentiment still acted even a century later is attested by the small metal flasks at Monza in North Italy, which came from Jerusalem to the West in the time of Gregory the Great. They manifestly endeavor to deviate from the real crucifixion, and stop short with suggestions; as where, in one instance, Jesus extends his arms in the manner of a crucified victim, though the cross itself is wanting; or, again, where only his head hovers above the cross.

During the transition from the early Christian to the Romanesque period, the reactive influences of the more primitive age still appear; Christ is represented as living, draped only with the loin cloth, his feet placed side by side. In another aspect, the increasing number of accompanying figures indicates an elaboration of the treatment; while also the long tunic occurs, though this exceptionally. In contrast with the West, Byzantine art favors both in this period and subsequently the representation of the dying Savior, as he succumbs in death's agony. In every instance his hands and feet are pierced, the feet resting on a step-fashioned cross-piece. The Romanesque epoch, during which the crucifixion was most extensively treated as a theme of painting or sculpture, adorns the head of Christ with a wreath or diadem; but there now also occur more and more frequent examples of the treatment of the Lord as dead or dying; in fact, there is a tendency toward sharpest realism. On the other hand, there still persists as a characteristic trait the composure of the feet side by side; and this custom is observed as far down as the middle of the thirteenth century.

A material transformation was brought about by the Gothic style, partly under the sway of religious individuality, partly through the realistic reaction of devotional plays. The kingly crown gives place to the crown of thorns; the effect of pain becomes visible in the bodily attitude, often most acutely so; the head is bowed, the body bent. A single nail now pierces or transfixes both feet, which are superimposed (for what is alleged to be better knowledge cf. F. Piper, *Einleitung in die monumentale Theologie*, Gotha, 1867, pp. 619 sqq.). The convulsive and tragical elements of the events are also reflected in the general setting. To this province belongs the German art of the sixteenth century, especially as illustrated in Dürer and Holbein. It aspires to historical truth, and is not repelled by what is ghastly. On the other hand, the Italian Renaissance mitigates the harsh tones by application of its ideal of beauty. The same tendency is followed in the main by the art evolution of the seventeenth and eighteenth centuries; while the so-called "Nazarenes" introduced an insipid sentimental tone into portrayals of the Passion, which has its exponents even to-day. The modern religious inclination seeks to enforce historic truth, and does not shrink from the sternest realism.

At the outset the other personages presented by the Gospel narrative appear only to a limited extent (John and Mary, and one or two soldiers); but, as the Middle Ages draw to a close, richly animated scenes are created from the accessory details; most notably so on the carved altars. The religious dramas were of conspicuous influence in this direction. However, during the Romanesque period as well, certain legendary or allegorical figures begin to group themselves about the cross. Personifications of the Church and the Synagogue occur: the former as *Victrix*, the latter as Vanquished (cf. Paul Weber, *Geistliches Schauspiel und kirchliche Kunst in ihrem Verhältnis erläutert an einer Ikonographie der Kirche und Synagoge*, Stuttgart, 1894, with illustrations). Adam and Eve, the primogenitors of sin, which the Savior expiated for them as well as others, kneel beside the cross; though usually Adam alone is seen, resting in his grave beneath the cross, or in the act of rising and uplifting his hand toward the Crucified. With reference to the grave on Golgotha, the skull and cross bones appear at the foot of the cross. Furthermore, in connection with Gen. iii. 15, a serpent is twined about the base of the cross. The chalice on which rests the Savior's foot, or which is fastened under the step, represents the Holy Grail. The chalice also is sometimes held in the hand of the Church, *Ecclesia*. At a quite early period, sun and moon are drawn into the scene, either in their natural semblance or personified; likewise, lamenting angels, God the Father, and the Holy Ghost on high. The popularity and wide circulation of the legend of Veronica (q.v.), again, accounts for the fact that the devout lady finds a place with especial frequency on the way to the place of execution, though sometimes as well in the vicinity of the Crucified.

The cross generally adheres to its traditional form. The medieval legends as to the wood of the cross became influential in approximating the cross in greater or less degree to the tree form. These observations attest the tremendous attractive power which the cross and the crucifixion exercised upon the religious temperament and upon ecclesiastical usage; and therewith, both directly and indirectly, upon art. See Cross and its Use as a Symbol.

Victor Schultze.

Bibliography: O. Zöckler, *Das Kreuz Christi*, Gütersloh, 1875, Eng. transl., London, 1877 ("sane and discriminating"); H. Fulda, *Das Kreuz und die Kreuzigung*, Breslau, 1878 (of great value); C. A. Zestermann, *Die bildliche Darstellung des Kreuzes und die Kreuzigung Christi*, 2 parts, Leipsic, 1867–68; T. Reil, *Die frühchristlichen Darstellungen der Kreuzigung Christi*, ib. 1904; *DB*, i. 528–529; *EB*, i. 957–961. For list of books on the Cross in Art see under Cross and its Use as a Symbol.

CRUCIGER (CREUZIGER, CREUTZINGER), KASPAR: The name of two German theologians.

1. Kaspar Cruciger the Elder: Luther's secretary and collaborator; b. at Leipsic Jan. 1, 1504; d. at Wittenberg Nov. 16, 1548. In 1513 he matriculated at Leipsic, where he heard the disputation between Eck and Luther. In 1521 he matriculated in theology at Wittenberg, and studied also mathematics and botany. In 1525 he became rector of St. John's School and pastor at Magdeburg, but in 1528 he returned to Wittenberg as professor of theology and minister at the Schlosskirche, where he remained with a few intermissions until his death. He assisted Luther in his translation of the Bible, gave instruction when Melanchthon and others were called away, and participated in theological debates and conferences. His most important public service was connected with the establishment of the Reformation in Leipsic (1539), which he carried through with the help of Myconius. The city council tried to keep him there, but Luther declared him indispensable to Wittenberg. The Schmalkald war and the Interim embittered his last years. He wrote exegetical and dogmatic works, most of which were published after his death. He had a knowledge of shorthand and thus preserved many of Luther's sermons. With Georg Rörer he edited the first volumes of the Wittenberg edition of Luther's Works (1539 sqq.).

2. Kaspar Cruciger the Younger: Melanchthon's successor at Wittenberg, son of the elder Kaspar Cruciger; b. at Wittenberg Mar. 19, 1525; d. at Cassel Apr. 16, 1597. In the discussions after 1570 he was one of the leaders of the Philippists, and was engulfed in their catastrophe in 1574. He was imprisoned and was banished from Saxony in 1576. After a short residence with the count of Nassau at Dillenberg he went to Hesse, and died as pastor and president of the consistory at Cassel.

(Ferdinand Cohrs.)

Bibliography: **For 1.** *CR*, xi. 833–841; O. G. Schmidt, *Caspar Crucigers Leben*, Leipsic, 1862; T. Pressel, *Caspar Cruciger*, Elberfeld, 1862; J. Köstlin, *Martin Luther*, 2 vols., Berlin, 1903. **For 2.** G. J. Planck, *Geschichte der Entstehung . . . protestantischen Lehrbegriffs*, V. ii. 626 sqq., Leipsic, 1799; H. Heppe, *Geschichte des deutschen Protestantismus*, ii. 312 sqq., Marburg, 1853.

CRUDEN, ALEXANDER: The author of "Cruden's Concordance"; b. at Aberdeen May 31, 1701;

d. in London Nov. 1, 1770. He studied at Marischal College, Aberdeen, and took the degree of M.A. (year not known). Indications of an unsound mind, from which he suffered more or less all his life, soon became evident and he was in confinement for a short time. In 1722 he went to London and found employment as tutor in Hertfordshire and the Isle of Man till 1732, when he opened a bookseller's shop in London, also acting as corrector of the press. He began the *Concordance* in 1736 and issued it the following year in quarto. It was not a success pecuniarily; he lost his business, suffered another attack of insanity, and was again put in an asylum. After a few weeks he escaped and in Mar., 1739, issued a curious pamphlet relating to his confinement, with the title *The London-Citizen exceedingly Injured, or a British Inquisition Displayed*. He instituted proceedings for damages, pleaded his own cause (unsuccessfully), and published a report of the trial dedicated to King George II. He was again in confinement for a short time in 1753. In 1754 he became proofreader for the *Public Advertiser* (daily newspaper); at the same time he was busy as general corrector of the press and labored diligently in revising the *Concordance*. The hard and regular work seems to have been beneficial to his health, and it was not necessary to send him again to the asylum. He supervised the printing of an edition of Matthew Henry's *Commentary*, and published a *Compendium of the Holy Bible, . . . Designed for Making the Reading more Easy* (1750); he compiled a *Scripture Dictionary*, which was published in two volumes at Aberdeen shortly after his death; it is said also that he wrote prefaces for many books, and he prepared the verbal index for Bishop Newton's edition of Milton (1749). He issued second and third editions of the *Concordance* in 1761 and 1769, and received considerable profit from them. The explanations of Scripture terms (omitted in some editions) were published separately by the Religious Tract Society (1840); they are strongly Calvinistic. Many stories are told of Cruden's eccentricities. He thought himself divinely appointed as the public censor, especially in regard to swearing and Sabbath keeping, and took the title "Alexander the Corrector." He went about London with a sponge, erasing obscene words on walls and other things which did not meet with his approval. He appeared as candidate for parliament in 1754, applied for knighthood, sought to marry the daughter of the Lord Mayor of London, and paid unwelcome and embarrassing addresses to other young ladies. To promote his schemes he issued several extraordinary pamphlets. But notwithstanding all this he was kind-hearted, benevolent, fearless in the discharge of duty, a useful citizen, and a humble, devout Christian; and he was honored and respected where he was fully known. He was a member of an Independent church in London. He gives much information about himself in his pamphlets, particularly the three which he called *The Adventures of Alexander the Corrector* (1754–55).

Bibliography. His life by Alexander Chalmers, written for the *Biographia Britannica* (1789), was reprinted in the 5th edition of the concordance; a memoir by Samuel Blackburn was prepared for the first octavo edition (1823); another by William Youngman is found in some editions. Consult *DNB*, xii. 249–251.

CRUSADES.

The Crusades were expeditions of Christian Europe in the twelfth and thirteenth centuries for the recovery of the Holy Land. They are a part of the thousand years' conflict between Christianity and Islam; yet they constitute in themselves a complete phase of historical development. They came at a time when the wave of Mohammedan conquest had been at a standstill for more than four hundred years, and the old fanatic zeal of Islam had given way to the pursuit of worldly interests and the fostering of that high culture which still constitutes its title to historic fame. In Christian Europe, on the contrary, religious feeling had been gaining in strength. There was a movement of revulsion from earthly interests, even of actual hatred for them, and a passionate longing for the felicities of another world and for a more intimate union with God. In this spirit of piety which strove to attain material vision of the Deity must be sought the true causes of the Crusades. An age which laid so much stress on sacred relics would as a matter of course be extraordinarily susceptible to the influence of the greatest of all relics, the Holy Land. The many pilgrims of the eleventh century may scarcely be regarded as precursors of the Crusades; yet the motives that animated them throw light upon the character of the later and greater movement. Had not thousands of individuals experienced the yearning for the heavenly Jerusalem, statecraft would not have found it possible at a later date to enlist great hosts for the recovery of the earthly capital.

As early as 1074, when Asia Minor passed into the hands of the Seljuk Turks, Gregory VII. had projected a war against the infidels, having also for its object reunion with the Greek Church. The plan was thrust into the background by the conflict with the emperor Henry IV. Urban II. (1088–99), who next took up the idea, was animated not so much by the political considerations of Gregory as by actual religious impulse. From the Church should come the impelling force; on the secular powers rested the actual execution of the plan. Before this, Norman knights had engaged in conflict with the infidel, and the conception of a crusade against the Saracen was therefore no absolute novelty to the nations of the West. The Byzantine emperor Alexius I. was quite aware of this when he turned to Urban for aid against the Turks in 1094, and met with a ready response from the general religious enthusiasm, from the ambitions of the Church, and from the lust for adventure and conquest. When the Greek ambassadors arrived Urban was preparing for the Council of Clermont;

1. The First Crusade, 1096–99.

and there before great throngs the pope first preached the crusade, Nov. 26, 1095, in words which have not come down, but which stirred the mighty multitudes to frenzied enthusiasm. The number of those who assumed the crusader's cross increased daily, and the movement, soon passing beyond papal restraint, seized upon the lower classes. The peasant exchanged his plow for arms and was joined by the dissatisfied, the oppressed, and the outcast; members of the lower clergy, runaway monks, women, children gave to this advance-guard of the crusading army the character of a mob, recognizing no leadership but that of God. This undercurrent of opposition to the pope gave rise to the legend, which is still current, that not Urban, but Peter the Hermit (Peter of Amiens) was the true representative of the crusading idea. Peter was one of the leaders of the fanatical bands, whose contribution to the enterprise was a story of an alleged personal appearance of Jesus, giving him commission to acquaint Christendom with the sad condition of the Holy Land. After the wildest excesses, in which the Jews appear as the principal sufferers at their hands, these tumultuous hosts found a pitiful end in Hungary and beyond the Bosporus.

The real crusading armies set out in 1096. They comprised the men of Lorraine under the brothers Godfrey, Eustace, and Baldwin of Bouillon; northern French under Robert of Normandy; Provençals under Raymond of Toulouse; and Normans of Italy under Bohemund and Tancred. The Christian cause suffered from dissensions among the leaders, not all of whom resembled Godfrey of Bouillon in his freedom from worldly motives, and it had to contend against the machinations of Alexius I., who was roused to a sense of danger to his realm by the presence of the Western armies. Nicæa was taken, the Sultan of Iconium was defeated at Dorylæum, and on June 3, 1098, Antioch was captured and on June 28 was successfully defended against the Sultan of Mosul; on July 15, 1099, Jerusalem was taken, and Godfrey of Bouillon was made Protector of the Holy Sepulcher. He died in July, 1100, and under his successors, Baldwin I. (d. 1118), Baldwin II. (d. 1131), and Fulk (d. 1143), the boundaries of the kingdom were extended through successful warfare. The kingdom drew strength from the influx of new crusading forces, from the presence of the Italian merchants who established themselves in the Syrian ports, and from the religious and military orders of the Templars and the Knights of St. John. But prosperity led to a weakening of the military spirit, and internal strife crippled the resources of the kingdom. On Christmas day, 1144, the capture of the strong frontier fortress of Edessa by the Emir of Mosul inflicted a serious blow on the Christian power.

The news of the fall of Edessa led to a second crusade (1147–49), headed by Louis VII. of France and Conrad III. of Germany. In spite of the lofty motives which animated the French king, the second crusade shows a waning of the spirit of enthusiasm which had brought about the first. The political danger involved in the triumph of the Mohammedan arms was a determining factor in the departure of the crusading armies, and Bernard of Clairvaux, the great preacher of this crusade, found it expedient to dwell upon the taking of the cross as a potent means in gaining absolution for sin and attaining grace.

2. The Second and Third Crusades, 1147–49, 1189–92.

Lack of harmony between the royal leaders and the treacherous policy of the Byzantines led to irremediable disaster. The German army was almost totally destroyed in Asia Minor during the winter of 1147–48, and the other crusading host succumbed to defeat and the climate in the summer of 1148. Baldwin III. by his unwise seizure of Ascalon in 1153 brought Egypt into the sphere of conflict and thus prepared the way for the fall of Jerusalem. Egypt after 1169 was ruled by the powerful Seljuks, whose great champion Saladin made it the object of his life to drive the Christian power from Palestine. The war was carried on in a half-hearted manner by the Christian princes. On July 4, 1187, Saladin won the battle of Hattin, and on Oct. 2 the Holy City surrendered. The Christian power was restricted to Antioch, Tripoli, Tyre, and Margat. In the third crusade (1189–92), to which the fall of Jerusalem gave occasion, Richard I. of England, Philip Augustus of France, and Emperor Frederick I., Barbarossa, participated. The German emperor was drowned at Salef in June, 1190; Acre was taken by Richard and Philip, but the two kings quarreled and Philip retired; and Richard left Palestine in 1192, after securing by treaty with Saladin the right for pilgrims to visit the Holy Sepulcher in small bands and unarmed.

The vital crusading spirit was now dead, and the succeeding crusades are to be explained rather as arising from the efforts of the papacy in its struggle against the secular power, to divert the military energies of the European nations toward Syria.

3. The Fourth Crusade, 1202–04.

A systematic agitation was carried on, and in 1201 a large army was collected which it was planned to transport on Venetian vessels to Egypt. The Venetians under their astute doge, Enrico Dandolo, succeeded in turning the crusading movement to their own purposes. The crusaders threw themselves against the Byzantines, Constantinople was taken and sacked (1204), and the empire was apportioned between Venice and the Christian leaders. The Latin empire at Constantinople was established. An outburst of the old enthusiasm led to the Children's Crusade of 1212, which Innocent III. interpreted as a reproof from heaven to their unworthy elders. By processions, prayers, and preaching, the Church attempted to set another crusade on foot, and the Fourth Lateran Council (1215) formulated a plan for the recovery of the Holy Land. A crusading force from Hungary, Austria, and Bavaria achieved a remarkable feat in the capture of Damietta in Egypt in 1219, but under the urgent insistence of the papal legate, Pelagius, they proceeded to a foolhardy attack on Cairo, and an inundation of the Nile compelled them to choose between surrender and destruction.

In 1228 Emperor Frederick II. set sail from

4. The Fifth, Sixth, and Seventh Crusades, 1228–70.

Brindisi for Syria, though laden with the papal excommunication. Through diplomacy he achieved unexpected success, Jerusalem, Nazareth, and Bethlehem being delivered to the Christians for a period of ten years. The papal interests represented by the Templars brought on a conflict with Egypt in 1243, and in the following year a Korasmian force summoned by the latter stormed Jerusalem. Europe's last efforts appear in the two unsuccessful crusades of Louis IX. of France, against Cyprus, Egypt, and Syria in 1248–54 and against Tunis in 1270. With the fall of Antioch (1268), Tripoli (1289), and Acre (1291) the last traces of the Christian occupation of Syria disappeared.

5. Power of Papacy Increased, also Intolerance.

First among the results of the Crusades is to be counted the great increase they brought about in the power of the Church and of the papacy. The achievements of the religious wars fell far behind expectations; but the idea became firmly fixed that the pope at the head of armed Christendom had effected the conquest of the Holy Sepulcher. It was he who gave the call to arms, who supplied the necessary means from the treasures of the Church, who showered on the warriors of the cross privileges and benedictions, and who led them on through his legates; and, though the actual work of battle fell to the secular princes, the latter were held firmly in the control of the hierarchy by their irrevocable crusader's vow. Through the instrumentality of his legates, who now became an important part in the ecclesiastical administration, the pope drew to himself increased authority within the Church. A more material source of strength was the riches which inured to the Church as a result of the sacrifices of individuals in providing themselves with the means for making the crusade. Princes and knights sold or mortgaged their estates, and the Church was the readiest and unchallenged purchaser in the open market. The popes drew a special profit from this state of affairs, for, whereas during the twelfth century the bishops were accustomed to contribute out of their funds toward the cost of the military expeditions, after the Lateran Council of 1215 these bounties were claimed by Rome as the supreme leader of the holy war and became the basis of a regular tax that was enforced throughout Europe long after the fall of the last Christian citadel in the East. Further, the crusades acted as a powerful incentive to the growth of the spirit of religious intolerance. From warfare against the non-believer, whether Mohammedan, Jew, or pagan, it was not a far step to war against the heretic. Here, too, Innocent III. appears as an epoch-maker when he ventured to turn the secular arm against the internal enemies of the Church and to preach a crusade of extermination against the Albigenses of southern France. The Inquisition with all its horrors could never have taken such deep root but for the awakening of religious passions which marked the Crusades. As an offset it can hardly be maintained that European knowledge profited by the wars with the Mohammedans. The introduction of the study of Aristotle in the West is to be ascribed rather to the friendly relations which prevailed between Christians and Saracens in Spain and Sicily. Nor is it absolutely certain that Western art was materially enriched by contact with Byzantium and Syria; the numerous *objets d'art* brought back as booty from the East did no more than influence the development of a decorative art by supplying models for imitation.

6. Devotion Stimulated, Absolution Extended.

On the other hand, it would be impossible to overestimate the stimulating effect of the Crusades on the spirit of devotion in Christian Europe. In the papal emissaries entrusted with the preaching of the crusade the first popular preachers of the Middle Ages are met with. The clerics left their churches and addressed the multitudes in the field and public squares; to them in large measure may be traced the fervent, imaginative eloquence of the later mendicant monks. The questionable practise of searching out localities supposedly connected with sacred tradition and the establishment therein of ceremonies endowed with peculiar efficacies now arises. The period is one of tradition-making, which up to the present day has plunged the geography of Palestine into confusion. The pilgrim who after the fall of Acre was shut off from the greatest shrine of Christian worship turned to the sacred places of the West or of his own land, and the creation of such centers and objects of devotion became an important function of the Church. The worship of relics extended enormously and the trade in holy remains was carried on in all conceivable forms and not without the grossest absurdities or deceptions. The body of legend increased and the Virgin became an especially favorite subject of presentation in narrative and art. It would also seem that the great importance of the rosary, which before this period appears prominently only in isolated instances, is to be regarded as dating from the thirteenth century, when it developed under the influence of the similar feature of Mohammedan worship known as *tasbiḥ*.

Of portentous importance was the effect wrought by the Crusades on the system of absolution. Originally immunity from the penalties of transgression was granted only to those who assumed the cross out of purely religious motives; but as early as Celestine III. (d. 1198) the mere contribution of money toward an expedition against the infidel was rewarded with at least partial remission, while Innocent III. granted complete remission to one who sent a substitute to the field. And inasmuch as one might be absolved from his crusader's vow on the payment of a sum of money, and absolution eventually was offered for such minor acts of piety as the mere listening to an exhortation to take the cross, it is evident that wide opportunities, indeed, were offered for escape from the penalties of sin.

The Crusades were not without effect on the Renaissance and the Reformation. Friendly intercourse with the Mohammedan world brought Europe into contact with accomplishments and virtues which were felt to be lacking at home. Men became aware of a moral system independent of

Christianity that was nevertheless worthy of respect.

7. The Renaissance and Reformation.

Theological disputations between Christian and Mohammedan revealed the fact that the Catholic dogma was not invulnerable. From the attention to the hitherto unsuspected merits of an opponent it was not a far step to a critical examination of one's own condition. In Germany suspicion of the motives of the Church in urging the wars against the Mohammedans and a reluctance to contribute toward the realization of the plans formulated by an ambitious papacy and carried on by self-seeking warriors became manifest. Thus the Church, which had made itself the leader of the Crusades, came to suffer the consequences of their ill success. Faith in papal absolutism waned; and a new religious spirit appeared, first in the sectaries (Cathari and Albigenses), and later in the Reformation. This spirit was fostered by the inspiration of that higher culture of which Frederick II. is the preeminent type, by the development of the sciences, and by the growth of commerce with the East, which enriched Europe and turned the attention of men from purely religious to material and cultural interests in the movement known as the Renaissance. (FRIEDRICH WIEGAND.)

BIBLIOGRAPHY: The best collection of sources are *Recueil des historiens des croisades*, 13 vols., Paris, 1841–85 (under the care of the Academy); J. Michaud, *Bibliothèque des Croisades*, 4 vols., Paris, 1829. Single sources are: Jean de Joinville, *Histoire de St. Louis IX.*, ed. A. Delboulle, Paris, 1882, Eng. transl., in *Bohn's Library*, London, 1848; Geoffroy de Villehardouin, *Histoire de l'empire de Constantinople*, ed. É. Bouchet, 2 vols., Paris, 1891, Eng. transl., in *Bohn's Library*, London, 1848; Ansbert, *Historia de expeditione Friderici . . .*, ed. J. Dobrowsky, Prague, 1827; Odo of Deuil, *De profectione Ludovici VII. in orientem*, ed. G. H. Pertz, in *MGH*, *Script.*, xxvi (1882), 59–73; *Historia* of William of Tyre, transl. by Mary N. Colom for the Early English Text Society, London, 1893; original documents in *Translations and Reprints from the Original Sources of European History*, vol. i., Philadelphia, 1902; H. von Sybel, *Hist. and Literature of the Crusades*, ed. Lady D. Gordon, London, 1861 (a compilation, not a translation of any one work, gives account of literature).

On the general history of the Crusades the best single work is still J. Michaud, *Histoire des Croisades*, 4 vols., Paris, 1856, Eng. transl., with preface and supplement, by H. W. Mabie, 3 vols., Boston, 1881. Other general works are: F. Wilken, *Geschichte der Kreuzzüge*, 7 vols., Leipsic, 1807–32; R. Röhricht, *Beiträge zur Geschichte der Kreuzzüge*, 2 vols., Berlin, 1874–78; B. Kugler, *Geschichte der Kreuzzüge*, Berlin, 1891; J. I. Mombert, *Short History of the Crusades*, New York, 1894 (popular); T. A. Archer and C. L. Kingsford, *The Crusades*, ib. 1895; J. M. Ludlow, *Age of the Crusades*, ib. 1897 (contains bibliography); L. von Ranke, *Weltgeschichte*, vol. viii., Leipsic, 1898; E. Heyck, *Die Kreuzzüge und das heilige Land*, ib. 1900; *Essays on the Crusades*, by D. C. Munro, C. Diehl, and H. Prutz, Burlington, 1903; L. Brehier, *L'Église et l'orient au moyen âge. Les croisades*, Paris, 1907; W. B. Stevenson, *The Crusaders in the East. A brief Hist. of the Wars of Islam with the Latins, 12.–13. Centuries*, Cambridge, 1907; Schaff, *Christian Church*, v. 1, pp. 211–295.

For the Kingdom of Jerusalem consult: R. Röhricht, *Geschichte des Königreichs Jerusalem, 1100–1291*, Innsbruck, 1898; C. R. Conder, *The Latin Kingdom of Jerusalem, 1099–1291*, London, 1897.

On individual Crusades consult: H. von Sybel, *Geschichte des ersten Kreuzzugs*, Leipsic, 1881; T. Wolff, *Die Bauernkreuzzüge*, Tübingen, 1891; B. Kugler, *Studien zur Geschichte des zweiten Kreuzzuges*, Stuttgart, 1866; E. Pears, *The Fall of Constantinople*, London, 1885; R. Röhricht, *Studien zur Geschichte des fünften Kreuzzuges*, Innsbruck, 1891; H. Klettke, *Robert of Marseilles, or the Crusade of the Children*, Philadelphia, 1883; G. Z. Gray, *Children's Crusade*, Boston, 1896; M. Schwob, *Children's Crusade*, ib. 1905.

CRUSIUS, CHRISTIAN AUGUST: German theologian; b. at Leuna, near Merseburg (10 m. s. of Halle), Jan. 10, 1715; d. at Leipsic Oct. 18, 1775. He entered the University of Leipsic in 1734, became professor of philosophy there, and in 1750 professor of theology. He was an independent follower of J. A. Bengel and an opponent of the Wolfian philosophy, founding all knowledge on positive revelation and seeking to prove that it harmonizes with reason. At the same time he intermingled mystic peculiarities, and thus constructed a strange typico-prophetical system of doctrine. While his colleague Ernesti explained the Scriptures in a purely grammatical way, Crusius followed the Church doctrine, which he interpreted in a mystical sense. Of his many writings the most important are *Hypomnemata ad theologiam propheticam* (3 parts, Leipsic, 1764) and *Kurzer Begriff der Moraltheologie* (2 parts, 1772–73). Here he opposes the divine will, known from revelation as moral principle, to the Wolfian principle of perfection. His "Prophetic Theology" was brought into notice in the nineteenth century by Hengstenberg and Delitzsch, who called attention to the fact that Crusius conceived of the essence and aim of prophecy in connection with the scheme of salvation, which no theologian before him had done with like emphasis. Crusius left the reputation of a learned, keen, original thinker and of a pure, pious, and mild character. Even in the great controversy which divided the University of Leipsic into "Ernestians" and "Crusians" he maintained his pious and mild manner, though there was no question that Ernesti's views were gaining the upper hand. PAUL TSCHACKERT.

BIBLIOGRAPHY: H. Döring, *Die Gelehrten Theologen Deutschlands*, i. 291–296, Neustadt, 1831; *ADB*, iv. 630–631; J. E. Erdmann, *Geschichte der Philosophie*, vol. iii., § 290, Berlin, 1870, Eng. transl., London, 1893.

CRUTTWELL, CHARLES THOMAS: Church of England; b. at London July 30, 1847. He studied at the Merchant Taylors' School, London, and St. John's College, Oxford (B.A., 1871), and was elected fellow of Merton College, Oxford, in 1870, where he was also tutor in 1875–77. He was curate of St. Giles's, Oxford, 1875–77, head master of St. Andrew's College, Bradfield, 1878–80, and of Malvern College 1880–85. He was rector of Sutton, Surrey (1885), Denton, Norfolk (1885–91), and Kibworth-Beauchamp, Leicestershire (1891–1901), as well as rural dean of Gartree, diocese of Peterborough (1892–1902). Since 1901 he has been rector of Ewelme, Oxfordshire, and was honorary canon of Peterborough Cathedral in 1897–1903, of which he has been residentiary canon since 1903, being also appointed proctor in convocation for the clergy of the diocese of Peterborough in 1900–05 and examining chaplain to the bishop of Peterborough in 1900. He has written *A History of Roman Literature* (London, 1877); *Specimens of Roman Literature* (1879; in collaboration with P. Banton); *Literary History of Early*

Christianity (2 vols., 1893); and *Six Lectures on the Oxford Movement* (1899).

CRYPT: An architectural term most frequently used to denote a subterranean story or division of a church. The word was early applied to the subterranean cemeteries of the Christians, the so-called catacombs, or, more properly, single passages and galleries of them in which martyrs or saints were buried. As it became customary to erect churches above the catacombs, just over the grave of a martyr, and with an opening under the altar which allowed the worshipers to look down into the grave, into the crypt, it was natural that afterward the name "crypt" should be transferred to similar excavations under the choir of the basilicas and churches of the Romanesque style, which sometimes were so extensive as to form whole subterranean churches, and often were used as places of interment for bishops. With the Romanesque style the crypts disappeared.

Bibliography: H. D. M. Spence, *White Robe of Churches*, pp. 77-90, New York, 1900.

CRYPTO-CALVINISTS: The term applied to those Germans who secretly held or were accused of holding the Calvinistic doctrine of the Eucharist. See Philippists.

CUDWORTH, RALPH: The most celebrated of the school of seventeenth century philosophers known as the "Cambridge Platonists" (q.v.); b. at Aller, in Somersetshire (12 m. s.w. of Wells), 1617; d. at Cambridge June 26, 1688. He entered Emmanuel College, Cambridge, in 1632, and, after taking his M.A. degree in 1639, became fellow and tutor of the college. In 1642 he entered the lists against the Catholic party with his first published work, *A Discourse concerning the True Nature of the Lord's Supper*, which he considers

Life.

to be that of a "feast upon a sacrifice," analogous to the feasts which followed the legal sacrifices among the Jews; not itself *sacrificium*, but, in Tertullian's language, *participatio sacrificii*. Soon after he published *The Union of Christ and the Church; in a Shadow*, in which he attempted to vindicate what he thought Protestants had too much lost sight of, the higher meaning of marriage. Young as he was, he had already mastered all the main sources of philosophy, medieval as well as classical, and quotes freely from the Neoplatonists and Cabalists, as well as from such modern Platonists as Vives and Pico della Mirandola (q.v.). In 1644 he was appointed master of Clare Hall by the Parliamentary visitors, and a year later was made regius professor of Hebrew, a position which his knowledge of Jewish literature and antiquities made congenial to him. It seems that he thought of leaving Cambridge in 1651, but the election to the mastership of Christ's College in 1654 settled him there anew. In spite of his close relations with the Commonwealth government, he was undisturbed at the Restoration, and was even presented in 1662 to the rectory of Ashwell in Herefordshire by Sheldon, archbishop of Canterbury, and made a prebendary of Gloucester in 1678. Academic and philosophic labors occupied the remainder of his life. Alarmed by the tendencies of the irreligious and deistic writers of the time, especially Hobbes, he essayed to meet them by a counter-philosophy which should go to the depth of human thought and belief. The most important part of what in his conception was intended to constitute one great whole was *The True Intellectual System of the Universe*, finished in 1671 but not published until 1678. Its full importance was not recognized until after its author's death; Le Clerc published extracts from it in 1703, and attracted to it the attention of Continental thinkers; in 1706 an abridged edition was published in London by Wise; and in 1733 Mosheim brought out a Latin version with valuable notes of his own, reproduced in the London edition of 1845. In this great treatise Cudworth combated the atheistic hypothesis.

Philosophical System.

He planned to set forth, against various forms of fatalism which appeared to him inconsistent with the true order of the universe, three great principles which should sum up religious and moral truth. These were (1) the reality of a supreme divine intelligence and a spiritual world, against the atomistic materialism of Democritus and Epicurus; (2) the eternal reality of moral ideas against the medieval Nominalists and their successors; and (3) the reality of moral freedom and responsibility in man against all pantheistic naturalism and stoicism. Of these the *Intellectual System* deals formally with the first only. To the later parts belong the *Treatise on Eternal and Immutable Morality*, posthumously published by Bishop Chandler in 1731, and the *Treatise on Free Will*, ed. Allen, 1838, as well as some two thousand folio pages of manuscript still lying in the British Museum. Though inferior in originality and clearness to Descartes and Hobbes, the writers with whose views his are most strongly contrasted, he went to the root of his side of the questions under discussion. As a philosopher he was not a pure Platonist; in metaphysics, indeed, he followed Plato and the Neoplatonists, but in natural philosophy the Atomists, and in that of religion Lord Herbert of Cherbury. His theological standpoint was determined partly by his philosophy, partly by the circumstances of his time. He asserted the necessity of revealed religion, but saw in philosophy a divine illumination. Averse from partisan strife, he held a middle course between the rigid High-churchmanship of the school of Laud and Independent fanaticism, combining the recognition, with the former, of the rightfulness of an ecclesiastical constitution and an order of worship, and with the latter of the necessity of inner light and an unswerving devotion to ethical ideals.

Bibliography: The principal authority is the preface to the ed. of Cudworth's Works, Jena, 1733, for which the materials were furnished probably by Thomas Baker. The best treatment of Cudworth's system is in J. Martineau, *Types of Ethical Theory*, ii. 396-424, London, 1886. Consult: J. Tulloch, *Rational Theology . . . in England in 17th Cent.*, ii. 193-293, Edinburgh, 1872; C. E. Lowrey, *The Philosophy of Ralph Cudworth*, New York, 1884; W. R. Scott, *Introduction to Cudworth's Treatise . . .*, London, 1891 (contains a life and an apology); *DNB*, xii. 271-272; also the works cited under Cambridge Platonists.

CULDEES. See CELTIC CHURCH IN BRITAIN AND IRELAND, III., 2, § 4.

CULM, BISHOPRIC OF: A bishopric in West Prussia, originally the southernmost in the territory of the Teutonic Order. It was constituted in 1243 by the legate of Innocent IV., Bishop William of Modena, and included the lands between the rivers Weichsel, Ossa, and Drewenz. The bishop's seat was originally Culmsee (85 m. s. of Danzig) and is now Pelplin (50 m. farther north). The first bishop was the Dominican Heidenreich (1245–1263), who encouraged colonization and, strongly supported by the Teutonic Order, built many churches. The bishop was the temporal as well as the spiritual ruler, but excercised his judicial and legislative rights through an appointed sheriff, who was also the military leader in case of need. As in the three other Prussian bishoprics founded during the supremacy of the Teutonic Order, the bishops recognized a certain not strictly feudal suzerainty in its heads, whose decisions were either taken in consultation with them or accepted by them on promulgation. Annual visitations (known as *synodi laicales*) were held by the bishop or his deputies; diocesan synods are known to have been held in 1438 and 1481; and provincial synods met in 1427 at Elbing and 1428 at Riga, under the metropolitan jurisdiction of which latter see Culm was placed by Alexander IV. in 1255. By the Peace of Thorn in 1466 Culm, with a part of Prussia, came under Polish rule, and the bishopric, henceforth a secular one, was to be subjected to the archbishop of Gnesen—though the last provision was not confirmed by the pope, and it was only after the see of Riga had perished in the Reformation that Bishop Peter Kostka (1577) sought union with Gnesen. The Reformation had been presaged in the fifteenth century by considerable Hussite and Wyclifite activity; and in the sixteenth, in spite of secular repressive measures, the Protestants rapidly increased in numbers, and won religious liberty in Thorn from King Sigismund in 1558. Most of the diocese came under Prussian rule at the first partition of Poland in 1772 (Thorn not until the second in 1793), and the estates of the bishop, chapter, and monasteries were confiscated by the State, which undertook to pay over half the net annual revenues. The Protestant faith, which had been kept down under the Polish government, now spread once more under the Prussian crown, which has had possession of the district except when (1807–15) it formed a part of the duchy of Warsaw.

BIBLIOGRAPHY: *Urkundenbuch des Bistums Culm*, ed. C. P. Woelky, Danzig, 1884–87; F. Schulz, *Geschichte der Stadt und des Kreises Kulm*, Danzig, 1876–77.

CULVERWEL, NATHANAEL: An English philosophical writer, belonging to the school known as the "Cambridge Platonists" (q.v.); b. about 1615; d. not later than 1651. He became a pensioner of Emmanuel College, Cambridge, in 1633, B.A., 1636, and M.A., 1640, and was elected to a fellowship in 1642. His chief work, the *Discourse of the Light of Nature*, was published with several smaller treatises in 1652 (new ed., Edinburgh, 1857). It seems to have been suggested by the *De veritate* of his contemporary Lord Herbert of Cherbury (see DEISM, I., § 1), with whose views on epistemology he coincides to a remarkable degree, though controverting his attack upon Christianity from the side of reason. For grandeur and harmony of conception, as well as for rare insight and the spiritual rapture which is almost the only trace of the Calvinism in which he was apparently brought up, the book is one of the most striking productions of the Cambridge school. Its main theme is the use of reason and the special nobility of its function in the search after truth; a second part was projected, to deal with the conciliation of faith and reason, against the Socinians and other opponents of the Gospel of Christ.

BIBLIOGRAPHY: E. T. Campagnac, *The Cambridge Platonists, Selections from the Writings of . . . N. Culverwel*, Oxford, 1901; J. Tulloch, *Rational Theology . . . in England in 17th Cent.*, ii. 410–426, Edinburgh, 1872; *DNB*, xiii. 288–289.

CUMBERLAND PRESBYTERIAN CHURCH. See PRESBYTERIANS.

CUMMIAN (CUMEAN, CUMINE, CUIMINE): The name of several Irish monks, of whom the best known is Cuimine Ailbhe ("Cummian the Fair"), seventh abbot of Iona, 657–669. He wrote a life of St. Columba, which forms the basis of the third book of Adamnan's life of Columba as well as of some chapters in the preceding books. Colgan and others think that he was also the author of a letter on the Easter controversy addressed in 634 to Seghine, fifth abbot of Iona, while Lanigan and others think it impossible that an ardent advocate of the Roman Easter, like the author of this letter, can have been made abbot of Iona in the seventh century, and ascribe the letter to another of the same name. By whomever written, it is an able document; it shows familiarity with the Scriptures and the writings of the Fathers, quotes the decrees of councils, and displays mathematical powers of no mean order. The writer feels the insignificance of his land among the great nations of the world, and, referring to the stubbornness of his countrymen, ironically exclaims: "Rome is wrong; Jerusalem is wrong; Antioch is wrong; all the world is wrong; only the Irish and Britons know what is right." He had himself followed the old custom till about 630, and changed only after careful and thorough study lasting a whole year.

Certain writings known as the *Excarpsus*, the *Pœnitentiale Remense*, and the *Capitula judiciorum*, published by Wasserschleben and Schmitz in their works on the ancient penitential discipline, are traditionally ascribed to "Cummian," but nothing is known as to the identity of the author. The most probable date for the composition of the works is the first half of the eighth century. The *Excarpsus* circulated throughout the Frankish kingdom and in Italy, and was used in later penitential books as well as collections of canons before Gratian.

BIBLIOGRAPHY: The life of Columba is in *ASM*, i. 342–349, and in De Smedt and De Backer, *Acta sanctorum Hiberniæ*, pp. 845–870, Edinburgh, 1888; the letter in Ussher, *Veterum epistolarum Hibernicarum sylloge*, Dublin, 1632, *Works*, iv. 432–444, whence it is copied in *MPL*, lxxxvii. 969–978; for the other works named consult: F. W. H. Wasserschleben, *Bussordnungen*, 72, 460 sqq., Halle, 1851; H. J. Schmitz, *Bussbücher und Bussdisziplin*, 602 sqq., Mainz, 1883. For life of Cummian consult: J. Colgan, *Acta sanctorum Hiberniæ*, Louvain, 1645, 408-411; Lanigan, *Eccl. Hist.*, ii. 396-402.

CUMMINS, GEORGE DAVID: Bishop and one of the organizers of the Reformed Episcopal Church; b. near Smyrna, Kent County, Del., Dec. 11, 1822; d. at Lutherville, near Baltimore, June 26, 1876. He was graduated at Dickinson College, Carlisle, Pa., 1841; served as a Methodist preacher for two years, but changed to the Protestant Episcopal Church and was ordained deacon in 1845. He became assistant minister at Christ Church, Baltimore, 1846; rector of Christ Church, Norfolk, Va., 1847; of St. James's, Richmond, 1853; of Trinity, Washington, 1855; of St. Peter's, Baltimore, 1858; of Trinity, Chicago, 1863. In 1866 he was consecrated assistant bishop of Kentucky. He was a leader of the "Evangelical" or "Low-church" party of his communion, and favored a revision of the prayer-book. In 1873 he attended the meeting of the Evangelical Alliance in New York and officiated at a joint communion service held there. For this act he was sharply criticized, and, as a result, a month later formally withdrew from the Episcopal Church, declaring that he could no longer countenance by his presence the ritualistic practises of certain churches of his diocese, that he had lost all hope of rectification of abuses by the Church, and that he must take his place where he could give open expression of Christian brotherhood without alienating those of his own household of faith. Conferences with others whose position or views were similar to his own followed, and the result was the organization in Dec., 1873, of the Reformed Episcopal Church (q.v.), of which he became senior bishop.

Bibliography: Mrs. G. D. Cummins, *Memoir of G. D. Cummins*, New York, 1878.

CUNEIFORM INSCRIPTIONS. See Inscriptions, II.

CUNIBERT, cū'ni"bār": Bishop of Cologne; d. about 660. He was educated in the cathedral school of Treves and became archdeacon in that city. He received the bishopric of Cologne before 626, probably by royal appointment. In 626 or 627 he took part in the Synod of Clichy and in the Synod of Reims under Sonnatius (627-630). After the retirement of Arnulf of Metz (629 or 630) he became very influential in politics at the court of the Merovingian kings Clothaire II., Dagobert I., and especially Sigebert III. (632-656), who was not yet of age. He was active in spiritual and secular affairs, for instance, in the division of the public treasury (638), in founding monasteries like those of Cougnon, Stablo, and Malmedy (642-650), in different donations and acquisitions of the Church of Cologne, also in the missionary activities among the Frisians. After the death of King Sigebert III. Cunibert seems to have retired to his bishopric, but in 660 he probably reassumed his political position under King Childeric II. He must have died soon afterward. Later he was honored as saint.

(A. Hauck.)

Bibliography: Rettberg, *KD*, i. 296, 535, ii. 602; Friedrich, *KD*, ii. 295; Hauck, *KD*, i. 377-378.

III.—21

CUNITZ, AUGUST EDUARD: Alsatian Protestant; b. at Strasburg Aug. 29, 1812; d. there June 16, 1886. After completing his theological education in his native city, he visited Göttingen, Berlin, and Paris, and in 1837 entered the Protestant Seminary as privat-docent. In 1864 he became professor of New Testament exegesis, and eight years later was transferred to the newly established University of Strasburg. His work was devoted for the most part to church history, and especially to the period of the Reformation. He collaborated with G. Baum and E. Reuss in editing the complete works of Calvin (59 vols., Brunswick, 1863-1900), and wrote the historical commentary for the first ten volumes, which contain the Reformer's correspondence. He also completed the edition of the *Histoire ecclésiastique des églises réformées au royaume de France*, begun by Baum and attributed to Beza (3 vols., Paris, 1883-89). From 1847 to 1855 he and Reuss edited the *Strassburger Beiträge zu den theologischen Wissenschaften*. He also wrote *De Nicolai decreto de electione pontificum Romanorum* (Strasburg, 1837); *Considérations historiques sur le développement du droit ecclésiastique protestant en France* (1840); *Historische Darstellung der Kirchenzucht unter den Protestanten* (1843); *Ueber die Amtsbefugnisse der Konsistorien in den protestantischen Kirchen Frankreichs* (1847); and *Ein katharisches Rituale* (Jena, 1852).

(A. Erichson†.)

CUNNINGHAM, JOHN: Church of Scotland; b. at Paisley, Renfrewshire, May 9, 1819; d. at St. Andrews Sept. 1, 1893. He studied at Glasgow (1836-40), and Edinburgh (1840-45), was ordained in 1845 to the ministry of Crieff, Perthshire, and in 1886 was appointed principal of St. Mary's College, St. Andrews. He was one of the first Scotch Presbyterians to introduce instrumental music into his church, and also manifested his liberal views in other ways. In 1886 he was chosen moderator of the general assembly of the Church of Scotland. He wrote *The Church History of Scotland from the Commencement of the Christian Era to the Present Century* (2 vols., Edinburgh, 1859); *The Quakers from their Origin till the Present Time* (London, 1868); *A New Theory of Knowing and Being Known, with Some Speculations on the Border-Land of Psychology and Physiology* (Edinburgh, 1874); *Episcopary, Presbytery, and Puritanism in Scotland, 1572 to 1660 A.D.* (St. Giles' lectures; 1881); and *The Growth of the Church in its Organization and Institutions* (Croall lectures; London, 1886).

CUNNINGHAM, WILLIAM: 1. Scotch theologian; b. at Hamilton (10 m. s.e. of Glasgow), Lanarkshire, Oct. 2, 1805; d. in Edinburgh Dec. 14, 1861. He studied at Edinburgh; was licensed in 1828; settled as minister in Greenock in 1830; was translated to Trinity College Church, Edinburgh, in 1834; appointed professor in the New College in 1843, and principal in 1847. He threw himself with great energy into the strife in the Church of Scotland, which began to become earnest about the time of his settlement in Edinburgh. Both his ecclesiastical learning and his debating power found a splendid field, as the strife advanced, in conflict with such learned men as Lord Medwyn and Sir William Hamilton. When appointed professor he was requested by the General Assembly to go to America and learn the methods of study pursued there, and this led to many warm friendships. In theology Dr. Cunningham was a thorough Calvinist. His works (chiefly posthumous) were: *Historical Theology* (2 vols., Edinburgh, 1862); *The Reformers and the Theology of the Reformation* (1862); *Discussions on Church Principles* (1863); *Sermons from 1828 to 1860* (1872); *Lectures on Subjects Connected with Natural Theology* (London, 1878).

Bibliography: R. Rainy and J. Mackenzie, *Life of W. Cunningham*, Edinburgh, 1871; *DNB*, xii. 321–323.

2. Church of England; b. at Edinburgh Dec. 29, 1849. He studied at Edinburgh (M.A., 1870), and Gonville and Caius and Trinity Colleges, Cambridge (B.A., 1873), was ordered deacon in 1873, and ordained priest in 1874. He was curate of Horningsea, Cambridgeshire, 1873–74, a licensed preacher in the diocese of Chester 1875–79, and curate of St. Mary the Great, Cambridge, 1879–93, as well as chaplain of Trinity College 1880–91. He was elected a fellow and lecturer of Trinity College in 1887, and vicar of St. Mary the Great, Cambridge, and has also been rural dean of Cambridge since 1894 and honorary canon of Ely and honorary fellow of Gonville and Caius Colleges, Cambridge, since 1896. He was likewise proctor of the diocese of Ely from 1891 to 1906, and Lady Margaret preacher to the University of Cambridge in 1905, while academically he has been Hulsean lecturer in 1885, professor of economic science in King's College, London, 1891–97, and lecturer in economic history in Harvard University in 1899. In theology he was at first a Presbyterian, but became dissatisfied with that system both for ecclesiastical and theological reasons, and is now a decided High-churchman. He has written *The Epistle of St. Barnabas* (London, 1877); *St. Austin and his Place in the History of English Thought* (1886); and *The Gospel of Work* (1902).

CUNNINGHAM LECTURES: A lectureship on a foundation created by a bequest of £2,000 by Dr. W. Binny Webster to perpetuate the memory of the Rev William Cunningham (q.v.). They are delivered annually in Edinburgh, the appointment to the lectureship is made for not less than two nor more than three years, the incumbent is by preference a professor or minister of the Free Church of Scotland, and each series must consist of not less than six lectures The first series was delivered in 1864 by Robert A. Candlish on the subject *The Fatherhood of God* (London, 1866). The subjects thus far discussed have all been concerned with Christian history and doctrine or with the Bible. A full list of the lecturers and their subjects may be found in L. H. Jordan, *Comparative Religion*, pp. 566–567, New York, 1905.

CURATE: A name applied primarily to a parish priest, as having the care (cure) of souls. In the strict canonical use of the term, it designates the holder of a *beneficium curatum* (see Benefice), who is thus directly charged with the cure of souls. Priests who are merely confessors are not properly designated as *curati*, since their function is limited to the administration of the sacrament of penance. On the other hand, the chaplains of institutions may be so called when they are bound to assist the parish priest in the discharge of his pastoral duties. In modern English usage (though the strict ancient meaning occurs in the rubrics of the prayer-book) the name curate is commonly applied to unbeneficed clergy who assist the rector or vicar of a parish; "perpetual curate," however, was until recently the legal title of a priest who had sole charge of a district not organized as a regular parish (see Chaplain). (E. Friedberg.)

CURCI, CARLO MARIA: Italian Jesuit; b. at Naples Sept. 4, 1809; d. at Careggi (3 m. n. of Florence) June 9, 1891. He was educated at Naples and Rome among the Jesuits, and entered the order Sept. 14, 1826. In its defense he wrote his *Fatti ed argomenti* (Naples, 1845), directed against the attacks of the *Prolegomeni* of Vincenzo Gioberti, and in 1850 he founded at Naples and edited for three years the *Civiltà Cattolica*, a religious and political review, which soon became the organ of the Jesuits and the Vatican. In 1870 he defended the temporal power of the pope, but in the preface to his *Lezione essegetiche e morali sopra i quattro Evangeli* (5 vols., Florence, 1874–76) he urged the pope to become reconciled with the kingdom of Italy. Emphasizing the same idea in a letter addressed to Pius IX. and in his book *Il moderno dissidio tra la chiesa e l'Italia* (1877), he was expelled from his order and was not readmitted until a few days before his death. In 1879 he submitted a general declaration of obedience to the Church, but in 1881 he again advocated his former views in his *La nuova Italia ed i vecci zelanti* (1881). This work, as well as the still bolder *Il Vaticano regio, tarlo superstite della chiesa cattolica* (1883), was put upon the Index, and the author was suspended from all ecclesiastical functions; but after the publication of his *Lo Scandalo del vaticano regio* (1884) he was forced to recant. His chief works, in addition to those already mentioned, are as follows: *La questione romana nell'assemblea francese* (Paris, 1849); *La demagogia italiana ed il papa-re* (Naples, 1849); *La natura e la grazia* (2 vols., Rome, 1865); *Il Libro di Tobia esposto in lezioni* (1877); *Il Nuovo Testamento volgarizzato ed esposto in note essegetiche e morali* (3 vols., Naples, 1879–80); *Il Salterio volgarizzato dall'Ebreo ed esposto in note essegetiche e morali* (Turin, 1883); and *Di un socialismo cristiano nella questione operaia e nel conserto selvaggio degli moderni stati civili* (Rome, 1885).

Bibliography: The first portion of his *Memorie*, extending to 1849, was published at Florence in 1891; F. H. Reusch, *Der Index der verbotenen Bücher*, pp. ii., 858, 862, 1137, 1166, Bonn, 1885.

CURETON, WILLIAM: Semitic scholar; b. at Westbury (11 m. w. of Shrewsbury), Shropshire, 1808; d. in London June 17, 1864. He studied at Christ Church, Oxford (B.A., 1831; M.A., 1833; B.D. and D.D., 1858; D.D., hon., Halle); was curate of Oddington, Oxfordshire, chaplain of Christ Church, chaplain in ordinary to the queen

(1847), canon of Westminster and rector of St. Margaret's (1849). He was sublibrarian at the Bodleian Library from 1834 to 1837, when he became assistant keeper of manuscripts at the British Museum. Up to this time he had devoted himself particularly to Arabic, but the receipt of many new Syriac manuscripts from the monastery of St. Mary Deipara, not far from Cairo, turned his attention to Syriac. In the collection he discovered certain copies of the letters of Ignatius, and published *The Ancient Syriac Version of the Epistles of St. Ignatius to St. Polycarp, the Ephesians, and the Romans*, with extracts from the epistles collected from various writers (text, transl., and notes, London, 1845), maintaining that here was the original and genuine text; this view being attacked (see IGNATIUS OF ANTIOCH), he published *Vindiciæ Ignatianæ* (1846); and, in 1849, the *Corpus Ignatianum, a complete collection of the Ignatian Epistles in Syriac, Greek, and Latin*. Another discovery, and that by which his name is best known, was that of the "Curetonian Gospels," a fragmentary Syriac version, unlike the Peshito, and, in Cureton's opinion, representing the original of Matthew more closely, published (text and transl.) in *The Remains of a very Ancient Recension of the Four Gospels in Syriac hitherto unknown in Europe* (1858). Other Syriac works were: *The Festal Letters of Athanasius* (1848; Eng. transl., by Henry Burgess, in Pusey's *Library of the Fathers*, 1854); *The Third Part of the Ecclesiastical History of John, Bishop of Ephesus* (1853; transl. by Payne Smith, 1860); *Spicilegium Syriacum, containing Remains of Bardesan, Meliton, Ambrose, and Mara bar Serapion* (text, transl., and notes, 1855); *Eusebius's History of the Martyrs in Palestine* (text and transl., 1861). He also published *Fragments of the Iliad from a Syriac Palimpsest* (1851). *Ancient Syriac Documents relative to the Earliest Establishment of Christianity in Edessa and the Neighboring Countries* appeared posthumously, edited by W. Wright (1864). In Arabic he published the text of Shahrastani's "Mohammedan Sects" (2 vols., London, 1842–46); the commentary on Lamentations of Tanchum ben Joseph of Jerusalem (1843); the *Pillar of the Creed of the Sunnites* by al-Nasafi (1843); and the catalogue of Arabic manuscripts in the British Museum (1846).

CUREUS, cū-rē'ûs, **JOACHIM**: German theologian of the Reformation period, whose original name was Scheer; b. at Freystadt (45 m. n.w. of Liegnitz), Silesia, Oct. 23, 1532; d. at Glogau (35 m. w.n.w. of Liegnitz) Jan. 21, 1573. From 1550 to 1554 he was at the University of Wittenberg, where he came at once under Melanchthon's influence. Returning to his native town to teach in the school, he worked there for a while in the spirit of Melanchthon to make his pupils love the Scriptures as well as their lessons. Meantime he began to study medicine, and spent two years (1557–59) at Padua and at Bologna, where he became a doctor of medicine. The rest of his life was spent as town physician at Glogau. He made his name known as a medical writer in 1567 by his treatise *De sensu et sensibilibus*, and as a historian in 1571 by his *Gentis Silesiæ annales*. Vögelin published his *Formulæ precum e lectionibus dominicalibus* in the year of his death; it is interesting especially for the view of the Lord's Supper expressed in his Eucharistic prayer. Of greater consequence was the *Exegesis perspicua et ferme integra de Sacra Cœna*, which he had written against Heshusen in 1562 and circulated anonymously in manuscript. The year after his death, however, Vögelin published it, pretending that it came from Geneva, and circulated the edition cautiously in Wittenberg, and especially at Heidelberg and in France. Its distinction between Luther's real teaching and the expressions which had fallen from him in the heat of controversy, its appeal to the martyrdoms of the Calvinists as testimonies to the "celestial verity" for which they had died, and its opposition to ubiquity, *manducatio oralis*, and reception by the unbelieving, stirred up much feeling and brought down heavy penalties and ultimate exile upon Vögelin.

(G. KAWERAU.)

BIBLIOGRAPHY: The early *Vita* was by J. Ferinarius, Liegnitz, 1601, reproduced in C. F. Heusinger, *Commentatio de J. Cureo*, Marburg, 1853, and M. Adami, *Vitæ Germanorum medicorum*, pp. 197–216, Heidelberg, 1620. Consult H. Heppe, *Geschichte des deutschen Protestantismus*, i. 159 sqq., 438 sqq., Marburg, 1852.

CURIA.

Curia is a comprehensive term used in the phrase *Curia Romana*, "the Court of Rome," for the entire system of officials of various kinds and degrees who compose the administration of the pope. He may be regarded in various lights—as bishop of Rome; as metropolitan of a province comprising eight dioceses; as primate of the Roman West; or, according to Roman Catholic teaching, as the successor of Peter, prince of the apostles, and centerpoint of all Christendom. Until recently he was also the temporal ruler of the States of the Church (see PAPAL STATES), and the Curia included a number of secular officials whose duties related to this aspect of their chief's position.

1. The Cardinals. Originally, just as an ordinary metropolitan has no subordinate officials as such, but makes use of those attached to his own see, the pope's assistants in not only his metropolitan, but also his primatial action, were the presbyters who gathered about him as bishop of Rome. The bishop of Rome had no special church, or, in the modern phrase, no cathedral; in the oldest period known the city was divided into districts, each with its own principal church. In charge of each of these *tituli* was a priest who represented the bishop, and who, as placed over such an important church, bore very early the name *incardinatus*, *cardinalis*. The meetings of this *presbyterium* were known either as synods or as consistories, and in them all important affairs relating to the administration not only of the local church, but of the primacy, were considered. According to the Pontifical of Damasus (d. 384) the city had been divided by Pope

Marcellus (308) into twenty-five "titles"; and from the first the deacons who had charge of the seven charitable districts, said to have been laid out by Clement I., were associated with them as cardinals. Under Pope Stephen III. (IV.) (d. 771) the suburban bishops were added to the number, which, however, varied much at different periods. In the twelfth century it seldom rose above thirty; in the thirteenth it went as low as seven; the Council of Basel (1431–49) fixed it at twenty-four; in 1516 there were only thirteen cardinals; under Pius IV. (d. 1559) once as many as seventy-six. Sixtus V. (1585–90) finally settled the number at seventy, corresponding to the elders of Israel chosen by Moses. These were to include the six "suburbicarian bishops" (of Ostia, Porto, Frascati, Sabina, Palestrina, and Albano), fifty cardinal priests, and fourteen cardinal deacons. All the seventy places are, however, rarely filled at any one time.

According to the present law, a cardinal is "created" by the pope, his eligibility depending on the same conditions as in the case of a bishop, with a special provision against the nomination of a person of illegitimate birth, even though subsequently legitimated. He must have been for a year at least in minor orders, and have no children or grandchildren, even by a previous lawful marriage, nor must he have any near relation (in the first or second degree of the canonical computation) among the existing cardinals. All nations are supposed to be considered in making the selections, but in modern times Italians have always been in a large majority. Until comparatively recent years certain European sovereigns had a prescriptive right to suggest the creation of one cardinal each to represent their interests at the capital of Christendom; these were known as crown cardinals. The creation takes place originally in a secret consistory, and is then proclaimed in a public one. Sometimes a cardinal may be created and his name not published for some time, but reserved *in petto*, as the phrase is.

The cardinals take rank immediately after the pope, of whom they are the electors. Though in theory any one otherwise eligible, even a layman, may be chosen, Urban VI. (1378) was the last pope who was not a cardinal. They have as insignia the broad red hat with pendent tassels, conferred by Innocent IV. in 1245, the red robe (by Paul IV., 1464), and the title of "Eminence" (Urban VIII., 1630). They have the privilege of a quasiepiscopal jurisdiction within their own "titles," may wear pontifical vestments there, and, if they are at least priests, may confer the tonsure and minor orders on their subordinates and members of their household. The senior cardinal bishop is dean of the sacred college. During a vacancy of the papacy they attend to necessary administrative details, and proceed as soon as possible to the election of a new pope (see POPE). The cardinal camerlingo (answering to the archdeacon in the historical development of Western dioceses) early received charge of the general internal administration under the pope. He was assisted by the vice-camerlingo or *governatore* for criminal jurisdiction, the *auditor cameræ* for civil jurisdiction, and the *tesoriere* for the custody of property. The cardinal vicar (analogous to the archpresbyter in the early chapters) attended to the local episcopal functions of an ordinary diocesan bishop. For the special administration of the "power of the keys," the pope has, like other bishops, a member of what may be called his chapter, the cardinal penitentiary.

2. Officials of State.

Down to 1815 the States of the Church were regarded as, what indeed they were originally, simply estates held by the pope as a landowner, and as such he administered the *patrimonium Petri*, in so far as the nobility did not interfere or the people of Rome preserve their ancient independence. When the outlying provinces known as legations were acquired, they preserved in large measure their former constitutions, the pope merely sending a legate to assume the chief government and transmit the revenues to Rome. As long as this "patrimonial" system prevailed the cardinal camerlingo had great influence and was practically minister of the interior and head of the department of finance (the *camera apostolica*). Toward the end of the fifteenth century, when the popes became more and more normal secular sovereigns of this territory, a minister who should represent the monarchical principle developed by degrees—called at first the cardinal-nephew, or, when this designation was inappropriate, cardinal-patron, now cardinal secretary of state. He gradually absorbed a good many of the functions of the cardinal camerlingo, took command of the legate governors and of the papal troops, and also fulfilled the functions of a minister of foreign affairs, not only in purely secular, but in ecclesiastical matters. When, after 1815, modern ideas began to be applied to the organization of the States of the Church, the business of this office increased so much that in 1833 it was divided, the former secretary of state confining himself mainly to foreign affairs, and another secretary of state for internal affairs being created, though subordinate to the original official.

3. Judiciary and Administration.

At the beginning of the sixteenth century legal questions were dealt with by the *Rota*, the highest court of the States of the Church; questions of government by the college of cardinals assembled in consistory; questions of conscience by the cardinal penitentiary and the office known as *Pœnitentiaria* under him; while the pope had an office called *Signatura*, with certain advisory assessors (*referendarii*) for matters requiring his personal signature. The last was divided, according to the two classes of papal action —spiritual administration and justice—into the *Signatura gratiæ* and *justitiæ*, which became later two distinct bodies. For the keeping of an accurate record and checking financial abuses, the chancery (*Cancellaria apostolica*) was organized out of the earlier body of notaries; and the *Dataria* grew up for the purpose of countersigning and registering the vast mass of grants of benefices, etc. These, with the secretariate of briefs, which originally served mainly for the pope's private correspondence, constituted the system at the time of the Council of Trent. Those of them which now exist as active institutions of the Curia are the College of Cardinals, the *Pœnitentiaria*, the *Dataria*, the secretariate of briefs, and the chancery.

Their position has, however, been altered to a considerable extent by the erection of a number of permanent committees of cardinals for definite branches of business. All these "congregations," besides the cardinals strictly composing them (of whom the head is called the prefect), have a number of expert subordinates who have a voice, though not a vote, in their meetings, and really do the detailed work. These are usually called consultors, sometimes qualificators, relators, etc. The Congregation of the Inquisition, of which the pope himself is prefect, is the oldest congregation, founded in 1542 in consequence of the Reformation, for the repression of all sorts of heresy. It was reenforced by the Congregation of the Index under Paul V., to supervise the publication of books (see CENSORSHIP AND PROHIBITION OF BOOKS). On the proclamation of the decrees of the Council of Trent, 1564, Pius IV. established the Congregation of the Council for the enforcement of these decisions; and Sixtus V. in 1587 gave it the express right to decide questions (not of a dogmatic nature) which might arise in regard to their interpretation. At the same time he erected three more, the Congregation of Bishops and Regulars, for the oversight of bishops and monastic orders in general and in their mutual relations; the Congregation of Rites, for the supervision of public worship in all its details, canonization, etc.; and the Congregation of the Consistory, for the preparation of business to come before the whole body of cardinals. In 1622 was added the Congregation *de Propaganda Fide*, for the centralizing of missionary work among both the heathen and non-Catholics, and for the government of the Church in non-Catholic countries. In 1626 originated the Congregation of Ecclesiastical Immunities, for the protection of the rights of the Church in relation to the State; after 1815 a large part of its business was transferred to the Congregation on Extraordinary Ecclesiastical Affairs. In 1669 was erected the Congregation of Indulgences and Relics; and others have since been founded, sometimes for a temporary purpose. In most current business these various bodies are competent to decide independently, in accordance with their faculties and their traditional practise; only the most important affairs come before the pope personally.

4. Congregations.

The requirement that every petitioner shall appear either in person or by proxy before the body with which he has business has led to the gradual evolution of a vast system of petty diplomacy, in which personal influence and experience count for much. For many centuries each diocese had its agents accredited to the Curia, the same one frequently representing several bishops. They attended not only to the matters brought up by the bishop himself, but also to all that came through him, such as requests for dispensations. The minor details were left in the hands of a subordinate official called *spedizionere*. The diminutionin the volume of business after 1808, and the establishment of embassies of a modern type in Rome, through which many bishops found themselves for the time obliged to treat with the Holy See, led by degrees to the effacement of the distinction between the agent and the *spedizionere*; and the official who discharges both functions, now that the bishops treat once more directly with the pope, is commonly known as a solicitor of pontifical briefs. See CONSISTORY; PAPAL STATES; and POPE, PAPACY. (J. F. VON SCHULTE.)

5. Diplomatic Agents and Solicitors.

BIBLIOGRAPHY: The best single volume is P. Hinschius, *Kirchenrecht der Katholiken . . . in Deutschland*, vol. ii., Berlin, 1871-78, to be supplemented by reference to F. H. Vering, *Lehrbuch des katholischen . . . Kirchenrechts*, Freiburg, 1876. Consult also: J. H. Bangen, *Die römische Curie*, Münster, 1854; F. Grimaldi, *Les Congrégations romaines*, Sienna, 1890; L. Lector, *Le Conclave*, Paris, 1894; idem, *L'Election papale*, ib. 1896; A. Pieper, *Zur Entstehungsgeschichte der ständigen Nuntiaturen*, Freiburg, 1894; P. A. Baart, *The Roman Court*, New York, 1895 (useful); A. R. Pennington, *Papal Conclaves*, London, 1897; W. Humphrey, *Urbs et orbis: the Pope as Bishop and as Pontiff*, ib. 1899 ("the purpose . . . is to set forth the Papacy in action"): P. M. Baumgarten, *Der Papst, die Regierung und die Verwaltung der heiligen Kirche in Rom*, Munich [1904]; D. Sladen, *The Secrets of the Vatican*, London, 1907; N. Hilling, *Procedure at the Roman Curia*, ib. 1907; and the annual semiofficial publication, *Gerarchia cattolica*.

CURIONE, cū-ri"o-nē', CELIO SECONDO: Italian Reformer; b. at Ciriè (13 m. n.w. of Turin) May 1, 1503; d. at Basel Nov. 24, 1569. Early left an orphan, relatives had him carefully educated, especially in the classics. A monk of the Augustinian monastery at Turin provided him with Luther's writings, and these and Melanchthon's *Loci theologici* led him into freer paths. With two like-minded friends he undertook to cross the Alps to meet Erasmus and the Germans, but the bishop of Aosta obstructed their way and sent Curione to the monastery of San Benigno. At a festival at which relics were usually shown he put a Bible into the shrine with the superscription: "This is the ark of salvation." When it was discovered he saved himself by flight. In 1530 he was teacher in Milan, then at Casale, where he became intimately associated with Fulvio Pellegrini, called Morato, the father of Olimpia Morata (q.v.), famous in the history of the Italian Reformation. He went to Pavia, where he spent some years at the university teaching grammar and rhetoric. Being obliged to leave in 1538 by the Inquisition, he went to Venice, where he felt "in a safe haven of rest." At the instance of Morato he was called to Ferrara, and afterward removed to Lucca in 1541. The following year became decisive for Curione and many other friends of the Reformation in the Italian peninsula. On the same day (June 10, 1542) on which he dated the preface to a work, *De liberis pie christianeque educandis*, he wrote to Morato that he was no longer safe. In July the bull *Licet ab initio* was published, which inaugurated a general persecution, and in August men like Bernardino Ochino and Peter Martyr Vermigli (qq.v.) had already taken to flight. Curione escaped when the bailiffs stood before his door, left his family, and crossed the Alps. After serving a long time as private tutor, he was appointed professor at Basel in 1547. In the mean time he composed his best-known work, *Pasquillus ecstaticus* (Basel, c. 1544; enlarged ed., Geneva, 1544), a severe satire on the utterances of papacy in form of a dialogue between Pasquino and Marferio. He followed eagerly the reformatory movement in his native country, translated the *Considerazione* of Juan de Valdés (Basel, 1550), and composed a work on doctrines, *Christianæ religionis institutio* (1549). In secret he corresponded with the representatives of a radical Protestantism among the Italians, and in 1550 he took part in the so-called "council" of the Anabaptists in Venice, though he nowhere stated or defended the views expressed there. In his work *De amplitudine regni Dei* (1554) he deviated from rigid Calvinism in the doctrine of predestination, but in 1559 he asserted his undeviating orthodoxy in a public confession of faith.

K. BENRATH.

BIBLIOGRAPHY: The main source is the *Oratio panegyrica* by J. N. Stupanus, Basel, 1570; his *Epistolarum selectorum libri duo*, together with the *Opera* of Olimpia Morata, were published, Basel, 1570. The best modern treatment is by C. Schmidt, in *ZHT*, 1860, pp. 571–634. Consult also J. Bonnet, *La Famille de Curione*, Basel, 1878.

CURRIER, CHARLES WARREN: Roman Catholic; b. at St. Thomas, Danish West Indies, Mar. 22, 1857. He studied at the Redemptorist College, Roermond, Holland (1871–74), and the Redemptorist College, Wittem, Holland (1874–80). He was a foreign missionary in Surinam, Dutch Guiana, 1880–81, and a missionary in the United States 1881–92 and 1897–1900, holding various parishes in the interval. From 1900 to 1905 he was rector of St. Mary's, Washington, D. C., and in 1905–06 was connected with the Bureau of Catholic Indian Missions, Washington. He has written *Carmel in America* (Baltimore, 1890); *History of Religious Orders* (New York, 1894); *Dimitrios and Irene, or The Conquest of Constantinople* (1894); *Church and Saints* (New York, 1897); *The Rose of Alhama* (1898); *Mission Memories* (Baltimore, 1898); *The Divinity of Christ* (1898); and *The Mass* (1899).

CURTIS, EDWARD LEWIS: Presbyterian; b. at Ann Arbor, Mich., Oct. 13, 1853. He studied at Yale College (B.A., 1874) and Union Theological Seminary (1879), and spent two years in Germany, chiefly at Berlin; was instructor of Old Testament literature in McCormick Theological Seminary, Chicago, 1881–84, professor of the same, 1884–91, when he went to Yale Divinity School in the same capacity.

CURTIS, WILLIAM ALEXANDER: Church of Scotland; b. at Thurso (65 m. n. of Elgin), Caithnesshire, Scotland, Mar. 17, 1876. He studied in Edinburgh (M.A., 1897; B.D., 1901), and in Heidelberg, Leipsic, and Oxford in 1901–03. Since the latter year he has been professor of systematic theology at the University of Aberdeen. In 1903 he became a member of the Church of Scotland and General Assembly's committee on the education of ministers and on probationers, and in 1906 was made a member of the same body's committee on the Formula of Subscription to the Confession of Faith. In theology he is an Evangelical Protestant of liberal sympathies, and has written *Religion, Yesterday, To-day, To-morrow* (Edinburgh, 1903).

CURTISS, SAMUEL IVES: Congregationalist; b. at Union, Conn., Feb. 5, 1844; d. in London, Eng., Sept. 22, 1904. He was graduated at Amherst College 1867, and at Union Theological Seminary, New York, 1870. The years 1872–78 he spent in Germany, studying at Bonn and Leipsic and serving as pastor of the American Chapel in Leipsic, 1874–78. In 1878 he became professor of Biblical literature in Chicago (Congregational) Theological Seminary, and in 1879 became professor of Old Testament literature and interpretation. He translated several works from the German and wrote *The Levitical Priests* (Edinburgh, 1877); *Ingersoll and Moses* (Chicago, 1879); *Franz Delitzsch: a Memorial Tribute* (Edinburgh, 1891); and *Primitive Semitic Religion To-day* (New York, 1902).

CURTIUS (KORTE, KORTHEIM, KORTMANN), VALENTIN: Reformer in Rostock and Lübeck; b. at Lebus (5 m. n. of Frankfort-on-the-Oder) Jan. 6, 1493; d. at Lübeck Nov. 27, 1567. He studied first at Lübeck, matriculated in theology at Rostock, 1512, and soon entered the Minorite monastery of St. Catherine, where he became reader. Won for the Reformation through Joachim Slüter, he became minister at the Church of the Holy Spirit in 1528, and in 1531 at St. Mary's. In opposition to Slüter, he favored the retention of some Latin hymns. On account of his opposition to the people's party led by Dr. Johann Oldendorp, he was obliged to leave Rostock in 1534. Where he went first is uncertain, but for many years, first as deacon, after 1545 (?) as chief pastor, he was stationed at St. Peter's in Lübeck, then the center of orthodox Lutherdom in North Germany. He was city superintendent there from 1554 until his death.

Curtius took a prominent place in the confessional contentions after Luther's death. While still officiating as pastor he interpellated Melanchthon concerning the *Liber Augustanus* (Melanchthon's answer of July 21, 1548, in *CR*, vii. 75 sqq.); he participated in the conference of the Lübeck ministry against Lorenz Mörsken; in 1551 he charged Melanchthon with novelty in doctrine (answer, *CR*, vii. 756 sqq.); in 1553 he signed the *Sententia* of the ministry against Georg Major in favor of Flacius; in 1554 as the first act of his superintendency he expelled the Belgic-French Calvinists under John a Lasko, whom Mary Tudor had driven from London.

Curtius led the ministry in the Osiandrian and Crypto-Calvinistic controversies, and often was its representative in conventions and disputations, as at Koswig and Wittenberg (1557), Mölln (1558), Brunswick (Feb., 1561), and Lüneburg (July, 1561). He was the author of the short but important *Formula consensus de doctrina evangelii et administratione sacramentorum* (the so-called Lübeck Formula of Feb., 1560, considered authoritative till 1685; in C. H. Starcke, *Lübeckische Kirchen-Historie*, pp. 196–197, Hamburg, 1724), and the comprehensive *Protestatio contra synodum Tridentinam* (in Starcke, pp. 208–243), occasioned by the pope's invitation of Lübeck to the council, Apr. 22, 1561; it attempts to prove the council unlawful on seven grounds: (1) because called by the pope and not by the emperor; (2) because the pope, rejected by the Lutherans as their enemy, could not be their judge; (3) because it should be held in Germany; (4) because the pope is himself a party to the case; (5) because the laity is excluded; (6) because the object is to crush the Evangelicals, not to find truth; (7) because its norm is papal laws, not the Bible. Curtius's entire library was destroyed by fire and some of his writings may have perished at that time.

(FERDINAND COHRS.)

BIBLIOGRAPHY: G. J. Planck, *Entstehung . . . unseres protestantischen Lehrbegriffs*, vi. 57 sqq., 285 sqq., Leipsic, 1800; H. Heppe, *Geschichte des deutschen Protestantismus*, i. 123 sqq., Marburg, 1852.

CUSA, NICHOLAS OF (NIKOLAUS CRYFTZ or KREBS; *Nicolaus Cusanus*): Born at Cues on the Moselle (25 m. n.e. of Treves) 1401; d. at Todi (24 m. s. of Perugia) Aug. 11, 1464. He was the son of a sailor and attended the school of the Brethren of the Common Life at Deventer. Then he studied law at Padua, as well as Greek, Hebrew, philosophy, mathematics, and astronomy. Having been ordained, he was sent in 1432 as representative of the archbishop-elect Ulric of Treves to the Council of Basel. As the pope had not confirmed the election of Ulric, and Nicholas had to represent the claims of his superior, he naturally joined the antipapal party; but when a disruption of the council took place, he sided in 1437 with the minority which upheld the papal claims. His new associates soon entrusted him with important diplomatic missions, including one to Constantinople, whence he accompanied the Greek emperor to take part in the negotiations for reunion at Florence. After a short rest in his native land, where he finished the important work *De docta ignorantia*, he entered the service of the pope as legate and devoted his energy especially to opposing the position of the council. His work was recognized in 1449 by his nomination as cardinal. In 1450 he was made archbishop of Brixen, and sent to Germany with extraordinary authority as visitor of the whole German Church. He traveled through Germany, held synods everywhere, reconstructed and "reformed" with great energy. He was less successful in his own diocese. Archduke Sigmund of the Tyrol was ill disposed toward him from the beginning, and was still further alienated when he claimed for his bishopric feudal supremacy over the Tyrol. When Nicholas attempted to reform the monasteries Sigmund protected the disobedient nuns and monks. At Easter, 1460, the duke imprisoned him. Upon his release he went to Rome, and returned no more to Germany. For the rest of his life he was constantly occupied in literary or political matters. His property and library he left to the hospital founded by him at Cues, where various relics of him, including manuscripts, are still to be seen.

Life.

Nicholas of Cusa may be regarded either as a scholar or as a churchman. Strongly influenced by the humanist movement, he stood opposed to scholastic theology, not to Christian dogma, which with its rich philosophical content serves him as both the basis and the outcome of his original speculations, resting upon Neoplatonic ideas and deriving a little from Augustine and Dionysius the Areopagite. God is the endless unity, the absolute superlative, at once the greatest and the least; the world, on the other hand, is the realm of the comparative, the greater and the lesser. The world is the *ens* under the form of contradictions; God is the identity of all contradictions, possibility and actuality at the same time. As absolute activity, will, and knowledge he is the triune God. He is absolutely transcendent; we know of him only that he is unknowable (hence the titles of some of Nicholas's works, *De docta ignorantia*, *Idiota*, etc.). Thus philosophy ends in mysticism. On the way of faith through knowledge to vision we become "sons of God." What is new in his philosophy is mainly the mood in which it is written, one of optimism rejoicing in the world, thirst for and joy in knowledge, which turns as much to the works of the ancients as to nature. Though it is not carried out to its logical conclusions, his system contains rich germs of future development. Giordano Bruno called him "divino" and appealed to him as his forerunner. Modern scholars have pointed out his affinity with Leibnitz, Kant, Fichte, and Hegel, and assigned a place to him as a leading representative of Renaissance philosophy, at the point where the modern development begins. He was also a mathematician and astronomer of some importance. At Basel he proposed the correction of the Julian calendar. His conception of the universe is not the Ptolemaic: the planets, even the earth, move each in its own sphere without a common local center.

Philosophy.

In regard to the constitution of the Church, in the work dedicated to the Council of Basel, *De concordantia catholica*, he still advocates a moderate conciliarism. He made little use of dangerous historical discoveries, like the spuriousness of the Donation of Constantine; he is far removed from the "destructive radicalism" of Marsilius of Padua. Since he regarded papacy as a necessary and divine institution, and was an enthusiastic believer in the unity and infallibility of the Church, in his struggle against the pope his hands, like those of similar thinkers at the time, were tied. Thus, e.g., he says that the pope can neither dissolve nor prorogue the council, but that the council must conduct itself toward him "without passion, and with the greatest meekness." The unity of his character lies in the practical domain. From beginning to end he was a reformer, as the word was then understood. His moral ideal, the imitation of Christ, was the catchword of the time. That he was nevertheless a good medieval Catholic may be seen from the fact that he could not conceive of the reform of the Church without restoring the full power of the hierarchy. But he tried also to reform the papal court by a strict supervision of morals. What he did in Germany toward awakening religious feeling, promoting the moral education of the people, raising the standard of learning and fidelity to duty among the clergy, has already been referred to.

Churchmanship.

In the reform of the monasteries, Busch, Van Hejlo, and others were fellow workers of his. It is characteristic of the time and significant of the final outcome of these reforming efforts that the Wilsnack pilgrimage soon after obtained papal sanction. Although his real life-work had, therefore, no lasting success, and there is no justification for setting him up as a true Catholic "reformer" against the "revolution" of the next century, no one will deny to his character the respect which belongs to his strenuous and unflagging labors for what he believed to be the right. R. SCHMID.

BIBLIOGRAPHY: There are two principal editions of the *Opera* of Cusanus, one by Faber Stapulensis, 3 vols., Paris, 1514, the other by Petri, 3 vols., Basel, 1565. On his life consult: F. A. Scharpff, *Der Cardinal . . . Nicolaus von Cusa*, vol. i., Mainz, 1843; J. M. Düx, *Der deutsche Cardinal Nicolaus von Cusa*, 2 vols., Regensburg, 1847–1848. For his philosophy consult: F. A. Scharpff, *Nicolaus von Cusa als Reformator in Kirche, Reich und Philosophie*, Tübingen, 1871; R. Falckenberg, *Grundzüge der Philosophie des Nicolaus Cusanus*, Breslau, 1880; M. Glossner, *Nikolaus von Cusa und M. Nizolius als Vorläufer der neueren Philosophie*, Münster, 1891; O. Kästner, *Der Begriff der Entwicklung bei Nikolaus von Kues*, Bern, 1896. On other phases of his activity consult: T. Stumpf, *Die politischen Ideen des Nikolaus von Cues*, Cologne, 1865; J. Uebinger, *Die Gotteslehre des Nikolaus Cusanus*, Paderborn, 1888; Pastor, *Popes*, i., passim.

CUSH, cush, CUSHITES: A tribal and place name appearing frequently in the Old Testament, in the versions generally rendered "Ethiopia," and until recently supposed always to refer to a region south of Egypt. Since the decipherment of the cuneiform inscriptions, and a more thorough examination of the historical inscriptions of Assyria, Babylonia, and Arabia, it has been discovered that the form may represent two other regions and peoples: (1) the inhabitants of a region east of central Babylonia, who were known as Kasshites or Kosshites (Gk. *Kossaioi*) and ruled Babylonia between the seventeenth and twelfth centuries B.C. (see BABYLONIA, VI., 5); (2) a land and people in northern Arabia. The discovery of the existence of the land of Muzri in Arabia and the supplementary discovery that the Hebrew text confused the country with Egypt (Heb. *Miẓraim*) have cleared up many difficulties of exegesis.

An examination of the passages where the words Cush, Cushite, and Cushites occur reveals four classes: (1) those which indicate a region in Africa; (2) those best explained by an Arabian locus; (3) those which point to an East-Elamitic situation; and (4) those which are in themselves indecisive or may be satisfied with either of two interpretations.

Cush in Africa.

In the first class are II Kings xix. 9 (cf. Isa. xxxvii. 9); II Chron. xii. 3; Esther i. 1, viii. 9; Ps. lxviii. 32; Isa. xviii. 1; Jer. xiii. 23, xlvi. 9; Ezek. xxix. 10, xxx. 4–5; Nah. iii. 9; Dan. xi. 43. These are so obvious as to require no discussion.

In the second group Num. xii. 1, mentioning the Cushite wife of Moses, is to be compared with Ex. ii. 16, 21, where the wife of Moses is called a Midianite, a term frequently used in the Old Testament to denote Arab nomads. While the presence of an Ethiopian woman in the camp is not absolutely precluded, the probabilities are greater that by "Cushite woman" a native of Cush in Arabia is meant, since the name is that of a district not far from the locus of the story. In II Sam. xviii. 21–32 the R. V. differs from the A. V. for the better, rendering *Kushi* "the Cushite" while the latter renders it as a proper name, though it has the gentilic ending and seven times out of eight has the article.

Cush in Arabia.

After David's conquest of the nomadic tribes of the border the historic probabilities greatly favor the presence in his army of an Arab rather than of an Ethiopian. II Chron. xxi. 16 is quite unambiguous when once the eyes are opened to the existence of the Arabian Cush. The phrase "the Arabians who are beside the Cushites" (Ethiopians) is to be construed rather of those living in the same region than of peoples separated by the Red Sea and a stretch of desert, particularly since Ethiopia must have been beyond David's sphere of vision. II Chron. xiv. 9–15 has until recently been a passage difficult to explain. The catalogue in verse 15 of the spoil of the conquered "Ethiopians" ("tents of cattle, sheep, and camels") suits the situation of a nomadic people such as the Cushites of Arabia were, but is incongruous in the case of a people fighting under Egyptian leadership. Moreover, no place for Zerah is found among the Pharaohs, since neither Osorkon I. nor II. fits the case. A victory by Asa over Egypt is historically improbable, but conquest of a nomadic foe is within the bounds of probability, especially as the beginnings of a new migration from Arabia took place in the period in which Asa lived. The Cushite in this passage is almost certainly Arabian. Isa. xliii. 3 must also be taken as Cush in Arabia. The three regions mentioned are *Miẓraim* (read *Miẓri*), *Kush*, and *Seba* (cf. xlv. 14, where read "the labor of Mizri, and merchandise of Cush and the Sabeans"). "Ebed-melech the Ethiopian" occurs in Jer. xxxviii. 7–12. The name is Semitic, and is intelligible if borne by an Arabian Cushite, not easily explained if borne by an African Ethiopian. Amos ix. 7 is to be taken in the same way. The reference in the passage is to the control by Yahweh of the migrations of the nations, and mention of the Arabian Cushites was particularly appropriate in view of the restlessness of the Arabs at the time in question. Habakkuk iii. 7 is beyond dispute; "Cushan" is a word formed from Cush like Ithran from Jether and Kenan from Kain, and is in parallelism with Midian, which can mean only Arabian tribes.

The third class of passages is more difficult. In Gen. ii. 13 the entire environment is Babylonian, and Cush is placed in connection with Eden (cf. the Sumerian name for Babylonia, *Edin*, "the plain," see BABYLONIA, I.) and the river Gihon, now generally identified with the Kerkhah. This locates the Cush of the passage where the home of the Kasshites was situated, relieves the passage of exegetical difficulties insuperable under the supposition that Ethiopia in Africa is meant, and requires no disturbance of the consonantal text. In Gen. x. 6–8 (cf. I Chron. i. 8–10) Cush is brother of Egypt (Mizraim), Put (either southeast of Egypt, or, as claimed by Glaser, in Arabia), and Canaan, and father of Seba (South Arabia), Havilah (North-east Arabia), Sabta (as yet unlocated, though claimed for Arabia by Glaser, *Skizze*, ii. 252, Berlin, 1890), Ramah (Regma on the Persian Gulf, cf. Ptolemy, *Geographike*, vi. 7, 14; the Septuagint reads *Regchma*, *Regma*, and in Ezek. xxvii. 22 *Rama* or *Ragma*), Sabteca (still unlocated), and Nimrod (Babylonia and Assyria).

The East-Elamitic Cush.

Apart therefore from Egypt (*Miṣraim*, which may be an error for *Miṣri*), the entire aspect of Cush in the passage is eastward of the Red Sea, and Ethiopia in Africa is out of the question. Consequently either the Arabian or the Elamitic Cush is indicated, while the weight of authority is inclining toward the latter. Zeph. ii. 12, iii. 10 receive new light and relief by seeing in Cush the Elamitic region. The passages deal with the oppressors of the Hebrews during the Assyrian age, when Egypt had not been active in Palestine. Moreover, in ii. 13 Assyria and Nineveh are mentioned as in the north.

On the fourth class of passages dogmatism is unbecoming. While Winckler sees the Arabian Cush in Ps. lxxxvii. 4 and Isa. xx. 2–5, in the latter passage reading *Miṣri* for *Miṣraim*, the case is not altogether clear. In Isa. xi. 11 for "Pathros" the Septuagint reads "Babylonia." In that case Cush stands altogether in an eastern environment between Elam and Babylonia, the location of the Kasshites. In the Masoretic text Cush is placed between Pathros (perhaps the region immediately east of Egypt) and Elam, which would suggest the Arabian Cush. But, on the other hand, *Miṣraim* may be an error for *Miṣri*. The arrangement of the names in the passages is not such as to afford a basis for conclusive reasoning, except that Ethiopia in Africa can hardly be meant. On Ezek. xxxviii. 5 no pronouncement can be delivered, for the text is undoubtedly corrupt.

Cush is also the name of an individual mentioned in the superscription of Ps. vii., and Cush occurs as the name of two individuals: an ancestor of Jehudi, Jer. xxxvi. 14, and the father of Zephaniah, Zeph. i. 1. GEO. W. GILMORE.

BIBLIOGRAPHY: E. Glaser, *Skizze und Geschichte und Geographie Arabiens*, ii. 326 sqq.; H. Winckler, *Alttestamentliche Untersuchungen*, pp. 146 sqq., Berlin, 1892; idem, *Altorientalische Forschungen*, vols. ii., iv., vii., ib. 1894–1898; A. H. Sayce, "*Higher Criticism*" *and the Monuments*, London, 1894; Schrader, *KAT*, pp. 69, 71, 91, 94, 137, especially 144–148, 172, Berlin, 1902.

CUST, ROBERT NEEDHAM: Church of England layman; b. at Cockayne Hatley (42 m. n. of London), Bedfordshire, England, Feb. 24, 1821. He studied at Eton, Trinity College, Cambridge, the East India Company's College at Haileybury, and the College of Fort William, Calcutta, graduating from the last-named institution in 1844. He was present at the battles of Mukdi, Firuzshah, and Sobraon in 1845–46, and at the close of the Sikh campaign was placed in charge of a new province in the Punjab. There he filled in succession every office in the judicial and revenue departments, and was rapidly promoted until 1867, when he resigned and returned to England, after having been a member of the Viceroy's Legislative Council and Home Secretary to the Government of India in 1864–65. Since his resumption of residence in England he has devoted himself to scientific research, philanthropy, and magisterial and municipal duties, declining reappointments in India. He is member and officer in many scientific, philanthropic, and religious societies and a prolific writer; of his many books special mention may be made of the following: *Draft Bill of Codes Regulating Rights in Land and Land-Revenue Procedure in Northern India* (London, 1870); *Modern Languages of the East Indies* (1878); *Pictures of Indian Life* (1881); *Modern Languages of Africa* (2 vols., 1883); *Poems of Many Years and Many Places* (2 vols., 1887–97); *Three Lists of Bible Translations Actually Accomplished* (1890); *Africa Rediviva* (1891); *Essay on the Prevailing Method of the Evangelization of the Non-Christian World* (1894); *Common Features Which Appear in All Forms of Religious Belief* (1895); *The Gospel-Message* (1896); *Memoirs of Past Years of a Septuagenarian* (Hertford, 1899); *Œcumenical List of Translations of the Holy Scriptures to 1900* (London, 1900); and *Linguistic and Oriental Essays* (7 vols., 1880–1904).

CUTHBERT, SAINT: Bishop of Lindisfarne; d. on Farne Island (2 m. from Bamborough, Northumberland) Mar. 20, 687. He was of Scotch origin, probably from the neighborhood of Dunbar. While still a boy, employed as a shepherd, he thought that he saw one night the soul of Aidan carried to heaven by angels, and thereupon went to the monastery of Old Melrose and became a monk (651). His fame for piety, diligence, and obedience was soon great. When Alchfrid, king of Deira, founded a new monastery at Ripon Cuthbert became its *præpositus hospitum* or entertainer of guests. Alchfrid, however, adopted Roman usages, and in 661 the Scottish monks returned to Melrose, where Cuthbert was made prior. He spent much time among the people, ministering to their spiritual needs. After the Synod of Whitby (q.v.) he seems to have accepted the Roman customs, for his old abbot, Eata, then at Lindisfarne, called him to introduce them there. It was an ungracious task, but Cuthbert disarmed opposition by his loving nature and patience. In 676 he adopted the solitary life and retired to a cave. After a time he settled on one of the Farne Islands, south of Lindisfarne, and gave himself more and more to austerities. At first he would receive visitors and wash their feet, but later he confined himself to his cell and opened the window only to give his blessing. After nine years he was prevailed upon to return to Lindisfarne as bishop and was consecrated at York by Archbishop Theodore and six bishops, Mar. 26, 685, but after Christmas, 686, he returned to his cell. Cuthbert's fame after his death steadily grew and he became the most popular saint of North England. Numerous miracles were attributed to him and to his remains. He was buried at Lindisfarne. In 875 the Danes took the monastery and the monks fled, carrying with them Cuthbert's body, in obedience to his dying injunction. After seven years' wandering it found a resting-place at Chester-le-Street until 995, when another Danish invasion led to its removal to Ripon. Then the saint intimated, as was believed, that he wished to remain in Durham. A new stone church was built, the predecessor of the present grand cathedral, and there the body has remained since 999, not, however, without being several times disturbed in succeeding centures.

BIBLIOGRAPHY: The writings which have been attributed to Cuthbert do not now exist and there is little reason to believe that they ever did. Two lives by Bede are in *MPL*, xciv. 575-596, 729-770, and in Stevenson's *Bedæ opera historica minora*, pp. 1-137, 259-317, London, 1841. Several lives and other tracts may be found in the publications of the Surtees Society of Durham, i., viii., li., lxxxvii., 1835-91. Consult also Bede, *Hist. eccl.*, iv. 26-32. Consult: R. Hegge, *The Legend of St. Cuthbert*, London, 1663, reprinted, Sunderland, 1816, Durham, 1828; J. Raine, *St. Cuthbert, with an Account of the State in which his Remains were found upon the opening of his tomb in Durham Cathedral in 1827*, Durham, 1828; C. Eyre, *The History of St. Cuthbert*, London, 1849; F. L. Catcheside, *Life of St. Cuthbert*, London, 1879; A. C. Fryer, *Cuthberht of Lindisfarne*, Edinburgh, 1880; E. Consitt, *Life of St. Cuthbert*, London, 1887; J. B. Lightfoot, *Leaders of the Northern Church*, London, 1890; W. Bright, *Chapters of Early English Church History*, pp. 214-216, 239-240, 300-306, 372-388, Oxford, 1897; *DCB*, i. 724-729; *DNB*, xii. 359-362.

CUYLER, THEODORE LEDYARD: Presbyterian; b. at Aurora, N. Y., Jan. 10, 1822; d. in Brooklyn, N. Y., Feb. 26, 1909. He studied at Mendham, N. J., Princeton College (B.A., 1841), and Princeton Theological Seminary (1846), and was stated supply at Burlington, N. J. (1846-49), pastor of the Third Presbyterian Church, Trenton, N. J. (1849-53), Market Street Reformed (Dutch) Church, New York City (1853-60), and the Lafayette Avenue Presbyterian Church, Brooklyn (1860-1890). In 1890 he resigned to become a minister at large. He was particularly active in temperance and philanthropic work. In theological position he was a moderate Calvinist. He made a large number of contributions to religious periodicals, many of which have been gathered up into volumes. Of his separate publications may be mentioned *Pointed Papers for the Christian Life* (New York, 1878); *From the Nile to Norway* (1881); *Newly Enlisted, or, Talks to Young Converts* (1889); *How to be a Pastor* (1891); *Recollections of a Long Life* (1902); *Our Christmas-Tides* (1904).

CYNEWULF (KYNEWULF, CYNWULF): Besides Cædmon the only Anglo-Saxon poet whose name is known. He flourished in the second half of the eighth century and was probably a Mercian (cf. *Anglia*, xvii., pp. 106 sqq., Halle, 1894). His knowledge of Latin indicates that he may have studied in a monastery school, but of his life nothing is known except what he tells himself in his poem *Elene* (v. 1236 sqq.). He long roamed about as wandering minstrel and took part in battles and voyages over the sea. Then, when he was well along in years, something changed his life, he renounced the world, and in the quiet of a monastery or hermitage he produced four poems, entitled *Fata apostolorum*, *Crist*, *Juliana*, and *Elene*, into which he interwove his name in runic letters, thus attesting his authorship. They are all religious narratives, based on legend with the exception of the *Crist*, which is in three parts, treating of the threefold coming of Christ (birth; resurrection and period on earth to the ascension; the last judgment). Traces of the veneration of saints and of Mary appear. Cynewulf's art is predominantly subjective, his poetry is often lyrical, sometimes dramatic, but never epic. His lively descriptions of battles and voyages remind of his early life, and he is fond of alliteration and rime. Many other poems have been attributed to Cynewulf, of which a *Death of Guthlac* has the best claim to genuineness. A collection of ninety-six *Riddles* belongs to his time, but there is no evidence that all or any of them are his. (R. WÜLKER.)

BIBLIOGRAPHY: The text of Cynewulf's poems is in C. W. M. Grein's *Bibliothek der angelsächsischen Poesie*, ed. R. Wülker, 3 vols., Cassel and Leipsic, 1883-98. The *Crist*, ed. with transl. I. Gollancz, London, 1892; also ed. A. S. Cook, transl. by C. H. Whitman, Boston, 1900. The *Elene*, ed. C. W. Kent with notes and glossary, Boston, 1889; Eng. transl. by R. F. Weymouth, Boston, 1888, J. M. Garnett, Boston, 1889, Jane Menzies, Edinburgh, 1895 (a metrical transl.), and J. H. Holt, New York, 1904, *Yale Studies in English*, no. xxi. Consult: C. ten Brink, *Geschichte der englischen Litteratur*, i. 64-65, Berlin, 1877, Eng. transl., pp. 186-189, New York, 1883; R. Wülker, *Grundriss zur Geschichte der angelsächsischen Litteratur*, pp. 147-217, Leipsic, 1885; H. Morley, *English Writers*, ii. 193-248, London, 1888; G. Herzfeld, *Die Rätsel des Exeterbuches und ihr Verfasser*, Berlin, 1890; M. Trautmann, *Kynewulf, der Bischof und Dichter*, Bonn, 1898.

CYPRIAN.

Flees During the Decian Persecution (§ 1).
Controversy Over the Lapsed (§ 2).
Controversy Concerning Heretic Baptism (§ 3).
Persecution Under Valerian (§ 4).
Cyprian's Writings (§ 5).

Cyprian (Thascius Cæcilius Cyprianus), bishop of Carthage and an important early Christian writer, was born probably at the beginning of the third century in North Africa, perhaps at Carthage, where he was educated from his early childhood; d. a martyr at Carthage Sept. 14, 258. His original name was Thascius; he took the name Cæcilius in addition in memory of the presbyter of that name to whom he owed his conversion. He belonged to a provincial pagan family and became a teacher of rhetoric. He was baptized probably in 245 or 246. He soon gave a part of his fortune to the poor, imposed upon himself austere penances, and devoted himself to the study of the Bible and the earlier Christian writers, especially Tertullian. In the early days of his conversion he wrote an *Epistola ad Donatum de gratia Dei*, a treatise on the vanity of idols (if this work is genuine), and controversial works against the Jews. Not long after his baptism he was ordained deacon, and soon afterward presbyter; and in 248 he was chosen bishop of Carthage.

After much hesitation he yielded to the stormy demand of the people, but a part of the presbyters soon formed an opposition party, hampered him in all his efforts, and even spread evil reports about him. At first Cyprian treated them with wise consideration, and asked their advice; but he soon had to use sharper measures. He was strict with priests and consecrated virgins who had broken the moral law. During th· Decian persecution (Jan.,

250, to Apr., 251; see DECIAN) he saved himself by flight, though his official income was sequestrated.

1. Flees During the Decian Persecution.

His secret departure was indeed interpreted by his enemies as cowardice and infidelity, and they hastened to accuse him at Rome. The Roman clergy (the see was vacant at that time) wrote to Cyprian in terms of disapproval. Cyprian rejoined that he fled in accordance with visions and the divine command. From his place of refuge he ruled his flock with earnestness and zeal, using a faithful deacon as his intermediary.

2. Controversy Over the Lapsed.

The persecution was especially severe at Carthage; many Christians fell away, but afterward asked to be received again into the Church. Their request was early granted, no regard being paid to the demand of Cyprian and his faithful clergy, who insisted upon earnest repentance; the arrogance of the confessors became more and more unbearable. Their intervention allowed hundreds of the Lapsed (q.v.) to return to the Church. Cyprian censured all laxity toward the lapsed, refused absolution to them except in case of mortal sickness, and desired to postpone the question of their readmission to the Church to more quiet times. A schism broke out in Carthage. One Felicissimus, who had been ordained deacon by the presbyter Novatus during the absence of Cyprian, opposed all steps taken by Cyprian's representatives. Cyprian deposed and excommunicated him and his supporter Augendius. Felicissimus was upheld by Novatus and four other presbyters, and a determined opposition was thus organized. When, after an absence of fourteen months, Cyprian returned to his diocese he called a council of North African bishops at Carthage, to consider the treatment of the lapsed and the schism of Felicissimus (251). The council in the main sided with Cyprian, and condemned Felicissimus. The *libellatici*, i.e., Christians who had made or signed written statements that they had obeyed the behest of the emperor, were to be restored at once upon sincere repentance; but such as had taken part in heathen sacrifices could be received back into the Church only when on the point of death. Afterward this regulation was essentially mitigated, and even these were restored if they repented immediately after a sudden fall and eagerly sought absolution; though clerics who had fallen were to be deposed and could not be restored to their functions. The followers of Felicissimus elected Fortunatus as bishop in opposition to Cyprian; and the followers of the Roman presbyter Novatian, who refused absolution to all the lapsed and had elected Novatian as bishop of Rome in opposition to Cornelius, secured the election of a rival bishop of their own at Carthage, Maximus by name. Novatus now left Felicissimus and followed the Novatian party. But these extremes strengthened the influence of the wise, moderate, yet firm Cyprian, and the following of his opponents grew less and less. He rose still higher in the favor of the people when they witnessed his self-denying devotion during the time of a great plague and famine. He comforted his brethren by writing his *De mortalitate*, and in his *De eleemosynis* exhorted them to active benevolence, while he gave the best pattern in his own life. He defended Christianity and the Christians in the treatise *Ad Demetrianum* against the reproach of the heathens that Christians were the cause of the public calamities.

3. Controversy Concerning Heretic Baptism.

But Cyprian had yet to fight another battle, in which his opponent was the Roman bishop Stephen. The matter in dispute was Heretic Baptism (q.v.). Stephen declared baptism by heretics valid if administered according to the institution either in the name of Christ or of the holy Trinity. Cyprian, on the other hand, believing that outside the Church there was no true baptism, regarded that of heretics as null and void, and baptized as for the first time those who joined the Church. When heretics had been baptized in the Church, but had temporarily fallen away and wished to return in penitence, he did not rebaptize them. Cyprian's definition of the Church was too narrow; this led him to wrong inferences and made him in this respect the connecting-link between his teacher, the rigorist Tertullian, and the Donatists who appeared later in North Africa. The majority of the North African bishops sided with Cyprian; and in the East he had a powerful ally in Firmilian of Cæsarea. But the position of Stephen came to find general acceptance. While, however, Cyprian defended his position with wisdom and dignity, Stephen showed a blind, blunt zeal; and there appears in his letters the claim of superiority of the Roman See over all bishoprics of the Church. To this claim Cyprian answered that the authority of the Roman bishop was coordinate with, not superior to, his own. Stephen broke off communion with Cyprian and Carthage, though perhaps without going as far as a formal excommunication of Cyprian. Modern Roman Catholic writers make a special effort to show that the controversy concerned only a question of discipline, not of doctrine.

4. Persecution Under Valerian.

At the end of 256 a new persecution of the Christians under Valerian broke out, and both Stephen and his successor, Xystus (Sixtus) II., suffered martyrdom at Rome. In Africa Cyprian courageously prepared his people for the expected edict of persecution by his *De exhortatione martyrii*, and himself set an example when he was brought before the Roman proconsul Aspasius Paternus (Aug. 30, 257). He refused to sacrifice to the pagan deities and firmly professed Christ. The consul banished him to the desolate Curubis, whence he comforted to the best of his ability his flock and his banished clergy. In a vision he saw his approaching fate. When a year had passed he was recalled and kept practically a prisoner on his own estate, in expectation of severer measures after a new and more stringent imperial edict arrived which demanded the execution of all Christian clerics. On Sept. 13, 258, he was imprisoned at the behest of the new proconsul, Galerius Maximus. The day following he was examined for the last time and sentenced to die by the sword. His only answer was "Thanks be to God!" The execution was carried out at once in an open place near the city. A vast multitude followed Cyprian on his last journey. He removed his garments without assistance, knelt down, and prayed. Two of his clergy blindfolded him. He ordered twenty-five gold pieces to be given to the executioner, who with a trembling hand administered the death-blow. The body was interred by Christian hands near the place of execution, and over it, as well as on the actual scene of his death, churches were afterward erected, which, however, were destroyed by the Vandals. Charlemagne is said to have had the bones transferred to France; and Lyons, Arles, Venice, Compiègne, and Rosnay in Flanders boast the possession of the martyr's relics.

Besides a number of epistles, which are partly collected with the answers of those to whom they were written, Cyprian wrote a number of treatises, some of which have also the character of pastoral letters. His most important work is his *De unitate ecclesiæ*. In this, which makes the one episcopate, not of Rome, but of the Church at large, the foundation-stone of the Church, occur the following statements: "He can no longer have God for his Father who has not the Church for his mother; . . . he who gathereth elsewhere than in the Church scatters the Church of Christ" (vi.); "nor is there any other home to believers but the one Church" (ix.). The most famous saying of Cyprian, usually though inadequately translated "Outside the Church there is no salvation," is found in Epist. lxxii. *Ad Jubajanum de hæreticis baptizandis*, "Quia salus extra ecclesiam non est." His work *De oratione dominica* is an adaptation of Tertullian's *De oratione;* he also worked over Tertullian's *De patientia* in his work *De bono patientiæ*. The following works are of doubtful authenticity: *De spectaculis; De bono pudicitiæ; De idolorum vanitate* (which may perhaps belong to Novatian); *De laude martyrii; Adversus aleatores; De montibus Sina et Sion*. The treatise entitled *De duplici martyrio ad Fortunatum* was not only published for the first and only time by Erasmus, but was probably also composed by him and fathered upon Cyprian.

5. Cyprian's Writings.

Posterity has had less difficulty in reaching a universally accepted view of Cyprian's personality than his contemporaries. He combined loftiness of thought with an ever-present consciousness of the dignity of his office; his earnest life, his self-denial and fidelity, moderation and greatness of soul have been increasingly acknowledged and admired. He was the type of a prince of the Church. The glory of his courageous and edifying martyrdom can not be extinguished by the earlier charges of cowardice. As a writer, however, he was in general by no means original or especially deep.

K. LEIMBACH†.

BIBLIOGRAPHY: The *Opera* of Cyprian have been frequently published. Early editions are, e.g., by Andreas, Rome, 1471; by Erasmus, Basel, 1520; by Fell, Oxford, 1682; *MPL*, vol. iv. The best ed. is by W. Hartel, in *CSEL*, 3 vols. They have been translated into Eng. by W. Marshall, London, 1717, and a transl. of the genuine and disputed works is in *ANF*, v. 264-576. A bibliography is in *ANF*, Index vol., pp. 59–63.

The basis for a life is in the *Vita Cæcilii Cypriani*, attributed to the deacon Pontius, printed in *ASB*, Sept., iv. 325–332, in *MPL*, iii., and in Hertel's ed. of the *Opera*, ut sup., iii., xc. sqq. Auxiliary sources are the letters of Cyprian. For more modern treatment consult: F. W. Rettberg, *Thascius Cæcilius Cyprianus*, Göttingen, 1831; C. E. Freppel, *S. Cyprien et l'église d'Afrique*, Paris, 1873 (Roman Catholic, ultramontanistic); B. Fechtrup, *Der heilige Cyprian*, Münster, 1878; O. Ritschl, *Cyprian von Karthago*, Göttingen, 1885; E. W. Benson, *Cyprian, his Life, Times, Work*, London, 1897 (the work of a lifetime); G. A. Poole, *Life and Times of Cyprian*, latest ed., 1898; J. A. Faulkner, *Cyprien the Churchman*, Cincinnati, 1906; Neander, *Christian Church*, vols. i.–ii., passim; Schaff, *Christian Church*, ii. 842–849; Krüger, *History*, pp. 280–304; Harnack, *Litteratur*, i. 688–723, II. i., passim; *DCB*, i. 739–755.

On literary and philosophical questions connected with Cyprian's works consult: J. Pearson, *Annales Cypriani*, Oxford, 1682, reprinted in Fell's ed. of the *Opera Cypriani*, ut sup. (a work of great merit and permanent worth); T. Zahn, *Cyprian . . . und die deutsche Faustsage*, Erlangen, 1882; Le Provost, *Étude philosophique et littéraire sur S. Cyprien*, Paris, 1888; K. Goetz, *Geschichte der cyprianischen Litteratur*, Basel, 1891 (valuable); idem, *Die Busslehre Cyprians*, Königsberg, 1895; W. Sanday and C. H. Turner, in *Studia biblica et ecclesiastica*, iii. 217–325, Oxford, 1891; A. Harnack treats of the Letters in *Theologische Abhandlungen Carl von Weizsäcker gewidmet*, pp. 1–36, Freiburg, 1892; H. von Soden, *Die Cyprianische Briefsammlung*, in *TU*, xxv. 3 (1903).

CYPRIAN, ERNST SALOMON: One of the few learned defenders of orthodox Lutheranism in the middle of the eighteenth century; b. at Ostheim (5 m. s.w. of Aschaffenburg), Franconia, Sept. 22, 1673; d. in Gotha 1745. He studied at Leipsic and at Jena; in 1698 followed his friend Andreas Schmidt to Helmstedt; became professor extraordinary of philosophy 1699; in 1700 went as director to the *Gymnasium academicum* at Coburg; Frederick II. of Gotha called him in 1713 into the upper consistory, and Frederick III. appointed him its vice-president in 1735. While at Helmstedt he wrote against Arnold's *Kirchen- und Ketzerhistorie*, and in 1719 against Romanists who began encroachments after the peace of Ryswick and Rastatt. But his chief exertion was in opposition to the movement toward union between Reformed and Lutherans by Frederick William I. of Prussia. He wrote three pamphlets, *Abgedrungener Unterricht*, etc. (1722), *Authentische Rechtfertigung*, etc. (1722), and *Das Urtheil englischer Theologen von der Synode zu Dortrecht und ihrer Lehre* (1723), which by their rich historical illustrations give considerable information about the whole question.

(GEORG MÜLLER.)

BIBLIOGRAPHY: J. M. Schröckh, *Lebensbeschreibungen berühmter Gelehrten*, II. iii. 377, Leipsic, 1767; G. Frank, *Geschichte der protestantischen Theologie*, ii. 287, ib. 1865; *ADB*, iv. 667–669.

CYPRUS. See ASIA MINOR, X

CYRAN, SAINT. See DU VERGIER DE HAURANNE, JEAN.

CYRENIUS. See QUIRINIUS.

CYRIACUS, sir-ai'a-cus (= Lat. *Dominicus*, "belonging to the Lord"): The name of several saints, a patriarch of Constantinople, and a number of bishops.

1. Saints: No less than eleven saints of the name are mentioned in the *Acta sanctorum*. They include (1) a deacon of Rome, who is said to have been condemned to the galleys under Diocletian, to have escaped to Sapor, king of Persia, and to have been beheaded under Maximian. His day is Aug. 8. (2) An alleged pope, who is said in the Ursula legend (twelfth century) to have resigned the papal chair to follow that saint and her company of virgins (see URSULA, SAINT), and suffered martyrdom with her at Cologne. A pope of the name is otherwise unknown, and the story is very possibly a development of that of the Roman deacon just mentioned.

2. Cyriacus: Patriarch of Constantinople 595–606, succeeded John IV. and, like him, assumed the title of "Ecumenical Patriarch"; a synod at Constantinople confirmed the title. But it was highly displeasing to Gregory I. of Rome, and he protested violently, writing letters to Cyriacus, to the other patriarchs of the East, and to the emperor Maurice, and denouncing the title as scandalous, criminal, perverse, worthless, even anti-Christian and diabolic (Jaffé, *Regesta*, 1470, 1474, 1476, 1477, 1683, 1905 [vol. i., Leipsic, 1885, pp. 176 sqq.]). When Phocas, a rude and coarse soldier, dethroned Maurice in 602, Cyriacus crowned him; but a disagreement soon arose and Gregory did his best to enlist Phocas on his side. Whether Phocas really issued an edict declaring Rome *caput omnium ecclesiarum*, as is asserted, is uncertain. At any rate, Cyriacus died (Oct. 7, 606) before it was issued.

3. Cyriacus: Metropolitan of Carthage, lived in the latter half of the eleventh century and was one of the last Christian bishops of northern Africa. He refused to perform uncanonical consecration, and for this reason some of his flock accused him before the Saracenic emir, who tortured him in a cruel manner. He addressed himself to Gregory VII. and received letters of consolation and exhortation from the pope. Later, in 1076, Gregory commended him to Servandus, a newly consecrated bishop of Hippo Regius. (O. ZÖCKLER†.)

BIBLIOGRAPHY: 1. (1) *ASB*, Aug., ii. 327–340; *Analecta Bollandiana*, ii. 247–258. (2) *ASB*, Oct., ix. 101 sqq.; F. W. Rettberg, *KD*, i. 112 sqq., 638; J. J. I. von Döllinger, *Die Papstfabeln des Mittelalters*, pp. 45 sqq., Munich, 1863; *DCB*, i. 756–758.

2. *ASB*, Oct., xii. 344–351; Nicephoras Callistus, *Hist. eccl.*, xviii. 40–42; Theophanes, *Chronographia*, i. 446 sqq., in *CSHB*, xxvi., Bonn, 1839; letters of Gregory the Great, bk. vii. 4–7, 31, ix. 68, xiii. 40; Baronius, *Annales*, ad an. 506 sqq.; M. le Quien, *Oriens Christianus*, i. 67, Paris, 1740; R. Baxmann, *Die Politik der Päpste*, i. 129 sqq., Elberfeld, 1868.

3. Gregory VII., *Registrum*, i. 22–23, iii. 19; P. Jaffé, *Regesta*, ad an. 1073, Sept. 15 (nos. 4793–94); and 1076, June (no. 4994).

CYRIL OF ALEXANDRIA: Archbishop of Alexandria; d. there June 27, 444. His early life is known only from notices in Socrates and a few elsewhere. He was a nephew of the archbishop Theophilus, whom he accompanied in 403 to Constantinople to attend the synod *Ad Quercum* (see CHRYSOSTOM, § 4).

Life and Character. When the uncle died, Oct. 15, 412, Cyril succeeded him in his see. The government was not pleased with this choice. It feared, not without reason, that the new bishop would show too much independence; and, indeed, on every occasion Cyril proved that he was master in Alexandria. He closed the churches of the Novatians, expelled the Jews from the city in spite of the opposition of the prefect Orestes, and when soon afterward Nitrian monks insulted the prefect in the open street, he praised their leader as a martyr. He did not order the murder of Hypatia (q.v.), but his lector and the parabolani, who were guilty of it, were well aware that the female philosopher was an eyesore to the archbishop. His restless, violent conduct, which excited the masses, seems to have hurt him at the court. Theodosius II. as well as Pulcheria listened to him rather than to the prefect. For the rest of the archbishop's life, which is closely connected with the dogmatic controversies of the times, see NESTORIUS. From the very beginning Cyril opposed Nestorius. It was the climax in his life when the emperor confirmed the deposition of his opponent which he had decreed at the Synod in Ephesus in 431, whereas he retained his office, though the Syrian bishops had declared him also deposed. His administration shows the Alexandrian bishops at the height of their power and influence, from which they were thrown by the pretentious but short-sighted and incapable Dioscurus (see EUTYCHIANISM; MONOPHYSITES). Among the Greeks Cyril is commemorated on June 9, among the Latins on Jan. 28. Leo XIII. promoted him in 1883 to the rank of *doctor ecclesiæ*.

In general Cyril's literary activity was in the dogmatic and exegetical field. In his homilies and epistles dogmatic subjects are often touched upon. As an apologist Cyril became famous by his refutation of the attack of the emperor Julian upon Christianity, in thirty books, of which only the first ten are extant entire, eleven to twenty in fragments. The dogmatico-polemical literary activity of the archbishop was very comprehensive.

Literary Activities. At the head stand the writings on the doctrine of the Trinity composed before the Christological controversy. The controversy itself caused a large number of treatises against Nestorianism. The results of the exegetical labor of the patriarch are contained in the seventeen books "On Worship in Spirit and in Truth," in the thirteen books of "Elegant Expositions" on the Pentateuch, as well as in numerous commentaries on the Old and New Testaments. The typico-allegorical interpretation, characteristic of the Alexandrian school in opposition to the Antiochian school, is very prominent in Cyril's exegesis. The most important work in that direction is the comprehensive commentary on the Gospel of John.

As regards his teaching, Cyril not unjustly bears the title of "Seal of the Fathers," as the one who finally fixed the true doctrine of the Trinity. Great as is his glory in that direction, the question has often been raised whether his Christology does not contain traces of a relationship with Apollinarianism, which he himself opposed from conviction (see APOLLINARIS OF LAODICEA). At any rate, his Christology approaches very near the limit which separates orthodoxy from Monophysitism. It rests on the suppositions of the older Alexandrians (Athanasius) and the Cappadocians by which they knew themselves in agreement with Apollinaris against every theory that denied the substantial unity of the incarnate Redeemer with the second person of the Trinity. Looking at the personality of the Redeemer, the energetic assertion of the unity of the person resulted from it indeed, but also a reckless neglect of the individual man in him. The God-Logos remained, with the human nature which he has assumed, the same one inseparable subject which he was before. The "physical union" is "not confounded," though both natures are to be distinguished "in theory alone." The attacks to which this view was exposed on both sides Cyril could only meet by giving to the idea of "nature" a meaning which disregards everything individual. In this way alone does the assertion become explicable that before the incarnation two natures existed, the divine and the human, but after the incarnation only one, the definite divine-human nature, or, as Cyril expressed it in the words of the creed regarded by him as Athanasian, but in reality composed by the hated Apollinaris, "one nature of God the Logos made flesh." The nature is here only thought of as "common." Christ is no *man* like Paul and Peter; he is the author of a new humanity. Nevertheless, Cyril makes all dependent on the Redeemer's assuming the perfect human nature. But Cyril's assertions do not help over the contradiction that this Redeemer in spite of his "rational soul" had no free will, but was "inflexible in mind." They are, indeed, not intended for that, because by his use of the idea of nature Cyril did not need to take exception to the "perfect man," like Apollinaris. He could speak the easier in favor of a mutual communication of the properties of the divine and human nature in the Redeemer (*communicatio idiomatum*), and thus avoid the danger of a fusion at least for his belief. The "in two natures" of the Chalcedonian formula of 451 found no support in Cyril's Christology. But his Christology overcame that formula, for the Byzantine theologians who had to interpret it did so by explaining the doctrine of the two natures according to Cyril's teaching of one nature (see LEONTIUS OF BYZANTIUM; MONOPHYSITES).

Significance for Doctrine.

G. KRÜGER.

BIBLIOGRAPHY: The *Opera* of Cyril, ed. J. Aubert, appeared in 7 vols., Paris, 1638, new ed., 1737, reproduced in *MPG*, lxviii.-lxxvii. An edition of the fragments of the commentary on Luke from the Syriac by R. P. Smith was issued Oxford, 1859, Eng. transl., 2 vols., 1859, and of the same from another MS., by W. Wright, London, 1874; P. E. Pusey edited the commentary on the twelve minor prophets, 2 vols., Oxford, 1868, a selection of the theological works, 2 vols., ib. 1875-77, transl. of the commentary on St. John, ib. 1838, and a text and transl. of the *Three Epistles*, ib. 1872. The commentary on John in Eng. transl. was published anonymously, 2 vols., London, 1874-85. On the life of Cyril consult: *ASB*, Jan., ii. 843-854; Abbé Rambouillet, *Le Pape Pélage I., S. Cyrille . . . et l'infallibilité*, Paris, 1870; A. Largent, in *Revue des questions historiques*, xii (1872), 5-70; J. Kopallik, *Cyrillus von Alexandrien*, Mainz, 1881; A. Rohrmann, *Die Christologie des heiligen Cyrill von Alexandrien*, Heidelberg, 1902; E. Weigl, *Die Heilslehre des heiligen Cyrill von Alexandrien*, Mainz, 1905; Schaff, *Christian Church*, iii. 942-949. Bibliographies are found in S. F. W. Hoffmann, *Bibliographisches Lexikon*, i. 484-494, Leipsic, 1838; U. Chevalier, *Répertoire des sources historiques*, pp. 533-534, 2588, Paris, 1877-88.

CYRIL OF JERUSALEM: A distinguished theologian of the early Church; d. 386. Little is known of his life before he became bishop; the assignment of the year 315 for his birth rests on mere conjecture. He seems to have been ordained deacon by Bishop Macarius of Jerusalem about 335, and priest some ten years later by Maximus. Naturally inclined to peace and conciliation, he took at first a rather moderate position, distinctly averse from Arianism, but (like not a few of his undoubtedly orthodox contemporaries) by no means eager to accept the uncompromising term *homoousios*. Separating from his metropolitan, Acacius of Cæsarea (q.v.), a partizan of Arius, Cyril took the side of the Eusebians, the "right wing" of the post-Nicene conciliation party, and thus got into difficulties with his superior, which were increased by Acacius's jealousy of the importance assigned to Cyril's see by the Council of Nicæa. A council held under Acacius's influence in 358 deposed Cyril and forced him to retire to Tarsus. On the other hand, the conciliatory Council of Seleucia in the following year, at which Cyril was present, deposed Acacius. In 360 the process was reversed through the metropolitan's court influence, and Cyril suffered another year's exile from Jerusalem, until Julian's accession allowed him to return. The Arian emperor Valens banished him once more in 367, after which he remained undisturbed until his death, his jurisdiction being expressly confirmed by the Second Council of Nicæa (381), at which he was present.

Life and Character.

Though his theology was at first somewhat indefinite in phraseology, he undoubtedly gave a thorough adhesion to the Nicene orthodoxy. Even if he does avoid the debatable term *homoousios*, he expresses its sense in many passages, which exclude equally Patripassianism, Sabellianism, and the Arian formula "There was a time when the Son was not." In other points he takes the ordinary ground of the Eastern Fathers, as in the emphasis he lays on the freedom of the will, the *autexousion*, and his imperfect realization of the factor so much more strongly brought out in the West—sin. To him sin is the consequence of freedom, not a natural condition. The body is not the cause, but the instrument of sin. The remedy for it is repentance, on which he insists. Like many of the Eastern Fathers, he has an essentially moralistic conception of Christianity. His doctrine of the Resurrection is not quite so realistic as that of other Fathers; but his conception of the Church is decidedly empirical—the existing catholic Church form is the true one, intended by Christ, the completion of the Church of the Old Testament. His doctrine on the Eucharist is noteworthy. If he sometimes seems to approach the symbolical view, at other times he comes very close to a strong realistic doctrine. The bread and wine are not mere elements, but the body and blood of Christ.

Theological Position.

His famous twenty-three catechetical lectures (Gk. *Katēchēseis*), which he delivered while still a presbyter in 347 or 348, contain instructions on the principal topics of Christian faith and practise, in rather a popular than a scientific manner, full of a warm pastoral love and care for the catechumens to whom they were delivered. Each lecture is based upon a text of Scripture, and there is an abundance of Scriptural quotation throughout.

Catechetical Lectures. After a general introduction, eighteen lectures follow for the *competentes*, and the remaining five are addressed to the newly baptized, in preparation for the reception of the communion. Parallel with the exposition of the creed as it was then received in the church of Jerusalem are vigorous polemics against pagan, Jewish, and heretical errors. They are of great importance for the light which they throw on the method of instruction usual in that age, as well as upon the liturgical practises of the period, of which they give the fullest account extant. (T. Förster†.)

Bibliography: The *Opera* of Cyril were edited by A. A. Touttée, Paris, 1720, in *MPG*, xxxiii., and by G. C. Reischl and J. Rupp, 2 vols., Munich, 1848–60. A translation of selected works is in *NPNF*, 2d series, vii. 1–183, with valuable introduction. The "Catechetical Lectures" were translated for the *Library of the Fathers*, Oxford, 1838. *Five Lectures on the Mysteries*, in Greek and Eng. and Lat. and Eng., ed. H. de Romestin, appeared, Oxford, 1887. Sources for a life are in Socrates, *Hist. eccl.*, ii. 28, 40; Sozomen, *Hist. eccl.*, iv. 25 (both in *NPNF*, 2d series, vol. ii.). Consult: *ASB*, March, ii. 625–633; G. Delacroix, *S. Cyrille de Jérusalem, sa vie et ses œuvres*, Paris, 1865; J. Mader, *Der heilige Cyrillus . . . in seinem Leben und seinen Schriften*, Einsiedeln, 1891; Schaff, *Christian Church*, iii. 923–925.

CYRIL LUCAR.

Early Life (§ 1).
Patriarch of Alexandria and Constantinople (§ 2).
Efforts for Protestantism (§ 3).

Cyril Lucar (Gk. *Kyrillos Loukaris*), patriarch of Constantinople 1620–38, was born at Candia, Crete, Nov. 13, 1572; d. at Constantinople June 26, 1638. After studying in his native island, he went to Venice and Padua, where he doubtless heard Cremonini and Piccolomini, and came under the influence of Maximos Margunios, whom he had met while living in Crete as a monk, and who was an enthusiastic advocate of the union of the Greek and Roman Churches. Through Margunios, Cyril became acquainted with such Western scholars as David Höschel and Friedrich Sylburg, yet he never came wholly under the sway of Occidental views.

1. Early Life. His training was philosophical and logical, rather than theological. He completed his studies in 1594, and in May, 1595, was syncellus at the court of Meletios Pegas, patriarch of Alexandria. From 1595 to 1602 he resided abroad, and in 1596 was rector of the Russian academy at Vilna. During this period he took part in the numerous conferences for union in Poland and Lithuania as the representative of the patriarch of Alexandria, but the statement that he visited Geneva and Wittenberg, and for a sum of money embraced Protestantism, is apocryphal, as is his alleged acceptance of Roman Catholicism.

Meletios Pegas died at latest a few months before May, 1602, and with Cyril's appointment as his successor the first period of the latter's life closes. As yet there was no trace of Protestant influence. The second part of Cyril's career is marked by a gradual break with Roman Catholicism and an approximation to Protestantism, together with an ever-increasing desire to reform his own Church.

2. Patriarch of Alexandria and Constantinople. He was energetic in his administration and did not shrink from a conflict with the ecumenical patriarchs. During his frequent tours he preached many sermons, but unfortunately few of them are accessible, although a large number are extant in the manuscripts of the library of the priory of the Holy Sepulcher at Constantinople. According to his own statement, he became a convert to Protestant doctrines after three years of study, but the exact date is uncertain. In 1611 he was characterized by an English traveler as "a friend of the Reformed Church," and two years later, shortly after declining the ecumenical patriarchate because he was unwilling to pay the price demanded for it, he was obliged publicly to defend himself against the charge of Lutheranism (June 4, 1613). It is not improbable, therefore, that this was the period of his conversion, especially as he was then receiving Protestant books, and made special mention of one by Arminius, with whose teachings he expressed much sympathy, especially with regard to the doctrine of the Holy Ghost, baptism, and the Eucharist; he avoided the tenets on free will, justification by faith, and predestination. On the other hand, his correspondence with the Dutch statesman David Le Leu de Wilhem shows his lack of knowledge of the principles of the Reformation, an ignorance doubtless due in great measure to the fact that hitherto he had been practically restricted to the writings of the Arminians. His hopes of reform within the Greek Church had now been abandoned. To this same period belong several brief polemics against the Roman Catholics, one of which is interesting as showing that Cyril sought to appeal solely to the Bible in defense of his position. As patriarch of Alexandria, moreover, he published a "Pragmatic Compend against the Jews" (Constantinople, 1627). On Nov. 4, 1620, he became patriarch of Constantinople, and in this position was still more courted by the Protestant powers, especially the Dutch, while Jesuit dislike of him increased. In 1623 he was banished for the first time, though not until after his official status had obliged him to canonize Gerasius the Younger in 1622. It should also be noted that he set up in Constantinople the press imported from England by Nikodemos Metaxas about 1527, but it was destroyed by the Turks.

The third period of Cyril's life began with the arrival of the Calvinistic Antoine Leger of Piedmont, who was sent by the clergy of Geneva in 1628. At that time the patriarch seems to have felt the need of strengthening his position with the Protestants.

3. Efforts for Protestantism. As early as 1616 he had entered into correspondence with George Abbot, archbishop of Canterbury, and later sent him the famous *Codex Alexandrinus*, possibly as a means of gaining English sympathy. Instead of contenting himself with giving instruction to Cyril and his clergy and waiting for the Reformed tenets to be introduced among the people by their own priests, Leger undertook an immediate Calvinistic propaganda. Within a year after his arrival he urged that the Bible be translated into the vernacular, and it accordingly appeared at Geneva in 1638, the Romaic version being prepared by Maximos Kalliupolites with the assistance of Cyril. Leger likewise advocated the establishment of schools (which soon decayed) and proposed the preparation of a catechism, although it is unknown whether this was done. In 1629 Cyril published at Constantinople his famous "Confession of the Christian Faith" (Eng. transl., London, 1629), which is essentially Calvinistic, but approximates as closely as possible the language and creed of the Greek Church. The reception accorded the confession in Constantinople is unknown, although in 1636 Meletios Pantogallos, archbishop of Ephesus, wrote in its defense. On the other hand, it evidently roused much opposition and, despite the fact that the majority did not understand it, its author and his adherents were branded as heretics. A synod also examined the work, but failed to condemn the patriarch, whereupon his opponents summoned Georgios Koressios to Constantinople to dispute with Leger, and the Swiss theologian left the city in 1636. Cyril had long been surrounded by opposition and had been repeatedly banished and as often recalled. On the eve of an expedition of the Sultan Murad against the Persians he was accused of attempting to rouse the Cossacks, and the Sultan accordingly had him strangled and thrown into the sea. His friends found the body and buried it far from Constantinople, where it remained many years before it could be brought back to the capital.

That the Protestant movement did not end with the death of Cyril is shown by the synods held at Constantinople (1638), Jassy (1642), Jerusalem (1672), and again at Constantinople (1691). It is also evident that the Reformed tendency found a large number of sympathizers, although Cyril's successors were not in harmony with his views. Meletios Pantogallos, the archbishop of Ephesus mentioned above, on the other hand, was driven from Constantinople and forced to take refuge in Holland. The patriarch Neophytos III. of Constantinople, in like manner, was an adherent of Cyril, as were Sophronios, metropolitan of Athens, and the patriarchs Parthenios the Younger and Theophanes of Jerusalem. Among the monks and minor clergy Cyril's followers were numerous, including Maximos Kalliupolites, the translator of the Bible; Nathanael Konopios, who went to Oxford after the death of Cyril and prepared a Greek version of Calvin's "Institutes"; Acbatios of Cephallenia; Nikodemos Metaxas; Eugenios Aitolos; and, above all, the Calvinist Johannes Karyophylles, as well as a number of minor characters.

(PHILIPP MEYER.)

BIBLIOGRAPHY: The sources are (1) the correspondence collected in E. Legrand, *Bibliographie Hellénique*, 4 vols., Paris, 1894-96 (of the first importance); (2) T. Smith, *An Account of the Greek Church . . . under Cyrillus Lukaris*, London, 1680; idem, *Miscellanea*, ib. 1690; idem, *Collectanea de Cyrillo Lucario*, ib. 1707 (contains A. Leger's *Fragmentum vitæ C. Lucarii*); (3) J. Aymon, *Monumens authentiques de la religion des Grecs*, The Hague, 1708. Consult: A. Pichler, *Der Patriarch Lucaris und seine Zeit*, Munich, 1862; A. Mettetal, *Études historiques sur . . . Cyrille Lucar*, Paris, 1869; *KL*, ii. 716, iii. 455, 1021, iv. 1380, v. 1251, vi. 1359-60.

CYRIL AND METHODIUS.

Of the two "Apostles to the Slavs," Cyril (originally named Constantine) died in 869; Methodius, in 885. They were the sons of a subordinate military officer named Drungarius, born at Thessalonica, of Greek descent, but acquainted with Slavonic. The *Vita Cyrilli* has a marked preference for the number seven; according to it, Cyril or Constantine was the youngest of seven brothers, at seven years of age gave himself to the pursuit of heavenly wisdom, at fourteen was left an orphan. An influential official, possibly the eunuch Theoctistes, brought him to Constantinople. Photius is said to have been among his teachers; Anastasius mentions their later friendship, as well as a conflict between them on a point of doctrine. After the completion of his education Cyril took orders, and seems to have held the important position of *chartophylax*, or secretary to the patriarch and keeper of the archives, with some judicial functions also. After six months' quiet retirement in a monastery he began to teach philosophy and theology. In this period may fall his controversy with the deposed iconoclast patriarch John. The *Vita* also speaks of a journey into Mohammedan territory, and discussions with the inhabitants; and precisely at this time the difference between Christianity and Mohammedanism had become more sharply marked. The *Vita* connects his anti-Jewish polemics with his mission to the Chazars, a Finnish-Turkish tribe on the Sea of Azof under a Jewish king who allowed Jews, Mohammedans, and Christians to live peaceably side by side. It is uncertain how far we may trust the account of this journey, undertaken at the emperor's bidding; but Dümmler has pointed out that the description of perils incurred from the Hungarians corresponds closely to what is known from other sources of their activity in those regions at this exact time. According to the *Vita*, Cyril found at Cherson an opportunity to learn the Hebrew and Samaritan languages, and, according to the Italian *Legenda*, also that of the Chazars. Anastasius says that he described his discovery of the bones of Saint Clement in a *Storiola*, a *Sermo declamatorius*, and a *Hymnus*, the first two of which Anastasius translated into Latin. Since Cyril, out of modesty, omitted to mention his own name, it may be inferred that the account extant in Slavonic, but no doubt originally Greek, comes from one of these works, probably from the *Sermo declamatorius*. The statement that Methodius accompanied him on the mission to the Chazars is probably a later growth. Methodius, a man of great practical energy, had already acquired a position of political importance, presumably the governorship of the

1. Early Life of Cyril.

Slavonian part of the empire; later, he became abbot of the famous monastery of Polychron.

But both brothers were now to enter upon the work which gives them their historical importance. An independent Slavonic principality had been established by Rostislav, duke of Moravia; and to maintain this independence it was necessary to assert also the ecclesiastical independence of his state, which had been, at least externally, Christianized from the German side. Hauck accepts the statement of Theotmar that Rostislav expelled the Teutonic clergy at the beginning of his contest with the Franks. He then turned

2. Mission to the Slavs.

to Constantinople to find teachers for his people. It is obvious that the opportunity to extend Byzantine influence among the Slavs would be there; and the task was entrusted to Cyril and Methodius. Their first work seems to have been the training of assistants. The assertion that Cyril now undertook his translation of part of the Bible contradicts the statement of the *Legenda* that it had already been made before his undertaking of the Moravian mission; and the oldest Slavonic documents have a southern character. Cyril is designated by both friends and opponents of contemporary date as the inventor of the Slavonic script. This would not exclude the possibility of his having made use of earlier letters, but implies only that before him the Slavs had no distinct script of their own for use in writing books. The so-called Glagolitic script can be traced back at least to the middle of the tenth century, possibly even into the ninth; it presupposes a man of some education as its originator, and is evidently derived principally from the Greek, but also partly from the Latin cursive. The Cyrillian script is undoubtedly later in origin, and apparently was first used in Bulgaria. It is impossible to determine with certainty what portions of the Bible the brothers translated. Apparently the New Testament and the Psalms were the first, followed by other lessons from the Old Testament. The *Translatio* speaks only of a version of the Gospels by Cyril, and the *Vita Methodii* only of the *evangelium Slovenicum*; but this does not prove that Cyril did not translate other liturgical selections (see Bible Versions, B, XVI., § 1). The question has been much discussed which liturgy, that of Rome or that of Constantinople, they took as a source. Since, however, the opposition objected only to the liturgical use of the Slavonic language, not to any alleged departure from the Roman type of liturgy, it is probable that the Western source was used. This view is confirmed by the "Prague Fragments" and by certain Old Glagolitic liturgical fragments brought from Jerusalem to Kief and there discovered by Sresnewsky—probably the oldest document for the Slavonic tongue; these adhere closely to the Latin type, as is shown by the words "mass," "preface," and the name of one Felicitas. In any case, the circumstances were such that the brothers could hope for no permanent success without obtaining the authorization of Rome.

Accordingly, they went to Rome after three and

a half years of labor, passing through Pannonia, where they were well received by the chieftain Kozel. The account of a discussion in Venice on the use of Slavonic in the liturgy is doubtful. But there is no question of their welcome in Rome, due partly to their bringing with them the relics of Saint Clement; the rivalry with Constantinople, too, as to the jurisdiction over the territory of the Slavs would incline Rome to value

3. Appeal to Rome.

the brothers and their influence. The learning of Cyril was also prized; Anastasius calls him not long after "the teacher of the Apostolic See." The ordination of the brothers' Slav disciples was performed by Formosus and Gauderic, two prominent bishops, and the newly made priests officiated in their own tongue at the altars of some of the principal churches. Feeling his end approaching, Cyril put on the monastic habit and died fifty days later (Feb. 14, 869). There is practically no basis for the assertion of the *Translatio* (ix.) that he was made a bishop; and the name of Cyril seems to have been given to him only after his death.

Methodius now continued the work among the Slavs alone; not at first in Moravia, but in Pannonia, owing to the political circumstances of the former country, where Rostislav had been taken captive by his nephew Svatopluk, then delivered over to Carloman, and condemned in a diet of the empire at the end of 870. Friendly relations, on the other hand, had been established with Kozel on the journey to Rome. This activity in Pannonia, however, made a conflict inevitable with the German episcopate, and especially with the bishop of Salzburg, to whose jurisdiction Pannonia had belonged for seventy-five years. In 865 Bishop Adalwin is found exercising all episcopal rights there, and the administration under him was in the hands of the archpriest Richbald.

4. Methodius as Bishop.

The latter was obliged to retire to Salzburg, but his superior was naturally disinclined to abandon his claims. Methodius sought support from Rome; the *Vita* asserts that Kozel sent him thither with an honorable escort to receive episcopal consecration. The letter given as Adrian's in chap. viii., with its approval of the Slavonic mass, is a pure invention. It is noteworthy that the pope named Methodius not bishop of Pannonia, but archbishop of Sirmium, thus superseding the claims of Salzburg by an older title. The statement of the *Vita* that Methodius was made bishop in 870 and not raised to the dignity of an archbishop until 873 is contradicted by the brief of John VIII., written in June, 879, according to which Adrian consecrated him archbishop; John includes in his jurisdiction not only Moravia and Pannonia, but Servia as well. The archiepiscopal claims of Methodius were considered such an injury to the rights of Salzburg that he was forced to answer for them

5. Methodius and the Germans.

at a synod held at Regensburg in the presence of King Louis. The assembly, after a heated discussion, declared the deposition of the intruder, and ordered him to be sent to Germany, where he was kept a prisoner for two years and a half. In spite of the strong representations of the *Conversio Bagoariorum et Carantanorum*, written in 871 to influence the pope, though not avowing this purpose, Rome declared emphatically for Methodius, and sent a bishop, Paul of Ancona, to reinstate him and punish his enemies, after which both parties were commanded to appear in Rome with the legate. The papal will prevailed, and Methodius secured his freedom and his archiepiscopal authority over both Moravia and Pannonia, though the use of Slavonic for the mass was still denied to him. His authority was restricted in Pannonia when after Kozel's death the principality was administered by German nobles; but Svatopluk now ruled with practical independence in Moravia, and expelled the German clergy. This apparently secured an undisturbed field of operation for Methodius; and the *Vita* (x.) depicts the next few years (873–879) as a period of fruitful progress. Methodius seems to have disregarded, wholly or in part, the prohibition of the Slavonic liturgy; and when Frankish clerics again found their way into the country, and the archbishop's strictness had displeased the licentious Svatopluk, this was made a cause of complaint against him at Rome, coupled with charges regarding the *Filioque*. Methodius vindicated his orthodoxy at Rome, the more easily as the creed was still recited there without the *Filioque* clause, and promised to obey in regard to the liturgy. The other party was conciliated by giving him a Swabian, Wiching, as his coadjutor. When relations were strained between the two, John VIII. steadfastly supported Methodius; but after his death (Dec., 882) the archbishop's position became insecure, and his need of support induced Goetz to accept the statement of the *Vita* (xiii.) that he went to visit the Eastern emperor. It was not, however, until after his death, which is placed, though not certainly, on Apr. 6, 885, an open conflict eventuated. Gorazd, whom he had designated as his successor, was not recognized by Stephen VI., and was soon expelled, with the other followers of Methodius.

(N. Bonwetsch.)

Bibliography: Some first-hand sources are collected in *ASB*, March, ii. 12–25, and Oct., xi. 168–171. For others consult: J. Friedrich, in *Sitzungsberichte der kaiserlich-bayerischen Akademie, philosophisch-philologische und historische Classe*, part 3, pp. 393–442, Munich, 1892; E. Dümmler, in *Archiv für Kunde österreichischer Geschichtsquellen*, xiii (1854), 145–199; idem and F. Miklosisch, in *Denkschriften der königlich-kaiserlichen Akademie der Wissenschaften, philosophisch-historische Classe*, xix. 214–246, Vienna, 1870; *MGH, Script.*, xi (1854), 1–14. Consult: J. Dobrowsky, in *Abhandlungen der böhmischen Gesellschaft der Wissenschaften*, viii. 2, Prague, 1823; W. Wattenbach, *Beiträge zur Geschichte der christlichen Kirche in Mähren und Böhmen*, Vienna, 1849; J. A. Ginzel, *Geschichte der Slawenapostel Cyrill und Method*, Leitmeritz, 1857; A. Würfel, *Das Leben und Wirken der heiligen Apostel Cyrill und Method*, Prague, 1863; L. Léger, *Cyrille et Méthode*, Paris, 1868; J. Martinov, in *Revue des questions historiques*, xxviii (1880), 369–397, xxxvi (1884), 110–166, xli (1887), 220–232; D. Rattinger, in *Stimmen aus Maria-Laach*, xxii. 38–52, 157–169, 400–410, Freiburg, 1882; A. d'Avril, *S. Cyrille et S. Méthode*, Paris, 1885; N. Bonwetsch, *Cyrill und Method*, Erlangen, 1885; B. Bretholz, *Geschichte Mährens*, I. i. 64 sqq., Brünn, 1893; L. K. Goetz, *Geschichte der Slavenapostel Cyrill und Method*, Gotha, 1897; Pastrnek, *Dějiny slovansk. apošt. Cyr. a Meth.*, Prag, 1902; J. Franko, in *Archiv für slavische Philologie*, xxviii. 229 sqq.

CYRUS THE GREAT (also called Cyrus the Elder, to distinguish him from Cyrus the Younger, son of Darius II., killed at Cunaxa, 401 B.C.): Founder of the Persian Empire; b. about 600 B.C.; d. in July, 529 B.C. He belonged to the elder line of the Achæmenidæ, which became extinct with the death of his son, Cambyses. Herodotus and Ctesias relate that he was of humble origin; but from inscriptions still preserved it is evident that he was of royal descent. In his cylinder inscription he designates his predecessors up to Teispes as kings of Anshan, which by some has been interpreted as Susiana, by others as the ancestral seat of the Achæmenidæ. He ascended the throne in 559, but not as an independent ruler, being forced to recognize Median overlordship. However, in 550 he conquered the last of the Median kings, Astyages, captured Ecbatana, in 546 assumed the title "king of Persia," and gained for the Persians dominion over the Iranian peoples. An alliance was formed against Cyrus by Crœsus of Lydia, Nabonidus of Babylon, and Amasis II. of Egypt; but before the allies could unite Cyrus had occupied Sardis, overthrown the Lydian kingdom, and taken Crœsus prisoner (546 B.C.). In 538 there followed the occupation of Babylon by Cyrus. According to the Babylonian inscription this was in all probability a bloodless victory (see Babylonia, VI., 7, § 3). From the list of countries subject to Persian rule given on the first tablet of the great Darius inscription of Behistan, written before any new conquests could have been made except that of Egypt, the dominion of Cyrus must have covered all Hither Asia and reached as far eastward as the borders of India. According to Herodotus and Ctesias, Cyrus met his death in the year 529, while warring against tribes northeast of the headwaters of the Tigris. He was buried in the town of Pasargadæ. Both Strabo and Arrian give descriptions of his tomb, based upon reports of men who saw it at the time of Alexander's invasion. The tomb northeast of Persepolis, which has been claimed as that of Cyrus, is evidently not his, as its location does not fit the reports.

Cyrus was distinguished no less as statesman than as a soldier. His statesmanship came out particularly in his treatments of newly conquered peoples. By pursuing a policy of generosity, instead of repression, and by favoring the local religion, he was able to make his new subjects his enthusiastic supporters. A good example of this policy is found in his treatment of the Jews in Babylon.

(B. Lindner.)

Cyrus figures in the Old Testament as the patron and deliverer of the Jews. He is mentioned twenty-three times by name and alluded to several times more, viz.: II Chron. xxxvi. 22 (twice), 3; Ezra i. 1 (twice), 2, 7, 8, iii. 7, iv. 3, 13, 14, 17, vi. 3; Isa. xliv. 28, xlv. 1; Dan. i. 21, vi. 28, x. 1. From these statements it appears that Cyrus, king of Persia, was the monarch under whom the captivity of the Jews ended, for in the first year of his reign he was prompted of Yahweh to make a decree that the temple in Jerusalem should be rebuilt and that such Jews as cared to might return to their land for this purpose. Moreover, he showed his interest in the project by sending back with them the sacred vessels which had been taken from the temple and a considerable sum of money to buy building materials with. After the work had been stopped by enemies of the Jews it was recommended under the exhortations of the prophets, and when the authorities asked the Jews what right they had to build a temple they referred to the decree of Cyrus. Darius, who was then reigning, caused a search for this alleged decree to be made, and it was found in the Babylonian archives (Ezra vi. 2), whereupon Darius reaffirmed the decree and the work proceeded to its triumphant close. Daniel was in the favor of Cyrus, and it was in that year of Cyrus that he had the vision recorded in his tenth chapter.

Bibliography: Herodotus, *Hist.*, i. 95, 108–130, 177–214; Ctesias, *Persica*, vii.–xi.; transl. of the Cyrus and Nabonidus Inscriptions, *Records of the Past*, new series, v. 144 sqq., London, 1882. Consult: F. Justi, *Geschichte des alten Persiens*, Berlin, 1879; T. G. Pinches, in *TSBA*, vii., 1880; V. Floigl, *Cyrus und Herodot*, Leipsic, 1881; J. V. Prasek, *Medien und das Haus des Kyaxares*, Berlin, 1890; E. Schrader and F. Peiser, in *Keilinschriftliche Bibliothek*, iii. 2, pp. 120 sqq., iv. 258 sqq., Berlin, 1892–1896; T. K. Cheyne, *Jewish Religious Life After the Exile*, New York, 1898; G. F. Unger, in *Abhandlungen der kaiserlichen bayerischen Akademie*, 1. Classe, vol. xvi., part 3; *DB*, i. 541–542; *EB*, i. 978–982.

CYSAT, RENWARD, AND THE COUNTERREFORMATION IN SWITZERLAND.

Situation After the Battle of Kappel (§ 1).
Carlo Borromeo and the Jesuits (§ 2).
Various Agencies (§ 3).

The battle of Kappel in 1531 (see Zwingli, Huldreich) had obstructed the advance of the Reformation in the Swiss Confederacy and brought about a reactionary subscription to the Roman faith. The majority of the thirteen cantons as then organized belonged to the Roman Church (Lucerne, Schwytz, Uri, Unterwalden, Zug, Soleure, Fribourg); two were on a footing of religious equality (Glarus, Appenzell); while only four (Basel, Bern, Schaffhausen, Zurich) were strictly Protestant. **1. Situation After the Battle of Kappel.** The last four, however, were superior in actual power and in intellectual forces to the remaining cantons all together. The Roman cantons had the advantage of a closely compact situation, and the original cantons were bordered on the south by the entirely or still predominantly Roman districts of Valais, Ticino, and Grisons; the other Roman jurisdictions, also (Fribourg, Soleure, diocese of Basel, Saint Gall), separated the Protestant cantons. Prior to the Council of Trent the status of the Roman Church in these her subject jurisdictions was by no means more hopeful than elsewhere; the spirituality and with it the entire existence of the Church was everywhere in a state of melancholy decline; only the support of the governing powers and the conservative disposition of the people at large constituted the mainstay of Catholicism in these democratic little communities.

The Counterreformation found two centers in Switzerland: in the diocese of Basel (see Jacob Christoph, Bishop of Basel) and in the original cantons, where the chief center was Lucerne. Here Ludwig Pfyffer, the mayor—the "Swiss King"—(d. 1594) and Renward Cysat, the modest town clerk (b. 1545; d. Mar. 16, 1614), were the life of the movement, the former of greater public renown, though the latter in his many-sided activity as statesman, man of letters, ecclesiastical zealot, and friend of the Jesuits is the more distinctively typical figure. Originally an apothecary, but broadening himself with extensive culture, especially in languages, Cysat became "underclerk" of Lucerne in 1570; and from 1575 till his death he was town clerk. His office, which conjointly with that of the mayor was the most important with regard to the public affairs of the town and State, gave him a right to exert a partial influence over the ecclesiastical and political concerns of Lucerne. His office was not subject to annual mutation, and through his hands all documents of any consequence had to pass. As "Roman notary" from 1570 various channels of communication were opened up for him with spiritual dignitaries and even with the Curia; and as early as that very year, 1570, he came thus into closer touch with Carlo Borromeo (q.v.), cardinal and archbishop of Milan.

Borromeo's journey to Switzerland in 1570 is the external starting-point of the Counterreformation for that country. It was Borromeo's indefatigable activity which secured in the same year the enactment of the Council's resolutions, and incited to measures for ameliorating the evil **2. Carlo Borromeo and the Jesuits.** condition of the clergy; later (1579) he founded in Milan a Swiss College (*Collegium Helveticum*) for the education of worthy Swiss clerics. He now gave his stimulating counsel at Lucerne, and continued afterward in communication with the leading men of the Roman districts. Through the efforts of Pfyffer and Cysat a Jesuits' College was instituted at Lucerne in 1574, and the Jesuits' activity soon bore fruits; by means of the school they influenced youth; and, by their strict example, the clergy and the life of the community. Voluntary liberality increased, new churches were built; processions, festival plays, ecclesiastical feasts soon again played an extensive part in public life. The municipal authorities everywhere supported the Jesuits' purposes; and negligent priests were disciplined by temporal magistrates. In 1579 Bishop Bonomi of Vercelli came to Lucerne as papal nuncio, and the seven Roman cantons and the dioceses of Constance and Basel were placed under his jurisdiction. By visitations, by founding a Capuchin convent at Altdorf, which became a point of departure for many further foundations, and a Jesuits' College at Fribourg he promoted the Counterreformation; in fact, by these measures and especially by his advocacy of a league contracted in 1579 between the bishop of Basel and the Roman cantons he became so odious to the Protestant cantons that in 1580 he was rudely insulted in the jurisdiction of Bern. This incident, which came near causing civil war, and Bonomi's doubtless warranted and yet not quite unobjectionable encroachment upon affairs in the diocese of Coire led to his recall in Sept., 1581. Not until 1586 did Bishop Santonio of Tricarico arrive as new nuncio at Lucerne; since that time this Swiss appointment of the nuncio's office has been permanent.

The work of ecclesiastical renovation by this time was well organized: the supervision and exercise of discipline rested in the nuncio's hands; the education of the clergy was carefully regulated, and the schools were organized anew. In these matters the Jesuits' activity proved eminently effectual. Both Jesuits and Capuchins were fruitfully diligent in the cure of souls. The increasing number of their colleges and convents affords the best demonstration of their ever-enlarging labor; in 1581 there arose a Jesuits' College in Fribourg; at Puntrut in 1588; in Valais, 1607; while the Capuchins established themselves at Stans in 1582, at Lucerne in 1583, in Schwytz in 1585, in Fribourg in 1586; in Soleure, Sitten, and Appenzell, 1588; and in Zug, 1597. Cysat was widely active in connection with the founding of Jesuits' colleges. The temporal authorities of the Roman cantons supported all these cooperative agencies, and directed their external policy to the same object. Opposition to the Protestant cantons led to a closer cohesion of the Catholic associates in faith; in 1579 a union was ratified between the seven Roman cantons and the bishop of Basel; and in Oct., 1586, the "Golden League" of the Catholic Confederates for the defense of their faith came into being; an alliance was sought with France, but above all with Spain and Savoy. The league with Spain took effect in May, 1587, thus incorporating the Roman cantons in the great Catholic alliance between the League in France, Philip II., Savoy, and the Curia. More than once the danger of civil war was imminent in Switzerland. But no blood was shed from that time, and the events of Reformation and Counterreformation went on side by side from the end of the sixteenth century.

3. Various Agencies.

WALTER GOETZ.

BIBLIOGRAPHY: A. P. von Segesser, *Rechtsgeschichte der Stadt und Republik Luzern*, vols. iii.-iv., Lucerne, 1857-1858; idem, *Ludwig Pfyffer und seine Zeit*, 3 vols., Bern, 1880-82; B. Hidber, *Renward Cysat*, in *Archiv für schweizerische Geschichte*, vols. xiii., xx., Zurich, 1863, 1876; *KL*, iii. 1307-08.

CZERSKI, JOHANN. See GERMAN CATHOLICISM.

D

D: The symbol employed to designate the Deuteronomic school of writers whose work, according to the critical school, is found not only in Deuteronomy, but in the historical books from Judges to II Kings, except Ruth. See HEBREW LANGUAGE AND LITERATURE, II., § 4.

DABNEY, ROBERT LEWIS: American Presbyterian (Southern); b. in Louisa County, Va., Mar. 5, 1820; d. at Austin, Tex., Jan. 3, 1898. He studied at Hampden-Sidney College, Va., and the University of Virginia (M.A., 1842), and was graduated at Union Theological Seminary, Hampden-Sidney, Va., in 1846. He was then a missionary in Louisa County, Va., 1846-47, and pastor at Tinkling Spring, Va., 1847-53, being also head master of a classical school for a portion of this time. From 1853 to 1859 he was professor of ecclesiastical history and polity and from 1859 to 1869 adjunct professor of systematic theology in Union Theological Seminary, Va. He then became full professor of the latter subject and held this position until 1883, when he was appointed professor of mental and moral philosophy in the University of Texas. In 1894 failing health compelled him to retire from active life, although he still lectured occasionally. He was copastor of the Hampden-Sidney College Church 1858-74, also serving Hampden-Sidney College in a professorial capacity on occasions of vacancies in its faculty. During the vacation of 1861 he was chaplain of the Virginia troops in the Confederate army, and in the following year was chief of staff to "Stonewall" Jackson in the brilliant Valley Campaign. While at the University of Texas he practically founded and maintained the Austin School of Theology, and in 1870 was moderator of the General Assembly of the Presbyterian Church, South. In theology he was a conservative. He wrote *Memoir of Rev. Dr. Francis S. Sampson* (Richmond, 1855), whose commentary on Hebrews he likewise edited (New York, 1857); *Life of General Thomas J. Jackson* (1866); *Defense of Virginia and the South* (1867); *Treatise on Sacred Rhetoric* (Richmond, 1870); *Theology, Dogmatic and Polemic* (1871); *Sensualistic Philosophy of the Nineteenth Century Examined* (New York, 1875); *Practical Philosophy* (Mexico, Mo., 1896); and the posthumous *Penal Character of the Atonement of Christ Discussed in the Light of Recent Popular Heresies* (Richmond, 1898). A number of his shorter essays have been edited by C. R. Vaughan under the title *Discussions* (vols. i.-iii., Richmond, 1890-92; vol. iv., Mexico, Mo., 1897).

BIBLIOGRAPHY: T. C. Johnson, *Life and Letters of Robert Lewis Dabney*, Richmond, 1903.

DACH, SIMON: German religious poet; b. at Memel (72 m. n.e. of Königsberg) July 29, 1605; d. at Königsberg Apr. 15, 1659. He studied at Memel, Königsberg, Wittenberg, and Magdeburg, attaining proficiency in the use of the classic languages, the cultivation of which in poetic form constituted his most grateful occupation through life. Returning to Königsberg, he matriculated at the university, where he devoted himself to theology and philosophy, and in 1633 was attached to the Cathedral school, of which he became associate rector in 1636. In 1639 he became professor of poetry in the university.

Dach was the most gifted member of a group of Prussian theologians, scientists, and poets commonly known as the Königsberg School, and comprising, among others, Robert Robertin, Michael and Andreas Adersbach, Christof Caldenbach,

Johann Baptist Faber, Christof Wilkow, Erasmus Landenberg, Michael Behm, and Georg Mylius. Throughout the poetical works of this group, religious or secular, runs the constant theme of the mutable and transitory nature of life, expressed in verse which shows more or less skill, yet reveals, especially in its numerous pastorals and songs of friendship, little sincerity or poetic fire. Dach alone rises above the level of his age to a height where he stands comparable with Gerhardt. His secular poems were written to order under the stress of pressing poverty, and show all the faults of this class of composition. A striking exception, however, is the song *Anke van Tharau* written in Plattdeutsch. It has become a popular folk-song. In his religious poems, however, Dach finds his true sphere. Sincerity of emotion, a simple fulness of faith and confidence in the justice of providence in the midst of a world of turmoil and uncertainty characterize them; in expression, melody, and deftness of rhythm and rime they are not unworthy of comparison with the productions of a higher age. That a surprisingly small number of his sacred songs have been retained in the Evangelical hymnals is due partly to the fact that, as poems written for special occasions, they reveal the quiet spirit of meditation rather than the sonorous swing of the hymn. His collected poems were published by Oesterley at Stuttgart in 1877.

(H. Jacoby.)

Bibliography: H. Stiehler, *Simon Dach*, Königsberg, 1896; C. v. Winterfeld, *Der evangelische Kirchengesang*, vol. ii., Leipsic, 1845; G. G. Gervinus, *Geschichte der deutschen Dichtung*, vol. iii., Leipsic, 1872; K. Goedeke and J. Tittmann, *Deutsche Dichter des siebenzehnten Jahrhunderts*, ib. 1876; Julian, *Hymnology*, pp. 276-277.

D'ACHERY, JEAN LUC. See Achery, Jean Luc d'.

DA COSTA, IZAAK: Dutch poet and Christian apologist; b. at Amsterdam Jan. 14, 1798; d. there Apr. 28, 1860. His parents were wealthy Jews of Portuguese descent who had departed in faith, though not in practise, from the hereditary belief, and were opposed to the political and social ideals of French revolutionism. At an early age Da Costa acquired a love for Greek literature which remained with him throughout life, and later the influence of the scholar and poet Willem Bilderdijk, to whom the elder Da Costa entrusted the education of his son, molded his entire career. In 1816 Da Costa entered the University of Leyden, and took his doctorate in law in 1818, and in philology in 1821. Bilderdijk had accepted a professorship at Leyden, and there his unobtrusive but persistent inculcation of the principles of the Christian faith won Da Costa from the teachings of Voltaire's deism to a fervent belief in the Gospel. In Oct., 1822, he was baptized, and he then devoted himself with characteristic zeal to the service of his new faith, bringing to the task an earnestness of conviction, a disregard of public opinion, and a gift for literary expression that were destined to exert a formative influence on the subsequent religious history of the Netherlands. The genius of the time was one of inoffensive neutrality between religion and secular culture, but men were inclined to interpret religion in the spirit of that secular culture. In 1823 Da Costa published at Leyden his *Bezwaren tegen den geest der eeuw*, in which he combated the complacent belief of his contemporaries that the nineteenth century was destined to surpass all that had gone before. As a period of decline in faith, morals, toleration, and humanitarianism, he chose rather to call it the age of slavery, unbelief, superstition, and darkness; *De Sadduceën*, published in the following year, was in the main an exposition of the same theme, comparing the theology of his own time and the Arminianism of the seventeenth century with the Sadduceeism of the days of Christ. Da Costa thus became the apologist of the old simple faith and orthodoxy, and this not alone in his prose works but in his poems, which are warm with the spirit of the old singers of the Bible. The bold position he assumed subjected him to virulent attacks by the press, and he was regarded with suspicion by the police. With the revolution of 1830, however, an event which he had predicted with almost prophetic foresight, adherents began to flock to him. From that time to the end of his life his zeal remained unabated in the furtherance of the cause of the new orthodoxy; and though the forces he had set in motion soon came to be directed by other hands, he may be called the prophet of the new movement, while others developed his principles.

Aside from his activity as an author, Da Costa conducted classes in the study of the Bible, lectured frequently throughout the country, and was identified with every movement favorable to the cause of religious revival. His poetical works were published by J. P. Hasebroek at Haarlem in 1861; his theological writings were issued two years later by H. J. Koenen. Of these the principal are: *Voorlezingen over de eenheid en overeenstemming der Evangeliën* (2 vols., Leyden, 1840; Eng. transl., *The Four Witnesses*, London, 1851); *Paulus* (2 parts, 1846); *Israël en de Volken* (1849; Eng. transl., *Israel and the Gentiles. Contributions to the History of the Jews from the Earliest Times to the Present Day*, London, 1850); and *Beschouwingen van dei Handelingen der Apostelen* (3 parts, 1856–58).

(J. A. Gerth van Wijk†.)

Bibliography: W. G. C. Bijvanck, *De jeugd van Is. da Costa*, 2 vols., Leyden, 1894–96; H. J. Koenen, *Levensbericht van Mr. Is. da Costa*, ib. 1860; G. J. Vos, *Geschiedenis der vaderlandsche kerk*, ii. 184–272, Dordrecht, 1882; A. Pierson, *Oudere Tijdgenooten*, pp. 1–35, Amsterdam, 1888; J. Reitsma, *Geschiedenis van de hervorming en de hervormde kerk der Nederlanden*, Groningen, 1893.

DAGON: A deity of the Philistines, perhaps the principal god of that people. He had temples at Gaza (Judges xvi. 21 sqq.) and Ashdod (I Sam. v. 1–2; I Macc. x. 82–85, xi. 4). The location of the temple mentioned in I Chron. x. 10 is not given. Indications are found in place-names, pointing to the worship of a deity with this name over a wider territory than that occupied by the Philistines. Thus a Beth-dagon is mentioned Josh. xv. 41, which is possibly the modern Beit-Dejan (6 m. s.e. of Joppa); there is a place of the same name 7 m. e. of Nablus and another near Jericho. The inscription of Eshmunazar of Sidon speaks of Dor and Joppa as seats of the worship of Dagon. A seventh century Phenician seal is known on which is an inscription read Baal-Dagon; and this is corroborated by the testimony of Philo Byblios to the effect that Dagon was worshiped elsewhere than in Phenicia and that he was worshiped by other Semites to the East. This is confirmed by the fact that a king of Isin (see BABYLONIA, VI., 3, § 4) is named Ishme-Dagan, while that of the Amarna Tablets is by a Dagan-takala—the name of the deity entering as an element in both names.

The meaning of the word and the form of Dagon's image are cognate questions still under discussion. Some see in the word a diminutive of affection formed from the Semitic *dag*, " fish " (cf. *shimshon*, " little sun "), and affirm that the form was that of a fish with the head and hands of a man. To this theory the statement in I Sam. v. 4, " only Dagon (i.e., the fishy stump) was left to him," is made tributary, and the explanation is given that after the human head and hands were broken off, only the fish-like form was left. With this agree the reports from the Greek age of the worship on the Philistine coast of a deity half fish and half man. Philo Byblios derives the name from a Semitic root *dagan*, " grain," and makes of the god a deity of agriculture (*Zeus arotrios*). With this fits in well the ear of grain on the Phenician seal mentioned above, though the argument is not strongly cogent. Both of these derivations seem to have warrant in early Semitic, if not in Sumerian worship, as in the case of Ea (see BABYLONIA, VII., 2, § 3), a deity derived from the water, and of the Oannes or Odakon of Berosus, who was pictured as part man, part fish. A Babylonian god Dagon was known, and the Arabic *dagn*, " fruitful rain," suggests a connection with agriculture. Sayce, Delitzsch, and Schrader agree in finding a pre-Semitic origin for the deity. In Greco-Roman times a goddess Derceto (Atargatis) was known, also connected with agriculture, who may have been the consort of Dagon but is not to be confounded with him.

Nothing is known of the form of the cult except that the worshipers avoided stepping on the threshold of the temple—a custom which has its parallels elsewhere. Possibly, though not certainly, allusion is made to this in Zeph. i. 9.

GEO. W. GILMORE.

BIBLIOGRAPHY: A. H. Sayce, *Higher Criticism and the Monuments*, pp. 325-327, London, 1894; F. Delitzsch, *Wo lag das Paradies?* Leipsic, 1881; G. F. Moore, *Commentary on Judges*, pp. 358-359; Schrader, *KAT*, p. 358; P. Jensen, *Kosmologie der Babylonier*, pp. 449-456, Strassburg, 1890. Earlier material is found in: J. Selden, *De dis Syris*, ii., chap. iii., London, 1617; F. C. Movers, *Die Phönizier*, i. 143-144, 590, Bonn, 1841; P. Scholz, *Götzendienst und Zauberwesen*, pp. 238-244, Regensburg, 1877. Consult also: *DB*, i. 544; *EB*, i. 983-985; Menant, in *RHR*, xi (1885), 295-301.

DAILLÉ, dê''yê' (DALLÆUS), JEAN: French Protestant; b. at Chatellerault (160 m. s.w. of Paris), department of Vienne, Jan. 6, 1594; d. at Charenton (an eastern suburb of Paris, where the Protestants met for worship after 1606; see ABLON) Apr. 15, 1670. He studied philosophy at Poitiers and at Saumur. In 1612 the governor of the last-named city, the celebrated Du Plessis-Mornay, made him tutor of his grandsons. With his pupils he traveled in Italy (1619), and at Venice made the acquaintance of Fra Paolo Sarpi. In 1623, after his pupils had passed their examination, he became chaplain at Mornay's château La Forêt. His benefactor having died soon after, Daillé returned to Saumur, where he prepared Mornay's memoir for the press and was appointed preacher. In 1626 he was called as minister of the Paris congregation at Charenton. He belonged to the liberal party, took an active part in the Calvinist synods, and was a moderator of the last Synod of Loudun. His most important works were *Traité de l'employ des Saints-Pères pour le jugement des différents qui sont aujourd'hui en la religion* (Geneva, 1632; Eng. transl., *A Treatise concerning the Right Use of the Fathers in the Decision of the Controversies that are at this Day in Religion*, London, 1651 and 1675; reissued 1841); *Apologie des églises réformées où est montrée la nécessité de leur séparation d'avec l'église Romaine, contre ceux qui les accusent de faire schisme en la Chrestienté* (Charenton, 1633; Eng. transl., *An Apologie for the Reformed Churches*, 1653); *La Foy fondée sur les Saintes Écritures, contre les nouveaux Méthodistes* (1634); *De la créance des pères sur le fait des images* (Geneva, 1641).

G. BONET-MAURY.

BIBLIOGRAPHY: Sources are: J. Daillé, *L'Abrégé de la vie de J. Daillé*, Geneva, 1671 (by his son); E. and É. Haag, *La France protestante*, ed. H. L. Bordier, vol. v., Paris, 1886; Lichtenberger, *ESR*, iii. 557-562.

DALAND, WILLIAM CLIFTON: Seventh-day Baptist; b. at New York City Oct. 25, 1860. He was graduated at the Brooklyn Polytechnic Institute in 1879 and Union Theological Seminary in 1886. While in the Seminary he changed from the Baptists to the Seventh-day Baptists. He held pastorates at Leonardsville, N. Y. (1886-91), Westerly, R. I. (1891-96), London (1896-1900), and again at Leonardsville (1900-02). Since 1902 he has been president of Milton College, Milton, Wis., where he is also professor of philosophy and English. He was recording secretary of the Seventh-day Baptist Missionary Society in 1891-96. In theology he is a Trinitarian in the sense of the Apostles' Creed, and philosophically is a moderate Calvinist, although an Arminian practically. As regards authority, his views are " Bibliocentric," and he accepts the conclusions of a moderate and reverent criticism. He has published an annotated translation of the *Song of Songs* (Leonardsville, N. Y., 1887).

DALE, JAMES WILKINSON: American Presbyterian; b. at Cantwell's Bridge (Odessa), New Castle County, Del., Oct. 16, 1812; d. at Media, Pa., Apr. 19, 1881. He was graduated at the University of Pennsylvania, 1831; studied theology at Andover, 1832-33, at Princeton, 1833-34, and was graduated at Andover, 1835; he also studied medicine (M.D., University of Pennsylvania, 1838) with a view to more efficient service as a missionary in India, but financial difficulties of the American Board prevented his departure; he was agent of the American Bible Society for Pennsylvania, 1838-1845; pastor at Ridley and Middletown, Pa., 1845-1866, at Media, 1866-71, at Wayne, 1871-76. He issued many sermons and labored zealously in behalf of total abstinence. His reputation was made, however, by his elaborate works on baptism, viz.: *Classic Baptism* (Philadelphia, 1867); *Judaic Baptism* (1869); *Johannic Baptism* (1871); *Christic and Patristic Baptism* (1874). A condensed statement of his views, which were in favor of pedobaptism and sprinkling, may be found in *The Cup and the Cross* (1872).

Bibliography: J. Roberts, *Memorial of James Wilkinson Dale*, Philadelphia, 1886.

DALE, ROBERT WILLIAM: Congregationalist; b. at London Dec. 1, 1829; d. at Birmingham Mar. 13, 1895. He studied at Spring Hill College, Birmingham (M.A., University of London, 1853), and was associate pastor of Carr's Lane Congregational Church, Birmingham, 1853–59, after which he was sole pastor until his death. In 1869 he was chairman of the Congregational Union of England and Wales and in 1877 was Lyman Beecher lecturer at Yale. In 1885 he was appointed by the crown a member of a committee for investigating the working of the English system of elementary education. He was likewise a governor of King Edward VI.'s School, Birmingham, and in theology was liberal and an advocate of conditional immortality. His publications embrace *Life and Letters of the Rev. John Angell James* (London, 1861); *The Jewish Temple and the Christian Church* (1865); *Christ and the Controversies of Christendom* (1869); *The Holy Spirit in Relation to the Work of the Ministry, the Worship, and the Work of the Church* (1869); *The Ten Commandments* (1871); *Protestantism, its Ultimate Principle* (1874); *The Atonement* (1875), a book which has had a remarkable reception; *Nine Lectures on Preaching* (Lyman Beecher lectures; 1877); *Impressions of America* (New York, 1878); *The Evangelical Revival, and Other Sermons* (London, 1880); *Epistle to the Ephesians, its Doctrine and Ethics* (1882); *The Laws of Christ for Common Life* (1884); *Manual of Congregational Principles* (1884); *Impressions of Australia* (1889); *The Old Evangelicalism and the New* (1889); *The Living Christ and the Four Gospels* (1890); *Fellowship with Christ and Other Discourses* (1891); *Christian Doctrine* (1894); *Christ and the Future Life* (1895); *The Epistle of James and Other Discourses* (1895); and *Essays and Addresses* (1899). He likewise edited *The English Hymn-Book* (Birmingham, 1875).

Bibliography: A. W. W. Dale (his son), *Life of R. W. Dale of Birmingham*, London, 1898.

DALMAN, GUSTAF HERMAN: German Lutheran; b. at Niesky (11 m. n.n.w. of Görlitz), Silesia, June 9, 1855. He studied at the Moravian school in his native town and the Moravian theological seminary at Gnadenfeld, where he was professor of Old Testament exegesis and practical theology 1881–87. In 1887 he left the Moravians for the Lutherans, studied at Leipsic (Ph.D., 1887), and until 1902 was professor and later director of the Institutum Delitzschianum at Leipsic. He was privat-docent 1891–96 and since 1896 has been associate professor of Old Testament exegesis in Leipsic. Since 1902 he has been on furlough in Palestine as president of the German Evangelical Archeological Institute, and was also appointed honorary Swedish consul for Palestine and Damascus in 1903. In theology he "belongs to no party of any description, and tries to unite Evangelical Christian faith with scientific progress." Of his numerous publications may be mentioned: *Studien zur biblischen Theologie* (2 parts, Berlin, 1889–97); *Jesaja 53, das Prophetenwort vom Sühnleiden des Heilsmittlers* (Leipsic, 1890); *Kurzgefasstes Handbuch der Mission unter Israel* (Berlin, 1893); *Grammatik des jüdisch-palästinischen Aramäisch* (Leipsic, 1894); *Eben Ezer, Gedenkbuch der Familie Julius Marx* (1897); *Aramäisch-neuhebräisches Wörterbuch zu Targum, Talmud und Midrasch* (2 parts, Frankfort, 1897–1901); *Christentum und Judentum* (Leipsic, 1898; Eng. transl., *Christianity and Judaism*, by G. H. Box, Oxford, 1901); *Die Worte Jesu mit besonderer Berücksichtigung des nachkanonischen jüdischen Schrifttums und der aramäischen Sprache*, i. (Leipsic, 1898; Eng. transl., *The Words of Jesus Considered in Light of Post-Biblical Jewish Writings and the Aramaic Language*, by D. M. Kay, Edinburgh, 1902); and *Palästinischer Diwan* (Leipsic, 1901). He edited the monthly *Berith Am* from 1893 to 1902 and the annual report of the *Deutsches Evangelisches Institut für Altertumswissenschaft des heiligen Landes* since 1905.

DALMATIC. See Vestments and Insignia, Ecclesiastical.

DALTON, HERMANN: German Reformed; b. at Offenbach (4 m. s.e. of Frankfort) Aug. 20, 1833. He studied at Marburg, Berlin, and Heidelberg 1853–56, and was pastor of the German Reformed church in St. Petersburg 1858–59. In the latter year he retired from active life, and has since resided in Berlin. In 1868 he was created a consistorial councilor, and in 1876 founded the Evangelical city mission in St. Petersburg. His writings include: *Nathanael, apologetische Vorträge über einzige Punkte des Christentums* (St. Petersburg, 1861); *Geschichte der reformierten Kirche in Russland* (Gotha, 1865); *Immanuel, der Heidelberger Katechismus als Bekenntnis- und Erbauungsbuch* (Wiesbaden, 1870); *Reisebilder aus dem Orient* (St. Petersburg, 1871); *Johannes Gossner, ein Lebensbild aus der Kirche des neunzehnten Jahrhunderts* (1874); *Johannes von Muralt, eine Pädagogen- und Pastorengestalt der Schweiz und Russlands aus der ersten Hälfte des neunzehnten Jahrhunderts* (Wiesbaden, 1876); *Johannes a Lasco, Beitrag zur Reformationsgeschichte Polens, Deutschlands und Englands* (Gotha, 1881; Eng. transl. by M. J. Evans, London, 1886); *Reisebilder aus Griechenland und Kleinasien* (Bremen, 1884); *Ferienreise eines evangelischen Predigers* (1886); *Beiträge zur Geschichte der evangelischen Kirche in Russland* (4 vols., Gotha and Berlin, 1887–1905); *Die evangelische Kirche in Russland* (Leipsic, 1890); *Offenes Sendschreiben an den Oberprokureur des russischen Synods, Herrn Wirklichen Geheimrat Konstantin Pobedonosieff* (1890; Eng. transl., *On Religious Liberty in Russia. Open letter*, 1890), *Auf Missionspfaden in Japan* (Bremen, 1895); *Indische Reisebriefe* (Gütersloh, 1899); *Aus dem Leben einer evangelischen Gemeinde* (1901); *Daniel Ernst Jab-*

lonski (Berlin, 1903); and *Lebenserinnerungen* (2 vols., 1906–07).

DAMASCENUS (DAMASKINOS) THE STUDITE: The most important popular writer of the Greek Church in the sixteenth century. He came from Thessalonica, was a disciple of Theophanes Eleabulkos in Constantinople, and a member of the Studite monastery (see ACŒMETI); he became bishop of Lite and Rhendine, and in 1573 was metropolitan of Naupactus and Arta. His chief work was the "Treasury" (1st ed. probably 1570; 2d ed., 1589; many later eds., down to the present), containing thirty-six sermons or homilies, with seven ethical treatises by Joannikios Kartanos (q.v.). The addresses are written in the popular speech of the time and based upon Bible texts or saints' lives. The aim is practical rather than theological, and Damascenus does not disdain now and then to please his hearers by a joke. So far as his theology appears, he is strongly orthodox. He avoids polemics, except sometimes against the Jews.

(PHILIPP MEYER.)

DAMASCUS: Perhaps the oldest city in Syria. Its name appears in the principal early tongues of the region (Heb. *Dammeśk*, *Darmeśek*, and *Dummeśek;* Egyptian *Timasku*, *Saramasku;* Assyr. *Dimashki* and *Dimashka;* Arab. *Dimashk*, *Dimishk el-Sham*, or *el-Sham*). It lies east of Mt. Hermon in 33° 32′ n. lat., 36° 18′ e. long., 133 m. n.n.e. of Jerusalem and about 60 m. e. of the Mediterranean, at an altitude of 2,260 feet, at the western end of the exceedingly fertile plain of the Ghuta (a hollow sheltered by hills and watered by the Barada and the Awaj), along the principal branch of the Barada ("Abana," II Kings v. 12; Gk. *Chrysorrhoas*). It is about a mile in length from east to west and half a mile from north to south, with a suburb of continuous buildings on the south nearly a mile in extent, thus presenting in contour the shape of a mallet with its handle. Its site is nearly level, it is walled, only the foundations of most of the wall being ancient, and it gives entrance by seven gates. Its location on a plain unusually rich in its products of fruits in many varieties, of grains and other products useful in the arts and manufactures, and its situation on great trade routes have combined not only to prolong its life, but to cause its speedy recovery from the many disasters which have befallen it in the course of history. It has been famed at different times for its wines, its wool products (Ezek. xxvii. 18), its silk (Amos iii. 12, R. V. margin; cf. the "damask" of commerce), and its "Damascus blades." Besides a part of the wall for which an early date is claimed, there is no ancient structure. It is likely that the Ommiad Mosque is situated on the site of the old Church of St. John, which took its name from the fact that it was supposed to be the repository of the head of John the Baptist. The conjecture has been offered that this was on the site of an early temple.

The history of the city has been very varied. It is first mentioned in connection with Abraham, Gen. xiv. 5, xv. 2. In the fifteenth century B.C. it figures as one of the conquests of Thothmes III., and at the same time its name is found in the Amarna Tablets, while in the thirteenth it is claimed as a part of the territory of Rameses III. According to II Sam. viii. 3 sqq. (cf. I Chron. xviii. 5 sqq.) it was included in the realm of David, but must have been lost to the Hebrews soon after, according to I Kings xi. 23–25. It appears later to have become the head of the Syrian confederacy which opposed for so long the westward march of the Assyrian empire (see ASSYRIA, VI., 3, §§ 7 sqq.), and the power which was centered there was almost continuously antagonistic to the Hebrew kingdoms. A Rezon son of Eliadah appears to have made himself king in the time of Solomon. A king named Ben-hadad helped Asa against Baasha (I Kings xv. 16–21), and the same king or one of the same name defeated Omri and established a trading station in Samaria (I Kings xx. 34), while a son had to yield under defeat the same privilege to Ahab in Damascus. In a later campaign against the same power Ahab met his death (I Kings xxii.). In the years 854, 850, and 847 the forces of Damascus under a Ben-hadad were defeated by Shalmaneser II., yet the city seems to have recovered and, under a king whose name was also Ben-hadad, besieged Samaria (II Kings vi.–vii.). The throne was soon after seized by Hazael (II Kings viii. 15), who defeated Jehoram (II Kings viii. 28–29), and was defeated by Shalmaneser II. in 843 and 840. Yet the same speedy recovery so often shown by the city enabled its king to regain territory from Israel east of the Jordan and even to threaten Judah (II Kings xii. 17–18) and to continue hostile operations against Jehoahaz and Jehoash (II Kings xiii. 3, 25). In 803 a king of Damascus whose name is given in the inscriptions as Mari was assailed by Ramman-nirari III., and Israel seized the opportunity to recover territory east of the Jordan (II Kings xiv. 28). In 773 the battering of the Assyrians was renewed, in 740 the ruler Rezin paid tribute to Tiglath-Pileser III. (cf. II Kings xv. 19 sqq., xvi. 7 sqq.), who took the city in 733, killed Rezin, deported the inhabitants, and introduced Assyrian colonists. In 732 Ahab visited the city to pay homage to the Assyrian overlord. In 713 Damascus was again found in an anti-Assyrian league and was again crushed in the defeat at Karkar. Under the Persians the city was made a seat of provincial government. When the region came under the sway of Alexander he issued coins from the city; but after his empire was divided Damascus was compelled to yield the chief place in importance to Antioch, though it was often a secondary capital. In 85 B.C. it fell into the hands of Aretas the Nabatæan. It was occupied in 65 by the Romans, and seems to have been ruled by an ethnarch for another Aretas in the time of Paul (II Cor. xi. 32). According to the testimony of coins, between 34 and 62 A.D. the city was not under Roman control. Christianity seems to have made an early entrance into the city, most likely through Jewish converts (Acts ix. 1 sqq.), and in Christian history the place is famous as the place where or near which Paul was converted. A bishopric was erected there, the incumbent of which took rank after the patriarch of Antioch. In 635 A.D. it became the residence of Mu'awiya, the first Ommiad calif. During the crusades it was frequently the object of attack, was captured by the Mongols in 1260, plundered by the Tatars in 1300, and taken by the Turks under Selim in 1516, since which date it has been the capital of a Turkish province, except for the period 1832–41, when it was under Egyptian control. The present population is not accurately known, estimates varying from 160,000 to 180,000, of whom about 100,000 are Mohammedans, about 5,000 Jews, 22,000 Orthodox Greeks, and the rest are distributed among the Christian sects. See ARAM, ARAMEANS, §§ 9–10.

GEO. W. GILMORE.

BIBLIOGRAPHY: J. L. Porter, *Five Years in Damascus*, London, 1855; W. K. Kelly, *Syria and the Holy Land*, chaps. xv.–xvi., ib. 1844; P. Schaff, *Through Bible Lands*, pp. 361 sqq., New York, 1878; Mrs. Macintosh, *Damascus and its People*, London, 1882; M. F. von Oppenheim, *Vom Mittelmeer zum persischen Golf*, i. 49–86, Berlin, 1899; Schürer, *Geschichte*, iii. 117 sqq. et passim; Eng. transl., passim.

DAMASUS: The name of two popes.

Damasus I.: Pope 366–384. He was born in 305, probably in Rome, the son of a priest of the Church of St. Laurence. After the death of Liberius, he was elected bishop by a part of the Church, while another faction chose the deacon Ursinus. Damasus could secure recognition only after a conflict marked by bloodshed, which lasted two years on account of the uncertain attitude of Valentinian I.; and even after the suppression of the disturbances the party of Ursinus maintained their opposition, to the point of schism. During these troubles clerics had been summoned before secular judges, and torture had even been used. On complaint being made, Valentinian issued a rescript, the substance of which is known from Ambrose (*Epist.*, xxi. 2); it is summed up in the phrase "that priests should judge priests." Rade thinks that the emperor meant to declare a fundamental division between secular and ecclesiastical jurisdiction; but this is too much to infer from the words. It was only an express recognition of the disciplinary power of bishops and councils, as it had been previously recognized in practise, and limited to questions of faith, morals, and contests over ecclesiastical offices. The appeal of the Roman council of 378 or 379 to Gratian was, in view of the occasion, an attempt to secure not extension, but recognition of the disciplinary power of the Roman See, which was practically nullified as long as imperial officials declined to enforce the sentence of ecclesiastical tribunals. This the council asked that they should be instructed to do, and Gratian agreed. There appears nothing in all this to support the contention of Rade and Langen that the Western bishops at least were subject to the tribunal of the pope; and the imperial decrees mentioned above can scarcely be cited as triumphs of the policy of Damasus. In fact, he does not seem to have known how to use either these or the famous edict of Theodosius (Feb. 27, 380), or the third canon of the Council of Constantinople in 381, as means to the elevation of Rome's ecclesiastical position—which, indeed, was actually damaged by his conduct in the Antioch controversy (see MELETIUS OF ANTIOCH), and did not again make progress until the pontificate of Siricius. In dogmatic conflicts Damasus remained steadfast in the traditional Roman policy. He opposed the Arians, and took strong measures against the Luciferians. It was during his pontificate that the understanding was reached between the Old and Young Nicene parties in the East; but he rather hindered the *rapprochement* than helped it, taking the side of the strict old orthodox party in the schism of Antioch. Basil of Cæsarea tried in vain to get him to acknowledge Meletius. A Roman synod of 382 renounced communion with Flavian. The measures taken by Damasus against Arianism in Italy were not very successful. Apparently as early as 369 he had condemned Auxentius of Milan at a council of Italian bishops, but the sentence was not executed by the secular authorities; Auxentius remained bishop until his death, and only in the election of Ambrose to succeed him did orthodoxy come into power. He was more successful in his repeated pronouncements against Apollinarianism, which was condemned in Roman councils of (probably) 377 and 381. Damasus was not lacking in learning, and did a good work by setting on foot a revision of the Latin Bible. He wrote a (lost) treatise on virginity and a number of metrical inscriptions for the catacombs, on which he bestowed intelligent care. He died Dec. 11, 384.

(A. HAUCK.)

BIBLIOGRAPHY: The *Opera* of Damasus are in *MPL*, xiii., and his *Epigrammata*, ed. M. Ihm, were published, Leipsic, 1895. Consult: *Liber pontificalis*, ed. Duchesne, i. 212, Paris, 1886, and ed. Mommsen in *MGH*, *Gest. pont. Rom.*, i. 82–84; Jaffé, *Regesta*, i. 37; M. Rade, *Damasus, Bischof von Rom*, Freiburg, 1882; Hefele, *Conciliengeschichte*, vols. i.–ii.; Bower, *Popes*, i. 83–107; Milman, *Latin Christianity*, i. 108–110. Consult also B. Hölscher, *De Damasi hymnis*, Münster, 1858.

Damasus II. (Poppo): Pope 1047–48. After the premature death of Clement II., Poppo, bishop of Brixen, was nominated to succeed him by Henry III. at Christmas, 1047. He was conducted to Rome in the following summer, consecrated July 17, and died Aug. 9.

(A. HAUCK.)

BIBLIOGRAPHY: Jaffé, *Regesta*, i. 528; J. Langen, *Geschichte der römischen Kirche . . . bis Gregor VII.*, Bonn, 1892; Hauck, *KD*, iii. 593; Bower, *Popes*, ii. 343; Milman, *Latin Christianity*, iii. 239.

DAMIAN, SAINT. See COSMAS AND DAMIAN, SAINTS.

DAMIANI, PIETRO. See PETER DAMIAN, SAINT.

DAMIANUS: Jacobite patriarch of Alexandria; b. in Syria July, 578; d. June 12, 605. He succeeded Peter IV. as patriarch of Alexandria in 578 under circumstances which were probably of a turbulent character. Controversies between the Jacobites and Paulites (the latter the adherents of Bishop Paul the Black of Antioch, d. probably 585) ensued and passed over into Egypt. On a journey in Syria and to Constantinople Damianus endeavored to frustrate peace negotiations which had already commenced. The Jacobite patriarch Peter of Antioch was consecrated by him in Alexandria (580 or 581), and later a controversy arose between the two which is known as a phase of the tritheistic controversy (see TRITHEISM); Damianus defended a position similar to that of Sabellianism (q.v.). On two Coptic ostraca a writing of Damianus is mentioned with the title *Kērugmata* (cf. Crum, *Coptic Ostraca*, London, 1902, no. 18, p. 7).

G. Krüger.

Bibliography: The sources are: John of Ephesus, *Hist. eccl.*, iii. 4, 33, 38, 41–45, 60, Syriac and Eng. transl. by W. Cureton, London, 1853; Timotheus, *De receptione hæreticorum*, in *MPG*, lxxxvi.; Sophronius, *Epistola ad Sergium*, in *MPG*, lxxxvii.; and Severus, in J. B. Asseman, *Bibliotheca orientalis*, ii. 70 sqq., Rome, 1721. Consult: J. P. N. Land, *Joannes, Bischof von Ephesus*, pp. 136–139, Leyden, 1856; C. W. F. Walch, *Historie der Ketzereien*, viii. 687, Leipsic, 1778; A. von Gutschmid, *Kleine Schriften*, ii. 498–499, ib. 1890.

DAMIEN, FATHER. See Venster, Joseph de.

DANCERS (DANSATORES, CHORIZANTES): A set of wild enthusiasts in the fourteenth and fifteenth centuries, whose peculiarities offered one of those strange mixtures of physical, spiritual, and moral elements to be found in the popular life of the Middle Ages. They made their appearance at Aachen in the summer of 1374, coming from southern Germany, and then spread eastward to Cologne, southward to Metz, and westward into Hainault. Their membership was numbered by thousands, of both sexes, and almost exclusively from the lower classes. They danced madly through the streets and in and out of the churches for hours at a time, until they were completely exhausted. They paid no attention to the amazed spectators, their minds being taken up with the contemplation of the most fantastic visions. Sometimes they imagined that they were wading in a stream of blood, to get out of which they leaped wildly in the air; others saw heaven opened and Christ upon his throne. The morbid mental condition which undoubtedly underlay these actions took the form of the popular notions of the day. It is probable that in many cases it was only simulated, and that lazy rascals joined and imitated the Dancers to get a share in the gifts which were freely bestowed upon them; and these excited mobs offered a natural breeding-ground for immorality of all kinds. The clergy and the people at large, however, sought no natural psychological explanation of the phenomena, but regarded the dancers as demoniacs; the priests attempted to help them by exorcism, while the populace was inclined to attribute their misfortune to unworthy priests, whose baptism had not sufficient validity to expel the demons. The dancers in their delirium invoked St. John Baptist, which may be connected with the fact that the outbreak occurred while the old popular celebration of his festival at midsummer, with its many excesses, was still observed. A similar epidemic occurred at Strasburg in 1418. Here it was customary to invoke St. Vitus for the cure of the malady, on account of the old tradition which has led to the application of the name " St. Vitus's dance " to the disease technically known as chorea.

(A. Hauck.)

Bibliography: J. F. C. Hecker, *Die grossen Volkskrankheiten des Mittelalters*, ed. A. Hirsch, pp. 143–193, Berlin, 1865, Eng. transl. of earlier edition, pp. 81–138, London, 1846 (where the authorities are given and reference made to similar phenomena elsewhere); *Encyclopædia Britannica*, xxiii. 60, s.v. " Tarantism "; P. Frédéricq, *Corpus documentorum inquisitionis Neerlandicæ*, i. 231 sqq., Ghent, 1889; idem, *De secten des geeselaars en der dansers in de Nederlanden*, Brussels, 1897.

DANCING: Dancing as a religious observance occupied an important place in the ceremonies of all ancient religions. It is connected with sacred processions (as in the Babylonian and Egyptian festivals) and with community rites at the altar, the sacred tree, or the sacred stone (cf., e.g., the account of such dances which comes from Cyprus, M. H. Ohnefalsch-Richter, *Kypros, die Bibel und Homer*, Berlin, 1893, Eng. transl., London, 1893, plates lxxxiii. 6, cxxvii. 4, etc.). In the Mohammedan festival at Mecca the march around the Kaaba still remains the culminating point of the celebration. The Old Testament reports that at the great Baal sacrifice on Mt. Carmel the priests went " limping " around the altar (I Kings xviii. 26, R. V. margin), and mention is made also of dancing around the golden calf (Ex. xxxii. 19). Sacred processions fell into disuse in the worship of Yahweh after the ark was transferred to Solomon's Temple; but the bringing of the ark into the Temple (I Kings viii. 1 sqq.) and its conveyance to Zion (II Sam. vi. 5) were accomplished in the manner usual in sacred processions. David and all Israel danced before the ark. Processions and dances without the ark formed an important part of festal celebrations (cf. the description of such a procession in Ps. lxviii. 25), at triumphal festivals (Ex. xv. 20; Judges xi. 34), and at the annual festival at Shiloh (Judges xxi. 21). Indeed, the whole celebration takes its name from them, the Hebrew *ḥagg* signifies the festival procession or dance. This remained true till the latest period of Jewish history. For the Psalmist the dance around the altar was part of the proper praise of God (Ps. cxlix. 3, cl. 4). On the evening of the feast of atonement the celebration was closed by dances of the maidens of Jerusalem in the vineyards (Taanit iv. 8). A peculiarity of the feast of tabernacles was the processions of those carrying branches of citron and palm around the altar of burnt offering, and even more especially the torch-dances of the most prominent men on the night between the first and second days of the festival.

Naturally, dancing also formed a part of the secular festivals (Jer. xxxi. 4, 13; Matt. xi. 17; Luke vii. 32, xv. 25), and at the banquets of the nobles dancing women could not have been lacking (cf. the Egyptian customs), although they are mentioned nowhere in the Old Testament (but note the dance of the daughter of Herodias, Matt. xiv. 6).

I. Benzinger.

Bibliography: John Spencer, in B. Ugolinus, *Thesaurus antiquitatum sacrarum*, xxxii. 1133, 34 vols., Venice, 1744–1769; R. Voss, *Der Tanz und seine Geschichte*, Berlin, 1868; F. Delitzsch, *Iris*, pp. 189–206, London, 1889; W. Smith, *Dictionary of Greek and Roman Antiquities*, ii. 592–594, ib. 1891; H. B. Tristram, *Eastern Customs*, pp. 207–210, ib. 1894; Mrs. L. Grove, *Dancing*, ib. 1895; M. Emmanuel, *La Danse grecque antique, d'après les monuments figurés*, Paris, 1876; *DB*, i. 549–551; *EB*, i. 998–1001; *JE*, iv. 424–426.

DANEAU, dā"nō' (DANNÆUS), LAMBERT: French Protestant; b. at Beaugency-sur-Loire (15 m. s.w. of Orléans) 1530; d. at Castres (80 m. w. of Montpellier) Nov. 11, 1595. He was of Roman Catholic family, began the study of law at Orléans, went to Paris in 1547, and returned to

Orléans in 1552, where he studied four years with Anne du Bourg and obtained the degree of *doctor in utroque jure* 1559. For a long time he was inclined toward Protestantism, and the death of his master, Du Bourg, decided him to go to Geneva in 1560, where he made the acquaintance of Calvin and adhered to the Reformed Church. In 1561 he became pastor at Gien, where he remained till St. Bartholomew's day. From 1574 he was professor at Geneva and in 1581 was granted citizenship. The same year he was called to the University of Leyden and became minister of the Walloon Church there. But when he tried to organize it on the Genevan model he met with much difficulty and had to leave Leyden the following year. For a year he was professor and preacher in Ghent, then at Orthez, and at Lescar (1591). In 1593 he was called to Castres. Daneau was one of the most celebrated theologians of the sixteenth century; he belonged to the extreme Calvinist party, and wrote many works on philosophy, jurisprudence, and theology, including *Methodus Sacræ Scripturæ in publicis tum concionibus utiliter, atque intelligenter tractandæ* (Geneva, 1570); *Les Sorciers, dialogue très utile et nécessaire pour ce temps* (1574); *Briève remontrance sur les jeux de sort* (1574); *Traité des danses auquel est amplement résolue la question, à savoir s'il est permis aux Chrétiens de danser* (1579); *Traité de l'estat honneste des Chrestiens en leur accoustrement* (1580); *Orationis Dominicæ explicatio* (1582); *Apologia seu vera et orthodoxa orthodoxorum Patrum sententia, defensio ac interpretatio de adoratione carnis domini nostri Jesu Christi* (1583). G. BONET-MAURY.

BIBLIOGRAPHY: P. de Félice, *Lambert Daneau*, Paris, 1882; Nicéron, *Mémoires*, xxvii. 21-36; É. and E. Haag, *La France protestante*, ed. H. L. Bordier, vol. v., Paris, 1886.

DANIEL, APOCRYPHAL ADDITIONS TO. See APOCRYPHA, OLD TESTAMENT, A, IV., 3.

DANIEL, BOOK OF.

I. Divisions and Contents: The book named after the prophet Daniel divides into narrative (i.-vi.) and prophecy (vii.-xii.). The first division contains six stories: (i.) the fortune of the four Hebrew youths at the court in Babylon, (ii.) Nebuchadrezzar's dream, (iii.) the episode of the golden image, (iv.) the second dream of the king, (v.) Belshazzar's feast, (vi.) the episode of Daniel in the lions' den. The second division contains four visions: (vii.) that of the four beasts, (viii.) of the ram and the goat, (ix.) the interpretation of Jeremiah's (Jer. xxv. 12, cf. xxix. 10) seventy weeks as seventy year-weeks, (x.-xii.) Daniel's final vision, dealing with the last things. Besides this the Septuagint and Theodotion have as additions chap. iii. the Prayer of Azariah and the Song of the Three Children, The Story of Susanna, and the Story of Bel and the Dragon (see APOCRYPHA, A, IV., 3). Inasmuch as the Story of Susanna was certainly written in Greek, and the other additions probably so, they have no bearing upon the canonical book and show merely to what extent the person of Daniel was used by the Jews of the Greek world.

II. Interpretation: One of the oldest witnesses to the Book of Daniel is I Macc. i. 54, where the heathen altar erected by Antiochus Epiphanes is called the "abomination of desolation" (cf. Dan. ix. 27, xi. 31, xii. 11), thus connecting these verses with the time of this king. Similarly, the Sibylline Oracles (iii. 394 sqq.) allude to Dan. vii. 7, which is referred to Antiochus Epiphanes and his successors. Again, the queer rendering of Dan. ix. 24 sqq. in the Septuagint points to the supposition that the events there mentioned had been fulfilled under that king. Ephraem Syrus (*Opera*, Rome, 1732-46, ii. 206, 214, 232), probably following Jewish tradition, construed the fourth kingdom (Dan. ii., vii.) as the Greek Empire, the little horn (Dan. vii.) as Antiochus Epiphanes; the resurrection (Dan. xii.) is referred figuratively to the revival of the religious spirit, but Dan. ix. 25-26 to Christ, in agreement with Christian interpretation. Julius Hilarianus, at the end of the fourth century, in his *De mundi duratione*, computed from this verse that the end of the seventy weeks coincided with the reign of Antiochus. But this oldest interpretation was displaced by another.

1. Fourth Kingdom Greece.

In the New Testament the description of the last grievous days before the Messianic deliverances are referred to the future in the eschatological sense (cf. II Thess. ii. 4 with Dan. xi. 36; Rev. xi. 2, 3, xii. 6, 14, xiii. 5). Christ himself, in picturing the parousia of the Son of Man (Matt. xxiv. 20), made use of Dan. vii. 13. From Matt. xxiv. 15, 16 and Luke xxi. 5, 6, it appears that Rome has taken the place of Greece. It was no doubt understood by Josephus in this way. With but few exceptions, the patristic exegetes followed this later interpretation. Though differing much in particulars (thus for Dan. ix. 25-26 Jerome enumerates nine different computations, while Fraidl in the fifteenth century registers no less than 107), the fundamental conception is the same. So Hippolytus refers the first world-power (Dan. ii., vii.) to Babylonia, the second to Persia, the third to Greece, the fourth to Rome. The ten horns (Dan. vii.) belong to the future, the little horn is Antichrist. The anointed one in Dan. ix. 25 sqq. is the high priest Joshua, after whom comes Christ, 434 years having intervened. The last year-week is eschatological; between the sixty-second and the final week Hippolytus inserts Christianity; Dan. xi. he interprets historically, but the two kings in verses 25 sqq. are Alexander Balas and Ptolemy Philometer; at Dan. xi. 36 his exegesis makes a bold leap, referring what follows to the eschatological future and the coming Antichrist. This method of interpretation found a strong opponent in Por-

2. Fourth Kingdom Rome.

phyry (see NEOPLATONISM). In book xii. of his extensive work against Christianity Porphyry discussed the Book of Daniel, and placed its author in the time of Antiochus Epiphanes. To prove his position, Porphyry gave abundant extracts from Greek authors; these were used liberally by the Fathers (so Jerome on Dan. xi.), but otherwise his work had no influence. The patristic view dominated the Middle Ages. Only a few Jewish exegetes had a different conception; thus Saadia and Ibn Ezra saw the Mohammedan empire in the fourth world-power. But all, Christians and Jews, Catholic and Protestant, agreed that the book was written during the Exile. That Uriel Acosta, in the seventeenth century, agreed with Porphyry in calling it a forgery made little impression. Semler made the statement anew; but only through the investigations of Corrodi (1783), Bertholdt (1806–1808), and especially of Gesenius and Bleek did criticism come to its own. In a short time the recognition that the historical vision of the book does not go beyond Antiochus and that its author lived during his reign became universally accepted among liberal-minded scholars. Among orthodox theologians this revival of Porphyry's view met with strong opposition, especially in the apologies of Hengstenberg and Hävernick. For a while Franz Delitzsch took a middle position, but finally recognized the book as a product of the times of the Seleucidæ.

3. Return to Earlier View.

Thus far mention has been made only of those who held to the unity of the book; but it is necessary to notice the endeavors made to separate it into parts. Some orthodox theologians used this method to save at least part of the book as exilic. The oldest exponent of this theory of a composite Daniel is Spinoza, who saw in Dan. viii.–xii. a genuine work and suggested from linguistic data that Dan. i.–vii. were taken from chronological works of the Chaldeans. B. Newton pointed out that Dan. vii.–xii. were written in the first person, consequently they alone had claims to genuineness. This view found a champion later in August Köhler. Essentially different is Orelli's treatment; he contends that originally the four kingdoms were Babylonia, Medo-Persia, Macedonia, and Rome, and that a Jew living in the troublous times of Antiochus thought he had discovered under Antiochus Epiphanes the fulfilment of the old prophecies of Daniel, and extended the book to make the reference evident to his contemporaries. Zöckler found one interpolation of Maccabean date (Dan. xi. 5–45); J. P. Lange found two (Dan. x. 1–11, 44, xii. 5–13); Meinhold held the part written in Aramaic to be exilic, that written in Hebrew Maccabean; Lagarde held that chap. vii. was written in Roman times (69 A.D.).

4. Decision Affected by Views on Unity.

III. **The Unity:** The totally different results at which the opponents of the book's unity arrive create but little faith in their method. That the book is partly Hebrew, partly Aramaic, would prove something only if the parts differed also in contents. But this is by no means the case. Dan. ii. 4, where the Aramaic begins, is part of a coherent narrative; vii. belongs with viii. and not with ii.–vi. The question why two languages are used can not be conclusively answered; altogether unsatisfactory is the explanation that the author used the Aramaic because he thought it the language employed by the speakers, for then he forgot himself until he came to viii. 1! The simplest explanation is that a lacuna in the original Hebrew was filled in at a later time from an Aramaic translation. The use of the first person in vii.–xii. has little weight as ground for partition for the reason that it is hedged in by the use of the third person. Therefore internal grounds alone can help in deciding whether exilic documents are incorporated or whether a (late) author designedly used as a part of his art the pretext of possession of genuine prophecies. Similarly the affirmation of a "tendency" is not to be used as ground for partition, for this appears in both parts alike. Thus the main question remains, whether or not the book everywhere in its description of the future has the same horizon.

1. The Two Languages and Use of First Person.

The investigation must begin with viii. and xi. In viii. the book itself gives a clear interpretation. The ram with the two horns refers to the kings of Media and Persia, the goat is Greece (viii. 20, 21). The great horn of the goat is the first Greek king (Alexander the Great). After his death the kingdom is divided, and the Ptolemies and Seleucidæ enter. Chapter xi. gives a detailed outline of the political relations between the kings of the north and of the south, that is, between the Seleucidæ and the Ptolemies; xi. 21 sqq. refers to Antiochus, xi. 25 sqq. describes his first campaign against Egypt (179 B.C.), xi. 29 sqq. relates his second campaign (168 B.C.); and the "ships of Chittim" refers to the arrival of Popilius Lænas to aid Egypt. In anger on account of the failure of his Egyptian campaign, Antiochus revenged himself against the Jews by eliminating their daily worship and setting up a heathen altar in the temple (cf. Dan. xi. 39 sqq. with I Macc. i. 47 sqq., 57, 62). That from Dan. xi. 36 to the end of the chapter another king is meant is impossible. The final destruction of the king and the expression "at that time" denote the end of the history and the beginning of Messianic times. If we examine now chap. ii. it appears undeniable that the fourth kingdom, first of iron, later of iron and clay, with its many futile attempts at union through matrimony, can refer only to Greece. It is objected that history knows only one world-power between the Babylonian and the Macedonian; however, the question is not one of history, but of the author's view, and he has two kingdoms, the Median and the Persian (vi. 1, ix. 1, x. 1). Since the boundaries of the two nations join, they appear in chap. viii. as a relative unit in the ram with the two horns. As thus chaps. ii., viii., and xi. have the same horizon, the supposition is that this is true also of chap. vii. Here the ten horns of the fourth animal create some difficulty. Lagarde has seen here ten Cæsars, but as he had to count in Antoninus and to connect Vespasian with the little horn (to whom

2. The Author's Key.

it is impossible that vii. 24, 25 refer), his theory must be rejected; but the question remains whether the ten horns may not be brought into connection with ten Grecian rulers. This is so easy that the only difficulty is to decide among the many possible combinations at which Nestle, Von Gutschmid, Gunkel, and others arrive. There remain for examination only the celebrated conclusions to chap. ix. Here the evil prince is by general agreement no other than Antiochus, who is similarly described in vii. 25, viii. 23 sqq., xi 31. That he is to reign half a week (3½ years) agrees with vii. 25, xii. 7, and his reign precedes that of the Messiah (chap. xi.); thus his horizon is limited to the Greek period. The anointed one is not Cyrus (Isa. xlv.), but a ruling high priest; the sixty-two weeks embrace post-exilic times under the guidance of a line of legitimate high priests, the end of which period is marked by the removal of this line, probably in the person of Onias III.; the last year-week is that during which Antiochus Epiphanes did away with the daily service. Comparison of these 7 x 62 years with the time between 536 B.C. and 170 gives sixty-eight years too many, but one has only to read Josephus to appreciate the labors and difficulties of a Jewish historian of his time and the futility of seeking a perfectly satisfactory reckoning.

IV. The Date: The result of an unbiased investigation of the book is therefore that the described period nowhere goes beyond that of Antiochus; thus the question as to the time of its composition is settled. Nearly all the Old Testament prophets join the time of the end closely to their own times. A similar expectation is expressed in Daniel, but only from the moment when the power of Antiochus had reached its zenith. According to Biblical analogy, the book was written at a time when the description of the future takes on the character of other prophetical books; while the minute, unprophetical description of the period between the Exile and Antiochus must be taken as a description of past events. Such passages as viii. 13, 19, xii. 6 sqq., 11 imply that the question which concerns the author is how long the terrorism of Antiochus is to last. In complete accord with this are the directions (viii. 26, xii. 4) to the exilic Daniel to seal the book, by which the author indicates that up to his time the book was unknown.

1. Antiochus the Terminus ad Quem.

This result is justified by a number of weighty considerations. That the book in the Hebrew canon is not among the "prophets," but among the "writings" is intelligible only if it were written at a time when the canon of the Prophets was already formed. Absolutely impossible is the hypothesis of the book's origin in exilic times when the total unhistoricity of the description of exilic times is compared with the correctness of the later history (cf. Dan. i. 1 with Jer. xxxvi. 9, 29). Every detail of the earlier period is unhistorical; Belshazzar was not the son of Nebuchadrezzar (Dan. v. 22), was not king (v. 1); Babylon was not conquered, but surrendered voluntarily to Cyrus (not to Darius, as the book has it). Aramaisms and Grecisms in the Aramaic sections are marks of a later age. That it was used by I Macc. matters little, as the latter was composed in 106 B.C.; still less weight has Josephus' story that Alexander the Great had read the book, for this is denied by the book itself (Dan. viii. 26, xii. 4).

2. Narrative Unhistorical.

V. The Value: A result which demands recognition is that it could have been composed only in the reign of Antiochus Epiphanes. Only by this knowledge is it possible to see the greatness of the book. The time must be still further limited. One totally misunderstands the character of the book if he thinks of it as written after the cleansing of the temple in 165 B.C. Everything which the book contains of comfort and promise is pure hope, for the whole book was composed at a time of extremest need. It is evident that the author did not know the eastern campaign of Antiochus; the third campaign against Egypt is a pure prophetic picture (Dan. xi. 40 sqq.); from the author's calling the Maccabean insurrection "a little help" Kuenen rightly concludes that Judah's victory over Lysias in 165 B.C. was unknown; and viii. 14 is, like ix. 24, a Messianic expectation. From this point of view the vacillation in the length of the reign of terror (3½ years, vii. 25, ix. 27, xii. 7; 1,150 days, viii. 14; 1,290 days, xii. 11; 1,335 days, xii. 12) is most easily understood; they are pure surmises or computations which can not be verified because the key is lacking. The greatness of the book consists in the fact that its author drew all promises out of his own faith. And in this hope he was not deceived, for the following year, through the cleansing of the temple and the death of the tyrant, brought a relative fulfilment of his promises, just as in earlier days the return from exile was a relative fulfilment of the promises of Deutero-Isaiah. This relative salvation the author has seen alongside of an absolute Messianic one, and in this vision of the future lies the particular and lasting value of the book. Odd and uncouth though his reading of history is, his vision of the age to come is deep and full of meaning. He did not try to support himself and his contemporaries by detailed and glaring sensual pictures, but he gave comfort through the rebirth of pure prophetic thought. After the fourth world-kingdom had run its full demonic course the longed-for judgment was to come (vii. 10), and with it the end of the history of revelation and that of man (ix. 24); thereupon was to come the divine kingdom from Heaven (vii. 27), without limit in time or space (ii. 44), in the glory of which even the pious dead should participate, while the worldly recreants would receive their due (xii. 2).

1. The Author's Faith.

It is more difficult to take a position respecting the narratives of the first part. One soon sees, however, that they can serve only as the materialization of the same faith as has created the vision of the future. This by no means excludes use of sources; on the other hand, even if one could point out everywhere a direct reference to Antiochus, this by no means makes it pure fiction. There is much that points to the use of older ma-

2. Use of Sources.

terial. The name Daniel occurs elsewhere (Ezra viii. 2); in Ezekiel it is placed between Noah and Job (Ezek. xiv. 14, xxviii. 3). Comparing Eusebius's *Præparatio evangelica*, ix. 41 with Dan. iv. one may conclude that the author of Daniel used here a Babylonian legend. The same may be true for chap. v., since he did not get the names of Belshazzar and Darius from the Bible; the latter personality he undoubtedly found in Darius Hystaspis, but why he saw in this Persian king a Mede is unknown. (F. Buhl.)

VI. Critical Objections Answered: None of the historic statements of Daniel can be invalidated. Alleged errors are as follows: (1) No secular historian names Belshazzar, therefore Belshazzar never existed. But in 1854 Belshazzar was found in the monuments. (2) Daniel calls Nebuchadrezzar king before Nabopolassar died. But so does Jer. xxvii. 6; Nebuchadrezzar was admitted to co-sovereignty. (3) Daniel terms a gild of wise men "Chaldeans," a use unknown till four centuries after the exile. But Herodotus (i. 181, 185) in the same century with Daniel uses the same term.

1. Major Objections.

(4) Belshazzar was not king, nor was he the son or grandson of Nebuchadrezzar. But somebody was left in command at Babylon when Nabonidus led out the army to Sippar. Who but his oldest and favorite son? Exercising royal authority, Belshazzar was king as much as was Nebuchadrezzar in similar circumstances. The queen mother (Dan. v. 11) said Nebuchadrezzar was Belshazzar's father (or grandfather). Probabilities sustain her truthfulness, thus: Eril-Merodach, Nebuchadrezzar's son, succeeded his father, and was succeeded by Neriglissar because he had married a daughter of the great king, the legitimate successor being Neriglissar's son. The son of Neriglissar dying, how came Nabonidus to occupy the throne in turbulent Babylon, unchallenged for seventeen years? If he had married another daughter of Nebuchadrezzar, then his son Belshazzar was grandson of Nebuchadrezzar, and legitimate heir, and the prophecy of Jer. xxvii. 6–7, "Nebuchadrezzar, his son, and son's son," was fulfilled. (5) Dan. i. 1, "third year," is inconsistent with Jer. xxxvi. 9, xlvi. 2, "fourth or fifth year." This, if true, would eliminate the conjectured Maccabean fabricator, for a fabricator with Jeremiah before him (Dan. ix. 2) would not contradict Jeremiah in the first sentence of his romance. But there is no inconsistency. (6) The annalistic tablet of Cyrus intimates that Babylon was taken easily. This agrees with Daniel (v. 30, 31), but there must have been some struggle, for the tablet says "the king's son died," and Daniel says "that night Belshazzar was slain." The tablet says further that the city yielded to Gobryas—Cyrus not appearing for several weeks—and that Gobryas was made governor and appointed other governors; all of which corresponds to Darius the Mede who "received" the kingdom and appointed satraps, etc. (Dan. v. 30, vi. 1). Cyrus had other conquests to make, and left a subordinate king in Babylon, wisely appointing a Mede. Abydenus and Æschylus say that the first ruler of the city was a Mede, and the scholiast of Aristophanes mentions a Darius who reigned before Darius Hystaspis. (7) There are three Greek words in Dan. iii. 5. They are the names of musical instruments, and these carry their native names with them. (8) Part of the Book of Daniel is in Aramaic, ii. 4–vii. But so is Ezra iv. 8–vi. 18. Ezra too was brought up in Babylon. His Aramaic is "all but identical" (Driver) with Daniel's. Aramaic was the vernacular. Each writer drops into it upon slight suggestion, Ezra upon quoting an Aramaic letter; Daniel upon quoting the frightened Chaldeans. The tablets from Nippur in course of decipherment by Professor Clay are in point; the business contracts are written in Babylonian cuneiform, the labels or dockets on the back are in Aramaic, for quick reference by the clerks in the office.

As to the other "historic inaccuracies," as Daniel's being too young for Ezekiel to have known—he was forty, possibly fifty years old when Ezekiel wrote of him; as to his not knowing how to spell the name Nebuchadrezzar—he spells it as Kings, Chronicles, and Ezra do and as Jeremiah does half the time.

2. Minor Objections.

On the other hand, there was a Daniel, eminent, wise, and godly enough to be linked with Noah and Job (Ezek. xiv. 14, 20). There is no Daniel but the man whose book is under consideration and whom Jesus called a prophet (Matt. xxiv. 15). The incident narrated by Josephus (*Ant.*, XI. viii. 5), that Alexander saw Daniel's mention of himself, is confirmed by the fact that, while Alexander destroyed every city in Syria friendly to Persia, he spared and greatly favored Jerusalem. He consulted the shrines at Gordium and Amon. Why not Jerusalem? The only shadow of a shade upon the historicity of Daniel is the omission of his name in Ecclesiasticus (200 B.C.). But other names are omitted and Daniel, the person, certainly existed prior to or contemporaneously with Ezekiel. The Book Ecclesiasticus is itself a witness to the antiquity of the Book of Daniel; though it presented the dominant type of Jewish thought at the time the canon was forming, it was not admitted to the canon because it was not ancient enough. Daniel was admitted. Daniel is not listed in the division called the "Prophets" (see CANON, I., 1, § 4). The reason probably was to satisfy the scruples of those rabbis who objected to prophecy delivered outside the Holy Land. Ezekiel was admitted, says Rabbi Jarchi, because his first prophecy (Ezek. xvii.) was delivered in Jerusalem. The Aramaic version interpolates "in the land of Israel" in pursuance of this scruple (Ezek. i. 3). There is no mention of Nebuchadrezzar's madness (Dan. iv.) in secular history. Nebuchadrezzar recovered, which accounts for the prudent silence of court historiographers; but Nebuchadrezzar himself in his Standard Inscription, after the usual royal boasts, records: "Four years . . . the seat of my kingdom in the city . . . which . . . did not rejoice my heart. In all my dominions I did not build a high place of power; treasures I did not lay up. In Babylon buildings for myself and my kingdom I did not lay out. In the worship of Merodach, my lord, I did not sing praises. I did not furnish his altars, nor clear canals." To those who do not believe that miracles ever occurred, the fiery furnace and the lion's den will seem incredible, but it is not incredible that a writer in the exile believed them. The "atmosphere" of the book betrays its place of origin. "The more I read Daniel," says Lenormant, "the more I am struck with the truth of the tableaux of the Babylonian court traced in the first six chapters." The tablets now undergoing decipherment show a people given over to superstition, magic, and talismans. The naiveté of truth appears in the mention that the Chaldeans spoke in Aramaic. They were frightened. There was no time for the composition of a reply in the court language. The unconscious revelation of the emergence of Law as superior even to the will of kings, when the Persian power came in. "The law of the Medes and Persians, which altereth not," shows contemporaneity. The simplicity of truth appears through all. The book is "sealed" at its close. This means: it is ended, or, it is attested, or, it is such that, as in Isa. xxix. 10–14, some will pretend they can not understand. All these are true of Daniel.

JOSEPH D. WILSON.

BIBLIOGRAPHY: The earlier commentaries are mostly worthless; few of the modern ones are much better. In English the best by far and of the highest intrinsic value is S. R. Driver, in *Cambridge Bible for Schools*, 1900. Consult also the commentaries by A. Bevan, Cambridge, 1892; J. D. Prince, London, 1899; K. Marti, Tübingen, 1901; and C. H. H. Wright, *Daniel and its Critics*, London, 1906. Discussion of critical problems are in Driver, *Introduction*, chap. xi.; A. H. Sayce, "*Higher Criticism*" *and . . . the Monuments*, pp. 495–537, London, 1893; G. Behrmann, *Das Buch Daniel*, Göttingen, 1894; *DB*, i. 551–557; *EB*, i. 1001–15; *JE*, iv. 430–432. Particular questions are treated in J. Meinhold, *Die Composition des Buches Daniel*, Greifswald, 1884; idem, *Beiträge zur Erklärung des Daniel*, Leipsic, 1888; A. Kamphausen, *Das Buch Daniel und die neuere Geschichtsforschung*, ib. 1892; H. Gunkel, *Schöpfung und Chaos*, pp. 266–270, 323–335, Göttingen, 1895; C. Bruston, *Études sur Daniel*, Paris, 1898. On the unity consult: A. von Gall, *Die Einheitlichkeit des . . . Daniel*, Giessen, 1895; G. A. Barton, in *JBL*, xvii (1898), 62–86. On the seventy weeks: F. Fraidl, *Die Exegese der 70 Wochen in der alten und mittleren Zeit*, Graz, 1883; Van Lennep, *De 70 jaarweken van Daniel*, Utrecht, 1888. For the text: Hebrew is by A. Kamphausen, in *SBOT*, New York, 1896; best LXX. text by Swete, *Old Testament in Greek*, vol. iii., Cambridge, 1896. Consult: M. Löhr, in *ZATW*, xv (1895), 75 sqq., 193 sqq., xvi (1896), 14 sqq.; A. Bludau, *Die alexandrinische Uebersetzung des Buches Daniel*, Freiburg, 1897.

DANIEL, ELECTOR OF MAINZ, AND THE COUNTERREFORMATION IN THE EICHSFELD.

His General Policy (§ 1).
Severe Measures in the Eichsfeld (§ 2).
The Results (§ 3).
Events After Daniel's Death (§ 4).

Daniel Brendel of Homburg (b. 1523; d. 1582) became elector of Mainz in 1555—to the chagrin of the citizens—by a majority of one vote over the palgrave Reichardt, who had Protestant leanings. His official policy was determined openly and mainly by political, rather than by religious considerations. He sought to maintain a good understanding with his powerful neighbor of the Palatinate, though at a later period he appears more reserved than at first; he discreetly abstained from intermeddling in French and Netherlandish affairs; and in imperial transactions he allied himself closely with Emperor Maximilian II. That this policy was not prompted by ecclesiastical indifference is witnessed by measures in other connections: in 1561 Daniel founded a Jesuit college at Mainz, and he furthermore expressed his regard for the Jesuits by presents, by admitting them to the cathedral pulpit, by founding a school, by patronizing a Jesuit confessor, and by the stimulus he gave to other spiritual princes toward founding Jesuit colleges. In only one part of his archbishopric—in the so-called Eichsfeld region, between Thuringia and the Harz country—did Daniel carry through the Counterreformation; in the electorate proper (Mainz and its vicinity), Protestant elements continued to be tolerated, even in the government and in the elector's official household. The Reformation had quite early penetrated the Eichsfeld, especially by way of Erfurt, and about the middle of the sixteenth century the entire district was fairly Protestant. At the outset Daniel, like his predecessors, tolerated this state of affairs; but afterward, albeit with a regard to the rights of sovereignty duly drawn up and subscribed for him by the Protestant nobility, he interfered with rigor.

1. His General Policy.

To subdue a disobedient vassal, he betook himself to the Eichsfeld in June, 1574, with a considerable array of troops, and accompanied by two Jesuits. The nobleman in question was quickly overcome, and the Protestant preachers were driven out of the two towns, Duderstadt and Heiligenstadt. Since the elector proceeded only against the towns, and at the same time granted freedom of conscience to the territorial knighthood, any general resistance to these extraordinary measures was for the time being averted. A zealous convert, Lippold of Stralendorf, was entrusted, as temporal chief officer, with the prosecution of the work thus begun; and the spiritual commissioner, Heinrich Bunthe, was of equally strict Catholic sentiments. At the beginning of 1575 they were joined by the Jesuit Elgard and other Jesuits despatched to the elector by the Curia. Elgard soon made himself indispensable, and measures animated by a spirit heretofore unknown in the Eichsfeld rapidly multiplied. At Duderstadt they sought to take the churches from the Protestants; visitations began alike in the towns and in the country, that is, within the sphere of the knightly patronages; the Protestant clergy were driven away, and ecclesiastical burial was refused to their adherents. Against this manner of procedure the knightly estate of the district now rose up, reenforced by the neighboring princes of Hesse and electoral Saxony, but without effectual results; still more energetic measures were prosecuted in favor of the Counterreformation. A fresh importation of Jesuits ensued; the dispersion of the Protestant clergy continued; the frequenting of outside Protestant churches and participation in the communion according to the Lutheran rite were forbidden; and even very secular methods were applied to render the population submissive, such as the prohibition of the export of Duderstadt beer.

2. Severe Measures in the Eichsfeld.

The victory of the Roman party at the Diet of Regensburg, 1576, led to new oppressions of the Protestants. The still remaining Protestant preachers were driven away; the churches were forcibly withdrawn from Protestant worship and were consecrated anew; the people were forced to attend mass with the aid of the electoral officers and their troops. As time passed, indeed, it happened again and again that upon withdrawal of the temporal power the Roman clergy who had been introduced by force were at once expelled, while parsonages and churches again were occupied by the returning Protestant preachers. In spite of all their prospective advantages, the number of converts remained very small; where no Protestant service could be longer observed, the people got along without spiritual provision entirely or traveled for miles to take part in secret worship or in Protestant worship still tolerated for want of repressive power. The elector's arrangement, however, was enforced by the sanction of the emperor Rudolph, who admonished the Council of Duderstadt to obey the elector; nor did the intervention of Protestant electors have any effect.

When Daniel died in 1582 very little had been gained for the Roman Church. The Roman clergy, to be sure, were everywhere present; divine service, baptisms, marriages, and burials were enforced according to Roman rite; but the people at large remained almost solidly loyal to

3. The Results.

the Protestant faith. In only one place, perhaps, was a somewhat firmer basis gained for the Counter-reformation. A Jesuit school had been opened in Heiligenstadt in 1575; in 1581 a well-endowed college with seven alumni scholarships was erected by the elector; and the neighboring Evangelical peasants had to contribute bond-service thereto. The school at first attracted more scholars from the surrounding districts than from the Eichsfeld itself; but the scholastic festivities, with their cleverly chosen allurements, the public presentation of Biblical dramas, in the course of time won candidates for instruction from the home town and country as well. The Jesuits were never discouraged by the failure of their plans or intimidated by the odium exhibited against them.

Daniel's successor, Wolfgang of Dalberg (1582–1601), continued the work already begun; the same coercive measures with their merely momentary results were applied over and over again, while all complaints and petitions of the knighthood met with the same negative answer. The knighthood proper, however, were now allowed the liberty of Protestant worship behind closed doors, though not for their dependent subjects. At the beginning of the Thirty Years' War (1618) conditions had changed somewhat; the Jesuit school in Heiligenstadt had gradually exerted its

4. Events After Daniel's Death.

influence; this town had again become predominantly Roman Catholic, and in like manner throughout the district the Protestants had been driven back. In Duderstadt alone there still persisted a secret band of Protestants who remained steadfast through all the military oppressions, and eventually secured their right of existence. During the first period of the war the quartering of imperial troops and Tilly's soldiers was one means employed to distress the Protestants and bring them into subjection; subsequently there came respites of better times with the Swedish troops. It was decreed at the Peace of Westphalia (1648) that the status of Jan. 1, 1624, should be in force with respect to church affairs—a ruling not exactly favorable to the Protestants. Public Protestant worship, however, was allowed in Duderstadt, and a dozen noble parishes received freedom of religious practise by the terms of the Peace. Oppression of the Protestants at the hands of electoral officers, however, did not cease till the termination of the electoral state of Mainz and the incorporation of the Eichsfeld into the kingdom of Prussia.

WALTER GOETZ.

BIBLIOGRAPHY: N. Serarius, *Res Moguntiacæ*, i. 862 sqq., Frankfort, 1722; H. Heppe, *Die Restauration des Katholisismus . . . auf dem Eichsfelde*, Marburg, 1850; W. Burghard, *Die Gegenreformation auf dem Eichsfelde, 1575–79*, vols. i.–ii., ib. 1890–91; L. von Wintzingeroda-Knorr, in *Schriften des Vereins für Reformationsgeschichte*, Nos. 36, 42, Halle, 1892–93; H. Moritz, *Die Wahl Rudolfs II.*, Marburg, 1895.

DANN, CHRISTIAN ADAM: Lutheran; b. at Tübingen Dec. 24, 1758; d. at Stuttgart Mar. 19, 1837. He was of Huguenot descent, and studied at Balingen, later at the cloister-school at Blaubeuren, and after 1777 in his native city. In 1793 he was called to a deaconry in Göttingen, in 1794 as assistant at St. Leonhard in Stuttgart. In 1812 he was transferred to Oeschingen, a village twelve miles from Tübingen, and in 1817 to Mössingen, near Stuttgart. He was recalled to Stuttgart in 1824, first to the cathedral church, one year later to St. Leonhard, where he preached eleven years to crowded congregations. From his youth he was under the influence of Bengel and Pietism. A strong champion of the ethical demands of the Gospel in the lax times of the Napoleonic wars, he had a deep, stern conviction of sin. Christianity was to him essentially an "institution of pardon, atonement, and compensation." The Christ of the Gospels was not only his constant example, but also mediator and redeemer. In the Eucharist he found "the most intimate blessed union with Christ." He wrote a large number of occasional tracts on various subjects—among the rest against cruelty to animals and vivisection. With Rieger he founded in 1811 the charity organization of Stuttgart. He labored long for a revision of the hymnal, which finally appeared, five years after his death; it contains the most beautiful of his hymns, "Gekreuzigter, zu deinen Füssen!"

BIBLIOGRAPHY: *Denkmal der Liebe für den vollendeten C. A. Dann*, Stuttgart, 1837; A. Knapp, in *Gesammelte Werke*, vol. ii., ib. 1875; *Der Christenbote*, l (1880), 204.

DANNHAUER, JOHANN CONRAD: Lutheran teacher of Spener; b. at Köndringen (10 m. n. of Freiburg) Mar. 24, 1603; d. at Strasburg Nov. 7, 1666. He began his education in the gymnasium at Strasburg and was the master of a thorough philosophical training before he commenced his theological work in 1624. He continued his studies at Marburg, Altorf, and Jena, lecturing at the same time on philosophy and linguistics and winning recognition at Jena by his exegesis of the Epistle to the Ephesians. Returning to Strasburg in 1628, he entered upon an active career as administrator, teacher, and theologian. Made seminary inspector in 1628, he became in the following year professor of oratory, and in 1633 professor of theology, pastor of the cathedral, and president of the ecclesiastical assembly. Although the judgment of his contemporaries, Bebel, Spener, and others, placed him in the front rank of the theologians of the time, Dannhauer has received scant justice at the hands of posterity. The influence exerted upon Spener by his teacher must not be underestimated because of the formal tone of the poem dedicated by the founder of the Pietists to his teacher's memory. Their relations were certainly not characterized by the warmth of personal friendship, but were rather in the nature of an intercourse based on common interests. Dannhauer ordained Spener, and in all probability secured for him the post of private tutor at the court of the elector palatine. Spener, in return, seems to have been connected with the preparation of the second edition of the *Hodosophia* for the press and to have acted as critic of another work of Dannhauer's which has not yet been identified. The estrangement between the two was apparently caused by Dannhauer's nephew, Balthasar Bebel, who was in control of the theological faculty at Strasburg at the time of the publication of Spener's *Pia desideria*. Dannhauer was a prolific writer, his principal works being as follows: *Hodosophia christiana sive theologia positiva* (1649); *Katechismusmilch oder Erklärung des kirchlichen Katechismus* (1657–78) and *Liber conscientiæ apertus sive theologia conscientiaria* (1662–67).

(F. Bosse.)

Bibliography: The best source is J. Reisseisen, *Strassburgische Chronik, 1657–77*, ed. R. Reuss, Strasburg, 1879. Consult: E. L. T. Henke, *Georg Calixtus*, Halle, 1853; *ADB*, iv. 745–746; P. Grünberg, *P. J. Spener*, vol. i., Göttingen, 1893.

DANOVIUS, dā-nō'vi-ūs, **ERNST JAKOB**: Lutheran; b. at Redlau or Kleinkatz (near Danzig) Mar. 12, 1741; d. at Jena Mar. 18, 1782. He was educated at Danzig, Helmstädt, and Göttingen, and in 1765 accompanied Abbot Schubert to Greifswald as tutor to his sons. Thence he was called to the rectorate of the Johannisschule at Danzig, and in 1768 went to Jena. His specialties were New Testament exegesis, symbolics, moral theology, and, most of all, dogmatics, but he felt little sympathy with historical theology. His point of view may be characterized as modern supernaturalism, substituting for inspiration a miraculous guidance of God, which gave protection against all error, yet by no means denying the human element in the sacred writings. He avoided the excessive concepts of the divine likeness, denied that original sin was actual guilt in the descendants of Adam, and identified justification, in the widest sense of the term, with predestination. Danovius was prevented from giving expression to his views both by his faculty and by the government, and when he finally enunciated them in two Christmas programs of 1774–75 he was publicly opposed by the theological faculty of Erlangen. He defended himself in a number of pamphlets (*Drei Abhandlungen von der Rechtfertigung des Menschen vor Gott*, Jena, 1777, and *Kurze Erklärung über die neue von D. Seiler der Lehre von der Rechtfertigung halber herausgegebene Schrift*, 1778). While he desired a union with the Reformed, and while he did not regard their doctrines of the absolute decree and irresistible grace or their views of the Lord's Supper as grounds of hindrance, he feared their teaching concerning the incarnation, since it rendered doubtful the efficacy of the meritorious works and death of Christ.

The delivery of Danovius was admirable in the professorial chair, though unpopular in the pulpit, but his literary style was crabbed, and he wrote slowly and with difficulty. His melancholy nature, aggravated by excessive work, led him to take his own life. In addition to the works already mentioned and a number of programs, he wrote *Schreiben an Herrn D. Semler, dessen neuere Streitigkeiten betreffend* (Jena, 1770) and *Super libro Torgensi Censura Holsato-Sleswicensis variis observationibus illustrata* (1780). He also edited the *Opuscula* of J. D. Heilmann (1774–77), and made a translation of a work by A. J. Roustan (pastor of the Swiss church in London) under the title *Briefe zur Vertheidigung der christlichen Religion* (Halle, 1783). (G. Frank†.)

Bibliography: C. G. F. Schütz, *Leben . . . des E. J. Danovius*, appendix to A. J. Roustan, *Briefe zur Vertheidigung der christlichen Religion*, Halle, 1783; G. Frank, *Geschichte des Rationalismus*, pp. 111 sqq., 127–128, Leipsic, 1875.

DANTE, dān'tê *or* dan'te, **ALIGHIERI**, ā"lî-gî-ê'rî.

I. Life.
  Education and Early Life (§ 1).
  Florentine Parties (§ 2).
  Dante's Banishment (§ 3).
  His Wanderings. Later Life (§ 4).
II. Literary Works.

I. Life: Dante, the greatest poet of Italy and one of the greatest of the world, was born at Florence between May 18 and June 17, 1265, and died at Ravenna Sept. 14 (13?), 1321. The name Dante is a contraction of Durante. He was the son of a notary. Nothing is known of his schools or teachers. Stories of his studies at the universities of Bologna, Padua, and Paris lack confirmation. He was an omnivorous reader, and compassed most of the learning of his age. He was a master of Latin, but knew neither Greek nor Hebrew. He was versed in dialectic, rhetoric, grammar, arithmetic, geometry, astronomy, and music, and in the Provençal and Old French literature. He drew, and had some knowledge of painting.

1. Education and Early Life.

He was thoroughly acquainted with the writings of Aristotle, through Latin translations, and derived from him his whole system of physics, physiology, and meteorology. He was familiar with the Bible, and with the writings of Aquinas, Bonaventura, and Albertus Magnus, and with those of Ambrose, Jerome, and Augustine. He knew Ptolemy and Euclid in astronomy and mathematics, and was not ignorant of the Arabian philosophers Averroes and Avicenna. Of the Latin classical writers he shows an acquaintance with Vergil, Cicero, Lucan, Horace, Ovid, Livy, and Statius. At the age of nine he saw for the first time Beatrice, the daughter of Folco Portinari, for whom he conceived an ardent passion which stimulated his poetical genius and found its last expression in the *Divina Commedia*. Their intercourse was confined to occasional salutations, and she married in 1287 and died in 1290. Dante, some time before 1298, married Gemma Manetto Donati, who bore him four children.

2. Florentine Parties. The party divisions in Florence in Dante's time were twofold, one Italian, the other local. The former was between Guelfs and Ghibellines, the latter between *Bianchi* and *Neri* ("Whites and Blacks"). The Guelfs, the popular party, were represented by the burghers and trade-gilds. The Ghibellines represented the aristocracy and the soldiery. Dante was originally a Guelf and a White. Later he passed over to the Ghibellines, but finally broke away from both parties. During Dante's earlier life the power was gradually shifting from the nobles to the people. In 1289 the Tuscan Ghibellines were routed at the battle of Campaldino (June 11), where Dante served as a soldier, as he did a little later at the siege and capture of the Pisan castle of Caprona by the Florentines and Luccans. The revolution of 1293 overthrew the grandees, and the democratic character of the constitution was confirmed by the reforms of Giano dell: Bella, a noble with popular sympathies. Thenceforth the nobles were excluded from the office of prior. However, they continued their intrigues, which were now promoted by the newly elected pope, Boniface VIII. (1294), who aimed to concentrate in himself all authority, temporal and spiritual. The control of Tuscany was an important means to this end.

Without membership in one of the industrial gilds no one could hold office. Dante was enrolled in the Gild of Physicians and Apothecaries in 1295, and in 1300 became one of the priors, in whom the executive power of the State was lodged. The division between the Whites and the Blacks—the Cerchi and Donati—now came to the front. The Cerchi represented the democracy, and the Donati the pope and his policy. A fight took place between the two factions. Boniface despatched a legate to Florence, nominally

3. Dante's Banishment. as a pacificator, really to support the Blacks. Dante with the signory refused his overtures. As the disturbance continued, the priors banished the leaders of both factions. Corso Donati went to Rome and appealed to Boniface, who selected as his tool Charles of Valois, brother of Philip the Fair of France. He sent him to Florence with an armed force, on the pretense of restoring peace, and his arrival was the signal for a ferocious attack upon the Whites by the Blacks. Dante's house was sacked. The priors were deposed. On Jan. 27, 1302, Dante was pronounced guilty of extortion, embezzlement, and corruption; of resistance to the pope and Charles; and of assisting to expel the Blacks, the servants of the Church. With four others he was banished for two years, condemned to pay a heavy fine, and excluded from holding office thereafter. On Mar. 10 a second sentence was pronounced, forbidding him to return to Florence on penalty of being burned.

It is impossible to follow the track of Dante's wanderings. It appears that, after the proscription, in 1302, 1303, and 1306, three attempts were made by the banished Whites to enter Florence. In the first and probably in the second of these Dante took part; but he soon broke finally with his associates, and thenceforth was a

4. His Wanderings. Later Life. party by himself. His first refuge was with the Scaligers at Verona, after which he wandered over the greater part of Italy. He was at Padua in 1306, and the same year with the Malaspini at Lunigiana. He was also at Mantua. It has been claimed that he resided in Paris, and that he visited England and Flanders. After the death of Henry VII., in 1313, he appears at Lucca. In 1316 the Government of Florence offered amnesty to political exiles, and Dante was granted permission to return on condition of undergoing the public penance of a malefactor. The offer was indignantly refused. In the latter years of his life he resided chiefly with Guido da Polenta at Ravenna, but was for a considerable time at Verona with Can Grande della Scala. He was invited to go to Bologna to receive the poet's crown, but declined. He was sent as an ambassador to Venice by Polenta, upon whom the Venetians had made war. Shortly after his return he died, and was interred near the church of San Francesco.

II. Literary Works: (1) The *Vita Nuova*: The story of his passion for Beatrice in prose, interspersed with brief poems. It explains the part which Beatrice plays in the *Commedia*. (2) The *Convivio or "Banquet"* (the form *Convito* is later): Projected in fourteen treatises, only four of which were written; a philosophical commentary on three of Dante's own *Canzoni*. It treats of questions of geography, astronomy, etymology, and dialectics, but also of philosophy, patriotism, and nobility of soul. (3) *Canzoniere*: Minor poems, songs, ballads, and sonnets. (4) *De monarchia*: In Latin, in three books. Monarchy is the normal, divinely instituted form of government. The Roman Empire is invested with universal monarchy by the decree of God, and is perpetuated in the Hohenstaufens. The normal administration of human affairs is through two coordinate agents, the Empire and the Church. The pope and the emperor are equally God's vicars. (5) *De vulgari eloquentia*: A treatise in Latin. It examines the fourteen dialects of Italy, and discusses the meter of the *canzone*, giving rules for the composition of Italian poetry. Four books were projected, of which only two were written. (6) *Epistles*: Number and authenticity much disputed; fourteen have been attributed to Dante, and ten are doubtfully accepted as genuine. (7) *De aqua et terra*: A treatise in Latin. Dante's authorship has been generally denied, but some modern scholars, notably Professor Edward Moore, believe it to be authentic. The question discussed is: Can water in its own sphere or natural circumference be in any place higher than the dry land or habitable part of the earth? (8) The *Bucolic Eclogues:* Two Epistles in Latin hexameters, to Giovanni del Vergilio, who blamed Dante for not writing the *Commedia* in Latin, and urged him to compose Latin poems, and to come to Bologna to receive the poetic crown. (9) The *Divina Commedia:* It is written in *terza rima*, and the theme is Dante's journey through hell, purgatory, and paradise. The poem is called *Commedia*, because although it begins horribly with hell, it ends happily with paradise. The epithet "Divine" was a later addition of admirers. Dante says that the subject of the work, taken literally, is the state of souls after death, regarded as a matter of fact. Taken allegorically, it is man, so far as by merit or demerit in the exercise of free will he is exposed to the rewards or punishments of justice. The astronomical and geographical elements of the poem are derived from the Ptolemaic system of astronomy and from the geographical writings of Orosius (4th cent.). Hell and purgatory are treated as geographical facts. Hell is directly beneath Jerusalem, the center of the land-hemisphere. It is a hollow inverted cone, the interior circumference of which is divided into nine concentric ledges, each devoted to the punishment of a distinct class of sinners. At the apex of the cone, the center of gravity, Lucifer is fixed in eternal ice. Purgatory is a lofty conical mountain rising from an island in the southern hemisphere. Its lower section, antepurgatory, is traversed by a spiral track of three rounds, which terminates at the gate of St. Peter. Above this is purgatory proper, which consists of seven concentric terraces, on each of which one of the seven deadly sins is expiated. At the summit of the mountain is the earthly paradise, the original Eden, where is the river Lethe, whose waters obliterate the memory of sin and sorrow, and the river Eunoe, which restores the memory of good actions.

The poem consists of three parts, *Inferno, Purgatorio, Paradiso.* In Apr., 1300, Dante finds himself astray in a rough and gloomy forest. Emerging from this, he attempts to ascend a hill, but is driven back by three ravenous beasts. He is met by the shade of Vergil, who proposes to conduct him through hell and purgatory, and then to commit him to the charge of Beatrice, who will guide him through paradise. On the evening of Good Friday, Apr. 8, they enter the gate of hell, and, passing through the successive circles, reach the apex, pass the center of gravity, and ascend to the island of purgatory. Through antepurgatory they reach the gate of St. Peter, are admitted, and traverse the successive terraces. At the summit Dante sees a magnificent symbolic vision of the triumph of the Church. Beatrice appears, and Vergil vanishes. Having been plunged in Lethe, and having drunk of Eunoe, Dante mounts with Beatrice through the nine heavens to the empyrean, where he beholds the bliss of the glorified, and the blessed Trinity.

It is preeminently a moral and religious work. It is the story of the human soul in its relation to God. In the conditions of departed souls which it portrays it reflects the multiform aspects of the life of men and women of all ranks, stations, and employments, from the emperor to the peasant. It is the consummate expression of medievalism in the thirteenth and fourteenth centuries. The range of allusion is vast and wonderful in its variety. The portrayal of human character and human passion is vivid and subtle. The poet's intense, pervading moral purpose divests of vulgarity even the hideous details of the *Inferno*. He is a plain speaker, but no word or picture ever appeals to a sensual instinct. Under his dominant conception of man as the inheritor of a moral destiny, distinctions of time, race, and position disappear, and classic heroes and mythological monsters mingle with popes, martyrs, and Christian emperors. His biting satire respects neither civil nor ecclesiastical dignity. The poem is packed with similes, allegories, portraits, historical and personal references, and theological and philosophical disquisitions. It is intensely personal, often egotistic, revealing the poet's consciousness of his own genius, tinged with bitterness of spirit, yet displaying the sympathy and the tenderness of a great soul. Dante is impatient of vagueness. He is intensely realistic. Every space is measured, every region mapped, every dimension recorded. His similes are chosen without regard to their source, with the single view of illustrating his thought; and the most grotesque images appear amid the very sublimities of heaven. With his wonderful sense of form he unites a delicate sense of color and sound.

M. R. VINCENT.

BIBLIOGRAPHY: Lists of literature are: C. de Batines, *Bibliografia Dantesca*, 2 vols., Prato, 1845–46, supplemented by C. F. Carpellini, 1866, by B. della Lega, 1883, and by Guido Biagi, 1888; G. J. Ferazzi, *Manuale Dantesco*, 5 vols., Bassano, 1865–77 (useful, but confused in arrangement); T. W. Koch, *Dante in America*, Cambridge, Mass., 1896 (for the Dante Society); W. C. Lane, *Dante Collections in the Harvard . . . and Boston . . . Libraries*, Boston, 1890; W. M. Rossetti, *Bibliography of the Works of Dante*, London, 1905.

General and introductory critical works are: G. A. Scartazzini, *Dante Handbuch*, Leipsic, 1892, Eng. transl., London, 1893; H. C. Barlow, *Critical, Historical and Philosophical Contributions to the Study of Dante*, 2 vols., ib. 1864–65; E. Moore, *Studies in Dante*, 3 series, ib. 1896–1903 (very valuable); F. X. Kraus, *Dante, sein Leben und sein Werk*, Berlin, 1897. More popular works are: M. F. Rossetti, *A Shadow of Dante*, Edinburgh, 1884; R. W. Church, *Dante and Other Essays*, London, 1888; J. A. Symonds, *Introduction to the Study of Dante*, ib. 1890; L. Ragg, *Dante and His Italy*, ib. 1907. On Dante's astronomy, geography, and chronology consult E. Moore, in *Dante Studies*, vol. iii., London, 1903, and his *Time References in the Divina Commedia*, ib. 1887.

Biographical works: The biographies by Boccaccio and Bruni are translated by P. H. Wicksteed, in *A Provisional Transl. of the Early Lives of Dante*, Hull, 1898; a critical résumé of the five early biographies is by E. Moore, *Dante and his Early Biographers*, London, 1880. Consult further: F. X. Wegele, *Dante Alighieri's Leben und Werke*, Jena, 1879 (valuable); G. A. Scartazzini, *Dante Alighieri*, Frankfort, 1879.

Dictionaries and concordances are: L. G. Blanc, *Vocabolario Dantesco*, Leipsic, 1852; Donato Bocci, *Dizionario . . . della Divina Commedia di Dante Alighieri*, Turin, 1873; G. A. Scartazzini, *Enciclopedia Dantesca*, Milan, 1896–99, continued by A. Fiamazzo, 1905 (supplement includes the Latin works; valuable); P. Toynbee, *Dictionary of Proper Names and Notable Matters in . . . Dante*, London, 1898 (useful); E. A. Fay, *Concordance of the Divina Commedia*, Boston, 1894 (very valuable); E. Sheldon and A. C. White, *Concordanza delle opere . . . di Dante*, ib. 1905 (also indispensable).

Editions deserving notice are: The superb quarto of G. G. Warren Lord Vernon, in which the four earliest editions of Foligno, Jesi, Mantua, and Naples (15th cent.), ed. A. Panizzi, are arranged in parallel columns, London, 1858 (only 100 copies printed); the two Aldine editions of 1502 and 1515; the Giuntina and Della Crusca editions are the chief of the 16th cent. editions; for students the edition of Padua, 1822, reprinted, 1 vol., 1850, is excellent; a beautiful edition, with variant readings, is that of C. Witte, Berlin, 1862. Convenient texts are: P. Fraticelli, Florence, 1879; the *Temple Dante*, London, 1902; and the Oxford text of E. Moore, 3 vols., ib. 1902, in fine open type.

Of commentaries, the earlier ones are: Jacopo della Lana, 1321–28; the Ottimo, 1334; P. di Dante, 1340; Benvenuto da Imola, 1379; Boccaccio, 1373; Francesco da Buti, before 1406 (all important); the chief one of the 18th cent. is by P. B. Lombardi (many editions, of which the Padua, 1822, 5 vols., ed., is very fine). Later commentaries are by N. Tommaseo, Turin, 1837, . . . 1869; P. Fraticelli, Florence, 1852 and often; G. A. Scartazzini, Leipsic, 1874–1890, 3d minor ed., 1899 (indispensable); W. W. Vernon, 2 vols., London, 1897 (based on Benvenuto da Imola); M. R. Vincent, New York, 1904 (transl. and commentary). Of English translations the following (in verse) are noteworthy: H. Boyd, London, 1802; H. F. Cary, ib. 1814 (more than 20 editions); C. B. Cayley, ib. 1851; H. W. Longfellow, Boston, 1863 (often printed); E. H. Plumptre, London, 1886; T. W. Parsons, Boston, 1893; K. H. Haselfoot, London, 1899; M. R. Vincent, New York, 1904; (and in prose) J. Carlyle, London, 1849; A. H. Butler, ib. 1892; C. E. Norton, Boston, 1901; H. Oelsner and P. H. Wicksteed, London, 1901–02; H. F. Tozer, ib. 1904.

The above entries relate chiefly or entirely to the *Divina Commedia*. Of his other works referred to in the above article these editions and translations may be mentioned: (1) *Vita Nuova*: "The New Life," ed. A. d'Ancona, Pisa, 1884; Eng. transl. by T. Martin, London, 1862, 4th ed., 1904; C. E. Norton, Boston, 1867, 10th impression, 1895; D. G. Rossetti, London, 1874 and often; C. S. Boswell, ib. 1895; text and transl. by L. Ricci, ib. 1903. (2) *Convito*: "The Banquet," transl. by E. P. Sayer, London, 1887; by Katharine Hillard, ib. 1889. (3) *Canzoniere*: "Lyric Poems," ed. P. Fraticelli, Florence, 1861–62; transl. by D. G. Rossetti, London, 1861, new ed. 1892, by E. H. Plumptre (with his transl. of the *Divina Commedia*, 2 vols., London, 1886–87). (4) *De Monarchia*: "On Monarchy," ed. C. Witte, Berlin, 1862; Eng. transl. by F. J. Church, London, 1879; by A. Henry, ib. 1904. (5) *De vulgari eloquentia*: Eng. transl. by A. G. Ferrers Howell, London, 1890. (6) Epistles, ed. P. Fraticelli, Florence, 1862; Eng. transl. by P. H. Wicksteed, London, 1898; by C. S. Latham, Boston, 1904. (7) *De aqua et terra*: transl. by C. H. Bromby, *A Question of the Water and the Land*, London, 1897. (8) *Eclogæ*: *Bucolic Eclogues*, Eng. transl. by P. H. Wicksteed (in his *Provisional Transl. of the Early Lives of Dante*), London, 1898. In general, P. Toynbee, *In the Footprints of Dante, A Treasury of Verse and Prose from the Works of Dante*, London, 1907.

DANZ, däntz, **JOHANN TRAUGOTT LEBERECHT**: Church historian; b. at Weimar May 31, 1769; d. at Jena May 15, 1851. He was educated at Weimar, Jena, and Göttingen, and became teacher at the gymnasium and normal school in his native city. Through the influence of Herder he went to Jena in 1798 as rector of the municipal school. He became privat-docent at Jena in 1804, assistant professor of theology in 1810, full professor in 1812, and retired in 1837. His theological tendency was that of a Biblical rationalist, and he postulated that both the rationalist and the supernaturalist could practise the true religion of Christ. Like Herder, he was characterized by breadth of learning and by skilful presentment of the most diverse themes. His most important theological book was his *Lehrbuch der christlichen Kirchengeschichte* (2 vols., Jena, 1818–26), of which he made compendiums in his *Kurzgefasste Zusammenstellung der christlichen Kirchengeschichte* (1824) and in his *Kirchengeschichtliche Tabelle* (1838). He also prepared an edition of the *Bibliotheca patristica* of Johann Georg Walch (1834), with which his own *Initia doctrinæ patristicæ* (1839) was closely connected, and he dedicated to Pope Gregory XVI. his edition of the *Libri symbolici ecclesiæ Romano-Catholicæ* (Weimar, 1836). He likewise wrote an *Encyklopädie und Methodologie der theologischen Wissenschaften* (1832) and an *Universalwörterbuch der theologischen Litteratur* (Leipsic, 1843), having already summarized practical theology in his *Grundriss der Wissenschaften des geistlichen Berufs* (Jena, 1824). He was, moreover, the author of a curious *Versuch einer allgemeinen Geschichte der menschlichen Nahrungsmittel* (Leipsic, 1806) and a philological work entitled *Antilexilogus* (Jena, 1842). (G. Frank†.)

Bibliography: *Annales academiæ Jenensis*, ed. H. C. A. Eichstadius, pp. 13 sqq., Jena, 1823; *Neuer Nekrolog der Deutschen*, 1851, i. 374–382.

DAPONTE, dä-pen'tê (secular name, **Constantinos**), **CÆSARIUS**: Greek monk and poet; b. (on the island of Skopelo, 15 m. n. of Eubœa, in the Ægean) 1713 (1714?); d. in the monastery Xiropotamu, on Mount Athos, 1784. He received a good education in Bucharest through the favor of Prince Racovitza. As secretary to Prince Maurogordatos he came into conflict with the Turkish authorities and was imprisoned for some years. Becoming a monk in 1753, he adopted the name Cæsarius, and entered in 1757 the monastery in which he died. He is the greatest poet of the New Greek Church. Of his works (all in É. Legrand, *Publications de l'école des langues orientales vivantes*, Paris, 1886) the following are important from a theological standpoint (for his historical works cf. *TLZ*, 1893, pp. 422 sqq.): "Woman's Looking-glass" (2 vols., Leipsic, 1766); its secular companion, "Woman's Lantern," the contents of which are given by Lambros in his "Catalogue of the Greek MSS. on Mt. Athos" (Athens, 1888, i. 221); "Honesty of Character" (Venice, 1770); "The Spiritual Table" (Venice, 1778, not seen by Legrand); the book for the people, "Exposition of the Divine Service" (Vienna, 1795). Exceedingly interesting is "The Garden of Graces" (edited by É. Legrand, *Bibliothèque grecque vulgaire*, vol. iii., Paris, 1881). His monastery preserves the MSS. of his later works in autograph. (Philipp Meyer.)

Bibliography: É. Legrand, *Publications de l'école des langues orientales vivantes*, 1st series, vols. xiv., xv., Paris, 1880–81 (Daponte's work on the Four Years' War is given).

DARBY, JOHN NELSON: The most prominent among the founders of the Plymouth Brethren, whence they are sometimes (especially on the continent of Europe) called "Darbyites" (see Plymouth Brethren); b. in London Nov. 18, 1800; d. at Bournemouth Apr. 29, 1882. He was graduated at Trinity College, Dublin, in 1819 and was called to the Irish bar about 1825; but soon gave up the law, took orders, and served a curacy in Wicklow until, in 1827, doubts as to the Scriptural authority for church establishments led him to leave the Church altogether and meet with a little company of like-minded persons in Dublin. In 1830 he visited Paris, Cambridge, and Oxford, and then went to Plymouth, where an assembly of Brethren was shortly formed, and the town soon lent its name to the movement. James L. Harris, perpetual curate of Plymstock, resigned his living to unite with them and, in 1834, started the *Christian Witness*, their first periodical. Darby became an assiduous writer, and published his *Parochial Arrangement Destructive of Order in the Church* in the first volume of the *Witness*, and his *Apostasy of the Successive Dispensations* (afterward published in French as *Apostasie de l'économie actuelle*) in the same paper in 1836. Dissensions among the Brethren had already begun, and Darby was accused of departing from their original principles.

Between 1838 and 1840 Darby worked in Switzerland. In the autumn of 1839 an influential member of the congregation at Lausanne invited him thither to oppose Methodism. In March, 1840, he came, and obtained a hearing by discourses and a tract, *De la doctrine des Wesleyens à l'égard de la perfection*. His lectures on prophecy made a great impression, and he soon gathered young men round him at Lausanne, with whom he studied the Scriptures. The fruit of these conferences was his *Études sur la Parole*, a work which appeared in English as *Synopsis of the Books of the Bible* (5 vols., London, 1857–67). Many congregations were formed in Cantons Vaud, Geneva, and Bern. Certain of his followers started a periodical, *Le Témoignage des disciples de la Parole*.

When, by Jesuit intrigues, a revolution broke out in Canton Vaud (Feb., 1845), the Darbyites in some parts of Switzerland suffered persecution, and Darby's own life was in jeopardy. He returned to England the same year, but his heart seems ever to have turned toward Switzerland and France. Thenceforth he took a more active lead among the English Brethren, with the result that they became split into two parties, the Darbyites or exclusives and the Bethesda or open brethren. In 1853 he visited Elberfeld and again in 1854, when he translated the New Testament into German. He was also in Germany in 1869, when he took part in a translation of the Old Testament into German. He visited Canada and the United States in 1859, 1864–65, 1866–68, 1870, 1872–73, and 1874. About 1871 he went to Italy, and in 1875 to New Zealand. He visited also the West Indies. Between 1878 and 1880 he was much occupied with a translation of the Old Testament into French, in connection with which he sojourned long at Pau. He had already made a French translation of the New Testament in 1859.

Darby was a most voluminous writer on a wide range of subjects—doctrinal and controversial, devotional and practical, apologetic, metaphysical, on points of scholarship, etc. His *Collected Writings* (incomplete) have been published by W. Kelly in thirty-two volumes (London, 1867–83). They include *Irrationalism of Infidelity* (1853), a reply to Newman; *Remarks on Puseyism* (1854); *The Sufferings of Christ* (1858) and *The Righteousness of God* (1859), two works which produced much controversy; *Analysis of Newman's Apologia* (1866); *Familiar Conversations on Romanism*, written between 1870 and 1880; *Meditations on the Acts of the Apostles*, composed in Italian; *Letters on the Revised New Testament* (1881), in which he criticized the revisers principally in respect to the aorist tense, a subject he had previously discussed in the preface to an English translation of the New Testament (2d ed., 1872). He was a hymn-writer and edited the hymnal in general use among the Brethren. A volume of his *Spiritual Songs* was published in London in 1883, and three volumes of his letters in 1886–89.

BIBLIOGRAPHY: W. B. Neatby, *Hist. of the Plymouth Brethren*, London, 1901 (best on both Darby and the Plymouth Brethren); F. Estéoule, *Le Plymouthisme d'autrefois et le Darbyisme d'aujourd'hui*, Paris, 1858; W. H. Dorman, *The Close of 88 Years of Association with J. N. Darby*, London, 1866; Stokes, in *Contemporary Review*, Oct., 1885, pp. 537–552; S. W. Duffield, *English Hymns*, pp. 403–405, New York, 1886; Julian, *Hymnology*, pp. 279–280; *DNB*, xiv. 43–44; and the literature under PLYMOUTH BRETHREN.

D'ARCY, dār'si, **CHARLES FREDERICK**: Church of Ireland, bishop of Ossory; b. at Dublin Jan. 2, 1859. He studied at Trinity College, Dublin (B.A., 1882), and was curate of St. Thomas, Belfast (1884–90), rector of Billy, County Antrim (1890–93), rector of Ballymena, with Ballyclug, County Antrim (1893–1900), and dean of St. Anne's Cathedral and vicar of Belfast (1900–03). He was examining chaplain to the bishop of Down 1892–1903, chaplain to the Lord Lieutenant of Ireland 1895–1903, prebendary of Connor in Connor Cathedral 1898–1900, prebendary of St. Patrick's Cathedral, Dublin, 1902–03, and Donellan lecturer in the University of Dublin 1897–98. In 1903 he was consecrated bishop of Clogher and in 1907 was translated to Ossory, Ferns, and Leighlin. Theologically he is interested in the philosophic expression of Christian doctrine and in the relation of religion and science, while he expects important results from recent criticisms of idealistic forms of thought and from the criticism of the New Testament. He has written *A Short Study of Ethics* (London, 1895); *Idealism and Theology* (1899); and *Ruling Ideas of Our Lord* (1901).

DARGAN, EDWIN CHARLES: American Baptist; b. at Springville, Darlington County, S. C., Nov. 17, 1852. He was educated at Furman University, Greenville, S. C. (M.A., 1873), and at the Southern Baptist Theological Seminary, then at Greenville, S. C., now at Louisville, Ky. (full graduate, 1877). He has been pastor of Baptist churches in Roanoke County, Va. (1877–81), of the First Baptist Church, Petersburg, Va. (1881–87), the Baptist Church at Dixon, Cal. (1887–88), the Citadel Square Baptist Church, Charleston, S. C. (1888–92), professor of homiletics in the Southern Baptist Theological Seminary (1892–1907), and, since June, 1907, pastor of the First Baptist Church, Macon, Ga. He has also been a member of various boards and other organizations of his denomination. He is "Evangelical and conservative in general theological views" and "Calvinistic in type of theology." His principal works are: *Ecclesiology* (Louisville, 1897; revised ed., 1905); *A History of Preaching, from A.D. 70 to 1572* (New York, 1905); *The Doctrines of Our*

Faith (Nashville, 1905); and *Society, Kingdom, and Church* (Philadelphia, 1907). He also published a commentary on Colossians (Philadelphia, 1890), and edited J. A. Brodus's *Preparation and Delivery of Sermons* (New York, 1898).

DARIUS, da-rai'us: The name given to several kings in the Old Testament. The earliest form of the word is given in the old Persian inscriptions as *Darayava(h)ush*, "up-holding-weal."

1. Darius the Mede (Dan. vi. 1 sqq., xi. 1), according to Dan. ix. 1, was son of Ahasuerus. These passages, in their mention of this king, raise the question of the authenticity of Daniel (q.v.). Dan. vi. 1, in connection with v. 28 sqq., makes Darius at the age of sixty-two the immediate successor of Belshazzar, who is the immediate predecessor of Cyrus as ruler of the Medo-Persian Empire according to Dan. vi. 2, 8, 26, 29. But according to the Ptolemaic canon, Cyrus the Persian succeeded Nabonidus, the last Chaldean king, and this is confirmed by the annals of Nabonidus and by the clay cylinder of Cyrus (cf. E. Schrader, *Keilinschriftliche Bibliothek*, III. i., Berlin, 1890). A kingdom of Cyrus immediately after the fall of the Chaldeans was known to Berosus, Ctesias, Alexander Polyhistor, Strabo, and other ancient historians. In full accord with these facts is another, viz., that Cyrus ruled Babylon nine years, and died 529 B.C., so that the beginning of his reign over that city coincides with the fall of Nabonidus. There seems therefore little ground for a defense of the historicity of the Book of Daniel in this particular. A hypothesis which has been supposed to relieve the difficulty identifies Darius the Mede with the Cyaxares II. of Xenophon's *Cyropædia*. Josephus (*Ant.*, X. xi. 4) is held to warrant making Cyaxares the son and successor of Astyages and uncle of Cyrus (Xenophon, *Cyropædia*, I. v. 2). Then, as the general of Cyaxares (= Darius), Cyrus took Babylon, married the daughter of Cyaxares, and became his heir. But this introduces new difficulties, since Dan. ix. 1 makes Ahasuerus (Xerxes) the father of Darius. Other hypotheses fail as signally to relieve the difficulty. Schrader (*KAT*, p. 437) explains the difficulty best by suggesting that the representation running through Daniel of some Median interregnum between Nabonidus and Cyrus leans upon an indistinct recollection of the once great power of the Medes, and refers to a later Darius.

2. Darius, son of Hystaspes, of the Achæmenidæ, king of Persia 521–485 B.C. He is best known through the ten well-known trilingual cuneiform inscriptions (original in Persian, and two versions). The most important of these, the rock-inscription of Behistan, reports in detail the overthrow by Darius of the magian Gaumata (the Pseudo-Smerdis of the Greeks) and his campaign against other rebels. In the inscription Darius appears as a prince zealous in piety; in other sources he is praised for the benefits he conferred upon the Persian Empire during a fortunate reign. In the second and fourth years of his reign the prophecies of Haggai (i. 1, 15) and several of Zechariah (i. 1, 7; vii. 1) were dated; in his second year (Ezra iv. 24) the work of rebuilding the temple was recommenced and finished in his sixth year (Ezra vi. 15).

3. Darius Codomannus (336–330 B.C.), the "king of the Medes and Persians" conquered by Alexander. He must be the Darius of Neh. xii. 22, since the Jaddus there named is necessarily the one mentioned by Josephus (*Ant.*, XI. viii. 4) as high priest under Alexander. (E. KAUTZSCH.)

BIBLIOGRAPHY: M. Duncker, *Geschichte des Alterthums*, iv. 254 sqq., Leipsic, 1877; F. Spiegel, *Die altpersischen Keilinschriften*, ib. 1881; G. Rawlinson, *Seven Great Monarchies*, New York, 1900; *DB*, i. 558–559; *EB*, i. 1016–17; and the literature under DANIEL, BOOK OF; and PERSIA.

DARLINGTON, JAMES HENRY: Protestant Episcopal bishop of Harrisburg, Pa.; b. at Brooklyn, N. Y., June 9, 1856. He studied at the University of the City of New York (B.A., 1877) and Princeton Theological Seminary (1880). He was licensed by the Presbytery of Newark 1879; but was ordered deacon and ordained priest in 1882 in the Protestant Episcopal Church, and from 1883 to 1905 was rector of Christ Church, Bedford Avenue, Brooklyn, as well as archdeacon of Brooklyn in 1896–98. In 1905 he was consecrated bishop of Harrisburg. He was lecturer in New York University in 1902–03. He has written *Pastor and People* (Brooklyn, 1902), and has edited *The Hymnal of the Church* (New York, 1900).

DATHE, dā'te, JOHANN AUGUST: Oriental scholar; b. at Weissenfels (20 m. s.w. of Leipsic), Prussian Saxony, July 4, 1731; d. at Leipsic Mar. 17, 1791. He studied at Wittenberg, Leipsic, and Göttingen; was professor at Leipsic from 1762. His chief work was a Latin translation of the entire Old Testament, with notes, one of the results of his labors in preparing his lectures (6 vols., Halle, 1773–89); the translation is free, exegetical, and somewhat paraphrastic, aiming to give the sense in good Latin, which occasioned the remark that Dathe made the prophets talk like Cicero. He also edited the *Psalterium syriacum* of Erpenius (Halle, 1768), the *Grammatica* and *Rhetorica* of the *Philologia sacra* of Glassius (Leipsic, 1776), and Walton's *Prolegomena* (1777). His minor works appeared posthumously, edited by E. K. F. Rosenmüller under the title *Opuscula ad crisin et interpretationem Veteris Testamenti spectantia* (Leipsic, 1796).

DATHENUS, dā-thī'nus, PETRUS (Pieter Daten): Flemish Reformer; b. at Cassel (27 m. n.w. of Lille) in the present Department of Nord, France, 1531 or 1532; d. at Elbing (34 m. e.s.e. of Danzig), West Prussia, Mar. 17, 1588. While still a youth, in the Carmelite monastery at Ypres, the new ideas took possession of him, and he became a zealous champion of Evangelical truth in West Flanders. Because of persecution he fled to England with others, but a similar fate met him under Mary Tudor. Johannes a Lasco called him to Frankfort, where he was installed pastor of the Flemish congregation, Sept., 1555, by Micronius. Here he suffered much from the Lutheran clergy, incited by Joachim Westphal of Hamburg. On Apr. 23, 1561, the magistrates forbade the congregation to worship after their fashion in spite of the intercession of the elector Frederick III. and Philip of Hesse. Part moved to England, some went home (where most of them perished in the Inquisition), and the rest found a shelter through the elector in the monastery of Gross Frankenthal, which soon became a flourishing industrial city. As court preacher of the Palatinate Dathenus served in many political missions, and became leader of the foreign congregations. In the cause of union he translated the Heidelberg Catechism and the Psalms of Clément Marot, revised the Confession of Guy de Brès, and composed a liturgy. Recalled to Holland through the compromise of the nobility in 1566, he participated in field-preaching and presided at the synod at Antwerp in May. In 1567 the Inquisition drove him again to the Palatinate, and with the count palatine John Casimir he went as field-preacher to France. In Nov., 1568, he was moderator in Wesel, in 1571 at the Frankenthal debate, in 1577 at the conference at Frankfort. Called to Ghent in 1578, he was imprisoned there for eight months and again driven into exile. Thenceforth he lived as physician at Husum, Stade, Danzig, and Elbing. (F. W. CUNO†.)

BIBLIOGRAPHY: H. ter Haar, *Specimen historico-theologicum P. Datheni vitam exhibens*, Utrecht, 1858; H. Q. Janssen, *Petrus Dathenus*, Delft, 1872.

DAUB, KARL: German theologian; b. at Cassel Mar. 20, 1765; d. at Heidelberg Nov. 22, 1836. He studied in his native city and at Marburg, where he became privat-docent in 1791, lecturing on philology, philosophy, and theology. Suspected of Kantianism in theology, he was transferred in 1794 to a school at Hanau as professor of philosophy, but in the following year was called to Heidelberg as professor of theology. His position was primarily Kantian, and in this spirit he wrote his *Lehrbuch der Katechetik* (Heidelberg, 1801), insisting on an ethical basis of religion, a sharp distinction between legalistic religion and the religion of reason, an emphasis on the practical import of the Bible, and a rejection of the supernatural. Yet even in this book there are traces of dissatisfaction with the Kantian position, and in the *Heidelberger Studien*, which he edited in collaboration with Georg Friedrich Creuzer after 1805, he acknowledged his conversion to the principles of Schelling. He now regarded religion as purely objective, and assuming distinct forms according to racial and individual characteristics. Christianity is a folk-religion, represented on the side of cult by Roman Catholicism, and on the side of doctrine by Protestantism; any unification of these two elements into a single Church would lead, in his opinion, to the destruction of the German nation. This change of view is fully developed in his *Theologumena* (1806) and *Einleitung in das Studium der Dogmatik* (1810). Rejecting both supernaturalism and rationalism, he assumed a speculative basis, implying by this term that the concept of God must form the foundation, while religion is the revelation of God in the soul of man, and attains perfection only in Christianity. Since, from his premises, Daub could assume no origin of the world from God as separate from the divinity, he was obliged to define the universe as having only the appearance of being. Creation was construed, in Platonic fashion, as the fall, and the Atonement was, accordingly, the reconciliation of the world to God, a process which was metaphysical rather than ethical. In his interpretation of the historic Christ Daub regarded the definitions of the Bible and the Church concerning the personality and deeds of Christ as symbolic statements of the general cosmical and metaphysical process, while, on the other hand, the personality and deeds of Jesus of Nazareth were taken as historical and were regarded as the perfection of the concept of incarnation and atonement.

The weak point of Daub's system was his ignoring of the problem of evil, and he was thus led to still another stage of development, which was represented in *Judas Ischarioth, oder Betrachtungen über das Böse im Verhältniss zum Guten* (2 parts, 1816–18), which, in a sense, forms the direct antithesis of his former views. The historical, hitherto practically ignored, now received full recognition, and he became obsessed with the concept of evil as a positive factor of destruction to such an extent that he approximated Gnostic dualism. The necessity of reconciling his theory of evil with the tenets of speculative philosophy obliged him to advance the hypothesis that evil is an actual, though false, "miracle," which is opposed by the fivefold positive "miracle" of the primal good in God, his ideational realization in the creation and order of the world, and finally the restoration of good in a world estranged from God through his incarnation and the absolute sinlessness of Christ, the Son of God. With all its eccentricities, this book was the ablest work of its author.

The final position of Daub was strongly Hegelian, and the result of Hegelian speculation and orthodox theology was, in his case, the reincarnation of a medieval scholastic. A long period of literary quiescence followed, until the publication of his *Dogmatische Theologie jetziger Zeit* (1833), in which he pitilessly revealed the weaknesses of the theology of the time. Extravagantly blamed and as extravagantly praised, the work is marred by the same lack of historic sense and impartiality which detract from the value of his other works. A far more pleasant impression is gained from his *Theologische und philosophische Vorlesungen*, edited after his death by T. W. Dittenberger and P. C. Marheinecke (7 vols., Berlin, 1838–44), although even these are not altogether free from his characteristic faults. (M. A. LANDERER†.)

BIBLIOGRAPHY: C. Rosenkranz, *Erinnerungen an Daub*, Berlin, 1837; K. P. Fischer, *Versuch einer Charakteristik (F. von Baaders) Theosophie und ihres Verhältnisses zu den Systemen Daubs*, Erlangen, 1865.

D'AUBIGNÉ. See MERLE D'AUBIGNÉ.

DAUGHERTY, dōн'er-ti, **JEROME:** Roman Catholic; b. at Baltimore Mar. 25, 1849. He was educated at Loyola College, Baltimore, and in 1865 was admitted to the Society of Jesus. He studied also at Frederick, Md., and at Woodstock, Md., and in 1872 became a member of the faculty of Georgetown University, where he subsequently continued his theological studies. He taught at St. Francis Xavier's College, New York City (1881–82), and was director of schools at Boston University (1882–84), professor at Loyola College (1884–85), vice-president of Gonzaga College, Washington,

D. C. (1885–89), professor at the College of the Holy Cross, Worcester, Mass. (1889–1900), and assistant to the provincial of the Society of Jesus at New York (1900–01). In 1901–05 he was president of Georgetown University, chancellor at Fordham University 1905–07, and professor of mathematics at Woodstock College since 1907.

DAUT, JOHANN MAXIMILIAN: German mystic; the date and locality of his birth and death are unknown (c. 1690–1737). A journeyman shoemaker of Frankfort, he belongs in the line of visionaries who at the beginning of the eighteenth century declared an impending judgment. At the command of God, as he declared, he published in 1710 his *Helle Donnerposaune*, and also, according to some, a French version, wherein he predicted woes especially for Frankfort and threatened the empire and other countries with destruction, from which only a little flock, after the conversion of the Turks, Jews, and heathen, were to escape to celebrate the "marriage-feast of the Lamb." His invectives were especially severe against the Lutheran clergy. Driven from Frankfort, he went in 1711 with a certain Boomen to the mystic Ueberfeldt in Leyden. With him he soon quarreled and wrote also against him, calling his party "Judas brethren," but later he became reconciled, having his home at Schwarzenau in Wittgenstein. At Giengen on the Brenz and at Geislingen, near Ulm, he and Tennhardt, a wig-maker, gained so great a following among the peasantry that the council of Ulm, Sept. 19, 1712, issued an edict against them. The account of his conversion given by Johann Frick is in error. To his writings belong the *Geistliche Betrachtungen* (1711), full of chiliastic and mystic ideas, and the *Harmonie der Zeiten und Werke Gottes*. About 1735 he revoked his *Donnerposaune*. (A. HAUCK.)

BIBLIOGRAPHY: J. G. Walch, *Einleitung in die Religions-Streitigkeiten*, ii. 794, v. 1051, Jena, 1733–36; C. M. Pfaff, *Introductio in historiam theologiæ* . . . , ii. 372, Tübingen, 1720; Burger, *Exercitatio de sutoribus fanaticis*, Leipsic, 1730.

DAVENPORT, CHRISTOPHER: English Roman Catholic; b. in Coventry, Warwickshire, 1598; d. in London May 31, 1680. At the age of fifteen, with his elder brother, John (q.v.), he entered Merton College, Oxford; influenced by a Roman priest, he went to Douai (1615) and Ypres (1617), and joined the Franciscans; he took degrees in divinity at Salamanca. Under the name of Franciscus a Sancta Clara he went to England as a missionary and became chaplain to Queen Henrietta Maria. He devoted himself with some success to the attempt to reconcile the churches of England and Rome and lived on terms of cordial intimacy with many of the Anglican clergy during the reign of Charles I. The civil war caused him to leave England, but only for a short time; he was not molested during the Commonwealth, and at the Restoration was restored to court favor and his position as chaplain to the queen. He was a learned man, of winning manners, and liberal in his views. His chief work was a *Paraphrastica expositio articulorum confessionis Anglicanæ* (printed first separately and then as an appendix to a volume called *Deus, natura, gratia*, Lyons, 1634; reprinted with translation, 1865), intended to show that the English articles and Roman doctrine are not essentially antagonistic. A two-volume edition of his works appeared at Douai, 1665–67.

BIBLIOGRAPHY: A. à Wood, *Athenæ Oxonienses*, ed. P. Bliss, vol. iii., 4 vols., London, 1813–20; J. Gillow, *Bibliographical Dictionary of English Catholics*, ii. 24–28, London (1885); *DNB*, xiv. 108–109.

DAVENPORT, JOHN: One of the founders and first minister of the New Haven colony; b. at Coventry, Warwickshire, England, 1597 (baptized Apr. 9); d. in Boston Mar., 1670 (the day of the month is variously given as the 11th, 13th, 15th, and 16th). He was graduated from the University of Oxford (B.A., 1615; M.A. and B.D., 1625); was chaplain at Hilton Castle (12 m. n.e. of Durham) for about six months, 1615–16; went to London, where he became curate of St. Lawrence Jewry, 1619, and vicar of St. Stephen's, Coleman street, 1624. He won great regard by his faithfulness to duty in 1625, when the city was devastated by the plague. In 1626 he joined in a scheme to purchase impropriations (church property in the hands of laymen) and use the profits to maintain ministers in various parts of the kingdom, and was one of twelve feoffees (trustees) entrusted with the care of the funds raised for the purpose. The plan was considered by Laud and others a movement in the interest of non-conformity, suit was brought against the feoffees, and in Feb., 1633, the association was dissolved as illegal and the impropriations which had been purchased were confiscated. In 1629 Davenport helped to obtain the charter for the Massachusetts Bay colony, gave £50 toward the expense, and his name was first on the committee to draw up instructions for the colonists. He took alarm when Laud (who had long been suspicious of him) was appointed archbishop in 1633, and late in the year went to Holland, where he became copastor with John Paget of the English church in Amsterdam. He did not approve of the baptism of children whose parents were not church-members, controversy arose between the two pastors on the subject, and after less than six months Davenport gave up preaching in public, but continued to hold meetings in his house. He returned to England about the beginning of 1637, decided to follow the advice of John Cotton and others to go to New England, and landed in Boston June 26. He was well received there, but in Apr., 1638, went to Quinnipiac (New Haven), as minister of the new colony. He approved of the provision in its constitution, which was settled in June, 1639, limiting the franchise and eligibility to office to church-members, and was one of the "seven pillars of state" who were charged with the government. In 1642 he declined an invitation to attend the Westminster Assembly, and in 1661 helped to shelter the regicides Whalley and Goffe. The New Haven colony was absorbed in Connecticut in Jan., 1665, contrary to his wishes; and dissatisfaction with his position after the event induced him to accept a call from the First Church in Boston in September. He was a leader of the opposition to the Half-Way Covenant, and this caused a split in the church when he was installed in Dec., 1668, and the formation of the Old South Church. He wrote comparatively little. Of most interest are *The Saint's Anchor-hold in All Storms and Tempests* (London, 1661) and *The Power of Congregational Churches Asserted and Vindicated* (1672).

BIBLIOGRAPHY: F. B. Dexter, in the *Papers of the New Haven Colony Historical Society*, ii (1877), 204–238; Cotton Mather, *Magnalia*, bk. iii., vol. i., chap. iv., pp. 321–331, Hartford, 1855; B. Brook, *Lives of the Puritans*, iii. 446–451, London, 1813; *DNB*, xiv. 110–111.

DAVID.

Discussion of Sources (§ 1).
Early Life (§ 2).
Early Rule (§ 3).
Domestic and Administrative Difficulties (§ 4).
Services to the Cultus (§ 5).
Character (§ 6).

David was the second king of Israel, and ruled, according to the traditional computation, about 1055–15 B.C.; according to Kamphausen (*Chronologie*, Bonn, 1883), 1010–978 B.C. He was a son of Jesse of Bethlehem, of the tribe of Judah. The Book of Ruth names the grandparents of Jesse, Boaz and the Moabitess Ruth. The main source for the life of David is the books of Samuel and Kings. The books of Chronicles give additions aiming to emphasize David's services to the cultus.

1. Discussion of Sources.

In the books of Samuel the prophetical historiography prevails, and his political and military activity is treated only in a summary way, since the religious interest predominates. The narrative of David's earliest life is less uniform, and the sources are not adjusted throughout. In the statements about his reign the narrative is uniform, following almost contemporaneous sources. The post-Biblical notices (e.g., the statements of Josephus) have little historical value.

2. Early Life.

David was first anointed secretly at Bethlehem by Samuel (I Sam. xvi. 1–13). On that occasion he appears as the youngest of eight sons (I Sam. xvi. 10, xvii. 12); according to I Sam. xvi. 14–23, David went to the court of Saul to banish by his harp the evil spirit of the king, and was made Saul's armor-bearer. In I Sam. xvii. he appears again as shepherd-boy, who with his sling kills Goliath of Gath. It is difficult to harmonize xvii. 55–58, where Saul does not know David, with chap. xvi. But no doubt there were different sources (see SAMUEL, BOOKS OF). It is noteworthy that in the Septuagint, *cod. Vat.*, verses 55 sqq., together with xviii. 1–5, also xvii. 12–31, are wanting. It is debated whether the Septuagint omitted these passages for the sake of avoiding the difficulty or whether they came later into the canonical text. Even in the latter case they may belong to an ancient book on David. At any rate, David's victory over the gigantic Philistine, which is also attested by the Septuagint, may not be rejected as unhistorical, continued as it is by I Sam. xxi. 9, xxii. 10. Whether this Philistine was really called Goliath (see PHILISTINES), which some deny on account of II Sam. xxi. 19 (cf. I Chron. xx. 5), is unimportant. David's fame made Saul distrustful (I Sam. xviii. 6–9). He denied to him his daughter Merab, whom he had promised to the victor, and only reluctantly gave his second daughter Michal, who loved David (I Sam. xviii. 17–27). He often threatened David's life (I Sam. xviii. 11, xix. 10–17). Even Saul's son Jonathan, who was warmly attached to David, could not influence the father in his favor; but he made with David a covenant of friendship (I Sam. xviii. 3–4, xx., xxiii. 16–18). Here, too, the narrative is not harmonious, and the simpler rendering of the Septuagint is perhaps nearer the original, according to which Merab had never been promised to David and Saul cast his javelin at the singer once only. David for a time sought refuge with Samuel in the colony of the prophets, but soon had to leave (I Sam. xix. 18–xx. 1). The assistance granted by Ahimelech the priest at Nob became detrimental to the latter and his whole house (I Sam. xxi.–xxii.; see DOEG). David first went to the Philistines (I Sam. xxi. 10–15), and then made his abode in the cave Adullam in Judah. Here he became the leader of a band of 400 men and supported himself by bold attacks upon the enemies of his people and by tribute levied upon the owners of land and herds (I Sam. xxii. 1–2, xxiii., xxv.). His life in the hill and desert country of Judah was restless and dangerous. Saul drove him from one hiding-place to another, and, though the king was twice in his power, David magnanimously saved him (I Sam. xxiii.–xxvi.).

When David was no longer able to maintain himself in Judah he offered his services to King Achish of Gath, who gladly accepted this reenforcement and gave him the city of Ziklag (Zuheilikah, six hours and a half southwest of Bet-Jibrin) for a residence; he was supposed to fight against the Judeans, but in reality he attacked their enemies, the Geshurites, Gezerites, and Amalekites (I Sam. xxvii.). A year later Achish asked David to join him in a campaign against Israel, but the other princes of the Philistines insisted that David be sent back (I Sam. xxix.). Ziklag had meanwhile been plundered by the Amalekites, but David recovered the booty (I Sam. xxx.). The Israelites were defeated at Mount Gilboa, and Saul and his son Jonathan were slain (I Sam. xxxi.). In his "Song of the Bow" (II Sam. i.) David has beautifully immortalized the general mourning and his personal grief for his friend.

Encouraged by divine direction, David took his place in the land of Judah, and made his abode in Hebron, where the Judeans proclaimed him king (II Sam. ii. 1–4). At first he was king over Judah only for seven years and six months (II Sam. ii. 11, v. 5). The northern tribes were induced by Abner,

3. Early Rule.

Saul's captain, to swear allegiance to Ishbaal (more generally called Ish-bosheth), a son of Saul who resided at Mahanaim in the East Jordan land (II Sam. ii. 8–9). Abner tried to subject Judah to him, but was defeated by Joab, David's captain (II Sam. ii. 10–32). Abner afterward negotiated with David and offered to him the rule of all Israel, but was murdered by Joab (II Sam. iii. 6–27). Ish-baal was slain soon after (II Sam. iv. 1–8). David did not approve of the murder of Abner and punished those who slew Ishbaal (II Sam. iii. 28-39, iv. 9-12). All Israel then did homage to David, but he seems to have continued his residence at Hebron (II Sam. ii. 11, v. 5; I Chron. xxix. 27). David soon perceived the necessity of making his seat at some central point, and with shrewd foresight selected the Jebusite fortress Jerusalem, which was taken by Joab in a bold attack (II Sam. v. 1-12). To this new center David transferred also the ancient national sanctuary, the ark of the covenant, and showed his humble adherence to his God (II Sam. vi.). His reign was spent in numerous wars against the neighboring peoples. By repeated victories he broke the power of the Philistines (II Sam. v. 17-25, viii. 1-13, xxi. 15-22), and warred successfully with the Ammonites, who were in league with the Syrians, i.e., with Damascus, and the king of Zobah (in cuneiform inscriptions Zubit) (II Sam. viii. 3-8, x. 15-19). His army had experienced champions in the "mighty men" under the command of Abishai, Joab's brother (II Sam. xxiii. 8-39; I Chron. xi. 10-47; see ABISHAI), and David himself was surrounded by a body-guard whose name points to a Philistine origin (see CHERETHITES AND PELETHITES). With the organization of the army is no doubt connected the census which the prophet Gad censured as an offense for which David humbled himself (II Sam. xxiv.; I Chron. xxi.).

4. Domestic and Administrative Difficulties.

Successful as were David's undertakings abroad, he experienced heavy affliction at home, the result of his own sins. His most disgraceful fall was the adultery with Bath-sheba and the removal of Uriah, her husband (II Sam. xi.), for which he was called to account by the prophet Nathan (II Sam. xii.). The Eastern custom of polygamy was also detrimental to the kingdom, proved by the dissensions of the royal family, connected with which was the attempt of Absalom to supplant his aging father on the throne. After scheming for years, Absalom imagined that the time had come to usurp the royal power. From Hebron, where he had been proclaimed king, the usurper advanced with his followers toward Jerusalem. To save the capital, David went with his choice troops to Mount Olivet. On this sad retreat David exhibited magnanimity and presence of mind, and revealed an honest, deep piety. Absalom, spending his time in celebration of victory, missed his opportunity. With a great multitude he pursued his father over the Jordan, but lost the victory and his life in the "wood of Ephraim" (II Sam. xv.-xxiii.). Though the people were still dissatisfied, David was honorably brought back to Jerusalem (II Sam. xix.) and reigned in peace unto his end. When, shortly before his death, his son Adonijah sued for the favor of the people and was supported even by Joab and Abiathar, this plan was frustrated by David at the advice of Nathan and Bath-sheba, who had Solomon anointed king (I Kings i.).

5. Services to the Cultus.

The king, a lover of song, had always given special care to the cultus. He was seriously considering the idea of building a worthy sanctuary on Mount Zion, where the ark of the covenant was. But the prophet Nathan revealed to him, that this was not to be done by him, but by his successor, adding the promise that God would build for himself a home and enter into a paternal relation with his seed. The Chronicler ascribes to David the organization of Levitical chanting (I Chron. xv. 16-24; cf. xxiii.).

6. Character.

David's character has been differently estimated. In subsequent times he was considered by his people and by the greatest prophets the pattern of a king after the heart of God; some modern writers by giving a one-sided prominence to his weaknesses and sins have made a caricature of him (Bayle, Tindal, Voltaire, Reimarus, and others). He was the most gifted of all the kings of Judah. It needed his courage and presence of mind, his direction and endurance, to unite under one royal scepter the jealous tribes. How he spared his people is learned from II Sam. xxiii. 17; how the people loved him, from 1 Sam. xviii. 16; II Sam. xviii. 3, xxi. 17. His imperial virtues were fruits of the childlike, devout piety which David preserved as the deepest secret of his strength unto his end. Many things with which he is personally reproached may be explained from the notions and customs of his time, e.g., the cruelty to conquered enemies (II Sam. viii. 2, xii. 31). His sincerity toward Saul's family is shown by his lamentation, II Sam. i. (cf. I Sam. xxiv. 7). The incident related in II Sam. xxi. must be understood from the notions of the time concerning the necessity of an atonement which the whole family had to make for blood innocently shed. The same is true for the last words of David (I Kings ii.) concerning Joab's death. The unanimous agreement of tradition that David was the gifted author of psalmody is evidence that his love of God was sincere. The opinion which in recent times ascribes not one psalm to David is regarded by some scholars as arbitrary skepticism (cf. James Robertson, *The Poetry and the Religion of the Psalms*, Edinburgh, 1898). For the development of the kingdom of God he did more than many a prophet. In contradistinction to Saul, he showed that the true greatness of the anointed of the Lord consists in his relation to God, and thus mediated to the later prophets the lofty idea, which they bring out in their prophecies: that of the perfect Son of David, an idea which David himself represented only in an imperfect manner. See PSALMS; PSALMODY.

C. VON ORELLI.

BIBLIOGRAPHY: Besides the appropriate sections in the works on the History of Israel mentioned under AHAB, consult: A. Köhler, *Lehrbuch der biblischen Geschichte*, II. i. 184-188, 373, Erlangen, 1884 (an able characterisation); L. P. Paton, *Early Hist. of Syria and Palestine*, New York, 1901. Of commentaries the two best are K. Budde, *Richter und Samuel*, pp. 210-276, Giessen, 1890; H. P. Smith, in *International Critical Commentary*, New York, 1899. Other works worth consulting are: C. R. Conder, *Scenery of David's Outlaw Life*, in *PEF, Quarterly Statement*, 1871, pp. 41-48; J. J. Stähelin, *Das Leben Davids*, Basel, 1866 (useful for Oriental parallels cited); L. von Ranke, *Weltgeschichte*, i. 1, Leipsic, 1881; E. Meyer, *Geschichte des Alterthums*, i. 361 sqq., Stuttgart, 1884; A. Kamphausen, in *ZATW*, vi (1886), 43 sqq.; T.

Cheyne, *Devout Study of Criticism*, part 1, London, 1892; S. A. Cook, *Critical Notes on O. T. History; the Traditions of Saul and David*, ib. 1907; G. Beer, *Saul, David, Salomo*, Tübingen, 1907; *DB*, i. 560–573; *EB*, i. 1019–35. For David's family and list of his mighty men: J. Marquardt, *Fundamente israelitischer und jüdischer Geschichte*, Göttingen, 1896.

DAVID OF AUGSBURG: Franciscan mystic; b. at Augsburg about 1215; d. there Nov. 19, 1272. Of the life of David very little is known. He was master of the novices in the Franciscan settlement at Regensburg founded in 1226, and after 1243 probably also in Augsburg. Either alone or in company with his famous pupil and friend, Berthold of Regensburg (q.v.), he went about preaching and wrote his treatises for the novices. It is difficult to state which these treatises were, since the *Epistola fratris David* and the introduction prefixed to the Augsburg edition of 1596 are wanting in other manuscripts, and all tractates for the novices are found also among the works of Bonaventura. Indeed, the very first of these treatises, *De exterioris hominis reformatione*, is among Bonaventura's writings with the title *De institutione novitiorum*, and also, in a more original form, among the works of Bernard of Clairvaux, with the title *Opusculum in hæc verba; ad quid venisti?* It is therefore debatable how much in this tractate really belongs to David. The second and third treatises, *De interioris hominis reformatione* and *De septem processibus religiosi*, belong undoubtedly to David, though they are also printed among Bonaventura's works with the title *De profectu religiosorum*. To David also belongs the fourth book found in manuscript and extant in Bonaventura's works as *De institutione novitiorum*. To the treatises for novices belong also the two German tractates *Die sieben Vorregeln der Tugend* and *Spiegel der Tugend*, whereas the other German treatises ascribed by Pfeiffer to David are undoubtedly spurious. The two German treatises are pearls of German prose; the Latin tractates are verbose. On account of these writings Preger called David a mystic. There is no doubt that he was mystic in tendency, but in the main this tendency is shown only in two larger sections of the *Interioris hominis reformatio* (ix.–xv.) and the *Septem processus* (xxxv.–xli.). David is too sober to be a true mystic; with him the principal things are the practical injunctions in which he refers to the pattern of Christ, especially to meekness, humility, and love. For a time David successfully served the Inquisition. The fruit of his experience appears in the treatise *De inquisitione hæreticorum*. Here he shows himself a child of his time. The heretics are foxes and wolves, who are neither to be refuted nor opposed with spiritual weapons, but are to be annihilated, and in such a hunt hunger, torture, lies, and treachery are allowed. In the last decade of his life he composed an "Exposition of the Rules of the Order of the Minorites," in which he tried to mediate between the clerical body and the community, but actually came to the point of view of the community. It is to be regretted that his sermons which John Trithemius had seen are lost. His characteristic was a sober common sense which was averse to everything untrue and exaggerated. His importance lies mainly in his activity as preacher and in his silent work of educating the rising generation of monks, of whom Berthold of Regensburg was the most prominent. E. LEMPP.

BIBLIOGRAPHY: The *De inquisitione*, ed. W. Preger, appeared in *AMA*, xiv. 2 (1879), 181–235. Consult: F. Pfeiffer, *Deutsche Mystiker des 14. Jahrhunderts*, vol. i., Leipsic, 1845; W. Preger, *Geschichte der deutschen Mystik*, i. 268 sqq., ib. 1874; E. Lempp, in *ZKG*, xix (1898), 15 sqq.

DAVID, CHRISTIAN. See UNITY OF THE BRETHREN.

DAVID OF DINANT or DINAN: Pantheistic philosopher; supposed to have been born either at Dinant (on the Meuse, 15 m. s. of Namur), Belgium, or at Dinan (14 m. s. of St. Malo) in Brittany; d. after 1215. He is said to have enjoyed the favor of Pope Innocent III. (1198–1216) because of his subtle dialectics. At the provincial council of 1210 held at Paris, which condemned Amalric of Bena (q.v.), the *Quaternuli* of David was also ordered to be burned, and in 1215 the reading of extracts from David's work was prohibited in the University of Paris. David fled from France, and the further events of his life are unknown. Albertus Magnus finds the basis of David's teaching in the identity of everything real in the absolute. David distinguished three kinds of things, corporeal, spiritual, and divine substances. For each of the three kinds he assumed a general, indivisible principle; for the corporeal, a primitive "stuff"; for the spiritual, the spirit; for divine things: God. Between these three principles no distinction can exist; each can be conceived of only as an undifferentiated entity, and the three must accordingly be identical. The details of his system and sources of his pantheistic teaching can not be ascertained with certainty. At all events, he is not dependent on Amalric of Bena, but was rather influenced by Aristotelian writings and Jewish and Moorish comment on them. Some thoughts of Giordano Bruno and Spinoza show a relationship to the pantheistic system of David's. HERMAN HAUPT.

BIBLIOGRAPHY: J. H. Krönlein, *De . . . Davidis de Dinanto doctrina*, Giessen, 1847; W. Preger, *Geschichte der deutschen Mystik*, i. 184–191, Leipsic, 1874; *Mémoires de l'académie des inscriptions et belles lettres*, xxvi. 2 (1870), 467–498 (by C. Jourdain); B. Hauréau, *Mémoire sur la vraie source des erreurs attribuées à David de Dinan*, in *Mémoires de l'académie*, ut sup., xxix. 2 (1879), 319–330; O. Bardenhewer, *Die pseudoaristotelische Schrift über das reine Gute*, pp. 212 sqq., Freiburg, 1882; J. E. Erdmann, *Geschichte der Philosophie*, i. 352, Berlin, 1896, Eng. transl., London, 1893; F. Ueberweg, *Geschichte der Philosophie*, pp. 208–212, Berlin, 1898, Eng. transl., i. 388–402, New York, 1874; Neander, *Christian Church*, iv. 445–448.

DAVID JORISZOON. See JORIS.

DAVID, SAINT: The patron saint of Wales. All that is known of him is that he died about 601, that he was bishop of Menevia (St. David's) in southwest Wales, and that he presided at two synods of the Welsh Church, the later of the two being held in 569 (cf. Haddan and Stubbs, *Councils*, i. 116–118). His legendary and fictitious history makes him metropolitan archbishop of Wales, consecrated at Jerusalem, ascribes to him numerous foundations, and says that he extirpated Pelagianism in Wales at the synods already referred to; it is well decked out with miracles, visions, and the like. He was popular in both Wales and Ireland, where many churches were dedicated to him. His day is Mar. 1.

Bibliography: W. J. Rees, *Lives of the Cambro-British Saints*, pp. 102–144, 402–448, Llandovery, 1853; *DCB*, i. 791–793; *DNB*, xiv. 113–115.

DAVIDIS, FRANCISCUS.

Franciscus Davidis (Ferencz David), a Unitarian of Transylvania, was born at Klausenburg (Kolozsvar; 72 m. n.n.w. of Hermannstadt), Hungary, 1510 (?); d. at Deva (37 m. s.w. of Karlsburg) Nov. 15, 1579. He was probably of Saxon descent. Franciscus, the episcopal vicar of Weissenburg, enabled him to study theology at Wittenberg. From 1551 to 1552 he was rector of a school in Bistritz. Later he accepted the Lutheran faith and was called to Petersdorf (Peterfalva) as first Evangelical preacher. In 1555 he became rector in Klausenburg, in 1556 also superintendent of the Evangelical Hungarian Church in Transylvania. He soon became the champion of the Reformation in his country, following Melanchthon and combating Calvinism. The state assembly of Thorenburg in 1558 permitted only the Lutheran and the Catholic religion, but the controversies continued without interruption, especially on the doctrine of the Lord's Supper, and the Calvinistic party headed by Peter Melius (q.v.) gained many adherents among the nobility. Davidis himself, anxious to maintain and increase his influence, turned toward Calvinism. From the discord of confessions resulted a separation of nationalities, the Saxons under their superintendent Matthias Hebler remaining faithful to Lutheranism, and the Hungarians under Melius and Davidis accepting Calvinism; after 1564 both parties were legally acknowledged. Davidis became Calvinistic superintendent, and soon afterward court preacher of the sovereign John Sigismund Zápolya.

1. Services as a Reformer.

At this time an irresistible current of Unitarian doctrines from Italy Switzerland, and especially from Poland, made its way into Transylvania, and the controversies turned from the Lord's Supper to the doctrine of the Trinity and the person of Christ. Davidis, again following the current of the time, accepted the new doctrine and was chiefly influential in introducing Unitarianism at the court, and at the University of Klausenburg. In 1566 he attacked the doctrine of the Trinity in a disputation with Peter Károlyi, rector of the university in Klausenburg. A number of conventions were held, treatises were written, and the controversies assumed greater and greater dimensions, Davidis and Melius becoming the most passionate opponents. Davidis and Georgius Blandrata (q.v.), court physician of the prince, succeeded in winning the majority of the nobility over to Unitarianism; and in 1567 the prince placed at their disposal a printing-press at Weissenburg. The state assembly held at Thorenburg in 1568 granted entire freedom in matters of religion, and in the same year a great disputation was held at Weissenburg with Peter Melius and Peter Károlyi on the one side and Davidis and Blandrata on the other. The controversies were continued at synods and in treatises. In 1568 the Unitarian Church was constituted independently with Davidis as bishop. Its adherents were almost exclusively of the Hungarian and Czech population, with Klausenburg and Weissenburg as their strongholds.

2. Adoption of Unitarianism.

The fundamental thoughts of Davidis's doctrine were that the Reformation must be placed upon a broader basis, and the ceremonies and articles of faith must be reduced to the simplicity of apostolic times. The main obstacle to such a reform is the scholastic doctrine of the Trinity, a product of Greek philosophy, and the source of all idolatry in the Church. There is no triune God, but only one God, the Father and Creator of the universe; to him alone divinity in the full sense is to be ascribed. Christ was born of Mary in a supernatural manner. The Son of God exists eternally in the divine decree; but in reality he is not born from eternity, but has originated only with the incarnation of Christ. The Holy Spirit is not the third person of the Trinity, but the power that emanates from the Father and is communicated to us through the Son for our sanctification. Davidis spread his doctrines abroad in Latin and Hungarian writings, in catechisms, sermons, and Latin distichs. But the predominance of Unitarianism in Transylvania was of but short duration. Zápolya, the reigning prince, died in 1571, and his successor, Stephen Báthory, a Roman Catholic, called the Jesuits into the country. Most of the Unitarians took the part of Caspar Békes, a pretender, and were involved in his utter defeat in 1575. Báthory immediately removed all Unitarians from the court, and their publications were subjected to a severe censorship; all innovations in religion were threatened with excommunication and punishment by the sovereign. Davidis, however, received important aid from Unitarians of foreign countries who sought refuge in Transylvania, as, for instance, Johann Sommer of Saxony, and Jacob Palæologus, an exile from Poland. Báthory succeeded in winning some of the Unitarians, especially Blandrata, over to his political cause. A separation from his wife injured Davidis's authority, and the liberties of the Unitarians were more and more restricted.

3. Theology.

To make matters worse, Davidis's position became so radical that he rejected the worship of Christ altogether. A controversy then ensued between him and Blandrata, who, belonging to the more moderate party, invoked the aid of Faustus Socinus. The latter came in person from Basel. Davidis expressed his views in four theses *De non invocando Jesu Christo in precibus sacris*. He held a synod with his adherents at Thorenburg, where he decreed the *Non-adoratio*. Thereupon Blandrata and Socinus effected his suspension from office

4. Controversies.

and imprisonment until a general synod should request him to revoke his heresy. In June of the same year a disputation took place at a synod in Thorenburg; and in July Davidis was tried at Weissenburg in the presence of the sovereign, condemned as innovator and blasphemer, and thrown into prison for life at the mountain-fortress of Deva.

5. Influence.

His party did not disappear. Although Blandrata succeeded for the moment in winning the Unitarian divines over to an adorantistic confession of faith and in reintroducing the ceremonies of baptism and the Lord's Supper, there separated themselves from these *New Unitarians* the adherents of Davidis as *Old Unitarians* or *Davidists* or *Non-adorantes*, and from the latter again there originated the sect of the Sabbatharians, thus completing the circle from Catholicism through Lutheranism, Calvinism, Unitarianism, Non-adorantism to a sect in which Christianity closely approached Judaism. Davidis's literary works were occasioned by his controversies, the most important being *De falsa et vera unius Dei Patris, Filii et Spiritus Sancti, cognitione libri duo* (Weissenburg, 1567) and *Refutatio scripti G. Majoris* (1569). The latter treatise was occasioned by his controversy on the Trinity with G. Major of Wittenberg. Davidis also wrote in Hungarian "On the Divinity of the One God-father and His Blessed Holy Son Jesus Christ" (1571).

K. Holl.

Bibliography: The best monograph, unfortunately only in Hungarian, is Elek Jakob, *David Ferencz Emléke*, 2 vols., Budapest, 1879. Consult: F. C. Baur, *Die christliche Lehre von der Dreieinigkeit*, iii. 144 sqq., Tübingen, 1843; O. Fock, *Der Socinianismus*, Kiel, 1847; P. Bod, *Hist. Hungarorum eccl.*, ed. L. W. E. Rauwenhoff and J. J. Prins, i. 397–457, Leyden, 1888 (history of Unitarianism in Hungary); J. H. Allen, *Hist. of Unitarians*, pp. 60–68, 105–112, New York, 1894. On the communion controversy: K. Landsteiner, *J. Palaologus*, Vienna, 1873. A statement of Davidis's principles is in *Opera J. Palaeologi*, Basel, 1581. Consult *KL*, iii. 1421–23; *ADB*, iv. 787.

DAVIDISTS: Followers of David Joris. See Joris.

DAVIDS, THOMAS WILLIAM RHYS: English student of comparative religion and Buddhist scholar; b. at Colchester (51 m. n.n.e. of London), Essex, May 12, 1843. He studied at Breslau (Ph.D., 1865), and entered the Ceylon Civil Service in 1866. In 1877 he became a barrister at the Middle Temple, London, and in 1883 was appointed professor of Pali and Buddhistic literature at University College, London. Since 1904 he has also been professor of comparative religion at Victoria University, Manchester. In 1882 he founded the Pali Text Society, of which he has since been president, also editing its *Journal* and other publications. He was Hibbert lecturer in 1881, and has been secretary and librarian of the Royal Asiatic Society since 1887. He has written, edited, or translated: *Ancient Coins and Measures of Ceylon* (London, 1877); *Buddhism* (1878); *Buddhist Birth-Stories*, i. (1880); *Lectures on the Origin and Growth of Religion as Illustrated by Some Points in the History of Buddhism* (Hibbert lectures; 1881); *Buddhist Suttas*, in *SBE*, xi. (Oxford, 1881); *Vinaya Texts*, ib. xiii., xvii., xx. (in collaboration with H. Oldenberg; 1881–85); *The Questions of King Milinda*, ib. xxxv. (1890); *Buddhism, Its History and Literature* (New York, 1896); *Dialogues of the Buddha* (London, 1899); and *Buddhist India* (1902). He is also the editor of the Sacred Books of the Buddhists, for which he edited *Dialogues of the Buddha* (London, 1899) and the *Digha-Nikâya* (1899), while to the *Journal of the Pali Text Society* he contributed an edition of the *Sumañgala Vilâsini* in collaboration with J. E. Carpenter (London, 1886).

DAVIDSON, ANDREW BRUCE: United Free Church of Scotland; b. on the farm of Kirkhill, parish of Ellon (15 m. n. of Aberdeen), Aberdeenshire, 1831 (probably Dec., although the exact date is uncertain); d. at Edinburgh Jan. 26, 1902. He studied at Marischal College, Aberdeen (M.A., 1849), taught in the Free Church school of Ellon until 1852, and was graduated at New College, the divinity hall of the Free Church, Edinburgh, in 1856. He filled several pulpits temporarily, but never held a charge. In 1858 he was appointed assistant to John Duncan, professor of Hebrew in New College, and in 1863 became full professor of Oriental languages and Duncan's colleague. After the latter's death in 1870 Davidson was sole professor until 1900, when he was senior colleague. He was an admirable Biblical scholar and critic, and a famous teacher. He was a member of the Old Testament Company of Revisers. He preached occasionally and with great acceptance, but reluctantly and preferably in obscure places. His literary work was relatively small in amount, but superior in quality. In addition to editing for *The Cambridge Bible for Schools* the volumes on Job (Cambridge, 1884), Ezekiel (1892), and Nahum, Habbakuk, and Zephaniah (1896), as well as Isaiah for *The Temple Bible* (London, 1902), he wrote: *Outlines of Hebrew Accentuation, Prose and Poetical* (London, 1861); *A Commentary on Job* (Edinburgh, 1862), which covers only the first third of the book; *Introductory Hebrew Grammar* (1874; 17th ed., 1902); *The Epistle to the Hebrews with Introduction and Notes* (1882); and *Hebrew Syntax* (1894; 3d ed., 1905). After Davidson's death his colleague, J. A. Patterson, issued his *Biblical and Literary Essays* (1902); *Old Testament Prophecy* (1902); and two volumes of sermons, *The Called of God* (1902; with a biographical introduction by A. T. Innes) and *Waiting upon God* (1903); while Principal S. D. F. Salmond edited his *Theology of the Old Testament* (1904).

DAVIDSON, RANDALL THOMAS: Archbishop of Canterbury and primate of all England; b. at Edinburgh Apr. 7, 1848. He studied at Trinity College, Oxford (B.A., 1871), was curate of Dartford, Kent, 1874–77, and chaplain and private secretary to the archbishops of Canterbury Tait (1877–82) and Benson (1882–83). He was dean of Windsor (1883–91), became bishop of Rochester 1891, was translated to the see of Winchester 1895, and consecrated archbishop of Canterbury 1903. He was domestic chaplain to the Queen 1883–91, and clerk of the closet to the Queen 1891–1901, and to the King 1901–03, a prelate of the Order of the Garter 1895–1903, while in 1904 he was created a Grand Commander of the Victorian Order. He has written *Life of Archbishop Tait* (2 vols., London, 1891; in collaboration with W. Beecham) and *The Christian Opportunity* (1904), and has edited *The Lambeth Conferences of 1867, 1878, and 1888* (London, 1889).

DAVIDSON, SAMUEL: English Congregationalist; b. at Kellswater (4 m. s. of Ballymena), County Antrim, Ireland, Sept. 23, 1807; d. at London Apr. 1, 1898. He was graduated at the Royal Academical Institution, Belfast, in 1832. Three years later he was appointed professor of Biblical criticism at Belfast to the General Synod of Ulster, and retained this position until 1841, when he became a Congregationalist. In 1842 he was appointed professor of Biblical literature and ecclesiastical history in the Lancashire Independent College, Manchester. He resigned in 1857, on account of opposition to his views of inspiration, and in 1862 was elected Scripture examiner in London University, and removed to London. He was a member of the Old Testament Revision Committee. His theology was rationalistic. In addition to translations he wrote: *Sacred Hermeneutics* (Edinburgh, 1843); *Ecclesiastical Polity of the New Testament* (London, 1848); *Treatise on Biblical Criticism* (2 vols., Edinburgh, 1852); *The Hebrew Text of the Old Testament Revised from Critical Sources* (London, 1855); *The Text of the Old Testament Considered, with a Treatise on Sacred Interpretation, and a Brief Introduction to the Old Testament Books and the Apocrypha* (1856; vol. ii. of the tenth edition of T. H. Horne's *Introduction to the Critical Study and Knowledge of the Holy Scriptures*); *An Introduction to the Old Testament, Critical, Historical, and Theological* (3 vols., 1862-1863); *An Introduction to the New Testament* (2 vols., 1868); *On a Fresh Revision of the English Old Testament* (1873); *The Canon of the Bible* (1876); and *The Doctrine of Last Things Contained in the New Testament, Compared with the Notions of the Jews and the Statements of the Church Creeds* (1882).

Bibliography: *Autobiography and Diary*, with selection of letters, edited by his daughter, Miss A. J. Davidson, Edinburgh, 1899.

DAVIES, JOHN LLEWELYN: Church of England; b. at Chichester Jan. 26, 1826. He studied at Trinity College, Cambridge (B.A., 1848; M.A., 1851), where he was fellow 1851-59. He was curate of St. Anne's, Limehouse, 1851-52, vicar of St. Mark's, Whitechapel, 1852-56, and rector of Christ Church, St. Marylebone, 1856-89, and rural dean 1882-88. Since 1888 he has been vicar of Kirkby-Lonsdale, Westmorelandshire. He was honorary chaplain to Queen Victoria 1876-81, chaplain in ordinary 1881-1901, and is an honorary chaplain to King Edward VII., while he has been principal of Queen's College for Ladies, London, one of the founders of the Workingmen's College, London, and chairman of the committee of the New Hospital for Women. He was select preacher at Oxford in 1881, Hulsean lecturer at Cambridge in 1890, and Lady Margaret preacher at the same university ten years later. In theology he is a follower of F. D. Maurice. Among his numerous publications may be mentioned: *Morality According to the Sacrament of the Lord's Supper* (London, 1865); *Epistles of St. Paul* (1866); *The Gospel and Modern Life* (1869); *Homilies, Ancient and Modern* (2 vols., 1884); *Social Questions from the Point of View of Christian Theology* (1885); and *Workingmen's College, 1854-1904* (1904).

DAVIES, SAMUEL: Presbyterian; b. near Summit Ridge, New Castle County, Del., Nov. 3, 1724; d. in Princeton, N. J., Feb. 4, 1761. He studied at Samuel Blair's School at Fagg's Manor (Londonderry), Chester County, Pa.; was ordained in 1747 and sent to Hanover County, Va., where his position was difficult and delicate owing to opposition on the part of the authorities to dissenters. In 1753-54 he was in England, with Gilbert Tennent, soliciting funds for the College of New Jersey (Princeton), and while there secured a royal declaration that the Act of Toleration extended to Virginia. Returning to America, he organized the first presbytery in Virginia in 1755. In 1759 he succeeded Jonathan Edwards as president of Princeton. He was an eloquent preacher, admired in England as well as in America.

Bibliography: His sermons were printed in five volumes, London, 1767-71; the best Am. edition, 3 vols., New York, 1846, has an essay on his life and times by Albert Barnes, and a separate *Memoir* was published at Boston in 1832. Consult also E. H. Gillett, *History of the Presbyterian Church*, chaps. vii., viii., Philadelphia, 1864.

DAVIES, THOMAS WITTON: English Baptist; b. at Nantyglo (16 m. n.w. of Newport), Monmouthshire, Feb. 28, 1851. He studied at the Baptist colleges at Pontypool and Regent's Park, University College and Manchester College, London (B.A., London University, 1879), and the universities of Berlin, Leipsic (Ph.D., 1898), and Strasburg. He was minister of the High Street Baptist Church, Merthyr-Tydfil (1879-81); professor of Hebrew, classics, and mathematics in the Baptist college at Haverfordwest (1881-91); principal and professor of theology in the Midland Baptist College, Nottingham (1891-98); and lecturer in Arabic and Syriac at University College, Nottingham (1896-98). Since 1898 he has been professor of Semitic languages in the University College of North Wales, Bangor, and was also professor of Old Testament literature in the Baptist College, Bangor, 1898-1906. In doctrinal theology he is in the main Evangelical, and in criticism is an adherent of the Graf-Wellhausen school. He has written: *Oriental Studies in Great Britain* (Woking, 1892); *Magic, Divination, and Demonology Among the Hebrews and Their Neighbours* (London, 1897); *The Scriptures of the Old Testament* (in Welsh, Wrexham, 1900); *Heinrich Ewald, Orientalist and Theologian, 1803-1903: A Centenary Appreciation* (London, 1903); and *Psalms 73-150 with Introduction and Commentary* (in *The Century Bible*, 1906).

DAVIS, JOHN D.: Presbyterian; b. at Pittsburg, Pa., Mar. 5, 1854. He studied at the College of New Jersey (B.A., 1879), the University of Bonn (1879-80), Princeton Theological Seminary (1880-1883), and the University of Leipsic (1884-86). He has been instructor in Hebrew in Princeton Theological Seminary (1883-84 and 1886-88), and professor of Hebrew and cognate languages (1888-92), of Semitic philology and Old Testament history

(1892–1900), and Oriental and Old Testament literature (since 1900), in the same institution. In theology he is Calvinistic, and in Old Testament criticism is a conservative. He has written *Genesis and Semitic Tradition* (New York, 1894) and *A Dictionary of the Bible* (Philadelphia, 1898).

DAVISON, WILLIAM THEOPHILUS: English Wesleyan; b. at Bath, Somersetshire, Oct. 5, 1846. He was graduated at London University in 1869, held various pastorates 1868–81, was for ten years professor of Biblical literature in Richmond College, Surrey, was professor of theology in Handsworth College, Birmingham, until 1904, and in 1905 returned in a similar capacity to Richmond College. He is a member of the faculty of theology in London University, and in 1901 was president of the Wesleyan Methodist Conference. He has written: *Praises of Israel* (London, 1893); *Wisdom Literature of the Old Testament* (1895); *The Lord's Supper* (1895); *Strength for the Way* (1902); and *Psalms* in *The Century Bible* (1903).

DAWSON, SIR JOHN WILLIAM: Canadian Presbyterian layman; b. at Pictou, N. S., Oct. 13, 1820; d. at Montreal Nov. 19, 1899. He studied at the College of Pictou and the University of Edinburgh (B.A., 1846). In 1850 he was appointed superintendent of education in Nova Scotia, and three years later was made professor of geology and principal of McGill College and University, Montreal, holding this position until he retired as professor emeritus in 1893. He was the first president of the Royal Society of Canada in 1883, of the American Association in 1884, of the British Association in 1886, and of the American Geological Society in 1893. He was made a Companion of the Order of St. Michael and St. George in 1882, and two years later was knighted. In theology his position was conservative. He wrote more than twenty books, of which those of special theological interest are: *The Bible and Science* (London, 1875); *The Origin of the World According to Revelation and Science* (1877); *Facts and Fancies in Modern Science: Studies of the Relation of Science to Prevalent Speculations and Religious Belief* (Philadelphia, 1882); *Egypt and Syria, Their Physical Features in Relation to Bible History* (London, 1886); *Modern Science in Bible Lands* (1888); *Modern Ideas of Evolution as Related to Revelation and Science* (New York, 1890); and *Eden Lost and Won: Studies of the Early History and Final Destiny of Man as Taught in Nature and Revelation* (London, 1896).

DAWSON, WILLIAM JAMES: English Congregationalist; b. at Towcester (45 m. n.e. of Oxford) Nov. 21, 1854. He studied at Didbury College, Manchester, and entered the Wesleyan ministry in 1875. He held pastorates at Wesley's Chapel, City Road, London, and at Glasgow and Southport until 1892, when he became a Congregationalist and was appointed minister of Highbury Quadrant Church, London, resigning this position in 1905 to become an evangelist. He has lectured widely on literary and historical topics, and in 1891 was a delegate to the Methodist Ecumenical Conference at Washington, D. C. He has written: *Arvalon* (London, 1878); *A Vision of Souls* (poems; 1884); *Quest and Vision: Essays on Life and Literature* (1886); *The Threshold of Manhood* (1889); *The Makers of Modern Poetry* (1890); *The Redemption of Edward Strahan: A Social Story* (1891); *The Church of To-morrow* (1892); *Poems and Lyrics* (1893); *The Making of Manhood* (1894); *The Comrade-Christ* (sermons; 1894); *London Idylls* (1895); *The Story of Hannah* (1896); *The House of Dreams* (1897); *Through Lattice Windows* (1897); *The Endless Choice and Other Sermons* (1897); *Table Talk with Young Men* (1898); *Judith Boldero: A Tragic Romance* (1898); *Makers of Modern Prose* (1899); *Savonarola: A Drama* (1900); *The Doctor Speaks: Episodes in the Experiences of John Selkirk, M.D.* (1900); *The Man Christ Jesus* (1901); *The Quest of the Simple Life* (1903); *The Reproach of Christ and Other Sermons* (1903); *The Evangelistic Note* (1905); *Makers of English Fiction* (1905); and *The Forgotten Secret* (1906).

DAY, THE HEBREW: The civil day was reckoned by the Hebrews from sunset to sunset, so that the day began at that time both on ordinary occasions and on Sabbaths and feasts. In this matter the Hebrews were in accord with the Athenians, and the Greeks in general, as well as with the Germans; and this mode of reckoning goes well with the habits under a cult of the moon (see MOON, SEMITIC CONCEPTIONS OF). Yet according to Delitzsch and Dillmann (in their commentaries on Genesis i. 5), the reckoning indicated in Gen. i. 5 sqq. is not to be taken as from evening to evening, but after the Babylonian fashion, from morning to morning. Excepting only the seventh day, the days of the week had no proper names, that system of designation which gave the days the names of the sun, moon, and planets being rejected because of heathen associations.

For the divisions of the day, besides the ordinary terms of dawn, morning, midday, and evening, there were in use such expressions as "the heat of the day" (Gen. xviii. 1), "the height of the day," or "the perfect day" (Prov. iv. 18), and "the cool of the evening" (Gen. iii. 8). The reckoning by hours does not appear in the Old Testament until the book of Daniel, when the word used is Aramaic. In the New Testament the reckoning by hours is customary, the first hour is sunrise and the sixth is midday (cf. Matt. xx. 1 sqq.), though it is debatable whether the Gospel of John does not follow the Roman civil mode by reckoning the hours from midnight (cf. John xix. 14 and xviii. 28 with Matt. xxvii. 45; Mark xv. 25, 33; Luke xxiii. 44). The hour, dependent upon the sun and the seasons, varies in the latitude of Palestine from forty-nine to seventy-one minutes in length. A sun-dial (doubtless an obelisk with steps), which marked the hours as the shadow passed, was used by Hezekiah (II Kings xx. 9–10). The night was divided by the Hebrews into three watches (Lam. ii. 19; Judges vii. 19; Ex. xiv. 24). In New Testament times the Roman division of the night into four watches was employed (Mark xiii. 35), though the Talmudists retained the earlier division into three watches. (C. VON ORELLI.)

Bibliography: C. L. Ideler, *Handbuch der . . . Chronologie*, i. 80 sqq., Berlin, 1825; C. Wieseler, *Chronologische Synopse der vier Evangelien*, pp. 410 sqq., Hamburg, 1843, Eng. transl., Cambridge, 1877; Benzinger, *Archäologie*, pp. 202-203; Nowack, *Archäologie*, i. 214-215; *DB*, i. 573; *EB*, i. 1035-38.

DAY OF THE LORD (Heb. *Yom Yahweh*, "Day of Yahweh"): A complex prophetic concept brought into connection with Hebrew Messianism and later used with eschatological significance. The full expression "day of the Lord" is not always used, the terms "the day," "that day," "the day of trouble," "the great and terrible day," "that time," and other like phrases being interchangeable with it. Indeed, the word "day" itself, in Hebrew as in Arabic, often had a sinister content and was equivalent to "day of battle" (cf. Isa. ix. 4). The idea undergoes so great development in the history of Messianism that no general description of it applies to any one period. Its fundamental and abiding characteristic is that it is the time of the manifestation of Yahweh as savior of (the actual or the ideal) Israel by the punishment of his enemies, when his benign purposes for that people will be accomplished. In its physical aspects it is a day of terrifying phenomena, all nature partaking of the awe inspired by the presence of the Creator and showing that awe in heaven by the darkening or falling of the heavenly bodies and on earth by quakes and cataclysms and by the unbounded terror of the nations. The idea seems to have originated in the popular mind as a nationalistic ideal, founded not in ethics but in the crude religious ideas concerning the effect of the covenant by which Yahweh was conceived as bound to help his people simply because they were his people and served him alone.

This day had from the very beginning and always retained two sides (cf. Mal. iv. 1-2), judgment (of Israel's and therefore of Yahweh's enemies, later of the wicked) and redemption (of Israel, later of the righteous). It was taken into the circle of prophetic ideas by Amos, who lifted it out of the nationalistic and unethical by the startling announcement that the day involved not (as the people assumed) the punishment of Israel's enemies, but of Israel itself because of its offenses against a righteous God. Sinners were the enemies of Yahweh and not the Gentiles as Gentiles, and on them the troubles of the day would fall. With this representation Hosea agreed, and Isaiah and Micah applied the same reasoning to Judah. In these cases the precedent, ever faithfully followed, was set of stating the purpose of the day to be the establishment of a righteous people. While the ethical element thus introduced remained dominant, it was frequently united with the nationalistic element, so that while the judgment was to discriminate between Israel and its enemies, it did so on the assumption that Israel was righteous while the enemy was wicked. The exact form which the conception took fluctuated according to the external conditions and the view of the individual prophet. Thus in Nahum and Habakkuk, dealing with times when Israel was oppressed, the view-point is national and the judgment is to be against the (wicked) Assyrians and in favor of (righteous) Israel. In Zephaniah an advance is made, and the day of the Lord becomes a world-judgment; but this is a corollary of the conception of Yahweh as not merely God of Israel, but God of the whole earth (i. 8-13, ii. 1-6, iii. 8). In the later prophets this is accomplished by an assembling of the peoples (Isa. xlv. 20; Zech. xii. 3; Joel iii. 2), when judgment is meted upon them. In Jeremiah the day is once more primarily against Judah, though other nations are involved (i. 18, xxv. 15-24; xxv. 27-33 is a later interpolation). Already in Jeremiah the idea is becoming denationalized and individualized, the cause of judgment being not collective or national, but individual, and in Ezekiel this is fully accomplished. The Messianic kingdom was to be introduced by this day, and a regenerate Israel was to survive. According to the exilic prophets, the day inaugurated the Messianic kingdom, but the guilt was largely individual. Haggai (chaps. ii.-iii.) and Zechariah (i. 15, ii.) returned again to the nationalistic ideal, but their position was reversed by Malachi. Up to this point the judgment was conceived as taking place and the kingdom being established on the earth, and this kingdom was earthly in character. This was changed in Isa. lxv.-lxvi. (before 400 B.C.), where a new heaven and a new earth is introduced—a fruitful suggestion for further development. Joel (c. 350 B.C.) exhibits the day in all its terror (ii. 30-31), but returns to the nationalistic view-point (iii. 1-2, 9-21), and the same idea prevails in Zech. xii.-xiv. (of about the same date as Joel). In Isa. xix. (c. 300) a universalism of worship of Yahweh (which is merely illustrated by mention of Egypt, Assyria, and Israel) is ushered in by "that day." In Daniel (166-165) the result of the coming of the day is the overthrow of the world-kingdoms, the establishment of the kingdom of the Messiah, in which will share the righteous dead of Israel, raised from the grave. Here first appears the resurrection of the individual, Ezekiel's resurrection (chap. xxxvii.) being national. In the earlier Pseudepigrapha (q.v.) a great development takes place, in part through the doctrine that Sheol (see Hades) is a place of punishment for the wicked, heaven appearing by contrast as the abode of the blessed (foreshadowed in the Old Testament in Ps. xlix. 15, lxxiii. 24). The resurrection is generalized, the wicked being raised for final condemnation, the righteous for participation in the new kingdom. Complete transcendentalizing does not take place, since sometimes the new Jerusalem is localized on earth, at other times it is a heavenly city. In these earlier books "the day" ushers in the Messianic kingdom. In the later Pseudepigrapha the earthly Messianic rule is only the temporary prelude to the real kingdom of God, and "the day" with the final judgment comes at its close. While the representation varies in different books, development takes place on the whole along these lines. In the Gospels the day is implicit, and is involved in the parusia (Mark viii. 38 and parallels) which is to be heralded by the same cataclysmic phenomena as accompany the day of Yahweh in the Old Testament (Mark xiii. 7-8, 24-27). In Paul the "day of Yahweh" has become the "day of our Lord

Jesus Christ" (I Cor. i. 8). See ESCHATOLOGY; and HADES. GEO. W. GILMORE.

BIBLIOGRAPHY: The best book is R. H. Charles, *Critical Hist. of the Doctrine of a Future Life*, pp. 85 sqq. et passim, London, 1899. Consult further the literature on O. T. theology and Messianic prophecy, e.g., H. Schultz, *O. T. Theology*, ii. 356 sqq., Edinburgh, 1892; C. A. Briggs, *Messianic Prophecy*, pp. 487–490 et passim, New York, 1898; idem, *Messiah of the Gospels*, pp. 309 sqq., ib. 1894; P. Volz, *Jüdische Eschatologie von Daniel bis Akiba*, Tübingen, 1903; A. B. Davidson, *Theology of the O. T.*, pp. 374 sqq., ib. 1904; *DB*, i. 574, 434 sqq., 440, iii. 377, iv. 771; *EB*, ii. 1348 sqq.

DAY, CHARLES ORRIN: Congregationalist; b. at Catskill, N. Y., Nov. 8, 1851. He was graduated at Yale in 1872, and Andover Theological Seminary in 1877. He was a city missionary at Montreal 1877–78, and pastor at Williamsburg, Mass., until 1884. He then spent a year in postgraduate study at the Yale Divinity School, after which he was pastor at Brattleboro, Vt., until 1898, when he became chaplain of the First Vermont regiment at Chickamauga during the Spanish-American war. From 1898 to 1901 he was secretary of the Congregational Educational Society, and since the latter year has been president of Andover Theological Seminary and Bartlet professor of homiletics and practical theology.

DAY, JEREMIAH: Congregationalist, ninth president of Yale College; b. in New Preston, Conn., Aug. 3, 1773; d. in New Haven Aug. 22, 1867. He was graduated at Yale 1795, and the same year succeeded Timothy Dwight (q.v.) as principal of the Greenfield Academy; was tutor at Williams 1796–98, at Yale 1798–1801; was elected professor of mathematics and natural philosophy at Yale 1801; succeeded Timothy Dwight as president in 1817; resigned in 1846. Besides a series of mathematical text-books, he wrote *An Inquiry Respecting the Self-determining Power of the Will*, a refutation of Cousin (New Haven, 1838), and *An Examination of President Edwards on the Will*, a conciliatory and apologetic defense of Edwards (1841).

BIBLIOGRAPHY: A memorial address by President T. D. Woolsey is in *The New Englander*, xxvi (1867), 692–724.

DAYANAND, dā"yā-nānd', **SARASWATI**, sā"rās-wā'tī: Hindu reformer and founder of the Arya Samaj (see INDIA, III., 3); b. of Shivite Brahmanic parentage at Mori, a town in the n.w. of Kathiawar, in 1827; d. at Ajmere Oct. 30, 1883. He early began the orthodox course of study, and by the time he had reached fourteen years of age had committed to memory a Sanskrit dramatic work, a Sanskrit vocabulary, the whole of the Yajur-Veda, and part of other Vedas. He very early felt the inconsistency between the religious ideas of the Vedas and those connected with the worship of Shiva, and he reluctantly yielded to his father's insistence upon performance of the idolatrous rites of Shiva. On one occasion, when thus taking part in this worship, the ceremonies having continued long into the night, his father and others fell asleep. While watching the idol the boy saw a mouse take away an offering that had been made to it. Suddenly the inconsistency of worshiping God in the form of a stone so overpowered him that he left the temple, and never again worshiped an idol. Death in his family led him into deep thought of the meaning of life, and he determined to break away from external form and find the true path through the efforts of the soul. His parents, thinking the boy too meditative, determined on his marriage. The preparations were nearly completed when he silently left his home by night, and never returned from his wanderings in search of some one who could guide him to the truth. At last, in Nov., 1860, he found a welcome at Mathura, with a religious teacher named Swami Virjananda Saraswati. With this profound scholar of the Vedas, who had been blind from infancy, Dayanand studied the Vedas for four years. At the conclusion of his education Virjananda sent him forth to spread the enlightenment gained from the Vedas. In obedience he traveled over India, visiting especially places of pilgrimage where he denounced idolatry and the superstitions of Hinduism. In 1872 he visited Calcutta and met Devendranath Tagore (see TAGORE, DEVENDRANATH) and Keshav Chandra Sen (see SEN, KESHAV CHANDRA), leaders in the Brahma Samaj movement (see INDIA, III., 1), with whom he had long and earnest conversations. In 1874 he arrived in Bombay, and after some months of effective labor organized the Arya Samaj, Apr. 10, 1875, extending it in 1877 in the course of a lecture tour in the Punjab. In 1883 he visited the Maharaja of Jodhpur. There he was greatly disturbed by the revelry and dissipation that marked the court life, and like John the Baptist rebuked the Maharaja to his face, as a consequence of which he was poisoned by a woman whom he had offended by his rebuke.

Dayanand Saraswati taught the inspiration of the Vedas as the pure fountain of all true knowledge. He looked upon the forms of popular Hinduism as the result of ignorance through a falling away from the teachings of those books. He taught the personality of God as the sole object of worship. God and the soul are related as pervader and pervaded. The eternal and distinct substances are God, soul, and matter; salvation is the state of emancipation from birth to death. He denounced the system of caste and the worship of idols.

JUSTIN E. ABBOTT.

BIBLIOGRAPHY: Three of Dayanand's works have been translated: *The Ocean of Mercy*, Lahore, 1889; *The Five Great Duties of Dayanand Saraswati*, Ajmere, 1897, and *A Hand-book of the Arya Samaj*, Arya Tract Society, 1906. Consult: Arjan Singh, *Dayanand Saraswati*, Lahore, 1901; Bawa Chhajju Singh, *The Life and Teachings of Swam Dayanand Saraswati*, ib.; and literature under INDIA.

DEACON.

I. In the New Testament: The term "deacon" (Gk. *diakonos*, "servant, attendant, minister," Lat. *diaconus;* also Gk. *diakōn*, Lat. *diacones* [pl.]

in Cyprian and synodical decrees) in its generic sense is used of all ministers of the Gospel as servants of God or Christ (I Thess. iii. 2; I Cor. iii. 5; II Cor. vi. 4, xi. 23; Col. i. 7, iv. 7; I Tim. iv. 6), also of magistrates (Rom. xiii. 4). In a technical sense it denotes the second and lower class of congregational officers, the other class being the presbyter-bishops. Deacons first appear in the sixth chapter of Acts (under the name of the "seven"), and afterward repeatedly (as Phil. i. 1; I Tim. iii. 2, 8, 12). The word *diakonia*, "ministry," is also used frequently of the apostles (Rom. xi. 13) and others.

1. Origin of the Diaconate.

Like the presbyterate (see PRESBYTER), the Christian diaconate had a precedent in the Jewish synagogue, which usually employed three officers for the care of the poor (cf. Lightfoot, *Horæ Hebraicæ*, ad Acta, vi. 3). Vitringa and some others wrongly derive it from the *ḥazzan* (Gk. *hypēretēs*, Luke iv. 20; John vii. 32), who was merely a sexton or beadle. As related in Acts vi. 1–6, the office grew out of a special emergency in the congregation of Jerusalem, in consequence of the complaint of the Hellenists, or Greek Jews, against the Hebrews, or Palestinian Jews, that their widows were neglected in the daily ministration (Gk. *diakonia*) at the common love-feasts (Agapæ). Hence the apostles, who had hitherto themselves attended to this duty, instructed the congregation to elect from their midst seven brethren, and ordained them by prayer and the laying on of hands. The diaconate, therefore, like the presbytero-episcopate, grew out of the apostolic office, which at first embraced all the functions and duties of the ministry—the ministry (*diakonia*) of tables and of the word (Acts vi. 2, 4). Christ chose apostles only, and left them to divide their labor under the guidance of his Spirit, with proper regard to times and circumstances, and to found such additional offices in the Church as were useful and necessary.

The "seven" elected on this occasion were not extraordinary commissioners or superintendents (Stanley, Plumptre, W. L. Alexander, McGiffert, pp. 78–79, Friedberg, p. 13, Sohm, and others), but deacons in the primitive sense of the term; for although they are not called "deacons" in the Acts (which never uses this word), their office is expressly described as one of "ministry" (*diakonia*) or "serving at the tables." Exegetical tradition is almost unanimously in favor of this view, and many of the best commentators sustain it (as Meyer, Alford, Hackett, Lange-Lechler, Jacobson, Howson and Spence, Stokes in the *Expositor's Bible*, on Acts vi. 3; also, very emphatically, Lightfoot, *Philippians*, pp. 185 sqq.). In the ancient Church the number seven was considered binding; and at Rome, for example, as late as the middle of the third century, there were only seven deacons, though the presbyters numbered forty-six (Eusebius, *Hist. eccl.*, vi. 43; Harnack, *TU*, ii., pp. 92, 97. The number seven was given up in Rome under Honorius II. [1124–30] and eighteen deacons were then appointed, to twelve of whom was given the care of the poor, while six served as papal assistants at the altar. Sixtus V. in 1586 finally fixed the number of cardinal deacons at fourteen). There is indeed a difference between the apostolic and the ecclesiastical deacons, which is acknowledged by Chrysostom, Œcumenius, and others; but the latter were universally regarded as the legitimate successors of the former—as much so as the presbyters were the successors of the presbyter-bishops of the New Testament—notwithstanding the changes in their duties and relations. The deacons in the Apostolic Age are closely associated with the presbyter-bishops and always are subordinate to them. This close association and subordination are maintained in the subapostolic age and later.

2. Duties in the New Testament Time.

The diaconate was instituted first for the care of the poor and the sick. But this care was spiritual as well as temporal, and implied instruction and consolation as well as bodily relief. Paul counts helps and ministrations (Gk. *antilēpseis*) among the spiritual gifts (I Cor. xii. 28). Hence the appointment of such men for the office of deacons as were of strong faith and exemplary piety (Acts vi. 3; I Tim. iii. 8 sqq.). The moral qualifications prescribed by Paul are essentially the same as those for the bishop (presbyter). Hence the transition from the diaconate to the presbyterate was easy and natural. Stephen preached, and prepared the way for Paul's ministry of the Gentiles; and Philip, another of the seven deacons ot Jerusalem, subsequently labored as an Evangelist (Acts viii. 5–40, xxi. 8). But they did this in the exercise of a special gift of preaching, which in the Apostolic Age was not confined to any particular office. The patristic interpreters understand the passage in I Tim. iii. 13 of promotion from the office of deacon to that of presbyter; but "the good standing" which is gained by those who "have served well as deacons" refers to the honor rather than to the promotion. The liberty of the Apostolic Church should not be confounded with the fixed ecclesiastical order of a later age.

II. In the Roman Catholic Church: After the departure of the apostles, during the mysterious period between 70 and 150 A.D., where information is so scant, that change in the ecclesiastical organization must have taken place which is found pretty generally established toward the close of the second century. The Didache knows only two classes of officers for the local churches, bishops and deacons;

1. Change in Position after the Apostolic Age.

they were to be elected by the congregations, and are to receive honor "together with the prophets and teachers" (xv. 1–2). Ignatius mentions deacons as a necessary part of the governing body of the local church. With him the bishops are raised above their fellow presbyters, and later they were regarded as successors of the apostles; the presbyters, at first simply pastors and teachers, were clothed with sacerdotal dignity ("priests"), which in the New Testament appears as the common property of all Christians; and the deacons became Levites, subject to the priests. They are often compared to the Levites of the Old Testament. These three officers constituted the three clerical orders (*ordines majores* or *hierarchici*) in distinction from the laity.

An act of ordination marked the entrance. No one could become a bishop without passing first through the two lower orders; but in some cases a distinguished layman, as Cyprian or Ambrose, was elected bishop by the voice of the people, and hurried through the three ordinations. The subdeacon was later associated with the deacon and was declared a member of the "major orders" by Innocent III. (1198–1216; cf. Friedberg, *Kirchenrecht*, p. 150; see ORDERS, HOLY). In fact, the Roman Catholic Church and the canon law have never formally decided whether the episcopate is a distinct order or not. The Council of Trent did not decide the question, although it speaks of the hierarchy of bishops, priests, and deacons (Schaff, *Creeds*, ii. 186–187). The schoolmen, including Peter Lombard (*Sent.*, IV. xxiv. 9), Hugo of St. Victor (*De sacramentis*, II. ii. 5), Thomas Aquinas (*Supplementum*, xxxvii. 2, ed. Migne, iv. 1056), and Bonaventura (*Breviloquium*, vi. 12, ed. Peltier, vii. 327), say again and again that the episcopate is not a distinct order, but an office or function. They regarded the presbyters, deacons, and subdeacons as constituting the three major orders. The prevailing view to-day in the Roman Catholic Church, if not the universal one (so Hergenröther, *Lehrbuch des katholischen Kirchenrechts*, pp. 208–209, Freiburg, 1888), is that the episcopate is a distinct order and that the subdeaconate is not.

2. Duties in the Later Church.

The deacons continued to be the almoners of the charitable funds of the congregation. Jerome calls them "ministers of the tables, and of widows." They had to find out and to visit the aged, the widows, the sick and afflicted, the confessors in prison, and to administer relief to them under the direction of the bishop. But in the course of time this primary function became secondary, or passed out of sight, as the sick and the poor were gathered together into hospitals and almshouses, the orphans into orphan asylums, and as each of these institutions was managed by an appropriate officer. Another duty became the prominent one—viz., to assist in public worship, especially at baptism and the holy communion. Justin Martyr (*Apol.*, lxv.; *ANF*, i. 185) says the deacons distributed the bread and wine at the Eucharist after they were blessed by the presiding officer, and also carried them to the sick. They arranged the altar, presented the offerings of the people, read the Gospel, gave the signal for the departure of the unbelievers and catechumens, recited some prayers, and distributed the consecrated cup (in the absence of the priest, the bread also), but were forbidden to offer the sacrifice. Preaching is occasionally mentioned among their privileges, after the examples of Stephen and Philip, but very rarely in the West. Hilary the Deacon (Pseudo-Ambrose), in his commentary on Eph. iv. 11, says that originally all the faithful preached and baptized, but that in his day the deacons did not preach. In some cases they were forbidden, in others authorized to preach. The *Pontificale Romanum*, however, defines their duties and privileges with the words "it is the duty of a deacon to minister at the altar, to baptize, and to preach." They stood near the bishops and presbyters, who were seated on their thrones in the church, and they were deputies and advisers of the bishops and often sent on confidential missions. This intimacy gave them an advantage and roused the jealousy of the presbyters. The Apostolic Constitutions (ii. 44; *ANF*, vii. 416) calls the deacon "the bishop's ear and eye and mouth and heart and soul, that the bishop may not be distracted with many cares." The archdeacon (q.v.) occupied a position little inferior to that of the bishop and hence he is called "the bishop's eye." He transacted the greater part of the business of the diocese. The canonical age for the deacon's order was set in 385 by Siricius, bishop of Rome, at thirty and later it was twenty-five, according to Num. viii. 24; the Council of Trent reduced it to twenty-three (Sess. xxiii. 12).

III. In the Protestant Churches: In the **Church of England** and the **Protestant Episcopal Church** of the United States deacons form one of the three sacred orders, as in the Greek and Roman churches. The canons require the age of twenty-three years before ordination. Deacons are permitted to perform any of the divine offices except pronouncing the formula of absolution and consecrating the elements of the Lord's Supper. In practise the diaconate is merely a stepping-stone to the priesthood. So the deacons are what in other churches are called candidates for the ministry or licentiates. The archdeacon in England is a priest and a permanent officer next after the bishop, with a part of the episcopal power and jurisdiction: he is *ex officio* examiner of candidates for holy orders, and has a seat in convocation. The institution dates from Lanfranc, archbishop of Canterbury, the first prelate who appointed an archdeacon in his diocese (1075).

In the **Lutheran** Church "diaconus" is merely a title, inherited from the Roman Church, of assistant clergymen and chaplains of subordinate rank. They are often called second or third preacher or pastor. Luther desired the restoration of the apostolic deacons for the care of the poor and the church property (*Works*, ed. Walch, xiii. 2464). In the last century the name, like the feminine form, "deaconess," was applied in Germany to members of certain fraternities, organized and trained for general Christian service (see IV., below, and the article DEACONESS, III.).

In the **Reformed** churches the apostolic diaconate was revived, as far as circumstances would permit, with different degrees of success. In the Reformation of the Church of Hesse (1526) it was prescribed that each pastor (*episcopus*) should have at least three deacons as assistants in the care of the poor. The Church of Basel in 1529 made a similar provision. Calvin regards the diaconate as one of the indispensable offices of the Church, and the care of the poor (*cura pauperum*) as their proper duty ("Institutes," bk. iv., chaps. 3, 9). The Reformed confessions acknowledge this office (*Conf. Gallicana*, art. xxix.; *Conf. Belgica*, art. xxx. and xxxi.). In the Dutch and German Reformed churches the deacons are "to collect and to distribute the alms and other contributions for the relief of the poor, or the necessities of the congregation, and to provide for the support of the ministry of the Gospel." The Presbyterian Church in the United States of America teaches, in its form of government (chap. vi.): "The Scriptures clearly point out deacons as distinct officers in the church, whose business it is to take care of the poor, and to distribute among them the collections which may be raised for their use. To them, also, may be properly committed the management of the temporal affairs of the church." [In accordance with this principle, deacons are a normal part of the machinery of the local churches and receive ordination, though they are not members of the church session (the governing body of the local church; see PRESBYTERIANS). The Reformed Presbyterian Church has held (1878) that the office is open to women, and in several presbyteries they have been ordained to this service.]

In the **Congregational** or **Independent** churches the deacons are very important officers, and take the place of the lay elders in the Presbyterian churches. At first the Pilgrim Fathers of New England elected ruling elders; but the custom went into disuse, and their duties were divided between the pastor and the deacons. Cf. H. M. Dexter, *Congregationalism of the Last Three Hundred Years*, Boston, 1876, pp. 131 sqq.

In the **Methodist Episcopal** Church the deacons constitute an order in the ministry, as in the Episcopal Church, but without the *jure divino* theory of apostolical succession. They are elected by the annual conference, and ordained by the bishop. Their duties are, "(1) To administer baptism, and to solemnize matrimony; (2) To assist the elder in administering the Lord's Supper; (3) To do all the duties of a traveling preacher." Traveling deacons must exercise their office for two years before they are eligible to the office of elder. Local deacons are eligible to the office of elder after preaching four years. (PHILIP SCHAFF†) D. S. SCHAFF.

IV. The Modern Associations of Deacons in Germany: Like the similar deaconesses' organizations (see DEACONESS, III.), these fraternities for Christian service are an outgrowth of the movement within the Protestant Church of Germany usually known as the "Innere Mission" (see INNERE MISSION). But this work, however much it might be regarded as incumbent on all, can not be so well done by untrained volunteers as by professional workers who devote their whole lives to it and receive the requisite special education. It was the "Innere Mission" which for the first time among German Protestants clearly perceived this truth and undertook to train such workers. The epoch-making dates are 1833, when the *Rauhes Haus* was founded for male workers, and 1836, when the first home for deaconesses was established at Kaiserswerth.

The *Rauhes Haus*, at Horn near Hamburg, was established by Johann Hinrich Wichern (q.v.) as a rescue-home for neglected children. The original foundation speedily expanded into a community, where the children dwelt in "families" or groups, each group constituting a unit for the purposes of moral, intellectual, and manual training. The "housefather" associated with himself in the administration of the work a number of assistants; and, as the work expanded and the number of institutions increased, the necessity arose of a normal training for the instructors. The *Rauhes Haus* became therefore a seminary for the training of workers in the field of the "Innere Mission," its early candidates coming almost exclusively from the humbler classes and comprising men whose simple piety and Christian spirit of self-sacrifice and devotion to duty qualified them admirably for this service. Wichern gave the name of "Brethren" to his first associates. In the execution of his wider plans he came into conflict with the authorities of the *Rauhes Haus* who regarded with mistrust the departure from the original idea of an institution for children, and he was finally allowed to proceed with his plans for a brotherhood only on condition that he should assume the financial risks of the venture. His devoted labors brought their reward; means were soon obtained for the establishment and maintenance of the fraternity which Wichern sought to organize on the model of the medieval Brothers of the Common Life so far as that was possible under modern conditions. He did not attempt to revive the office of deacon as it existed in the primitive Church, and only reluctantly did he assent to the use of the term "deacon," which to him connoted a person officially set apart by the Church, while "brother" bore a more secular and independent signification.

1. Johann Hinrich Wichern.

Wichern supplied the model upon which all later institutions of a similar nature have been founded, which differ from the original only in the general use of the name deacon, and in the wider scope of work which the necessities of other times produced. By the side of those institutions whose field embraced every phase of Christian charity, others arose devoted to particular branches of work. Thus in southwestern Germany there are institutions for the training of teachers for the poor, dating from the period of predominantly educational interest which saw the rise of the "Innere Mission." Further, there are associations for lay preaching and others whose special field lies among the German Protestants scattered in Catholic countries (see DIASPORA). The inner organization is practically the same everywhere, consisting of a clerical chief executive who exercises control over the educational and administrative work, and a *curatorium* or committee of trustees in whom the property of the institution is vested. Common also are the conditions for admission, of which a summary of the regulations prevailing in the *Rauhes Haus* may serve as an illustration. Applicants must be of unblemished reputation, and masters of some trade or profession upon which in case of emergency they may fall back; admission for the purpose of acquiring a trade or profession is not tolerated. Candidates must be between the ages of twenty and thirty, unmarried, and must have completed their term of military service. They must be prepared to yield absolute obedience

2. Extension of Wichern's Work. Conditions of Admission.

to the head of the house, submit to all tasks imposed upon them, and look upon their office not as a temporary calling, but as their mission in life. The course of training lasts three years, with an extension to five or six for those handicapped by a lack of the requisite educational qualifications, or preparing themselves for positions of responsibility in the service of the "Innere Mission." Candidates are not allowed to determine beforehand to which branch of the work they will devote themselves, and must be ready to pursue their work for a part of the time in affiliated institutions. The documents that must accompany applications for admission are comprehensive and deal minutely with the facts of the applicant's life and his moral and spiritual history, including the testimony of physicians, pastors, and parents or guardians. The greater number of candidates for admission are from the artisan and peasant classes.

The chief aim of the training to which candidates are subjected is the formation of steadfast Christian character, and in this respect the relations of the head of the house toward his associates and assistants are among the most decisive factors. The standard of intellectual acquirements set up is approximately that of the elementary school teacher or lower government official. In addition, however, there is the special knowledge of the main principles of pedagogy and of the history of education, studied chiefly in the form of biography, together with a mastery of catechetical methods.

3. Training.

The specialization of function must also be kept in view so that the needs of the future colporteur, instructor for the feeble-minded, or elementary teacher may be provided for. The problem presented is by no means a simple one, in that it involves the training of students possessing the education of the child with the experience of the youth or the full-grown man. Practical work is carried on side by side with theory, and every house of deacons stands in close connection with one or more relief institutions—rescue-homes, hospitals, asylums for the feeble-minded, homes for epileptics, etc. An important element is the religious life of the brotherhoods. Some satisfy their needs by attendance at the churches of the community of which they form a part, while others possess chapels of their own. The training of a brother once completed, he is detailed to outside duty, his graduation and dismissal being marked by a solemn service. The regulations of the *Rauhes Haus*, which may be taken again as typical, provide that on the acceptance by a brother of an office to which he is recommended by the head of the house he is pledged to render conscientious service and not to abandon his post without seeking the advice of the head of the house; failure to do so will exclude him from further appointment. A brother who abandons the service of the "Innere Mission" ceases thereby to be a member of the fraternity. From the foregoing it is apparent that the brotherhoods possess their spiritual center in the deacons' houses. The truth is briefly expressed in the following summary from the regulations of the *Rauhes Haus*: "The brethren of the *Rauhes Haus* are gathered in fraternal communion about the *Rauhes Haus* as a center, and their aim is to come to the aid of the community by devoting themselves to the welfare of those who have been estranged from the Church and its teachings. In belief and practise they live within the bounds of the Evangelical Church, to whose ordinances they submit themselves."

While the problem of the cooperation and communication is not a serious one with the minor fraternities, it is a weighty one in the case of the *Rauhes Haus*, whose branches are found in all parts of Germany.

4. Organization. Wide Extent of the Work.

Here conferences embracing the organizations of the various provinces are held every year, in addition to which special conferences and general conventions are held from time to time at the *Rauhes Haus*. With regard to their spheres of activity, every house has its special field. At the *Rauhes Haus* special emphasis was laid in the beginning upon rescue work; Duisburg devoted itself primarily to the care of the sick; the summoning of Wichern to Berlin led to the rapid rise of mission work in the prisons. From many deacons' houses members have been called to positions as colonial and home missionaries, superintendents of labor colonies, heads of other houses, etc. A complete list of institutions wherein the members of the brotherhoods have been active would include rescue-homes, orphan asylums, homes for destitute children, workhouses, hospitals, asylums for the feeble-minded, the insane, and the epileptic, industrial schools, apprentices' lodging-houses, city and harbor missions, penal institutions, and institutes for the cure of alcoholism. (Theodor Schäfer.)

Bibliography: I. J. B. Lightfoot, *Commentary on Philippians*, pp. 179 sqq., London, 1878; E. Hatch, *Organisation of the Early Christian Church*, pp. 25 sqq., Oxford, 1888 (the preceding are the two authoritative discussions); R. Sohm, *Kirchenrecht*, Leipsic, 1892; F. J. A. Hort, *Christian Ecclesia*, London, 1897; A. C. McGiffert, *Apostolic Age*, pp. 76–77, 667 sqq., New York, 1897; T. M. Lindsay, *Church and the Ministry in the Early Centuries*, pp. 154-155, 194–195, London, 1902; W. Lowrie, *The Church and its Organisation*, pp. 370–383, ib. 1905; Schaff, *Christian Church*, i. 59 sqq.; A. Harnack, in *TU*, ii. 5, pp. 57–103, 1886; *DB*, i. 574–575; *EB*, i. 1038–40; and the various treatises on the *Didache* (q.v.).

II. and III. J. N. Seidl, *Der Diaconat in der katholischen Kirche*, Regensburg, 1884; A. J. Binterim, *Denkwürdigkeiten*, i. 335–386, Mainz, 1825; J. C. W. Augusti, *Denkwürdigkeiten*, xi. 194 sqq., Leipsic, 1830; Bingham, *Origines*, book ii., chap. 20; *DCA*, i. 526–533; *KL*, iii. 1660-1674; and for modern practise, the *Book of Discipline* of the various denominations.

IV. Important sources of knowledge are the *Monatsschrift für Diakonie und Innere Mission*, and *Monatsschrift für Innere Mission*; also *Aktenstücke aus der Verwaltung des evangelischen Oberkirchenraths*, vols. iii.–iv., Berlin, 1856–57 (contain accounts of Fliedner, Wichern, Jakobi, and others prominent in the movement). Consult: P. Schaff, *Germany, its Universities, Theology and Religion*, chap. xxxviii., Philadelphia, 1857; J. Wichern, *Das Rauhe Haus und die Arbeitsfelder der Brüder des Rauhen Hauses, 1833–83*, Hamburg, 1883; idem, *J. H. Wichern und die Brüderschaft des Rauhen Hauses*, ib. 1892; G. Uhlhorn, *Die christliche Liebesthätigkeit*, iii. 347 sqq., 365 sqq., Stuttgart, 1890.

DEACONESS.

I. In the Apostolic Age: The function dates from the earliest period of the Church, though the technical term in the feminine form, "deaconess" (Gk. *diakonissa;* Lat. *diaconissa, diacona*), does not occur till a later period. Phœbe was a deaconess in the church of Cenchrea, the masculine form, *diakonos*, being applied to her (Rom. xvi. 1; transl. "servant" in Eng. versions). The women whose names are given in Rom. xvi. 12 were probably of the same class. It is not probable that there was a distinct order of deaconesses in the Apostolic Church in the modern sense. Nevertheless, Paul's mode of referring to Phœbe implies that she was recognized at Cenchrea and by himself as having a special work and authority. It is possible that deaconesses are referred to in I Tim. iii. 11. If so, they were distinguished from the "widows" (I Tim. v. 3–16), who were not to be enrolled in that class till they had reached sixty years of age. From the earliest times the need must have been felt of a special class of women who should devote themselves to Christian service at times of baptism, visit the parts of the houses set aside for females, and perform other duties. While Phœbe is the only person in the New Testament distinctly called a deaconess, there are indications, as in the case of Dorcas (Acts ix. 36) and other cases, that woman's service was held in high esteem by the Church and had a distinctive character.

II. In the Patristic Age: The earliest reference in the subapostolic age to women functionaries in the Church is by the younger Pliny in his letter (x. 96) to Trajan about 110 A.D. He speaks of "young women who are called *ministræ*"; that is, "deaconesses." The notices in the literature of the second and third centuries are very rare before the Apostolic Constitutions, which contain frequent references to both the widows and deaconesses and directions for their work and induction into office. When the Apostolic Constitutions were written the widows and deaconesses were distinct bodies (ii. 26; *ANF*, vii. 410), and the widows occupied a position inferior to the deaconesses and are enjoined to be in subjection to them (iii. 7). Different rules are given for the consecration of each (vii. 19, 25). On the one hand, it is not clear that in the second century this distinction was maintained. On the other hand, it is clear that in the fourth century the order of widows was abandoned, while the order and term of deaconesses remained. The Council of Nicæa (325) speaks only of "deaconesses." The Council of Orléans (533) speaks of the "widows who are called deaconesses."

1. Deaconesses and Widows.

In the literature of the second century, with the exception of the passage in Pliny, there is no reference to the deaconess by name and no distinct reference to any class but the widows. When Tertullian, at the beginning of the third century, speaks of "virgins" and distinguishes them from the "widows" (*De virginibus velandis*, ix.; *De monogamia*, xi.; etc.) he does not seem to have in mind a class of functionaries in the Church. Ignatius in his letter to Symrna (xiii.; cf. Lightfoot, ii. 322 sqq.) speaks of "virgins who are called widows," and Polycarp in his letter to the Philippians (iv.; Lightfoot, ii. 912) calls "the prudent widows" the altar of God. This expression, which is also used in the Apostolic Constitutions (ii. 26), was interpreted to mean that the women devoted themselves to prayer and holy thoughts. Polycarp is speaking of widows in their official relation, as he mentions them before deacons and priests. At the beginning of the third century the institution of widows seems to have been widely prevalent. Clement (*Hom.*, xi. 36, *Recognitiones*, xv.) and Tertullian refer to them repeatedly. Lucian in his "Death of Peregrinus" also speaks of aged widows who ministered to Peregrinus in prison, bringing orphans with them. But a change took place and in the middle of the third century the "widows" at Rome were simply a class of poor women dependent upon the support of the Church (Eusebius, *Hist. eccl.*, VI. xliii. 11).

While the order of widows was given up in the West, it continued to flourish in the East. But they can not be followed beyond the time of composition of the Apostolic Constitutions. The term "widow" seems to have been dropped. On the other hand, the deaconess comes into prominence and is mentioned in the conciliar decisions of the East and the West and in the legislation of Justinian (*Novellæ*, vi. 6, cxxiii. 30; cf. G. Pfannmüller, *Die kirchliche Gesetzgebung Justinians*, Berlin, 1902, pp. 72 sqq.). In the West, Ambrose, commenting upon I Tim. iii. 11, declared that women were forbidden to hold office in the Church, and Jerome in commenting upon Rom. xvi. 1 and I Tim. iii. 11 (the quotations are given by Uhlhorn, p. 408) speaks of women functionaries as still existing in the East and gives the impression that they had ceased to exist in the West. However, there seem to have been deaconesses in Gaul as late as the sixth century, as attested by the Second Council of Orléans in 533. An inscription at Ticinum, dated 539, bears the name of the "deaconess (*diaconissa*) Theodora" (Uhlhorn, p. 409). Deaconesses continued in the Eastern Church down to the eighth century. The terms "deaconess" and "archdeaconess" were used as designations of the officers in convents and they are still found in the twelfth century at Constantinople aiding in the communion.

The reason why the orders of widows and deaconesses fell into desuetude is in part the abuses of the Montanists, who allowed women to preach, while Montanus himself went about with two women, a thing which gave much scandal. Some of the heretics, following Simon Magus, were mixed up with prophetesses who were supposed to be subjects of revelation and taught contrary to the teaching of Paul. Other reasons were the moral dangers besetting such women. Rules were required distinctly forbidding clerics of the lower orders to visit widows and deaconesses without special permission from the bishop or priest and then not without an attendant (Synod of Hippo, 393; cf. Hefele, *Conciliengeschichte*, ii. 58). Still other reasons were the growth of monastic houses for nuns which offered a safe refuge as well as a distinct religious and clerical calling for women, and the cessation of the need of female ministries after adult baptism gave way to infant baptism.

The age at which women might enter the class of widows was reduced from sixty (*Apostolic Constitutions*, iii. 1). Tertullian (*De virginibus velandis*, ix.) tells of a virgin who had been admitted into the order of widowhood at the age of twenty, but speaks of it as a notorious irregularity. The Theodosian code of 390 (cf. Hefele, ut sup., ii. 519) required obedience to the Pauline rule requiring the age of sixty. As for the

2. Age.

deaconesses, the Council of Chalcedon (451; canon xv.; cf. Hefele, ut sup.) allowed their consecration at the age of forty, but only after probation. The Justinian code (*Novellæ*, cxxiii. 13) likewise prescribed the age of forty. In case a deaconess married, both she and her husband were to be anathematized. According to the Justinian code, if she married or allowed herself to be seduced, she became liable to the death penalty and the man suffered death by the sword (Pfannmüller, ut sup., p. 72). Olympias (d. 420), the deaconess of Constantinople praised by Chrysostom and to whom he addressed seventeen letters, became a widow at eighteen and seems to have immediately entered upon diaconal functions.

The statement of the Apostolic Constitutions (iii. 15) is regulative of the functions of these women: "A deaconess is to be ordained for the ministrations toward women." She is called the assistant or minister of the deacon (viii. 28). She was to be sent to do certain services for which it was distinctly ordered that the deacon should not be sent (iii. 15). At baptism she assisted the presbyter "for the sake of decency" (viii. 28). The bishop was instructed to anoint only the head of a

3. Duties.

woman and the anointing of the other parts was left to the deaconess (iii. 15). A change, however, took place and this custom was deliberately set aside. The Synod of Dovin in Armenia (527; Hefele, ut sup., p. 718) forbade the ministry of deaconesses at baptism. The prohibition probably grew out of the unwillingness to allow to women even the appearance of performing clerical services. Tertullian (*De baptismo*, xvii.) allowed laymen to baptize, but expressly forbade women both to baptize and to teach. The Apostolic Constitutions (iii. 9; also Origen, Homily on Isa. vi.) state expressly that deaconesses were not to serve at the altar, and forbid them to teach and baptize or in any wise perform the functions of the priest. Another duty of the deaconess was to stand at the entrance to the church through which the women passed to their own place in the auditorium to greet those that entered, to show them seats, and to preserve order (*Apostolic Constitutions*, ii. 57).

Roman Catholic scholars in interpreting the patristic statements on the induction of the deaconess into office deny that there was any rite of ordination. This interpretation has plainly in its favor the nineteenth canon of the Council of Nicæa (Hefele, ut sup., i. 427), which distinctly states that "the deaconesses are without any imposition of hands and are to be ranked with the laity." The Synod of Laodicea, a generation or two later, which speaks of *presbutides* and *prokathēmenai*, that is, female presbytids (not presbyters; cf. Epiphanius, lxxix.) and overseers, seems to deny them official position in the Church, but the meaning of the passage is vague (cf. Hefele, i. 757). On the other hand, there are plain statements that a rite of ordination was performed. There was an imposition of hands (Epiphanius, ut sup.), and such imposition was made by the hands of

4. Ordination.

the bishop and in the presence of the presbytery, the deacons, and those already belonging to the order of deaconesses (*Apostolic Constitutions*, viii. 19). The code of Justinian treats of their ordination (cf. Pfannmüller, ut sup., p. 72). The form of prayer used on such occasions is given in the Apostolic Constitutions (viii. 20). The Synod of Orange in 441 (canon xxvi.; Hefele, ii. 295) forbade the further ordination of women and allowed them only the consecration imparted to the laity. By the Synod of Epao in 317 (Hefele, ii. 684) such ordination was forbidden in all Burgundy. Similarly the Second Synod of Orléans in 533 (Hefele, ii. 758) denied to women "on account of the weakness of their sex" the diaconal benediction. This would seem to have been of the same nature as ordination to the diaconate. During the Middle Ages the heretical sects ordained deaconesses (cf. Döllinger, i. 186, 203, and elsewhere).

III. In the Protestant Churches.—1. The Earlier Period: The Reformers made no provision for the official recognition of women as functionaries in the Church. Among the rare notices of deaconesses are those in connection with the Church of Wesel from 1575 to 1610 and the Puritan church of Amsterdam. One of the first acts of the Church of Wesel was to decide to employ women. After long delay the Synod of Middelburg in 1581 pronounced against the proposition "on account of various inconveniences which might arise out of it, but in times of pestilence and other sicknesses where any service is required among sick women which would be indelicate to deacons they ought to attend to this through their wives or others whose services it may be proper to engage." The conclusions drawn up by Thomas Cartwright (q.v.) and Walter Travers as the result of several confessions of Puritan ministers in 1575 contained a clause "touching deacons of both sorts, namely men and women." Both were to be chosen by the congregation and "to be received into their office with the general prayers of the whole Church" (cf. D. Neal, *History of the Puritans*, i., New York, 1855, p. 140). In Gov. Bradford's *Dialogue* it is stated that there was one deaconess "who visited the sick, relieved the poor, and sat in a convenient place in the congregation, with a little birchen rod in her hand, and kept little children in great awe from disturbing the congregation. She did frequently visit the sick and weak, especially women, and if there were poor she would gather relief for them of those that were able, or acquaint the deacons, and she was obeyed as a mother in Israel and an officer of Christ" (A. Young, *Chronicles of the Pilgrim Fathers*, Boston, 1841, pp. 445–446). Early American Congregationalism recognized the office and ordered the "ancient widows (where they may be had) to minister in the Church, in giving attendance to the sick, and to give succor unto them, and others in the like necessities" (*Cambridge Platform*, 1648, vii. 7). This theory was not put in practise (cf. W. Walker, *History of the Congregational Churches in the United States*, New York, 1894, p. 230). The Mennonites of Holland seem to have had the custom of appointing deaconesses to serve among the sick and poor and do other Christian and charitable work.

2. The Nineteenth Century: No more important feature characterizes the recent history of Protestantism than the development of woman's public activity in the Church. Woman's work among women and for women in the various missionary organizations and in other bodies is in the direct line of the diaconal work of Phœbe and other female "helpers" of the early Church. Some of the Protestant bodies have given official recognition to the vocation of the congregational deaconess in one form or another, without, however, sanctioning an order of deaconesses in the sense that the order of deacons is sanctioned. It is difficult to make a sharp distinction when an ecclesiastical body commends training-schools for deaconesses and yet denies their election and setting apart to their office by the individual congregation.

a. Germany: The organization and official training of women for Christian work in the Protestant Churches were developed in the early half of the nineteenth century, and found their first embodiment in the institution of deaconesses founded by Pastor Theodor Fliedner (q.v.), which has been the model for similar organizations throughout the Protestant world. This institution was founded in 1836 at Kaiserswerth on the Rhine, near Düsseldorf. Fliedner was not moved in the first instance by the pious idea of reviving the apostolic order of female helpers, although he believed it to have been in existence in primitive times. He was animated by practical considerations to meet a pressing need of his day, the proper care of the sick and the training of neglected children. A feeling existed in certain pious German circles that the Church needed an

1. Origin. Theodor Fliedner.

order of trained women, similar to the sisterhoods of the Roman Catholic Church. This feeling found expression in a pamphlet published by Pastor Klönne of Bislich near Wesel in 1820, entitled "The Revival of the Deaconesses of the Ancient Church in our Ladies Societies." In 1835 the pious Count Adalbert von der Recke-Volmerstein began the publication of a periodical "Deaconesses, or Life and Labors of the Handmaids of the Church in Teaching and Training and in Nursing the Sick." It was Fliedner, however, who gave practical embodiment to this feeling. Before 1836, on his visits to Holland in 1823 and 1832, he was struck with the employment of deaconesses among the Mennonites. They were appointed by the official boards of the churches and did their work without remuneration. In his description of his experiences in Holland he wrote: "This praiseworthy early Christian institution of deaconesses should be revived by other Protestant communions." He was also struck, on his visit in England in 1832, with the contrast between the fine architecture of the hospital buildings and the incompetency of the attendants within. Impressed by the need of trained women, after these visits he prepared a constitution for "the Order of Deaconesses for the Rhenish Provinces," which was signed in the house of Count Stolberg at Düsseldorf, 1836. In October of the same year the first deaconess, Gertrud Reichard, entered the Institute. Two years later it sent the first deaconesses to the city hospital of Elberfeld.

The Institute has grown to large proportions. It educates three kinds of deaconesses. The first class devote themselves to the care of the sick, the poor, and the fallen in Magdalen asylums. The second dedicate themselves to teaching; the third class aid ministers in parish-work. The fundamental conditions of admission are Christian character and a strong constitution. Other rules are that candidates must be of suitable age, must be unmarried or widows, and must consecrate themselves for five years to the office. Candidates are accepted on probation for a year. The Kaiserswerth deaconesses take no vows, wear no crucifixes, and are distinguished by a simple and distinctive, but not necessarily uniform, dress. The internal organization of the houses comprises as a rule a clergyman as rector and chaplain, assisted by a woman superior, of whom the former exercises general administrative control, while the more intimate details of domestic economy are in the hands of the sister superior. In a few institutions the influence of Roman Catholic models may be discerned in that the clergyman acts only in the capacity of spiritual adviser to the sisterhood. The Kaiserswerth institutions lay stress upon their form of organization. The time of training lasts from two to six years according to the attainments of the women on entering the Institute and according to their aptness. The instruction includes a thorough course of training in Biblical knowledge. At the close of the term of preparation the deaconesses are consecrated by a fitting ritual and with the laying on

2. The Kaiserswerth Institute.

of hands, and promise obedience and fidelity in their work.*

The Kaiserswerth Institute supplies not only many hospitals, orphanages, and other establishments in Germany with deaconesses, but has under its control hospitals in foreign lands, e.g., in Jerusalem (founded 1851), Constantinople (1852), Smyrna (1853), Alexandria (1857), Florence (1860), Cairo, etc.

3. Other Institutions.

In 1861, at the twenty-fifth anniversary of the Kaiserswerth Institute, the number of daughter institutions in Germany, Austria, Bohemia, Hungary, Holland, France, England, Scandinavia, Italy, and the United States was twenty-seven. Among the earlier ones were the home in Paris (1841), St. Loup near Lausanne (1841), Strasburg (1842), Dresden and Utrecht (1844), Bern, and Bethany in Berlin (1845), Stockholm (1849), Riehen near Basel (1852), Stuttgart (1854), St. Petersburg (1859), Copenhagen (1863). In 1904 there were in Germany forty-six institutions connected with the Kaiserswerth mother house. The yearly expenditure of the mother house averages 700,000 marks. A triennial conference of homes has been instituted. Many institutions have become members of the association which are not the direct daughters of the Fliedner mother house, for example the Milwaukee Lutheran Deaconesses' home. In 1905 the conference included seventy-five institutions with 14,501 deaconesses.

Independent deaconesses' institutions have also been founded in different cities of Germany which have adopted the Kaiserswerth idea, e.g., the Elizabeth hospital and Deaconesses' home in Berlin founded by Gossner in 1840; Sarepta in Bielefeld (1860), where the eminent philanthropist Friedrich von Bodelschwingh assumed the superintendency in 1872; in Neuendettelsau by the philanthropist Wilhelm Löhe (1854); Stuttgart (1865); Altona (1867); etc. The Moravians established one at Niesky in 1842. The Methodists of Germany agitated the matter in the sixties and in 1876 opened their first house at Frankfort and then in Berlin (1883), Hamburg (1886), Magdeburg, Munich, Vienna, Strasburg, Zurich, and other cities. They also have a home in Gothenburg, Sweden, founded 1900. The Evangelical Association in Germany has homes at Berlin (1887), Hamburg (1888), Strasburg (1889), Elberfeld (1890), Stuttgart (1896), and Carlsruhe (1900). The German Baptists have the deaconesses' home, Bethel, in Berlin (1887).

b. **England:** The influence of Kaiserswerth upon the Protestant Churches of England and Scotland resulted in a general discussion of the subject of deaconesses and in the establishment of deaconesses' institutions. With Elizabeth Fry and Florence Nightingale (qq.v.) the permanent efforts at organization may be said to have begun, and they came under the immediate influence of Pastor Fliedner and the Kaiserswerth work. Miss Nightingale went through a thorough course of training at Kaiserswerth before taking charge of the female sanitarium in London, and Mrs. Fry, after a visit to the German town, established the first English institution for the training of nurses in London in 1840. In 1846 Fliedner brought four deaconesses to the German hospital in London.

A new development was furnished in the sisterhoods established within the pale of the Anglican Church. These were due in some measure to the Anglo-Catholic movement led by Pusey and the Tractarians, and it is not improbable that with the high reverence which this party had for Roman Catholic institutions they would have established sisterhoods even if the deaconess movement had not gone before.

1. Sisterhoods.

The first Protestant sisterhood was established or consecrated by Dr. Pusey in 1847 in Park Village near London. The same year

* More detailed information is given in the article *Diakonen- und Diakonissenhäuser* by Theodor Schäfer in the Hauck-Herzog *RE* as follows:

The conditions for admission are the same to the minutest degree for all establishments, and an extract from those of the house at Altona may serve as an example. The future deaconess must be of unblemished reputation, and is required to offer evidence of the facts of her life and her relations to family, employers, and all others under whose authority or influence she may have come. Sound health is a requirement, but it is recognized that women of slight physical constitution have shown themselves capable of excellent service in charitable work. Eighteen and thirty-six are set as the age-limits, but the rule may be waived in exceptional cases. Candidates are supposed to possess a common school education, and it is desirable that they shall have had some experience in housework. The documents to be submitted in applying for admission comprise a short autobiography of some minuteness, evidence of permission granted by parents or guardians, a testimonial of moral character supplied by the applicant's pastor, medical, baptismal, and confirmation certificates. Statistics have shown that the great bulk of candidates come from the peasant and artisan classes and the class of small officials, but large numbers, too, are the children of clergymen, professors and teachers, merchants, and landed proprietors.

Successful applicants are retained conditionally for a few weeks, after which they enter upon a year of actual probation. During this year the neophyte is brought to a thorough understanding of the conditions confronting her in her future calling, the chief object being to discern the existence of inclination and adaptability for the work. In most houses the hospital is the first and most important school of practise. Parallel with practise in the hospital runs theoretical instruction under the direction of the head physician. Where necessary, instruction is given also in elementary subjects. The religious side is not neglected; in many institutions a few hours are devoted every week to religious instruction in which as many of the younger sisters as can be spared from their daily work participate. Under the head of religious instruction is included instruction in the theory and history of charitable work, while the religious factor proper is supplied by a study of Bible history and geography, church history, the catechism, and the liturgy.

After the completion of the probationary year the candidate is admitted to the novitiate, and after a further training, ranging from two to six years, there follows the dedication. In this the deaconess promises obedience, faithfulness, and devotion in her chosen calling and to remain in it so long as it shall please the Lord to allow her. This is not a vow such as is taken in the Roman Catholic orders. From the day of her dedication the neophyte has full rights of membership in the sisterhood. She has become the daughter of the house which is to be her actual home through life, her guide, and her provider in sickness and in old age. Long before her dedication, the future deaconess may be despatched on service to any post which the authorities of her house may select; and such service is in fact a part of her preparation. She is never assigned to any permanent position, but is subject to whatever arrangements the sisterhood may make for her services. Marriage is not allowed for practical reasons purely. The list of institutions wherein the deaconesses have been active includes hospitals, poorhouses, orphan asylums, elementary schools, industrial schools, rescue-homes, homes for fallen women, and prisons.

Priscilla Lydia Sellon organized the Sisterhood of Mercy at Devonport, binding herself with three other ladies to an association for the relief of the sufferings of the poor. They adopted a uniform dress, the use of the cross, etc. They founded at Devonport a house of destitute children, a "House of Peace" for older girls, and an industrial school. Miss Sellon was addressed as mother superior. Since then many sisterhoods with various names have been founded in the Church of England, e.g., the Sisterhood of St. John the Baptist at Clewer, founded in 1849, which devoted itself more especially to the reformation of fallen women. The difference between the sisterhoods of the Church of England and the order of deaconesses consists in this, that the sisterhood leans in its organization to the convent as its model. The sisters take vows, live strictly in communities, acknowledge a mother superior, and often find refuge in the sisterhood for the sake of pious devotion more than for philanthropic activity.

The deaconess idea as carried out at Kaiserswerth was formally commended by Dr. Tait, then bishop of London, in his charge May 2, 1850. From 1858 to 1871 woman's work was the subject of animated discussion in the convocation of Canterbury. In 1861 Bishop Tait invested Elizabeth Catherine Ferard (d. 1883) with the office of deaconess, and it was generally regarded as a revival of the apostolic office. Miss Ferard had been trained at Kaiserswerth and with the aid of Dean Champneys and others opened the deaconesses' institution of North London, a diocesan institution founded on the Kaiserswerth model. In 1871 rules were laid down for diocesan deaconesses' homes and signed by the archbishop of Canterbury and eighteen bishops. The first principle sets forth "that a deaconess is a woman set apart by the bishop under that title for service in the Church. She is at liberty to resign her commission as deaconess or may be deprived of it by the bishop." She was to be an auxiliary to the pastorate, and not a conventual. Dean Howson contended for this idea and he saw it prevail. The institution was taken up as a diocesan matter and in 1904 there were deaconesses' homes in the dioceses of Canterbury, Chester, Ely, London, Salisbury, Winchester, Llandaff, Exeter, and Rochester. There are also deaconesses' institutions in Lichfield, Durham, and Worcester. The Mildmay institutions with the deaconesses' home as the center were due to the zeal and organizing power of William Pennefather, an English clergyman. The beginning was made at Barnet in 1860, and the institutions moved to Mildmay in 1864. The deaconesses' department has three branches, medical work, parish work, and foreign mission work. The Institution has stations in Malta, Jamaica, and Hebron. While the Mildmay institutions were founded by Anglicans, they are not intended to be strictly denominational. The only mother house in England belonging to the Kaiserswerth group is Tottenham, North London, founded in 1877 by Dr. Michael Laseron, a converted Jew, and his wife, and aided by Samuel Morley with a gift of £7,000. Dr. Laseron was very successful in training deaconesses. The institution supplies a number of hospitals, including one in Sierra Leone.

2. Deaconesses in the Church of England.

The Wesleyans of England have been active in promoting the work of the deaconess. In 1888 the Rev. Hugh Price Hughes (q.v.) formed an organization called "The Sisters of the People" with a home near the British Museum, named Catherine House after his wife; in 1891 it was removed to larger quarters in Viceroy Street. The sisters do all kinds of mission work, visit the poor, conduct midnight missions, teach in kindergartens, etc. The Wesleyan Deaconesses' Institution was founded in 1890 by the Rev. T. B. Stevenson, and has two training-schools, Newburn House, London, N. E., and Calvert House, at Leicester. The deaconesses are stationed in all parts of England and are employed chiefly in parish work. The institution has stations in New Zealand, South Africa, and Ceylon. There are three departments of work contemplated by the training: the teaching and care of children, nursing the sick, and home and foreign mission work. The training includes Biblical and medical instruction, and lasts a year. The Institution was formally adopted by the Wesleyan Conference in 1902. The following extract from an official report gives an idea of the Wesleyan conception of the deaconess and her work:

3. Wesleyan Deaconesses.

> What is a Wesleyan deaconess? One who belongs to the Order so-called, governed by the Council, and sanctioned by the Wesleyan Methodist Church. But her work is not sectarian, and she may by arrangement serve other than Methodist churches. . . . The work of the deaconess is anything that the cause of Christ and the poor demand. She is nurse, teacher, visitor, even preacher when necessary. She is a helper in sorrow and a rescuer from all sin. Her work varies in every locality.

c. **Scotland:** Fliedner visited Scotland in 1846 and met Chalmers. In 1886 the Church of Scotland took the matter of deaconesses' work seriously in hand, and in 1887 the Assembly commended the establishment of deaconesses' training-schools and more especially the Edinburgh House, a home for deaconesses established the same year. Dr. Archibald H. Charteris was the most influential person in bringing about this consummation. St. Ninian's Hospital is connected with the home. The first deaconess was installed in office Dec. 9, 1888. The work is incorporated in the constitution of the Established Church, which not only commended the training of deaconesses, but established rules for their admission, garb, etc.

d. **America:** Practically all denominations in the United States have adopted in one form or another the special training of women for Christian work. Some have made the work of the deaconess a part of their constitution, or have officially recognized the deaconess as a local church official or functionary appointed by the local church. The fathers of the deaconess movement in the United States were the Rev. W. A. Passavant and the Rev. W. A. Muhlenberg (qq.v.), the former a Lutheran, the latter an Episcopalian of Lutheran birth. The Lutheran Church first recognized the Kaiserswerth movement. At the age of twenty-four Dr. Passavant was sent as a delegate to the meeting in London in 1846 which resulted in the foundation of the Evangelical Alliance, and he afterward visited Kaiserswerth. In his annual report of Jan. 1, 1847, Fliedner said, "We have been urgently requested to send deaconesses from here to North America." In 1849 he accompanied four deaconesses to Pittsburg, where they were stationed in a hospital already opened by Dr. Passavant and dedicated July 17, 1849, Fliedner being present. On May 28, 1850, the first American deaconess, Katherine Louisa Marthens, trained under Dr. Passavant, was consecrated (cf. Späth, p. 25). Dr. Passavant was not successful in building up a permanent deaconesses' home in Pittsburg, and the enterprise was given up because women did not come forward for the work and for other reasons. The Passavant hospital in Pittsburg still employs deaconesses, as do the affiliated institutions for epileptics in Rochester, N. Y., and for orphans at Zelienople, Pa. The hospital at Jacksonville, Ill., formerly employed them. The Mary J. Drexel Home in Philadelphia, opened in 1888, is a Lutheran institution and occupies the finest building consecrated to deaconesses' work in America. It was founded by Dr. Lankenau as a memorial to his wife, and associated with the German Lutheran hospital of Philadelphia, of which Dr. Lankenau was treasurer. This deaconesses' home was started in 1884. In 1894 it was brought into organic relation with the Lutheran Church and joined the group of the Kaiserswerth institutions. The deaconesses labor in kindergartens and hospitals and in parish work. The Milwaukee Deaconesses' Home was established in 1891, Dr. Passavant having founded a hospital in that city in 1863, of which his son, the Rev. R. W. Passavant, was made director in 1900, but lived less than a year to administer the office. There are other Lutheran deaconesses' homes connected with the various branches of American Lutheranism:—in Baltimore (founded 1895), Omaha (Swedish, 1887), Brooklyn (founded by Mrs. Boers, wife of the Norwegian consul, 1883), Minneapolis (Norwegian, 1888), Chicago (1900), Buffalo, and St. Paul. In most cases, if not in all, these institutions were organized with the aid of one or more deaconesses from Germany or Scandinavia. In 1905 the Mary J. Drexel, Milwaukee, and Omaha houses had respectively 47, 19, and 22 deaconesses, and 25, 13, and 15 probationers. The sixth annual conference of the "Evangelical Lutheran Deaconesses' Motherhouses in the United States" was held in Milwaukee in 1905.

1. The Lutherans.

The Protestant Episcopal Church followed the Lutherans in the deaconesses' work in America. In 1843 Rev. W. A. Muhlenberg, then rector of the Church of the Holy Communion, New York city, organized a sisterhood, which, however, was not formally constituted till 1852, when a house was erected adjoining the church. A dispensary was started and developed into St. Luke's Hospital. The second organization was the Sisterhood of the Good Shepherd in Baltimore, formed into a community in 1863, but its history dates back to 1855, when, with the approval of the bishop of the diocese, the Rev. Horace Stringfellow of St. Andrew's Church inaugurated the movement. A sister superior stands at the head of the community. The Sisterhood of St. Mary in New York was founded in 1865, five sisters being consecrated to their work Feb. 2, by the bishop of the diocese in St. Michael's Church. The sisters take vows and none but members of the Protestant Episcopal Church are admitted to these bodies. The Sisterhood of St. Mary is probably the most influential in the Episcopal Church. It carries on an extensive work in New York and beyond. The Sisterhood of St. John was established in Washington in 1867. The Sisterhood of St. John the Baptist (New York, 1881) is a branch of the similar body in England. The Sisterhood of All Saints was transferred from London to Baltimore in 1891, and the Sisterhood of St. Margaret from East Grinstead, Eng., in 1873 to Boston. The Sisterhood of the Holy Childhood of Jesus was established by the Rev. C. C. Grafton in Providence, R. I., in 1882. The Protestant Episcopal Church has not officially approved the sisterhoods, but it has given approval to the deaconesses' organizations and the office of deaconess. In 1864 a diocesan deaconesses' institution was formed in Mobile, Ala. On Feb. 11, 1872, Bishop Littlejohn of Long Island consecrated six to the office of deaconess in St. Mary's Church, Brooklyn. The General Convention of the Episcopal Church had before it for a number of years the subject of woman's work and the question of reviving the primitive order of deaconess. In 1889 action was taken by the Triennial Convention and a "Training School for Deaconesses" was opened by Bishop Potter in New York in 1890 and placed under the jurisdiction of the Rev. W. R. Huntington and Grace Church. It provides a course of training covering two years. Matriculants must be of the age of eighteen. After the course they are at liberty to labor under the direction of a bishop or to join an association of deaconesses or a sisterhood. Similar institutions have been begun in Philadelphia and in Toronto, Canada. The deaconess idea has also found incorporation in the English colonies under the charge of the Anglican episcopate (cf. Golder, pp. 464 sqq.).

2. The Protestant Episcopal Church.

The Methodists of the United States have done more than any other American denomination to utilize the movement started by Pastor Fliedner and to modify it according to their needs. By action of the General Conference in 1888, due especially to Rev. J. M. Thoburn, afterward bishop of India, the deaconess is recognized as an official of the Church (cf. Wheeler, pp. 269 sqq.). She takes no vows; "her duties are to minister to the poor, visit the sick, pray with the dying, care for the orphan, seek the wandering, comfort the sorrowing, save the sinning, and, relinquishing wholly other pursuits, to devote herself in a general way to such forms of Christian labor as may be suited to her abilities." Each annual conference through a board, composed partly of women, exercises oversight over the work and issues diaconal certificates to women properly accredited. In 1900 the General Conference perfected the law of the Church on this subject. The bishops are now a general deaconesses' board, having general supervision over all deaconesses' work throughout the Church. One of its duties is to authorize new deaconesses' homes. The committee of the annual conferences is continued as established by the conference of 1888. Deaconesses are licensed and consecrated to their office after two years of continuous probationary service and an examination. They must be twenty-three years of age and unmarried. The work of the deaconess is thus an integral part of the discipline of the Methodist Church. There is also in the Methodist Church "The Deaconesses' Bureau of the Woman's Home Missionary Society" and "The Methodist Deaconesses' Society," with headquarters in Chicago. The "Chicago Training School for City Home and Foreign Missions" was established as early as 1885 by Mrs. Lucy Rider Meyer. In 1890 the first deaconesses' home, under that distinctive name, was opened in Detroit by Mrs. Jane Bancroft Robinson, who was instrumental in opening similar homes in Philadelphia, Baltimore, Buffalo, Pittsburg, Los Angeles, and other cities. The "Elizabeth Gamble Deaconesses' Home and Christ's Hospital" was founded in 1888 in Cincinnati. The "Lucy Webb Hayes Deaconesses' Home and National Training School" was founded in Washington in 1889 and has associated with it the Sibley Hospital (1894). The same year a training-school was founded in New York. One of the largest houses in the Methodist Episcopal Church and in the United States is the "Rebecca Deaconesses' Home and Asbury Hospital" in Minneapolis, founded in 1891. At the present time there are over one hundred deaconesses' homes and training-schools in the United States under the care of the Methodist Church. It has also deaconesses' homes in Madras, Calcutta, Lucknow, and other cities of India. In 1902 the value of their properties was $2,402,000.

3. The Methodists.

The German Reformed Church has a home in Cleveland, founded 1892. The Evangelical Association has one in St. Louis (1890). The German Methodists have homes in Cincinnati (Bethesda, 1891), St. Paul (the "Elizabeth Haas Deaconess Home," 1891), Chicago (the "German Deaconesses' Institute," 1892), Louisville (1895), Kansas City (1897), and elsewhere. The United Brethren incorporated the deaconess office and idea into their discipline in 1891. The Congregationalists of Illinois secured a charter for "the American Congregational Deaconesses' Association" in 1901 and established a training-school in Chicago. The first organization in the Baptist Church was the "Baptist Deaconesses' Society of the City of New York," organized 1895. The first deaconess was ordained after a full course of study in 1897. The deaconesses wear a special garb and are called sisters. The Christian Church under the lead of Rev. A. M. Harvuot established a "Training School for Pastoral Helpers" in Cincinnati in 1890, now removed to Des Moines and connected with Drake University. The Presbyterian Church, North, in 1899 refused to recognize the special office of the congregational deaconess, but several churches have elected and set apart deaconesses by a special form of consecration. In accordance with action of the General Assembly in 1892, which commended the establishment of institutions and training homes for the instruction of godly women duly recommended by sessions and presbyteries for practical Christian work, a training-school for deaconesses was opened in connection with the First Presbyterian Church of Baltimore in 1903. The Presbyterian Church, South, in 1879 provided for the recognition of godly women in church work by the sessions, and in 1906 the synod of the United Presbyterian Church sanctioned congregational deaconesses. Lastly, a class of interdenominational deaconesses' homes may be mentioned, such as the "German Deaconesses' Home" in Cincinnati founded in 1888; the "Protestant Deaconesses' Home" in Indianapolis (1894); and the "German Deaconesses' Home" in Buffalo (1895). For a further presentation of the work of women in the Church see the article WOMAN'S WORK.

4. Other Denominations.

D. S. SCHAFF.

BIBLIOGRAPHY: On I. and II.: Bingham, *Origines*, books i., ii., iv.; L. Thomassin, *Vetus et nova ecclesiæ disciplina*, I. iii., chaps. 47–50, Paris, 1728; A. J. C. Pankowski, *De diaconissis commentatio*, Regensburg, 1866; T. Zahn, *Ignatius von Antiochien*, pp. 580–587, Gotha, 1873; G. Uhlhorn, *Die christliche Liebesthätigkeit*, 3 vols., Stuttgart, 1881–90, vol. i, *In der alten Kirche*, 1881, Eng. transl., *Christian Charity in the Early Church*, New York, 1883, vol. ii. *Im Mittelater*, 1884, vol. iii, *Seit der Reformation*, 1890; J. B. Lightfoot, *Apostolic Fathers*, ii. 322–324, 913 sqq., London, 1885; J. J. I. Döllinger, *Beiträge zur Sektengeschichte des Mittelalters*, Munich, 1890; the Commentaries on Romans, especially Lange's, New York, 1869, and by Sanday and Headlam, in *International Critical Commentary*, New York, 1895; works on the Apostolic Age, such as Schaff, *Christian Church*, i. 499, cf. iii. 259–262; *DCA*, i. 532–535.

III.: The classical work on Deaconesses in the modern Church is T. Schäfer, *Geschichte der weiblichen Diakonie*, 3 vols., Stuttgart, 1887–94. Consult: Florence Nightingale, *The Institution of Deaconesses*, London, 1851; Mrs. Jameson, *Sisters of Charity*, ib. 1855; P. Schaff, *Germany, its Universities, Theology and Religion*, chap. xxxviii., Philadelphia, 1857; J. S. Howson, *Deaconesses*, London, 1862; idem, *The Diaconate of Women in the Anglican Church*, ib. 1886; J. M. Ludlow, *Woman's Work in the Church*, ib. 1865; H. C. Potter, *Sisterhoods and Deaconesses*, New York, 1873; A. Späth, *Phœbe the Deaconess*, Philadelphia, 1885; H. Wheeler, *Deaconesses Ancient and Modern*, New York, 1889; Jane M. Bancroft, *Deaconesses in Europe*, ib. 1889; L. R. Meyer, *Deaconesses*, ib. 1889; H. J. Cooke, *Mildmay, the First Deaconess Institution*, London, 1892; J. M. Thoburn, *The Deaconess and Her Vocation*, New York, 1893; G. M. Maynard, *Pictures of Mildmay*, London, 1895; C. Robinson, *The Ministry of Deaconesses*, ib. 1898; C. Golder, *Hist. of the Deaconess Movement in the Christian Church*, New York, 1903; G. H. Gerberding, *Life and Letters of W. A. Passavant*, Greenville, Pa., 1906; Livinia L. Dock and Mary A. Nutting, *A History of Nursing*, 2 vols., New York and London, 1908; the *Reports* of the Conferences of the Evangelical Lutheran Mother-houses in the United States. A concise review of the modern movement is given in the *Addresses, Reports, Statements . . . of the National Council of Congregational Churches of the United States, 1907*, pp. 202–308, Boston, 1907.

DEAD SEA. See PALESTINE.

DEAN: A word which comes from the Latin *decanus*, originally a military term, designating the leader of a *decania* or body of ten soldiers. It early acquired the general meaning of overseer of a small number of inferiors, and was used in households for the overseers of slaves, subsequently in Constantinople for police officials. In ecclesiastical usage there are: (1) Monastic deans, whose authority extended over ten novices (Augustine, *De moribus ecclesiæ*, i. 31). (2) Deans (also called archpresbyters) appointed by a bishop to visit and oversee a part of his diocese, having supervision of the official and private conduct of the priests, presiding (from the ninth century on) at their district conventions, etc. A dean of this sort was dependent upon the archdeacon (Friedberg, *Kirchenrecht*, 188–189; see ARCHDEACON AND ARCHPRIEST). (3) Deans of cathedrals are recognized cathedral officers as early as the eighth century. In the Church of England the dean is the next ecclesiastic to the bishop. Deaneries of the "old foundation" (those older than the Reformation) are elective; those of the "new foundation" (created by Henry VIII.) are appointed by the crown. The jurisdiction of the dean is supreme in his cathedral in all matters except those which affect doctrine. The deans of Westminster and Windsor are independent of all superior ecclesiastical authority. (4) The rural deans of England are clergymen appointed by the bishop "to execute the bishop's processes and inspect the lives and manners of the clergy and people within their jurisdiction" (Phillimore, *Ecclesiastical Law*). "The dean and chapter" is the name given in England to the body electing a bishop. (5) In the Lutheran Churches the title dean is for the most part synonymous with superintendent (q.v.), but sometimes signifies a subordinate official. In the Reformed Churches a dean is an overseer of clergy or the head of a classis in France. The oldest cardinal is usually the dean of the Sacred College, presides in the consistory in the pope's absence, confers upon a newly elected pope the orders he may not have received, and presides at the pope's coronation. D. S. SCHAFF.

BIBLIOGRAPHY: J. G. Hofmann, *De decanis et decanissis*, Wittenberg, 1739; P. Baldauf, *Das . . . Decanatamt*, 6 vols., Graz, 1836; P. Hergenröther, *Römisches Kirchenrecht*, Freiburg, 1905; *KL*, iii. 1430–32; *DCA*, i. 537–539; Bingham, *Origines*, books i., iv., v., vi., viii.

DEATH.

1. Various Representations. Among the Greeks, *Thanatos*, or death, was represented as a god, and the twin-brother of sleep (Hesiod and Homer). They endeavored to exclude all that is revolting from the idea. The representation of it, however, at a later period, under the figure of a priest in sable garments, cutting the hair from the heads of the dying to offer it to the gods of the underworld, betrays the natural dread of death common to the race. The Romans brought forward prominently the awful features, describing death as a pitiless divinity, pale, and haggard of aspect, furnished with black wings, etc. The mythologies of northern nations presented him under the figures of a fowler spreading his net, or a reaper with sickle in hand, or a skeleton. In the Scriptures also death is personified, and described as intelligent (Job xxviii. 22), as sitting on a pale horse (Rev. vi. 8), or cast with hell into the lake of fire (Rev. xx. 14). Scripture expresses a universal sentiment of mankind when it calls death the king of terrors (Job xviii. 14), and an occasion of suffering and fear (Ps. lv. 4; Heb. ii. 15). But it also speaks of it as a release from pain (Job iii. 17), the passage to a better life (II Cor. v. 4), as "being gathered to one's people" (Gen. xxv. 8), a taking-down of the pilgrim's temporary tent (II Cor. v. 1), a sleeping with the fathers (I Kings ii. 10), or with Christ (I Cor. xv. 18; I Thess. iv. 13–15), a departure (Phil. i. 23; II Tim. iv. 6), a dissolution of the earthly house (II Cor. v. 1), and a rest (Rev. xiv. 13).

There are three kinds of death mentioned in the Scriptures—physical death, spiritual death, and the second or eternal death. Physical death is the dissolution of the body into its component parts.

2. Three Kinds of Death Mentioned in Scripture. The spirit takes its flight (Eccles. xii. 7), and the body passes back into the dust from which it was taken (Gen. iii. 19; Eccles. iii. 20). The time of this dissolution is known to God only (Ps. xxxi. 15; Matt. xxv. 13). It must be regarded as a benignity for the righteous man (Num. xxiii. 10; Rom. vii. 24), but as a dread calamity to the impenitent, whom it ushers to his own place (Acts i. 25), and for all as "the night in which no man can work" (John ix. 4). Spiritual death is a state of sin and darkness, in which man is alienated from God, the fountain of life and light (I John i. 5), and consequently destitute of true spiritual life. The whole world, at the coming of Christ, was sitting in the shadow of this death (Luke i. 79). All men, without exception, are dead in trespasses and sins (Eph. ii. 1, 5; Col. ii. 13; cf. Luke xv. 32). Our Lord became subject unto the death of the body, but was always in communion with the Father, and free from sin. The entrance upon a life of faith is called arising from the dead (Eph. v. 14), or becoming alive unto God (Rom. vi. 11). Spiritual death is not a stagnant condition, but a progressive state, the heart becoming more hardened, the eyes more blind (John xii. 49; Rom. i. 21), the conscience seared as with a hot iron (I Tim. iv. 2), and the pleasure in lust and hatred of God increased (Rom. i. 26–31). The second or eternal death (Rev. ii. 11; xx. 6, 14; xxi. 8) signifies the final loss of the power and opportunity to repent and turn to God. The personality is not destroyed; but God's image is wholly defaced, and heavenly blessedness forfeited. This terrible doom of the second death is described under the figure of an exclusion from what is good (Rev. xxii. 15; cf. Matt. xxv. 30), and of a lake burning with fire and brimstone, into which the finally impenitent are cast (Rev. xx. 14, xxi. 8). Those who overcome (Rev. ii. 11), and are partakers of the "first resurrection" (regeneration, cf. Eph. v. 14, etc.), shall in no wise be hurt of it (Rev. xx. 6). The same idea is expressed by the words "perishing" (John iii. 15), "eternal punishment" (Matt. xxv. 46), "destruction" (Phil. iii. 19), "everlasting destruction" (II Thess. i. 9), and "corruption" (Gal. vi. 8).

3. The Origin of Death.

Sin and death are indissolubly associated in the Old and New Testaments. Death is not merely the natural fruit of sin (Jas. i. 15), but its just punishment or wages (Gen. ii. 17; Rom. vi. 23), and expression of the divine wrath (Ps. xc. 7–10; Rom. ii. 5–8). We are subject to it because we are subject to the law of sin, and in virtue of our union with Adam (Rom. v. 17; I Cor. xv. 22). It has been denied by Pelagius and the Socinians that physical death was included in this penalty. The body is regarded as having been mortal before the fall. This view is in contradiction to what seems to be the plain meaning of the words, "In the day thou eatest thereof thou shalt surely die" (i.e., begin to die, or become mortal—Gen. ii. 17), when read in the light of the curse in Gen. iii. 19, "Unto dust thou shalt return." Although our first parents did not actually return to dust the very day they sinned, nevertheless, the principle of death then began to work in them (Augustine, *De peccatorum meritis*, i. 21).

4. The Abolition of Death.

Christ has abolished death (II Tim. i. 10). This has been accomplished by the defeat of him who had the power of death (Heb. ii. 14), and the spoliation of the kingdom of darkness (Eph. iv. 8; Col. ii. 15). Christ could not be holden of death (Acts ii. 24), and triumphantly rose from the grave. The dead were raised by his word of power (Mark v. 41; Luke vii. 15; John xi. 44). He quickens with new spiritual life whom he will (John v. 21; Eph. ii. 5), so that moral death has no more dominion over us (Rom. vi. 9). He that believeth is "passed from death unto life" (John v. 24). The death of the body becomes, for those thus spiritually revived, a sleep (I Thess. iv. 14) and a rest from labor (Rev. xiv. 13), from which they shall be raised to an estate of eternal blessedness (II Cor. xv. 21, 22; I Thess. iv. 13–16). The sea then (Rev. xx. 13), as well as all earthly graves, shall give up their dead. And so effective is this quickening power of Christ that they who are raised by him can nevermore die (Luke xx. 36); and so perfect is the life in heaven that there is no death there (Rev. xxi. 4).

5. The Condition of Death.

The states following the moment when the bodily organs cease to perform their functions are treated in other articles (see GEHENNA; HADES; HEAVEN; PURGATORY; RESURRECTION OF THE DEAD; etc.). The body of Jesus saw no corruption. It is a pious belief held in the Roman Catholic Church that this was true also of the body of Mary. The belief was stated at an early period, and in its most popular form comes through Juvenal, bishop of Jerusalem, who told it to the emperor Marcian at Chalcedon, 451. Whether the soul sleeps at the death of the body until the general resurrection was answered negatively by Calvin in his tract *Psychopannychia* (written at Orléans 1534 against some of the Anabaptists who held to that opinion). John XXII. denied the doctrine of the immediate beatific vision of the blessed dead. His successor declared this view heresy. The Westminster Shorter Catechism (question xxxvii.) states the doctrine that the bodies of the dead rest in their graves till the resurrection, but that their souls do immediately pass into glory. This was the view of the Reformers. D. S. SCHAFF.

BIBLIOGRAPHY: For the Biblical side: F. Delitzsch, *System der biblischen Psychologie*, Leipsic, 1861, Eng. transl., Edinburgh, 1865; J. T. Beck, *Umriss der biblischen Seelenlehre*, Stuttgart, 1871; H. Schultz, *Alttestamentliche Theologie*, 2 vols., Göttingen, 1896, Eng. transl., London, 1892; W. Beyschlag, *Neutestamentliche Theologie*, 2 vols., Halle, 1895, Eng. transl., Edinburgh, 1896. On the general aspect consult: F. Splittgerber, *Tod, Fortleben und Auferstehung*, Halle, 1869; J. J. G. Wilkinson, *Origins and Issues of Life and Death*, ib. 1885; A. Schopenhauer, *Ueber den Tod und sein Verhältniss zur Unzerstörbarkeit*, Leipsic, 1886; J. C. Bellett, *The Dead in Christ*, London, 1887; A. Sabatier, *Essai sur la vie et la mort*, Paris, 1892; H. M. Alden, *A Study of Death*, London, 1895; L. Bordeau, *Le Problème de la mort*, Paris, 1900; C. du Prel, *Der Tod, das Jenseits*, Jena, 1901. For the literary treatment consult: P. Bornstein, *Der Tod in der modernen Litteratur*, Leipsic, 1900.

DEATH, DANCE OF: A famous subject of art, especially in the fifteenth century. Death, in the figure of a skeleton, is depicted in the company of representatives of every class of society. The fell enemy is represented in the most various attitudes; now harshly tugging at the victim, and now gently leading him; now walking arm in arm, and now beating him. An hour-glass is usually found somewhere in the pictures. The Dance of Death was painted on the walls and windows of churches, on house-fronts, in illuminated books, and on bridges. Among the oldest representations are those of Minden (1383), Dijon (1436), and Basel (1441); the principal ones are those of Basel, Bern, and Erfurt. The subject was also frequently represented in England, as at Croydon, Salisbury Cathedral, Stratford-on-Avon, and elsewhere. Moral and descriptive verses were frequently printed below the pictures, and usually closed with such a sentence as, "Death awaits all." Hans Holbein is the only painter of fame associated with these curious works of art, who, however, never went farther than to make sketches. These were engraved on wood by Lützelburger, and appeared at Lyons (1538). As might be expected, they were characterized by humor and poetic imagination. The Dance of Death was also represented on the stage; at least two cases are well attested, one before Philip the Good of Burgundy at Bruges in 1449 (called a *certain jeu, histoire et moralité sur le fait de la danse macabre*), and one at Besançon in 1453.

D. S. SCHAFF.

BIBLIOGRAPHY: A very full list of books is given under "Dance of Death" in the *British Museum Catalogue*. Consult: G. Peignot, *Recherches sur les Danses des Morts*, Paris, 1826; F. Douce, *The Dance of Death*, London, 1833; G. Kastner, *Les Danses des Morts*, Paris, 1852; *Dance of Death by Hans Holbein, with introductory Note by A. Dobson*, London, 1872; W. Sulmmann, *Die Totentänze des Mittelalters*, Nordlingen, 1892; [J. J. Berthier], *La plus Ancienne Danse Macabre au Klingenthal à Bâle*, Paris, 1896; A. Götte, *Holbeins Totentanz und seine Vorbilder*, Strasburg, 1897; E. K. Chambers, *The Mediaeval Stage*, 2 vols., Oxford, 1903; W. Combe, *The English Dance of Death; from the Designs of T. Rowlandson by the author of "Doctor Syntax,"* new ed., 2 vols., New York, 1903.

DEBORAH, deb'o-rū *or* dē-bo'rū ("Bee"): The name of two women of the Bible.

1. The nurse of Rebekah who accompanied her from Mesopotamia to Canaan when she married Isaac.

2. Prophetess and Judge: She belonged to one of the northern tribes and was the wife of a certain Lappidoth. While the Canaanites occupied the open country, she acted as prophetess and judge on Mount Ephraim. When for twenty years the country had been oppressed by the enemy Deborah proclaimed a war of liberation. She ordered Barak of Kedesh in Naphtali with 10,000 men from the tribes of Zebulon and Naphtali, who, according to Judges v. were joined by others, to encamp on Mount Tabor and to attack the hostile general who was about to gather his forces in the valley of Kishon. Barak consented only when Deborah declared her readiness to go with him; she predicted, however, that on account of this timidity, he would yield the prize of victory to a woman. Of the subsequent battle there are two independent records, each distinguished by peculiar details, which supplement each other: the prosaic narrative in Judges iv. and Deborah's song of victory, chap. v. From the two it appears that, by the attack of the Israelitic infantry, the army of the enemy was completely beaten at Taanach and Megiddo. A thunder-storm threw the Canaanitic chariots into confusion, and the violent downpour caused the overflow of the river Kishon, which became the grave of the heavily equipped, disorderly mass (Ps. lxxxiii. 9). This may have happened in the narrow pass of Haritieh. Sisera fled on foot over the northern mountain, and came to the tent of Jael, who belonged to a branch of the Kenites tenting near Kedesh in Naphtali (cf. Josh. xix. 37). The unhappy general arrived exhausted and found a hospitable reception in the tent of Jael, but also a disgraceful death at the hand of his hostess. Thus, in accordance with the utterance of the seer, Jael anticipated the pursuing Barak. The assertion of Wellhausen that the prose narrative in chap. iv. is only a version of the song is refuted by the fact that the narrative mentions many details wanting in the song, and makes no use of many things peculiar to the latter. The contradictions which some have thought they discovered between chaps. iv. and v. are doubtful. The position of Jabin, "king of Canaan," at Hazor in the narrative might give rise to objection, since no reference is made to him in the song, whereas Sisera, his general (according to iv. 2), seems in the song to have the household of a prince. On this account many suppose that Jabin did not originally belong to the narrative, but was incorporated from Josh. xi. 1. But the song (v. 19) speaks of kings of Canaan who took part in the battle, and it is conceivable that the king of Hazor was their head, whereas another of these "kings," Sisera, commanded in the field. Other alleged contradictions between chaps. iv. and v. are of no importance. The song of triumph which Deborah sang after this decisive victory bears so much the stamp of originality that the critics almost unanimously recognize in it an authentic testimony. Language and style are peculiar and ancient. The narrative betrays the cutting wit as well as the holy seriousness which was peculiar to the new nation. Alongside of the stormy savageness of the time, there appears in Deborah a tender, genuinely female sense, which comes out in the singer and the "mother in Israel." For the critical treatment of the history of Israel this ancient song is of great importance.

C. von Orelli.

Bibliography: Of the highest importance is G. F. Moore, *Commentary on Judges*, New York, 1895. Consult: G. A. Cooke, *Hist. and Song of Deborah*, London, 1892; H. Winckler, *Altorientalische Forschungen*, ii. 192, iii. 291, Leipsic, 1894; K. Budde, *Actes du dixième congrès d'orientalistes*, ii (1896), 20 sqq.; J. Marquart, *Fundamente israelitischer und jüdischer Geschichte*, pp. 1-10, Göttingen, 1896; D. H. Müller, *Actes du dixième congrès d'orientalistes*, iv (1898), 261 sqq.; *DB*, i. 578-579; *EB*, i. 1047-48; *JE*, iv. 490.

DECALOGUE.

The decalogue is the fundamental moral law of Jews and Christians. The words which, according to Ex. xx. 1; Deut. iv. 12, 13, v. 4, 19-23, God spoke at Sinai to the assembled Israelites, given Ex. xx. 2-17 and, in slightly different form, Deut. v. 6-78, are called the decalogue. These, according to the plain statement of Deut. iv. 13, v. 19, ix. 10, 11, x. 4, and the implication of Ex. xxiv. 12, xxxi. 18, and other passages, God had written upon the two tables of stone which became part of the contents of the ark of the covenant.

1. Names and Character.

The name generally given to this code is "the ten commandments"; the Old Testament calls them the "ten words" (Ex. xxxiv. 28; Deut. iv. 13, x. 4; cf. Ex. xxiv. 3), because they possessed a preeminent excellence, spoken as they were to the people by their God. They alone were written on the two tables, which received the name "tables of the covenant," while the box in which they were deposited was called the "ark of the covenant," since they were the "witness" of the covenant (see Covenant) made on Mount Sinai. The decalogue is an independent and complete code, expressing the relations existing between the Creator and created man. The mass of laws which make up the codes of Israel may be considered the unfolding of the ethical-religious idea expressed in the ten words. The prohibition to worship other gods and to make images have a place only in antiquity, and the commandment concerning Sabbath-observance steps outside the purely ethical sphere and demands a cult which in Deuteronomy is applied to Israel. Again the ten commandments have reference to external acts only, the prohibitions outnumber the precepts, the threats and promises are limited to this life; nevertheless, the form is such as to be able to receive the whole content of the New Testament concepts of the divine will. As the Christian sees in the Yahweh of the Old Testament the God who in Jesus revealed himself as Father, so he finds stated in the decalogue the fact that God is the only good to be desired, that the material must be kept apart from the spiritual, and that there is a Sabbath after life's week of toil and travail. While it is the people as a whole who are addressed by the code, the commands come also to the individual; so Christians, to whom this tribal law has become the law of humanity, refer it to every individual within the range of its voice.

About the division of the decalogue churches differ: the Jews count Exod. xx. 2 as the first commandment, 3–6 as the second, and 17 is consequently the tenth; the Greek and Reformed churches make 3 the first, 4–6 the second, and 17 the tenth; the Roman and Lutheran churches see in 3–6 one commandment and in 17 two commandments. The oldest witness favors the second view, held by Josephus and Philo, and this is undoubtedly the correct one; there is no reason for seeing in 17 two commandments, moreover, the text forbids division; verse 2, though a highly important statement, is not a commandment, and

2. Divisions and Original Form.

4–5 may well on internal grounds be taken as independent of verse 3. The Samaritans have after Exod. xx. 17 and Deut. v. 18 another commandment, borrowed from Deut. xxvii. 2–7 and xi. 30, and wrongly affirm that the Jews have only nine commandments. The decalogue is divided in Exodus generally into nine, and in Deuteronomy always into ten sections. While the division into nine sections is certainly as old as the other, it has no necessary connection with that into ten "words." It is noteworthy that the prohibition to covet is nowhere divided into two verses. That there were two tables is witnessed by all the sources except E. It may be surmised that each contained five "words," and putting the fifth (Ex. xx. 12) on the first table gives excellent balance, the first table containing the commandments of piety, the second those of probity. Less attractive is the arrangement of Augustine and Calvin, who place the fifth commandment on the second table as enjoining performance of duties toward fellow men. The difference in length in the commandments is remarkable; and since this seems due to the addition of explanations, threats, or promises, the conviction is forced that originally the decalogue contained ten short sentences about as follows, which alone the designation "ten words" truly fits: (1) Thou shalt have no other gods besides me, (2) Thou shalt not make unto thee any image, (3) Thou shalt not take the name of Yahweh thy God in vain, (4) Remember the Sabbath day to keep it holy, (5) Honor thy father and thy mother, (6) Thou shalt not kill, (7) Thou shalt not commit adultery, (8) Thou shalt not steal, (9) Thou shalt not bear false witness against thy neighbor, (10) Thou shalt not covet thy neighbor's house. In this form the decalogue may easily have been written on two stone tables.

Among the additions certain expressions occur frequently, or only, in Deuteronomy, but this does not involve that these additions have been imported into Exodus from Deuteronomy. For, to the additions which the two statements have in common, Deuteronomy has others which

3. Variations in Expressions.

mark it as the younger, and has besides a different vocabulary in the fourth, ninth, and tenth commandments. Changes are evidently not wilful; they are due rather to the fact that at the time of the Deuteronomist the text was still fluctuating. In common with other peoples of antiquity, Israel cared very little for verbal correctness, and thus it need not cause surprise that they did not end these discrepancies by consulting the original tables, since they were difficult of access. Notable in this connection is the commandment concerning Sabbath-observance. E bases it on the creation week, D on the exodus from Egypt; it is difficult to believe that D would have dropped the former, had it stood in his copy. However, the conclusion that the reference to creation was incorporated into the decalogue later is by no means certain; while the common view now is that it is a postexilic enlargement on the basis of Gen. ii. 1–4a, the expressions in the decalogue do not agree with those in Genesis (cf. W. Lotz, *Quæstiones de historia sabbati*, Leipsic, 1883, 94–100).

The Mosaic origin of the decalogue, at least in the shorter form, is admitted by Delitzsch, Dillmann, Lemme, König, Kittel, Driver, and others. But Nöldeke as early as 1869 declared that view extremely doubtful, and lately Wellhausen, Stade, Cornill have rejected it, while Smend and H. Schulz have lost faith in it. The main argument has always been that the prohibition to making

4. Mosaic Origin.

images could not date back to Moses, since the worship of Yahweh under the form of images persisted in the northern kingdom, and in Judah was found at least until Solomon. But it is pure assumption that, while the image-worship existed, it was not displeasing. As far as is known, the true champions of the Yahweh-religion always stood for imageless worship, and where the ark stood, at Shiloh and at Jerusalem, there was no image (on the ephod, I Sam. xxi. 9; see Ephod). But that the mere existence of the prohibition would make image-worship impossible and would cause Jeroboam to refrain from introducing calf-worship no one would affirm who considers what even to-day is possible in the Christian Church. The other argument against the Mosaic origin is that the fourth commandment presupposes settlement in Canaan. While the Sabbath rest has less meaning when applied to nomads than when related to agricultural conditions, it must not be forgotten that Israel at Moses's time was not wholly nomadic. Again, it is urged that the mode of thought is that of the prophets, and is not met in preprophetic time. But it is not certain that the prophets invented the ethical standard; and, inasmuch as their teachings in complicated and developed form far surpass what in the decalogue is given in the most simple and fundamental precepts, the latter can not be the mere precipitate of the former. It is the narrative of E in which the decalogue in Exodus is found. That the writings of P contained it is denied by no one, though the doubtful opinion is advanced by Wellhausen, Jülicher, Budde, and others, that J had a different Sinaitic decalogue, namely Ex. xxxiv. 14–26. But while it is possible on good grounds to have the conviction that the decalogue as an inheritance of the Mosaic time has stood in all Pentateuch sources, others, such as Meissner, Steuernagel, and Staerk, on religious-historical and philological grounds have denied that even E contained it. (W. Lotz.)

Bibliography: The subject is treated in most of the critical works on the history of Israel and the introduction to the O. T. Consult: A. Kuenen, *Origin and Composition of the Hexateuch*, London, 1886; R. Kittel, *Geschichte der Hebräer*, 2 vols., Gotha, 1888–92, Eng. transl., London, 1895–96; B. Bäntsch, *Das Bundesbuch*, Halle, 1892; H. Schultz, *Alttestamentliche Theologie*, 2 vols., Göttingen, 1896, Eng. transl., London, 1892; E. König, *Einleitung in das A. T.*, Bonn, 1893; A. Dillmann, *Alttestamentliche Theologie*, Leipsic, 1895; W. H. Green, *Higher Criticism of the Pentateuch*, New York, 1895; C. A. Briggs, *Higher Criticism of the Pentateuch*, pp. 242 sqq., New York, 1897; C. H. Cornill, *Einleitung in das A. T.*, Tübingen, 1905, Eng. transl., Lond., 1907; H. L. Strack, *Einleitung in das A. T.*, Munich, 1898; C. Caverno, *The Ten Words*, Boston, 1899; R. Smend, *Alttestamentliche Religionsgeschichte*, Freiburg, 1899; J. Wellhausen, *Composition des Hexateuchs*, Berlin, 1899; J. E. Carpenter and G. Harford-Battersby, *The Hexateuch*, 2 vols., London, 1900; S. A. Cook, in *The Guardian*, Dec. 17, 1902 (on a new papyrus with early text); *DB*, i. 580–582; *EB*, i. 1049–51; *JE*, iv. 492–498. Earlier homiletical literature is given in J. F. Hurst, *Literature of Theology*, pp. 149, 164, 392, 528, New York, 1896. Consult also L. Lemme, *Die religionsgeschichtliche Bedeutung des Dekalogs*, Breslau, 1880.

DECIUS, di'shi-us, **CAIUS MESSIUS QUINTUS TRAJANUS**: Roman emperor 249–251; b. near Sirmium about 200, of a Roman or Romanized family; d. in the marshes of Dobrudja, Rumania, in the summer or autumn of 251. He began his career in the army, became governor of Dacia and Mœsia under Philippus Arabs, and was placed in command of the forces sent to crush the Gothic invasion. Discouraged by its defeats, the Danubian army proclaimed him Augustus in 249, and his victory at Verona, in which the emperor Philippus fell, won him the throne in the same year. Decius was essentially a soldier, also eager to revive and strengthen the moral and religious forces which still existed, but he lacked political insight, and was unable to secure permanent results during his brief reign. A new inroad of the Goths soon recalled him from Italy and Rome to the Danubian countries, where he fell after a series of disastrous battles.

In the course of his turbulent reign Decius began a persecution of the Christians, which endangered the Church more than any which had preceded it. The religious policy of Philippus, who had favored the Christians, may have made the new emperor regard them as his opponents, but a stronger motive was his personal anti-Christian bias, based on his adherence to the ancient faith, and directed primarily against the clergy. It is also probable that the censor Valerian, who later became emperor, and was in high favor with Decius, was active in this persecution, and as chief civil magistrate was required to carry it through. It is with justice, therefore, that Christian tradition combines the name of the emperor with that of his chief officer. It is even possible that Valerian was the real leader. The repression, which seems to have begun about the end of 249, and which lasted, at least in part, until Decius fell, was premeditated from the very first, while the uniformity of its execution is shown by the reports from North Africa, Rome, Egypt, and Asia Minor. All, without exception, were commanded to offer sacrifice. In case of refusal, however, further proceedings were left to the discretion of the judge, and the penalties which were inflicted ranged from light punishment to death, sometimes in such cruel forms as starvation, burning, and stoning. The only uniformity observed was the desire to kill the chief clergy, and many bishops, as at Rome, Antioch, and Jerusalem, suffered martyrdom, while others saved themselves by flight. The attitude of the laity was, on the whole, a feeble one. Origen was tortured, and the general picture of devastation is described by the Roman presbyters with the words (Cyprian, *Epist.*, xxx. 5): "Look upon almost the whole world devastated, and observe that the remains and the ruins of the fallen are lying about on every side." These conditions gave rise to the difficult problem of the attitude of the Church toward the lapsed, among whom the so-called *libellatici* now appeared for the first time in the history of the persecution of the Christians (see Lapsed); yet beside those who wavered the Church could also point to many courageous, steadfast souls.

In view of its destructive effect the Decian persecution has always been regarded as one of extraordinary severity. Nevertheless, this persecution was not general in scope, although it was intended to be so. In many places the imperial edicts were disregarded, and in others executed only formally. The turbulent political conditions of the period forbade strenuous and uniform action, and the Decian persecution was, consequently, merely transitory. Victor Schultze.

Bibliography: The sources are, from the Roman side, *Prosopographia imperii romani sæc. i.–iii.*, part ii., ed. H. Dessau, p. 368, Berlin, 1897; from the Christian side, Cyprian, *De lapsis*, Eng. transl., in *ANF*, v. 437–447; and Eusebius, *Hist. eccl.*, vi. 40–42, Eng. transl., in *NPNF*, 2d series, i. 281–286. Consult: L. S. le N. de Tillemont, *Mémoires . . . ecclésiastiques*, iii. 2, pp. 123 sqq., Brussels, 1695; E. G. Hardy, *Christianity and the Roman Government*, London, 1894; H. Schiller, *Geschichte der römischen Kaiserzeit*, i. 2, pp. 804 sqq., Gotha, 1883; J. A. F. Gregg, *The Decian Persecution*, Edinburgh, 1897; L. Pullan, *Church of the Fathers*, pp. 156 sqq., New York, 1905; Neander, *Christian Church*, i. 130–136; Schaff, *Christian Church*, ii. 60–63; Gibbon, *Decline and Fall*, ii. 113–114.

DECIUS, NIKOLAUS: According to P. J. Rehtmeyer—*Kirchengeschichte der Stadt Braunschweig* (5 vols., Brunswick, 1707–15), iii. 19—translator or adapter of the *Gloria in excelsis*, the *Sanctus*, and the *Agnus* into Low German verse; d. Mar. 21, 1541 (?). About 1519 he was provost in Steterburg, near Wolfenbüttel; after his conversion to Lutheranism, 1522, teacher in Brunswick; and finally preacher in Stettin. Attempts to identify him with a Nicolaus a Curia who was preacher in Stettin about 1523 and with others are not convincing. (Ferdinand Cohrs.)

DECLARATION OF INDULGENCE: An act of Charles II. of England, whereby he suspended all penal laws against both Roman Catholics and dissenters, Mar. 15, 1672. A royal proclamation of the same king, issued ten years earlier, promising modification of the severity of the Act of Uniformity (q.v.), is sometimes called the First Declaration of Indulgence. The king's motive in both cases was believed to be a desire to favor Roman Catholics and revive the royal prerogative of dispensing with the execution of laws, and opposition arose even among Protestant dissenters. Strong antagonism developed in parliament, the legality of the king's action was questioned, and the declaration was recalled Mar. 8, 1673. Another declaration of indulgence was issued by James II., Apr. 4, 1687, granting full religious liberty to all his subjects. The same opposition developed, and the king failed to obtain parliamentary sanction even from a packed parliament. The king reissued the declaration Apr. 22, 1688, and ordered all clergy to read the declaration in their pulpits. But the order was generally disobeyed and called forth a protest written by Archbishop Sancroft (q.v.) and signed by himself and six other bishops, for which they were committed to the Tower (June 8); they were acquitted by jury when brought to trial at the end of the month. On the same day the invitation was despatched to William of Orange to become king of England.

Bibliography: The Declaration of James II. is reproduced in Gee and Hardy, *Documents*, pp. 641–644. Consult: T. B. Howell, *Complete Collection of State Trials*, vol. xii., London, 1809–28; G. D'Oyly, *Life of William Sancroft*, ib. 1840; W. H. Hutton, *The English Church, 1625–1714*, pp. 184–227, ib. 1903; Robinson, *European History*, ii. 256–259.

DECREE, DECRETAL: In the canonical sense the latter is an authoritative rescript of a pope in reply to some question. The original name was *decretale constitutum* or *decretalis epistola;* afterward *decretalis*. A *decree* is a papal ordinance enacted with the advice of the cardinals, but not as response to an inquiry.

DECRETUM GRATIANI. See Canon Law.

DEFENDER OF THE FAITH (*Defensor fidei*): A title borne by English sovereigns. It was first conferred by Leo X. on Henry VIII., as a reward for his *Assertio septem sacramentorum*, in the bull *Ex supernæ dispositionis* (Oct. 11, 1521), and confirmed by Clement VII. on Mar. 5, 1523. After the breach with Rome it was recognized by Parliament in "An Act for the Ratification of the King's Majesty's Stile," 35 Henr. VIII. (A. Hauck.)

DEFENDER OF THE MARRIAGE-TIE (*Defensor matrimonii*): An official in every diocese in the Roman Catholic Church deputed, according to the bull *Dei miseratione* of Benedict XIV. (Nov. 3, 1741), to prevent by all proper means the dissolution of the marriage-tie where proceedings to that end have been begun. The office was instituted in America by the Third Plenary Council of Baltimore in 1884.

DEFILEMENT AND PURIFICATION, CEREMONIAL.

I. Defilement: In order to define what Old Testament purification covers, it is necessary first to describe what is there declared to defile or make impure.

1. The Region of Polluting Existences: Certain animals polluted if they were eaten (see Dietary Laws of the Hebrews). Unclean animals might

1. Animals.

be brought to God neither as free-will offerings (Gen. viii. 20) nor as firstlings (Num. xviii. 15) nor as tithes (Lev. xxvii. 32), but contact with living unclean animals is not forbidden.

In the case of women in childbirth (Lev. xii.) the cause of uncleanness is not the fact of giving birth, but the condition resulting which resembles that of the menses. The duration of the unclean-

2. Women in Childbirth.

ness is seven or fourteen days followed by thirty-three or sixty-six days, according as the child is male or female, during the whole of which period (forty or eighty days) the woman is barred from approach to things holy. The period of seven or fourteen days involves a completer or more "contagious" impurity than that of the remaining thirty-three or sixty-six days. The manner of purification of person and clothing by washing is as in the menses (cf. Lev. xv. 11, 16–18, 21, 27).

Leprosy (not always the real leprosy; cf. P. Haupt, *Babylonian Elements of the Levitic Ritual*,

3. Leprosy.

pp. 64–65, 1900), during its continuance, defiled the person or thing with which it came into contact. "House-leprosy" defiled any who entered the house pronounced leprous by the priest.

Certain secretions of the human body (Lev. xv.), such as unhealthy secretions from the male organ (vv. 1–12), defiled by contact with the person afflicted. The case in vv. 16–18 is peculiar; noc-

4. Bodily Secretions.

turnal emissions polluted things which they touched (verse 17); the man who had the emission polluted persons whom he touched, e.g., the wife by his side. Lev. xix. 20 reprehends the lying together of persons of different stations in life (a freeman and a bondmaiden). In the earlier instance (Lev. xv. 18) sexual intercourse is not involved by the phrase "lie with" (cf. Lev. xv. 24 with xx. 18; in the former passage the phrase carries only the meaning "being in the same bed," while the latter passage makes sexual intercourse under the circumstances named a capital offense). The section Lev. xv. 16–18 deals with involuntary emission and does not involve defilement through sexual intercourse. This (correct) interpretation was the view of the Masoretes and of Luther (the latter translates "the woman near whom such a one lies"); but another view, that verse 18 made sexual intercourse a defilement became common among the Jews. The Old Testament makes the sexual act only relatively polluting; for example, before performing a religious act or touching a sacred object (cf. Ex. xix. 15; I Sam. xxi. 5–6; I Cor. vii. 5), just as drinking of wine was not absolutely and always forbidden to the priests, but only when sacred functions were to be performed. A woman's menses (Lev. xix. 19–24) rendered her unclean for seven days, anything that she touched till the evening, and the husband who occupied the bed with her while she was in that condition for seven days. Any other issue of the kind carried the same disability.

5. Death. Death rendered unclean. The dead body of unclean beasts made him that touched them unclean for one day (Lev. xi. 8, 24–25, 28). Lev. xi. 29–38 names eight varieties of creeping animals the dead bodies of which defiled things and persons, except fountains, cisterns, and seed, unless the last were soaking in water. These animals were generally found near human habitations. The body of a clean beast which had died, i.e., was not slaughtered in the legal way, defiled for the day him that touched or ate it (Lev. xi. 39–40; cf. Ex. xxii. 31; Lev. xxii. 8). A corpse rendered unclean for seven days him who touched it, defiled the tent and any who entered it, as well as any uncovered vessel which was in the tent (Num. xix. 11–14). Contact with a corpse in the open, with a human bone or a grave, defiled for seven days; and whoever engaged in the purification of such a defiled person was himself unclean till the evening (Num. xix. 7–8, 10, 21–22).

6. Booty. Booty taken from Gentiles rendered unclean for seven days (Num. xxxi. 23–24). This impurity of booty differed from that of heathen lands (Amos vii. 17), which was rather unholiness and did not render unclean the Hebrew who dwelt there.

2. The Character of this Impurity: This depends on the meaning of the Heb. *tame*, "unclean," which is connected with the ideas "submerged," "besmirched," "concentrated," hence "dark," "gloomy."

1. The Hebrew Tame. The usage involves both external impurity and that of the spirit (Is. vi. 5; Gen. xxxiv. 5; Num. v. 13; Lev. xviii. 19). The actions described in these passages are "abominations," as was the Moloch cult. The word is used of immorality and irreligion, and takes in both express abominations and such unsanctity as that of a heathen land (cf. II Kings v. 17–19) and its population. The synonyms of *tame* give various consonant meanings, such as "degraded," "soiled," "smirched," applicable in both the physical and the moral spheres, just as the antonym *kodhesh* refers to both physical and moral states.

2. Impurity not Simply Physical. Considerations which decide the character of uncleanness are the following. Impurity was not simply physical, since the usual sources of the evil did not belong to the region of this impurity. Yet defilement of a bed might be wrought by a corpse or by excrement, and ablutions were a partial means to holiness. The ultimate thought was relation to the deity. In the case of childbirth the distinction between absolute and relative impurity was based on the flow of blood, and in the menses stoppage of the flow *ipso facto* restored purity so far as the basis was physical. Even then impurity had for Israelites a moral-religious significance, since for the reestablishment of purity a religious rite was performed (e.g., Lev. xii. 6–8). That a spring or cistern or seed for sowing was not contaminated by a dead unclean beast proceeded from the thought that the spring and the seed renewed themselves, while the body of water in the cistern was relatively large. Against the merely physical character of uncleanness can be alleged the fact that through eating of creeping things the soul was thought to be defiled (Lev. xi. 43), and the fact that the impurity of a woman is regarded as more absolute than that of a man. This appears in the doubling of the period of impurity after the birth of a girl as compared with that following the birth of a boy, and in the circumstance that issue from a woman defiles for seven days, from a man only one (Lev. xv. 18, 24). Yet washing or aspersion with water and searing with fire point to the external character of the impurity. On the other hand, the Old Testament teaches that animals and things inanimate suffer under man's culpability.

3. But Religious-Ethical-Esthetic. Impurity had then the significance of a religious-ethical abnormality. But this was not all, since it was not always mere psychological immorality. Impurity is sometimes called baseness or sin, which, however, did not communicate itself as contagion nor was it purged exactly through sacrifice. It is noteworthy that the person who came into contact with the sin-offering of the Day of Atonement was not called unclean (Lev. xvi. 24, 26, 28), as was he who touched the ashes which purified from contact with the dead (Num. xix. 7, 8, 10). If then impurity has an ethical-religious character, it has also an external character as a secondary factor. It is best to gather these qualities in one phrase, and to speak of impurity as religious-ethical-esthetic.

3. Antiquity and Development of the Idea in Israel: From those prophetical writings the date of which is certain the following is gathered, those passages where unclean is taken in a mere religio-ethical sense, and as not immediately belonging here, being put in brackets: [Amos: unclean is the land outside of Palestine (vii. 17).] Hosea: Israel shall eat unclean things in Assyria (ix. 3–4); [Israel is defiled on account of irreligion and immorality (3).] [Micah: uncleanness (i.e., abomination) causes destruction (ii. 13). Isaiah: the Israel of the time of salvation will defile his former idols (xxx. 22).] Jeremiah: the houses of Jerusalem shall be defiled as the place of Tophet (xix. 13). This defilement was brought about by Josiah (II Kings xxiii. 10), since he defiled the high places in the cities of Judah, not by physical defilement (as II Kings x. 27), but as, in the case of the altar at Bethel (II Kings xxiii. 15–16), by bones out of the sepulchers. [Israel has polluted himself by idolatry (Jer. ii. 23), and his land (ii. 7, vii. 30, xxxii. 34). Lamentations: polluted with blood (iv. 14–15).] In Ezekiel are parallels to I. 1: food baked with dung of man is unclean (iv. 12–13); the menstruating woman is mentioned (xxii. 10); the defiled land is compared to her uncleanness (xxxvi. 17); that which dieth of itself, or is torn in pieces, is unclean (iv. 14)]; Yahweh's house is defiled by bones out of the sepulchers (ix. 7, xliii. 7); priests may defile themselves only in the case of the death of father, mother, son, daughter, brother, or unmarried sister (xliv. 25); [the sanctuary and Jerusalem are defiled by idols (v. 11, xiv. 11, xxii. 3, 15, and often); ancient Jerusalem is defiled by blood (xxiv. 9, 11); uncleanness and apostasy together (xxxix. 24); the neighbor's wife is defiled by adultery (xviii. 6, 11, 15, xxii. 11); God pronounces Israel unclean because of sin (xx. 26); but will cleanse Israel (xxxvi. 25, 29, xxxvii. 23); finally the soul becomes polluted by uncleanness (iv. 14)]. Ezekiel laments over the priests who made no difference between the unclean and the clean (xxii. 26), and makes it a special duty of the priests to teach this difference (xliv. 23). Deutero-Isaiah: The uncircumcised and unclean shall come no more into Jerusalem (Isa. lii. 1); "touch no unclean thing" (11); the unclean shall not be in the land in the Messianic time (xxxv. 8). Haggai: A dead body defiles (ii. 13). Since the oldest literary monuments of Israel contain essentially the same laws of uncleanness as are contained in Lev. xi.–xv., Num. xix., there can be no question that Israel's views concerning purifications are, for the most part, very old.

1. Evidence in the Prophetic Writings.

4. Ethnic Analogies: Among the **Aryans** the impurities described in the Hindu Manu-shastra have an esthetic, not a religious-esthetic, character. **Greeks** and **Romans** used lustrations after contact with the dead (Vergil, *Æneid*, vi. 229), and reckoned hair, wool, and nail-parings as impurities. Spiegel, Justi, and Tiele regard **Persian** conceptions as differing in starting-point and area from the Hebrews', though Hitzig ascribes to Persian thought a considerable influence upon Old Testament religion. That **Babylonians** made a distinction between clean and unclean is proved, and on specified days certain kinds of meat were unlawful. Regulations existed also concerning contact with the dead and resulting disability, also concerning sexual relations. The **Sabeans** and **Arameans**, according to Chwolson, prohibited as food the flesh of the camel and of animals which had incisors in both jaws, also of swine, dog, and ass, except in the yearly swine-sacrifice. They refused also doves, birds of prey, and certain vegetables. Those afflicted with certain diseases were considered unclean. Emission and the menses received attention from them, and contact with a corpse necessitated purification. Prayer was forbidden those in an impure state. Among the northern **Mandæans** distinctions were made as to clean and unclean animals, the woman who had given birth to a child was isolated, contagious diseases were defiling, and the results of nocturnal emissions and the menses were similar to those among the Hebrews. Of the **Syrians** Lucian reports (*De dea Syria*, liv.) that swine were neither eaten nor sacrificed. Fish they eschewed, since Derceto had the form of a fish, and doves, because Semiramis had been transformed into a dove. Uncleanness for a day resulted from the breach of some of these taboos. **Phenicians** also had distinctions as to kinds of animals fit for food, but in respect to birds their distinctions were not those of the Hebrews. In the mystic sacrifice they offered men, dogs, and swine (Smith, *Rel. of Sem.*, 220–221). In northwestern **Arabian** inscriptions directions with respect to sexual relations, contact with a corpse and a menstruating woman are found. **Egyptians** feared to eat doves, ascribed uncleanness to certain plants, and in general had the distinction between clean and unclean.

The result of this inquiry is, therefore, that, while the Hebrews inherited a stock of notions upon the subject, comparison shows that in their religion they developed these notions along lines of their own choosing.

5. Origin of the Old Testament Doctrine of Uncleanness: The idea of the Old Testament is that in the specified objects actual uncleanness inheres, but not that the result is absolute and necessary psychological irreligiousness and immorality. While symbolical interpretations have from time to time been offered (e.g., Barnabas, *Epistle*, x.; Philo, *De agricultura Noæ*, xxv.–xxxi.; Clement of Alexandria, *Pædagogus*, iii.; Kurtz, *Opferkultus*, pp. 7–8, Mitau, 1862), such an interpretation is not indicated in the Old Testament and is not consistently applicable. The view has been advanced that the object was to protect the dwelling of God from approach by a man in a condition unbecoming a worshiper, or that Israel was by the laws concerning purity separated and differentiated from other peoples. But these replies simply put the question a stage farther back. The explanation has been given that the regulations arose from fear of contagion, from disgust or natural abhorrence or instinctive revulsion. But these explanations do not cover all the facts, particularly the omissions (for example, of a contagious disease like the plague). Physiological motives are insufficient. Riehm and Schlottmann have brought the subject into relation with sin; but the relationship of sin to uncleanness is a late notion, coming out in Ezekiel. As Giesebrecht remarks (*Grundzüge der israelitischen Geschichte*, p. 111, Leipsic, 1903), "the conceptions clean and unclean have nothing immediately to do with the ethical." Others have brought in the two factors of final being, birth and death, procreation and corruption, origin and end, with the idea that the ethical opposition to absolute holiness inherent in these relegates them to the sphere of the sinful and impure (e.g., G. F. Oehler, *Alttestamentliche Theologie*, §§ 123–124, Tübingen, 1873–74). But this theory is met by the objection that the new-born child was never regarded by the Hebrews as unclean. The principal idea in the Old Testament conception of uncleanness was the relation to death apparent in the given phenomena. The opposition

1. Unsatisfactory Explanations.

2. The Principal Idea the Relationship to Death.

between the holy living God and the death which results from a sickness is thoroughgoing, and in insensate and finite things that corruption was considered inherent which is the opposite of God. In particular it may be remarked that since the disgust at blood, the seat of the life, was an old inheritance, it follows that those animals were not regarded as fit for food which devoured other animals in their blood; and a similar line of reasoning applies to the unclean birds of prey or carrion. The loss of blood at childbirth seemingly puts the mother into connection with death-phenomena—the issue of the vital fluid. The delimitation of the areas of cleanness and uncleanness through the action of instinctive repulsion and disgust reveals the basis of uncleanness in a religious-ethical-esthetic relationship. An unpleasant odor (like that of the camel) or repugnant habits or appearance may have helped to put some animals in the class of unclean. The derivation of the Old Testament presentations about unclean beasts from religious-historical, demonistic, and totemistic origins, which derivation is approved by Stade, Benzinger, Frey, and Matthes, simply refers the matter to an earlier stage.

II. Purification.—1. The Removal of Uncleanness: For unclean beasts there is no purification. The woman in childbirth.—For seven or fourteen days respectively (i.e., after the birth of a boy or a girl) the woman is as thoroughly unclean as in the time of her menstruation; and, after washing herself and her clothes, she is clean from positive impurity, but not from negative impurity (i.e., keeping aloof from holy things and from the sanctuary), which can be removed only by presenting a lamb one year old as a burnt-offering, and a young pigeon or turtle-dove as a sin-offering; but, if she be poor, a pigeon or a turtle-dove suffices for the burnt-offering also (Lev. vii. 6–8).

1. Women in Child-birth.

In cases of leprosy, he who has shown a doubtful symptom of leprosy on his body has only to wash his garments; garments affected with leprosy must be burned; garments or stuffs which showed only doubtful signs of leprosy are to be washed (Lev. xiii. 6, 34, 52, 54, 55, 57–58). At the purification of the leper, one of the two clean live birds is to be killed over a vessel containing spring water; the other is to be dipped in the mixed blood and water, together with cedar-wood, hyssop, and a crimson thread or band. The fluid is then sprinkled upon the convalescent seven times, and the living bird is allowed to fly away. The convalescent then washes his garments, shaves his hair, and bathes, as he is to do again on the seventh day. Of the blood of the lamb killed as trespass-offering the priest sprinkles upon the top of his right ear, upon the thumb of his right hand, and upon the great toe of his right foot; then some of the oil is sprinkled seven times toward the holy place. Next the ewe-lamb is presented as a sin-offering, and the second he-lamb as a burnt-offering, accompanied by the usual bloodless oblation of the flour. In case of poverty, for the sin-offering and burnt-offering two turtle-doves or two young pigeons are accepted (Lev. xiv. 4–32). A leprous house is to be broken down, and he who slept or ate in it must wash his garments. But, if the house is declared clean, its purification is effected as described above (Lev. xiv. 4–7, 45–53).

2. Leprosy.

A man with a discharge, after recovering is to wash his garments, and bathe in running water; he presents two turtle-doves or two young pigeons, one for a sin-offering and the other for a burnt-offering. Persons defiled directly or indirectly by such a person have only to wash their garments, and bathe their bodies. Earthen vessels touched by the patient must be broken; wooden ones rinsed with water. Nocturnal accidents render the persons unclean till the evening, when they must bathe, while all stained garments require washing (Lev. xv. 5–18). For the menstruating woman no purification is indicated; but the persons indirectly defiled by her must wash garments and person (Lev. xv. 21–22). Since, however, the irregular issue of blood on the part of the woman is regarded only as temporary, different from the regular issue, having the same defiling qualifications, it may be taken for granted that the lawgiver intended the same purificatory laws for the menstruating woman as for the one afflicted with an irregular issue of blood (Lev. xv. 25–26, 29–30).

3. Emissions.

Whoever carries the carcass of unclean animals must wash his garments; the objects upon which a carcass accidentally falls, such as utensils of wood, garments, or skins, require cleansing by being left in water till the evening; earthen vessels, ovens, and stoves must be broken. Carrying the carcass of a clean animal requires washing of garments (Lev. xi. 25, 28, 32, 33, 35, 40). Defilement from a corpse requires a red heifer without spot, and upon which never came yoke. The ashes of the burned heifer are put into running water, which becomes the water of abomination, i.e., the water appointed for the purification of uncleanness (in this sense the word *may niddah*, Num. xix. 9, is to be taken). With this water, those who have become defiled directly or indirectly for a dead person, as well as the house of the dead and its vessels, are to be sprinkled, by means of hyssop, on the third and seventh day after the defilement; and on the seventh day the person shall purify himself, and wash his clothes. The latter must also be done by him who prepares, keeps, and uses the ashes. The officiating priest, as well as the man who burned the red heifer, have, besides, to bathe their flesh in water (Num. xix. 1–8, 10, 12–13, 17–21). The Nazirite who became defiled by a sudden death was to shave his head on the seventh day, offer two doves or young pigeons, one as a sin-offering, the other as a burnt-offering, and a lamb as a trespass-offering, and lose the time passed in Naziritic separation before his defilement (Num. vi. 9–12).

4. Dead Things.

Of the booty taken from heathen nations every thing that may abide the fire is to go through it, and must be purified with the water of separation; all that abideth not the fire is to go through the water; and a person touching such booty must wash his clothes on the seventh day (Num. xxxi. 23).

5. Booty.

3. Underlying Conceptions: The destruction of unclean things, in whatever form or manner, needs no explanation. Going through fire is easily understood, since fire is often mentioned as a purifying means (Ps. xii. 6). That water should be used for removing the ethico-esthetic impurity is a matter of course; and it is possible that "living" water is meant, even where it is not expressly stated. The sin and burnt sacrifices required of the woman after childbirth, the leper, the man having a running issue, and the woman having an issue of blood, have their usual signification. In the purification of the leper all materials and actions show the great step which the person to be purified took from the awful nearness of death to the gladsome communion of untroubled life. In removing the impurity caused by the touch of a dead person the red color of the cow, as symbol of the source of life, being in the blood, must be considered. As a yoke had never come upon her, she was the emblem of virgin energy. Cedar-wood, crimson thread, and hyssop, which were also used, represent emblems of incorruptibility, medicine against impurity, and symbol of life.

III. Postcanonical Development: When, in the time of Ezra, Israel undertook to observe even the laws concerning clean and unclean according to the Pentateuch, the scribes assumed clearly to define, not only the laws in the canon, but also inferences deduced from them. These rules and regulations are found in the treatises *Ḥullin, Niddah, Ṭebul Yom, Ohalot, 'Abodah Zarah* (ii. 6), *Miḳwa'ot, Yadayim* (see TALMUD). Evident among the restrictions were those against entering the house of a Gentile (cf. John xviii. 28; Acts x. 28), which resulted in defilement like that caused by contact with the dead, accounted for on the supposition of the burial of abortions in the house. The idea of a heathen land's conveying a like impurity finds support in Amos vii. 17, cf. Num. xxxi. 23. Water was used, as well as fire, in purifications; but the hand-washing, of which much appears in the New Testament, is not an Old Testament phenomenon. But not all Israelites took part in these rigorous purificatory efforts. Religious indifference led to laxness (Tobit i. 10–11), while overscrupulousness led to the formation of special societies, the most rigorous of which was that of the Chasidim (q.v.).

That the Old Testament ideas of impurities and purifications existed before and after the time of Christ is seen from I Macc. i. 62–63; II Macc. vi. 18, vii. 1–2, xi. 31; Tacitus, *Hist.*, v. 4–5. The sixth part of the Mishnah (compiled about 180 A.D.) shows a development of the Old Testament purificatory laws. But partly in consequence of the declarations of Christ—though he did not abolish the ideas of his times concerning clean and unclean (Matt. viii. 4; Luke xvii. 14) when dealing with unconverted persons—concerning the spirituality of the Old Testament religion and morals (Matt. v. 17, 21 sqq., vii. 12, xi. 30, xii. 8, xv. 11); partly in consequence of the work of the Holy Spirit, who reminded the disciples of the new spiritual foundation of the Christian religion (John xiv. 26), and showed to Peter in a vision that the difference of food has lost its authority in the Christian eon of salvation (Acts x. 15), Jewish Christians were at a very early period converted to eat with Gentile Christians, by receiving Christ as the new living lawgiver (Gal. ii. 12–20). The departure of this Jewish-Christian part of the first Christians from Jerusalem, and the destruction of the temple, became, at least to the less rigorous among them, a guide to regard the *lex ceremonialis* of the Old Testament (cf. Heb. ix. 1) as perfected, i.e., spiritualized, in Christianity. The Church of Christ knows, it is true, that death is the wages of sin (Rom. vi. 23), and groans to be relieved from the body of this death (vii. 24); but she does not regard the death of the body as the evil most to be avoided, but the spiritual and everlasting death (Matt. viii. 22; Luke ix. 60). "Let the dead bury their dead: but go thou and preach the kingdom of God." See for ethnic parallels COMPARATIVE RELIGION, VI., 1, c.

E. KÖNIG.

BIBLIOGRAPHY: From the comparative side the best three books are: J. G. Fraser, *Golden Bough*, especially i. 323–325, ii. 204–233, 304–309, London, 1900; E. B. Tylor, *Primitive Culture*, especially ii. 25–27, 431–433, ib. 1891; F. B. Jevons, *Introduction to the History of Religion*, pp. 57–58, 75–78, 102, 116–127, ib. 1896. For the Semitic world consult: Smith, *Rel. of Sem.*, 122, 324 sqq., 447–448; idem, *Kinship*, chap. viii., 304–311 et passim; D. Nielsen, *Die altarabische Mondreligion*, pp. 204–208, Strasburg, 1904; M. J. Lagrange, *Études sur les religions sémitiques*, pp. 140 sqq., 161, 237, 395 sqq., Paris, 1905. For other regions consult: F. C. Movers, *Die Phönizier*, 2 vols., Bonn, 1841–56; D. A. Chwolson, *Die Ssabier*, i. 146 sqq., St. Petersburg, 1856; L. Krehl, *Religion der vorislamischen Araber*, pp. 30–34, Leipsic, 1863; F. Spiegel, *Eranische Altertumskunde*, ii. 144–145, ib. 1873; F. Justi, *Geschichte des alten Persiens*, pp. 144–145, ib. 1879; P. E. Lucius, *Der Essenismus*, Strasburg, 1881; E. Westermarck, *History of Human Marriage*, chaps. xiv.–xv., London, 1894; A. Wiedemann, *Die Toten und ihre Reiche im Glauben der alten Aegypter*, pp. 25 sqq., Leipsic, 1900; Wellhausen, *Heidentum*, pp. 113 sqq.

On the custom of the Hebrews consult: H. Ewald, *Altertümer des Volkes Israel*, pp. 192 sqq., Göttingen, 1866, Eng. transl., pp. 142 sqq., Boston, 1876; W. Baudissin, *Studien zur semitischen Religionsgeschichte*, ii. 20 sqq., 90 sqq., Leipsic, 1878 (important discussion); Benzinger, *Archäologie*, § 72; Nowack, *Archäologie*, ii. 287 sqq.; J. Frey, *Tod, Seelenglaube und Seelenkult im alten Israel*, pp. 127, 137 sqq., Leipsic, 1898; Matthes, in *ThT*, 1899, pp. 293 sqq.; V. Zapletal, *Totemismus und die Urreligion Israels*, pp. 81 sqq., Freiburg, 1901; W. Bousset, *Religion des Judentums*, pp. 202 sqq., Berlin, 1903; K. Marti, *Geschichte der israelitischen Religion*, Stuttgart, 1903; the commentaries on Exodus, Leviticus, and Deuteronomy; and the works on O. T. theology.

DEFINITOR: An official of religious orders who, according to the reformed constitutions of the Middle Ages, stood at the head of a district (*definitio*). The orders consisted of congregations, which were divided into *definitiones*, each including a certain number of monasteries. The heads of the houses were subject to the definitor, the latter to the provincial, and the provincial to the general.

DEGRADATION: A severe penalty inflicted upon delinquent clerics by the ancient ecclesiastical discipline (see JURISDICTION, ECCLESIASTICAL). By the end of the twelfth century the doctrine of the indelible character of holy orders had been generally accepted; and in connection with it and with the struggle of the Church for clerical immunities the earlier penalty of deposition was divided into what was now called deposition (the removal of a cleric from his office and benefice with the prohibition of the exercise of his orders) and degradation, which, in addition, withdrew from him all the privileges of the clerical state. The *degradatio verbalis* involved the pronouncement of the former penalties, and was performed by the bishop with the assent of the chapter in the case of the minor orders, of three bishops in that of deacons, and of six bishops, mitered abbots, or other dignitaries in that of priests. The solemn *degradatio actualis* went further and involved the observance of special formalities—the stripping of the culprit of his vestments, the shaving of the head to obliterate the tonsure, and the scraping of the thumbs and fingers as if to remove the unction bestowed at ordination. These ceremonies were supposed to take place in the presence of the secular authority, to whose jurisdiction the delinquent, as now no more than a mere layman, was then handed over.

DE HÆRETICO COMBURENDO: A writ for the burning of heretics by the secular power after they had been condemned by the ecclesiastical power. It was issued in England under Henry IV. in 1401; expanded under Henry V. in 1415; repealed in the twenty-fifth year of Henry VIII. (1534), and again in the first year of Edward VI. (1547); revived in the first year of Mary (1553); repealed in the first year of Elizabeth (1559), and finally in the twenty-ninth year of Charles II. (1678). In its original form it was directed against the Lollards, and was the earliest step taken by Parliament in their suppression, but was afterward used against Protestants in general. It solemnly abjures them to abstain entirely from preaching or otherwise circulating their "new doctrines and wicked, heretical, and erroneous opinions"; orders them to give up the books which advocate the same; threatens them with imprisonment for disobedience if they refuse; and on their condemnation by the ecclesiastical authorities lays it upon the secular authorities to burn them.

Bibliography: The full text of the writ is given in Gee and Hardy, *Documents*, pp. 133–137. Consult: J. Gairdner, *The English Church in the 16. Century*, pp. 146, 231, 249, 346, 362, London, 1903; J. H. Overton, *The Church in England*, i. 300, 418, ii. 19, ib. 1897.

DEISM.

The term "Deism" properly denotes a belief in deity that is rational and universal, in contrast to Atheism and Pantheism (qq.v.), on the one hand, and to uncritical Theism (q.v.), on the other. Deism, which originated in England, represented an effort to find a standard of religious truth by which the conflicting claims of individual creeds and the pretensions of supernatural revelation might be tested, and which should harmonize with the metaphysical results of the new sciences. It is in this sense that "natural religion" and the term "natural" itself are so intimately bound up with the history of Deism (see Natural Theology). Since the habit was to regard religion as a system of metaphysics, the desired standard of truth was sought in a metaphysics that should be universally cognizable and whose validity might be tested by the facts of experience. The development of Deism in consequence is closely bound up with the development of sensualism and mechanism, and with the struggle between the a priori philosophy and empiricism, as well as with the development of the theory of morals which at the same time had succeeded in emancipating itself from the sway of theology and sought to lay its foundations upon epistemology and psychology (see Ethics). Since the entire conception of natural religion is nothing but a restatement of the Stoic *lex naturæ* (see Natural Law), Deism may be taken as the point of departure for the employment of the epistemological and psychological methods in the philosophy of religion. At the same time, in the attempt to decide between the conflicting claims of particular revelations, Deism made its chief problem the study of the historical connection between natural religion and revelation, and became a philosophy of the history of religion in which the relation of elemental truth, as determined by the mind, to Christian revelation and to pagan truth was fixed on purely rational lines. Criticism of historic Christianity and the recognition of the relative truth contained in other creeds led to the abandonment of the system of the philosophy of history at first adopted and made way for the modern principles of the philosophy of religion.

As a contributory force, with Puritan radicalism, to the opposition with which the Anglican Church was confronted, Deism was naturally at odds with respectable conservatism in the State, the Church, and the world of literature and learning. Not till Hume and Gibbon took them up did the problems of Deism attain full scientific treatment in lasting and really literary form. Far more profound was the influence it exercised on French literature. The real tendency of Deism is best expressed in the name "freethinkers," which its advocates adopted; by their opponents they were designated as Naturalists on account of their opposition to supernatural revelation.

I. England: The beginnings of Deism appear in the seventeenth century. Its main principles are to be found in the writings of Lord Herbert of Cherbury (d. 1648), one of the most original thinkers of his century, who devoted the calm evening of a life spent in a military and diplomatic career to a search for a standard and a guide in the conflicts of creeds and systems. He was a friend of Grotius, Casaubon, and Gassendi, and during a long sojourn in France made himself acquainted with the thought of Montaigne, of Bodin, and especially of Charron. His works are: *De Veritate* (Paris, 1624); *De religione Gentilium errorumque apud eos causis* (London, 1645); and two minor treatises, *De causis errorum* and *De religione laici*. The first

1. Lord Herbert of Cherbury.

work advances a theory of knowledge based upon the recognition of innate universal characteristics on the object perceived, and rigidly opposed to knowledge supernatural in its origin and determinable only by strife and conflict. The second work lays down the common marks by which religious truth is recognized. These are a belief in the existence of the Deity, the obligation to reverence such a power, the identification of worship with practical morality, the obligation to repent of sin and to abandon it, and, finally, divine recompense in this world and the next. These five essentials (the so-called "Five Articles" of the English Deists) constitute the nucleus of all religions and of Christianity in its primitive, uncorrupted form. The variations between positive religions are explained as due partly to the allegorization of nature, partly to self-deception, the workings of imagination, and priestly guile.

Herbert's influence disappeared in the storms of the Puritan Revolution, and Deism found the most important impetus supplied to its progress in ecclesiastical circles. The learning of the Renaissance had served to incline the clergy of the Establishment to a moderate rational theology, and in the conflict between Puritans and Anglicans, and between Roman Catholics and Protestants, it became common to invoke Reason as arbiter. Later Deists could appeal to the arguments of leading theologians, as well as to those of the Cambridge Platonists (q.v.), who, in their conflict against the sensualism of Hobbes, exalted the authority of moral intuitions. The Revolution served to intensify the growing feeling against what was arbitrary in religion, and emphasized the demand for subjective independence in the field of reason and the need of unity in the realm of practical morality.

Antagonism to theological supernaturalism stands out as the most conspicuous characteristic in the system of Hobbes (d. 1679; see Hobbes, Thomas), inspired by the teachings of the new mathematical and natural sciences. The different religions are explained as the product of human fear interpreting natural phenomena in anthropomorphic form, or, in their higher aspects, as the outcome of reflection on causal relation in the universe.

2. Hobbes and Others.

Miracles and revelations are in themselves improbable, and may be most easily explained as the imaginings of the ignorant. Positive religion is the creation of the State, and the sovereign justly possesses unconditional power to enforce its prescriptions, for only in this way can religious strife be avoided. Between religion thus naturally explained and a prophetic and Christian revelation Hobbes, nevertheless, attempted to mediate; he mentions as the means that might lead to such a reconciliation the rational interpretation of miracles, the differentiation between the inner moral sense of Scripture and mere figurative expression, and the historical criticisms of Biblical sources. The entire apparatus of Rationalism is here to be found, limited only in its application. Further, Spinoza's *Tractatus theologico-politicus* (1670) and Bayle's *Dictionnaire* (1695–97) were effective in shaping the character of Deism. Of no small importance, also, was the rise of a literature of comparative religion and the publication of ethnographical studies and works of travel. China, Arabia, Egypt, Persia, India, savage nations even, were brought within the horizon of religious investigation. Philosophy, beginning with Locke's theory of knowledge, and natural science, with Newton's theory of gravitation, contributed to the opposition with which dogma was confronted. Yet their attitude was not one of hostility to religion, which they sought rather to utilize for the purpose of establishing the desired universal standard of truth. Newton and Boyle succeeded in reconciling the creed of the Church with their mechanical metaphysics; and this union remained characteristic of England, so that even men like Priestley and Hartley did not shrink from supporting their materialistic theories by theological arguments. We have here the blending of a sensualistic epistemology, a mechanical-teleological metaphysics, a historical criticism, and an aprioristic ethics whose product in the shape of natural religion was destined first to undermine Christianity, then to compete with it, and finally to supplant it.

These various tendencies could not show themselves fully under the ecclesiastical restraint of the Restoration, yet they appear clearly enough in the writings of Charles Blount (d. 1693), usually placed second to Herbert in the lists of Deists.

3. Charles Blount.

Like his predecessor, Blount dwells on the conflict between rival religions, and finds a standard of adjustment in a fusion of Herbert's theory of universal characteristics with Hobbes's prescription by the State. Like Hobbes and Spinoza, he touches serious problems of Biblical criticism at this early date. Freedom from prejudice is his boast; he asserts the supernatural character of Christianity on the basis of its miracles, after he has already rendered them dubious by parallels with non-Christian miracles. His works were: *Anima mundi* (London, 1679), *Great is Diana of the Ephesians* (1680), and *The Two First Books of Philostratus concerning the Life of Apollonius Tyaneus, published in English with notes* (1680).

The Revolution of 1688, the establishment of the freedom of the press in 1694, the political favor that was bestowed on the new tendencies in theology, in opposition to the stricter Anglicanism which was tainted with Stuart partizanship, were conditions favorable to the development of the seed that had already been planted.

4. John Locke.

Parallel with the liberalization of orthodox dogma, there ran a more radical development aiming at the attainment of a standard for the testing of the contents of revelation. Of surpassing importance in this direction was the influence and work of John Locke (d. 1704), who, in the field of theology, found his starting-point, like most prominent thinkers of the age, in the conflict of systems, doctrines, and practises. Out of his reflections on the data of experience he developed a mechanical-teleological metaphysics and an empirical-utilitarian ethics, the latter agreeing with the old idea of *lex naturæ* in that ethical experience merely confirms the connection established by a teleological government of the universe between certain acts and their consequences. In spite of his supernaturalist tendencies, Locke nevertheless maintained, in his *Letters on Toleration* (1689–92), that only rational demonstration, and not compulsion or mere assertion, can establish the validity of revelation. In the *Essay concerning Human Understanding* (1690) he had investigated the conception of revelation from the epistemological standpoint, and laid down the criteria by which the true revelation is to be distinguished from other doctrines which claim such authority. Strict proof of the formal character of revelation must be adduced; the tradition which communicates it to us must be fully accredited by both external and internal evidence; and its content must be shown to correspond with rational metaphysics and ethics. Revelation is revelation; but, after it is once given, it may be shown a posteriori to be rational, i.e., capable of being deduced from the premises of our reason. Only where this is possible is there a presumption in favor of the purely mysterious parts of revelation. Where these criteria are disregarded the way is open to the excesses of sects and priesthoods by which religion, the *differentia* of reasoning man, has often made him appear less rational than the beasts. Locke advances therefore the remarkable conception of a revelation that reveals only the reasonable and the universally cognizable. The practical consequences of the thesis are deduced in his *Reasonableness of Christianity as Delivered in the Scriptures* (1695), which aims at the termination of religious strife through the recovery of the truths of primitive, rational Christianity. From the Gospels and the Acts, as distinguished from the Epistles, he elicits as the fundamental Christian verities the doctrine of the Messiahship of Jesus and that of the kingdom of God. Inseparably connected with these are the recognition of Jesus as ruler of this kingdom, forgiveness of sins, and subjection to the moral law of the kingdom. This law is identical with the ethical portion of the law of Moses, which in its turn corresponds to the *lex naturæ* or *rationis*. The Gospel is but the divine summary and exposition of the law of nature, and it is the advantage of Christianity over pagan creeds and philosophies that it offers this law of nature intelligibly, with divine authority, and free from merely ceremonial sacerdotalism. To do this it requires the aid of a supernatural revelation, whose message is attainable through reason also, but only in an imperfect way.

5. Toland, Collins, and Others.

Deducing the full consequences of Locke's theory, John Toland (q.v.; d. 1722), in his *Christianity not Mysterious* (1696), maintained that the content of revelation must neither contradict nor transcend the dictates of reason. Revelation is not the basis of truth, but only a "means of information" by which man may arrive at knowledge, the sanction for which must be found in reason. Primitive Christianity knew nothing of mystery, whose sources are Judaic and Greek, and the original Christian use of the word *mysterium* conveyed no idea of that which transcended reason. The basis is thus laid for the critical study of early Christianity. Further problems of Biblical criticism and the distinction between the diverse parties in primitive Christianity are advanced in Toland's *Amyntor* (1699) and *Nazarenus; or Jewish, Gentile and Mahometan Christianity* (1718). In like manner, Anthony Collins (q.v.; d. 1729), in his *Discourse of Freethinking* (1713), developed the consequences of Locke's propositions. Revelation depends for its sanction upon its agreement with reason, and what is contrary to reason is not revelation. Practical morality is independent of dogma, which, on the contrary, has been the cause of much evil in the history of the world. Christ and the Apostles, the prototypes of the freethinkers, never made use of supernatural authority, but confined themselves to simple, rational demonstration. Collins's work elicited numerous replies; but none really made answer to his main thesis. After remaining silent for eleven years, Collins renewed the contest with a contribution on prophecy and miracles. Setting out from Locke's proposition that revelation was truth sanctioned by reason, he found it a simple step to reject prophecy and miracles as non-essential characteristics of religion, amounting at most to mere didactic devices. The mathematician William Whiston (q.v.; d. 1752) gave a new impulse to the controversy by the publication of *The True Text* (1722), in which the lack of real concordance between the New Testament interpretation of Old Testament prophecies is pointed out, and the prevailing allegorical method of reconciling such differences summarily rejected. The present form of the Old Testament is characterized as a forgery perpetrated by the Jews, and an attempt is made by Whiston to restore the original text. Collins, in his *Discourse on the Grounds and Reasons of the Christian Religion* (1724), agreed with Whiston as to the discrepancies between the two Testaments, but defended the allegorical method of interpretation. Thomas Woolston (q.v.; d. 1733) came to the support of Collins in this controversy over the Biblical prophecies; and when his opponents shifted their appeal from the prophecies to the miraculous acts of Jesus he applied his destructive allegorical method to those also, in his *Discourses on the Miracles of our Saviour* (1727–30).

Matthew Tindal (q.v.; d. 1733), in his dialogue *Christianity as Old as the Creation, or the Gospel a Republication of the Religion of Nature* (1730), produced the standard text-book of Deism. Proceeding from Locke's proposition of the identity of the truths of revelation with those of reason, he adduces a new array of arguments in support of that position.

6. Matthew Tindal.

The goodness of God, the vast extent of the earth, the long duration of human life on earth render it improbable that only to Jews and Christians was vouchsafed the favor of perceiving truth. We now have brought in the classic example of the three hundred million Chinese who surely could not all be excluded from the truth, and Confucianism begins to be extolled against much that is repugnant and harsh in the Mosaic law. Christianity, to be the truth, must find its substance in all religions; it must be as old as creation. The doctrines of the fall and of original sin can not stand, since it is irrational to believe in the exclusion from the truth of the vast majority of humanity. Tindal's position is orthodox to the extent that Judaism and Christianity are acknowledged as revelations, though revelations only of the *lex naturæ*, which is identified with natural religion, the primitive, uncorrupted faith, consisting in "the practise of morality in obedience to the will of God." An echo of the teachings of Tindal is found in Thomas Chubb (q.v.; d. 1747), whose *True Gospel of Jesus Christ* (1738) attempts to prove that what Jesus sought to teach his followers was but natural morality, or the law of nature.

7. Morgan, Annet, and Middleton.

Thomas Morgan (q.v.; d. 1743) continued Tindal's argument on its historical side in *The Moral Philosopher* (1737–40), displaying much originality in tracing the development of heathen religions, as well as of Judaism and Christianity. Abandoning the old method of deriving specific religions from priestly deception, he explains their rise through the gradual supplanting of the one God of the law of nature by a crowd of divinities connected with definite natural phenomena. The legislation of Moses, under Egyptian influences, imposed a rigid and nationally restricted form upon the *lex naturæ*, and the Jewish ritual and ceremonial is in essence a purely political institution. Full revelation of the law of nature came with Christ, who gave to the world in concentrated form the truth that had already been revealed to Confucius, Zoroaster, Socrates, and Plato. The protagonist of this divinely revealed truth after Christ was Paul, who, in his form of expression, indeed, was compelled to make concessions to the influence of Judaism, and in whom, therefore, much is to be taken figuratively. Peter, on the other hand, and the author of the Apocalypse misunderstood the import of the revelation of Christ and corrupted it in the spirit of Messianic Judaism. Persecution forced the two tendencies into union in the Catholic Church, and the Reformation has only partially succeeded in separating them. Morgan's argument results, therefore, in the rejection of the formerly assumed identity between the law of Moses and the *lex naturæ*, and the restriction of the latter, in the fulness of revelation, to Christianity. His conclusions were denied by William Warburton (q.v.) in *The Divine Legation of Moses* (1738–41). When the Christian apologists substituted for the argument from miracles the argument from personal witness and the credibility of Biblical evidence, Peter Annet (d. 1769), in his *Resurrection of Jesus* (1744), assailed the validity of such evidence, and first advanced the hypothesis of the illusory death of Jesus, suggesting also that possibly Paul should be regarded as the founder of a new religion. In *Supernaturals Examined* (1747) Annet roundly denies the possibility of miracles. Conyers Middleton (q.v.; d. 1750) in his later writings sought to bridge over the gulf between sacred and profane history, and to test them equally by the same method. His *Inquiry into the Miraculous Powers* (1748) demonstrates that the belief in miracles is common to primitive Christianity and heathen creeds, and that it developed to great proportions in the later life of the Church, so that one is there confronted with an endless succession of miracles to which belongs the same degree of credibility that the apologists attributed to the miracles of the Bible. Though special reference to the New Testament was omitted, Middleton propounded a question to answer which no serious attempt was made when he asked why credence should be granted to one faith that is denied to another.

The Deistic controversy died out in England about the middle of the eighteenth century. The Deistic literature had exhausted its stock of materials, while its tenets had never obtained a strong hold on the people. The cold, inflexible, rational supernaturalism of Paley (q.v.; d. 1805) was considered as the final settlement of these long conflicts. From the beginning, however, there had been a class of critics, representatives of the old Renaissance spirit, and inimical, therefore, to the Stoic and Christian ethics, who had only partially shared the views of the Deists, and in some ways had advanced to a position far beyond them. Shaftesbury (q.v.; d. 1713), in opposition to the utilitarian and supernaturalist ethics of Locke and Clarke, developed the conception of a strictly autonomous moral code having its basis in a moral instinct in man whose end is to bring individual and society to harmonious self-perfection. Bernard Mandeville (1733) adopted the Epicureanism of Hobbes and Gassendi, studied moral problems in the skeptical spirit of Montaigne and La Rochefoucauld, gave the preference to Bayle over the Deists, and developed empiricism into a sort of Agnosticism. He criticized the prevailing morality as a mere conventional lie. Christianity—which the Deists had wished, while reforming, to maintain—he declared impossible, not only as a religion, but as a system of morality. His *Free Thought on Religion* (1720) has caused him to be included in the ranks of the Deists; but his real position is brought out in the *Fable of the Bees* (1714). Henry Dodwell (q.v.; d. 1711), in *Christianity not Founded on Argument* (1742), attempted to demonstrate the invalidity of the rationalistic basis for Christian truth constructed by the Deists, from the very nature of the religious impulse, which, being opposed to rational argumentation, calls for the support of tradition and mystery, and finds fascination in the attitude of *credo quia absurdum*. The only proof proceeds from a mystic inner enlightenment; logical demonstrations like those of Clarke or the Boyle lectures are only destructive of religion. Bolingbroke (d. 1751) voices the French influence in a capricious and dilettante manner. Despising all religions as the product of enthusiasm, fraud, and superstition, he nevertheless concedes to real Christianity the possession of moral and rational truth; an advocate of freedom of thought, he supports an established church in the interest of the State and of public morals (*Letters on the Study and Use of History*, 1752; *Essays*, 1753).

8. Shaftesbury, Mandeville, Dodwell, Bolingbroke.

Far greater is the influence of David Hume (q.v.; d. 1776), who summarized the Deistic criticism and raised it to the level of modern scientific method by emancipating it from the conception of a deity conceived through the reason and by abandoning its characteristic interpretation of history.

9. Hume's Influence. He separates Locke's theory of knowledge from its connection with a scheme of mechanical teleology, and confines the human mind within the realm of sense perception. Beginning then with the crudest factors of experience and not with a religious and ethical norm, he traces the development of systems of religion, ethics, and philosophy in an ascending course through the ages. He thus overthrew the Deistic philosophy of religion while he developed their critical method to the extent of making it the starting-point for the English positivist philosophy of religion. Distinguishing between the metaphysical problem of the idea of God and the historical problem of the rise of religions, he denied the possibility of attaining a knowledge of deity through the reason, and explained religion as arising from the misconception or arbitrary misinterpretation of experience (*Dialogues Concerning Natural Religion*, written in 1751, but not published till 1779; *Natural History of Religion*, 1757). Against the justification of religion by other means than rational Hume directs his celebrated critique of miracles, in which to the possibility of miraculous occurrences he opposes the possibility of error on the part of the observer or historian. Human experience, affected by ignorance, fancy, and the imaginings of fear and hope, explains sufficiently the growth of religion. Hume's contemporaries failed to recognize the portentous transformation which he had effected in the character of Deism. The Scottish "common-sense school" saved for a time the old natural theology and the theological argument from miracles to revelation; but in reality Hume's skeptical method, continued by Hamilton and united to French Positivism by Mill and Browne, became, in connection with modern ethnology and anthropology, the basis of a psychological philosophy of religion in which the data of outward experience are the main factors (Evolutionism, Positivism, Agnosticism—Tylor, Spencer, Lubbock, Andrew Lang, etc.). In so far as Hume's influence prevailed among his contemporaries, it may be said to have amalgamated with that of Voltaire; the "infidels," as they were now called, were Voltairians. Most prominent among them was Gibbon (d. 1794), whose *Decline and Fall* offers the first dignified pragmatic treatment of the rise of Christianity. The fundamental principles of Deism became tinged in the nineteenth century with skepticism, pessimism, or pantheism, but the conceptions of natural religion retained largely their old character.

II. France: With other English influences Deism entered France, where, however, only its materialistic and revolutionary phases were seized upon, to the exclusion of that religiosity which had never been lost in England. French Deism stood outside of theology. The English writers who came to exercise the greatest influence were Hobbes, Locke, Shaftesbury, Pope, Bolingbroke, and Hume. Of the true Deists only Collins, the most critical and the least theological, became prominent.

1. Voltaire. Voltaire (q.v.; d. 1778) embraced the conception of natural religion with ardor, and entered into a polemic against intolerance in Church and State as well as against the philosophy of the Church and the prevailing religious Cartesianism (*Essai sur les mœurs et l'esprit des nations*, 1754–58; *Dictionnaire philosophique*, 1764). He derived his natural philosophy from Newton and Clarke, his theory of knowledge and his ideas on toleration from Locke, the main principles of his ethics from Shaftesbury, his critical method and the conception of natural religion from the Deists. All phenomena are explained historically by the interaction between man and his environment, and all things are governed by God acting only in accordance with natural laws. Natural morality and religion are not entirely innate ideas, but rather simple and universally prevalent conditions standing in need of development and following a course that leads through errors arising from ignorance and fear to an ultimate standard truth which is characterized as the "fruit of the cultivated reason." Deism is thereby emptied of all religious content and restricted to the field of morals and rational metaphysics. All that is essentially characteristic of human nature is the same everywhere; all that depends on custom varies. The chief influences for changes in the human mind are climate, government, religion, and in opposition to these one should seek to arrive at the underlying, undiversified unity. "Dogma leads to fanaticism and strife; morality everywhere inspires harmony." The rise of positive religions may be studied psychologically in children and savages. Fear and ignorance of the law of nature are the primary causes; the parallel growth of social groups and the need of authority cooperate. In China alone natural religion has escaped this pernicious development. India became the home of theological speculation, and influenced the religions of the West, of which the most important was Judaism as the parent of Christianity and Mohammedanism. Moses was a shrewd politician; the prophets were enthusiasts like the dervishes, or else epileptics; Jesus was a visionary like the founder of the Quakers, and his religion received life only through its union with Platonism. Voltaire's conception of the evolution of history entered deep into European thought.

By the side of the party of the *juste milieu* and of "good sense," of which Voltaire is the most prominent representative, there arose a school which carried the doctrines of mechanism and sensualism to their furthest consequences and evolved a philosophy of materialism.

2. The Encyclopedists. They removed from Deism the great factor of natural religion, retaining only its critical method as applied to the history of religion. The head of this school was Denis Diderot (q.v.; d. 1784), and its great organ of expression was the *Encyclopédie* (see ENCYCLOPEDISTS). The state censorship, however, compelled the projectors to call to their aid a number of contributors of conservative views and to bring their skeptical method to the task of defending the compromise between reason and revelation.

In this spirit the main religious topics were treated, but by a subtle infusion of the spirit of Bayle and the expedient of cross-references from these articles to topics which might be handled with greater freedom, Diderot succeeded in supplying the desired corrective.

It was the circle of Holbach (q.v.; d. 1789) that dared to apply the most extreme consequences of materialism to religious questions. Helvétius (q.v.; d. 1771) prepared the way with his *De l'esprit* (1758), in which he expounded a materialistic psychology and ethics. Their moral theories, deriving though they did from Hobbes and Hume, lost all connection with the position of Deism, which became for them a mere armory of weapons for the destruction of all religion with its consequences, intolerance and moral corruption. Holbach is undoubtedly the author of the *Système de la nature*, which appeared in 1770 as the work of Mirabaud. The *Système* is not original in ascribing the beginnings of religion to human hope and fear and to ignorance of the laws of nature. Fraud, ambition, and unhealthy enthusiasm have made use of it as a means of political and social influence and have succeeded in crystallizing its primitive emotions into positive creeds, within which animistic tendencies have been developed and subtilized into systems of metaphysics and theology—the sources of irrational intolerance. Christianity is but Galilean doctrines translated into Platonic metaphysics, and its theology to the present day hovers between the extremest anthropomorphism and the most abstract speculation. The natural religion of the Deists differs from the concrete religions only in that it proceeds not from fear and ignorance but from an optimistic interpretation of life; however, in attempting to prove by natural science the goodness of God and man and the adaptation of the world to the purpose of creation, it is but a half-matured critical method vainly endeavoring to reconcile the old irrationalism with the spirit of the new sciences. It is guilty of clinging to the naive view which regards the world as anthropocentric instead of recognizing the existence of laws to which man is indifferent—the purely causal, not teleological force of matter. Further, the whole scheme of identifying morality with religion—the psychological support of the Deistic position—is repudiated by Holbach, who defines morality as based solely on the natural law of self-preservation and self-perpetuation. Step by step Deism is thus stripped of its connection with revelation, with metaphysics, and finally with morality, and nothing is retained but its method of interpreting religion and its criticism of the facts of Christianity. From Holbach and his circle, and from the cognate group of the Encyclopedists, proceeded the so-called ideological school, who held the main problem of philosophy to be the analysis of the mental conceptions aroused by sensations from the material world (Condorcet, Sieyès, Naigeon, Garat, Volney, Dupuis, Saint-Lambert, Laplace, Cabanis, De Tracy, J. B. Say, Benjamin Constant, Bichat, Lamarck, Saint-Simon, Thurot, Stendhal). Out of this school, in turn, developed the positivism of Comte.

3. Holbach and the Theological School.

J. J. Rousseau (q.v.; d. 1778) gave quite a different tendency to Deism. Accepting in the main the sensualism of Locke and the metaphysics of Clarke and Newton, he maintains after the manner of Shaftesbury and Diderot a belief in inborn moral instincts which he distinguishes as "sentiments" from mere acquired ideas; he is true to the position of Deism in connecting this moral "sentiment" with a belief in God, and he protests against the separation between the two which the skepticism of Diderot had brought about. He was influenced by Richardson, as well as by Locke. "Sentiment" becomes the basis of a metaphysical system built up out of the data of experience under the influence of the Deistic philosophy, but redeemed from formalism by constant reference to sentimentality and emotion as the primary sources of religion. The nature of religion is not dogmatic but moralistic, practical, emotional. Rousseau, therefore, finds the essence of religion, not (like Voltaire) in the cultivated intellect, but in the naive and disinterested understanding of the uncultured. Conscious, rational progress in civilization, no less than supernaturalism in Church and State, is an outcome of the fall, when the will chose intellectual progress in preference to simple felicity. With Rousseau natural religion takes on a new meaning; "nature" is no longer universality or rationality in the cosmic order, in contrast to special supernatural and positive phenomena, but primitive simplicity and sincerity, in contrast to artificiality and studied reflection. In his scheme of the rise of religions he sets out from the common standpoint of the discrepancies and contradictions prevailing among historic creeds. Yet positive religion to him is not so much the product of ignorance and fear as the corruption of the original instinct through the selfishness of man, who has erected rigid creeds that he might arrogate to himself unwarranted privilege or escape the obligations of natural morality. Something of the true religion is to be found in every faith, and of all creeds Christianity has retained the greatest measure of the original truth, and the purest morality. So sublime and yet so simple does Rousseau find the Gospel that he can scarcely believe it the work of men. Its irrational elements he attributes to misconception on the part of the followers of Christ and especially of Paul, who had no personal intercourse with him. It was natural that between the advocate of such views and the party of the materialists strife should arise, and in fact Rousseau's religious influence in France was slight. On the rising German idealism, however, he exercised a mighty influence. (E. TROELTSCH.)

4. Rousseau.

BIBLIOGRAPHY: On the preparation for Deism in the *Aufklärung* ("enlightenment") consult: H. Henke, *Geschichte der christlichen Kirche*, vols. iv.–vi., Brunswick, 1804; K. Erdmann, *Die Aufklärung*, Hamburg, 1845; H. von Busche, *Die freie religiöse Aufklärung*, Darmstadt, 1846; F. C. Schlosser, *Geschichte des 18. Jahrhunderts*, 7 vols., Heidelberg, 1853–57; E. Henke, *Neuere Kirchengeschichte*, vol. ii., Halle, 1878; O. Pfleiderer, *Religions-Philosophie*, Berlin, 1896, Eng. transl., *Philosophy of Religion*, 4 vols, London, 1886–88.

Books which treat of Deism in general are: J. F. Hurst, *History of Rationalism*, New York, 1902; L. Noack, *Die*

Freidenker in der Religion, 3 vols., Bern, 1853-55; A. S. Farrar, *Critical History of Free Thought*, Lectures iv.-viii., London, 1863; C. J. Abbey and J. H. Overton, *Eng. Church in the 18th Century*, chap. iv., London, 1878 ("an admirable summary"); J. H. Overton and F. Relton, *The English Church (1714-1800)*, chaps. iii.-iv., London, 1906.

On English Deism the classic is J. Leland, *Deistical Writers*, 5th (best) ed. with Appendix by W. L. Brown, continuation by C. R. Edmonds, London, 1837. Consult: J. Hunt, *Religious Thought in England*, vols. ii.-iii., London, 1870; J. Cairns, *Unbelief in the 18th Century*, ib. 1881; L. Stephen, *Hist. of Eng. Thought in the 18th Century*, ib. 1881; E. Sayous, *Les Déistes anglais*, Paris, 1882; W. Arthur, *God without Religion; Deism and Sir James Stephen*, ib. 1887; W. E. H. Lecky, *Hist. of . . . Rationalism in Europe*, 2 vols., ib. 1899.

On Deism in France consult: C. Bartholmèss, *Histoire critique des doctrines religieuses modernes*, Strasburg, 1855; H. Taine, *Les Philosophes français du 19. siècle*, ib. 1867; F. Ravaisson, *La Philosophie française au 19. siècle*, ib. 1868; F. Picavet, *Les Idéologues*, ib. 1891; J. Texte, *Rousseau et les origines du cosmopolitisme littéraire*, ib. 1895.

On the German phase consult: K. R. Hagenbach, *German Rationalism*, Edinburgh, 1865; G. C. B. Pünjer, *Geschichte der christlichen Religionsphilosophie*, 2 vols., Brunswick, 1880-83, Eng. transl., Edinburgh, 1887; F. A. Lange, *Geschichte des Materialismus*, Leipsic, 1887, Eng. transl., 3 vols., London, 1877-81.

DEISSMAN, dais'mān, **GUSTAV ADOLF**: German Lutheran; b. at Langenscheid-an-der-Lahn, Nassau, Nov. 7, 1866. He studied at Tübingen (1885-88) and Berlin (1888), and the theological seminaries at Herborn (1889-90) and Marburg (1891-92). He became privat-docent at Marburg 1892; tutor in the Herborn theological seminary 1895; professor of New Testament exegesis at Heidelberg, 1897, and at Berlin, 1908. In 1906 he made an archeological tour of Asia Minor and Greece. His publications include a translation of IV Maccabees in E. Kautzsch's *Apokryphen und Pseudepigraphen des Alten Testaments* (Tübingen, 1900); *Die neutestamentliche Formel "in Christo Jesu"* (Marburg, 1892); *Johann Kepler und die Bibel: Ein Beitrag zur Geschichte der Autorität* (1894); *Bibelstudien: Beiträge, zumeist aus den Papyri und Inschriften, zur Geschichte der Sprache, des Schrifttums, und der Religion des hellenistischen Judentums und des Urchristentums* (1895; Eng. transl. by A. Griere, Edinburgh, 1901); *Neue Bibelstudien: Sprachgeschichtliche Beiträge, zumeist aus den Papyri und Inschriften, zur Erklärung des Neuen Testaments* (1897); *Briefe eines Herborner Classicus aus den Jahren 1605 und 1606* (Herborn, 1898); *Die sprachliche Erforschung der griechischen Bibel, ihr gegenwärtiger Stand und ihre Aufgaben* (Giessen, 1898); *Ein Original-Dokument aus der diokletianischen Christenverfolgung: Papyrus 713 des British Museum* (Tübingen, 1902; Eng. transl., "The Epistle of Psenosiris," London, 1902); *Evangelium und Urchristentum: Das Neue Testament im Lichte der historischen Forschung* (Munich, 1905); *Die Septuaginta-Papyri und andere altchristliche Texte der Heidelberger Papyrus-Sammlung* (Heidelberg, 1905); and *New Light on the New Testament, from Records of the Græco-Roman Period, Transl. from the Author's MS.* by *R. M. Strachan*, Edinburgh, 1907.

DELANY, WILLIAM: Irish Roman Catholic and president of University College, Dublin; b. at Leighlinbridge (12 m. n.e. of Kilkenny), County Carlow, Ireland, June 4, 1835. He was educated at Carlow College (1851-53), Maynooth College (1853-56), and the Gregorian University, Rome (1865-68), and entered the Society of Jesus in 1856, being ordained priest at Rome in 1866. He was professor in Clongowes-Wood College 1858-60 and in St. Stanislaus's College, Tullamore, 1860-65. In 1868-70 he was vice-president of the latter institution and its rector 1870-80; rector of St. Ignatius's College, Dublin, 1881-83; president of University College, Dublin, 1883-88, and since 1897. He was on the staff of the Gardiner Street Jesuit Church, Dublin, 1888-97. He has written *Lectures on Christian Reunion* (Dublin, 1896) and *Irish University Education* (1904).

DELITZSCH, dē'lich, **FRANZ**: Lutheran; b. at Leipsic Feb. 23, 1813; d. there Mar. 4, 1890. He came of Hebrew parentage; studied at Leipsic, and became privat-docent 1842; was called as ordinary professor to Rostock 1846; thence to Erlangen 1850; and back to Leipsic in 1867. In early life he was an adherent of the theology represented by Hofmann of Erlangen, but his Biblical criticism was freer than Hofmann's hyperconservative position would allow. He was as rich in spirit as in learning, though his theology was not free from theosophic influences, as is shown by his *System der biblischen Psychologie* (Leipsic, 1855; Eng. transl. Edinburgh, 1867). He especially distinguished himself as an exegete. At Rostock he wrote *De Habacuci prophetæ vita* (Leipsic, 1842), but his exegetical activity really commenced at Erlangen, where he prepared independently and in connection with Keil some of the best commentaries on the Old Testament which had been produced in Germany. These were soon translated into English and published at Edinburgh (Job, Ps., Prov., Cant., Eccl., Isa.). In their earlier editions they show the influence of Hofmann, but his "Commentary on Hebrews" (Leipsic, 1857; Eng. transl., 2 vols., Edinburgh, 1870) was written in defense of the old Protestant doctrine of atonement, as opposed to Hofmann's position. In spite of his confessional attitude, Delitzsch opposed the idea "of fencing theology off with the letter of the Formula of Concord," and when his colleague Kahnis was attacked, he published a defense of him (1863). He published in 1869 his *System der christlichen Apologetik*, which was followed by a Hebrew translation of the New Testament (1877; 11th ed. 1890), and, in connection with S. Baer, an edition of the Old Testament text, except Exodus-Deuteronomy (Leipsic, 1861-97).

The effect caused by the investigations of Wellhausen on his followers induced Delitzsch conscientiously to examine his own position with regard to the critical questions raised, and to give up whatever was not tenable. He published in Luthardt's *Zeitschrift*, 1880 and 1882, a series of articles on the Pentateuch which prepared the way for the fifth edition of his Genesis (1887), which he justly regarded as a new work. In the Introduction he made it clear that his position in relation to Old-Testament problems was in the main what it had been, and that the Bible, as the literature of a divine revelation, can not be permitted to be charged with a lack of veracity or to be robbed of its historic basis. In the fourth edition of his Isaiah (Leipsic, 1889, dedicated to Driver and Cheyne of Oxford; Eng. transl., 1890), and in his *Messianische Weissagungen* (Leipsic, 1890; Eng. transl., Edinburgh, 1891), the preface of which is dated five days before his death, a modification of his views also appeared. For those who took offense at his concession to the modern critical school he wrote *Der tiefe Graben zwischen alter und moderner Theologie. Ein Bekenntniss* (Leipsic, 1888; 2d ed., 1890). Besides the works already mentioned, he wrote: *Zur Geschichte der jüdischen Poesie* (Leipsic, 1836); *Wissenschaft, Kunst, Judentum* (Grimma, 1838); *Anekdota zur Geschichte der mittelalterlichen Scholastik unter Juden und Moslemen* (Leipsic, 1841); *Philemon oder das Buch von der Freundschaft in Christo* (Dresden, 1842); *Wer sind die Mystiker?* (Leipsic, 1842); *Das Sakrament des wahren Leibes und Blutes Jesu Christi* (Dresden, 1844; 7th ed., 1886); *Die biblisch-prophetische Theologie* (Leipsic, 1845); *Symbolæ ad psalmos illustrando isagogicæ* (1846); *Vier Bücher von der Kirche* (Dresden, 1847); *Vom Hause Gottes oder der Kirche* (1849); *Komplutensische Varianten zum alttestamentlichen Texte* (Leipsic, 1878); *Fortgesetzte Studien zur Entstehungsgeschichte der komplutensischen Polyglotte* (1886); *Iris. Farbenstudien und Blumenstücke* (1888). He took a lively interest in the conversion of the Jews, for whose benefit he translated the New Testament into Hebrew, and published works like *Jesus und Hillel* (Erlangen, 1867; 3d ed., 1871) and *Handwerkerleben zur Zeit Jesu* (Erlangen, 1868; 3d ed., 1878; Eng. transl., New York, 1883). He also defended them against anti-Semitic attacks and wrote *Ernste Fragen an die Gebildeten jüdischer Religion* (Leipsic, 1888; 2d ed., 1890), and *Sind die Juden wirklich das auserwählte Volk?* (Leipsic, 1889) against Jewish pretensions and invectives. In 1886 he founded at Leipsic a seminary in which candidates of theology are prepared for missionary work among the Jews, and which in memory of him is now called *Institutum Judaicum Delitzschianum*.

Bibliography: S. I. Curtiss, *F. Delitzsch*, London, 1891; H. V. Hilprecht, in *Old Testament Student*, vi. 209 sqq.; T. K. Cheyne, in *Academy*, xxxvii (1890), 169, and *Athenæum*, 1890, i. 308; W. Baudissin, in *Expositor*, 1890, pp. 465 sqq.; A. Köhler, in *Neue kirchliche Zeitschrift*, i. 234 sqq.

DELITZSCH, FRIEDRICH: German Assyriologist; b. at Erlangen Sept. 3, 1850. He studied at Leipsic, where he became associate professor of Semitic languages and Assyriology in 1877. In 1893 he was called to Breslau as full professor of the same subjects, and since 1899 has held a similar position in Berlin, in addition to being director of the Asiatic section in the Royal Museum. He has written *Assyrische Lesestücke* (Leipsic, 1876); *Wo lag das Paradies?* (1881); *The Hebrew Language Viewed in the Light of Assyrian Research* (London, 1883); *Die Sprache der Kossäer* (Leipsic, 1884); *Prolegomena eines neuen hebräisch-aramäischen Wörterbuchs zum Alten Testament* (1886); *Assyrisches Wörterbuch zur gesammten bisher veröffentlichten Keilschriftliteratur* (3 parts, 1887–90); *Assyrische Grammatik* (1889; Eng. transl. by A. R. S. Kennedy, London, 1889); *Geschichte Babyloniens und Assyriens* (Calw, 1891); *Beiträge zur Entzifferung und Erklärung der kappadokischen Keilschrifttafeln* (Leipsic, 1893); *Die Entstehung des ältesten Schriftsystems oder der Ursprung der Keilschriftzeichen* (1896); *Das Buch Hiob neu übersetzt und erklärt* (1902); *Babel und Bibel* (2 parts, 1902–03; Eng. transl. by C. H. W. Johns, London, 1903), which was based on lectures delivered before the Emperor of Germany and roused vehement opposition in certain conservative circles; *Die babylonische Chronik* (1906); and *Mehr Licht* (1907). He collaborates with Paul Haupt in editing the *Assyriologische Bibliothek* (Leipsic, 1881 sqq.) and *Beiträge zur Assyriologie und semitischen Sprachwissenschaft* (1889 sqq.).

DELLA VOLPE, FRANCESCO SALESIO: Cardinal; b. at Ravenna, Italy, Dec. 24, 1844. He studied at the seminary of Bertinovo, the Seminario Pio, Rome, and the Pontificia Accademia dei Nobili Ecclesiastici. At the age of thirty he became a privy chamberlain of Pope Pius IX., and five years later was appointed secretary of the Congregation of Indulgences. He became Maestro di Camera in 1886 and Majordomo in 1892. He was created cardinal *in petto* in 1899, although his appointment was not publicly announced until 1901, when he received the title of cardinal priest of Santa Maria in Aquiro. Since 1903 he has been prefect of the Congregation of the Propaganda.

DELUGE. See Noah.

DEMAREST, WILLIAM HENRY STEELE: Reformed (Dutch); b. at Hudson, N. Y., May 12, 1863. He studied at Rutgers College (B.A., 1883), and was graduated at the New Brunswick Theological Seminary in 1888. In the same year he was ordained to the ministry, and held pastorates at Walden, N. Y. (1888–97), and Catskill, N. Y. (1897–1901). From 1901 to 1906 he was professor of ecclesiastical history and church government in New Brunswick Theological Seminary, and in 1906 was elected president of Rutgers College, having already been acting president in 1905–06. He has written *History of the Church of Walden* (New York, 1893); *Outline of Church Government* (New Brunswick, N. J., 1903); and *Outline of Church History* (1904).

DE MENT, BYRON HOOVER: Baptist; b. at Silver Springs, Tenn., May 17, 1863. He was graduated at the University of Nashville in 1885, and studied at the University of Virginia (1888–90), and Southern Baptist Theological Seminary, Louisville, Ky. (1896–1900). He was professor of Greek and Latin in Doyle College, Doyle, Tenn., 1885–86, and from 1893 to 1896 was pastor at Lexington, Va. In 1900–03 he was pastor of the Twenty-second and Walnut Street Baptist Church, Louisville, Ky., and of the First Baptist Church, Waco, Tex., 1904–06. In 1903–04 he was professor of Hebrew and practical theology in Baylor University, Waco, and since 1906 has been professor of Sunday-school pedagogy in Southern Baptist Theological Seminary, Louisville, Ky. He was a member of the Texas Baptist Education Commission in 1903–06.

DEMETRIUS OF ALEXANDRIA. See ORIGEN, I., § 3.

DEMON, DEMONISM.

The Greek *daimon* (diminutive, *daimonion*), the original of the English "demon," did not connote necessarily the idea of evil. It was rather neutral, and might even be used as a synonym of *theos*, "god"; it was also generally employed to designate a tutelary genius (Lat. *lar, lemur, genius*), and came to be applied to any departed soul. In the Septuagint of the Old Testament, in the New Testament, and in Christian usage the connotation is sinister and always involves an evil spirit. The origin of the idea of demons lies far back in the empirical dualism of man's animistic conceptions, according to which all nature is peopled with spirits which are believed constantly to affect or control human acts and destiny (see COMPARATIVE RELIGION, VI., 1, a, § 4). Man's efforts may turn out to his satisfaction or to his disappointment, and he attributes the results to the assistance or hindrance of spirits whom he regards as good or bad according as they seem to assist or to thwart his efforts. This primitive bipartition of the spirit-world into good spirits (which may become angels) and bad (which become demons) persists through many stages of unfolding in civilization and in religion, and remains as a belief even in the period of enlightenment. Traces of animistic belief have not been wholly eradicated from the Old Testament; cf., e.g., the serpent of Gen. iii. which has speech, mentality, and evil purpose, and also the anointing by Jacob of the stone to which he attributed his wonderful dream (Gen. xxviii. 18). The narrative in Num. xxii. 22–34 presupposes a belief in the vocal power of animals, though the impression given by the narration is rather that of miraculous impartation of speech to an otherwise mute animal. The entire religious provenience out of which the Hebrew religion sprang is full of demonism (see ASSYRIA, VII., § 8; BABYLONIA, VII., 1, §§ 4–6). The Babylonian religion divided its spirits into good and bad. These were again classified and grouped, and to the classes and groups names were given, though in general the individual demons did not receive names. This is in accordance with the general law that only in the more developed stages do the spirits become so individualized as to be named. This appears in the Hebrew representation, where in the earlier writings individual spirits are merely referred without individualization to classes (cf. the unnamed "evil spirit" which tormented Saul, I Sam. xvi. 14–15, and the "evil spirit" which by divine commission came between Abimelech and the Shechemites, Judges ix. 23), while Satan, not at first as devil, but as one belonging to God's company, or at least admitted to his presence (Job i. 6 sqq.; Zech. iii. 1 sqq.), Azazel, and Asmodeus (see below) emerge as personal spirits possessing names only in the late (postexilic) literature. A wealth of demonic conceptions quite equal to the Babylonian is found also in the Arabic religion, according to which demons swarm in the regions of air, earth, and water, lying in wait for the unwary. The magic and incantations of Arabic folk-lore are hardly less prominent and numerous than those of Babylonia, and where these exist belief in demonology is sure to be found (see DIVINATION; and MAGIC).

1. Background of Demonology.

The characteristics of the demons in the Semitic sphere are like those of demons among other peoples. These beings, whose power is greatest during the hours of darkness, are responsible for ills of the flesh, of the mentality, and of the spiritual life. They cause disease, aberration of mind, and perverseness toward the gods; they control the atmosphere and bring storms; by their mastery of the waters they bring floods and destruction; they enter the bodies of human beings, are especially dangerous to women and children, and at the critical periods of life are alert to work them harm. They may be warded off by attention to the proper ritual, by the use of drugs and herbs, and by the potency of incantations and charms (the later Jews regarded the *shema*, "Hear, O Israel," of Deut. vi. 4 as a protection). Yet they may be welcomed by the individual and become so at home in his person that he becomes virtually one of their number. In accordance with their perverse nature, the demons have their dwelling-places in spots shunned by mortals—in the deserts, among ruins and in cities which have been destroyed by the enemy, among graves, in miasmatic morasses, and in like places. The demonology of the Old Testament and the New exhibits many of these traces. Yet it is to be observed that not even in its monotheism does the religion of Israel show a loftier elevation above the faiths of the surrounding peoples than in its demonology. The most numerous traces appear in the period of depression when national disaster had enforced contact with the pregnant demonism of Babylonians, Persians, and the invading Arabs. As a matter of course, the nature of demons is ever vaguely treated, and the exact notions about them are difficult to determine. Demons were regarded as not of flesh and blood (cf. Eph. vi. 12), yet they ate and drank, reproduced their kind, and might be wounded and killed. They were pictured with the passions and even the lusts of mankind (cf. Tobit vi. 14). They were above the laws of nature, and could transform themselves into various shapes, even into those of angels of light (cf. II Cor. xi. 14). In Judaism they were regarded as especially the opponents of the Messiah (see DEMONIAC). Their origin is seldom accounted for in popular belief. They come down as elemental spirits in the common belief of the people, and their number is added to as the souls of the departed become regarded as malignant. When an angelology develops, the angels are regarded as falling from their high estate and adding to the number of the demons. So in the earlier stages of the Hebrew religion demons are not accounted for; but in late Jewish works, especially in the Book of Enoch (see PSEUDEPIGRAPHA), the demons are largely derived from the episode narrated

2. Nature of Demons.

in Gen. vi. 1–4 or from the conceptions of the fall of the angels who thereby became demons. In the same region demonology developed *pari passu* with angelology, and a demonarchy with Satan and archdemons at the head were opposed to the hierarchy of God and the archangels and angels which left its traces in all Western and some Eastern literatures.

3. The Hebrew Se'irim and Shedhim.

The word *daimon* was introduced into the Biblical sphere through the Septuagint as a translation of the two Hebrew words *sa'ir* (pl. *se'irim*) and *shedh* (pl. *shedhim;* cf. Assyr. *shedu*, like the Gk. *daimon*, originally a word of neutral signification, found also in Phenician inscriptions, and possibly etymologically connected with *Shaddai*, one of the patriarchal names for God, e.g., Gen. xvii. 1, R. V., margin, and also with the Arabic *sa'id, sayyid*, " lord "). The former occurs Lev. xvii. 7 (A. V. " devils," R. V. " he-goats," margin " satyrs "); Isa. xiii. 21, xxxiv. 14 (A. V. and R. V. " satyrs," R. V. margin " he-goats "); and II Chron. xi. 15 (A. V. " devils," R. V. " he-goats," margin " satyrs "). *Shedh* (*shedhim*) occurs in Deut. xxxii. 17 and Ps. cvi. 37 (A. V. " devils," R. V. " demons "). In Isa. xiii. 21, regarded as exilic or later, the reference is to the desolate site of Babylon where repulsive creatures and dancing *se'irim* are to abide. The conception is evidently that of hairy goat-like creatures, not unlike the satyr or Pan of Greek myth; some varieties of the Arabic jinn are also represented as having somewhat of the same form (Wellhausen, *Heidentum*, pp. 151–152). This representation is in full accord with that of Isa. xxxiv. 14, also exilic or postexilic, in which the *sa'ir* cries " to his fellow " in Edom, which has become a waste inhabited by wolves and by the night monster (Heb. *lilith*, R. V. " night-hag," see below). Further, light is cast on the subject by the passage Lev. xvii. 7, which forbids sacrifice to the *se'irim*, here mentioned as the objects of worship. This worship may have been simply avertive, after the primitive fashion of bringing offerings to beings whose ill will it was desired to avoid. It is significant that the purpose of the entire passage is to proscribe sacrifice in " the open field "—i.e., apart from the dwelling-place—which may mean the desert, the assumed home of evil spirits. Similar in purport is Deut. xxxii. 17, where the fathers are said to have sacrificed to *shedhim*, and Ps. cvi. 37, in which case sons and daughters were the offerings presented. It is questionable whether these two cases are mere invidious comparison of false gods to demons (W. von Baudissin, in Hauck-Herzog, *RE*, vi. 4), since this comparison is not met again for several centuries, possibly not till apostolic times. The entire provenience of the passages and the ideas connected are best suited by the supposition that offerings of an avertive character are here referred to, and that not the heathen deities, but actual demons were conceived as objects of worship. The possible renascence of totemistic practises (probably under the influence of Arabic immigration) suggested by Ezek. viii. 10 and Isa. lxvi. 17 is in favor of this conclusion.

4. Other Hebrew Demonic Conceptions.

Mention of *lilith* (Isa. xxxiv. 14, A. V. " screech-owl," margin and R. V. " night monster," R. V. margin " Lilith ") has already been made. There can be no doubt of the Babylonian origin of this word. The god of Nippur was known as En-lil, " lord of spirits " (see BABYLONIA, VII., 2, § 2), and the Assyrian *lilu, lilutu* had the signification " sprites." The Semitic *lilatu*, " night," may be compared, and the fem. *Lilith* is named in the cuneiform inscriptions as an attendant of Namtar, the deity of plagues (see BABYLONIA, VII., 2, § 8). In late rabbinic literature *lilin* means female demons, and Lilith herself bears no slight part in legend and was conceived as living in the desert whence she emerged to make her attacks. A kindred conception is that of Prov. xxx. 15 (Heb. *'alukah*, A. V. " horseleech," R. V. margin " vampire," described as having daughters ever crying " give, give "), to which what is at least a parallel, if not a cognate conception, is found in the Arabic *'aluk*. The circumstances of the reference suit much better the conception of a demon than that of a horseleech, especially the circumstance of the insatiable daughters. Azazel (Lev. xvi. 8 sqq.) is the name of a demon whose home is in the desert, whose character and aims are opposed to those of Yahweh. The name has not yet yielded to investigations on the side of Hebrew philology, and is unique as being the one element of this character entering into the ritual of the Hebrews. Asmodeus, mentioned in Tobit, is either derived from Persian sources or is a literary imitation of a Persian conception. *Heylel* (Isa. xiv. 12), the " day star, fallen from heaven," is interesting as an early instance of what, especially in pseudepigraphic literature, became a dominant conception, that of fallen angels. The Septuagint translates by *daimonia* the *elilim* of Ps. xcv. 5 (A. V. and R. V. " idols," R. V. margin " things of naught "), probably rendering aright the conception of the author of this late psalm. It is not improbable that behind the " pestilence " and " destruction " of Ps. xci. 6 are animistic conceptions of mischief-working demons, and that they are not mere personifications. A belief closely akin to that in demons is referred to in the *obh*, " familiar spirit," of I Sam. xxviii. 7 sqq. In direct line with this and connecting the belief of the early Hebrews with that of surrounding nations are the *teraphim* (q.v.), the best explanation of which relates them to ancestral spirits that are sought among the graves (cf. Isa. lxv. 4; cf. Deut. xxvi. 14; Ps. cvi. 28). Etymologically connected with *teraphim* is the word *rephaim*, " giants," and this again connects the Hebrews with the beliefs of other peoples who speak of earlier inhabitants of their land as still remaining, though in the shape of elves, dwarfs, and fairies. In the Assyrian tongue the words *utukku* and *ukimmu* designated both a class of demons and also the spirits of the dead, and they are compared with *zakiku*, " wind," recalling the " spirits " mentioned above as unclassified (cf. Heb. *ruah*). The idea which underlies that of *rephaim* is unsubstantiality, and *ruhim* becomes a late Jewish word for demons. The Hebrew popular belief in demons is attested further by the many injunctions against sorcery which appear in the legislative and prophetic utterances. In ethnic custom one of the universally employed means of averting the harmful action of demons is the use of the magic word or act. The fact that the people needed this admonition so constantly speaks more strongly for the abiding belief in demons than the few specific references which are found. For the New Testament doctrine and for later Jewish belief in demons see DEMONIAC, §§ 1–4.

GEO. W. GILMORE.

BIBLIOGRAPHY: A. Kohut, *Angelologie und Dämonologie in ihrer Abhängigkeit vom Parsismus*, in *Abhandlungen für die Kunde des Morgenlandes*, iv., 1866; W. Baudissin, *Studien zur semitischen Religionsgeschichte*, i. 110–146, Leipsic, 1876; P. Scholtz, *Götzendienst und Zauberwesen*, pp. 133–137, Regensburg, 1877; J. T. de Visser, *De Daemonologie van het O. T.*, pp. 80–83, Utrecht, 1880; H. Schultz, *O. T. Theology*, London, 1892; R. Stube, *Jüdisch-babylonische Zaubertexte*, Halle, 1895; W. R. Newbold, *Demon Possession and Allied Themes*, in *New World*, Sept., 1897; E. Stave, *Ueber den Einfluss des Parsismus auf das Judentum*, pp. 235–280, Haarlem, 1898; Smith, *Rel. of Sem.*, pp. 119–120; *DB*, i. 590–594; *EB*, i. 1069–1074; *JE*, iv. 514–521. On Lilith consult: J. A. Eisenmenger, *Entdecktes Judentum*, ii. 413 sqq., Frankfort, 1700; W. Gesenius, *Jesaia*, i. 916–920, Leipsic, 1821. On ethnic demonology consult: F. Lenormant, *La Magie chez les Chaldéens*, Paris, 1874; J. Wellhausen, *Heidentum*, pp. 151 sqq.; J. L. Nevins, *Demon Possession and Allied Themes*, New York, 1895; E. B. Tylor, *Primitive Culture*, London, 1903. Consult also the literature under DEMONIAC.

DEMONIAC.

1. Jewish and New Testament Demonology.

A demoniac is one supposed to be possessed by a demon or evil spirit or by several demons. The name "demon" originated in Greek mythology and was introduced into the Bible and Christianity through the Septuagint translation of the Hebrew *se'irim* and *shedhim* (see the article DEMON for the Old Testament demonology). In postexilic Judaism demonology gained ground, either through foreign influence or by a recrudescence of primitive Semitic or Israelitic folk-lore. The New Testament reflects the current beliefs of its time. The demonic powers are represented as spirits, not flesh and blood (Eph. vi. 12); they can assume any form, even appearing as angels of light (II Cor. xi. 14); they dwell in ruins (Rev. xviii. 2), in tombs (Mark v. 1 sqq.), and especially in the desert (Matt. iv. 1 sqq., xii. 43). In the Talmud their generic name is *mazziḳin* ("injurers"). They lead men to sin (Enoch lxix. 4, 6), and return more readily to the sinner than to the righteous (Testament of Naphtali 8); yet it is possible to resist the devil (Eph. vi. 12; James iv. 7; I Pet. v. 8), and even to stop the way of the evil spirits by opposing them (Matt. xii. 43 sqq.). One who transgresses the commandments falls an easy victim to the demons (*Debarim rabbah* 4), although he is protected by the recitation of the Shema, or by the strict observance of other commandments (*Berako* 5a; *Pesiḳta* 187a). The devil and his hosts are the special foes of the Messianic kingdom (Rev. xii. 10). The mission of Jesus was the conquest of the "strong man" (Matt. xii. 29), although, according to Luke xxii. 3, I Cor. ii. 8, he apparently fell a victim to the evil one; yet, as he had expressed the conviction that he had cast out the kingdom of Satan by the spirit of God (Matt. xii. 26, 28), he inspired his disciples and all early Christianity with the consciousness of victory over the demons (Luke x. 17 sqq.). They, on the other hand, recognized Jesus as the Messiah (Mark i. 24, and frequently). According to Rev. xii., which is confirmed by allusions in the Pauline writings, the devil, having been cast down from heaven, is come to earth to work evil during the little time which still remained to him, and must be resisted continually, although he can win no real victory. The Pauline concept of the "rudiments of the world" (Col. ii. 20; cf. ii. 15; Rom. viii. 38; Eph. vi. 12) refers not only to the sovereigns of the Jews and the Gentiles (Gal. iii. 19; iv. 1–4, 8–9; Enoch lxxxix. 59–60), but also to the gods of the nations and of idolatrous Israel (Deut. xxxii. 17; Ps. xcv. 5, cvi. 37). This comparison of the pagan deities to *shedhim* recurs in postexilic Judaism (Enoch xix. 1; Rev. ix. 20), in the writings of Paul, and throughout ecclesiastical antiquity. Though Paul denied the existence of idols (I Cor. viii. 4 sqq.), declaring them dead (I Thess. i. 9) and no gods by nature (Gal. iv. 8), he expressly stated that the sacrifices offered to pagan deities were really given to devils (I Cor. x. 19 sqq.; cf. Justin, i. 5, 10, 12, 23, ii. 1, 12, 13; Tatian, *Oratio ad Græcos*; Tertullian, *Apol.*, xxii., xxiii., et passim; Origen, *Contra Celsum*).

2. New Testament Ideas Concerning Demoniacs.

The principal source for the Biblical view of demoniacs is the historical books of the New Testament. According to the general concept of the various passages, the demon enters into man as a second personality (Luke viii. 30), dwelling in him as in a house (Matt. xii. 44; Luke xi. 24), so that evil spirits dread to be banished into the abyss (Luke viii. 31), or (Mark v. 10) to be expelled from a land they love, preferring to inhabit the bodies of swine. The demon tortures man (Matt. xv. 22), driving him whither he would not go (Luke viii. 29). The demoniac is often so thoroughly possessed by the evil spirit that he lives in sepulchers and other lonely places, a danger to passers-by (Matt. viii. 28) and unable to be bound by even the strongest fetters (Mark v. 3–6); he even speaks as though he were himself the demon, using the plural when possessed by many evil spirits (Matt. viii. 29; Mark i. 24, v. 9; Luke iv. 34, viii. 28).

The manifestations of demoniac possession are extremely varied. The boy at the foot of the Mount of Transfiguration (Mark ix. 14–27) is represented as seized with convulsions, writhing on the ground, and foaming at the mouth. At the first attack the boy wallowed dumb upon the ground, nor did he cry out until the demon had been expelled, although the account of Luke (ix. 39) states that the child screamed at every attack, and that the evil spirit "bruising him, hardly departeth from him."

3. Symptoms of Possession. Both Mark and Luke record symptoms of epilepsy; the account in Matthew not only omits all these details, but especially characterizes the disease as lunacy (xvii. 15), thus giving a preferable explanation of the falling of the boy into fire and water, which has no specific cause in Mark, and is altogether lacking in Luke. The passage in Matthew is the more interesting since in iv. 24 he distinguishes "those which were possessed with devils, and those which were lunatic, and those that had the palsy." The demoniac met by Jesus in the synagogue at Capernaum (Mark i. 23–28) does not exhibit the characteristic foam of epilepsy, but shows symptoms of epileptic hysteria, especially as Luke iv. 35 notes that the fit did him no harm. It is evident, from a summary of the cases in Matthew and Mark, that such attacks were regarded as demoniac in origin, and to the same agency are ascribed the superhuman strength, the self-injury, the dwelling among tombs, the threatening gestures, and the nakedness of the demoniac of Gadara (Mark v. 2–5; Luke viii. 27–29). Other complaints of a less serious nature, however, are also referred to the agency of demons, such as dumbness (Matt. ix. 32; Luke xi. 14), or blindness and dumbness (Matt. xii. 22), although no mention is made of the expulsion of demons in the accounts of the healing of the dumb and the blind in Matt. ix. 27–31; Mark vii. 32, 37, viii. 22–26, x. 46–52. In like manner, Luke iv. 40–41 (cf. vi. 17–18, vii. 21) regards the curing of demoniacs as a special phase of healing, and in Acts viii. 7 demoniacs are distinguished from the paralytic and the lame. On the other hand, the woman bowed with "a spirit of infirmity eighteen years" was "bound by Satan" (Luke xiv. 11–16), and the fever of Peter's mother-in-law seems to have been believed to be demoniac (Luke iv. 38–39). The healings at Capernaum (Matt. viii. 16) were in the main exorcisms of demons, and these formed a large part of the activity both of Jesus (Mark i. 39) and of the Twelve (Mark iii. 14–15, vi. 7, 13; Matt. x. 8).

The gloom and asceticism of John the Baptist gained him the reputation of a demoniac (Matt. xi. 18; Luke vii. 33), and this charge was brought against Jesus himself (Matt. ix. 34, xii. 24; Mark iii. 22, 30; Luke xi. 15; John vii. 20, viii. 48, x. 20). Nor was it an easy matter to distinguish between spirits of evil and spirits of God (Matt. xxiv. 11, 24; I John iv. 1–3), so that the "discerning of spirits" was regarded as a special grace (I Cor. xii. 10, xiv. 29). Even a storm (Mark iv. 37–41; cf. Rev. vii. 1; Enoch lx. 11 sqq.; Jubilees ii.) was considered the work of demons. It is surprising, on the other hand, that moral defects and delinquencies are seldom represented as demoniac either by popular belief or by Jesus himself. Neither Matt. xi. 18; John vii. 20, viii. 48, 52, nor Luke xi. 24–26 admits of such an interpretation, the only passages really entering into consideration being Luke xxii. 3, 31 and the account of the temptation, where, however, Satan is rather the avowed opponent of all Messianic work than the principle of evil.

In the exorcisms of Jesus the demoniacs are agitated at his approach (Mark i. 23, iii. 11, v. 6, ix. 20), while the evil spirits, recognizing him as the Son of God, implore him not to torment them before their time (Matt. viii. 29). Such recognition,

4. Exorcism by Jesus. although rebuked by Jesus (Mark i. 25, iii. 12), receives its explanation in the supernatural power of perception possessed by the evil spirits, since by means of his Spirit God wrought through Jesus all his miracles, wonders, and signs. The rebuke of Jesus is sufficient in most cases to exorcise evil spirits (Matt. viii. 16; Mark i. 25, ix. 25), even at a distance (Mark vii. 29, 30). The successful exorcism of the demon is recognized by the quiet and repose of the patient (Mark v. 15, vii. 30), or by a loud cry from the person possessed (Mark i. 26), while the transfer of the demon from the man of Gadara to the swine in Mark v. 2–13 finds its probable explanation in the fright of the animals at the final paroxysm of the maniac. The historicity of Jesus' successful treatment of demoniacs is admitted in principle even by adherents of the critical school. Exorcisms were the order of the day and were expected from a Messianic prophet, and the chief proof for their historicity lies in statements of Jesus which represent their importance for himself and his activity as the Messiah (Matt. xi. 5; Luke vii. 22). It becomes clear from Matt. xii. 25–32 and Luke xi. 17–23 that Jesus believed not only in the existence of demons (cf. Matt. xii. 43–45; Luke xi. 24–26), but, like his contemporaries, in exorcism (Matt. xii. 27; Luke xi. 19). The expulsion of demons implied the debilitation and the destruction of the "kingdom of Satan" (Matt. xii. 26; Luke xi. 18), thus representing victories over the principle of evil in the dawn of the Messianic age (cf. Assumption of Moses x.). It is clear, from the allusion to the "strong man" in Matt. xii. 29, and Luke xi. 21–22, that Jesus deduced his victory over the demons from his previous conquest of Satan, their lord, in his temptation (cf. Luke x. 18–20).

The accounts of the Gospels receive their full explanation, however, only in the light of the history of religion, which shows that the belief in demoniac possession was not restricted to the time of Jesus

5. Exorcism in the Early Church. or to his surroundings. Exorcism continued to be practised in the early Christian Church (Acts v. 16, viii. 7). Of particular interest is the account of the "spirit of divination," in Acts xvi. 16–18. The narrative in Acts xix. 13–19, on the other hand, contains no exorcism in the strict sense of the term, but merely shows the power of the name of Jesus over those possessed with demons (cf. Mark ix. 38–39; Luke ix. 49). Jesus himself admitted the success of other exorcists and sanctioned them as helping to destroy the kingdom of Satan, so that the failure of the Jewish exorcists (Acts xix. 13–16) is an exception to the general rule. Although the epistles contain no direct statements concerning demoniacs and exorcisms, such beliefs must be attributed to Paul when he mentions among *charismata* the ability to discern between spirits (I Cor. xii. 10). The conviction that "the Son of God was manifested that he might destroy the works of the devil" (I John iii. 8) continued active in the early Church. Thus Irenæus (II. xlix. 3) asserts that certain exorcisms "mightily and truly expel demons"; while Tertullian put the belief in the form of a challenge (*Apol.*, xxiii.; cf. *De corona*, xi.; *De idolis*, xi.; Minucius Felix, xxvii.; Origen, *Contra Celsum*, vii. 4, viii. 58, etc.). While in the earliest period many Christians expelled evil spirits, exorcists are definitely mentioned as special officials of the Church as early as Cyprian (*Epist.*, xvi.; cf. the tenth canon of the Council of Antioch and the twenty-sixth of the Apostolic Constitutions). [The energumens (Gk. *energoumenoi*, "worked upon," "influenced," i.e., by an evil spirit) constituted a special class. They were not permitted to enter the church if they were violent, but were commanded to stand in the porch, so that they could hear the singing and prayers; and with them might be found lepers and persons of offensive lives (cf. the seventeenth canon of the Synod of Ancyra, 314; Hefele, *Conciliengeschichte*, i. 235–237); after the prayers they came in to receive the blessing of the bishop. If they were quiet, they were allowed in the church, yet separated from the catechumens, and listened to the sermon. They were also called *cheimazomenoi* ("storm-tossed"). The exorcists daily brought them food, laid their hands upon them, and prayed for them. After their recovery they kept a twenty to forty days' fast, then partook of the sacrament; a particular prayer was made for them by the priest, and their names were entered upon the church-records, with especial mention of their recovery.] The belief in demoniac possession and the power of exorcism has continued in the Church down to modern times. See BENEDICTION; SACRAMENTALS.

This phenomenon loses its singularity in view of its ethnic distribution. In the Old Testament a special instance is the evil spirit which troubled Saul after the spirit of God had departed from him, mentioned by Josephus (*Ant.*, VI. viii. 2, xi. 2) as a case of demoniac possession, and the lying spirit of I Kings xxii. 20–23. The cases of Judges ix. 23; II Kings xix. 7; Isa. xxix. 10 are more doubtful, but the underlying concept is clearly that of possession by evil spirits. Josephus expressed a firm belief in possession. According to him, in a case which he observed, the exorcist held to the patient's nose a ring containing under its seal one of the roots which Solomon had endowed with healing power, thus drawing the demon from the nostrils of the person possessed. The patient then fell down, and the exorcist conjured the demon not to return, commemorating Solomon, and pronouncing the incantations which he had composed. Jewish exorcists are mentioned by Jesus (Matt. xii. 27) as well as in Acts xix. 13–20, while Origen (*Contra Celsum*, I. xxviii., xxxviii.) declared exorcism an art which the Jews had learned from the Egyptians. Lucian (*Philopseudes*, xvii.) describes exorcists in terms which resemble those of the New Testament, mentioning particularly a Palestinian and an Arab conjurer. Especially famous were

6. Exorcism by Jews.

the exorcisms of Apollonius of Tyana (q.v.), although there is no foundation for Baur's view that they were imitations of the Gospel narratives.

Strong evidence for the wide-spread extent of the ancient belief in demoniac possession are the countless incantations still preserved, and the mass of magic papyri recently discovered. A distinct category is formed by the "Ephesian letters," a mixture of foreign and unintelligible names, including many Hebrew words and even verses from the Bible. In these formulas the Hebrew name of God and the name of Jesus recur with great frequency, both being regarded as especially potent.

In spite of the progress of modern thought and of the natural sciences, the primitive conception of all these things as supernatural has by no means been eliminated. In the Roman Catholic and orthodox Protestant churches it finds a strong support in the Scriptural narratives and in the general supernatural standpoint from which their exposition is approached. The natural view of these phenomena was first taken by the rationalist school, especially by Semler, and is to-day fully recognized in historical theology. Theologians are now willing to adimt their need of information on the underlying psychological facts at the hands of specialists, especially the medical men who in recent years have made careful study of phenomena of this class. The labors of Charcot, Richer, Snell, and others have led to a prevalence of the view that cases of so-called possession are usually to be regarded as acute hysteria, and the cures, the accomplishment of which is still possible, as the work of suggestion. This would have been all the more likely to operate effectively in the early days of Christianity, when powerful religious excitement and extreme submissiveness of faith would have offered the most favorable conditions for its exercise. (JOHANNES WEISS.)

7. Modern Explanations.

BIBLIOGRAPHY: On Biblical presentations consult: F. C. Conybeare, in *JQR*, 1896–97; W. Baudissin, *Studien*, part 1, Leipsic, 1876; G. Hafner, *Die Dämonischen des N. T.*, Frankfort, 1894; H. Laehr, *Die Dämonischen des N. T.*, Leipsic, 1894; R. Stube, *Jüdisch-babylonische Zaubertexte*, Halle, 1895; W. M. Alexander, *Demoniac Possession in the New Testament*, Edinburgh, 1902; *DB*, i. 590–594; 811–813; *EB*, i. 1069–74, ii. 1451–53; *JE*, v. 305–306. On the relationship of Christ to the subject consult: F. Nippold, *Die psychiatrische Heilthätigkeit Jesu*, Bern, 1889; idem, *Engels- und Satansidee Jesu*, ib. 1891; Schwartskopff, in *Zeitschrift für Theologie und Kirche*, 1897. For beliefs and practises of the Middle Ages cf. Schaff, *Christian Church*, v. 1, pp. 878 sqq.

On ethnic belief consult, besides the literature under COMPARATIVE RELIGION: A. Harnack, *Medizinisches aus der alten Kirchengeschichte*, in *TU*, viii. 4 (1892), 111 sqq.; J. L. Nevius, *Demon Possession*, Chicago, 1895 (Chinese phenomena); W. R. Newbold, *Demon Possession*, in *New World*, 1897, pp. 499 sqq.; W. M. Townsend, *Satan and Demons*, Cincinnati, 1902. The medical side may be consulted in J. M. Charcot, *Les Maladies du système nerveux*, 3 vols., Paris, 1886–87. Consult J. M. Charcot and P. Richer, *Les Démoniaques dans l'art*, Paris, 1887.

DEMPSTER, THOMAS: Scotch scholar; b. (according to his own not altogether trustworthy account) at Gliftbog, near Muiresk (32 m. n.w. of Aberdeen), Aberdeenshire, Aug. 23, 1579; d. at Bologna Sept. 6, 1625. He led an adventurous life as student at Pembroke Hall, Cambridge, at Paris,

Louvain, Rome, and Douai; and as teacher at Tournai, Paris, Toulouse, Nîmes, Pisa, and Bologna. He possessed a remarkable memory, and accumulated a great store of learning; was impetuous, contentious, and ill-mannered, and his personal character is not free from reproach. The best known of his writings (all in barbarous Latin) is the *Historia ecclesiastica gentis Scotorum* (Bologna, 1627; ed. David Irving for the Bannatyne Club, 2 vols., Edinburgh, 1829), a biographical dictionary of Scotchmen, remarkable for its fictions rather than its facts. He wrote also upon Roman antiquities, Etruria, etc., and edited and annotated Benedetto Accolti's *De bello a Christianis contra barbaros gesto* (Florence, 1623).

DENIO, FRANCIS BRIGHAM: Congregationalist; b. at Enosburg, Vt., May 4, 1848. He was graduated at Middlebury College, Middlebury, Vt., in 1871 and Andover Theological Seminary in 1879, and was ordained in 1881. He was instructor in New Testament Greek in Bangor Theological Seminary 1879–82, and has been professor of Old Testament language and literature since 1882. His theological position is moderate. His has written *Outlines of Old Testament Theology* (Bangor, Me., 1897) and *Supreme Leader; Study of the Nature and Work of the Holy Spirit* (Boston, 1900).

DENIS (DIONYSIUS), SAINT: First bishop of Paris and patron saint of France; d. a martyr at Paris either under Valerian (253–260) or Maximian (285–305). He is said to have gone to Gaul about 250, established himself on the island in the Seine now known as *La Cité* in Paris, and, with miracles attesting the divine favor, to have built a church there and ordered the church life. Persecution broke out, Denis was arrested with Rusticus, a priest, and Eleutherius, a deacon, and after cruel tortures the three were beheaded. They were buried where they fell on the heights of Montmartre (*Mons martyrum* according to tradition, though the original name was more likely *Mons Martis*). The place became a great resort of pilgrims, and wonders were wrought there. Thence in the seventh century the relics were transferred to the famous Abbey of St. Denis founded by Dagobert I.

In the first half of the ninth century Hilduin, abbot of St. Denis (q.v.), at the request of Louis the Pious, wrote a life of the saint (*MPL*, cvi. 23–50); and here, for the first time, St. Denis is identified with Dionysius the Areopagite. All the great activity which the Abbey of St. Denis developed in the field of French history from the ninth to the fourteenth century is centered in the idea that Dionysius the Areopagite (q.v.) is the patron saint of France. Abelard (q.v.) had his doubts; and it was not until the middle of the seventeenth century that Launoy (*De Areopagiticis Hilduini*, Paris, 1641, and *De duobus Dionysiis*, Paris, 1640) and Sirmond (*Dissertatio in qua ostenditur discrimen Dionysii Parisiensis et Dionysii Areopagitæ*, Paris, 1641) succeeded in exploding the audacious hypothesis. The shrine of St. Denis grew immensely rich, and the abbey became a storehouse packed with valuable historical memorials (cf. M. Félibien, *Histoire de l'Abbaye de Saint Denys*, Paris, 1706). During the Revolution it was plundered (Nov. 12, 1793) by a mob led by one of its own priests; and its relics, jewelry, etc., were carried on six carts into the Convention, where they disappeared. Denis is one of the Fourteen Helpers in Need (q.v.). His day is Oct. 9.

Bibliography: The early documents are printed in *ASB*, Oct., iv. 925–951; also, in part, ed. B. Krusch, *MGH*, *Auct. ant.*, iv., part 2 (1885), 101–105. Consult: J. E. Darras, *S. Denys l'Aréopagite*, Paris, 1863; E. Taillar, *Apostolat de S. Denys dans les Gaules en 250*, Amiens, 1868; F. Arbellot, *Études sur les origines chrétiennes de la Gaule*, part 1, Paris, 1881; A. Vidieu, *S. Denys l'Aréopagite*, Paris, 1884 (richly illustrated, but not historical).

DENISON, GEORGE ANTHONY: Church of England; b. at Ossington (6 m. n. of Newark), Nottinghamshire, Dec. 11, 1805; d. at East Brent (14 m. w. of Wells), Somerset, Mar. 21, 1896. He studied at Christ Church, Oxford (B.A., 1826), and was ordered deacon and ordained priest in 1832. Until 1838 he was curate to the bishop of Oxford, and then resigned his fellowship and became vicar of Broadwinsor, Dorset, and so remained until 1845, when he became vicar of East Brent, and also examining chaplain to the bishop of Bath and Wells, who in 1851 made him archdeacon of Taunton. In theology he was a High-churchman, and from 1854 to 1858 was unsuccessfully prosecuted for maintaining the doctrine of the Real Presence. From 1839 to 1870 he was prominent as a Church champion in the school controversy between the Church of England and the civil power, which resulted in the Elementary Education Act, the final and decisive victory of the civil power. He wrote *Proceedings against the Archdeacon of Taunton* (London, 1854); *Defence of the Archdeacon of Taunton* (1856); *Church Rate a National Trust* (1861); *Notes of my Life, 1805–78* (1878); and *Mr. Gladstone* (1885). He also translated Hadrianus Saravia *On the Holy Eucharist* (1855).

DENK (DENCK), HANS: Anabaptist; b. at Heybach (Habach; 30 m. s.w. of Munich) c. 1495; d. at Basel Nov., 1527. He studied at Ingolstadt, and in 1520 is found at Augsburg among the Humanists. Thence as a Protestant he went to Basel, was proof-reader and befriended by Œcolampadius, who secured for him the rectorship of St. Sebaldus' school in Nuremberg in the autumn of 1523. There he mingled with those who were dissatisfied with the dominant theology, and on the charge of heresy he was expelled from the city Jan. 21, 1525. Thenceforth he was a wanderer. He allied himself with the Anabaptists and his learning made him a valuable acquisition. He was expelled from Augsburg in Oct., and from Strasburg in Dec., 1526, from Worms in Aug., 1527. He is heard from as a leader of the Anabaptists in Augsburg, Nuremberg, and Ulm in 1527; but, weary of continued persecution and his enforced wanderings, he went to Basel in the fall of that year, threw himself upon the protection of Œcolampadius, who again befriended him and tried in vain to convert him to the established Protestant theology. The plague soon after released him from his troubles. By the Anabaptists he was highly honored; and even his detractors conceded his ability, personal high character, and scholarship. His translation of the prophetical books of the Old Testament with L. Haetzer (Worms, 1527) is still esteemed. His tracts are now extremely rare (cf. *Mennonitische Blätter*, xxx. 56). One is in the British Museum, *Was geredt seyn, das die Schrifft sagt, Gott thue und mache güts und böses* (1526). His principal works were reprinted in *Geistliches Blumengärtlein* (Amsterdam, 1680); his *Von der wahren Liebe* was republished by the Mennonite publishing house, Elkhart, Ind.

Bibliography: L. Keller, *Ein Apostel der Wiedertäufer*, Leipsic, 1882 (best); cf. idem, *Die Reformation und die älteren Reformparteien*, ib. 1885; idem, *J. von Staupitz und die Anfänge der Reformation*, ib. 1888. Consult also: G. E. Roehrich, *La Vie . . . de . . . Jean Denck*, Strasburg, 1853; C. Beard, *The Reformation of the 16th Cent.*, London, 1885; A. Baur, *Zwinglis Theologie*, ii. 175 sqq., Halle, 1889; H. Lüdemann, *Reformation und Täufertum*, pp. 53 sqq., Bern, 1896; A. H. Newman, *Hist. of Anti-Pedobaptism*, pp. 163, 242 sqq., Philadelphia, 1897.

DENMARK: A kingdom of northwestern Europe. The country proper covers an area of 15,289 square miles, with a population (1906) of 2,588,919. The Danish colonies comprise Iceland (q.v.), part of Greenland, the Faroe islands, and the islands of St. Thomas, St. Croix, and St. Jan in the Caribbean Sea. Since 1863 the Lutheran faith has been the established religion of Denmark, and the only one receiving the support of the State. The king must belong to this Church. Other denominations, however, are allowed full religious liberty, with no disabilities whatever. The census of 1901 shows the following distribution of the population according to creeds: Lutherans, 2,436,084; Roman Catholics, 5,373; Greek Catholics, 106; and Jews, 3,476. There are, besides, a small number each of Reformed, Protestant Episcopalians, Methodists, Catholic Apostolics (Irvingites), Baptists, and Mormons.

Ecclesiastical Division of Country.

The ecclesiastical divisions of Denmark comprise seven *stifter*, or bishoprics, as follows: (1) Zealand, (2) Funen (with the neighboring islands of Aero, Langeland, etc.), (3) Laaland and Falster, (4) Aalborg, (5) Viborg, (6) Aarhus, and (7) Ribe. Iceland constitutes a separate stift. The bishops, like the rest of the clergy, are appointed by the king; and upon them it devolves to ordain ministers and to inspect churches and schools. Under the Ministry of Public Instruction and Ecclesiastical Affairs the bishops constitute the highest ecclesiastical authority, officiating in some cases independently, in other cases in association with the secular head of the stift (the *stiftsamtmand*, or governor). Each stift is divided into *provstier* ("provostries"), Zealand having 18, Funen 11, Laaland and Falster 4, Aalborg 10, Viborg 9, Aarhus 13, and Ribe 8: total 73. Each *provsti* is superintended by a provost, who officiates as preacher also. He has to look after all ecclesiastical affairs within his precinct, and, together with the local *amtmand* and a member appointed by the School Commission, he supervises the parochial schools of his provostry (the eighteen secular divisions of Denmark are called *amts*—"counties"—each amt being governed by an *amtmand*). The amts within each stift are again ruled by a *stiftsamtmand*. Each provostry is divided into sognekald, the total number of which is about 1,070, each comprising one or two (rarely more) *sogns*, or parishes. Sognekalds of ordinary dimensions have each a minister who preaches alternately in the different parish churches. Large sognekalds, however, may have two officiating clergymen. The minister is also a school commissioner. The parish is thus the unit in the ecclesiastical organization of Denmark. By royal resolution of 1883 an ecclesiastical council was established, and the clergymen who are members of this body frequently assemble to discuss religious matters and questions pertaining to the affairs of the Church. The minister of each parish is, as already stated, a member of the school committee, and in this way the Church exercises a direct supervision over the parochial schools, of which there are nearly 3,000. The religious instruction given in the communal schools is based either upon Luther's smaller catechism or upon Balslev's version of the same.

Educational Institutions.

The Danish clergy receive their education at the University of Copenhagen, which has a theological faculty consisting of five ordinary professors. The curriculum includes Old and New Testament exegesis, dogmatics, ethics, and church history. There is also a theological seminary, in which two resident clergymen lecture on homiletics and catechetics, while a member of the juridical faculty expounds canon law. The Icelandic clergymen are mostly educated at the theological seminary in Reikiavik, although many frequent the University of Copenhagen. Several stipends are awarded by the Danish State for the promotion of theological studies.

While it was originally compulsory upon a Danish resident to frequent the church in his own parish, and to pay tithes and feast-offerings to the local clergyman, important laws modifying these obligations were enacted on Apr. 4, 1855, and Mar. 25, 1872. By the former legislation every citizen was granted the right to identify himself with any church according to his own choice, being obliged only to notify the local provost of the desired change. He would thenceforth have to pay to the minister of his home parish only the stipulated levies on real estate, produce, etc., while the feast-offerings were to go to the clergyman of his choice. The law of 1872 extended this grant so that a citizen may now have his church ceremonies (baptisms, funerals, weddings) conducted by an outside clergyman in the church of his own parish, provided, of course, that the church is not occupied for other purposes.

Inner Mission.

A Danish Society for the Inner Mission was founded in 1853, and has exerted a highly meritorious influence among the lower classes. Its activity received special impetus when Wilhelm Beck, minister of the parish of Oerslev on Zealand, became its head. Under his leadership the society was completely reorganized, and has since maintained a staff of about 120 missionaries, who conduct religious meetings especially for young men and women. The society has upward of 250 meeting-houses and a valuable free library. The Inner Mission is not merely an activity, but a religious trend; and if it should come to a breach between this society and the established Church, a sect would be created which might well be compared with the English Methodists. A local Society for the Inner Mission in Copenhagen (founded by the Rev. Mr. Frimodt in 1865) has a beautiful prayer-house, the Bethesda, where popular meetings are regularly held. The party founded by N. F. S. Grundtvig (q.v.) has been especially active in establishing the so-called *Folkehöjskoler* ("people's high schools"), which have won great and well-deserved recognition as educational mediums.

The Danish Society for Foreign Missions was founded in 1821. It has stations among the Tamils in India (established 1864; ten missionaries), in Dagusan and Port Arthur, China (1892; five missionaries), and in Syria (three missionaries). In western Greenland Christianity is so firmly established that one may speak of a Greenlandic Church there; but in the eastern parts the Danish State had no missionary until 1894, when a station was established at Angmagsalik. Among other societies the following may be mentioned: Danish Bible Society (founded 1814); the Society for Missions among Seamen (stations in Hamburg, London, Hull, and Newcastle); and the Society for Danish-American Missions, which supplies the Danish congregations of North America with preachers. (F. Nielsen.)

Bibliography: F. Nielsen, *Statskirke og Frikirke*, Copenhagen, 1883; H. G. Saabye, *Om Sekterne i Danmark*, ib. 1884; H. L. S. P. Koch and H. F. Rordam, *Danmarks Kirkehistorie, 1517–1848*, 2 vols., ib. 1889; T. J. A. Elmquist, *Kirken og dens hellige Handlinger*, Odense, 1892; E. A. F. Jessen, *Die Hauptströmungen des religiösen Lebens ... in Dänemark*, Gütersloh, 1895; T. Loegstrup, *Nordiske Missionaerer*, Copenhagen, 1897; F. S. O. A. Nygard, *Kristenliv i Danmark ... 1741–1840*, ib. 1897; A. V. C. Kjölbede, *Haandbog for den danske Folkekirke*, ib. 1899; *Studier og Aktstykker vedkommende de danske Östifters Historie*, ib. 1899; A. T. Jörgensen, *Den danske Folkekirkes Bekendelsesskrifter*, ib. 1900.

DENNEY, JAMES: United Free Church of Scotland; b. at Paisley Feb. 5, 1856. He was graduated at Glasgow University (M.A., 1879) and Free Church College, Glasgow (B.D., 1883). He was minister of East Free Church, Broughty Ferry, Fifeshire, from 1886 to 1897, and since 1897 has been professor of New Testament language, literature, and theology in the United Free Church College, Glasgow. He has edited for *The Expositor's Bible* Thessalonians (London, 1892) and II Corinthians (1894), and Romans for *The Expositor's Greek Testament* (1900). He has also written *Studies in Theology* (London, 1895); *Gospel Questions and Answers* (1896); *The Death of Christ* (1902); and *The Atonement and the Modern Mind* (1903); and has collaborated in *Questions of Faith; Lectures on the Creed* (1904).

DENNIS, JAMES SHEPARD: Presbyterian; b. at Newark, N. J., Dec. 15, 1842. He studied at Princeton (B.A., 1863), the Harvard Law School (1863–64), and Princeton Theological Seminary (B.D., 1867), and went as a missionary to Syria in 1868, studied at Sidon till 1872, and then made a brief visit to the United States. From 1873 to 1891 he was principal and professor of systematic theology at the Theological Seminary at Beirut. He returned definitely to the United States in 1891, and has since devoted himself to the promotion of foreign missionary work by the preparation of missionary literature and lecturing. He was Students' Lecturer on missions at Princeton in 1893 and 1896, and in 1900 was chairman of the committee on statistics of the Ecumenical Conference on Foreign Missions in New York City. He is a member of the Presbyterian Board of Foreign Missions. He is the author of Arabic theological treatises on the evidences of Christianity, on the science of Biblical interpretation, and on systematic theology, chiefly based on the works of Charles and Archibald Alexander Hodge. In English he has written *Foreign Missions after a Century* (Chicago and New York, 1893); *Christian Missions and Social Progress* (3 vols., 1897–1906); *Centennial Survey of Foreign Missions* (1902); and *New Horoscope of Missions* (1908).

DENS, PETER: Roman Catholic; b. at Boom (8 m. s. of Antwerp), Belgium, Sept. 12, 1690; d. at Mechlin, as archpriest of St. Rombold's cathedral, Feb. 15, 1775. He was the author of a *Theologia moralis et dogmatica*, which was often reprinted (e.g., 8 vols., Dublin, 1832), and much used as a textbook in Roman Catholic seminaries. Various books of extracts from this work exposing its alleged errors and immoralities have appeared from anonymous compilers (Dublin, 1836, 1851; Philadelphia, 1847; Boston, 1855). The best known of such publications is by J. F. Berg, *Synopsis of the Theology of Peter Dens* (Philadelphia, 1840; 4th ed., 1869).

DENUNCIATION: Properly, a making known, especially by public proclamation; hence, sometimes used of the publication of banns of marriage; commonly the word signifies in church usage a complaint before authority to initiate action by the latter. The *denunciatio evangelica* is the course recommended in Matt. xviii. 15–17, and is approved by the Church where applicable. When it fails the *denunciatio judicialis* follows and brings the case before the ecclesiastical courts; its form and procedure are regulated by the canon law (cf. book v., title 1, and commentators). The *denunciatio canonica* is the obligatory announcement of obstacles to a proposed promotion, ordination, or marriage. See Jurisdiction, Ecclesiastical.

DEPOSITION: A severe penalty inflicted upon delinquent clerics by the ancient ecclesiastical discipline (see Jurisdiction, Ecclesiastical), originally equivalent in practise to Degradation (q.v.), but now denoting the deprivation of the delinquent's office and benefice with the prohibition of the exercise of his orders. Unlike degradation, it may be removed, restoring the penitent offender to the exercise of his functions by a mere act of jurisdiction, without reordination. It does not remove the general clerical privileges of the delinquent nor absolve him from general clerical obligations; and the canon law assumes that he will be confined for the purpose of amendment in a monastery or house of correction. In the Protestant Churches generally, in accordance with their view of the nature of orders, the only sentence of this kind is the deprivation of a specific office. In the Church of England "deprivation" is the term commonly used whether for the taking away of a benefice (deprivation *a beneficio*) or the withdrawal of the right to exercise clerical functions (deprivation *ab officio*). In the American Episcopal Church the term "deposition" is used for the latter; it is pronounced by the bishop to whom the cleric is subject, and may be at his own request, for causes not affecting his moral character, or after trial for certain grave offenses.

DEPRIVATION. See DEGRADATION; DEPOSITION.

DEPUTATUS: The title of an office in the Greek and Roman Catholic Churches. According to Codinus, the third in the ninth pentad of officials of the *megalē ekklēsia* was termed *depotatos*, while the other lists name several *depotatoi* in addition to the one official of this name, who was the first and drew double pay. The first *depotatos* accompanied the bishop on the street to make room for him, and in the service the *depotatoi* escorted him to the pulpit and to the Holy Table, bearing the mantles and the candles. The *depotatos* was allowed to marry a second time, since he was ineligible for any higher order. It is doubtful whether this office still exists, since Chrysanthos (about 1700) seems to depend for his statements on books rather than on actual usage.

In the Roman Catholic Church *deputati* act in certain districts as the administrators of the *regiunculæ*, or subdivisions of large deaneries. They are usually subject to the dean and often act as his representatives, but occasionally they receive their orders immediately from the bishop, in which case the dean becomes merely first among his peers.

(PHILIPP MEYER.)

DE PUY, WILLIAM HARRISON: Methodist; b. at Penn Yan, N. Y., Oct. 31, 1821; d. at Canaan, Conn., Sept. 4, 1901. He was educated at Genesee College, Union University, and Mount Union College, and was professor of mathematics and natural philosophy in Genesee Wesleyan Seminary 1851–1855. He was associate editor of *The Christian Advocate* 1865–84, and editor of *The Methodist Year Book* 1866–80. He also edited *The People's Cyclopedia of Universal Knowledge* (3 vols., New York, 1882); *The People's Atlas of the World* (1886); and *University of Literature* (1896), and wrote *Threescore Years and Beyond: or, Experiences of the Aged* (New York, 1872); *Home and Health and Home Economics* (1880); and *The Methodist Centennial Year Book, 1784–1884* (1884).

DERESER, de-rē'ser, THADDÆUS ANTON: German Roman Catholic; b. at Fahr, in Franconia, Feb. 9, 1757; d. at Breslau July 16, 1827. He studied at Würzburg and Heidelberg, became priest at Mainz (1780), and was made professor of Oriental languages and Biblical interpretation at Bonn in 1783. He moved to Strasburg in 1791, returned to Heidelberg in 1797, and went to Freiburg in 1807. In 1810 he was made priest at Carlsruhe, but was dismissed the following year because of a funeral sermon over the Grand Duke of Baden. He then became professor and head of the episcopal seminary at Lucerne, but was removed in 1814, and in 1815 became professor in Breslau. He belonged to the liberal wing of his Church, and his *Commentatio biblica in effata Christi: Tu es Petrus* (Bonn, 1789) was put on the Index. He wrote Biblical commentaries, continued the Bible translation begun by Brentano (see BIBLE VERSIONS, B, VII., § 5), and published a Hebrew grammar (Freiburg, 1812), a German breviary, and a prayer-book.

DE ROSSI, GIOVANNI BALLISTA. See ROSSI.

DERVISH.

A dervish is a member of one of the orders which in Mohammedanism have some correspondence to the monasticism of Buddhism and Christianity. The name is Persian, but its derivation is disputed. The first syllable means "door," and the last is taken to mean either "sill" or "to beg." The sense derived in either case is "to be destitute" or "to be dependent (upon God)." The Arabic *fakir*, "poor," "ascetic," is the equivalent in general use. The word is often popularly misused to mean the tribes still in a nomadic state; it is also misapplied to beggars, jugglers, and to impostors.

The existence of the orders is due to the union of two general characteristics of religion, the ascetic and the mystic. Their formation was stimulated in early times by the example of the Christian monastics who were numerous in the lands conquered by the Moslems. They began by gathering about an individual whose mode of life had gained him repute for piety; a shelter was built for winter quarters, and developed into a monastery. The continuance of the institution is decided by several considerations, such as the prestige, religious and political, which the orders enjoy, a sincere devotional spirit which the exercises satisfy, the food for vanity furnished the individual members by a reputation for sanctity, and by the value placed upon the ecstatic condition sometimes induced by the exercises. The theology is usually mystical and pantheistic, and therefore heretical, and the orders are sometimes considered a protest against the scholasticism of orthodox Islam.

1. Origins and Objects of the Institution.

Mohammedan monasticism, however, differs much from Christian. The vows are relative, not absolute. They do not usually involve celibacy or poverty, obedience to the sheikh, or head of the house, being the essence of the vow. Even this may be retracted, and the dervish may withdraw from the order. The members are not required to reside at the monastery. Full membership involves a novitiate which may run from a year to four or five years, varying with the assumed fitness of the candidate. During his novitiate the candidate is under instruction, and learns the rules and ritual of the order. Very many do not pass beyond the

2. Character and Membership of the Orders.

novitiate. Most of the orders have what corresponds to a lay membership. Certain of the orders are in favor with certain professions or trades. Thus the fishermen of Egypt are nearly all members of the Kadariyah, and join in the religious processions, carrying colored fish-nets as banners. With some of the most prominent of the orders it is common for influential classes to become associated, doubtless that they may share in the prestige of those orders. Theoretically there is no distinction of rank within the orders except that of sheikh and members and novitiates. Practically individuals are differentiated; those supposed to be miraculously endowed are called walis: the begging friars go by the name of fakirs. The office of sheikh is in some orders hereditary; thus the rule of the Mawlawiyah has remained for nearly eight centuries in the family of the founder.

3. Number and Insignia of the Orders.

The number of orders is usually given as thirty-six, but this number is rather ideal than founded upon actual count. Some of the orders are divided into sects, and these are confounded with the orders. Each sect has its distinguishing insignia of cap or turban, girdle, cloak, rosary, and banner, its own color and method of wearing it. Sometimes the orders are distinguished simply by the number of gores in the cap. Theoretically the orders trace their origin to Ali, except three which claim to go back to Abu Bekr, and thence to Mohammed. The time of actual formation is unknown, but there is great probability that the first monastery was founded at Damascus about 772. The bloom of Mohammedan monasticism is to be placed in the twelfth to the fourteenth century, when most of the orders now in existence were founded. But the formation of orders has gone on continuously, one of the most influential being that of the Sanussites founded by Mohammed ibn Ali al-Sanussi in 1837, which has spread throughout the Mohammedan world, with headquarters in the desert between Egypt and Tripoli.

4. Names and Exercises of the Orders.

A number of these orders are noted both inside and outside the circle of Mohammedanism. The Mawlawiyah (founded by Jalal al-Din al-Rumi c. 1290) are known to travelers as the whirling or dancing dervishes from that part of their exercises which consists of the "mystic dance," a spinning movement continued often till unconsciousness or ecstasy supervenes. It is the order most popular among the Turks, many of the upper classes of whom are affiliated with it, and is the best endowed of all the orders. The Rufaiyah (founded by Ahmad al-Rufa'a c. 1190) are the "howling dervishes," especially popular in Egypt, a part of whose exercise consists of a chant or shout which generally consists of the Mohammedan formula "There is no God but Allah," sung while a swinging motion of the body is maintained. This exercise is also often continued till exhaustion and catalepsy result. The Kalandariyah (the "Calendars" of the Arabian Nights, founded c. 1350) are the wandering dervishes, really bound by a vow of poverty. The Nakshbendiyah (founded c. 1360) are influential, and their exercise is mainly that of contemplative devotion upon the names of Allah and the precepts of the order. The Baktashiyah (founded c. 1380) are celebrated because of the connection with them of the Janizaries. It is a military order, corresponding somewhat with the crusading Knights of the Temple or of St. John. The Kadiriyah (founded c. 1160), the Badawiyah (c. 1280), and the Ahmadiyah are most numerous in Egypt.

The exercises, varying with each order, are intended to be devotional. Some of them are repulsive in their effects and methods, and include self-mutilation with broken glass or sharp instruments, handling and even eating of serpents and scorpions. That they often produce a cataleptic condition makes them the more highly esteemed, since that condition is regarded as one of communion with higher powers, from which enlarged capacities and increased sanctity are supposed to result.

Geo. W. Gilmore.

Bibliography: J. P. Brown, *The Dervishes*, Philadelphia, 1868 (contains much material, but undigested); D. Ohsson, *Tableau général de l'empire Ottoman*, vol. ii., Paris, 1790 (gives a list of thirty-two orders with the dates of their founding, but is unreliable); J. Malcolm, *Hist. of Persia*, London, 1829; E. W. Lane, *Modern Egyptians*, 2 vols., ib. 1871; T. P. Hughes, *Dictionary of Islam*, articles *Faqir*, *Zikr*, ib. 1885; M. Ansiaux, *Les Confréries musulmanes*, Paris, 1891; O. Deport and X. Coppolani, *Les Confréries religieuses musulmanes*, ib. 1897; Père Petit, *Confréries musulmanes*, ib. 1899; S. M. Zwemer, *Arabia, the Cradle of Islam*, New York, 1900.

DESCARTES, dē''cārt', RENÉ.

1. As Student and Soldier.

René Descartes (*Renatus Cartesius*), French philosopher and mathematician, was born at La Haye (105 m. s.w. of Orléans) Mar. 31, 1596; d. at Stockholm, Sweden, Feb. 11, 1650. From 1604 to 1612 he attended the College of Jesuits at La Flèche, which had just been established (1604) by Henry IV., and in 1610 he was one of the twenty-four *gentilshommes* sent forth from that institution to receive the heart of the murdered king. From 1613 to 1617 he resided in Paris, devoting himself chiefly to the study of mathematics. The next four years he spent as a volunteer, serving successively under Prince Maurice of Nassau, Maximilian of Bavaria, and Count Boucquoi. After a further period of travel and study he settled in Paris in 1625. He was now recognized as one of the leading mathematicians of the day.

Late in 1628, after having taken part in the siege of La Rochelle, he left Paris and settled in Amsterdam the following spring.

2. Seclusion in Holland.

For the next twenty years he lived almost exclusively in Holland, developing and defending his philosophical theories, carrying on scientific investigations, and writing the works that have made him famous. His interests were varied, and in his correspondence not even phonetic spelling escapes his attention. During this period his place of abode, which he changed more than twenty times, was a secret known only to a few friends, particularly Marin Mersenne, his Paris correspondent. Descartes claimed that he was only seeking the quiet and seclusion necessary for study, but he was probably hiding from the Roman Catholic Church. Professedly an orthodox Catholic, he did not wish to offend the Church with a theory of matter out of harmony with the doctrine of transubstantiation, or with his equally objectionable theory of the earth's motion. Indeed, he was long deterred from publishing his work by the experience of Galileo (q.v.).

3. Publications. Controversies.

In Holland Descartes had made enthusiastic disciples; and under the leadership of Henri Reneri, and his successor at the University of Utrecht, Henri Le Roy (Regius), the new philosophy was triumphant. However, soon after the publication of the *Discours de la méthode* (Leyden, 1637) he began to experience opposition; and on the appearance of his *Meditationes de prima philosophia* (Paris, 1641), which was followed by his *Principia philosophiæ* (Amsterdam, 1644), he found himself the center of the most bitter theological controversies. He was attacked by Protestants and Catholics alike. Gisbertus Voetius (q.v.), who had become rector of the University of Utrecht in 1641, led the Calvinist opposition. He stopped the teaching of Descartes's doctrine, induced the city magistrates to take action against Descartes, and all but succeeded in having his works burned by the public hangman. Descartes finally had to appeal to the Prince of Orange to end the persecution to which he was being subjected by the Voetians. In a measure he escaped these troubles by two visits to France, where, in 1644, he conciliated his old teacher, Father Bourdin, who had led the Jesuit opposition against him, and in 1647 received a pension of 3,000 livres from the French king.

4. Death in Stockholm. Works Proscribed.

On the occasion of his last visit to France (1648), the lukewarm reception accorded him at the court, due to the disorders of the time, caused him to abandon the intention he had formed of settling in Paris, and in Sept., 1649, on the invitation of Queen Christina of Sweden, he set out for Stockholm to teach his philosophy to that eccentric sovereign. Less than four months after his arrival in Stockholm he succumbed to pneumonia. He died in the Roman Catholic faith and was buried in the Catholic cemetery in Stockholm. In 1667 his remains were reinterred with imposing ceremonies in St. Geneviève du Mont (the modern Panthéon), Paris, though the funeral oration prepared for the occasion was suppressed by the court. In 1819 his remains were removed to St. Germain-des-Prés, where they now rest. Despite the efforts of Descartes during his lifetime, and those of his friends after his death, to convince the Church of his orthodoxy, his works were placed on the Index at Rome in 1663, and in 1671 the teaching of Cartesianism at the University of Paris was prohibited by royal order. However, Cartesianism, which had now become an intellectual fad, remained the only philosophy of the day and continued to be taught in numerous private academies in Paris, and also in the Dutch universities.

5. His Skepticism. The Self and God.

The philosophical views of Descartes will be found in the three works mentioned above. In reflecting over his scholastic studies at La Flèche, he came to the conclusion that all generally accepted knowledge is open to doubt. From this sweeping indictment he reserved morals and religion; but it was inevitable that, once enunciated, skepticism, as a method, would be extended to these fields. Both Father Bourdin and Voetius foresaw this. Thus, rejecting all supposed knowledge, Descartes set about to build up a philosophical system *de novo*. He begins by establishing the reality of the self. In questioning the truth of everything he finds at least one fact that he can not doubt; viz., the very fact of doubting itself. This doubt, of course, is a form of thought; but before there can be any thought there must be a subject that thinks. Hence, his famous *cogito, ergo sum*, a modification of Augustine's *fallor, ergo sum*. From the reality of the self he then develops his proof of the existence of God. Among other innate ideas he finds the idea God, a perfect being, omniscient, omnipotent, infinite. Since an effect can not be greater than its cause, we ourselves, as finite beings, could not have produced this idea. In fact, only a perfect being could have produced it; but, since existence is an attribute of a perfect being, this being must necessarily exist—a form of Anselm's ontological argument, which was demolished by Kant (q.v.). In searching for the ground of the certainty of his knowledge regarding his own existence and that of God, Descartes finds that it lies in the clearness and distinctness of the idea. He then lays down the obscure and highly questionable rule that whatever is perceived clearly and distinctly must be true. Since he has already demonstrated that there is a God, God's veracity (another attribute of perfection) becomes the guaranty of our knowledge. Hobbes was the first to point out that this argument moves in a circle.

6. His Dualism. Ethics.

In addition to an infinite substance, or God, Descartes, retaining the dualism of the schoolmen, finds in existence two created substances, mind (*res cogitans*) and matter (*res extensa*). These are absolutely heterogeneous and not further reducible the one into the other. While the essence of the one is thinking, the only quality of the other is extension, such supposed qualities as color, odor, etc., being merely subjective. The difficulty in conceiving of any causal relation between these two incompatible kinds of being does not seem to have presented itself to Descartes. Since in the case of man there is apparently such a relation there must be some point of contact between the spatial body and the non-spatial soul. This point Descartes locates in the pineal gland. The body itself he regards as an automatic mechanism, so far as the functions of digestion, circulation, and the affections of love, hate, etc., are concerned; though the immaterial soul, which God has fused into the body, directs all conscious movements.

Animals he regards as soulless, mechanical automata which are moved by vital springs after the analogy of a watch. He denies that death is due to the departure of the soul from the body, holding, on the contrary, that the soul departs because the machine that we call the body has run down. In conformity to this mechanical view of animal life, Descartes and his followers practised vivisection freely, interpreting the cries of their victims as the creakings of breaking machinery. For Descartes the whole sensible world was a mechanism whose essential qualities were extension and mobility. Given these, he was ready to reconstruct a priori, and with mathematical exactness, the whole universe. The idea of necessity was so strong in him that in an unguarded moment he even identified God with the order of nature. He did not attempt a systematic treatment of ethics; but when he touches the subject, in his letters to Queen Christina and Princess Elizabeth and in *Les Passions de l'âme* (Paris, 1649), he follows Greek rather than Christian ideals. He counsels humility from practical considerations, and usually interprets moral obligation in a eudemonistic sense.

7. Estimate of His Work. Descartes is properly called the father of modern philosophy, for it was through him that the sway of scholasticism was finally broken and a new method and content given to philosophy. He stands at the head of the modern rationalistic development, both in philosophy and theology; and in his insistence on the importance of experiment he rivals Bacon as one of the founders of English empiricism. The rationalistic school that he established was practically dominant till the time of Kant; and, indeed, most speculation since Descartes has been an attempt to overcome the intellectual difficulties of his extreme dualism. If mind and matter are absolutely opposed to each other, how can they react on each other? This was the problem of Descartes' successors. Geulincx and Malebranche solved it with the theory of occasional causes (occasionalism), Leibnitz with his preestablished harmony, Spinoza with his *unica substantia*, or pantheism, others with materialism. Kant showed that the spatial, as well as the temporal, aspect of our experience is only a form of sense-perception. His German successors then took the further step to absolute idealism.

In the history of mathematics Descartes is famous as the founder of analytic geometry. He also systematized the use of exponents, and gave new significance to negative quantities. He was the first to hit upon the undulatory theory of light, afterward developed by his pupil Christian Huyghens; and in his view that the world was evolved from a chaotic state by vortical motions he anticipated the nebular hypothesis of Kant and Laplace. The most important Latin and French editions of Descartes's works are. *Opera omnia* (8 vols., Amsterdam, 1670–83; 9 vols., 1692–1701); *Œuvres* (13 vols., Paris, 1724–29; ed. Victor Cousin, 11 vols., 1824–26). The best English translations of the philosophical works are: *The Method, Meditations, and Selections from the Principles of Descartes*, by J. Veitch (London and Edinburgh, 1850–1853; new ed., New York, 1899); *The Philosophy of Descartes in Extracts from his Writings*, by H. A. P. Torrey (New York, 1892). A monumental edition of his works is now in preparation under the auspices of the French Academy (10 vols., Paris, 1897 sqq.). See MATERIALISM, § 5; and ELIZABETH, ALBERTINE.

HUBERT EVANS.

BIBLIOGRAPHY: On the life consult: A. Baillet, *La Vie de M. Des Cartes*, 2 vols., Paris, 1691; A. Prévost, *Œuvres . . . de Descartes, précédées d'une notice sur sa vie*, ib. 1855; J. Millet, *Descartes*, 2 vols., ib. 1867–70; W. Ernst, *Descartes*, Leips, 1869; C. J. Jeannel, *Descartes et la princesse Palatine*, Paris, 1869; J. P. Mahaffy, *Descartes*, Edinburgh, 1881; K. Fischer, *Geschichte der neueren Philosophie*, vol. 1, Heidelberg, 1897, Eng. transl., New York, 1887; Elizabeth S. Haldane, *Descartes*, London, 1905. On his philosophy consult: V. Cousin, in the *Œuvres* of Descartes, i. 1–80, Paris, 1824; J. B. Bordas-Demoulin, *Le Cartésianisme*, 2 vols., ib. 1843; F. X. Schmid, *René Descartes und seine Reform der Philosophie*, Nördlingen, 1859; F. Bouillier, *Hist. de la philosophie cartésienne*, Paris, 1868; C. Waddington, *Descartes et le spiritualisme*, ib. 1868; W. Cunningham, *The Influence of Descartes on Metaphysical Speculation in England*, London, 1876; F. Bowen, *Modern Philosophy*, pp. 22–37, New York, 1877; R. A. Meincke, *Descartes' Beweise vom Dasein Gottes*, Heidelberg, 1883; A. Barthel, *Descartes' Leben und Metaphysik*, Erlangen, 1885; G. Monchamp, *Hist. du cartésianisme en Belgique*, Brussels, 1887; E. Caird, *Essays on Literature and Philosophy*, Glasgow, 1892; G. F. Hertling, *Descartes' Beziehung zur Scholastik*, Munich, 1899; J. Iverach, *Descartes, Spinoza, the New Philosophy*, Edinburgh, 1904.

DESCENT OF CHRIST INTO HELL.

The sentence "He descended into hell" (Lat. *descendit ad inferna* or *ad inferos*), expressing a christological fact following the death and burial of Jesus, is found in the Apostles' Creed and the Athanasian Creed, but is lacking in the Niceno-Constantinopolitan Creed and the Old Roman Symbol. Its first official statement, as far as a date can be assigned, was formulated in 359 and 360 at synods at Sirmium in Pannonia, Nice in Thrace, and Constantinople, held under homoiousian influence. A few decades later it formed, according to the testimony of Rufinus (*Expositio symboli Aquileiensis*, xviii.), a part of the confession of the Church of Aquileia (see AQUILEIAN CREED). But it was taught much earlier by the most various writers of the Church. The older assertion that it was received into the confession to combat the Apollinarian heresy has long been refuted. It is simply the crystallization of an old unassailed Christian tradition.

The New Testament tells only that the soul of Jesus was for a time subject to the realm of the dead like that of any other man. According to Acts ii. 27, 31, the characteristic feature is not that

1. New Testament Data. he descended into Hades, but that he soon returned from it by his resurrection. Paul also assumes probably, in Rom. x. 7, Christ's real presence in the intermediate place of the deceased since he speaks of the "deep" (Gk. *abyssos*) in connection with the awakening of Christ. In Luke xxiii. 43 Christ assures the thief on the cross that he shall be with him in paradise, thus adding, according to the meaning of the word *paradeisos* in the current usage of the Jews, a further testimony that the soul of Jesus was in the realm of the dead, more particularly in that part of it which was destined for the just. But it must be observed that in these passages a descent into hell is not expressly taught, but is presupposed as something which naturally follows death.

Concerning the activity of Christ in Hades, the First Epistle of Peter (iii. 18 sqq. and iv. 6) has occasioned great dispute. According as the "spirits" (Gk. *pneumata*) have been understood to be the souls of deceased men or real spirits (i.e., fallen angels), and according as Christ, who descended to them, has been thought of as incarnate or preexisting, this passage has been interpreted in four different ways: (1) Christ preached after his death to the departed souls of the unbelieving contemporaries of Noah. Origen, Bengel, König, Güder, Usteri, and others assumed that the purpose of Christ's preaching in Hades was of a redeeming nature, while since Flacius and Calovius many Lutheran interpreters and dogmaticians have looked upon it as a damnatory manifestation of judgment against the rejected, in the evident effort to adopt the text of the Bible to the churchly conception of the descent as a triumph of Christ over the power of Satan. (2) Following Augustine, Thomas Aquinas, Beza, and many Reformed theologians after him, especially A. Schweizer, interpreted the passage as a sermon of Christ before his incarnation, which proceeded either from the mouth of Noah, the "preacher of righteousness" (II Pet. ii. 5), or coincides with the "long suffering of God" expressed in iii. 20. (3) Spitta tried to solve the problem by assuming that the Messiah before his incarnation, in the time before the flood, preached to the fallen angels, who, according to Gen. vi. 1 sqq., Enoch vi.-viii., united with the daughters of men and corrupted mankind. His words, according to Spitta, were identical with the announcement of punishment with which Enoch was entrusted according to the book bearing his name (xii. seq.), since in pre-Christian Judaism the representations of Enoch and the Messiah were frequently confused. (4) F. C. Baur shares the view of Spitta that Christ announced condemnation to the fallen angels, but not until after his awakening from the death on the cross. The fruit of the innocent suffering of Christ consists in the victory over these corrupting beings by which man is brought to God (I Pet. iii. 18).

It may, however, be proved from history that the passage I Pet. iii. 18 sqq. has not formed the basis for the development of the church doctrine of the saving activity of Christ in Hades. Among early Christian writers it is cited only by Origen, and, in very incidental manner, by Hilary of Poitiers, while other Old and New Testament passages are brought forward in great number. It is evident from Matt. xxvii. 52–53 that, in consequence of the death of Jesus and his descent into Hades which followed as a natural consequence, many departed saints were delivered from the bonds of death. There was a general belief in the old Church that the salvation accomplished by Christ was made available for the prophets and the pious men of the Old Testament in the time between Christ's death and his resurrection. Since the soul of Jesus with its inseparable divinity appeared in Hades, Satan was deprived of the sovereignty which he had exercised hitherto in an unlimited way in the nether world. There was a difference between the Occidentals and Orientals in regard to the question to whom the announcement of salvation referred. The Occidental Church confined it strictly to the patriarchs, prophets, and other believers of the Old Testament, while in the Oriental Church a more universalistic tendency made itself felt. The scholastics of the Middle Ages emphasized again and again that the salvation which Christ brought to Hades referred simply to the *limbus patrum*, and not to any persons who had died without faith or to the *limbus infantium*. According to the *Catechismus Romanus*, the soul of Christ descended into Hades while his body lay in the grave, not because he was subject to the law of man, as the older Church taught, but of his own will, in order to conquer the demons.

2. The Older Church Doctrine.

The Protestants rejected, with purgatory, also the *Limbus* (q.v.), and retained only two conditions after death; hence originated the tendency to identify Hades with hell; i.e., the place or condition of condemnation. The Lutheran Church adopted the thought of Luther, contained in his Torgau sermon (1533), according to which Christ in his whole personality, God and man, body and soul, really and truly descended into the hell of the damned and conquered the devil. The Formula of Concord stood on the same ground. Christ descended on the early morning of the resurrection, just before his appearance as the risen one on the earth. The interval between the crucifixion and the descent he had spent in paradise. The descent of Christ is considered the first stage in his exaltation (see JESUS CHRIST, TWOFOLD STATE OF), since then for the first time he made an unlimited use of his divine *idiomata* by triumphing over the power of Satan.

3. The Protestant Doctrine.

The Reformed theologians regarded the descent into hell as a figurative expression for the unutterable sufferings of Christ's human soul, which he endured in the last moments of his vicarious dying (Calvin, "Institutes," bk. ii., chap. xvi., §§ 8–21). It was a part of his humiliation, not, as in the Lutheran view, the first stage of his exalted state. Beside this view, others have been held concerning the meaning of the clause. It was only another way of saying that Christ was buried (Beza, Drusius, and others) or denoted the state of death regarded as an ignominious one for the Prince of Life (Piscator, Arminius, and others).

It was only in the period of the Enlightenment that the text in I Peter iii. attracted new attention in an exegetical respect. It was held that it implied a sermon of glad tidings to persons who had died without salvation. The rationalists looked upon it as well as upon the descent into Hades as a passing Jewish conception, while dogmaticians like De Wette, Marheineke, and Hase discovered in it as in a myth a permanent Christian idea.

Presupposing the actuality of an intermediate state, a great number of theologians have proclaimed this sermon of salvation on the part of Christ as an essential factor by means of which the universality of Christianity is realized. But in recent times the descent into Hades is treated with great reservation, if not entirely passed over.

4. Conclusion. In looking back upon the doctrine of the descent, we find that from the standpoint of the New Testament, as well as from that of the history of dogma, two distinct features stand in the foreground—the sojourn of Christ in Hades and the triumph over the powers of hell. The sentence of the Apostles' Creed, *descendit ad inferos*, relates primarily only to the former. If it is desired to connect a certain activity with Christ's sojourn, one may believe with the old Church that he carried life and salvation to the believers in Hades. But in so far as Hades, from which the patriarchs were to be delivered, was under the dominion of Satan, the prince of darkness was to be conquered, and this idea came to the foreground, since the interest in the fate of the patriarchs and pious men of pre-Christian times gradually diminished and the expression *inferi* became in the course of time in popular as well as theological representation the place of the damned and evil spirits. Finally, inasmuch as the assumption of a sermon of salvation to all deceased persons in the intermediate state is based upon the very questionable interpretation of a single Bible text and can hardly be harmonized with other passages (II Cor. v. 10; Gal. vi. 8; Rom. ii. 6; etc.), it is unjustly considered indispensable for the maintenance of the principle of divine justice and love; for the belief that God gives all men somehow an opportunity to obtain full salvation in Christ is independent of the definite way in which some think it is realized.

(M. LAUTERBURG.)

BIBLIOGRAPHY: J. A. Dietelmayer, *Historia dogmatica de descensu Christi ad inferos*, Nuremberg, 1741; E. Güder, *Lehre von der Erscheinung Christi unter den Todten*, Bern, 1852; A. Schweizer, *Hinabgefahren zur Hölle, als Mythus*, Zurich, 1868; C. Hodge, *Theology*, ii. 616–621, New York, 1871; F. Huidekoper, *The Belief of the First Three Centuries Concerning Christ's Mission to the Underworld*, ib. 1876; E. H. Plumptre, *The Spirits in Prison*, ib. 1885; C. H. H. Wright, *Biblical Essays: St. Peter's Spirits in Prison*, Edinburgh, 1886; J. M. Usteri, *Hinabgefahren zur Hölle*, Zurich, 1886; F. Spitta, *Christi Predigt an die Geister*, Göttingen, 1890; Briney, in *Christian Quarterly Review*, 1897; C. Brustow, *La Descente du Christ aux enfers*, Paris, 1897; A. C. McGiffert, *The Apostles' creed*, pp. 193 sqq., 1902; Schaff, *Creeds*, i. 14-23; the commentaries on I Pet. iii. 19-22 and iv. 6; Rufinus, *Commentarius in Symbolum Apostolorum*. Later text with notes by C. Whitaker, 3d ed., London, 1908; and the literature under APOSTLES' CREED.

DESERT, CHURCH OF THE. See CAMISARDS; COURT, ANTOINE; HUGUENOTS; RABAUT, PAUL.

DES MARETS, dê mā″rē′ (MARESIUS), SAMUEL: Representative of the Reformed polemic orthodoxy; b. at Oisemont (75 m. n.n.w. of Paris), Picardy, Aug. 9, 1599; d. at Groningen May 18, 1673. He studied in Paris, in Saumur under Gomarus, and in Geneva at the time of the Synod of Dort. He was ordained in 1620, and preached at Laon until a controversy with Roman Catholic missionaries, which led to an attack on his life (1624), forced him to leave. He became professor at Sédan (1625), pastor at Maestricht (1632), pastor and professor at Bois-le-Duc (1636), and at Groningen (1643), where he won a reputation that led to calls to Saumur, Marburg, Lausanne, and Leyden. He wrote more than one hundred works, including a *Systhema theologiæ* (Groningen, 1645; 4th and best ed., 1673, with an appendix giving a list of his writings), worked out in scholastic fashion, which was much used as a text-book. But his literary activity was chiefly polemical—against Roman Catholics, Socinians, Arminians, Amyraldism as represented by Dallæus, Chiliasm, etc.

(S. D. VAN VEEN.)

DESSERVANT. See CHAPLAIN.

DÉSUBAS, dê″sū″bā′. See MAJAL, MATHIEU.

DETERMINISM: The common name for all theories of the human will which represent it as absolutely determined by motives which lie entirely outside of it, thereby reducing its freedom to a mere delusion. There is a dogmatic determinism, which, in order to glorify the majesty of God, excludes all other causality from human action but God himself (Luther, *De servo arbitrio*); and there is a philosophical determinism, which explains all human actions as results of surrounding circumstances (La Mettrie; many modern so-called "social reformers"). There is a fatalistic determinism, which places God himself in the grip of an iron necessity (the ancient idea of Nemesis, Islam); and there is a pantheistic determinism, which makes even the faintest gleam of human freedom vanish into the darkness of a natural process (the Hindus, Stoicism, Spinoza). One of the most interesting forms under which determinism has appeared in theology is that which it received from Schleiermacher and his school. See WILL.

DEUSDEDIT, dê″us-dê′dit: The name of three men who figure in church history.

1. Pope 615–618. He was a Roman, chosen pope after the death of Boniface IV., 615, and consecrated Oct. 19. He died Nov. 8, 618. Nothing is known of his activity; miracles and spurious decretals are attributed to him, and he is honored as a saint on Nov. 8.

BIBLIOGRAPHY: *Liber pontificalis*, ed. Duchesne, i., pp. cclvi., 319, Paris, 1886; ed. Mommsen, in *MGH*, *Gest. pont. Rom.*, i. 160–167, Berlin, 1898.

2. Sixth archbishop of Canterbury and the first of English origin; d. at Canterbury July 14, 664. He was a West Saxon whose native name was Frithona, and succeeded Honorius as archbishop after an interval of a year and a half, being consecrated by Ithamar, bishop of Rochester, Mar. 26, 655. The insignificance of Canterbury in his time is shown by the fact that he consecrated only one English bishop (Damian, successor of Ithamar at Rochester); all others were consecrated abroad or by Celtic bishops. He was not present at the Synod of Whitby, and no mention is made of any one to represent him there. After his death the see remained vacant for some time.

Bibliography: The *Vita* by Gosalin is given in part in *ASB*, July, iv. 48-50. Consult: Bede, *Hist. eccl.*, iii. 20, 29, iv. 1; Haddan and Stubbs, *Councils*, iii. 99-113; *DNB*, xiv. 422.

3. Cardinal; d. about 1099. Of his earlier life it is related merely that he was once a monk in Todi. At the Roman November synod of 1078 he belonged to the clerics in the circle of Gregory VII. who agreed with Berengar of Tours. He is said to have been in Spain as legate of this pope; he was certainly in Germany, perhaps in the same capacity. It was probably also under Gregory VII. that he became a cardinal. The significance of Deusdedit lies primarily in his literary achievements on behalf of the Gregorian party. His *Liber canonum*, doubtless suggested by Gregory VII., was completed in 1087 (ed. P. Martinucci, Venice, 1869, and recently republished with detailed investigations by V. W. von Glanvell, *Die Kanonensammlung des Kardinals Deusdedit*, Paderborn, 1905). Deusdedit participated in the public questions of his time by composing in 1097 the *Libellus contra invasores et symoniacos* (*MGH, Libelli de lite*, ii., 1892, 300 ff.), important for its treatment of simony, investiture, and the value of sacraments administered by simoniac priests. Probably he is the author also of the so-called *Dictatus papæ Gregorii VII.* (*Gregorii VII. Reg.*, II. 55a). [Mann, *Popes*, i. 304, calls him "the best of the eleventh-century canonists."]

CARL MIRBT.

Bibliography: W. von Giesebrecht, *Münchener Historisches Jahrbuch*, 1866; E. Sackur, *Neues Archiv für die ältere deutsche Geschichtskunde*, xvi., xviii.; C. Mirbt, *Die Publizistik im Zeitalter Gregors VII.*, Leipsic, 1894; W. Martens, *Gregor VII.*, ib. 1894; G. Buschbell, *Die professiones fidei der Päpste*, Münster, 1896.

DEUTERONOMY. See HEXATEUCH.

DEUTSCH, doich, **SAMUEL MARTIN**: German Protestant; b. at Warsaw, Poland, Feb. 19, 1837. He studied at Erlangen and Rostock (Ph.D., 1857), and, after being for many years instructor in a gymnasium in Berlin, was appointed in 1885 associate professor of church history in the university of the same city. He has written *Die Lehre des Ambrosius von Sünde und Sündentilgung* (Berlin, 1867); *Drei Aktenstücke zur Geschichte des Donatismus* (1875); *Der Synode von Sens (1141) und die Verurteilung Abälards* (1880); and *Peter Abalard, ein kritischer Theolog des zwölften Jahrhunderts* (Leipsic, 1883). He edited K. R. Hagenbach's *Leitfaden zum Religionsunterricht* from the sixth to the ninth edition (Leipsic, 1881-1905).

DEUTSCHMANN, JOHANN: Lutheran theologian; b. at Jüterbogk (27 m. s. of Potsdam) Aug. 10, 1625; d. at Wittenberg Aug. 12, 1706. In 1657 he became extraordinary professor, and in 1662 ordinary professor at Wittenberg. During the syncretistic and pietistic controversies he represented the extreme orthodox Lutheranism; and opposed especially the younger Calixtus and the theology of the pietists. Against Spener, the leader of the pietists, he charged no less than 263 heresies. Being the son-in-law of the orthodox professor Calovius, he used the weak man as a blind tool in his hand. To his scientific fancies belonged the development of the so-called *Theologia paradisiaca*, i.e., that Adam, the patriarchs, and the whole Old Testament agreed with the Augsburg Confession and Formulas of Concord. To prove this, he published an *Antiquissima theologia positiva primi theologi Adami*, a *Symbolum apostolicum Adami*; and *Der christlutherischen Kirche Prediger—Beicht und Beichtstuhl von dem grossen Jehova-Elohim im Paradiese gestiftet*.

PAUL TSCHACKERT.

Bibliography: M. Ranfft, *Leben der chursächsischen Gottesgelehrten*, i. 243, Leipsic, 1742; *ADB*, v. 93.

DÉVAY, MÁTYÁS BIRÓ: Hungarian Reformer; b. about 1500 at Deva (140 m. n.e. of Belgrade), Transylvania; d. perhaps 1545 in Debreczin. Where he received his earlier education is unknown; some Hungarian authors call him a pupil of Grynæus at Ofen. Hungarian students of Transylvania at this time usually visited the University of Cracow, and Dévay with his fellow Reformer Kálmáncschi is matriculated there for the winter semester of 1523. On his return from Cracow two years later, he joined a monastic order, and is found in 1527 a zealous Roman Catholic priest, on the estate of Stephan Tomory. By this time the Reformation had made great progress in Hungary. Dévay was won over and went to Wittenberg to arm himself for its defense and propagation, and studied at the university for a year and a half, during which time he had free board and lodging with Luther. Returning well recommended by the great Reformers, he appears in the spring of 1531 in Ofen-Buda as minister of its Hungarian congregation, spreading the Reformation. He then wrote his *De sanctorum dormitione*, against the invocation of the saints, and fifty-two propositions in defense of the Reformation. As Hungary had no printing-press, the tracts circulated only in manuscript, and their contents are known only through his polemic works published later in other countries. Before the end of the same year he was called to Kaschau (Kassa) as preacher. Here his zeal for the Reformation aroused the wrath of the Roman clergy, and Thomas Szalaházy, bishop of Erlau, arrested him on higher orders, Nov. 6, 1531. Though the citizens resisted his arrest, he was imprisoned, first in Likava, then in Presburg, finally in Vienna. Here he suffered much, and was several times examined before the bitterest enemy of the Reformation, Bishop Faber. Released, he went again to Ofen, then under Ferdinand's rival John Zápolya, but his zeal led him into captivity, 1534-35. From Ofen he went under the protection of Count Nádasdy, a rich Hungarian magnate and an open and active Reformer, to Sarvar, where he used the count's splendid library in the composition of his Latin polemic treatises. Gregory Szegedy, provincial of the Franciscans in Hungary, a chief persecutor of Protestants, finally fulfilled his threat and replied to Dévay's tracts, already mentioned, under the title *Censuræ Fratris Gregorii Zegedini, O. F., in propositiones erroneas Matthiæ Dévay . . .* (Vienna, 1535). Dévay at once set himself to reply and toward the end of 1536 went to Germany to see to the publication of his rejoinder. In the spring he was at Wittenberg, enjoying the friendship of Melanchthon. Before fall his book was published in Nuremberg, with the title *Disputatio de statu in quo sint beatorum animæ post hanc vitam, ante ultimi judicii diem. Item de præcipuis articulis Christianæ doctrinæ*, and an introduction perhaps by Melanchthon or Grynæus. Returning soon after to Hungary, he joined Count Thomas Nádasdy and John Sylvester (Erdösi) in the endeavor to strengthen the Reformation by means of schools and a national literature. He wrote his *Orthographia Ungarica* (the first book printed in Hungary in the Hungarian language), in which he incorporated the fundamentals of Protestantism and the children's prayers from Luther's Shorter Catechism. During this time Dévay wrote a "Handbook of Religion" in Hungarian (2d facsimile ed., Budapest, 1897). Meanwhile the Turk had invaded Hungary in aid of Ferdinand's rival, whose party was hostile to the Reformation. Dévay and his comrades were forced to flee, and are found in Dec., 1541, in Wittenberg. Dévay took the opportunity of visiting Switzerland, and became a decided adherent to the Swiss doctrines, which at first surprised and later angered Luther. After about a year and a half he returned to Hungary and labored for a while in Miskolcz in Upper Hungary, then in Debreczin. (K. Révész.)

Bibliography: G. Bauhofer, *Geschichte der evangelischen Kirche in Ungarn*, Berlin, 1854; F. Balogh, *Geschichte der ungarisch-protestantischen Kirche*, Debreczin, 1882; P. Bod, *Hist. Hungarorum eccl.*, ed. Rauwenhoff, 3 vols., Leyden, 1889–90.

DEVELOPMENT, THEOLOGICAL AND HISTORICAL: The Evangelical Protestant theory maintains that Christianity objectively considered is perfect in Christ and the New Testament, but that its understanding and application is gradual, and progressing from age to age. The rationalistic theory holds that Christianity itself is imperfect, and will ultimately be superseded by philosophy or a humanitarian religion, or that reason will take the place of the Bible as a rule of faith and action. The theory advocated by Cardinal Newman, in his *Development of Christian Doctrine* (London, 1845), written just before he went over to Rome, but never indorsed by the Roman Catholic Church, is that the New Testament contained the germs of certain doctrines, i.e., those distinctive to the Roman and Greek Catholic Churches, which, under divine care, have been developed into their present shape. The reply to Newman's position is that, while descent from earlier formulas may be traced for many later doctrines, it does not follow that the development was always along legitimate lines. The Protestant criticism of Roman Catholic development is that the latter is often in a direction contrary to the spirit of the Gospel. See Doctrines, History of.

Bibliography: Philip Schaff, *What is Church History? A Vindication of the Idea of Historical Development*, Philadelphia, 1846; W. A. Butler, *Letters on the Development of Christian Doctrine in Reply to Mr. Newman's Essay*, Dublin, 1850; O. Pfleiderer, *Philosophy of Religion*, 4 vols., London, 1886–88; A. V. G. Allen, *Continuity of Christian Thought*, Boston, 1887; J. Kaftan, *Truth of the Christian Religion*, 2 vols., Edinburgh, 1894; J. Orr, *Progress of Dogma*, New York, 1901.

DEVIL.

I. The Old Testament Teaching: The Old Testament does not contain the fully developed doctrine of Satan (Heb. *Satan*, "adversary") found in the New Testament. It does not portray him as at the head of a kingdom, ruling over kindred natures and an apostate from the family of God. The belief in evil spirits is distinctly alluded to (see Demon). In the older books God is described as the source from which come influences noxious to man (Ex. viii. sqq., xii. 29); but there are not wanting references to evil spirits as evil agencies (I Sam. xvi. 14; I Kings xxii. 20 sqq.). In this connection the parallel statements of II Sam. xxiv. 1 and I Chron. xxi. 1 should be compared; it will be found that the same event is attributed in the first passage to God as its author, and in the second to Satan (cf. Luke xii. 5 and Heb. ii. 14).

The term "Satan" is used in the general sense of adversary (Ps. cix. 6 etc.), but more particularly also as the spirit of evil, who comes into collision with the plans of God, and plots the hurt of man. It is not definitely stated in the account of the fall that the serpent who tempted Eve was the devil, or his agent. The first identification of the two is in the Book of Wisdom (ii. 23–24; cf. II Cor. xi. 3; Rev. xii. 9), and it is taken for granted in the expression "that old serpent called the devil" (Rev. xii. 9; cf. John viii. 44). This inference is justified by the words which the serpent used, and agrees with the portrait of the devil as the tempter. Lev. xvi. 8 has been thought to contain a reference to Satan (see Azazel; Demon). In the Book of Job he is brought out as a distinct personality. He presents himself before Yahweh with the sons of God (i. 6), and, after questioning the motives of the patriarch, secures permission to tempt and torment him, but not to kill him (i. 12). In Zech. iii. 1 he is portrayed as standing at the side of Joshua the high priest to "resist" him (A. V.; A. V. marg. and R. V., "to be his adversary"). In the Book of Enoch and the Hebrew Apocrypha and Pseudepigrapha the doctrine of the personality of the devil is developed and grotesque features are introduced.

II. The New Testament Teaching: The New Testament is full of allusions to the personality and agency of the devil (Gk. *diabolos*, "calumniator"). He bears the titles of "tempter" (I Thess. iii. 5), the "wicked" or "evil one" (Matt. xiii. 19 etc.; cf. vi. 13), "Beelzebub" and "prince of devils" (Gk. *daimones;* Matt. xii. 24), "the prince of this world" (John xii. 31, xiv. 30, xvi. 11), "the god of this world" (II Cor. iv. 4), "prince of the power of the air" (Eph. ii. 2), the "dragon," and the "serpent" (Rev. xii. 9, xx. 2). He has a kingdom (Matt. xii. 26), which is hostile to the kingdom of Christ (Acts xxvi. 18), and dominates a realm of demons (Matt. ix. 34).

1. Names and Description.

Created one of the angels, he became an apostate (John viii. 44), and fell from heaven (Luke x. 18; Jude 6). He is the indefatigable adversary of the kingdom of good, but will ultimately be overthrown, and cast into everlasting fire (Matt. xxv. 41). No hope is set forth in the Scriptures of his redemption. He endeavored to seduce Christ himself (Matt. iv. 1), worked among the apostles (John xiii. 2), and worketh in the children of disobedience (Eph. ii. 2). Conversion is the passage and deliverance from his kingdom of darkness to the kingdom of light (Col. i. 13). He is restlessly sowing seeds of error and doubt in the Church (Matt. xiii. 39), blinding the eyes of them that believe not (II Cor. iv. 4), goes about as a roaring lion (I Pet. v. 8), and has the power of death (Heb. ii. 14). Christ has given a more definite description of him (John viii. 44) as a "murderer and liar." His chief characteristics are power and craft. He is as a "strong man" (Matt. xii. 29), and his subtlety (cf. Gen. iii. 1) is exhibited in treacherous snares (II Tim. ii. 26), wiles (Eph. vi. 11), and devices (II Cor. ii. 11), and the delusive shift of transforming himself into an angel of light (II Cor. xi. 14). The Book of Revelation is a sublime drama in which Satan is one of the chief figures.

2. The Belief of Jesus.

It was to undo the desolation, and destroy the works of Satan that the Son of God was manifested (I John iii. 8). It has been attempted to make him out to be a mere personification of evil, and to show that evil exists only as it is found in the human heart. Schleiermacher thinks that Jesus accommodated himself to the ideas and language that then prevailed in Judea, but did not himself regard Satan as a real and living person. Objection is made to this view that, if he were not a distinct personality, Christ would hardly use so strong language in speaking of him and would not bid the disciples beware of his craft and power. In the exposition of the parable of the tares Christ makes the didactic statement that the enemy who sowed them was the devil. Another view adopted by advocates of a humanitarian christology is that Jesus shared the ignorance of his age in ascribing certain maladies to demoniac influence and asserting the personality of the devil. A remark of Bernard Weiss is here apposite (*Die Religion des Neuen Testaments*, p. 121, Stuttgart, 1903): "The deeper the sense of sin is the more confidently is the supernatural power of sin, by which man is deceived and dominated, ascribed to a superhuman adversary of God, for sin can not be traced back to God. The Scriptures and Jesus take this fact for granted and give it the weight of their authority."

III. The Church Teaching: The Fathers agreed in representing Satan as an apostate angel. According to Origen the fallen angels, who sinned less grievously, are of most subtle constitution. The stars belong to them. The devil and the demons, who sinned most grievously, inhabit the air (F. Loofs, *Leitfaden zum Studium der Dogmengeschichte*, p. 127, Halle, 1893). At last even the devil will return to God and thus the "restoration of all things" (Gk. *apokatastasis pantōn*, Acts iii. 21; see APOCATASTASIS) be accomplished. The fall, however, may be repeated again in the course of the eons. In the development of the doctrine of the atonement (q.v.) from Irenæus on (cf. Schaff, *Christian Church*, ii. 585 sqq.) the satisfaction of Christ was regarded as a payment made not to God, but to the devil, who through the disobedience of our first parents acquired a right to us. Origen says sinful man is the devil's property (Loofs, p. 129). John of Damascus expressly rejected this theory (Loofs, p. 186). The second part of his system of theology devotes much space to the devil, and is in this respect a precursor of the medieval systems. In the West Augustine represented Christ's work as a redemption from the devil rather than as a reconciliation to God (Loofs, p. 220), but he gave the impulse to the later doctrine enunciated by Anselm. He pronounced the pagan gods demons (*De civitate Dei*, v. 12, xviii. 18). Like the good angels, the bad spirits have bodies and by God's permission have power to stir up storms and blast harvests, and they cohabit with men and women. They have no power to create new substances, but they have power to accelerate the growth of seeds and germs, and the development of potencies hidden to men, but known to their own shrewd senses. Gregory the Great (d. 604) went even to greater lengths than Augustine in giving experiences of demonic and diabolic influence. Harnack (*Dogmengeschichte*, iii. 235) has called him the "Doctor of angels and the devil." The popular belief in the devil and his immediate influence in antagonizing holy aspirations and practises had a copious illustration in the weird experiences of the hermits of the Thebaid and Chalcis. St. Anthony and other ascetics thought they had frequent encounters with him, and their cells were often turned into pandemonium by the shrieks and howls of the demons whom they imagined Satan called forth to torment them in their lonely solitude (cf. Schaff, *Christian Church*, iii. 147 sqq.; Charles Kingsley, *The Hermits*, London, 1868).

1. The Fathers.

2. The Middle Ages.

In the Middle Ages the devil and demonology were among the subjects which received most elaborate treatment. The leading schoolmen devote long sections filled with Scriptural quotation and argumentative reasoning to show the origin, the mode of existence, and the influence of the devil and the evil spirits. To these disquisitions of the study are added the popular stories which fill the pages of some of the most interesting tale-writers of all times. To schoolmen and compilers must be added another class of writers, men of liberal culture like Walter Mapes and John of Salisbury and Étienne de Bourbon of France (ed. A. Lecoy de la Marche, Paris, 1877). Mapes treats Ceres, Bacchus, Pan, the satyrs, and the fauns and dryads as fallen spirits, and represents the devil as himself bearing witness to the truth of this view (*De nugis curialium*, ed. T. Wright, ii. 14, London, 1850). John of Salisbury has no doubt about the fell alliance of demons with men and women and their power over the weather (*Polycraticus*, chaps. viii.-xiii.).

According to the medieval theology the devil is at the head of a realm of demons divided into prelacies and demonarchies. Pride was the cause of Lucifer's fall. The region where the devil was cast down is the tenebrous air, where, in pits of darkness, he and his followers are reserved till the day of final judgment, and not till then will their full degree of torment be meted out to them (Peter Lombard, ii. 6). Albertus Magnus, of all the schoolmen, speaks with most precision upon the locality. There are three zones or interstices in the air, and it is the middle zone which is inhabited by the devil and his angels ("Sentences," II. vi. 5, ed. Borgnet, xxvii. 152). There the tempests are bred and the hail and the snow are generated. There the demons start the clouds on fell missions and send forth the thunders and other natural terrors to frighten and hurt men. For until the time of their final torment they have power to trouble men (Thomas Aquinas, *Summa*, I. lxiv. 4; Peter Lombard, II. vii. 6). As for their mental power, the devil and his angels are more acute than men, and their long experience enables them to foretell the future. Albertus Magnus says they are far more shrewd in watching the stars and predicting future events than are the astronomers. The miracles they perform are for the most part legerdemain and juggleries by which they deceive and outwit. But, as Thomas Aquinas asserts (*Summa*, I. cxiv. 4), quoting Augustine, they have also supernatural power and cause sickness and death, blast the crops, produce all sorts of freaks upon the progeny of men, and make women sterile. About 1250 the witchcraft craze began to sweep through Europe. From the time when Gregory IX. issued his bull on the subject in 1233 the punishment for such satanic influence and heresy went side by side, for heresy also was considered the work of the devil (see INQUISITION). Thomas Aquinas gave full doctrinal statement to the popular view, declaring that all practisers of witchcraft and sorcery were in league with the devil, and advocated the penalty of death. From that time pope after pope issued orders not to spare those who were under the direct agency of the devil (see WITCHCRAFT).

The popular writers of the Middle Ages, Cæsarius of Heisterbach (*Dialogus*), Thomas Cantimpratensis (*Bonum universale de apibus*), and Jacobus de Voragine in his "Golden Legend," are full of the most marvelous postures and feats of the evil one and his minions. They saw them with their eyes. Usually they were clad in black. Sometimes they had the face of a woman and were veiled. The devil himself appeared in meetings of witches and other persons as a great black tom-cat but also as a dog, a Moor, and in other shapes.

3. Popular Notions.

Sometimes the demons had the forms of children with faces of iron. In convents the devil was a frequent visitor. Sometimes poor monks lost their minds through the devil's influence. Sometimes he imparted to them an unusual gift of preaching. The most gruesome of all these tales are those which represent the devil as tormenting the naked soul after death and driving his sharp claws into it (Cæsarius of Heisterbach, i. 32, v. 10, etc.). These stories were fully believed, and all these experiences are in accord with the principles laid down by the great schoolmen, Peter Lombard, Bonaventura, Thomas Aquinas, and Albertus Magnus. The schoolmen, following Anselm (who wrote a special treatise, *De casu diaboli*) in his *Cur deus homo*, set aside the old view that Christ's death and sufferings were a payment made to Satan. Thomas Aquinas (*Summa*, III. xlviii. 3) says, "Christ offered his blood, which is the price of our redemption, not to the devil, but to God."

The Reformation brought only partial relief from these harrowing medieval notions. In Protestant lands persecution went on for those who were supposed to be under the special influence of Satan. Luther threw his inkstand at the devil, and on one occasion when he was awakened by a noise from sleep he finally composed himself by saying, "I heard one walking on the floor above my head, but, as I knew it to be only the devil, I went quietly to sleep."

4. Luther.

He said, "Let a Christian know this, that he is sitting in the midst of devils, and that the devil is closer to him than his coat or shirt or even his very skin." Nevertheless, in the domain of theology Luther made an advance when he denied to the devil all right to us and power over us ("*Recht und Macht*"). Christ's death was not a payment to him, but to the wrath of God (cf. R. Seeberg, *Lehrbuch der Dogmengeschichte*, ii., Leipsic, 1898, p. 252).

In more modern times there have been theologians who have denied wholly the personality of the devil; for example, the German rationalists, beginning with the eighteenth century. Even Schleiermacher combated the view of a personal Satan (see above, II., § 2). Later theologians like Martensen, Nitzsch, Twesten, Julius Müller, Dorner, and others hold firmly to his personality. Martensen says he was "Christ's younger brother, and became God's adversary because he was not content to be second, but wanted to be first; because he was unwilling to bear the light of another, and wanted to be the light itself." Jakob Böhme says: "Lucifer envied the Son his glory; his own beauty deceived him, and he wanted to place himself on the throne of the Son." An attempt has even been made to fix the date of his apostasy. Lange thought it occurred on one of the days of the creative week; while Kurtz and others held that the formless and void chaos of the world (Gen. i. 2) was the result of Satan's fall. Whatever may be said of these theories, evangelical theologians agree in three points: (1) The possibility of Satan's apostasy is as conceivable as the fall of man; (2) The inveterate hostility of Satan to the kingdom of Christ makes the denial of eternal punishment on the ground of the divine compassion untenable; (3) In proportion as the Christian consciousness of sin is deep does the belief in the personal agency of Satan prevail. In the New Testament the apostles feel that they are participants in the struggle

5. Modern Views.

between the kingdom of Christ and the kingdom of Satan, and this conviction draws forth the vivid exhortations to fight manfully and with the armor of God, and to resist by prayer and vigilance. It may be said with Dorner that the conviction of a great struggle going on between the two kingdoms of darkness and light, a struggle in which we all may take part, is adapted to produce an earnest conception of evil, and develop watchfulness and tension of the moral energies. D. S. SCHAFF.

BIBLIOGRAPHY: Lists of literature (very partial) are found in M. Osborn, *Die Teufelsliteratur des xvi. Jahrhunderts*, Berlin, 1893; *Bibliotheca diabolica: A Selection of Books relating to the Devil*, New York, 1874.

On Biblical ideas consult the works on Biblical theology, particularly: H. Schultz, *O. T. Theology*, London, 1892; A. B. Davidson, *Theology of O. T.*, pp. 300–355, Edinburgh, 1904; W. Beyschlag, *N. T. Theology*, Edinburgh, 1896; *DB*, iv. 407–412; *EB*, iv. 4296–4300; *JE*, xi. 68–71.

On the Christian conception the works on dogmatics, especially those by J. P. Lange, ii. 569 sqq., Heidelberg, 1852; H. L. Martensen, pp. 213–231, Copenhagen, 1850, Eng. transl., Edinburgh, 1865; J. J. van Oosterzee, ii. 413–422, Utrecht, 1872, Eng. transl., New York, 1874; J. A. Dorner, ii. 188–217, Berlin, 1881, Eng. transl., Edinburgh, 1880–82. Also Harnack, *Dogma*, passim, consult Index. Special treatment in: R. Gilpin, *Demonologia sacra*, London, 1877; A. D. White, *Warfare of Science and Religion*, 2 vols., New York, 1898; J. Hansen, *Zauberglaube, Inquisition und Hexenprocess im Mittelalter*, Munich, 1900; idem, *Quellen und Untersuchungen des Hexenwahns und Hexenverfolgung*, Leipsic, 1901; Graf von Hoensbroech, *Das Papsttum in seiner kulturellen Wirksamkeit*, i. 207–380, ib. 1901.

On the general subject: G. Roskoff, *Geschichte des Teufels*, i. 175–186, Leipsic, 1869; M. D. Conway, *Demonology and Devil-lore*, London, 1871; F. T. Hall, *Pedigree of the Devil*, ib. 1883; E. H. Jewett, *Diabolology: The Person and Kingdom of Satan*, New York, 1890; P. Carus, *Hist. of the Devil*, Chicago, 1900 (disappointing); Faivre, *La Personalité du Satan*, Montauban, 1900; and the works cited under DEMON; and DEMONIAC.

DEVOLUTION, LAW OF: A law which provides for the filling of ecclesiastical offices in an extraordinary manner when those whose duty it is to fill a vacancy fail illegally to observe the proper time or violate the canonical rules. The earlier canon law knows of no devolution right. It arose with the development of a time limit for the filling of vacancies in ecclesiastical offices. At the Lateran council held under Alexander III. in 1179 (capitula 3, 8) it was enacted that all lower livings shall be filled within six months from the time they became vacant, and in case either the bishop or chapter are negligent, the one must act for the other; in case both are negligent, the metropolitan must fill the vacancy. Innocent III. extended this law at the Lateran Council of 1215, and in the collections of decretals and by doctrine and practise the institution was further developed. The present law of the Roman Catholic Church is this: in case the authority having the right of collation illegally fails to fill a vacancy within the prescribed time, or culpably transfers the office to an unworthy person, or violates the rules to be observed on such occasions, the next ecclesiastical superior has the collation *ipso jure*; he can resign his privilege and allow an appointment by another in due order; but in case he makes use of his right, the same rules apply to him as to the original collator, the difference being only in the person making the appointment. E. SEHLING.

DEVOTION: The response of man to God's revelation of himself. The impression of his reality is so strong upon us that we gaze in awestruck silence upon his incomparable majesty; and devotion is based on this conviction. Its object, the living and eternal God, is beyond and above this world; and hence this spirit has a tendency to shun the world, which may easily be exaggerated. We can not escape from the world, which is the product of our own living consciousness. When man tries, as in what is called mysticism, to grasp the idea of God without relation to this world, he attempts the impossible. This transcendental God can only be found of men when he draws near to them by revealing himself to them; and their devotion to him can only be their willingness to listen when he speaks. God reveals himself in the world about us, to each man in the mode of his own existence, and thus to each in a different way. Knowledge of God is a personal conviction to be gained by each soul for itself. This will not remove us from the world, or free us from the claims of environment. We are rather to find in the latter the source of the strength which is to enable us to realize the invisible and prepare us for the life beyond.

It has been said, as a reproach against religion, that it is much easier to be "devout" than to live a moral life. But this reproach is based upon a false conception of devotion, which is wholly different from mere idle dreaming or emotional enthusiasm. Devotion, while it brings with it the most entrancing delight, is a call to the greatest exertion of spiritual energy. The way to it is through the conscience. A man must know what he is to do and be. This condition once fulfilled, all about him perceive a power from above in him. He is conscious himself of the force of the right. His moments of realization testify for him to the presence of an invisible agent, and lead his thoughts to God.

To abide in the God who has thus revealed himself to us, in what for us are such undeniable facts, is devotion. The words in which others who stand in his presence tell of what they have realized are valuable means to it; they may kindle the fire—but they are not the flame itself. And so likewise the purpose of devotion is not fulfilled until it is translated into activity. It means the decision of the will in favor of good; and this brings light and order into man's ideas of his actual existence, of the significance of his individual position in the world. The realization of duty forces action. Where devotion does not issue in the activity proper to one's vocation the emotions felt fail of their effect. This is the case with some forms of Roman Catholic piety, in which devotion grows not out of a revelation made to the individual, but of the contemplation of traditional conceptions; in which intercourse with one's fellows and labor in the world are considered an interruption of intercourse with God. The Church is bound to proclaim that for the individual the divine revelation consists of the facts which he himself recognizes as indubitable parts of his own existence, such revelation does not necessarily come to him in the first place as facts formally orthodox. If it is given to us to see as such facts the person and office of Jesus Christ; then and then only may we become Christians and find in the devotion of Christians the beginning of a life of blessedness. (W. HERRMANN.)

DE WETTE. See WETTE, WILHELM MARTIN LEBERECHT DE.

DE WITT, JOHN: The name of two American clergymen. 1. Reformed (Dutch); b. at Albany, N. Y., Nov. 29, 1821; d. at Irvington, N. Y., Oct. 19, 1906. He was educated at Rutgers College (B.A., 1838) and the New Brunswick Theological Seminary, from which he was graduated in 1842. He was then pastor successively at Ridgeway, Mich. (1842–44), Ghent, N. Y. (1844–49), Canajoharie, N. Y. (1849–50), and Millstone, N. J. (1850–63). From 1863 to 1884 he was professor of Oriental literature at Rutgers College, and from the latter year until his retirement in 1892 was professor of Hellenistic Greek and New Testament exegesis in the same institution. He was one of the American Old Testament Revision Company from its foundation, and wrote *The Sure Foundation, and how to build on it* (New York, 1848) and *The Praise Songs of Israel, a new Rendering of the Book of Psalms* (1884).

2. Presbyterian; b. at Harrisburg, Pa., Oct. 10, 1842. He studied at Princeton (B.A., 1861), studied law for a year, and then theology at Princeton and Union seminaries, graduating in 1865. He held pastorates at Irvington-on-Hudson, N. Y. (1865–69), Central Congregational Church, Boston (1869–76), and Tenth Presbyterian Church, Philadelphia (1876–1882); was professor of church history in Lane Theological Seminary, Cincinnati, O. (1882–88); professor of Christian apologetics at McCormick Theological Seminary, Chicago (1888–92), and since 1892 has been professor of church history in Princeton Theological Seminary. In theology he adheres to the Reformed confessions. He has written: *Sermons on the Christian Life* (New York, 1885); *What is Inspiration?* (1893); and *History of Princeton University* (in *Princeton Sesquicentennial Volume*, 1896).

DEXTER, HENRY MARTYN: American Congregationalist; b. at Plympton, Mass., Aug. 13, 1821; d. at New Bedford, Mass., Nov. 13, 1890. He was of both Pilgrim and Puritan descent. He entered Brown University in 1836, but went to Yale in 1838, and was graduated there in 1840. After teaching a year in Rochester, Mass., he was graduated at Andover Theological Seminary in 1844. He was ordained first pastor of the Franklin St. Congregational Church, Manchester, N. H., Nov. 6, 1844, and was pastor of the Pine St. Church (now Berkeley Temple), Boston, 1849–67. He joined the staff of the *Congregationalist* in 1851, and was editor-in-chief, excepting during 1866, from 1856 until his death. In 1854 he drew up the memorable antislavery Nebraska Protest to Congress against the Missouri Compromise. In 1858 he was one of the founders of the *Congregational Quarterly*. In 1880 he was moderator of the National Congregational Council at Oberlin and, later, one of its Creed Commission. In 1884, with Dr. G. E. Day, he represented the American Home Missionary Society to the Independent Churches of Norway and Sweden, and in 1889 he was invited to preach the opening sermon before the first International Congregational Council, at London in 1890, but died before the appointed date arrived.

Dr. Dexter wrote many articles and volumes, and was an expert on Congregationalism and American Colonial history. His chief books are: *Congregationalism: What it is, Whence it is, How it Works, Why it is better than any other form of Church Government, and its Consequent Demands* (Boston, 1865); and *The Congregationalism of the Last Three Hundred Years as Seen in its Literature* (New York, 1880), the latter embodying his Southworth Lectures at Andover in 1877 and containing a valuable bibliography of 7,200 titles. He traveled extensively and made special studies abroad of the Pilgrim movement. His unfinished manuscript on this subject was edited and rewritten by his son Morton Dexter, and published as *The England and Holland of the Pilgrims* (Boston, 1905). MORTON DEXTER.

BIBLIOGRAPHY: A sketch of Dr. Dexter's life is in the *Proceedings of the Massachusetts Historical Society* for 1891; consult also W. Walker, *Hist. of Congregational Churches*, pp. 385–388, New York, 1894.

DEXTER, MORTON: Congregationalist; b. at Manchester, N. H., July 12, 1846. He was graduated at Yale in 1867 and Andover Theological Seminary in 1870. He was pastor of Union Congregational Church, Taunton, Mass., from 1873 to 1878, and was then associate editor of the *Congregationalist*, Boston, until 1901. He was secretary and treasurer of the committee of the Congregational National Council which erected and dedicated the memorial tablet to John Robinson on St. Peter's Cathedral, Leyden, Holland, in 1891, and he was a delegate to the first International Congregational Council held at London in the same year, and to the second at Boston eight years later. In theology he may be described as a Broad-church evangelical. He has written *The Story of the Pilgrims* (Boston, 1894) and *The England and Holland of the Pilgrims* (1905).

DIACONICON, dai"[or di"]a-con'i-con: A Greek word which denotes the semicircular extension on the southern side of the *bēma* in the Greek churches, corresponding to one on the north side which is known as *prothesis*. It is the place occupied by the deacons, and is used also for the custody of various things used in divine service. This use of the term was definitely established at least as early as the end of the Middle Ages. The word is also applied to a selection from the great Euchologion of the Greek Church which contains all the liturgical functions of deacons (officially called *Hierodiakonikon*), and to certain prayers in the Greek liturgy recited by the deacon.

(PHILIPP MEYER.)

DIALOGUS DE RECTA IN DEUM FIDE: A dialogue directed against the errors of the Marcionites, Bardesanites, and Valentinians. From the use of the name Adamantius for the speaker who maintains the orthodox position, it has passed under his name—a proof that the real author was unknown. The fact that Origen bore this name led Basil and Gregory of Nyssa to attribute the dialogue to him, and this view was wide-spread in the Middle Ages; but on both internal and external evidence it is untenable. The work was composed (according to i. 21) in a time of persecution; but the text was altered later (probably between 330 and 337) to suit changed circumstances. In the first of the five parts the discussion turns on the theory proposed by the Marcionite Megethius of three principles—the good God, the demiurge, and the evil principle. Megethius attempts in a large number of antitheses to show a distinction between the Old Testament Creator and the good God of the New. These the author probably took from an anti-Marcionite treatise, probably that used by Irenæus and Tertullian and identified with good reason with a lost treatise of Theophilus of Antioch. For the second dialogue, in which the Marcionite Marcus develops his extreme theory of a good God and an evil demiurge, the author had probably looked into Marcion's New Testament. In the third part, the Bardesanite Maximus brings up the questions of the origin of evil, the incarnation of the Word, and the resurrection of the body. For the first of these, which extends through the third and fourth dialogues, considerable parts are taken literally from the dialogue of Methodius of Olympus (q.v.) on the freedom of the will, unless both Methodius and this author borrowed alike from a treatise on matter purporting to have been written by Maximus. The fifth dialogue deals with the resurrection, and here again borrows from the *Aglaophon* of Methodius. The work was probably written in Syria, most likely at Antioch. It displays no great literary art.

(ERWIN PREUSCHEN.)

BIBLIOGRAPHY: The editio princeps, by J. R. Wetstein, Basel, 1674, is also in C. E. Lommatzsch, *Origenis Opera*, xvi. 254 sqq., Berlin, 1844, and *MPG*, x. The latest ed. is by Van de S. Bakhuyzen, Berlin, 1901. The Lat. transl. by Rufinus is edited by C. P. Caspari, *Kirchenhistorische Anecdota*, pp. 1 sqq., cf. pp. iii.–v., Christiania, 1883. Consult: T. Zahn, in *ZKG*, ix (1888), pp. 193–230; idem, *Geschichte des neutestamentlichen Kanons*, II. ii. 409–426, Leipsic, 1891; Krüger, *History*, pp. 245–247; *DCB*, i. 39–41.

DIASPORA (Gk. "a scattering, dispersion"): A term used in the New Testament and other literature about the beginning of the Christian era to denote the Jews living outside of Palestine after the Captivity (see ISRAEL); also applied to the Christians as the spiritual Israel among those of other faiths (Jas. i. 1; I Pet. i. 1; cf. Schürer, *Geschichte*, Eng. transl., II. ii. 31). The Moravians used the word to signify their friends living apart from them and in spiritual union with them, but not officially and constitutionally belonging to them. In modern German usage the term signifies any people living scattered among those of another faith, and more particularly a Protestant minority in a Roman Catholic region.

Special conferences have been instituted to increase the efficiency of the Diaspora pastor; e.g., the Conference of Rhenish Prussia, founded in 1858; the Conference of Posen, 1860; that of the Middle Rhine, 1868; of Westphalia, 1871; and of Upper Swabia, 1882. See GOTTESKASTEN, LUTHERISCHER; and GUSTAV-ADOLF-VEREIN.

(THEODOR SCHÄFER.)

DIATESSARON, dai"[or di"]a-tes'a-ron. See TATIAN; and HARMONY OF THE GOSPELS.

DIAZ, JUAN. See SPAIN, THE REFORMATION IN.

DIBELIUS, di-bé'li-us, **FRANZ WILHELM**: German Lutheran; b. at Prenzlau (58 m. n.e. of Berlin) Jan. 6, 1847. He studied in Berlin, was assistant pastor at the Berlin cathedral and inspector of the institute for the training of canons 1871–74, and pastor of the Annenkirche, Dresden, 1874–84. Since 1884 he has been city superintendent and first pastor of the Kreuzkirche in Dresden, and is also a councilor of the high consistory. His writings include: *Gottfried Arnold* (Berlin, 1873); *Die Einführung der Reformation in Dresden* (Dresden, 1889); *Die Kreuzkirche in Dresden* (1900); and *Vom heiligen Kreuz* (1903). He has edited *Beiträge zur sächsischen Kirchengeschichte* since 1882.

DICK, THOMAS: Scotch Secession Church; b. at Dundee Nov. 24, 1774; d. at Broughty Ferry (5 m. e. of Dundee) July 29, 1857. He studied at Edinburgh, and preached as a probationer for two years (1803–05); taught school for twenty years at Methven and Perth, and after 1827 devoted himself entirely to literature. He wrote a number of scientific, philosophical, and religious works in popular style, which had a large sale. Perhaps the best known were: *The Christian Philosopher, or the Connection of Science and Philosophy with Religion* (London, 1823); *The Philosophy of a Future State* (1828); *Celestial Scenery, or the Wonders of the Heavens Displayed* (1838); *The Sidereal Heavens* (1840); *The Solar System* (1840); and *The Practical Astronomer* (1845).

DICKEY, SAMUEL: Presbyterian; b. at Oxford, Pa., Nov. 27, 1872. He studied at Princeton (B.A., 1894), Princeton Theological Seminary (1897), and the universities of Berlin, Marburg, Erlangen (1897–99), Athens (1901), and Jena (1904). He was professor of classical and Hellenistic Greek at Lincoln University, Pa., 1899–1903; adjunct professor of New-Testament literature and exegesis at McCormick Theological Seminary, Chicago, 1903–05; full professor since 1905.

DICKINSON, JONATHAN: Presbyterian; b. at Hatfield, Mass., Apr. 22, 1688; d. at Elizabeth, N. J., Oct. 7, 1747. He was graduated at Yale in 1706, and in 1709 settled at Elizabeth (then called Elizabethtown). He covered an extensive field as preacher, serving regularly six or seven congregations. He was a man of general culture and read and practised medicine, in addition to his pastoral work. As a scholar and wise leader he was not excelled in the American Presbyterian Church in his time, and his name stands out in the early Presbyterian history of the middle colonies much as that of Jonathan Edwards does in New England. A strong Calvinist, he opposed a rigid subscription to the Westminster standards as a test of ordination. He was prominent in the adoption of the so-called Adopting Act of 1729 passed by the Synod of Philadelphia. It declined to make a literal subscription to the Westminster standards a condition of ordination, as the Presbytery of New Castle had asked should be done, and demanded that the candidate accept and approve of them "as being in all essential and necessary articles good forms of sound words and systems of Christian doctrine." In case he had any scruples he had a right to state them, and the synod or presbytery was to judge whether they concerned "articles not essential and necessary in doctrine, worship, and government." In the course of the discussion, Dickinson wrote in a letter that he regarded it "as the most glorious contradiction to subscribe chap. xx. of the Confession which calls 'God alone the Lord of Conscience' and then impose the rest of the chapters." He took a prominent part in the measures which led to the formation of the synod of New York (1745), the second synod of the Presbyterian Church in the United States. David Brainerd and Indian missions found in him a warm friend. He also took a deep interest in education, and was the most prominent among the founders of the College of New Jersey (Princeton University). Under his counsel a charter was received for the institution in Oct., 1746. His election as the first president was announced Apr. 27, 1747, and in May the college was opened in his house. He died the following autumn. He took the side of the Tennents and Edwards in favoring the evangelistic movement led by Whitefield.

Mr. Dickinson's defense of the Five Points of Calvinism in his *True Scripture Doctrine concerning some Important Points of Christian Faith, particularly Eternal Election, Original Sin, Grace in Conversion, Justification by Faith, and the Saints' Preservation, represented and applied in five discourses* (Philadelphia, 1741; Elizabethtown, 1793) is one of the soundest expositions of Calvinism which America has produced. His other works are *Four Sermons on the Reasonableness of Christianity* (Boston, 1732); *A Display of God's Special Grace* (1742); *Familiar Letters upon Subjects in Religion* (1745); *Vindication of God's Saving Free Grace* (1748). A complete edition of his *Sermons and Tracts* appeared at Edinburgh, 1793.

D. S. SCHAFF.

BIBLIOGRAPHY: W. B. Sprague, *Annals of the American Pulpit*, iii. 14-18, New York, 1858; the histories of the Presbyterian Church by C. Hodge, Philadelphia, 1839-1840; E. H. Gillett, ib. 1873; J. H. Patton, ib. 1887; R. E. Thompson, ib. 1895. Also J. Maclean, *Hist. of the College of New Jersey*, Philadelphia, 1877; John De Witt, in *Memorial Book of the Sesquicentennial Celebration of the Founding of the College of New Jersey*, pp. 348-352, New York, 1898.

DICKSON (DICK), DAVID: Scotch commentator; b. in Glasgow about 1583; d. 1663. He studied at Glasgow and taught philosophy there till 1618, when he was ordained minister of Irvine, Ayrshire; was deprived in 1622 for testifying against the Five Articles of Perth, but was permitted to return the next year; became professor of divinity at Glasgow 1640, in Edinburgh 1650; was ejected in 1662 for refusing to take the oath of supremacy. He was moderator of the General Assembly at Edinburgh in 1639. His commentaries include *Explications* upon the Psalms (3 vols., London, 1653-55), an *Exposition* of Matthew (1651), an *Explanation* of Hebrews (Aberdeen, 1635), and an *Exposition* of all the epistles (Latin, Glasgow, 1645; English, London, 1659). He also published *Therapeutica sacra, seu de curandis casibus conscientiæ circa regenerationem per fœderum divinorum applicationem* (London, 1656; Eng. transl., 1695) and *True Christian Love* (Edinburgh, 1655), a collection of short poems "to be sung with any of the common tunes of the Psalms," which includes the familiar *O mother dear, Jerusalem*.

BIBLIOGRAPHY: His life by R. Wodrow was prefixed to *Truth's Victory over Error*, Glasgow, 1752, and was reprinted by the Wodrow Society in *Select Biographies*, vol. ii., Edinburgh, 1847; a volume of his *Select Practical Writings* also contains a life by T. Thompson, Edinburgh, 1845; *DNB*, xv. 41-42; Julian, *Hymnology*, 293, 580.

DICKSON, WILLIAM PURDIE: Church of Scotland; b. at Pettinain (26 m. s.e. of Glasgow) Oct. 22, 1823; d. at Glasgow Mar. 9, 1901. He studied at St. Andrews (M.A., 1851), and after being minister of the parish of Cameron, Fife (1851-63), was professor of Biblical criticism (1863-73) and of divinity in the University of Glasgow. He was convener of the Education Committee of the Church of Scotland from 1874, and in that capacity had charge of the training colleges in Edinburgh, Glasgow, and Aberdeen, while after 1866 he was curator of the University of Glasgow library and superintended the preparation of the catalogue. He wrote *St. Paul's Use of the Terms Flesh and Spirit* (Baird lecture for 1883; Glasgow, 1883) and translated T. Mommsen's *History of Rome* (4 vols., London, 1862-66) and six volumes of H. A. W. Meyer's *Commentary on the New Testament* and revised the translation often (Edinburgh, 1873-80).

DIDACHE, doi′dak-ī *or* did′ak-ē.

I. Contents and Arrangement.
II. Title, Address, and Purport.
III. Transmission and Integrity.
IV. Language and Vocabulary.
V. Sources.
  Biblical Writings (§ 1).
  Barnabas (§ 2).
  Hermas and Jewish Writings (§ 3).
VI. The Author's Standpoint.
  The Author not an Ebionite (§ 1).
  Was He a Jewish Christian? (§ 2).
VII. Time and Place of Composition.
  Limits 70-160 A.D. (§ 1).
  Not Before 120 A.D. (§ 2).
VIII. History of the Document.
IX. The Witnesses.
X. Importance of the Work.

In a manuscript (written in 1056 by a notary, named Leon), discovered by Bryennios (q.v.) in the Jerusalem Convent at Constantinople, from which he edited in 1875 the complete epistles of Clement, there is found between the epistles of Clement and Ignatius a work of the size of the epistle to the Galatians entitled *Didache ton dodeka Apostolon*, which the discoverer published in 1883, showing at the same time that the work belongs to the first half of the second century and is identical with the "Teaching of the Apostles," which Clement of Alexandria, Eusebius, Athanasius, and other Fathers knew.

I. Contents and Arrangement: The work is divided into two, or perhaps three parts. The first contains precepts of Christian morality, and brief instructions for the specific ecclesiastical acts which gave Christian character to the Church (i.–x.); the second, directions for churchly intercourse and life (xi.–xv.); the closing chapter (xvi.) is an exhortation to be ready for the coming of the Lord. The first part, again, contains, i.–vi., under the form of a description of the "Two Ways," the way of life and the way of death, the laws of Christian morality; while vii. deals with baptism; viii. with fasting and daily prayer; and ix.–x. with eucharistic prayers. In regard to specific points: baptism should be preceded by fasting; the Lord's Prayer, given in the words of Matthew with slight alterations and with the doxology, should be said three times every day. The Lord's Supper should be partaken of only by the baptized; and the "prophets" were at liberty to use, instead of the eucharistic prayers given, such thanksgiving as they would. The second part lays down rules for the treatment of the teachers of the Divine Word and of the peripatetic brethren, and gives distinguishing tests of their character (xi.–xiii.), and also the usages each congregation should observe (xiv.–xv.).

II. Title, Address, and Purport: The manuscript has two titles: "Teaching of the Twelve Apostles" and "Teaching of the Lord through the Twelve Apostles to the Gentiles." By "the Gentiles" were meant the Christians who had come from heathenism, just as the epistle "to the Hebrews" was addressed to Christians who had come from Judaism. The document, consequently, is not addressed to catechumens—for it is not adapted to lead persons to Christianity, but to those already Christians, that they might learn from it how to conduct their lives upon Gospel principles, and what they were to impress on the newly won brethren [cf. Schaff's edition, pp. 15 sqq. The document is commonly quoted and referred to simply as the "Didache," which means the "Teaching"].

III. Transmission and Integrity: The present text has comparatively few errors, yet the appearance of the document in later recensions has raised suspicions whether it is so free from interpolations as it seems to be. Suspicions are caused only through derived works cited in patristic sources.

IV. Language and Vocabulary: The idiom is Hellenistic, more exactly the idiom of the Septuagint of the poetical books and of the Old Testament Apocrypha. There are numerous Hebraisms, but the Greek is better than that of Hermas. The style is simple, popular, and concise, while being somewhat rhythmical and liturgical. The document contains 2,190 words (about 10,700 letters), and 552 different words. Of these 504 are found also in the New Testament; 38 of the remaining 48, in the Septuagint, Barnabas, or other older Greek writers (cf. Schaff, ut sup., pp. 95–113).

V. Sources: There is no known primitive Christian writing which, with originality in arrangement and form, so combines dependence upon older writings. The author avows his dependence, for he seeks merely to set forth the teaching of the Lord through the twelve apostles, and finds no room for his own ideas. There are eight express quotations: two (xiv. 3, xvi. 7) are from the Old Testament (Mal. i. 11, 14; Zech. xiv. 5); five from the Gospels, introduced by certain formulas (viii. 2, ix. 5, xi. 3, xv. 3, 4), and one (i. 6) from some unknown "Sacred Scripture." The Old Testament

1. Biblical Writings.

is, moreover, frequently drawn upon in the first five chapters, the decalogue and the Wisdom literature (Prov., Eccles., Tobit) being used. The Old Testament alone is "Sacred Scripture"; of a New Testament Canon there is no trace. The author in the five cited passages does not draw from the written Gospel alone; throughout he weaves into his writing references and longer or shorter citations, twenty-three in all, from what he calls "the Gospel," which he presupposes his readers know. Seventeen of the twenty-three citations must be referred to Matthew; but other citations are plainly combinations of the text of Matthew and Luke, strikingly like the text of Tatian's *Diatessaron.* In the citations there is no trace of John's Gospel; but the eucharistic service is conceived on the lines of John vi. and xvii., without, however, directly borrowing anything. The Pauline Epistles are not cited, yet traces of acquaintance with them appear. More important are certain resemblances to Jude and II Peter. There is no trace of acquaintance with the Pastoral Epistles.

The much-disputed question, as to the relation of the "Teaching" to the Epistle of Barnabas and the Shepherd of Hermas, is thus to be answered: it is in the highest degree probable that Barnabas is prior to the "Teaching"; i. 1–2, ii. 2–7, iii. 7–vi. 2 of the "Teaching" agree substantially, if not verbally, with Barnabas xviii.–xx.; but the order of the phrases is different, and while that in Barnabas

2. Barnabas.

is confused, that in the "Teaching" is clear. In the description of the "Two Ways," the "Teaching" offers further (a) in i. 2–5 a series of evangelical sayings: (b) in i. 6 a fragment from an unknown other writing; (c) in iii. 1–6 a section imitated from the Old Testament proverbial literature; (d) in ii. 2–3, 5, 6, iii. 8, iv. 2, 8, 14 a series of additions to the sections common to it and to Barnabas. Barnabas, on the other hand, offers in the chapters in question only a couple of phrases (xix. 2, 3, 8), an unintelligible sentence (xix. 4), and some further words in xix. 10. Further, xvi. 1, 3–8 of the "Teaching" are confessedly a compilation of evangelical passages and Zech. xiv. 5, together with a tradition concerning Antichrist. Verse 2, however, is not so derived, but has in Barnabas IV, x. 9 an almost verbally exact parallel. Now, were Barnabas later, he would have appropriated the only verse in this passage of the "Teaching" which is peculiar. Hence it is probable that, since all the other verses of xvi. are borrowed, this verse (xvi. 2) is also borrowed. Moreover (and this appears still more decisive of the priority of Barnabas), the author of Barnabas is convinced that the last times have already come (iv. 3, 9); the author of the "Teaching," on the other hand, does not so hold. The decision therefore must be that the "Teaching" as it now is given in the Constantinopolitan manuscript is secondary to Barnabas, and is either dependent upon it or upon materials already used by Barnabas; and the possibility is excluded that Barnabas copied from the "Teaching" as it exists in the Constantinopolitan manuscript. [The priority of Barnabas is advocated also by Bryennios, Hilgenfeld, and Krawutzky in *KL*, whereas the priority of the *Didache* is strongly advocated by Zahn, Funk, Langen, Farrar, nearly all English and American writers on the subject. A third opinion is held by Lightfoot, Holtzmann, Massebieau, Lipsius, Warfield, McGiffert, that both Barnabas and the writer of the *Didache* drew from a common source which is lost.]

The relation between the "Teaching" and Hermas is more uncertain. There are only two parallels, "Teaching," i. 5; cf. *Mand.*, ii. 4–6, and the very doubtful one "Teaching," v.; cf. *Mand.*, viii. 4–5. That the "Teaching" had Hermas as a source may not be safely affirmed in view of the variations in these passages in different recensions; but the opposite is certainly excluded. [Schaff holds that the *Didache* is older than the Shepherd of Hermas; for in its brief parallel sections Hermas is likewise an enlargement of the simpler statements of the *Didache*; Schaff, pp. 121 sqq.] Lately, American, English, and French scholars have brought forward numerous parallels to i.–v. from Philo, Pseudo-Phokylides, the Sibylline books, and from the Talmud and Midrash. If, from these chapters, i. 3–6 be omitted, the remainder has almost nothing specifically Christian about it, and the little it has can be shown by the use of other original documents to be additions. Therefore it is an extremely probable conjecture that the "Two Ways" is a Jewish production, intended for proselytes, derived from the decalogue and an amplification of its commands, which along with the Old Testament has come over into the Christian Church.

3. Hermas and Jewish Writings.

VI. The Author's Standpoint: This much-discussed point is not settled. The "Teaching" has been regarded as a Jewish anti-Pauline Christian (Sabatier), as Jewish Christian, but not Ebionitic (Schaff), as anti-Pauline and Sadducean, heretical and anti-Christian (Churton), as Ebionitic, semi-Ebionitic, or anti-Ebionitic (cf. Krawutzky, *KL*, iii., 1869 sqq.), as Hellenistic-Christian, as anti-Montanistic and anti-Gnostic (Bryennios), as Montanistic (Hilgenfeld and Bonet-Maury), etc. To refute these different views is not necessary, but it is necessary to oppose the notion that the author of the "Teaching" was a Jewish Christian who belonged to a circle detached from Gentile Christians, and attached in some way to the Jews as a nation.

1. The Author not an Ebionite.

The facts are these: The author maintains silence upon circumcision and all other Jewish rites; in the two places where he mentions them he calls the Jews "hypocrites"; not a word is said of observing the Mosaic law; in the long eschatological section (xvi.), derived from Matthew, the passages referring to Jerusalem, the Jewish people, and the Temple are wanting, nor is there any mention of a glorious kingdom in Palestine, although the author presupposes a visible kingdom of Christ, as his belief in a double resurrection proves (cf. G. v. Lechler, *Apostolisches und nachapostolisches Zeitalter*, p. 592, Carlsruhe, 1885); Matthew and Luke, or a recension of them, and not the Gospel of the Hebrews, was used, perhaps also the Pauline Epistles; Jesus is not called the Son, but the God, of David; the book passed over into the use of the Catholic Church. These considerations exonerate the author from Ebionism. But some assert the Jewish-Christian but not anti-Pauline character of the author. Schaff (pp. 125 sqq.) has collected arguments as follows: only the Twelve, but not the Apostle Paul are named; but in this respect the author does not differ from many ordinary Christian authors before the closing of the New Testament Canon. The style and phraseology are Hebraistic; but that is not remarkable in view of the Jewish origin of Christianity and the use of the Old Testament in the Septuagint. The author calls the prophets "high priests," but this was the rule among Gentile Christians. He demands the first-fruits for the prophets; but so do Paul and the Gentile Christian Church of the earliest times, especially after Justin's day. He warns against fasting with the Jews on Monday and Thursday, enjoins fasts on Wednesday and Friday, and names Friday *paraskeuē*, "preparation." But even if the author had set the fasts upon the Jewish fast-days, this would have been no more a sign of Jewish Christianity than was the practise of the Quartodecimans. The author's discussion of the week in a religious sense explains the use of the Jewish names for the days, and he is entirely silent respecting the Sabbath. The injunction three times daily to repeat the Lord's Prayer is plainly adopted from Jewish custom. Besides what has been said above, it should be remarked that it is not known what hours for prayer were in the author's mind, and that, even if he had enjoined the Jewish hours, that would not have been specifically Jewish-Christian. The author conceives of Christianity substantially as the highest morality; he is a moralist in the better sense of the word, like James and Matthew. Consequently he must have been a Jewish Christian. To answer this argument would take too much space. The author does not attack the Jewish religion, as does Barnabas; but as a rule he attacks nobody. He not only lays stress upon the (Jewish-Christian) prohibition of meat offered to idols, but sets forth the observance of the Jewish dietary laws as the summit of Christian perfection. The prohibition of eating meat offered to idols was universal in the congregations in the empire from the end of the first century (cf. C. T. Keim, *Aus dem Urchristenthum*, pp. 88 sqq., Zurich, 1878); and, as for the second point, no one ever made such a claim, for by *brosis*, "food" (vi. 3), is most certainly meant, not the Jewish dietary regulation, but an ascetic restriction in the use of meat, as Schürer also maintains. The view-point of the author is that of common Gentile Christianity. His standpoint is very close to that of the author of the second epistle of Clement; he is not a Jewish Christian,

2. Was He a Jewish Christian?

not a follower of Paul, but a universalist, knowing no distinction between peoples; in his prayers acknowledging God, the creator of all things and Father of all men, who provides them with food and drink; he acknowledges Jesus, the son of God, the God of David, the vine of David, and the Lord who spoke by the prophets, and he awaits his coming; he also acknowledges the Holy Ghost, who has prepared those whom God called. He believes in the Old Testament and in the Gospel; he acknowledges baptism and the Lord's Supper as important acts; one becomes a Christian by baptism and remains a Christian by partaking of the eucharistic celebration.

VII. Time and Place of Composition: It has been placed in every decade from 50 A.D. to 190 A.D., and even as late as the fourth century. Generally the three generations 70–100, 100–130, 130–160 A.D. are the most favored. Internal evidence can not decide the time, because the "Teaching" is avowedly a compilation, and some of its sources are very old. External evidence proves that it must be before 165 A.D., for Clement of Alexandria knew it as "Scripture." A number of negative facts taken together show that it is earlier than 160 A.D.; it shows no traces of a New Testament Canon or of the authority of the Pauline Epistles; or of a *regula fidei* or of regular doctrinal instruction; or of a monarchical episcopate—prophets were the chief teachers and were not yet superseded by bishops; or of an ordered church service, like that to which Justin testifies; or of a regular administrator of baptism, while it gives the congregation authority to depose bishops and deacons; or of symbolical ceremonies accompanying baptism; or of a yearly Easter festival; or of prohibition of blood and things strangled; or of Montanism and the characterization of heretics. Other marks seem to fit better into the time 80–120 A.D. than 120–160 A.D., e.g., its treatment of apostles, prophets, and teachers. But care must be taken not to give definite dates to documents of primitive Christianity, for not all the steps are known of the development of Christianity during the empire till Catholic Christianity in most of the provinces, and in no province is the development fully known.

1. Limits 70–160 A.D.

Having set the limits for the "Teaching" between 70 and 160 A.D., the question may be asked whether there is anything to prove that it must have been written after some Christian generations had passed. With the greatest probability an affirmative answer may be given, as follows: Apostles and prophets no longer occupy their primitive unapproachable position, hence the strongest conservative measures are enjoined; respect for the prophets is declining, hence the exorbitant demand on the church and the severest menaces; mistrust of the "old prophets," who belong to a past generation. These are not the Old Testament but older Christian prophets; the present text shows in the "Two Ways" of i. certain diminution of evangelical demands, and in the appendix to the same, in vi., a contrast between a higher and a lower Christian morality; the injunctions about first-fruits, fixed prayers, and fasts, which in a Gentile Christian land is the indication of a later time; the injunction that since bishops and deacons minister to the congregations "the ministry of the prophets and teachers," therefore despise them not, can not apply to the primitive state of things; the regulation of fasting before baptism, and permission to pour; the eschatological closing section has not the glow which the prayers transmitted to the author have, and lacks the description of the glorious kingdom of Christ upon the earth.

2. Not Before 120 A.D.

These observations are strengthened by noticing the author's use of Matthew, and perhaps also Luke, in a comparatively late form; and the relation of the "Teaching" to Barnabas, which probably belongs to Hadrianic time (before Bar Kokba). All these considerations show that the writing can not with certainty be set earlier than 120 A.D. or earlier than 100 A.D. with any probability, but that the probable limits are 120 and 160 A.D., and within these limits the earlier dates are in most cases freer from difficulty than the later. Taken all in all, the "time of Hadrian" has the most probability in its favor. The place of composition was probably Egypt, as the external testimonies and the source seem to prove. The arguments for Syria, derived from mention of the bread "upon the hills" (ix. 4), and from the adoption of the "Teaching" with the "Apostolical Constitutions," are not decisive; for the mention occurs in a prayer most probably copied by the author, and the Syrian forger had the library of Eusebius at his command.

VIII. History of the Document: A book called "The Two Ways" was composed by Jews in the first century or perhaps earlier for the instruction of proselytes. It comprised what is found in the "Teaching," i. 1–3, ii. 2–v. 2, which passed over into the Christian Church, and was used as an address at baptism. The author of the Epistle of Barnabas incorporated this writing into his, without, however, knowing it as a "teaching of the Apostles." Another unknown Christian made the Jewish instruction a "teaching of the (twelve) apostles," and added vii.–xvi. This edition is now lost. The present one, the *Didache* of the Constantinopolitan manuscript, contains, in order to give evangelical coloring to the Jewish original, chap. i. 3–ii. 1, by which the tone of the "Two Ways" was wholly changed. This passage being an interpolation, the original form of the Christian "Teaching" may be put considerably earlier than the present recension.

IX. The Witnesses: Before Clement of Alexandria no direct use of the "Teaching" can be proved. On the other hand, Clement employs it in several places, and in one (*Stromata*, i. 20 = "Teaching," iii. 5) calls it "Scripture," counting it among the holy writings. Evidences of its use have been found in Origen (*Hom. vi. in lib. Jud.*; *De principiis*, iii. 2, 7), who also called it "Holy Scripture," but the quotation may have been taken from the Epistle of Barnabas. Eusebius (*Hist. eccl.*, III. xxv.) is the first to mention the book by name, "the so-called Teachings of the Apostles," and puts it among the *antilegomena*. Athanasius (*Epistola festalis*, xxxix., of the year 367) mentions the

"Teaching, so called, of the Apostles" among the books which are not canonical but useful for the instruction of catechumens. Rufinus repeats this statement of Athanasius (*Comment. in Symb. Apost.*, xxxvi.-xxxviii.), but in place of "Teaching, so called, of the Apostles," he puts "The Two Ways," or "The Judgment of Peter," or "According to Peter," for the "Teaching of the Apostles." Jerome (*De vir. ill.*, i.) likewise mentions "Peter's Judgment" among five apocryphal books ascribed to that Apostle. The last mention of the "Teaching of the Apostles," so far as present knowledge goes, was made in the ninth century by Nicephorus, who speaks of such a book as among the Apocrypha of the New Testament, and as consisting of 200 lines. The manuscript discovered by Bryennios numbers 203 lines.

X. Importance of the Work: From vii. to the end each section of the "Teaching" is a source of the first rank for the points it covers, baptism, fasts, prayers, the eucharist, apostles, prophets, teachers, Sunday, the episcopate and diaconate. But its greatest importance lies in the fact that it affords so much better an understanding of the organization of the earliest Christian churches, where the interest of early Christianity lay, and how it became in literary matters the heir of Judaism. (ADOLF HARNACK.)

BIBLIOGRAPHY: The literature on the Didache has become enormous. A list down to 1887 is given in *ANF*, Index vol., pp. 83–86; down to 1888 in P. Schaff, *The Teaching of the Twelve Apostles*, pp. 306–320, 3d ed., New York, 1890; and by Bäumer, in *Literarischer Handweiser für das katholische Deutschland*, xxvii (1888), 393–398, 425–430; and to 1900 by A. Ehrhard, *Die altchristliche Litteratur und ihre Erforschung*, i. 37–68, Freiburg, 1900. The editio princeps is by P. Bryennios, Constantinople, 1883; the best edition, at least in Eng., is by Schaff, ut sup., giving Greek text, Eng. transl., introduction, and discussions. Other good editions are by A. Harnack, Leipsic, 1884; R. D. Hitchcock and F. Brown, New York, 1885; P. Sabatier, Paris, 1885; H. D. M. Spence, London, 1885; F. X. Funk, Tübingen, 1887; J. R. Harris, Baltimore, 1887; J. B. Lightfoot, in *Apostolic Fathers*, London, 1893; J. Schlecht, Freiburg, 1900. Most of the foregoing contain translations in the tongue of the editor, besides notes, introduction, and discussions. Eng. transl. exists also in *ANF*, viii. 377–382, and in G. C. Allen, *The Teaching of the Twelve Apostles*, London, 1903. Many of the most important discussions are in periodicals, especially those of 1884–87. Discussions of especial worth are: J. R. Harris, *The Teaching of the Apostles and the Sibylline Books*, Cambridge, 1885; A. Harnack, *Die Apostellehre und die jüdischen beiden Wege*, Leipsic, 1886; C. Taylor, *The Teaching of the 12 Apostles with Illustrations from the Talmud*, Cambridge, 1886; B. B. Warfield, in *Bibliotheca Sacra*, 1886, pp. 100–161; J. Heron, *The Church of the Sub-Apostolic Age . . . in the Light of the Teaching of the 12 Apostles*, London, 1888; G. Wohlenberg, *Die Lehre der 12 Apostel in ihrem Verhältniss zum neutestamentlichen Schrifttum*, Erlangen, 1888; P. Batiffol, in *Studia patristica*, ii. 117–160, Paris, 1890; G. Salmon, *Introduction to . . . N. T.*, pp. 551–566, London, 1892; *DCB*, iv. 806–815; C. H. Hole, *The Didache*, London, 1894; L. E. Iselin, in *TU*, xiii. 1, 1895; J. Schlecht, *Die Lehre der 12 Apostel in der Liturgie*, Freiburg, 1901; T. Schermann, *Eine Elfapostelmoral*, Munich, 1903; Krüger, *History*, pp. 63–67.

DIDASCALIA. See APOSTOLIC CONSTITUTIONS AND CANONS.

DIDEROT, did"rō', **DENIS:** The most prominent of the Encyclopedists (q.v.); b. at Langres (150 m. s.e. of Paris) in Champagne Oct. 5, 1713; d. at Paris July 31, 1784. He was educated by the Jesuits, and, refusing to enter one of the learned professions, was turned adrift by his father and came to Paris, where he lived from hand to mouth for a time. Gradually, however, he became recognized as one of the most powerful writers of the day. His first independent work was the *Essai sur le mérite et la vertu* (1745). As one of the editors of the *Dictionnaire de médecine* (6 vols., Paris, 1746), he gained valuable experience in encyclopedic system. His *Pensées philosophiques* (The Hague, 1746), in which he attacked both atheism and the received Christianity, was burned by order of the Parliament of Paris. In the circle of the leaders of the "Enlightenment" Diderot's name became known especially by his *Lettre sur les aveugles* (London, 1749), which supported Locke's theory of knowledge. He attacked the conventional morality of the day, with the result (to which possibly an allusion to the mistress of a minister contributed) that he was imprisoned at Vincennes for three months. He was released by the influence of Voltaire's friend Mme. du Châtelet, and thenceforth was in close relation with the leaders of revolutionary thought. He had made very little pecuniary profit out of the *Encyclopédie*, and Grimm appealed on his behalf to Catherine of Russia, who in 1765 bought his library, allowing him the use of the books as long as he lived, and assigning him a yearly salary which a little later she paid him for fifty years in advance. In 1773 she summoned him to St. Petersburg with Grimm to converse with him in person. On his return he lived until his death in a house provided by her, in comparative retirement but in unceasing labor on the undertakings of his party, writing (according to Grimm) two-thirds of Raynal's famous *Histoire philosophique*, and contributing some of the most rhetorical pages to Helvétius's *De l'esprit* and Holbach's *Système de la nature*, *Système social*, and *Morale universelle*. His numerous writings include the most varied forms of literary effort, from inept licentious tales and comedies which pointed away from the stiff classical style of the French drama and strongly influenced Lessing, to the most daring ethical and metaphysical speculations. Like his famous contemporary Samuel Johnson, he is said to have been more effective as a talker than as a writer; and his mental qualifications were rather those of a stimulating force than of a reasoned philosopher. His own position gradually changed from theism to deism, then to materialism, and finally rested in a pantheistic sensualism (see DEISM, II., § 2). In Sainte-Beuve's phrase, he was "the first great writer who belonged wholly and undividedly to modern democratic society," and his attacks on the political system of France were among the most potent causes of the Revolution.

BIBLIOGRAPHY: *Œuvres complètes*, 20 vols., Paris, 1875–77; *Œuvres choisies*, 1884; A. Collignon, *Diderot, sa vie, ses œuvres, sa correspondance*, Paris, 1895; J. A. Naigeon, *Mémoires . . . sur . . . Denis Diderot*, ib. 1821; E. Salverte, *Éloge de Diderot*, ib. 1847; E. Bersot, *Études sur Diderot*, ib. 1855; L. Asseline, *Diderot*, ib. 1866; P. Duprat, *Les Encyclopédistes*, Brussels, 1866; K. Rosenkranz, *Diderot's Leben und Werke*, Leipsic, 1866; J. Morley, *Diderot and the Encyclopædists*, 2 vols., London, 1879; E. Scherer, *Diderot, étude*, Paris, 1880; F. Picavet, *Les Idéo-*

logues, ib. 1891; L. Ducros, *Diderot, l'homme et l'écrivain*, ib. 1894; J. Reinach, *Diderot*, ib. 1894; M. Tourneux, *Diderot et Catherine II.*, ib. 1899; *KL*, iii. 1704–13.

DIDON, di″dōṅ′, **HENRI**: Dominican; b. at Touvet (16 m. n.e. of Grenoble) Mar. 17, 1840; d. at Toulouse Mar. 13, 1900. In 1856 he entered the Dominican Order, and in 1861 went to Rome to complete his education. He was professor of theology in various Dominican monasteries, and in 1866 was Lenten preacher in London. In 1868–69 he was stationed at Nancy. He took part in the conferences at Marseilles in 1871–76, but his views favoring divorce resulted in his confinement for a year and a half in the convent of Corbara, Corsica. From 1890 until his death he was the director of the Collège Albert-le-Grand in Arcueil. He was famous for his pulpit eloquence. His writings include *L'Enseignement supérieur et les universités catholiques* (Paris, 1876); *La Science sans Dieu* (1878; Eng. transl. by R. Corder, London, 1882); *Indissolubilité et divorce* (1880); *Les Allemands* (1884; Eng. transl. by R. L. de Beaufort, London, 1884); *Vie de Jésus-Christ* (2 vols., 1891; Eng. transl., London, 1891); *La Foi en la divinité de Jésus-Christ* (1894; Eng. transl., London, 1894); *Deux problèmes religieux: Conférences de Nancy, 1868–69* (1896); *L'Éducation présente* (1898); and the posthumous *Lettres à Mlle. Th. V.* (1900) and *Lettres à un ami* (1902).

Bibliography: Roibère, *Un Moine moderne*, Paris, 1900; A. de Coulanges, *Le Père Didon*, ib. 1900; P. Gaffre, *Le Père Didon*, ib. 1902; J. de Romano, *Henri Didon*, ib. 1903; and St. Raynaud, *Le Père Didon, sa vie et son œuvre*, ib. 1904.

DIDYMUS, THE BLIND, OF ALEXANDRIA: One of the last teachers and masters of the Alexandrian catechetical school (see Alexandria, School of) and one of the most learned men of his time; b. probably 313; d. probably 398 (Palladius, *Hist. Laus.*, iv.; Jerome, *De vir. ill.*, cix.). He lost his sight when a child, but his excellent memory and great gifts enabled him to obtain much secular and religious learning (Rufinus, *Hist. eccl.*, ii. 7). For more than fifty years he labored in the catechetical school, and among his pupils were Jerome and Rufinus. Thoroughly orthodox on the trinitarian question, he had the misfortune of being suspected of Origenism. That he was condemned by the Fifth General Council (Second Constantinople, 553) for heresy is indeed not proved (cf. Hefele, ii. 859 sqq.; Eng. transl., iv. 294 sqq.), but the sixth and seventh councils (Third Constantinople and Second Nicæa, 680 and 787) rejected his supposed heresies. Of his dogmatic and exegetical writings the following are extant either wholly or in part, in the original or in translation: (1) "On the Trinity," 3 books composed in 379 or later; (2) a "Book on the Holy Spirit," extant in Jerome's translation (printed among Jerome's works, *MPL*, xxiii. 101–154), considered one of the best works of the ancient Church on the subject; (3) "Against the Manicheans," incomplete in the original, a refutation of Manicheism on logical and metaphysical grounds; (4) exegetical works, fragments of expositions of Genesis, Exodus, Samuel, Kings, Psalms, John, Acts, II Corinthians, and an exposition of the Catholic epistles extant in the translation of Epiphanius Scholasticus (q.v.). The genuineness of this translation has been questioned by E. Klostermann (*TU*, new series, xiii. 2, Leipsic, 1905) on the basis of the Greek fragments printed by J. A. Cramer in *Catenæ in epistolas catholicas* (Oxford, 1840). Of the lost writings the most noteworthy is the "Notes on Origen's 'Principles.'" Didymus was probably also the author of the last two books of the work against Eunomius ascribed to Basil the Great (cf. F. X. Funk, *Kirchengeschichtliche Abhandlungen*, ii., Paderborn, 1899, 291–329). Recently K. Holl (*ZKG*, xxv., 1904, 380–398) has claimed for Didymus the treatise *Adversus Arium et Sabellium*, ascribed to Gregory of Nyssa (in *MPG*, xlv. 1281 sqq.).

G. Krüger.

Bibliography: The works of Didymus are in *MPG*, xxxix. Consult: J. A. Mingarelli, *De Didymi commentariis*, Bologna, 1709, reprinted *MPG*, xxxix. 139–216; H. E. F. Guericke, *De schola quæ Alexandriæ floruit*, i. 92–97, ii. 83–95, 332–378, Halle, 1824–25; G. C. F. Luecke, *Quæstiones ac vindiciæ Didymianæ*, Göttingen, 1829–32; O. Bardenhewer, *Patrologie*, pp. 290–293, Freiburg, 1894; T. Leipoldt, *Didymus der Blinde von Alexandria*, Leipsic, 1905; *DCB*, i. 827–829.

DIDYMUS, GABRIEL: German Reformer; b. at Annaberg (in Saxony, 18 m. s. of Chemnitz) c. 1487; d. at Torgau (in Prussian Saxony, 70 m. s.s.w. of Berlin) May 1, 1558. His family name was Zwilling, translated Didymus. According to a doubtful tradition he studied first at Prague, but from the year 1502 pursued his studies at Wittenberg, where he joined the Augustinians. When in 1512 he matriculated in the University he had already joined the order and was an associate of Luther in the monastery. On gaining his bachelor's degree, Oct. 14, 1516, he was sent by Luther to Erfurt to continue his studies there (T. Kolde, *Joh. v. Staupitz und die deutsche Augustinerkongregation*, Gotha, 1879, p. 267; Luther's letter to Joh. Long, Mar. 1, 1517, De Wette, *Luthers Briefe*, Berlin, 1825–28, i. 52), but the following winter he returned to Wittenberg and took his master's degree Feb. 14, 1518. Nothing more is heard of him until he took the leadership among the innovators in the Augustinian monastery in the stormy days of 1521. He entered the pulpit, manifesting a spirit like Carlstadt's; a great sensation was made by his sermon of Oct. 6, in which for hours he inveighed against the worship and sacrifice of the host and the private mass, demanded that the Eucharist be served in both kinds, and declared that he would never read another mass (*CR*, i. 460; *ZKG*, iv. 325 sqq.). The "little insignificant one-eyed man" could hold his hearers, who saw in him another Luther; even Melanchthon was fascinated by him (*TSK*, 1885, 134). His appeal was successful, for the next Sunday the mass ceased to exist in the monastery—and the exodus of the monks followed. About Christmas Didymus began to preach the Reformation at Wittenberg. He went to Eilenburg, where in layman's garb he preached against the old worship, celebrated the Lord's Supper in German, putting cup and bread into the hands of the communicants (*ZKG*, v., 1882, 327). On Friday, Jan. 10, 1522, he preached in Wittenberg against images (*ZKG*,

v. 331 sqq.), and dared even to denounce from the pulpit Justus Jonas and Amsdorf. He was the associate of Carlstadt, but was also the first to submit to Luther's leadership on the latter's return (Luther's letter to W. Link, Mar. 19, 1522, De Wette, *Luthers Briefe*, ii. 150). Called to Altenburg on Luther's recommendation Apr. 17, 1522 (De Wette, *Luthers Briefe*, ii. 183 sqq.), he was compelled to leave, after a few months' useful service, on account of the Eilenburg events, when he returned to Düben. In the spring of 1523 he went to Torgau, where he thenceforth labored, respected and defended by Luther (De Wette, *Luthers Briefe*, iv. 581; v. 76, 492, 756). In the mean time he had come into conflict with the secular authorities, was deposed in 1549, but continued to live privately in Torgau and remained chaplain to the mother and wife of the Elector Moritz until his death. (T. Kolde.)

Bibliography: J. G. Terne, *Versuch zur sufficienten Nachricht von des Gabriel Didymus . . . Leben*, Leipsic, 1737; C. Knabe, *Die Torgauer Visitationsordnung von 1529*, Torgau, 1881; H. Barge, *Andreas Bodenstein von Karlstadt*, 2 vols., Leipsic, 1905, ii. 545-549 (reprints the complaint of the Augustinian monks in Wittenberg against his sermon of Oct. 6, 1521; cf. i. 313, and for other references passim. Barge calls him Zwilling).

DIECKHOFF, AUGUST WILHELM: German Lutheran theologian; b. at Göttingen Feb. 5, 1823; d. at Rostock Sept. 12, 1894. In 1847 he became lecturer in the theological faculty in Göttingen, in 1850 was inaugurated lecturer there; in 1854 became extraordinary professor of systematic and historical theology, in 1860 professor of historical theology in Rostock, where he remained until his death.

1. Life and Character.

In the years 1860-1864 he edited, with Kliefoth, the *Theologische Zeitschrift*. Beside his academical duties, in the performance of which his lectures on the history of evangelical doctrine during the Reformation left a lasting impression, he developed a great literary activity in the interest of a historic presentation of the genesis of the Lutheran doctrinal reform.

This began with his *De Carolostadio Lutheranæ de servo arbitrio doctrinæ contra Echium defensore* (Göttingen, 1850). In his first extensive work, on *Die Waldenser im Mittelalter* (Göttingen, 1857), he showed that the Evangelicalism of the Waldensian manuscript literature is a forgery of the seventeenth century and that in doctrine they stood on the ground of medieval Catholicism, and that it was the Lutheran Reformation which first broke radically with the false medieval doctrinal development.

2. Theological Writings.

Next appeared vol. i. of his largest work, *Die evangelische Abendmahlslehre im Reformationszeitalter* (Göttingen, 1854), a work which unfortunately he never completed; in this he treated of the doctrine as stated by Luther during the years 1517-23, by Carlstadt, Zwingli, Œcolampadius, and the Swabian Syngramma. The work is of lasting value, for it treats with decisive clearness the evolution of Luther's doctrines, setting forth both their merits and their defects. That Dieckhoff did not continue this study is undoubtedly due to the fact that his interest centered in the beginnings of the Reformation. Then too he was drawn into theological controversies. Against Hofmann he postulated that (1) faith attains certainty only in union with Scripture, (2) the content of the system of theological thought is given in the Word of God. Later he again attacked Hofmann and his school. In these otherwise valuable contributions his polemics is at times misleading and his dogmatic position confused.

The ecclesiastical-political questions of his time he studied with zealous attention. After the Vatican Council he published *Schrift und Tradition . . .* (1870), a clear and convincing refutation of Catholic objections to the evangelical doctrine of Scripture as they appeared in the work of Von Ketteler, the bishop of Mainz, entitled *Das allgemeine Konzil und seine Bedeutung für unsere Zeit* (Mainz, 1869). Then came questions nearer home—school supervision by the state, treated in his *Staat und Kirche* (Leipsic, 1872); civil marriage, which he attacked in *Die kirchliche Trauung* (Rostock, 1878) and in *Civilehe und kirchliche Trauung* (1880). In the last decade of his life he was drawn into the controversy raised in Germany by the ultra-Lutheran Missouri-Synod. In 1884, on account of a decision in favor of the Wisconsin-Synod,

3. Ecclesiastical Writings.

he was attacked by the Missourians, to whom he replied in *Der missourische Prädestinationismus und die Concordienformel* (1885) and *Zur Lehre von der Bekehrung und die Prädestination* (1886). These essays are of lasting importance since they give a clear view not only of Luther's predestinationism, but also of the teaching of the almost forgotten Lutheran theologian Laterman. On the other hand, his *Inspiration und Irrthumslosigkeit der heiligen Schrift* (Leipsic, 1891), directed against the Missouri extreme, brought him judicial censure. While in all these works he labored in his especial field, tracing the doctrines back to Luther's teaching, he wrote also a number of essays preparatory to these subjects. Worthy of mention are *Augustins und Luthers Lehre von der Gnade* (in *TZ*, i.), *Luthers Lehre von der kirchlichen Gewalt* (Berlin, 1865), and especially *Der Ablasstreit* (1866), wherein he showed how much Luther and the Reformation profited by the discussion about the sale of indulgences. Finally mention must be made of the work *Justin, Augustin, Bernhard und Luther* (Leipsic, 1882), developed from lectures in which he traced in masterly fashion the evolution of the Christian conception of the truth. He received a new inspiration from the rediscovery in 1876 of Luther's "Lectures on the Psalms." Here followed *Luthers Stellung zur Kirche vor 1517* (Rostock, 1883) and *Luthers Lehre in ihrer ersten Gestalt* (1887), the ripest fruit of all his investigation, expounding Luther's conception of "Faith." (K. Schmidt.)

DIEKAMP, FRANZ: Roman Catholic; b. at Geldern (65 m. s.w. of Münster) Nov. 8, 1864. He studied at Münster, Eichstätt, and Munich from 1882 to 1887; became chaplain at Camp, 1888; lecturer in the theological seminary at Münster, 1889; student at Munich, 1896; privat-docent for patrology and the history of dogmatics at Munich, 1898; associate professor, 1902, and full professor, 1904. He has written *Die Gotteslehre des heiligen Gregor von Nyssa* (Münster, 1896); *Hippolytos von Theben* (1898); and *Die origenistischen Streitigkeiten im sechsten Jahrhundert und das fünfte allgemeine Concil* (1899), and has edited the *Theologische Revue* since 1902.

DIEPENBROCK, MELCHIOR VON: Cardinal; b. at Bocholt (44 m. w. of Münster) Jan. 6, 1798; d. at the castle of Johannesberg at Jauernig (52 m. n.w. of Troppau) Jan. 20, 1853. In 1810 he was sent to the military academy of Bonn, but was soon expelled for insubordination. Permeated with the rising spirit of nationalism which inspired the Germany of the period, he became a lieutenant of militia and later entered a regiment of the line, serving in France and also in garrison-duty. Resigning on the advice of his superiors, he returned to his home, and was there converted by Michael Sailer, who was then professor at Landshut. He then studied at Landshut, and in 1819 decided to enter the priesthood, and studied at Mainz, Münster, and Regensburg, where Sailer had been a canon since 1821. On Dec. 27, 1823, Diepenbrock was ordained priest, and then entered on his duties as Sailer's secretary, devoting himself especially to the mysticism of the Middle Ages, the result being his *Heinrich Susos Leben und Schriften* (Regensburg, 1829) and the *Geistlicher Blüthenstrauss* (Sulzbach, 1829). When Sailer was consecrated bishop of Regensburg in 1829, Diepenbrock, after long hesitation, accepted a canonry, and under Bishop Valentine rose to be vicar-general. He soon resigned, however, and in a brief period of retirement prepared a translation from Hendrik Conscience under the title of *Vlämisches Stilleben* (Regensburg, 1845). He was consecrated prince bishop of Breslau on July 27, 1845. Within a year he found himself obliged to excommunicate all the "German Catholics" to check the disturbances which this movement caused in the diocese of Breslau, while in the revolution of 1848 he urged obedience to the government. On the other hand, he firmly advocated the independence of the Church as regards the State, and protested against the oath to support the constitution which was required of the clergy who held official positions. Only the conciliatory attitude of the State prevented serious controversies. A papal brief of Oct. 24, 1849, appointed him vicar apostolic for the Prussian Army. As prince bishop of Breslau Diepenbrock furthered the cause of monasteries, and encouraged Redemptorist and Jesuit missions among the laity. He was created cardinal by Pius IX. in 1850, and in this capacity became involved in a controversy with the Protestant general superintendent of Silesia, who complained of the missionary propaganda of the Roman Catholics, only to receive a sharp rebuff from Diepenbrock. (Heinrich Schmidt.)

Bibliography: Lives are by H. Förster, Regensburg, 1878; J. H. Reinkens, Leipsic, 1881; M. Röttscher, Frankfort, 1886; B. Boenisch, Oppeln, 1898; H. Finke, *Zur Erinnerung an Kardinal Melchior von Diepenbrock*, Münster, 1898.

DIES IRÆ. See Thomas of Celano.

DIESTEL, dis'tel, LUDWIG: Theologian and church historian; b. at Königsberg Sept. 28, 1825; d. at Tübingen May 15, 1879. He entered the University of Königsberg in 1844 to prepare himself for the clerical calling, and in Oct., 1847, went to Berlin; in 1848 he migrated to Bonn, where he became privat-docent in 1851, and there, during a residence of seven years, lived in intimate friendship with Ritschl. He was made extraordinary professor in 1858, and in 1862 went to Greifswald, where he held the chair of Old Testament exegesis. In 1867 he became professor at Jena, and in 1872 at Tübingen. After 1871 he was a member of the Halle committee for the revision of the Luther Bible. Diestel's work on the Old Testament was that of the theologian rather than of the philologist or textual critic. His fame rests chiefly on his *Geschichte des Alten Testaments in der christlichen Kirche* (Jena, 1869), a valuable storehouse of information on Old Testament exegesis and hermeneutics. The work may be characterized as a history of the study of the Old Testament in the Christian Church rather than as a history of the Bible in itself. Of especial importance is the division of the guiding principles in the correct method of investigation of the Old Testament into national, historical, and religious. Diestel's only independent works, in addition to the one already mentioned, were *Der Segen Jakobs in Genesis XLIX historisch erläutert* (Brunswick, 1853); *Ueber die Theokratie Israels* (Greifswald, 1864); and a revision of the fourth edition of August Knobel's commentary on Isaiah (Leipsic, 1872). (E. Kautzsch.)

DIETARY LAWS OF THE HEBREWS.

As with the symbolically elaborated religions of antiquity in general, the sacred laws of the Old Testament include prescriptions restricting the choice of meats and rules for preparing the same.

Many animals are described as unclean, neither to be sacrificed nor eaten by man, nor to be touched as carcasses; whereas, of those designated as clean for food, not all are allowed in sacrifice (Lev. xi.; Deut. xiv. 3-21). Animals appear to be grouped, in this connection, according to the primitive Hebrew arrangement, in four or five classes; and in several classes the enumeration of particular species is precluded by the expedient of general marks of distinction. Among quadrupeds, for instance, those are accounted clean which, in the first place, "part the hoof," and, in the second place, chew the cud. There are thus mentioned as edible in Deut. xiv. 4-5, the ox, sheep, goat, hart, gazel, roebuck, and certain species of antelope. On the other hand, those which lack one or both of these

1. Animals Allowed and Prohibited as Food.

distinguishing marks are unclean; such as the camel, rock-badger, hare, swine, together with "whatsoever goeth upon its paws" (Lev. xi. 27). Among aquatic animals, those are edible which have fins and scales; not those, however, which (like the eel) resemble the reptile family and exhibit no marked fish type at all. Among birds about nineteen to twenty-one species are prohibited as food; for the most part, birds of prey, such as the eagle, vulture, raven, owl, etc., which feed on carrion and filthy substances; marsh birds and water-fowls also, such as the stork, heron, pelican, and others, are prohibited; likewise the ostrich, or "desert bird." The bat is classed with birds, as the Arabs still class it. There is an additional prescription with reference to "winged creeping things" (insects), which are summarily prohibited with but one general exception (stated only in Lev.); namely, those are permitted as food "which have legs above their feet, to leap withal"; so that grasshoppers are thus allowed, together with three similar species (Lev. xi. 22). Among the "creeping things" which are unclean according to Lev. xi. 41, 42 special mention is made of the mole, mouse, lizard, and some similar but not certainly definable animals; together with the chameleon (Lev. xi. 29–30). It is also observed of these, in Lev. xi. 32–33, that they defile vessels, raiment, etc., as well as food, by contact when dead. Among "creeping things" which are an "abomination" mention is made (verse 42) of "whatsoever goeth upon the belly"; that is to say, snakes and worms. Mere touching of live "unclean" animals does not defile, but only to eat of them defiles; as is also true of touching or carrying their carcass; while, finally (on the ground adduced below), there is defilement in touching the dead body of clean creatures (see DEFILEMENT AND PURIFICATION, CEREMONIAL, I., 1, § 5), and in eating or carrying such creatures when fallen dead without being slaughtered (Lev. xi. 39). The consequences of transgressing these prescriptions and the necessary purifications are simple and not unduly oppressive. Whoever touches the carcass of unclean or clean beasts shall be unclean till evening; whoever carries such dead body, or even eats of it, and this of edible, or clean beasts as well, must furthermore wash his clothes (Lev. xi. 24–25, 28, 31, 39–40). With reference to polluted objects cf. Lev. xi. 32–33.

2. Origin and Significance of the Distinction.

The fact that the distinction between clean and unclean beasts extends as far back as the memories of the Hebrews is attested by the Jehovistic passages, wherein the distinction is traced to the deluge (Gen. vii. 2, viii. 20). The distinction was not first introduced by the Mosaic legislation, but was already at hand in popular usage; which, like all tribal customs, had religious authority. Moses simply imparted a more definite legal form to this usage, and brought it into relation with the worship of Yahweh. The dominating motive herein was not so much mere expediency, well adapted though these prescriptions were to exert a wholesome physical effect, as the feeling that a natural uncleanness pervaded the prohibited animals, from which the members of Yahweh's consecrated people should be kept clean (cf. Lev. xi. 44–45; Deut. xiv. 2–3). The people of the covenant are to keep themselves clean bodily, out of regard to the God who dwells in their midst, unto whom everything unclean is abhorrent. In the matter of practical determination of what was clean or unclean the law adjusted itself to the sentiment already operative among the people. It took account first of all of the natural aversion among them toward certain kinds of food and of the disgust for certain animals. This factor is more primitive than the superstition attached to it. Totemism and taboo have been advanced as hypotheses to explain the origin of this distinction (W. Robertson Smith). But totemism would lead merely to prohibition of some particular animal or animals, but by no means explain the separation of the animal world into two classes, of which the greater is accounted unclean. Moreover, the dietary regulation of the Israelites is very different from ethnic taboo regulations, whereby certain foods, animals, and fruits, consecrated to some divinity, are forbidden either entirely or at stated times to specified persons or classes. With the Israelites the distinction is easy to understand, because objectively grounded, in the light of the common human desire for cleanliness (see DEFILEMENT AND PURIFICATION, CEREMONIAL, I., 5).

3. Contributory Factors.

Nor was the popular intuition, prompted by sound natural sentiment, unworthy to be adopted by the Mosaic religion, to be more definitely regulated and made serviceable to the same. What at first glance appear to be surprising marks of distinction for the mammals are to be explained as follows: those quadrupeds which, being herbivorous, furnish the cleanest and most savory meat (hence meat appropriate for sacrifice as well, such as beef animals, sheep, etc.) have also supplied, as customary slaughter animals, the distinguishing marks for discrimination of doubtful animals (for example, game). So the real significance of the distinction is not to be sought in the marks, but in the qualities, just mentioned, which are associated therewith. Beasts "that go on their paws," however, are carnivorous, being chiefly beasts of prey and such as live on carrion, for which reasons they are much more liable to be characterized by offensiveness of every description than the standard animals; and they must have seemed especially unclean to the Israelites, to whom it was extremely offensive to swallow carrion, lacerated or strangled flesh, and the like. Neither is the motive to be disregarded that what is edible shall belong to some pronounced species of animal. This becomes apparent in the distinguishing marks of fishes; perhaps also in case of the bat, which, furthermore, makes its haunt in filthy holes; and in case of the ostrich, whose peculiar characteristics are enhanced by its singular mode of life. But Philo and other Jews of an allegorical bent, and after them the Church Fathers, sought some immediate moral basis or symbolic significance in all these prescriptions with an all too mystical refinement.

Essentially different in principle is the prohibition against consuming the blood and the fat of (clean or edible) animals. The blood is not unclean in itself; on the contrary, it is the precious vital fluid, which is offered to God as the worthiest portion of the animal creature. Life is from God and belongs to God. On account of its intimate relation to life, men shall not swallow the blood, but shall consecrate it to God. By this very property, too, blood is also the appropriate means of atonement, can intercede for men, can be offered to God in their place—"For the life of the flesh is in the blood: and I have given it to you upon the altar to make atonement for your souls" (Lev. xvii. 11). For this reason care must be observed in the slaying that the blood may escape. Nothing lacerated or smothered is allowed to be eaten, because in that case the blood has not properly escaped. This practise of avoiding to partake of blood is very ancient (Gen. ix. 4). It is sharply accentuated in various repetitions and portions of the Law (Lev. iii. 17, vii. 26–27, xvii. 10, xix. 26; Deut. xii. 16, 23–24, xv. 23; cf. Ezek. xxxiii. 25; I Sam. xiv. 32–33). Even the stranger who had settled in Canaan was forbidden to eat the blood (Lev. xvii. 10, 15), whereas in Deut. xiv. 21 the stranger is at least allowed the cattle "that dieth of itself." Whoever transgressed the commandment had to undergo the same course of expiation as in the case of the defilements noted above (Lev. xvii. 10, 15), or expect extermination by the band of God (Lev. xvii. 16, vii. 27). The blood of sacrificial beasts was brought to the altar; in other cases it was simply poured on the ground or covered with "dust." The avoidance of partaking of blood has become so natural to the Jews that the practise continues. The proviso that the blood of animals must properly escape in the slaughtering led to a complicated ceremonial, under rabbinical Judaism, with reference to the slaughter (purporting to follow the tradition mentioned in Deut. xii. 21). The slaying is to be despatched by a "Schächter" (Jewish butcher) who thoroughly understands the Talmudic regulations (cf. the Mishna tract *Hullin* and the penal laws in connection with partaking of blood, *Keritot*, K, 5; also Maimonides, *Yad ha-Hazakah, Hilkot Shehitah*; *Shulhan 'Aruk*, *Yore De'ah*; and on Jewish butchering, I. Hamburger, *Realencyklopädie für Bibel und Talmud*, ii. 1099 sqq.; *JE*, xi. 253 sqq.).

4. The Prohibition of Blood.

Like the blood, the fat of sacrificial beasts is forbidden to be eaten (Lev. iii. 17, vii. 25). Not the outer fat, which grows united with the flesh, is meant, but that deposited about the entrails, and especially about the kidneys, including in case of sheep the "fat tail" (Lev. iii. 9–10). But, far from being unclean, the fat is, in a certain sense, the "quintessence" of the body, and therefore the choicest portion, reserved by Yahweh for himself. Here, too, the standpoint is theocratic, not hygienic or sanitary. Moreover, Deuteronomy says naught of this prohibition.

5. The Prohibition of Fat.

There are two additional precepts in respect to food: (1) Gen. xxxii. 32, which, to be sure, is not a prescriptive rule, but states as a generally recognized usage in Israel that the hip sinew (*nervus ischiadicus*) of slaughtered animals was never eaten. (2) The express command not to "seethe a kid in its mother's milk" is found in the Book of the Covenant (Ex. xxiii. 19) and repeated Ex. xxxiv. 26 and Deut. xiv. 21. It is not necessary to assume that the intent here was to do away with some heathen sacrificial practise (Maimonides, Roskoff) or some other custom of superstitious intent (magical craft, Stade). It is more probable that this prohibition, like Lev. xxii. 28, Deut. xxii. 6–7 (cf., too, the Sabbath rest for beasts), enjoins a certain sparing of nature even in the animal world. In later times this prohibition was so far amplified by the Targum and rabbinical writers that meat might not be cooked in milk or butter at all; and this led to a punctilious classification of kitchen utensils, and to similar pedantries in vogue among modern orthodox Jews. The original significance of the matter is more correctly recognized by the Samaritans, who even now procure meat and milk from different districts.

6. Two Additional Restrictions.

In the New Testament the primitive Christian congregation is found for the most part loyal to the traditional precepts of Moses. But the distinction between clean and unclean animals, like other purificatory prescriptions that hedged Israel in, had to fall away if any closer touch was to ensue with the heathen world. The lesson was imparted to Peter (Acts x. 9 sqq.). Such abolition of barrier precepts, indeed, is intrinsically supported by the revelation fulfilled through Christ, which, by removing from the sinner his once burdening ban of uncleanness, purifies and sanctifies the whole creature. In this light the external distinction of clean and unclean loses its proper warrant of being. Especially to be noted is the canon of Matt. xv. 11, 17–20; Mark vii. 15, whereby dietary laws are already repealed in principle. In the primitive Christian Church the prohibition against partaking of blood was longest and most strictly maintained in force; and this, indeed, with reference to Gentile Christians as well as Jewish (Acts xv. 20, 29, xxi. 25), not as a distinctively Israelitic prohibition, but one reaching back even to Noah. In Tertullian's time the Church deemed itself still generally bound by that restriction (Tertullian, *Apol.*, ix.; *De monogamia*, v.; *De idolatria*, xxiv.; Eusebius, *Hist. eccl.*, v. 1). The Greek Church adhered to the same constantly (Second Trullan Council, canon lxvii.; Suicerus, *Thesaurus ecclesiasticus*, i. 113). In principle, however, this prohibition was done away with by the word of the Lord, Matt. xv. 11, as well as through the evangelic liberty proclaimed by the apostles, Paul especially (I Tim. iv. 3–4), as belonging to the "elements of the world" (Gal. iv. 3), which could serve only by way of preparatory instruction to the congregation of the faithful, who are told "all things are yours, and ye are Christ's."

7. The Christian Usage and Attitude.

C. von Orelli.

BIBLIOGRAPHY: A. Wiener, *Die jüdischen Speisegesetze*, Breslau, 1895; J. D. Michaelis, *Mosaisches Recht*, iv. 125–126, Biehl, 1777; H. Ewald, *Die Alterthümer des Volkes Israel*, pp. 192–212, Göttingen, 1866, Eng. transl., pp. 144–165, Boston, 1876; W. M. Thomson, *The Land and the Book*, 3 vols., New York, 1881–86; H. L. Strack, *Das Blut im Glauben und Aberglauben*, Berlin, 1900; *DB*, ii. 27–43; *EB*, ii. 1538 sqq.; *JE*, v. 431–433; and the literature under DEFILEMENT AND PURIFICATION, CEREMONIAL.

DIETENBERGER, JOHANNES: German Roman Catholic Bible translator; b. at Frankfort-on-the-Main c. 1475; d. at Mainz Sept. 4, 1537. He entered in early life the Dominican order, and in 1510 became prior of the Frankfort monastery. This office he held till 1524. In 1526 he became prior in Coblenz. He was among the theologians chosen to refute the Augsburg Confession in 1530. He was also one of the Dominican inquisitors, and as such had a part in the Reuchlin investigation. From 1533 till his death he was professor of theology at the University of Mainz. He is spoken of by his contemporaries, both Roman Catholic and Protestant, as one of the foremost men of his time, but he has been so much forgotten that the details of his life are not known, and the way in which the outline that is known has been stated is usually erroneous. He was a prolific author. Most numerous are his ascetic and polemical writings, but of greater permanent value are his translation of the entire Bible, for which his scholarship in Hebrew and Greek qualified him, but which was fiercely attacked by the Protestants as nothing more than a transcript of Luther's translation, and particularly his catechism which was one of the earliest of the kind known. The Bible version (Mainz, 1534) is of course from the Vulgate. It passed through forty editions. His catechism (Mainz, 1537) was also very popular and received the indorsement of numerous church bodies.

BIBLIOGRAPHY: H. Wedewer, *Johannes Dietenberger*, Freiburg, 1888; C. Moufang, *Die Mainzer Katechismen . . . bis zum Ende des 18. Jahrhunderts*, Mainz, 1878.

DIETRICH, di'tris, OF APOLDA: Author of a life of St. Elizabeth of Thuringia and another of St. Dominic. He is undoubtedly identical with Dietrich of Thuringia, but of his life is known only what may be gathered from the prologues to his works—that he was born probably about 1228 in Apolda, and became a Dominican in the monastery at Erfurt in 1247; he most likely died there after 1296. His two biographies are written not without skill, and display painstaking search after oral and written sources. The *Vita S. Elisabethæ* was written 1289 and printed in Canisius, *Lectiones antiquæ*, ed. Basnage, iv (Amsterdam, 1725), 116–152; it adds nothing to our knowledge of the saint's life, and the same is true of his *Vita S. Dominici* (latest ed. by A. Curé, Paris, 1887). Begun at the request of Munione da Zamorra, general of the order, Dietrich finished it under Nicholas Bocassinus, general 1296–98. He has incorporated oral tradition from Sister Cæcilia in Rome, and the German provincial Gerard, and has used the older biographies of the saint by Jordanus, Constantine, Humbert, Gerhard of Frachet, and the acts of the canonization.

(G. GRÜTZMACHER.)

BIBLIOGRAPHY: J. Quétif and J. Échard, *Scriptores ordinis prædicatorum*, i. 413 sqq., 453 sqq., Paris, 1719; G. Boerner, in *NA*, xiii (1888), pp. 472–491 (pp. 491–493 contain an edition of the *Vita*).

DIETRICH OF NIEHEIM (NIEM): Roman Catholic Reformatory writer at the time of the great Western schism (see SCHISM); b. in the diocese of Paderborn in Westphalia, probably at Nieheim (18 m. e.n.e. of Paderborn) between 1338 and 1348; d. at Maestricht Mar., 1418. A very industrious man, he labored for the removal of the schism and, like Pierre d'Ailly and Gerson in France, lifted up his voice in Germany in favor of a thorough reformation of the Church. At the time of the Council at Constance he was the greatest ecclesiastico-political publicist using the German tongue. All his life he is designated as a cleric of the diocese of Paderborn. He was not of noble birth, was educated outside of his native land, and traveled through Italy. Having studied jurisprudence, he obtained a position in the curia. In 1370 he was an officer in the papal court at Avignon, and in 1377, as *notarius sacri palatii* went with the curia to Rome. Under Urban VI. he obtained the important and lucrative offices of abbreviator and scriptor in the chancery. After the outbreak of the schism in 1378 he shared the vicissitudes of Urban VI., but he obtained rich livings, and under the next pope, Boniface IX. (1389–1404), he was appointed to the episcopal see of Verden on the Aller, in his native Lower Saxony. He occupied the see from 1395 to 1399, when he had to resign. In 1403 he was again in Rome and interested in the newly founded German Hospital dell' Anima. He took no part in the Council at Pisa (1409), as certain business took him to Germany. But he remained in the service of the curia till the flight of John XXIII. from the Council at Constance in 1415 induced him to sever his connection with the pope. At the Council of Constance he played officially no important part, but exercised considerable influence by his writings. It may be taken for granted that he composed at Constance the passionate libel which its first editor entitled *Invectiva in diffugientem . . . Johannem xxiii.* In this he holds before the pope a fearful list of sins committed, and destroys his moral character irretrievably In his official position Dietrich had the chance of observing the doings of the curia from 1377 to 1415, and, as he was well educated and strove to be honest, his records have almost the value of a source. There is at present no agreement concerning the genuineness of the writings attributed to him. The most important may be: (1) *Nemus unionis* (first printed Basel, 1566, as bk. iv. of the following work), treating of the union of the church; (2) *De schismate* (Nuremberg, 1536), a history of the schism to 1410; (3) *Historia de vita Johannis xxiii.* (Frankfort, 1420), also a history of the Council of Constance and Dietrich's day-book to 1416; (4) *Privilegia et jura imperii* (Basel, 1566), a history of the Holy Roman empire, after the fashion of Dante's political dreams. According to Erler, Dietrich did not write the works *De necessitate reformationis ecclesiæ*, *De modis uniendi ac reformandi ecclesiam*, and *De difficultate* *reformationis in concilio universali*, all of which belong to the time of the great Western schism.

PAUL TSCHACKERT.

BIBLIOGRAPHY: For a full list of editions of the works of Dietrich and of literature on him consult: Potthast, *Wegweiser*, pp. 1051–55 (indispensable as an aid to special study). The best review of his life and writings is G. Erler, *Dietrich von Nieheim*, Leipsic, 1887. Consult further: J. B. Schwab, *Johannes Gerson*, Würzburg, 1858; H. V. Sauerland, *Das Leben des Dietrich von Nieheim*, Göttingen, 1875; P. Tschackert, *Peter von Ailli*, Gotha, 1877; A. Fritz, *Zur Quellenkritik der Schriften Dietrichs von Niem*, Paderborn, 1886; O. Lorenz, *Deutschlands Geschichtsquellen*, ii. 152, 313–323, 371–374, 413–414, Berlin, 1887; H. Finke, *Acta concilii Constantiensis*, vol. i., Münster, 1896; *KL*, iii. 1747–49.

DIETRICH, VEIT: German Reformer; b. in Nuremberg Dec. 8, 1506; d. there Mar. 25, 1549. Though only a shoemaker's son, he went in 1522 to the University of Wittenberg, where he soon gained the affection of Melanchthon. Later he came in close touch with Luther, who advised him to forsake medicine for theology; he shared Luther's house and board, and became his amanuensis and secretary. As such he accompanied Luther to the debate at Marburg in 1529, in the following year he went with Luther to Coburg on the way to the Diet at Augsburg. In 1533 he appears as dean of the faculty of arts in Wittenberg. On Dec. 14, 1535, he became minister at St. Sebald's in Nuremberg, and shortly after married a lady of Nuremberg. He was Melanchthon's lifelong friend, and had his confidence, knew his thoughts, and shared his cares as no other did except Camerarius; while more anti-Roman than Melanchthon, he was his disciple rather than Luther's. He edited and translated into German a number of Luther's and Melanchthon's minor writings; it is charged that he proceeded very arbitrarily in editing, sometimes suppressing Luther's views or changing them completely. Of his own works (which were very numerous) the most popular was the *Summaria über das Alte Testament* (Wittenberg, 1541), an attempt to give briefly "what it is most necessary and useful that the young people and the common man should know of each chapter." In 1544, with Melanchthon's help, he rendered a like service for the New Testament (reprinted by the Evangelical Lutheran Synod of Missouri and Ohio, St. Louis, 1857).

(T. KOLDE.)

BIBLIOGRAPHY: G. T. Strobel, *Nachricht von dem Leben und den Schriften Veit Dietrichs*, Nuremberg, 1772; J. Voigt, *Briefwechsel der berühmtesten Gelehrten . . . der Reformation*, pp. 171–216, Königsberg, 1841; H. E. Jacobs, *Martin Luther*, New York, 1898; J. W. Richard, *Philip Melanchthon*, ib. 1898. Very numerous are the references to Dietrich in J. Köstlin, *Martin Luther*, Berlin, 1903.

DIEU, dyȫ, LUDOVICUS (LODEWIJK) DE: Dutch Orientalist; b. at Flushing, Holland, Apr. 7, 1590; d. at Leyden Nov. 13, 1642. He studied in Leyden, where, under J. Scaliger, Oriental studies had thriven. The Library of the "Athens of Holland" was rich in Oriental manuscripts, and Thomas Erpenius, who was with Daniel Colonius (van Ceulen) the teacher who most impressed him, saw to it that these treasures were well used. After completing his studies, in 1613 Dieu became pastor at Middelburg, in 1615 he removed to Flushing, and in 1617 took charge of the Low German congregation at Leyden, and served also as regent of the Walloon College until his death. He refused a call to the newly founded University of Utrecht, and also many other offers. He was a plain, reliable, and clear-eyed scholar, as a commentator he was highly esteemed, and was always active in the public weal. Because of the character of his studies and of his taste for linguistics he became an exegete, and employed in a new way, in the service of Biblical science, the translations from Oriental languages, especially those from the Syriac, the Arabic, and the Ethiopic, as well as his knowledge of Jewish literature. The study of Tremellius's Latin translation of the Syriac New Testament and the use of a translation into Hebrew of a part of the New Testament by Mercerus and Münster gave his zeal new impetus in the same direction. Further to equip himself he dived into the translations of Oriental literature furnished by his friend Heinsius, librarian in Leyden. The fruits of his labors he gathered partly in writings on linguistics, partly in notes on difficult Biblical passages. The exegetical works completed in this period are collected under the title *Critica sacra sive animadversiones in loca quædam difficiliora Veteris et Novi Testamenti* (Amsterdam, 1884), edited with good indexes.

In still another field Dieu's scientific work bore good fruit. Through a traveler to the Orient he got possession of some missionary tracts put into Persian by the Jesuit Jerome Xavier, and of a Life of Jesus and a Life of Peter, which were intended to bring to the "Mongols" the true word of God. He acquired a knowledge of Persian in order to examine the missionary methods of the Jesuits, and expressed disgust at the way in which they palmed off legends and falsehoods as truth. He proceeded to edit their works, added a Latin translation and valuable notes, and affixed a Persian grammar, that any one might investigate and see that he, a priest of science, fought with clean weapons. It is a missionary's duty, he taught, to learn the language, so as not to hinder the progress of the Gospel among the heathen.

(G. HEINRICI.)

BIBLIOGRAPHY: As an early source consult R. Simon, *Histoire critique du V. T.*, pp. 440 sqq., Amsterdam, 1678; idem, *Histoire critique des . . . commentateurs du N. T.*, pp. 787 sqq.; Rotterdam, 1693. Consult also Niceron, *Mémoires*, xv. 85 sqq.; A. J. van der Aa, *Biographisch Woordenboek der Nederlanden*, iv. 53, Haarlem, 1859.

DIGGLE, JOHN WILLIAM: Anglican bishop of Carlisle; b. at Pendleton (a suburb of Manchester) Mar. 2, 1847. He studied at Merton College, Oxford (B.A., 1870), and was ordained priest in 1872. He was curate at Whalley Range, Lancashire (1871-1872), All Saints', Liverpool (1872-74), St. John's, Walton, Liverpool (1874-75), and vicar of Mossley Hill, Liverpool (1875-96). He was canon of Carlisle and archdeacon of Westmorland (1896-1901), and examining chaplain to the bishop of Carlisle (1892-1901). He was rector of St. Martin's, Birmingham, in 1901-04, and archdeacon of Birmingham and rural dean in 1903-05. He was rural dean of Childwall in 1882-96, honorary canon of Liverpool in 1889-96, president of the Liverpool Council of Education in 1891, select preacher to the University of Oxford in 1898, and examining chaplain to the bishop of Worcester in 1902–05. In 1905 he was consecrated bishop of Carlisle. He has edited Bishop James Fraser's *University and Parochial Sermons* (London, 1887) and *Lancashire Life* (1889); and has written *Godliness and Manliness* (London, 1886); *True Religion* (1887): *Sermons for Daily Life* (1891); *Religious Doubt* (1895); and *Short Studies in Holiness* (1900).

DIKE, SAMUEL WARREN: Congregationalist; b. at Thompson, Conn., Feb. 13, 1839. He studied at Williams College (B.A., 1863), Hartford Theological Seminary (1863–65), and Andover Theological Seminary (B.D., 1866). He was pastor at West Randolph, Vt. (1866–77), and Royalton, Vt. (1879–82), and since 1881 has been corresponding secretary of the National League for the Protection of the Family, which was founded in that year under the name of the Divorce Reform League, largely as the result of his writings. He has lectured in many higher institutions of learning, and originated the home department of the Sunday-school. He sympathizes with the use of scientific methods in theology and polity. He is the author of numerous articles on divorce, the family, and country towns.

DILLER (DILHERR), MICHAEL: Reformer of Speyer; b., probably in the diocese of Speyer, in the early part of the sixteenth century; d. at Heidelberg 1570. He matriculated at Wittenberg in 1523, and shortly after 1529 was prior of the Augustinian monastery at Speyer, and preached there frequently. Being a pupil of Wittenberg, he preached justification from a strictly evangelical point of view, although he avoided polemics. He soon gained the confidence of the citizens of Speyer, and in 1538 the municipal council, recognizing the necessity of providing for regular evangelical preaching to prevent the people, who neglected the Roman Catholic service, from "sinking into depravity," requested Diller to hold regular services in his church. In 1540 the bishop became aware of this course, and commanded him to cease immediately, although he was obliged to acquiesce in the refusal of Diller, who was protected by the council. In Jan., 1541, the emperor Charles V. visited Speyer and forbade the council to permit Diller to deliver his sermons, since he "preached of justification and good works after the new fashion." Diller, who had left the city before the arrival of Charles, pleaded his cause before the council and continued his activity after the emperor's departure. Thus far Diller had made no changes in the form of the service, but previous to Easter of 1543 he preached against the mass and demanded that the cup be given to the laity. The bishop in vain asked the council to interfere, and it would seem that Diller now actually administered the Holy Sacrament in both kinds. During the emperor's attendance at the Diet of Speyer (Jan.–June, 1544) Diller was absent from the city, but he resumed his activity with fresh ardor after the adjournment of the diet. The council, encouraged by the course of events at the diet, not only protected him, but also decided to give him an assistant.

The success of the emperor in the Schmalkald War ended Diller's work and evangelical preaching in Speyer. Charles V. again visited the city, and Diller was obliged to leave. He went to Basel, and in 1553 accepted a call to Neuburg as court preacher to the palgrave Ottheinrich. There, in 1554, he cooperated in the introduction of the church-order. When Ottheinrich became elector of the Palatinate in 1556 Diller followed him to Heidelberg, and collaborated with Marbach and Stolo in the preparation of a church-order, Lutheran in type, which was adopted Apr. 4, 1556. He also assisted in the Baden church-order of 1556, took part in the same year in the ecclesiastical visitations in the Upper Palatinate and in the margravate of Baden, and was one of the most influential members of the council appointed to direct the Palatinate Church. The elector Frederick III., who succeeded Ottheinrich in 1559, likewise reposed full confidence in Diller. Throughout the doctrinal controversies of the period he labored for peace. Repelled by Heshusen and his sympathizers, he sided more and more with the Reformed, especially at the Conference of Maulbronn in 1564, although henceforth he rarely appeared in public. He does not seem to have engaged in literary activity. JULIUS NEY.

DILLMANN, (CHRISTIAN FRIEDRICH) AUGUST: German Lutheran theologian; b. at Illingen (17 m. n.w. of Stuttgart), Württemberg, Apr. 25, 1823; d. in Berlin July 4, 1894. He studied in the seminary at Schönthal, 1836–40; at Tübingen, 1840–45; was assistant pastor at Sersheim, Württemberg, 1845–46; traveled and studied, especially Ethiopic, at Paris, London, and Oxford, 1846–48; became repetent (i.e., tutor for three years) at Tübingen, 1848; privat-docent for Old Testament exegesis in the theological faculty, 1852; professor extraordinary of theology, 1853; professor of Oriental languages in the philosophical faculty at Kiel, 1854; professor of theology at Giessen, 1864; and at Berlin, 1869. He was distinguished for his cultivation of the neglected field of Ethiopic language and literature. As a critic he stood in opposition to the traditional treatment of the Old Testament, but was always guided by his perception of the historical principle. He received on this account the thanks of the late Dr. Delitzsch on the occasion of an address which was an answer to the latter's treatment of Old Testament theology, and replied in a spirit of warm cordiality and appreciation.

His publications embrace *Catalogus codicum orientalium MSS. qui in Museo Britannico asservantur. P. III. Codices Æthiopicos amplectens* (London, 1847); *Catalogus codicum manuscriptorum Bibliothecæ Bodleianæ Oxoniensis. P. VII. Codices Æthiopici, digessit A. Dillmann* (Oxford, 1848); *Liber Henoch, Æthiopice* (Leipsic, 1851); *Das Buch Henoch übersetzt u. erklärt* (1853); *Das christliche Adambuch des Morgenlandes, aus dem Aethiopischen übersetzt* (reprinted from Ewald's *Jahrbücher*, 1853); *Biblia Veteris Testamenti Æthiopica*, Tomus I. *Octateuchus*. Fasc. 1, *Genesin, Exodum, Leviticum* (1853). Fasc. 2, *Numeros et Deuteronomium* (1854). Fasc. 3, *Josua, Judicum et Ruth* (1855). Tomus II. Fasc. 1 et 2, *Libri*

Regum (1861 and 1871), vol. v. containing the *Apocrypha* (1894, but the missing vols. iii. and iv. will not appear); *Grammatik der äthiopischen Sprache* (1857, 2d ed., by C. Bezold, 1899; Eng. transl., 1907); *Liber Jubilæorum, Æthiopice* (1859); *Lexicon linguæ Æthiopicæ* (1865); *Chrestomathia Æthiopica cum glossario* (1866); *Liber Jubilæorum* (Kiel, 1859); for the *Kurzgefasstes exegetisches Handbuch* he edited *Hiob* (1869, 1891); *Genesis* (1882, 1886, 1892, Eng. transl., 2 vols., Edinburgh, 1897); *Exodus* and *Leviticus* (1880); *Numeri, Deuteronomium und Josua* (1886); *Jesaia* (1890); and posthumously, *Handbuch der alttestamentlichen Theologie* (Leipsic, 1895). He contributed also to Schenkel's *Bibel* or *Lexikon*, to Brockhaus' *Conversations-Lexikon*, and was associate editor of the *Jahrbücher fur deutsche Theologie*.

BIBLIOGRAPHY: W. Baudissin, *August Dillmann*, Leipsic, 1895; *Zur Erinnerung an . . . Dillmann*, Stuttgart, 1900.

DILTHEY, WILHELM: German philosopher; b. at Biebrich (3 m. s. of Wiesbaden) Nov. 10, 1833. He studied at Heidelberg and Berlin, was privat-docent in Berlin, and was appointed professor of philosophy at Basel in 1866. In 1868 he was called in the same capacity to Kiel, and in 1871 to Breslau. Since 1882 he has been professor of philosophy at Berlin. His writings include *Leben Schleiermachers* (Berlin, 1870); *Einleitung in die Geisteswissenschaften* (Leipsic, 1883); and *Das Erlebnis und die Dichtung* (1906).

DIMOERITES: According to Epiphanius (*Hær.*, lxxvii.), a name given to the followers of Apollinaris of Laodicea (q.v.), because, according to them, Christ had assumed only two of the three elements of the perfect human form, the *soma* and the *psychē alogos*, whereas the divine Logos himself took in him the place of the *nous*, the *psychē logikē*. G. KRÜGER.

DINTER, GUSTAV FRIEDRICH: German educator and theologian; b. at Borna (16 m. s.s.e. of Leipsic) Feb. 29, 1760; d. in Königsberg May 29, 1831. In 1773 he entered the Fürstenschule at Grimma, in 1779 the University of Leipsic. After serving as tutor he entered the ministry in 1787 as substitute at Kitscher, where his pastoral work, especially his untiring zeal for the education of the youth, made him greatly beloved. His success in training teachers for the lower schools led to his appointment as director of the normal school at Dresden in 1797. Because of ill health he returned to the ministry in 1807 at Görnitz, where he founded a progymnasium, which became famous as a training-school for the practical pursuits of life. He became member of the consistory and board of education in Königsberg, 1816; professor of theology, 1817. His *Schullehrerbibel* (9 vols., Neustadt, 1826-30) made a sensation. Starting with Semler's distinction between theology and religion, he sought in the Bible only that which, in his view, immediately belongs to religion; in this sphere, but not in science, the Bible should be the authority "To religion belong worthy conceptions of God, of Jesus and his work, of the sacredness of the moral law, of the worth and destiny of man, of the love of God even to the erring, of forgiveness of sins, of the help God renders us to be good," etc. Dinter repudiated strongly the charge that this is rationalism, and considered himself orthodox. In his method he was akin to Bahrdt, trying to reinterpret the language of the Bible in the spirit of his time, and believing that herein he followed Paul and Luther. His autobiography (Neustadt, 1829) gives the best key to his theology; it shows a vigorous, plain, jovial, practical, and sympathetic character. A complete edition of his writings was edited by J. C. B. Wilhelm (43 vols., Neustadt, 1840-51). (SANDER.)

DIOCLETIAN (Caius Valerius Diocletianus): Roman emperor 284-305; b. near Salona (3 m. n.n.e. of Spalato), Dalmatia, c. 225; d. there Dec. 3, 316. He was probably a slave by birth, but entered the army and rose to high rank, becoming consul and commander of the body-guards. After the death of Numerian he was proclaimed emperor by the legions near Chalcedon on Nov. 17, 284, and the assassination of Carinus in the following year left him sole emperor. He soon appointed his junior comrade Maximian Cæsar, and later made him co-regent, assigning him the Western half of the empire. A second division of the empire took place Mar. 1, 793, when two Cæsars were created, Caius Galerius Valerius Maximianus, who married Valeria, Diocletian's daughter, and Marcus Flavius Valerius Constantius. The reins of government remained in the hands of Diocletian, who was a born ruler, firmly convinced of the divinity of the imperial dignity. He possessed an interest in higher culture and was filled with a strong passion for building, though his refinement was but superficial and was frequently overborne by the savagery of his Illyrian blood.

In the latter part of the third century the Church was flourishing in consequence of its long peace, and many Christians were found in aristocratic society, in influential public positions, in the army, and even in the imperial household. Diocletian's wife, Prisca, and his daughter Valeria were at least catechumens. Shortly after his accession, however, Diocletian left no doubt as to his attitude toward Christianity by an anti-Manichean decree issued in Egypt and usually assigned to 287, forbidding all religious innovation under heavy penalty. The purging of the army by weeding out those who refused to sacrifice was the first measure directly planned to render the troops reliable. An ill-timed religious zeal offended the emperor and helped the anti-Christian party, headed by Galerius, who urged him on, despite his hesitation in fear of consequences. In the winter of 302-303 tedious conferences were held at Nicomedia, but it was only after the Milesian Apollo had been consulted that Diocletian yielded, though he insisted that no blood be shed. Galerius, however, overcame all his politic considerations and finally molded his religious policy. On Feb. 23, 303, the first edict was issued at Nicomedia. Christian freedmen were to be removed from public offices and were to lose their civic rights, while slaves were

The Diocletian Persecution.

deprived of the possibility of emancipation. The churches were to be demolished, the Scriptures were to be surrendered and burned, and religious meetings were prohibited. On the same day the destruction of the basilica of Nicomedia was begun and the Scriptures were publicly burned. Before the movement became general, however, a Nicomedian official scornfully tore the edict down, and the palace was twice set on fire, the incendiary, according to the Christians, being Galerius, who hoped thus to impel the emperor to more drastic measures. Rebellions broke out in Armenia and Syria, and were naturally laid to the charge of the Christians. That the latter resolved upon active resistance and rebellion lacks justification, although it is not impossible that individuals, either secretly or openly, aided the usurpers in the East. The effect, however, could not but be unfavorable upon Diocletian's mind. A second edict was issued, similar to that of Decius, decreeing the imprisonment of all the clergy. Diocletian's original injunction forbidding the effusion of blood was soon forgotten in the general tumult. The multitude of prisoners caused no little trouble, and a new decree enacted that the sacrifice required by the second edict should be exacted by all means. In 304 another edict universalized the decree concerning sacrifice and abolished the distinction between clergy and laity, aiming primarily to detach the latter, who were far inferior to the clergy in zeal for the Church. Patient persuasion was also employed, and steadfast refusal led to punishment, torture, and execution. In many cases the decree was only superficially enforced. The leading spirit in all these events was Galerius; Maximian was a minor figure; and Constantius, already in sympathy with the Christians, was as conservative as possible, contenting himself with the demolition of buildings.

The End of the Persecution.

On May 1, 305, Diocletian abdicated and forced Maximian to do the same. Their places were filled by the Augusti, Galerius and Constantius, the new Cæsars being Maximinus Daza, a nephew of Galerius, who received Syria, Palestine, and Egypt, and Severus, an uneducated officer of low birth, who received Italy, Africa, and Pannonia. The West remained peaceful, but in the East the persecution was rendered still more severe by the measures of Maximinus. Constantius died July 25, 306, and the army proclaimed his son Constantine Augustus. The ultimate outcome of rebellions and wars was the victory of Constantine at the Milvian Bridge, Oct. 28, 312, and soon afterward the so-called religious decree of Milan brought peace to the Church in the West (see CONSTANTINE THE GREAT). Meanwhile the situation had changed in the East; circumstances compelled Galerius to cease from persecuting, and toward the end of Apr., 311, he and his coregent issued an edict in which they admitted the inefficiency of their efforts to restore religious uniformity. This was the first decree which officially recognized the Christian religion in the Roman empire, although the vagueness of the clause, "yet so as that they offend not against good order," left a loophole for the State. In the autumn, however, when scarcely six months had elapsed, Maximinus, now being the oldest Augustus, renewed the persecution. Christians were inhumanly mutilated and executed. The customary funeral services in the cemeteries were forbidden, possibly on the pretext that they were a cloak for immorality; religious meetings and the building of churches were prohibited; and delegates of the cities petitioned for the exclusion of the Christians. The defeat and death of Maxentius, the insignificant but ambitious son of Maximian, who had overthrown Severus, suddenly changed the situation, and the victorious Constantine advised Maximinus to cease oppressing the Christians. The result was a circular letter addressed by Maximinus in the latter part of 312, prohibiting the use of violence against Christians. On Apr. 30, 313, Maximinus was defeated in Thrace by Licinianus Licinius and forced to retire to Nicomedia. There, where the persecutions had been begun, an edict of toleration was issued on June 13, proclaiming the principle of religious liberty with special regard to the Christians. Every invidious distinction which still existed was abolished, and all property, including the confiscated places of assembly, was to be restored at once to the Church as a legal person. Licinius assisted in rebuilding churches, while Maximinus retired beyond the Taurus and issued a new edict emphasizing his later measures. Soon afterward he died, imploring the help of Christ in his agony and despair. All memorials of him were destroyed by the victor, and his wife and children, together with the wife and daughter of Diocletian and other relatives and adherents of the fallen dynasty, were murdered with shameful barbarity. Thus ended the ten years of the Diocletian persecution.

In his retirement Diocletian witnessed all these events, but every effort to induce him to leave Salona for public life was in vain. After a long and painful illness he died, perhaps by his own hand, and was buried in the splendid mausoleum of his palace. The bitter hostility of Christian writers toward him is readily intelligible. He was the

Its Results.

cause of the longest and bloodiest persecution which the Church experienced, and its continuation by his successors was regarded as his legacy. In a rapid series of edicts of increasing severity this persecution oppressed the congregations and resulted in a refinement of cruelty which surpassed all that had gone before. The effect of the first decree, which interfered so deeply with civic life, was tremendous. The reaction, both contemporary and subsequent, against apostasy produced Donatism in Africa and Meletianism in Egypt, besides causing schisms of more or less importance in many other places. Flight was not considered apostasy by the Church, and it frequently afforded a means of safety, though there were many who endured torture, imprisonment, reproach, and death. The enthusiasm for martyrdom induced some to anticipate their trial by a self-chosen death, and women and virgins preferred suicide to dishonor. Self-accusation and violent denunciation of heathenism also took place, while life itself was considered less valuable than the safety of the Scriptures. The clergy of all ranks fell by scores, though the Roman bishop Marcellinus made an offering of incense. The rich growth of martyrological literature in prose and poetry and the cult of martyrs, which soon became both wide-spread and important, were but expressions of the feeling with which Christendom looked back upon its "soldiers of the faith."

VICTOR SCHULTZE.

BIBLIOGRAPHY: Sources most productive are Eusebius, *Hist. eccl.*, books viii.-ix.; Lactantius, *De mortibus persecutorum*. The best monograph is A. J. Mason, *The Persecution of Diocletian*, Cambridge, 1876. Consult: T. Bernhardt, *Diokletian in seinem Verhältniss zu den Christen*, Bonn, 1862; O. Hunziger, *Zur Regierung und Christenverfolgung . . . 303-313*, Leipsic, 1868; B. Aubé, *Histoire des persécutions de l'église*, 2 vols., Paris, 1875-78; G. Uhlhorn, *Der Kampf des Christenthums mit dem Heidentum*, Stuttgart, 1889, Eng. transl., New York, 1880; V. Schultze, *Geschichte des Untergangs des griechisch-römischen Heidentums*, 2 vols., Jena, 1887-92; P. Allard, *La Persécution de Dioclétien et le triomphe de l'église*, 2 vols., Paris, 1900; idem, *Les Dernières Persécutions du 3. siècle*, ib. 1897; E. Le Blant, *Les Persécuteurs . . . aux premiers siècles*, Paris, 1893; O. Seeck, *Geschichte des Untergangs der antiken Welt*, vol. i., Berlin, 1897; G. Boissier, *La Fin du paganisme*, 2 vols., ib. 1901; L. Pullan, *Church of the Fathers*, chap. xvi., New York, 1905; Neander, *Christian Church*, i. 147-155 et passim, ii. passim; Schaff, *Christian Church*, ii. 64-74; Gibbon, *Decline and Fall*, chaps. xiii.-xvi.; *DCB*, i. 833-836.

DIODATI, dî"o-dā'ti, GIOVANNI: Genevan Reformer; b. at Lucca June 6, 1576; d. at Geneva Oct. 3, 1649. His family was compelled by religious persecution to flee from Italy. He was a rigid Calvinist, and while still a young man was appointed to teach Hebrew in the Academy of Geneva (1597), and later became professor of dogmatics. As one of the Genevan deputies to the Synod of Dort in 1618, he took part in the compilation of the canons of that body. He translated the Bible into Italian (Geneva, 1607), his version meeting with a success comparable with that of Luther's German rendering. He also prepared a revision of the French translation which had been made by the pastors and professors of Geneva in 1588, enriching his work by valuable notes and elucidations (Eng. transl., *Pious Annotations upon the Holy Bible*, London, 1643). He translated into French Sarpi's *Historia del concilio tridentino* (1621) and Sir Edwin Sandys's *Relation of the State of Religion* (1626). Diodati was a remarkable preacher and one of the most distinguished defenders of the Reformed Church, while the ambition of his life was the conversion of his native land, and especially the republic of Venice, to his own creed.

EUGÈNE CHOISY.

BIBLIOGRAPHY: E. de Budé, *Vie de Jean Diodati*, Geneva, 1869; G. D. J. Schotel, *Jean Diodati*, The Hague, 1844; P. Plan, *Lettres trouvées, pages historiques sur un épisode de la vie de Jean Diodati*, ib. 1864; Maria Betts, *Life of Giovanni Diodati, Genevese Theologian*, London, 1905.

DIO"DO'RUS: Presbyter in Antioch, after 378 bishop of Tarsus; d. before 394. He was a native of Antioch, one of the most prominent theologians of the school of Antioch (q.v.), and on the dogmatic side its founder. After a general education at Athens he equipped himself as a theologian and orator by studying the writings of, and by personal intercourse with Eusebius of Emesa. His aim was twofold: to attain the fulness of ascetic perfection, and to be a champion of the Church's faith. He strove with all his energy to fulfil the monastic ideal, and the emperor Julian pointed to his wasted body as a proof of the displeasure of the gods. The state of the Church in Antioch called forth all his zeal as a presbyter. Not only had Julian, who made his winter quarters there after his return from the Persian campaign, restored the temple of Apollo and used all his influence to win the population back to paganism, but most of the heretical sects were strong there. It was the center of Arianism, and the Meletian schism had rent the Church in two. Diodorus was the leading defender of the Nicene faith. Naturally, therefore, his writings, of which the later Syrian Church still knew over sixty, were mainly controversial. They were directed against all the principal enemies of the Church, pagan, Jewish, and heretic. Of the philosophers he especially combated Plato, Aristotle, and Porphyry; among heretics the Manicheans, Eunomians, and Apollinarians, Sabellius, Marcellus, and Photinus. He employed, too, a very practical churchly activity against both pagans and Arians; and his success, while it raised up bitter enemies for him, made his name honored throughout the Eastern Church. Even as a layman, under Constantius, when the Arian Leontius occupied the episcopal chair of Antioch, with his friend Flavian, Diodorus had assembled the faithful by night for worship. When the gentle Meletius became bishop in 360 Diodorus supported him vigorously and watched over the welfare of the flock when the bishop was obliged by Arian enmity to flee, and went from house to house strengthening the devotion of the oppressed faithful. In 372 he was forced to join the banished Meletius in Armenia. Here he made friends with Basil the Great, and the orthodoxy of Cappadocia and of Antioch joined hands to insure the triumph of the Nicene faith. Six years later he was consecrated bishop of Tarsus by Meletius (378). In this capacity he took part in the Council of Constantinople (381), and is said to have brought about the choice of Nectarius as patriarch. The council gave him metropolitan jurisdiction over Cilicia. An imperial edict of 381 names him among the bishops who were to decide the question of Nicene orthodoxy and consequently of membership in the Catholic Church.

Life and Literary Activity.

By a curious turn of fate, he who had been honored as a pillar of the true faith by his contemporaries fell under suspicion of heresy not forty years after his death, as a result of the Nestorian controversy. In his anxiety to vindicate the significance of the human element in the person of Christ and in the Scriptures, threatened by an overstrained idealism, in controversy with Apollinaris Diodorus had put forth a theory of the relation of the two natures in Christ which seemed to dissolve the one divine-human Person into two. According to the fragments still preserved of the works called in question ("Against the Synusiasts" and "On the Holy Spirit"), he apparently distinguished between the Logos and the Son of David, one the Son of God by nature, the other by grace. Mary's son was not the Logos,

Theological Opinions.

but the man begotten of the Holy Spirit. Since the Logos is essentially perfect, what is read in Scripture (Luke ii. 52) of a development in the Savior can only relate to his humanity. The mystery of the Incarnation consists in the assumption of a perfect man by the Logos, and the relation of the two natures is that of the indwelling of the Logos in the man Jesus as in a temple. In consequence of this connection, the son of David may be called the Son of God, but only in a derived sense; adoration is due to the humanity of Christ, but only so long as the distinction of nature is borne in mind. The spirit of God dwelt also in the prophets, but only temporarily and in a smaller measure; in Christ he dwelt permanently and without measure. This ethic-dynamic view, based on the teaching of Paul of Samosata and Lucian, did not, of course, content Greek piety and orthodoxy. When partizan zeal drove out Nestorianism as heresy the blow could not but react on the Christology of the older Antiochian theologians. Thus Cyril of Alexandria in several treatises demanded the condemnation of Diodorus and Theodore of Mopsuestia; but the whole Syrian Church rose up to vindicate its revered teacher, and an imperial edict put an end to the dangerous business.

It was not till 499 that Bishop Flavian of Antioch, hard pressed by the Monophysites, ventured to pronounce an anathema on the writings of Diodorus and Theodore. No such condemnation, however, is found in the acts of the fifth general council (Second Constantinople, 553). But the suspicion of heresy clung to Diodorus, and most of his works perished. The Nestorians alone kept alive the memory of the man and the theologian as long as their own existence lasted. He must have been of considerable force in exegesis, following out the grammatico-historical principles of his school in a commentary covering nearly the whole Bible, which was marked by philological learning, independence of dogmatic prejudice, careful distinction of the Old and New Testament stages of revelation, clearness, and sobriety. Only a few fragments are scattered through the catenæ; most of what remains is in *MPG*, xxxiii., but needs sifting. Diodorus's mind was not creative, but one that combined extensive learning with strongly marked dialectic individuality. Even his opponents respected his zeal for the truth, and his life was without reproach. He has a special historical importance from the fact that he trained for the Church more than one of its prominent teachers. In his school were matured the two great Greek Fathers Theodore of Mopsuestia, in whom the theology of Antioch reached its completest form, and John Chrysostom. (A. HARNACK.)

BIBLIOGRAPHY: Sources are Jerome, *De vir. ill.*, chap. cxix.; Chrysostom, *Laus Diodori;* Socrates, *Hist. eccl.*, vi. 3; Sozomen, *Hist. eccl.*, viii. 2 (the two last-named in *NPNF*, 2d series, vol. ii.); and Theodoret, *Hist. eccl.*, iv. 22-24 (in *NPNF*, vol. iii.). Consult: *KL*, iii. 1765–68; *DCB*, i. 836-840.

DIOGNETUS, EPISTLE TO: An early Christian work, formerly preserved in a manuscript in the Strasburg Library, where it was included in a collection of the writings of Justin Martyr, with the heading "His [Epistle] to Diognetus." The manuscript perished in the siege of Strasburg in 1870. A late copy of it still exists at Leyden, from which Stephanus published it in 1592, and Sylburg in 1593. According to Otto, the manuscript belonged to the thirteenth or fourteenth century, and had a good original, though the copy was somewhat carelessly made. What seems to be a considerable hiatus is observed in the seventh chapter, and the present conclusion is probably not the original one.

The letter is addressed to one Diognetus, in answer to his question how Christianity may be distinguished from paganism and Judaism, why it came so late into the world, and whence its disciples draw their courage and contempt of the world. In answer to the first question, the author considers paganism as mere crude idolatry, admitting that the Jews have the advantage of a pure knowledge of God, though their material sacrifices and trivial ceremonial law are as foolish as the heathen system. In the second part he describes the Christian worship and ethics, and in the third explains the late arrival of this revelation by God's will, to let the world see how helpless mere human powers were to win the heavenly crown. When the measure of their sins was full he revealed himself by the Incarnation of his son, who, though sinless, paid the penalty of sin, so that men, now justified, might trust in the fatherly goodness of God. Hence springs the love which raises Christians so far above worldly rewards or penalties, and the fraternal devotion which makes their life on earth a foretaste of heaven.

There is no mention of the letter in any ancient writer, though here and there, as in Tertullian's *Apologeticus*, some scholars have thought they saw allusions to passages of it. No one seems to have known of it until the edition of Stephanus, nor does the epistle contain any indications from which a satisfactory conjecture as to its date or authorship can be made. Its attribution to Justin was originally accepted, but Semisch has demonstrated that it can not be his. The language and literary style are too correct; the attitude of the letter toward both Judaism and paganism is not at all Justin's; and in its cosmology there is no trace of his favorite thought of the operation of the "spermatic logos" in the non-Christian world.

There is less certainty, however, about the date of composition. While Semisch, Bunsen, and others adhered to Justin's period, attempts were made to throw it still farther back, with Ewald into the reign of Hadrian, or with Hefele into that of Trajan, or even into the first century. Hilgenfeld and Keim assign it to the second, and Zahn puts it between 250 and 310. A new stage of the investigation opened with the discovery of the "Apology" of Aristides, to which the letter stands in a secondary or derived relation, though not close enough for Aristides to have been the author, as Krüger thought. This relation helps to clear the ground for a decision as to the date, placing it between that of the "Apology" (from 138 to 161, probably 147) and that of Constantine. Seeberg is probably right when he supposes some time to have elapsed between the two works; and, on the other hand, the author of the Epistle does not seem to have been through a general persecution. About the beginning of the third century, then, will be a safe date. The importance of the Epistle has been much overestimated in the past. Its rhetorical force and smoothness have possibly helped to evoke this enthusiasm, which, however, has in large measure disappeared; and it contributes scarcely anything to our knowledge of the history of dogma.

(G. Uhlhorn†.)

Bibliography: Good editions are by C. Otto, Leipsic, 1852; O. von Gebhardt and A. Harnack, *Patrum apostolicorum opera*, I. ii. 154-164, Leipsic, 1878; B. L. Gildersleeve, in *Apology of Justin Martyr*, pp. 83-94, New York, 1877; F. X. Funk, in *Opera patrum apostolicorum*, i. 310-333, Tübingen, 1881. Eng. transl. may be found in B. Cooper, *Free Church of Ancient Christendom*, London, 1852, and in *ANF*, i. 25-30. A list of literature is given in *ANF*, Index vol., pp. 5-7. Consult: C. G. Semisch, *Justin Martyr*, i. 172 sqq., Breslau, 1840, Eng. transl., i. 84-193, Edinburgh, 1832; C. K. J. Bunsen, *Hippolytus*, i. 138 sqq., Leipsic, 1852, Eng. transl., London, 1852; G. H. H. Ewald, *Geschichte des Volkes Israel*, vii. 250 sqq., Göttingen, 1868; F. Overbeck, *Ueber den pseudo-justinianischen Brief an Diognet*, Basel, 1872; A. Hilgenfeld, *ZWT*, xvi (1873), 270-286; T. Keim, in *Protestantische Kirchenzeitung*, 1873, pp. 285-289, 309-314; T. Zahn, *GGA*, 1873, pp. 106-116; H. Kihn, *Der Ursprung des Briefs an Diognet*, Freiburg, 1882; J. A. Robinson, in *TS*, i. 1 (1891), 95-97; Kruger, *History*, pp. 135-137; idem, in *ZWT*, xxxvii (1894), 206-223; *KL*, iii. 1774-78; *DCB*, ii. 162-167.

DIONYSIUS, dai″o-nish′i-us: Pope 259-268. During the pontificate of Stephen (254-257) he took part in the controversy about heretical baptism, with his fellow presbyter Philemon addressing a letter to Dionysius of Alexandria. Elected bishop on July 22, 259, the edict of toleration of Gallienus soon enabled him to bring the Roman Church into order. He had a share in dogmatic development through his further dealings with his namesake of Alexandria, who had already been in communication with Sixtus II. concerning Sabellianism, and had been led by his zeal against this heresy to use expressions which seemed to reduce Christ to the position of a creature. Some Egyptian clergy brought the matter before Dionysius of Rome, who dealt with it in a synod and gave out a dogmatic pronouncement, of which a large section is preserved by Athanasius ("On the Council of Nicæa," xxvi.). It was no doubt addressed to Egyptian or Libyan bishops, and attacked the Sabellian teaching on one side, while on the other it rebuked anti-Sabellian extremes. At the same time he wrote to his namesake asking him to clear himself of the charges made against him, which resulted in the well-known "Retractations" of Dionysius of Alexandria (q.v.). Dionysius of Rome also wrote a letter of condolence to the Church of Cæsarea in Cappadocia when it was attacked by the Goths about 264, and sent representatives to ransom captive Christians. His name appears with that of Maximus of Alexandria, the successor of Dionysius, at the head of the bishops to whom the last council held in Antioch against Paul of Samosata addressed its synodical epistle (Eusebius, *Hist. eccl.*, VII. xxx.).

(A. Hauck.)

Bibliography: *Liber pontificalis*, ed. Duchesne, i. 157, Paris, 1886, ed. Mommsen, in *MGH*, *Gest. pont. Rom.*, i (1898), 36; R. A. Lipsius, *Chronologie der römischen Bischöfe*, Kiel, 1869; J. Langen, *Geschichte der römischen Kirche*, pp. 353, Bonn, 1881; Bower, *Popes*, i. 35-37; Milman, *Latin Christianity*, i. 91; Neander, *Christian Church*, i. 606-610, ii. 404; Schaff, *Christian Church*, ii. 570-571.

DIONYSIUS OF ALEXANDRIA (called the Great): Bishop of Alexandria; d. 264. A pupil of Origen, though but little younger than his teacher, he succeeded Heraclas in 231 or 232 as head of the catechetical school of Alexandria, and became bishop in 247 or 248. The Decian persecution soon fell upon him (250). Attempting to escape, he was arrested, but was unexpectedly set at liberty. He next appears writing to Novatian in the hope of restraining him, and his inclination toward mildness in discipline comes out in other letters. He took a similar conciliatory position in the controversy on heretic baptism; his own principles placed him on the Roman side, but he respected the views of his opponents and was unwilling to break off communion with them. In the persecution under Valerian (257) he was banished, first to Kephron in Libya and then to Kolluthion in the Mareotis district, and returned to Alexandria only after the edict of Gallienus (260), to suffer further trials from revolt, plague, and famine, of which he has left a vivid picture (in Eusebius, *Hist. eccl.*, vii. 22). In the spirit of the Alexandrian school, he assisted in the overthrow of Millenarianism. In the Trinitarian controversy he endeavored to uphold the Origenistic position as far as possible, but was carried beyond it by the course of the controversy and his own logic. His letters against Sabellianism contained expressions which were thought to decide in a contrary direction, and gave rise to accusations brought against him before Dionysius of Rome, to whom he justified himself in four books, partly explaining away or retracting the expressions complained of, and partly taking refuge in vague language. Before his death he took a decided stand against Paul of Samosata by letter, since his age and infirmity prevented him from attending the synod at Antioch. He was the most important of the disciples of Origen, and a worthy representative of the older Alexandrian school, though not enough of an independent thinker to understand and guide the doctrinal tendencies of his time. His importance in exegesis, after the manner of Origen, is shown by his short critical comparison of the Gospel and Revelation of John, undertaken with the purpose of demonstrating a diversity of authorship, and considered by some modern writers a still unsurpassed treatment of the question. The most important remains of his literary activity are his letters, which include at least six on the treatment of the Lapsed (q.v.), at least eight on the schism of Novatian, at least eight on heretic baptism, at least four on Sabellianism, a long series of annual Easter letters, and a number to individuals. Only fragments of certain letters are preserved, although Dionysius was the chief source used by Eusebius for the middle of the third century.

(A. Harnack.)

Bibliography: The Fragments of Dionysius are collected in M. J. Routh, *Reliquiæ Sacræ*, iii. 219-250, iv. 393-437, Oxford, 1846, and in *MPG*, x. Also, *Letters and Remains of Dionysius of Alexandria*, ed. C. L. Feltoe, Cambridge, 1904. Eng. transl. is in *ANF*, vi. 81-120 Literature is given in *ANF*, Bibliography, pp. 66–68. Sources are: Jerome, *De vir. ill.*, chap. lxix.; Athanasius, *De sententiis Dionysii*; Eusebius, *Hist. eccl.*, vi. 40 sqq. (cf. especially *NPNF*, 2d series, i. 281, note). Consult: F. Dittrich, *Dionysius der Grosse*, Freiburg, 1867; T. Förster, *De doctrina et sententiis Dionysii*, Berlin, 1865; Krüger, *History*, pp. 205–215; Harnack, *Litteratur*, i. 409–427, II, ii. 57–66 et passim; Neander, *Christian Church*, vols. i.–ii. passim; Schaff, *Christian Church*, ii. 800–803; *DCB*, i. 850–852; *KL*, iii. 1780–89.

DIONYSIUS THE AREOPAGITE.

Writings Ascribed to Dionysius (§ 1).
Proofs of Late Origin (§ 2).
Doctrine of the Soul (§ 3).
Doctrine of First Person of Trinity (§ 4).
Doctrine of the Universe (§ 5).
Doctrine of the Son (§ 6).
Doctrine of the Church (§ 7).

Dionysius the Areopagite was converted to Christianity by the sermon of Paul at Athens (Acts xvii. 34). According to Eusebius (*Hist. eccl.*, iii. 4, iv. 23) and the Apostolic Constitutions (vii. 46), he was the first bishop of Athens; a later tradition affirms that he suffered martyrdom there. His importance in church history depends upon the ascription to him of a series of remarkable writings in Greek, probably belonging to the fifth or sixth century, entitled "On the Heavenly

1. Writings Ascribed to Dionysius.

Hierarchy," "On the Ecclesiastical Hierarchy," "On the Names of God," and "On Mystical Theology," and ten letters, all evidently belonging to the same author. At the conference held in Constantinople (533), at the instance of Justinian, between the orthodox and the Severians, the latter quoted, among other ecclesiastical authorities, Dionysius the Areopagite against the Council of Chalcedon; and when the orthodox objected that Athanasius and Cyril certainly would have used such an authority against Nestorius, if he had existed and been known to them, the Severians asserted that Cyril had actually quoted the works of Dionysius in his books against Diodorus of Tarsus and Theodore of Mopsuestia, as might be seen from the copies of those books in the libraries of Alexandria. This is the first certain citation of the works supposed to be written by Dionysius, but after that time they are frequently mentioned. Severus himself, Monophysite patriarch of Antioch 512–518, often quotes them, as does Ephraem, orthodox patriarch of Antioch 527–545. Commentaries upon them were written by John of Scythopolis about 530, Sergius of Resaina (d. 536) translated them into Syriac, and Leontius of Byzantium cited Dionysius. In the Western Church Gregory the Great is the first who refers to these writings (*Hom.*, xxxiv.); but when the Byzantine emperor Michael the Stammerer sent a copy of them to Louis the Pious in 827 they soon became better known; and after the invention of Abbot Hilduin, combining Dionysius the Areopagite and St. Denis, the patron saint of the Franks, in one person (see DENIS, SAINT), they became quite celebrated. Johannes Scotus Erigena translated them into Latin at the instance of Charles the Bald, and was himself deeply influenced by them. In the Western Church, among the schoolmen, the Areopagite became a guide to mysticism and mystical theology. Hugo of St. Victor, Albertus Magnus, Dionysius the Carthusian, and others drew their inspiration from him. Corderius has shown how much, for instance, Thomas Aquinas owes to the Areopagite. The Platonists of the Italian Renaissance also appreciated him highly, as did other humanists, like John Colet.

The development, however, of literary criticism (under Laurentius Valla, Erasmus, and others) inevitably destroyed, first, the invention of Hilduin (the identification of Dionysius and St. Denis), and, second, the assumption of authorship in apostolic times. The internal evidences of a later date, besides the total absence of mention or quotation till the conference of Constantinople (533), were conclusive. The most decisive inter-

2. Proofs of Late Origin.

nal evidences are: the difference between the pompous and inflated style of the writings and the simplicity of the apostolic age; the use of theological terms which were not formed until the fourth century; references to an elaborately developed church ritual and church government; allusions to later persons and events, as, for instance, to the martyrdom of Ignatius and to "Clement the Philosopher" (Clement of Alexandria); and appeals to "ancient traditions." The defense of Roman Catholic theologians and the attempted vindication of the authorship of Dionysius the Areopagite were demolished by Daillé and Le Nourry.

The question then arose, By whom and at what time were these works written? A number of hypotheses were proffered, differing as widely as that of Baumgarten-Crusius, placing the author at Alexandria in the third century, and that of Westcott, placing him at Edessa at the beginning of the sixth century. The general outcome of critical inquiry is that the philosophical, and more especially the mystical, ideas expounded in these books presuppose the later development of Neoplatonism which was due to Proclus; and, as Proclus died 485, the date of the books seems to coincide nearly with the date of their first notice.

Dionysius distinguishes between a cataphatic (affirmative or positive) theology, in which truth is presented under the garb of a symbol of history, or of the traditionary teaching of the Church, and an apophatic (negative) theology, which dispenses with such media, in which also the initiated rises by contemplation or in the ecstatic

3. Doctrine of the Soul.

state to an immediate view of things divine. He distinguishes a direct movement of the soul, when its knowledge is conditioned by the various things outside of it; a spiral movement, when it aspires to penetrate divine knowledge by discursive thinking; and a circular movement, when it guides its united power to the Deity ("Names of God," iv. 9). Under the influence of deity it surrenders its own thinking and arrives at a condition of Ecstasy (q.v.) and the mystic view of God. There is here a strong resemblance to the teachings of Philo and the Neoplatonists.

Dionysius believes in the dogma of the Trinity, but his chief interest centers in the Father. The Father is for him the sole source of transcendent divinity; Jesus and the Holy Spirit are the offspring, bloom, and transcendent light ("Names of God," ii. 5, 7). The being of God *per se*, his real essence, can not be expressed, since it transcends all qualities. The Deity includes every perfection; it is the cause and essence of all being,

4. Doctrine of First Person of Trinity.

and yet it is above all being; it is without quality, yet transcends the highest conception of goodness; without a name, yet including every name. The highest principle is neither sensuous nor spiritual, has or is neither representation nor understanding nor reason, is neither One, deity, nor goodness, and yet is neither without essence nor without life, understanding or reason, since the negations also have to be denied. Just as apophatic theology, proceeding from the broad variety of things, by negation ascends to the highest cause and to mystic unity with the unspeakable, so cataphatic theology proceeds from above and descends to the variety of creatures. Accordingly God becomes sun, star, fire, water, and all being; as the all-comprehensive cause he is all in all because the cause has anticipated everything in itself. He is all in all, and yet not anything in any one thing. But not everything may be affirmed or denied of him in an equal degree. He is life and goodness in a more pregnant sense than light or star, and such affections as intoxication (Ps. lxxviii. 65, LXX.) or fits of anger are to be denied of him in a higher degree than the statements that he can be expressed or cognized.

But all being has proceeded from the nature of God. All emanation of being has its original exemplar in the development of the divine first cause into the hypostases of the Trinity; all fatherhood and sonship of godlike spirits and even of human beings proceeds from the original fatherhood and original sonship. The participation of all things in being is at the same time a partici-

5. Doctrine of the Universe.

pation in the good and the beautiful which is one with true being; the transcendent good and beautiful is the cause of all goodness and beauty and of all participation in the good and the beautiful ("Names of God," iv. 1 sqq.); but between cause and effect there is not the relation of entire equality. Here Dionysius shares Proclus's view concerning evil according to which all existing things have no real being, but are only privation, want, diminution of the good, since all being as such is good. If therefore the universe appears on the one hand as the product of the good, it is on the other hand also the product of the differentiating negation which penetrates the unity of the absolute. But this negation does not exist for God because in him all differences are done away with. God knows evil as good, and before him the causes of evil are powers working for the good ("Names of God," iv. 20). Correspondingly, the universe is placed under the view-point of existence in God as first cause; and also, as being finite and separate, under the view-point of striving toward God as the basis and aim of all creatures ("Names of God," i. 5, cf. "Heavenly Hierarchy," iv. 1). These two points of view find their expression especially in the doctrine concerning the hierarchy of being. Dionysius assumes descending derivation of the chain of beings, and a mediation for the ascension of all creatures toward unity with God. The highest spiritual beings, the angels, are in the antechamber, so to speak, of the transcendent Trinity, and have from it and in it their existence and likeness to God ("Names of God," v. 8). They are good and communicate their goodness to those below them (iv. 1). The hierarchy of angels contains three divisions: (1) seraphim, cherubim, thrones; (2) dominions, powers, forces; (3) principalities, archangels, angels.

The system of the heavenly hierarchy is followed by that of the earthly or rather ecclesiastical hierarchy. Here Dionysius has interwoven with his doctrine concerning the hierarchies the idea of redemption as a historical fact. God is salvation and redemption in so far as he not only guards the existing things from falling into nothingness, but also in so far as he redeems that which has departed from the right and suffered a diminution of goodness by an abuse of freedom of the will (ib. iv. 18). Dionysius looks upon the institutions of the Church as mysteries, "Jesus" is the cause of everything; he is the transcendent cause of the superheavenly beings ("Heavenly Hierarchy," iv. 4); in regard to his activity in the world, he is the transcendent One, the Logos, the principle of all hierarchy and theurgy. But the influence of Jesus upon the lower spheres is not like that of the angels. He

6. Doctrine of the Son.

became man; he subsisted among us perfect and without change ("Names of God," ii. 3). By stepping into earthly reality, the transcendent was not abolished or subjected to any change. The nature of Jesus became really and truly human, and he participated in all human conditions; but in physical conditions he was superphysical and under the conditions of being he was above being by possessing all human qualities, yet in a transcendent manner. Thus Dionysius depicts him as walking upon the sea because he was not subject to the laws of gravity. It is evident from the above that the incarnation of Jesus was not reduced to a mere semblance; but the divine in Christ assumes such a human reality that the human is elevated above itself and deified.

The Gospel is the announcement that God according to his goodness has descended to us and makes us like himself by uniting us with himself. Men had departed from true life and surrendered to evil-minded demons. According to secret (oral) tradition, Christ has broken the power of the demons over us, not by an act of might, but by a forensic negotiation with the devil, the head of the demons. But every effect of salvation is conditioned for each one by submitting to the sanctions of ecclesiastical hierarchy which, like the heavenly hierarchy, proceeds from the divine *Nous* as the principle of all hierarchy and divine efficacy, whose aim is love to God and to the divine, knowl-

7. Doctrine of the Church.

edge of being, vision, union, and deification. While the sanctions of material spirits secure pure and immediate knowledge of God, man needs symbolic veilings. The hierarchy of Old Testament law educated by means of obscure pictures and riddles for the spiritual service of God, and found its fulfilment in ecclesiastical hierarchy which stands midway between the heavenly and the legal and is based chiefly upon Scripture and tradition. The apostles were bound to communicate the supersensuous in sensuous pictures because man needs sensuous mediation. In every hierarchic transaction there are to be distinguished (1) the holy consecrations, (2) officiants, (3) candidates for consecration. The consecrating acts are (a) baptism, the symbol of regeneration which consists in cleansing and illumination; (b) communion, the symbol of the fact that Jesus unites us in his original divine unity, for illumination leads to union; (c) unction as completing communion. The estate of the officiants consists of three grades: (a) hierarch (i.e., bishop), (b) hiereus (priest-presbyter), (c) liturgist (i.e., deacon); the last performs the purifying acts of the hierarchy, the second the illuminating acts, and the first the completing acts. In the order of the consecrated there are distinguished (a) the lowest who under the supervision of the liturgist are first to be purified; (b) those that are illuminated, Christian laymen, guided by the priests; (c) the therapeutai, i.e., monks who by the hierarchy are guided to perfection and lead a life solely devoted to the One.

Dionysius was of decisive importance in the change of the Anatolian Church into a cult of mysteries in that he created its systematic basis. It was he who first expressed coherently those thoughts which afterward shaped the Christianity of that Church, the characteristic features of which were desire for learning and especially participation in the mysteries. (N. Bonwetsch.)

Bibliography: The editio princeps was issued in Florence, 1516; the whole works, with the *Scholia* of Maximus and Pachymerus are in *MPG*, iii.-iv. The "Mystical Theology," best edition by B. Corderius, with notes, Antwerp, 1634, reissued with enlarged notes, 2 vols., Venice, 1755-1756. The edition by John Colet of "The Heavenly Hierarchy" and "The Eccl. Hierarchy" with Colet's treatises was reissued and translated by J. H. Lupton, London, 1869; the *Works* were translated by J. Parker, ib. 1897. The fabulous *Acta sancti Dionysii Areopagitæ*, with commentary, are in *ASB*, Oct., iv. 696-797.

Consult: J. G. V. Engelhardt, *De origine scriptorum Areopagitæ*, Erlangen, 1823; idem, *De origine scriptorum Dionysii*, ib. 1823; E. von Muralt, *Beiträge zur alten Litteratur, Dionysius Areopagita*, St. Petersburg, 1844; F. Hipler, *Dionysius der Areopagiter*, Regensburg, 1861 (an epoch-making work); J. Niemeyer, *Dionysius Areopagita*, Halle, 1869; J. Fowler, *The Works of Dionysius especially in Reference to Christian Art*, London, 1872; J. Dräseke, in *ZWT*, 1882, pp. 300 sqq.; C. M. Schneider, *Areopagitica*, Regensburg, 1884 (defends authenticity); A. L. Frothingham, *Stephen bar Sudaili. The Syrian Mystic and the Book of Hierotheus*, Leyden, 1886; R. Foss, *Ueber den Abt Hilduin von St. Denys und Dionysius Areopagita*, Berlin, 1886; H. Koch, in *TQ*, 1895, pp. 353 sqq.; N. Nilles, in *ZKT*, 1896; Neander, *Christian Church*, vols. ii.-iv. passim; Harnack, *Dogma*, vols. i., iii.-vi. passim, see Index; *DCB*, i. 841-848 (a noteworthy article); *KL*, iii. 1789-96.

DIONYSIUS THE CARTHUSIAN (Dionysius van Leeuwen or Leuwis): Monk, ascetic, and theologian; b. at Rickel (40 m. e. of Brussels), Limburg, Belgium, 1402 or 1403; d. at Roermonde (45 m. n.w. of Cologne), Limburg, Holland, Mar. 21, 1471. Before he was twenty-one he obtained the dignity of magister at Cologne, and entered the Carthusian monastery of Roermonde. Complying with the strictest rules of his order or rather surpassing them, he continued his studies with indefatigable zeal and was highly honored by his contemporaries. Cardinal Nicholas of Cusa, when traveling through Germany as legate took him in 1451 as his companion (cf. F. A. Scharpff, *Der Kardinal und Bischof Nicolaus von Cusa*, p. 176, Mainz, 1843; J. M. Düx, *Der deutsche Cardinal Nicolaus von Cusa*, ii. 28, Regensburg, 1848). In 1459 Dionysius succeeded in bringing about a reconciliation between Duke Arnold of Gelderland and his rebellious son Adolphus. With great difficulties he founded the Carthusian monastery at Herzogenbusch between 1466 and 1469. The last years of his life he spent at Roermonde.

Dionysius is one of the most serious representatives of the Reformation of religious and ecclesiastical conditions in the fifteenth century. Heart and soul a monk, he practised asceticism and found his highest enjoyment in the ecstatic state. He was also one of the most learned theologians of his time, had an accurate knowledge of ecclesiastical affairs, and was an author of much versatility and productiveness. The list of his works (*Opera*, i., l.-lxx.) shows 187 titles, and the complete edition, it is estimated, will fill thirty volumes without the supplements. But he had no creative mind. His scientific labors are mostly rich collections of what others said before him with criticisms. His style is clear and simple. Of least importance are his voluminous exegetical works, which comprise the entire Scriptures. Of greater importance is his commentary on Peter Lombard, though here too the collection and criticism of different opinions is the main object. Without being a Thomist, Dionysius often gives preference to Thomas Aquinas, but he often differs from him where he follows Aristotle in favor of Neoplatonic-Dionysian conception, and shows in general an inclination toward mysticism. An independent exhibition of Christian doctrine is contained in the two books *De lumine Christianæ theoriæ*. Other dogmatic and apologetic writings are mentioned by Zöckler, 648 sqq. Ethics Dionysius treated not only in a *Summa de virtutibus et vitiis*, but also in a series of writings on the different states. What is here treated separately he collects with special reference to its application in preaching, in the two books *De regulis vitæ christianorum*. The many orations which are extant from him show that he was also actively engaged in preaching. Some of his writings are especially given to the devotion to Mary, in which he is as enthusiastic as Thomas a Kempis and others of his contemporaries. His mysticism produced an extensive commentary on Dionysius Areopagita and Johannes Climacus, besides some independent works, as *Inflammatorium divini amoris*, *De meditatione*, and others. Not a few of his writings are devoted to ecclesiastic reformatory efforts, as (besides the lost *De deformatione et reformatione ecclesiæ*) *De reformatione claustralium*; *De auctoritate generalium conciliorum*; *De doctrina scholarium*, etc. His reformatory ideas are on the whole the same as those of Gerson, whom he highly esteems. He is far removed from the thought that anything should be changed in the doctrine or general cultus and regulations of the Church, but for outwardly conspicuous defects, like frivolity, religious indifference, immorality in general, neglect of duty, ignorance and worldliness, especially of the priests, he has not only an open eye, but also a just appreciation. From the cooperation of the pope and an ecumenical council he expects the remedy. He assumes that the council in its proper duties, viz., of deciding controversial points of doctrine, of proceeding against a heretical pope or against one who gives too much offense, certainly stands above the latter; on the other hand, he yields to the pope a regular right of supervision over the Church as a whole, and says that in the things "wherein the papal rule and office is supreme the pope stands above a council and above all the Church" (*De auct. gen. concil.*, i. 27). Considering the ecclesiastical position of Dionysius and the character of his writings, it is easy to understand how in the sixteenth century they were appreciated as very timely and promotive of a conservative reform in opposition to the Reformation. On this account most of them were published at that time at Cologne by Loer and Blomevenna, and were often reprinted. A complete edition of his works was commenced at Montreuil in 1896 under the title, *Doctoris ecstatici Dionysii Cartusiani opera omnia in unum digesta ad fidem editionum Coloniensium cura et labore monachorum S. Ordinis Cartusiensis*, 30 vols., 1896–1905, of which all but vols. xxv.-xxvi. have appeared. S. M. DEUTSCH.

BIBLIOGRAPHY: The chief source is the biography by Dietrich von Loer, Cologne, 1530, reprinted with notes in *ASB*, March, ii. 245–255. Modern lives are by: Welters, Roermonde, 1882; D. A. Mougel, Montreuil, 1896. Consult also: W. Moll, *Johannes Brugmann*, i. 70–81, Amsterdam, 1854; K. Werner, *Die Scholastik des späteren Mittelalters*, IV. i. 134–137, 206–262, Vienna, 1887; O. Zöckler, in *TSK*, lviii. (1881), 648 sqq.; *KL*, iii. 1801–07.

DIONYSIUS OF CORINTH: Greek bishop. He was a contemporary of Soter of Rome (165–173 or 167–175), and was the author of epistles to various congregations. Among these letters Eusebius (*Hist. eccl.*, iv. 23) mentions the following: (1) to the Lacedæmonians, with exhortations to peace and unity; (2) to the Athenians, urging them to hold fast to the faith and to live according to the Gospel; (3) to the Nicomedians, with polemics against the Marcionite heresy; (4) to the congregation at Gortyna and the other Cretan churches, with a eulogy of piety and steadfastness; (5) to the congregation of Amastris and the other churches in Pontus; (6) to the Cnossians with admonitions against extreme asceticism; (7) to the Romans, with thanks for gifts and an admonition; (8) to Chrysophora. Four fragments of the epistle to the Romans have been preserved by Eusebius (ii. 21, iv. 23), and their contents bear eloquent testimony to the authority of the Roman Church. The admonition mentioned in (7) is identified by Harnack with the second epistle of Clement.

G. KRÜGER.

BIBLIOGRAPHY: The fragments of Dionysius's works are collected in M. J. Routh, *Reliquiæ Sacræ*, i. 175–201, Oxford, 1846, and translated in *ANF*, viii. 765 sqq. For his life consult: Eusebius, *Hist. eccl.*, iv. 22 sqq. (in *NPNF*, 2d series, i. 200 sqq., note 1); B. F. Westcott, *Hist. of Canon of N. T.*, pp. 185–190, London, 1855; [W. R. Cassels], *Supernatural Religion*, i. 218, 295, ii. 163–171, London, 1874–75; Neander, *Christian Church*, iii. 467, iv. 382; Harnack, *Geschichte*, i. 235–236, II. i. 313; Krüger, *History*, pp. 156–157; *DCB*, i. 849–850; *KL*, iii. 1798–1800.

DIONYSIUS EXIGUUS ("Dionysius the Little"): One of the most conspicuous men of the Latin Church in the sixth century; d. in Rome before 544. He was a Scythian by birth, came to Rome toward the end of the fifth century and became a monk there. Later authors call him an abbot. From the description given by his friend Cassiodorus (*Institutiones*, i. 23) he must have been a master in all monastic virtues, as his self-chosen surname indicates. He had also the polish of a man of the world, took great interest in learning, and was a famous teacher. He was in conflict with the popes of his time and was received into the peace of the Church only after his death. Probably he had associations with the "Scythian monks" who in 519 or 520 brought to Rome the so-called theopaschitic formula (see THEOPASCHITES). His chief importance rests on the fact that by translations he acquainted the West with Greek learning. Both his Greek birth and his position in Rome fitted him for that service. His works are: (1) A collection of canons in two recensions, containing the fifty apostolic canons, the canons of Nicæa, Ancyra, Neo-Cæsarea, Gangra, Antioch, Laodicea, and Constantinople, the twenty-seven canons of Chalcedon (xxviii.-xxx. are wanting), the twenty-one canons of Sardica, and the decisions of Carthage of 419. The two recensions differ by different positions of the canons of Chalcedon and a more complete version of the acts of Carthage in the second redaction. Cassiodorus testifies to the use of the collection in the Church of Rome. The first recension was edited by C. H. Turner in *Ecclesiæ occidentalis monumenta*, i, (Oxford, 1899); the second is in *MPL*, lxvii. (see CANON LAW, II., 3, § 3). (2) A collection of decretals containing an epistle of Siricius, twenty-one epistles of Innocent I., one by Zozimus, four belonging to the time of Boniface I., three by Celestine I., seven by Leo I., one by Gelasius, and one by Anastasius I. This collection also was soon made use of by the popes, and is first referred to in 534. (3) The "Easter-Table," a continuation of the ninety-five-year Easter-table of Cyril of Alexandria, which ended with 531. Dionysius took up the work in 525, repeated the last nineteen-year cycle of Cyril and added five others from 532. Hereby he introduced into the Latin Church the Alexandrian Easter computation, which had been customary in the East since the Council of Nicæa, while the West had till then followed the cycle of Victor, and thus he promoted not a little the unity of the Church. He won popularity by numbering the years not from the era of Diocletian, the impious persecutor of the Christians, but "from the Incarnation of the Lord." He placed the birth of Christ on Dec. 25, 754 a.u.c., and Mar. 25 of the same year he took as the day of the Incarnation (see ERA). His Easter-cycle was soon adopted by Rome, gradually also in other parts of Italy. Toward the end of the sixth century it was used in Gaul, and by the eighth century had come into general use in the British Church. Dionysius also translated letters and writings of Proterius of Alexandria, Proclus of Constantinople, Gregory of Nyssa, Marcellus of Emesa, Cyril of Alexandria, the *Vita* of Pachomius, and perhaps other works to which he was attracted by learned or ascetic interests. His works are in *MPL*, lxvii. H. Achelis.

Bibliography: L. Ideler, *Handbuch der . . . Chronologie*, vol. ii., Berlin, 1826; F. Maassen, *Geschichte der Quellen und der Litteratur des kanonischen Rechts*, i. 130 sqq., 422 sqq., Graz, 1870; F. Rühl, *Chronologie*, pp. 129 sqq., Berlin, 1897; *DCB*, i. 853-854 (noteworthy).

DIOSCURUS: Antipope 530. See Boniface II.

DIOSCURUS OF ALEXANDRIA. See Eutychianism.

DI PIETRO, dī pī-ē'trō, **ANGELO:** Cardinal; b. at Vivaro (near Tivoli), Italy, May 26, 1828. He studied at Rome, became vicar-general of the diocese of Tivoli, and was consecrated titular bishop of Nyssa in 1866 and appointed bishop coadjutor of Ostia and Velletri. In 1877 he was made titular archbishop of Nazianzum and appointed apostolic delegate to the Argentine Republic. He was then internuncio at Rio de Janeiro (1879–82) and nuncio at Munich (1882–87) and Madrid (1887–1893). He was created cardinal priest of Santi Alessio e Bonifacio in 1893, and shortly afterward was appointed prefect of the Congregation of the Council, while in 1902 he became prefect of the Congregation of Bishops and Regulars, and prodatarius five months later.

DIPPEL, JOHANN KONRAD (*Democritus Christianus*): German Pietist and alchemist; b. at Frankenstein (5 m. s. of Darmstadt) Aug. 10, 1673; d. at the castle of Wittgenstein (24 m. n.w. of Marburg) Apr. 25, 1734. At the age of sixteen he entered the University of Giessen and there rapidly gained note as an acute and fervid champion of orthodoxy against the rising influence of the Pietists, actuated in his course, however, more by the honor which the orthodox then enjoyed than by conviction. In after-days he ascribed to all adherents of the orthodox system the same insincerity of which he had been guilty. In 1693 he took his master's degree and for a time lived as a tutor in the Odenwald, continuing his polemic against the Pietists and hoping for a professorship at Giessen. Meeting with the coldest treatment from the authorities there, however, he went to Wittenberg, where his fortunes proved no better. At Strasburg his views made it impossible for him to establish any connection with the university, but he passed some time there lecturing on astrology and palmistry, preaching frequently in a spirit that showed the growing influence of Pietism, and leading a life which ultimately sent him back to his native place, a fugitive from his creditors. Now openly professing the tenets of Pietism, though with mercenary motives, he preached repeatedly before the court at Darmstadt, and in 1697 published at Giessen his satirical *Orthodoxia orthodoxorum*. At this time, however, occurred his sincere conversion to Pietism through the instrumentality of Gottfried Arnold (q.v.), whom he met at Giessen, and it is a testimonial to his final sincerity that he did not hesitate to sacrifice his chances for a professorship at the university by the publication of the work just mentioned.

With characteristic energy he devoted himself to the service of his new faith and, taking the destruction of orthodoxy as his mission, entered upon a fierce polemic that speedily made him famous. In 1698 appeared his *Papismus Protestantium vapulans* and this was followed in the course of the next two years by no less than fourteen controversial writings in which, with skilful variation, he expounded the same theme of morals versus dogma, Christianity versus ecclesiasticism, and orthopraxy versus orthodoxy. Embracing Arnold's views of church history, Dippel carried them to an extreme, and his pamphlets were naturally more popular than Arnold's heavy tomes. His views subjected him to persecution from the clergy and even from the mob, by whom his life was threatened. In 1702 the Consistory forbade him to publish any writings of a theological nature. After 1704 he lived in Berlin, devoted to researches in alchemy and deluded at one time by the conviction that he had solved the problem of transmutation. The discovery of Prussian blue was the accidental result of his studies. He was driven from Berlin through the machinations of J. F. Mayer, an inveterate enemy of the Pietists, and fled to Köstritz, which the princes of the line of Reuss had made a refuge for adherents of the new movement. Thence he went to Holland, lived for some time near Amsterdam, and after 1711 practised medicine at Leyden, bringing into therapeutic use the oil known by his name. His theological interests, however, were not neglected. He wrote the *Fatum fatuum* (Amsterdam, 1710) in defense of the freedom of the will against the teachings of the Cartesians, and in 1714 published at Amsterdam the *Alea belli Muselmannici*. In the same year he removed to Altona, in Sleswick-Holstein, where he lived until 1717 in honored peace. By an imprudent incursion into politics he aroused the hatred of high officials at court, and in 1719 was condemned to perpetual imprisonment. The full rigor of the sentence was not carried out, though for seven years he lived in semiconfinement on the island of Bornholm engaged in the practise of medicine. Released in 1726, he went to Sweden, plunged into politics, and was utilized by the nobles as an effective instrument against the hierarchy. He finally became physician to King Frederick I. In this position he did not neglect to promulgate his religious views, which, represented in final form in his *Vera demonstratio evangelica* (Frankfort, 1729) and making rapid progress in the country, aroused the clergy and brought about his banishment. Returning to Germany, he took up his residence at Liebenberg, near Goslar, and continued his studies in alchemy. Though he abstained entirely from theological controversy, the clergy compelled him to flee, and he found refuge with the count of Wittgenstein-Berleburg. His last years were largely taken up by a violent controversy with Zinzendorf over the nature of the Atonement. (F. Bosse.)

Bibliography: The one book is W. Bender, *Johann Konrad Dippel*, Bonn, 1882.

DIPTYCHS. See Liber Vitæ.

DISCIPLES OF CHRIST.

Origin (§ 1). Doctrinal Teaching (§ 2).
Statistics (§ 3).

The Disciples of Christ, or Christians, are a body of believers which dates as a distinct organization from the early part of the nineteenth century. In different parts of the United States teachers arose simultaneously among the religious denominations who pleaded for the Bible alone without human addition in the form of creeds or formulas of faith, and for the union of Christians of every name upon the basis of the apostles' teaching. James O'Kelly (q.v.) and others in Virginia and North Carolina, Barton W. Stone (q.v.) and his coadjutors in Kentucky, Walter Scott in Ohio, the Campbells in West Virginia (see Campbell, Alexander)—ministers of different denominations, unknown to each other, lifted up their voices against divisions in the body of Christ. In Aug., 1809, Thomas

1. Origin. Campbell, a Presbyterian minister in Washington County, Pa., formed "The Christian Association of Washington," and in September of the same year issued a remarkable *Declaration and Address*, deploring the tendencies of party spirit among Christians and the enforcement of human interpretations of God's Word in place of the pure doctrine of Christ. Commencing with the admitted truth that the Gospel was designed to reconcile and unite men to God and to each other, the address proceeded to consider the sad divisions that existed, and their baleful effects in the angry contentions, enmities, excommunications, and persecutions which they engendered; it set forth the object of the association "*to come firmly and fairly to original ground and take up things just as the apostles left them*," that, "*disentangled from the accruing embarrassments of intervening ages*," they might "*stand upon the same ground on which the Church stood at the beginning.*"

The principles of this address were cordially indorsed by Alexander Campbell, and in the following year (1810) he began publicly to urge them. The first organization was formed May 4, 1811, at Brush Run, Pa., with twenty-nine members; in 1813 this church united with the Redstone, and ten years after with the Mahoning Baptist Association. In 1823 Mr. Campbell began publishing the *Christian Baptist*, and his teachings began to attract universal attention. Opposition was aroused and his views were denounced as heterodox, but large numbers accepted them. Many new churches were organized under his labors and those of Walter Scott, and the Baptists began to declare non-fellowship with those who pleaded for the Bible alone, thus forcing these brethren to organize themselves into separate communities. This was in 1827, and from this time may be dated the rise of the people known as Disciples of Christ. In 1831 the followers of Barton W. Stone in Kentucky, and of Alexander Campbell in Virginia and Pennsylvania, united (see Christians, 2); for the next thirty-five years Mr. Campbell is the foremost figure in the movement.

In substantial agreement with all evangelical Christians, Disciples of Christ accept the divine inspiration of the Holy Scriptures of the Old and New Testaments; the all-sufficiency of the Bible as a revelation of God's will and a rule of faith and life; the revelation of God in threefold personality of Father, Son, and Holy Spirit as set forth by the apostles; the divine glory of Jesus Christ as the Son of God, his incarnation, doctrine, miracles, death as a sin-offering, resurrection, ascension, and coronation; the personality of the Holy Spirit, and his divine mission to convince the world of sin, righteousness, and judgment to come, and to comfort and sanctify the people of God; the alienation of man from his maker, and the

2. Doctrinal Teaching. necessity of faith, repentance, and obedience in order to salvation; the obligation of the divine ordinances of baptism and the Lord's Supper; the duty of observing the Lord's Day in memory of the resurrection of the Lord Jesus; the necessity of holiness on the part of believers; the divine appointment of the Church of Christ, composed of all who by faith and obedience confess his name, with its ministries and services for the edification of the body of Christ and the conversion of the world; the fulness and freeness of the salvation that is in Christ to all who will accept it on the New Testament conditions; the final judgment, with the reward of the righteous and punishment of the wicked.

The Disciples of Christ, however, have their distinctive position: (1) In their plea for restoration. Others have sought to reform the Church. The Campbells and their coworkers aimed to restore in faith, spirit, and practise the Christianity of Christ and his apostles as found in the pages of the New Testament. The need was not to recast any existing creed, or reform any existing religious body, but to go back of all creeds and councils, all sects and schools since the days of the apostles, and to take up the work as left by inspired men. To believe and to do none other things than those enjoined by our Lord and his apostles they felt must be infallibly safe, and for this to-day the Disciples continue to stand—the word of Christ and the body of Christ as in the beginning. (2) In the rejection of human creeds. They claim to stand strictly upon the original Protestant principle—the Bible, the whole Bible, and nothing but the Bible, the religion of Protestants. They affirm that the Sacred Scriptures as given by God answer all purposes as a rule of faith and practise and a law for the government of the Church; and that human creeds and confessions spring out of controversy and tend to division and strife. (3) In their emphasis upon the divine Sonship of Jesus. In place of all human confessions they would exalt that of Peter: "Thou art the Christ, the Son of the Living God." "What think you of Christ?" is the great question. "Thou art the Messiah, the Son of the Living God," is the great answer. "On this rock I will build my Church" is the great oracle. (4) In their division of the Word. They believe that of old, "Holy men of God spake as they were moved by the Holy Spirit," yet do not regard the

Old and New Testaments as of equally binding authority upon Christians. "God, who at sundry times and in divers manners spake in time past unto the fathers by the prophets, hath in these last days spoken unto us by his Son." A clear distinction is made between the Law and the Gospel, the old covenant and the new, and the New Testament, it is claimed, is as perfect a constitution for the worship, government, and discipline of the New Testament Church as the Old was for the Old Testament Church. (5) In the plea for New Testament names for the Church and followers of Christ. As the Bride of Christ, the Church should wear the name of the Bridegroom. Party names perpetuate party strife. "For while one saith, I am of Paul; and another, I am of Apollos; are ye not carnal?" Disciples do not deny that others are Christians, or that other churches are churches of Christ. They do not claim to be the Church of Christ or even a Church of Christ. They simply desire to be Christians only, and their churches to be only churches of Christ. Hence they repudiate the name "Campbellites." (6) As to the work of the Holy Spirit in conversion. Accepting the divine personality of the Holy Spirit and holding that in every case regeneration is begun, carried on, and perfected through his gracious agency, the Disciples claim the Divine Word is his instrument, the sinner is in no sense passive, regeneration is not a miracle, the Gospel is God's power unto salvation to every one that believeth, and men must hear, believe, repent, and obey the Gospel to be saved. (7) As to Christian baptism. Recognizing Christ alone as King, his Word only as authoritative and binding upon the conscience, and finding, as they would return to the order instituted by our Lord and his apostles, baptism commanded in order to the remission of sins and administered by a burial with Christ, they take it up as one of the items of the original divine system against all human systems. Baptismal regeneration they have never taught. They simply insist upon the purpose of baptism as set forth in the divine testimonies: Mark xvi. 16; Acts ii. 38; Acts xxii. 16. They would give the inspired answers to the question, "Men and brethren, what shall we do?" They would demand no other prerequisite to baptism than the confession of the whole heart in the personal living Christ. They would teach the believing penitent to seek through obedience the divine assurance of forgiveness; and in Scriptural surrender to the authority of Christ, and not in sensation, or vision, or special revelations, to find evidence of acceptance with God. (8) As to the Lord's Supper. The Disciples hold first to the weekly observance of this holy ordinance in all their assemblies. Of the Church in Troas we read: "On the first day of the week, when the disciples came together to break bread, Paul preached unto them," and following this apostolic model, Disciples teach that the Lord's Supper should be celebrated by the Lord's people on every Lord's Day; and, secondly, they emphasize and exalt this institution, not as a sacrament, but as a memorial feast—an act of worship in which all Christians may unite, and from which they have no right to exclude any sincere follower of our common Lord. (9) As to the Lord's Day. With the Disciples this is not the Sabbath, but a New Testament institution, consecrated by apostolic example, and to be observed in joyous and loving remembrance of the resurrection of the Lord Jesus. (10) As to the Church. The Disciples believe that the institution built by Christ, set forth by the apostles on Pentecost under the special guidance of the Holy Spirit, established upon the foundation of apostles and prophets, Jesus Christ himself being the Chief Corner-stone—the Church of Christ—is a divine institution; that sects as branches of the Church are unscriptural and unapostolic; and that the sect name and sect spirit and sect life should in every case give place to the unity of the spirit and the union and cooperation that distinguished the Church of the New Testament.

3. Statistics. The Disciples rank sixth among the religious bodies of America, and in the decade 1890–1900 increased eighty-four per cent. They have 11,000 churches and one and a quarter millions communicants. In Christian Endeavor Societies they rank third. They have a Home Missionary Society working in thirty-seven States, and their Foreign Missionary Society sustains 466 workers, 40 colleges and schools, and 18 hospitals in twelve different foreign lands. Their Christian Woman's Board of Missions does a large work in both home and foreign fields, and they have both a National Education Society and a National Benevolent Association. They publish fifty-five journals and support thirty-four colleges and seminaries of high grade, among which are Bethany College, Bethany, W. Va., founded by Alexander Campbell in 1840, and Hiram College, Hiram, O.

F. D. POWER.

BIBLIOGRAPHY: The sources first in importance are the writings of A. Campbell, partly collected in his *Works*, 6 vols., Cincinnati, n.d., to be supplemented by the *Debate with N. L. Rice*, ib. 1844, his *Popular Lectures and Addresses*, Philadelphia, 1863, and *The Christian Baptist*, a newspaper nearly the whole of which was written by Campbell. Valuable also is R. Richardson, *Memoirs of Alexander Campbell*, Cincinnati, 1868. Consult further: J. A. Williams, *Life of John Smith*, Cincinnati, 1870; W. Baxter, *Life of Walter Scott*, ib. 1874; J. S. Lamar, *Life of I. Errett*, 2 vols., ib. 1894; B. B. Tyler, *American Church Hist. Series*, vol. xii., New York, 1894; F. D. Power, *Sketches of our Pioneers*, St. Louis, 1899. On the doctrines of the Disciples consult: B. Franklin, *The Gospel Preacher*, Cincinnati, 1868; I. Errett, *Walks about Jerusalem*, ib. 1872; J. H. Garrison, *Old Faith Restated*, St. Louis, 1891; S. Lamar, *First Principles and Going on to Perfection*, Cincinnati, 1891; F. D. Power, *Bible Doctrine for Young Disciples*, St. Louis, 1899.

DISCRETION, YEAR OF: In ecclesiastical usage, the age at which a change of confession may be made. In countries which legislate on the subject (as the German states) it varies from fourteen to twenty-one.

DISEASES AND THE HEALING ART, HEBREW.

I. General Conditions in Palestine: The general hygienic conditions of the environment of the Israelites were good, and they appear to have been a healthy people (Ex. i. 10 sqq., 18 sqq.). Palestine is a country conducive to health, since the characteristics of the climate give to the human body a high degree of elasticity and firmness. The principal climatic disease is fever; the low-lying land, the mountain valleys, and the marshes are dreaded on account of the prevalence of malaria (tertian typhus). Inflammation of the eyes prevails as in Egypt, owing to the heat, which causes hyperemia of the brain, the nightly dews, and the sand-storms (cf. Lev. xix. 14; Deut. xxvii. 18; Matt. ix. 27, xii. 22, etc.). All these diseases, however, seem to have been kept within reasonable bounds.

II. Religious Ideas of Disease: The whole ancient Orient shared in the belief that disease was sent by the Deity. Among the ancient Babylonians disease signified that an evil spirit possessed the sick man and held him in its power. These evil spirits were numerous, different classes causing diseases of the head, fevers, the plague, etc. Healing was almost exclusively by means of exorcisms; it was necessary to gain the protection of some powerful divinity that by his help the evil spirits might be driven out. In Israel also this belief persisted, and Josephus asserts that in his time people employed various superstitious remedies (*Ant.*, VIII. ii. 5). The prevalence of this custom in more ancient times is proved by the many animadversions in the Old Testament against sorcery, which was used either for protection against disease or for its cure (see DRESS AND ORNAMENT, HEBREW, § 7, for ornaments used as amulets). Yahwism also shares this view of the supernatural origin of disease, but it always puts Yahweh in the place of the many gods and evil spirits. The angel of Yahweh smites the people with the plague (II Sam. xxiv. 16; II Kings xix. 35); leprosy (q.v.) is a "smiting" (*ẓara'ath*) from God. Indeed, the Israelites, explaining disease in this manner, made it unnecessary to look for natural causes. Still the conviction persisted that in certain maladies, such as mental derangement, epilepsy, and hysteria, evil spirits possessed the patient and tortured him. Even in the modern East no fundamental distinction is made between insanity and inspiration (I Kings xxii. 19 sqq.; II Kings iii. 15 sqq.). Saul was tormented by one of Yahweh's evil spirits (I Sam. xvi. 14), and the inspired prophets behaved like madmen (I Sam. xix. 18 sqq., xxi. 13 sqq.; II Kings ix. 11; cf. also the demoniacs of the New Testament and see DEMONIAC).

III. Healing and Healers: In spite of the views concerning the origin and nature of disease just noticed, the art of healing was practised at an early period. The Code of Hammurabi (see HAMMURABI AND HIS CODE) contains rules applying to the physician. In ancient Egypt also the art of healing had attained a high standard; there were specialists for diseases of the eye, of the teeth, etc. (Herodotus, ii. 84; cf. A. Erman, *Aegypten und aegyptisches Leben*, Tübingen, 1887, pp. 477 sqq., Eng. transl., London, 1894). Ex. xxi. 19 implies that there were physicians in Israel. As the sanctuaries were the centers of all knowledge, the priest was at the same time the physician. This is easily understood from the supposed origin of disease (ut sup.), according to which only the priests could effect a cure. In agreement with this the law (Lev. xiii.) gives a prescription that where leprosy was suspected the priest was to determine the character of the disease, a fact which implies that he was believed to be possessed of medical knowledge. How early there were professional healers outside of the priesthood is not known. In process of time, naturally, recourse to physicians became more general. Jeremiah (viii. 22) complains that the hurts of the nation could not be healed by a physician as could the wounds of men, and the Chronicler blames Asa for trusting too much in his physicians (II Chron. xvi. 12). Sirach praises in high terms the art of healing (Ecclus. xxxviii. 1 sqq.), and several recipes are preserved from this later period (cf. J. Lightfoot, *Horæ hebraicæ et Talmudicæ* on . . . Mark v. 26, Cambridge, 1663), while the baths of Tiberias and Callirhoë were used (Josephus, *Ant.*, XVII. vi. 5; *War*, I. xxxiii. 5). According to the Talmud (*Sheḳalim* v. 1–2) a physician was attached to the temple to treat abdominal diseases, because the priests, who went barefooted and were required to use frequent cold ablutions, were especially subject to such troubles, while *Sanhedrin* 17[b] recommends that there be a physician and a surgeon in every community. In the interest of science it was allowable to become unclean by touching a corpse. Several Talmudic teachers bore the title of doctor.

IV. Separate Diseases: Definite directions for ascertaining the character of diseases are given only in such cases as were considered ceremonially unclean. In all other cases it is almost impossible to determine the disease from the popular nomenclature because of the lack of complete and specific statement of the symptoms. Therefore only an unsystematic list of the diseases mentioned in the Old Testament can be given.

The name leprosy (q.v.), *ẓara'ath*, includes not only leprosy proper (*Lepra Arabum*), but also other maladies with like symptoms (Lev. xiii. 1 sqq.; cf. xiv. 56). Four forms of disease are

1. Diseases of the Skin.

enumerated which in their incipient stages might be taken for leprosy: *seth*, *sappaḥath*, *bahereth*, *netheḳ* (Lev. xiii. 2 sqq.). For the diagnosis only certain negative signs are mentioned. If the hair on the skin at the places affected does not become white, if the affected parts of the skin do not appear depressed, and if the affected area does not spread, then the disease is not unclean (verses 6, 39). In the laws for the priests three other skin-diseases are mentioned, *garabh*, *yallepheth*, and *ḥeres*, which render the victims ineligible for the priesthood. The Biblical description of this malady is insufficient for identification. Of all these names only *seth* can be explained as "rising," and implies a swelling of the skin in contradistinction to a depression of the affected skin, the characteristic sign of leprosy. *Sappaḥath* seems (Isa. iii. 17) to attack especially the head. *Bahereth* is with some probability connected with *bahar* ("to shine") and is supposed to refer to light spots and bald places on the dark skin (cf. Lev. xiii. 4). This suggests vitiligo, a skin-disease in which the pigment disappears from parts of the epidermis. These eruptions may appear over the whole body without any previous injury to the skin (Lev. xiii. 2), or where there has been a boil (verse 18) or a burn (verse 24). *Netheḳ* is sometimes regarded as a mild disease (Lev. xiii. 31–34), and at others considered to be the same as the *ṣara'ath* of the head and beard (Lev. xiii. 30). *Garabh* (LXX. *psora agria*, Vulg., *scabies*) and *yallepheth* (LXX. *lichēn*, Vulg., *impetigo*) seem to indicate an incurable disease, as they exclude the patients from the priesthood (Lev. xxi. 20). They are generally considered to be the itch or herpes. *Ḥeres* (LXX. *knēphē*, Vulg., *prurigo*) was also regarded an incurable disease, as were the plague and Egyptian boils (Deut. xxviii. 27).

2. The Malady of Job.

In connection with these skin-diseases Job's malady may be mentioned. This is generally considered to have been real leprosy. Some think of *lepra Arabum* or *elephantiasis Græcorum*, others of *elephantiasis Arabum*, or pachydermia, a disease of the lymphatics and blood-vessels, especially of the lower extremities. If, however, the account of Job's sufferings might lead to the belief that he was afflicted with several distinct maladies, it must not be forgotten that the recital is not the clinical history of a disease, but a poet's description. However, the people of Israel were threatened with this very malady, the same name being employed (*sheḥin ra'*, Job ii. 7) as for one of the most severe pestilences (Deut. xxviii. 27, 35), and this passage may have been present to the mind of the poet when describing Job's sufferings. For the various symptoms of Job's malady as given by the author of the book cf. Job ii. 7, vii. 3–5, xvi. 8, 13, 16, xvii. 7, xix. 17–20, xxx. 17, 27, 30.

3. Pestilence.

Pestilence (*debher*) is regarded in the East as the most destructive of all diseases (Lev. xxvi. 25; Deut. xxviii. 21; II Sam. xxiv. 13, 15; I Kings viii. 37; Jer. xiv. 12; Hos. xiii. 14). The name in itself signifies simply "destruction"; the same may be said of the name *ḳeṭebh* (Deut. xxxii. 24; Ps. xci. 6; Hos. xiii. 14). A still more common designation is *maweth*, "death" (Job xxvii. 15; Jer. xv. 2; *Thanatos* in LXX. of Deut. xxviii. 21; Rev. vi. 8, xviii. 8; cf. the medieval expression, the Black Death). The names correspond with the definition of the plague given by Galen: "If many people in a place are attacked by the same malady, then it is an epidemic; if, however, many people die of that malady, it is the plague" ("Commentary on Book iii. of Hippocrates's Epidemics").

4. The Bubonic Plague.

The foremost place must be given to the bubonic plague, which was known in the Orient from the earliest times (cf. Pliny, *Hist. naturalis*, iii. 4; Cyprian, *De mortalitate*). The details given in the Old Testament accord with the symptoms of this disease. In the description of the malady of the Philistines, *'ophalim*, "boils," are mentioned as characteristic (I Sam. v. 6–12), hence five golden images of boils were given as votive offerings (I Sam. vi. 4–5). Among the severe pestilences with which the people of Israel are threatened (Deut. xxviii. 27) the bubonic plague is mentioned. The pestilence which befell the Israelites as a result of David's census is not particularly described, but was evidently the plague. The conception of the angel of Yahweh who smites the people (II Sam. xxiv. 16) is repeated in the account of the destruction wrought in the camp of Sennacherib (II Kings xix. 35; Isa. xxxvii. 36). The recital of Herodotus has long been regarded as of similar origin with the Old Testament account. He narrates that a multitude of field-mice gnawed the quivers, shield-straps, and bowstrings of the Assyrians, and the disarmed warriors were forced to seek safety in flight. That mice are symbols of the plague is proved by the fact that the Philistines offered, besides the five golden images of boils, five golden mice, as symbols of the plague (I Sam. vi. 4).

5. Symptoms and Characteristics of the Plague.

The bubonic plague has its name from the usual location of the boils which characterize it, appearing generally in the neighborhood of the groin, rarely in the armpits, at the nape of the neck, or behind the ear, and taking the form of round swellings, sometimes as large as a hen's egg. Death often occurs very quickly, even before these external signs of the disease have developed. The bacillus of the plague has been discovered only very recently. Pliny (*Hist. naturalis*, iii. 4) connects its appearance with the inundation of the Nile, when this and heavy rains are followed quickly by hot weather. In severe epidemics as much as ninety per cent of the cases result fatally; with the course of the epidemic, however, the percentage of mortality decreases. So far no effectual remedy has been found; the best precautionary measures against the disease are the ordinary regulations of sanitation, by means of which the spread of the plague has been greatly restricted even in Egypt, where it is endemic. Such precautionary measures were unknown to the Israelites; the cremation of the bodies of those who died of the plague (Amos vi. 10) has nothing to do with regulations of this kind. The "murrain" which swept away the beasts has no connection with the bubonic plague (Ex. ix. 3; cf. Ps. lxxviii. 50; Ezek. xiv. 21), which is a disease of men; animals seem to be immune, with the exception of rats, which play an important part in the spread of the plague. Hezekiah's illness is also considered by many to have been the plague (II Kings xx. 7; Isa. xxxviii. 21, *sheḥin*), being brought into causal connection with the above mentioned Assyrian plague. But any chronological connection is rendered impossible by the fact that Hezekiah's illness took place at the time of Merodach-baladan's embassy.

6. Diseases of the Sexual Organs.

As diseases of the sexual organs caused ceremonial uncleanness, the law offers more abundant details regarding them (Lev. xv.; cf. Num. v. 2; II Sam. iii. 29). The prescriptions concern the issues of men and women and the menstruation of women. A particularly severe case of the latter which Jesus cured is mentioned in the synoptics (Matt. ix. 20; Mark v. 25; Luke viii. 43). Syphilis has been identified by some among the maladies described in Lev. xv., and also in the illness of Abimelech (Gen. xx. 17; cf. F. Buret, *Syphilis in Ancient and Prehistoric Times*, London, 1892). It can not, however, be proved that the Hebrews knew this disease. The description of the malady of Herod the Great, in Josephus (*Ant.*, XVII. vi. 5; *War*, I. xxxiii. 5), suggests syphilis, but in this case there may have been cancerous or other sores.

7. Diseases of the Nervous System.

Lameness is often mentioned in the Old Testament. The word *pisseḥ* is always used in reference to the legs (cf. II Sam. iv. 4; Job xxix. 15; Prov. xxvi. 7; Isa. xxxv. 6); only in I Kings xiii. 4 sqq. is the term applied to the arm. Next to the blind, the lame are considered the most miserable of beings (II Sam. v. 6; Isa. xxxiii. 23; Jer. xxxi. 8). The lame were ineligible for the priesthood (Lev. xxi. 18). The New Testament alludes often to palsy and lameness (*paralytikoi, paralysis, choloi*). Among those whose affliction was considered humanly incurable and who came to Jesus and the apostles in search of a cure the palsied occupied a foremost place (Matt. iv. 24; Mark ii. 3; Luke v. 18; John v. 5 sqq.; Acts viii. 7). Their cure was one of the signs of the Messianic kingdom (Luke vii. 22). A case of hip-disease is mentioned Luke xiii. 11. Naturally nothing is said of the cause of paralysis; it is incidentally mentioned that Mephibosheth's lameness resulted from a fall when he was five years old (II Sam. iv. 4 sqq.). The Greek *paralytikos* includes every disease in which the patient loses freedom of movement in any part of his body by reason of relaxation or contraction of the muscles. This may result from gout or apoplexy or from spinal disease. Still, in Acts viii. 7, the *chōloi* are differentiated from the *paralytikoi*. Atrophy of the limb affected frequently accompanied this paralysis (cf. I Kings xiii. 4; Zech. xi. 17; the *cheir ksēra*, "withered hand," of Matt. xii. 10; Luke vi. 8 and the "withered" of John v. 3).

8. Special Cases.

Recently the illness of Antiochus (II Macc. ix. 5, 9) has been explained as spinal paralysis. After he had suffered from abdominal disease (verses 5 sqq.) accompanied by excruciating pains, he fell from his chariot and sustained a fracture of the spine. In consequence paralysis set in, inflammation developed in the paralyzed parts, and worms were produced from the dead flesh; but this account contains unreliable material. A case of apoplexy, a disease not rare in the East, is suggested in the account of Nabal's death, ascribed to a sudden fright while in a state of intoxication. But it is useless to seek by special researches to fix the medical status of such a "stroke of God" as that of Nabal, that of Uzzah (II Sam. vi. 7), or that of Ananias and Sapphira (Acts v.). In the stroke which befell Alkimos some have supposed a case of tetanus, and the same holds good of "sick of the palsy, grievously tormented" of Matt. viii. 6 (cf. Luke vii. 2).

9. Epilepsy.

Epilepsy, while not mentioned in the Old Testament, is often alluded to in the New. The Greek designation *seleniazomenoi* (literally "moonstruck"; A. V., "lunatic"; R. V., "epileptic"; Matt. iv. 24, xvii. 15; cf. Mark i. 23 sqq., ix. 17–18; Luke ix. 38 sqq.) owes its origin to the idea that the disease was due to the moon. In the New Testament period this illness was attributed to demoniac possession (Mark ix. 18), though Matthew usually distinguishes between the possessed and the lunatics (iv. 24, see DEMONIAC). The symptoms described in Mark ix. 17; Luke ix. 38 sqq. are those which characterize epileptic fits; violent spasms shake the patient, he falls to the ground, froths at the mouth, gnashes his teeth, howls, he often casts himself into the water or into the fire, and generally he becomes emaciated. The great number of cases of demoniac possession described in the New Testament are explained by modern medical science as caused by autosuggestion, the sufferers being under the delusion that they were the prey of evil spirits.

10. Mental Diseases.

At no time was a fundamental distinction made in the East between inspired prophets and men suffering from mental derangement. Insanity was rarer in the Orient than in modern civilization; nevertheless, it is quite often mentioned, and the actions and appearance of the insane were well known (Deut. xxviii. 28–34; cf. I Sam. xxi. 14; II Kings ix. 20; Prov. xxvi. 18; Zech. xii. 4). Two cases are described very minutely, that of Saul and that of Nebuchadrezzar. Saul's malady suggests melancholia (I Sam. xvi. 14 sqq., xviii. 10 sqq., xix. 9 sqq.) alternating with madness. But the very meager information given in the Old Testament does not reveal in Saul's case the symptoms which modern psychiatry requires in determining a case of melancholia, even putting aside all the legendary features of the recital. To the hallucination of Nebuchadrezzar (Dan. iv. 29 sqq.) that he was an animal many parallels exist in the so-called lycanthropy. But there is no real proof that Nebuchadrezzar ever led a life like a beast's; these details are mere adornment of the account (but see DANIEL, BOOK OF, VI.). Medical men of sober judgment diagnose Nebuchadrezzar's malady as a form of megalomania accompanied by visions, delusions of the senses, and a morbid fear of persecution, this phase of excitement being followed by a phase of extreme depression, physical as well as mental. But the Biblical historian knows nothing of this, and, as the event is not historical, to seek for the true medical definition of this malady is superfluous.

11. Diseases of the Abdomen, Bones, and Eyes.

The only case of disease of the abdominal organs mentioned is that of Joram (II Chron. xxi. 15, 18 sqq.). His malady is explained by the medical authorities as diarrhea, or as a rupture of the intestines with its various complications. The account in the Old Testament is much too generalized as to details for the formation of any positive opinion in the case. Caries (Heb. *raḳabh*) is often mentioned, but only as a symbol of destruction (Prov. xii. 4; Hos. v. 12; Hab. iii. 16). Rickets is, according to present medical science, the chief predisposing cause of spinal curvature and is assumed in every case of hunchback, except such as result from spinal disease caused by a tuberculous condition. Gout may have been the disease of some of the paralytics of the New Testament. The illness of Asa (I Kings xv. 23; II Chron. xvi. 12) is also explained as gout, and great age and the duration of his illness make this seem probable; the details, however, are so indefinite that nothing more than a conjecture may be hazarded. The commonness of blindness in the East has already been noticed. The causes are the lack of cleanliness, the prevailing dust, the intense brightness of the sunlight, the flies and other insects, and the failure to treat properly the eyes when disease has once developed. The law takes the blind under its special protection (Lev. xix. 14; Deut. xxvii. 18), although they were excluded from the priesthood (Lev. xxi. 18). There is frequent mention of miraculous infliction and removal of blindness (Gen. xix. 11; II Kings vi. 18–19; Zech. xii. 4, etc.). Cure by medical treatment was regarded as impossible; and as the healing of Tobit (Tob. ii. 10, xi. 2 sqq.) is given as a miracle, it is unnecessary to discuss the curative properties of gall.

12. Fevers and Sunstroke.

A great number of Hebrew words designate a disease by the "burning" which accompanies it (*ḳaddaḥath*, Lev. xxvi. 16; *dalleḳeth*, Deut. xxviii. 22; *ḥarḥur*, Deut. xxviii. 22; *resheph*, Deut. xxxii. 24). It can not be determined whether these names refer to as many different kinds of fevers; in any case, climatic fevers are included among them. It is as difficult to determine the character of the "great fever" of Peter's mother-in-law (Luke iv. 38) and the fever of the nobleman's son, John iv. 46. According to Josephus (*Ant.*, XIII. xv. 5), Alexander Jannæus suffered for three years from intermittent fever. The "consumption" mentioned in connection with fevers (*shaḥepheth*, Lev. xxvi. 16; Deut. xxviii. 22) signifies great debility and emaciation. Sunstroke (*makkath shemesh*) is often mentioned (II Kings iv. 19; Ps. cxxi. 6; Jonah iv. 8; Judith viii. 3), and is even to-day much dreaded in the plains of the Jordan. It is difficult to discriminate in individual cases between genuine sunstroke and heat-prostration caused by the overheating of the body.

I. Benzinger.

Bibliography: The literature of the subject is given in W. Ebstein (see below); A. Pauly, *Bibliographie des sciences médicales*, Paris, 1874; and J. Pagel, *Historisch-medizinische Bibliographie*, Berlin, 1898. Consult: J. R. Bennett, *The Diseases of the Bible*, London, 1887; T. Shapter, *Medica sacra; or a Short Exposition of the More Important Diseases Mentioned in the Sacred Writings*, ib. 1834; J. P. Trusen, *Darstellung der biblischen Krankheiten*, Posen, 1843; J. B. Friedreich, *Zur Bibel: naturhistorische, anthropologische und medizinische Fragmente*, 2 vols., Nuremberg, 1848; G. Böttger, *Die Arzneikunst bei den alten Hebräern*, Dresden, 1853; J. D. Tholozan, *Une épidémie de peste en Mésopotamie en 1867*, Paris, 1869; idem, *Hist. de la peste bubonique en Mésopotamie*, ib. 1874; idem, *Hist. de la peste bubonique au Caucase, en Arménie et en Anatolie*, ib. 1876; idem, *La Peste en Turquie*, ib. 1880; L. Kotelmann, *Die Geburtshilfe bei den alten Hebräern*, Marburg, 1876; Oppler, in *Deutsches Archiv für die Geschichte der Medizin*, 1881, pp. 62 sqq.; H. Ploss, *Das Weib in der Natur- und Völkerkunde*, Leipsic, 1885; C. C. Bombaugh, *The Plagues and Pestilences of the Old Testament*, in *Johns Hopkins Hospital Bulletin*, iv (1893), 04 sqq.; J. Preuss, in Virchow's *Archiv*, cxxxviii (1894), 261 sqq.; idem, in *Wiener medizinische Wochenschrift*, 1898, pp. 570 sqq.; U. Passigli, *Un' antica pagina d'igiene alimentare*, Florence, 1897; idem, *L'Allattamento; saggio di pediatria biblica*, Bologna, 1898; idem, *La Prostituzione e le psicopatie sessuali presso gli Ebrei all' epoca biblica*, Milan, 1898; idem, *Le Cognizioni ostetrico-ginecologiche degli antichi Ebrei*, Bologna, 1898; W. Ebstein, *Die Medizin im A. T.*, Stuttgart, 1901; idem, *Die Medizin im N. T. und im Talmud*, ib. 1903; *DB*, iii. 321–333; *EB*, i. 595–507, 1104–06, iii. 2833–34, 3005–09, 3675–3677. Interesting side-lights are cast by Mary Hamilton, *Incubation or the Cure of Disease in Pagan Temples and Christian Churches*, London, 1906.

DISIBOD, SAINT: Founder of the monastery of Disibodenberg, in the diocese of Mainz, in Bavaria, near the border of Rhenish Prussia (10 m. s.w. of Kreuznach). All that is certainly known concerning him is that he was an Irishman; he died most probably in 674. His "life" by the Abbess Hildegarde of Bingen (d. 1179) is too rhapsodical and fantastic to be considered a historical document. It states that when he was a young man at home "great scandals" prevailed in Ireland; some rejected Christianity, others adopted heresies or Judaism; some relapsed into paganism, others desired to live "like beasts, rather than men." For many years Disibod struggled against these evils; at last, tiring of the thankless toil, he left home, and, after long wanderings, with a few companions settled on the hill by the Glan in Alemannia; when he had learned the language he preached to the people, and he lived there for thirty years in high esteem. The monastery was abandoned and the church in ruins when Willigis became archbishop of Mainz in 975. He renewed the foundation as a canonry, and Archbishop Ruthard brought back the monks in 1108. In 1259 the monastery passed under the control of the Cistercians. In 1559 it was finally abandoned. Extensive ruins still mark the site.

Bibliography: *ASB*, July, ii. 581–599, and *MPL*, cxcvii. Consult: Lanigan, *Eccl. Hist.*, iii. 113–115; Falk, in *Der Katholik*, lx (1880), i. 541–547. For the monastery consult: F. X. Remling, *Geschichte der Abteien und Klöster in Rheinbayern*, i. 14–51, Neustadt, 1836; Rettberg, *KD*, i. 587–580.

DISPENSATION: In the practise of the Roman Catholic Church the suspension in a particular case of a rule of the canon law, or the exemption from the consequences usually following the transgression of an established rule. As early as the fifth century the bishops of Rome assumed the right of deviating from the decrees formulated by the ecumenical councils where such departures involved a mere abandonment of detail without injury to the essence of canonical prescription, or were found necessary for the preservation of the spirit of the law. Similar powers were exercised by the provincial synods and bishops; but from the middle of the eleventh century the reference of applications for exemption (q.v.) to the bishop of Rome became general, and once the supreme legislative power of the pope had been established the highest power of dispensation was deduced therefrom. In theory the exercise of this function was justified only by the welfare or necessities of the Church, but in practise the papal discretion became absolute. After the fourteenth century the practise became a source of papal revenue; for though theoretically the grant of exemption was not purchasable, yet the charges connected with the administration of this department fell upon the applicant and were made heavy for the express purpose of discouraging frequent recourse to this mode of evading the law. The Council of Trent confirmed the pope in possession of his absolute power, unlimited even by the decrees of a general council, and sanctioned the exercise of the dispensatory power by others than the pope, but only in cases of extreme necessity or where the aim is some benefit for the Church admitting of no delay.

Upon the principle that the power of dispensation follows from that of legislation, the pope alone may grant exemption from a universal law or a law of limited application emanating from the pope or a general council. Dispensations *in foro externo* are issued through the office of the *Dataria*, and those *in foro interno* by the *Pœnitentiaria;* the former requiring in every case the papal decision, the latter only in certain exceptional cases. The formal modes of granting dispensation are in *forma commissaria*, whereby a mandate is addressed to the territorial bishop authorizing him after due investigation to act in the name of the pope; or in *forma gratiosa*, wherein the act of concession is addressed directly to the petitioner, a favor extended, however, only in such exceptional cases as that of sovereigns or bishops. The acceptance of the grant of dispensation by the petitioner is not necessary to render it efficacious.

The independent exercise of the power by the bishops is restricted to cases specified in the *Corpus juris* and established by the Council of Trent, outside of which the papal authorization is necessary. Such authorization (*facultates;* see Faculties) is conferred for a regular number of years and within a prescribed sphere of action. The doctrine that bishops may make use of the power of dispensation in emergencies where communication with Rome is impossible or hazardous finds its sanction in a constructive papal authorization. Bishops and provincial and diocesan synods possess the independent power of dispensation in the matter of rules and regulations of local validity; here too, however, the papal authority may intervene.

(P. Hinschius†.)

Bibliography: M. A. Stiegler, in *Archiv für katholisches Kirchenrecht*, Mainz, 1897–98; H. Brandhuber von Etschfeld, *Ueber Dispensation und Dispensationsrecht*, Vienna, 1888; E. Friedberg, *Das geltende Verfassungsrecht der evangelischen Landeskirchen*, Leipsic, 1888. Consult also J. H. Blunt, *Dictionary of Doctrinal and Historical Theology*, pp. 205–206, London, 1870.

DISSELHOFF, JULIUS AUGUST GOTTFRIED: Successor of Fliedner at the head of the Kaiserswerth home for deaconesses (see Fliedner, Theodor; and Deaconess, III., 2, a, §§ 2–3); b. in Soest, Westphalia, Oct. 24, 1827; d. near Simmern (26 m. s.w. of Coblenz) July 14, 1896. He entered the University of Halle in 1846. In the national student movement of 1848 he represented the royalistic old Prussian side, and was Halle's delegate to the parliament at Eisenach. In 1850 he became Fliedner's assistant in Kaiserswerth; in 1853 pastor at Schermbeck, near Wesel, where he established a basket factory for the unemployed in his own parsonage, and showed great talent as an organizer. On the call of Fliedner, in 1855 he returned to Kaiserswerth, thenceforth his field of labor. His careful study *Gegenwärtige Lage der Kretinen, Blödsinnigen und Idioten* (Bonn, 1857) led to the founding of several asylums for the insane. In 1859 appeared his collections of sermons (*Geschichte des Königs Sauls. David, Ruth, Paulus*) and his epic poem *König Alfred;* in 1860, *Neue Weisen*—the last two works under the pseudonym Julius von Soest. He traveled much in the interest of Kaiserswerth, visiting the Orient five times, and founded the orphanage "Zoar" in Beirut in 1861. During the wars of 1864, 1866, and 1870–71 he led the Kaiserswerth deaconesses in the field and organized their work. After Fliedner's death (1865) he became the head of the latter's institutions. With the publication of his *Wegweiser zu J. G. Hamann* in 1871 he bade farewell to his favorite literary studies and devoted himself henceforth for thirty years to his allotted work. When he entered the field he found 115 stations and 327 sisters; he left double the number of stations and 953 sisters.

(Diodat Disselhoff.)

Bibliography: The *Kaiserswerther Kalender* for 1898 contains a brief sketch of his life. Consult: J. Disselhoff, *Pastor Julius Disselhoff, zum Gedächtniss*, Kaiserswerth, 1896.

DITTRICH, FRANZ: Roman Catholic; b. at Thegsten (near Heilsberg, 41 m. s.e. of Königsberg) Jan. 26, 1839. He studied at Braunsberg, Rome, and Munich, and was ordained to the priesthood in 1863. In 1866 he became privat-docent at Braunsberg, where he was appointed associate professor of theology. In 1873 he was promoted full professor, and since 1903 has also been provost of the cathedral of Ermland. He is a member of the Prussian house of deputies. He was editor of the *Mittheilungen des ermländischen Kunstvereins* (Braunsberg, 1870–75), and has written *Dionysius der Grosse von Alexandrien* (Freiburg, 1867); *Observationes quædam de ordine naturali et morali* (Braunsberg, 1869); *Regesten und Briefe des Cardinals Gasparo Contarini* (1881); *Gasparo Contarini, eine Monographie* (1885), *Abriss einer Lehre der Unterziehung und des Unterrichts* (1890); *Nunciaturberichte Giovanni Morones vom deutschen*

Königshofe (Paderborn, 1892); and *Geschichte des Katholizismus in Altpreussen von 1525 bis zum Ausgange des achtzehnten Jahrhunderts* (2 vols., Braunsberg, 1901–03).

DIVINATION.

Divination is the supposed art of discovering the will of the gods, of forecasting the future from indications ascribed to them, or of deciding from phenomena supposedly supernatural the correct course of action to be followed. Three principles lie at the root of divination: (1) belief that Deity is willing to reveal to his worshipers both his own will and directions for a correct method of procedure for their advantage; (2) persistent longing to read the future; (3) belief that natural events have a significance for man akin to the principles of magic (see MAGIC; and COMPARATIVE RELIGION, VI., 1, § 5). The art is confined to no one stage of civilization. It exists in primitive and tribal religion, is always a part of the official cults of developed faiths, and persists as a superstition under Christianity, even receiving churchly sanction.

I. In Ethnic Religion: In the stage when man imagined that volition and power resided in things now held to be only material he worshiped them as superhuman, not only in power, but also in knowledge. As a characteristic of early religion is to expect from the objects of its worship a *quid pro quo* in the direction of man's wants (cf. Gen. xxviii. 20–22), the belief obtained that, from objects conceived to possess wisdom greater than man's, knowledge of the future could be gained if the right methods were pursued. Human perceptions were early sufficiently keen and human reasoning was sufficiently logical to look for indications of the future or for directions as to conduct in methods suited to the observed character of the object consulted. Hence men fancied they heard answers to queries or indications of divine will in the leaves of a sacred tree, in the waters of a sacred stream, in the surf on the shore, etc. Individuals claimed superior ability in reading these omens, and diviners developed as a class. Inventive genius came into play, and methods of consulting superhuman powers were devised. Observed sequences were read as cause and effect, and a repetition of the first or its artificial production was believed to insure repetition of the other. Thus a pseudo-science or fictitious art developed with its established canons. Along with other consequences of animistic belief there was unfolded the idea of exchange of souls, the doctrine of possession or obsession of human bodies by spirits to impart information (cf. the phrase "familiar spirits"), the ability of the dead (enlarged in knowledge by passing the gates of death) to share this knowledge with the living, and also the power of the human spirit to wander from the body in search of wisdom. Moreover, persons in abnormal states of mind (see ECSTASY), or with minds diseased ("demoniacs"; see DEMONIAC) or defective (idiots), or with unusual physical characteristics (as albinos), were considered channels of divine communication and were employed in divinatory art. Where observation had shown that a certain environment produced abnormal states of mind, that environment was sought, or a person inhabited a particular place to act as the medium between the oracle god and the inquirers, and the utterances were accepted as inspired. Such utterances proceeded from the Cumæan and Delphic oracles, at the shrines of which mephitic gases produced ecstatic effects. This condition, expressed by the Greek *mania*, "prophetic frenzy," developed the technical term *mantikē* or *mantikē technē*. The dream was also believed to be of superhuman sending and to have significance as an index of divine will. Hence dreams were induced by the drinking of decoctions brewed by the knowing, or by sleeping on a spot haunted by divinity or in a temple. The art of reading dreams grew, and persistently survived in advanced stages. Instruments for use in divination were taken from sacred objects and employed in all the ways which the ingenuity of man could devise.

1. Animistic Basis.

How various were the methods employed is only suggested by the following (incomplete) list of names applied to some of the methods. Hydromancy is divination by water (e.g., the roar of the waves, the flow of an intermittent spring, or the movement of water poured into a cup, the latter also called culicomancy); xylomancy, rhabdomancy, and belomancy used sacred trees or parts of them, or arrows made from them (compare the modern "dowsing" with a forked twig of hazel); empyromancy employed fire; geomancy used soil from a sacred spot or supposed motions of the earth; asteromancy employed the motions of stars and planets or meteors; capnomancy drew its conclusions from the appearance or motions of clouds (cf. I Kings xviii. 44); cleromancy or sortilegium was the casting of lots by stones, dice, or other objects; ornithomancy used the flight or voices of birds; ichthyomancy observed the movements of fishes; oneiromancy interpreted dreams; necromancy professed to use the dead or ancestral images; logomancy depended upon the chance utterance of a word (cf. I Sam. xiv. 8–10); axinomancy employed an ax; coscinomancy used the oscillations of a suspended sieve, and dactylomancy employed a ring in the same manner; cheiromancy has survived in almost its old form of reading the lines on the hand; scapulomancy or omoplatoscopy read the fissures caused on the shoulder-blade of a sacrificial animal by exposing it to fire; haruspication used many methods, including the inspection of the liver or entrails of slain victims (hepatomancy or hepatoscopy and splanchnomancy). Among the Romans arose the *Vergilianæ sortes*, in which the *Æneid* was opened and a passage selected by chance was interpreted with reference to the point at issue. Later the Bible took the place of the *Æneid* for this purpose (bibliomancy). Especially noteworthy is the Ordeal (q.v.) to decide innocence or guilt. Such methods have been employed among all peoples, the articles depending upon the environment; e.g., the Tongans

2. Names and Methods.

and Samoans use coconuts as the sieve and ring are used elsewhere. The employment of the lot is universal, and many nations have deities who preside over the cast.

In all the foregoing two characteristics appear: (1) Divination is in general under the patronage of religion. On the other hand, among many peoples there exists a distinction between legitimate and forbidden. Thus necromancy, or commerce with the dead, is often forbidden. (2) All methods are regarded by science as marked by a total inconsequence of data and results. Thus the lack of connection between the aspect of the planet Mars simply from its color and peace and war is sufficiently obvious, and is asserted to exist between all the methods of divination and the supposed results.

II. In the Bible: The Pentateuch legislates in all the codes against divination as practised among the surrounding peoples. The earliest code permits no sorceress in Israel (Ex. xxii. 18); the Deuteronomist (xviii. 10–11) forbids the people to suffer among them diviners, enchanters, necromancers, charmers, wizards, and those who have familiar spirits; the Levitical Code (Lev. xix. 31) forbids approach to those who have familiar spirits and to wizards. An indication earlier than the codes of prohibition of these means is found in I Sam. xxviii. 3. Yet the assumption in early Old Testament books is not that these means were not successful, but that they were not permissible to Israel (e.g., the magicians of Egypt wrought duplicates of some of the signs and plagues, Ex. vii. 11, 22, viii. 7, 18, etc.). That diviners wrought actively in the surrounding nations is assumed (e.g., ut sup. and in I Sam. vi. 2, Ezek. xxi. 21, etc.), just as it is assumed in the Balaam passages and II Kings i. 2–3 that prophecy and the utterance of oracles existed outside Israel. The means legitimated in the Old Testament are: the dream, coming to Hebrew and to heathen alike, to Joseph and to Pharaoh and his servants (Gen. xx. 3, 6, xxviii. 12 sqq., xxxi. 24, etc.; Judges vii. 13 sqq.; I Kings iii. 5 sqq.; Job xxxiii. 14–16; Dan. vii. sqq., and frequently); the lot (Josh. xv. sqq.; I Sam. xiv. 41; see LOTS, HEBREW USE OF); Urim and Thummim (q.v.); the ephod (q.v.; I Sam. xxx. 7); and the living voice of the prophets. I Sam. xiv. 8 gives a case of logomancy. But there are indications that, as late as the time of the Judges, at least sacred trees were employed as oracles (Judges iv. 5, a very clear case in the light of ethnic usage; cf. verse 10). The dream is emphasized in the Old Testament, and the Pentateuchal narrator E has great fondness for it; the interpretation of the dream was a divine gift among the Hebrews as among many other nations (Gen. xli. 16, 38; Dan. ii. 28, 47, iv. 18). That in prophetic times in Israel there was either persistence of old methods or else adoption of them from the surrounding peoples is indicated by Hos. iv. 12, where rhabdomancy or xylomancy is referred to, and probably by several passages in Ezekiel. In the New Testament indications are given by the dream (Matt. i. 20, ii. 12 sqq., xxvii. 19; Acts x. 9–16, xi. 4–10) and the sacred lot (Acts i. 23–26).

III. Under Christianity: Divination entered the Christian Church from two sources: (1) with the membership which, recruited from paganism, brought with it practises customary under heathenism; (2) forms of decision sanctioned by the Scriptures tended to continue so far as they were available, together with those which non-canonical Judaism had practised. In particular, use of divination for the detection of criminals was especially persistent and continued till modern times. A strong tendency toward the continued use of divination is proved by the fact that church synods found it necessary to legislate against it. Thus canon lxii. of the Synod of Elvira (305–306) requires that augurs who have become Christians renounce their calling before being admitted to membership in the Church; the Synod of Ancyra (314) condemns the *manteuomenoi*, "those who employ the mantic art," to five years' penance; the Fourth Synod of Carthage (398) excommunicates those who practise divination. The legislation of the period grows increasingly severe up to and including the Theodosian Code (ix. tit. 16, leg. 4). The Synod of Vannes denounces the use of the lot. But, as is frequently the case, the theory and the practise of the Church were at variance. To the common mind the fact that things were sacred (such as the wafer of the Eucharist, the emblem of the cross, and the Scriptures) seems to have justified their use in this manner, and this tendency spread upward from the common people to the clergy. The employment of the lot as based upon both Old Testament and New Testament usage and the application by Jews of the method of the *Vergilianæ sortes* to the Old Testament were carried over into the Christian Church as early as the fifth century. In parts of the West the lot entered into Christian codes (Ripuarian Code, xxxi. 5) and was sanctioned by early Irish synods (*Excerptiones*, ascribed to Egbert of York, ed. Thorpe, ii. 108). In France a dispute among the bishops of Poitiers, Arras, and Autun over the possession of the relics of St. Liguaire was decided at the altar by the lot in favor of Poitiers. The use of the Bible as in the *Vergilianæ sortes* to divine by was condemned by Augustine, though he regarded it as a less evil than consulting demons (*Epist.*, lv., *ad Januarium*, xxxvii., *NPNF*, 1st ser., i. 315). The synods in Gaul in the fifth century found it necessary to threaten the clergy with penalties for resort to divination; yet Gregory of Tours (*Hist. reg. Franc.*, iv. 16) relates that in the presence of a concourse of bishops and priests at a celebration of the mass at Dijon the Gospels and Epistles were solemnly consulted regarding the fortunes of a son of Lothair I. Especially did the Ordeal (q.v.) as an appeal to God to indicate the guilty receive the practical sanction of the Church by the presence and often the participation of Church dignitaries and officials. The use of the Bible and the key (another form of bibliomancy) was particularly persistent. A key was loosely fastened to the Bible at Ps. l. 18, the Bible made to revolve, while names of suspects were mentioned, and he at whose name the book fell was regarded as guilty. The latest case known of use of this method occurred at a trial in 1867 in London. The weighing of a person against the Bible to determine his guilt or innocence is known to have occurred as late as 1759 at Aylesbury, England. GEO. W. GILMORE.

BIBLIOGRAPHY: Classical works are Cicero, *De divinatione;* Lucian, *De astrologia;* Cornelius Agrippa, *De occulta philosophia.* For the ethnic side consult: E. B. Tylor, *Primitive Culture*, i. 78–81, 117–133, ii. 155, Boston, 1874; F. B. Jevons, *Introduction to Hist. of Religion*, London, 1896; J. G. Frazer, *Golden Bough*, ii. 355, iii. 342, London, 1900; Mary Hamilton, *Incubation*, London, 1906. For the Biblical side consult: C. A. Briggs, *Messianic Prophecy*, §§ 4–8, New York, 1902; H. Schultz, *Old Testament Theology*, ii. 322, London, 1892; S. R. Driver, *Commentary on Deuteronomy* (on Deut. xviii. 10), New York, 1895; Smith, *Rel. of Sem.*, pp. 194, 246, 407, 427. For divination under Christianity consult: H. C. Lea, *Superstition and Force*, pp. 93–370, Philadelphia, 1878; S. Baring-Gould, *Curious Myths of the Middle Ages*, pp. 55 sqq., London, 1884; H. C. Bolton, *The Counting-out Rhymes of Children*, London, 1888. A quite full list of the "mancy's" from Bolton is given in *The New International Encyclopædia*, "Superstition," xvi. 347, New York, 1904.

DIVORCE.

I. History of Divorce Law and Custom: Recent research has disclosed among rude peoples elaborate systems of unwritten law covering, often in an orderly way, most of the divisions commonly associated with "civilized" jurisprudence. This is especially true of divorce. Among barbarous, even savage, races appears a careful attention to detail, a stability, and a respect for equity in the social rules relating to the dissolution of marriage, which Western prejudice is hardly prepared to find; while other races commonly looked upon as civilized, but hitherto relatively non-progressive, such as the Chinese, are quite capable of teaching us valuable lessons in this regard.

1. Among Existing Backward Peoples. As to the right or freedom of divorce, five classes of peoples may be differentiated: (1) The marriage bond is lax and readily dissolved at the pleasure of either the man or the woman. Such is the case among a large number of American, African, Asiatic, and Oceanic tribes; e.g., among the Makassars and Buginese, the Alfurese of Minehasa, and the Point Barrow Eskimo. (2) At the other extreme are peoples with whom wedlock is absolutely indissoluble; for the sacramental nature of marriage is affirmed, not exclusively in Christian lands, but among races standing on a very low plane of culture; e.g., with certain Papuans of New Guinea, the Veddahs of Ceylon, and the Niassers of Batu death alone is sufficient to dissolve the nuptial tie. (3) Sometimes the only method is mutual agreement except in case of life-assault, as among the Karo-Karo of Sumatra; or the husband may put away the wife for serious misconduct, as in West Victoria, but then only when she has no children and the tribal chiefs give their consent. (4) Very commonly the man alone has absolute right of divorce, putting away the woman when he likes, without assigning any reason, or on the most frivolous grounds. Theoretically this is true of some parts of China; but practically with the more advanced Chinese, as among the ancient Aztecs, the wife, under the influence of Confucius, enjoys the privilege of separation in several important contingencies; while under the existing law of Islam she has a quite limited right of divorce through purchase or by judicial decree. (5) Finally, among many rude races the woman has great liberty of divorce, leaving the man at pleasure or on the slightest pretext. The lot of the married woman among barbarous or even savage tribes is not always so dark as it is frequently painted (cf. the usages of the American Indians and others). In general, divorce among backward peoples, even where great liberty is allowed, is far less frequent than is popularly believed. Their conservatism is remarkable. Very commonly custom frowns upon divorce after children are born. The usages regarding the legal effects of divorce are particularly enlightening. One is almost as often surprised by the reasonableness and stability of early institutions as he is shocked at their harshness or injustice. In the disposal of the children or the division of the property after the marriage is dissolved principles of natural equity and justice are frequently observed which constitute a rebuke to the laws sanctioned by some modern Christian societies. It appears to be practically a universal rule among uncivilized races that the repudiated wife or the woman who legally puts away her husband shall return to her own family or clan, whose duty it is to receive her.

2. Earlier Christian Doctrine. According to the spirit of the earliest Christian teaching, divorce, properly so called, is strongly condemned, though by a strict interpretation of its letter it may not be wholly forbidden. Between the first assertion of the new doctrine and the final triumph of the canonical theory of absolute indissolubility of the marriage bond intervenes a struggle of twelve hundred years. The various utterances of the New Testament relating to the subject are disjointed and confusing in their details (for Hebrew and Jewish customs see FAMILY AND MARRIAGE RELATIONS, HEBREW, § 7). Many vital questions are either completely ignored or else left in such obscurity as to open the way for wide divergence of doctrine and the bitter controversies of the Reformation period. For four centuries the Bible passages were debated by the Fathers and the councils. Nearly all were agreed that divorce is forbidden except for the one cause mentioned by Matthew (v. 32); but not all conceded the equal right of the sexes in this regard. There was a like want of harmony touching the lawfulness of remarriage after divorce. Finally Augustine's interpretation prevailed—that adultery is the only Scriptural ground of separation; but even this does not dissolve the nuptial tie. Moreover, he reproaches those who, following the letter of Matthew's text, for this offense would allow the man, but not the woman, the right of repudiation, with violating the great principles of Christian teaching by disregarding the equality of the wedded pair.

These views were adopted by the Eleventh Synod of Carthage in 407 (canon viii.; Hefele, *Conciliengeschichte*, ii. 101), which thus anticipated the final settlement of the canon law.

3. The Canon Law. Theory and Practice. Before that settlement, however, centuries of compromise intervened. From Constantine to Justinian the divorce legislation of the Christian emperors was practically untouched by the essential doctrines of the Church; while in dealing with the newly converted Teutonic peoples the rigid Augustinian rules were relaxed in diverse ways. In England and in Gaul, as proved in the most convincing way by the penitentials, full divorce with remarriage was allowed on various grounds. Authority had to yield perforce to social expediency. Not until 1164, in the fourth book of Peter Lombard's "Sentences," is found the first clear recognition of the "seven sacraments," including that of marriage. The theory of the sacramental nature of wedlock had two consequences which involved the whole medieval problem of separation and divorce. First was the dogma of the indissolubility of the marriage bond, and, second, the exclusive jurisdiction of the Church in matrimonal causes. Accordingly, in theory, divorce proper is entirely eliminated from the mature law of the Western Church. Inconsistently, however, in the canons the word "divorce" is used in two senses, neither of which harmonizes with its ancient and right meaning as a complete dissolution of the bond of true wedlock. First the term *divortium a mensa et thoro* means a separation of husband and wife which does not touch the marriage tie. Secondly, the term *divortium a vinculo matrimonii* is commonly employed to designate, not the dissolution of a valid union, but the judicial declaration of nullity of a spurious marriage which on account of some impediment is void, or at least voidable, from the beginning. There was another inconsistency far more important in its consequences. In effect absolute divorce was tolerated by the canon law, as that law existed on the eve of the Reformation. Theological subtlety had devised two exceptions to the rule that a genuine marriage can not be dissolved. First is the *casus apostoli* or *privilegium Paulinum*, by which the Christian convert, if abandoned by his infidel spouse, is permitted to contract a new marriage. By the second exception, the Church violated the theory, sanctioned since Peter Lombard, that a contract *de præsenti*, or in words of the present tense, constitutes a valid marriage whether followed by actual wedded life or not; for the mature doctrine of the canon law, still obeyed by the Roman Church, allows the unconsummate marriage *de præsenti* to be dissolved through papal dispensation or *ipso facto* by taking holy orders.

Thus, accepting the Church's own definition of marriage, divorce *a vinculo* did not quite disappear from the canon law; and in effect there was a far more prolific source of full divorce. In reality, when rationally considered, the decree of nullity was a divorce proper. By this means a wide liberty of divorce existed in the Middle Ages, although it existed mainly for those who were able to pay the ecclesiastical lawyers and courts for finding a way through the tortuous mase of forbidden degrees and other impediments. Abundant opportunity for this was afforded in a characteristic way by theological refinement. By persistently sustaining the validity, though not the legality, of clandestine precontracts *de præsenti*—contracts formed without witnesses, parental consent, official celebrant, or record—the Church invited social anarchy. In a divorce procedure masquerading under the guise of an action to nullify spurious marriages lurked the germs of perjury and fraud. Before the Reformation the voidance of alleged false wedlock on the ground of precontract or forbidden degrees of affinity, spiritual relationship, consanguinity, or some other canonical pretext had become an intolerable scandal in Christendom.

By the leaders of the Reformation the mother Church was accused of fostering vice by professing

4. Protestant Doctrine. The Rise of Civil Divorce. a doctrine too severe; and at the same time she was bitterly reproached with a scandalous abuse of her jurisdiction through which in effect the forbidden degrees had become an open door to divorce for the use of the rich and powerful. With the rejection of the sacramental theory of marriage it was inevitable that a more liberal interpretation of the Scriptural precepts should be accepted; while ultimately the rise of civil divorce was assured. A great impulse was then given to the development of social control through the State. The Protestant doctrine of divorce, like the Protestant conception of the form and nature of wedlock, was shaped mainly by the thought of Martin Luther. In his dictum, "marriage is a worldly thing," lay the germs of future civil marriage and of its counterpart, civil divorce. Liberty of divorce is the fruit of the Reformation; and from the start it has been especially favored by the more extreme sects. While Luther and some other Reformers sanctioned temporary separations, there was a strong tendency at first entirely to reject perpetual divorce *a mensa et thoro* as being a "modern invention" unknown to the primitive Church; but eventually this was allowed. On the other hand, two causes of full divorce—adultery and malicious desertion—were admitted by Luther and his immediate followers. Rather than further multiply the number of permissible grounds of absolute dissolution of wedlock, an effort was made by hard logic to broaden the definition of desertion so as to give to it a wide range without seeming to transgress the letter of the Scriptural authority. In this way, for instance, *sævitia*, or cruelty, was included; as also was "refusal of conjugal duty," thus eventually giving rise to the doctrine of "quasidesertion." More extreme theologians, like Lambert of Avignon and Martin Butzer, Milton's teacher, went almost as far as the modern statute-maker in multiplying the permissible grounds of divorce. Yet even the most radical thinkers of the sixteenth and seventeenth centuries to a large extent still appealed to authority rather than to reason and experience in their attempts to solve a great social problem. Only gradually, after three centuries of struggle, has civil divorce, on rational grounds sanctioned and regulated by the State, been almost universally established throughout the civilized world. In England—more conservative than Protestant Germany—no immediate change in the canon law of divorce was effected by the Reformation; for the liberal provisions of the commission of Edward VI. failed of adoption. Except by parliament, full divorce was not granted. Until 1857 the sole relief obtainable in the courts was the ecclesiastical decree of separation from bed and board; and this was allowed only for two causes, adultery and cruelty.

Among the Independents and Puritans advanced Protestantism bore its legitimate fruit. By these sects in the new world civil marriage, and therefore civil divorce, were instituted. The American type of liberal divorce legislation had its birth in the New England colonies. Before the Revolution in the five Southern provinces not a single instance of either full or partial divorce has been discovered. Courts with competent jurisdiction were not created; and there were no statutes on the subject. The only relief from bad marriages was through informal or parol separation; and, contrary to the English practise, separate alimony without divorce was sometimes granted, even by the county courts. The case is somewhat different for the middle colonies. A few marriages were dissolved by the legislature in Pennsylvania. Civil divorce through arbitration or judicial decree existed in New Netherlands under the Dutch régime. For some years after the English took possession there is evidence of the survival of arbitration in cases of separation, and of marital reconciliation managed and recorded by the courts. With the exception of this practise, judicial divorce *a vinculo* ceased in New York with the English conquest, and it was not revived until the act of 1787. Subsequent to the meeting of the first assembly in 1683 there is no clear evidence of legislative divorce. On the other hand, Cadwallader Colden declares that previous to 1689 the "governors of New York took on them the power of granting divorces"; and this seems to be an entirely unique instance of executive decree.

5. Civil Divorce and New England Puritanism.

A farmore liberal policy prevailed in the Northern colonies. In most respects throughout New England from the outset the broad modern doctrines of the *Reformatio legum* of the commission of Edward VI., though even now not wholly accepted in the mother country, were put in force by Puritan and Separatist alike. The most advanced ideals of Protestantism were realized. The American conception of divorce as belonging not to the criminal, but exclusively to the civil, jurisdiction had its birth in the seventeenth century. For more than 100 years in the New England colonies the canonical decree of separation from bed and board—which the early Reformers were inclined to reject—was practically, though not wholly, abandoned; while, on the other hand, a dissolution of the bond of matrimony, with right of remarriage, was freely granted for adultery, desertion, and even on other grounds. For Massachusetts the records are but partially preserved. Between 1639 and 1692 forty actions for divorce or annulment have been discovered; while between 1739 and 1776 at least 107 such suits were tried by the courts. The complete record, doubtless, would disclose many more. From 1650 onward Rhode Island authorized divorce *a vinculo*. This colony was much afflicted by the evil of legislative divorce. During nearly the entire provincial period the assembly, side by side with the courts, acted on divorce petitions. The divorce legislation of Connecticut gained surprisingly early maturity. In the middle of the seventeenth century no society in the world, with the possible exception of Holland, possessed a system so modern in character. Separation from bed and board was rejected. Reasonable grounds for absolute divorce were sanctioned. Husband and wife were treated with even justice; and, although legislative divorce was permitted and liable to abuse, the greater part of the litigation seems always to have been entrusted to the regular courts.

II. European Divorce Legislation: During the seventeenth century, almost simultaneously in Holland and America, the foundation of modern divorce law was laid. In its original form the law of 1792, instituting civil divorce in France, practically sanctioned free dissolution of wedlock at the pleasure of the parties. The natural result was a vast number of decrees. Accordingly, in 1803 the *Code Napoléon* substituted a more conservative provision, allowing absolute divorce for five causes. The law of 1803 was abrogated in 1816, and civil divorce was restored only in 1884; but the liberal policy of France, as expressed in the *Code Napoléon*, undoubtedly has had a powerful influence on the extension of civil marriage and divorce throughout Europe. The act of 1884 sanctions absolute divorce, on the petition of either spouse, for adultery, cruelty, and condemnation to infamous penalty, if at the same time the penalty be corporal; while separation from bed and board is still permitted.

Previous to 1900 the laws of divorce in German lands were complex, obscure, and well-nigh past finding out. The conditions were probably as unsatisfactory as they are in the United States. By the imperial code of 1900 absolute divorce is sanctioned for five causes: (1) adultery; (2) attempt on the life of either spouse by the other; (3) malicious desertion; (4) "when either spouse has been guilty of grave violation of the obligations based on the marriage or of so deeply disturbing the marital relation through dishonorable or immoral behavior that the continuance of the marriage can not be expected from the other;" and (5) insanity (*Geisteskrankheit*) of three years' standing. It may reasonably be doubted whether any "omnibus clause" in the laws of American States gives wider discretion to the court than does the fourth of these grounds. The law, however, appears to be conservatively administered; for the number of divorces is rapidly decreasing. In 1899 9,563 decrees were granted; while in 1901, under the new code, the number had sunk to 8,037.

By the present law of England three forms of separation are recognized; and jurisdiction is vested wholly in the civil courts. Full divorce may be granted for the adultery of either spouse; but the woman is treated with grave injustice. For while the husband may secure an absolute divorce on account of the simple adultery of the wife, the wife is unable to free herself from an unfaithful husband unless his infidelity has been coupled with such cruelty as "would have entitled her to a divorce *a mensa et thoro*"; or "with desertion, without reasonable cause, for two years and upward"; or with certain other aggravating offenses. Since 1860 the decree *nisi* has been in force, with the right of the king's proctor to intervene. Secondly, the law allows a decree for "judicial separation" with the same force and the same consequences as the former ecclesiastical sentence *a mensa et thoro*, which was abolished in 1857. In the third place, the existing law provides for what is commonly called "magisterial separation," through which, by the issue of "protection," "maintenance," and "separation" orders, the court is able to secure to a deserted wife the enjoyment of her own property, with a just share in the delinquent partner's goods; and to protect the woman against a brutal husband's violence. In England, as in European countries generally, few divorces are granted as compared with the United States; but the divorce rate is rising. The number mounted from 127 in 1860 to 390 in 1887. In France, for each 1,000 marriages celebrated, fourteen divorces were decreed in 1885 and twenty-four in 1891, the population showing a very small increase. A similar movement is shown by the statistics for Holland and Sweden, and even for Roman Catholic states like Belgium and Bavaria.

III. Divorce Legislation in the United States: Under the Federal Constitution the States within their respective borders have exclusive control of matrimonial and divorce legislation. Congress has conferred the same power upon the organized Territories; but it legislates directly for the District of Columbia and Alaska. Therefore at present (1907), including Porto Rico and Hawaii, there are in force fifty-two distinct divorce codes whose provisions are often conflicting, although in many of their vital features they are slowly approaching a common type. Jurisdiction belongs to the civil courts. Formerly the granting of divorces by the legislatures was a wide-spread evil. In nearly all the States, directly or indirectly, it is now prohibited by constitutional enactment; and since 1886 Congress has put a stop to it in the Territories.

1. Statutory Grounds of Divorce.

Except between 1872 and 1878, divorce has never been provided for by statute in South Carolina. In the other fifty-one States—using "States" to include the districts, Territories, and insular possessions—full divorce is permitted, while in twenty-three States separation from bed and board is likewise allowed. Moreover, in seven jurisdictions the courts are authorized to decree separate maintenance, which is virtually the same as separation from bed and board. The number of legal causes of divorce *a vinculo* varies from one (adultery) in New York, District of Columbia, and (practically) in North Carolina (1905), to fourteen in New Hampshire. Several of these grounds reveal the tendency to abandon authority and to treat divorce purely as a social problem. Thus forty-two States have admitted drunkenness (intoxication, intemperance) as a proper cause for dissolving the marriage tie. Failure to provide for wife or family is recognized by twenty-one codes. Vagrancy of the husband is a cause in Missouri and Wyoming. By the statute of Rhode Island a marriage may be dissolved when either spouse is guilty of "habitual, excessive, and intemperate use of opium, morphine, or chloral"; and a similar law exists in Maine, Massachusetts, Mississippi, and Porto Rico.

2. Remarriage After Divorce.

In eighteen States no restraint is placed on the immediate remarriage of either party with another. Elsewhere restrictions are put upon one or both of the persons either as a penalty or to allow time for proceedings in error or on appeal. Thus, in case of adultery, marriage with the accomplice during the life of the former spouse is forbidden in Louisiana, Pennsylvania, and Tennessee; while such a union is absolutely prohibited in Delaware. In South Dakota and New York the defendant guilty of adultery may not marry any person during the life of the aggrieved; although in New York, on certain conditions, the court may remove the restraint. By the criminal code of Florida, the guilty defendant may not rewed. Under the act of 1901, in the District of Columbia the defendant is absolutely prohibited from remarriage, unless with the former spouse. In several States the placing of a temporary or perpetual restriction on further wedlock is left to the court's discretion. Such is the case in Michigan, Mississippi, Virginia, and Alabama; while in Georgia the question is left to the jury, subject to the court's revision. Three of the New England States discriminate against the defendant. Since 1878, in Vermont, the libelee may not marry any person other than the libelant for three years, unless the latter dies. Since 1883 the statute of Maine forbids the party obtaining the decree to rewed in two years without the court's permission; while during that period the adverse party is absolutely restrained; nor at any later time may he remarry without the court's consent. In Massachusetts since 1881 the offending person, without petition to the court, may remarry only after two years. Moreover, Massachusetts, following the English precedent, has adopted the decree *nisi*; and in principle her example has already been followed by Maine (1883), Oklahoma (1893), Rhode Island (1902), New York (1902), and California (1903). Nine commonwealths of the West, foregoing any attempt to impose a penalty, are content to fix a period within which neither person may marry again; and usually, if proceedings in error or on appeal be instituted, the restraint is extended to final judgment, or to thirty days beyond it, as in Kansas and Oklahoma. This term of delay varies from three months in North Dakota to one year in Colorado and Wisconsin. On the other hand, two Western States are more stringent, discriminating against the guilty person. Thus Illinois (1905) requires such a person to wait two years, and Montana (1905) three years; while in those commonwealths one year and two years respectively are the period for the aggrieved. An anomalous condition of the law should be noted. Owing to the want of precision and uniformity in the legislation of the States the restraints placed on the marriage of divorced persons are practically futile. In 1829 the supreme court of Massachusetts (in Putnam v. Putnam, 8 Pick., 433–435) decided that if a man, "being a resident in this State, for the sake of evading the law goes into a neighboring State where such a marriage is valid, and is there married and immediately returns and continues to reside here, the marriage is valid here, and after his death his widow is entitled to dower in his estate." This precedent was followed by New York in 1881 (Van Voorhis v. Brintnall, 86 N. Y., 18), Washington in 1900 (Willey v. Willey, 22 Wash., 115–121), and California in 1903 (Estate of Wood, 137 Cal., 129). The prevailing doctrine of the courts appears to be that a marriage good where it is contracted is good everywhere; but there are opposing decisions.

3. Residence and Notices.

Bad laws relating to residence and notice are the chief source of clandestine divorce in the United States. Notice to the defendant through publication in the newspapers, still quite generally permitted, is especially capable of abuse; but in recent years a number of States have enacted rigorous statutes governing notice when personal service can not be had. The provisions regarding residence are conflicting, lax, and wanting in precision. They invite migration for divorce. At present the term of previous residence for the plaintiff, or at least for one of the parties, varies from six months to five years; but the prevailing period is one year, at least twenty-eight commonwealths, under various conditions, having that requirement. Massachusetts, in particular, has a very stringent and carefully drawn statute which in principle may serve as a model for other States.

4. American Statistics.

The government report, compiled under the direction of Hon. Carroll D. Wright and published in 1889, contains fairly complete statistics, drawn from a careful analysis of the manuscript court records in all the States and Territories for the twenty years, 1867–86, inclusive. In the entire country during this time 328,716 petitions for full or partial divorce were granted. From 9,937 decrees in 1867 the number rose to 11,586 in 1871, 14,800 in 1876, 20,762 in 1881, and 25,535 in 1886; thus, comparing the last year with the first, showing an increase of 157 per cent, while the population grew but sixty per cent during the same two decades.

Again—to express the result in terms of the divorce rate—in 1867, it is estimated, there were 173 divorces to 100,000 married couples, while in 1886 the number had risen to 250. As a matter of fact, in the last-named year the average divorce rate in the United States was higher than for any other country collecting statistics, except Japan. Of the whole number of divorces during the period 112,540 were granted to the husband, and 216,176 to the wife. Among the principal causes, at each stage of the wedded life, only for adultery were more decrees granted on the husband's petition than on that of the wife. But the relative number granted on the wife's petition varies greatly; from 39.3 per cent in North Carolina to 77.9 in Nevada. These figures are one indication of the relative significance of the divorce problem to women.

Important generalizations may be drawn from the available divorce statistics. In the United States, as in Europe, the divorce rate is higher in the city than in the country. Willcox (*A Study of Vital Statistics*, in the *Political Science Quarterly*, viii., 1893, pp. 76, 77) has demonstrated that the average divorce rate for the whole country, like the marriage rate everywhere, sinks in hard times and rises on the restoration of business. The report of 1889 shows that the evil of migration for easy divorce, due to the lack of uniformity of State laws, is greatly exaggerated by popular opinion. It seems probable that not more than two or three per cent of all divorces are secured by persons migrating to other jurisdictions for the purpose. As early as 1889, the Rev. Samuel W. Dike, of Auburndale, Mass., secretary of the National League for the Protection of the Family, to whom especially is due the inception of the great government report, declared that "the establishment of uniform laws is not the central point" of the divorce problem. Moreover, since 1900 the action of the Federal and certain State courts is significant. In a number of cases arising in various States they have declared null and void decrees secured in jurisdictions where the plaintiffs were not *bona fide* residents, even when they had dwelt in such jurisdictions for the statutory term prescribed as a condition for obtaining a divorce. Thus both the statutes and the courts are distinctly discouraging the "divorce colony." In certain places, however, the evil of migration for divorce has been very pronounced. Previous to the reform legislation of 1899, probably the most flourishing divorce colonies in the world were those at Fargo and Mandan, N. D. In 1899, in Morton County, containing Mandan, there was one divorce to 1.11 marriages (cf. J. L. Coulter, *Marriage and Divorce in North Dakota*, in the *American Journal of Sociology*, xii., Nov., 1906, p. 412).

It appears, likewise, that to some extent the evil of lax administration of divorce laws is exaggerated by popular opinion. The report shows that in seventy counties scattered over twelve States about thirty per cent of all petitions for divorce were rejected. But here also there are extreme or exceptional cases. In North Dakota, between 1900 and 1903, 87.4 per cent of all actions were successful. There is a prevailing notion that a large number of persons who seek divorce do so in order at once to contract new marriages. Unfortunately there are no collected statistics adequate to settle this question. Such foreign statistics as are available show that restriction upon the remarriage of divorced persons would not in a large degree affect the divorce rate. They indicate that within the first two or three years after dissolution of marriage divorced men are not much more inclined to remarry than are widowers, while during the same period a greater number of divorced women than widows renew the nuptial ties. Whether the number of divorces is greatly influenced by legislation is a question which has given rise to decided differences of opinion. In 1883 Bertillon took the position that statutes extending the causes of divorce or relaxing the procedure in divorce suits have little influence "upon the increase in the number of decrees." For the United States, at any rate, this view can not be entirely sustained. The divorce movement is indeed mainly dependent upon social forces which lie far beyond the reach of the legislator. Yet it seems almost certain that there is a margin, very important though narrow, within which he may wisely exert a restraining influence. He can create a legal environment favorable to reform. Good divorce laws—laws which are clear, certain, and simple, laws which can not be evaded, which are not a "dead letter," laws which express the best results of social experience—constitute such an environment, and they may even greatly lower the divorce rate, as conclusively proved by the experience of North Dakota. They may check hasty impulse and force individuals to take time for reflection. They may also by securing publicity prevent manifold injustice in the granting of decrees.

In Europe the divorce rate is rising, while the marriage rate is falling. The same is doubtless true of the United States. It is by no means creditable to the American people that with eleven exceptions—the six New England commonwealths, Ohio, Indiana, Michigan, California (1905), and Iowa (1906)—the States are making no effective provision for the collection or publication of divorce statistics.

5. American Legislative Reform, 1887–1907.

At present there is no means of determining the average rate for the whole country; but every practical reformer and student of social ethics will rejoice that Congress has already provided for a second report on marriage and divorce, covering the period since 1886. The report, doubtless, will show substantial progress. Indeed, there is much hasty and misdirected criticism of American divorce laws that ignores the remedial legislation of the last twenty years. Within this period the foundation of what some time may become a common and effective divorce code for the whole Union has slowly been laid. More and more in their essential features the divorce laws of the States are duplicating one another, and they are becoming better. Little by little, as a detailed examination of the whole body of enactments reveals, more stringent provisions for notice to the defendant have been made, longer terms of previous residence for the parties required, and more satisfactory conditions of remarriage after the decree prescribed; while the more dangerous "omnibus clauses" in the list of statutory grounds have been repealed. At least eight States now severely punish the soliciting of divorce business. Moreover, saner opinions regarding the true nature and the real sources of the divorce evil are beginning to prevail.

IV. Nature of the Divorce Problem: The divorce movement, an almost universal incident of modern civilization, signifies underlying social evils vast and perilous. To the student of history it is perfectly clear that this is but a part of the mighty movement for social liberation which has been gaining in volume and strength ever since the Reformation. According to the sixteenth-century Reformer, divorce is the "medicine" for the disease of marriage. It is so to-day in a sense more real than Adam Smith or Heinrich Bullinger (q.v.) ever dreamed of. Certain it is that a detailed study of American legislation produces the conviction that, faulty as are our divorce laws, our marriage laws are far worse; while our apathy, our carelessness and levity touching the safeguards of the matrimonial institution are well-nigh incredible.

Nowhere in the field of social ethics, perhaps, is there more confusion of thought than in dealing with the divorce question. Some people look upon divorce as an evil in itself; others regard it as a "remedy" for, or a "symptom" of, social disease. To the Roman Catholic and to those who believe with him divorce is a sin, the sanction of "successive polygamy," of "polygamy on the instalment plan." At the other extreme are those who, like Milton and Humboldt, would allow marriage to be dissolved freely by mutual consent, or even at the desire of either spouse. According to the prevailing opinion, however, as expressed in modern legislation, divorce should be allowed, with more or less freedom, only under careful state regulation. Yet divorce is sanctioned by the State as an individual right; and there may be occasions when the exercise of that right becomes a social duty. The right, of course, is capable of abuse. Loose divorce laws may even invite crime. Nevertheless, it is fallacious to represent the institution of divorce as in itself a menace to social morality. It is a result, and not a cause; a remedy, and not the disease.

This is the principle upon which rests the whole modern theory of social control. In the Western world the extension of the sphere of secular legislation practically to the whole province—the whole outward or legal province—of marriage and divorce is a fact of transcendent interest. In this regard the Reformation marks the beginning of a social revolution. Luther's dictum that "marriage is a worldly thing" contained within it the germ of more history than its author ever imagined. The real trend of evolution has not at all times been clearly seen or frankly admitted; but from the days of Luther, however concealed in theological garb or forced under theological sanctions, however opposed by reactionary dogma, public opinion has more and more decidedly recognized the right of the temporal lawmaker in this field. As a result, in the United States, not less clearly than elsewhere in countries of Western civilization, marriage, divorce, and all the institutions of the family are emerging as purely social institutions, to be dealt with according to human needs. Definitively the State seems to have gained control of matrimonial administration. Yet it must be conceded that the influence of legislation in curing social disease is very restricted. Apparently if there is to be salvation, it must come through the vitalizing, regenerative power of a more efficient moral, physical, and social training of the young. The fundamental causes of divorce lie far beyond the reach of the statute-maker. They are rooted deeply in the imperfections of human nature and the social system, particularly in false sentiments regarding marriage and the family. Beyond question, the chief cause of divorce is bad marriage laws and bad marriages. The conviction is deepening that for the wise reformer, who would elevate and protect the family, the center of the problem is marriage and not divorce.

The remedial influence of good statutes may be relatively small, still the legislator has a very important task to perform. In particular it seems worth while to strive for more uniform laws in the States. Ideally a common code embracing the entire body of matrimonial laws is desirable, if it may be gained without too great a sacrifice of local control; for it would conduce in many ways to social order. The earlier movement to secure a Federal statute under an amendment to the national constitution has been abandoned by practical reformers. Instead, it has been thought best to strive for the adoption of a model statute by the separate States. Such a statute, relating mainly to procedure, with a view to checking clandestine divorce, was adopted in 1899–1900 by the Conference of State Commissions on Uniform Legislation. But a more comprehensive effort than that was started by the "National Congress on Uniform Divorce Laws." At its Washington session, Feb. 19–22, 1906, after an enlightening discussion, this body, composed of delegates from forty States, adopted a series of seventeen resolutions upon which is based "an act regulating annulment of marriage and divorce" agreed upon by the Congress at its Philadelphia session in November of the same year. The act contains careful provisions for residence and notice. The decree *nisi* is provided for. Both partial divorce and absolute divorce are sanctioned. Divorce *a vinculo* is permitted, on the suit of the aggrieved spouse, for (1) adultery; (2) bigamy; (3) conviction and sentence for crime, "followed by a continuous imprisonment for at least two years or, in the case of indeterminate sentence, for at least one year"; (4) extreme cruelty; (5) wilful desertion for two years; (6) habitual drunkenness for two years. Divorce from bed and board is authorized for the same six causes and also for "hopeless insanity of the husband." Draft-acts providing respectively for the "return of statistics relating to divorce proceedings" and for the "return of marriage statistics" were also submitted by the Congress. In its first resolution the Congress declares that "no federal divorce law is feasible." Moreover, it is significant of its right understanding of the problem that the body urges a like effort to secure a uniform marriage law. See Marriage.

Bibliography: For the history of divorce among backward peoples consult: A. H. Post, *Afrikanische Jurisprudenz*, Oldenburg, 1887; idem, *Entwicklungsgeschichte des Familienrechts*, ib. 1890; T. Araki, *Japanisches Eheschliessungsrecht*, Göttingen, 1893; E. Westermarck, *Hist. of Human Marriage*, London, 1894; P. G. von Möllendorff, *Das chinesische Familienrecht*, Shanghai, 1895; E. Alabaster, *Notes and Commentaries on Chinese Criminal Law*, London, 1899; G. E. Howard, *Hist. of Matrimonial Institutions*, vol. i., chap. v., Chicago, 1904 (where the authorities are cited in full).

On divorce under the canon law consult: H. Geffcken, *Ehescheidung vor Gratian*, Leipsic, 1894; A. Esmein, *Le Mariage en droit canonique*, 2 vols., Paris, 1891; J. Freisen, *Geschichte des canonischen Eherechts*, Paderborn, 1893; Howard, ut sup., vol. ii., chap. xi. (where the authorities are cited). Compare H. Benecke, *Die strafrechtliche Lehre vom Ehebruch*, Marburg, 1884; the standard Catholic treatises of A. Cigoi, *Die Unauflösbarkeit der christlichen Ehe*, Paderborn, 1895; and especially J. Perronne, *De matrimonio*, Paris, 1861. For England consult: F. Pollock and F. W. Maitland, *History of English Law*, vol. ii., Cambridge, 1895.

For the Reformation period consult: A. L. Richter, *Beiträge zur Geschichte des Ehescheidungsrechts in der evangelischen Kirche*, Berlin, 1858; and Richter's edition of the *Kirchenordnungen des sechzehnten Jahrhunderts*, 2 vols., Weimar, 1846 (the legislation of the evangelical churches on marriage and divorce). These ordinances are analysed by O. Goeschen, *Doctrina de matrimonio*, Halle, 1848; and by H. C. Dietrich, *Evangelisches Ehescheidungsrecht*, 1892. Luther's utterances are compiled by H. L. von Strampff, *Dr. Martin Luther: Ueber die Ehe*, Berlin, 1857.

For England, very convenient handbooks are: W. Ernst, *Treatise on Marriage and Divorce*, London, 1880; N. Geary, *Law of Marriage and Family Relations*, ib. 1892. The modern French law is treated by E. Kelly, *The French Law of Marriage, Marriage Contracts, and Divorce*, ib. 1895.

For the United States and for divorce problems in general consult: C. D. Wright, *Report on Marriage and Divorce in the United States, 1867–86*, Washington, 1889, reprinted, 1897; idem, in *The Christian Register*, lxx (1891), 655–658; S. W. Dike, *Reports of the National Divorce Reform League*, and *Reports of the National League for the Protection of the Family*, 1886–1906; idem, in *Political Science Quarterly*, iv (1889), 206–214; idem, in *Century Magazine*, xxxix (1890), 385–395; idem, in *Publications of the American Statistical Association*, i (1889), 206–214; idem, in *Andover Review*, Dec., 1893; idem, in *Congress of Arts and Science*, vii. 707–720; T. D. Woolsey, *Divorce and Divorce Legislation*, New York, 1881; J. Bertillon, *Étude démographique*, Paris, 1883; idem, in *Journal of the Statistical Society*, xlvii (1884), 519–526; A. P. Lloyd, *Law of Divorce*, Baltimore, 1887; D. Convers, *Marriage and Divorce in the United States*, Philadelphia, 1889; W. L. Snyder, *Geography of Marriage*, New York, 1889; F. Adler, in *The Ethical Record*, ii (1889), 200–209, iii (1890), 1–7; J. P. Bishop, *New Commentaries on Marriage, Divorce and Separation*, 2 vols., Chicago, 1891; E. Janes, in *New Englander and Yale Review*, 1891, pp. 395–402; C. H. Pearson, *National Life and Character*, chap. v., New York, 1894, answered by J. H. Muirhead, in *International Journal of Ethics*, vii (1896), 33–35; H. C. Whitney, *Marriage and Divorce*, Boston, 1894; J. C. Richberg, in *Publications of the Michigan Political Science Association*, i., no. 4, 1895; W. F. Willcox, in *Political Science Quarterly*, viii (1893), 69–96; idem, *The Divorce Problem*, New York, 1897; J. Bryce, *Studies in Hist. and Jurisprudence*, London, 1901; H. Hirsh, *Tabulated Digest of Divorce Laws*, New York, 1901; W. B. Bailey, *Modern Social Conditions*, ib. 1906; and especially *Proceedings of the National Congress on Uniform Divorce Laws*, Harrisburg, 1906, and the pamphlet containing the model statutes since published by the Congress.

In this article, through the generous permission of the

publishers, some passages have been freely taken by the author from the following writings: *Marriage and Divorce*, in the *Encyclopedia Americana*, x.; *Social Control and the Function of the Family*, in *Congress of Arts and Science*, vii. 697-706; *The Problem of Uniform Divorce Law in the United States*, in *The American Lawyer*, xiv (1906), 15-17; *Divorce*, in Bliss's *Encyclopedia of Social Reform* (new ed., 1908); and *History of Matrimonial Institutions* (3 vols., Chicago, 1904), where a systematic bibliography for every phase of the subject may be found.

GEORGE ELLIOTT HOWARD.

DIX, MORGAN: Protestant Episcopalian; b. in New York City Nov. 1, 1827; d. there Apr. 29, 1908. He was graduated at Columbia College in 1848, and the General Theological Seminary in 1852. He was ordered deacon in 1852, ordained priest in 1853, was assistant rector of St. Mark's, Philadelphia (1853-55), was a curate of Trinity Church, New York City, until 1859, when he became assistant rector and rector in 1862. He was president of the Standing Committee of the Diocese of New York, a trustee of many institutions, and a member of numerous important committees. He wrote *Manual of the Christian Life* (New York, 1857); *Commentary on Romans* (1864); *Commentary on Galatians and Colossians* (1866); *Lectures on the Pantheistic Idea of an Impersonal-Substance Deity as Contrasted with the Christian Faith Concerning Almighty God* (1865); *Book of Hours* (1865); *Lectures on Two Estates—Wedded in the Lord, Single for the Kingdom of Heaven's Sake* (1872); *Historical Lectures on the First Prayer Book of King Edward VI.* (1881); *Lectures on the Calling of a Christian Woman* (1883); *Memoir of John A. Dix* (2 vols., 1883); *The Gospel and Philosophy* (1886); *The Seven Deadly Sins* (Lenten sermons; 1888); *Lectures on the Authority of the Church* (1891); *Three Guardians of Supernatural Religion* (Paddock lectures; 1891); *The Sacramental System Considered as the Extension of the Incarnation* (Paddock lectures; 1893); *Harriet Starr Cannon, First Mother Superior of the Sisterhood of St. Mary* (1896); *Good Friday Addresses* (1898); and *History of the Parish of Trinity Church* (4 vols., 1898-1906).

DIXON, AMZI CLARENCE: Baptist; b. at Shelby, N. C., July 6, 1854. He studied at Wake Forest College, Wake Forest, N. C. (B.A., 1874), and held pastorates at Warsaw, N. C. (1875-76), Chapel Hill, N. C. (1878-81), Asheville, N. C. (1881-1884), Immanuel Baptist Church, Baltimore, Md. (1884-91), Hanson Place Baptist Church, Brooklyn (1891-1901), Ruggles Street Baptist Church, Boston (1901-07), and Moody Church, Chicago (since 1907). In theology he is orthodox. He has written *The True and the False* (Baltimore, Md., 1890); *Milk and Meat* (sermons, New York, 1893); *Lights and Shadows of American Life* (Chicago, 1898); *Present Day Life and Religion* (Cleveland, O., 1905); *Evangelism Old and New* (New York, 1905); and *The Young Convert's Problems and their Solution* (1906).

DIXON, RICHARD WATSON: Church of England; b. at Islington, London, May 5, 1833; d. at Warkworth (26 m. n. of Newcastle), Northumberlandshire, Jan. 23, 1901. He studied at Pembroke College, Oxford (B.A., 1857), and was ordered deacon in 1858 and ordained priest in the following year. After being curate at St. Mary-the-Less, Lambeth (1858-61), and of St. Mary's, Newington-Butts (1861-63), he was second master of Carlisle High School (1863-68) and minor canon and honorary librarian of Carlisle Cathedral (1868-75). He became vicar of Hayton-cum-Talkin, Cumberlandshire, in 1875, and of Warkworth in 1883. In 1874 he became an honorary canon of Carlisle and from 1879 to 1883 was rural dean of Brampton, while from 1885 until his death he was rural dean of Alnwick and after 1891 was also examining chaplain to the bishop of Newcastle. While at Oxford he was associated with William Morris and Edward Burne-Jones in editing *The Oxford and Cambridge Magazine*, advocating the Preraffaelite movement, and also wrote besides several volumes of verse: *Second Peak Prize Essay on the Maintenance of the Church of England as an Established Church* (1873); *Life of James Dixon, Wesleyan Minister* (1874; a biography of his father); his most important work, however, was his *History of the Church of England from the Abolition of the Roman Jurisdiction* (6 vols., 1877-1902). This work takes high rank by reason of its learning, research, and attractive style. It extends from 1530 to 1570. The last two volumes were posthumous and edited by Henry Gee, who has prefaced them by a biographical sketch. In the last year of his life he was made by his university a doctor of divinity, and by his college an honorary fellow.

BIBLIOGRAPHY: Besides the sketch by Gee, ut sup., consult *DNB*, supplement, ii. 139-140.

DOANE, WILLIAM CROSWELL: Protestant Episcopal bishop of Albany; b. at Boston, Mass., Mar. 2, 1832. He studied at Burlington College, Burlington, N. J. (B.A., 1850), where he was a professor 1850-63. He was ordained to the priesthood in 1856, and was rector of St. Mary's, Burlington (1859-63), St. John's, Hartford, Conn. (1863-1867), and St. Peter's, Albany, N. Y. (1867-69). In 1869 he was consecrated first bishop of Albany. He has been instrumental in building the Cathedral of All Saints, Albany, and established in the same city St. Agnes' School for Girls, the Child's Hospital, and St. Margaret's House for Babies, the St. Christina Home (for training servants) at Saratoga, and the Orphan House of the Holy Savior at Cooperstown, founding the Sisterhood of the Holy Child Jesus to take charge of these institutions. In theology he is a conservative High-churchman. He has written a life of his father, Bishop G. W. Doane of New Jersey (5 vols., New York, 1860); *Mosaics, Being Comments on the Collects, Epistles, and Gospels of the Christian Year* (1882); *Sunshine and Play-Time* (poems; 1893); *The Manifestations of the Risen Jesus* (Oxford, 1898); and *Rhymes from Time to Time* (Albany, 1901).

DOBSCHUETZ, deb″shûts′, ERNST (ADOLF ALFRED OSKAR ADALBERT) VON: German Protestant; b. at Halle Oct. 9, 1870. He studied at Leipsic, Halle, and Berlin (Ph.D., 1893), and in 1893 became privat-docent for New Testament theology at Jena, where he was appointed associate professor in 1899. Since 1904 he has been professor of the same subject at Strasburg. He has written *Studien zur Textkritik der Vulgata* (Leipsic, 1894); *Die urchristlichen Gemeinden* (1902; Eng. transl. by G. Bremner, London, 1904); *Ostern und Pfingsten, eine kritische Studie zu I Kor. xv.* (Leipsic, 1903); *Probleme des apostolischen Zeitalters* (1904); and *Das apostolische Zeitalter* (Halle, 1905).

DOCETISM, do-sí'tism: A heresy which appears in the most varied forms and aspects, but may be generally defined as the theory which would merge the truth and reality of Christ's human nature in a mere fantom. The Docetæ, as a distinct sect, are mentioned by Clement of Alexandria (*Strom.*, iii. 13; vii. 17), who names as the founder Julius Cassianus (see ENCRATITES); by Serapion of Antioch (Eusebius, *Hist. eccl.*, vi. 12); and by Hippolytus (*Philosophoumena*, viii. 8–11; cf. x. 16). The latter has preserved a detailed record of these sectaries, which on the whole may be trustworthy, but can not be considered entirely reliable. Their fundamental idea is that current in the Gnostic systems. The aim is to describe the divine process of development, the history of the spirit of God, who, himself forever the same, suffered himself to be limited by a material existence in order to withdraw himself from it as fruit. From the first *archē*, which appears here under the image of the seed of the fig, out of which develops the world-tree, emanate at first three, finally thirty eons. They form the intelligible nature (*hē noētē physis*), pure light, comprising in itself the primitive forms (*tas apeirous ideas*) of all living. Its light shines into the chaos, and becomes the cause of everything created because it impresses the everlasting ideas upon that which has been formed. To separate darkness from light, the third of the primeval eons created the firmament, the *stereōma* (Gen. i. 5). It separated itself as living fire, and became the great archon, the god of fire, who spoke out of the bush, the lord over the ideas who had confined them in the bodies and made them wander as souls when they grew cold therein. To redeem these and to end their wandering, the "only begotten son," produced by the thirty eons, came upon this earth. He took upon himself the extremest darkness, the flesh, and was born of Mary. In the water of the Jordan this Jesus received the seal of the body born of the virgin, so that, after putting off the body created by the archon and being nailed to the cross, his soul may not be found naked, but be enabled to put on the *soma anti tēs sarkos ekeinēs* (cf. John iii. 5, 6), imprinted in the water of baptism. The human souls, all somehow related to Jesus, exert themselves for him in different ways. So the different sects can know their own Jesus only in part; the Docetæ alone know the whole Jesus.

G. KRÜGER.

BIBLIOGRAPHY: G. Salmon, in *Hermathena*, xi (1885), 389–402; idem, in *DCB*, i. 865–870 (valuable); E. W. Möller, *Geschichte der Kosmologie*, pp. 323–335, Halle, 1860; A. Hilgenfeld, *Ketzergeschichte des Urchristentums*, pp. 546–550, Leipsic, 1884; H. Staehelin, in *TU*, vi. 3, 1891; L. Pullan, *The Church of the Fathers*, pp. 46, 51, New York, 1905; Harnack, *Dogma*, i. 256–259, ii. 276 sqq., 370, iii. 16, iv. 138 sqq. et passim. Consult also the literature under HIPPOLYTUS.

DOCTOR: The Latin word for "teacher," employed in various ways in academic and ecclesiastical usage. The **Doctors of the Church** (*Doctores ecclesiæ*) are certain of the Church Fathers (q.v.) who bear the title by "express declaration of the Church" (i.e., conferred by the pope or by a general council) because of their "orthodox teaching, holiness of life, and eminent erudition." As early as 1298 the following had thus been pronounced Doctors of the Church: of the Greek Fathers, Athanasius, Basil the Great, Gregory Nazianzen, Chrysostom, and Cyril of Alexandria; of the Latins, Ambrose, Jerome, Augustine, and Gregory the Great. Since 1298 the names have been added of Hilary of Poitiers, Petrus Chrysologus, Leo the Great, Isidore of Seville, Peter Damian, Anselm of Canterbury, Bernard of Clairvaux, Thomas Aquinas, Bonaventura, Francis of Sales, and Alfonso de' Liguori.

The title "doctor" with a descriptive adjective or equivalent expression was also popularly given to many scholars or churchmen of the Middle Ages, including some who filled no professorial positions. Some of the commoner of these titles with the name of the bearer are as follows: *Doctor admirabilis*, Roger Bacon; *doctor angelicus*, *communis*, or *cherubicus*, Thomas Aquinas; *doctor beatus et fundatissimus*, Ægidius de Columna; *doctor christianissimus*, Jean Gerson; *doctor christianus*, Nicholas of Cusa; *doctor doctorum*, Anselm of Laon; *doctor evangelicus*, John Wyclif; *doctor illuminatus*, Raymond Lully; *doctor illuminatus et sublimis*, Johannes Tauler; *doctor invincibilis et singularis*, William of Occam; *doctor irrefragabilis*, Alexander of Hales; *doctor marianus*, Anselm of Canterbury and Duns Scotus; *doctor mellifluus*, Bernard of Clairvaux; *doctor planus et utilis*, Nicholas of Lyra; *doctor resolutissimus*, William Durand; *doctor scholasticus*, Abelard, Peter Lombard, and others; *doctor seraphicus*, Bonaventura; *doctor subtilis*, Duns Scotus; *doctor universalis*, Albertus Magnus. For more complete list cf. the *KL*, iii. 1867–69.

DOCTRINAIRES, doc"tri"nārz. See CHRISTIAN DOCTRINE, SOCIETY OF.

DOCTRINE, HISTORY OF.

The history of Christian doctrines as a department of theological study was inaugurated by S. G. Lange of Jena in his *Ausführliche Geschichte der Dogmen* (Leipsic, 1796), which came down to Irenæus. This was followed by W. Münscher's *Handbuch der christlichen Dogmengeschichte* (4 vols., Marburg, 1797–1809), extending to Gregory the Great, and J. C. W. Augusti's *Lehrbuch der christlichen Dogmengeschichte* (Leipsic, 1805). Of course, much had been written previously regarding the history of particular dogmas and controversies. The present article deals with the rise and development of the history of doctrines and the lessons taught by a century of work in this department respecting its idea, task, method, and scope.

As early as the time of Irenæus (by way of opposition to Gnostic innovations) stress was laid upon the continuity of the doctrinal teachings of the elders from the apostolic age. Athanasius constantly appealed to the Fathers in support of his positions in conflict with Arius and others. Vincent of Lerins (d. 450) declared that "the ancient consensus of opinion of the holy fathers ought to be most diligently sought out and followed" (*Commonitorium*, i. 28). Naturally non-catholic parties also sought and found support for their views in earlier Christian literature. Abelard (d. 1142), in his *Sic et non*, by arraying authority against authority on all important doctrines demonstrated the necessity of freely applying the mind to the solution of theological problems. The harmonizing of patristic authorities was one of the tasks of scholasticism. The Renaissance brought with it disparagement of authority and recognition of the possibility of progress in the apprehension of truth. The Reformation interrupted for the Evangelicals the continuity of doctrinal tradition. The adoption of the Scriptures as the sole authority gave free course to investigation in the history of doctrine. Melanchthon could say in his *Loci* (1521): "Immediately after the founding of the Church, Christian doctrine was ruined by the Platonic philosophy." Yet Luther and Melanchthon alike, alarmed by the undesirable consequences of too rigorous an insistence on Scripture authority by Anabaptists, felt it necessary to defend the doctrinal definitions of the first four general councils as authoritative interpretations of Scripture and necessary inferences therefrom. The Magdeburg Centuriators (1559–74) assumed that from the fifth century (in part from the second) there was a progressive obscuration of evangelical truth, not seriously hindered by isolated "witnesses" who appeared from time to time. The stimulus given by the Reformation to historical research and the vast amount of material thus brought to light made possible such works as that of the Jesuit Petavius, *De theologicis dogmatibus* (Paris, 1644–50), and the *Instructiones historico-theologicæ de doctrina Christiana* (Amsterdam, 1645) by the Scotch theologian John Forbes of Corse. Early Lutheran theologians did little more in the history of doctrine than to gather rich patristic materials for polemical purposes on the various *loci* of their dogmatic systems. Examples of this kind of work are Gerhard's *Loci* (Jena, 1610–25) and Quenstedt's *Theologia Didactico-polemica* (Wittenberg, 1685). It was not until Pietism and the Enlightenment (q.v.) had shattered faith in the absolute correctness of Lutheran orthodoxy that "heretical" systems began to be studied on their merits and that doctrine history could become a distinct department of study. Gottfried Arnold's *Kirch- und Ketzer-Historie* (1st ed., 1699–1700; most complete ed., 3 vols., Schaffhausen, 1740–42) brought to light and treated sympathetically a vast amount of authentic material regarding dissenting parties from the first century to his own time. His disposition to give to "heretics" their due was to some extent shared by Mosheim and C. W. F. Walch. Walch, Ernesti, Semler, and Planck have been regarded, along with Lange and Münscher, as the fathers of doctrine history.

1. Early Attempts at Doctrine History.

Leaving out of consideration Roman Catholic works, which (with the exception of those of Bach and Schwane) are based upon the dogmatic assumption of the identity of dogma during all the centuries, four groups of works from Münscher to F. Nitzsch (*Grundriss der christlichen Dogmengeschichte*, vol. i., Berlin, 1870) and Harnack (*Lehrbuch der Dogmengeschichte*, 3 vols., Freiburg, 1886–90; Eng. transl., 7 vols., Boston, 1895–1900) may be advantageously distinguished. Works of the Münscher type which conceive of the history of doctrines as the history of the multiform changes which Christianity (as doctrine or dogma) has undergone up to the present time constitute the first group. Münscher, though learned and accurate, failed completely to understand the reasons and significance of changes and had no proper appreciation of times and persons. The same may be said of Lentz and Bertholdt. This method may be designated the rationalistic-pragmatic. The supernaturalistic modification of this method (Münter, Augusti) avoided the offensive extravagances of pragmatism and recognized as legitimate for their time a mass of opinions no longer acceptable, but made little advance in method. Under the influence of the romanticism and religious earnestness of the awakening (Schleiermacher) the vision for the abiding and common in all the diversified forms of doctrine was sharpened (Neander and his school). Deep appreciation of all Christian character as the embodiment of the new life introduced by Christ is what gives coherence to Neander's work. This is true in a measure of Hagenbach, and in a larger measure of Baumgarten-Crusius, whom Hase called the "historian of the religious spirit." These historians agree in distinguishing between "general" and "special" history of doctrines, in discarding the distinction between "dogmas" (authoritatively formulated doctrines) and opinions on doctrine set forth by any one whomsoever in any way whatever (their aim having been in many cases to discredit dogma by demonstrating its instability), and in ignoring Roman Catholic doctrinal development since 1517. Niedner's work is peculiar in its combination of the history of philosophy and that of theology, and in its discrimination between the doctrines of the schools and those of the Churches, yet it undeniably belongs to this group.

2. Four Groups of Histories. The Münscher Group.

The second group, introduced by Baur's monograph on the doctrine of the Atonement (1838), is characterized by the dominance of the Hegelian philosophy. Baur, like his predecessors, was concerned about the whole mass of changes in doctrinal teaching that have occurred from the apostolic time to the present. He saw in the manifold changes the logical development according to inner laws of a substantially unchanged whole. Every doctrine is to him a development of the Christian idea, inevitable in its time. The history of dogmas has to do as well with the multiplicity of dogmas as with the unity of the dogma. He followed his predecessors in distinguishing between a general and a special history of doctrines, and in taking little account of

3. The Hegelian Group.

the development of Roman Catholic dogma since 1517. Marheineke applied the Hegelian method in producing an orthodox counterpart to Baur's work, abandoned the distinction between general and special history of doctrines, limited the scope of dogma to public definitions, identified the substantial contents of the Christian religion with the teachings of Christ and the apostles, and limited doctrine history to the time between the apostolic age and the completion of the formation of the ecclesiastical symbols. To the Hegelian school likewise belonged Meier and Noack.

4. Engelhardt and Gieseler. To a third group, in which doctrine history is conceived as a historic-genetic representation of the coming into existence of the doctrinal ideas of the various Christian Churches, belong Engelhardt's *Dogmengeschichte* (1839) and Gieseler's lectures. Both were free from Hegelian influence. Engelhardt had much in common with the group next treated, Gieseler with the Münscher type. Engelhardt's peculiarity appears in his comparative treatment of the Lutheran, Roman Catholic, and Reformed dogmas, and his brief survey of the doctrinal movements in the various Churches since the definition of doctrines in the great symbols. Gieseler's definition of dogma is noteworthy: "Christian dogma is not doctrinal opinion, not the pronouncement of any teacher, but doctrinal statute. The dogmas of a church are those doctrinal propositions which it declares to be the most essential contents of Christianity." While he held that a complete doctrine history embraces the development of dogmas in all Christian Churches, he paid little attention to the development of doctrines in the Greek Church after its separation from the Roman, or in the Roman Catholic Church after the Protestant revolt.

5. The Confessional Lutheran Group. The last group of the older writers on the history of doctrines is the confessional Lutheran, whose aim was to show the complete doctrinal agreement of the Book of Concord with divine revelation. Engelhardt and Marheineke prepared the way for this type of doctrine history. Kliefoth, deeply immersed in Hegelianism, marked out its program. Kahnis embodied this idea in his *Kirchenglaube*. Schmid's brief treatise (1860) was of the same character. The most important work of this group is that of Thomasius (1874–76). The second edition of Thomasius by Bonwetsch and Seeberg belongs rather to the preceding group.

6. Nitzsch and Harnack. Side by side with these four groups stands the uncompleted work of Nitzsch, who, though he had a narrow conception of dogma, yet aimed to make intelligible the present position of Christian theology, including the influence of Schleiermacher. The one-sidedness of the Hegelian construction of history is eliminated by sound historical realism, and the separation of general and special dogmatics is abandoned. Nitzsch's work is the mature resultant of the older development of doctrine history. But Harnack's famous text-book begins a new section of the history of the discipline. While building on the foundations laid by Nitzsch, Thomasius, and Ritschl, he has created an epoch in the study of the history of doctrines by materially increasing knowledge of the subject, by his living grasp of the objects of investigation, and by his brilliant and highly interesting literary presentation. His abandonment of any schematic arrangement of the materials and his sole regard to genetic connections, his appreciation of the "tenacity" of dogma and the inner logic of its development, and his effort to understand individual dogmas as parts of the conception of Christianity as a whole may be regarded as contributions of abiding value. The more recent text-books of the writer [F. Loofs] and of R. Seeberg (2d ed., vol. i., 1907, vols. ii.–iii. in preparation), though dependent on Harnack's, are not without distinctive features.*

7. The Idea and Task of Doctrine History. The question as to the light thrown on the idea, task, method, and scope of doctrine history by a century of study can only be answered personally and briefly. The writer regards Harnack's conception of doctrine history as only individually justified. Dogma is for Harnack not a generic idea, but the particular doctrinal ideas that have formed themselves on the basis of the ancient world. Ancient dogma, with its objectivity formally independent of the faith of the individual, is of a wholly different kind from any modern evangelical system, while Roman Catholic dogma still bears this purely objective character. It is therefore instructive to discover the rise of ancient dogma and to trace its further development until it is dissolved in heterogeneous new formations or has found a homogeneous continuation to the present. As there is no dogma on the idea of dogma, Harnack can not be fairly reproached for publishing his doctrine history of the ancient Church under the title *Dogmengeschichte*. Another question is whether the interest that theology has in doctrine history inheres in this special idea of dogma or in the generic idea. Is the term dogma to be used to designate the entire body of doctrines commonly held by a church, or is it to be limited to statements of doctrine made in earlier times by ecclesiastical authority, to which adherence is obligatory? Stange, without sufficient ground, charges Harnack, Kaftan, and Loofs with innovation in using the term in the generic sense; for most of the older writers (Hollatz, Marheineke, Gieseler, Rothe, Biedermann, Nitzsch, etc.) allow the legitimacy of this usage. Seeberg and Heinrici agree with Loofs in defining the history of dogmas as the history of the rise, development, and eventual change of church conceptions of doctrine in Christianity as a whole or in its various denominations.

On the method of this discipline two views have recently been set forth, that of Bernouilli and others, who insist that doctrine history can attain to the

* The editor of this article may be allowed to express the highest admiration of Loofs's *Leitfaden* as a masterpiece of condensed wisdom on the subject. But the 4th ed. (1906) has 1,002 pages. It contains an amount of pertinent quotation from the sources greater than is to be found in many larger works. A. H. N.

highest results only by dealing with the matter from the religio-historical point of view, and that of Stange (following Baur), who thinks that it should be treated purely as a history of ideas, praise and blame being completely eliminated, and every phase of doctrine being regarded as part of a process. As a matter of fact, every historian has some sort of standpoint, and pure objectivity is out of the question. Still, it is no disqualification in the historian of dogmas to be imbued with Evangelical principles and to be a master of dogmatics. The better he understands current dogmas the better should he be able to understand the process by which they have been reached. As regards the starting-point and the closing-point of the history of dogmas, the question at issue is whether it should begin with the teachings of Christ and the apostles and end with the present, or begin with the earliest ecclesiastical formulations and end with the latest. Against making the teachings of Christ and the apostles the starting-point is the fact that New Testament theology is in itself so large and complicated a subject and contains so many elements of controversy as to require separate treatment. The historian of dogmas must base himself upon the most assured results of New Testament criticism, exegesis, and theology, rather than attempt to make New Testament theology a part of his field. Certainly, the history of dogmas does not end with the Formula of Concord, the Westminster Confession, or any other symbol; but is it possible to discern surely between modern dogmatics and dogmas? Therefore the history of dogmas may stop with the latest ecclesiastical formulations of dogmas.

8. Method and Scope.

The relation of the history of doctrines to other theological disciplines, especially to symbolics and church history, can not be adequately treated here. The former can be more advantageously treated in the article SYMBOLICS. The history of dogmas is undoubtedly a part of church history, and the question is how far the former should be eliminated from lectures and text-books on church history and reserved for separate treatment. (F. LOOFS.)

BIBLIOGRAPHY: On the conception of history of doctrine consult: K. Daub, in *Zeitschrift für speculative Theologie*, i. 1 (1836), 1–60, i. 2, pp. 63–132, ii. 1 (1837), 88–161; T. F. D. Kliefoth, *Einleitung in die Dogmengeschichte*, Parchim, 1839; C. F. Kling, in *TSK*, xiii (1840), 1051–1152, xiv (1841), 749–852, xvi (1843), 217–259; J. E. Kuhn, in *TQ*, 1850, pp. 249–253; F. Niedner, in *ZHT*, xxi (1851), 579–678; F. C. Baur, *Die Epochen der kirchlichen Geschichtsschreibung*, Tübingen, 1853; G. Frommel, *Introduction à l'hist. des dogmes*, Dôle, 1895; G. Krüger, *Was heisst und zu welchem Ende studiert man Dogmengeschichte?* Freiburg, 1895; C. A. Bernouilli, *Die wissenschaftliche und die kirchliche Methode in der Theologie*, ib. 1897; C. Stange, *Das Dogma und seine Beurteilung in der neueren Dogmengeschichte*, Berlin, 1898.

The works on the history of doctrine earlier than the nineteenth century are given in Hauck-Herzog, *RE*, iv. 752. Later works, in addition to those indicated in the body of the article, are as follows: L. Berthold, *Handbuch der Dogmengeschichte*, 2 vols., Erlangen, 1822–23; F. O. Baumgarten-Crusius, *Kompendium der christlichen Dogmengeschichte*, 2 vols., Leipsic, 1840–46; C. G. H. Lentz, *Geschichte der christlichen Dogmen in pragmatischer Entwickelung*, 2 vols., Helmstedt, 1834–35; J. C. W. Augusti, *Lehrbuch der christlichen Dogmengeschichte*, Leipsic, 1835; H. Klee, *Lehrbuch der Dogmengeschichte*, 2 vols., Mainz, 1837–38; D. F. Strauss, *Die christliche Glaubenslehre in ihrer geschichtlichen Entwickelung*, 2 vols., Tübingen, 1840–41; P. Marheineke, *Christliche Dogmengeschichte*, Berlin, 1849; J. M. A. Ginoulhiac, *Hist. du dogme catholique*, 3 vols., Paris, 1852–62; L. Noack, *Die christliche Dogmengeschichte nach ihrem organischen Entwicklungsgange*, Erlangen, 1853; J. C. L. Gieseler, *Dogmengeschichte*, Bonn, 1855; A. Neander, *Christliche Dogmengeschichte*, Berlin, 1857; E. Haag, *Hist. des dogmes chrétiens*, 2 vols., Paris, 1862; J. Schwane, *Dogmengeschichte*, 4 vols., Münster, 1862–90; K. Beck, *Christliche Dogmengeschichte*, Tübingen, 1864; K. F. A. Kahnis, *Der Kirchenglaube historisch-genetisch dargestellt*, Leipsic, 1864; J. Zobl, *Dogmengeschichte der katholischen Kirche*, Innsbruck, 1865; F. C. Baur, *Lehrbuch der Dogmengeschichte*, Tübingen, 1867; J. Bach, *Dogmengeschichte des Mittelalters*, 2 vols., Vienna, 1873–75; T. C. Crippen, *Popular Introduction to the Hist. of Christian Doctrine*, Edinburgh, 1883; A. V. G. Allen, *The Continuity of Christian Thought*, Boston, 1884; W. G. T. Shedd, *Hist. of Christian Doctrine*, New York, 1884; H. C. Sheldon, *Hist. of Christian Doctrine*, ib. 1886; G. Thomasius, *Die christliche Dogmengeschichte*, 2 vols., Erlangen, 1886–89; H. Schmid, *Lehrbuch der Dogmengeschichte*, Nördlingen, 1887; K. R. Hagenbach, *Lehrbuch der Dogmengeschichte*, Leipsic, 1888, Eng. transl. of 4th ed., 2 vols., New York, 1861–62; C. H. Tuthill, *Origin and Development of Christian Dogma*, London, 1888; F. Bonifas, *Hist. des dogmes de l'église chrétienne*, 2 vols., Paris, 1889; A. Harnack, *Grundriss der Dogmengeschichte*, 2 parts, Freiburg, 1889–91, Eng. transl., *Outlines of a History of Dogma*, London, 1893; R Seeberg, *Lehrbuch der Dogmengeschichte*, 2 vols., Erlangen, 1895–98, 2d ed., 1907 sqq.; idem, *Grundriss der Dogmengeschichte*, Leipsic, 1905; G. P. Fisher, *Hist. of Christian Doctrine*, New York, 1896; J. Orr, *Progress of Dogma*, London, 1901; J. Turmel, *Hist. de la théologie positive*, Paris, 1904.

DODANIM: According to Gen. x. 4, one of the four sons of Javan (q.v.). The question of identification is complicated by the question of the correct reading in this passage and in the parallel (I Chron. i. 7). In Genesis the Hebrew manuscripts, the Targums, Vulgate, and Peshito read *Dodanim;* the Samaritan, Septuagint, and Lucian read *Rodanim* (*Rodioi*), thus agreeing with most of the Hebrew manuscripts of I Chron. i. 7 (where, however, Lucian and Ben Asher read Dodanim). Compare the R. V. with the A. V. F. Brown (*Hebrew and English Lexicon*, p. 187, New York, 1906) reads *Rodanim*. To explain the two forms which the manuscripts thus attest, the conjecture has been made that the author of Gen. x. obtained his information concerning Greek peoples from Phenician travelers, that he possibly wrote *Dardanim* (cf. Gk. *Dardanoi*, "Trojans"), and that the "r" was subsequently misread as "w" (o), the word thus appearing as *Dodanim*. Later writers (this theory proceeds), composing after the name *Dardanoi* had disappeared from use, would naturally use "Rhodians," which was the form the (late) Chronicler employed as attested by the manuscripts. If, however, *Rodanim* be the correct reading in Genesis, this explanation is unnecessary. Against this reading are the early authorities as cited above; in favor of it are the later date of Gen. x. and the far greater probability of mention of Rhodians than of Dardanians in that period. If *Dodanim* be the original reading, it is impossible to say what part of the Greek people the author had in mind. The reading *Rodanim* gives a simple and direct solution, referring to the inhabitants of Rhodes. GEO. W. GILMORE.

BIBLIOGRAPHY: B. Stade, *De populo Javan parergon*, Giessen, 1880; and the Bible dictionaries on the word.

DODDRIDGE, PHILIP: English non-conformist; b. in London June 26, 1702; d. at Lisbon Oct. 26, 1751. As early as 1716 he began to think of adopting the ministry as a profession, but declined an offer of a university education and subsequent provision in the Established Church, preferring the freedom of non-conformity. His theological education was directed by Samuel Clarke (q.v.) and the Independent John Jennings. He became minister at Kibworth, Leicestershire, in 1723, without ordination or profession of faith; two years later he removed to the neighboring town of Market Harborough and entered into a joint pastorate with David Some; and he refused several offers which seemed likely to limit the theological liberty to which he clung so ardently. In some sense taking up the work of the deceased Jennings, he became the first head of a new academy at Market Harborough, and, on accepting a call to a pastorate at Northampton six months later, removed his school thither, being ordained by eight ministers in the following March. In the same year appeared his first publication, *Free Thoughts on the Most Probable Means of Reviving the Dissenting Interest.* This expressed his ideal of unity in essentials and freedom in non-essentials, with a view to bringing all non-conformists together on a common ground. He was an inspiring, if not a very systematic teacher, and was busy in many good works, including a scheme which has been described as the first non-conformist project of foreign missions (1741). His multifarious works were collected in ten volumes (Leeds, 1802-05). The best-known of them with the exception of his hymns are *The Rise and Progress of Religion in the Soul* (London, 1745) and *The Family Expositor, or a Paraphrase and Version of the New Testament, with Notes* (6 vols., 1739-56). His hymns (370 in number) were published by his friend Job Orton at Salop, 1755, and were re-edited, with a collation of Doddridge's manuscripts, by his great-grandson, J. D. Humphreys (*Scriptural Hymns*, London, 1839). Among the best-known are "Awake, my soul, stretch every nerve," "Grace, 'tis a charming sound," and "O happy day, that fixed my choice."

Bibliography: The *Works* (ut sup.) contain the *Memoirs*, by Job Orton, expanded greatly in *Biographia Britannica*, ed., Kippis, 1793. The best source is the *Correspondence and Diary of Philip Doddridge*, ed. J. Doddridge Humphreys (his great-grandson), 5 vols., London, 1829-1831. The best life is by C. Stanford, London, 1881. Consult the lives by J. Stoughton, London, 1851; J. R. Boyd, New York, 1860; D. A. Harsha, Albany, 1865; and the notices in *DNB*, xv. 158-164; S. W. Duffield, *English Hymns*, pp. 364-366, New York, 1886; and Julian, *Hymnology*, pp. 305-306.

DODS, MARCUS: United Free Church of Scotland; b. at Belford (44 m. n.w. of Newcastle), Northumberland, England, Apr. 11, 1834; d. at Edinburgh, Apr., 1909. He studied at Edinburgh (M.A., 1854) and New College, Edinburgh (1854-1858), and was ordained to the ministry in 1864. He was pastor of Renfield Free Church, Glasgow, until 1889, when he was appointed professor of New-Testament theology in New College, Edinburgh, of which he was principal after 1907. He wrote *The Prayer that Teaches to Pray* (Edinburgh, 1863); *The Epistles to the Seven Churches* (London, 1865); *Israel's Iron Age* (1874); *Mohammed, Buddha, and Christ* (1877); *Handbook on Haggai, Zecharia, and Malachi* (Edinburgh, 1879); *Isaac, Jacob, and Joseph* (London, 1880); *Handbook on Genesis* (Edinburgh, 1882); *Commentary on Thessalonians* (1882); *The Parables of Our Lord* (2 vols., London, 1884-85); *The First Epistle to the Corinthians* (1889); *Introduction to the New Testament* (1889); *Erasmus, and Other Essays* (1891); *Why be a Christian?* (1896); *How to become like Christ* (1897); *The Gospel according to St. John* (in *The Expositor's Greek Testament*; 1897); *Genesis, John, and I Corinthians*, in *The Expositor's Bible* (1888-91); *Forerunners of Dante* (Edinburgh, 1903); and *The Bible, its Origin and Nature* (Bross lectures; 1905). He also translated the "Apology" of Justin Martyr and the three books of Theophilus of Antioch to Autolycus, in Clark's *Ante-Nicene Christian Library* (Edinburgh, 1865), and edited the English version of J. P. Lange's *Life of Christ* (6 vols., 1864), and the writings of St. Augustine (15 vols., 1872-76).

DODWELL, HENRY: English theologian; b. at Dublin Oct., 1641; d. at Shottesbrooke, Maidenhead (26 m. w. of London), June 7, 1711. He was a fellow of Trinity College, Dublin, but was obliged to resign because he was not prepared to take orders (1666), and settled in London (1674). He wrote in defense of the Anglican Church, and made such a reputation that he was appointed Camden professor of history at Oxford in 1688, but lost the position in 1691, by refusing to take the oath of allegiance to William and Mary. He defended the nonjuring bishops, declaring those "schismatics" who submitted, and himself left the Anglican communion, but in 1710, on the extinction of the nonjuring line of bishops, returned to it. His works were numerous, particularly in the various departments of classical literature, and attest great industry and learning, but little judgment. He is remembered for his assertion, in his *Dissertationes in Irenæum* (Oxford, 1689), that the New Testament demoniacs were epileptics, and for his *Epistolary Discourse concerning the Soul's Immortality* (London, 1706), in which he connected immortality with Baptism.

Bibliography: The *Life* by F. Brokesby, London, 1715; J. Darling, *Cyclopædia bibliographica*, pp. 938-939, London, 1854; S. A. Allibone, *Critical Dictionary of Eng. Literature*, Philadelphia, 1891; *DNB*, xv. 179-181.

DOEDERLEIN, dö'der-lain: The family-name of several German theologians.

1. **Johann Alexander Döderlein**: B. at Weissenburg (27 m. s.e. of Anspach) Feb. 11, 1675; d. there Oct. 23, 1745. His most important work was *Antiquitates gentilismi Nordgaviensis* (Nuremberg, 1734).

2. **Christian Albert Döderlein**: B. at Seyringen (40 m. s.w. of Nuremberg) Dec. 11, 1714; d. at Bützow (18 m. s.w. of Rostock) Nov. 4, 1789. He was professor of theology at Rostock and Bützow, and published *De Thaletis et Pythagoræ theologica ratione* (Göttingen, 1750); *Vermischte Abhandlungen aus alten Theilen der Gelehrsamkeit* (Halle, 1755); *Von dem rechten Gebrauch und Misbrauch der menschlichen Vernunft in göttlichen Dingen* (Bützow, 1760); *Commentatio de Ebionæis e numero hostium divinitatis Christi eximendis* (1769); *Ueber Toleranz*

und Gewissensfreiheit (Wismar, 1776); *Theologische Abhandlungen über den ganzen Umfang der Religion* (4 vols., 1777–89); *Ueberzeugender Beweis von der wahren Gottheit des Sohnes Gottes* (1789).

3. **Johann Christoph Döderlein**: B. at Windsheim (30 m. n.w. of Nuremberg) Jan. 20, 1745; d. at Jena Dec. 2, 1792. He studied at the University of Altorf, and at the age of twenty-two became deacon in Windsheim. Gaining recognition by his *Curæ criticæ et exegeticæ* (Altorf, 1770), he received in 1772 a professorship at Altorf, and ten years later was called to Jena. His chief exegetical works were his *Esaias* (Altorf, 1775) and his translation of Proverbs (1778). His most important book was his *Institutio theologiæ Christianæ* (1780), which marks a transition to the modern critical method, since, as he himself said, he took into consideration new interpretations and the results of individual systems of thought with special regard to the requirements of the time, though he did not feel justified in going beyond the Bible or in inventing new doctrines. He likewise urged caution in the choice of arguments, and emphasized the need of quality rather than of quantity in their selection. The same principles were advocated in the *Theologische Bibliothek*, which he edited at Leipsic from 1780 until his death. (K. R. Hagenbach†.)

DOEDES, dō-ē'dēs, JACOBUS ISAAK: Dutch theologian; b. at Langerak, a village in the province of South Holland, Nov. 20, 1817; d. at Utrecht Dec. 17, 1897. In the year 1830 he entered the Latin school at Amsterdam, and in 1834 the University of Utrecht, where he founded the lifelong friendship with his fellow student J. J. van Oosterzee. On June 16, 1841, he attained the doctorate, and his thesis, *Dissertatio Theologica de Jesu in Vitam reditu* (Utrecht, 1841), appeared also in Dutch under the title *De Opstanding van onzen Heer Jezus Christus, in hare zekerheid en belangrijkheid voorgesteld* (Utrecht, 1844). In 1841 he passed his ministerial examination, and while waiting for a charge he wrote the prize essay *Verhandeling over de Tekstkritiek des Nieuwen Verbonds* (Haarlem, 1844). In 1843 he was installed pastor at Hall, in the province of Gelderland, and soon after became an editor of the *Jaarboeken voor wetenschappelijke Theologie*, 10 vols., 1845–54. A study of the subject of baptism and the Lord's Supper led to the writing of *De leer van den Doop en het Avondmaal op nieuw onderzocht.* I. stuk, *Het Avondmaal* (Utrecht, 1847). About this time came his encounter with C. W. Opzoomer, professor of philosophy at Utrecht, who had taken the field against van Oosterzee in behalf of the "infidel philosophy," contending that "scientific infidelity" must make war upon the "miraculous history of Christ and the dogmas founded upon it." That miracles are impossible is assumed as the starting-point for all investigation. Against such an assumption Doedes contended in *Het recht des Christendoms tegenover de wijsbegeerte gehandhaafd* (Utrecht, 1847), a work the sober, historic tone of which gained the admiration even of his opponent, who spoke highly of his "clear, intelligent, and true language."

This apology was partly the cause of his call as pastor to Rotterdam in 1847, where he labored for twelve years with such zeal and success that he is still gratefully remembered. In connection with his pastorate he issued catechetical manuals on the doctrine of salvation and Biblical history which have gone through many large editions and have been translated into the Malayan and the Javanese. Though much occupied in Rotterdam with pastoral work, he yet found time for the sciences, as the *Jaarboeken voor wetensch. Theologie* bears ample witness. Prof. van Hengel in Leyden attacked in 1847 his doctrine of the Eucharist, to whom Doedes replied in his *Aphorismen over de leer des Avondmaals* (*JWT*, 1848, vi. 1). His *Exegetische Studiën over I Pet. iii. 18–iv. 6* (*JWT*, 1848, vi. 2), a contribution to the Petrine conception of the Lord's death, resurrection, and preaching to the imprisoned spirits, is still worth reading. In 1853, in collaboration with N. Beets and Chantepie de la Saussaye, he edited the periodical *Ernst en Vrede*. In the period 1849–1855 he published at Utrecht his *Evangeliebode* in seven volumes. Besides this he put forth several collections of sermons. As a true Protestant he was drawn into the so-called "April disturbance" of 1852; the tone of Pius IX. in his allocution of March 7, 1853, led him to write *De Allocutie van Paus Pius IX. ter aankondiging van het herstel der Bisschoppelijke hierarchie in de Nederlanden, met eene historische toelichting* (Utrecht, 1853).

In 1859 he was called to the chair of theology at Utrecht. His inaugural address, *Oratio de critica studiose a theologis exercenda* (Utrecht, 1859), was bitterly attacked and ridiculed by A. Pierson and the poet P. A. de Génestet, to whom Doedes only sparingly replied one and two years after in the opening addresses *Modern of Apostolisch Christendom?* (Utrecht, 1860) and *De zoogenaamde Moderne Theologie eenigszins toegelicht* (Utrecht, 1861). He characterized the liberty of teaching in the Church as an ecclesiastical absurdity which would lead only to the enslaving of the Church. Against his colleague C. W. Opzoomer he defended the position that choice must be made between a consistent naturalistic philosophy and the Gospel, and that choice of the first leads to an irreconcilable warfare with the latter (*Oud en Nieuw! De leus der Christelijk-orthodoxe Theologie*, Utrecht, 1865). The best commentary to his work as a professor is found in the presence of his pupils in chairs of New Testament exegesis—van Manen in Leyden, Baljon in Utrecht, van Rhijn in Groningen, and Brandt in Amsterdam. He wrote a number of handbooks for academic use: *Hermeneutiek voor de Schriften des N. Verbonds* (Utrecht, 1866; translated into English from the 2d ed. by G. W. Stegmann, Jr., Edinburgh, 1867); *Inleiding tot de Leer van God* (Utrecht, 1870; 2d ed., 1880); *De Leer van God* (Utrecht, 1871); *Encyclopedie der Christelijke Theologie* (Utrecht, 1876; 2d ed., 1883). His standard work, written with much sagacity and fairness, is *De Nederl. Geloofsbelydenis en de Heidelbergsche Katechismus, als belydenisschriften der Ned. Herv. Kerk in de 19e Eeuw, getoetst en beoordeeld* (2 vols., Utrecht, 1880–81). This work brought him into conflict with Dr. A. Kuyper. Of surpassing interest are the recollections of a rich and favored long life which he gives in his *1843–1893 Biografische Herinneringen* (Utrecht, 1894).

(S. D. VAN VEEN.)

BIBLIOGRAPHY: Besides the autobiography, ut sup., valuable material may be found in A. W. Bronsfeld, *Een theologisch Klaverblad*, Rotterdam, 1897; J. M. S. Baljon, in *Stemmen voor Waarheid en Vrede*, Feb., 1898.

DO'EG: An Edomitic servant of Saul, who witnessed David's interview with Ahimelech (I Sam. xxi. 7), and later betrayed the priest (I Sam. xxii. 9–10). The infuriated king sent for the accused and his fellow priests and ordered their slaughter. As Saul's body-guard hesitated, Doeg, at the king's order, murdered the eighty-five priests (Septuagint, "305"; Josephus, *Ant.*, VI. xii. 6, "385"). Saul (or Doeg) then annihilated the priestly city Nob, Abiathar alone escaping to David (I Sam. xxii. 11–23). That Doeg, though an Edomite, is found among Saul's servants has numerous analogies in history (II Sam. xi. 3, xxiii. 37; I Chron. xi. 46, xxvii. 30–31). According to I Sam. xxi. 7, Doeg was at Nob, "detained before Yahweh"; of the surmises aiming to explain his detention—for the keeping of a vow, for concealment (contradicted by xxii. 22), as a recent proselyte, or for levitical uncleanness—Hitzig's (*Begriff der Kritik*, Heidelberg, 1831, 82) is best, viz., that Doeg had been quarantined for suspected leprosy (cf. Lev. xiii. 1 sqq.). In I Sam. xxi. 7 Doeg is called "the chiefest of Saul's herdsmen"; as this expression in the Hebrew is very strange, and the Septuagint seems to follow a different text (also in xxii. 9), Graetz's proposal may be right—to read "runners" (*haraẓim*) for "herdsmen" (*haro'im*; cf. Wellhausen, *Text der Bücher Samuelis*, Göttingen, 1871, 125). Psalm lii. refers to the betrayal of Doeg, according to the superscription; but it is not certain that the superscriptions rest on old tradition; they are now generally regarded as an accommodation to the text of Samuel. (E. KAUTZSCH.)

DOELLINGER, JOHANN JOSEF IGNAZ VON.

Johann Josef Ignaz von Döllinger, church historian and leader of the Old Catholic movement, was born at Bamberg Feb. 28, 1799; d. at Munich Jan. 10, 1890. He entered the University of Würzburg in 1816 and devoted himself to the study of history, philology, and the natural sciences, chiefly botany, mineralogy, and entomology; the last-named science he followed in exhaustive fashion for quite thirty years. In 1817 he chose the priesthood as a profession, influenced by the converts Eckhart, Werner, Schlegel, Stolberg, and Winkelman. In the summer of 1818 he continued his studies under the theological faculty of Würzburg. Out of deference to his father's wishes he took up the study of law at Würzburg in 1819, but he resumed his theological studies at Bamberg in the autumn of 1820 and continued there until Easter, 1822. On Mar. 22, 1822, he was ordained priest. His ideal of life at this time was not a professorship, but a rural pastorate with sufficient income for the formation of a library and with opportunity for study. Accordingly, in November he went as chaplain to Marktscheinfeld in Mittelfranken.

1. Youth and Education.

2. Early Labors as a Professor.

In Nov., 1823, he was chosen professor of church history and ecclesiastical law in the lyceum of Aschaffenburg. Here originated his first work, *Die Eucharistie in den drei ersten Jahrhunderten* (Mainz, 1826), still considered a model treatise. On account of it he was honored with a doctorate of theology by the faculty at Landshut. In the autumn of 1826 he was called to a professorship of church history and ecclesiastical law at the newly opened University of Munich. Here he became intimate with Franz von Baader, and in 1827 made also the acquaintance of Görres. Both Baader and Görres believing that a publication for the promotion of Roman Catholic interests was a necessity, Döllinger was drawn into journalistic activity. A little later, he devoted himself again to his church history, portions of which appeared from 1833 to 1838 (Eng. transl., *A History of the Church*, 4 vols., London, 1840–42). In 1836 he visited England. His relations with that country, for which he had the greatest sympathy, never ceased. Year after year he had a colony of young English students under his own roof. In 1837 he became chief librarian of the University, and in 1838, as newly installed member of the Academy of Sciences, he delivered the opening address on *Muhammed's Religion* (published at Regensburg, 1838). About this time he began to gather material for a history of the heresies of the Middle Ages, for which he made journeys to Holland, Belgium, and France.

3. Activities as Catholic Apologist.

When in 1838 King Ludwig I. ordered all soldiers to kneel before the host the Protestants sought exemption for themselves on conscientious grounds. The king, however, stood firm, maintaining that the bending of the knee was merely a military act. Döllinger published articles on the question, at first anonymously, which called forth sharp replies from the Protestants and were not altogether acceptable to the Roman Catholics (see KNEELING CONTROVERSY IN BAVARIA). His work on the Reformation (*Die Reformation, ihre innere Entwicklung und ihre Wirkungen*, 3 vols., Regensburg, 1846–48) received little attention in the stormy years of 1847–48. In 1853 he published at Regensburg *Hippolytus und Kallistus* (Eng. transl., Edinburgh, 1876). Döllinger was considered in these years an Ultramontane, but he himself expressed himself publicly against such a characterization. And, indeed, he was right, if one understands by Ultramontanism the Jesuitical system. That system he never learned.

In 1843 Harless gave expression to his views on the controversy concerning the immaculate conception of the virgin, and Döllinger answered that the Church permits a difference of opinion regarding a subordinate question concerning which there is no tradition and nothing is revealed. His hearers, in 1847, presented him with an address on his birthday, and in acknowledging his thanks he spoke upon the significance of a German Catholic, or national church, and pointed out as its special mission the conservation of theological learning. As they conceived it, the principal mission of himself and his friends was, not only to maintain freedom of faith and conscience, but also the independence of Church and State, with a similar basis for all religious societies. The opposition to him, which began in 1849, because of his national church tendencies never waned. The archbishop of Munich, Count Reisach, a Jesuit scholar, denounced him, and, on the whole, he was regarded at Rome with the greatest mistrust.

4. Beginnings of Break with Rome.

Meantime Döllinger had projected a comprehensive church history, and in connection therewith had collected material for a history of the popes. In 1857 there appeared at Regensburg as part thereof *Heidenthum und Judenthum, Vorhalle zur Geschichte des Christenthums* (Eng. transl., *The Gentile and the Jew in the Courts of the Temple of Christ*, 2 vols., London, 1862 reprint), and in 1860 *Christenthum und Kirche in der Zeit der Grundlegung* (Eng. transl., *The First Age of Christianity and the Church*, 2 vols., 1866). Besides this he busied himself with a history of the heresies of the Middle Ages, and upon many journeys to Italy drew from wide sources. In 1857 he finally made his often planned journey to Rome. The attempts of the Italians for a United Italy appeared to him to have miscarried. Even Napoleon III. seemed to be weakening. Without an ecclesiastical state the control of the Church was believed impossible; and the Jesuits insisted upon the necessity of such a state as a part of the Catholic faith. At Easter of 1861 certain ladies of the nobility requested him to say something regarding the situation. In response he gave his Odeon lectures, in which he considered the possibility of the fall of the Papal State. The nuncio left the hall in the middle of the discourse, and the Roman Catholic world was thrown into great excitement. Napoleon had the substance of the lectures transmitted to him by telegraph. Döllinger published the lectures with an explanatory introduction in *Kirche und Kirchen, Papstthum und Kirchenstaat* (Munich, 1861, Eng. transl., *The Church and the Churches, or the Papacy and the Temporal Power*, London, 1862), and even Pius IX. was appeased by the flattering picture of himself which it contained. Meanwhile a severe conflict broke out between the Jesuits and the German theologians. No unscholastic theologian or philosopher was accepted as trustworthy, no theological faculty as Catholic, which was not held by the Jesuits.

5. Position upon the Temporal Power.

Many German theologians considered that a conference of scholars was necessary, and Döllinger was induced to issue the call. It cost, however, endless trouble to bring it about. But on Sept. 28, 1863, Döllinger opened the conference with his celebrated address, *Die Vergangenheit und Gegenwart der katholischen Theologie*. This was the signal for a stormy outbreak on the part of the Jesuits against Döllinger, and, indeed, it was clearly evident that a reconciliation between them and the German theology was now impossible. The breach widened rapidly and a most vigorous fight on paper took place, in which the Jesuits' organ at Rome participated. In the syllabus of 1864 the lectures of Döllinger were put under the ban. No less objectionable was his *Papstfabeln des Mittelalters* (Munich, 1863; Eng. transl., *Fables respecting the Popes in the Middle Ages*, London, 1871; New York, 1872), in which he criticized the Donation of Constantine and elaborated on the heresy of Pope Honorius I. This was regarded as directed immediately against papal infallibility. In Aug., 1866, Döllinger's friend Bishop Weis of Speyer wrote to Rome that there had lately appeared in Munich a school of theologians who strove to lower the authority and rule of the apostolic chair, and especially to oppose the doctrine of the infallibility of the pope. Archbishop Manning in London on Feb. 25, 1866, wrote to Rome that Döllinger was writing against the prerogatives of the holy chair. Archbishop Scherr of Munich considered it to be the best solution of all the difficulties, if Döllinger should die of the attack of pneumonia from which he was then suffering.

6. Widening of Breach with Rome.

Nothing definite concerning the purpose of the approaching Vatican Council (q.v.) was known until the *Civiltà Cattolica* in Feb., 1869, raised the curtain through the correspondence of Cardinal Antonelli. Thereupon Döllinger again took up his pen and published in the Augsburg *Allgemeine Zeitung* a series of articles, collected in August into a book, *Der Papst und das Konzil*, under the pseudonym of Janus (Eng. transl., *The Pope and the Council*, London, 1869). He opposed pope and council, and the work displayed such knowledge of papal history that it was immediately suspected that the author could be none other than Döllinger. At the same time he issued the so-called Hohenlohen Theses, and followed shortly with his anonymous *Erwägungen für die Bischöfe des Konzils über die Frage der Unfehlbarkeit*, at once translated into French and sent to the bishops. Both writings, however, gave the sources insufficiently, and therefore were quite useless for ignorant or poorly instructed bishops. Cardinal Schwarzenberg urged upon Döllinger that, at least as a private individual, he should attend the Council; but he preferred to remain in Munich, where he published regularly in the *Allgemeine Zeitung* *Briefe vom Konzil*, based upon material furnished him from Rome, each of which fell as a bomb in Rome. *Einige Worte über die Unfehlbarkeitsaddresse* and *Die neue Geschäftsordnung im Konzil* were articles which still more militated against

7. The Vatican Council, his Excommunication.

him in Rome, so that already he was called a heretic. Bishop Ketteler of Mainz, and other bishops of the minority, in an open letter addressed to him begged of him to keep silent. He complied and on July 18, 1870, the personal infallibility of the pope and his universal episcopacy were declared an article of faith. Döllinger declined to give up what he had hitherto taught, and on Apr. 18, 1871, Archbishop Scherr, himself an opponent in the Council of infallibility, caused his excommunication to be declared from the Chancel. Döllinger acknowledged the fact of excommunication, but pronounced it unrighteous and therefore futile. He considered himself and his associates as still Roman Catholics. He opposed the organization of a separate church, but soon threw in his lot with the Old Catholics (q.v.).

8. Relations with Old Catholics.

It now became clear to Döllinger that the Roman Church could not possibly be the Catholic one as conceived by Christ and described by St. Paul. The very highest aim of Christlike development was to unite the now divided Christian communions. These thoughts had been long harbored by Döllinger, and he had already given public expression to them. With some of his Old Catholic friends he now elaborated them in seven lectures upon the *Wiedervereinigung der christlichen Kirche* (published in English, *Lectures on the Reunion of the Churches*, London, 1872; German, Munich, 1888). He attended the second Old Catholic congress at Cologne in the autumn of 1872, where union conferences were arranged to be held in 1874 and 1875, at Bonn, under Döllinger's direction. Meantime he waited to see what attitude the church authorities would take. But he soon found, as he says, "indolence and political considerations do not permit the church authorities to do anything." However, he comforted himself with the thought that he had at least raised anew the idea of a union of all Christian communions. He took part in all difficult and weighty questions of the sessions of the Munich Old Catholics Committee.

9. Gradual Retirement.

His position at the head of the university, where, at the celebration of its 400th anniversary (1872), he was a shining figure, together with his duties in connection with the Academy of Sciences made unusual demands upon him, so that, gradually, his age began to make itself felt. In 1873 he was appointed president of the academy. He delivered his academical lectures, speaking even two months before his death, at the age of ninety, with his accustomed intellectual and physical vigor concerning the downfall of the temporal power. But finally he began to retire from activities. With the help of Professor Reusch he published (Bonn, 1887) an edition of Bellarmine's autobiography, which he had long had in hand, and his Jesuitica under the title, *Geschichte der Moralstreitigkeiten in der römisch-katholischen Kirche seit dem sechszehnten Jahrhundert mit Beiträgen zur Geschichte und Charakteristik des Jesuitenordens* (2 vols., Nördlingen, 1889); shortly before his death appeared *Beiträge zur Sektengeschichte des Mittelalters* (2 vols., Munich, 1890). His *Akademische Vorträge* were published in 3 vols., Nördlingen, 1888–91 (Eng. transl., *Studies in European History: being Academical Addresses*, London, 1890; *Addresses on Historical and Literary Subjects*, 1894; and his *Kleinere Schriften* were edited by Professor Reusch, Stuttgart, 1890).

10. Final View of Reformation.

At last Döllinger understood better how to appreciate Luther, "that titan of the spiritual world." When, in 1851, he wrote his sketch of Luther he had read only a few of his writings. Later he studied them all, and then he modified greatly his former judgments. The events of 1870 enabled him to take a still deeper view. In an academical lecture (1882) on the Reformation he makes this confession: "I must admit that, for a greater portion of my life, what occurred in Germany from 1517 to 1552 was an impenetrable riddle, and, moreover, a subject of sorrow and pain. I saw only the fact of the separation, the two halves of the nation, divided as by the sharp blows of a sword, standing inimical to each other. Since I have examined more closely the history of Rome and of Germany in the Middle Ages, and since the experiences of these later years have so illumined the subjects of my research, I now believe that I understand what was so enigmatical and I adore the ways of Providence, in whose almighty hand the German nation became an instrument—a vessel in the house of God, and not one unto dishonor." (J. Friedrich.)

Bibliography: Lives are by J. Friedrich, 3 vols., Munich, 1899–1901; E. Melzer, Danzig, 1889; Louise von Kobell, Munich, 1891; idem, Eng. transl., *Döllinger's Conversations*, London, 1892; E. Michael, Innsbruck, 1894. Consult also the literature cited under Old Catholics and Vatican Council.

DOERHOLT, BERNHARD: Roman Catholic; b. at Bockum Jan. 23, 1851. He studied at Innsbruck (1871–72), Münster (1872–76), and Rome (1876–79), and in 1892 became privat-docent for dogmatic theology at Münster. Since 1899 he has been associate professor of the same subject, and has written *Lehre von der Genugtuung Christi* (Paderborn, 1891); *Entwicklung des Dogmas und der Fortschritt in der Theologie* (Münster, 1892); and *Das Taufsymbolum der alten Kirche nach Ursprung und Entwicklung* (Paderborn, 1898).

DOGGETT, LAURENCE LOCKE: Congregationalist; b. at Manchester, Ia., Dec. 22, 1864. He studied at Oberlin College (B.A., 1886), Oberlin Theological Seminary (B.D., 1890), and the universities of Berlin (1893–94) and Leipsic (1895). He entered Y. M. C. A. work, and was assistant State secretary for Ohio 1890–93 and State secretary 1895–96. Since 1896 he has been president of the International Young Men's Christian Association Training School at Springfield, Mass. He has written *History of the Young Men's Christian Association* (vol. i., New York, 1896); *History of the Boston Young Men's Christian Association* (Boston, 1891); and *Life of Robert R. McBurney* (Cleveland, O., 1902).

DOGMA, DOGMATICS.

I. Meaning and Scope: The explanation of the word "dogma" goes back to an old usage of good Greek, in which *dokei moi* and *dedoktai* mean not only "it seems to me" or "it pleases me," but also "I have definitely determined something so that it is for me an established fact." Hence *dogma* has the significance of a firm, and especially a public resolution, *decretum*. Thus the words are found in the Septuagint and in the New Testament to designate firm enactments in the sphere of practical conduct; governmental decrees (Esther iii. 9; Dan. ii. 13, vi. 8–10; Luke ii. 1); apostolic regulations (Acts xvi. 4); and the Mosaic ordinances (Col. ii. 14; Eph. ii. 15). Hence also the use of the word by philosophers, especially the Stoics, to denote established declarations of truth and doctrinal formulation which by virtue of their firm validity serve in turn as the basis and norm both for further concrete scientific investigations and conclusions and for concrete precepts pertaining to practical conduct. Accordingly the term may be applied both to such sentences as contain ethical principles and to such as refer to objective existences, to God and the world. The name "dogma" was then transferred to propositions in which the basal truths of ethics and religion are established and which are derived from a divine revelation. Josephus designates the content of the sacred books of Judaism as "dogmas of God" (*Apion*, i. 8). Ignatius likewise (*Ad Magnes*, xiii.) speaks of "the dogmas of the Lord and of the apostles," the context referring especially to ethical norms and commandments. According to Origen (*De principiis*, iv. 156), Christ is "the interpreter of the saving dogmas of Christianity." These very propositions then came to be called, with reference to the validity which they have for the Church, *ecclesiastica dogmata*. (On this use of the word among the ancients cf. especially W. Schmidt, *Christliche Dogmatik*, i., *Prolegomena*, Bonn, 1895.)

1. Meaning and Use of "Dogma."

2. A Dogma an Established Truth.

According to this usage and in the light of recent discussions as to the meaning of the word "dogma" and therefore also of "dogmatics" (cf. the doctrinal works of Hahn, K. J. Nitzsch, Schenkel, A. Schweizer, Biedermann, Kahnis, and Nitzsch's *Dogmengeschichte*), it should be definitely borne in mind that, in the language of the ancient Christians, as in that of the philosophers, "dogma" never denotes a view or doctrine which is to be regarded as a mere opinion, but always one that is to be regarded as established—at least for those who support it. The same is true (e.g., in Origen) of the heretical dogmas, just in so far as they are held as firm convictions. When, therefore, an ecclesiastical writer speaks with precision of dogmas, he means, even without the express addition of *ecclesiastica*, those statements of doctrine which for the body of Christians to which he belongs are established as unimpeachable truths.

3. Basis of the Certainty of Dogmas.

The term "dogma" itself gives no information either as to the reason why the truths expressed in the dogma have such certainty and stability or as to the authority upon which their validity is supposed to rest. That church dogmas rest upon the authority of divine revelation is hinted at in the designation "dogmas of God" or "of Christ"; and all the deliverances of the Church have this implication. Then, just because the Church truly and correctly derived its dogmas from the revelation contained in the Scriptures, it leaned for support upon the authority that belonged to its very self, but it did not call the propositions dogmas on the ground that it established them by its own authority, but only because of the firm validity which they must have as "dogmas of God." It is a mistake to define dogma in general as a judgment resting essentially "upon personal authority" (Kahnis), nor does it belong to the conception of dogma that it should have an "authority binding in the sphere of civil law" (Schenkel). Too much significance has also been given by some recent theologians (including Lobstein, who is opposed by W. Schmidt) to a sentence of Basil (*De spiritu sancto*, xxvii.) according to which "the dogma is observed in silence, but the kerygmata are proclaimed to all the world." [For a discussion of the meaning of the term "dogma" and an example of the Ritschlian view of the basis of its authority see P. Lobstein, *Einleitung in die evangelische Dogmatik* (Freiburg, 1897; Eng. transl., Chicago, 1903).]

Starting therefore from the sense which the word "dogma" acquired in ecclesiastical and theological usage, dogmatics may be defined as the scientific exhibition of the established religious truth which the Christian community acknowledges and confesses to have been derived from divine revelation. Its content, accordingly, embraces all Christian truth so far as it exists in the Church in the form of doctrine; or the whole doctrine of the life in God, as it is mediated by Christ—of the relation in general in which we and all the world about us stand to God; of the relation which subsists between him and us by virtue of sin; of redemption and real communion with God effected by Christ, and of the nature of this God who determines us for his fellowship; of the person and efficacy of the Redeemer, Christ, and of the future acts of God which are to bring about the perfection of that life for humanity and the world. To this content, however, belong also the basal declarations concerning the aims and tasks which are set for us by virtue of the vocation given by God, concerning the ethical attitude of soul that God demands of us and that fits those living in God—in general, the truths concerning the ethical and the ethically good. To this discipline, therefore, belongs, as a subject for scientific treatment, that whole domain which the catechism treats in a non-scientific fashion. It is, however, usual in present terminology to make a fundamental distinction between dogmatics and ethics; the former pertains to God and the relation in which he places himself toward us, to the redemptive facts and the *ordo salutis* appointed by him, and to the future completion promised by him; whereas ethics pertains to one's own personal relation, that is to say, the relation of one's will to God and his requirements of us. The name *theologica dogmatica*, or "dogmatics," arose only after this division of the sciences had begun—after the middle of the seventeenth and especially after the first half of the eighteenth century—in harmony with the more definite sense that then prevailed of the distinction between the science of dogmas and that of ethics or morals. Schleiermacher gave his influence in behalf of the term *Glaubenslehre*. [The term *Glaubenslehre*, however, implies that the basis of authority has been changed from an objective to a subjective source, i.e., the Christian consciousness, the characteristic of which is faith.]

4. Dogmatics, Definition and Content.

But the conception and task of dogmatics must be still more precisely fixed in an essential particular in accordance with the prevailing usage of the term. If it is the task of the dogmatist to set forth that which according to the conviction of a religious body constitutes religious truth and is recognized as such by it, it might still be possible to leave out of account the dogmatist's personal faith or conception of truth. But the Christian Church demands that its dogmatists shall give only such representations of its faith as can serve for the further proclamation of Christian truth. Such a task, however, can be performed only by one who agrees with the faith of the congregation and shares its religious life. "Christian dogmatics," therefore, commonly means specifically such a treatment as purports to set forth what is religious truth not only for a Church, but also for the writer. Accordingly, it can not properly be subsumed under "historical theology" (as is the case in Schleiermacher, although in *Der Christliche Glaube* he aimed not only at "a historical, but at the same time at an apologetic" treatment). But taking the term in the stricter sense, the question may still be raised, whether the dogmatist, while standing with conviction for the doctrinal views of his Church, may not and should not at the same time labor for a development and purification of the church doctrine. The answer will depend upon the double question, how far a Christian Church can find itself justified in the opinion that it has already completely appropriated and developed the truth, and how far its individual members are bound to ascertain and express the truth of religion independently; or, as Roman Catholicism requires, to submit to the authority of the Church. Thus it is possible for a dogmatist, besides reproducing the doctrines of his Church's symbols, to exhibit that which actually constitutes at a given time the content of the Church's faith. [For an able and satisfactory discussion of this subject, setting forth the Christian Church as the "subject" of dogmatics, but not the faith of the Church as the "object" of dogmatics, see A. Kuyper, *Encyclopædia of Sacred Theology* (Eng. transl., by J. H. de Vries, London, 1898).]

5. The Individual Element in Dogmatics.

Again, the question may be asked at the outset, whether dogmatics in the sense of declarations of doctrinal truths belongs to Christianity at all; and, in particular, whether they can, and must be still maintained. If the answer be negative, dogmatics continues to have justification only as a historic science; that is, no longer as an exhibition of the actual faith of the Church, but only as the exhibition of that which Christian Churches once upon a time established and think they must to a large extent still maintain. The question has become a pressing one only in recent years. It is indisputable that the words of Jesus and his apostles aimed to present with special emphasis objective truths concerning God, the Redeemer, the way of salvation, etc.; to have them apprehended by the religious subjects by reason of the influence upon the inner life; and upon the basis of this apprehension to build up a Church and plant new life. What a summary of such truth is to be found even in the simple testimony that Jesus is the Christ, the Son of the living God, and that in his name there is salvation and life. The Roman Catholic and old Protestant orthodoxy had no doubt about the right and obligation to formulate what it recognized as the content of divine revelation into declarations and confessions of faith and doctrinal propositions, and claimed for them unconditional validity. The old rationalism demanded the right of freely criticizing at all times the doctrinal deliverances the Church had sanctioned, and challenged also the supernatural character of the Biblical revelation. But it, too, admitted that the perception and recognition of objective truths belongs to the very essence of religion, and of Christianity in particular; that at least certain basal truths concerning God, man, and the world must,

6. Dogmas Essential to Christianity.

precisely on rational grounds, be continually taught in the Church.

If, however, religion be considered as essentially a matter of feeling (Schleiermacher), it is not enough to say that certain conceptions as to the source of the feeling, as to the feeling subject, and the factors producing the feeling must be combined, and that the religious life of a community always and necessarily produces a certain uniformity in such conceptions. For one might simply ignore the question whether those conceptions have objective truth or reality back of them. But the case is different, not only when religion and Christianity are made to consist essentially in perceptions and knowledge —which even the old orthodoxy did not assert—but also when true religious experience, no matter how essential feeling may be, realizes itself, after all, only in a definite inner practical attitude. It is a question of being able to come to the enjoyment of communion with God and life in him, of losing this ability through sin, and of having it restored in a definite attitude on our part to actual deeds and ordinances of God. For the fellowship of the religious life, moreover, not only mutual incitement and harmony of subjective feelings are necessary, but common devotion to God and the Redeemer, and mutual encouragement and help in that whole relation; and this is possible only when there is agreement as to those basal truths, and when the leaders of the common worship and edification have fixed confessional formulas of doctrine. To renounce such fundamental dogmas would be to sign the Church's death warrant, to seal the ruin of Protestantism.

7. Sources and Norms of Dogma.

But the most important question is that concerning the sources out of which, and the norms according to which dogmas are to be formed. It is precisely by those norms that the dogmatist must test the dogmatic material lying before him in the Church, unless, indeed, he simply confines himself to the historical task of setting forth a given stage of doctrinal development. Even the Roman Catholic dogmatists have never confined themselves merely to the ecclesiastical formulations of doctrine, but have always had recourse to the testimony of Scripture and tradition. We are here dealing with that basal question of dogmatics, about which there are now the most serious disputes within the Protestant theology. Roman Catholic dogmatists, going back to Scripture and tradition, must none the less bind themselves to the Fathers and tradition, and give the actually existing Church, as she is represented in the totality of her bishops (indeed, according to the Vatican decree, in the one infallible pope), the infallible decision as to what is really the content and sense of Scripture and tradition. Evangelical Protestant dogmatists find nowhere a tenable ground for the authority of such ecclesiasticism. Against this they place the authority of the Scriptures, which are deemed sufficiently perspicuous for believers. Luther, to be sure, had exercised a free criticism as to the constituent parts of the traditional documents of revelation; but the old orthodoxy lacked a clear consciousness as to the principles of dogmatic procedure. Moreover, the old dogmatists distinguished between *articuli puri*, which are to be derived exclusively from special revelation, and *articuli mixti*, which as to content, indeed, must likewise be taken from the Scriptures, but which may find confirmation in the universal religious consciousness supported by general revelation. The Bible is therefore not merely the highest and only norm by which all doctrinal statements must be tested, but the revelation it contains is, in an absolute sense, the very principle of theological knowledge. None the less, in spite of the Reformation, tradition in the form of a scholastic philosophizing continued to exert a far-reaching influence. Rationalism and supranaturalism, accordingly, subjected the dogma to a new testing and purifying. At the same time the doctrine of inspiration is so transformed that an unconditional infallibility can no longer be claimed in behalf of all statements contained in Scripture.

8. Fundamental Questions.

But even under the most radical criticism Scripture retains a certain unique normative authority. The views differ greatly, however, on the question as to what gives Scripture its peculiar documentary value and how far this value extends. It is by no means enough to say that we here find the Christian truth in its original form and that we must accept it thus. For the question is whether this first form was not the lowest stage in a process of development, or whether Schleiermacher's dictum (cf. his *Darstellung des theologischen Studiums*, Berlin, 1830, p. 83) is here valid, that the earliest conditions of a historical development, before there has been any chance of collision with adverse forces, most purely represent its peculiar spiritual essence. Another question must be raised as to the date of the New Testament books; namely, whether they belong to the origin of Christianity or are themselves the product of a development that extended, as Baur claimed, to the end of the second century. Furthermore, does the power of the Scriptures differ only in degree or also in kind from that of other writings? Finally, there is the main question, whether in any event the sum and substance of the truth recorded in the Bible, namely, Jesus the Son of God, is so represented in these books as the perfect revelation of God and as the Redeemer that we can recognize him as such and that we must acknowledge him as such in obedience to the demands of our inmost nature when once it is brought under the power of this representation.

9. Relation of Scripture to the Inner Life.

We thus come to the relation of Scripture to the inner life. It is only through a personal experience of the influence of the Christ here portrayed that the right conception of the aim and core of that revelation is obtained. The right conviction as to the higher character of those writings can be obtained only when their very content in this manner attests itself to the heart, when their spirit with its peculiar originality, sublimity, power, freshness, and simplicity makes itself known in experience, and when at the same time this their spiritual peculiarity is understood in the light of the external and internal historical connection in which they stand to the original revelation of Christ and the life that has proceeded from him. In order, therefore, to establish the content of the faith, the dogmatist must also deal with those processes of the inner life by which faith is produced in the first instance; just as moral philosophy or ethical theology must deal with such subjective considerations without being able by external authorities or historical proof or logical deduction to establish the matter for those who deny knowledge and experience of the corresponding subjective processes. Much, too, will depend upon the answer to the question, whether the value of Scripture differs only in degree from that of other products of the genuinely Christian spirit, and whether the effect of the Spirit upon the Biblical writers pertains only to the sphere of morals and religion, and thus leaves room for the influences, defects, and progressive character of general human culture. Upon all such topics dogmatists differ greatly. Frank, e.g., in his *System der christlichen Gewissheit* (2 vols., Erlangen, 1870–73), seeks to deduce from the inner experience of the regenerate man itself all the principal elements of Christian truth revealed in the Bible and recognized in the Church confession; whereas Cremer and Beck derive the truth only from the revelation of Scripture approving itself to the conscience.

10. Conclusions. Thus then the dogmatist must objectively reproduce the ecclesiastical confession and forms of doctrine as they appear above all in the official symbols; he must establish any departures therefrom which he may choose to make, and at the same time show with what right he can as a dogmatist still regard himself as belonging to his particular body. At the same time he is bound to try to advance Christian truth by working at the original sources with the highest degree of independence. The very spirit of loyalty will make it his duty to purify the Church and her doctrine. The scientific character of dogmatics, moreover, necessitates a sharply methodical mode of thought, an analysis into its constituent elements, and the establishment of every individual element of doctrine in its relations to the whole. Reason itself will here have to admit, however, that in the attempt to ascend from the finite limitations in which man moves there are no perfectly adequate categories for God and his relation to man. Instead of trying to overcome this fact, it is far more expedient freely to use anthropomorphisms in dogmatics.

11. Relation to Philosophy. But while doctrinal theology as such draws from the divine revelation, the scientific dogmatist will also deal with the independent philosophic attempts that have been made to know God in his relations to us, whether by way of cosmological or moral philosophizing or by the processes of thought itself (Hegel). But that which thus proceeds from a conscience and a self-consciousness that is not yet specifically Christian can be truly and correctly interpreted only by the Christian revelation and experience; and so far the old orthodox dogmatists and also Kaftan rightly affirm that reason in dogmatics has only *usus formalis*. At the same time the actual influence of philosophy and particular philosophies even upon dogmatists who deny the fact is perfectly clear; e.g., in Schleiermacher may be seen the mighty influence of Schelling's philosophy of identity and of Spinoza's attempts to express the thoughts of the pious consciousness concerning God.

II. History of Protestant Dogmatics.—1. In Germany: The Evangelical Protestant Reformation was bound by virtue of its original spirit to lead to all these problems and questions. But only gradually, through the strife of opposing tendencies did the real task of Evangelical Christian dogmatics reveal itself. The new doctrine of the

1. The Fifteenth and Sixteenth Centuries. Reformation pertained in the first instance to the very heart of dogmatics and ethics, to the essence of the salvation that has appeared in Christ, and in particular to the mode of appropriating it. The dogmas of the Trinity and the person of Christ were accepted without criticism in the traditional form (Melanchthon's *Loci*, 1521). The next generations gave the new Christian dogmatics more and more of a scholastic character: e.g., Chemnitz, in his *Loci*, published in 1591; Hutter, *Compendium locorum theologicorum*, 1610; Calovius, *Systema locorum theologicorum*, 1655–77; and Quenstedt, *Theologia didactico-polemica*, 1685; Johann Gerhard, in his *Loci* of 1610–21, the most valuable production of the Lutheran orthodoxy, revealed a far more energetic religious spirit, and Hollatz, the last important representative of the old Lutheran orthodoxy, in his *Examen theologicum acroamaticum*, 1707, showed Pietistic influences. In the Reformed Church the development of dogmatics proceeds essentially from Calvin's *Institutio Christianæ religionis* (1536; final edition 1559). The development here, too, leads to a period which may be characterized as scholastic, but the process is not shut up within itself as was Lutheranism. Arminianism is a departure. Coccoius takes the content of faith from Scripture. See below, 2.

2. Influence of Pietism. The deep and powerful practical religious movement of Pietism reacted against those learned theologies which asserted the divine authority of Scripture indeed, but treated its content in the way of barren and dead forms of conception. To stimulate and establish a living and true faith, Spener and his followers pointed to the inner assurance of the Biblical truth through the Holy Spirit for every one who would open his heart to its influence. But there was here no endeavor to make this truth, its validity for faith, and its relation to knowledge of the world the object of a strictly scientific treatment. Dogmatists influenced by Pietism, such as Breithaupt (*Institutiones theologiæ dogmaticæ*, 1723), Anton, Freylinghausen, and Rombach, sought, by going back to Scripture, to simplify the ecclesiastical doctrines in the direction of a practical religious tendency. And more strictly scientific theologians, like Buddeus (*Institutiones theologiæ dogmaticæ*, 1723) and Pfaff (*Institutiones theologiæ dogmaticæ et moralis*, 1723), who made more of the historical development, show the new warmth and simplicity. The Biblical tendency fostered by Pietism won a peculiar power and independence in Württemberg, exemplified in Bengel (d. 1752), M. F. Roos (*Die christliche Glaubenslehre*, 1774; new ed. by J. T. Beck, 1845), and Beck himself, the most important and influential of these dogmatists.

The next great turn in the history of Protestant dogmatics came from a quarter opposed to Pietism; the philosophy of Leibnitz and Wolff, and later of Kant. Wolff's first and most influential disciple among the dogmatists was S. J. Baumgarten, who went out from Pietism (d. 1757; his *Evangelische Glaubenslehre* was published by Semler in 1759–60). Wolff's influence was at first apparent only in the method of rational demonstration, then in the preference given to those truths which can be apprehended by the natural reason, and in the slighting and weakening of the other dogmas. Then Semler employed an important Biblical and historical criticism against the ecclesiastical dogmas. Still using the Bible as a recognized higher source of truth, rationalism gave a new turn to the difficult propositions. Then, when the Wolffian and at the same time the English and French philosophy and the "Enlightenment" (q.v.) threatened to issue in downright rationalism with no strictly ethical spirit, Kant, asserting the absolute character of the categorical imperative and its assurance as to the existence of God, gave this rationalism a most powerful ethical impulse. None the less, the rationalists themselves learned little from Kant and continued to put all trust in their God-given reason. But also the supranaturalism gave a wrong treatment of Christian truth and of religious truth in general. It hoped by dialectic processes to establish not only the existence of God, but also a higher source of the Sacred Scriptures, and thence the reality of the miracles there recorded (which, however, are admitted to be incomprehensible), and also the truthfulness of the Biblical statements (likewise transcending reason) concerning God, the essence of Christ, the Trinity, etc.; at the same time, in opposition to the former orthodoxy, it sought as much as possible to confine itself in its dogmatics to the actual statements of Scripture. The most serious lack in the case of this rationalism and this supranaturalism is that—in F. Nitzsch's phrase (*Lehrbuch der evangelischen Dogmatik*, Freiburg, 1889, p. 31)—of a "sense of immediacy"; that is, of a knowledge of the significance of immediate perception and experience for faith and its certitude. Here belong, on the one hand, the systematic works of Töllner (1775); Döderlin (1780); then, revealing Kantian influences, Tieftrunk (1791); H. P. K. Henke (1793); Eckermann (1800); Wegscheider (1817; 8th ed., 1844); and Ammon (1803; 4th ed., 1830); on the other hand, Reinhard (1801), Storr (after 1793; a representative of the Württemberg Biblicism), Knapp (1826), A. Hahn (1827), and Steudel (1835).

3. Influence of Leibnitz, Wolff, and Kant.

A powerful awakening of the sense for the immediate, which became the most important factor for a new period in the history of dogmatics, was introduced by the transition from the eighteenth to the nineteenth century with the great political agitations which deeply reacted upon thought and feeling. Schleiermacher, proceeding from Moravianism and well schooled in philosophy, sought, in opposition to the intellectualism of the rationalistic and the supranaturalistic movements, to make the pious self-consciousness of the Church the basis of the system of doctrine. Like the original Pietism, his movement opposed a learned orthodoxy and at the same time strengthened the confessional church spirit. In the philosophy of that day, though Kant was willing to give validity to the content of religious faith only in the postulates of the practical reason, Jacobi at least taught a direct knowledge, according to the feelings, of the supersensuous and the divine through a believing reason just as the objects of sense perception are recognized by the senses. From Jacobi Fries adopted the view that reason as the faculty of ideas grasps these by way of feeling or presentiment. De Wette (*Ueber Religion und Theologie*, 1817) followed him. Nevertheless, at that time the Schelling-Hegel philosophy of the speculative reason gained the ascendency, and it was in the forms of this thinking that Daub and Marheineke thought they could state the true content of the Christian faith (Daub, *Theologumena*, 1806; *Einleitung in das Studium der Dogmatik*, 1810; Marheineke, *Grundlehren der christlichen Dogmatik*, 1819 and 1827; *System der christlichen Dogmatik*, after his death, 1847). Among the learned theologians Schleiermacher was most influential in remolding dogmatics by reason of his determination to make the system express the pious feelings or the pious self-consciousness (*Der christliche Glaube*, 1821; *Reden über die Religion*, 1799). He also influenced dogmatists who in opposition to him made it the task of dogmatics to represent the divine realities attested by the feelings as objectively true, and to ground them in reason; and he cooperated with those who had a different understanding from his of the inner processes of the soul and who found in these the workings of God and of the divine revelation in Christ and in the Biblical testimonies.

4. Schleiermacher and his Contemporaries.

In more recent dogmatics must be noted first of all a simple Biblical tendency now more effective in scientific theology than before. A chief representative is the above-named Beck, who is unique not only in that with perfect trust in the self-evidencing character of Scripture he sought to take the content of faith purely from this source, but also in that he would, on principle, have nothing to do with the views of Schleiermacher, church orthodoxy, philosophy, or Biblical criticism. This new ecclesiastical and confessional interest is to be seen also in H. Schmidt's *Dogmatik der evangelisch-lutherischen Kirche* (1843), which had the merit of once more systematically presenting the actual content and the veritable treasures of the old and forgotten orthodoxy.

5. Biblical Tendency of Beck and H. Schmidt.

While Rothe, Lange, Martensen, Dorner, and

others continued in the steps of Daub and Marheineke, the Hegelian left threatened in Strauss (*Christliche Glaubenslehre*, 1840) to dissolve the Christian views, but the Hegelians Biedermann and Pfleiderer opposed him. Kant influenced anew Lipsius and, above all, A. Ritschl.

6. Ritschl. Kaftan, a follower of Ritschl (cf. his *Wesen der christlichen Religion*, 1881), was also attracted by the positivism of Comte. Ritschl has been since Schleiermacher the most effective factor in the development of dogmatics. His basal characteristic is his emphasis upon the ethical, upon the will, as against the metaphysical. At the same time Christianity as the only true religion is expressly derived from revelation, from the objective manifestation of God and his will in the person of Christ. All "mysticism" is abhorred. It can not be known in what inner relation of life and essence Christ stood to God, though by virtue of his work as revealer he may also be called "God." The conception of the kingdom of God reminds of Kant, as also the peculiar dogmatic juxtaposition of the kingdom of God and redemption as two foci of an ellipse. Ritschl never built his dogmatic ideas into a complete and homogeneous system. Among his pupils the chief progress was made in the direction of a decided recognition of the immediacy of the Christian experience; especially in Herrmann who, though in a lesser measure than Kaftan, makes room for mysticism. The school has developed opposing parties (cf. G. Ecke's *Die theologische Schule A. Ritschls*, Berlin, 1897).

With reference to their attitude to the Biblico-ecclesiastical body of doctrines modern dogmatists may be divided into two classes, the more conservative and the more radically critical, though the line of division can not be sharply drawn. Prominent among the former are K. F.

7. Conservative School of Modern Dogmaticians. Nitzsch (*System der christlichen Lehre*, 1829, which also embraces ethics); Julius Müller (though he published no dogmatics); H. Voigt (*Fundamentaldogmatik*, 1874); Rothe, more speculative, though not basing the convictions of faith upon speculation (*Zur Dogmatik*, 1863, which makes the science a historical critical discipline); J. P. Lange (*Christliche Dogmatik*, 1849–52, more suggestive and fantastic than strictly philosophic); Martensen (*Christliche Dogmatik*, 1850, mystical, more attractive than acute); I. A. Dorner (*System der christlichen Glaubenslehre*, 1879, 1886, among other peculiarities a basing of the certitude of faith upon an inner immediate perception); Runze (*Grundriss der evangelischen Glaubens- und Sittenlehre*, 1883); and H. Plitt (*Evangelische Dogmatik nach Schrift und Erfahrung*, 1863). In connection with the Biblicist Beck already mentioned stand his fellow countrymen Reiff (*Christliche Glaubenslehre als Grundlage der christlichen Weltanschauung*, 1873–1876) and W. Gess (*Christi Person und Werk*, 1870–1887). In North Germany this tendency is best seen in Cremer (*Dogmatische Prinzipienlehre*, in Zöckler's *Handbuch der theologischen Wissenschaften*, iii., Nördlingen, 1885) and Zöckler, whose academic labors, however, pertain more to history than dogmatics (*System der Glaubenslehre*, in the same volume, a scientific reproduction of the doctrine of the Lutheran Church). Here, too, belong M. Kaehler (*Wissenschaft der christlichen Lehre*, 1883, 1893, a concise systematic treatment of the Christian doctrines as the content of the self-evidencing Biblical revelation), W. Schmidt (*Christliche Dogmatik*, 1895–98), and F. A. B. Nitzsch (*Lehrbuch der evangelischen Dogmatik*, 1892, 1896; critical yet conservative). Of all these only Lange belonged to the Reformed Church. To this same confession belonged Ebrard (*Christliche Dogmatik*, 1852), who, however, took an independent attitude toward confessional differences. This is even more the case with Böhl (*Dogmatik auf reformiert kirchlicher Grundlage*, 1887). Specifically Lutheran and specifically polemic against the Reformed theology and against the Union are Philippi (*Kirchliche Glaubenslehre*, 1854 sqq.), Vilmar, Thomasius (*Christi Person und Werk, Darstellung der evangelisch-lutherischen Dogmatik*, 1852 sqq.), Luthardt (*Kompendium*, 1865), Kahnis (*Die lutherische Dogmatik historisch-genetisch dargestellt*, 1861–68; 1874), F. H. R. Frank (*System der christlichen Gewissheit*, 1872; *System der christlichen Wahrheit*, 1878–81, 1885). At the same time Thomasius and the rest of this group have no hesitation in departing from the Lutheran orthodoxy; Gess, e.g., in respect to kenosis, Kahnis in trinitarian subordinationism and in an approximately Reformed view of the Lord's Supper; and least of all does A. von Oettingen in his *Prinzipienlehre* (1897) reproduce Lutheranism in the sense of the old orthodoxy.

In the other more critical group—though its members are not to be charged offhand with the guilt of a "negative criticism"—

8. The More Radical School of Modern Dogmaticians. stands the Reformed theologian A. Schweizer (*Christliche Glaubenslehre nach protestantischen Grundsätzen*, 1863–72, 1877, to be distinguished from his *Glaubenslehre der evangelisch-reformierten Kirche*, 1844–47). Schenkel in his *Christliche Dogmatik vom Standpunkte des Gewissens aus dargestellt* (1859) does not clearly show the difference between his "conscience" and Schleiermacher's pious "self-consciousness." His *Grundlehren des Christentums* (1877) is more rationalistic. Close to De Wette stands Hase, more eminent in historical theology than in dogmatics (*Evangelische Dogmatik*, 1826, 1870). Against Strauss and in behalf of Hegelianism labored Biedermann (*Dogmatik*, 1869) and Pfleiderer (*Grundriss*, 1880, 1886), although the former abandoned Hegel's attempt to deduce the content of truth from thought itself. Lipsius (*Lehrbuch der evangelischen protestantischen Dogmatik*, 1876, 1893) rejects the Hegelian claim of a dialectic knowledge of the absolute, and also the validity of the church doctrines; but as against Ritschl's protest against metaphysics he regards some declarations about God and supramundane realities as possible and necessary, and goes back to self-consciousness and the immediacy of the mystic elements in religion and faith. At first sight, indeed, the content of the faith of the Church thus seems seriously threatened; but he shows an unmistakable endeavor to establish the self-evidencing truth of the inner experience, and to guard against a false distinction between the person of Christ and the "principle" of theological knowledge. Ritschl greatly influenced Hermann Schultz (*Grundriss der evangelischen Dogmatik*, 1890) and Kaftan (*Dogmatik*, 1897, and *Zur Dogmatik*, 1904), who more than Ritschl seeks to accept the full content of the faith that is based upon the historical revelation of God. He also gives a proportionate treatment to factors which Ritschl put into the background; he discusses the relation of Christ's essence to God as a "fact of nature," and puts a due estimate upon the inner working of God in the believer. The Ritschlian left has as yet produced no important works of a truly dogmatic content and character. (J. Köstlin†.)

9. Troeltsch. Ernst Troeltsch, professor of systematic theology at Heidelberg, has as yet published no comprehensive work on dogmatics, but by his monographs (*Die Absolutheit des Christentums und die Religionsgeschichte*, Tübingen, 1902; *Das Historische in Kant's Religionsphilosophie*, Berlin, 1904; *Politische Ethik und Christentum*, Göttingen, 1904; etc.) has attracted attention and provoked criticism. He maintains the absoluteness of Christianity as resting on divine revelation, yet insists that, having been drawn by modern historical science into the stream of religious evolution, its relativity and limitation must be recognized. As sustaining historical relations Christianity is a relative phenomenon; for one who has had personal experience of communion with God in Christ it is the absolute religion. But the study of comparative religion leads to recognition of the fact that the devotees of other religions may have a similar experience and an equal right to consider their religions absolute. (Cf. critique of Troeltsch's *Absolutheit* by Hermann, in *TLZ*, 1902, 364 sqq., and summary of Troeltsch's views by G. B. Foster, in his *Finality of the Christian Religion*, Chicago, 1906, pp. 42–46.)

2. The Reformed Churches: Reformed dogma owes its content and form to Calvin. Zwingli's dogmatic views were most systematically presented in his *Uslegen und Grund* of his sixty-seven articles (1523). In his exposition of art. vi. he seeks

1. Zwingli and Calvin. to prove from Scripture that God's promises of salvation in Christ were made to the whole human race, the only condition being personal acceptance. Calvin's fundamental dogma was that of the absoluteness of the divine predestination, involving the certainty of the salvation of the elect and the inevitableness of the eternal destruction of the non-elect. The first edition of the "Institutes" (1536) was really an apology for Protestantism and by no means a systematic treatise on theology. In the final edition of 1559 it was expanded and divided into four books—Knowledge of God the Creator, Knowledge of God the Redeemer, the Law, the External Means for Salvation. The Scriptures alone are regarded as absolutely authoritative. Calvin's doctrine became dogma in various confessions of faith, catechisms, and the like.

Calvin's predestination dogma was assailed with vigor by Bolsec, Pighius, Castellio, and others. Socinianism may be regarded as in part a reaction against Calvinism. Several of Calvin's followers

2. Calvin's Successors. (Beza, Gomarus, Piscator, Chamier, and others) went far beyond Calvin in making God directly and absolutely the author of sin (supralapsarianism). Their views gained considerable acceptance and, with Socinianism and other influences, called forth Arminianism by way of reaction. The position of Arminius was clearly expressed in the remonstrance of 1610 and in the works of Episcopius, Uitenbogaert, and, later and more moderately, by Limborch. The Synod of Dort (1618–19) reaffirmed in strong language the dogmatic teachings of Calvin, while carefully avoiding supralapsarianism. Piscator reacted to Arminianism. The Scotch theologian John Cameron (d. 1625) originated in the Saumur school (1618 onward) a mode of theological thought involving important modifications of the Calvinistic system. He maintained that, notwithstanding the fall and hereditary sin, there remains in man, after his understanding has been enlightened by divine revelation, enough of good to enable him to lay hold upon salvation. Among the most noted of Cameron's disciples were Joshua Placeus (d. 1665), Moïse Amyraut (d. 1664), and Louis Cappel (d. 1658). Opposed to the Saumur school was that of Sédan, where Daniel Chamier (d. 1621) and his disciples maintained polemically a rigorous Calvinism.

In the Netherlands, Gisbertus Voetius (q.v.; d. 1676) upheld Calvinism after the Synod of Dort (*Selecta disputationes theologicæ*, 5 vols., Utrecht, 1648). Johannes Cocceius (q.v.; d.

3. The Netherlands. 1669) became important for dogmatics through his application of the historical method to it and the resultant scheme of divine covenants (the federal theology). F. A. Lampe (d. 1729), professor in Utrecht, brought the influence of German Pietism powerfully to bear upon Dutch theological thought. As a means of settling controversies that had arisen, it was arranged that in each university the professor of systematic theology should be a Voetian, that of exegetical theology a Coccejan, and that of practical theology a Lampean. This placing of three types of Reformed theological thought on a basis of equality, together with the wide influence exerted by such learned Arminian (Remonstrant) teachers as Peter Limborch (d. 1712) and Johannes Clericus (d. 1736), meant a complete breakdown of rigorous Calvinism as the authoritative form of Christianity in the Protestant Netherlands. It enjoyed a revival in the nineteenth century under the leadership of Isaak da Costa (d. 1860), Abraham Capadose (d. 1874), G. Groen van Prinsterer (d. 1876), and others, and has been extended and perpetuated by A. Kuyper, G. J. Vos, and others. A Platonizing, mystical type of Reformed theology, influenced by Schleiermacher, led by P. W. van Heusde (d. 1839) and including J. F. van Oordt, Hofstede de Groot, and others, had its center at Groningen (see Groningen School). J. J. van Oosterzee (d. 1882) represents a position intermediate between the rationalistic mysticism of the Groningen school and the somewhat rigorous Calvinism of Kuyper and the separatists. Extreme rationalism of the German type had become so far dominant in Holland by 1876 that the theological faculties of the universities were transformed into faculties of religions, the aim being to place Christianity upon the same basis as other religions and to encourage freedom in dealing with religious problems. Among the eminent leaders of liberalism in the Dutch Reformed Church may be mentioned A. Kuenen (d. 1891), C. P. Tiele, and P. D. Chantepie de la Saussaye, who have worked chiefly in the fields of Biblical criticism, comparative religion, and the philosophy of religion.

4. Switzerland. In Switzerland, Beza's influence withstood for some time the inroads of more liberal types of thought. The Helvetic Consensus, embodying uncompromising Calvinism, was adopted (1675) by the Swiss churches as a protest and defense against the Saumur and Coccejan types of thought. The Consensus proved too rigorous for the time and was abandoned by Zurich (1685), Geneva (1708), and Bern (1722). François Turretin, one of its authors, had to contend with his own more liberal colleagues, Jean Mestrezat and Louis Tronchin, in Geneva. He was fighting a losing battle, but he succeeded in putting the Calvinistic theology as interpreted and applied by the Synod of Dort, with elaborate refutation of earlier and later more liberal forms of thought and sharp antagonizing of Roman Catholicism and Lutheranism, in a thoroughly and minutely wrought out scholastic form, worthy of the great dialecticians of the Middle Ages. His *Institutio theologiæ elencticæ* (Geneva, 1679–85) is still the most complete exposition of fully developed Calvinism and has exerted a wide-spread influence on later Reformed dogmatics. His son, J. A. Turretin (d. 1737), led in the abolition of the Helvetic Consensus and, under the influence of Cameron and the Saumur school and of English latitudinarianism, labored for a union of the Reformed and Lutheran Churches. He insisted that only fundamentals should be made terms of communion, and that only doctrines necessary to salvation should be regarded as fundamental. Like-minded and similarly influenced by English and German thought was Benedict Pictet (d. 1724). Calvinism vanished from Geneva, which soon became a center of French rationalism (Voltaire, Rousseau, and others). A temporary revival of Calvinism (from 1817 onward; see HALDANE) found its chief representative in Alexandre Vinet, but his writings were practical rather than dogmatic. Pietism made its influence felt in Basel during the late eighteenth and early nineteenth centuries. Zurich, where De Wette labored (1822 onward), was swayed by German rationalism.

8. England: The Thirty-nine Articles of the Church of England represent moderate Calvinism, or, perhaps more correctly, the type of thought developed by Melanchthon. English Puritans maintained a rigorous type of Calvinism, some even of the conforming Puritans being hyper-Calvinistic (supralapsarian) in their teachings.

1. To the Revival of the Eighteenth Century. In the reaction against Puritanism Romanizing theologians like Archbishop Laud (d. 1644) and Richard Montagu (d. 1641) developed a type of doctrine closely approximating the Semi-Pelagianism (Semi-Augustinianism) of the Council of Trent, commonly designated Arminianism. Both Arminianism and Socinianism greatly influenced English thought during the revolutionary period (1641–60). John Milton (*De doctrina Christiana*, ed. and transl. by C. R. Sumner, Cambridge, 1825) taught Arian Christology and Arminian anthropology. John Hales (d. 1656) had been converted to Arminianism at the Synod of Dort. William Chillingworth (d. 1644) became imbued with Pelagianism through consorting with the Jesuits. At Cambridge there grew up during the Cromwellian period the so-called Cambridge Platonists (q.v.), whose mysticism was based on the Jewish cabala and Neoplatonic writings. Their Christology was essentially Sabellian. The latitudinarianism of the time of William and Mary (John Tillotson, d. 1694; Gilbert Burnet, d. 1715) was due in part to Arminian and Socinian influence and in part to the syncretism that prevailed so widely on the Continent among Lutherans and Reformed alike, or, more correctly, to the changed philosophical conceptions and modes of thought of which all alike were expressions. By way of reaction against dominant latitudinarianism High-church dissidents (nonjurors) developed an ascetical, mystical type of thought and life, and a Romanizing dogmatics and apologetics, resembling Jansenism without its rigorous Augustinianism (Charles Leslie's *Short and Easy Method with the Deists*, London, 1698; William Law's *Serious Call to a Devout and Holy Life*, London, 1724). Deism (q.v.) may be regarded as a revival and adaptation of Stoicism, which identified God with the nature of things and sought a purely natural basis for religion and morality. Against Deists and Arminians High-churchmen like Joseph Butler (d. 1752), Daniel Waterland (d. 1740), and William Warburton (d. 1779) ably defended revealed religion and the supernatural in Judaism and Christianity.

2. The Eighteenth and Nineteenth Centuries. The evangelical revival brought about fresh combinations of dogmatic thought. John Wesley with a substratum of High-church Semi-Pelagianism became imbued with the old evangelical Semi-Augustinianism, or Arminianism. George Whitefield preached a thoroughgoing type of Calvinism. Moderate Calvinism, with little attempt at philosophical representation, became the theology of the Low-church or evangelical party in the Church of England. The philosophy of Kant and Hegel was brought to bear upon English theological thought by S. T. Coleridge, father of the Broad-church movement. English Broad-churchmen have followed closely in the footsteps of German radical thought; but few have devoted their attention to dogmatics proper. Their favorite field is Biblical and historical criticism. An intensely Romanizing mode of thought and life, with deep aversion to Protestantism and to Calvinism in particular and a strong tendency toward Semi-Pelagianism and Jesuitical methods of thought and of work, appeared, by way of reaction against aggressive liberalism and evangelicalism, in the Oxford or Tractarian movement (see TRACTARIANISM). The *Theological Institutes* of Richard Watson (6 parts, London, 1823–29) has been much used by Methodists in both England and America. It presents evangelical Arminianism in a popular and effective way. W. B. Pope's *Compendium of Theology* (3 vols., London, 1875) is a more scholarly exposition of Christian doctrine from the Methodist point of view. The more recent works of J. S. Banks (*The Development of Doctrine from the Early Middle Ages to the Reformation*, London, 1901) and J. A. Beet (*Manual of Theology*, London, 1906) show the influence of liberal thought. John Gill (*A Body of Doctrinal and Practical Divinity*, London, 1769) was the first Baptist to attempt a comprehensive exposition of Christian doctrines—with the possible exception of the General Baptist Thomas Grantham, whose *Christianismus primitivus* (London, 1688) partook of the nature of a dogmatic work. Gill taught a rigorous (supralapsarian) Calvinism, which was assailed by Andrew Fuller (d. 1815) in several works. Fuller was influenced by Jonathan Edwards, and his type of thought became well-nigh normative for Baptists in both England and America.

4. Scotland: The early Scottish symbols prepared by John Knox and his associates were strictly Calvinistic, as were the writings of all influential Scottish Presbyterians for more than a century after the beginning of the Reformation (Henderson, Rutherford, Gillespie, and others). After the Revolution (1688) "Moderatism" and "Evangelicalism" were arrayed against each other. The Moderates were affected by Socinian modes of thought and had much in common with English latitudinarians. They produced no great theological works and were for the most part wanting in initiative. Thomas Erskine, of Linlathen, a layman (d. 1870), rebelled against Calvinistic dogma as immoral and inculcating unworthy conceptions of God, and taught an evangelical mysticism with great earnestness and zeal (*Internal Evidence*, Edinburgh, 1820; *Unconditional Freeness of the Gospel*, 1828; *The Brazen Serpent*, 1831; *Spiritual Order*, 1871). Erskine was no doubt influenced by Coleridge, and in turn greatly influenced J. McLeod Campbell, who in 1831 was deposed from the ministry for teaching general redemption and related doctrines (*The Nature of the Atonement, and its Relation to the Remission of Sins and Eternal Life*, Cambridge, 1856). The distinctive feature of his view is that not the bearing of penalty, but adequate repentance is requisite to divine forgiveness, and that Christ on behalf of humanity adequately repented of sin. Thomas Chalmers, the greatest Scottish religious leader since Knox, devoted more attention to practical problems than to matters of doctrine. His *Institutes of Theology* (Edinburgh, 1849) represents moderate Calvinism vitalised by a profound sense of the obligation of world-wide evangelisation and social reform. Thomas Carlyle did much to popularise German advanced thought in Scotland. The higher criticism has secured general recognition. Names that may be mentioned of the past and the present generation are A. B. Davidson, A. B. Bruce, Robert Flint, James Denney, Robert Rainy, George Adam Smith, H. R. Macintosh, W. P. Patterson, T. M. Lindsay, James Lindsay, W. R. Smith, Marcus Dods, and S. D. F. Salmond.

5. America: Early New England theology was strictly Calvinistic. A Socinianized Arminianism had become widely prevalent by 1733, to the destruction of evangelistic zeal (cf. J. White, *New England's Lamentations . . . the Decay of the Power of Godliness; the Danger of Arminian Principles, etc.*, Boston, 1734, and Jonathan Edwards, *Thoughts on the Revival in New England*, 1742). Jonathan Edwards (d. 1758) was the first American theologian to make important contributions to dogmatics and may be regarded as the most important theologian that America has produced. He presented Calvinistic doctrine in all its rigor in opposition to the current Arminianism. His application of Locke's philosophy, which hitherto had seemed to minister to deism, to the refutation of the Arminian doctrine of free will (*An Essay on the Freedom of the Will*, Boston, 1754) awakened great interest in Europe as well as in America. Joseph Bellamy (d. 1790) in the spirit of Edwards defended Calvinism against antinomianism and Arminianism (*True Religion Delineated*, Boston, 1750). Samuel Hopkins (d. 1803) propagated a harsher form of Edwardsian Calvinism (*A System of Doctrines Contained in Divine Revelation*, Boston, 1793). Nathanael Emmons (d. 1840) presented the doctrine of divine sovereignty in still harsher form than Hopkins. See NEW ENGLAND THEOLOGY.

1. The Early Calvinistic Theology.

Universalism was taught in New England by John Murray (from 1770) on the basis of the then generally accepted thesis that Christ died for all. The Socinianized Arminianism which called forth the modified Calvinism of Edwards and his disciples was carried by opposition to the Great Awakening (see REVIVALS OF RELIGION) to Unitarianism (Chauncy, Ware, Buckminster, Channing, and others). Nathanael W. Taylor (d. 1858) sought to eliminate from the theology of Edwards and Hopkins the features which were especially objectionable to Unitarians. His theology had much in common with original Arminianism and more perhaps with Amyraldism. C. G. Finney (d. 1875) taught the sinner's plenary ability to repent, made regeneration an act of the will rather than a special work of the Holy Spirit, and insisted upon the perfectibility of regenerate human nature in the present life. Horace Bushnell (d. 1876) popularised in America the views of Schleiermacher and Coleridge and presented in a fresh form the moral influence theory of the atonement.

2. Universalism, Unitarianism, and Later Types.

The influence of New England theology on American Presbyterianism, resulting in the formation of the "New School" party and in disruption, appears in H. B. Smith (d. 1877). Next to Edwards he was probably the profoundest theologian that America has produced. He combined the theology of Edwards and Taylor with that of Schleiermacher, Tholuck, and Neander, and was as much interested in church history as in dogmatics. What is known as the Princeton School, whose most eminent representatives have been Charles Hodge (d. 1878), A. A. Hodge (d. 1886), and B. B. Warfield, as the "Old School" party, has consistently defended historical Calvinism of the Synod of Dort and the Westminster type against all competing types of thought. Union Theological Seminary of New York City is the most prominent representative of the more liberal Presbyterianism. The following works are by Baptists: J. L. Dagg, *A Manual of Theology* (Charleston, 1857; thoroughly Calvinistic); A. Hovey, *Manual of Systematic Theology and Christian Ethics* (Boston, 1877; Philadelphia, 1880; moderately Calvinistic, influenced by New England theology and to some extent by German thought); A. H. Strong, *Systematic Theology* (Rochester, 1886; new and enlarged edition, 1907; characterized by Neoplatonic modes of thought derived from Lutheran sources; no longer maintains the inerrancy of Scripture, accepts the evolution philosophy, and seeks a *via media* on the will between Calvinism and Arminianism); J. P. Boyce, *Abstract of Systematic Theology* (Louisville, 1887; presents the Princeton theology); W. N. Clarke, *An Outline of Christian Theology* (Boston, 1894; liberal, expressing as a Baptist the type of teaching of Schleiermacher, Coleridge, and the "New Theology"). C. A. Beckwith, *Realities of Christian Theology* (Boston, 1906), and William Adams Brown, *An Outline of Christian Theology* (New York, 1906), represent liberal and modern views by a Congregationalist and Presbyterian respectively. See FUNDAMENTAL DOCTRINES OF CHRISTIANITY.

8. Presbyterians and Baptists. Late Works.

A. H. NEWMAN.

BIBLIOGRAPHY: The important works are nearly all mentioned in the body of the article, while the literature of another branch of the subject is represented in DOCTRINE, HISTORY OF, q.v. For methods and contents consult: C. Lagrange, *Le Christianisme et la méthode expérimentale*, Lausanne, 1883; H. B. Smith, *Introduction to Christian Theology*, New York, 1883; J. Drummond, *Introduction to the Study of Theology*, London, 1884; R. Kübel, *Ueber das Wesen und die Aufgabe einer bibelgläubigen Theologie*, Stuttgart, 1889; W. L. P. Cox, *The Scientific Study of Theology*, London, 1893; H. Wendt, *Die Aufgabe der systematischen Theologie*, Göttingen, 1894; A. Cave, *Introduction to Theology and Its Literature*, pp. 493 sqq., Edinburgh, 1896; G. Wobbermin, *Die Grundprobleme der systematischen Theologie*, Berlin, 1899; idem, *Theologie und Metaphysik*, ib 1901; F. Buisson and C. Wagner, *Libre pensée et protestantisme libéral*, Paris, 1903; L. Emery, *Introduction à l'étude de la théologie protestante*, pp 162-184, Lausanne, 1904.

To be added to works in the text are: W. G. T. Shedd, *Dogmatic Theology*, 3 vols., New York, 1888-94; J. Miley, *Systematic Theology*, 2 vols., ib. 1892-94; E. V. Gerhart, *Institutes of the Christian Religion*, ib. 1893; J. Orr, *Christian View of God and the World*, Edinburgh, 1893; L. F. Stearns, *Present Day Theology*, New York, 1893; W. DeW. Hyde, *Outlines of Social Theology*, ib 1895; J. Caird, *Fundamental Ideas of Christianity*, Glasgow, 1899; A. Bouvier, *Dogmatique chrétienne*, 2 vols., Paris, 1903; H. C. Sheldon, *System of Christian Doctrine*, New York, 1903; H. L. Martensen, *Den christelige Dogmatik*, Copenhagen, 1904; H. E Jacobs, *A Summary of Christian Faith*, New York, 1905; O. A. Curtis, *The Christian Faith . . . in a System of Christian Doctrine*, ib. 1905; A. Dorner, *Die Entstehung der christlichen Glaubenslehren*, Munich, 1906; P. Geiermann, *A Manual of Theology for the Laity*, New York, 1906 (Roman Catholic); J. A. Moehler, *Symbolism; or, Exposition of the Doctrinal Differences between Catholics and Protestants as evidenced by their Writings*, London, 1906; J. Wilhelm and T. A. Scannell, *A Manual of Catholic Theology*, vol. i., ib. 1906; M. Valentine, *Christian Theology*, 2 vols., Philadelphia, 1907; G. L. Young, *Fundamental Christology*, Boston, 1907; M. S. Terry, *Biblical Dogmatics*, New York, 1907.

DOGS: Dogs are only exceptionally domestic animals in Palestine, but are useful as scavengers (Ex. xxii. 31). For this reason they are protected and valued, although regarded as unclean. They are extremely noisy, particularly at night (Ex. xi. 7; Judith xi. 19), but do not bite unless molested (Prov. xxvi. 17). Rabies is rare. The street-dog has always been a type of everything low (Prov. xxvi. 11), and is placed in the same category with swine (Isa. lxvi. 3; Matt. vii. 6; II Pet. ii. 22; cf. Horace, *Epist.*, I. ii. 26; II. ii. 75). It is a mark of humility to call oneself a dog in the presence of a superior (I Sam. xxiv. 14; II Sam. ix. 8; II Kings viii. 13—in the first two passages read *tame'*, "unclean," instead of *meth*, "dead"), and the greatest insult to call another a dog (I Sam. xvii. 43; II Sam. xvi. 9). A supreme misfortune was to be devoured by dogs in the field after death (I Kings xiv. 11, xvi. 4; and often). On account of his wantonness the name of "dog" became a designation for men addicted to unnatural vices and for the male *ḳedheshim* (Deut. xxiii. 18; the Gk. *kunaidos*, cf. *kynes*, "dogs," Rev. xxii. 15). With the Jews of later times "dogs" was a favorite name for the heathen (Niddah 77a; Baba Kamma 49a; Matt. xv. 26; Mark vii. 27). The uncleanness of the dog among the Hebrews, in its ritual aspect, is connected with the fact that by other Semitic peoples he was regarded as a sacred or at least a sacrificial animal (cf. Smith, *Rel. of Sem.*, 291 sqq.). The Hebrews made a limited use of the dog, e.g., as a sheep-dog (Job xxx. 1; Isa. lvi. 10); whether in hunting is doubtful (Prov. xxx. 31; cf. the commentaries). Dogs are mentioned as companions only in later times (Tobit v. 16, xi. 4; Matt. xv. 26–27).

I. BENZINGER.

BIBLIOGRAPHY: S. Bochart, *Hierozoicon*, i. 769 sqq., Leipsic, 1793; *DB*, i. 615–616; *EB*, i. 1124–26; *JE*, iv. 630–632; V. Zapletal, *Der Totemismus und die Religion Israels*, p. 38, Freiburg, 1901.

DOLCINO, dol-chî'no: A leader of the Apostolic Brethren; b. in the diocese of Novara in the thirteenth century; burned at the stake at Vercelli June 1, 1307. He joined the Apostolic Brethren (q.v.) in 1291 [and in 1300, after the execution of Segarelli, became their head. His denunciations of the Church brought him into frequent conflict with the Inquisition, but he invariably escaped condemnation. He sought refuge in Dalmatia, and remained there until 1304, when he emerged from concealment, and] at the head of a large army waged a guerrilla warfare for several years against the troops which opposed him in the districts of Novara and Vercelli. After many vicissitudes, he was finally defeated by the bishop of Vercelli on Mar. 23, 1307, and was executed with his "spiritual sister," Margareta.

Dolcino sent three letters from Dalmatia to his followers and to all Christians, of two of which long extracts are preserved. The first was written in Aug., 1300, shortly after the death of Segarelli. It opens with declaration of the spiritual and apostolic character of Dolcino's community, and asserts that he, as its head, had received revelations from God. He then recounts the persecutions which had driven him to take refuge in flight, and describes four stages of the development of the lives of the saints on earth, each good in the beginning, and each degenerate at the close and therefore superseded by a new and better régime. These epochs were the period from the patriarchs of the Old Testament to Christ; when marriage was necessary to replenish the earth; from Christ to Pope Silvester and the emperor Constantine, when celibacy was better than wedlock and poverty preferable to wealth; from Silvester and Constantine to the time of Dolcino, when papal power and wealth had been requisite rather than apostolic poverty, although love for God and for one's fellow man had so far cooled that even the rules of Benedict and the still more rigid regulations of Francis and Dominic had proved unavailing to check the increasing degeneracy; from Dolcino to the end of the world, when the apostolic ordinances of life were to be renewed, and all things were to be in common. Dolcino then declares that he and his followers should be considered liars if the events which he foretold did not take place within three years. King Frederick of Sicily would be elected emperor, would set up new kings, and sweep Pope Boniface and all his creatures from the face of the earth, while peace would rule among all Christians. A new pope would be sent by God and would rule over the Apostolic Brethren, and all priests and monks who had divinely escaped the sword would now join them. Like the apostles of the early Church, they would receive the gift of the Holy Ghost and would spread throughout the world, while the emperor Frederick, the pope, and the new kings would remain until a time known to Dolcino, when Antichrist would appear and rule.

Three years elapsed without the fulfilment of the prophecies, and in Dec., 1303, two months after the death of Boniface VIII., Dolcino issued the second letter, in which he practically repeated his assertions. Within three years, according to Isa. xvi. 14, the wicked would be rooted out, the pope and his cardinals would be destroyed in the following year (1304), and in the next all priests, monks, and nuns who persisted in their iniquity would disappear, after which, under the rule of Frederick and the pope chosen of God, the Apostolic Brethren would be free from all oppression, would be joined by all who were truly spiritual, would receive the Holy Ghost, and regenerate the Church. See Apostolic Brethren.

(Hugo Sachsse.)

Bibliography: Muratori, *Scriptores*, ix. 425 sqq., 25 vols., Milan, 1723–51; F. C. Schlosser, *Abälard und Dulcin*, Gotha, 1807; J. Krone, *Frà Dolcino und die Patarener*, Leipsic, 1844; L. Mariotti, *Frà Dolcino and His Times*, London, 1853; G.S.A.S., *Frà Dolcino*, Milan, 1889.

DOLE, CHARLES FLETCHER: Unitarian; b. at Brewer, Me., May 17, 1845. He was graduated at Harvard in 1868, and Andover Theological Seminary in 1872. After being professor of Greek at the University of Vermont 1873–74, he was pastor of Plymouth Church, Portland, Me., 1874–76, and since 1876 has been minister of the First Congregational (Unitarian) Society at Jamaica Plain, Boston. In theology he designates himself a "minister of the religion that is behind and beneath all the names." He has written *The Citizen and the Neighbor* (Boston, 1884); *Early Hebrew Stories* (1886); *Jesus and the Men About Him* (1888); *The American Citizen* (1891); *The Golden Rule in Business* (New York, 1895); *A Catechism of Liberal Faith* (Boston, 1895); *The Coming People* (New York, 1897); *Luxury and Sacrifice* (1898); *The Young Citizen* (Boston, 1899); *The Theology of Civilization* (New York, 1899); *The Problem of Duty* (1900); *The Religion of a Gentleman* (1900); *Noble Womanhood* (Boston, 1900); *The Smoke and the Flame* (1901); *From Agnosticism to Theism* (1903); and *The Spirit of Democracy* (New York, 1906).

DOMICELLUS: A canon who had not a seat and a voice in chapter, but enjoyed certain incomes. See Canon; and Chapter.

DOMINIC, SAINT, AND THE DOMINICAN ORDER.

Dominic was born at Calaroga, a village of Old Castile in the diocese of Osma, 1170; d. at Bologna Aug. 6, 1221. That his father belonged to the noble family of Gusman, as many Dominican writers assert, can not be proved. At seven he was sent to his uncle, archpriest of Gumiel d'Izan, to be educated, and at fourteen went to study philosophy and theology at Palencia, where celebrated teachers were already lecturing, though the university was not founded until 1209.

1. St. Dominic. He soon distinguished himself by his progress in study and by his devotion and charity, selling his books to help the poor. Between 1194 and 1199 he became a canon and later subprior in the cathedral chapter of Osma, which had been reformed under the Augustinian rule. In 1203 he was taken by his bishop, Diego de Azevedo, as companion on a journey, probably to the court of Guy of Lusignan in southern France, on the commission of Alfonso VIII., to ask for a wife for his son Ferdinand. The embassy went again to receive the princess and conduct her to Spain; but she died before their arrival. Diego took Dominic with him to Rome, where the latter requested Innocent III. to relieve him of his bishopric that he might go as a missionary to the Saracens. The pope refused; and on a third journey through southern France Diego and Dominic met at Montpellier (1204) the Cistercian abbots, Arnold of Cîteaux, Peter of Castelnau, and Raoul, who had been entrusted by Innocent with the mission to the Albigenses. Diego urged that the heretics should be converted by the preaching of poor apostolic men, who should renounce all pomp and luxury. This method, so different from the one in vogue, was approved by the legates. Diego and Dominic, and others, went out two by two, barefoot, without retinue, to preach and dispute in the nobles' castles, in the effort to win back the Cathari and Albigenses to the Church. But heresy was too wide-spread and deep-rooted in the south of France for much impression to be made by these few laborers in the Montpellier district alone. To have a base for the work, Diego founded a convent of nuns at Prouille, in the diocese of Toulouse, into which in 1206 eleven high-born ladies were received, nine of them converts.

After Diego had returned to his diocese, where he died in 1207, Dominic carried on the work with zeal and energy. He introduced the rule of Augustine and strict observances into the convent of Prouille. In 1208 Peter of Castelnau was murdered, and Innocent III. proclaimed a crusade against the Albigenses (see NEW MANICHEANS, II.). Dominic apparently took no part in this, but continued his work in the old spirit, supported by the higher clergy. He declined several bishoprics offered to him, to remain true to his mission, feeling called to devote his whole life to showing that the Church had a heart still for the poor misled folk who were alienated from its fold. In 1215 Bishop Fulco of Toulouse assigned one-sixth of the diocesan tithes to the support of his work, and took Dominic to Rome to the Lateran Council, there to seek confirmation from the pope for the foundation of a new order. The council had just ruled against the multiplication of orders, and Innocent, while taking the convent of Prouille under his protection, advised Dominic to choose some established rule for his associates. After his return they talked the matter over and chose the Augustinian rule with the institutions of the Premonstratensians; the new brotherhood would thus be a society not of monks, but of canons regular, with the special purpose of defending the faith and combating heresy by preaching (whence the official name, *ordo prædicatorum*, "order of preachers"). Dominic recognized the necessity of learning for this end, and sent his six companions, who had no technical training, to the theological school at Toulouse.

He was in Rome from Sept., 1216, to Easter, 1217, and obtained from Honorius III. the confirmation of his new order. According to the bulls, it was not originally a mendicant order, but adhered to the older conception of the vow of poverty, as forbidding only the possession of property by the individual, not by the community. Nor was it at first distinguished from the old canons regular by assuming a universal character; it was several years before papal briefs instructed archbishops, bishops, and other prelates to allow the brothers to preach in their dioceses, assume the cure of souls, and hear confessions. At the feast of the Assumption, 1217, Dominic sent out his associates in all directions. He fixed his eyes especially on the three centers of intellectual life, Paris, Rome, and Bologna. Matthew of Paris with seven brothers went to the first-named, where they occupied the monastery of Saint Jacques in 1218 (hence the popular French name for the order, Jacobins). Dominic went to Rome with some of his younger disciples, and sent two brothers thence to Bologna in 1218. Two more were left behind at Prouille and two at Toulouse; four went to Spain, where they had little success—it was not until the founder himself visited Spain (1218) that two houses, one for men at Seville and one for women at Madrid, came into existence. On a visit to Paris in 1219 he found thirty brothers; five years later the number was 120. Toward the end of that year he was again in Rome, where the pope gave him the difficult commission of assembling in a convent all the scattered nuns who were living uncloistered in Rome. Supported by Cardinal Hugo of Ostia, the later Gregory IX., he succeeded in his task, and founded the convent of San Sisto for them, while he and his brothers occupied the monastery of Santa Sabina near the pope's palace. This proximity led to his noticing the careless lives of the papal retainers, who spent their time in drinking and dicing; he got them together and gave them regular spiritual conferences. From this fact grew the story that the pope appointed him *magister sacri palatii*—an office the existence of which is first demonstrable under Gregory IX., though later it was regularly conferred on a Dominican; it acquired great importance in the time of Leo X., when its holder was made the official censor of books.

2. His New Order.

The first general chapter of the order was held at Bologna in 1220, when it became a mendicant order by the decision to renounce all property and fixed incomes. Although its founder died solemnly cursing those who should bring temporal possessions into his order, the vow of poverty was never pushed to its extreme limit among them, and they thus escaped the dissensions which rent the Franciscan order over this question. No objection was ever raised against the possession of churches and convents, though the oldest constitutions (1228) prescribe that these shall be small and plain. A laxer conception of poverty was not long in making its way; though the later constitutions still formally ruled out *possessiones et reditus*, the prohibition was not observed, and Martin V. abrogated it in 1425 for certain houses, and Sixtus IV. in 1475 and 1477 for the whole order.

After a journey through northern Italy, Dominic returned to Bologna, where he won for the order Master Conrad, the first provincial of Germany (see CONRAD OF MARBURG). His last sojourn in Rome was in the winter of 1220–21. The second general chapter met in Bologna May, 1221, and decided that future meetings should take place yearly, alternately in Bologna and Paris, a provision which fell into disuse. At this chapter, if not before, the constitution was completed.

3. Its Constitution.

It distinguishes the order sharply from the older ones. It is organized from the top, where stands a master-general, of far more power than the abbots-general of earlier organizations. In conformity with the universal character of its mission, the vow of *stabilitas loci* is omitted, and that of obedience is made immediately to the general. He is chosen for life by the general chapter, and selects his own *socii*, or counselors. Each province is governed by a prior-provincial chosen for four years by the provincial chapter, which also names four definitors to assist him, as representatives of the whole body. Each house chooses its own head, called prior. The decisions of the general chapter have the force of law when they have been passed at two successive chapters. After the chapter of 1221 Dominic undertook one more journey through northern Italy, got as far as Venice, and returned to Bologna to die on Aug. 6, 1221. At this time the order numbered sixty houses, divided into eight provinces—Toulouse, Provence, France, Rome, Lombardy, Spain, England, and Germany. Dominic was buried in the church of St. Nicholas at Bologna, in the presence of Cardinal Hugo of Ostia, who afterward, as Pope Gregory IX., canonized him (1234). His tomb was afterward beautified by Niccolò Pisano and Michelangelo.

It is difficult to arrive at a satisfactory characterization of the man. He has left no written works, and his biographies, while very full on his miracles, make no attempt to reproduce the distinctive features of his personality. He was undoubtedly a noble character. Sincere piety and equally sincere belief in the truth of the Church's teaching and claims, gentle sympathy for all, heretics as well as orthodox, strictness in self-discipline, and wonderful energy are traits which stand out clearly in his life.

4. Its Development.

After Dominic's death his order spread with remarkable rapidity. At the general chapter of 1228 four new provinces arose—Greece, Poland, Denmark, and Palestine. The four earliest successors of the founder were skilful organizers who knew how to develop and adapt to new conditions the principles given to them. Jordanus, a Saxon (1222–37), codified the constitutions for the first time in 1228; he traveled widely through all the provinces of the order, and met his death by shipwreck after a visit to Palestine. The third general was the distinguished canonist Raymond of Peñaforte, of a noble Spanish family; he resigned his office in 1240, after revising and completing the constitutions. The fourth was a North German, John of Wildeshausen (1241–52), and the fifth a Frenchman, Humbert of Romans (1254–64), who rendered great services to the educational system of the order. The purpose of its very existence being the combating of heresy and strengthening of faith by means of preaching, study was insisted on as a primary requisite. The Dominican order was the first which required study as an essential means to the attainment of its special end, and regulated it minutely by rule. This, of course, was confined to the priests, who found it possible to devote themselves wholly to their ministry since the lay brothers relieved them of household tasks. Eight years were spent in this study after the completion of the novitiate; its system followed that of the University of Paris. After 1248 each province had its own *studium generale*, or university. Theology had naturally the first place, but the liberal arts soon began to be taught; Raymond of Peñaforte paid special attention to the teaching of Greek, and erected schools in the Spanish and North African houses for the study of Hebrew and Arabic. Theology was first taught from the "Sentences" of Peter Lombard, but by the end of the thirteenth century the *Summa* of Thomas Aquinas was taking their place, and the general chapter of 1315, by requiring his works to be found in every monastery, marked his final triumph.

The rapid growth of the order was due not alone to its qualities, but also to the protection of powerful friends among the kings and nobles, and to the lavish privileges which the popes conferred upon both them and the Franciscans. The Dominicans had the advantage, however, in being preferred, if not exclusively chosen, as inquisitors *hæreticæ pravitatis*. When Gregory IX. began, in 1232, to replace the episcopal inquisition by officials appointed directly by the pope, he usually chose the Preaching Friars, on account of their theological learning. When the secular arm was placed at the disposition of the Church, Frederick II. offered his protection in 1239 to the Dominicans as inquisitors, and in 1255, at the request of Louis IX., Alexander IV. named the Dominican provincial and the Franciscan guardian as inquisitors-general for France. (See INQUISITION.)

5. Achievements and Controversies.

The growth and privileges of the order aroused enmity in more than one quarter. From the end of the thirteenth century many of the cities in which the mendicants, unlike the older orders, built their houses, began to show hostility. Some of the older orders, especially the Cistercians and Carthusians, displayed a spirit that was anything but brotherly toward them, and the higher secular clergy resented their intrusion into the organized cure of souls, so that Innocent IV. was obliged in 1254 to limit their privileges, allowing them to preach and hear confessions only with the assent of the parish priest. The universities were at first unfriendly, and tried to bar out the Preaching Friars. The famous contest in Paris was terminated in favor of the Dominicans in 1259, and it was not long before they occupied the theological chairs in Bologna, Padua, Vienna, Cologne, Prague, Oxford, and Salamanca. The greatest of the scholastics, Thomas Aquinas, and his many-sided teacher, Albertus Magnus, are but two out of many distinguished theologians produced by the order in the later Middle Ages. It did not confine itself to the cultivation of learning, but did much for the religious training of the common people. One of the most popular preachers of a little later day was the Spanish Dominican Vincent Ferrer (q.v.). They were active in the missionary field, appearing at the court of Kubla Khan in 1272, and accomplishing much in the still heathen parts of Europe; the conversion of the Lithuanians, completed in 1386, was their work. Their services to art were very considerable. Two of them designed the church of Santa Maria Novella in Florence, the purest and most beautiful example of Tuscan Gothic. Here, at San Marco, and at Santa Caterina in Pisa painting was cultivated

III.—31

with great success in the fourteenth and fifteenth centuries, the last flowering, under mystical illumination, of the school of Giotto was seen in the work of Giovanni du Fiesole, better known as Fra Angelico (d. 1455).

The mendicant orders had at first stood together against the monks, the secular clergy, and the universities; but before the end of the thirteenth century jealousy brought discord. The partisans of Thomas Aquinas on one side and Duns Scotus on the other made the controversy between Thomists and Scotists traditional (see IMMACULATE CONCEPTION). The Dominicans themselves were divided in the great Western Schism (see SCHISM), and only reunited by Martin V. in 1418. Worldliness made its inroads, and theological subtlety was pushed to absurd extremes. The conflict of the humanist Reuchlin with the Cologne inquisitor Jakob von Hoogstraten and the *Epistolæ obscurorum virorum* (q. v.) show how the order had declined from its early zeal for learning by the beginning of the sixteenth century. The Counterreformation owed its results not to the Preaching Friars, but to the new order of the Jesuits, whom the Dominicans steadily opposed on several questions of internal policy and belief. In the great controversy about grace (1588–1611) they stood for a moderate Augustinianism against the Semi-Pelagianism of the Jesuit Molina. In the moral controversy the two orders became theological parties, the Jesuits at the end of the sixteenth and beginning of the seventeenth centuries almost always defending Probabilism (q.v.), while the Dominicans adopted probabiliorism as their view. The most violent conflict, however, arose in the mission-field. The Jesuits had had it almost to themselves in the era of the Counterreformation, except in America, where the Preaching Friars had been active, and one of the noblest of missionaries, Las Casas (d. 1566), had not only sought the conversion of the Indians of Mexico, but protected them from the greed and cruelty of the Spaniards. They came to China after the Jesuits had already occupied the field; they opposed and soon denounced at Rome the "accommodation" (q.v.) of the rival order, and after a long struggle won the victory in 1782—though the downfall of Christianity in China followed almost immediately.

The secularizing policy of Joseph II. (d. 1790) diminished still further the number of convents which the Reformation had spared; the same thing took place in Germany, and the Revolution suppressed the order in France, until it was restored by the eloquent advocacy of Lacordaire in 1840. Great progress was made under the generalship of Alexander Vincent Jandel, a Frenchman (d. 1872), who published a revised constitution in 1872, the most important change being the limitation of the general's term, which Pius VII. in 1804 fixed at six years and Pius IX. in 1862 at twelve. The general has resided since 1272 at Santa Maria sopra Minerva in Rome. Fifty-two provinces are named in the new constitutions, but several of these are merely nominal. There are about 300 houses, with some 3,000 members. Under Pope Leo XIII., a great admirer of Thomas Aquinas, the order once more assumed importance by its influence on theological learning. There have been four Dominican popes: Innocent V. (d. 1276), Benedict XI. (d. 1304), St. Pius V. (d. 1572), and the learned Benedict XIII. (d. 1730).

6. Present Condition.

Two houses of the female branch of the order, that of Prouille and San Sisto at Rome, arose in the founder's lifetime. Their rule prescribed confinement to the cloister, ascetic practises, the contemplative life, and employment of time as far as possible analogous to that of the brothers; the obligation of poverty was for obvious reasons not as strictly imposed on them. New houses were at first founded wherever the order spread, and were under the direction of the provincial. As their number grew, this produced difficulties and interfered with the work of the friars, who got themselves released from this charge in 1252, though they were obliged to reassume it two years later, as the female houses were suffering from the separation. Only a few remained under episcopal care. They followed in the main the fortunes of the friars. At first wholly contemplative, they devoted themselves later to the education of girls; and their rule was correspondingly mitigated. At present there are about ninety houses of the "second order," with some 1,500 inmates. For the "third order," composed of confraternities of people living in the world, see TERTIARIES; CONFRATERNITIES, RELIGIOUS. (G. GRÜTZMACHER.)

7. The Sisters.

BIBLIOGRAPHY: Early lives of Dominic are collected in *ASB*, Aug., i. 358–658; some of the same, with others not included, are in J. Quétif, *Scriptores ordinis prædicatorum*, ed. J. Echard, i. 1–56, Paris, 1719. The *Vita* by Dietrich of Apolda (c. 1296 A.D.), ed. A. Curé, Paris, 1887. Consult: E. Caro, *St. Dominique et les Dominicains*, Paris, 1853; J. B. H. Lacordaire, *Vie de S. Dominique*, ib. 1882, Eng. transl., London, 1883; A. T. Drane, *Hist. of St. Dominic*, ib. 1891; J. J. Berthier, *Le Testament de S. Dominique*, Freiburg, 1892; M. J. Rousset, *Der heilige Dominicus*, Freiburg, 1899; T. Alemany, *Life of St. Dominic with Sketch of the Dominican Order*, New York, n.d.

On the order, for sources consult: *Monumenta ordinis fratrum prædicatorum historica*, now in course of publication at Rome, 1896 sqq.; *Acta capitulorum . . . prædicatorum*, ed. C. Douais, Toulouse, 1894. Further: W. G. D. Fletcher, *Black Friars of Oxford*, Oxford, 1882; C. F. R. Palmer, *Notices of the Friar Preachers of the Eng. Province*, London, 1884; *Friar Preachers of Leicester*, Leicester, 1884; A. T. Drane, *Hist. of Catherine of Siena and her Companions*, London, 1887; idem, *Spirit of the Dominican Order*, ib. 1896; B. M. Reichert, in *Historische Jahrbücher*, 1897, ii. 363–374; B. A. A. Wilberforce, *Dominican Missions and Martyrs in Japan*, London, 1897; M. D. Chapotin, *Histoire des Dominicains de . . . France*, Rouen, 1898; Franziska Raphael, *Der Geist des Dominicaner Ordens*, Dulmen, 1901; J. Herkless, *Francis and Dominic and the Mendicant Orders*, New York, 1901; E. G. Gardner, *Saint Catherine of Siena*, London, 1907; Heimbucher, *Orden und Kongregationen*, i. 540 sqq.; Currier, *Religious Orders*, pp. 271–283; Neander, *Christian Church*, vol. iv. passim (valuable); Schaff, *Christian Church*, v. 1., pp. 519 sqq.

DOMINICALE, do-min"i-kē'lī: A white linen cloth used by women when receiving the Lord's Supper; either a napkin, upon which the bread was laid instead of upon the bare hand, or the veil which women generally wore in the house of God.

DOMINICAL LETTER: A letter used to indicate Sunday in ancient calendars, which marked the first seven days of the year by the letters A–G and repeated them for every succeeding week. The same letter thus designated Sunday throughout the year except in leap-years, when the dominical letter changed from A to G, B to A, etc., after Feb. 28 (in some calendars after Feb. 24). It is used in finding the date of Easter of any given year. See CALENDAR, THE CHRISTIAN, § 4; EASTER, I., 3.

DOMINIS, MARCO ANTONIO DE: Archbishop of Spalato (on the coast of Dalmatia, 160 m. s.e. of Triest); b. of a noble Venetian family on the island of Arbe (80 m. s.e. of Triest), off the Dalmatian coast, 1560; d. at Rome Sept. 8, 1624. He was professor of mathematics at Verona, Padua, and Brescia, and was appointed bishop of Zengg (on the coast of Croatia, 10 m. n. of his native island) in 1596, and two years later archbishop of Spalato and primate of Dalmatia and Croatia. His position was a difficult one owing to the conflict between the curia and the republic of Venice; and the complications in which he was involved led him to thorough canonical, historical, and dogmatic studies which later bore fruit in the publication of the *De republica ecclesiastica.* The incompatibility between a strong tendency toward an episcopal system and the autocratic rule of the pope induced him to resign his office, to withdraw from the Roman Church, and to separate himself from his friends and country. In the *Consilium profectionis,* which he published (London, 1616; also in part i. of the *De republica ecclesiastica*) to explain his conduct, he expresses his dissatisfaction with the position of the bishops under the pope, declares that the Roman Church in doctrine and polity has fallen from the purity of Christian antiquity, professes to be actuated by the love of Christ and the truth, and says that he hopes to promote the reunion of Christendom (chaps. xii., xiii., xx.). By way of Venice, Switzerland, and Heidelberg he went to England, arriving Dec. 16, 1616. At St. Paul's in London he joined the Anglican Church, and in 1618 was made master of the Savoy and dean of Windsor. The same year he published in London *The Rocks of Christian Shipwreck,* a book of popular character, previously published at Heidelberg in Italian (*Scogli del naufragio christiano*). It was a polemic intended to warn and admonish his countrymen, and at the same time a keen Biblical and patristic critique of the chief Roman doctrines and institutions. Meanwhile he had completed his chief work, the *De republica ecclesiastica libri* (3 parts, i., London, 1617; ii., 1620; iii., Frankfort, 1658; books viii. and xx. were never printed). With much learning he treats of the hierarchical order, the power of the Church, the rights of the laity, the decision of questions of faith, jurisdiction, church property and liberties; the difference between priests and bishops he makes not one of ecclesiastical functions, but of jurisdiction and relation to the Church in general, from which, rather than from the pope, the episcopal power is derived and by which it is conferred through the election by the Christian congregation. To the early part of his stay in England belongs also the *Papatus Romanus seu de origine, progressu atque extinctione ejus* (London, 1617), which was inspired, according to the preface, by King James I. He carried on correspondence with such men as Hugo Grotius and Paolo Sarpi, and published the latter's *Historia del concilio Tridentino* (the manuscript of which he had brought with him from Venice), with additions, in 1619, dedicated to James I.

After the good reception accorded to De Dominis in England and the polemical activity he had displayed, great surprise was occasioned in [Jan.] 1622, by the news that he intended to return to Italy. The reasons he gave in a letter to the king —advancing age, the raw air of England, etc.— were evidently only pretexts. He was warned of danger to himself in his purpose; but nevertheless he went back, trusting to the protection of his former friend, Pope Gregory XV. He received absolution only after a threefold recantation, including an appearance in public in St. Peter's with a rope about his neck and in penitential garb. His literary activity naturally took a new direction. As an offset to the *Consilium profectionis* he published *Reditus ex Anglia consilium* (Rome, 1623; Eng. transl., Liége, 1623; London, 1827), in which he explains his apostasy as due to a twofold disorder, brought on by his own conceit and vindictiveness toward his superiors, and condemns all his polemical writings of the earlier period. His retractation made no impression, however, and the book scarcely attempts to refute the material brought together previously in so great abundance. Gregory XV. died July, 1623, and the case of De Dominis was reopened. Before it was decided, however, he died in prison. On Dec. 20, 1624, his body was carried to the Church of Santa Maria sopra Minerva, his picture and a sack containing his books were placed beside it, and a conclave deprived him of all ecclesiastical honors, confiscated his property, and handed him over to the civil authorities for execution of sentence; his body was publicly burned on the next day. His books were naturally already on the Index. It has been asserted that he was sent to England by Paul V. to convert the king and bishops and was ill treated when he returned to Rome because he did not succeed (cf. J. W. Jaeger, *Historia ecclesiastica saeculi decimi septimi,* i., Hamburg, 1709, p. 382, dec. iii., lib. ii., cap. xv.). His works not already mentioned include *A Sermon Preached in the Mercers' Chapel, London* (London, 1617) and a *Tractatus de radiis visus et lucis in perspectivis et iride* (Venice, 1611), in which he came near giving the true scientific explanation of the rainbow. Opinions concerning De Dominis differ. His ability and learning are unquestioned; but his honesty has been seriously impugned by Protestants as well as Roman Catholics. It is said that he obtained the copy of Sarpi's *Concilio Tridentino* surreptitiously, published it without the author's consent, and made unjustifiable alterations and additions. His conduct in England is said to have been shamelessly avaricious.

K. BENRATH.

BIBLIOGRAPHY: *Trajano Boccalini lettera al Sgr. Mutio,* in *La bilancia politica di tutte le opere di Trajano Boccalini,* iii. 7–40, Castellana, 1678; R. Neile, *Marco Antonio de*

Dominis, his Shiftings in Religion, London, 1624; L. Veith, *De vita . . . de Dominis*, appended to his *Edm. Richeri Systema*, Mechlin, 1825; F. A. Reusch, *Der Index der verbotenen Bücher*, ii. 401–404, Bonn, 1885; H. Newland, *The Life and Contemporaneous Church History of Antonio de Dominis*, Oxford, 1859; *KL*, iii. 1949–50.

DOMINUS. See DOMUS.

DOMITIAN, do-mish'i-an (**TITUS FLAVIUS DOMITIANUS**): Roman emperor 81–96; b. at Rome Oct. 25, 51; d. there Sept. 18, 96. The son of the emperor Vespasian and Flavia Domitilla, he succeeded his father Sept. 13, 81. He ruled at first in an autocratic, but zealous and intelligent manner, and strengthened the life and the ordinances of religion. Aristocratic opposition, however, especially of the senatorial body, awakened in him a distrust which was fostered by informers and quickly led to bloody executions, particularly in 95–96. The result was a reaction, culminating in a conspiracy to which the emperor fell a victim.

In 96 Domitian instituted repressive measures against the Christians, and though his policy was both brief and of limited extent, its execution was severe and cruel. The distress of the Roman congregation was increased by the quick and unexpected character of the blow. One of its most prominent members, Flavia Domitilla (q.v.), was banished, and her husband, the consular Flavius Clemens, was put to death. It is not impossible that the ex-consul Manius Acilius Glabrio (q.v.) also suffered as a Christian. The causes which led to the stringent measures against the Christians are unknown, but they were probably connected with the contemporary political executions; the emperor's distrust extended to the firmly organized congregation which stood aloof from public life, yet had members in the higher social circles and even the hostile aristocracy which surrounded him. His self-deification, which resulted in such official and unofficial designations as *theos*, *Deus*, *Dominus et Deus*, *Zeus eleutheros*, and *Jupiter*, as well as his systematic attempts to regenerate the ancient cults, must also be taken into consideration. Since there is no reliable tradition to show that the persecution extended beyond Rome, and since Tertullian knows only of a brief period of oppression (*Apol.*, v.), the numerous martyrdoms mentioned by the historian Bruttius and the banishments to which Tertullian alludes were doubtless limited to Rome.* The measures taken by Domitian, according to Hegesippus, against the relatives of Jesus, who were denounced, imprisoned, and carried to Rome as members of the royal house of David, were inspired, on the other hand, simply by political considerations connected with the relations between the government and the Jews. The emperor questioned the prisoners solely regarding their political affiliations and finally dismissed them as politically harmless. It is incorrect to assume, with Hegesippus, that this affair caused a cessation of the persecution of the Church, for there was no persecution of the Church *per se*. VICTOR SCHULTZE.

* If, as is commonly admitted, the Apocalypse was written during the reign of Domitian, and the reigning emperor was associated by the writer with Nero (Rev. vi. 9 sqq., xvii. 5, 8, 11, etc.), it would seem reasonable to infer that the persecution extended beyond Rome, or at least that a wide-spread persecution seemed imminent. A. H. N.

BIBLIOGRAPHY: J. B. Lightfoot, *Apostolic Fathers*, i. 104 sqq., London, 1890 (collects the sources); H. Schiller, *Geschichte der römischen Kaiserzeit*, i. 520 sqq., Gotha, 1883; F. Pichemayr, *T. Flavius Domitianus*, Amberg, 1889; W. M. Ramsay, *Church in the Roman Empire*, pp. 259–263, London, 1893; E. G. Hardy, *Christianity and the Roman Government*, pp. 85 sqq., ib. 1894; L. Pullan, *Church of the Fathers*, New York, 1905; Schaff, *Christian Church*, i. 427–428. For the life of Domitian consult Suetonius, Eng. transl. by A. Thompson, revised by T. Forester, pp. 479–505, London, 1896.

DOMITILLA, FLAVIA: According to Dio Cassius (lxvii. 14; cf. Suetonius, *Domitian*, xv.), a niece of the emperor Domitian, married to her cousin, the consul Flavius Clemens; both were condemned for "atheism" (or "Judaizing") in 96 A.D., Clement was beheaded, and Domitilla was banished to the island of Pandateria (in the Tyrrhenian Sea; the modern Ventotene, about half-way between Ponza and Ischia). The acts of Nereus and Achilleus, and Eusebius, who quotes from a heathen writer Bruttius (*Hist. eccl.*, iii. 18; *Chron.*, in *MPG*, viii. 605), represent Domitilla as a niece of Flavius Clemens and the place of her banishment as Pontia (Ponze; so also Jerome, *Epist.*, lxxxvi. [cviii.] *ad Eustochium*, *NPNF*, 2d ser., vi. 197). Some have thought that there were two Domitillas, but it is more natural to suppose that the two accounts, though discrepant, refer to the same person. One of the oldest catacombs, on the Ardeatine Way, near Terracina, is called *Cœmeterium Domitillæ* or *Cœmeterium Nerei et Achillei*. See CLEMENT OF ROME, § 2.

BIBLIOGRAPHY: Mommsen, in *CIL*, vi. 172; F. X. Kraus, *Roma sotterranea*, p. 43, Freiburg, 1872; G. B. de Rossi, *Bullettino di archeologia cristiana*, 2d ser., vi (1875), 69–71; J. S. Northcote, *Roma sotterranea*, pp. 69–70, ib. 1879.

DONALDSON, SIR JAMES: Church of Scotland; b. at Aberdeen Apr. 26, 1831. He studied at Aberdeen (B.A., 1849), New College, London (1849–51), and the University of Berlin (1851). He was tutor of Greek in Edinburgh University 1852–54, rector of the high school at Stirling 1854–56, classical master and rector of the Edinburgh High School 1856–81, professor of humanity in Aberdeen University 1881–86, and is now principal and vice-chancellor of St. Andrews University and principal of the United College of St. Salvator and St. Leonard. He was knighted in 1907. His books include: *A Critical History of Christian Literature and Doctrine from the death of the Apostles to the Nicene Council* (3 vols., London, 1864–66); and *The Westminster Confession of Faith and the Thirty-Nine Articles of the Church of England: The Legal, Moral, and Religious Aspects of Subscription to Them* (1905). With Alexander Roberts he edited *The Ante-Nicene Christian Library* (24 vols., Edinburgh, 1867–72).

DONATION OF CONSTANTINE.

Contents of the Document (§ 1).
Its History (§ 2).
Origin (§ 3).
Present State of the Discussion (§ 4).

The "Donation of Constantine" is the name traditionally applied, since the later Middle Ages, to a document purporting to have been addressed by Constantine the Great to Pope Sylvester I., which is found first in a Parisian manuscript (*Codex lat.* 2777) of probably the beginning of the ninth century. Since the eleventh century it has been used as a powerful argument in favor of the papal claims, and consequently since the twelfth it has been the subject of a vigorous controversy. At the same time, by rendering it possible to regard the papacy as a middle term between the original and the medieval Roman Empire, and thus to form a theoretical basis of continuity for the reception of the Roman law in the Middle Ages, it has had no small influence upon secular history.

1. Contents of the Document.

After a remarkable introduction (chap. i.), the emperor promises a "clear narration" of the marvels which the apostles Peter and Paul have wrought through the "supreme pontiff and universal pope" Sylvester (ii.); but before proceeding to this he gives (iii.–iv.) the confession of faith which Sylvester has taught him, and admonishes all nations to accept it and adore the Christ whom "our universal father" Sylvester preaches. He goes on (vi.–x.) to give the history of his conversion, baptism, and deliverance from leprosy by Sylvester, in terms which agree substantially with the Sylvester legend (see SYLVESTER I., POPE), and asserts his desire to show his gratitude for the benefits of Peter. Accordingly, in agreement with his "satraps," the senate, and the Roman people, he recognizes the primacy of the vicar of the Prince of the Apostles, and intends to raise his see above all earthly thrones (xi.). Accordingly he sanctions (xii.) the precedence of the "see of Peter" over Antioch, Alexandria, Constantinople, and Jerusalem, and decrees (xiii.) that the church founded by himself near the Lateran palace shall be honored as the "head and summit of all the churches in the whole world," stating at the same time that he has built churches to Peter and Paul, and endowed them with his possessions in Judea, Greece, Asia [Minor], Thrace, Africa, and Italy. He hands over (xiv.) the Lateran palace to the pope, and allows him to use the imperial diadem and the other insignia of empire. The Roman clergy (xv.) are also distinguished by senatorial rank and eligibility to the patriciate and consulate; he gives the pope the exclusive right to confer holy orders upon senators. He asserts (xvi.) that Sylvester has refused to wear the imperial diadem over the tonsure, and therefore he himself has set the white miter with his own hand upon the pope's holy brow. In order (xvii.) that the papal throne may not be of low esteem, he leaves to the pope the power and jurisdiction, "in imitation of our sovereignty," over the city of Rome and "all provinces, places, and cities of Italy or of the western regions," confining his own sovereignty to the East, where he intends to build up a capital for himself at Byzantium. He lays (xix.) a solemn obligation upon his successors, "satraps," the senate, and all peoples of the earth to leave these provisions intact, and invokes an eternal curse upon those who violate them. He proclaims (xx.) that he has signed the decree with his own hand and laid it upon the body of St. Peter, closing with the imperial signature and the date.

2. Its History.

It is a controverted question whether Adrian I., in his letter of May, 778, to Charlemagne (Jaffé, *Regesta*, 2423) refers to this document. The passage (line 9) in which he alludes to Constantine and Sylvester seems to imply a knowledge of it, but lines 18 sqq. more easily bear the opposite construction. The *Codex Parisinus*, however, is positive evidence that it was known at Saint Denis early in the ninth century, perhaps before 793. The next oldest testimonies to it also belong to the Frankish kingdom—the pseudo-Isidore, Ado of Vienne, and Hincmar of Reims. On the other hand, no Roman references to it during the ninth or tenth century are met. Two Frankish popes, Gregory V. and Sylvester II., are the first to base certain territorial claims upon it. These excited such vigorous imperial opposition that the chancellor of Otto III., Leo of Vercelli, boldly asserts that the document is a Roman forgery. Another Frankish pope, Leo IX., brought it up half a century later, using it in a controversy with Byzantium so energetically that it was not again forgotten. Peter Damian cites it against the antipope Cadalus of Parma, and Gregory VII. alludes to it in the oath which he tenders to Herman of Salm, a claimant of the empire (1081). Anselm of Lucca and Cardinal Deusdedit include it in their collections of canons. The publicists of the early twelfth century use it as the basis for far-reaching conclusions; in a word, by this period it is known everywhere and employed as a valuable weapon in the strife with the civil power, whose representatives were forced to take it into account. As a rule, they contented themselves with denying, not its authenticity, but the conclusions drawn from it. This line of argument was inconclusive. The first to attack the validity of the document itself was the republican party in Rome, under Arnold of Brescia's influence; one of his adherents, a jurist, maintained in 1151, in a disputation with Gerhoh of Reichersberg, that it was invalid because Constantine was baptized or rebaptized in the Arian heresy, and a year later they went further, declaring the whole thing a lie and a heretical fable, and supporting their contention by historical arguments, as that Constantine, according to the pseudo-Isidore, had already been baptized before he came to Rome. But these utterances made little impression. Frederick Barbarossa and his partizans did not attack the authenticity of the document; and the popes of the later twelfth and the thirteenth centuries appealed with increasing confidence to it. The Waldenses, Cathari, and Apostolic Brethren, on the other hand, stoutly maintained that the Donation had marked a step away from the original purity of the Church, in the direction of Antichrist, with whom some of them even identified Sylvester. At the end of the thirteenth century the lawyers of Philip the Fair took up once more the Arnoldist line, and denied its legal validity. Their theory found considerable approbation in the University of Paris, and soon spread throughout Western Europe. Their arguments, however, were of a scholastic type, and the possibility of the document being a mere forgery is not mentioned until the rise of historical criticism in the fifteenth century. Nicholas of Cusa came (1432-33) to the conclusion that Constantine never made any such donation; Laurentius Valla gave a brilliant demonstration of its spuriousness in 1440, and Reginald Pecock came independently to the same conclusion in 1450. For a century longer, however, in spite of their arguments, the general belief in its authenticity continued to prevail among the great body both of ecclesiastics and lawyers, so that it is not surprising that Luther first learned of its spuriousness from Hutten's edition of Valla's treatise. The defense of the authenticity ceased on the Roman Catholic side when Baronius abandoned it, as far as the external form went, in 1592—though he and his successors attempted, up to the beginning of the nineteenth century, to maintain the accuracy of its substance.

3. Origin. Since the admission of the spuriousness of the document, the most diverse views have prevailed as to its real origin. The Roman Catholic writers thought it Greek (Baronius) or Frankish (Thomassin, Zaccaria, Cenni); the Protestants (Freher, Schröckh) believed that it originated in Rome. The dates assigned to its composition ranged from the pontificate of Stephen II. (757-767) to c. 963. In the first edition of his *Papstfabeln des Mittelalters* (Munich, 1863) Döllinger demonstrated conclusively that it was not Greek, but Western. Between 1882 and 1884 Grauert subjected the structure and vocabulary to a more searching examination than it had ever received, concluding that it originated on Frankish soil soon after 840. In the course of the vigorous discussion aroused by this theory Friedrich propounded a new view in 1889, that the document consists of an older part, written before 653, and a later, added by Paul I. not later than 754.

4. Present State of the Discussion. The net result of all these modern examinations, including that of Loening in 1890 and of Martens still more recently, gives a substantial agreement on certain propositions: (1) The Donation is a forgery. (2) It is the work of one man or period. (3) The forger has, however, made use of older material, including, for chaps. vi.-x., a version of the Sylvester legend not now extant, but current in Rome in the eighth century; for iii.-iv., an ancient confession of faith; and for the opening and closing chapters, genuine Byzantine imperial documents. (4) The forgery originated in Rome, between 752 and 778; whether under Paul I., Stephen II., or Adrian I. is still disputed. As to the purpose of its composition, Scheffer-Boichorst believes it to have been the exaltation of St. Sylvester; but for this a new legend, not a legal document, would have been the natural means to employ. The form adopted shows that the forger had in mind to confirm or make possible certain legal claims of the Roman Church. The recognition of the pope as a potentate equal in rank to the emperor, the attribution of senatorial rank to the Roman clergy, dominion over all the provinces of Italy or of "the occidental regions"—these were not things seriously claimed or contended for by the Roman Church of the eighth and ninth centuries. The probability is that the forger, as happened in other cases, not venturing clearly to designate the object aimed at, enveloped it in sufficiently vague circumlocution. In this case it would seem obvious that the tendency of the forgery is visible in the seventeenth and following chapters, relating to the donation of territory. But since the popes of that period made no pretensions to sovereignty over the whole of Italy, the special design would have been to provide a firm basis for their claims to the part which they did desire, the exarchate of Ravenna. It is accordingly probable that the document was meant to serve as a weapon in their conflict for the possession of this, and specifically to be laid before the Frankish court. Reasoning from this, the simplest solution of the date problem is the view that it was composed shortly before Stephen II.'s departure from Rome on Oct. 14, 753. This date offers the least difficulty in regard to both external and internal evidence, and is consonant with the history of the document, which makes its first appearance in the abbey of Saint Denis, where Stephen spent the winter of 754, and is found there between two letters (whose authenticity is, indeed, questioned) from Zacharias, Stephen's predecessor, and Stephen himself.

(H. Böhmer.)

Bibliography: The best text is given by K. Zeumer, in *Festgabe für Rudolf von Gneist*, Berlin, 1888; a transl. is given in Henderson, *Documents*, pp. 319-329. Consult: J. J. I. von Döllinger, *Die Papstfabeln des Mittelalters*, pp. 72-125, 2d ed., Stuttgart, 1890, Eng. transl., *Fables Respecting the Popes of the Middle Ages*, London, 1871; R. Pecock, *The Repressor of over much Blaming of the Clergy*, ed. C. Babington, *Rolls Series*, No. 19, vol. ii., pp. 351-366; A. Bonneau, *La Donation de Constantin*, Lisieux, 1879; Gmelin, *Das Schenkungsversprechen und die Schenkung Pippins*, pp. 36-37, Vienna, 1880; J. Friedrich, *Die constantinische Schenkung*, Nördlingen, 1889; W. Martens, *Die falsche Generalkonsession Konstantins*, Munich, 1889; idem, *Beleuchtung der neuesten Kontroversen über die römische Frage unter Pippin und Karl dem Grossen*, iii. 151 sqq., ib. 1898; F. Gregorovius, *Rome in the Middle Ages*, ii. 359-362, London, 1894; T. Hodgkin, *Italy and her Invaders*, vii. 135 sqq., Oxford, 1899.

DONATISM.

1. Origin. Donatism, a schismatic movement which originated in the African Church early in the fourth century, was an outcome of the Diocletian persecution, as the persecutions of Decius and Valerian had given birth to Novatianism. In the former persecution the demand for the delivery of the sacred books of the Christians made the question of their duty a complicated one; a compromise with the government might both insure the bishop's personal safety and protect his flock, but it was very like apostasy. The conduct of Mensurius, bishop of Carthage, is told in his correspondence with Secundus of Tigisis, the primate of Numidia. He adopted the expedient of leaving heretical writings to the persecutors in the churches, which satisfied the proconsul; and he censured those who courted martyrdom by declaring themselves in possession of sacred books and refusing to surrender them. Secundus, on the other hand, extolled the latter class as martyrs, and refused his approval to any concession. Light is thrown upon the words of Mensurius by the accusations brought against him and his archdeacon Cæcilianus in the Acta of Saturninus and his companions, which are Donatist at least in their present form. Mensurius had evidently taken pains to check anything which could call forth a more acute persecution, and opposed the extravagant reverence shown to confessors. Though it is uncertain how far the accusations against Cæcilianus, showing passionate hatred of him, are true, he had clearly been imprudent. The latent fundamental opposition in the Carthaginian Church was thus tinged with personal bitterness, which broke out severely on the death of Mensurius. There is a difference of opinion as to the circumstances under which the actual breach came to pass. The moderate party seems to have at once elected Cæcilianus to succeed Mensurius and to have taken order for his consecration without waiting for the primate, probably thinking to gain the advantage of a *fait accompli* and insure his recognition outside of Africa; but the manner of the proceeding gave occasion for forcible objections on the part of the faction hostile to Cæcilianus and of the Numidian bishops. The latter sent to Carthage as *interventor* (administrator of the see) Bishop Donatus of Casæ Nigræ, who was the real founder of the schism. According to the most reliable authorities, he was sent before Cæcilianus's consecration, to intervene in the factional strife in the name of the Numidian bishops, and perhaps to put off decisive action until their arrival. His openly declared hostility to Cæcilianus only made the latter's party more active and determined. Donatus consecrated Majorinus as bishop, and seventy of the Numidian bishops, assembled at a council in Carthage, summoned Cæcilianus before them, refusing to acknowledge him even when he expressed his readiness to undergo a second consecration.

Though personal differences were the active causes of the Donatist schism, its extent and duration show that there were deeper grounds. The opposition between the rigorist and the moderate attitudes had been widely at work and the spread of this purely local schism into one which had destructive consequences for the whole African Church was also due largely to the new relations between Church and State which began at this time.

2. The Actual Breach. In 313 the emperor Constantine gave a subsidy (equivalent to over $80,000) to Cæcilianus and his party; he called the attention of his representatives in Africa to the schism, and directed that exemption from taxation should apply only to the clergy of Cæcilianus's party. These measures forced the Donatists to appeal formally to Constantine, and he referred the matter to Melchiades, bishop of Rome. Ten bishops of each party were to appear with Cæcilianus in Rome; three Gallic and fifteen Italian bishops were to act with Melchiades as assessors. As the Roman bishop had from the first maintained friendly relations with Cæcilianus, who had priority of consecration also in his favor, it is not surprising that the award recognized him as the lawful bishop. Donatus was treated as the real defendant, and excommunicated on a charge of having rebaptized lay people and reconsecrated bishops who had lapsed in the persecution. The way of reconciliation was smoothed for the bishops of Majorinus's party by permission to retain their sees; where there were two bishops in one see, the senior was to hold it and a diocese to be found elsewhere for the other. The letters of Constantine to Ælafius (called also *Ablabius* or *Ablavius*), vicar of Africa, and to Chrestus, bishop of Syracuse, show that the Donatists complained they had not had a full and fair hearing in Rome. The emperor ordered a new hearing at Arles in 316, of which an account is given in the report made by the bishops there assembled to Sylvester of Rome, and in the canons passed by the synod. The African practise of rebaptizing schismatics, applied by the Donatists to the adherents of Cæcilianus, was disallowed, and the Roman custom of mere laying on of hands sanctioned. The Donatist accusation that Felix of Aptunga, the consecrator of Cæcilianus, had been a *traditor* (one who gave up the sacred books to the heathen; see LAPSED), which had been only incidentally considered, took a prominent place here; but the synod decided that only those against whom *traditio* could be proved by official documents should be considered guilty, and that even in those cases orders conferred by them were valid. A section of the Donatists yielded to these decisions; but the remainder appealed once more to the emperor, and he summoned the principal witnesses and representatives of both parties to him at Rome. When Cæcilianus did not appear Constantine thought of sending delegates to try the case in Africa, or even of going thither himself, but finally transferred the hearing to Milan. Here both Cæcilianus and his opponent Donatus (called " the Great " by his adherents to distinguish him from Donatus of Casæ Nigræ), who had succeeded Majorinus as claimant of the see of Carthage, were present. The decision was once more in favor of Cæcilianus; but the emperor forbade both contestants to return to Africa, sending two bishops as delegates in the hope of restoring peace.

When these efforts proved fruitless he took up in earnest the repressive measures which he had already threatened. Orders were sent out to take their churches away from the Donatists, which meant the use of force, as they were unlikely to surrender them peaceably. Blood was shed in

3. Repressive Measures against Donatists. taking possession of a church in Carthage, and persecution, regarded as a mark of the true Church, only increased the fanaticism of the Donatists. They assured the emperor that they would never hold communion with " the rogue " Cæcilianus, and he was so far impressed that he revoked his order and allowed the banished bishops to return. The schismatic party made the most of this reprieve, and a council of 270 of their bishops sat for two months undisturbed in Carthage (before 340). Still, their organization was practically confined to Africa, though they had one community in Spain and another in Rome itself.

The situation changed on Constantine's death. Constans, to whom Africa fell, adopted severe measures to restore the unity of the Church, after offers of money had been scornfully rejected by Donatus's orders. But this time the schismatics met force with force. Another Donatus, bishop of Bagæ, enlisted the dangerous fanatics known as Circumcelliones (q.v.) in support of their cause. The date of this persecution has not been determined; it must have been between the Synod of Sardica, which attempted to enter into some kind of relations with Donatus, and the death of Constans—possibly in 342. The schismatic bishops, including Donatus himself, were once more banished, and their churches given over to the followers of Cæcilianus. His successor, Gratus, in a council at Carthage, gave thanks for the restoration of unity as a work well pleasing to God, and lauded the servants of God, Paul and Macarius, through whom it had been brought about. The rebaptism of those who had received the sacrament according to the orthodox formula was forbidden, and all veneration of Donatist martyrs strictly prohibited.

Under Constantius the Donatists fared no better. Donatus died in exile, and was succeeded by the Spaniard Parmenianus. But when Julian permitted the return of Athanasius and other bishops who had been expelled by the semi-Arian court party, the Donatists demanded the same treatment, which they gained, as well as the restoration of the churches; the latter only after armed conflict with the catholics in some cases. Whole communities were won for the schism during this period of toleration; but with Julian's death began a new epoch of imperial repression. Valentinian forbade rebaptism; Gratian, soon after his accession, and still more definitely in 378, prohibited all gatherings of heretics—in 379 specifically of the rebaptizers, i.e., the Donatists. These regulations could not at first be enforced in Numidia, and Donatism, maintained for a while an unbroken outward front.

4. Decay of the Sect.

The inner decay of the sect had, however, already begun. It undoubtedly owed its long existence in Africa not only to its more or less nationalist position, but to the wise leadership for seventy-five years of Donatus the Great and Parmenianus. The qualities of Donatus were recognized even by his opponents; he was a man of deep learning, of eloquence, and of undaunted courage. His work was well continued by Parmenianus, against whose writings the work of Optatus (q.v.) is specially directed. Tychonius, however, who was one of the most prominent members of the sect and has left a lasting name in the history of exegesis, rejected the extreme views which had prevailed and pronounced against rebaptism. Parmenianus addressed a warning to him, and on his contumacy he was excommunicated by a Donatist synod. He does not seem to have formed any distinct party; when that of the Rogatists, who held similar moderate views, was formed is not clear, though they were persecuted by the pagan king Firmus in 372 or 373 through Donatist influence. Of much more significance was the split caused by the Maximianists soon after Primianus had succeeded Parmenianus in 392. He belonged to the moderate side, and was accused by the deacon Maximianus, a relative of Donatus, of surrendering the old principles of the sect. The extremists called a synod at Cabarsussi in 393, deposed him, and elected Maximianus in his place, while an opposition synod at Bagæ, three times as large, adhered to Primianus and excommunicated Maximianus. By secular aid the churches of the Maximianists were taken from them, but some of them still existed at the time of the conference of Carthage in 411.

5. Opposition of Augustine.

Whatever the effect of these dissensions may have been, there can be no doubt of the influence exerted by the most powerful and determined enemy of Donatism, Augustine (q.v.), who for almost twenty years devoted himself to the recovery of its members. In his see city of Hippo they were the majority, and displayed bitter hostility to the Church, which suffered from the violence of the Circumcelliones. By personal conference and by literary activity he tried to win back the schismatics; but when conciliatory measures, such as those of the Synod of Carthage in 401 and 403, seemed to have little effect an appeal was made to the secular power in 404. Strict laws brought a number of Donatist communities, with their bishops, into the Church; but after the relaxation of this severity in 409 they began to relapse. A deputation of catholic bishops obtained an imperial order for a conference at Carthage which the Donatists were required to attend, though they could have but little doubt of its issue in the temper of the government. It took place in May, 411, between 286 catholic and 279 Donatist bishops, Augustine and Petilianus being the chief speakers on the two sides. After a three days' debate the imperial representative, Marcellinus, decided against the Donatists, and the laws were once more strictly enforced against them. In 414 and 415 attendance at their meetings was forbidden on pain of death, all civil rights were taken from them, and special commissioners were charged with the execution of these measures. The writings which Augustine controverted show clearly enough how far this system of making peace was from really attaining its object. But the common danger from the Vandals probably brought Donatists and catholics nearer together, and the gradual influence of Augustine's teaching doubtless contributed much to the weakening of the schism. The remnants of the sect which were found as late as well into the Byzantine period finally yielded to fresh repressive measures on the part of the government.

The fundamental question discussed in the debate just referred to concerned the holiness of the Church as conditioned by the moral state of its members. Novatianism had reduced its original stipulations to the demand that the lapsed should not be restored; Donatism had gone a step farther and limited its requirements to the quality of the bishops. Both sides appealed to Cyprian, who had declared lapsed bishops incapable of performing their functions and had favored rebaptism, indeed, but whose whole conception of the Church had regarded its holiness as resting on its provision with the means of grace.

6. Doctrinal Positions of the Two Parties.

The schismatics laid down the principle that no one could give what he had not—sanctification, the Holy Spirit. They regarded persecution as stamping them with the note of the true Church, and the friendship of earthly rulers as proving the opposite of the catholics; their community, requiring holiness of its bishops and members, was alone the true bride of Christ. The catholics, on their side, distinguished between heretics and schismatics, though they accused the Donatists of teaching some heretical doctrines. Thus they still designated their opponents brethren, and acknowledged their baptism; but Optatus calls their organization only a quasichurch, because it is not the catholic. True catholicity is lacking to them because they are confined to one region, not spread throughout the world; apostolicity is lacking because they have cut themselves off from the apostles' fellowship. Augustine strongly emphasizes the unity of the Church in the spirit of love. He does not insist so much on subordination to the episcopate as does Cyprian; but he considers the Donatists to show their lack of essential Christian love, of the Spirit, by the very fact of their separation from the one Church. Though, as an ethical teacher, he demands personal holiness from the Church's officers not less urgently than the Donatists, he calls it holy because it possesses and communicates the spirit of love, even though all its members do not walk perfectly in that spirit. His belief in that inseparable connection between the catholic Church and the means of grace led him into his conviction that brotherly duty toward those without required him to "compel them to come in" (Luke xiv. 23). (N. Bonwetsch.)

[The failure of all efforts to allay the Donatist controversy was due in large measure to the absolutely uncompromising spirit of the Donatists and to the impracticability of their demands. They would have no fellowship with any individual or body of Christians who would not join with them alike in the charges that they made against Mensurius, Cæcilianus, Felix of Aptunga, etc., and in the condemnation of the alleged acts. Further, they disfellowshiped all who would not disfellowship Cæcilianus, Felix, and their direct supporters. Most of them refused to recognize the validity of baptism received at the hands of any bishop or presbyter outside of the Donatist communion, and insisted on the rebaptism of all who came into their fellowship from without. Catholics could harmonize with them only by making a complete surrender, repudiating their baptism and ordination, and disfellowshiping all other catholics. A. H. N.]

Bibliography: Sources are: Eusebius, *Hist. eccl.*, x. 5–7 (the notes of McGiffert to the Eng. transl. in *NPNF*, 2d series, i. 380 sqq., are noteworthy); Augustine, the anti-Donatistic writings, brought together and translated in *NPNF*, 1st series, iv. 369–651; Optatus Melevitanus, *De schismate Donatistarum*, ed. Du Pin, with rich illustrative material, Paris, 1700, printed in *MPL*, xi. (cf. vol. viii.), a good edition also in *CSEL*, vol. xxvi.; early notes on the schism are collected in M. J. Routh, *Reliquiæ sacræ*, iv. 275 sqq., 5 vols., Oxford, 1846–48. Consult: C. W. F. Walch, *Historie der Ketzereien*, vol. iv., Leipsic, 1768; F. Ribbeck, *Donatus und Augustinus*, Elberfeld, 1858; C. Bindermann, *Der heilige Augustinus*, ii. 366 sqq., iii. 178 sqq., Greifswald, 1869; S. M. Deutsch, *Drei Aktenstücke zur Geschichte des Donatismus*, Berlin, 1875; D. Völter, *Der Ursprung des Donatismus*, Freiburg, 1883; O. Seeck, in *ZKG*, x (1889), 505; K. Müller, *Kirchengeschichte*, i. 178–179, Freiburg, 1892; W. Thümmel, *Zur Beurtheilung des Donatismus*, Halle, 1893; T. Hahn, *Tychonius Studien*, in *Studien zur Geschichte der Theologie und Kirche*, vol. vi., part 2, Leipsic, 1900; J. McCabe, *St. Augustine and his Age*, chap. xi., New York, 1903; L. Pullan, *Church of the Fathers*, ib. 1905; Schaff, *Christian Church*, iii. 360–370; Neander, *Christian Church*, ii. 182 sqq.; *KL*, iii. 1969–79; *DCB*, i. 881–896; Harnack, *Litteratur*, i. 744 sqq., II. i. 453–458; idem, *Dogma*, iii. passim, v. 38 sqq., 140 sqq., 162.

DONATUS, do-nē'tus, VESONTIENSIS: Bishop of Besançon; b. about 594; d. after 657. He was the son of the Frankish duke Waldelenus, and was educated in the monastery of Luxeuil. He was consecrated bishop of Besançon about 625 and was a zealous promoter of the monastic life, founding the cloister of Palatium (later St. Paul) before the walls of the city, while his brother Namelenus established a second monastery and his mother, Flavia, the nunnery of Jussanum (Joussan-Moutier). For the latter Donatus drew up a special rule which is of interest since it served as the model, together with the rule of St. Columban, for the rules of Cæsarius and Benedict of Nursia. Donatus took part in the synods of Clichy, 626 or 627, Reims (?), between 627 and 630; and Châlons-sur-Saône, between 639 and 654. His name appears for the last time on a document of 657. (A. Hauck.)

Bibliography: *ASB*, Aug., ii. 197–200; E. Löning, *Deutsches Kirchenrecht*, ii. 433, Strassburg, 1878; F. O. Seebass, *Columban von Luxeuil Klosterregel*, pp. 37–38, Dresden, 1883.

DONNE, JOHN: Clergyman and poet, dean of St. Paul's; b. in London 1573; d. there Mar. 31, 1631. He studied at Hart Hall, Oxford (M.A. by convocation, 1610), and in 1592 was admitted to Lincoln's Inn. He immediately became an intimate of the intellectual leaders of the time and had soon won for himself a great reputation as a wit and poet. In 1596 he took part in the expedition to Cadiz, under the Earl of Essex, and on his return was appointed secretary to the Keeper of the Great Seal. About 1600 he lost this position through a clandestine marriage with a niece of the lord keeper. As early as 1592 he had renounced the Roman Catholic faith, and in 1610 he published in London *Pseudo-Martyr*, a treatise against Catholicism. He wrote the book at the suggestion of James I., and it is probable that he was well paid for it. This was followed (1610 or 1611) by *Conclave Ignatii, sive ejus in nuperis inferni comitiis inthronizatio* and an English *Ignatius his Conclave; or his Inthronization in a Late Election in Hell* (1611). Both works were republished later with titles changed. The original Latin is now extremely rare. As his sovereign was unable to do anything for him immediately in the way of political preferment, Donne continued in civil pursuits till 1615, when he took orders. He was urged to do this by James, who immediately made him royal chaplain. On the insistence of the king the University of Cambridge reluctantly conferred the degree of doctor of divinity on Donne in March of the same year. Many livings were offered him throughout the country, but he preferred to remain in London. However, in 1616 he accepted the rectory of Keyston, in Huntingdonshire, and later in the same year that of Sevenoaks. He never resided in either parish, remaining in London, where he was appointed divinity reader of Lincoln's Inn. During the next few years he came to be recognised as one of the first preachers of his time, and in 1621 he was appointed dean of St. Paul's. He was chosen prolocutor of the convocation in 1623, and again in 1624. In the spring of the latter year he was given the rectory of Blunham, in Bedfordshire, and the vicarage of St. Dunstan's-in-the-West, London. Donne's ability as a preacher continued to increase, and his popularity grew in proportion. He surpassed all others; and, indeed, the editor of his last sermon claims that Donne finally surpassed even himself. This sermon, called by Donne "Death's Duel," was preached just five weeks before his death. He was buried in St. Paul's.

At present Donne's reputation rests on his poetry. He wrote much verse, but it was usually handed around in manuscript, little of it being published in his lifetime, though his poems were greatly admired by his contemporaries. A collection of his poetry was published in 1633. It contains satires, elegies, epigrams, letters, etc. He is usually classified as a "metaphysical poet," and occupies an important place in English literature. He set a style in English poetry that continued dominant till the time of Dryden; and even in Browning's ruggedness and obscurity may be detected the influence of Donne. His sermons were published in various forms, including three volumes edited by his son, John Donne the Younger (London, 1640, 1649, 1660). As many as 180 are now known. They are marked by poetic, imaginary, and philosophic insight, and with Donne's other literary works constitute a memorial of great industry and rare talents.

Bibliography: A very full list of his works is given after the extended sketch of his life in *DNB*, xv. 223 sqq. Besides the volume of eighty sermons, mentioned below, two others, one containing fifty and the other "six-and-twenty" (really only twenty-four), were issued by his son, London, 1649–60; an edition of his *Poems* was also issued by his son, ib. 1650 and often, who published also *Essayes in Divinity*, ib. 1651, and a collection of *Letters*, ib. 1651 The best edition of the *Poems* is by Grosart in 2 vols., ib. 1872 The *Works*, ed. H. Alford, 6 vols., Oxford, 1839, are poorly put together. His *Life*, by Izaak Walton, was issued first in the *LXXX. Sermons* of Donne, published by his son, London, 1640, and the best edition, containing "careful and learned notes," is by H. K. Causton, 1855.

DONNELL, ROBERT: Cumberland Presbyterian; b. in Guilford County, N. C., Apr., 1784; d. at Athens, Ala., May 24, 1854. His parents early moved to Tennessee. He offered himself in 1806 to the so-called "Council" of the Cumberland Presbytery, who encouraged him to exercise his gifts as a catechist and exhorter. He preached independently of ecclesiastical connection, and for the most part in Alabama, until 1811, when he placed himself under the care of the newly organized Cumberland Presbytery. From that time on he labored incessantly, in Tennessee, Alabama, and western Pennsylvania, organizing many churches, and winning the position of a leader in his denomination. He was a member of the committee appointed in 1813 to draw up a confession of faith and discipline for the Cumberland Presbyterian Church. He was the author of *Thoughts on Various Subjects* (Nashville, 1852).

Bibliography: Lowry, *Life of Rev. Robert Donnell*, Nashville, 1867; R. Beard, *Biographical Sketches of Some of the Early Ministers of the Cumberland Presbyterian Church*, 2 vols., Nashville, 1867.

DONNELLAN (DONNELAN) LECTURES: A lectureship named after "Mrs. Anne Donnelan, of the parish of St. George, Hanover Square, in the County of Middlesex, Spinster," who bequeathed to Dublin University £1,243 "for the encouragement of religion, learning and good manners, the particular mode of application being entrusted to the Provost and Senior Fellows." The income was appropriated as salary of a lecturer in divinity, to be chosen annually on Nov. 20th from among the Fellows, at which time the subject was determined. The lectures in each series are not less than six in number, and one-half of the salary is paid on delivery of the lectures, the rest when at least four are published. During a number of years no appointments have been made, some of those made have been declined, and many of the lecturers have failed to publish. The following is believed to be a complete list of those which have appeared in print:

1794. T. Ebington, *The Proof of Christianity . . . from the Miracles recorded in the New Testament*, Dublin, 1796.

1797, 1801. R. Graves, *The Divine Origin of the Jewish Religion proved from the . . . Last Four Books of the Pentateuch*, 2 vols., London, 1807.

1815–16. F. Sadleir, *The Various Degrees of Religious Information Vouchsafed to Mankind*, in his *Sermons and Lectures*, 3 vols., Dublin, 1821–24.

1818. W. Phelan, *Christianity provides . . . Correctives for . . . Tendencies to Polytheism and Idolatry*, in his *Remains*, ed. J. Jebb, London, 1832.

1821, 1824. J. Kennedy, *The Researches of Modern Science . . . demonstrate the Inspiration of . . . Scripture*, 2 vols., ib. 1826–27.

1823. F. Sadleir, *The Formulas of the Church of England Conformable to the Scriptures*, Dublin, 1824.

1838. J. H. Todd, *The Prophecies Relating to Antichrist in . . . Daniel and St. Paul*, ib 1840.

1839. J. H. Todd, *The Prophecies Relating to Antichrist in the Apocalypse of St. John*, ib. 1846.

1851. M. O'Sullivan, *The Hour of the Redeemer*, ib. 1853.

1852. W. Lee, *Inspiration of the Holy Scriptures*, ib. 1854 (often republished)

1853. W. de Burgh, *The Early Prophecies of a Redeemer*, ib. 1854.

1854. C P. Reichel, *The Nature and Offices of the Church*, London, 1856.

1855. J. Byrne, *Naturalism and Spiritualism*, Dublin, 1856.

1855–56, 1859. J. MacIvor, *Religious Progress*, London, 1871.

1857. J. C. MacDonnell, *The Doctrine of the Atonement deduced from Scripture*, ib. 1858

1858. J. Wills, *The Antecedent Probability of the Christian Religion*, Dublin, 1860

1860. W. Atkins, *Pastoral Duties*, London, 1861.

1861. W. P. Walsh, *Christian Missions*, Dublin, 1862

1862. W. de Burgh, *Messianic Prophecies of Isaiah*, ib. 1863.

1863. A. G. Ryder, *Scriptural Doctrine of Acceptance with God*, ib. 1865.
1869. A. Daunt, *Person and Offices of the Holy Spirit*, ib. 1874.
1871–72. J. Leech, *The Epistle to the Hebrews*, ib. 1874.
1875–76. F. F. Carmichael, *Jesus Christ*, ib. 1876.
1877. J. H. Jellett, *The Efficacy of Prayer*, London, 1878.
1877–78. J. Quarry, *Religious Belief*, Dublin, 1880.
1878–79. G. A. Chadwick, *Christ Bearing Witness to Himself*, London, n.d.
1879–80. T. Jordan, *The Stoic Moralists and the Christians*, Dublin, 1880.
1880–81. C. H. H. Wright, *The Book of Koheleth*, London, 1883.
1882–83. H. Jellett, *Thoughts on the Christian Life*, ib. 1884.
1883–84. J. W. Murray, *Christian Vitality*, Dublin, 1884.
1884–85. R. T. Smith, *Man's Knowledge of Man and of God*, London, 1886.
1887–88. W. Lefroy, *The Christian Ministry*, ib. 1890.
1888–89. J. H. Kennedy, *Natural Theology and Modern Thought*, ib. 1891.
1889–90. T. S. Berry, *Christianity and Buddhism*, ib. 1891.
1891–92. T. L. Scott, *The Visions of the Apocalypse*, ib. 1893.
1892–93. W. M. Foley, *Christ in the World*, Dublin, 1894.
1897–98. C. F. Darcy, *Idealism and Theology*, London, 1899.
1898–99. E. J. Hardy, *Doubt and Faith*, ib. 1899.
1899–1900. M. Kaufmann, *Social Development under Christian Influence*, Dublin, 1900.
1900–01. G. R. Wynne, *The Church in Greater Britain*, London, 1901.
1901–02. J. O. Hannay, *The Spirit and Origin of Christian Monasticism*, ib. 1903.
1902–03. L. A. H. T. Pooler, *Studies in the Religion of Israel*, ib. 1904.
1903–04. F. W. Macran, *English Apologetic Theology*, ib. 1905.
1906–07. H. J. Dukinfield Astley, *Prehistoric Archæology and the O. T.*, Edinburgh, 1908.

DONOSO CORTÉS, JUAN FRANCISCO MANUEL MARIA DE LA SALUD: Marquis de Valdegamas, Spanish author and statesman; b. at Valle de la Serena (near Castuera, 135 m. s.w. of Madrid), in Estremadura, May 9, 1809; d. in Paris May 3, 1853. He studied law in Salamanca and Seville and settled in Madrid, where he engaged in literature and politics. In the revolution of 1832 he took the part of Isabella against Don Carlos. He entered the Cortes in 1835. About this time he established a newspaper, the *Avenir*, in which he published many articles of political and historical character. He continued to give his enthusiastic support to Isabella and accompanied her on her flight to England in 1840. On her return to Spain in 1843 he was appointed secretary and tutor for the young queen. In 1848 he was sent as ambassador to Berlin, but returned to Madrid in the same year. He immediately reentered the Cortes, where, in Jan., 1848, he startled his party and his country with a bitter denunciation of all liberal principles and the demand for a dictatorship. In 1851 he proclaimed the absolute supremacy of the Roman Catholic Church in his *Ensayo sombre el catolicismo, el liberalismo y el socialismo*. This essay, an eloquent and brilliant plea for the ideas of Gregory VII. and Innocent III. against modern tendencies, was immediately translated into French and German, and, a few years later, into English. *Essay on Catholicism, Liberalism and Socialism, in Their Fundamental Principles*, Philadelphia, 1862; another transl., Dublin, 1874. At the close of his career, he was ambassador at Paris for two years. A collected edition of his works in five volumes, including a biography by Tejado, was published at Madrid in 1855. A French edition appeared in Paris in 1858.

BIBLIOGRAPHY: Besides the biography by G. Tejado, mentioned above, there is a sketch from the Italian of G. E. de Castro in the Philadelphia translation and an excellent sketch in *KL*, iii. 1982–85.

DONUS (DOMNUS): Pope Aug., 676–Apr., 678. All that is known of him is that he was a Roman by birth, that he adorned certain churches in Rome, and that he banished the Syrian monks from Rome. The Donus II. assigned by some lists to 974 did not exist, but is due to a misreading of the title *Domnus (dominus) papa* as a proper name.

BIBLIOGRAPHY: *Liber pontificalis*, ed. L. Duchesne, i. 348, Paris, 1886, ed. T. Mommsen, in *MGH, Gest. pont. Rom.*, i (1898), 192; Mann, *Popes*, I. ii. 20–22.

DOOLITTLE, THOMAS: Non-conformist; b. at Kidderminster (15 m. n. of Worcester) 1631 or 1632; d. in London May 24, 1707. As a boy he was converted under the preaching of Richard Baxter. He studied for the ministry at Pembroke Hall, Cambridge, and in 1653 became pastor of the parish of St. Alphage, London Wall, London. He received Presbyterian ordination and soon became popular as a preacher. When the Uniformity Act was passed in 1662 he declared himself a non-conformist and opened a boarding-school which he maintained in different localities till 1687, and after this time he continued privately to prepare pupils for the ministry.

After the great fire in London in 1666 Doolittle was one of the non-conformist preachers who defied the law by erecting meeting-houses in the ruins. For a while he was not disturbed; but, when he insisted on preaching, his meeting-house was seized and he fled to escape arrest. On the indulgence of Mar. 15, 1672, he took out a license for his meeting-house; but this was revoked the next year, and it was not till the Toleration Act of 1689 that he was allowed to resume services at his old church. While popular as a preacher, and influential as a tutor, Doolittle was neither a scholar nor an original thinker. Among the most popular of his works were: *A Treatise concerning the Lord's Supper*, London, 1665; *A Call to Delaying Sinners*, 1683; and *A Compleat Body of Practical Divinity*, 1723, folio.

BIBLIOGRAPHY: The *Memoirs* were prefixed to the *Body of Practical Divinity*, ut sup.; *DNB*, xv. 236–238.

DOORKEEPER. See OSTIARIUS.

DORA, SISTER. See PATTISON, DOROTHY WYNDLOW.

DORCHESTER, DANIEL: Methodist; b. at Duxbury, Mass., Mar. 11, 1827; d. at West Roxbury, Mass., Mar. 13, 1907. He studied at Wesleyan University, Middletown, Conn. (1848–1851), and held pastorates in Connecticut 1847–55, and in Massachusetts 1858–89. He was presiding elder of the districts of Worcester 1865–68, Lynn 1874–77, and North Boston 1882–85. In 1854 he was elected to the State Senate of Connecticut, and in 1855 was appointed chairman of a committee to investigate the condition of the feeble-minded. In 1882 he was elected to the Massachusetts Legislature for Natick, and from 1889 to 1893 was superintendent of Indian Schools of the United States. After 1893 he lived in retirement at Melrose and West Roxbury, Mass. He wrote *The Concessions of Liberalists to Orthodoxy* (Boston, 1878); *The Problem of Religious Progress* (New York, 1881); *Why of Methodism* (1887); *Christianity in the United States* (1888); *Romanism versus the Public School System* (1888); and *Christianity Vindicated by its Enemies* (1896).

DOREMUS, SARAH PLATT (HAINES): Reformed (Dutch) philanthropist; b. in New York Aug. 3, 1802; d. there Jan. 29, 1877. In 1821 she married Thomas C. Doremus, a wealthy merchant of New York, and seven years later began philanthropic work for Greek women during the Greco-Turkish war. In 1835 she took an active interest in the Canadian Grande Ligne mission, later becoming president of a society for the furtherance of this work. In 1840 she commenced to hold Sunday services in the female wards of the Tombs in New York, and on the formation of the Woman's Prison Association, two years later, she became one of its managers and was its president after 1863. In 1841 she became a manager of the New York City and Tract Mission, and nine years later aided in the foundation of the House and School of Industry, of which she was elected president in 1867. She was also one of the founders of the Nursery and Child's Hospital in 1854, and in 1855 was one of the prime movers in the establishment of the Woman's Hospital in New York, the first of its kind in the world, of which she became president in 1864. In 1860 she aided materially in the establishment of the Woman's Union Missionary Society; in 1866 she helped to organize the Presbyterian Home for Aged Women, and in 1876 she was one of the committee to form the Gould Memorial in behalf of Italo-American schools. But it was as the friend of every American Protestant foreign missionary and one who kept open house for them so long as her husband's means allowed that her memory will be longest preserved.

Bibliography: *In Memoriam of Mrs. Doremus*, Edinburgh, 1877.

DORNER, AUGUST JOHANNES: German Protestant, son of Isaak August Dorner (q.v.); b. at Schiltach (30 m. n.e. of Freiburg) May 13, 1846. He studied in Göttingen, Tübingen, and Berlin (Ph.D., 1867), and, after being *Vikar* to the German congregation in Lyons and Marseilles (1869) and traveling in the Orient (1870), was lecturer at Göttingen 1870–73. He then visited the United States, and on his return was professor and co-director of the theological seminary at Wittenberg 1874–89. Since 1889 he has been professor of systematic theology at Königsberg. He has edited his father's *System der christlichen Sittenlehre* (Berlin, 1885) and *Briefwechsel zwischen H. L. Martensen und I. A. Dorner* (2 vols., 1888), and has written *De Baconis philosophia* (Berlin, 1867); *Augustinus, seine theologische und seine religionsphilosophische Anschauung* (1873); *Ueber die Principien der Kantischen Ethik* (Halle, 1875); *Predigten vom Reiche Gottes* (Berlin, 1880); *Kirche und Reich Gottes* (Gotha, 1883); *Das menschliche Erkennen* (Berlin, 1887); *Das menschliche Handeln* (1895); *Grundriss der Dogmengeschichte* (1899); *Grundriss der Encyklopädie der Theologie* (1901); *Zur Geschichte des sittlichen Denkens und Lebens* (Hamburg, 1901); *Grundriss der Religionsphilosophie* (Leipsic, 1903); *Grundprobleme der Religionsphilosophie* (Berlin, 1903); *Individuelle und soziale Ethik* (Leipsic, 1906); and *Die Entstehung der christlichen Glaubenslehren* (Munich, 1906).

DORNER, ISAAK AUGUST.

One of the foremost German theologians of the nineteenth century; b. at Neuhausen ob Eck. (60 m. s.s.w. of Stuttgart), Württemberg, June 20, 1809; d. at Wiesbaden July 8, 1884. His father was pastor at Neuhausen. He studied in the Latin school at Tuttlingen, the collegiate seminary at Maulbronn, and the University of Tübingen (1827–32). For two years he assisted his father as pastor, then became repetent in theology (1834) and professor extraordinary (1838) at Tübingen. In 1835 his colleague David Friedrich Strauss (q.v.) published his *Leben Jesu*, and Dorner was induced in 1839 to issue his *Entwickelungsgeschichte der Lehre von der Person Christi*, a work of directly opposite tendency, in which the historical Christ of the Gospels is traced through the ages of the Church as the greatest fact in Christian thought and experience. This work determined Dorner's place among theologians and doctrinal historians, and was a most effectual answer to Strauss and his mythical theory. The work was afterward greatly enlarged and improved by an exhaustive study of the sources from the Apostolic Age down to the kenosis controversy (see Christology; Kenosis), and appeared in a second edition as *Die Lehre von der Person Christi* (4 vols., Stuttgart, 1846–56; Eng. transl., *History of the Development of the Doctrine of the Person of Christ*, 5 vols., Edinburgh, 1861–63).

1. Early Life. Professorship at Tübingen.

From 1839 to 1843 Dorner was professor in Kiel. His principal writing during this period was the dogmatic treatise dedicated to Claus Harms (q.v.), *Das Princip unserer Kirche nach dem innern Verhältniss seiner zwei Seiten betrachtet* (Kiel, 1841). In this work he maintained that the so-called material and formal principles of the Reformation—i.e., justification by faith, and the supreme authority of Scripture—were to be considered as two pillars inseparably joined, so that each stands with and through the other. This was his word of comfort to those distressed by Strauss. No criticism can alter the fact that the primitive Church did record in the New Testament, by means of the Spirit proceeding from Christ, its impressions and experiences of Christ's salvation. On the other hand, faith holds fast to the written word. For the Christ whom faith

2. Professor at Kiel.

Bibliography: *ASB*, Feb., i. 771–776; Aldhelm, *De laudibus virginitatis*, ed. J. A. Giles, pp. 62–63, Oxford, 1843; Dom Fea, *Breve vita di S. Dorotea*, Turin, 1889.

2. Dorothea the Recluse was born at Montau, near Marienwerder (45 m. s.s.e. of Danzig), 1347; d. at Marienwerder 1394. She lived in Danzig with her husband until she was forty-four, and had nine children. Then she devoted herself to a solitary ascetic life, inhabiting a cell adjoining the cathedral of Marienwerder in 1393 and 1394, and following a rule which she said was divinely revealed to her. Miracles occurring at her grave and the universal veneration induced the grand master of the Teutonic Order and the clergy of the neighborhood to begin proceedings for her canonization; but these were stopped when it came out in 1404 that she had sharply criticized the Order and predicted its downfall. The people, however, continued to revere her and regarded her as the patron saint of Prussia.

(J. J. Herzog†.)

Bibliography: Early *Vitæ* by different authors are collected in *ASB*, Oct., xiii. 493–575. Consult F. Hipler, *Meister J. Marienwerder und die Klausnerin Dorothea von Montau*, Leipsic, 1865.

DORT, SYNOD OF: The largest and, next to the Westminster Assembly, the most imposing of all synods of the Reformed Churches, convened by the States General of the Netherlands at the instance of the Calvinists to try to settle the disputes between the latter and the "Remonstrants," or followers of Jacobus Arminius (see Arminius; Remonstrants). It met at Dort (Dordrecht, on an island in the Meuse, 10 m. s.e. of Rotterdam) Nov. 13, 1618, and adjourned May 9, 1619. The Dutch churches of the provinces sent thirty-five clergymen and a certain number of elders; the States General were represented by six deputies; the academies by Gomarus and Polyander of Leyden, Thysius of Harderwyk, Lubbertus of Franeker, and Walæus of Middelburg. Foreign countries had been invited to participate, and twenty-seven delegates were present from the Palatinate (Abraham Scultetus and others), Nassau, Hesse (Georg Cruciger), East Friesland, Switzerland (J. J. Breitinger and Jean Diodati), England, and Scotland. [The English representatives appointed by King James I. were George Carleton, bishop of Llandaff (afterward of Chichester); John Davenant, bishop of Salisbury; Samuel Ward, professor at Cambridge; Joseph Hall, afterward bishop of Exeter and Norwich (who left during the sessions and was replaced by Thomas Goad); and Walter Balcanquall, a Scotchman and chaplain of the king.] Anhalt was not invited, Brandenburg declined to be represented, and four delegates chosen by the National Synod of France were forbidden to leave the country by Louis XIII. Jan Bogerman, pastor at Leeuwarden, was elected president, H. Faukelius and J. Rolandus were appointed assessors, and F. Hommius and S. Damman secretaries. The Remonstrants had chosen sixteen clergymen and the Leyden professor Simon Episcopiu to represent them. As they were late in arriving the first sessions were devoted to a discussion of a new translation of the Bible, and it was agreed that three members should undertake the Old Testament, and three others the New; it was then declared that the Heidelberg Catechism should be expounded in sermons in all the churches.

Constitution and Organization.

Not until Dec. 6 and the twenty-second session was the main business of the gathering reached. The Remonstrants were told that they could merely express their opinions and the Synod would pronounce judgment. Against this they immediately protested. Episcopius in an eloquent speech said that they had all come of their own accord, and that they should not be accused of heterodoxy; while they were ready to discuss the dogmas in question, they would not submit to any human power or belief, but only to the word of God in the Holy Scripture. Their status in the Synod was discussed for many days, but finally the delegates of the States General decided that they had nothing to do but to defend their beliefs; the Synod must decide at the end. The Remonstrants then submitted successively written statements in defense of each of the Five Articles (see Remonstrants). They were asked to put in writing their objections to the Confession, at first refused to do so, but finally complied. The members of the Synod and of the States General sometimes addressed them very bruskly. Matters grew worse when the question arose whether the Remonstrants could speak against the convictions of their opponents. They unanimously refused to go on if they should not be allowed to do so, and it was decided to submit the question to the States General; in the mean time the Remonstrants must remain in Dort. Thus ended the year 1618. On Jan. 3, 1619, the Remonstrants were informed of the decision, which sustained the majority of the Synod, and they again declared that they could not accept it. It was decided to proceed without them. They tried to bring about a reconciliation by offering to answer any question submitted to them in writing, but the president rejected their proposal. On Jan. 18 (the fifty-seventh session) they were finally asked if they would submit, and answered decidedly "no." Bogerman delivered a passionate speech, exclaiming, "You have begun with lies and you end with lies," and concluding "*Dimittimini, ite, ite.*" The net result of six weeks' time was that the Remonstrants were expelled, while they were commanded not to leave Dort.

Proceedings, and Expulsion of the Remonstrants.

The Synod now divided in groups which met in the morning to formulate their opinions about the doctrines of the Remonstrants, while they met in the afternoon for discussion. In the 125th session it was voted that the Five Articles of the Remonstrants were contrary to the doctrine of the Reformed Church, and that their objections to the Confession and the Catechism were not supported by the authority of Scripture. A committee was appointed to express the final decision in the form of canons, which were adopted and

Decision of the Synod.

signed by all at the 136th session (Apr. 23). The doctrine of absolute predestination was maintained, though not acceptable to the supralapsarians. It was now decided at Bogerman's suggestion to depose the Remonstrants from their positions, and the provincial synods, the classes, and presbyteries were directed to execute the sentence. The Confession and Catechism were considered in presence of the foreign delegates and were found to agree in every respect with Scripture. Finally Conrad Vorstius (q.v.) was declared unworthy of his position as professor of theology on account of his heretical writings.

On May 6 the members of the Synod marched in procession to the cathedral of Dort, where Bogerman delivered a Latin address and the secretaries read the canons against the Remonstrants. Three days later they met for a formal farewell to the foreign delegates at a banquet tendered by the city authorities of Dort. The Dutch delegates met again from May 13 to May 29 to consider certain ecclesiastical affairs.

For two centuries the decision of the Synod of Dort was the basis of the Reformed Church in Holland, and the *Canones Dordracenses* gave it a peculiar character; for what they stated concerning predestination differed as much from Calvin's *Institutiones* as from the Helvetian Confession and the *Consensus Genevensis*. H. C. Rogge†.

Bibliography: For the original records consult: *Acta synodi . . . Dordrechti*, Dort, 1620; *Acta et scripta synodalia Dordracena ministrorum remonstrantium Herderwici*, ib. 1620; *Canones Synodi Dordracena, cum notis D. Tileni*, Paris, 1622. Consult: J. Halesius, *Hist. concilii Dordraceni*, Hamburg, 1724; M. Graf, *Beyträge zur Kenntniss der Geschichte der Synode von Dordrecht*, Basel, 1725; B. Glasius, *Geschiedenis der . . . Synode . . . te Dordrecht*, 2 vols., Leyden, 1860–61; Schaff, *Creeds*, i. 512–523 (history), iii. 550–597 (the canons, in Lat. and Eng.); Moeller, *Christian Church*, iii. 410–415 (lucid). The Canons of the Synod of Dort are part of the symbolical books of the Reformed (Dutch) Church in America, and are officially published by that denomination (New York).

DOSITHEOS, dō-sī'thē-os, OF JERUSALEM: Patriarch of Jerusalem 1699–1707, and one of the most important figures of the modern Greek Church. He reformed the cloisters by a strict insistence on their communal life, erected churches, took great interest in the Holy Sepulcher, and defended the holy places against the claims of the Roman Catholics and the Armenians. He extirpated the Protestant tendency which had entered the Church through Cyril Lucar (q.v.), and opposed in his "Manual" (Bucharest, 1690) Johannes Karyophyllis, the logothete of Constantinople, who taught a Calvinistic doctrine of the Lord's Supper. He assailed the Roman Catholic Church both in practise and by the publication of such controversial works as the "Book of Absolution" (Jassy, 1692), the "Book of Love" (1699), and the "Book of Grace" (1705). His chief objects of attack were the union, the procession of the Holy Ghost, and the light of Mount Tabor. His chief work was his posthumous "History of the Patriarchs in Jerusalem" (Bucharest, 1715), in which he gave the entire history of the Greek Church and dogma, together with savage polemics against other Churches. Despite its lack of criticism, the book is valuable for its material where Dositheos drew from sources accessible to him alone, and it thus forms a Greek counterpart to the Annals of Baronius and the Magdeburg Centuries.

(Philipp Meyer.)

Bibliography: E. Legrand, *Bibliographie hellénique*, 4 vols., Paris, 1894–98, and the works cited under Jerusalem, Synod of.

DOSITHEUS, dō-sith'e-us, THE SAMARITAN: A false Messiah among the Samaritans, and founder of a religious sect. Very little is known of him; and the uncertainty of the reports is increased by his being confounded with an older Dositheus, the teacher of Zadok, who founded the sect of the Sadducees. He was probably a contemporary of Jesus, or perhaps a little later. In those days of great religious excitement he presented himself to the Samaritans as the prophet promised in Deut. xviii. 18 (which passage, according to Samaritan doctrine, is the only true Messianic prophecy ever given) and as the Son of God (Origen, *Contra Celsum*, i. 57, vi. 11; *ANF*, iv. 421, 578). His doctrines can not be definitely determined. He seems to have laid stress upon the precepts of the law (Epiphanius, *Hær.*, i. 13) and gave to the words concerning the Sabbath in Ex. xvi. 29 a ridiculously literal interpretation (Origen, *De principiis*, IV. i. 17: "Each one must remain until the evening in the posture, place, or position in which he found himself on the Sabbath-day; i.e., if found sitting, he is to sit the whole day, or if reclining, he is to recline the whole day," *ANF*, iv. 366). The number of his followers was probably never great, but they lasted into the sixth century. Theophilus, a Persian, wrote against them in the fourth century (Assemani, *Bibl. Orient.*, i. 42), and in 588 Dositheans and Samaritans disputed in Egypt over Deut. xviii. 18 (cf. Photius, *Bibl. cod.*, 230).

(G. Uhlhorn†.)

Bibliography: J. L. von Mosheim, *Institutiones historiæ Christianæ*, i. 376–389, Helmstadt, 1739 (the fullest account, cf. Eng. transl., ed. W. Stubbs, i. 86, London, 1863); C. W. F. Walch, *Historie der Ketzereien*, i. 182 sqq., Leipsic, 1762; A. Hilgenfeld, *Die Ketzergeschichte des Urchristenthums*, pp. 155 sqq., Leipsic, 1884; Harnack, *Litteratur*, i. 152 sqq.; *DCB*, i. 902–904.

DOSKER, HENRY ELIES: Presbyterian (Southern Branch); b. at Bunschoten (25 m. s.e. of Amsterdam), Holland, Feb. 5, 1855. He studied at the Latin school, Harlingen, Holland, the gymnasium of Zwolle, Holland, Hope College, Holland, Mich. (B.A., 1876), New Brunswick Theological Seminary, and McCormick Theological Seminary, Chicago (B.D., 1879). After pastorates at Ebenezer (1879–82) and Grand Haven, Mich. (1882–86), he was lector of historic theology in the Western Theological Seminary, Holland, Mich., until 1888, and then pastor in the same city till 1894. He was then appointed professor of church history in Western Theological Seminary, and since 1903 has been professor of the same subject in the Presbyterian Seminary of Kentucky, Louisville, Ky. He edited *Hope*, the magazine of Hope College, 1894–1903, and was associate editor of the *Presbyterian and Reformed Review* 1898–1902. Since 1903 he has been an editorial contributor to the *Christian Observer*, Louisville, Ky.

In theology he is a firm Calvinist of the type of the Dutch Free University of Amsterdam. He has written *De Zondagschool* (Kampen, Holland, 1882); *Dr. A. C. Van Raalte* (1893); and *Outlines of Ecclesiastical History* (Holland, Mich., 1901).

DOUAI, dū"ē': A town of France, department of Nord, 20 m. s. of Lille and 110 m. n.n.e. of Paris. In the sixteenth century it belonged to Spain, and a university was founded there by Philip II. in 1562. In 1568 Cardinal William Allen (q.v.) opened in connection with the university a college or seminary for English Roman Catholics, which, during the first five years of its existence, sent more than one hundred missioners into England. In later years many of the Catholic gentry of England were educated there, and the college produced about one hundred doctors of divinity and 160 martyrs. In consequence of the political and religious disturbances in the Low Countries it was removed to Reims in 1578, but returned to Douai in 1593. The college was supported by private subscription at first, received a monthly pension of 100 gold crowns from Pope Gregory XIII. in 1575, and an annual appropriation of 2,000 ducats from Philip II. after its removal to Reims. Allen continued at its head till 1588, when he was succeeded by Richard Barrett. Douai became French territory in 1667, and both university and college were suppressed during the French Revolution (1793).

Bibliography: The "Records of the English Catholics," edited by fathers of the Congregation of the London Oratory, vol. i., *The First and Second Diaries of the English College, Douay*, London, 1878; vol. ii., *Letters and Memorials of William Cardinal Allen*, 1882; A. Bellesheim, *Wilhelm Cardinal Allen und die englischen Seminare auf dem Festlande*, Mainz, 1885; Léon Legrand, *L'Université de Douai, 1530–1790*, Douai, 1888; G. Cardon, *La Fondation de l'université de Douai*, Paris, 1892. For the Douai Bible see Bible Versions, English.

DOUCHOBORS. See Dukhobors.

DOUEN, EMMANUEL ORENTIN: French Protestant; b. at Templeux-le-Guérard (Somme) June 2, 1830; d. at Paris July 9, 1896. His parents in 1833 removed to Lemé (Aisne), and there his education was begun. Later he studied at Saint-Quentin, from 1840 to 1849 at Lille, and the next four years at the University of Strasburg, where he particularly distinguished himself in Hebrew. From 1853 to 1861 he was pastor of the Protestant church of Quincy-Ségy (Seine-et-Carne). A disease of the larynx compelled him to give up preaching, and he accepted the position of agent of the Protestant Bible Society of Paris. He was a prolific author, but only the titles of those books which are likely to have interest for a later generation will here be given (for a full list down to 1882 see *ESR*, vol. xiii., p. 62); *Clément Marot et le Psautier huguenot* (2 vols., Paris, 1878–79), a work published at the expense of the State; *Les premiers pasteurs du Désert* (2 vols., 1879), decreed a prize by the French Academy; *Étienne Dolet* (1881); *La Révocation de l'édit de Nantes à Paris, d'après des documents inédits* (3 vols., 1894).

DOUGLAS, GEORGE CUNINGHAM MONTEATH: United Free Church of Scotland; b. at Kilbarchan (8 m. s. of Dumbarton), Renfrewshire, Mar. 2, 1826; d. at Bridge of Allan (2 m. n. of Stirling), Stirlingshire, May 24, 1904. He studied at Glasgow and New College, Edinburgh, and after being pastor at Bridge of Weir, Renfrewshire (1852–57), was professor of Hebrew and Old Testament exegesis at the Free Church College, Glasgow, until 1892. From 1875 until 1892 he was also principal of the same institution. He was one of the Old Testament revisers from 1870 to 1884. He translated J. C. F. Keil's *Lehrbuch der historisch-kritischen Einleitung in die Schriften des Alten Testaments* (2 vols., Edinburgh, 1869–70), prepared the notes to Judges, Joshua, and the six intermediate minor prophets in *Handbook for Bible Classes* (3 vols., 1881–90), and wrote *Why I still believe that Moses wrote Deuteronomy* (Edinburgh, 1878); *A Short Analysis of the Old Testament by Means of Headings to the Chapters* (Paisley, 1889); *Isaiah One and his Book One* (London, 1895); and *Samuel and His Age* (1901).

DOUMERGUE, ÉMILE: French Reformed; b. at Nîmes (30 m. n. of Montpellier) Nov. 25, 1844. After the completion of his education he was editor of *Le Christianisme au dix-neuvième siècle* (1872–1880), and was also assistant pastor of the Reformed church at Paris and chaplain of the municipal high schools in the same city (1878–80). Since the latter year he has been professor of church history at Montauban. He has written *L'Unité de l'Église Réformée de France* (Paris, 1875); *La Veille de la loi de l'an X (1763–1802)* (Paris, 1879); *La Création et l'évolution* (1883); *Essai sur l'histoire du culte réformé, principalement au seizième et au dix-neuvième siècle* (1890); *L'Autorité en matière de foi et la nouvelle école* (Lausanne, 1892); *Le Réveil national* (Montauban, 1894); *Jean Calvin: Les Hommes et les choses de son temps* (Lausanne, vol. i., 1899, vol. ii., 1902, vol. iii., 1905—more to follow, a monumental work, intended to be exhaustive); *Une Poignée de faux: La Mort de Calvin et les Jésuites* (1900); and *Lausanne au temps de la Réformation* (1903).

DOVES: Many species of wild doves are found in Palestine. The rock-dove (*columba livia* and *columba Schimperi*) builds its nest in the clefts of the rocks and cliffs (Jer. xlviii. 28; Ezek. vii. 16; Cant. ii. 14). In wooded regions dwell ring-doves (*columba palumbus*), which build their nests in the trees; many of them winter in Palestine and fly north in the spring. The stock-dove, or wood-pigeon, is rarer. Of turtle-doves the most common is the ordinary turtle-dove (*turtur auritus*), a migratory bird (Jer. viii. 7), which appears in April in great numbers (Cant. ii. 11 sqq.). More rare is the laughing-dove (*turtur risorius*), which frequents the neighborhood of the Dead Sea; and the smaller *turtur senegalensis*, which prefers to build in the palm-trees. By the ancient Israelites (Lev. v. 7) and also by the pre-Israelitic inhabitants of Palestine not only the common house-dove, but also more choice varieties were domesticated (cf. Ps. lxviii. 13, the description of a rarer variety) Dove-cotes are mentioned Isa. lx. 8, and Josephus (*War*, V. iv. 4) speaks of a number of small towers for tame doves which stood in the garden of Herod's palace. In the account of the deluge the dove appears as a domesticated bird. The figurative language of Old Testament poetry often speaks of the dove, mentioning its simplicity (Hos. vii. 11), its swiftness (Ps. lv. 6; Hos. xi. 11), and its plaintive cooing (Isa. xxxviii. 14, lix. 11; Ezek. vii. 16; Nahum ii. 7); in Canticles the dove is used as a type of the loved one (ii. 14, v. 3, vi. 9). The comparisons are easily understood, but it must not be forgotten that the dove was sacred to Astarte and was, therefore, anciently the object of great honor and care. The dove was frequently offered as a sacrifice; it was, indeed, the legal offering for purification (Lev. xii. 6 sqq., xv. 14–15; Num. vi. 10), and, among the poor, often took the place of a greater sacrifice (Lev. v. 7, xii. 8, xiv. 22 sqq.). For the symbolical use of the dove in Christian art see SYMBOLISM.

I. BENZINGER.

BIBLIOGRAPHY: Lucian, *Dea Syria*, liv.; H. B. Tristram, *Natural Hist. of the Bible*, pp. 211–220, London, 1867; B. Lorentz, *Die Taube im Alterthume*, Leipsic, 1886; *DB*, i. 619–620; *EB*, i. 1129–30; *JE*, iv. 644–645; *DCG*, i. 492. On the dove as a symbol consult: *DCA*, i. 575–576 and references there; *New International Cyclopædia*, vi. 254–256.

DOW, LORENZO: Methodist; b. at Coventry, Conn., Oct. 16, 1777; d. at Georgetown, D. C., Feb. 2, 1834. He received only the most elementary education, but determined to become a Methodist preacher, and after being rejected by the Connecticut Conference in 1796 was finally appointed, three years later, to the Cambridge Circuit, N. Y. Within the year he was transferred to Pittsfield, Mass., and Essex, Vt., but had no official relations with his sect after 1799, although he continued to preach its characteristic tenets throughout his life. Believing that he had a special message for the Roman Catholics of Ireland, he visited Great Britain in 1799 and 1805, where the violence of his harangues exposed him to personal danger. During this time he introduced camp-meetings into England, thus beginning a controversy which resulted in the formation of the Primitive Methodists (see METHODISTS). In 1802 he preached in the Albany district, N. Y., and in 1803–04 delivered the first Protestant sermons in Alabama. In 1807 he was in Louisiana. The latter years of his life were devoted to fanatical attacks on the Jesuits. He was well known as "Crazy Dow," on account of his long hair and beard, peculiar clothing, and habit of swaying as he preached, but his addresses were characterized by a sarcasm, wit, and fearless courage which gained him throngs of hearers. Among his numerous writings, many of which were issued under the pseudonyms of "Cosmopolite" and "Lorenzo," mention may be made of his *Polemical Works* (New York, 1814); *The Stranger in Charlestown, or the Trial and Confession of Lorenzo Dow* (Philadelphia, 1822); *A Short Account of a Long Travel, with Beauties of Wesley* (1823); and the posthumous *Journal and Miscellaneous Writings* (ed. J. Dowling, New York, 1836) and *History of a Cosmopolite, or the Writings of the Rev. Lorenzo Dow, containing his Experience and Travels in Europe and America up to near his Fiftieth Year* (Cincinnati, 1851).

BIBLIOGRAPHY: *The Dealings of God, Man, and the Devil, as Exemplified in the Life, Experience, and Travels of L. Dow, together with his Writings complete*, 2 vols., Cincinnati, 1875.

DOW, NEAL: Temperance worker; b. at Portland, Me., Mar. 20, 1804; d. there Oct. 2, 1897. He studied at the Friends' Academy, New Bedford, Mass., and engaged in mercantile and manufacturing pursuits. He early became an advocate of rigid restriction of the liquor traffic, and entered political life in 1839 as chief engineer of the Portland fire department. He was elected mayor of Portland in 1851 and 1854, and during his first term drafted a bill "for the suppression of drinking-houses and tippling-shops," which was presented to the legislature on the day before its adjournment and carried without change on the following day (May 31, 1851). This law is still in force in its original form. Dow was a member of the Maine legislature 1858–59, and in 1861 was commissioned colonel of the 13th Maine Volunteers and assigned to the department of the Gulf. A few months later he was commissioned brigadier-general and placed in command of the forts at the mouth of the Mississippi and subsequently of the district of Florida. He was severely wounded at the battle of Port Hudson in 1863, and was captured the same night and confined for eight months in Libby Prison and Mobile before being exchanged for Fitz Henry Lee. He visited England in 1857, 1866, and 1874 at the invitation of the Temperance Alliance of the United Kingdom, and devoted himself for the remainder of his life to the furtherance of the total abstinence movement, traveling extensively and contributing frequently to magazines and newspapers in support of his principles. He was the Prohibition candidate for President of the United States in 1880, but received only 10,305 votes. Four years later he was instrumental in adding an amendment to the Maine constitution forever prohibiting the manufacture, sale, or keeping for sale of intoxicating beverages, and directing the legislature to compel a rigid enforcement of the amendment.

BIBLIOGRAPHY: *Reminiscences of Neal Dow; Recollections of 80 Years*, Portland, 1898.

DOWDEN, JOHN: Anglican bishop of Edinburgh; b. at Cork, Ireland, June 29, 1840. He studied at Queen's College, Cork, and Trinity College, Dublin (B.A., 1861), and was ordained priest in 1865. He was curate of St. John's, Sligo (1864–1867), incumbent of Calry, Sligo (1867–71), chaplain to the lord lieutenant of Ireland (1870–74), and assistant at St. Stephen's Chapel of Ease, Dublin (1871–74). He was Pantonian professor of theology (1874–87) and canon of St. Mary's Cathedral, Edinburgh (1880–86), and in 1886 was consecrated bishop of Edinburgh. He was Donellan lecturer at Dublin in 1884, and select preacher at the same university in 1886, 1894, and 1895. He has written *The Celtic Church in Scotland* (London, 1894); *Outlines of the History of the Theological Literature of the Church of England from the Reformation to the close of the Eighteenth Cen-*

tury (1897); *Helps from History to the True Sense of the Minatory Clauses of the Athanasian Creed* (1897); and *The Workmanship of the Prayer Book* (1899); and has edited *The Annotated Scottish Communion Office* (London, 1884); *The Correspondence of the Lauderdale Family with Archbishop Sharp, 1660–1677* (Edinburgh, 1893); and *The Chartulary of the Abbey of Lindores* (1903).

DOWIE, JOHN ALEXANDER: Founder of the Christian Catholic Apostolic Church in Zion (q.v.); b. at Edinburgh, Scotland, May 25, 1847; d. at Zion City, Ill., Mar. 9, 1907. He was educated in the schools of his native city, and from 1860 to 1868 was engaged in business in Adelaide, Australia. Returning to Scotland, he studied for two years at the University of Edinburgh, and in 1870 was ordained to the Congregational ministry in South Australia. He held successive charges at Alma and Sydney, but in 1878 retired from the Congregational body. Meanwhile he had become convinced that he possessed the gift of divine healing, and in 1882 removed to Melbourne, where he built a "tabernacle" and established the International Divine Healing Association. After working in Australia for six years, during which time he conducted a large number of missions, he went to the United States, where he labored for two years on the Pacific Coast. In 1890 he removed to Evanston, Ill., and in 1893 transferred his headquarters to Chicago. In 1896 he established the Christian Catholic Church in Zion, of which he made himself "general overseer," repeatedly antagonizing various Protestant denominations, and in 1901 founded Zion City on the shores of Lake Michigan, 42 m. n. of Chicago, in which he sought to prove the practicability of his teachings. There he gained immense power and influence, announced himself as "Elijah the Restorer," became the idol of his followers, and in 1904 he appointed himself "first apostle." Outside Zion City, however, his success was less. An attempt to introduce his views in New York in 1904 ended in failure, and visits to London in 1903 and 1904 were equally unproductive. Beneath his apparent supremacy opposition began to develop, criticism being leveled particularly against his financial administration of Zion City. Charges were also made that he held views conducive to immorality, and during his absence, on account of ill health, in Mexico in 1905 he was deposed from his office at Zion City. He thereupon returned to Zion City and vigorously opposed his deposition, finally securing at least a partial vindication by a court order, which also made provision for his support.

Bibliography: R. Harlan, *John Alexander Dowie and the Christian Catholic Apostolic Church in Zion*, Evansville, Wis., 1906.

DOWLING, JOHN: Baptist; b. in Pevensey (13 m. s.w. of Hastings), Sussex, England, May 12, 1807; d. in Middletown, N. Y., July 4, 1878. He taught school in England till 1832, when he came to America. For many years he was pastor in New York City, and he also preached in Providence, Philadelphia, and Newark. He became widely known by his *History of Romanism* (New York, 1845, and later editions).

DOXOLOGY. See Liturgical Formulas.

D'OYLY, GEORGE: Church of England; b. at London Oct. 31, 1778; d. there Jan. 8, 1846. He studied at Corpus Christi College, Cambridge (B.A., 1800), and was elected fellow in 1801. He was ordered deacon in 1802 and ordained priest in the following year, and after being curate to his father for a few months became curate of Wrotham, Kent, in 1804. From 1806 to 1809 he was moderator in the University of Cambridge, and in 1811 was appointed Hulsean Christian advocate. In 1813 he became domestic chaplain to the archbishop of Canterbury, and in 1815 was presented to the vicarage of Hernhill, Kent. Before he could take up his residence there, however, he was made the successor of his father at Buxted, Sussex. From 1820 until his death he held the rectories of Lambeth, Surrey, and Sundridge, Kent. He was treasurer of the Society for Promoting Christian Knowledge, a member of the London committee of the Society for the Propagation of the Gospel, one of the main agents in the establishment of King's College, London, and select preacher at Cambridge in 1809, 1810, and 1811. He published *Two Discourses preached before the University of Cambridge on the Doctrine of a Particular Providence and on Modern Utilitarianism* (Cambridge, 1811); *Letters to Sir W. Drummond Relating to his Observations on Parts of the Old Testament in his "Œdipus Judaicus"* (London, 1812); *Remarks on Sir W. Drummond's "Œdipus Judaicus"* (1813); *An Essay on the Doctrine of Assurance, as Maintained by Some Modern Sects of Christians* (1814); *Life of William Sancroft, Archbishop of Canterbury* (2 vols., 1821); *Sermons* (1827); and the posthumous *Sermons* (edited, with a memoir, by his son, C. J. D'Oyly, 1847). He is best known, however, for the annotated Bible (3 vols., London, 1814) prepared in collaboration with Richard Mant (q.v.).

DRABIK, dră'bîk, **MIKULÁŠ** (*Nicolaus Drabicius*): Moravian mystic and prophet; b. at Strasnitz (13 m. s.s.w. of Hradisch) Dec. 5, 1588; d. at Presburg (34 m. e.s.e. of Vienna) July 17, 1671. He was educated in his native town, and in 1616 was ordained by the Bohemian Brethren and appointed pastor at Drahotusch. When the non-Catholics were exiled in 1627 he left Moravia with them and found a refuge in Lednitz. His addiction to liquor and his disobedience of the regulations of the Brethren resulted in his deposition from the clergy. Thereupon he devoted himself to the study of the prophets of the Old Testament and, in 1643, set himself up as a prophet. His revelations were based on dreams and on conversations with a divine voice, and are characterised by a bitter hatred of the house of Austria rather than by religious apocalyptics. In 1650 he received fresh inspiration when Comenius was sent by the Bohemian exiles in Poland to their Moravian brethren. The accession of Charles X. of Sweden again inspired Drabik with new hopes, and he went to Holland, where Comenius published his

Lux in tenebris (n.p., 1657). To the very last his prophecies foretold the speedy downfall of Austria and the return of the Brethren. In 1671 he was seized, together with the leaders of the conspiracy of Wesseleny, with which he had had nothing to do, and was executed on a charge of lese-majesté.

(P. KLEINERT.)

BIBLIOGRAPHY: [A. Comenius], *Historia revelationum*, Amsterdam, 1659; G. Arnold, *Kirchen- und Ketzerhistorie*, iii. 353 sqq., 4 vols., Frankfort, 1700-15; P. F. Grünenberg, *De Nicolao Drabitio neopropheta*, Altorf, 1721; P. Kleinert, in *TSK*, 1898; and the literature cited under COMENIUS.

DRACHMAN, BERNARD: Jewish rabbi; b. in New York City June 27, 1861. He studied at Columbia College (B.A., 1882), the universities of Breslau and Heidelberg (Ph.D., 1884), and the Jewish theological seminary at Breslau. He received the rabbinical diploma at Breslau in 1885, and has been rabbi of the Congregation Oheb Sholom, Newark, N. J. (1885-87), the Congregation Beth Israel Bikkur Cholim, New York City (1887-1889), and the Congregation Zichron Ephraim in the latter city since 1889. In 1886 he was one of the founders of the Jewish Theological Seminary of New York, in which he was professor of Biblical exegesis, Hebrew grammar, and Jewish philosophy 1887-1902, and dean 1889-1902. On the establishment of the Jewish Theological Seminary of America in 1902 he was appointed professor of the Bible and rabbinical codes. He was the founder of the Jewish Endeavor Society. In theology he is an adherent of Orthodox Judaism. He has written *Die Stellung und Bedeutung des Jehuda Hajjug in der Geschichte der hebräischen Grammatik* (Breslau, 1885) and *From the Heart of Israel* (New York, 1905); and has translated *The Nineteen Letters of Ben Uziel, from the German of Samson Raphael Hirsch* (New York, 1899).

DRACONITES, drā-cō-nī'tēs, **JOHANNES** (Johann **Drach, Trach;** also **Carlstadt,** from his native town): German Reformer and Biblical scholar; b. at Carlstadt (14 m. n.w. of Würzburg) 1494; d. at Wittenberg Apr. 18, 1566. He entered the University of Erfurt in 1509, and after taking his master's degree in 1514 lived there as a prominent member of the circle of young poets and enthusiasts led by Eobanus Hessus. Erasmus was the object of their admiration, and in 1520 Draconites traveled to the Netherlands to make the acquaintance of the great scholar. With the advent of Luther, however, he found a new leader, his devotion dating particularly from the Reformer's visit to Erfurt in Apr., 1521. In June of the same year he was expelled from his office of canon of the cathedral church because of his open adherence to Luther's teachings, but violent demonstrations by the populace and students led to his reinstatement.

Early Life to 1534.

To him was ascribed the instigation of the antisacerdotal riots of June, 1521, which led to a definite cleavage between the Evangelical and Roman Catholic elements. An outbreak of the plague drove him to Wittenberg in the same month, and there he pursued the study of Hebrew, but the following year he accepted the pastorate of Miltenberg on the Main. In dogma and practise he approached closely to the Wittenberg model, and thus gained the enmity of the local Roman Catholics, though the majority of the inhabitants were on his side. Cited to appear before the commissary of the archbishop of Mainz, he refused to obey, and was excommunicated. At the urgent entreaty of his parishioners, he fled from threatening danger in Sept., 1523, and lived at Wertheim, Nuremberg, Erfurt, and Wittenberg, whence he addressed epistles of consolation to the inhabitants of Miltenberg, where the old system had been reestablished by force. In 1525 Draconites became pastor at Waltershausen near Gotha, and in the following year was made inspector for the district of Tenneberg. Owing to the frequent conflicts in which the performance of his duties involved him, he resigned in 1528 and retired to private life at Eisenach, actuated partly by the desire to devote himself to the preparation of a polyglot Bible. His retirement was regarded with suspicion by his friends, and the charge of heresy was brought against him, but he held to the Evangelical faith in spite of efforts to win him away, and in his defense published *Bekenntnis des Glaubens und der Lehre* (Erfurt, 1532).

In 1534 Draconites became pastor and professor at Marburg, and labored with zeal in both fields. His publications during this period include Biblical commentaries, sermons, and devotional works. He renewed his friendship with Eobanus Hessus, and in 1540 pronounced the funeral oration over his friend, and later edited his letters (*Epistolæ familiares Eobani Hessi*, Marburg, 1543).

His Professorial Career.

A noteworthy feature of his activity was his successful missionary labor among the Jews. He was present at the Diet of Frankfort in 1536, signed the Schmalkald articles in the following year, and in 1541 attended the negotiations at the Interim of Regensburg. A letter addressed to the authorities of that town exhorting them to adopt Lutheranism attracted the dangerous attention of Granvella, whom, however, he eluded. At this time he came into conflict with Thamer, a member of the University of Marburg, on the relation of faith and penitence. Thamer enjoyed the protection of the young landgrave, and after a pastorate of fourteen years Draconites left Marburg in Oct., 1547. For a while he lectured at Lübeck on the prophets, and in 1549-50 published there a long-contemplated work on Messianic prophecy under the title *Gottes Verheissungen von Christo Jesu.* His reputation as a Hebrew scholar brought him a call to a chair in the University of Rostock, where at different times he held the rectorate. In 1557 he was made superintendent of Rostock, and as such was plunged into the bitter controversy between the civic authorities and the clergy, whose champions were Heshusen and Eggerdes. His liberal interpretation of the laws of the Sabbath again brought upon him the charge of antinomianism, and in 1560 he was glad to abandon the conflict on receiving from Duke Albert of Prussia the offer of the presidency of the see of Pomerania, while he also welcomed the new position as an opportunity for bringing to completion his contemplated polyglot Bible.

Under leave of absence he proceeded to Wittenberg and there remained to the end of his life, enjoying the revenues of his Prussian office until removed by the duke in 1564. His *Biblia Pentapla* began to appear at Wittenberg in 1563, and by 1565 he had published Gen. i.–v., Psalms, Proverbs, Isaiah, Malachi, Joel, Zechariah, and Micah. The Hebrew text was presented in very large type, and beneath each word appeared the translation in Aramaic, Greek, Latin, and German, while passages which he regarded as Messianic were printed in red. The value of the work is small, however, because of the radical changes which he made in the text of his versions, and its completion was found impracticable.

His Life at Wittenberg.

(G. Kawerau.)

Bibliography: The older literature is indicated and worked over by J. Moller, *Cimbria litterata*, ii. 167–173, Copenhagen, 1744. Of great service is G. T. Strobel, *Neue Beiträge zur Litteratur*, iv. 1, pp. 1–136, Nuremberg, 1793. A short biography by G. Kawerau is in *Beiträge zur bayerischen Kirchengeschichte*, iii. 247 sqq., Erlangen, 1897. For his life in Erfurt consult: C. Krause, *Helius Eobanus Hessus*, vol. i., Gotha, 1879; in Miltenberg, O. Albrecht, *Die evangelische Gemeinde Miltenberg und ihr erster Prediger*, Halle, 1896; in Waltershausen, C. Polack, *J. Drach*, in *Zeitschrift des Vereins für thüringische Geschichte*, vii (1890), 211 sqq.; in Marburg, K. W. H. Hochhuth, *T. Thamer und Landgraf Philipp*, in *ZHT*, 1861, pp. 165 sqq.; in Rostock, O. Krabbe, *Die Universität Rostock*, p. 501, Rostock, 1854; for the later portion of his life, J. Voigt, *Briefe der berühmtesten Gelehrten mit Herzog Albrecht*, pp. 216–234, Königsberg, 1841; for his work on the Bible, L. Diestel, *Geschichte des A. T. in der christlichen Kirche*, Jena, 1869.

DRACONTIUS, dra-cen'shi-us, **BLOSSIUS ÆMILIUS**: Christian poet; b. in Africa; flourished in the latter half of the fifth century. His poem in honor of a foreign ruler (possibly the emperor of the East) aroused the anger of the Gothic king Gunthamund (484–496), who confiscated his property and imprisoned him. He vainly endeavored to regain the royal favor by his elegy *Satisfactio*; his *De laudibus Dei* was also written in prison. The latter poem is devoted to the divine creation and preservation and redemption of the world, and to man's love for God. In his youth, or at least before his imprisonment, Dracontius wrote brief secular poems, epics based on Hellenic legends (*Hylas*, *Medea*, *Raptus Helenæ*, and *Orestis Tragœdia*), two epithalamia, and rhetorical themes (*Verba Herculis*, *Deliberativa Achillis*, and *Controversia de statua viri fortis*). The two Christian poems, which breathe a devotional spirit, evince linguistic and metrical skill, and show extensive knowledge of the Bible and of profane literature. Only the first part of the *Laudes Dei*, the *Hexaëmeron creationis mundi*, was known to Isidore of Seville (*De vir. ill.*, xxiv.), and this portion was first edited (poorly) by Bishop Eugenius II. of Toledo. At the wish of the Visigothic king Chindaswinth (642–649), Eugenius also prepared a wretched edition of the *Satisfactio*. The true Dracontius first became known through Arevalo.

K. Leimbach†.

Bibliography: The best edition of the *Carmina minora* is by F. de Duhn, Leipsic, 1873; of the *Carmina*, including the *Satisfactio*, by F. Arevalo, Rome, 1791. The *Hexaëmeron*, ed. J. B. Carpzov, appeared Helmstadt, 1794; the *Raptus Helenæ* is in the *Appendix ad opera edita*, by A. Mai, Rome, 1871; the *Orestes Tragœdia*, ed. R. Peiper, Wratislav, 1875. Consult: C. Rossberg, *In Dracontii carmina minora*, Stade, 1878; idem, *Materialien zu einem Commentar über die Orestis tragœdia*, Hildesheim, 1888–1889; W. S. Teuffel, *Geschichte der römischen Litteratur*, ed. L. Schwabe, pp. 1220–24, Freiburg, 1886; J. B. Pitra, *Analecta sacra et classica*, i. 176–180, Paris, 1888; W. Meyer, in *Sitzungsberichte der Berliner Akademie*, 1890, pp. 257–296; *DCB*, i. 905–907.

DRAENDORF, drēn'dorf, **JOHANNES**: German Reformer; b. at Schlieben (30 m. s.e. of Wittenberg) 1390; burned at the stake at Heidelberg Feb. 17, 1425. He was of noble descent, and was educated at Dresden by the magistri Peter and Frederick. He completed his studies at the universities of Prague and Leipsic, and in 1417 was ordained to the priesthood in Bohemia. He traversed middle and southern Germany as an itinerant preacher subsequent to 1421, and at Speyer collaborated with the school-director Peter Turnow of Tolkemit on a manifesto in which he vehemently assailed the abuse of excommunication and the temporal power of the clergy. In 1424, when the imperial city of Weinsberg was put under ban and interdict, Dråndorf endeavored to incite the city and its allies to open rebellion against ecclesiastical control. The municipal council invited him to visit the city, but he was arrested by the elector palatine Louis III., and in Feb., 1425, was brought before the Inquisition at Heidelberg. He frankly acknowledged that he held to the Utraquistic doctrine of the communion indulgences, and that he was opposed to the taking of oaths, to the mass, the doctrine of the infallibility of the councils, the temporal jurisdiction and power of the clergy, papal primacy, the mendicant orders, excommunication, and the like. His religious system seems to have been the result of a combination of Waldensian, Wyclifite, and Taboristic elements.

Herman Haupt.

Bibliography: J. E. Kapp, *Kleine Nachlese . . . zur Erläuterung der Reformations-Geschichte nützlicher Urkunden*, iii. 1–60, Leipsic, 1730; Krummel, in *TSK*, xlii (1869), 130–144; H. Haupt, *Hussitische Propaganda in Deutschland*, in *Historisches Taschenbuch*, series 6, vii. 263–266; idem, *Waldenserthum und Inquisition im Südöstlichen Deutschland*, pp. 68–71, Freiburg, 1890; idem, in *Zeitschrift für die Geschichte des Oberrheins*, new series, xv. 479 sqq.

END OF VOL. III.

Zeitfracht Medien GmbH
Ferdinand-Jühlke-Straße 7
99095 Erfurt, Deutschland
produktsicherheit@kolibri360.de